LAROUSSE

THE SECOND WORLD WAR

IN COLOUR

LAROUSSE

THE SECOND WORLD WAR IN COLOUR

CHANCELLOR PRESS

Originally published under the title *La Seconde Guerre Mondiale en coulers*

General editor , Philippe Masson

English translation by Angela M.Wootton and John Bailie
Historical and technical advice by T.C. Charman

First published 1985 by The Hamlyn Publishing Group Limited
part of Reed International Books

This 1991 edition published by
Chancellor Press
Michelin House
81 Fulham Road
London SW3 6RB

ISBN 1 85152 150 X

Produced by Mandarin Offset
Printed in Hong Kong

Introduction

It is now 52 years since the outbreak of the Second World War. Yet the interest aroused by this devastating conflict, which led to the deaths of 50 million people, shows no sign of slackening, as is proved by the regular stream of publications covering all aspects of the war which continue to find an enthusiastic public response. This interest is amply justified by the unprecedented scale of the conflict, whose outcome continues to have a profound effect on today's world.

In fact, quite unlike the events of 1914–18, the Second World War was fought on a truly global scale. Military operations were not confined to Europe: they also took place in North Africa, the Near East and the Far East. The war at sea was not restricted to northern waters, the Mediterranean and the Atlantic: it reached as far as the Indian Ocean and the Pacific.

The conflict was also marked by a return to the war of movement after the costly stalemate of 1914–18. Nazi Germany's resounding victories up to 1942 were made possible by the techniques of the Blitzkrieg – the close support between tanks and aircraft – and the Allied victory over the Axis powers in 1945 was to be achieved by the use of the same methods on a much vaster scale. The war was also notable for the employment of combined operations – which helped in the landings of the Anglo-American forces in France and Italy and helped to ensure the victory of the United States in the Pacific.

One further striking feature of the conflict was the evolution of air warfare. The aircraft progressed far beyond its tactical role – the close support of armies in the field of battle – and was increasingly used for strategic bombing. The enemy's homeland, hitherto considered an inviolable sanctuary, became a legitimate target, and it was the fate of Germany and Japan to experience the full horrors of bombing – culminating in the dropping of atomic bombs on Hiroshima and Nagasaki.

New weapons systems made their appearance. The aircraft-carrier reduced the battleship to a secondary role. The high-performance submarine of 1945 heralded the nuclear-powered vessel of today. From the machines which came into service at the end of the war – jet aircraft, rockets, V1 and V2 missiles – are derived the most sophisticated weapons in use in the armies of the 1980s, while radar and sonar have revolutionized methods of detecting hostile forces.

The war was also characterized by the mobilization of the manpower and economic resources of the belligerents who had to tackle the problem of creating mass armies. It was not just a question of bringing together millions of men, but also of feeding them and equipping them in the context of a complete transformation in the economy. It was also important to keep up the morale both of the fighting men and the people at home, while at the same time undermining the enemy's. In an ideological confrontation of regimes with fundamentally opposed ideas, propaganda, benefiting from the development of press and radio, attained sufficient importance to merit the name of a psychological weapon.

The Second World War also provided a vivid illustration of man's inhumanity to man: the concentration camps, the systematic extermination of the Jews, the terror bombing of towns and the sufferings of people whose countries were occupied by a ruthless enemy.

In short, the Second World War marks an important stage in the history of mankind. It put the seal on the decline of Europe which began in 1919. Despite the postwar economic recovery Europe was no longer able to influence the course of events directly or to shape its own future.

Although there was, strictly speaking, no 'division of the spoils' at Yalta and Potsdam, a polarized world, dominated by two nuclear superpowers, the United States and the Soviet Union, is a direct result of the war. By its victory over all forms of fascism, the war consolidated the strength of the liberal democracies, at the same time giving a strong stimulus to communism which discovered a remarkable field for expansion in eastern Europe and in the Far East. The war was, in addition, the indirect cause of the vast process of decolonization, which was not completed until the 1960s.

Seen from this viewpoint the present work differs markedly from existing publications about the Second World War. It is based on an entirely new concept: the use of colour photographs from the period. The majority of these photographs have been selected, after painstaking research, from the archives of all the countries which took part in the war. Bearing in mind the fact that the process of colour photography was still in its early stages, the reader will be able to judge for himself the remarkable quality of most of them, notably those of German or American origin. This unique pictorial record is not restricted to scenes of actual fighting or to photographs of war leaders. It also provides coverage of the daily lives of ordinary people from behind the front lines, as well as striking reproductions of posters or paintings. There are some 60 full-page photographs which are included for their human interest as much as for their visual impact.

The book has, however, a second claim to originality. The various topics are treated alphabetically for easy reference and each picture is accompanied by clear, concise captions, which not only describe what is happening but place the event in the context of the war as a whole. A selection of all-colour maps enables the reader to follow the evolution of the conflict in the different theatres of operations.

Contents

Picture Acknowledgements

Anonymous/unidentified 120, 142 top, 243 top, 335 top; Archives Idées et Editions 98 bottom, 107, 122 bottom, 170 bottom, 215 top, 229 top, 243 bottom, 251 bottom, 258, 274; Archives *Paris-Match* 86 top; Archives Tallandier 79 top, 109 top, 131 top, 167 top right, 261 top; Archives Tallandier (Private collection) 75 top; Archives Tallandier–*Signal* 140 top; Associated Artists 26 centre left, 84 bottom; Australian War Memorial 63 bottom; Bibliothek für Zeitgeschichte, Stuttgart 75 bottom, 140 bottom, 211 bottom right, 240 bottom, 283 left, 284, 286 top, 325 top; Bibliothek für Zeitgeschichte, Stuttgart–Archives Idées et Editions 162 top, 208 bottom, 321 top left, 322 top; Bibliothèque Nationale–Archives Tallandier 106 centre right; Bildarchiv Preussischer Kulturbesitz 32 top, 43 top, 44 top, 44 bottom, 74, 106 bottom, 112 right, 115 top, 117 bottom, 118 top right, 118 bottom, 128 bottom, 132 top, 132 bottom, 133, 135 left, 137 bottom, 143 bottom left, 144, 146 bottom, 148 top, 150, 152 top, 152 bottom, 155 bottom, 158 top, 160 bottom, 161 centre, 167 top left, 167 bottom, 181, 183, 184 top, 184 centre, 185 top, 194 top, 194 bottom, 196 centre right, 197 left, 197 right, 198, 199 top, 200 bottom, 214 top, 214 bottom, 217 centre, 219 right, 235 bottom, 265, 280 bottom, 282 top, 287 bottom, 291 top, 299, 308, 313 bottom, 314 top, 314 bottom, 319 bottom, 320 top, 321 top right, 321 bottom, 322 bottom, 327 bottom, 332, 334 left; Bridgeman Art Library 62 bottom; Bundesarchiv 42 centre, 96 top, 276 top; Bundesarchiv Koblenz 128 top left; Bundesarchiv–Wehrmacht 306 top; Collection Chiaselotti–Archives Tallandier 72 bottom; Collection Delagarde 51 top, 71 bottom, 80 top, 80 bottom, 128 top right, 179 top, 211 bottom left, 234 bottom, 330 top; Collection Rieussec 29 top right, 116 left; Domenica Del Corriere–Archives Idées et Editions 178 top; Domenica Del Corriere–N. Marchand–M. Rieussec 174 top; Erwitt, Elliott–Magnum 63 top; Eyerman–*Time Life*–Colorific! 209 bottom; Fox Photos Ltd 154 top, 160 top, 164 top; *Il Dagherrotipo* 24 top, 24 bottom, 70 bottom, 291 bottom, 315 right, 316 bottom; Imperial War Museum, London **Front cover** (main picture), 23 top, 23 bottom, 29 bottom, 30 top, 32 centre, 33 top, 35 bottom left, 42 bottom, 46 bottom, 47, 48 left, 55 centre, 57 bottom, 79 bottom, 94 top, 100 bottom, 108, 113 top, 122 top (W. Russell), 124 bottom, 125 top, 138, 153, 154 left, 154 bottom, 156 top, 157, 172 top, 172 bottom, 173 top, 186 top, 195 bottom, 196 top, 201 bottom, 208 centre, 212 top, 213, 215 bottom, 217 bottom, 228 top (A. Gross), 256 bottom, 257, 259 top, 259 bottom, 262 bottom, 268, 269, 275 bottom, 276 bottom, 279, 282 bottom (A. Gregson), 285 bottom, 292 bottom, 293, 294, 305 top, 305 bottom, 306 bottom left, 307, 317 centre, 317 bottom, 318, 323 bottom, 324 top, 328 top, 329 top, 331, 335 bottom; Imperial War Museum–E. Tweedy–Archives Idées et Editions 170 top; Jaeger H.–*Time Life* 36 bottom; Jaeger H.–*Time Life* – Colorific! **Front cover** (top left), 37 bottom, 38, 41, 46 top, 65, 77 bottom, 78 top, 83 top, 84 top right, 89 top, 89 bottom, 102 top, 115 bottom right, 123 bottom, 124 top, 161 top, 162 bottom, 174 right, 180 centre, 199 bottom, 216 bottom, 222 top left, 223 top right, 235 centre, 246, 247 top, 247 centre, 247 bottom, 248 top, 248 bottom, 251 top, 261 centre, 266 left, 270 top, 272 top, 275 centre, 278 centre left, 283 right, 297 top, 298 bottom, 319 top; Joubert L.–Archives Tallandier 262 centre; Jourdes–Edimages 295 top; Kessel D.–*Time Life* – Colorific! 35 top, 224 bottom, 233 top, 239 top; Larousse 49 top, 71 top, 72 top, 76 bottom, 77 top, 91 top, 103 bottom, 139 top, 143 centre right, 158 bottom, 188 left, 201 top, 212 centre right, 302 bottom, 312 centre; Larousse–Collection Tallandier (© S.P.A.D.E.M.) 35 bottom right; Larousse–*Signal* 21 bottom left, 22, 26 centre right, 26 bottom, 30 bottom, 50 left, 50 right, 55 bottom, 56, 57 top, 58 top, 58 bottom, 59, 60 top left, 64, 66, 67 top, 67 bottom, 68, 69 top, 69 bottom, 82 left, 90 bottom, 92, 94 bottom, 95 bottom, 101, 103 top right, 106 centre left, 111 bottom, 112 left, 115 left, 116 right, 126 bottom, 139 bottom, 141 bottom, 147 top, 163 top, 163 bottom, 165, 173 bottom, 180 top left, 188 top, 196 bottom left, 202 top right, 202 bottom, 209 top right, 210 bottom, 212 bottom left, 222 top right, 223 top left, 252 top, 255 top, 256 centre right, 261 bottom, 277 bottom, 289, 290 top left, 301 bottom, 310 top, 317 top, 324 bottom, 325 bottom, 326, 327 top, 329 bottom; Lauros-Giraudon 39 bottom, 104 bottom, 244 bottom left, 252 bottom right; Lemaire J. 242 top; Levchine (N. Marchand–M. Rieussec) 113 bottom; Marchand N.–Archives Idées et

Editions 73 bottom; Marchand N.–*L'Expresso* – M. Rieussec 298 top; Marchand N.–Rieussec M. 99 right, 155 top, 168, 174 bottom left, 203 top, 234 top, 236 bottom, 241, 256 top left, 273 top, 285 top, 320 bottom; Marine Corps, Defense Department–Archives Tallandier 203 bottom, 204, 223 bottom; MARS 330 bottom; MARS–© Airborne Forces Museum, Hampshire 55 top; MGM 102 bottom; Mydans C.–*Time Life* – Colorific! 48 right, 177 top, 191, 218 bottom, 220 bottom; Ott A. 42 top; Parimage 29 top left, 31, 61, 91 bottom, 99 left, 118 top left, 119, 252 centre left, 306 bottom right, 313 top; Photri 34 top, 78 bottom, 81, 82 right, 90 centre, 121 top, 136 bottom left, 137 top, 156 bottom, 164 right, 193 top, 210 top, 230 bottom, 233 bottom, 240 centre, 250 bottom left, 253 bottom, 271 top, 286 bottom, 287 top, 300, 312 top; PIA 87 bottom; Popperfoto 36 top, 84 left, 85, 90 top, 126 top, 149, 159 top, 166, 219 bottom left, 260 top, 270 centre right, 270 bottom left, 278 top, 281 top, 295 bottom, 323 top, 328 bottom; Preston N.–*Time Life* – Colorific! 309 bottom; Private collection 182 left, 316 top; Robert Hunt Library 76 top, 159 bottom, 182 right, 184 bottom right, 264 bottom, 272 bottom, 302 top, 333 top; Roger-Viollet 28 bottom; Scherschel F.–*Time Life*–Colorific! 179 bottom, 229 bottom, 242 bottom; *Signal*–Collection Tallandier 21 top, 21 bottom right, 87 top left; Silk G.–*Time Life*–Colorific! 40 bottom, 49 bottom, 147 bottom; Sirman L.–Camera Press–Parimage 136 bottom right; Snark International 73 top, 86 centre, 87 top right, 155 centre; Snark International–Bibliothèque Nationale 98 top; Snark International–Imperial War Museum 249 top; S.P.A.D.E.M. (Royal Museum of Army and Military History, Brussels) 72 centre right; Stackpole P.–*Time Life* – Colorific! 121 bottom; Time Life–Colorific! 28 top, 216 top, 225 bottom, 250 top left, 271 bottom, 292 top, 296, 297 bottom, 333 bottom; Tweedy E.–Archives Idées et Editions 164 bottom, 334 right; Twentieth Century Fox–Archives Idées et Editions 236 top; Ullstein–Camera Press–Parimage 51 bottom, 91 centre right; UPI 93 top, 111 top, 208 top; US Air Force 26 top, 62 top, 130 top, 130 bottom; US Air Force–Archives Idées et Editions 27 bottom, 32 bottom, 131 centre right, 131 bottom, 141 top, 161 bottom, 237, 240 top; US Air Force–N. Marchand–Archives Idées et Editions 27 centre, 178 bottom, 182 top, 290 top right; US Army **Back cover**, 40 top, 88, 93 bottom, 109 bottom, 110, 151 top, 169 bottom, 177 bottom, 187 bottom left, 205 bottom, 217 top, 232, 238, 245 top, 245 bottom, 253 top, 263 top, 290 bottom, 311 bottom; US Army–Archives Idées et Editions **Front cover** (top centre left, top centre right and top right), 27 top, 45, 52, 53, 54 top, 54 bottom, 83 bottom, 96 centre, 100 top, 104 top, 105 top, 105 bottom, 106 top, 107, 125 bottom, 129 top, 148 bottom, 151 bottom, 169 top, 171, 176, 189, 190 top left, 190 right, 190 bottom left, 192, 200 top, 202 top left, 205 top, 206, 207, 211 top, 226, 230 top, 231, 244 bottom right, 249 bottom, 254, 255 bottom, 262 top, 264 top, 266 right, 273 bottom, 277 top, 281 bottom, 288 top, 303 bottom, 304, 311 top, 312 bottom; US Army–Archives Tallandier 43 bottom, 60 centre, 97, 275 top, 278 bottom right; US Army–N. Marchand–Archives Idées et Editions 129 bottom, 145 top, 145 bottom, 146 top, 159 centre, 220 top, 227, 267, 280 top, 315 left; US Army–N. Marchand–M. Rieussec 175, 180 bottom, 263 bottom; US Navy 25, 33 bottom, 34 bottom, 70 top, 123 top, 185 bottom, 186 bottom, 193 bottom, 218 top, 221 top, 224 top, 239 bottom, 244 top; US Navy–Archives Idées et Editions 117 top, 187 right, 221 bottom, 225 top, 225 centre, 228 bottom, 310 bottom; Vandivert W.–*Time Life* – Colorific! 86 bottom; Vigne J.–*Signal* 209 top left; Vigne J.–Wehrmacht 60 bottom, 95 top, 127, 188 bottom, 195 top, 222 bottom, 301 top, 303 top, 309 top; Zucca A.–Archives Tallandier 37 top, 39 top, 103 top left, 114 top, 114 bottom, 134, 135 right, 136 top, 142 bottom, 143 top, 187 top, 235 top, 250 centre right, 260 bottom, 288 bottom.

Europe from 1919 to 1923

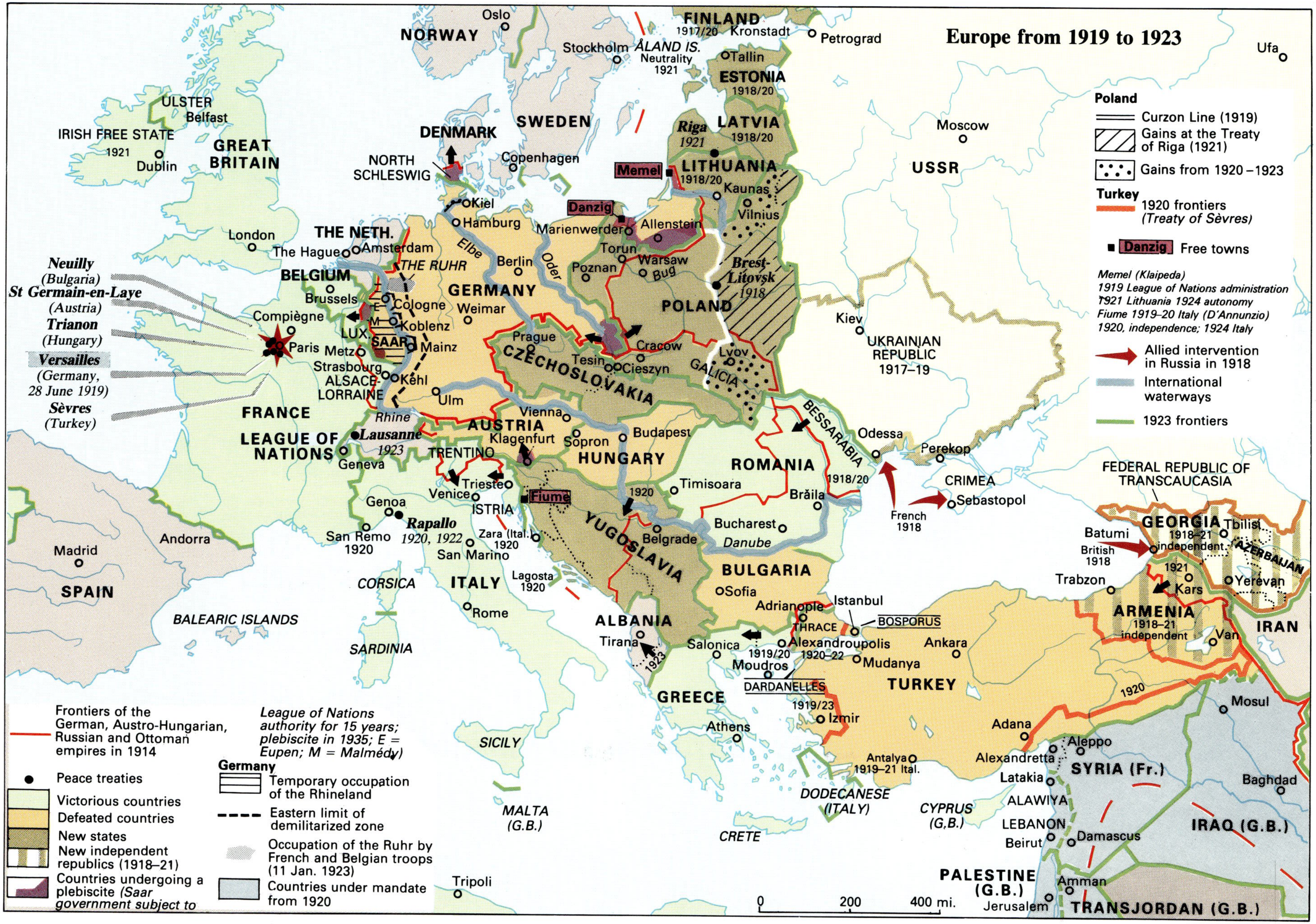

Dictatorships in Europe from 1920 to 1939

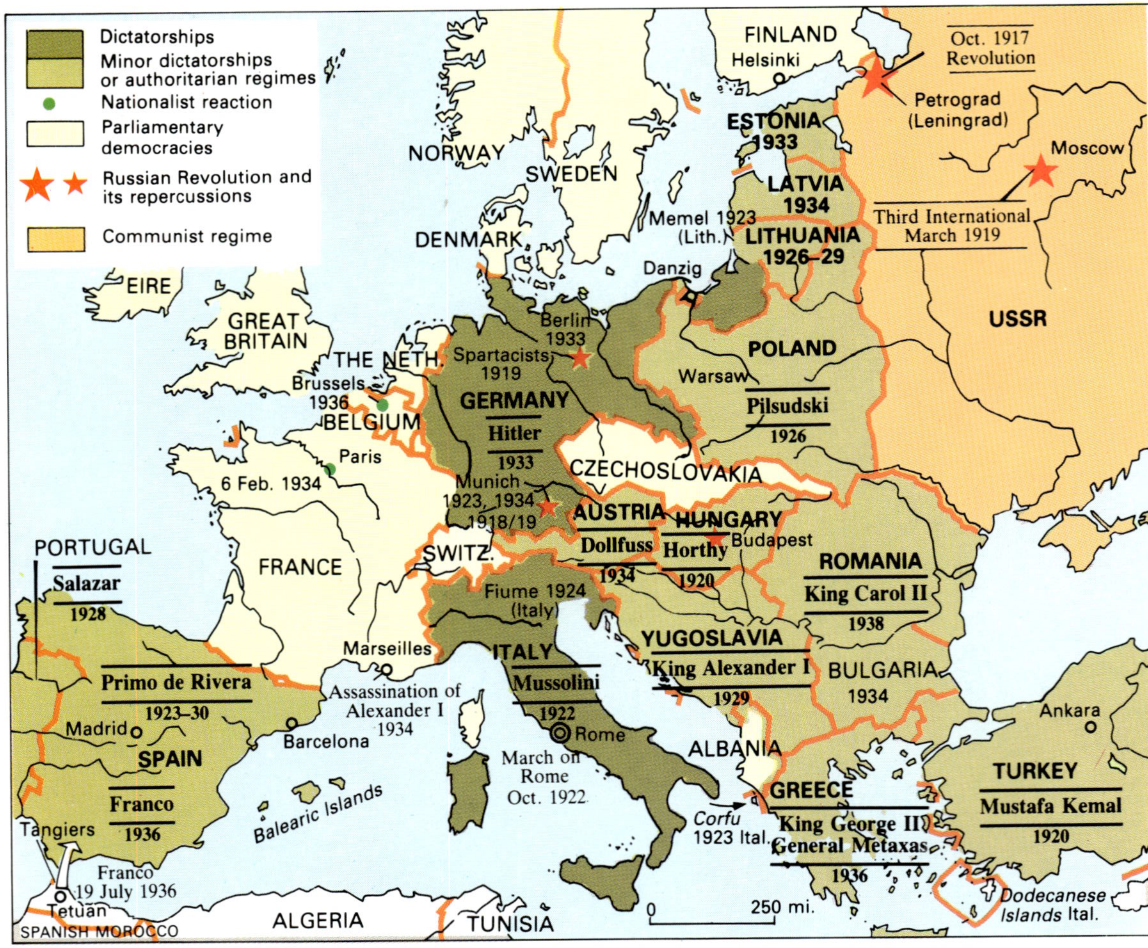

Dictatorships in Europe from 1920 to 1939

The Blitzkrieg in Europe

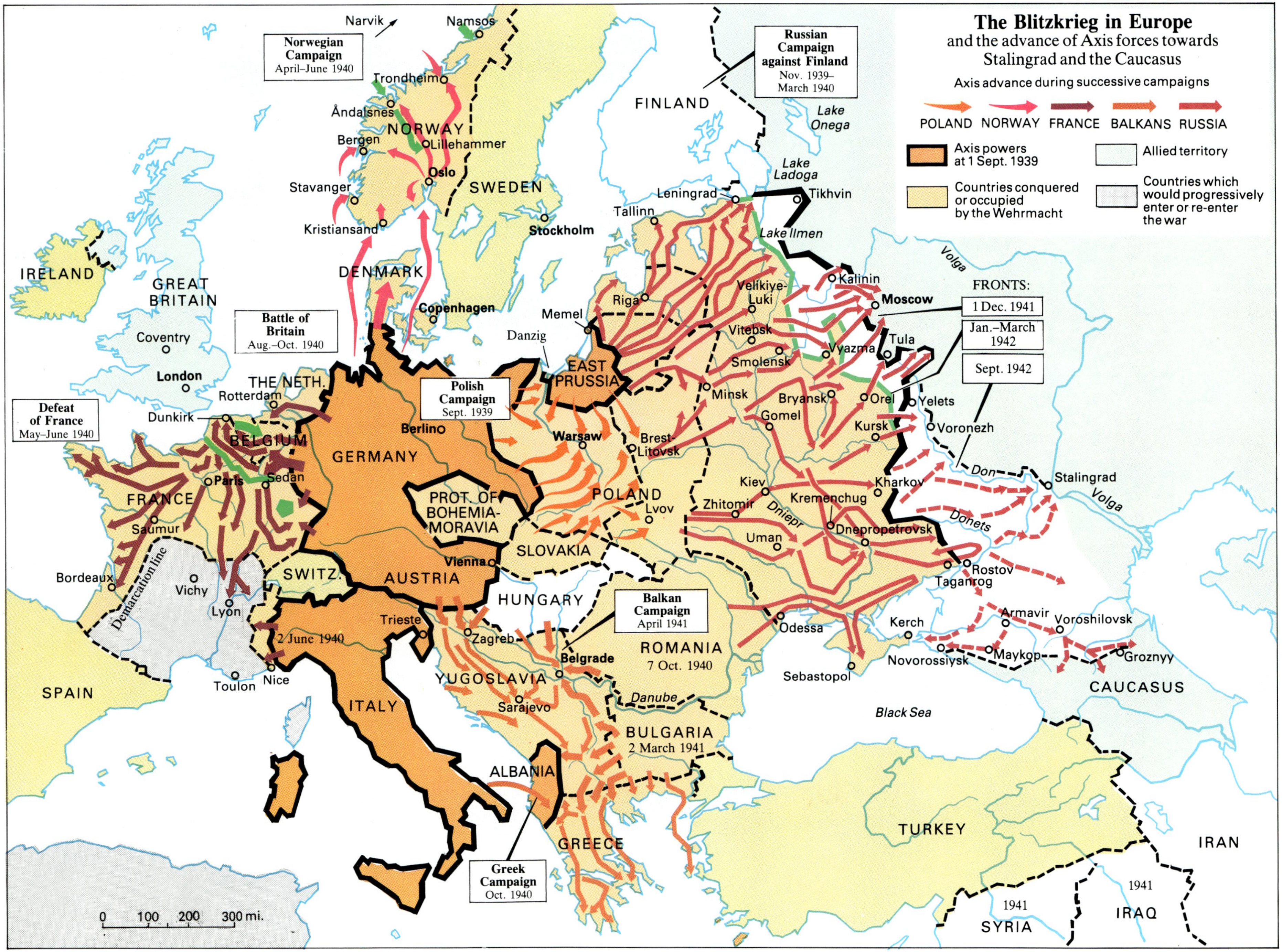

The Height of Axis Power in 1942

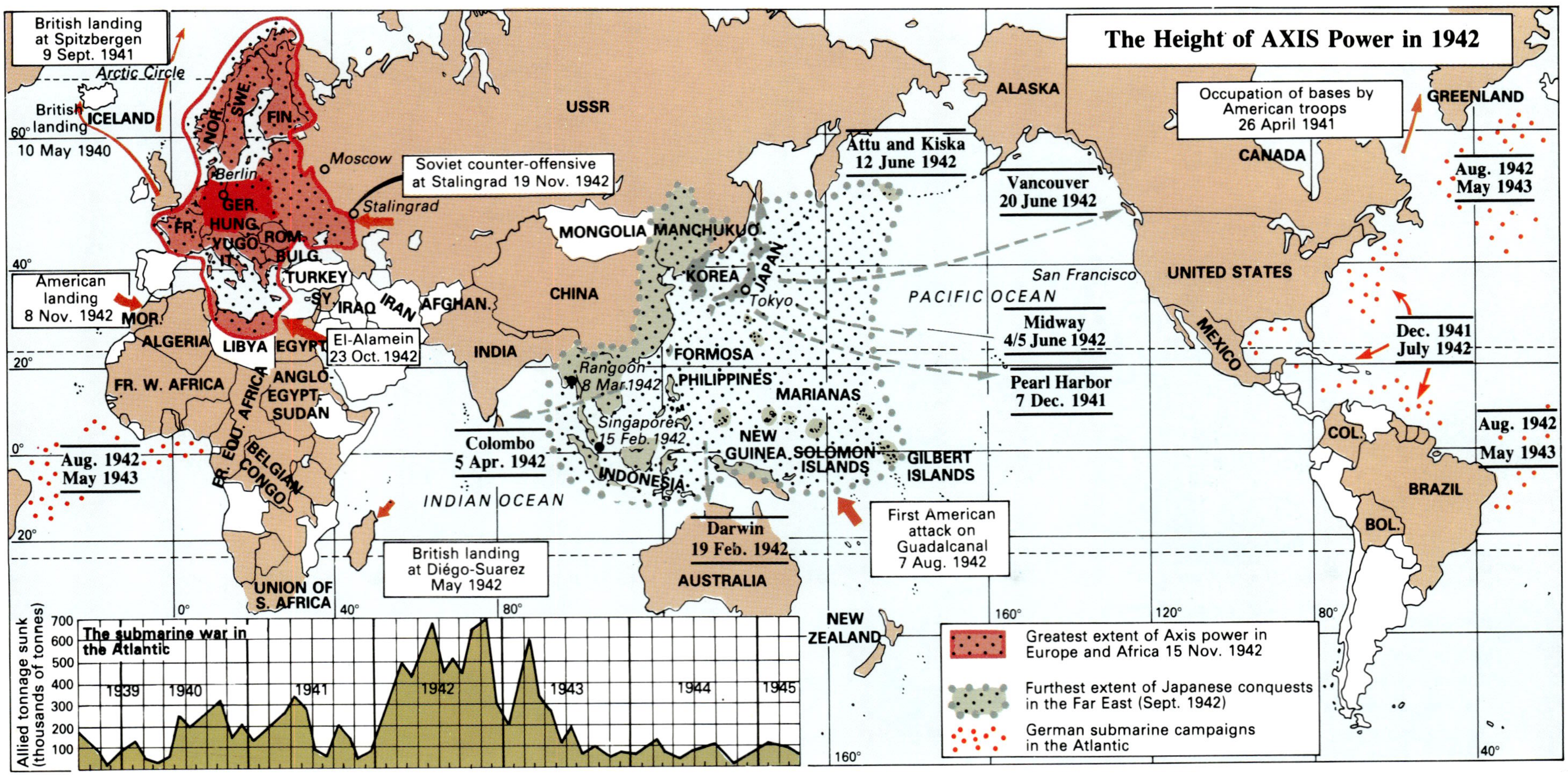

The Japanese Offensive 1941-42

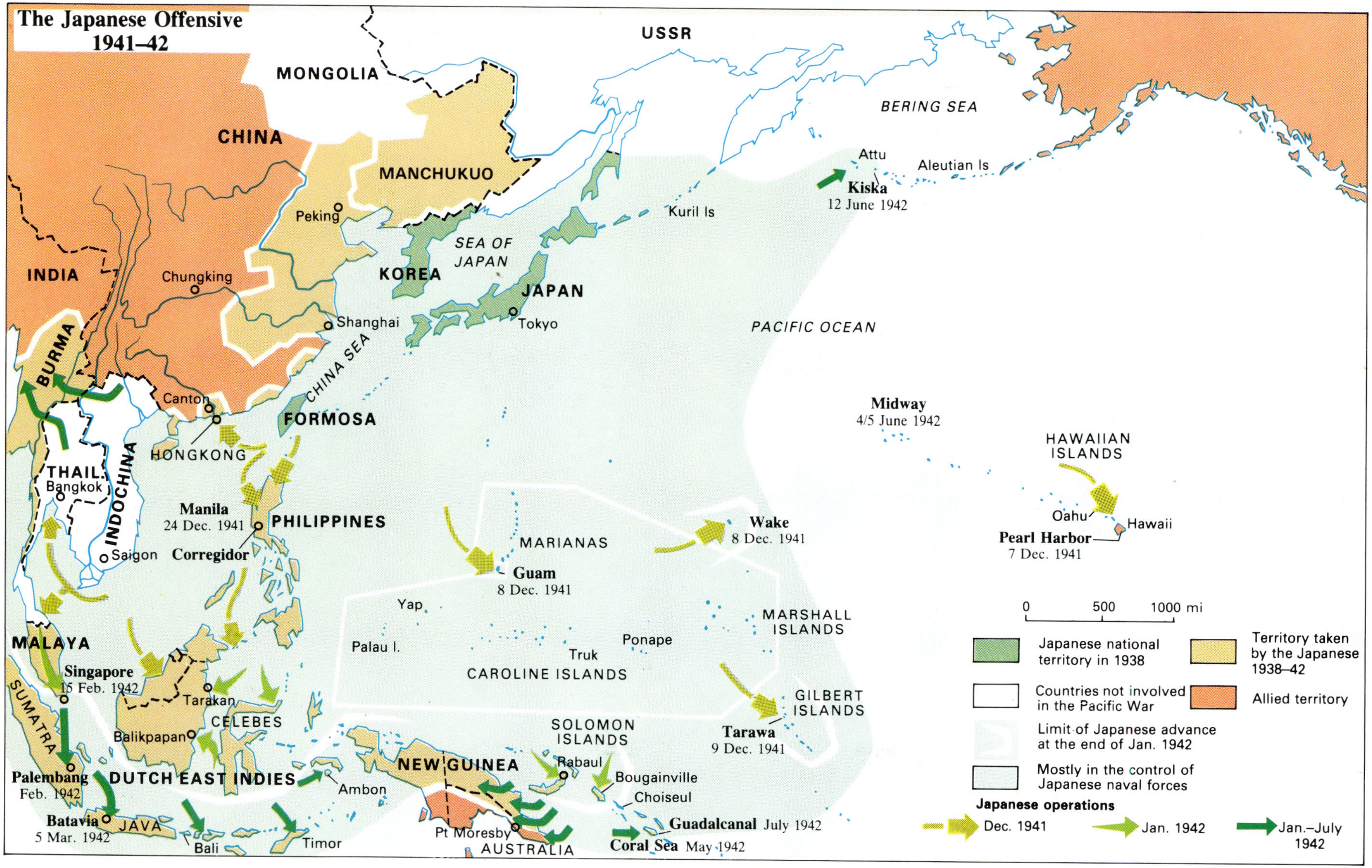

The American Reconquest of the Pacific 1943-45

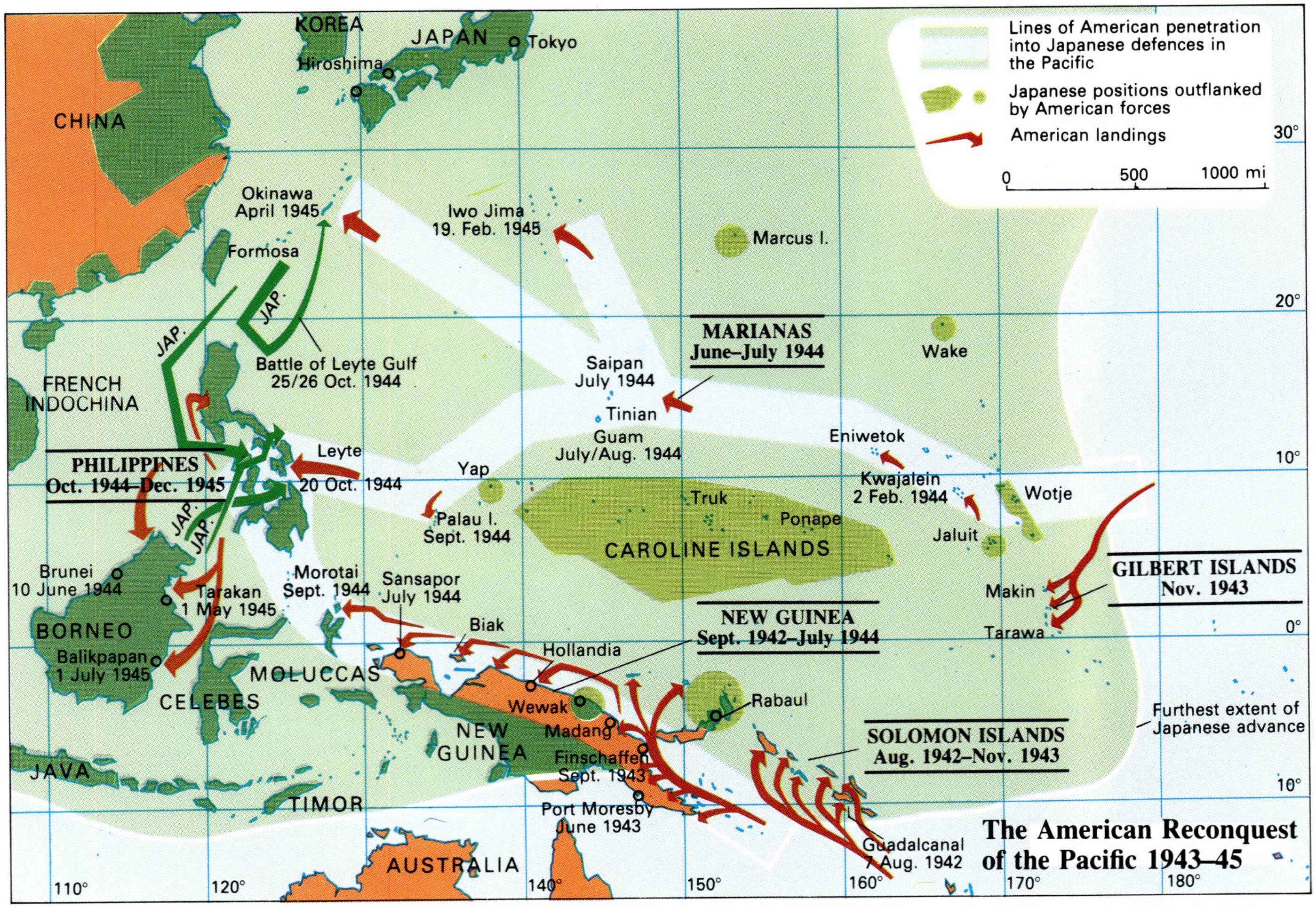

The Liberation of France and Western Europe

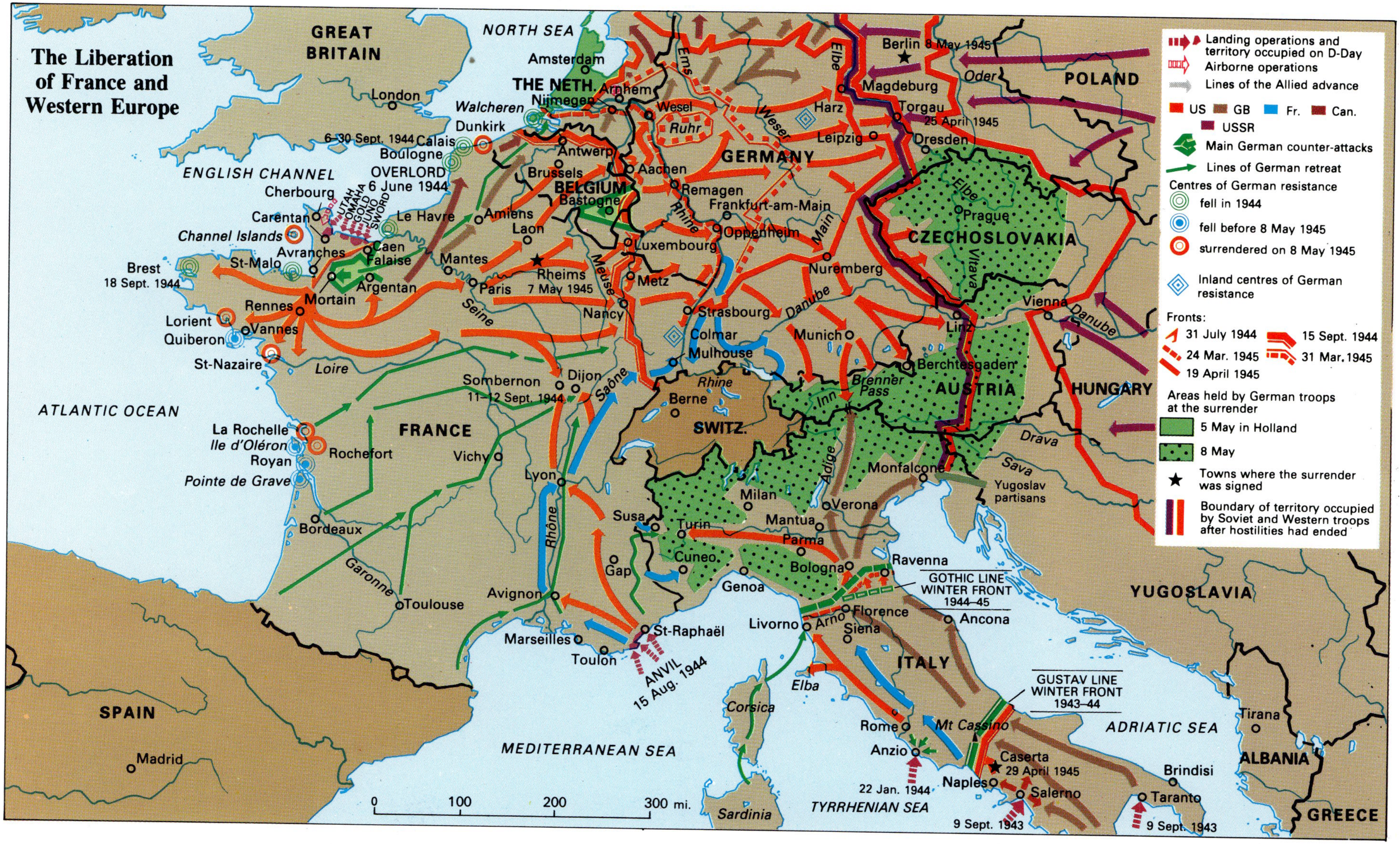

The Liberation of Europe

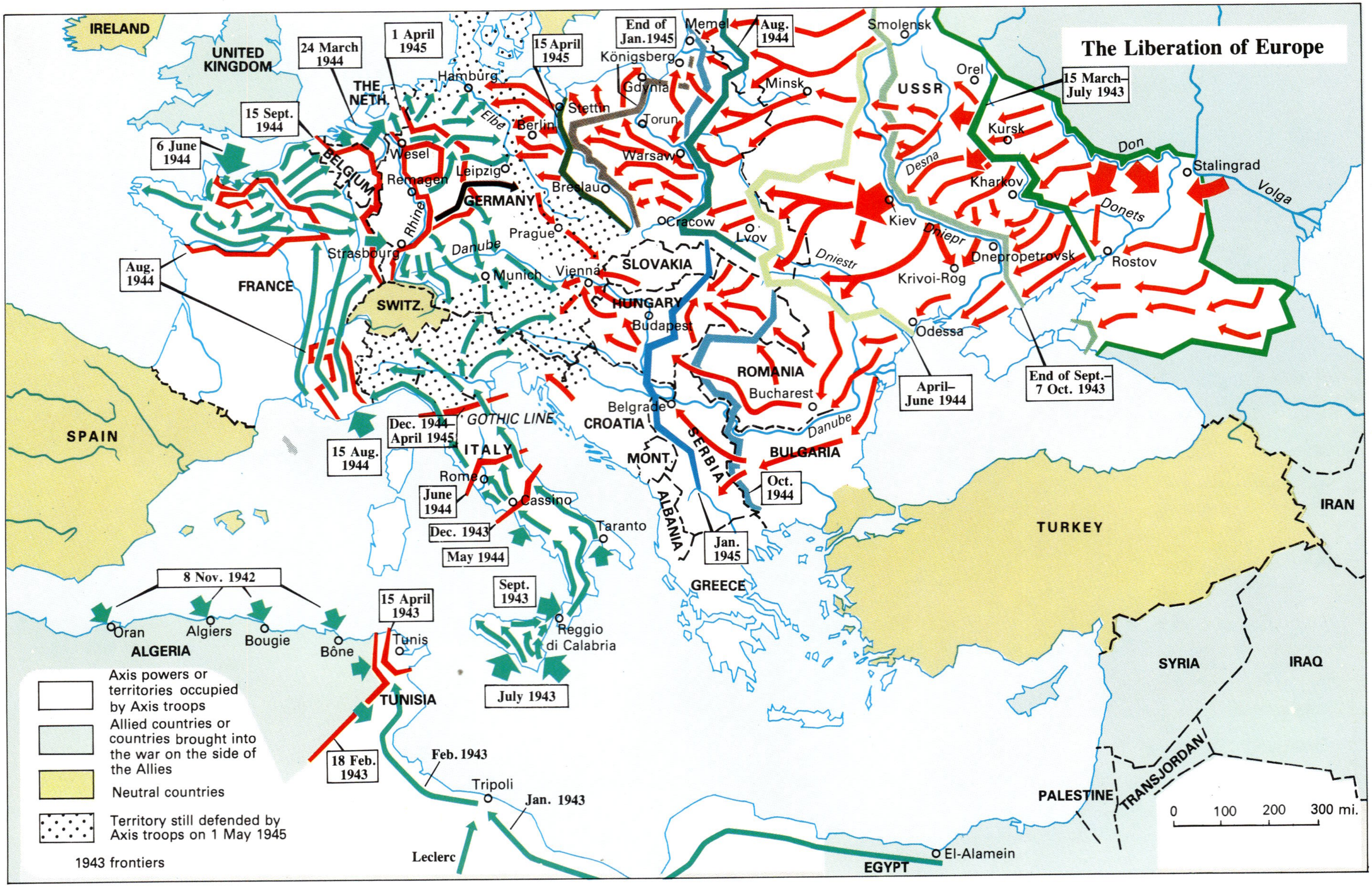

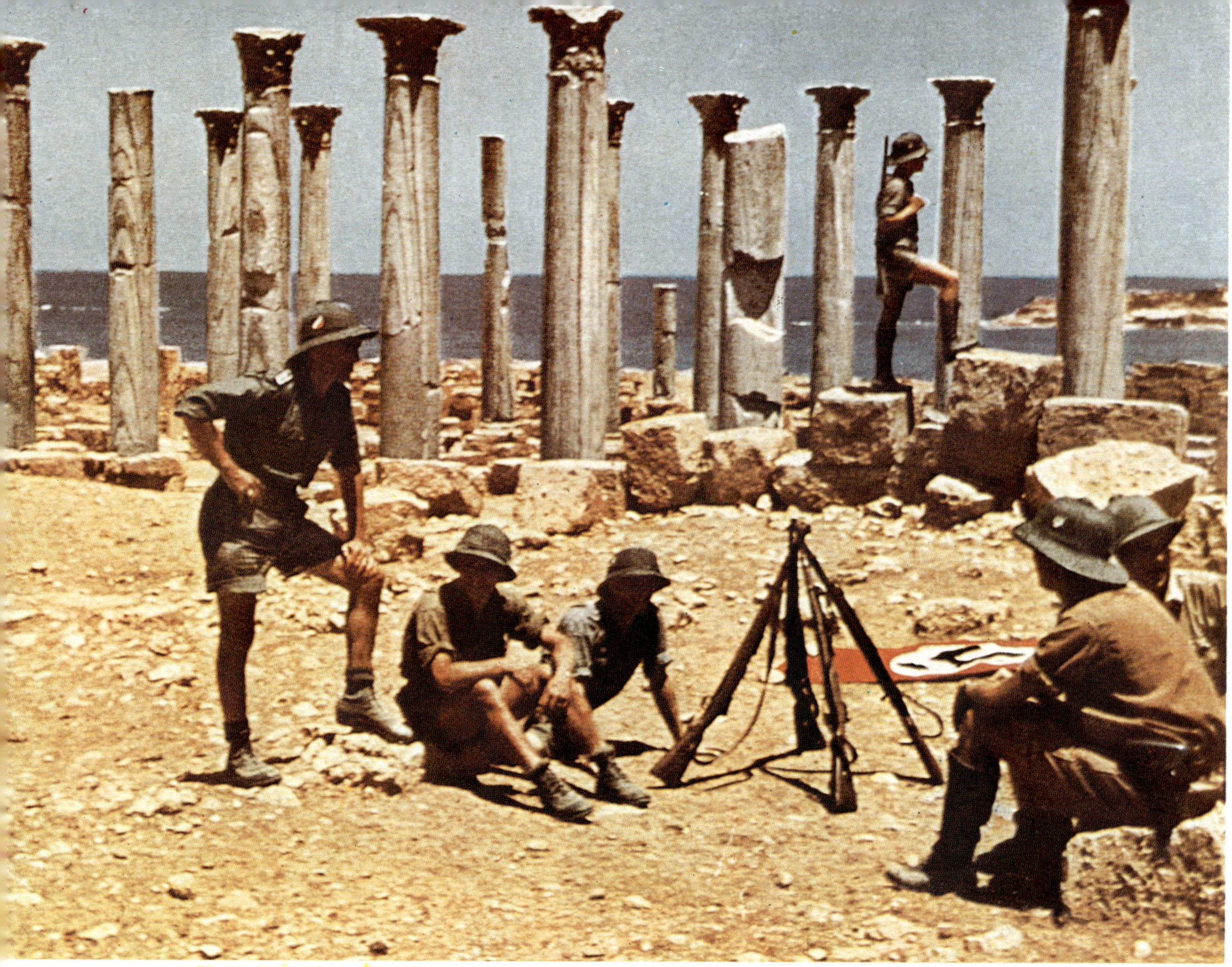

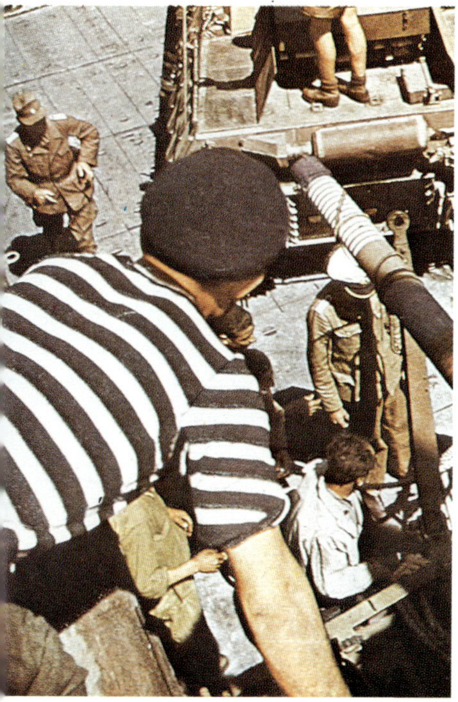

The Afrika Korps. To prevent an Italian collapse in North Africa, Hitler decided to send the Afrika Korps to Libya at the beginning of 1941. Thus, the first elements of the 5th Light Division, an armoured regiment with 150 tanks, disembarked at Tripoli in Feb. 1941. They had had an unhindered sea crossing since the Luftwaffe was bombing Malta very heavily at the time.

Above
A group of soldiers of the Afrika Korps among the ruins of a classical temple in Apollonia in Cyrenaica. The soldiers destined for Libya, whose special equipment for desert warfare included khaki uniforms, pith helmets and cloth boots, had previously undergone special training in the sandy heathlands of Brandenburg.

As soon as they arrived in Africa the two major formations of the Afrika Korps, the 15th and the 21st Panzer divisions, stabilized the situation in Libya, pushing the British back towards the Egyptian border and besieging Tobruk. Rommel, at the head of the Afrika Korps, was to show that the desert was particularly suitable for the conduct of tank warfare. Here a German officer is seen examining British positions through binoculars.

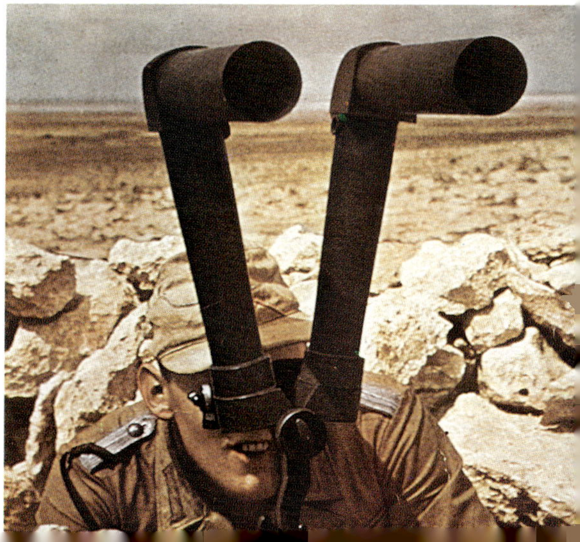

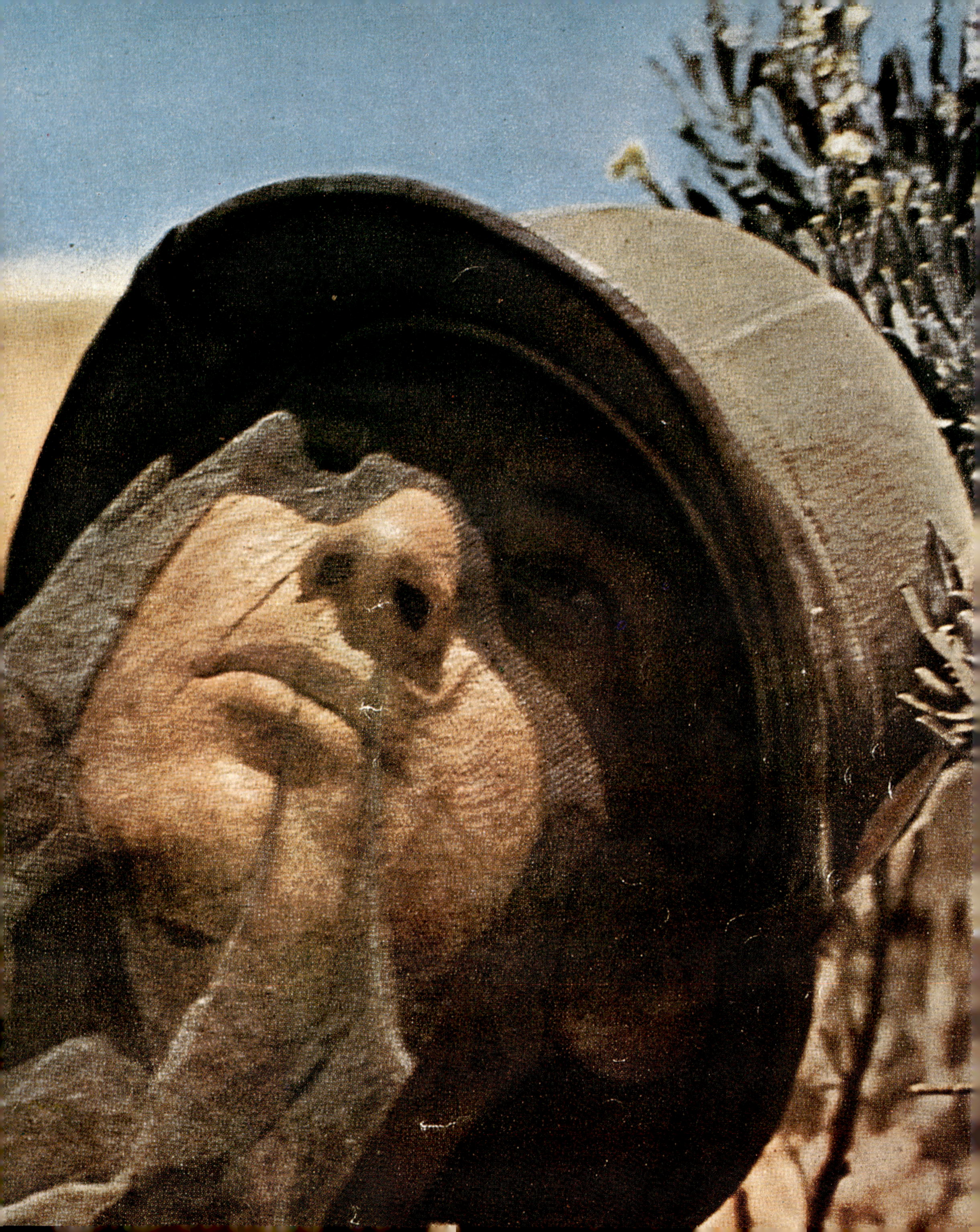

The Afrika Korps. The face of the German soldier in Africa.

Airborne forces. First used by the Germans in 1940 during the offensive in the west and then in the attack on Crete in June 1941, these were immediately copied by the British and the Americans. Here we see a descent from a metal training tower during parachute training in Britain.

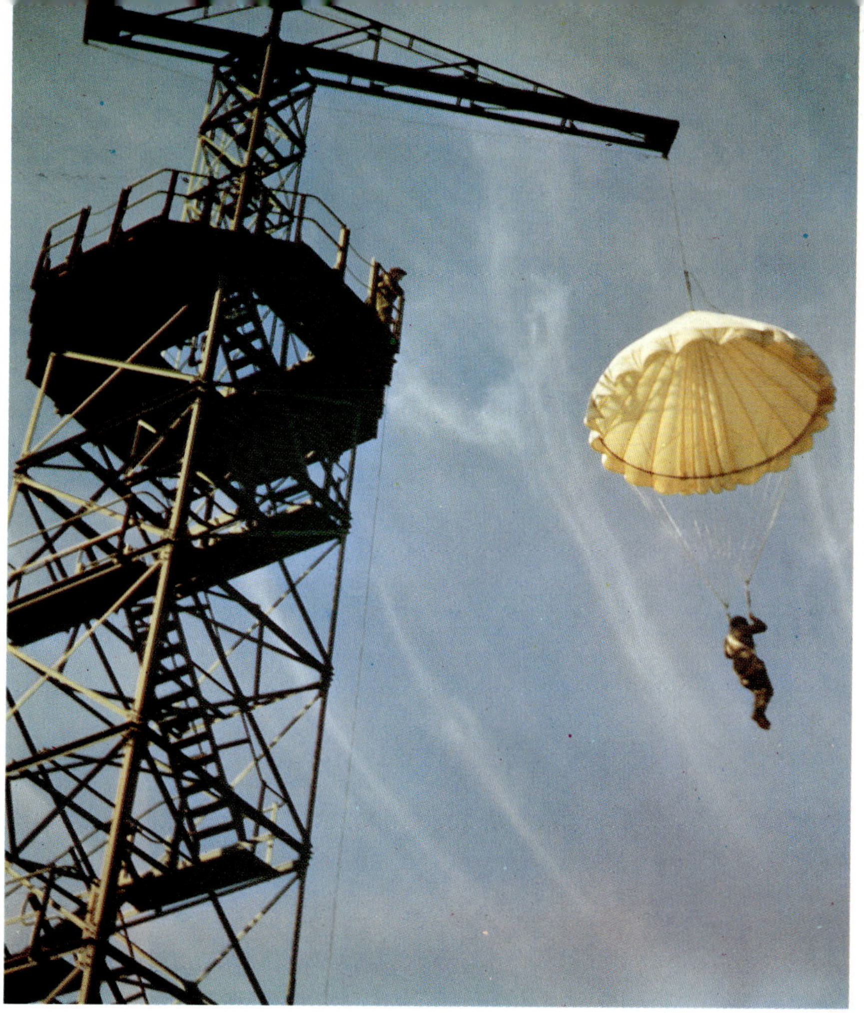

From 1940 onwards the Germans used two kinds of airborne forces – as paratroops and in gliders, and the British took their inspiration from this. In the major landing operations, like Sicily and Normandy, and at Arnhem, they used gliders which had the great advantage of being able to land in a particular place and the capacity to transport heavy weapons, mortars, anti-tank guns and so on.

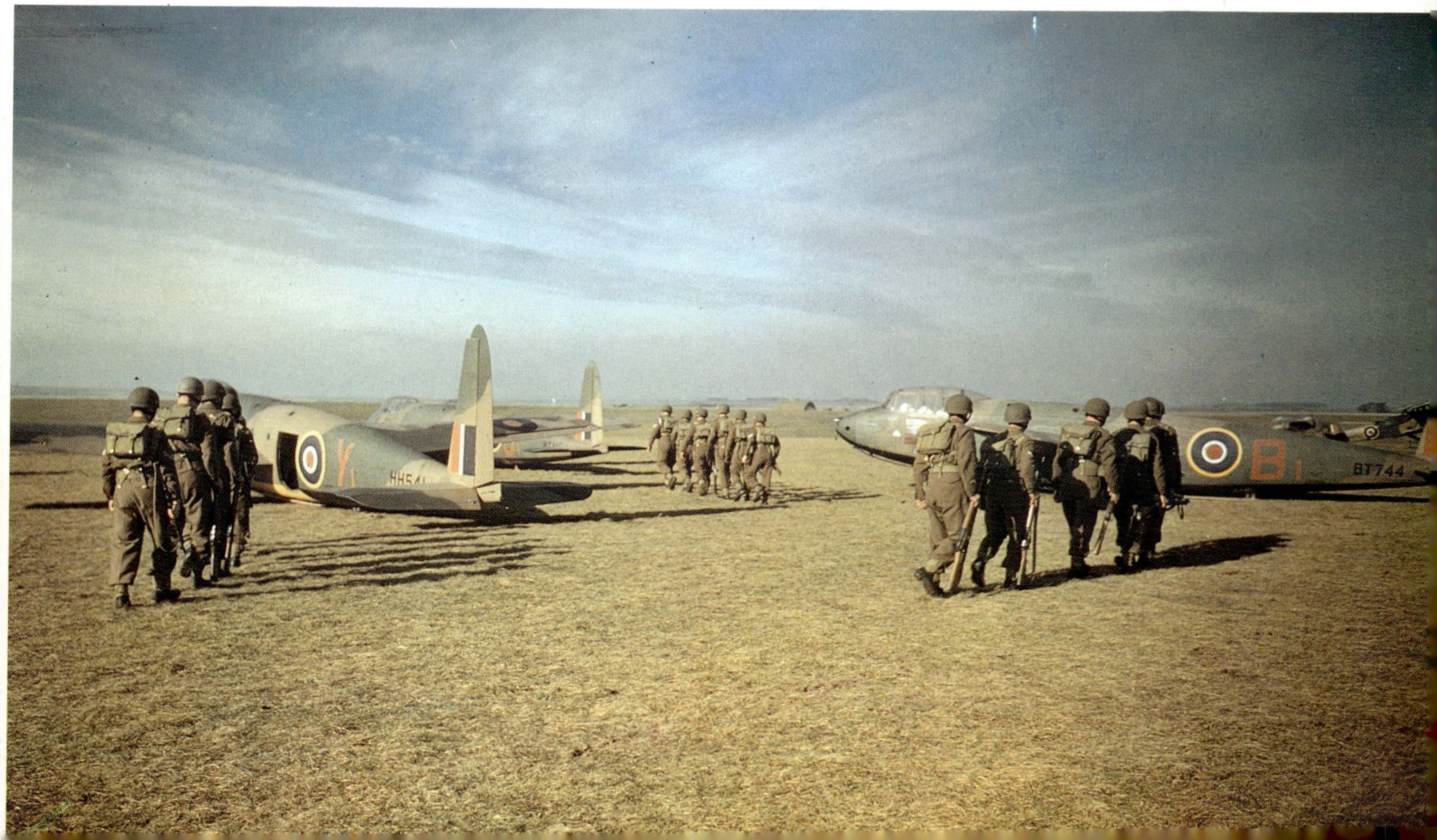

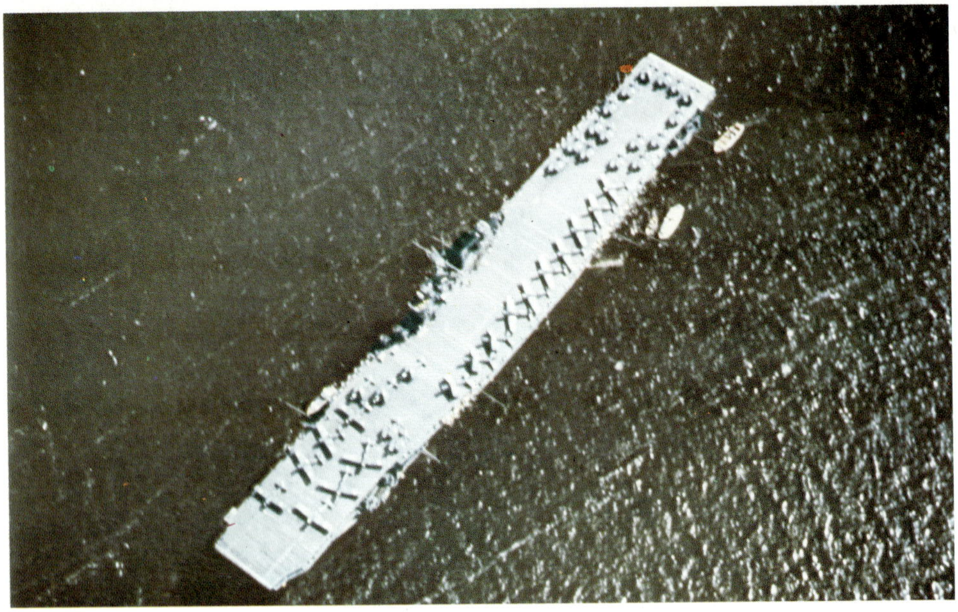

An American aircraft carrier. On the deck are Grumman F4F Wildcat fighters with folding wings.

Left
The Aircraft Carrier. An aerial view of the 27,500-ton American heavy aircraft carrier *Wasp*, belonging to the *Essex* class. During the Second World War aircraft carriers were to play a conspicuous role. In 1939–40 only the really large navies, such as those of Britain, the United States and Japan, possessed aircraft carriers. However, for lack of actual combat experience, they played a subordinate role to the battleship, which remained 'the capital ship' of the battle fleets. The aircraft carrier was basically restricted to reconnaissance missions. In extreme necessity its aircraft might be able to inflict damage on an enemy battleship in order to slow it down sufficiently to bring it within gun range of the heavily armed warships. The battle of Cape Matapan (March 1941) and the destruction of the *Bismarck* (May) bore this out.

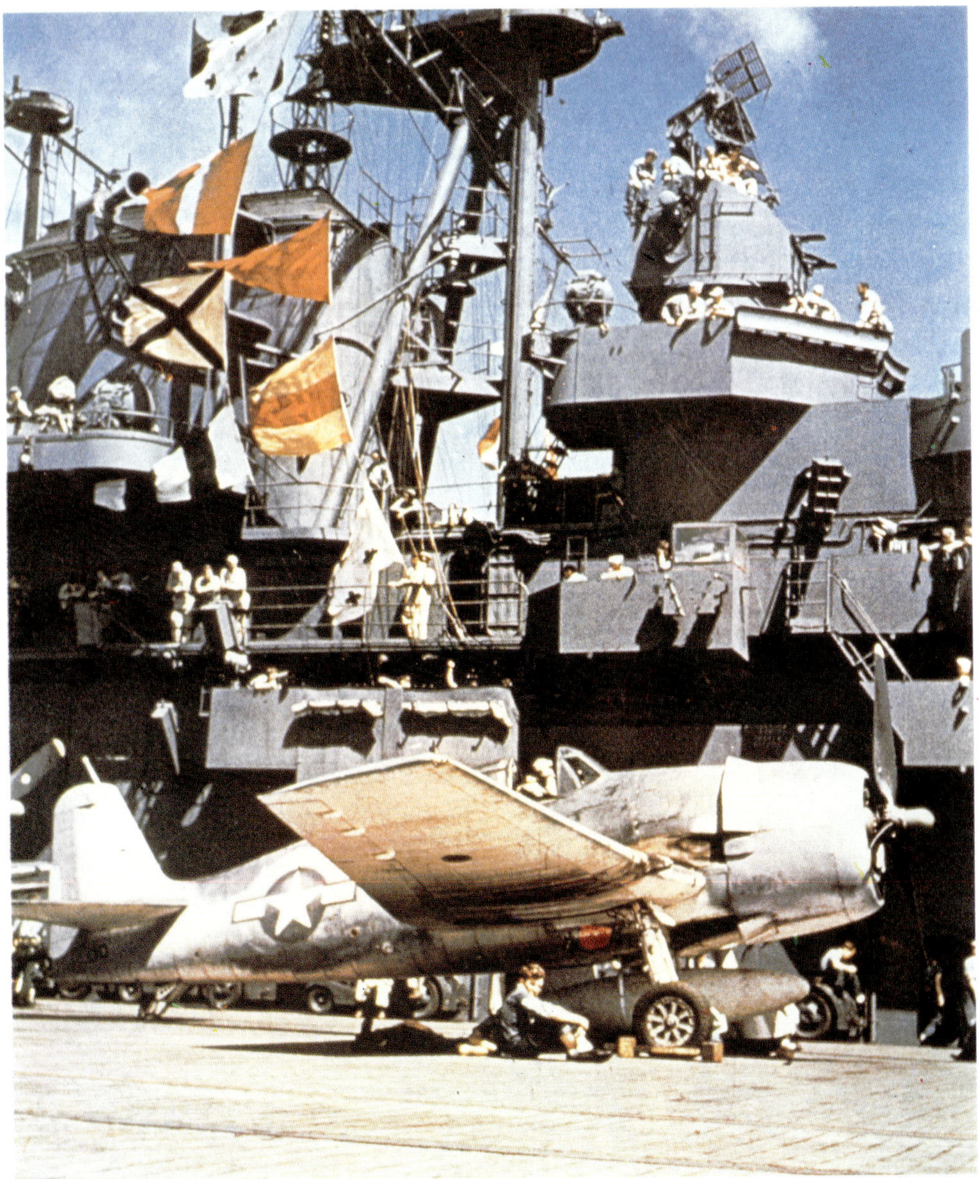

It was not until 1942 and the battles of the Coral Sea and, especially, Midway that it was fully realized how effective the aircraft carrier could be as an attacker and a destroyer over a range of as much as 300 miles (500 km). From that time onwards the aircraft carrier became the spearhead of the battle fleets. At the centre of powerful task forces, it reduced the battleship to a secondary role with a protective function, in collaboration with cruisers and destroyers, which were also responsible for anti-aircraft and anti-submarine defence. In the photograph a Grumman F6F Hellcat fighter-bomber, one of the finest products of the American aircraft industry between 1943 and 1945, is ready for take-off from the deck of an *Essex*-class aircraft carrier.

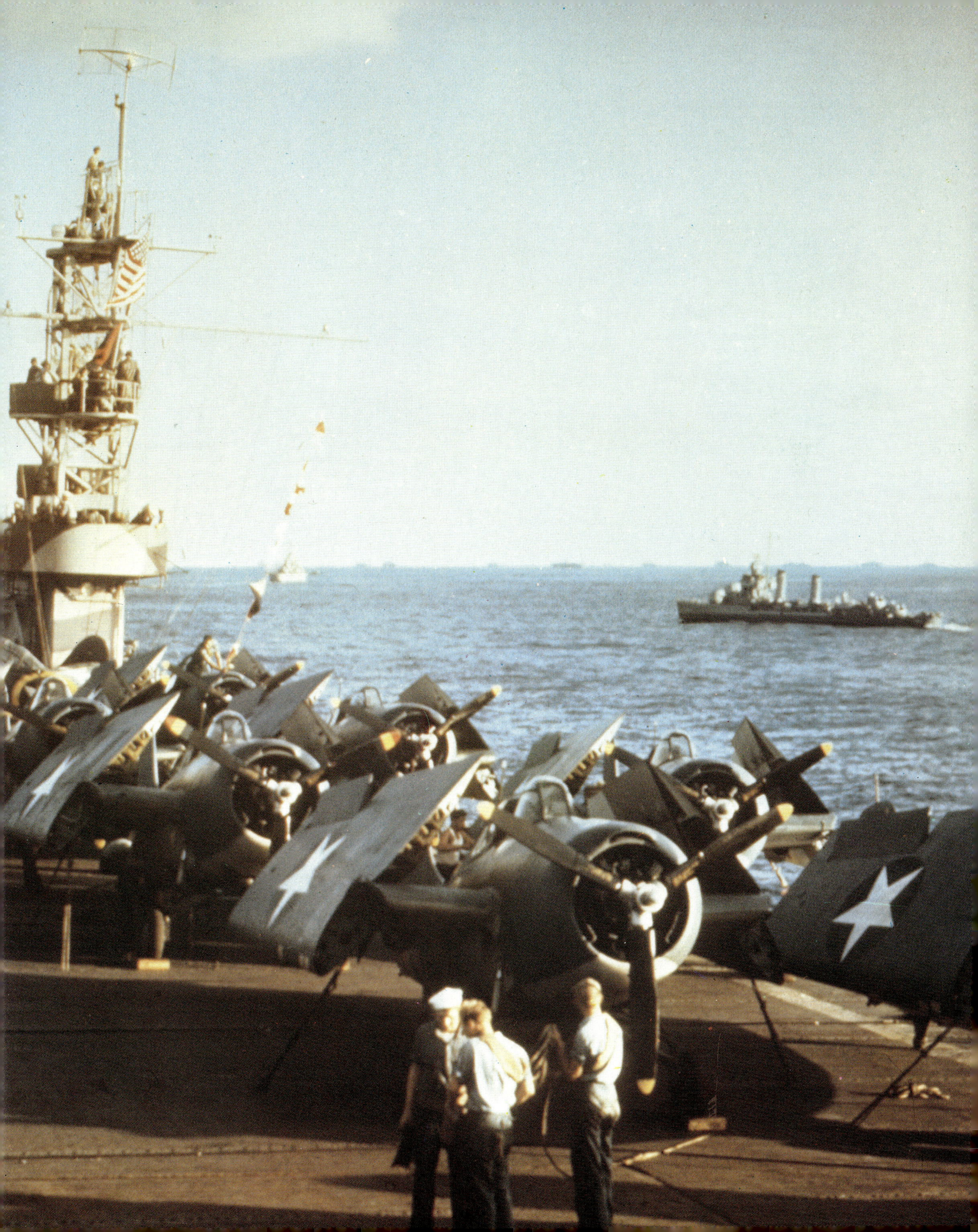

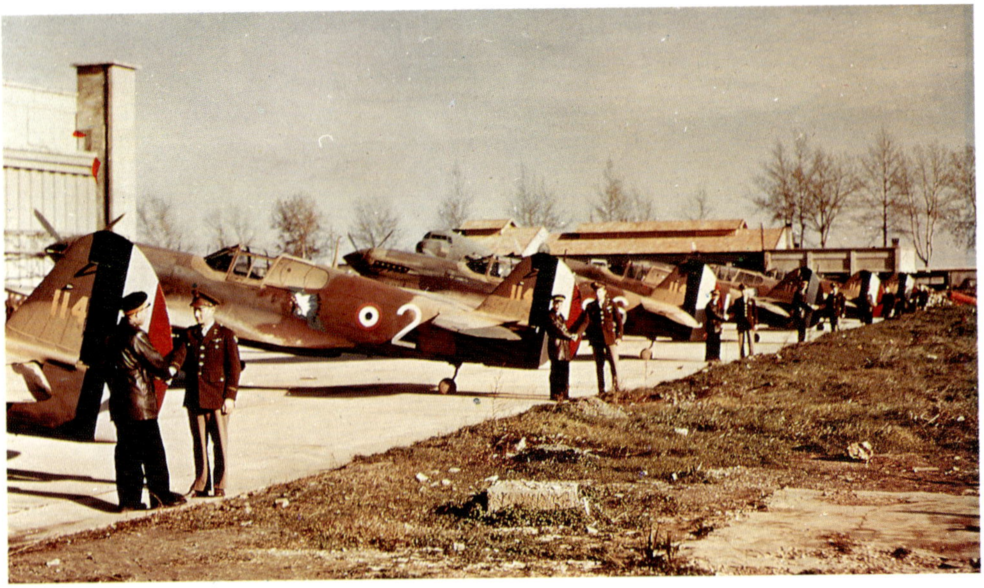

The French Air Force. Following Operation Torch, the Allied landings in North Africa in Nov. 1942, the French Air Force in North Africa rejoined the struggle against the forces of the Axis. However, in view of the age of its aircraft and equipment the Allies refused to use it in Tunisia. At the Casablanca conference they decided on a plan to re-equip it, involving 1000 aircraft, of which 500 were to be fighters and 300 bombers. Here American airmen are seen handing over Curtiss fighters to French pilots at Algiers.

The Italian Air Force. Although he intended to conduct a parallel campaign in the Mediterranean, Mussolini could not resist the temptation of taking part in the Battle of Britain. Thus it was that the Corpo aero-italiano, consisting of 80 BR20 bombers and 50 CR42 and Fiat G50 fighter aircraft, installed itself near Brussels in Oct. 1940. In fact it took part in only ten or so night raids on southeast England. It was recalled as early as Jan. 1941, when the situation in Greece and Libya deteriorated.

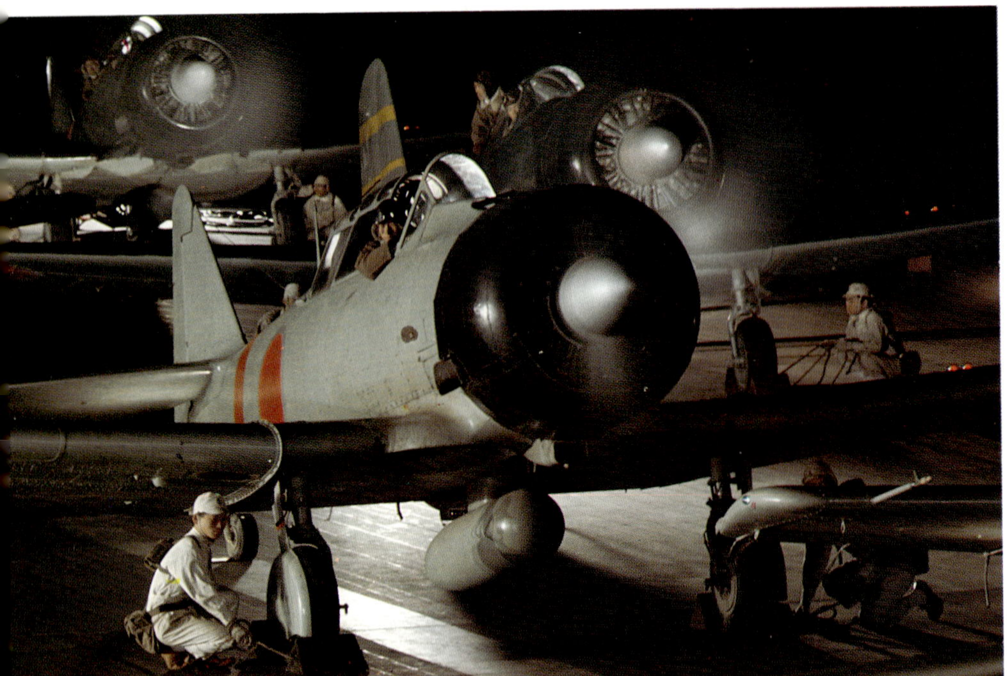

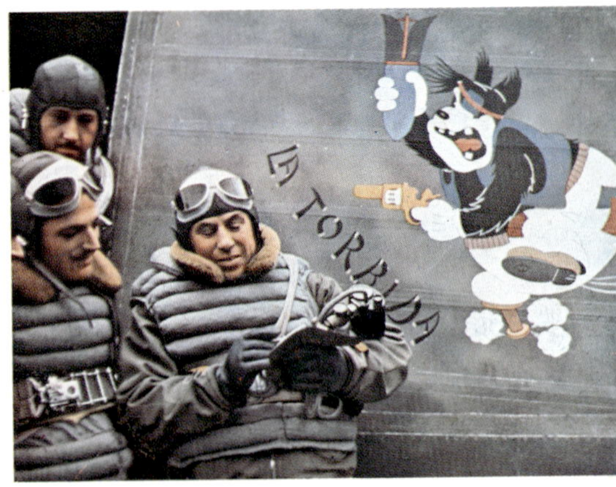

The Japanese Air Force. In Dec. 1941, at the time of the attack on the United States at Pearl Harbor and on southeast Asia, Japan possessed an efficient first-line air force which was experienced in combat. In fact, there were two separate air forces, one attached to the army and the other to the navy. Here a Mitsubishi Zero fighter is seen about to take off from the flight deck of the aircraft carrier *Akagi*. In reality, this aircraft is a scrupulous reconstruction made long after the war in connection with the film *Tora-Tora-Tora* which depicted the Pearl Harbor operation.

The Soviet Air Force. As a result of the surprise of the German attack and the inferior quality of much of its equipment, the Soviet Air Force was seriously put to the test in 1941–42. However, at the end of 1942 there was a recovery, linked with the appearance of excellent aircraft such as the Ilyushin Il-2 Stormovik and the Yakovlev Yak-9. At the time of the Battle of Kursk the Soviet Air Force could stand on equal terms with the Luftwaffe. In this photograph can be seen the wreck of a Soviet fighter which had been seriously damaged by a German fighter and was obliged to make a forced landing in a village during the summer of 1943.

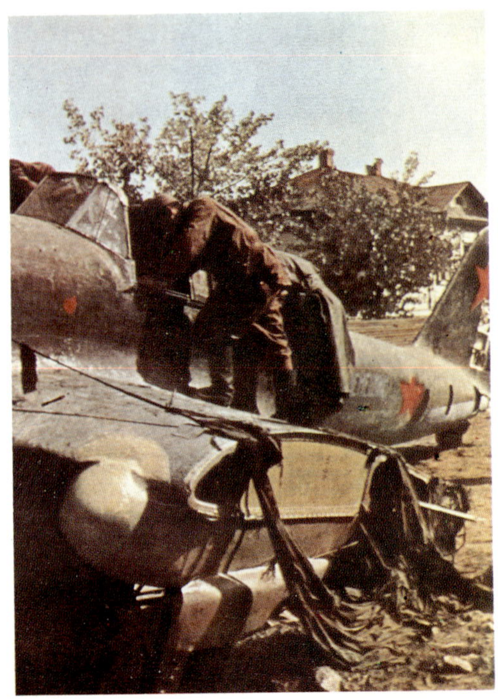

The US Army Air Force. At the time of the attack upon Pearl Harbor in Dec. 1941 the US Army Air Force did not even possess 3000 front-line aircraft. During the subsequent years it was to undergo a remarkable development. At the time of the Japanese surrender it had more than 75,000 aircraft and a total of 2,400,000 men. However, its losses had been heavy: 23,000 aircraft and 122,000 crew members. In this photograph ground crew are preparing to load incendiary bombs on to a medium bomber. Such bombs were to have devastating effects upon German and Japanese towns.

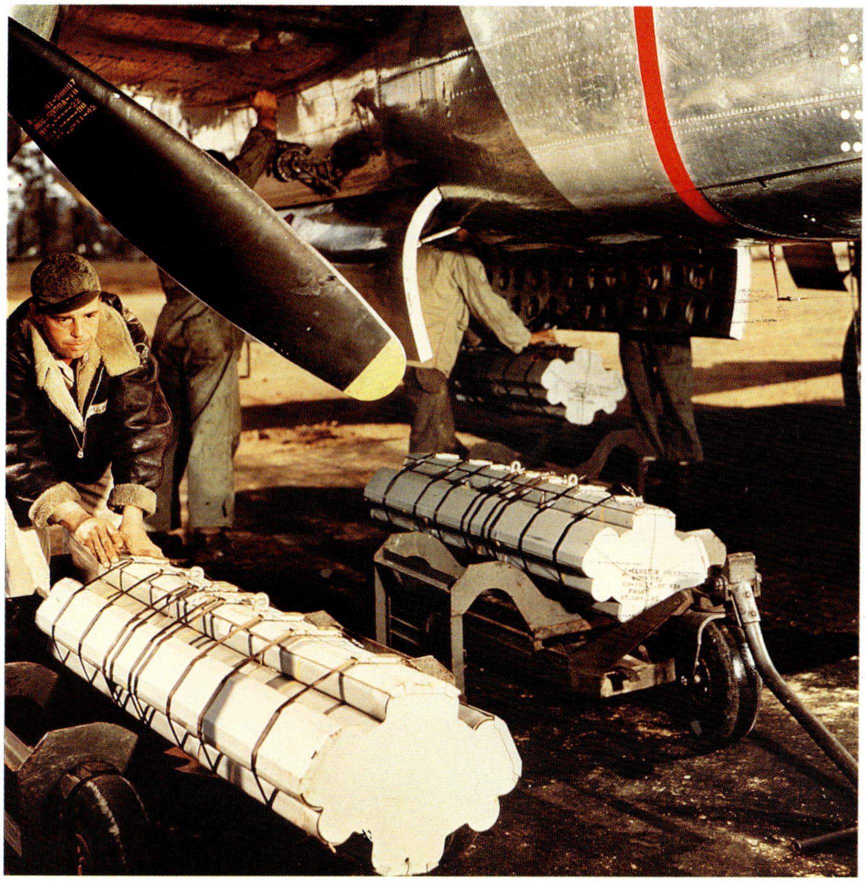

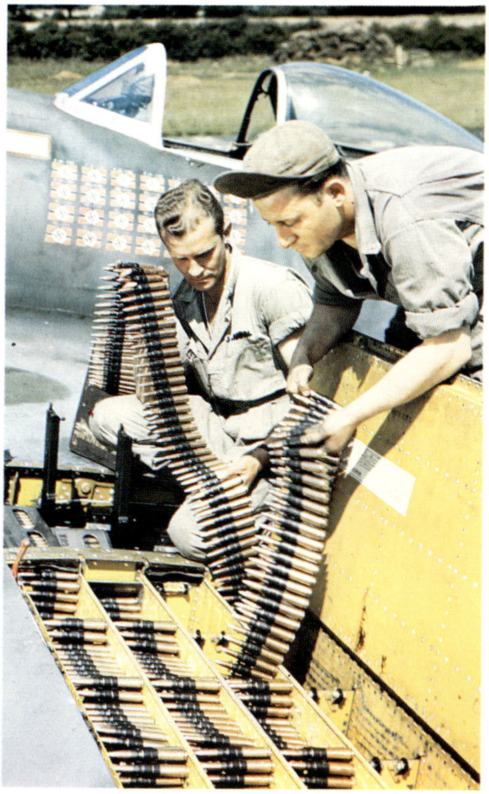

During its astonishing development and despite the remoteness of the United States from the theatres of operations, the US Army Air Force did not in any way stint on the fighter aircraft required for the protection of bombers, for attacking enemy aircraft and for the support of troops on the ground. Here armourers are examining a box containing belts of 12.7 mm cartridges intended for the machine guns of fighter planes. On the fuselage of the aircraft in the background each swastika indicates a victory.

In accordance with the principles laid down just before the start of the conflict, at the time of Pearl Harbor the US air force attached very great importance to strategic bombing carried out by powerful four-engined bombers. Quite apart from the Boeing B-17, known as the 'Flying Fortress', one of the most widely used aircraft was the Consolidated B-24 Liberator. This heavy bomber required, as the photograph shows, a crew of at least nine: pilot and copilot, navigator, bomb-aimer, radio operator, engineer-mechanic and three gunners. Among these crews losses were particularly severe. The raids over Germany alone cost the US strategic bomber force the lives of 70,000 men.

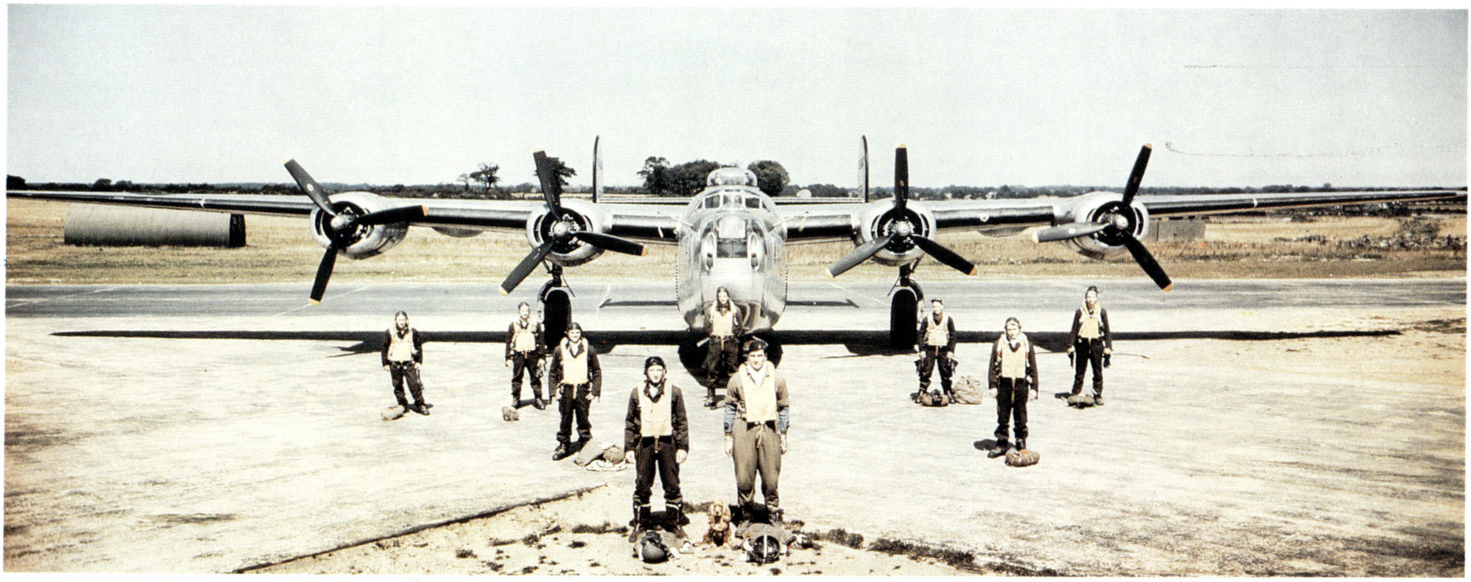

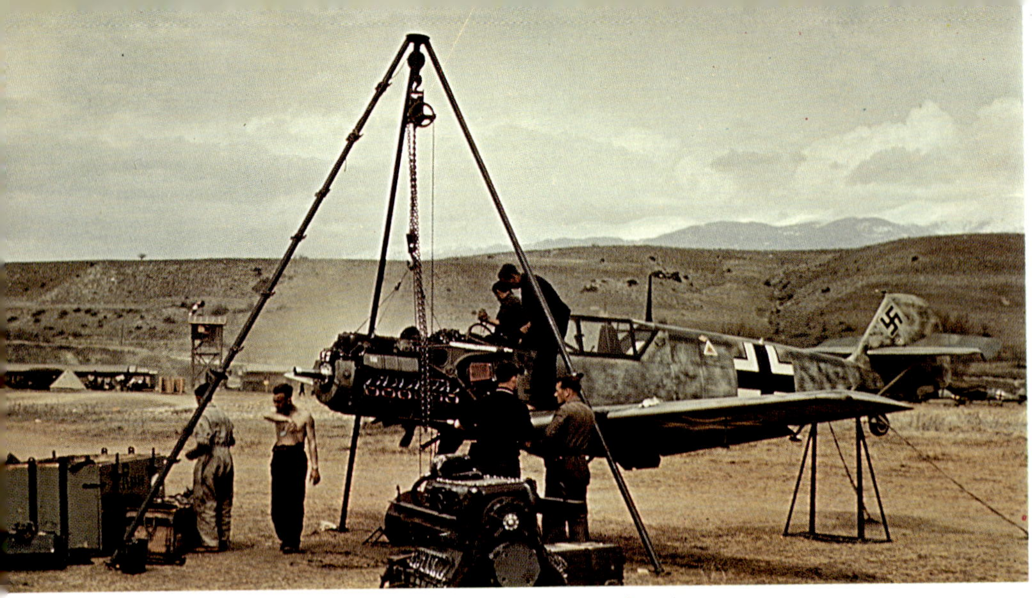

Air warfare: airfields. In the course of the Second World War the maintenance crews of the various air forces had to operate at many latitudes. Here, a group of Luftwaffe ground crew are seen on an airfield in Libya. They are about to change the engine of a Messerschmitt Bf-109 fighter with the aid of a maintenance gantry.

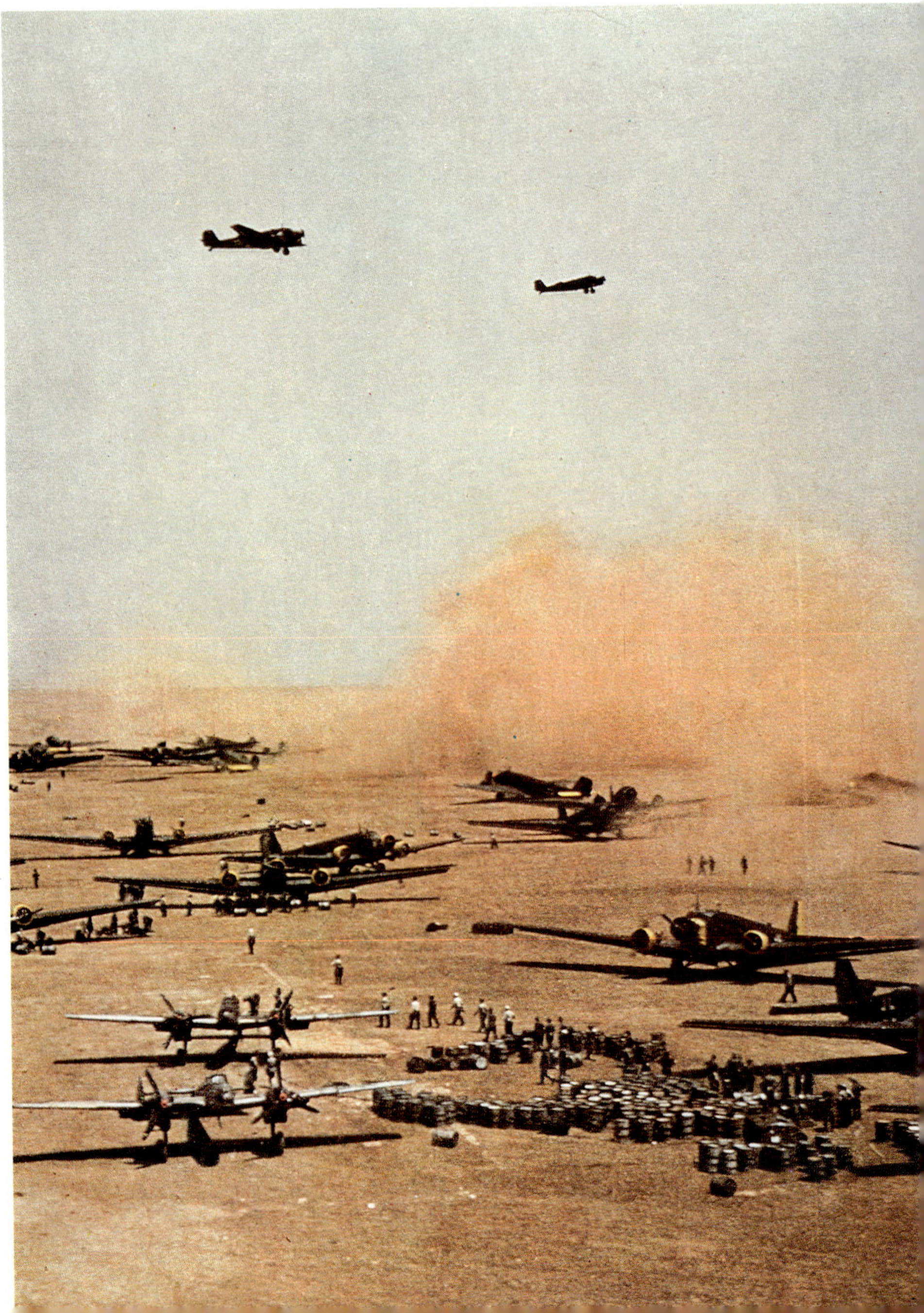

A group of German aircraft assembling on an airfield in the Cyrenaica area of Libya during the summer of 1941. Apart from two Messerschmitt Bf-110 fighter 'destroyers' in the foreground, these planes are mainly Junkers Ju-52s. These three-engined machines, derived from a pre-war commercial aircraft and used for bombing in the Spanish Civil War, became known as the Luftwaffe's 'maid of all work' on all fronts. They were used for dropping parachutists, for the medical service and for transporting reinforcements and supplies. Sturdy and able to use the most rudimentary airfields, the Junkers Ju-52 was handicapped by its slow speed and its lack of armament which made it an easy prey for fighters.

Air warfare: bombers and fighters. German Messerschmitt Bf-110 twin-engined fighters. In the course of the Polish and French campaigns the Bf-110 was used successfully in ground attack missions. However, during the Battle of Britain it was ineffective as a fighter and showed itself to be too slow and lacking in manoeuvrability compared with its British counterparts. Nevertheless, it was later to be used to good effect in night-fighter operations.

Right: A German Junkers Ju-87 or Stuka light bomber releasing its bombs. The Stuka (*Sturzkampfflugzeug* = dive bomber) was the famous bomber aircraft used in Spain and during the campaigns of 1939–40. It was the principal instrument of the German victories of the Blitzkrieg, in which, operating in conjunction with tanks, it made plain the decisive role of tactical air power. The action of the Stukas was rendered even more terrifying by the use of sirens which sounded as they dived. On the Russian front the 'Stuka' was a formidable tank destroyer.

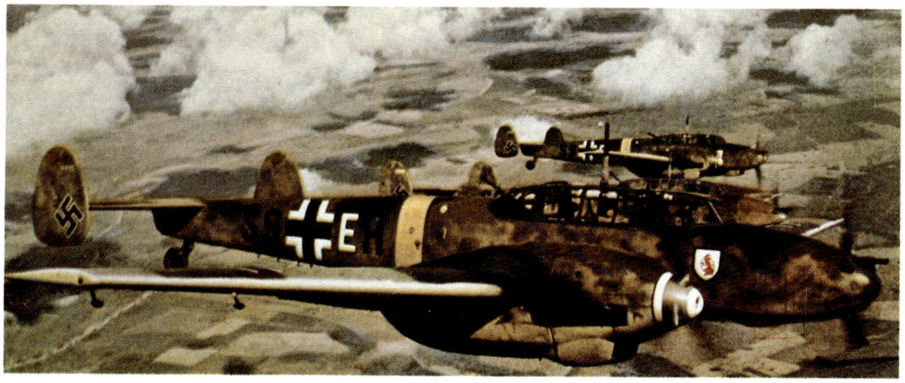

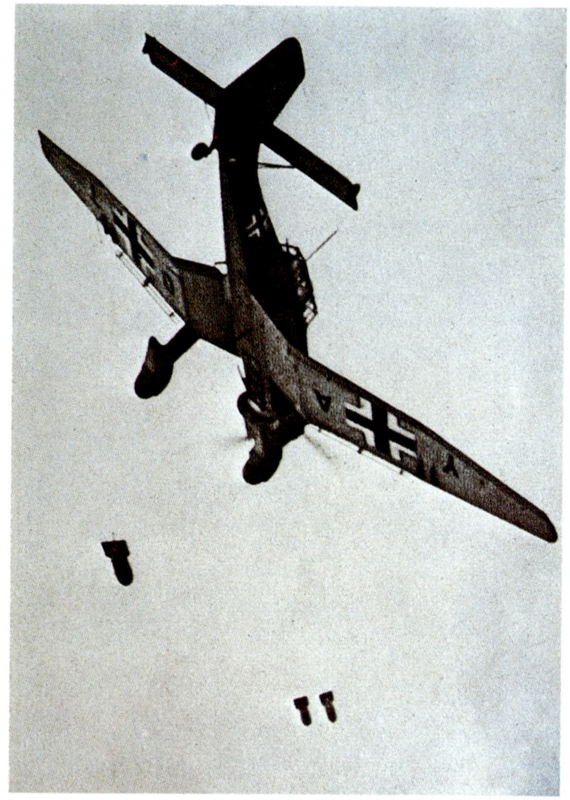

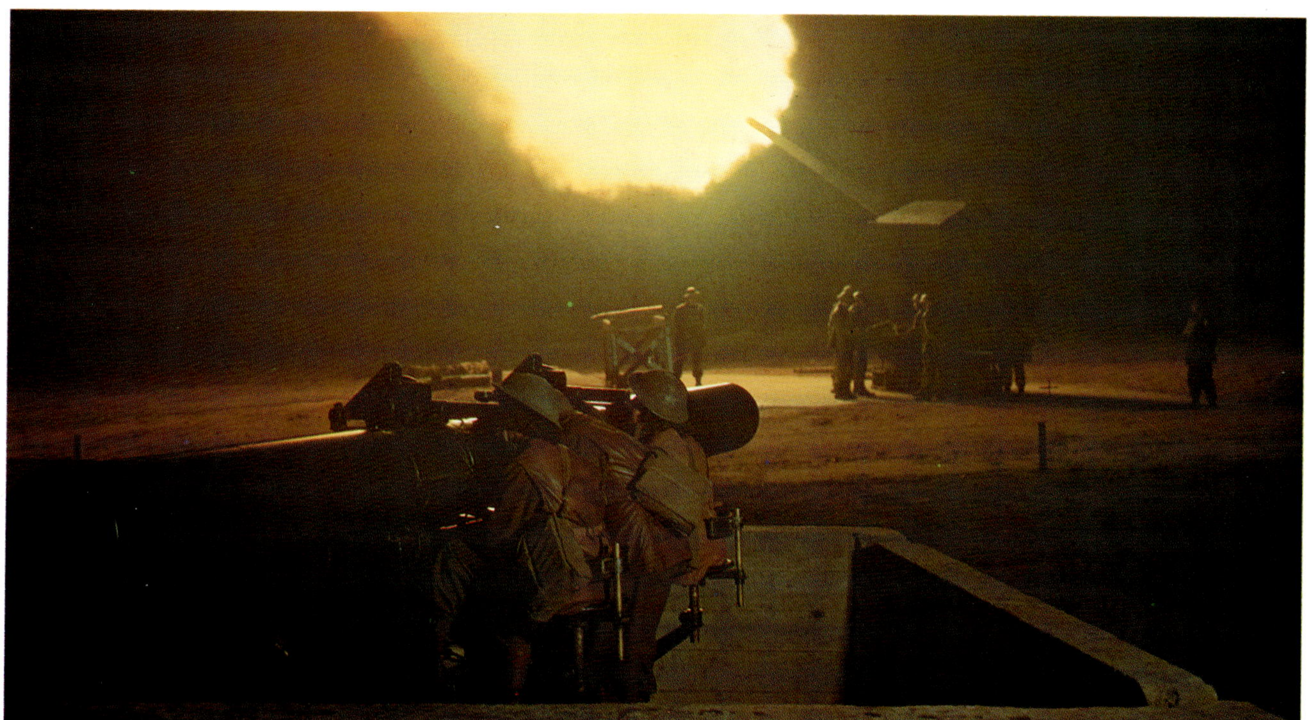

Air warfare: anti-aircraft defence. A British coastal anti-aircraft battery in a naval turret in action at night during 1944. In the foreground is the range-finder which indicates the distance of the target.

Opposite
A squadron of German Junkers Ju-87 Stuka ground–attack aircraft.

Air warfare: bombers and fighters. *Right*: British Lancaster heavy bombers. The Lancaster was the most famous and the most successful of the RAF's heavy bombers. From 1942 to 1945 it was used intensively in strategic bombing operations against Germany. *Below*: A German airfield with Stukas being armed. The ugly lines of the aircraft are emphasized even more by the shark's mouth decoration. The bombs were brought on special trolleys which lifted them into place on the bomb racks fixed under the fuselage behind the radiator cowling. This rack was swung forward when the bomb was released, enabling the bomb to fall clear of the propeller. The Ju-87B series Stuka, which was used in Poland and France in 1939–40, could carry one 1100 lb (500 kg) bomb under the fuselage or one 550 lb (250 kg) bomb under the fuselage and four 110 lb bombs under the wings.

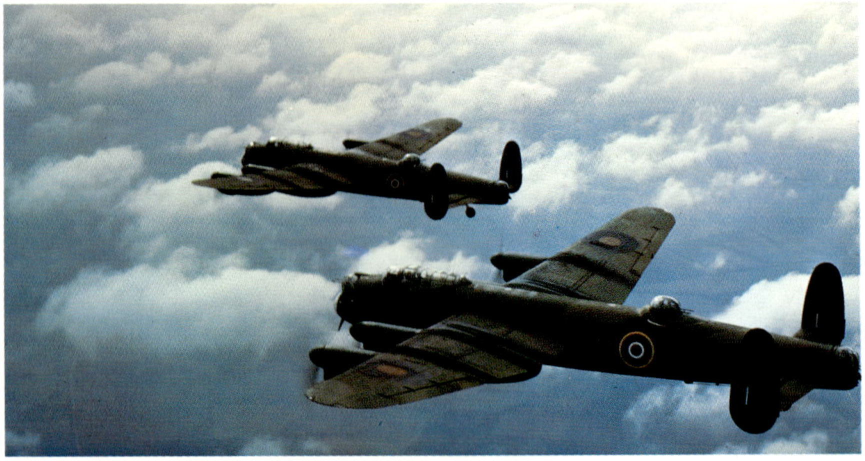

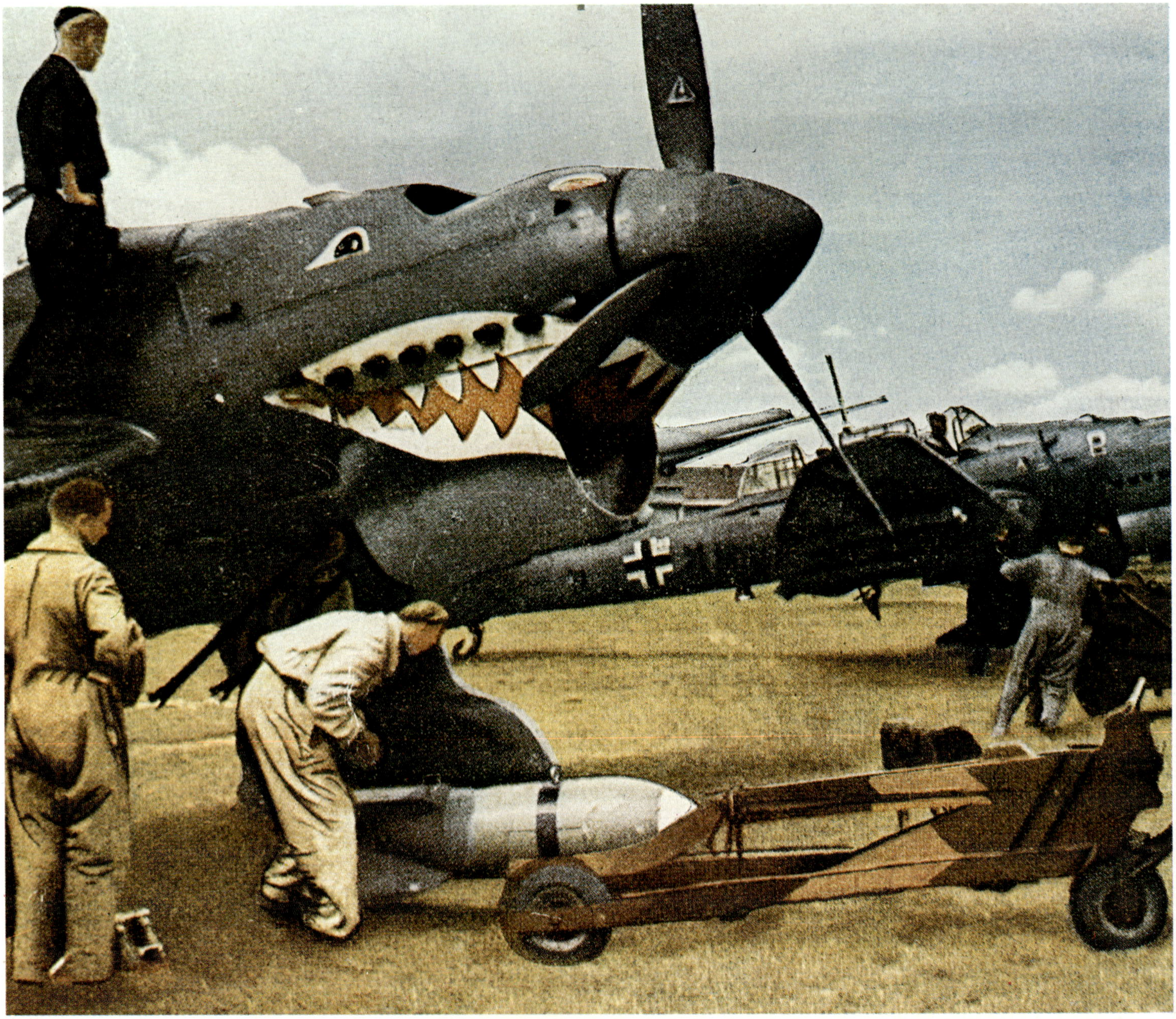

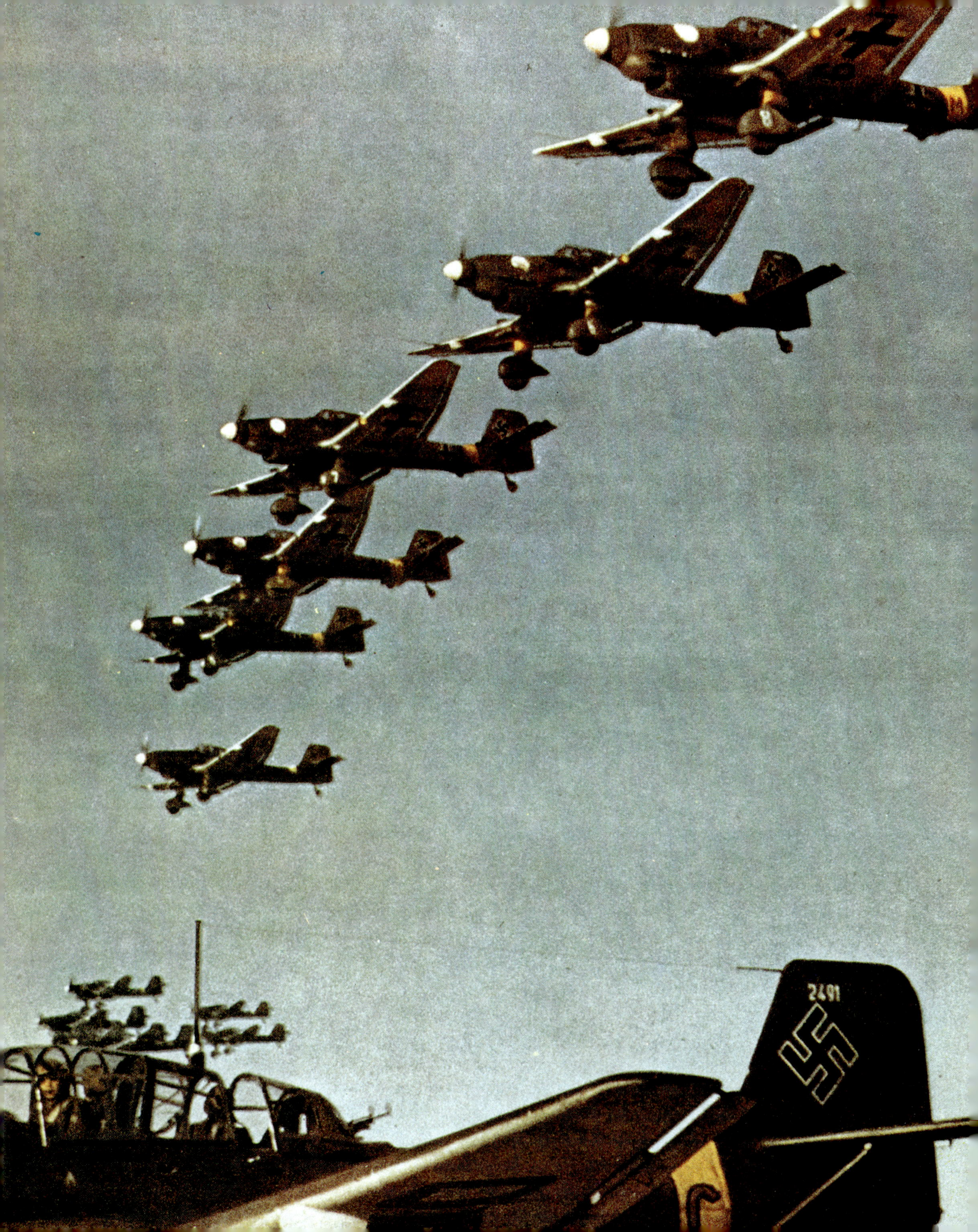
2491

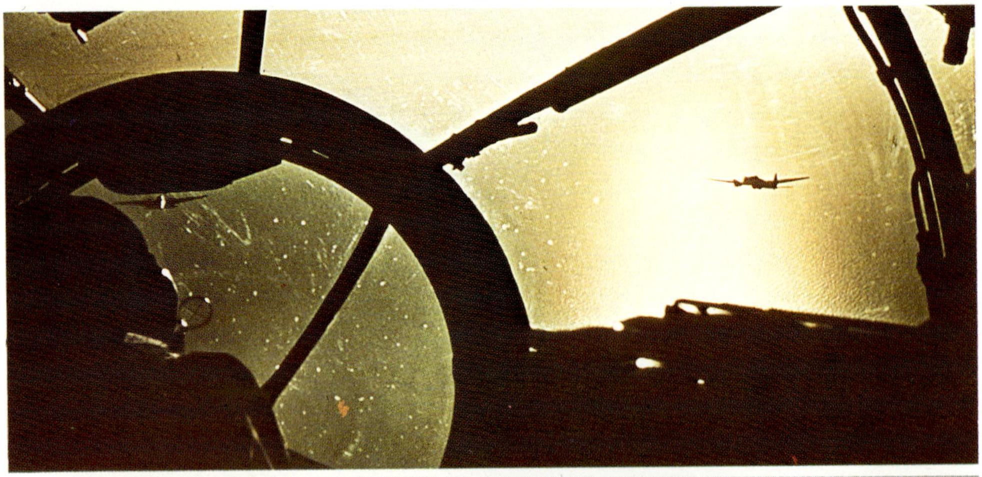

An aircraft seen from the pilot's seat of a Heinkel He-111, looking through the glass nose. Tried out during the war in Spain, the Heinkel He-111 was one of the Luftwaffe's best tactical bombers during the campaigns in Poland and France. However, the weakness of its defensive armament was responsible for serious losses during the Battle of Britain. Weighing 18,700 lb (8500 kg), the Heinkel He 111 could carry two tons of bombs at 270 mph (435 km/h). More than 5000 were built from 1934 to 1944, in several versions – bombers, torpedo-carrying and reconnaissance.

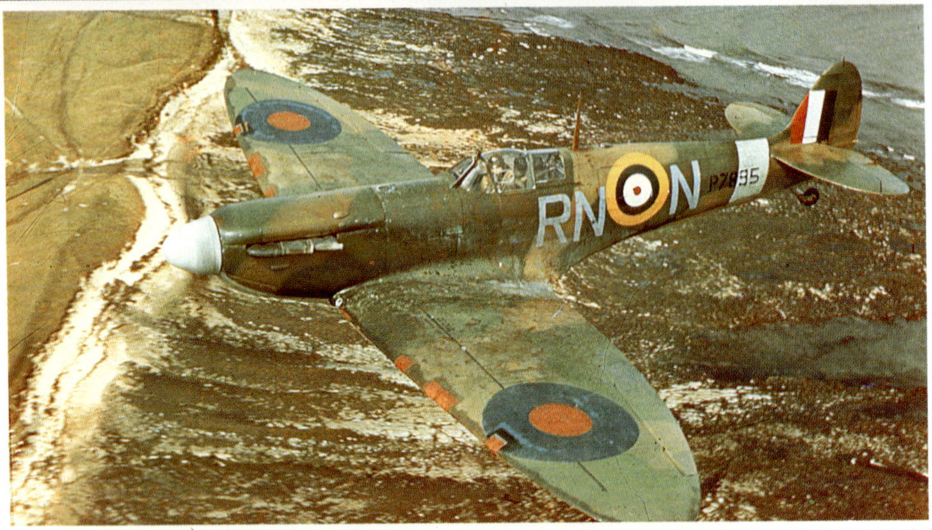

Armed with eight machine-guns and able to reach 360 mph (580 km/h), the Supermarine Spitfire, in action at Dunkirk and during the Battle of Britain where it successfully countered German fighters, was one of the most famous British aircraft of the Second World War. Nearly 25,000 were built between 1937 and 1947. The Spitfire, to which improvements were continually being made, was used as a fighter, a fighter-bomber and a reconnaissance aircraft. Quite apart from the RAF and Commonwealth countries, it was used to equip the US Army Air Force, and the Soviet, Egyptian, Portuguese and Turkish air forces. A naval version, the Seafire, entered service in 1941. One of them is seen here over the French coast.

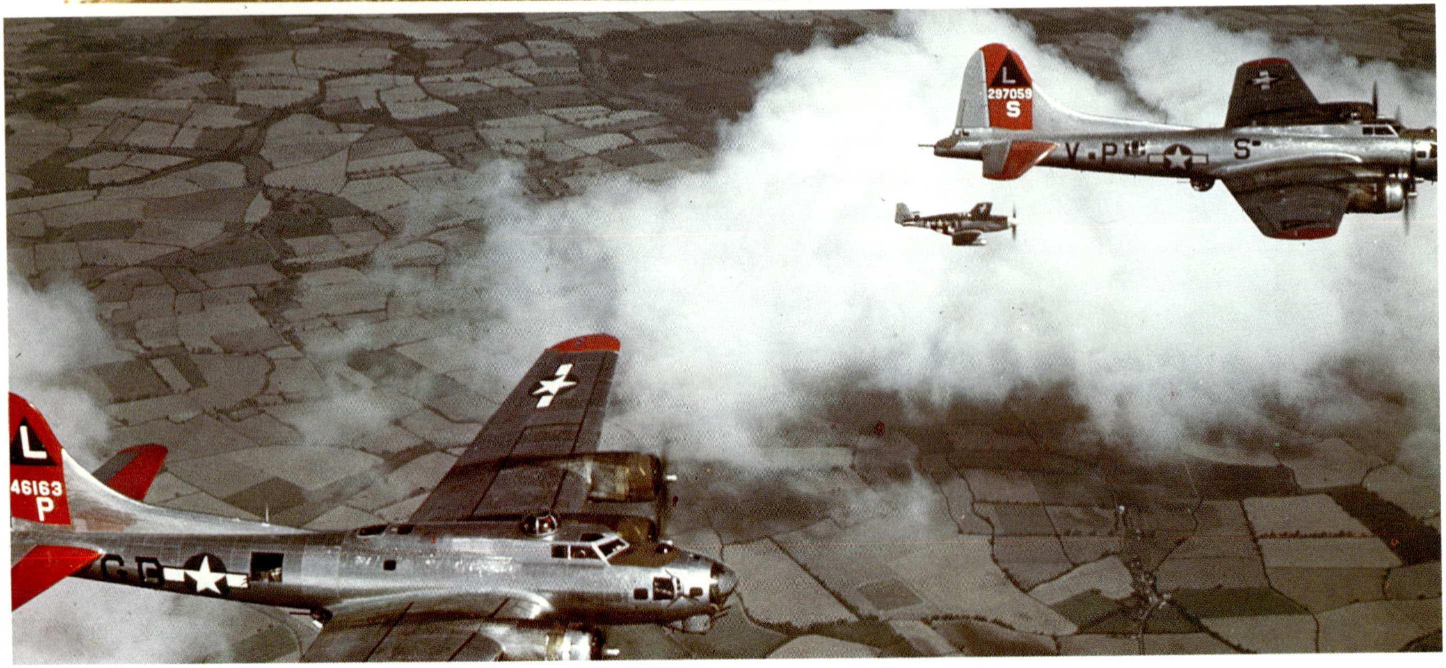

From the summer of 1942 American Boeing B-17s were, together with the Liberators, the constituent element of the US Army Air Force's formations of strategic bombers operating over Europe. Equipped with an impressive defensive armament, these aircraft carried out destructive raids on industrial centres, but suffered heavy losses from anti-aircraft defences and German fighters. For this reason they had to undergo various modifications and were unable to be completely effective until they were accompanied by Mustang escort fighters, equipped with extra fuel tanks for long-range flying. A Mustang can be seen in the background of this photograph.

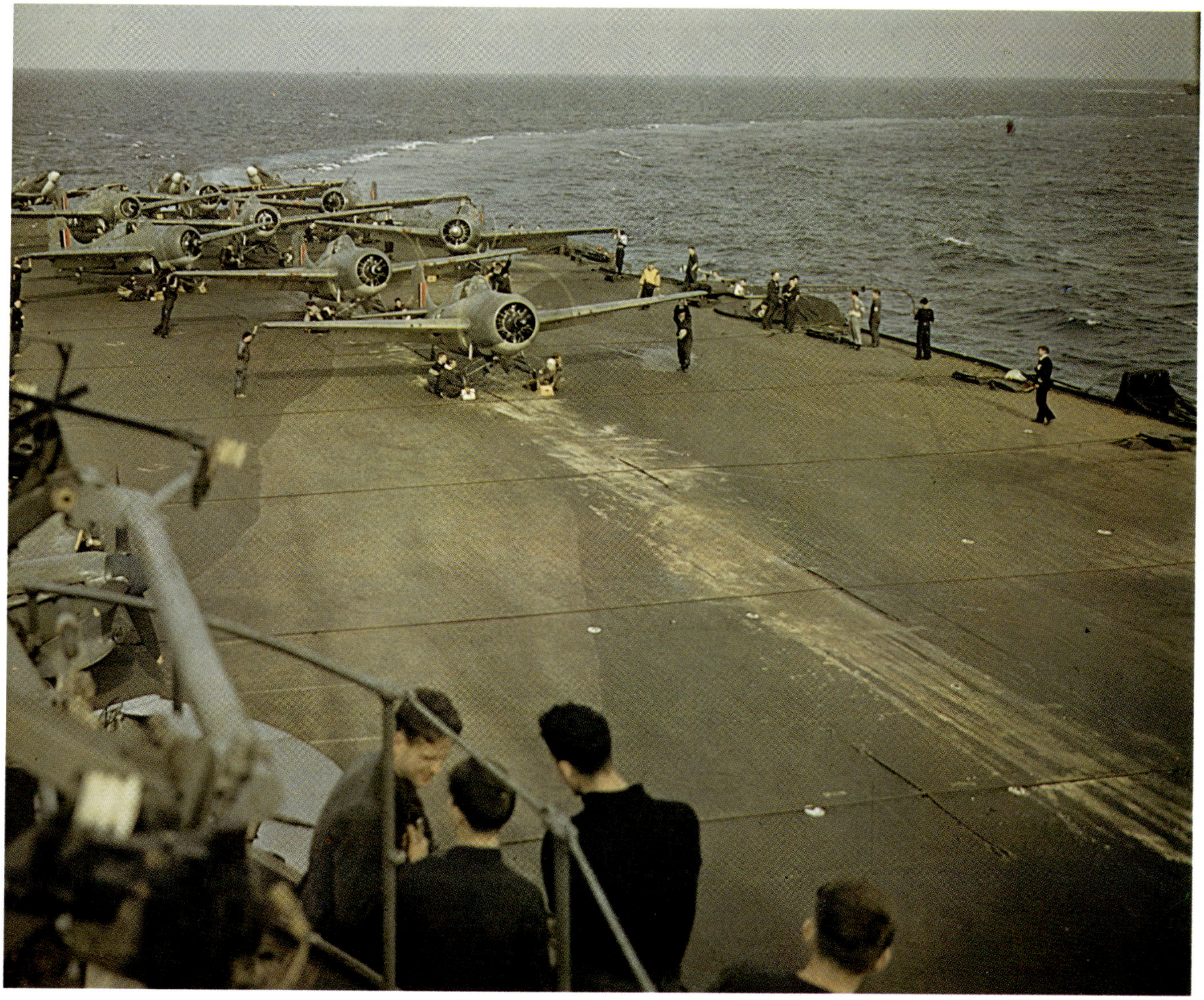

Air warfare: naval aircraft. *Above*: The flight deck of a British *Illustrious*-class aircraft carrier off Tunisia in 1942. Several of the aircraft are American-built Grumman F4F Wildcats. A number of these planes, supplied by the United States under the lend-lease agreement, saw service with the British forces with the designation of Martlet-11. *Right*: The US aircraft carrier *Enterprise*, nicknamed by naval historians the 'survivor of the Pacific', after it had escaped the disaster of Pearl Harbor and, although damaged many times, had successfully gone through the whole of the war in the Pacific. It took part in almost all the major operations of the naval air war against Japan.

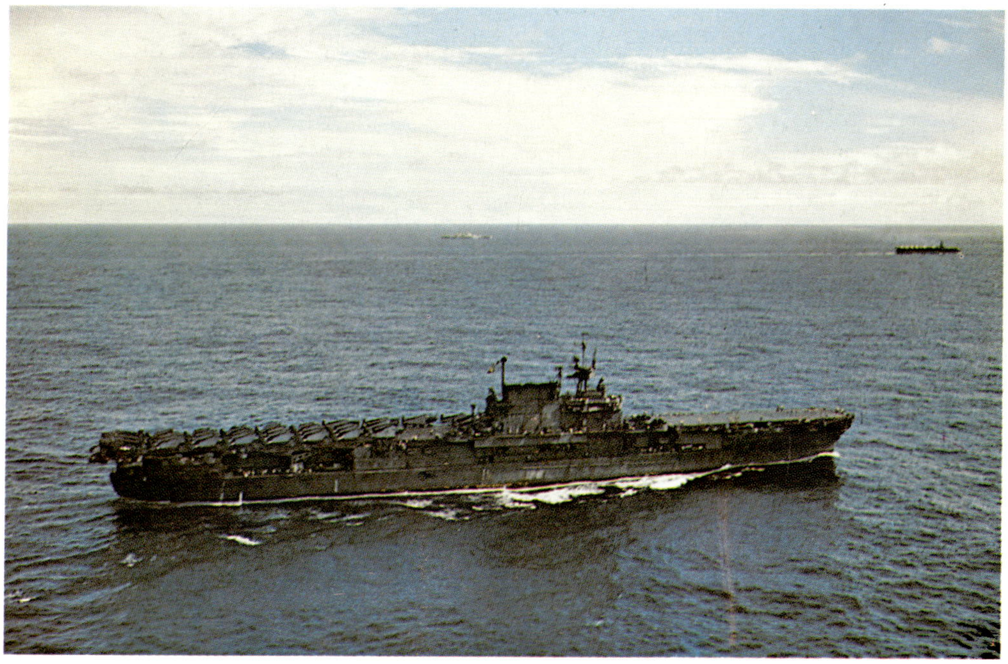

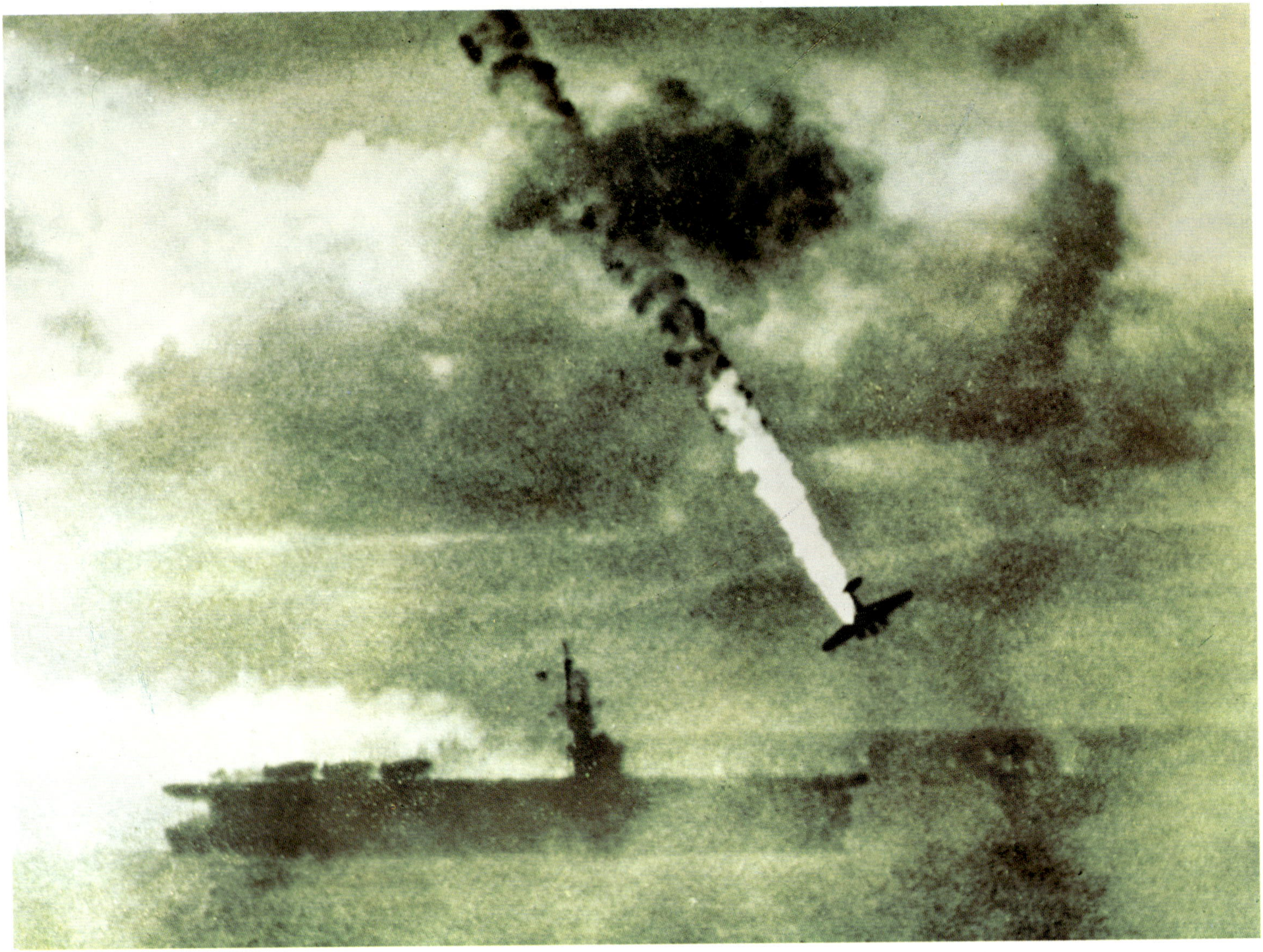

Air warfare: naval aircraft. *Above*: A Japanese kamikaze suicide aircraft, which has been hit by American anti-aircraft fire, is about to crash into the sea near a US escort carrier of Rear-Admiral Sprague's squadron during the Battle of Leyte Gulf (25 Oct. 1944). *Right*: The wreck of a Japanese Zero fighter shot down in the Solomon Islands in 1942. The Mitsubishi 12 Shi A6M type O Zeke or Zero was the most famous and the most numerous Japanese aircraft of the Second World War. Up to 1943 it outclassed the American fighters and formed the basic element of Japanese naval air forces. Exceptionally manoeuvrable, it was superior to all other aircraft in dogfights.

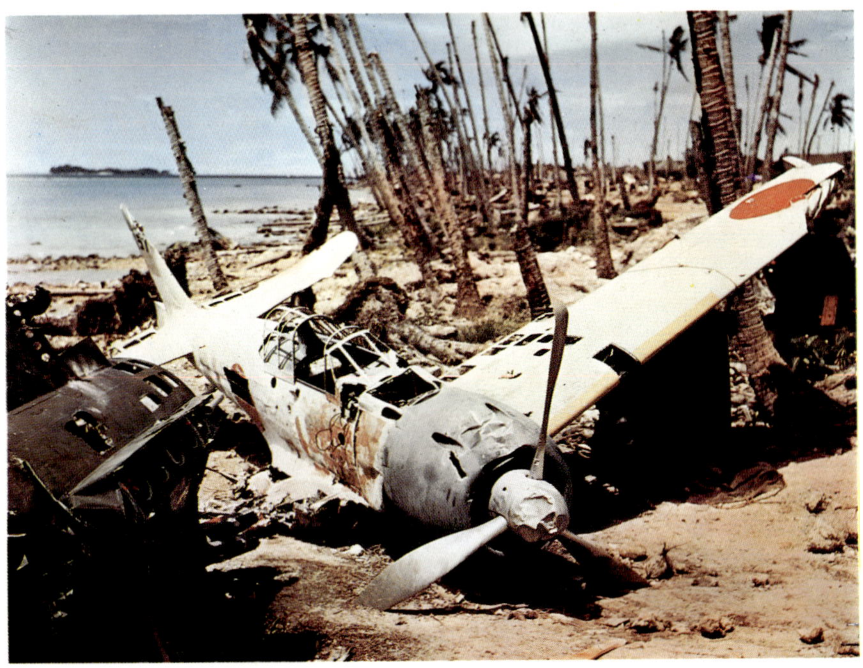

The Aleutian Islands. Throughout the Pacific war the Aleutians were only a secondary theatre of operations. Nevertheless, in June 1942 the Japanese occupied the islands of Kiska and Attu as a diversionary action during the Battle of Midway. They obtained no advantage from this and it was for purely political reasons that the Americans re-occupied these two islands a year later.

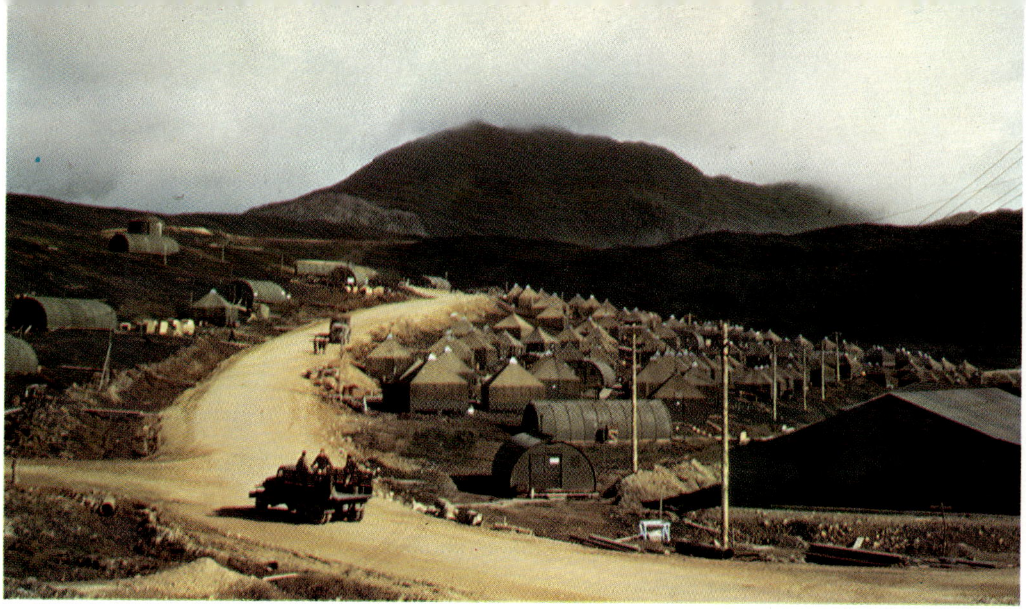

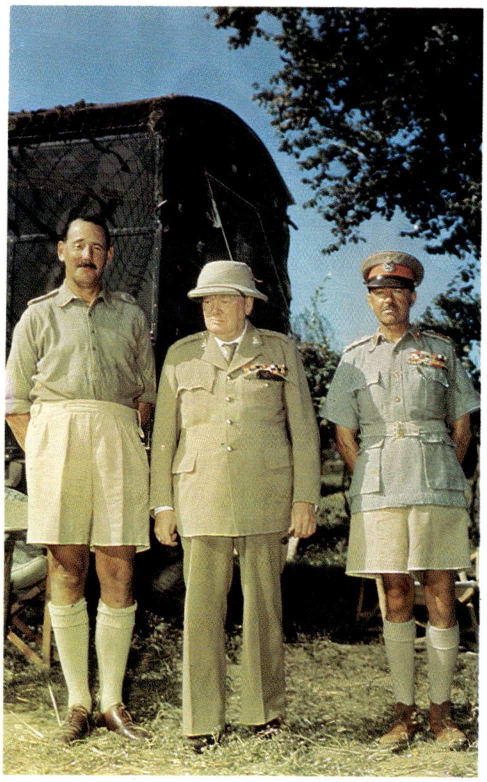

Field Marshal Alexander (on Churchill's left). After handling the difficult retreat in Burma, Alexander, who was a fine tactician and diplomat, served as Commander-in-Chief of the Allied forces in the Middle East in 1942–43 and played an important part in the recovery at El Alamein. From Feb. 1943, as deputy to Eisenhower, he commanded operations in Italy until the end of the war, constantly aware of the lack of men and supplies which would otherwise have permitted him to bring the Italian campaign to a decisive conclusion. In this picture, taken in 1944, there can also be seen General Leese, the commander of the 8th Army in Italy.

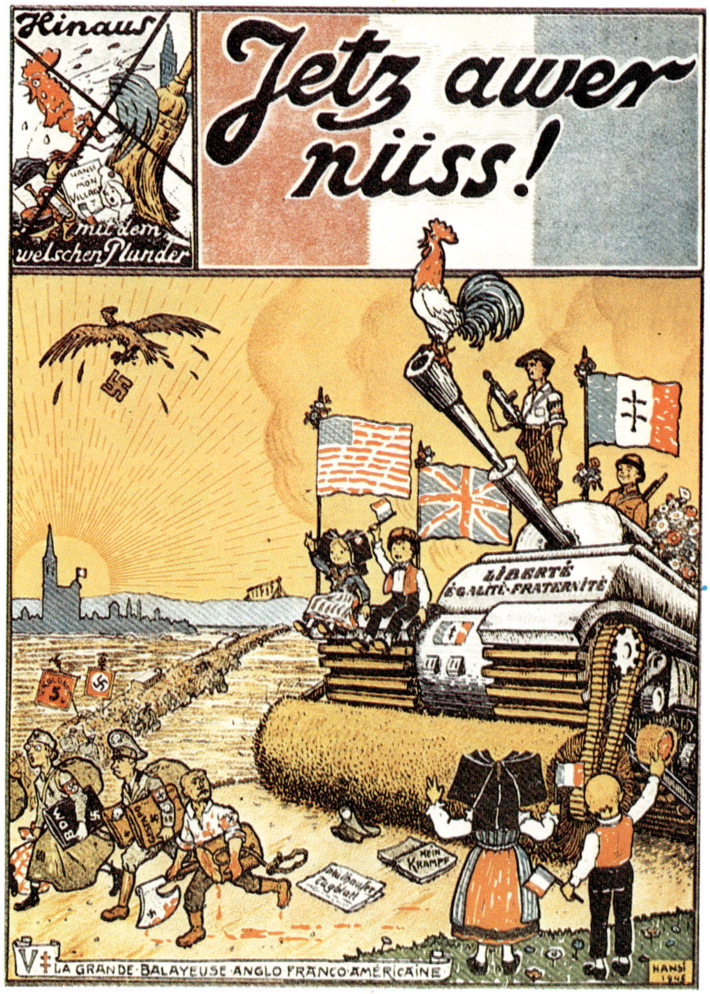

The Alsace campaign. The liberation of Colmar, the last large town in Alsace still held by the Germans at the beginning of 1945, only came about after more than ten days of fierce fighting. It took four divisions of De Lattre de Tassigny's 1st French Army and a whole United States army corps to break German resistance in the 'Colmar pocket'. A week after the Allies had entered Colmar, virtually the whole of Alsace was liberated. This event provided an opportunity for Hansi, the veteran cartoonist, who had personified Alsace's resistance to German oppression before the First World War, to display the joy of the liberated people of Alsace and to evoke the horrors of the Nazi occupation.

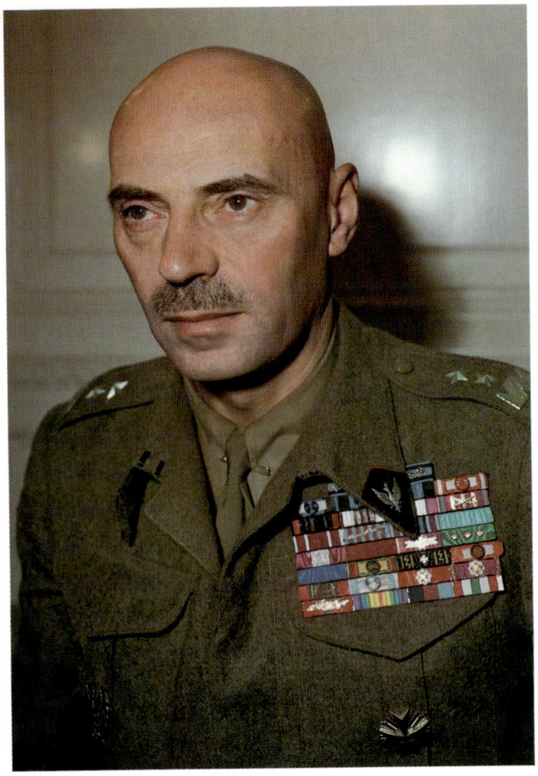

Anders. By late 1943 the homeless Free Polish army had been trained for combat in Palestine and joined the British army in Italy as the Polish II Corps, under the leadership of Lt-Gen. Wladyslaw Anders. Having fought courageously in the capture of Monte Cassino in May 1944, suffering heavy casualties, the Poles withdrew for a time in order to rebuild their forces. Later Anders led the Polish Corps into the Adriatic sector and liberated Bologna. After the death of Sikorski in July 1943, Anders was looked to by the Poles as their leading soldier.

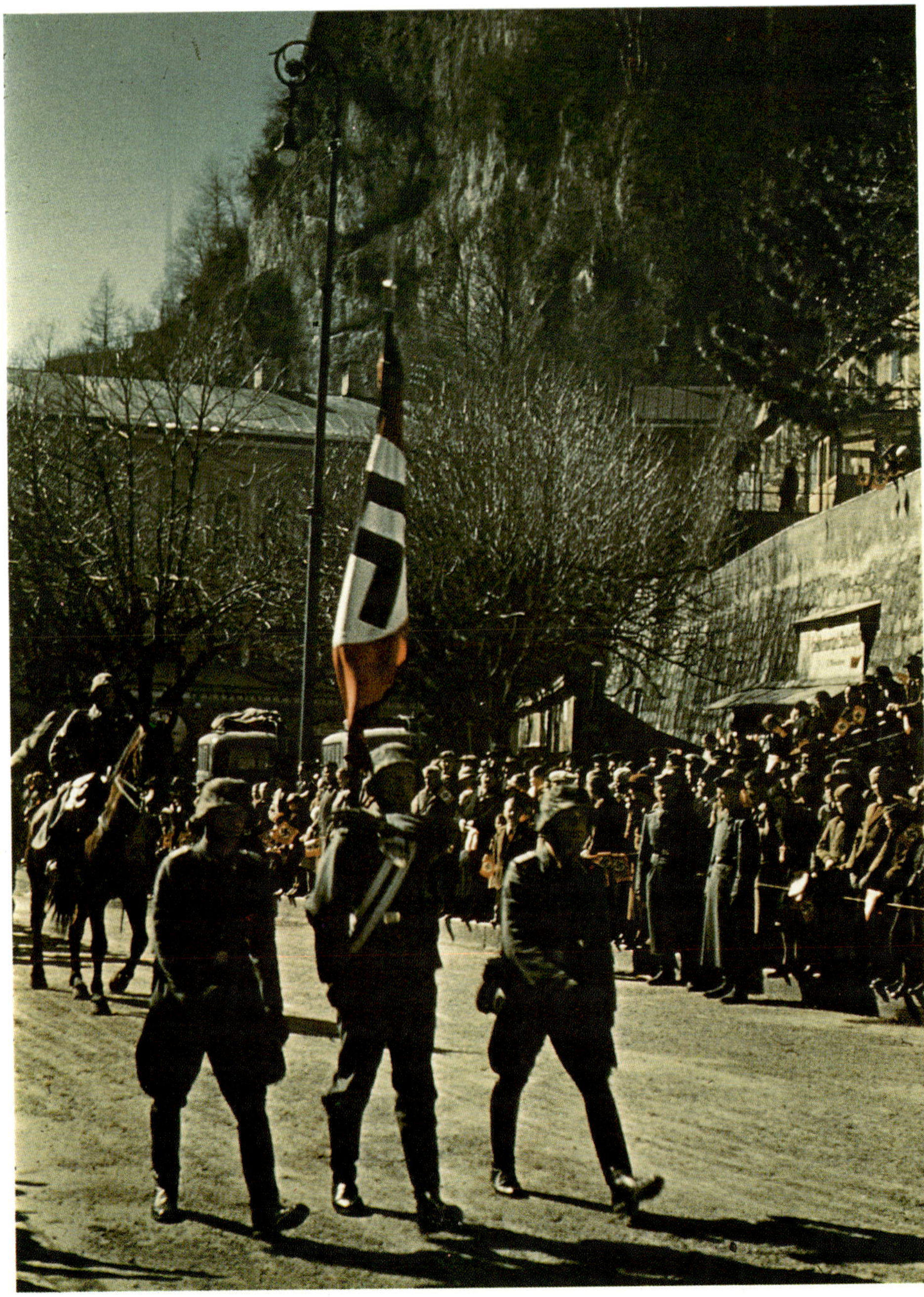

The *Anschluss*. It was as a consequence of a large-scale intimidatory manoeuvre that Hitler was able to bring about the *Anschluss*. German troops entered Austria on the morning of 12 March 1938. They occupied the whole of the country without meeting resistance and were warmly received by the population in general. In spite of this flagrant violation of the Treaty of Versailles the *Anschluss* did not provoke the slightest reaction from France or from Britain. Nor did it bring any from Mussolini in Italy, who had, however, reacted with a demonstration of force at the time of the first attempt at an *Anschluss* in 1934.

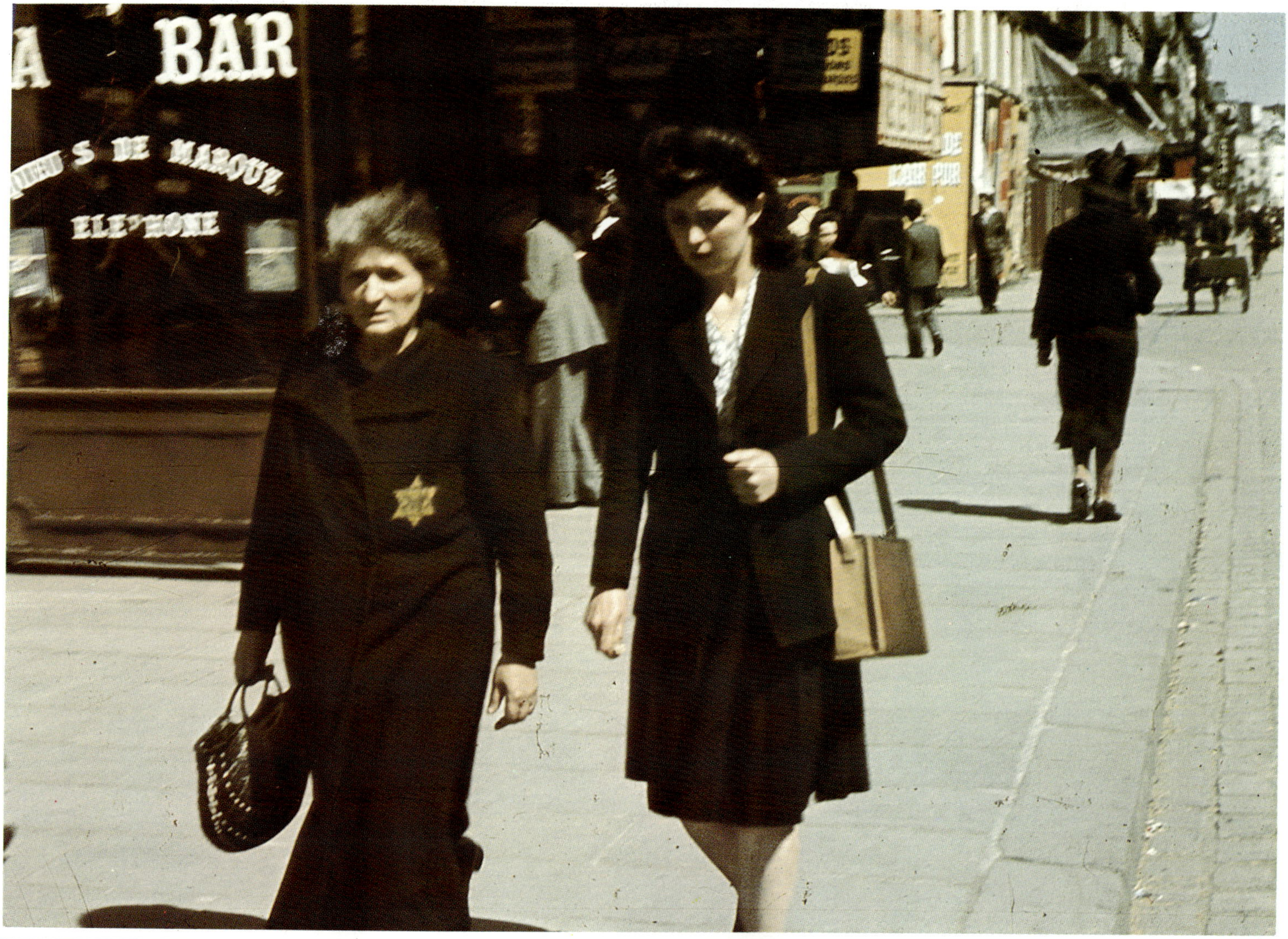

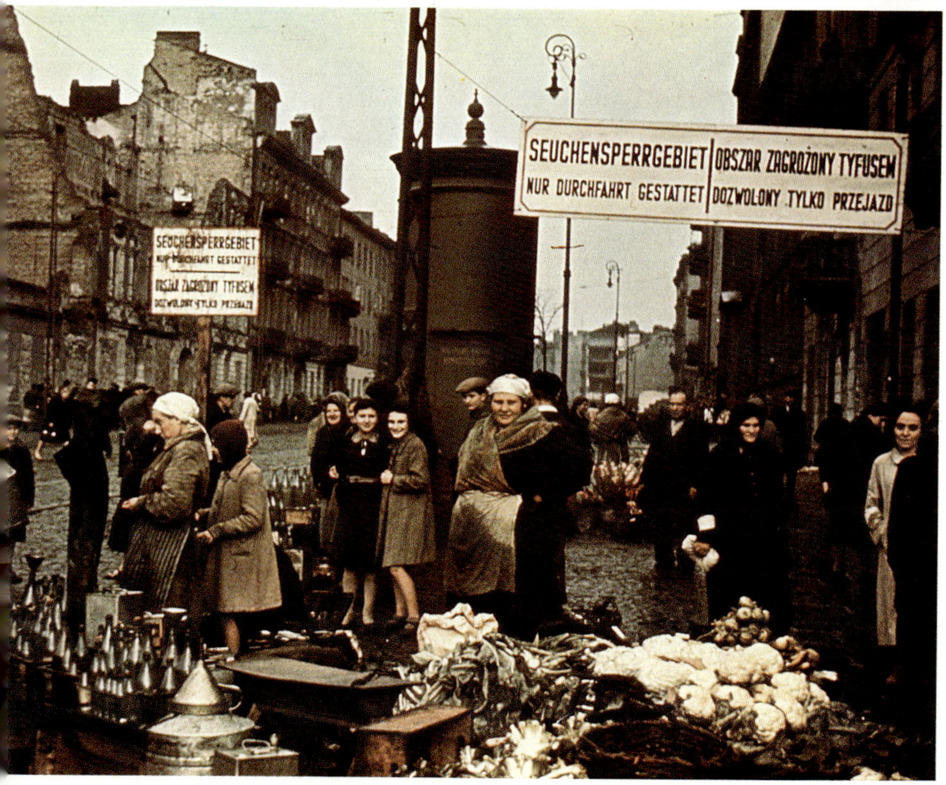

Anti-semitism in France. From 1942 the Germans began to carry out a systematic anti-semitic policy on a European scale. Thus in the occupied zone of France the wearing of a yellow star with the word *Juif* (Jew) in black letters was made obligatory by an order of the military government dated 29 May 1942. In July the first arrests were made in Paris, followed by internments at Drancy and soon by deportations. It was in fact the first stage of the 'final solution' as it affected France.

Anti-semitism in eastern Europe. In countries such as Poland the Germans exploited the particularly fierce anti-semitism of the local population. As early as 1940 the whole Jewish population was herded together in the already existing ghettos. Thus more than 350,000 people were crowded into the one in Warsaw. The starving population strove to survive by working in a number of workshops controlled by the Germans or by devoting themselves to numerous small businesses and trades, as can be seen in this photograph. The first systematic deportations began during the summer of 1942. The final 'liquidation' of the Warsaw ghetto ended in an uprising by the last survivors, which was only crushed in May 1943 after a month of fighting.

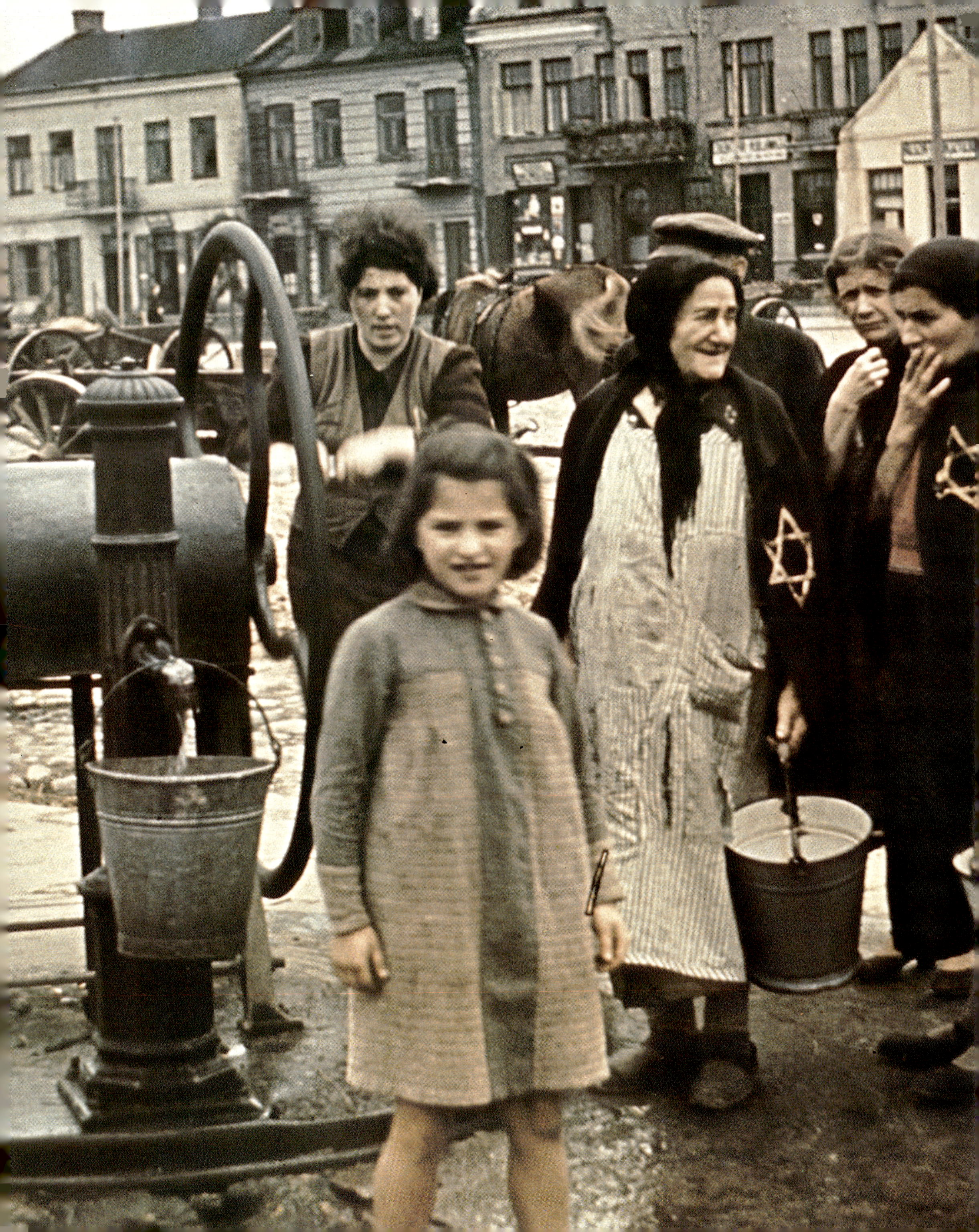

Opposite
Anti-semitism in eastern Europe. The ghetto of Kutno in Poland.

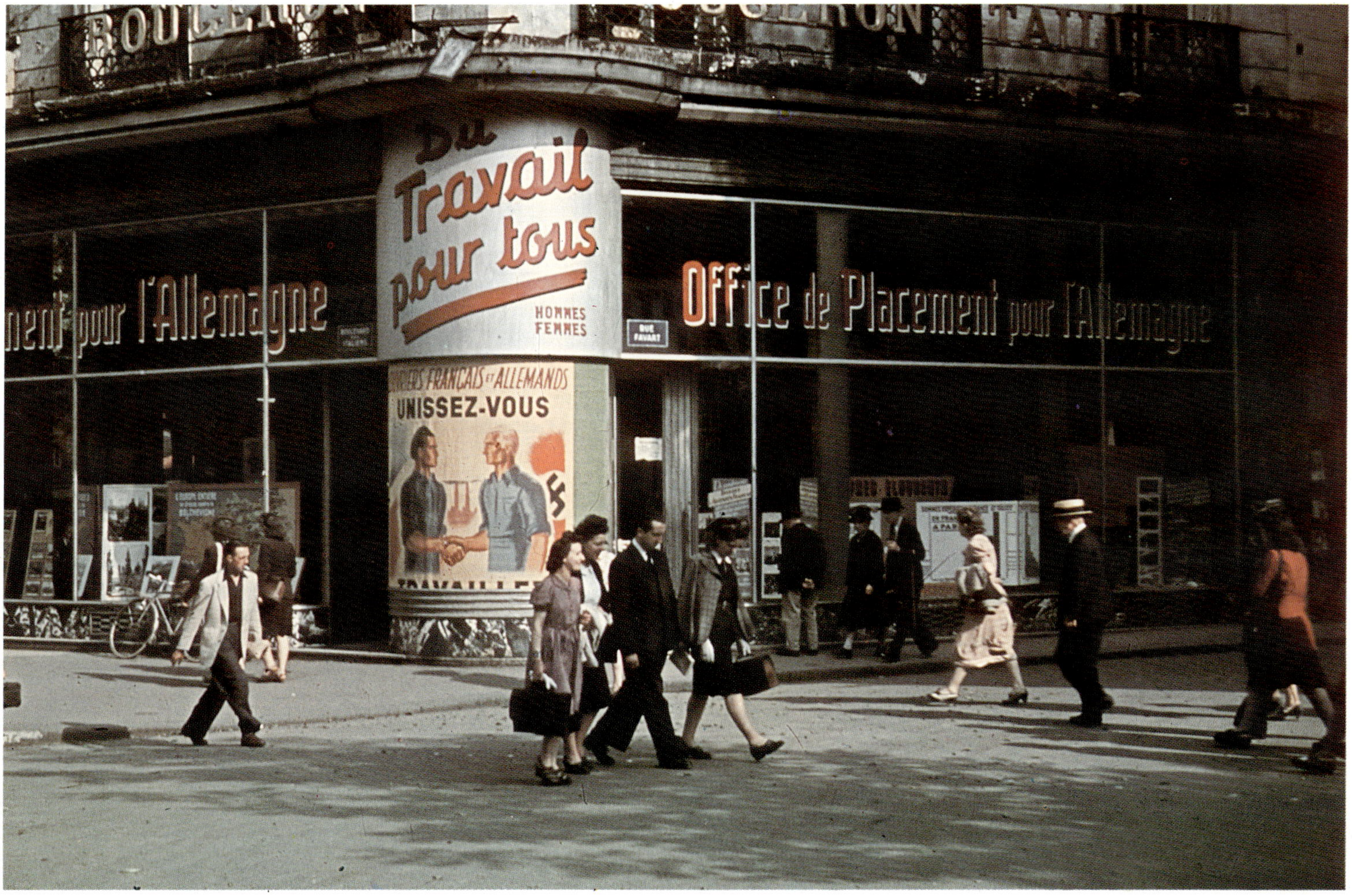

The *Arbeitsdienst* (Labour Service). In a Paris without cars pedestrians pass the German employment office in the Boulevard des Italiens. Up to 1942 the Germans did not undertake any forced recruitment of labour in the countries of western Europe. They were content to make a large number of businesses work on their behalf or to call for volunteers for the factories of the Reich, promising them high salaries and the same social advantages as those enjoyed by German workers.

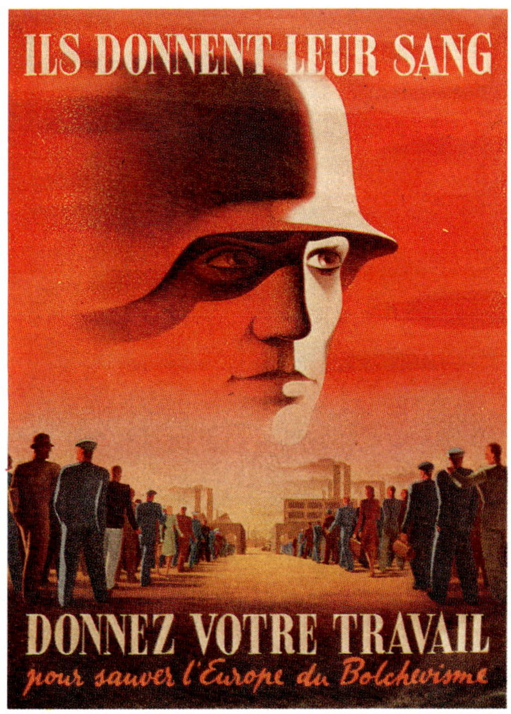

From the spring of 1942 the difficulties on the eastern front and the need to make up for the losses of the Wehrmacht led the Germans to try to recruit workers in western Europe. The Reich 'Plenipotentiary for Labour Allocation' Fritz Sauckel, still hesitating to use coercive methods, carried out an enormous propaganda campaign in favour of voluntary labour in Germany. One of the most widespread themes was the solidarity of European peoples in the struggle against Bolshevism. However, this method produced only very meagre results. (A poster from the Musée de la Guerre).

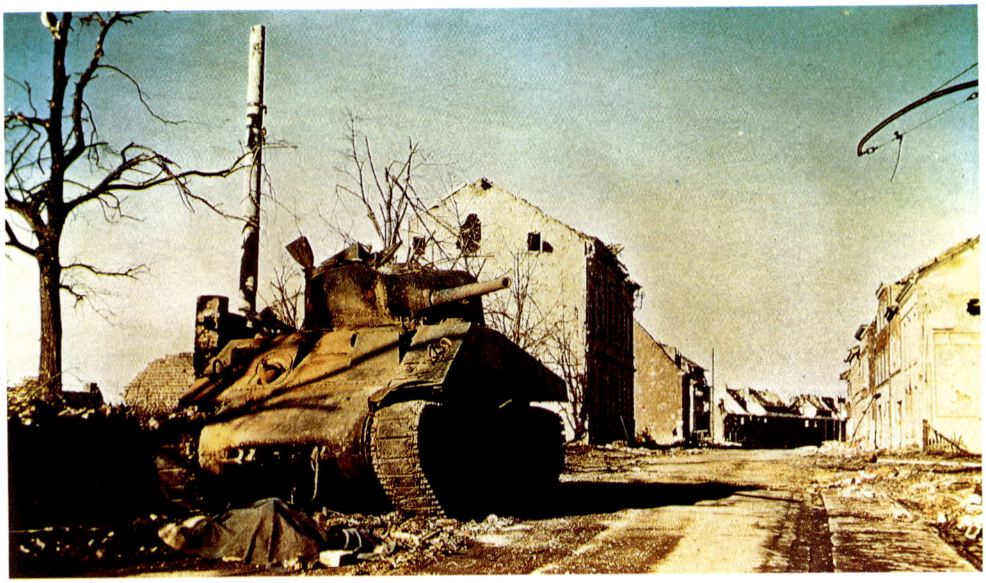

The Ardennes offensive. Launched on 16 Dec. 1944 by three German armies, the offensive 'to save the fatherland' was a terrible shock to the Allied commanders. Although they resisted fiercely the American forces yielded in the centre of the line and the Germans advanced rapidly towards Houffalize and Bastogne. This picture shows a destroyed American Sherman tank at the entrance to a village. The body of one of the tank crew is lying under a cloth.

At the end of Dec. 1944 the threat of the German offensive was averted. However, it took a month of effort by Anglo-American forces to push back the enemy and reduce the Ardennes pocket completely. The fighting took place in intensely cold weather and snowstorms hindered the advance of tanks, which still had to take account of mines laid by the Germans. The Wehrmacht's last offensive cost the Allies about 80,000 men and the Wehrmacht itself about 100,000.

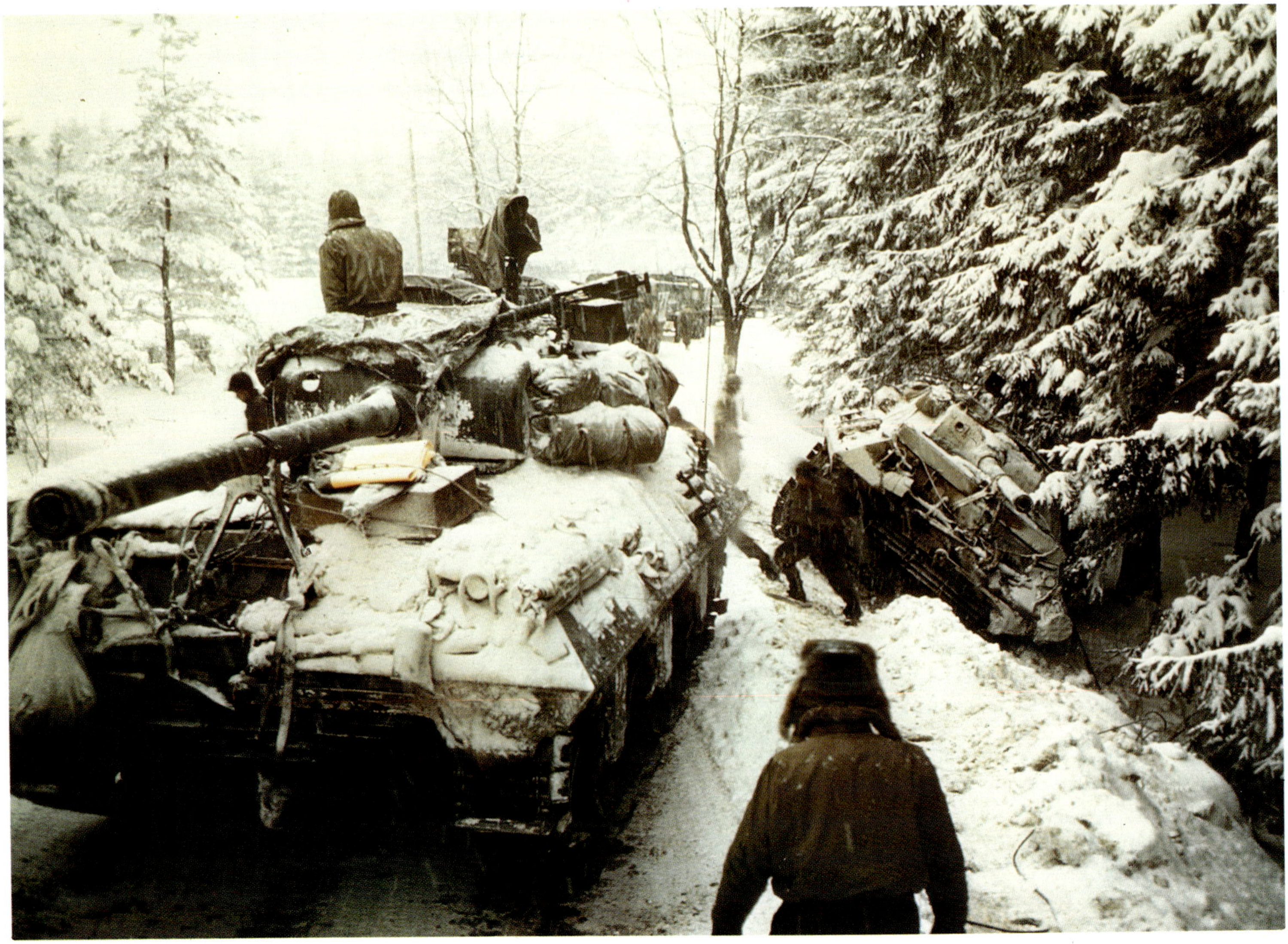

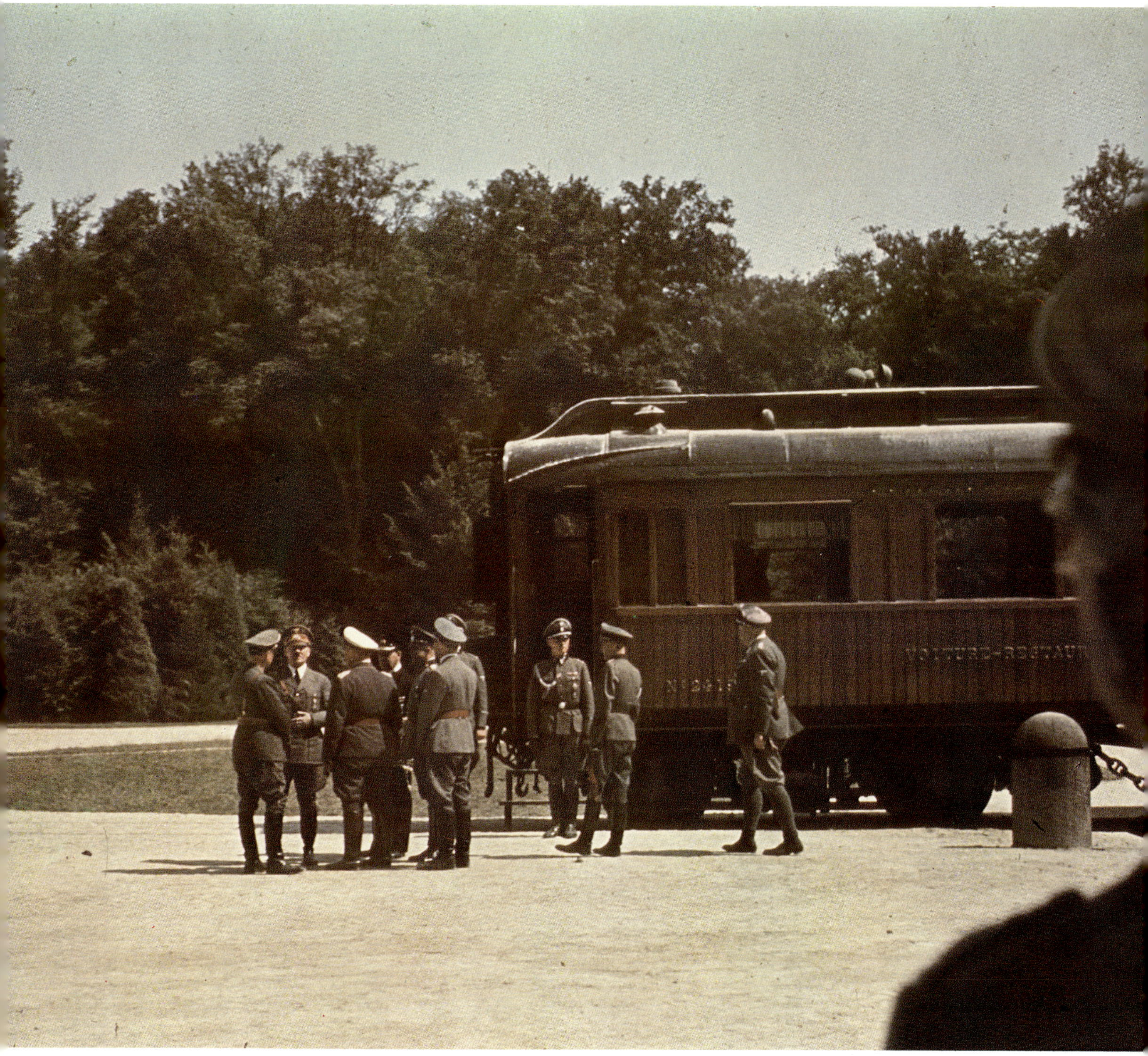

The Armistice of June 1940. Hoping to wipe out the 'shame' of 1918, Hitler required that the armistice of 22 June 1940 should be signed at Compiègne in the same railway carriage in which Foch had received the German delegation on 11 Nov. 1918. However, in variance with this precedent, the Germans forced the French to accept a military delegation led by General Huntziger. The French army was thus compelled to recognize its defeat.

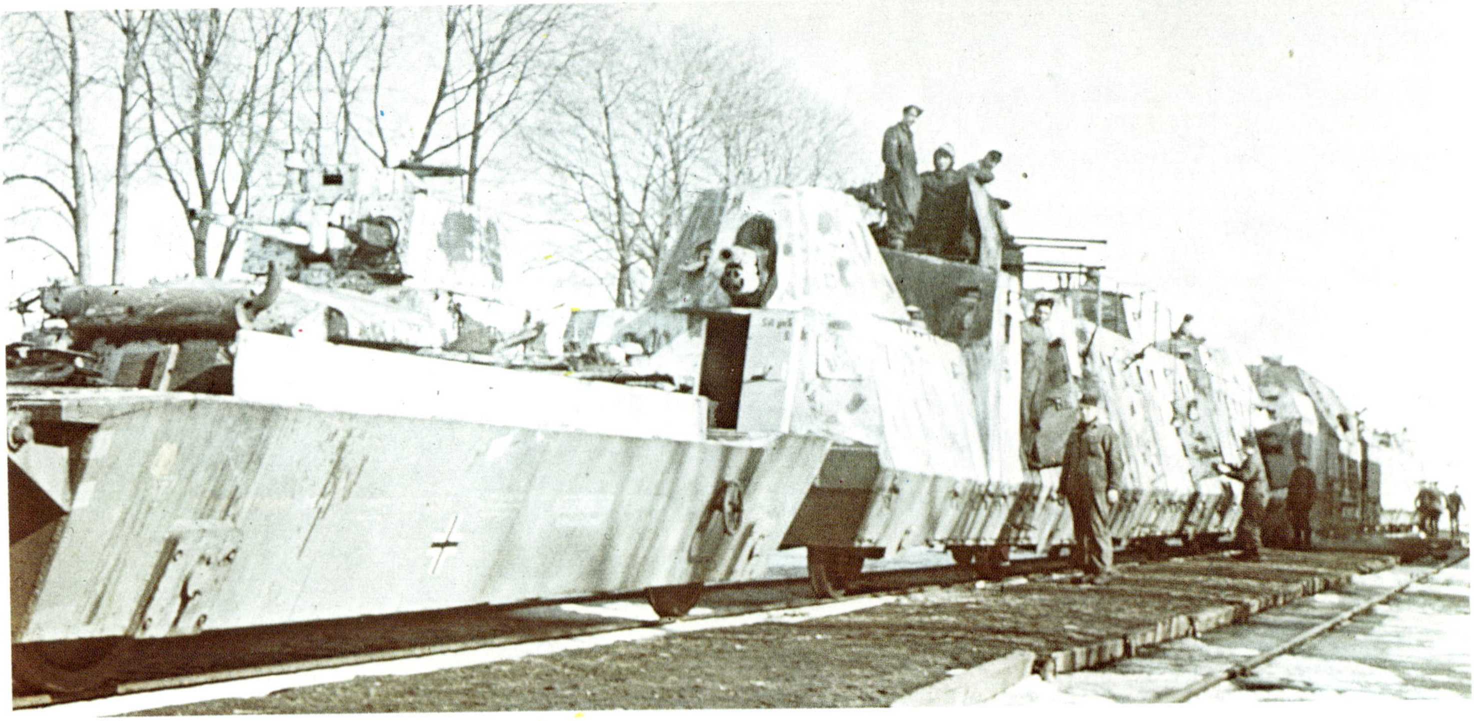

Armoured trains. These were mainly used by the Soviet forces, because of the poor quality of the roads, but the Germans were not slow to employ them on the eastern front to protect their lines of communication against attacks by partisans and to provide fire support for their troops. These armoured trains comprised, as this Wehrmacht photograph shows, flat wagons carrying tanks and light anti-aircraft guns, protected by steel panels, or medium-calibre guns in turrets. A command wagon had radio and fire control equipment.

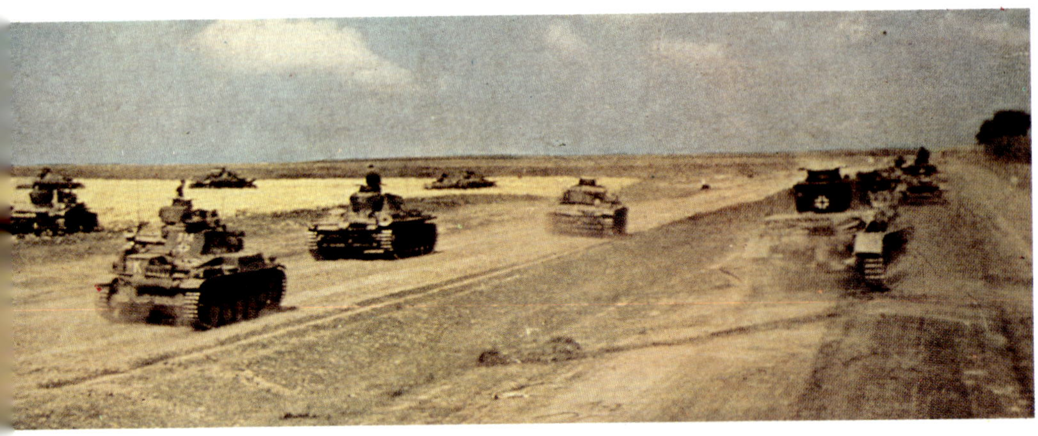

Armoured warfare. German type PzKpfw III tanks in action on the eastern front in the summer of 1941. In the first phase of the campaign, the German armoured forces, experienced in combat after two years of war, easily outclassed the Soviet tanks in manoeuvrability. However, the first encounters with the KV-1 and, particularly, the T-34 tanks were to be an unpleasant surprise. The German high command was obliged to give urgent consideration to the development of new types of tanks and this led to the introduction of the Tiger and the Panther, which entered service in 1942 and 1943 respectively.

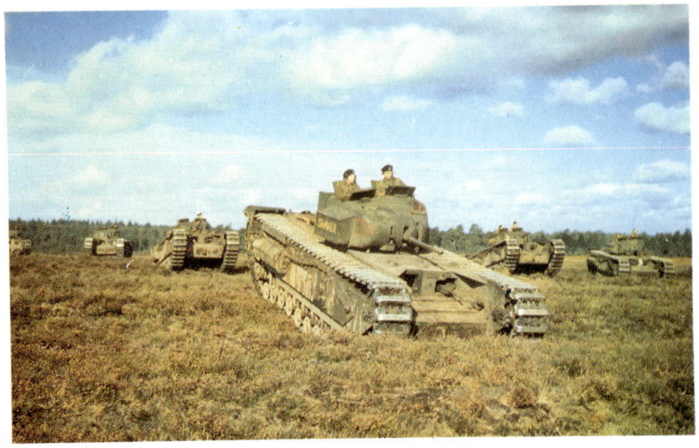

Throughout a large part of the war the British stayed faithful to the concept of the tank intended for infantry support. Thus the Churchill tank (in an early version) had a 2 pdr gun in the hull intended for the destruction of smaller fortifications, and a light 2 pdr/40 mm gun in the turret. This gun was seen to be inadequate in use against German tanks and it proved necessary to replace it, firstly with a 6 pdr and then with a 75 mm gun. This change brought about the disappearance of the gun in the hull.

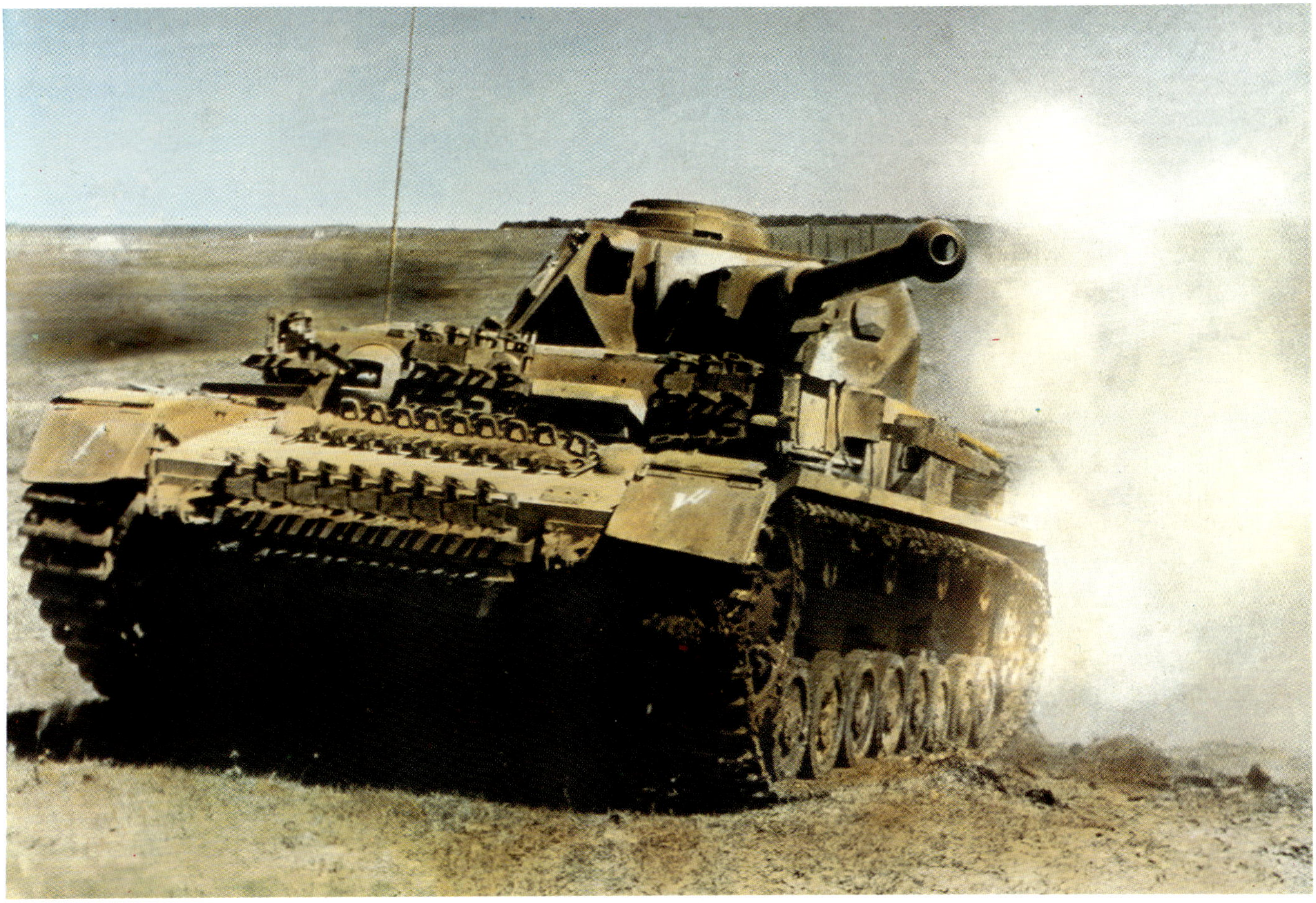

The German PzKpfw IV, originally conceived in 1937, was the backbone of the German armoured divisions throughout the Second World War. It underwent a number of modifications, keeping pace with the appearance of formidable adversaries, such as the Soviet T-34 and the Anglo-American Churchill and Sherman. Here a PzKpfw IV is seen in action at the close of the German offensive in the Caucasus. It has reinforced armour and a 75 mm long-barrelled high-velocity gun.

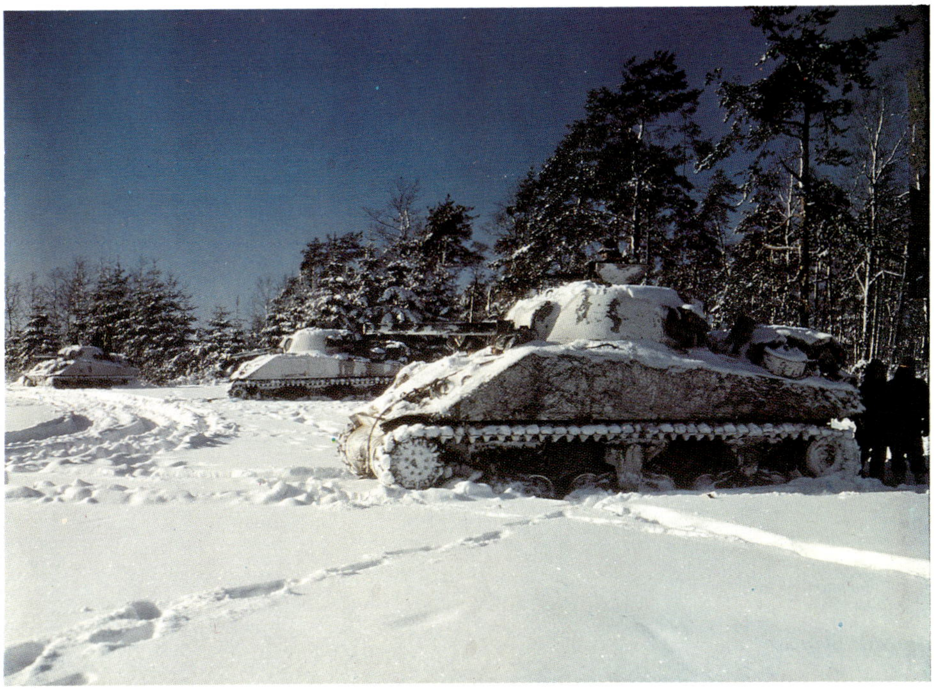

Weighing 32.6 tons, the American Sherman tank was standard equipment for many Allied divisions in the major European campaigns. It was armed with a 75 mm gun, a .50 in. (12.7 mm) anti-aircraft machine gun and two light machine guns. 50,000 Shermans were built but it showed itself inferior to the later German tanks such as the Tiger and the Panther. It proved necessary to rearm the Shermans with a heavier gun while waiting for the Pershing tank to enter service. This picture shows three of these tanks outside Saint-Vith during the Battle of the Ardennes in Jan. 1945.

Loading ammunition on to a PzKpfw II German tank on the Terek front at the time of the German offensive in the Caucasus in Sept. 1942. The photograph is interesting in that it underlines the importance of the logistic support for armoured divisions as part of a war of movement. The Panzers' capacity for action was in fact closely dependent on the provision of petrol, ammunition and spare parts. These large formations also included breakdown repair tanks, which could carry out repairs while under enemy fire.

Soviet heavy tanks of the 'Kliment Voroshilov' KV-1 class moving along the Unter den Linden in May 1945 after the Battle of Berlin. The Brandenburg Gate can be seen in the background. Despite their power and the thickness of their protective armour, these tanks proved to be vulnerable in street fighting. The *Panzerfaust*, in particular, inflicted heavy damage on them. Hundreds of Russian tanks were destroyed and nearly 300,000 men killed or wounded before the Red Army could take possession of Berlin.

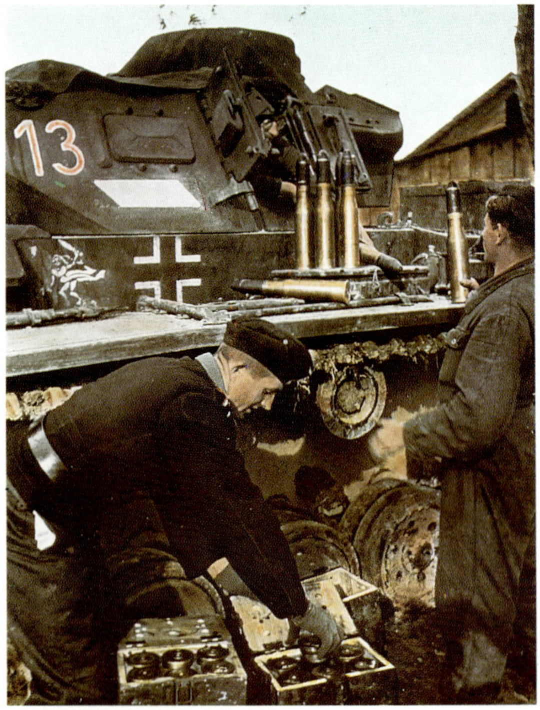

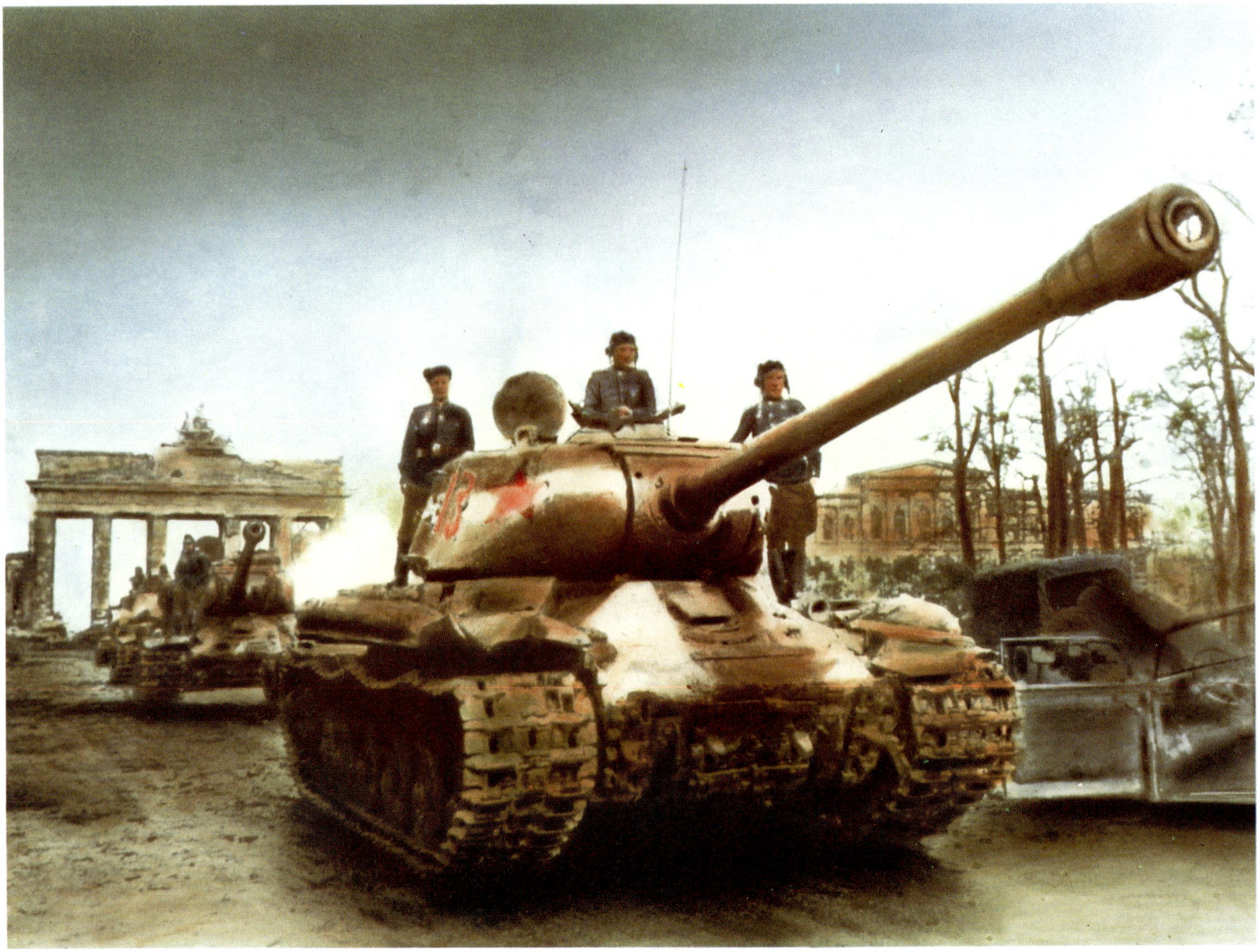

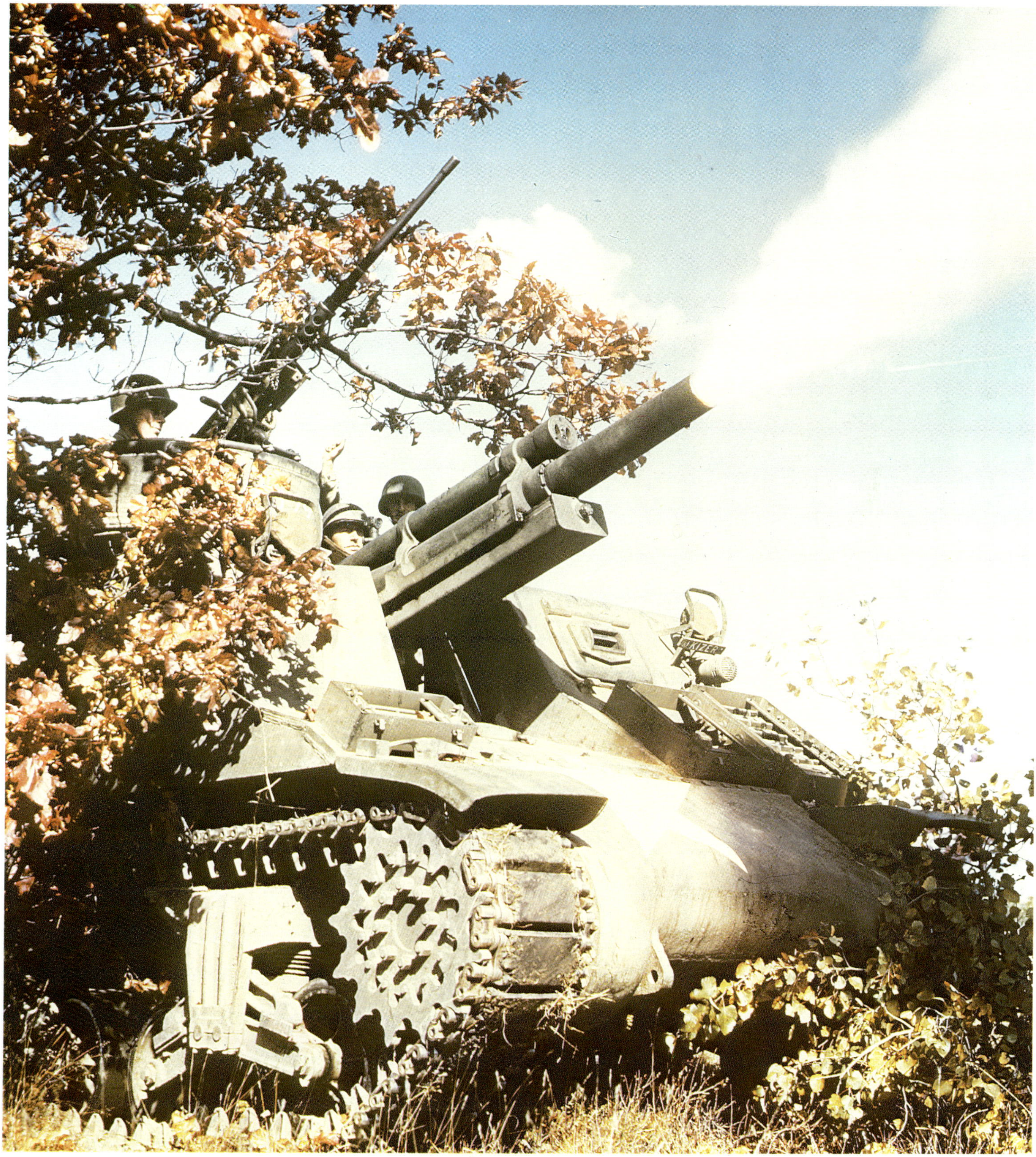

From 1942 to 1945 American Sherman tanks, of which nearly 50,000 were built, formed the basis of Allied armoured units. Apart from the tank itself, equipped with a 75 mm and later a 76 mm gun, the chassis of the Sherman was used for tank destroyers, for breakdown repair tanks and also for self-propelled artillery such as the 155 mm 'Long Tom' and, particularly, for the 105 mm M7 howitzer, seen here in the photograph. These howitzers considerably increased the fire power of armoured divisions.

The British Army. Young soldiers of a gun crew at work.

The Belgian Army. With a strength of 22 divisions on 10 May 1940 the Belgian army, surprised by the strength of the German attack, was unable to make a stand on the Albert Canal and the River Meuse. As a result of the collapse of the French army's centre between Namur and Sedan, it was forced into an almost uninterrupted retreat towards the Scheldt and the Lys. Threatened by encirclement and subject to constant attacks, it was compelled to surrender on 28 May 1940 in spite of heroic resistance. In this picture, taken some hours after the surrender, a line of Belgian lorries passes a horse-drawn artillery column of the German army.

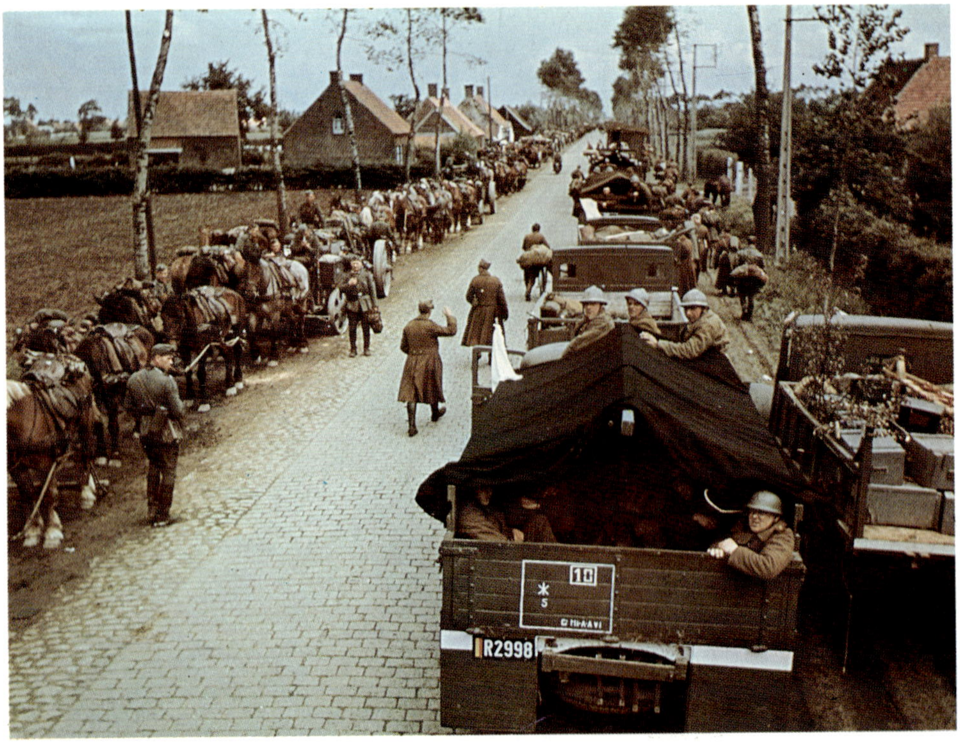

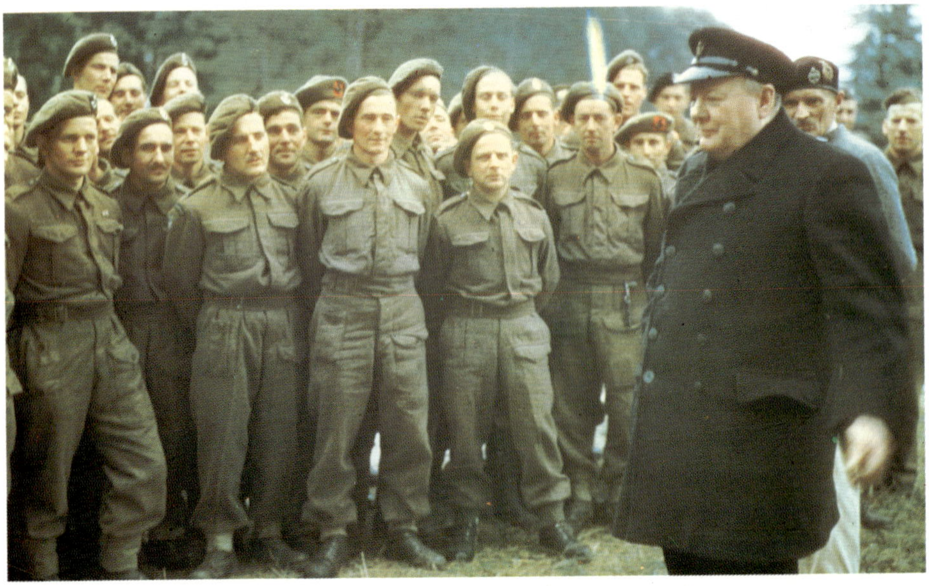

The British Army. On 27 July 1944, at the time of the battle of Caen, Churchill, accompanied by Montgomery, reviews a group of British soldiers. With the tradition of a sea power Great Britain had only a small professional army at the beginning of the war but by 1945 it had expanded to reach a strength of nearly 3 million. All the same this was a relatively weak effort in comparison with other major military powers. The needs of industrial mobilization and the vast development of the Navy and the Royal Air Force had restricted the growth of the British army, in spite of the major contribution of the colonies and the dominions.

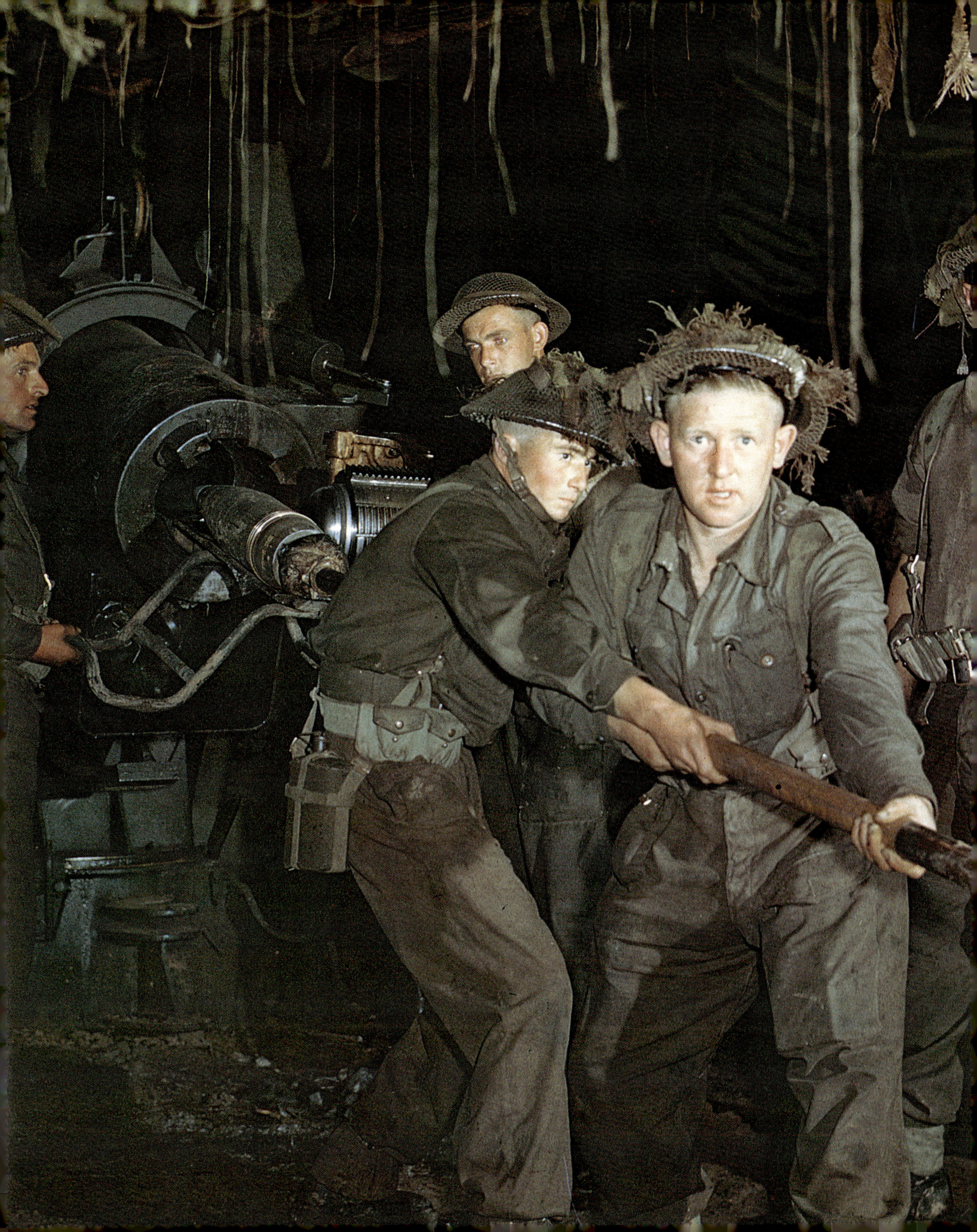

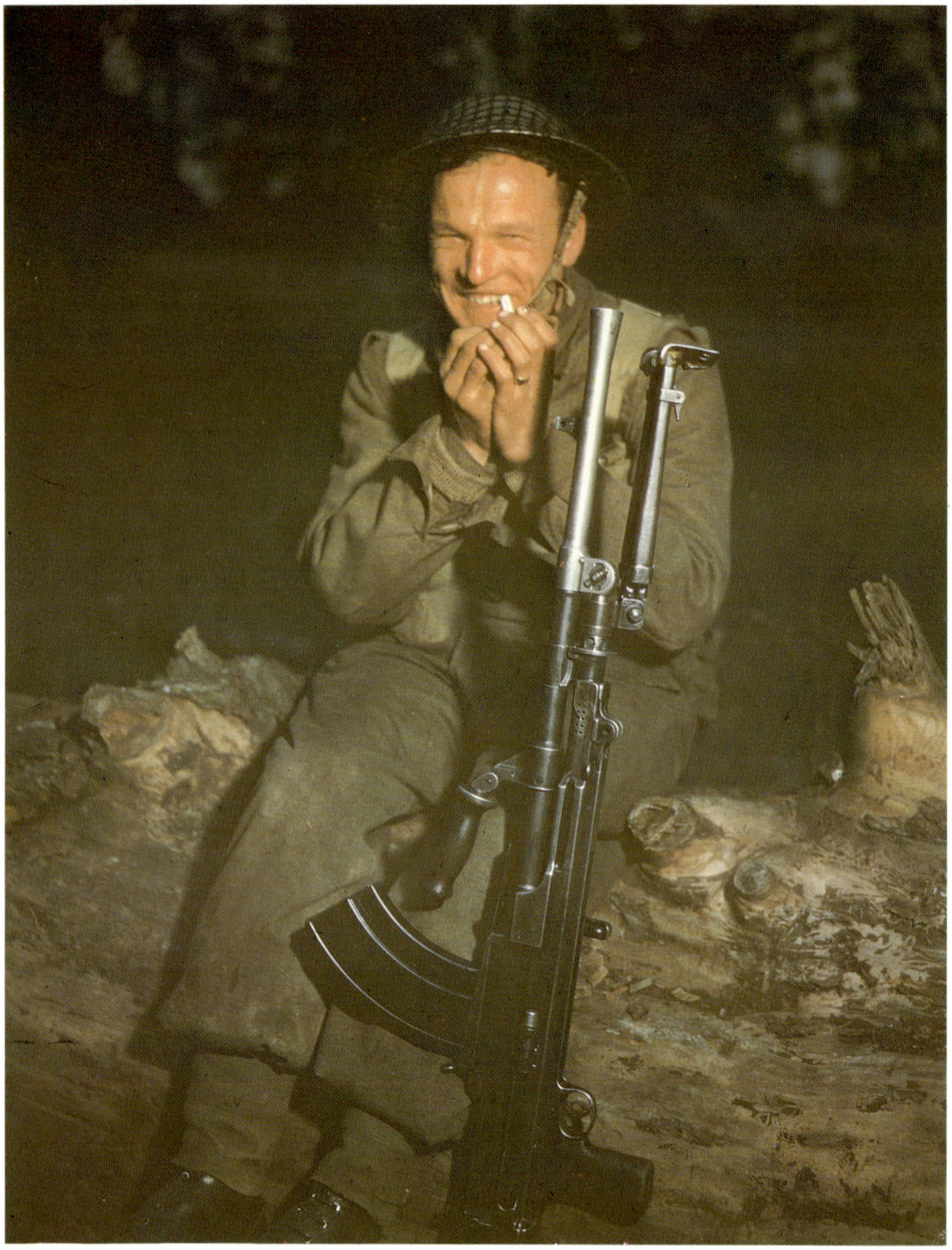

Throughout the conflict the British soldier showed his traditional qualities of good humour, calmness and tenacity in defence and methodical caution in attack. In operation in all the major theatres – Europe, North Africa, the Far East – the British army, in large part improvised, was a veritable kaleidoscope of the Empire. In the great victory at El Alamein in Oct. 1942 New Zealand, Indian, South African and Australian as well as British troops took part.

The Chinese Army. At the end of the conflict the Chinese army, with more than 300 divisions, was one of the largest in the world. However, it only had about 30 modern units, entirely equipped by the Americans via the air lift over the Himalayas. In spite of its size the role of the Chinese army was only minor. Generalissimo Chiang Kai-shek was keen to spare his troops, with a view to using them to crush the Communists after the war.

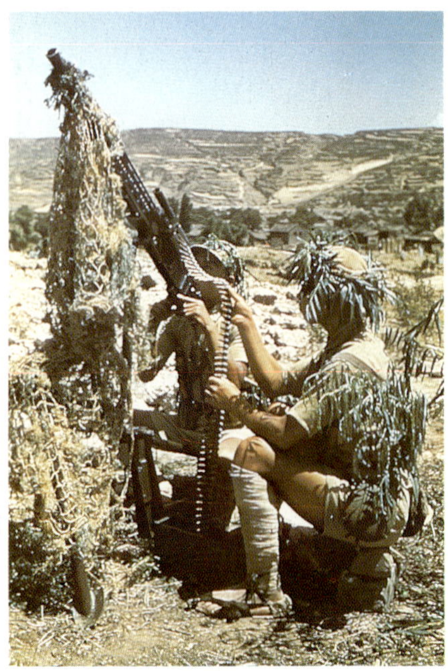

Right
The French Army. In 1939 the French army was still considered to be one of the best in the world. However, it suffered from outdated military doctrines, the legacy of 1917–18. Aircraft and tanks were dispersed along the whole front and the great majority of armoured vehicles were essentially seen as a means of infantry support, as this picture demonstrates. (A painting by A. Brenet in the Musée de la Guerre.)

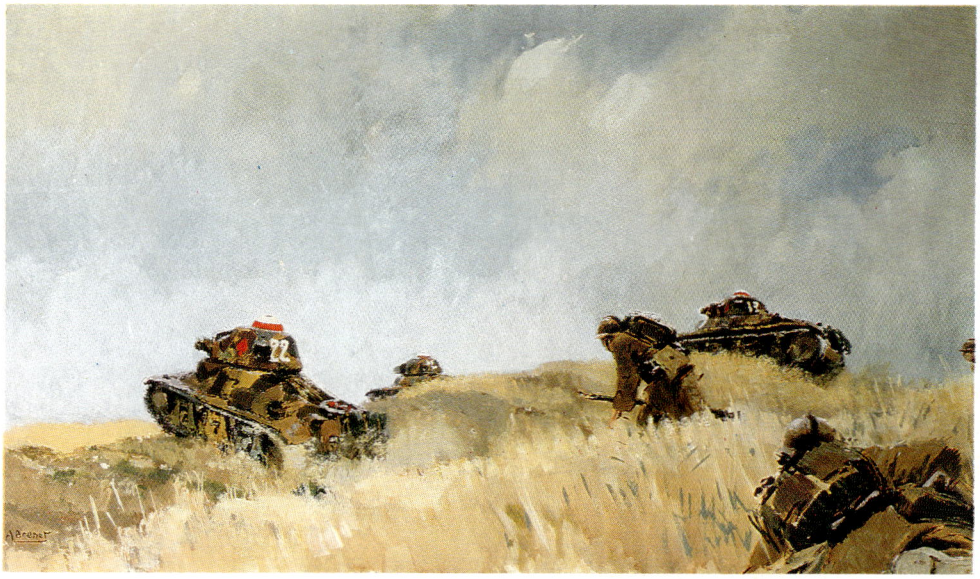

Below
From 1943 France was able to establish its military prestige once again thanks to the Army of Africa which was rearmed by the Americans. This army, composed mainly of units of Muslim soldiers commanded by French officers, played a major role in the breaking of the German front (Gustav Line) in Italy in May 1944 but this was not achieved without fierce fighting. This picture shows how a column fell victim to a murderous ambush on leaving the town of Esperia near Monte d'Oro.

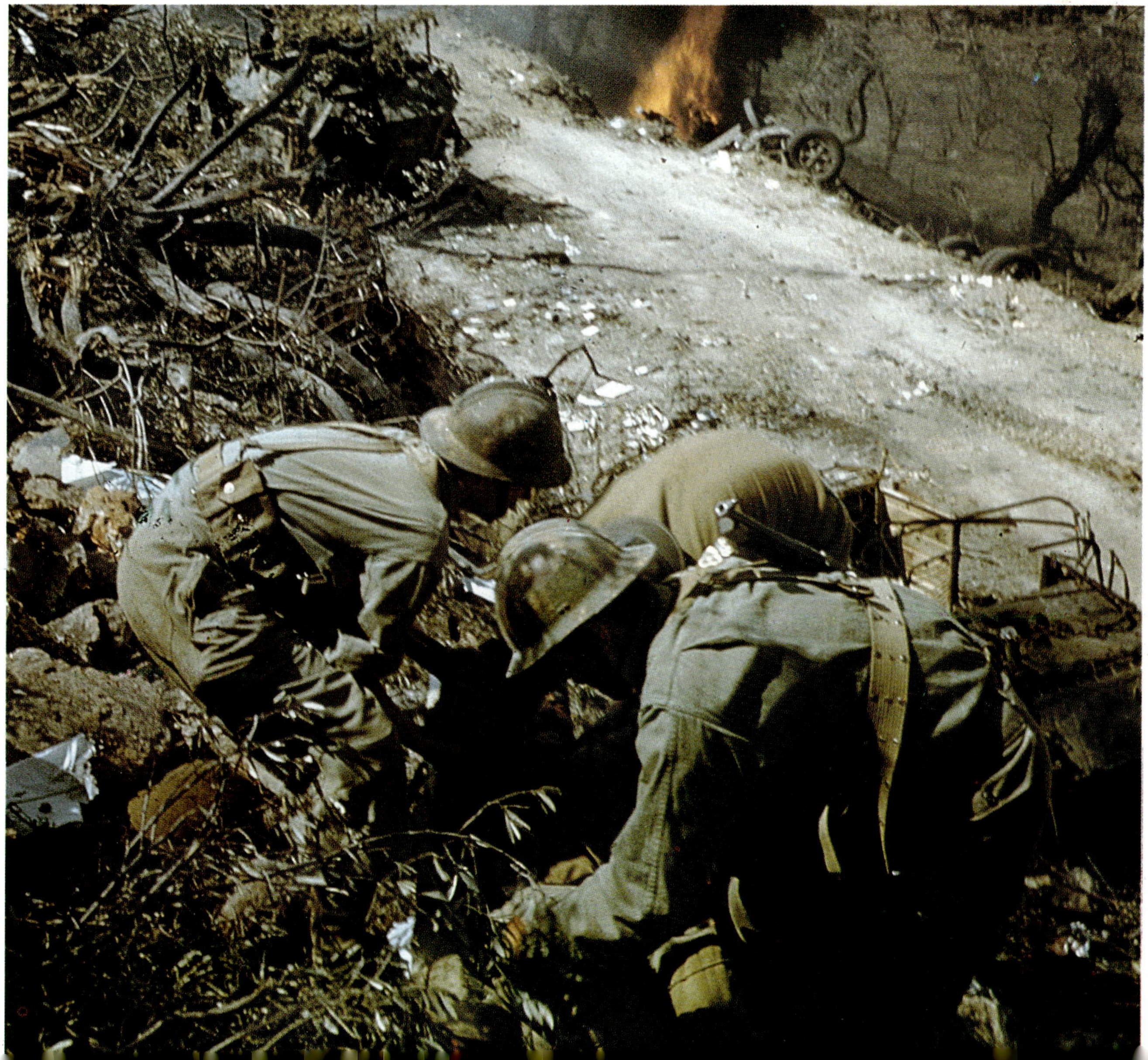

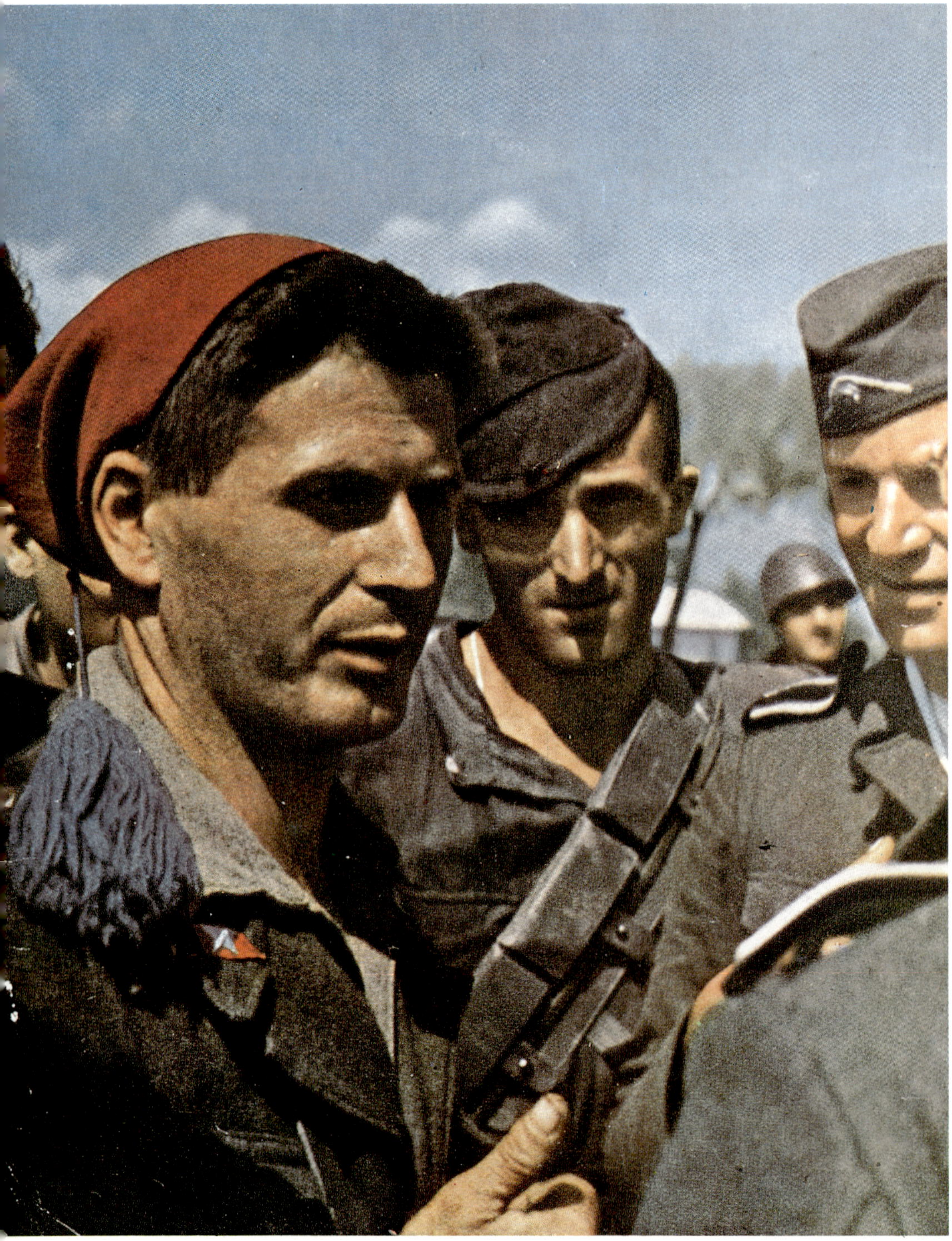

The Italian Army. In spite of being chronically under-equipped the Italian army saw action in Albania, in Africa and even in Russia. At the beginning of the war on the eastern front Mussolini sent an expeditionary corps of nine divisions, among which were the famous Bersaglieri units (see picture). Lacking heavy equipment, the Italian units were routed on the Don in the winter of 1942–3 and eventually repatriated to Italy.

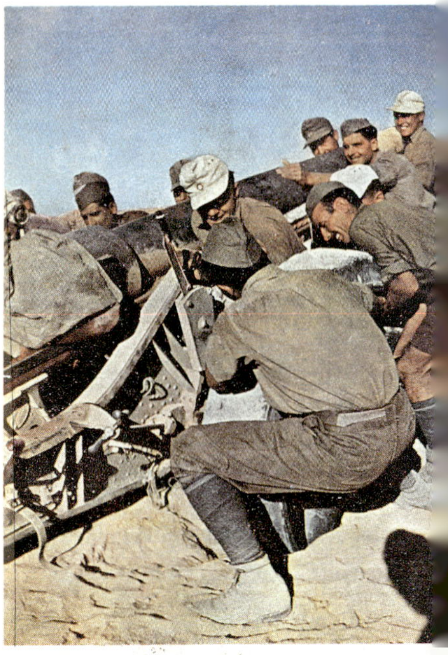

Italian soldiers setting up a gun in the firing position with the help of Germans from the Afrika Korps. Impressive on paper, with more than 70 divisions, the Italian army suffered from serious deficiencies in materials, leadership and morale, which caused a series of unfortunate reverses. However, certain units such as the Ariete, Littorio and Folgore divisions distinguished themselves in action.

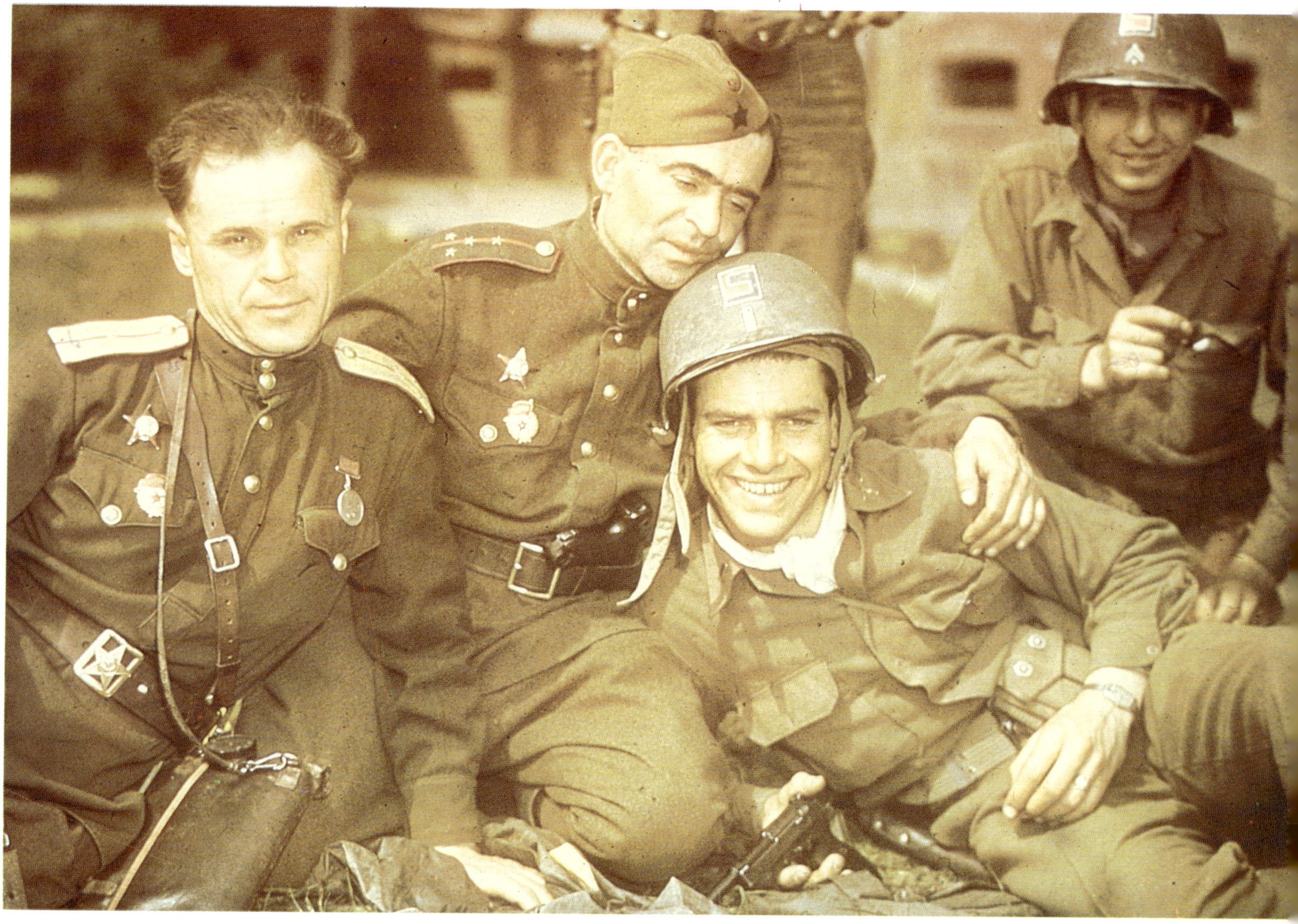

The Red Army. Russian and American soldiers fraternizing when units of both armies met on the Elbe near Torgau in April 1945. After four years of fighting the Soviet army had become a remarkable instrument of war. Following the early disasters in 1941, Stalin did not hesitate to re-establish the privileges and authority of the officer corps, which got its epaulettes back and was permitted to receive decorations recalling the Tsarist era, such as the Order of Suvorov.

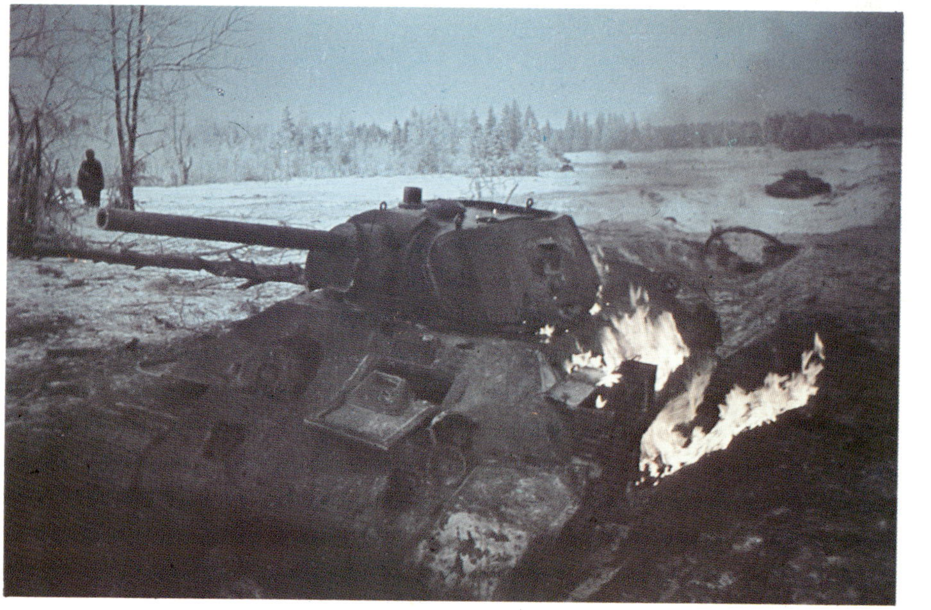

In the end it was only at the cost of terrible losses in men and materials that the Red Army was able to seize victory from the hands of the German forces. Tens of thousands of tanks were destroyed and the losses in men reached 12 million. Here a T-34, one of the Red Army's best tanks, is seen burning on a snow-covered slope.

Opposite
The US Army. A member of an engineer unit armed with a flame-thrower.

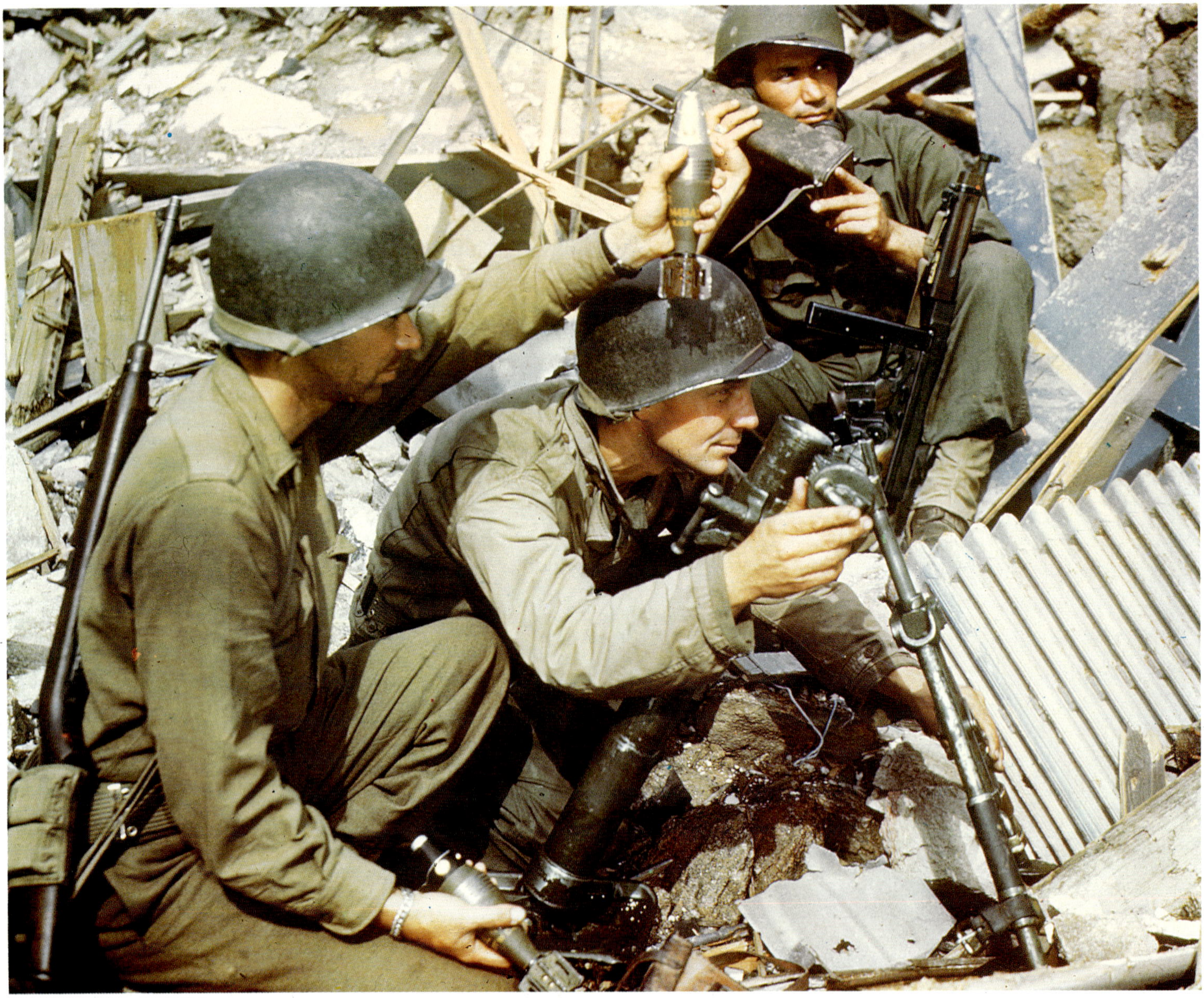

The US Army. An American infantry mortar in operation during the fierce fighting which was to end with the liberation of the port of Saint-Malo (Aug. 1944). The US army underwent a remarkable development during the course of the war. In 1939 its effective strength did not even reach 200,000 men, which made it 16th in order of size in the world. Despite determined efforts to rectify the situation, it still had only 37 divisions at the time of Pearl Harbor, or scarcely a sixth of the German army. The real spurt did not take place until after the Japanese attack and the launching of the very ambitious Victory Programme, which was in fact to be only partly carried out. Of the 215 divisions planned, only 91 were actually set up. Despite its abundant equipment and its decisive part in the fighting on all fronts, the US army as a whole, and particularly its operational fighting units (battlefield units and support units), was never able to reach the manpower level of the Wehrmacht or the Red Army.

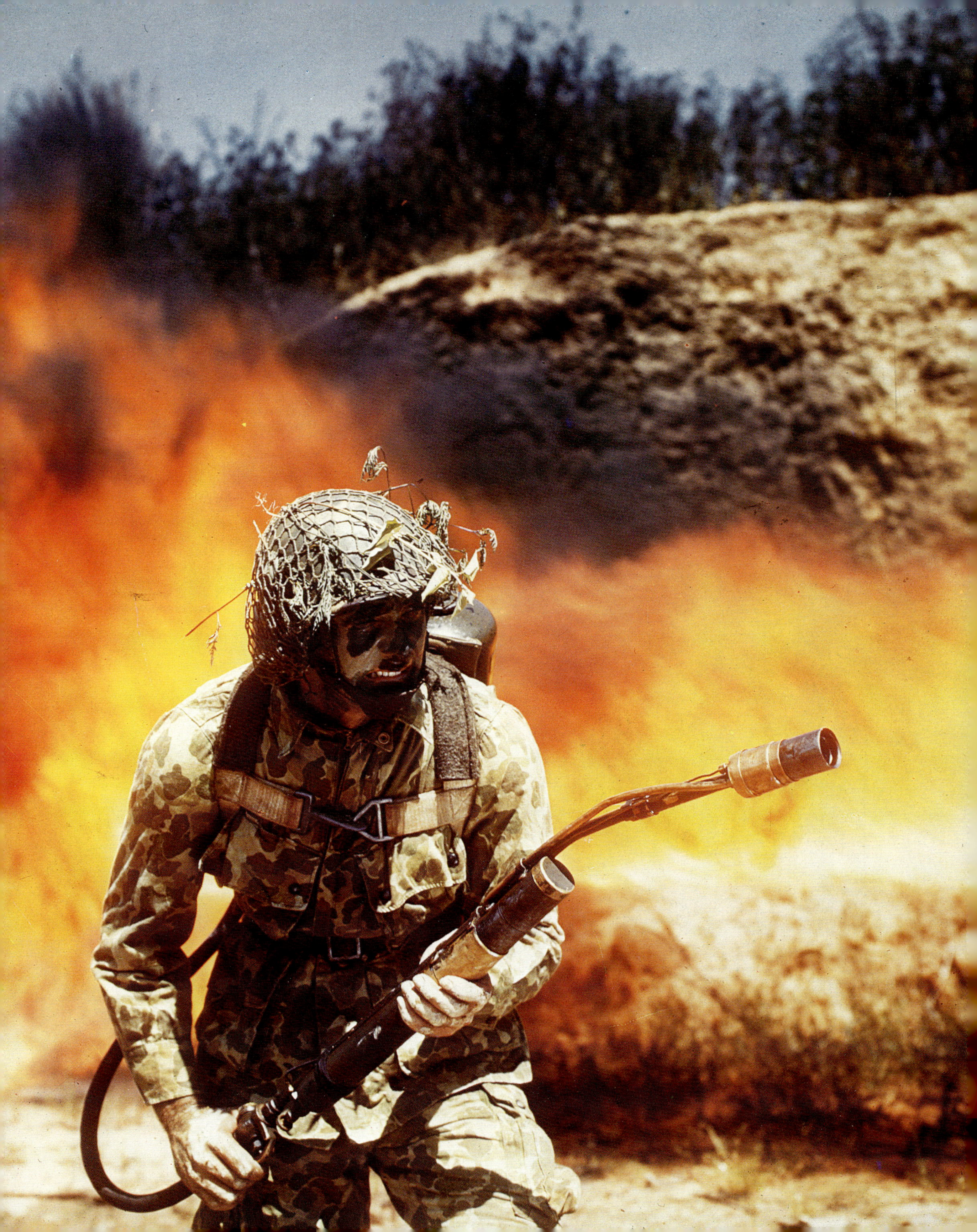

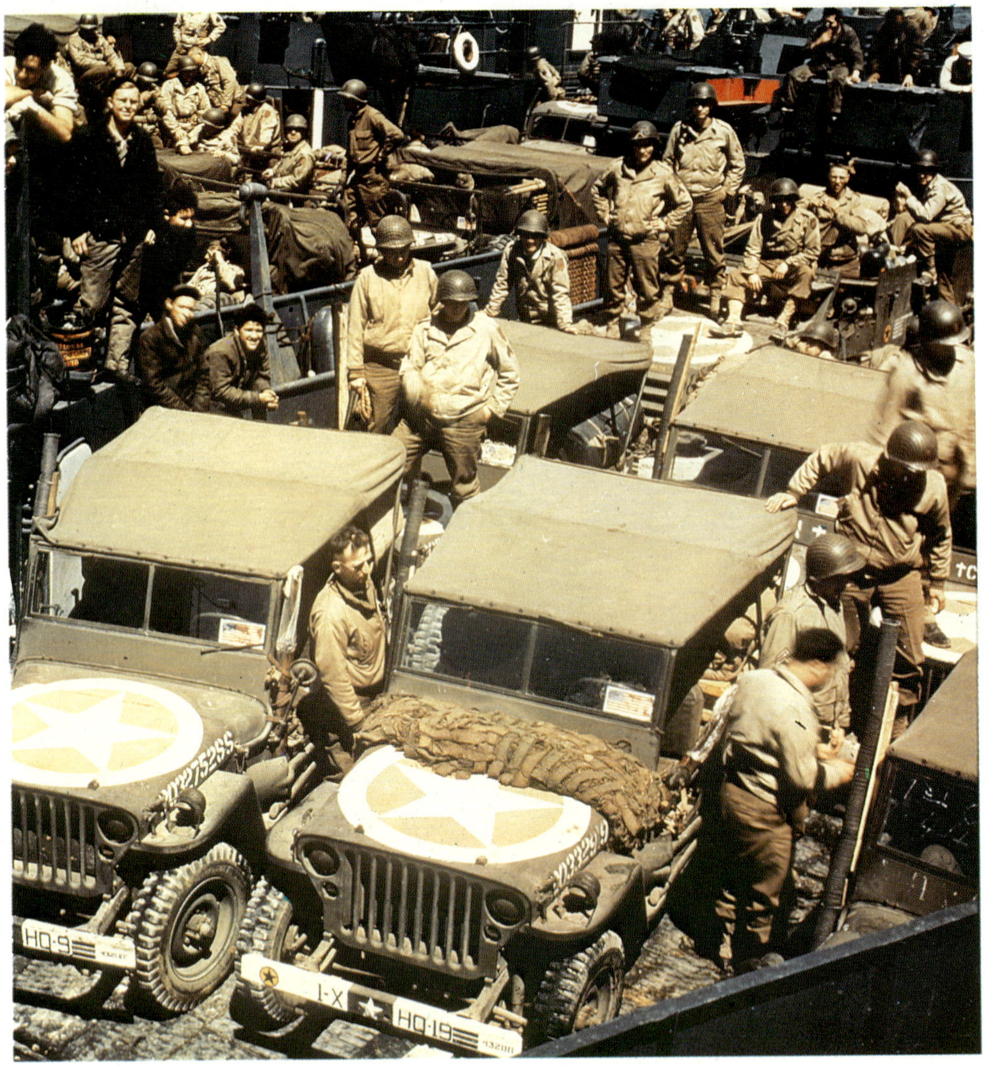

American soldiers with their Jeeps embarked on board landing craft in a port on the south coast of England on the eve of the Normandy landing. In view of the strategic position of the United States, separated from the principal theatres of war by two oceans, the US army could not be put where it was required without the use of long-distance transport by sea and amphibious operations. In March 1945, near the end of the war in Europe, out of 8 million men belonging to the US army, 2,750,000 were still in the United States, 3,500,000 were engaged in the European theatre and 1,450,000 in the Pacific and Asia.

An American artillery convoy on an English road on the eve of the launching of Operation Overlord (June 1944). Unlike the German army or the Red Army, which in 1945 still had many units which were horse-drawn or on foot, the US army of the Second World War, relying on abundant resources of oil and a powerful automobile industry, was fully mechanized. It possessed more than 3 million vehicles, of which more than 600,000 were Jeeps, 800,000 GMC lorries and 150,000 heavy lorries, etc. Although this superiority in materials enabled the Allies to move very rapidly in France and Belgium after the breakthrough at Avranches (31 July 1944), the very speed of their advance confronted the Americans with the new problems in logistics bound up with the lengthening of lines of communication. Difficulties in transport and in the supplying of petrol contributed to the standstill on the front in the autumn of 1944.

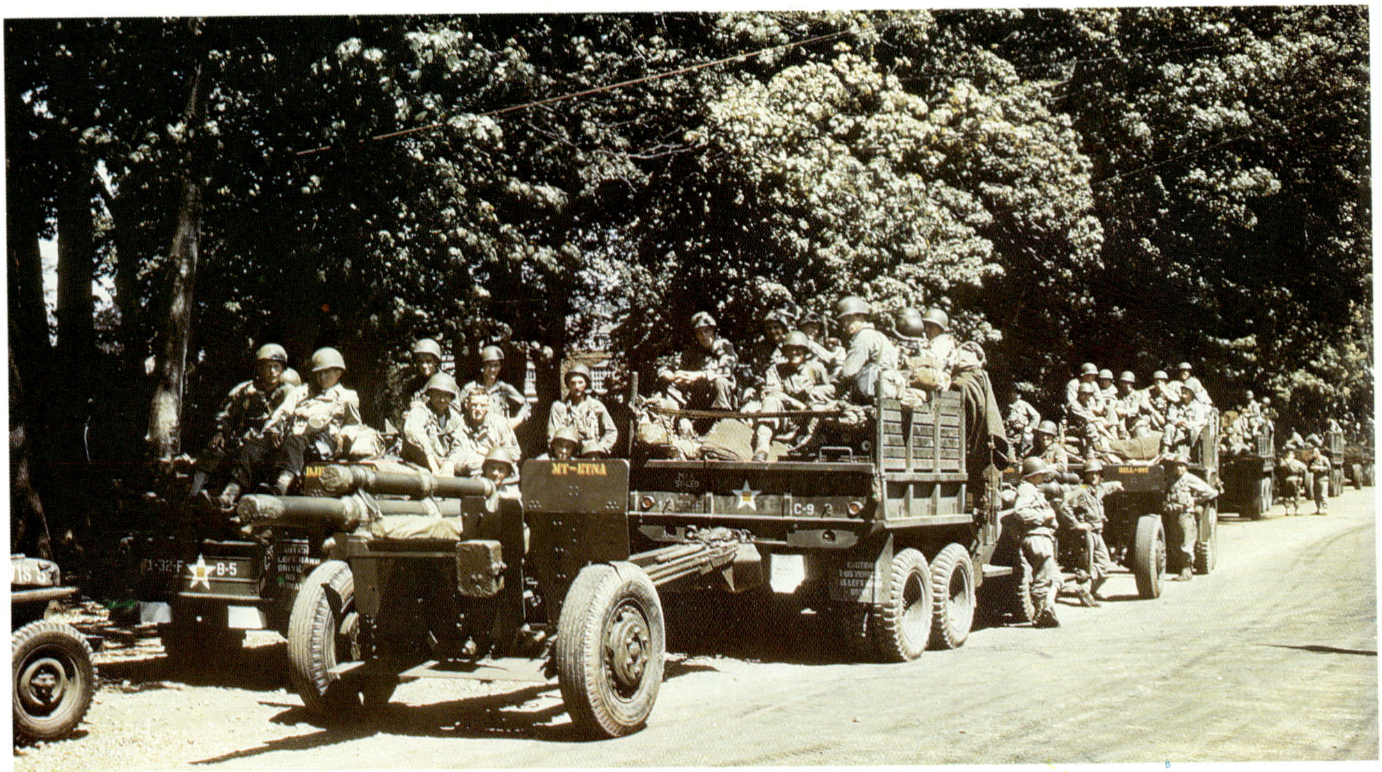

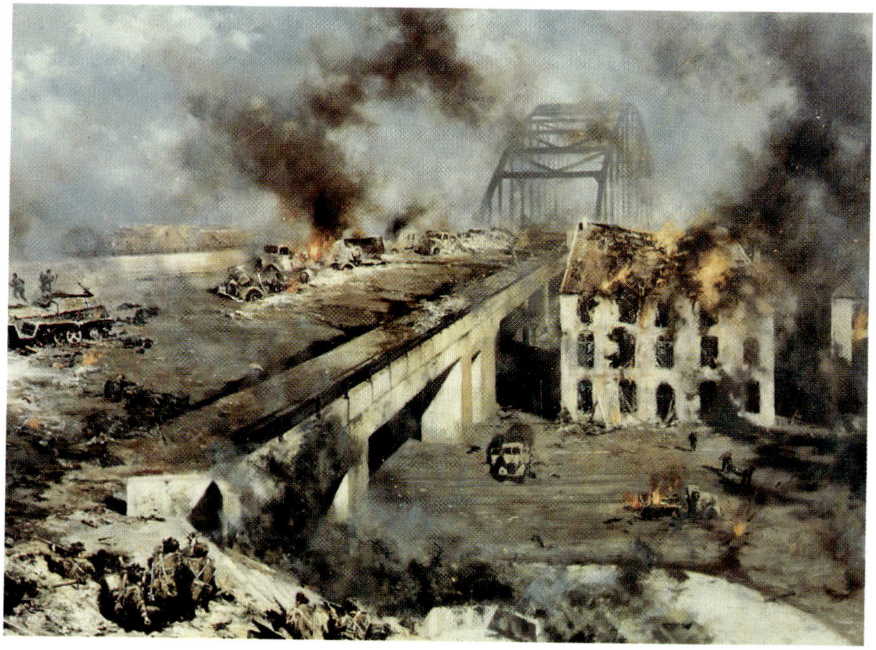

Arnhem. Codenamed Operation Market Garden, the plan to invade Germany by way of the Ruhr, was centred on the mistaken belief that the Germans were weak in the Arnhem area of the eastern Netherlands. The scheme involved taking five major bridges by dropping airborne divisions. The British paratroops at Arnhem landed in gliders some way from the bridge and were unfortunate enough to encounter an SS Panzer division. After a week of fierce fighting resulting in severe British casualties, it was decided to evacuate the surviving troops across the Rhine, 1100 having been killed and 6400 taken prisoner out of the original 10,000. Painting of Arnhem Bridge by David Shepherd.

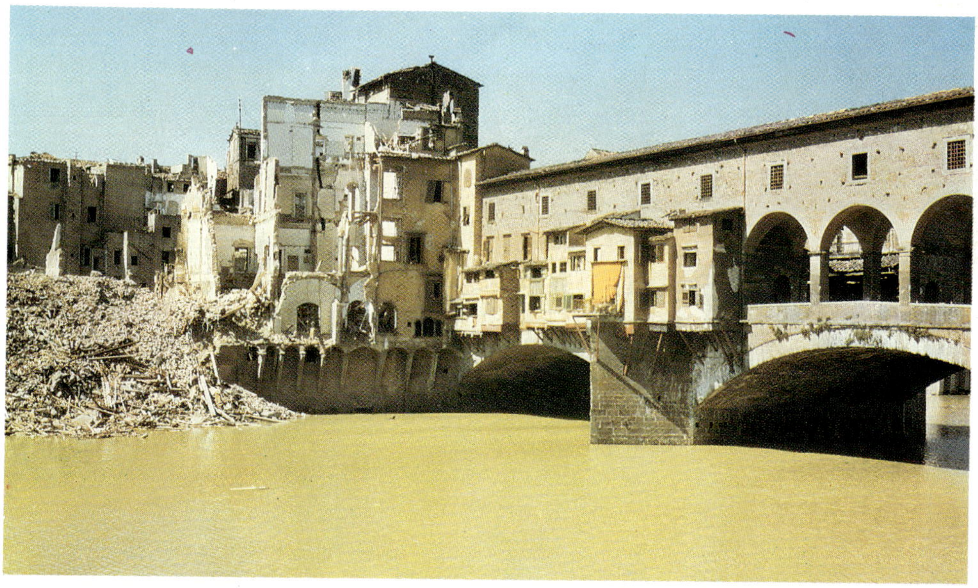

Art. Throughout the Italian campaign the various armies had the feeling, as Kesselring put it, that they were fighting in the galleries of a museum. Both the Germans and the Allies set up special units, such as the American MFAA (Monuments, Fine Arts and Archives), which were charged with the preservation and restoration of historic buildings. When the Germans evacuated Florence in Aug. 1944 Hitler forbade the destruction of the Ponte Vecchio. The Germans blew up the buildings commanding access to it in order to slow up the crossing of the Arno by the Allies.

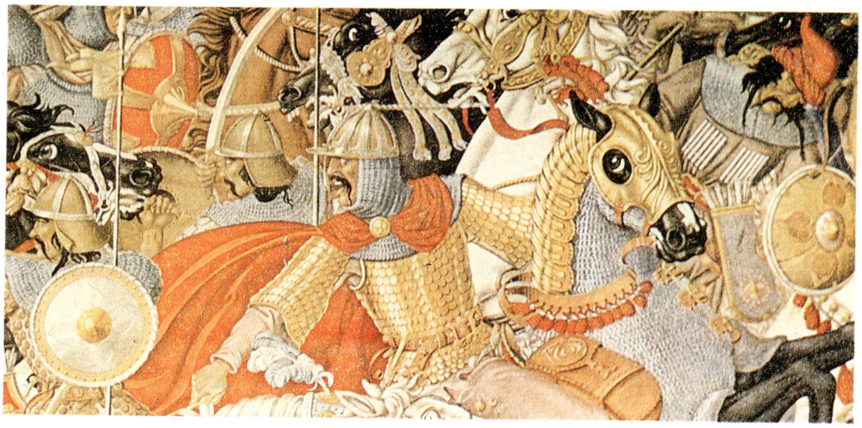

In 1942 at the time when the outcome of the war on the eastern front was becoming uncertain, Hitler ordered the cartoons of eight great tapestries for the Reich Chancellery from the painter Werner Heiner. These were to represent the battles in which the German people had staked its existence in the past, such as Arminius's victory over the Romans or the 'Battle of Hungary' after which the Mongol hordes withdrew.

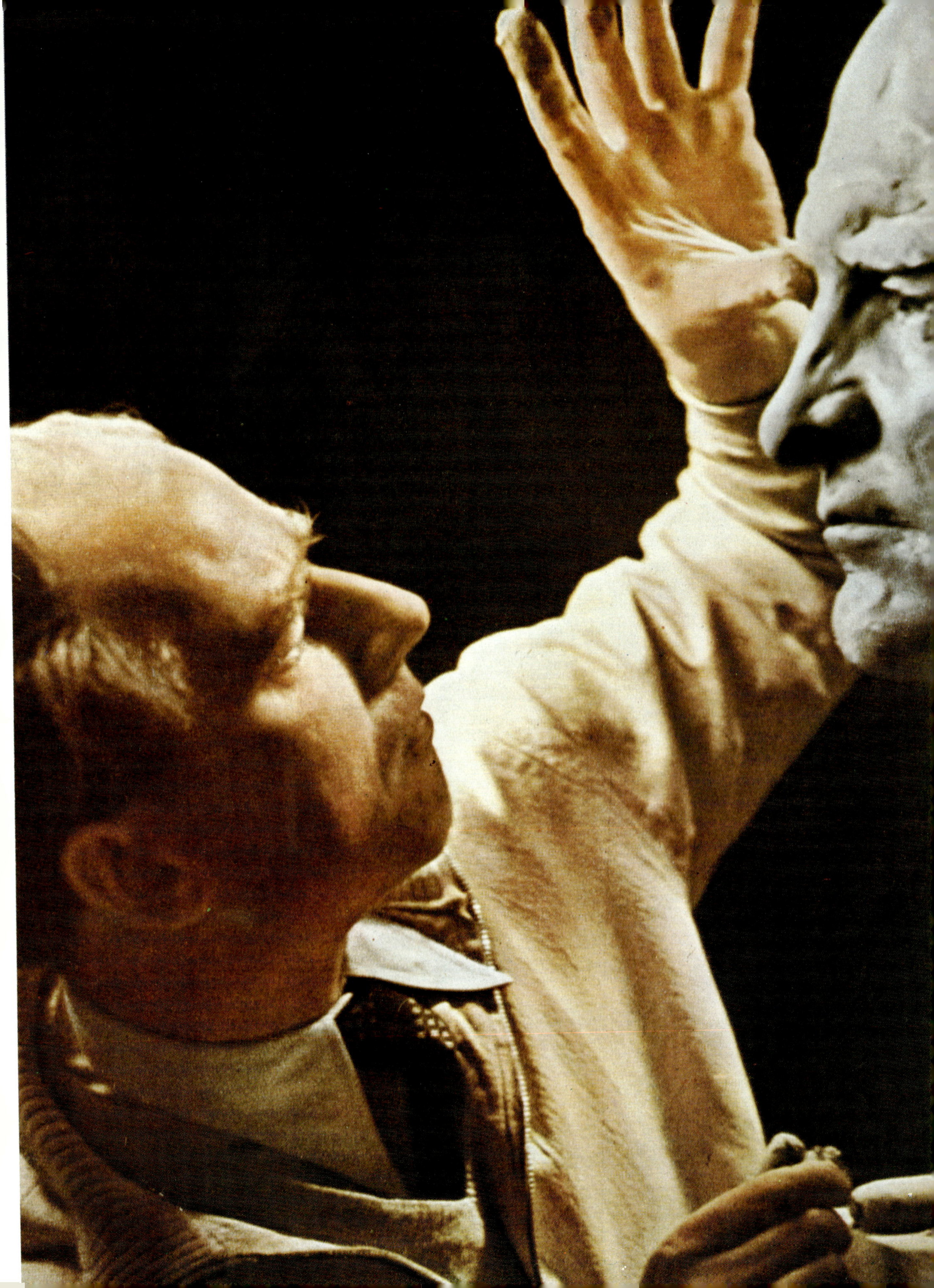

Art. A photograph of Arno Breker, the Third Reich's official sculptor, with a bust of the SS General, Sepp Dietrich.

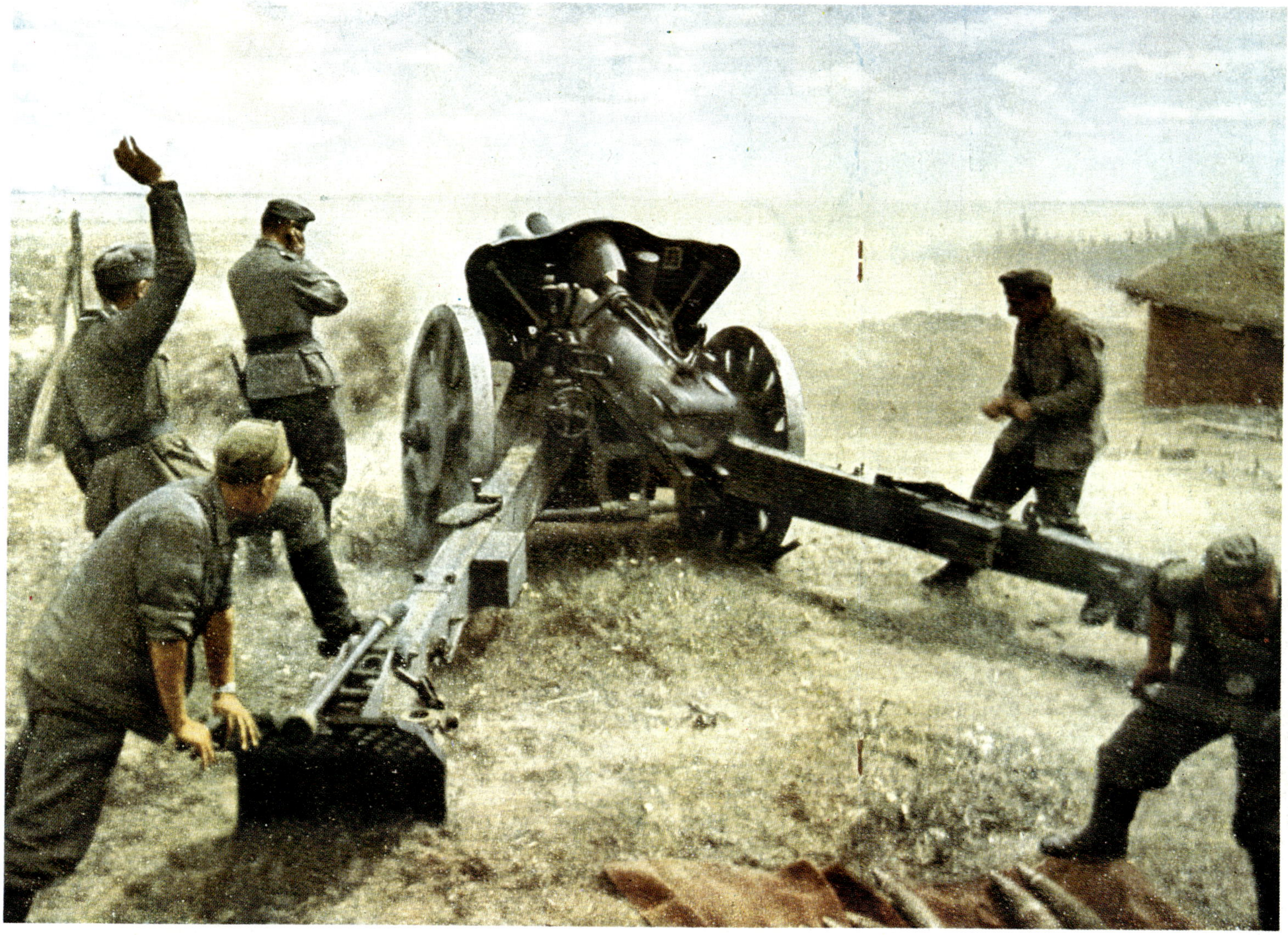

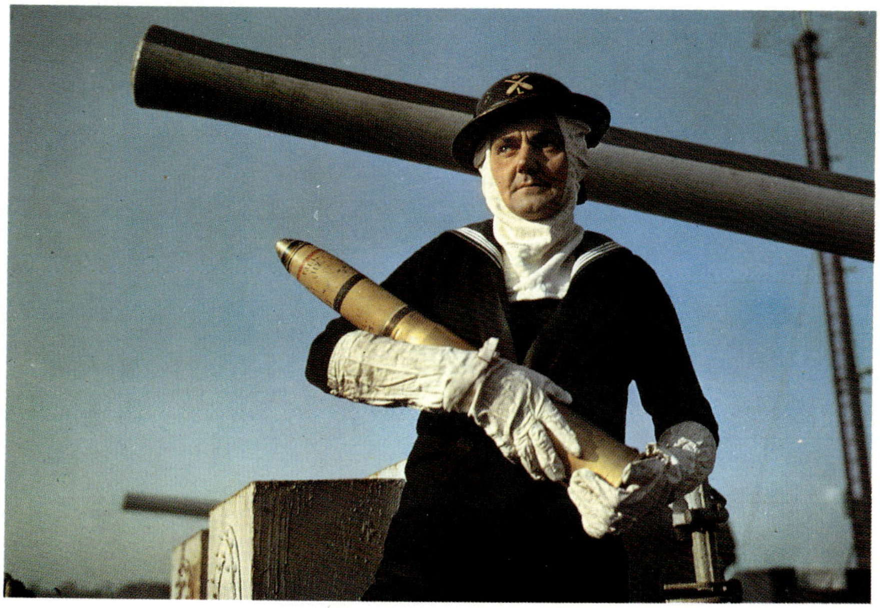

Artillery. With the return to a war of movement linked to the effectiveness of the tank–aircraft combination, artillery did not occupy the privileged place during the Second World War which it had held from 1914 to 1918. Nevertheless, it retained an essential tactical importance, especially in the Red Army, or at times when positions had become stabilized. Here a German 105 mm howitzer is seen in action on the Russian front during the summer of 1943.

Naval artillery. In spite of the increasing importance of air power, the guns of the major surface ships played a decisive role throughout the war. The big guns took part in the preparation of combined operations, while the anti-aircraft guns, which were continually being strengthened, provided defence against air attack. Here a British gunner is seen, wearing the well-known 'antiflash' hood and gloves. These were intended as protection against burns which might be caused if flames blew back when the breech of the gun was opened.

Opposite
On the lookout for aircraft from a German submarine somewhere in the Atlantic.

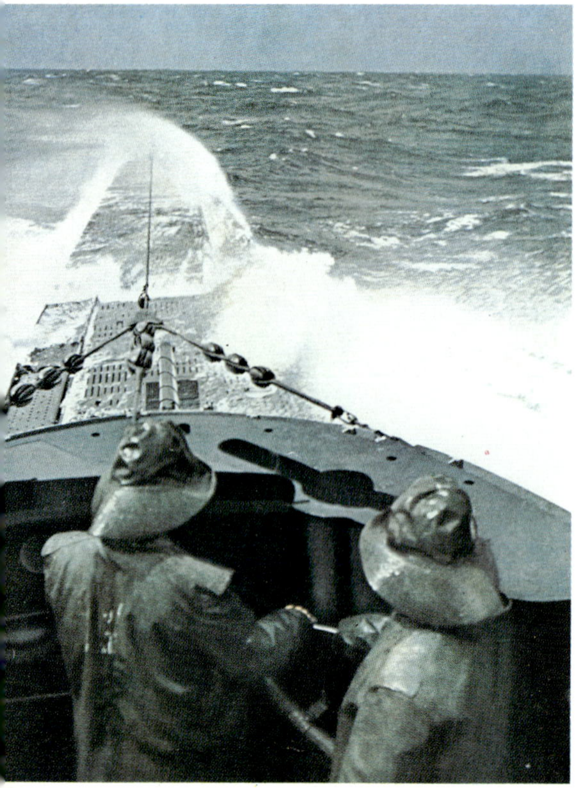

The Battle of the Atlantic. A German submarine on patrol off the Cape of Good Hope during the winter of 1942–43. The Battle of the Atlantic affected an area far beyond the ocean itself and spread into Arctic waters as well as into the Indian Ocean. In the course of a desperate struggle lasting 56 months, it was the U-boats which inflicted the lion's share of the losses on Allied trade, sinking ships amounting to a total tonnage of over 12 million. However, 784 submarines were themselves lost and out of 40,900 men in the U-boat service nearly 30,000 perished.

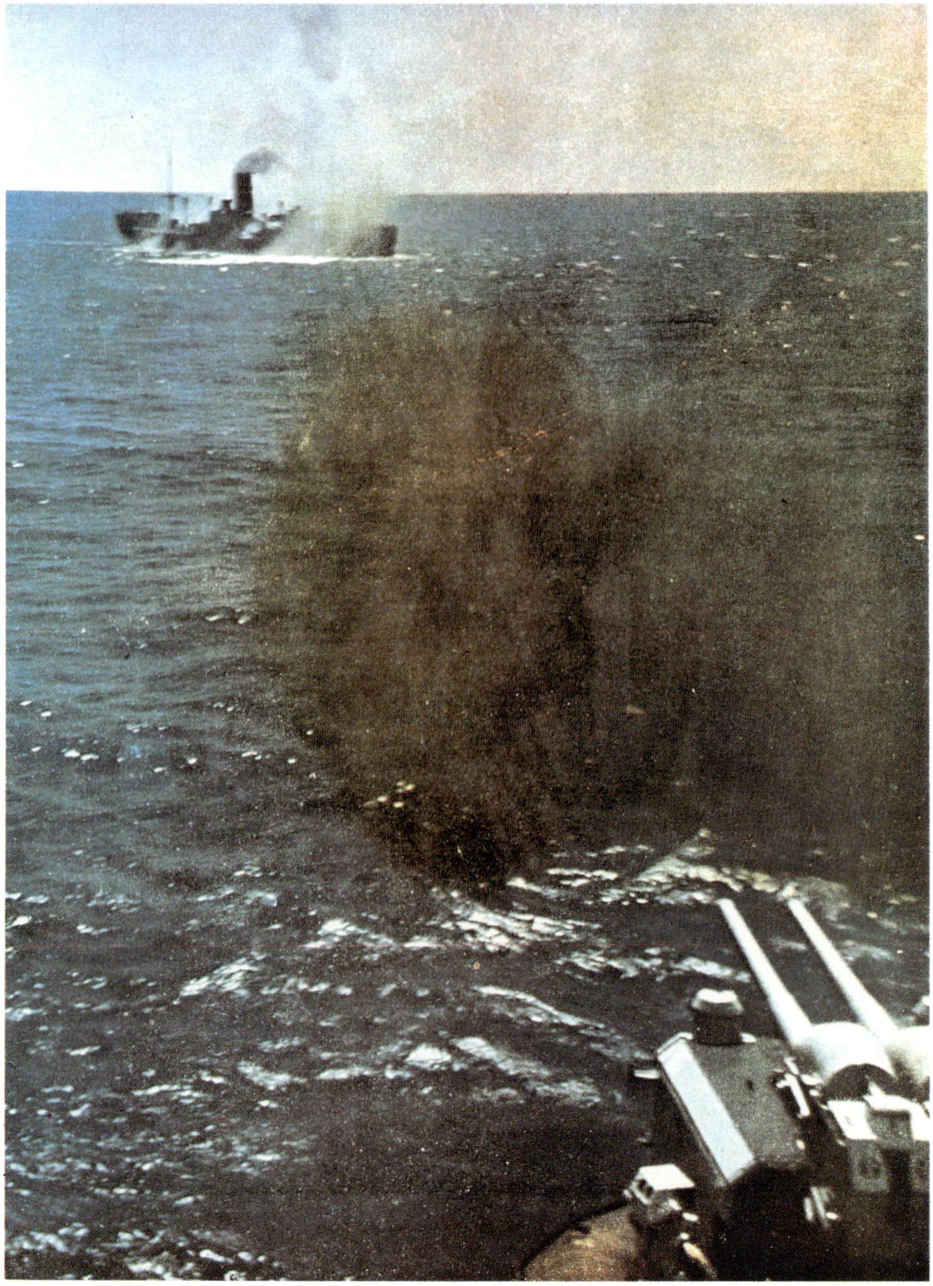

In conformance with the doctrine evolved on the eve of the war, the German navy's major surface ships took part in the Battle of the Atlantic. The battle cruisers *Scharnhorst* and *Gneisenau* made several long-range patrols from the French port of Brest. However, these only produced mediocre results and, after the sinking of the *Bismarck* in May 1941, the German high command had no hesitation in moving its major ships to Norway, beyond the range of Allied aircraft.

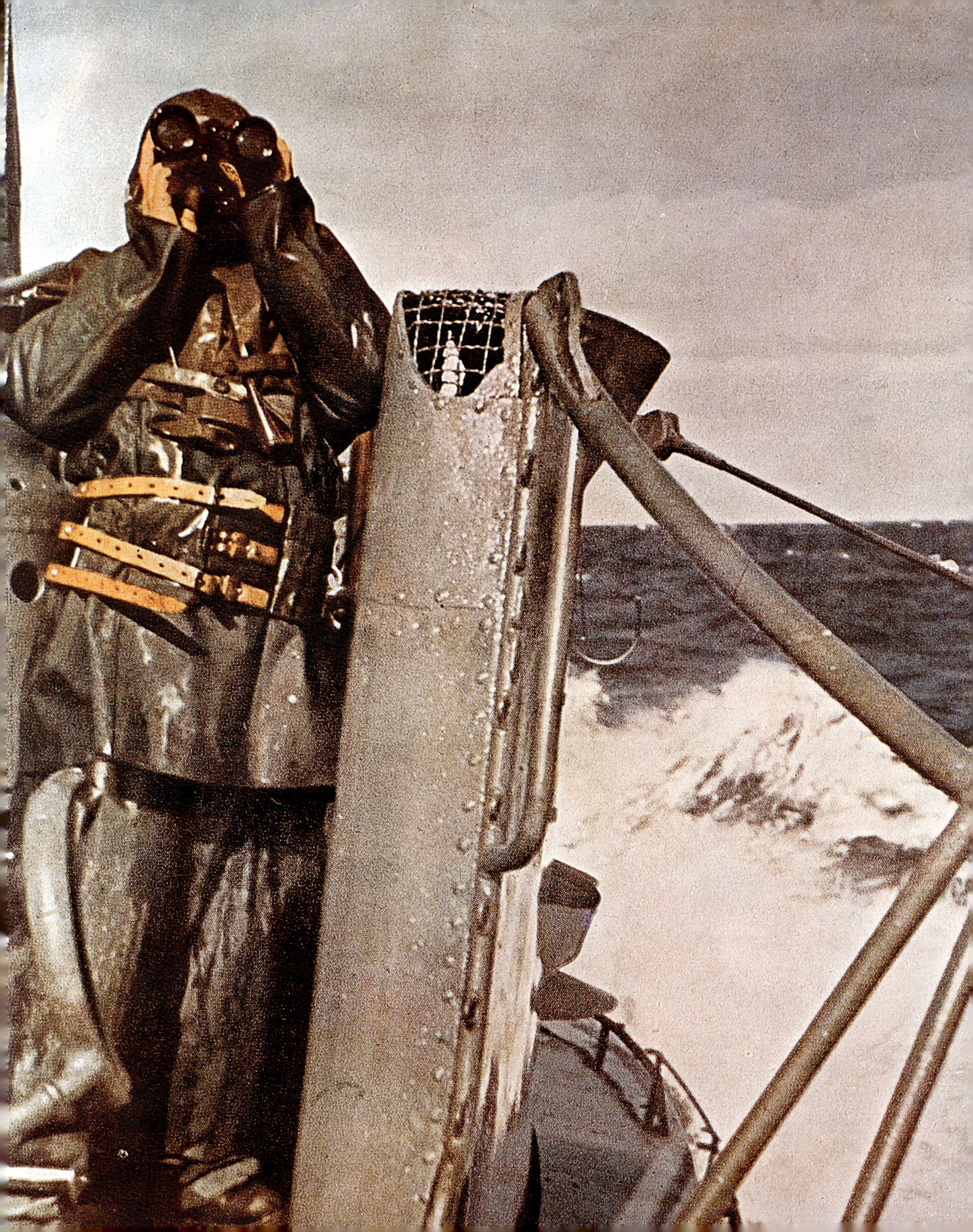

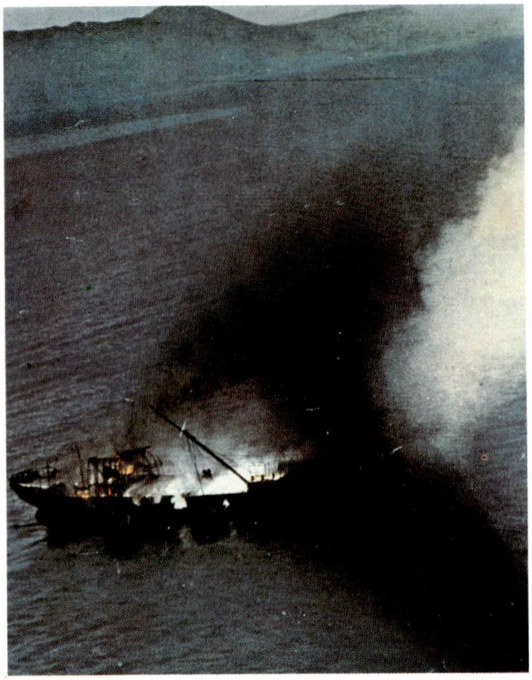

An Allied merchant ship being attacked by a German aircraft in European waters. The Luftwaffe also took part in the attacks on lines of communication, using its long-range four-engined bombers, the Focke-Wulf Condors, which were based at Bordeaux and Stavanger. These aircraft had the additional task of locating convoys and signalling their position to the submarines.

The Atlantic Coast pockets. After the Normandy front had been broken the German high command organized islands of resistance or 'pockets' round the Atlantic coastal ports, with the intention of crippling Allied supply routes by sea. Thus, the taking of Brest was a costly operation for the American army. In the same way Colonel von Aulock, the German commander of Saint-Malo, was able to hold up the US 83rd Infantry Division outside the town for a fortnight. This picture shows an American anti-tank gun attempting to reduce one of the strong points on the small fortified island of Grand-Bé, the old pirate stronghold, in Aug. 1944. Dunkirk, Lorient, Saint-Nazaire and Royan held out until the end of the war.

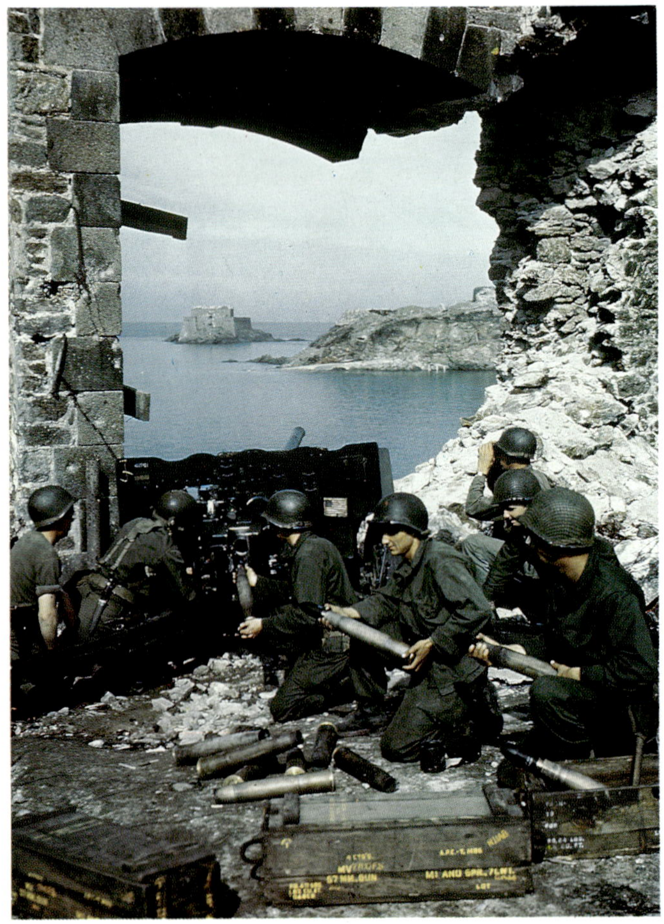

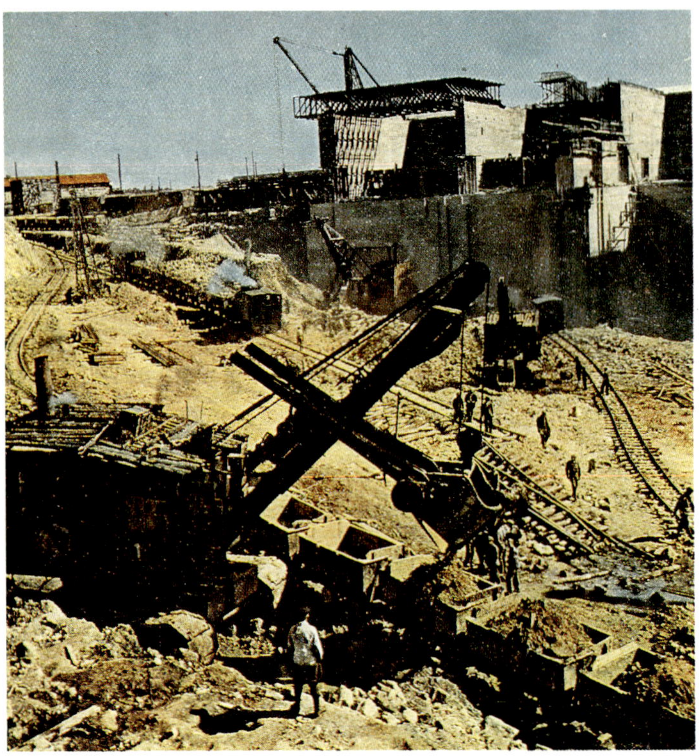

The Atlantic Wall. From 1942, with the prospect of an Allied landing in mind, the Germans began to fortify the western coasts of occupied Europe. Christened 'the Atlantic wall' by German propaganda, the thickness of this 'wall' was in fact very variable. Only the areas considered most vulnerable such as ports, submarine bases and the coast of the Pas-de-Calais were very heavily fortified. The work was carried out by the Todt Organization, using local firms or forced labour.

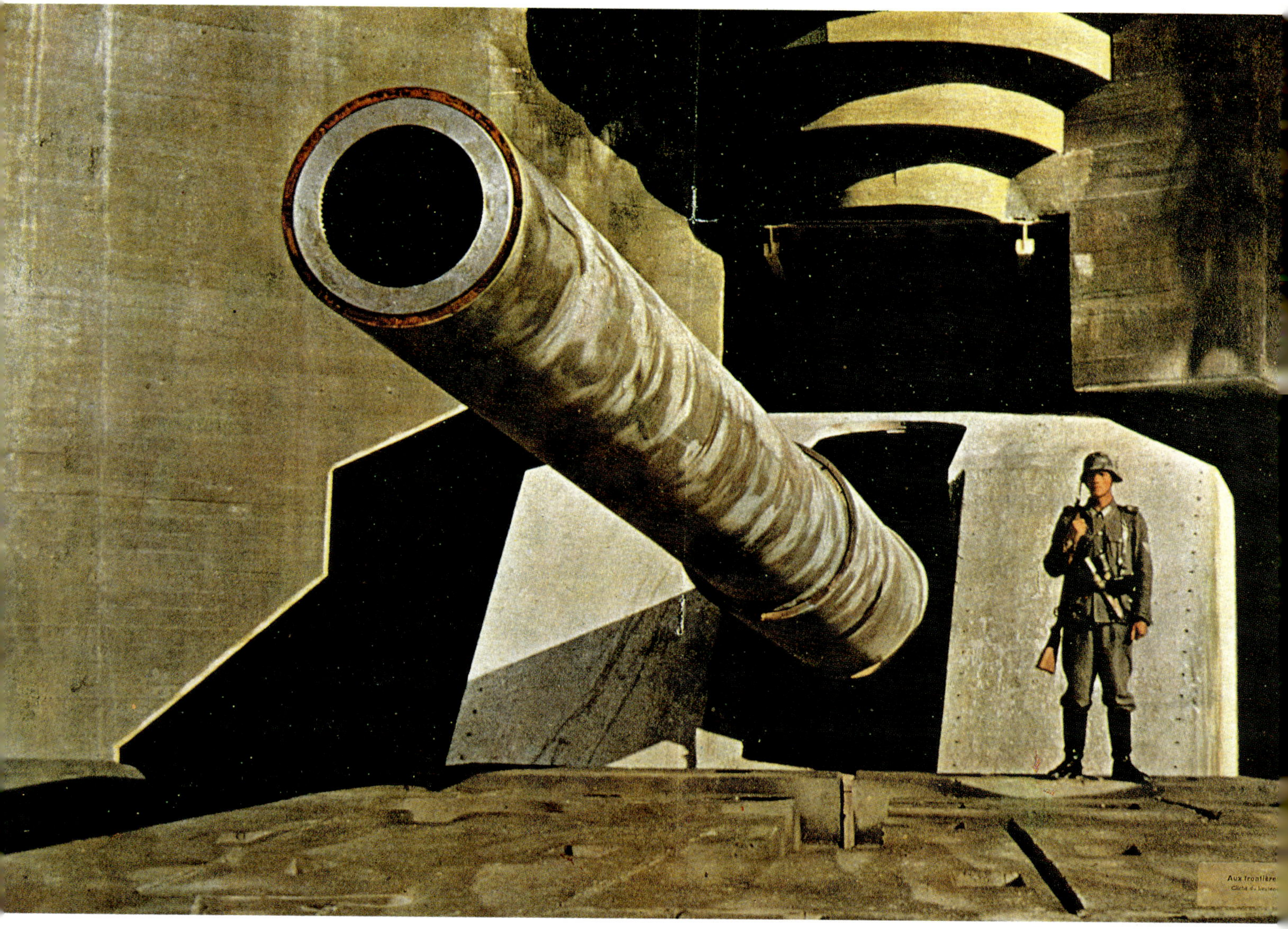

Convinced that an Allied landing could only come at the narrowest part of the Channel, the Germans constructed impressive defences in the coastal area of the Pas-de-Calais. These fortifications included in particular enormous naval guns such as the 406 mm (16 in.) Lindemann battery, seen in this picture, which was one of the most photographed objects of the war. The range of these guns was such that they could reach Dover and they were also intended to prevent British shipping from passing through the Dover Straits.

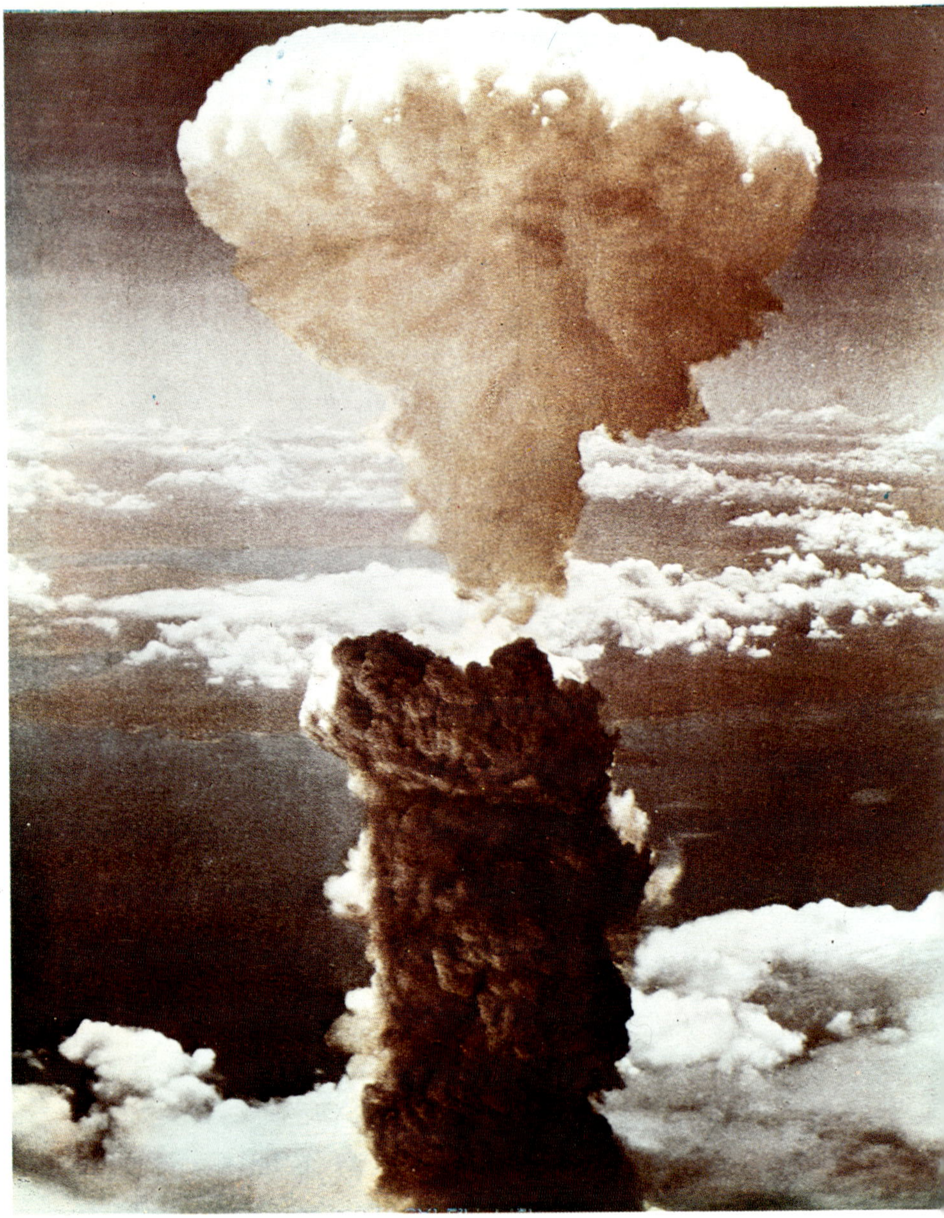

The atomic bomb. The explosion of the atomic bomb above Nagasaki on 9 Aug. 1945 was accompanied by a mushroom cloud which rose to a height of 49,000 ft (15,000 m). The bomb, christened 'Fat Man' because of its shape, consisted of a ring of 64 detonators which simultaneously expelled plutonium elements in such a way that a supercritical mass was obtained. It weighed more than five tons and was 13 feet (4 m) long.

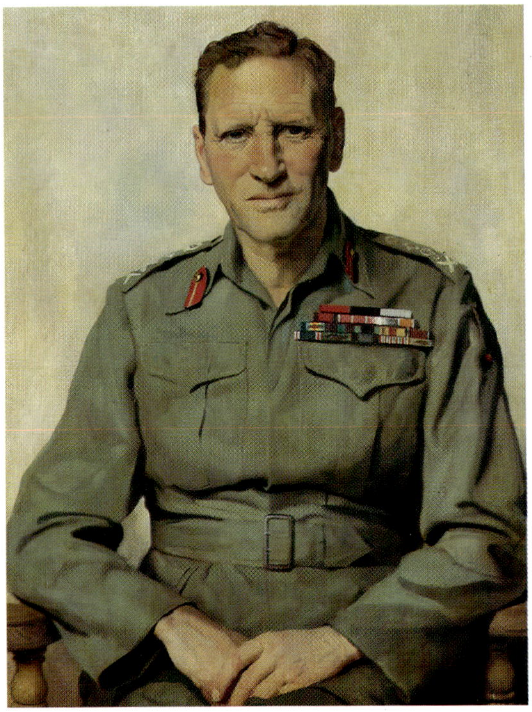

Auchinleck. A highly respected commander in the British Army, he was appointed by Churchill to replace Wavell in the Middle East in June 1941. British fortunes there were at a low ebb, and Field Marshal Sir Claude Auchinleck set about planning Operation Crusader, a response to Rommel's defeat of the British Battleaxe Operation. Crusader led to the relief of Tobruk, but following a strategic withdrawal by the British, Rommel retook Tobruk after renewed fighting in June 1942. Despite the decisive Allied victory at Alam el Halfa two months later, Churchill did not forgive Auchinleck for the fall of Tobruk and had him replaced by Alexander. Painting by James Gunn. Wellington College, Berks.

Auschwitz. Set up in May 1940, Auschwitz-Birkenau was the largest and most notorious of the concentration camps. It consisted of three main camps and a number of smaller ones and included a complex of buildings used for the systematic extermination of prisoners in gas chambers and the cremation of their remains. More than a million people, mainly Jews, died at Auschwitz.

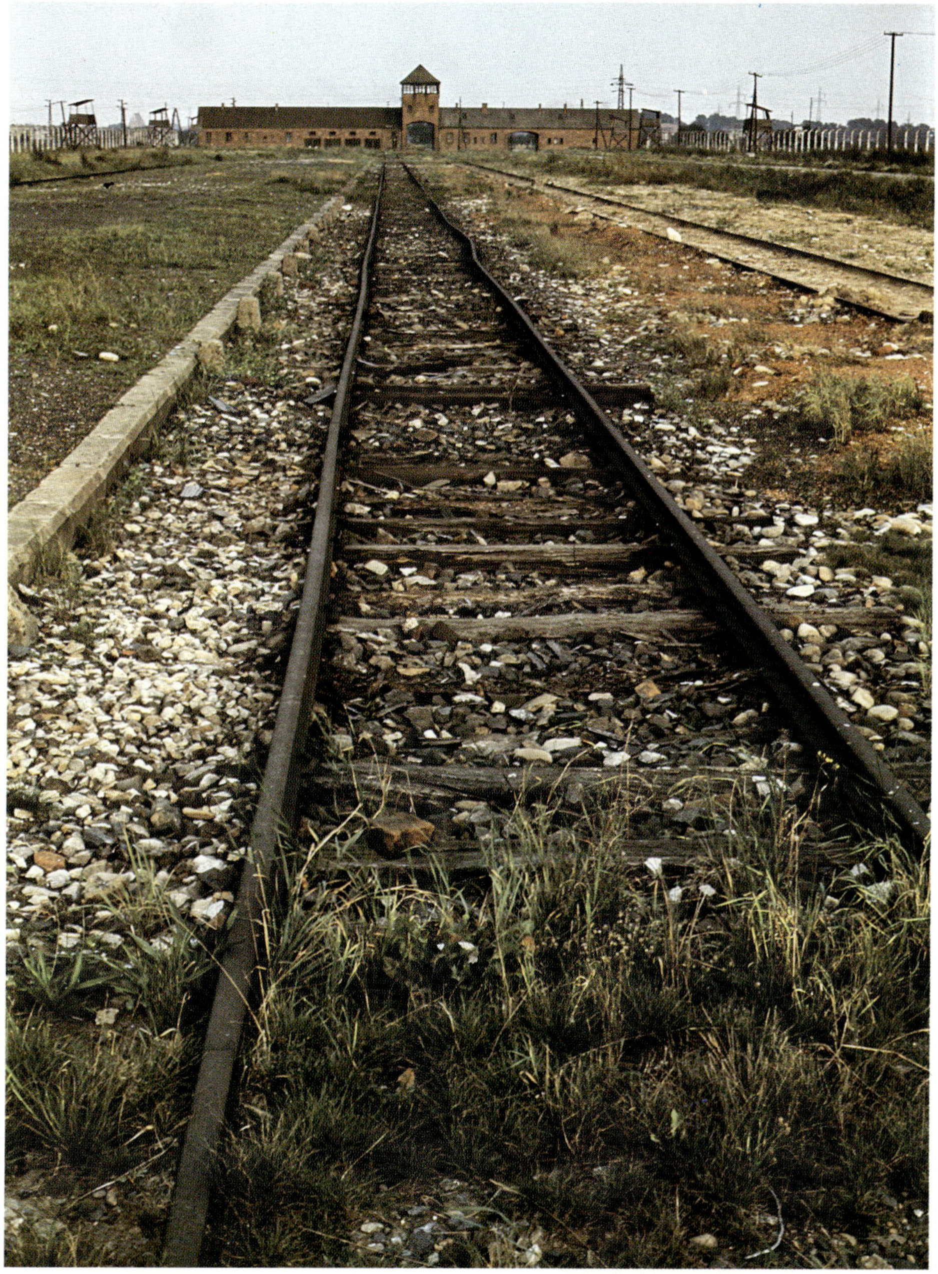

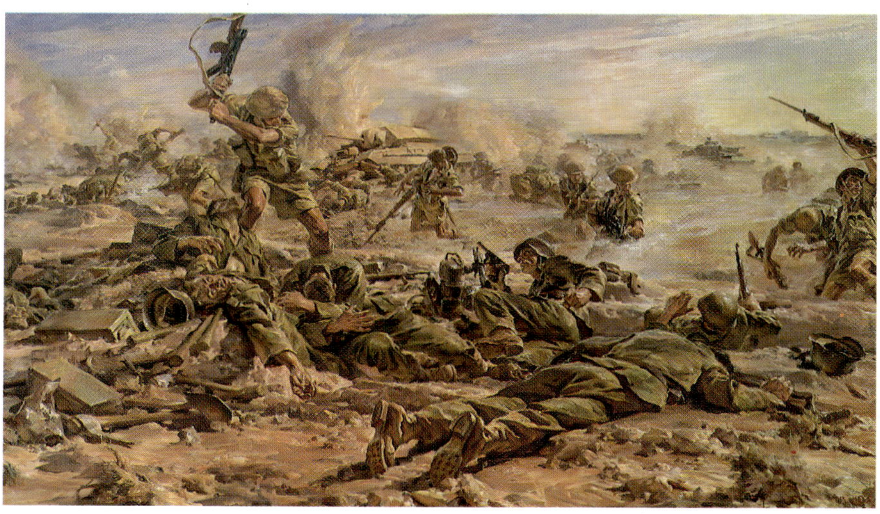

Australia. Within a few hours of Britain's declaration of war on Germany, Australia unhesitatingly followed suit. Australian troops were posted to the Middle East, and were engaged in Cyrenaica during 1940. Following the Japanese attacks in the Pacific, Australia lost 22,000 prisoners in Malaya and Indonesia and had few well-prepared troops left at home. Two divisions were transferred from the Middle East and it was decided to seek close co-operation with the US. The Japanese navy having been defeated, Australian troops began to clear the Japanese from New Guinea and adjacent islands, followed by campaigns intended to destroy the Japanese forces in Bougainville, Sarawak and Borneo. The atom bombs in Aug. 1945 ended the war without the need for these campaigns to be pursued further. Throughout the war, Australians flew with the RAF and served in the Royal Navy. This painting by Ivor Hele depicts Australian troops in action in Egypt in Sept. 1942. Australian War Memorial.

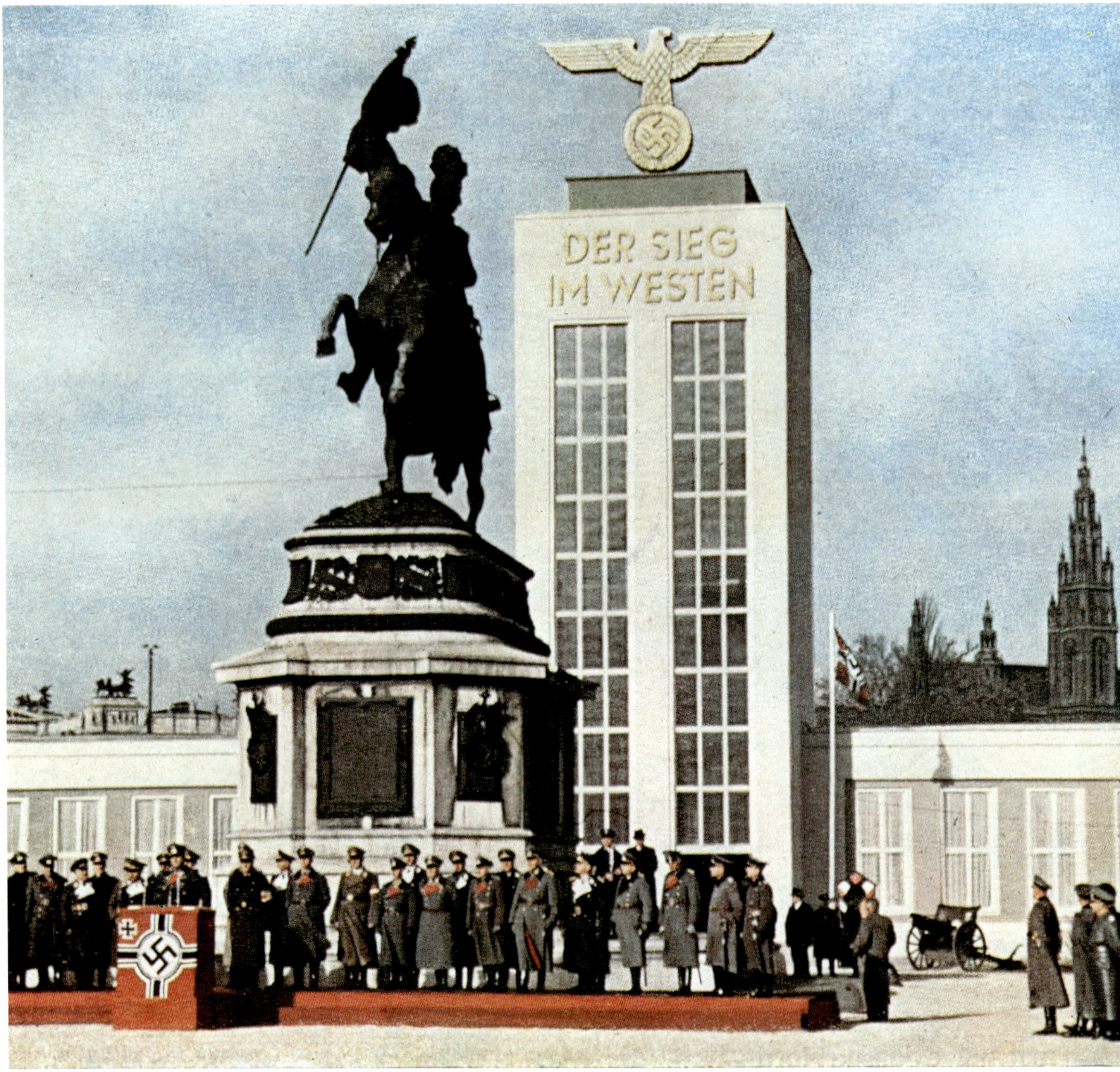

Austria. Following the *Anschluss* Austria was completely integrated into the Reich, simply forming the *Ostmark* or 'eastern march', divided into seven provinces or *Gaue*. In exchange for Austria's abandonment of all political freedom, the German government developed its economic potential and introduced measures intended to end unemployment. From 1939 it lauded the courage of the Austrian contingents in the Wehrmacht. Thus during the winter of 1940–41 on the Heldenplatz (Hero Square) in the heart of Vienna, dominated by the statue of Napoleon's adversary the Archduke Karl, Göring and Field-Marshal List opened an exhibition celebrating the victory in the west and stressing the part played in Norway by Austrian mountain troops.

The Axis. Agreed on in Oct. 1936, the Rome–Berlin Axis was strengthened by Hitler's visit to Rome in May 1938. On this occasion Hitler and his suite were present, with Mussolini and other Fascist leaders, at Italian army manoeuvres at Santa Marinella near Rome. At these manoeuvres a number of failings could not be concealed and this increased Hitler's resolve to give his partner only a secondary role and to exclude Mussolini from major decisions.

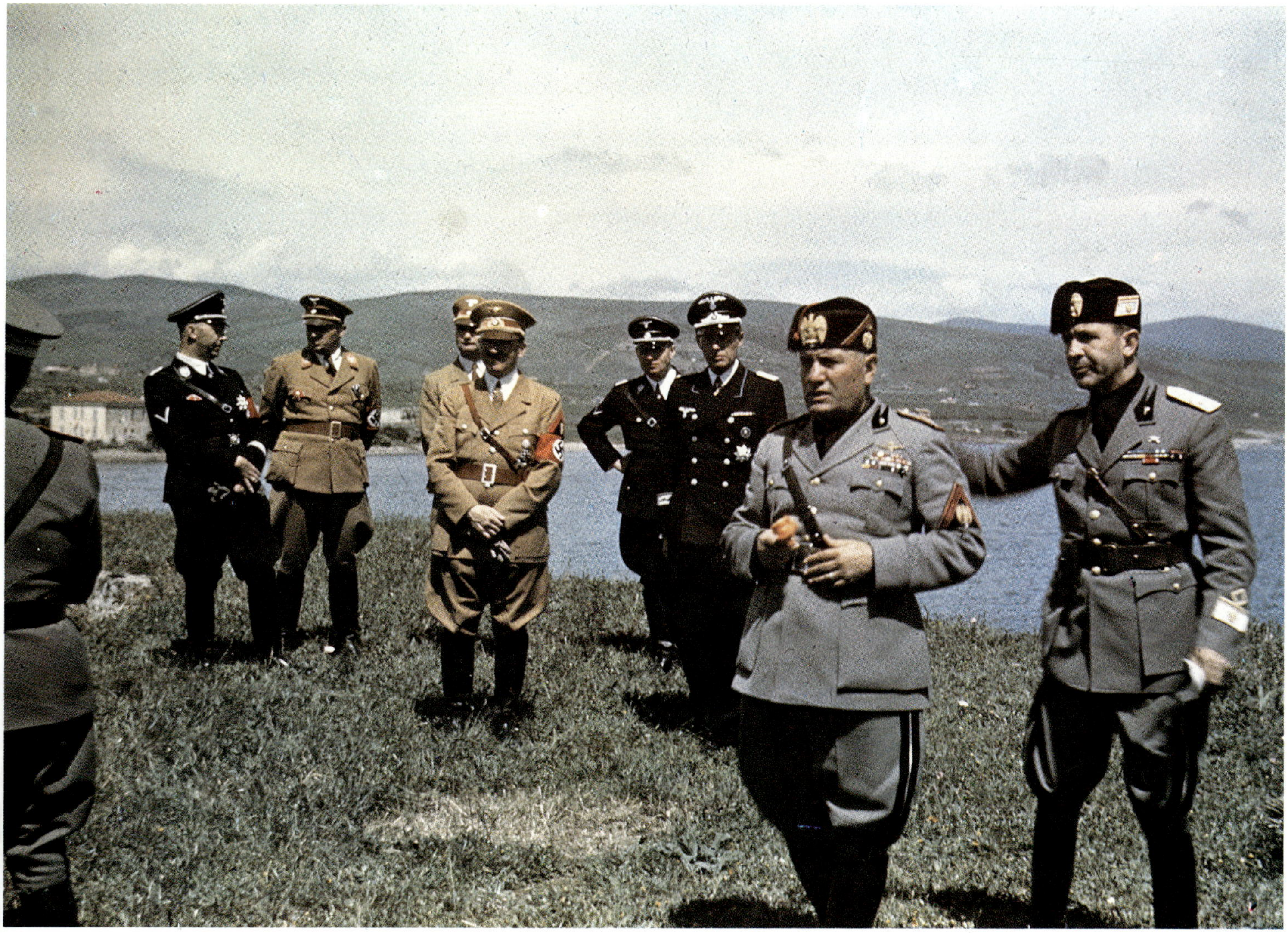

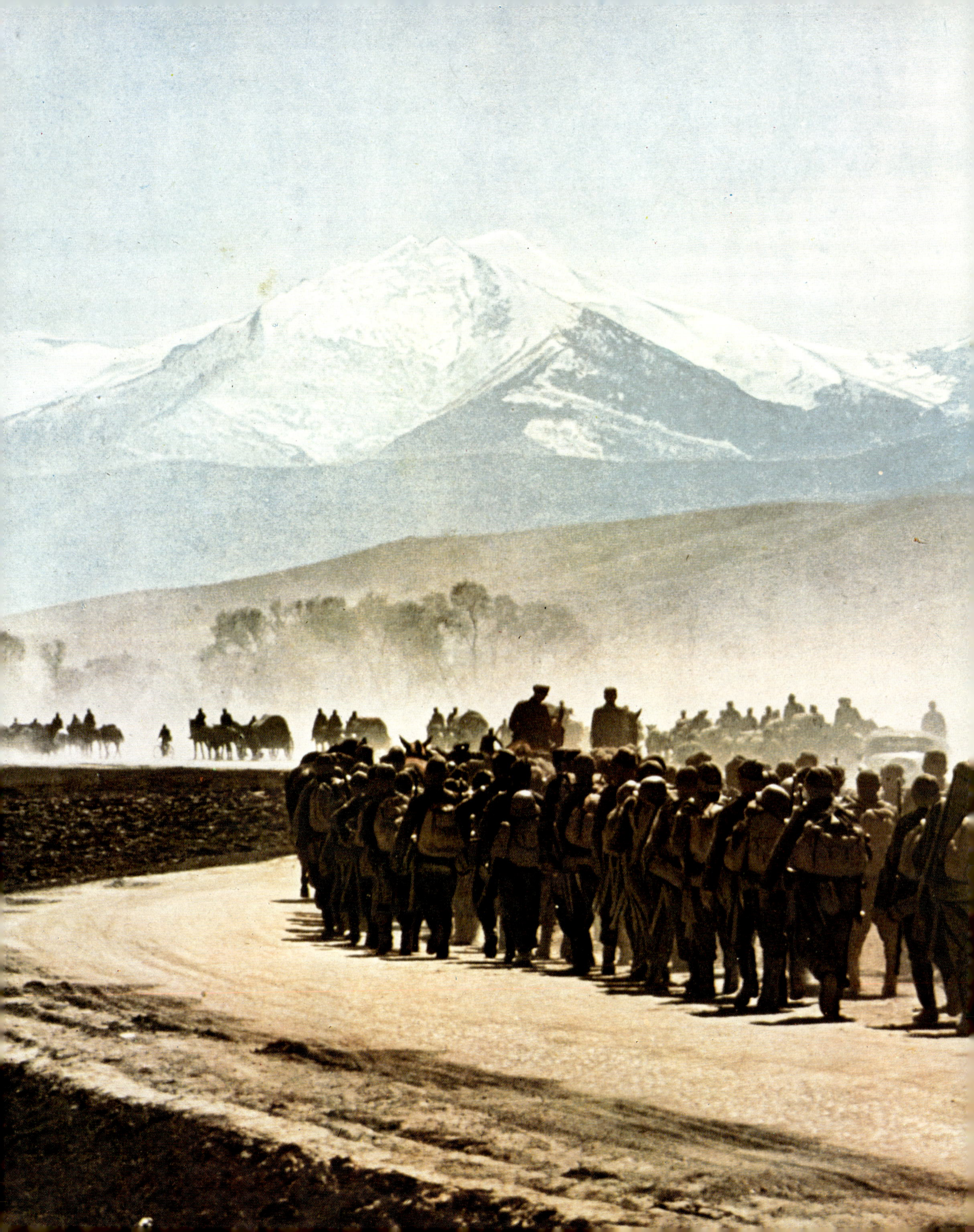

The Balkan campaign. *(Opposite)* A column of German troops at the foot of Mount Olympus in Greece in April 1941.

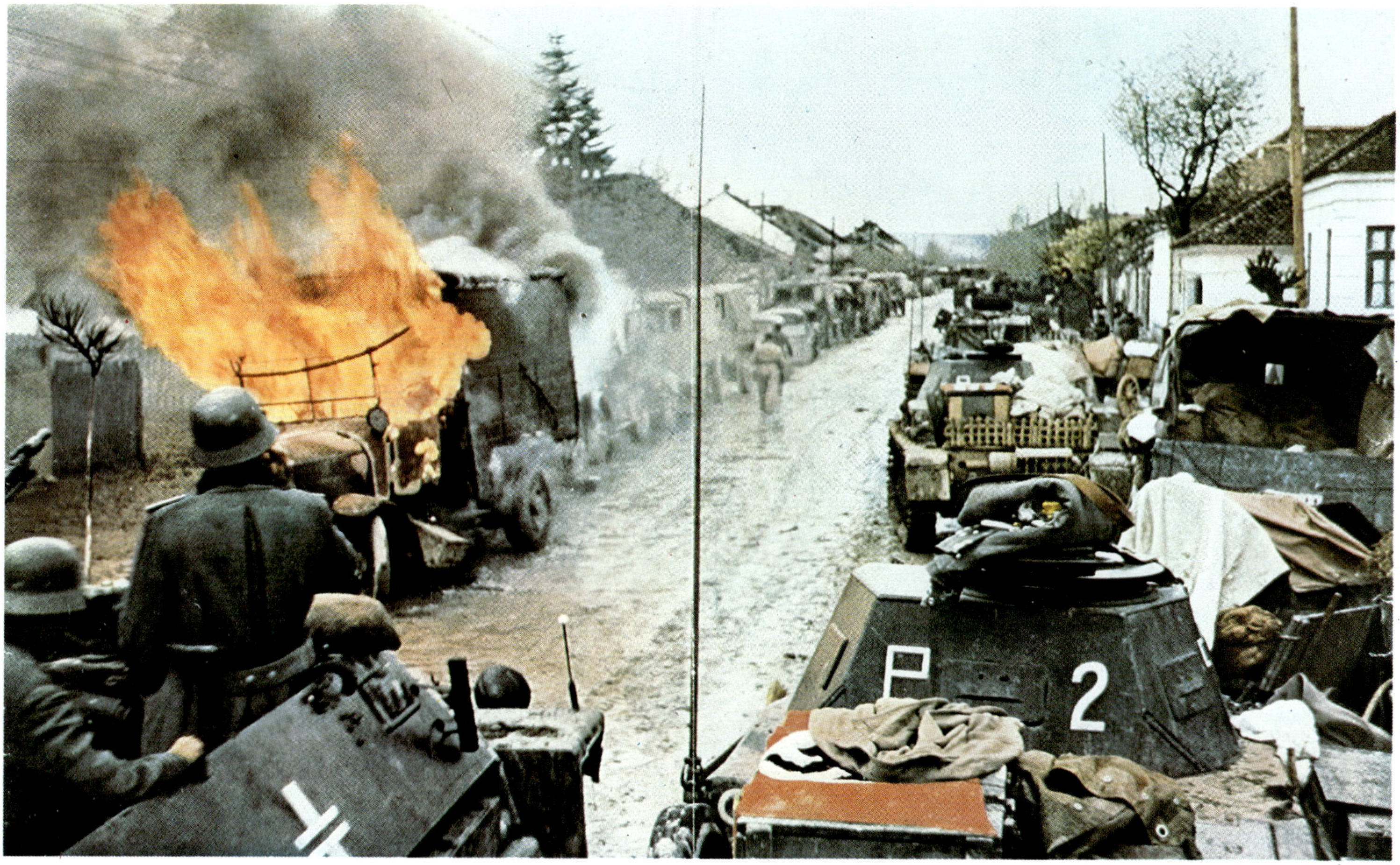

The Balkan campaign. Once again this demonstrated the Wehrmacht's tactical skill. Beginning on 6 April 1941, the campaign in Yugoslavia was over by 13 April, when the troops in Belgrade surrendered. In this picture of a road in Serbia a German motorized column is passing a totally disabled Yugoslavian convoy. Nevertheless, the German victory in Yugoslavia was incomplete. Partisans led by General Mihajlović quickly organized themselves in mountainous areas.

German and Bulgarian 'brotherhood in arms' during the Balkan campaign in the spring of 1941. Having joined the Axis Tripartite Pact on 1 March 1941, Bulgaria seized the chance, to the detriment of Yugoslavia and Greece, to regain territories lost in 1919. Thus it recovered part of Thrace and, with the islands of Lemnos and Tenedos, direct access to the Aegean Sea.

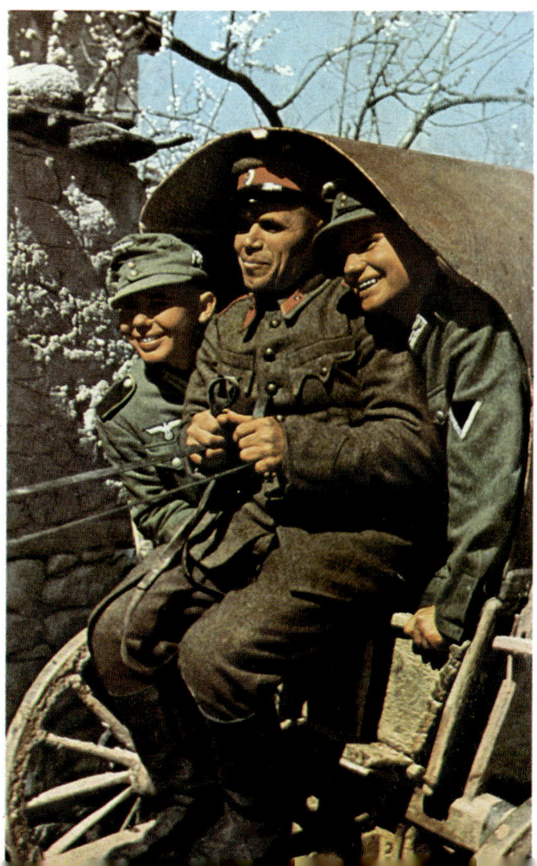

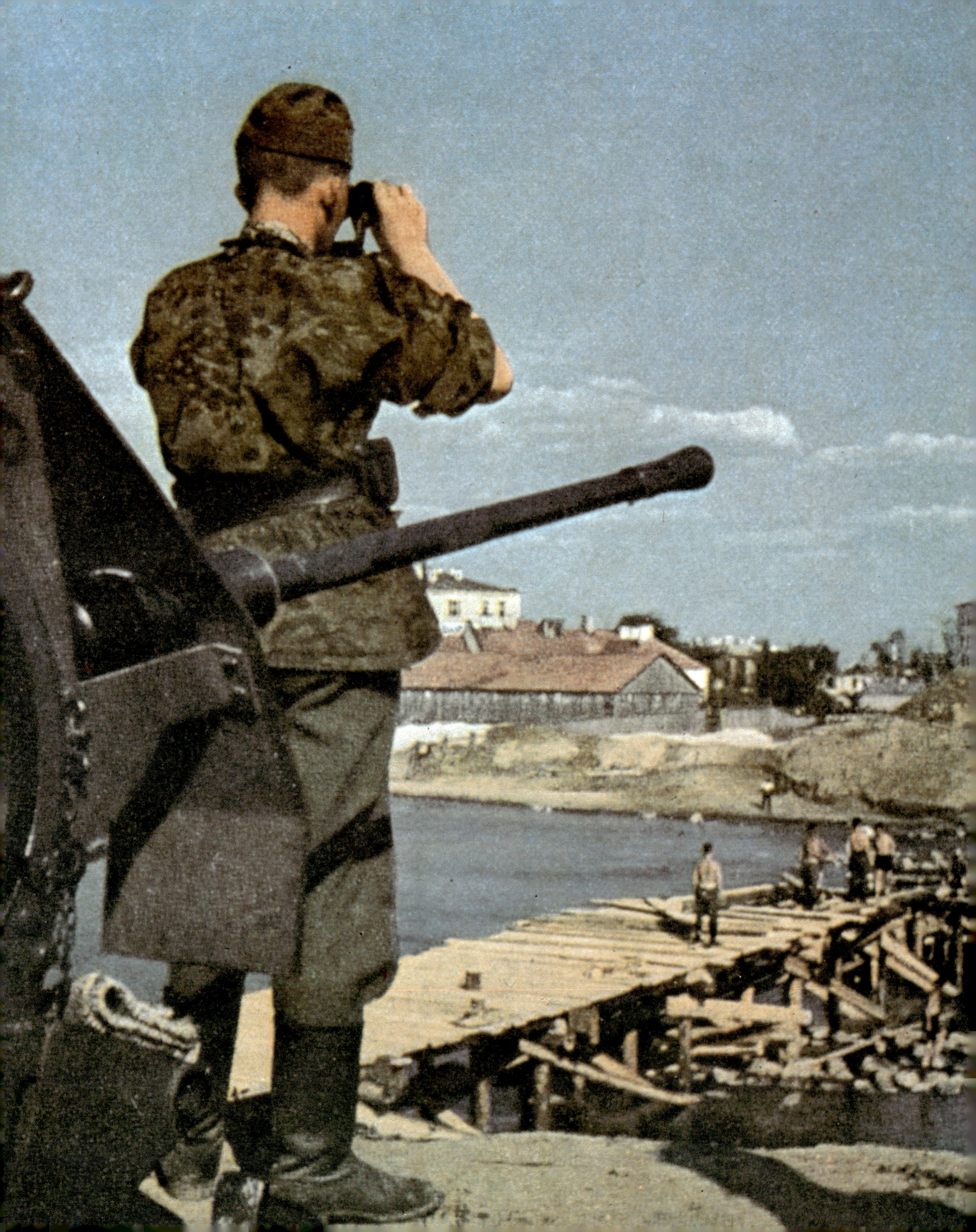

The Baltic states. Construction of a bridge across the Velikaya river on the border of Latvia by troops of the Waffen SS.

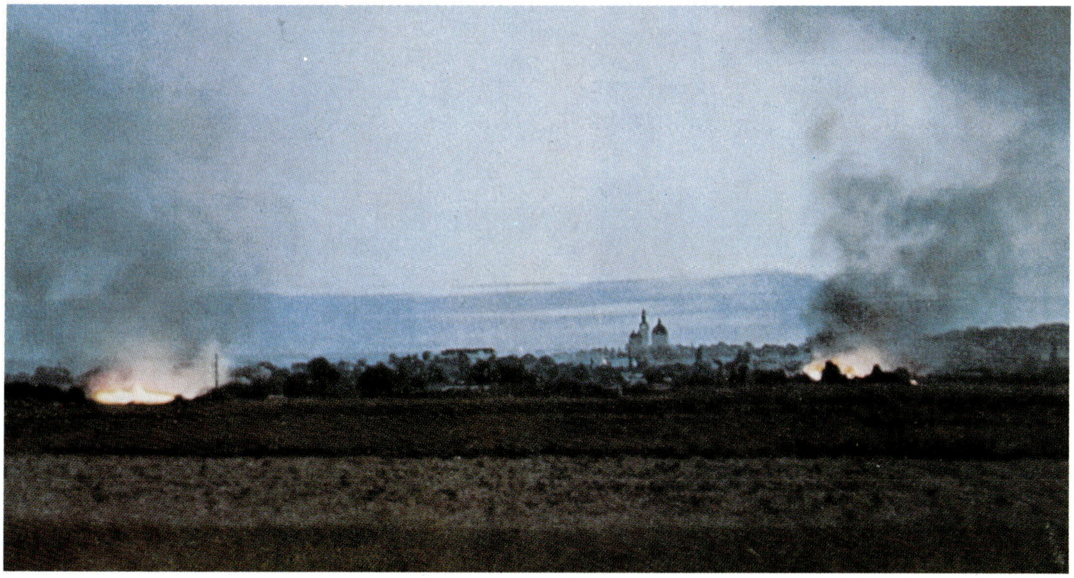

The Baltic states. At dawn on 22 June 1941, the day of the launching of Operation Barbarossa, German artillery opens fire on Tauroggen, a town on the border between Lithuania and East Prussia. Like Estonia and Latvia, Lithuania had known only a brief 20-year period of independence. By virtue of the Soviet-German pact of Aug. 1939 the three Baltic states had come into the Soviet Union's sphere of influence and had been annexed by the USSR in the summer of 1940.

Some hours after the capture of Tauroggen a German soldier examines a marker post placed by the Soviets on the East Prussian border. With lettering in Russian and Lithuanian the notice indicates the existence of a no man's land 800 metres wide. Lithuania, which formed part of the Reichskommissariat 'Ostland', was occupied by the Red Army once again in 1944 and made an integral part of the Soviet Union, in spite of the majority of the population's strong desire for independence.

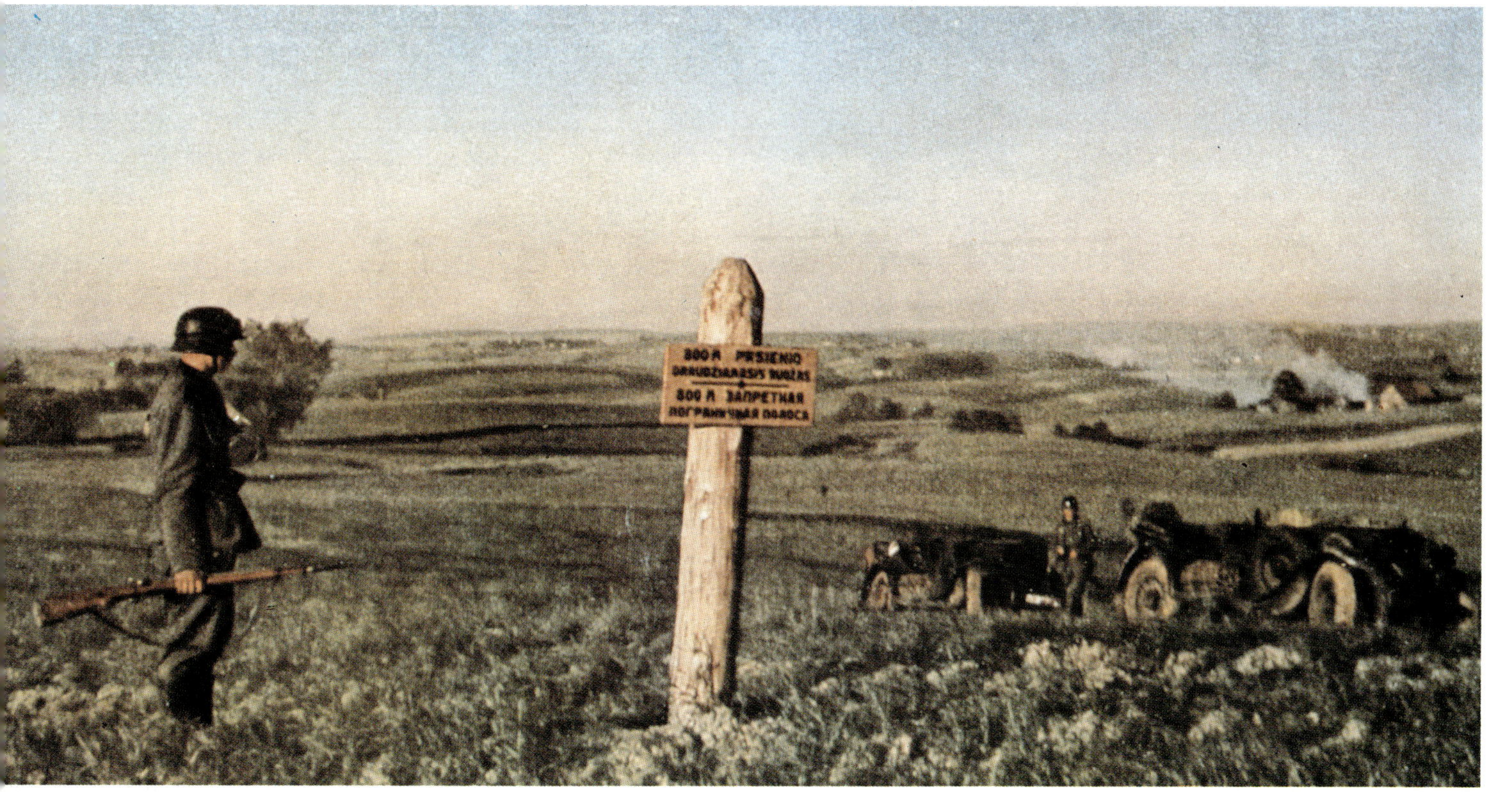

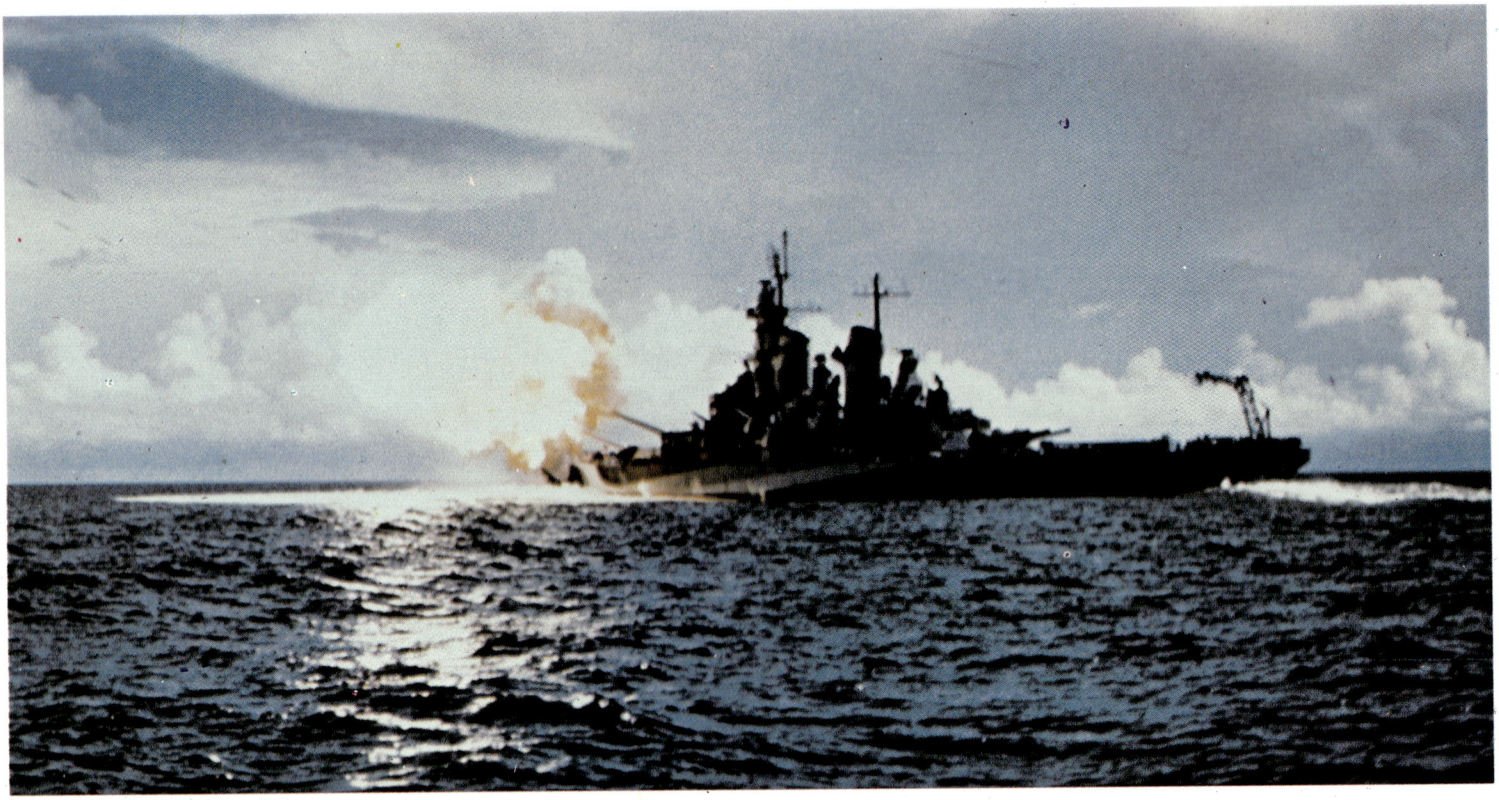

The Battleship. Still regarded as the 'capital ship' of the war fleets in 1939, by the middle of the war the battleship had been relegated to a secondary role in favour of the aircraft carrier. However, it remained considerably important because of the supporting fire it could provide when landings took place and because of its formidable anti-aircraft defences. In 1945 the US Navy possessed four fast battleships of the *Missouri* class. With a displacement of 45,000 tons, these splendid ships were armed with nine 16in. (406mm) guns and a considerable number of anti-aircraft weapons. The *Missouri* (photograph) took part in the operations at Iwo Jima and Okinawa.

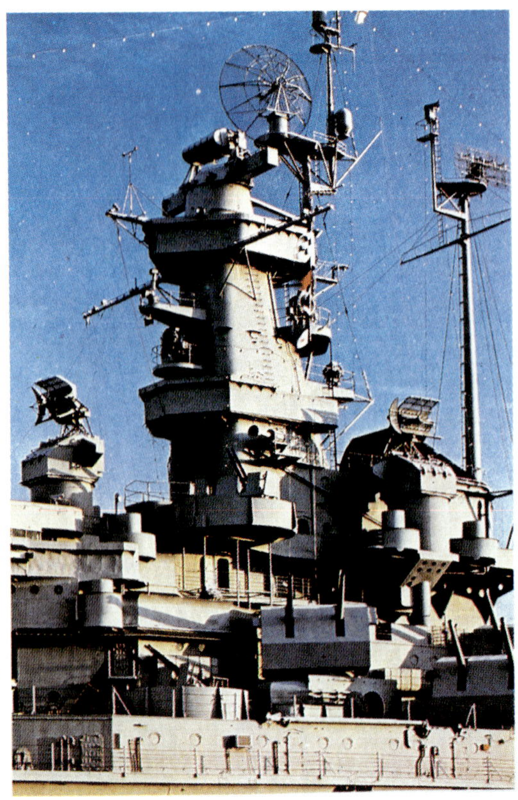

Already, on the eve of the conflict, battleships had very different outlines from those of the First World War. The military or tripod masts were replaced by towers or turret masts protecting the bridge and surmounted by the fire control turret of the main armament. This arrangement was to be copied on older vessels which had been refitted, such as the American battleship *Arizona*, heavily damaged at Pearl Harbor. During the course of the war, the superstructures of warships bristled with radar aerials used for navigation or for direction of fire.

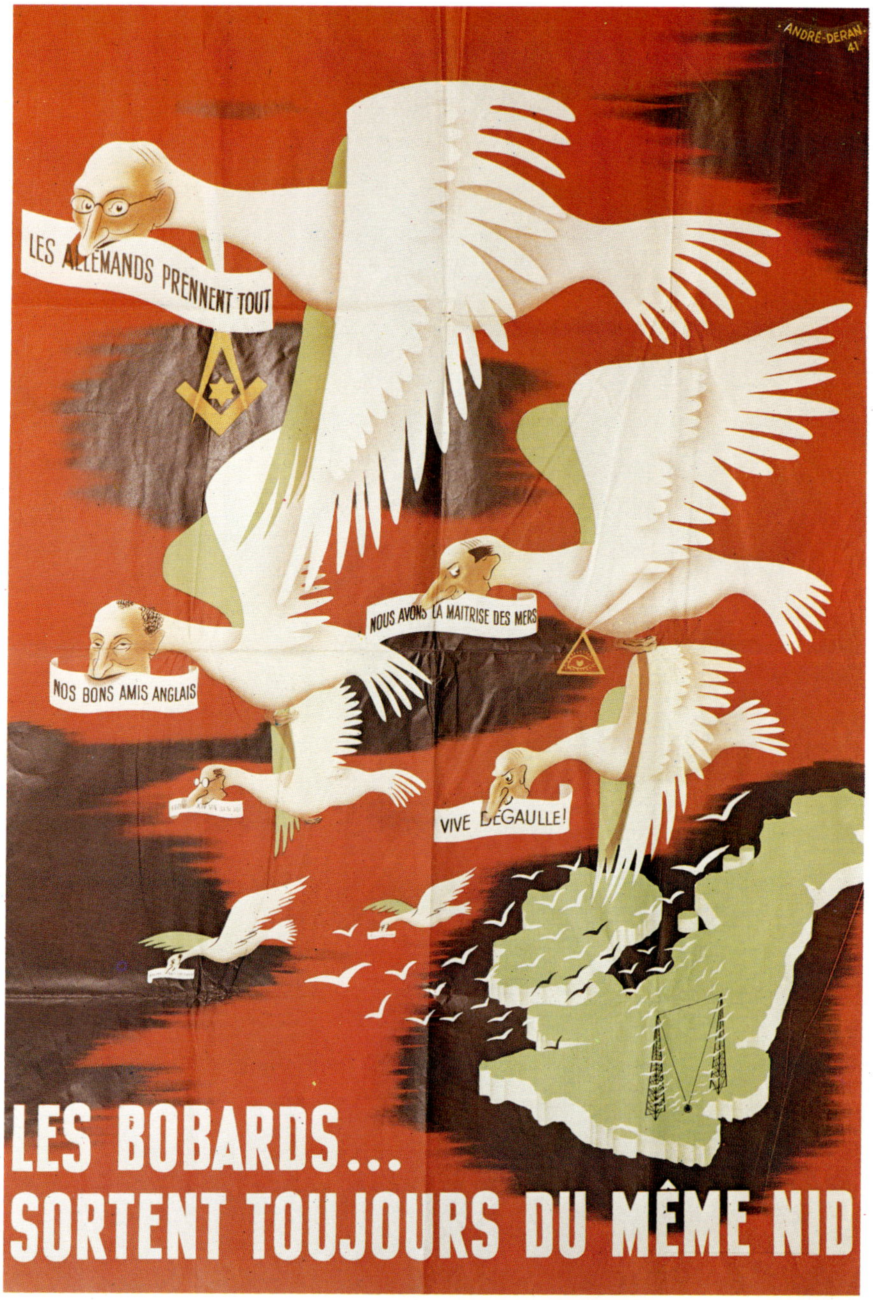

The BBC. With the German victory in Europe, the BBC's foreign-language broadcasts expanded considerably from 1941. Their aim was to sustain the morale of the populations in occupied countries and to send messages to the resistance. The German authorities and civilian governments in the occupied countries tried to counter the increasing influence of the BBC, but without much success. This poster by André Deran, published in occupied France, denounces 'British tall stories'. (From the collection of the Comité d'histoire de la 2e Guerre Mondiale.)

Bedell Smith.General Bedell Smith, christened 'bulldog' by Churchill, was Eisenhower's Chief of Staff from 1943 to 1945. In view of the commander in chief's reluctance to meet German representatives, it was Bedell Smith who had the privilege of signing the document of German unconditional surrender at Rheims on 7 May 1945. After the war Bedell Smith was US ambassador to Moscow, director of the CIA and then in 1954 under-secretary of state.

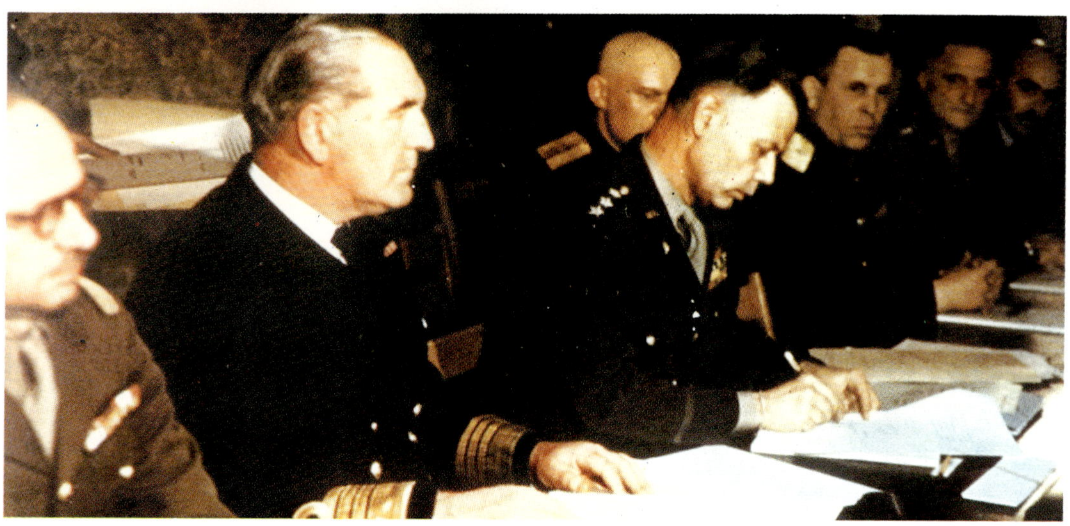

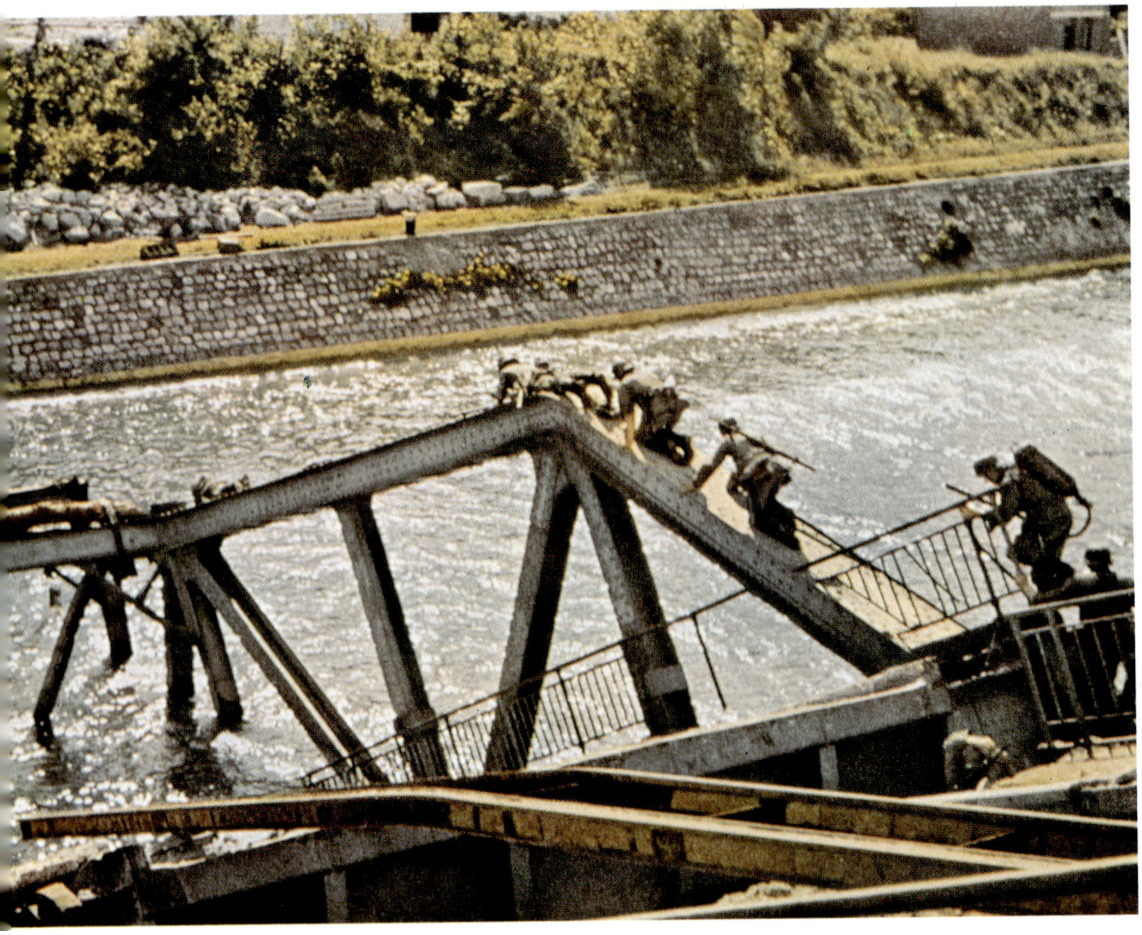

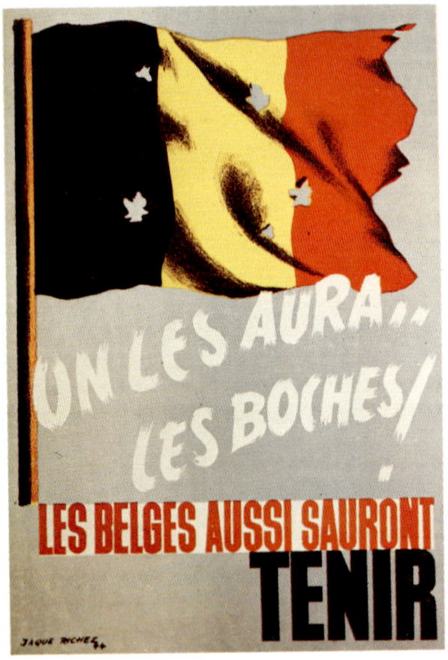

Belgium. In 1940 the Belgian high command hoped to contain or at least delay the Germans along a line resting on the fortress of Eben-Emael and the Albert Canal. In fact this line of resistance was broken in less than 48 hours. Here German infantry are seen crossing the Albert Canal, using the girders of a bridge which has previously been destroyed by Belgian army engineers. (From the Bibliothèque du Musée de l'Armée, Paris.)

A resistance movement was born in Belgium right at the beginning of the German occupation. It included people of various political viewpoints and manifested itself in the form of maquis in the wooded and hilly Ardennes, in acts of sabotage and the passing on of intelligence reports. It also found expression in a significant clandestine press and the publication of posters, like this one by J. Richez, which appeared on walls in 1944.

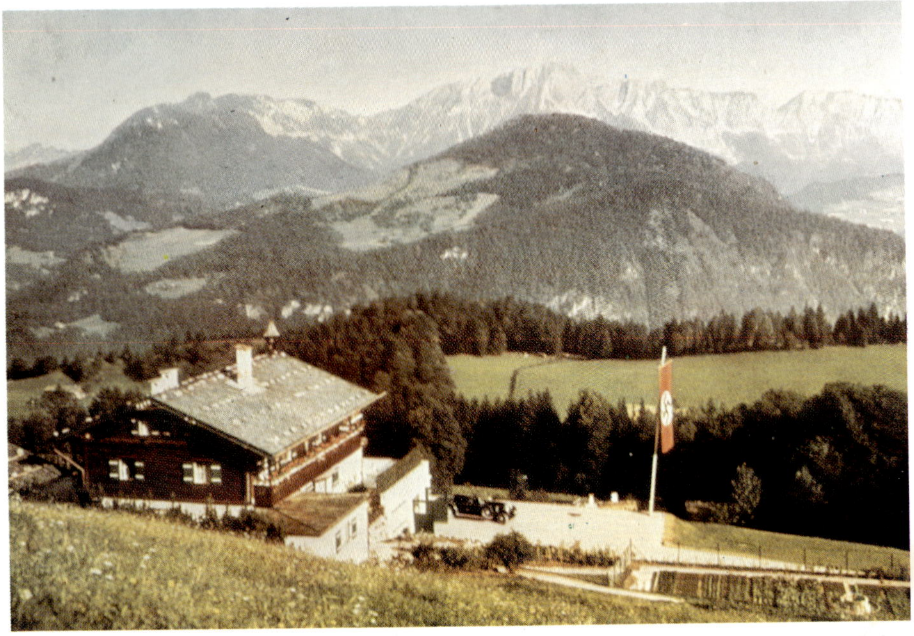

Berchtesgaden. After the Nazis came to power, Hitler had the Berghof, an estate and chalet on the Obersalzberg which dominates Berchtesgaden, enlarged and rebuilt in accordance with his own designs. Adjacent to the central chalet were villas intended for major Nazi dignitaries. An SS barracks, a hotel for prominent guests and a military command post were also added. Hitler's private retreat, the 'Eagle's Nest', was built at a height of 6250 ft (1900 m) on a neighbouring mountain spur, with an impressive view over the Bavarian Alps. At the Berghof Hitler was to receive Schuschnigg, the Austrian chancellor, Chamberlain, the British prime minister, Count Ciano, the Italian foreign minister, Admiral Horthy, the regent of Hungary, and Admiral Darlan, the foreign minister of Vichy France. The Berghof, which had been badly damaged by bombing, was eventually demolished by the Americans in 1945.

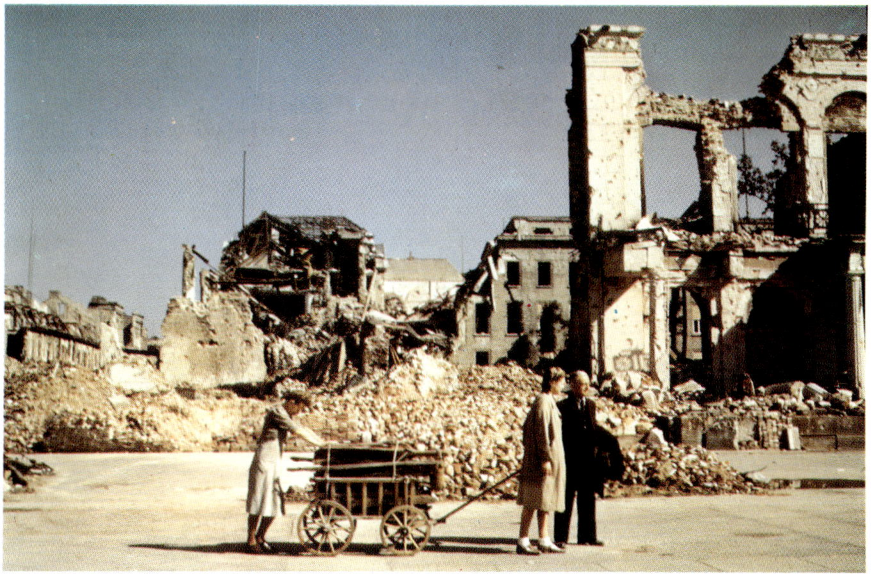

The Battle of Berlin. On the eve of the war Hitler had entrusted his architect, Albert Speer, with the task of changing the architectural aspect of Berlin completely by constructing a series of grandiose buildings, among them the famous Reich Chancellery. The building work was of course interrupted by the war and from 1942 Berlin was the target of devastating air raids carried out by the RAF, and later by the US Army Air Force as well. To this substantial damage was added that caused by the battle for the German capital in April 1945. The ruins of Dr Goebbels' Propaganda Ministry are seen here.

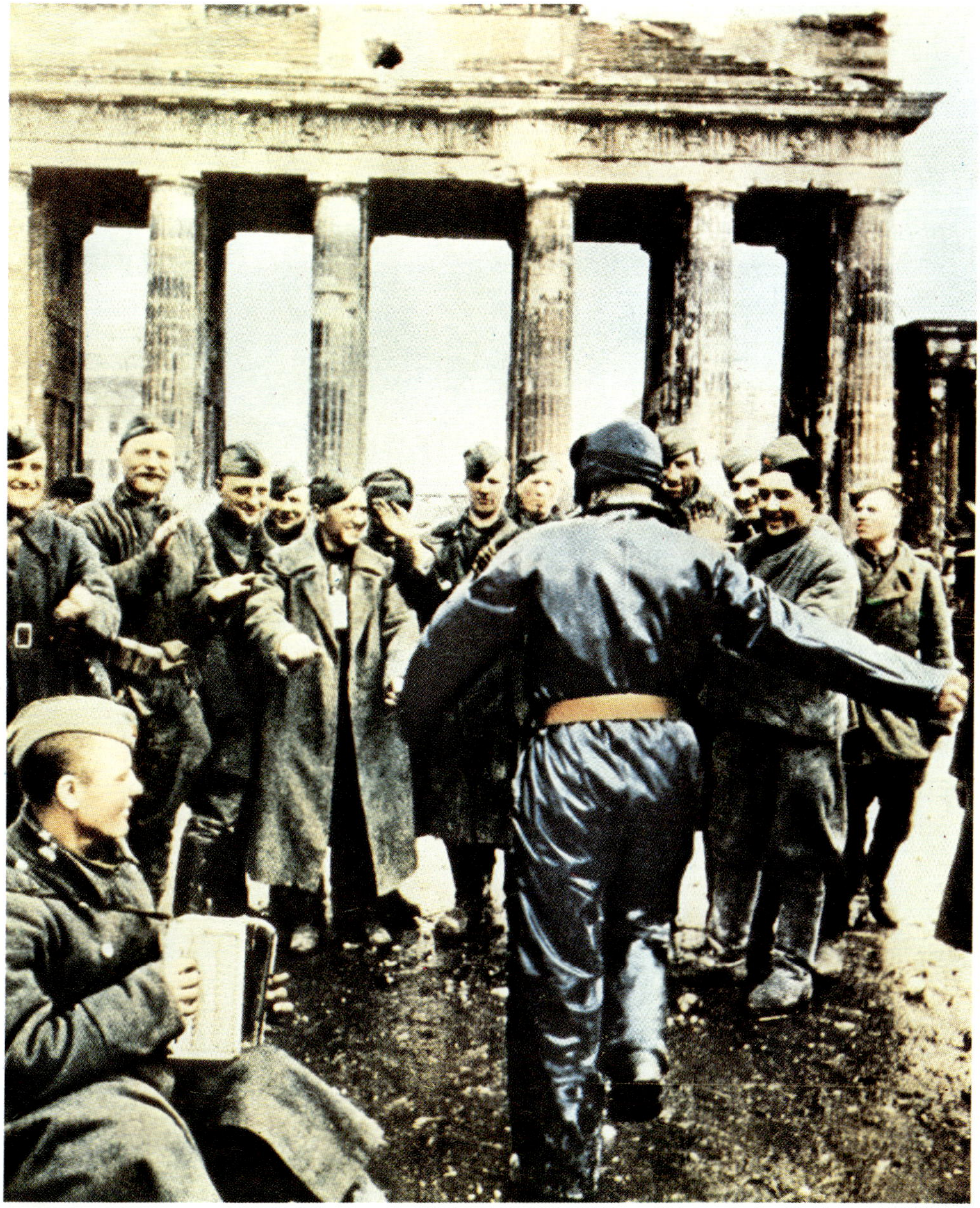

A group of Soviet soldiers celebrating victory in front of the Brandenburg Gate in Berlin. Giving up the idea of going to Berchtesgaden, Hitler had finally decided to stay in Berlin and to make the city into a second Stalingrad, in the foolish hope of breaking the offensive capability of the Red Army. This obstinacy led to a fierce battle which lasted from 22 April to 2 May 1945 and which ended with the suicide of the Führer, the destruction of the garrison and the devastation of the capital city. The Battle of Berlin alone cost the Red Army more than 300,000 men, 2000 tanks and 500 aircraft.

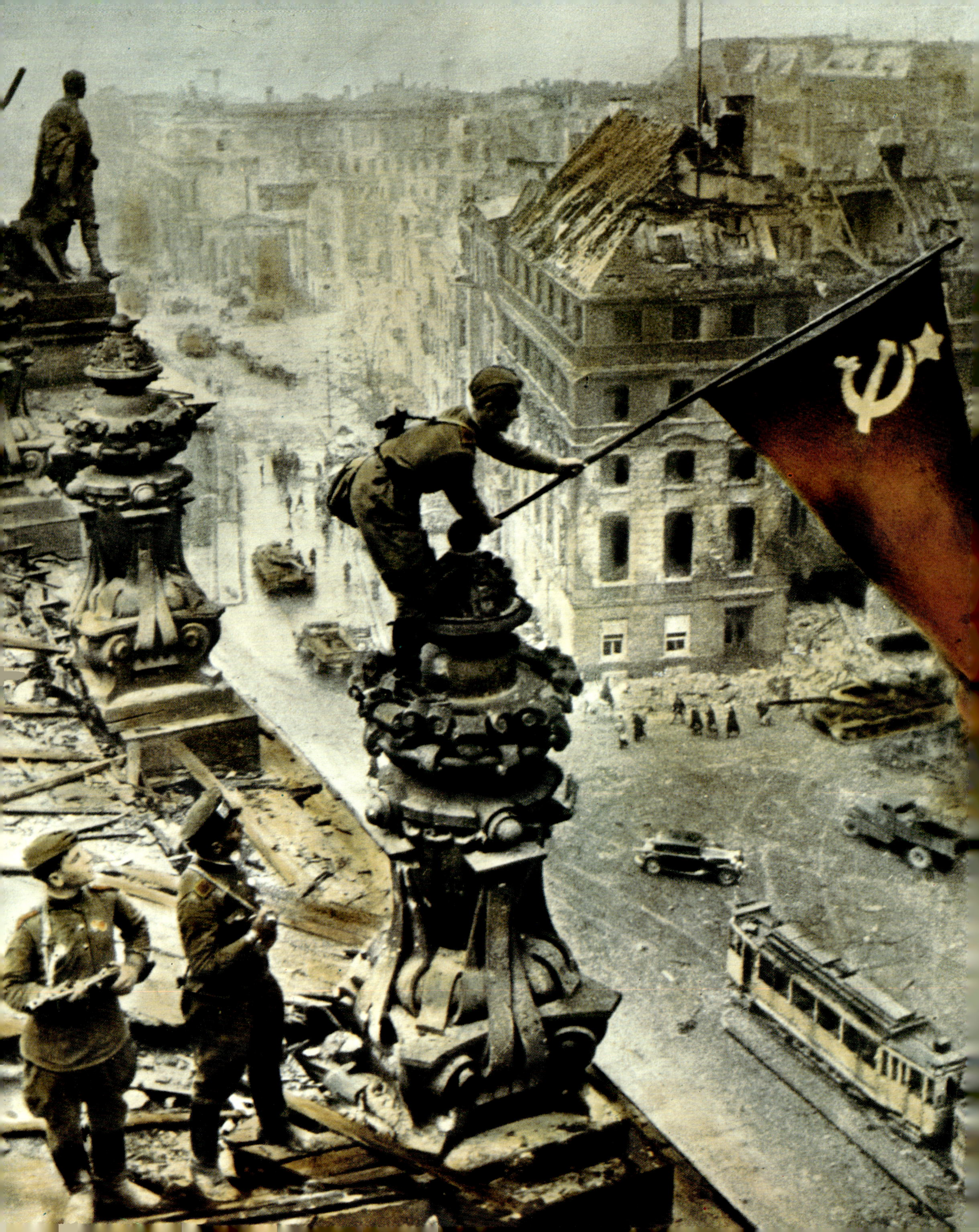

The Battle of Berlin. This still from a film shows Soviet soldiers raising the red flag on the top of the Reichstag.

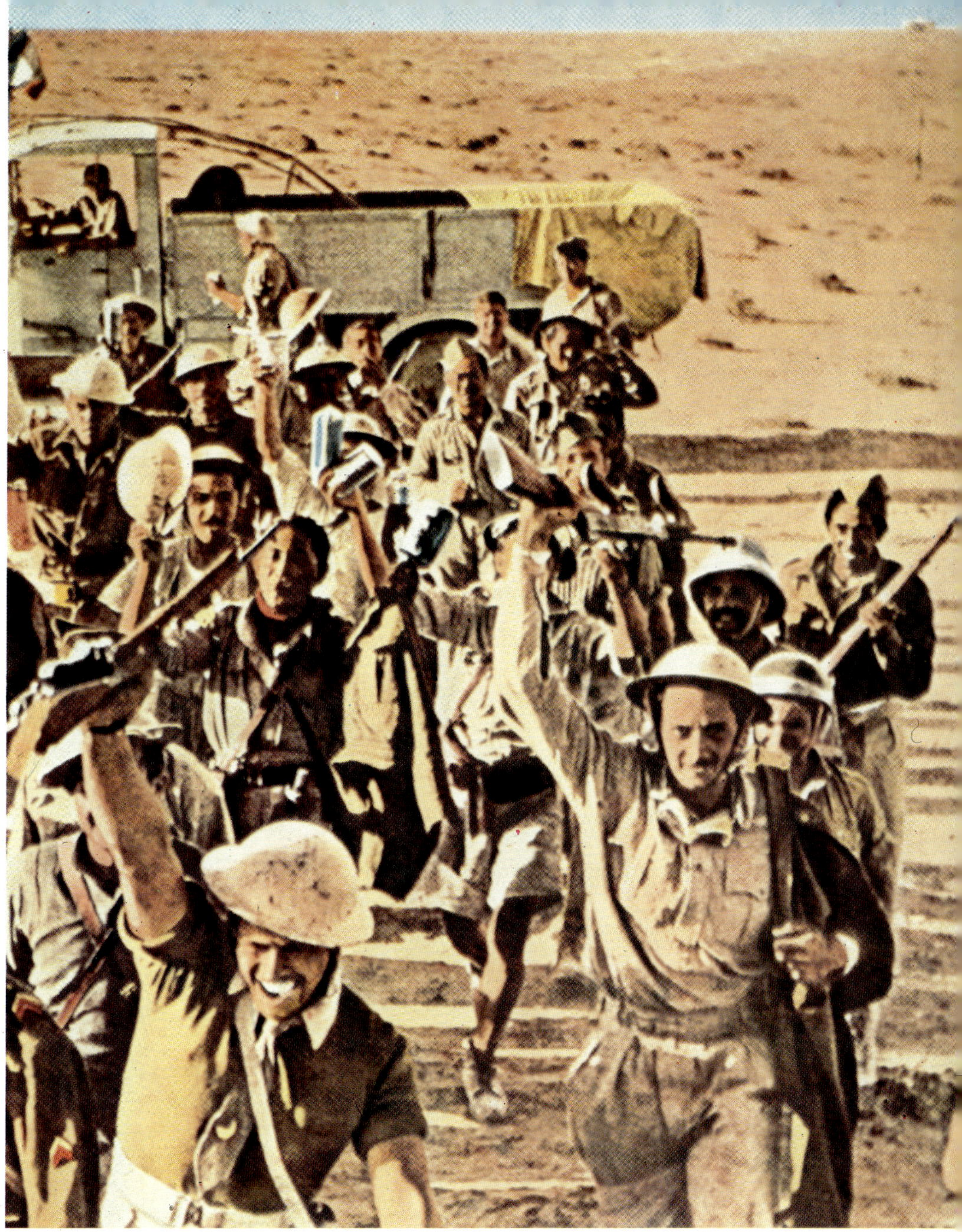

Bir Hakeim. At Gazala in the spring of 1942 Rommel achieved a resounding victory over the British 8th Army, pushing it back towards Egypt and capturing Tobruk. Nevertheless, during this battle the 1st Free French brigades commanded by General Koenig resisted magnificently at Bir Hakeim from 2 to 10 June, delaying the German advance and enabling the British forces to recover. At the end of a night sortie the remains of the garrison succeeded, as this picture shows, in reaching the Allied lines.

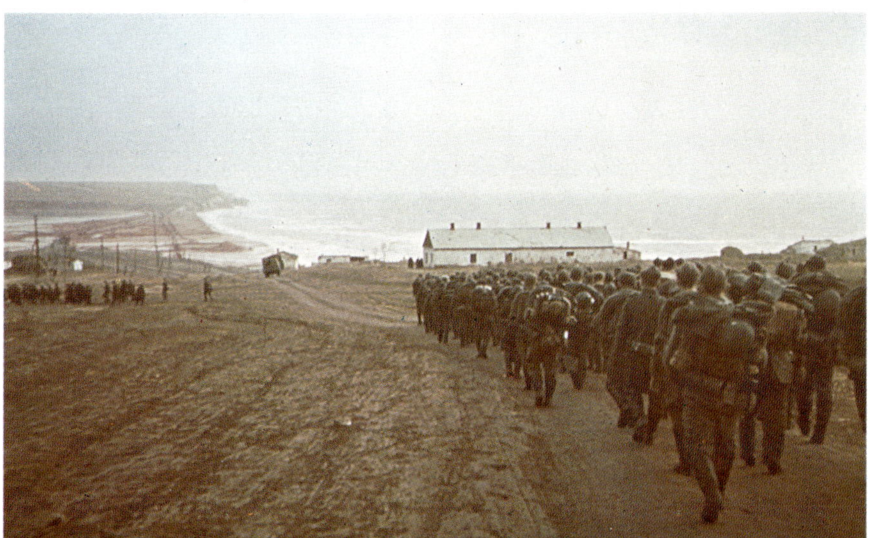

The Black Sea. During the Russo–German war the shores of the Black Sea were the scene of fierce fighting. Having occupied Odessa and the Crimea during 1941, the Germans endeavoured to secure complete control of the area during the summer of 1942 by storming Sebastopol and occupying Novorossyisk. However, they did not succeed in capturing Poti and Batum. It was only during the early months of 1944 that the Red Army was able to repossess this coastal area. The photograph records the advance of German soldiers during the summer of 1942.

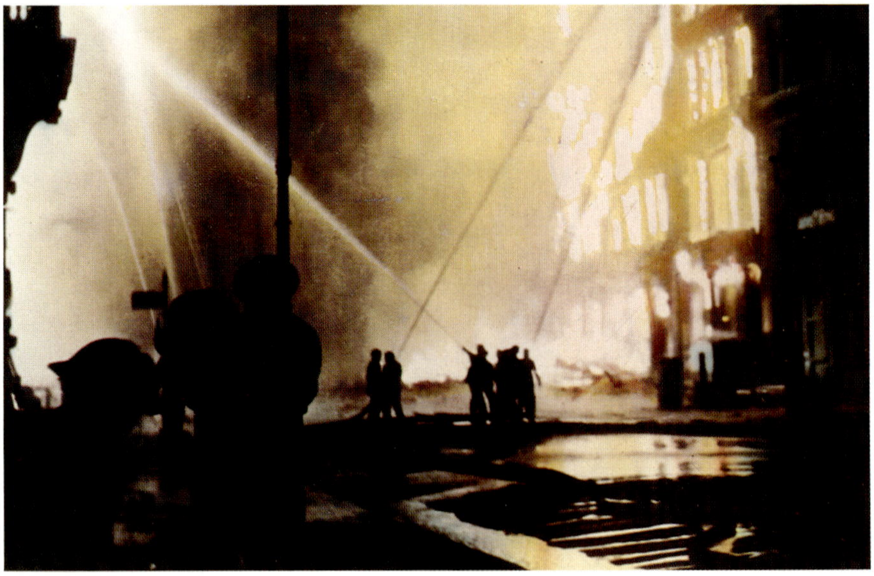

The Blitz. During the Battle of Britain in the summer of 1940, German bombing concentrated on aircraft factories and Fighter Command airfields, but on 7 Sept., the Germans altered their tactics and launched a major daylight raid against London, following this with afternoon and night attacks on the docks. These attacks were nicknamed 'The Blitz' by the British. Night raids on London continued and in October were extended to Liverpool, Manchester, Birmingham and other major towns. On 14 Nov. Coventry suffered a very heavy bombing attack from 450 planes, inflicting thousands of civilian casualties. Bombing continued right through the winter of 1940–41, petering out in the late spring.

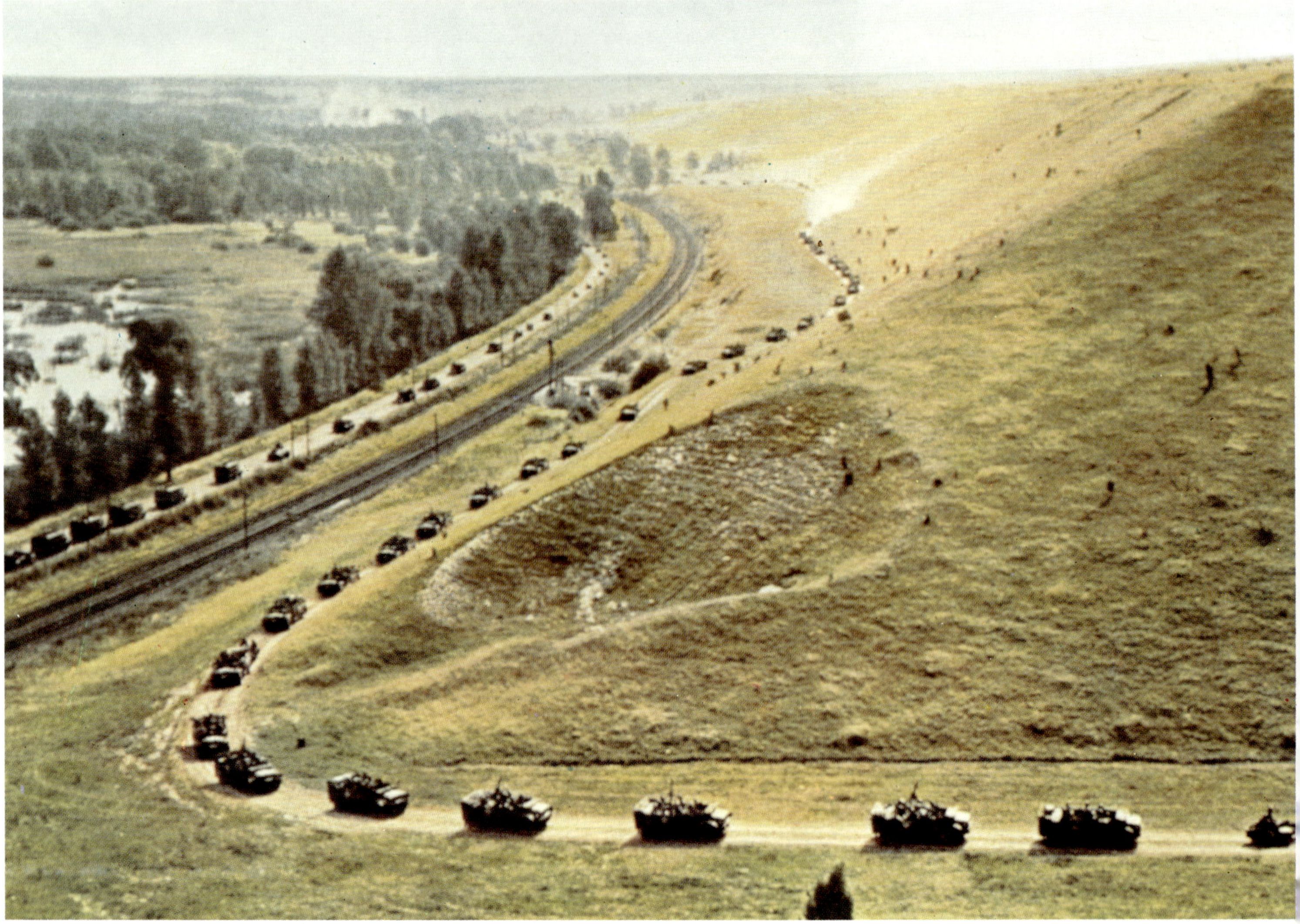

Blitzkrieg ('lightning war'). First used in Poland and further proved in the course of the French campaign of 1940, the Blitzkrieg owed its success to the action of strong armoured formations, operating closely with aircraft, which were able to make surprise breakthroughs on narrow fronts and to follow these up quickly. This system meant that armies which had stayed faithful to the doctrines of 1917–18 were caught off guard, since they could only conceive of an attack as being preceded by a formidable artillery preparation and being based on the slow and methodical advance of infantry supported by tanks. Here a German motorized division is seen advancing in Belgium in May 1940. (From the Bibliothèque du Musée de l'Armée.)

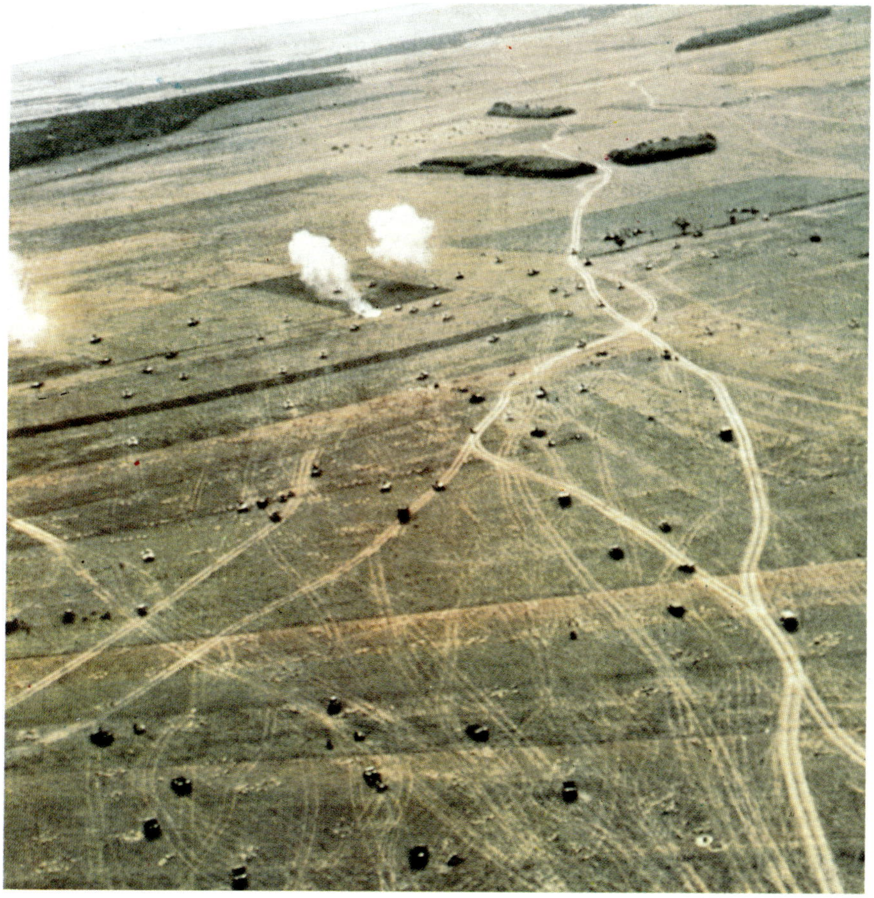

A German armoured division deployed on the northern French plain in June 1940. In contrast to the French army, in which more than half the tanks were dispersed among major infantry units, all the German tanks were grouped in 10 armoured divisions. Each of these Panzer divisions formed a small 'independent army' of great strength and mobility, consisting of about 250 tanks and linked with battalions of motorized infantry, anti-tank, anti-aircraft and engineer units. The armoured division also operated in close liaison with powerful air fleets which acted as 'flying artillery'. (From the Bibliothèque du Musée de l'Armée.)

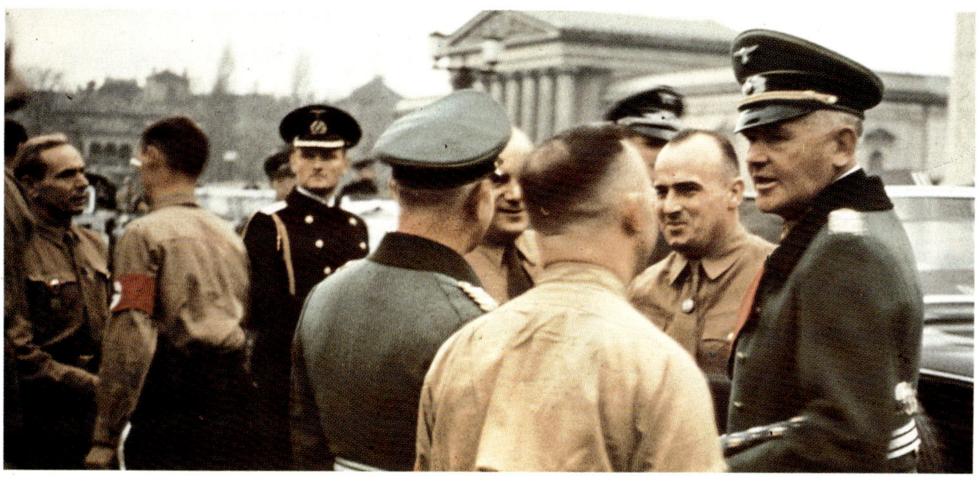

Field-Marshal von Blomberg. Appointed Minister of the Reichswehr just before Hitler came to power, Blomberg was the creator of the new German army, involved in the reintroduction of conscription and the creation of armoured divisions, and this gained him the rank of field-marshal. Learning of Blomberg's misgivings in regard to his expansionist policies, Hitler seized the pretext of the marshal's second marriage to a woman of dubious reputation to retire him and thus reinforced his personal ascendancy over the army.

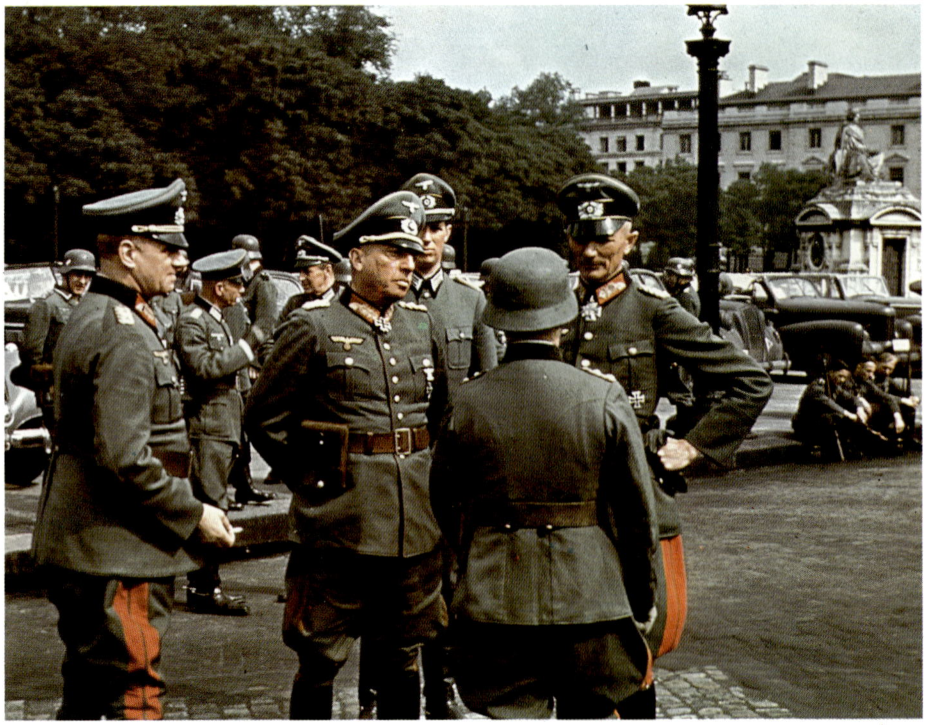

Field-Marshal von Bock. Having already distinguished himself in Poland, Bock played a decisive part at the head of Army Group B, advancing into Holland and holding the best of the Allied forces in Belgium in order to facilitate the forcing of the Meuse. With about 50 divisions at his disposal, he then broke the Somme front and advanced towards Rouen and Compiègne. It was he (on the right in this picture) who had the privilege of presiding over the entry of German troops into Paris on 14 June 1940. Disagreeing with Hitler over the conduct of operations on the eastern front, Bock was relieved of his command in July 1942 at the time of the advance on Stalingrad.

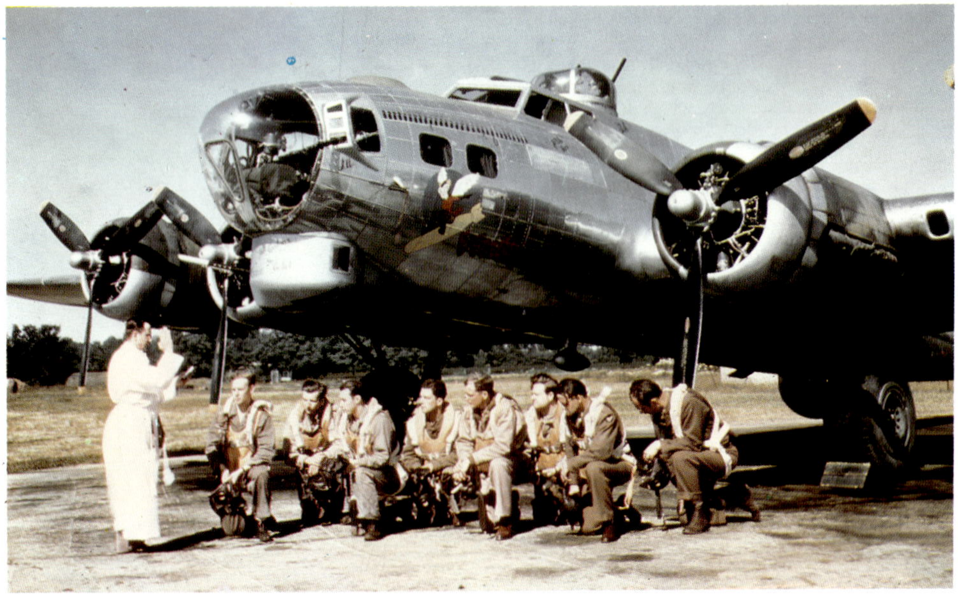

The Boeing B-17. A chaplain blessing the crew of an American Boeing B-17 G heavy bomber before their departure on a mission. Together with the B-24 Liberator, the B-17 or 'Flying Fortress' formed the spearhead of the US Army Air Force in its raids over Europe from 1942 onwards. It was designed to operate by day in massive formations, carrying out precision raids on major industrial installations. In spite of an impressive armament based on heavy machine guns its losses were considerable and it was only fully effective when escorted by Thunderbolt or Mustang fighters, which protected the bomber formations against German fighter attacks.

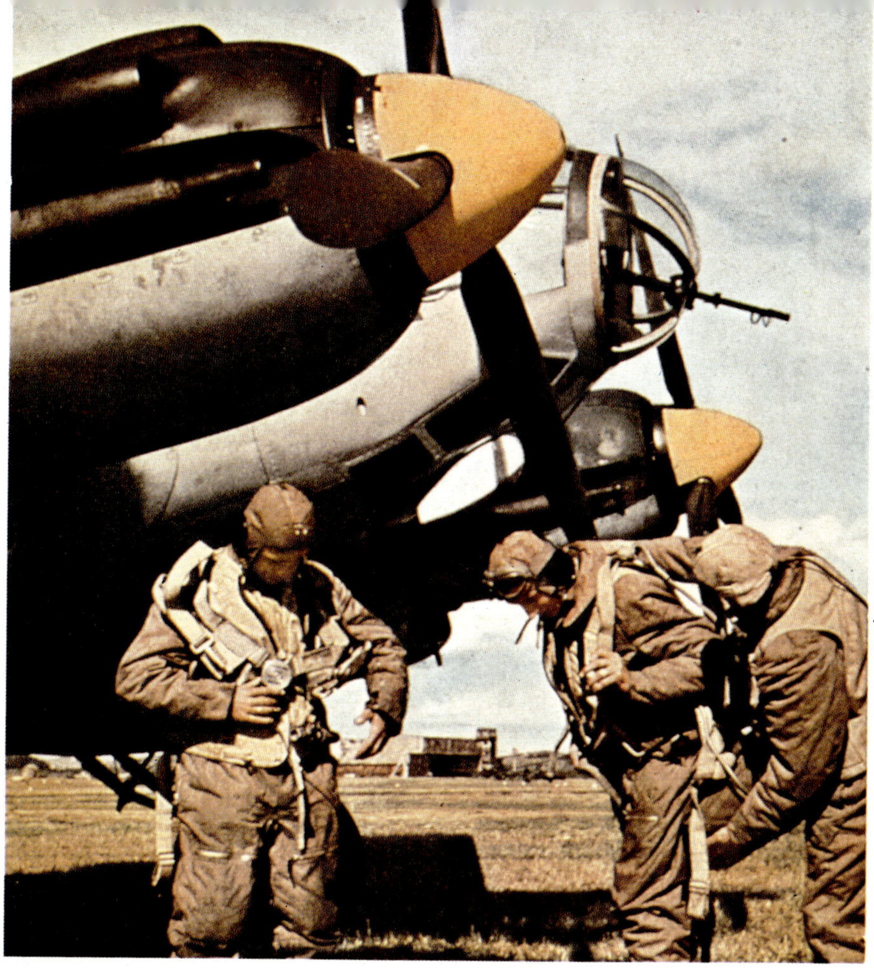

Bomber aircraft. The crew of a Heinkel He-111 preparing to leave on an operation. In the first years of the war the He-111 was one of the German air force's best bombers. It was a twin-engined tactical support aircraft intended to operate in conjunction with armoured divisions. On the other hand, in raids on targets in England during the Battle of Britain it was seen to be inadequate since it lacked power and range. Originally it had been planned that the Luftwaffe should have a strategic air arm equipped with heavy bombers. This idea was, however, abandoned as early as 1939, since priority was given to the Blitzkrieg concept.

In conformance with the theory developed by Trenchard before the outbreak of war, from 1941 the RAF undertook strategic night raids on Germany, which were intended to disorganize the economy of the Reich and to undermine the morale of the civilian population. The four-engined Short Stirling bomber (in the picture) was the main instrument of this offensive up to the end of 1942. At the outset these raids lacked precision and German anti-aircraft defences and night fighters caused heavy losses. It was not until 1944 that the raids became fully effective. They were then aimed at targets of economic significance such as the transport system and the petrol industry and by that time radio-navigation systems and H2S radar were in use in aircraft.

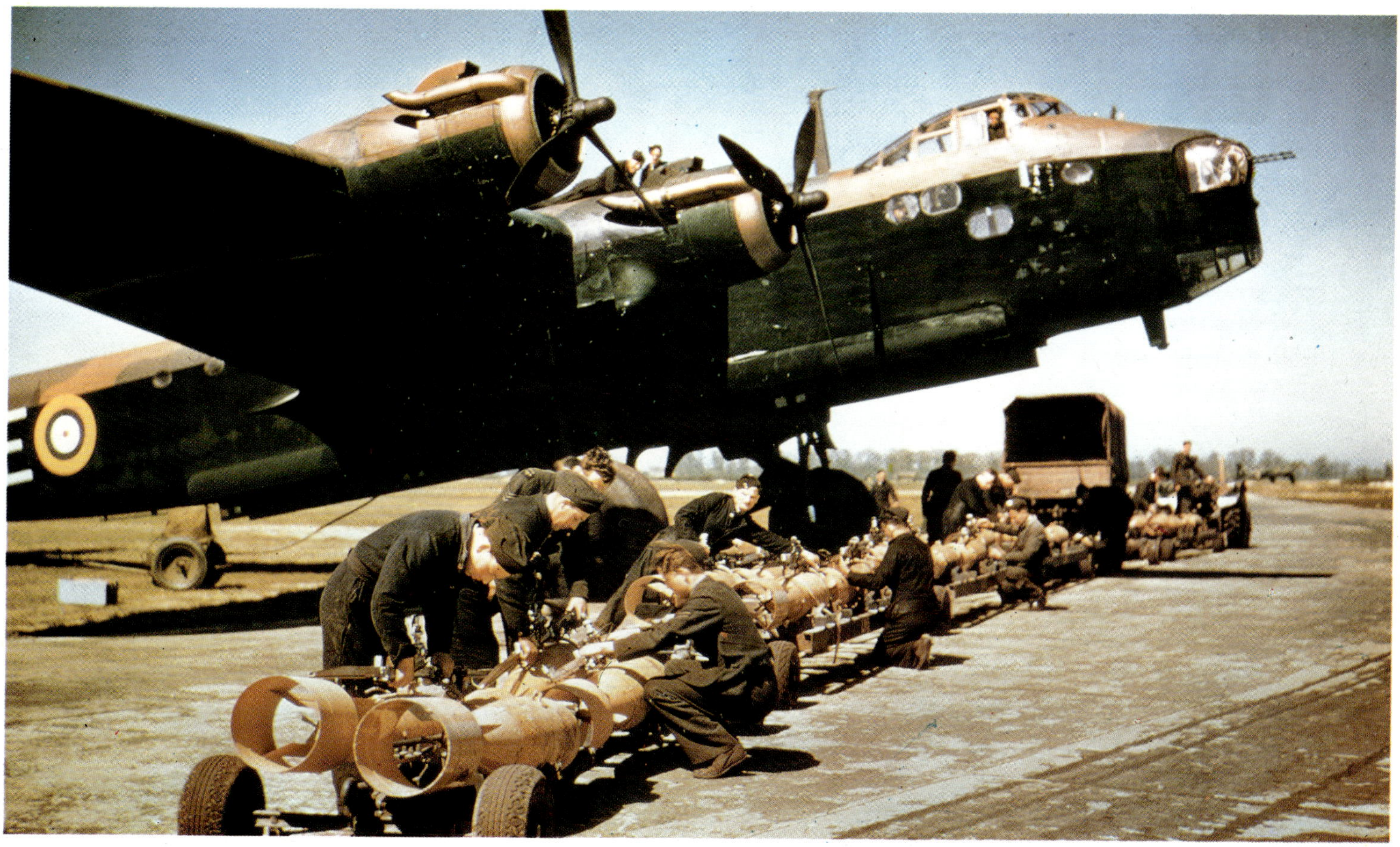

Opposite
The effects of aerial bombing. Ruins in Nuremberg.

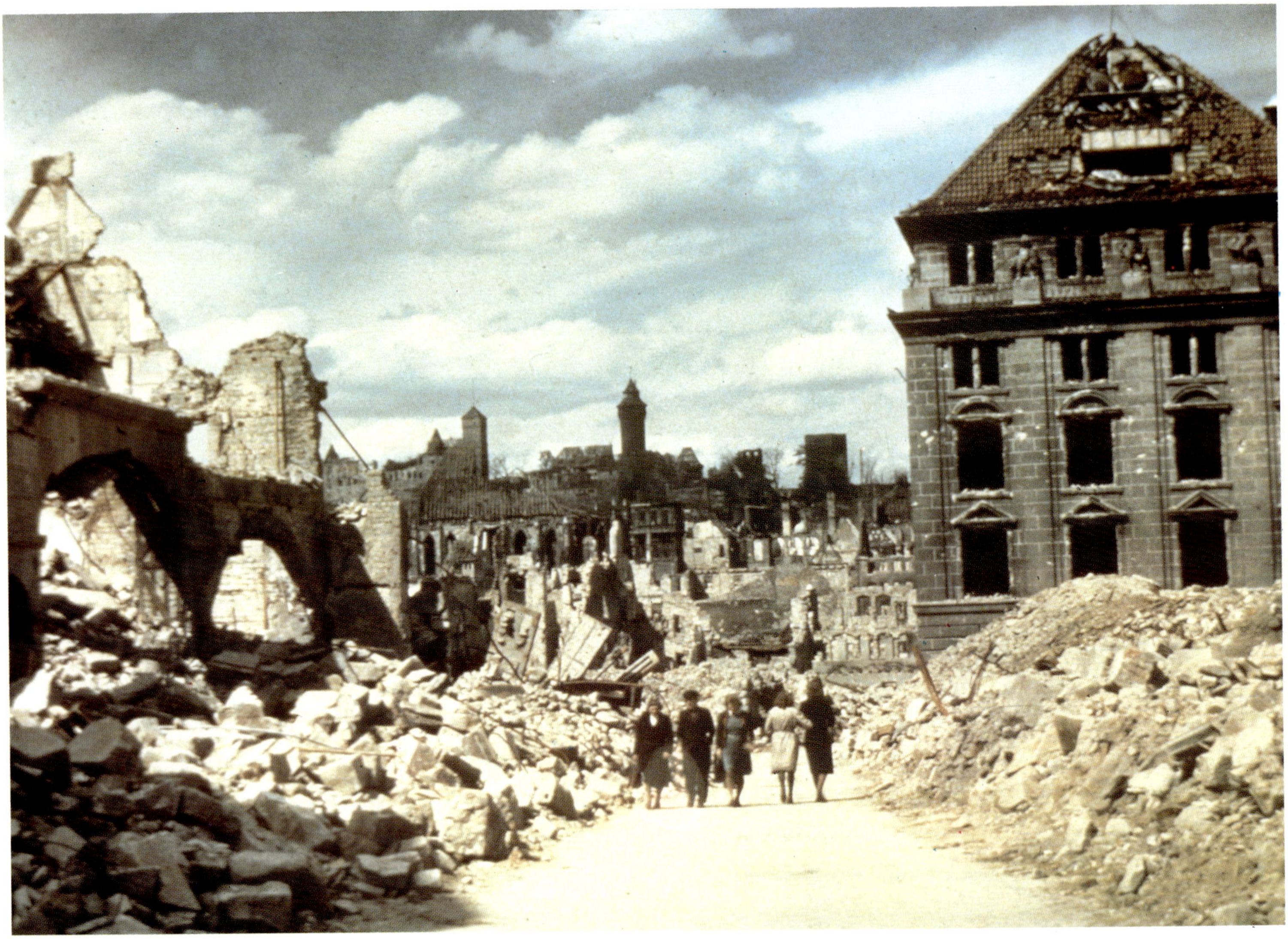

The effects of aerial bombing. During the major part of the conflict the RAF directed its raids on the centres of German cities in the hope of disorganizing industrial production and of undermining civilian morale. This objective was only very partially attained. Nevertheless, these raids, mainly carried out with incendiary bombs, had devastating effects, ravaging the historic centres of old medieval cities such as Lübeck, Bremen, Münster and Frankfurt-am-Main. This picture shows the ruins of the old town centre of Nuremberg.

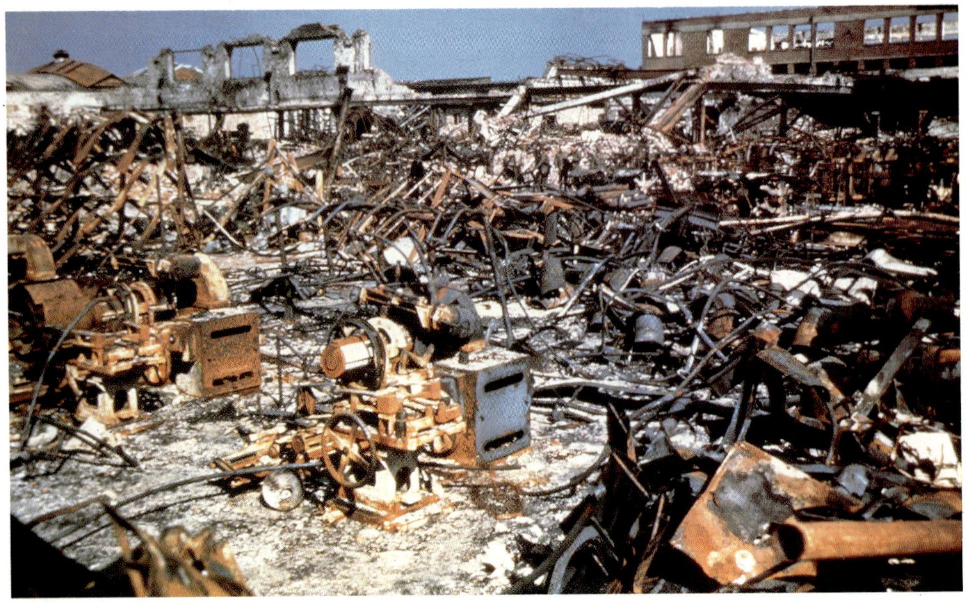

Up to early 1944 neither the British area raids by night nor the American raids by day produced decisive results in regard to the Reich's major arms factories. The adoption of H2S radar and the appearance of the escort fighter changed this situation radically, enabling destructive raids to be made on major installations such as railway marshalling yards, aircraft factories and oil refineries. This picture of the ruins of the Dunlop factory in Hanover gives an idea of the effectiveness of aerial bombing at the end of the war.

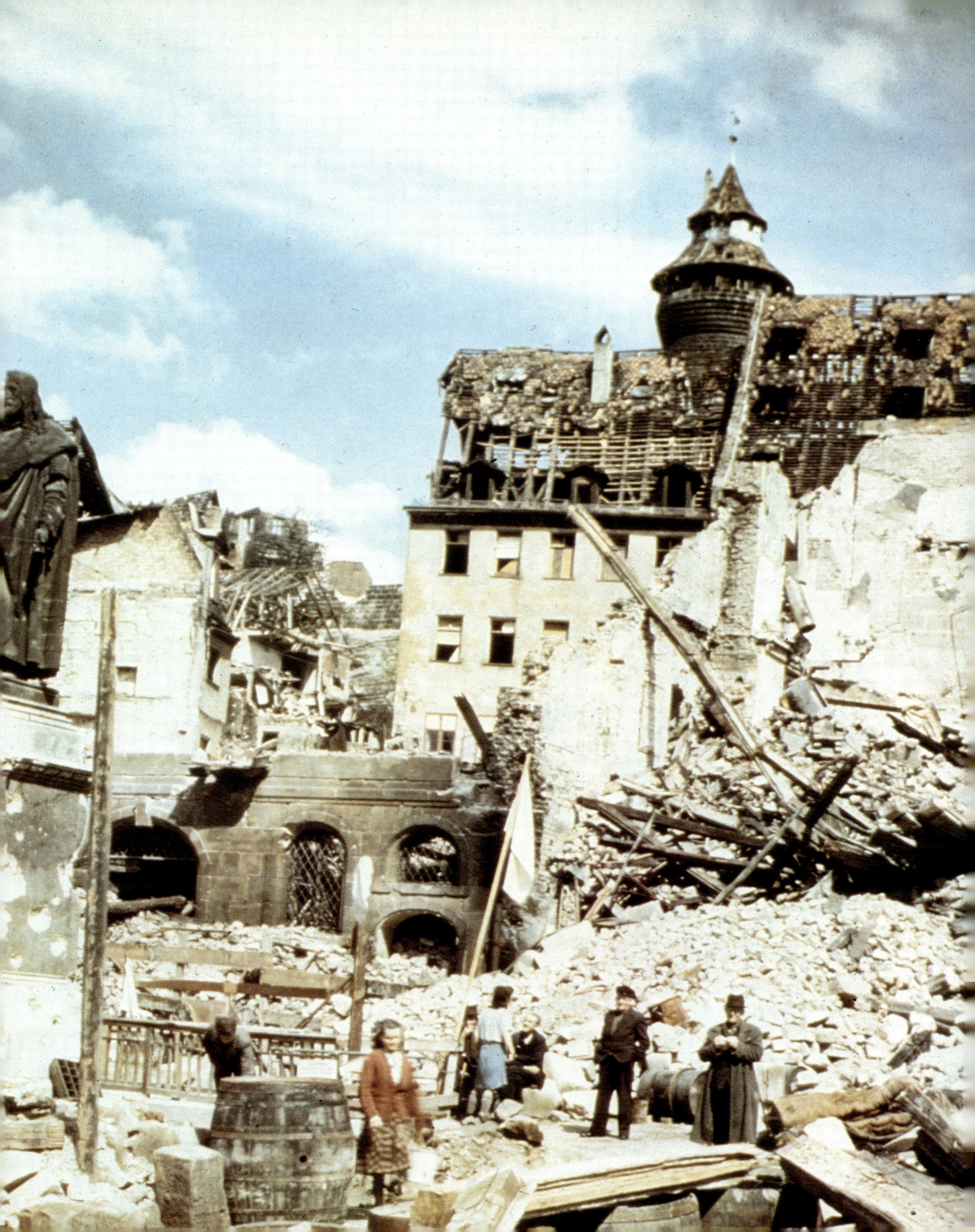

Below
Bombs. A bomb dropped by a German aircraft on Soviet positions in 1944. Since their air force was basically tactical, the Germans in particular used relatively light bombs, weighing from 110 lbs to 4400 lbs (50 to 2000 kg). The most widely used were 1100 lb (500 kg) fragmentation bombs and penetration bombs of 500 to 1000 kg (1100 to 2200 lbs). Also employed were 'container' bombs of 1100 lb, which held 120 incendiary projectiles of about 2 lbs each.

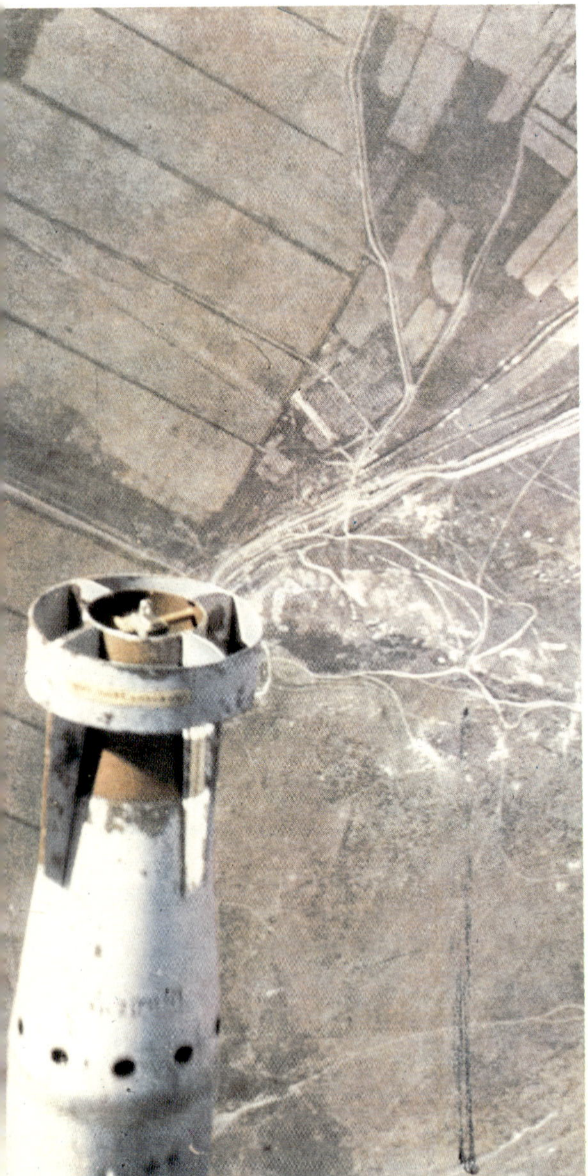

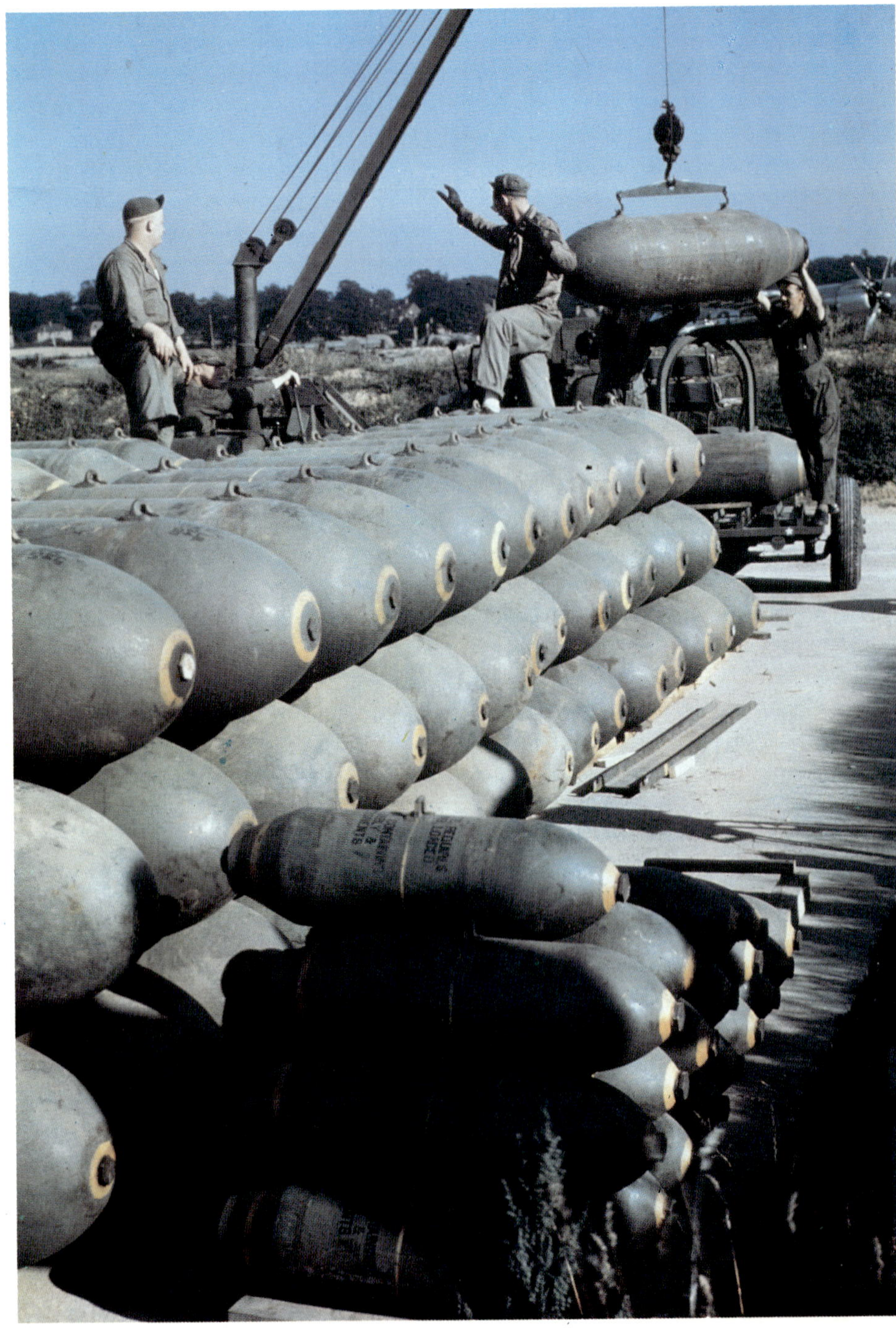

On an American airfield ground crew are stacking 1100 lb (500 kg) bombs (in the background) and incendiary bombs (in the foreground). As the RAF and USAAF developed into major forces they were to use bombs on a massive scale. In five years nearly 2,700,000 tons were dropped on Europe, 1,350,000 tons on Germany alone. In the attacks on towns it was the mixture of explosive and incendiary bombs which showed itself to be the most effective, since it was this which started devastating fires.

Martin Bormann. A member of the Nazi party from 1927, he quickly became one of the regime's key figures, particularly after Rudolf Hess's flight to England in May 1941. He was made head of the Chancellery and a member of the Council of Ministers and the government and then in April 1943 given the title of Secretary to the Führer. He disappeared in 1945 at the time of the fall of Berlin. It is thought that a skeleton found in Berlin many years after the end of the war may have been Bormann's. The man remains an enigma and some people have maintained that he was a Soviet agent.

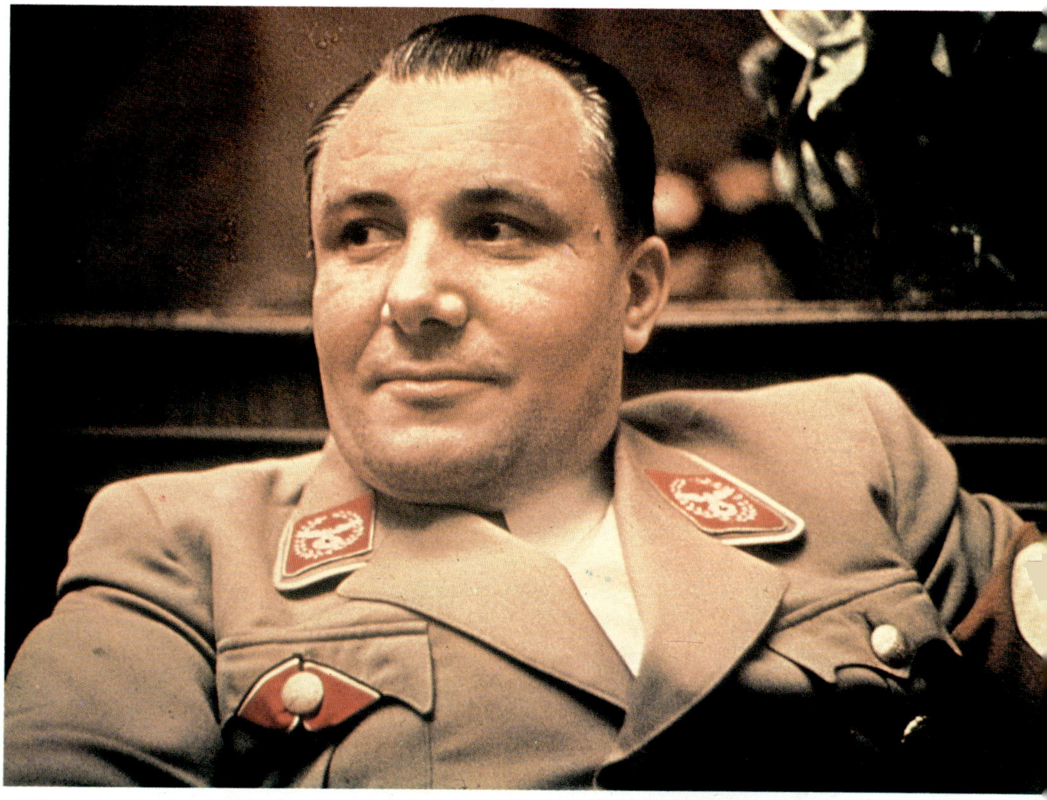

Bougainville. US marines landed on Bougainville on 1 Nov. 1943. This was part of the Battle of the Solomons, the objective of which was to remove the Japanese threat to the northern coast of Australia. In spite of heavy losses the Japanese navy was unable to relieve the island. The Americans set up a strong air and naval base on Bougainville and were content to contain the remains of the Japanese garrison. This 'rotting' or 'wearing down' policy involved sporadic fighting up to the end of the war. Here an American 81 mm M1 infantry mortar is being prepared for firing.

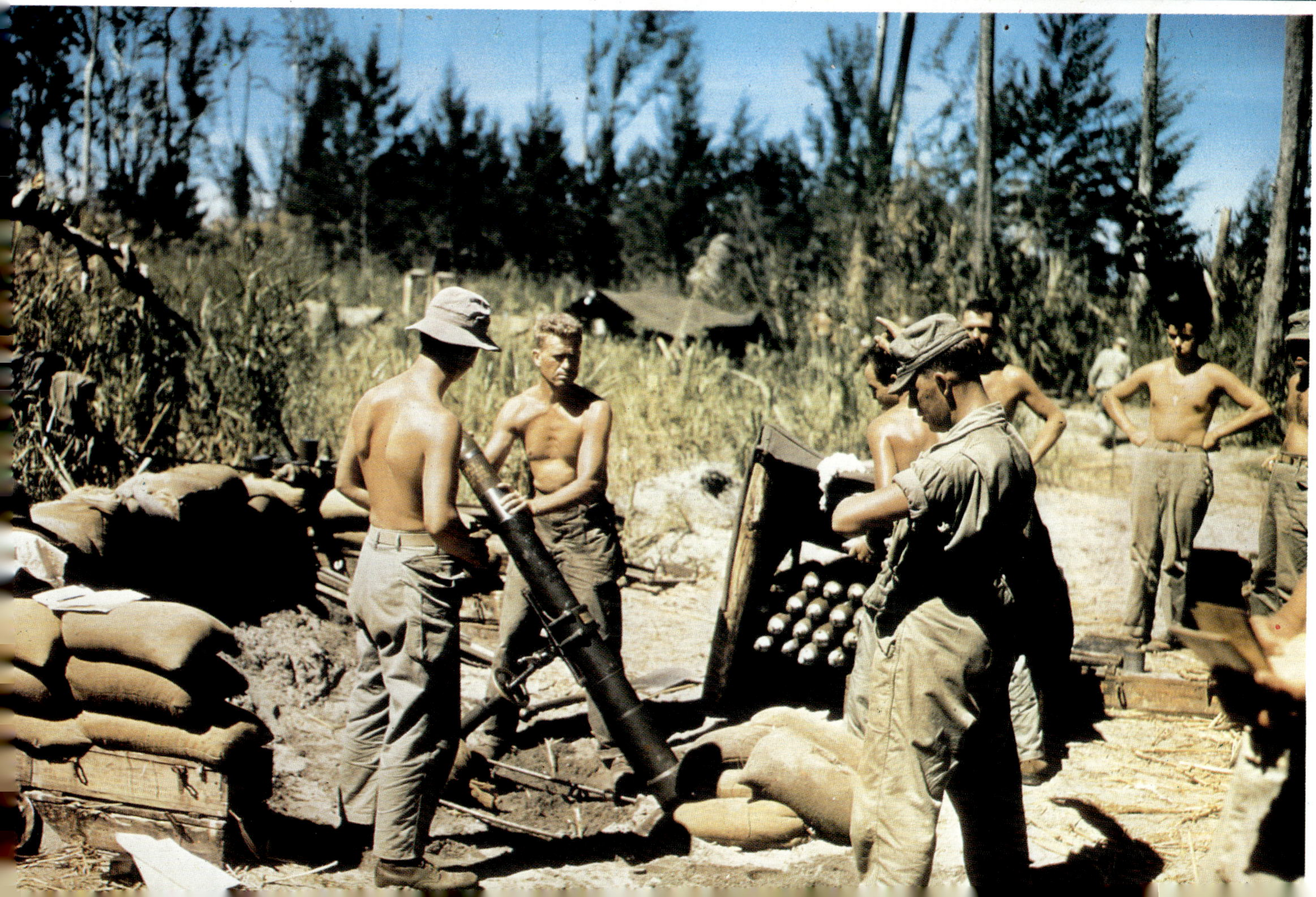

Opposite
The Battle of Britain. King George VI and Queen Elizabeth inspecting damage at Buckingham Palace in Sept. 1940.

Bradley. A quiet and calm man, General Omar Bradley (*far left*) was one of the most respected commanders of the war. Having participated in the invasion of North Africa, and of Sicily in 1943, his greatest contribution to the Allied victory was as commander of the US landings on D-Day in June 1944. The Ardennes offensive, launched by the Germans in Dec. 1944, took his men completely by surprise, but Bradley did not panic and he was able to prevent the Germans achieving a decisive breakthrough.

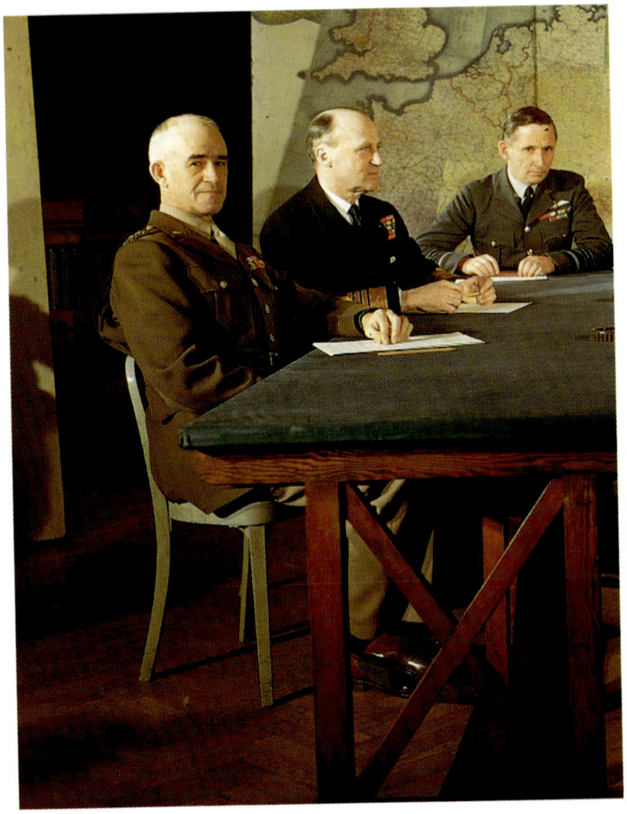

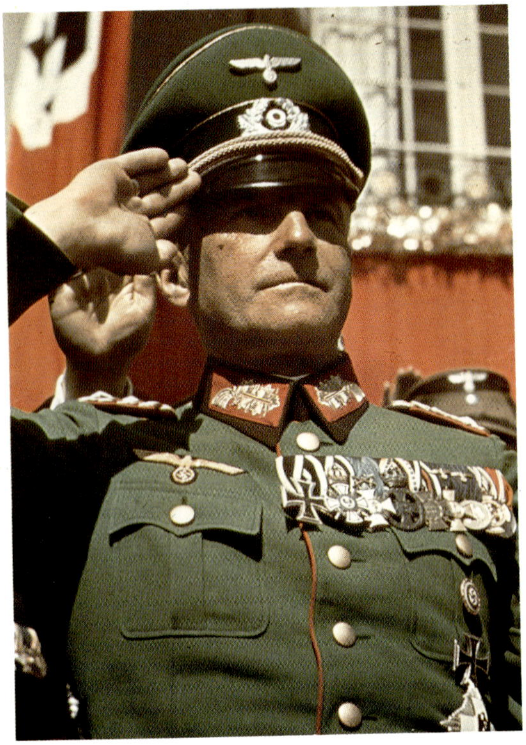

Field-Marshal von Brauchitsch. A member of an old Prussian family, von Brauchitsch succeeded General von Fritsch as head of the German army in Feb. 1938. In this post he was to have the privilege of conducting the Polish and French campaigns under the close control of Hitler. Having prepared the plan of attack on the USSR, he found himself in disagreement with the Führer at the time of the Battle of Moscow. He was sacked on 19 Dec. 1941 and it was then that Hitler assumed command of the German army, which he kept until the very end of the war.

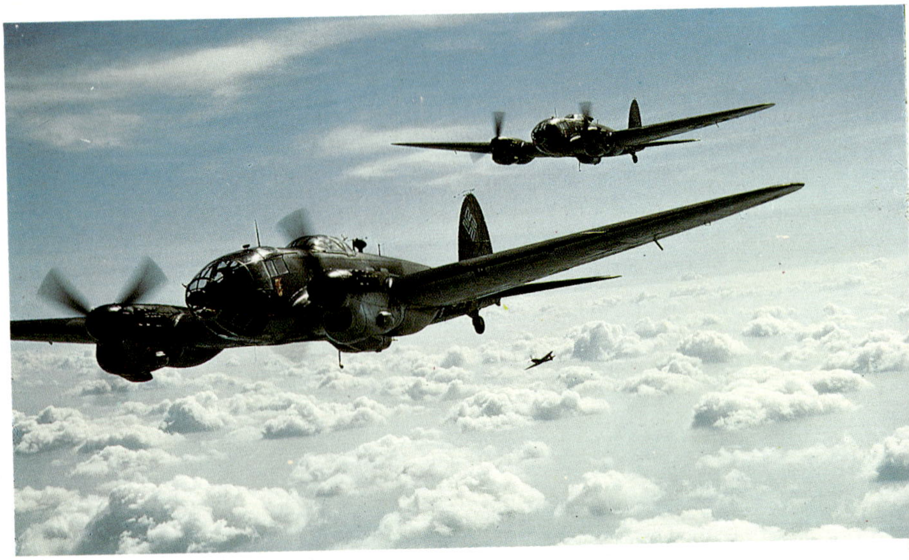

The Battle of Britain. The Heinkel He-111 bomber, as shown in this scene from the feature film *Battle of Britain*, was one of the aircraft used most frequently by the Luftwaffe during the battle. Tried out in Spain, this twin-engined aircraft could carry a maximum bomb load of 2 tons and had a top speed of 250 mph (400 km/h). Conceived as a tactical support aircraft, the Heinkel He-111 lacked range and was under-armed, which meant that its performance in operations over England was much below expectations.

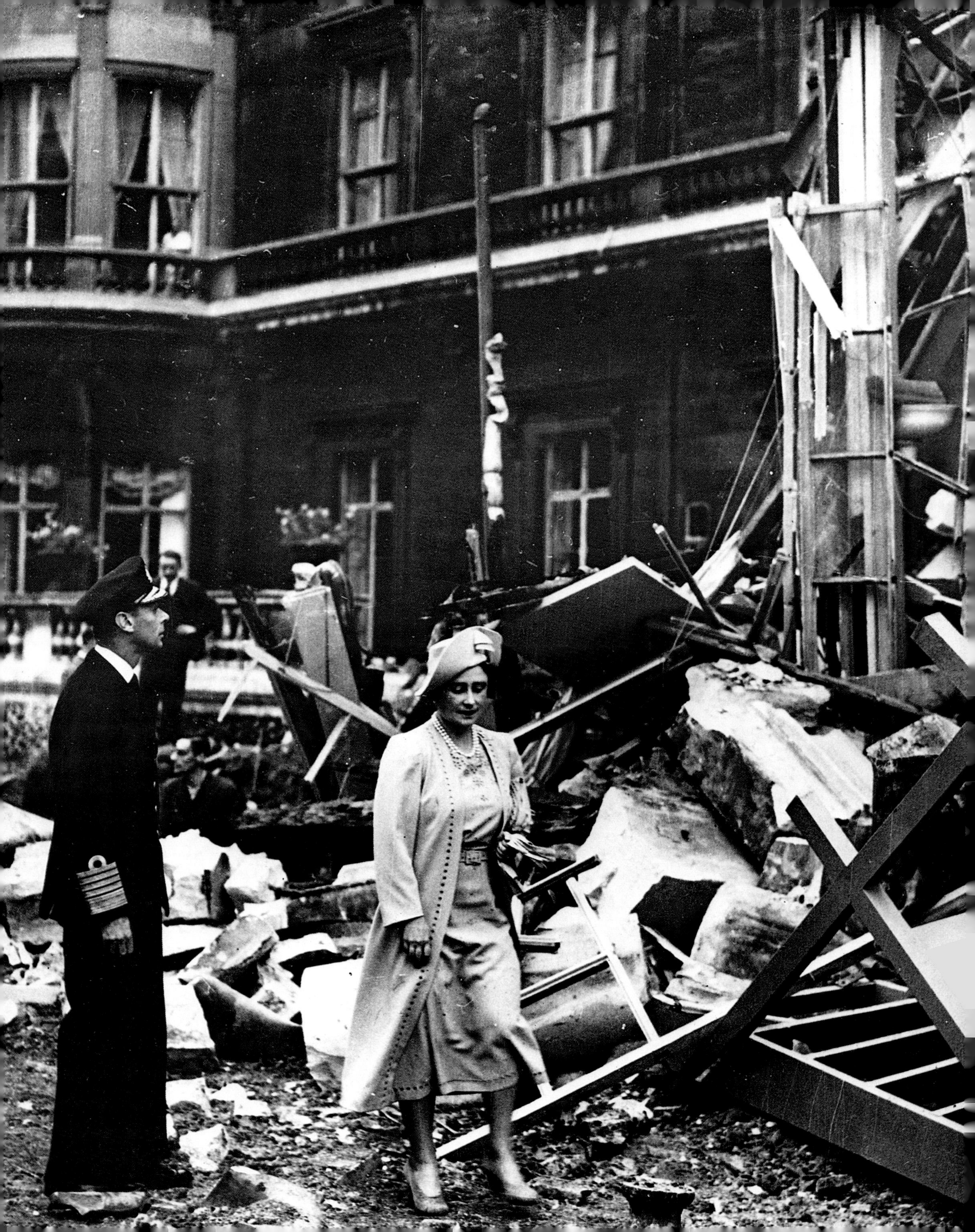

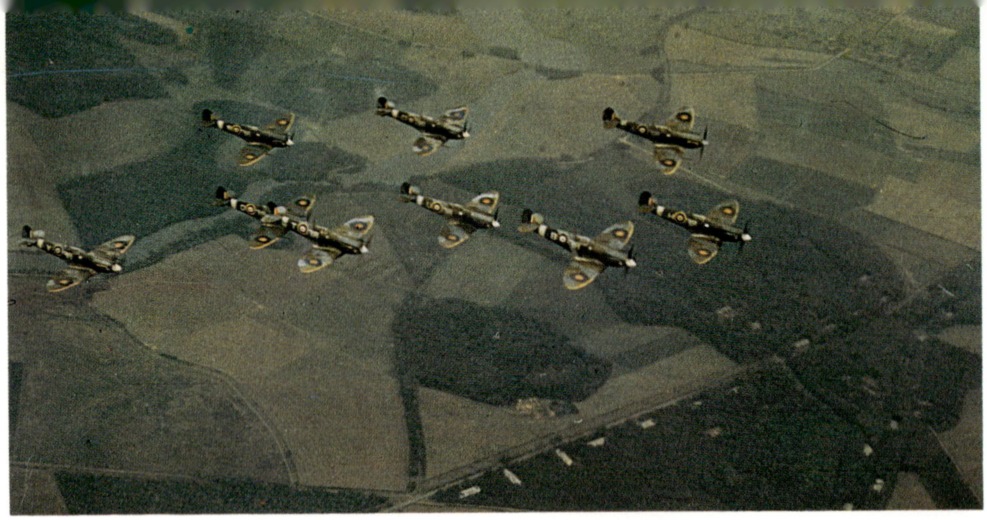

With the Hurricanes, Spitfires formed the spearhead of the British fighter force during the Battle of Britain. At the start of the battle the British pilots flew in close formation, as can be seen in this picture, while the Luftwaffe pilots flew in much looser formations, as a result of lessons learned during the Spanish Civil War. It took the British several weeks to adapt to these tactics which enabled the aircraft to manoeuvre more easily and which were shown to be very effective.

During the summer of 1940 the British took the threat of a German landing very seriously. To support the regular army, which had yet to recover from the evacuation at Dunkirk, the government looked to the volunteers of the Home Guard, who trained enthusiastically – if occasionally somewhat awkwardly – under the indulgent or mocking gaze of the rest of the population. (A painting by E. Ardizzone.)

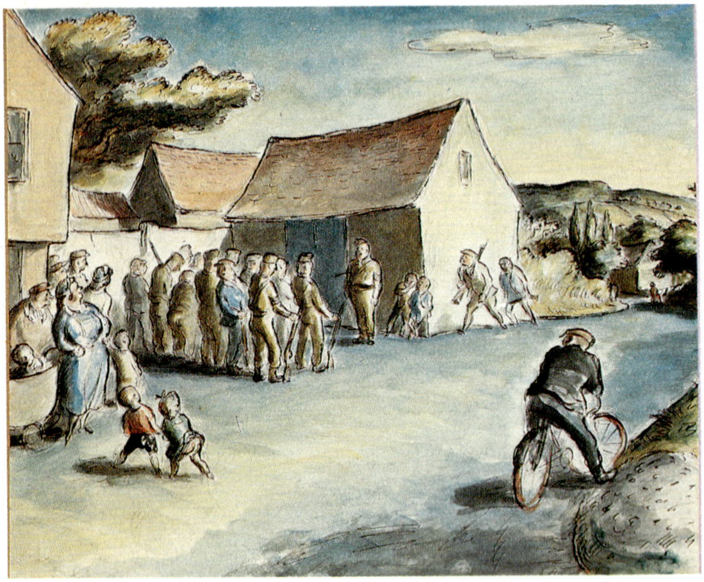

After 7 Sept. 1940 the Luftwaffe ceased its attacks on airfields and aircraft factories owing to faulty estimates of the results obtained. It concentrated its efforts against towns, particularly against London. The air raids affected the docks, the City and the working class areas of the East End in particular, causing extensive damage and heavy loss of life. These raids, which continued up to May 1941, did not succeed in paralysing the life of the capital nor did they bring about the collapse of British morale.

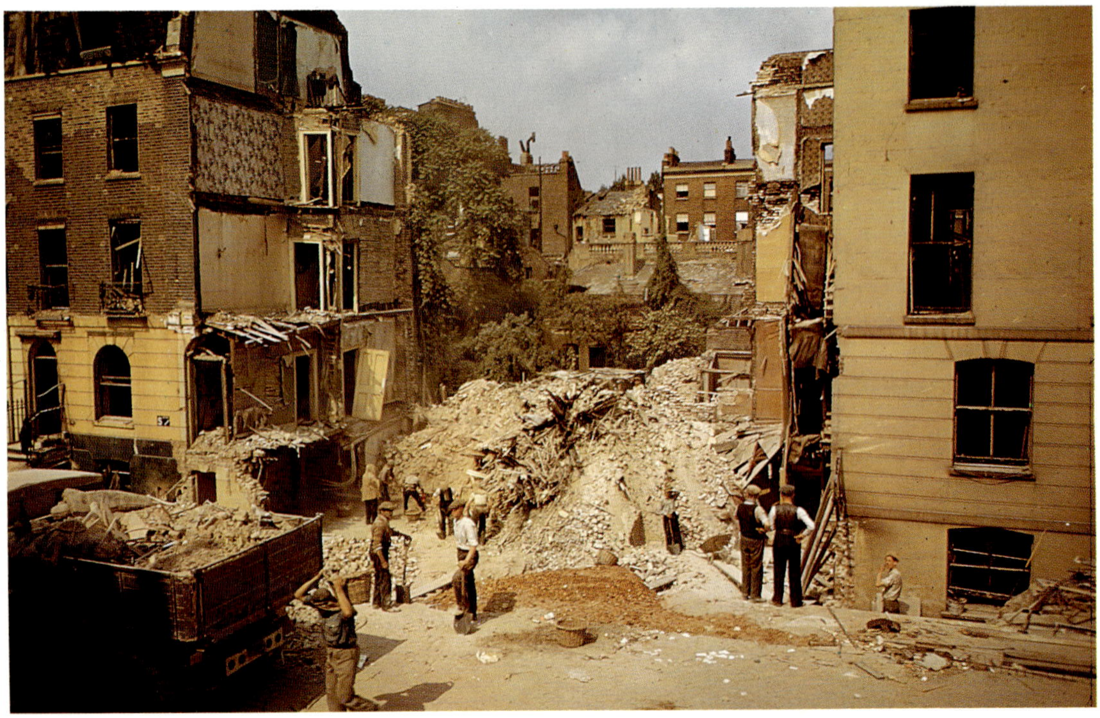

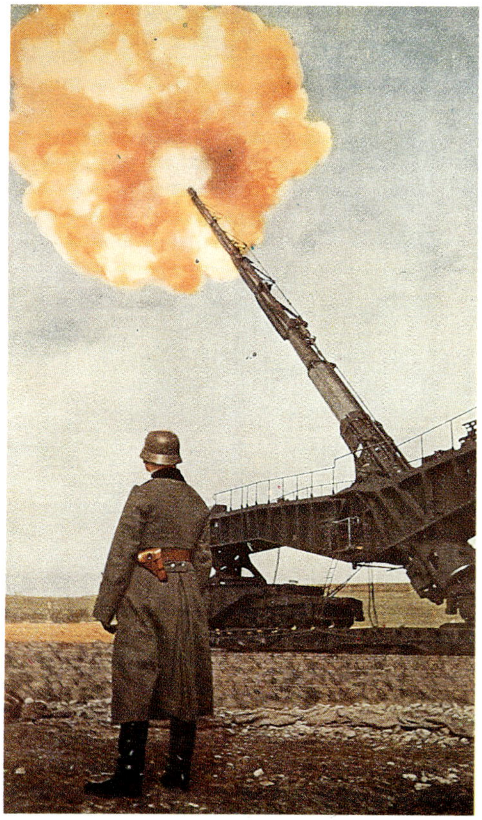

Left: As soon as they had occupied the French coast the Germans installed heavy long-range artillery in the Pas-de-Calais which was capable of hitting Dover and the surrounding area. These guns were intended to protect the landing of an invasion force, once air superiority had been gained by the Luftwaffe. After the Battle of Britain they served especially to hinder British sea traffic in the Channel and to represent potential opposition to any Allied landing on that part of the French coast.

Right: During the Battle of Britain the British used barrage balloons on a large scale in air defence. These balloons were generally operated by members of the Women's Auxiliary Air Force. Barrage balloons were used by most of the belligerents and proved to be quite effective. Barrages round towns and important factories prevented bombers from attacking at low level and thus avoiding radar surveillance and anti-aircraft fire. (A painting by Laura Knight.)

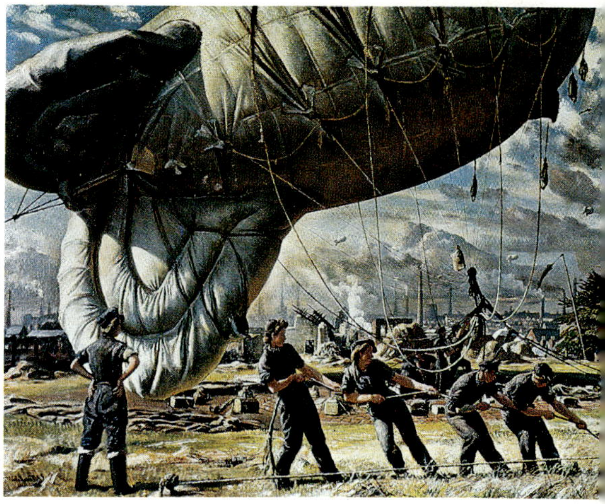

Brittany. Resistance forces had appeared in Brittany early on and in Aug. 1944 several thousand resistance fighters played an active part in the liberation of the region in liaison with American forces. Among the most active resistance units was the 'Tito company' of the maquis at Callac in the Côtes-du-Nord. With a strength of 130, from 1941 onwards this formation carried out an increasing number of attacks and acts of sabotage against German units and was able to save numerous Allied airmen. (A drawing by Anthony Gross in the collection of the Imperial War Museum.)

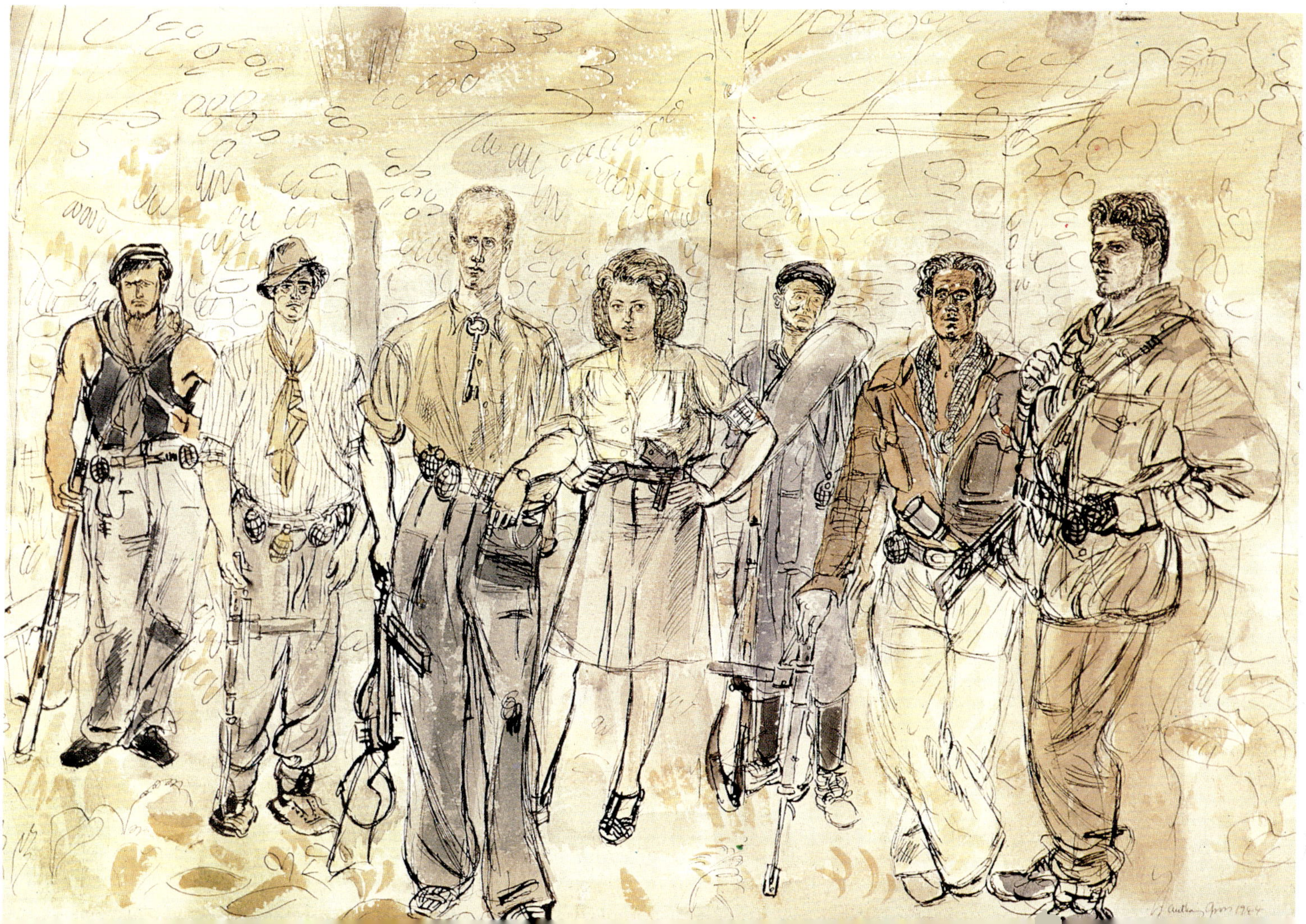

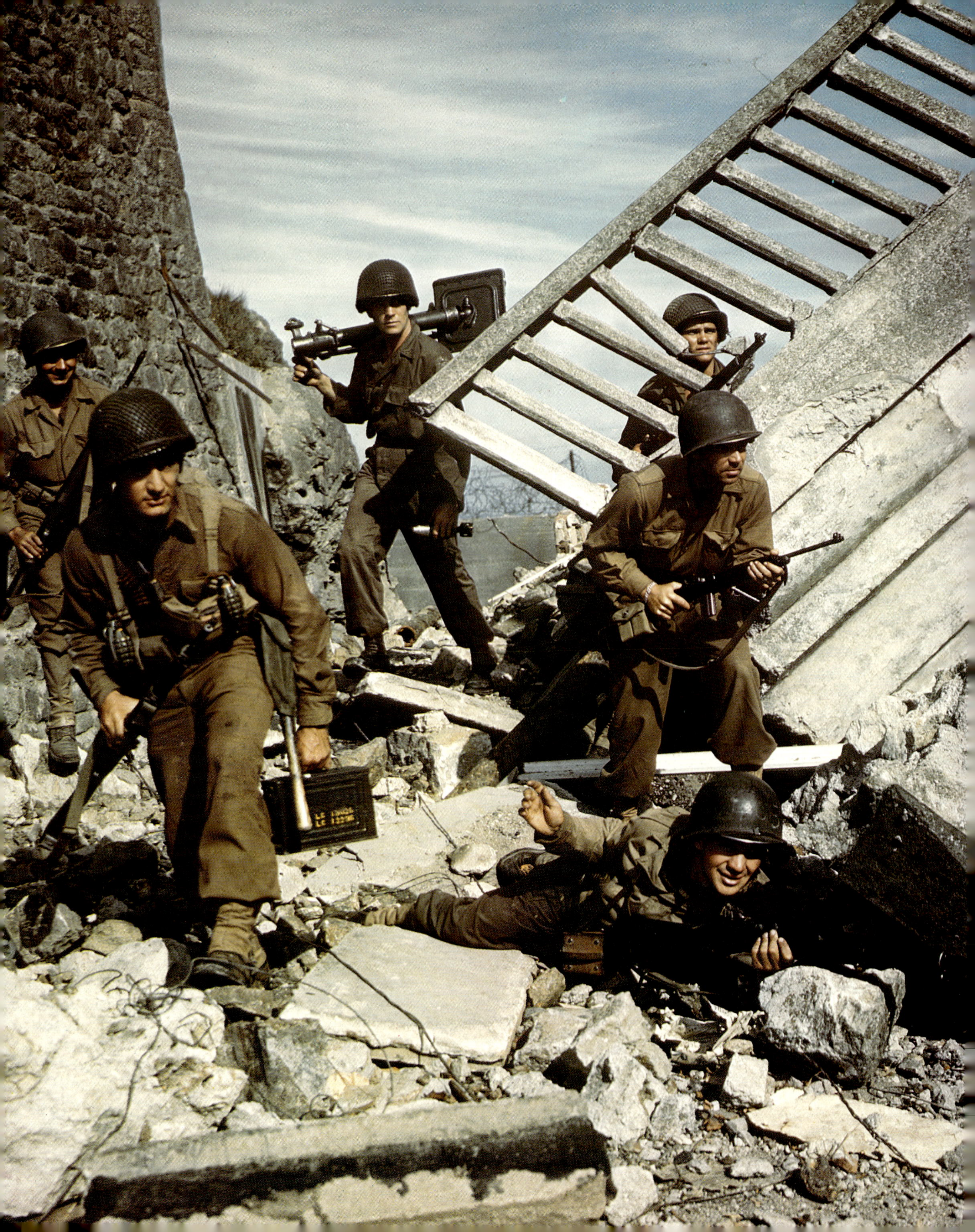

Opposite
Brittany. US infantry on the outskirts of Saint-Malo.

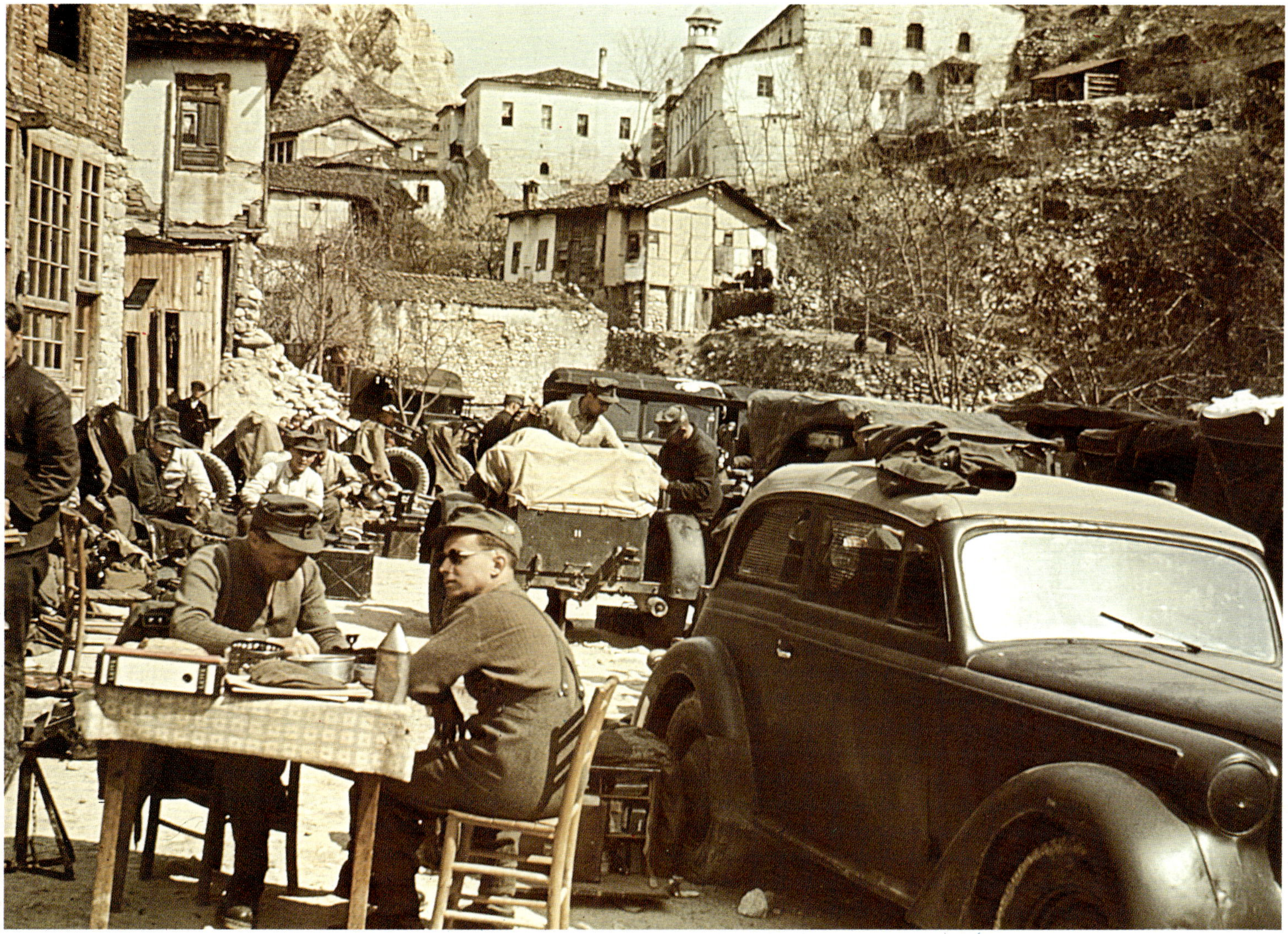

Bulgaria. German mountain troops in a small town in Bulgaria. By joining the Axis Tripartite Pact on 1 March 1941, the government in Sofia permitted ten divisions under the command of General von List to enter Bulgaria. As a result of the Wehrmacht's attack on Yugoslavia and Greece the government hoped to recover the territories lost after the First World War. The participation of Bulgarian troops in the Balkan campaign enabled these objectives to be reached, including the recovery of a part of Thrace, with access to the Aegean Sea.

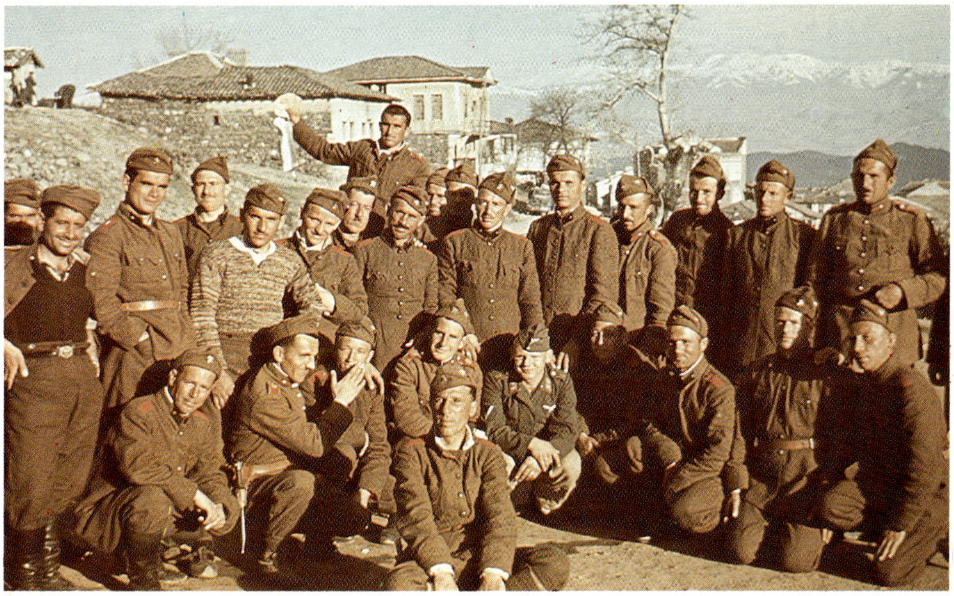

In the spring of 1941 Bulgarian troops (in the picture) had taken part in the attack on Yugoslavia and Greece at the side of the Germans. However, in spite of having joined the Axis, the Bulgarian government would not commit itself against the USSR. In 1944 the USSR declared war on Bulgaria. In 1946 the monarchy was abolished and a people's republic established.

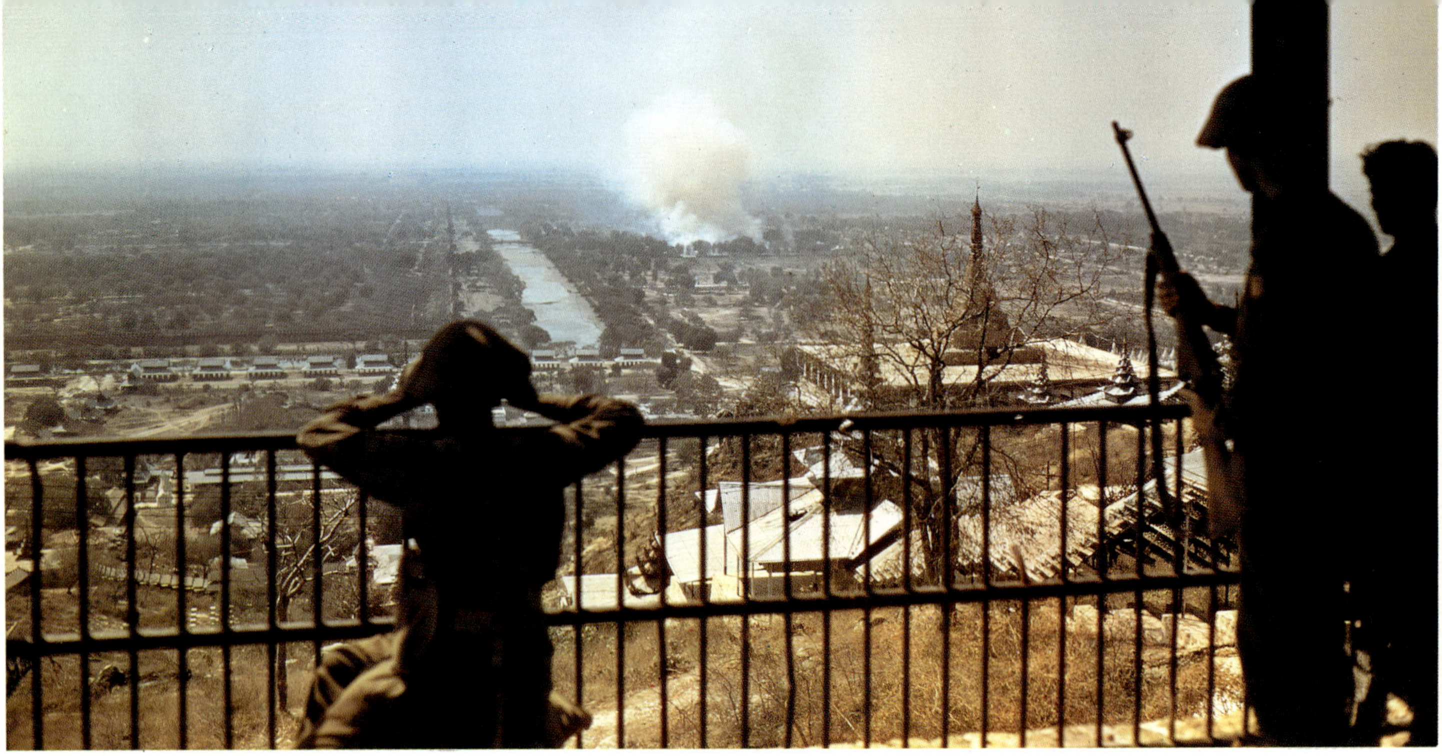

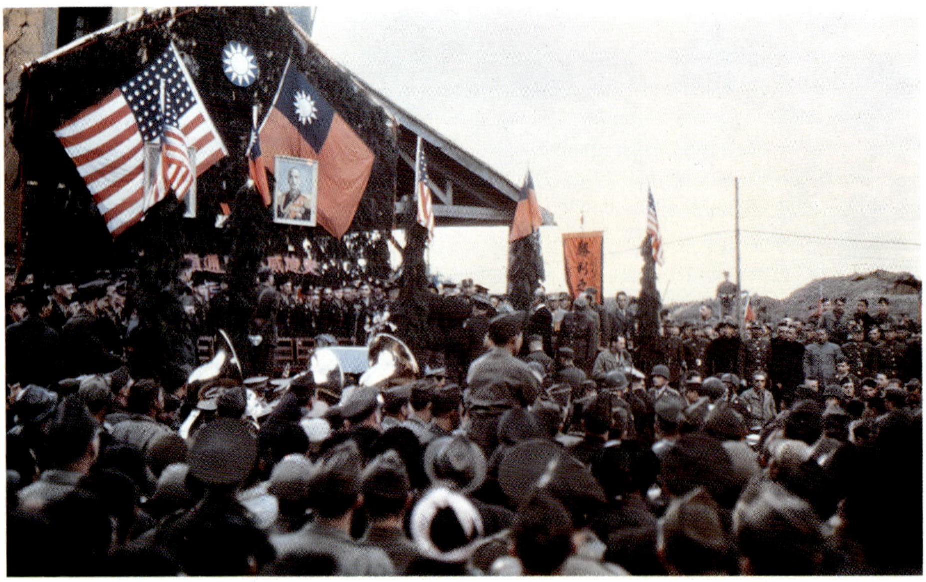

The Burma campaign. During the early months of 1942 the Japanese conquered Burma, thus reaching the gates of India and isolating China. It was only in 1944 that the reorganized British army, together with American and Chinese troops, was once again in a position to take an initiative and to reoccupy Burma. Here we see the liberation of Mandalay in March 1945. British soldiers observe the bombardment of Fort Dufferin from the balcony of a temple on Pagoda Hill which overlooks the city.

The Burma road. Nationalist China's last supply route, the Burma road, was cut in 1942 by the Japanese invasion. To break the Chinese isolation, the American general, Joseph Stilwell, undertook to open a new road linking Ledo in India to the former Burma road across north Burma, from which it would be necessary to drive the Japanese. The building of the road, in mountainous terrain and under enemy fire, took over a year. When the first convoy to travel by this road arrived in China in Feb. 1945 the Chinese and American allies were able to celebrate their joint exploit.

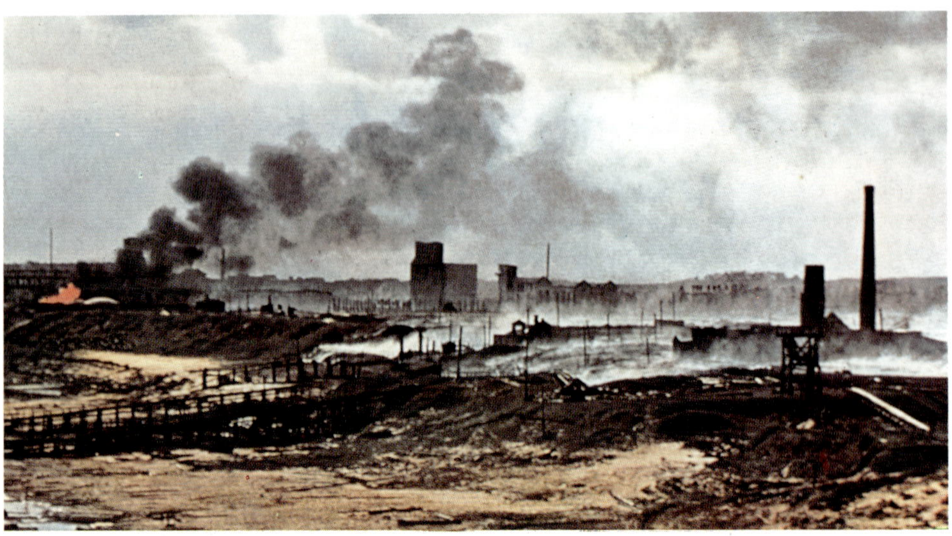

Byelorussia. During the summer of 1941 Byelorussia had the sad distinction of serving as the theatre of the Blitzkrieg waged by the Wehrmacht following the German attack on the USSR. The Germans occupied the whole territory of this Soviet republic in less than a fortnight, capturing Vitebsk on 10 July. As this picture shows, they occupied a ruined city, which had been set on fire by the Red Army in order to hold up the enemy.

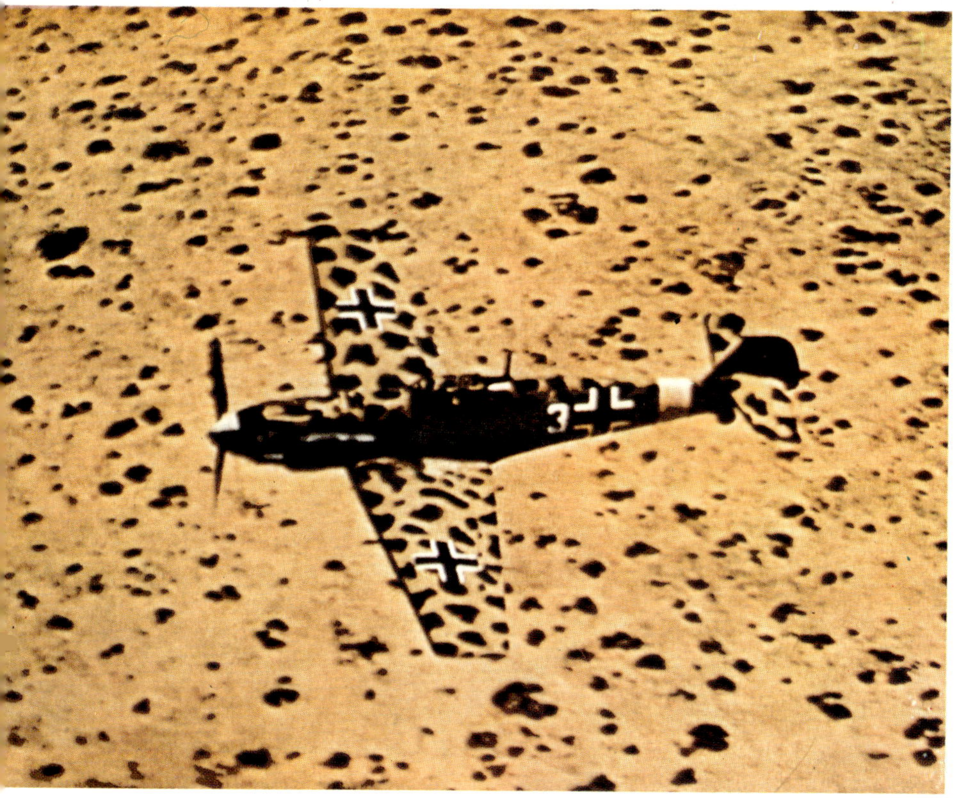

Camouflage. During the Second World War camouflage was to gain considerable importance and become virtually a science. It affected not only land forces but also naval vessels, painted in ways intended to cause mistakes in identification or in estimates of distance or speed. Aircraft were also involved. The Luftwaffe's aircraft on the eastern front were painted white for winter operations. Bombers and night fighters were regularly painted black. For day missions the undersides of wings and fuselages were painted grey or blue and the upper parts of the aircraft were painted in a colour to correspond to the nature of the terrain to be flown over. In this picture can be seen a Messerschmitt Bf-109 camouflaged so that it blends in successfully with the Libyan desert. (From a collection of the Bibliothèque du Musée de l'Armée.)

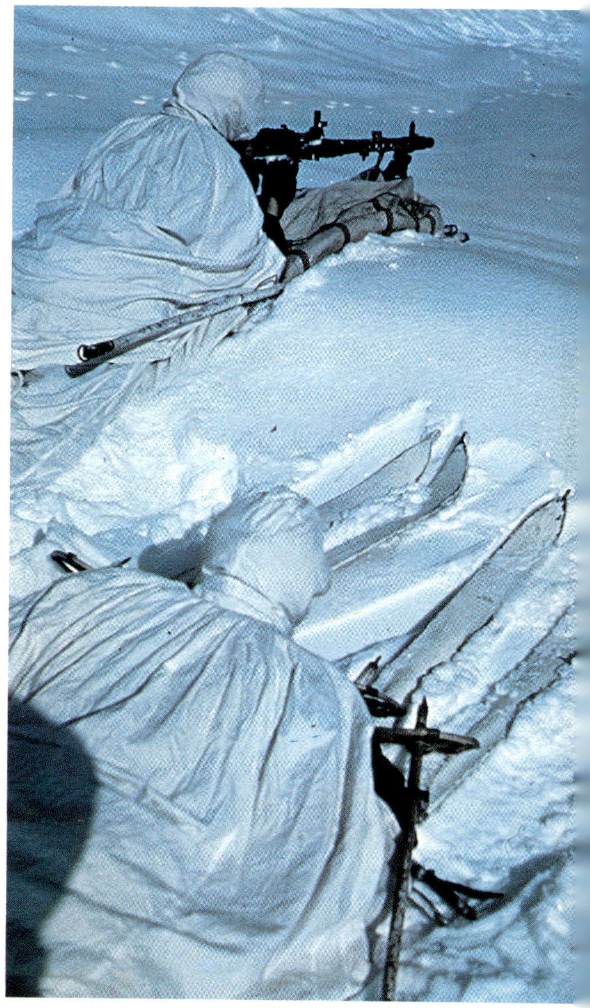

Contrary to the old tradition in which the soldier went into battle and on to the parade ground in the same uniform, modern armies have continually developed camouflage methods in order to try to limit the effects of artillery firepower and to confuse observers in the air and on the ground. Apart from inconspicuous uniforms of field grey or khaki, camouflaged battle dress appeared first in 1940, worn by German paratroops. As can be seen in this picture, the soldiers of the Wehrmacht wore white overalls and helmet covers during the Norwegian campaign and these were to reappear during the war on the eastern front. The soldiers of the Afrika Korps, on the other hand, had a sand-coloured uniform. British commandos on night operations even blackened their faces and hands so as to blend into the darkness more effectively.

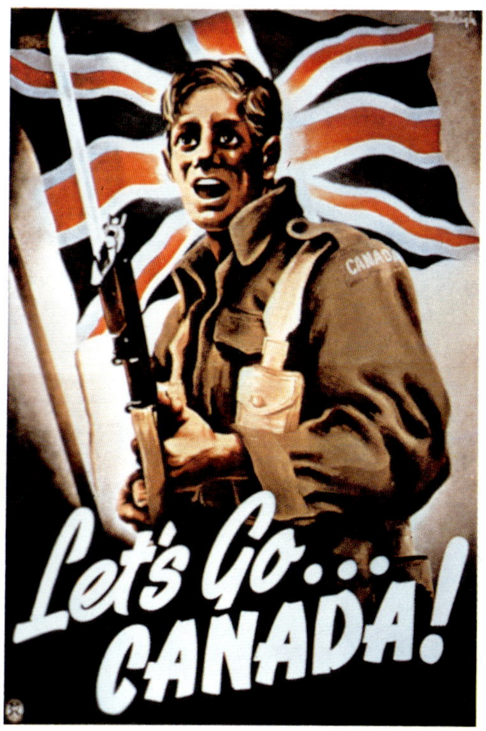

Canada. This wartime poster emphasizes Canada's important role during the Second World War. Although Canada was very seriously unprepared at the beginning of the conflict, its war effort was considerable. It mobilized more than a million men, who were involved in most of the theatres of war. Its shipyards and factories produced more than 500,000 tons of shipping, 50,000 armoured vehicles, 800,000 motor vehicles and more than 15,000 aircraft. At the end of the war, Canada, whose financial links with the United States had become very close, appeared as a great industrial power and the standard of living of its population had much increased.

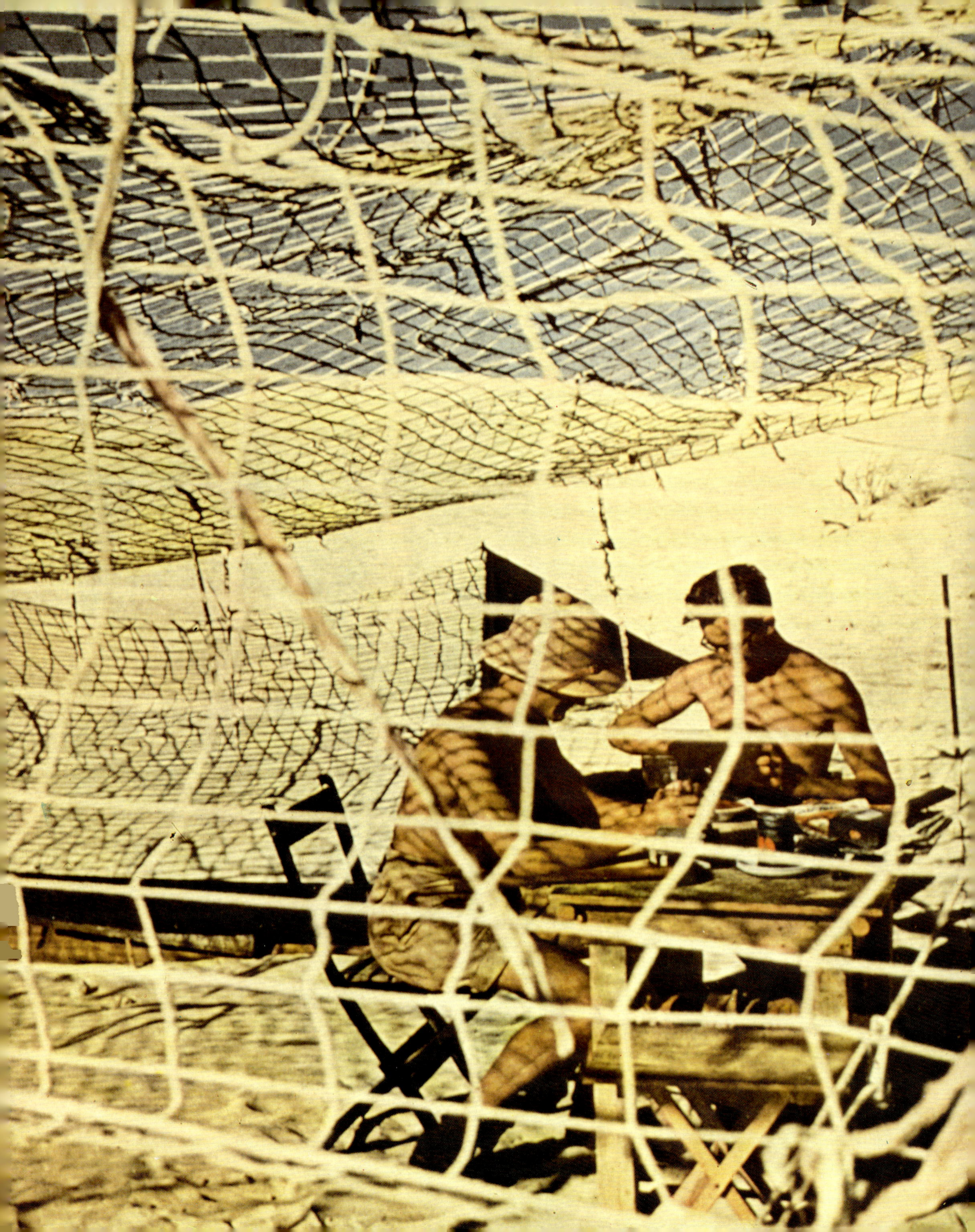

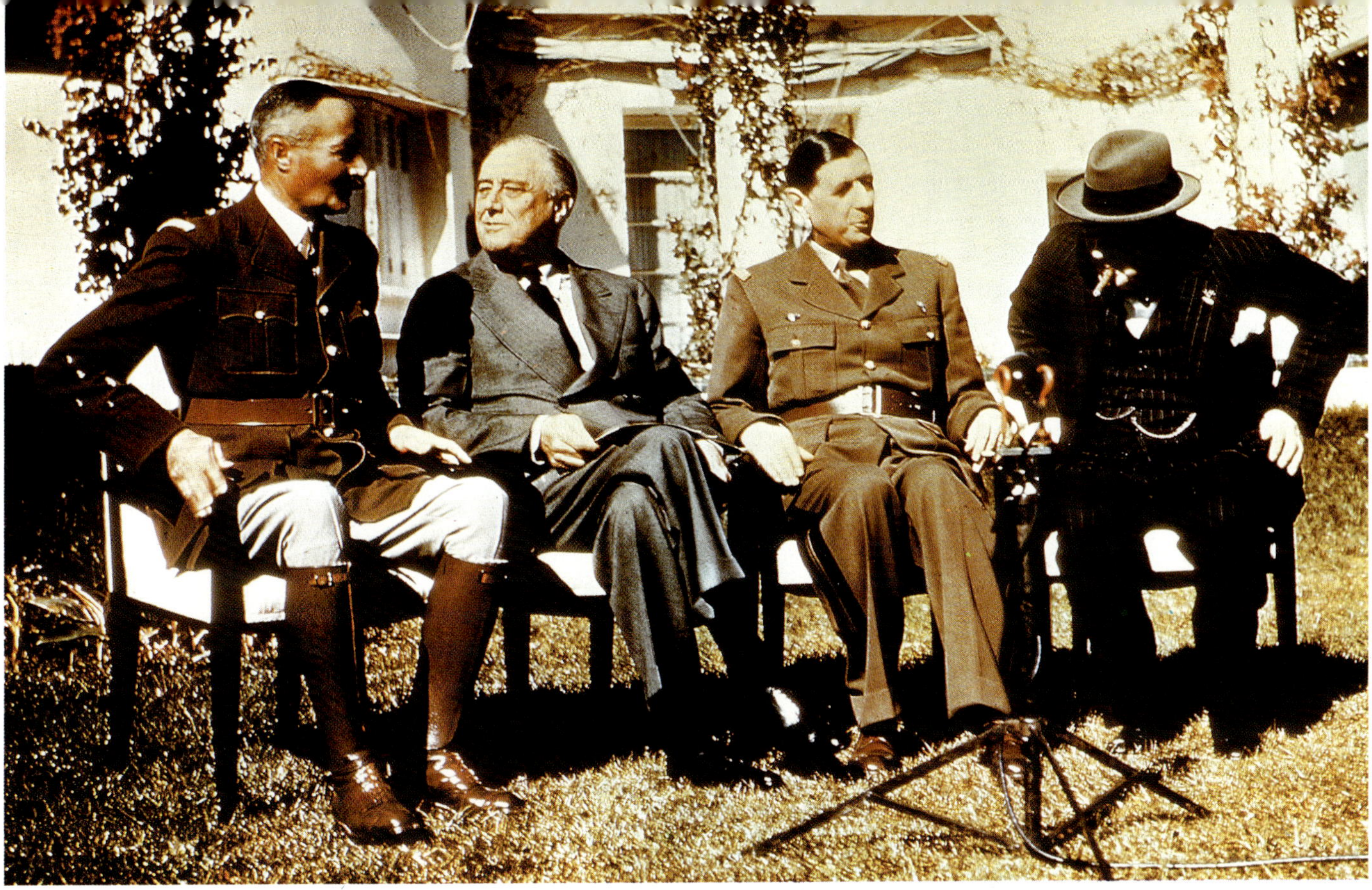

The Casablanca conference. Held in Jan. 1943, this was one of the most important Anglo-American meetings of the entire war. Accompanied by their staffs, Churchill and Roosevelt took the decision to put all their efforts into winning the Battle of the Atlantic, to step up the bombing of Germany, to complete the conquest of North Africa and to land in Sicily in the summer of that year. Also, it was at Casablanca that Roosevelt put forward the idea of 'unconditional surrender'. Finally the two allies tried to bring about a reconciliation between Giraud and de Gaulle, who embodied two different aspects of French 'legitimacy'. The attempt at reconciliation failed, notwithstanding the forced smiles which the two French generals put on for the photographers.

Cassino. The small town of Cassino and Monte Cassino crowned by the famous monastery were to be one of the most important localities of the Second World War. From Jan. to May 1944 the Allied forces in Italy – Americans, British, Free French, New Zealanders and Poles – made three unsuccessful attempts to capture this obstacle which commanded the road to Rome. All three attacks were broken by the heroic resistance of German paratroops and mountain troops. This picture shows a British anti-aircraft gun among the ruins of Cassino town and, in the background, the ruins of the Benedictine monastery, which was completely destroyed in the US Army Air Force and RAF air raid of 15 Feb. 1944.

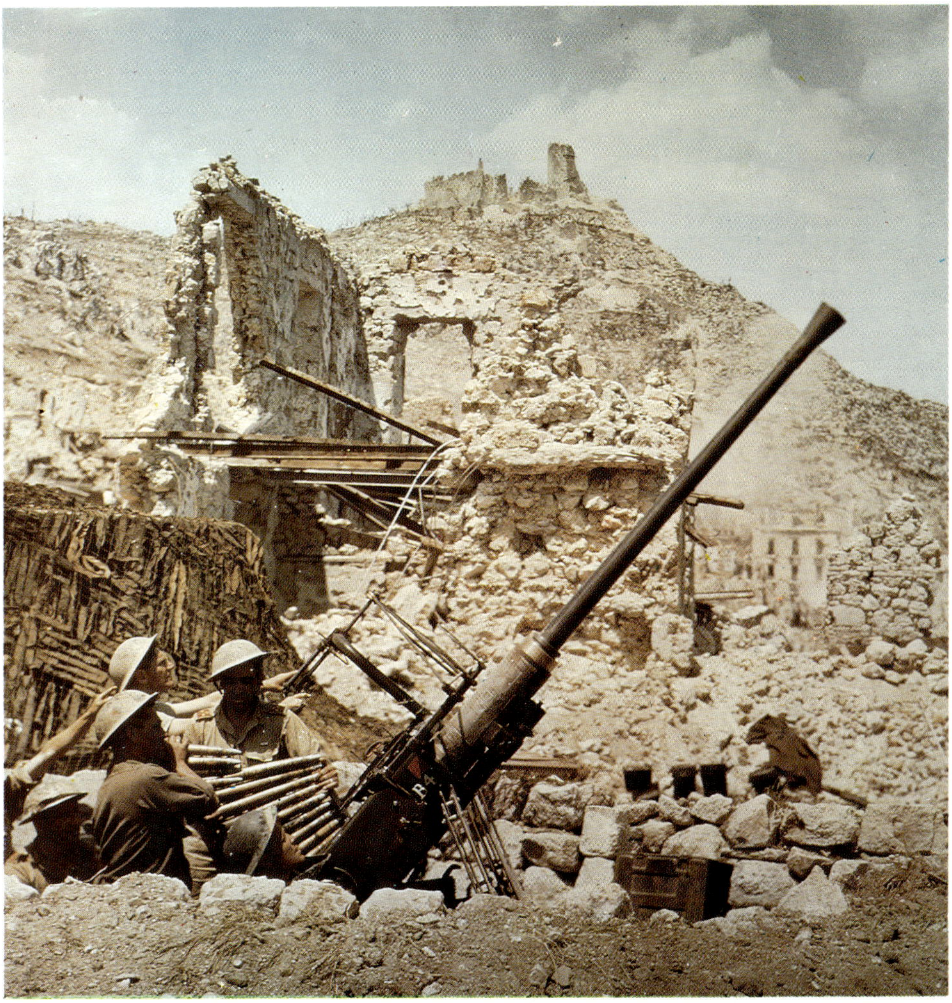

Opposite
Camouflage. A German command post in the desert, concealed from enemy view.

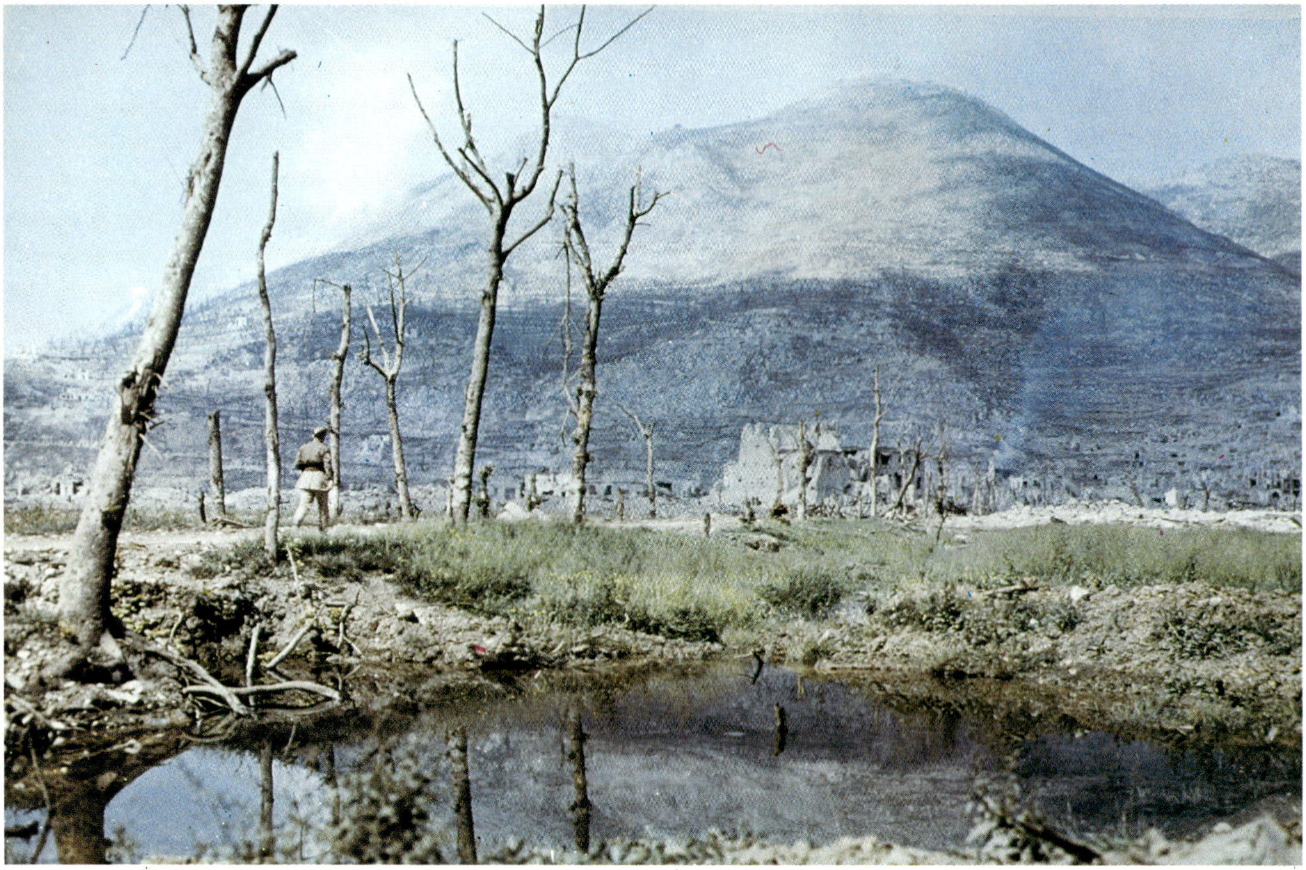

The battlefield of Cassino in Feb. 1944 at the time of the Allied bombing of the monastery. It was over this difficult terrain, cut by the course of the Rapido river, that the US II Corps fought the first phase of the battle. The Americans were unable to make a successful crossing of the river, which was in flood, although their attack had been preceded by an intense air and artillery bombardment. They were crushed by machine-gun and artillery fire, which was directed most effectively from observation posts on the mountain. However, contrary to the belief of the Allied forces who were in action at Cassino, the Germans were not occupying the monastery, and it became clear that its destruction, a disaster from an aesthetic viewpoint, had in fact been unnecessary.

The Caucasus. After the crossing of the Don and the taking of Rostov at the end of July 1942, the German divisions of List's Army Group A advanced towards the Caucasus and its oilfields. During this advance German forces (in the picture) crossed the immense steppes of the Kuban, one of the Soviet Union's major grain-producing areas, without meeting much resistance at all. They also reached the Black Sea at Novorossyisk and the oilwells at Maikop, which the Russians had set on fire.

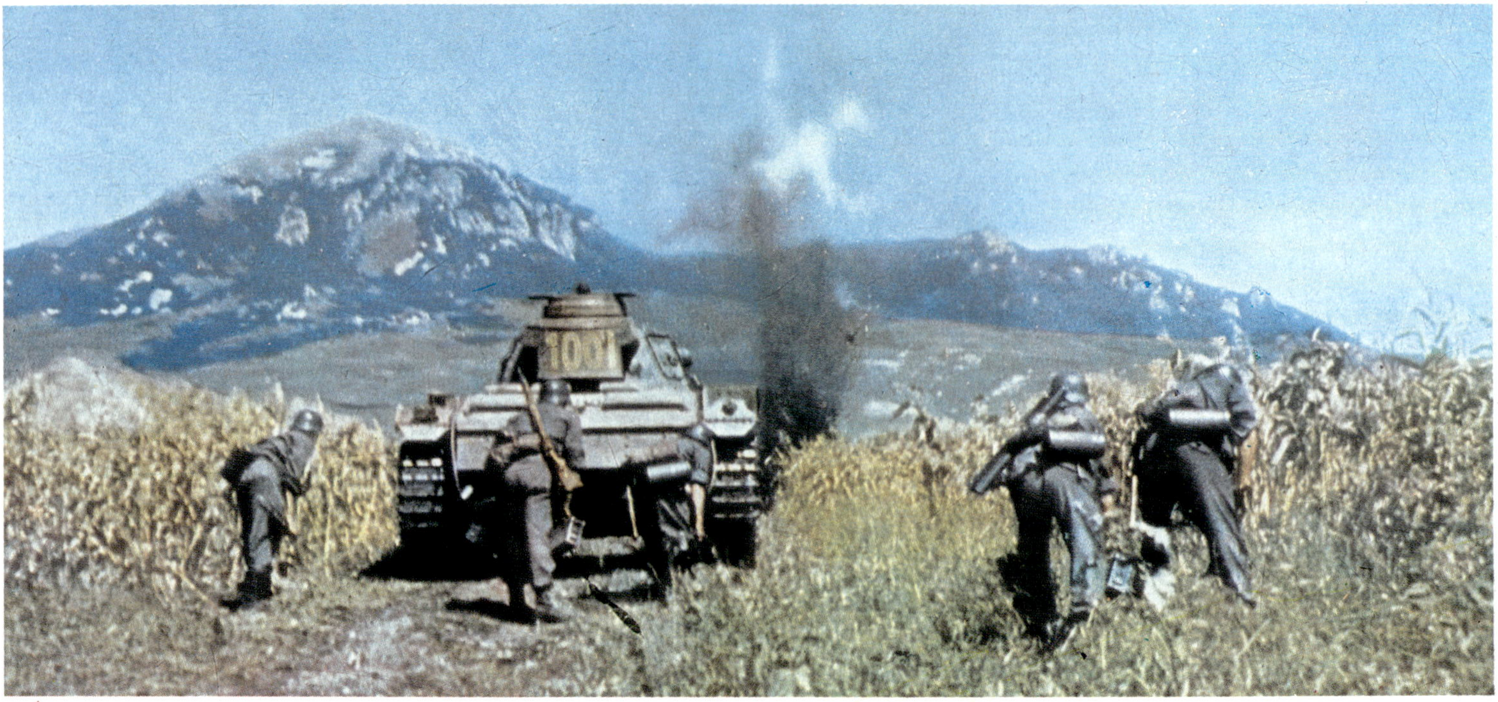

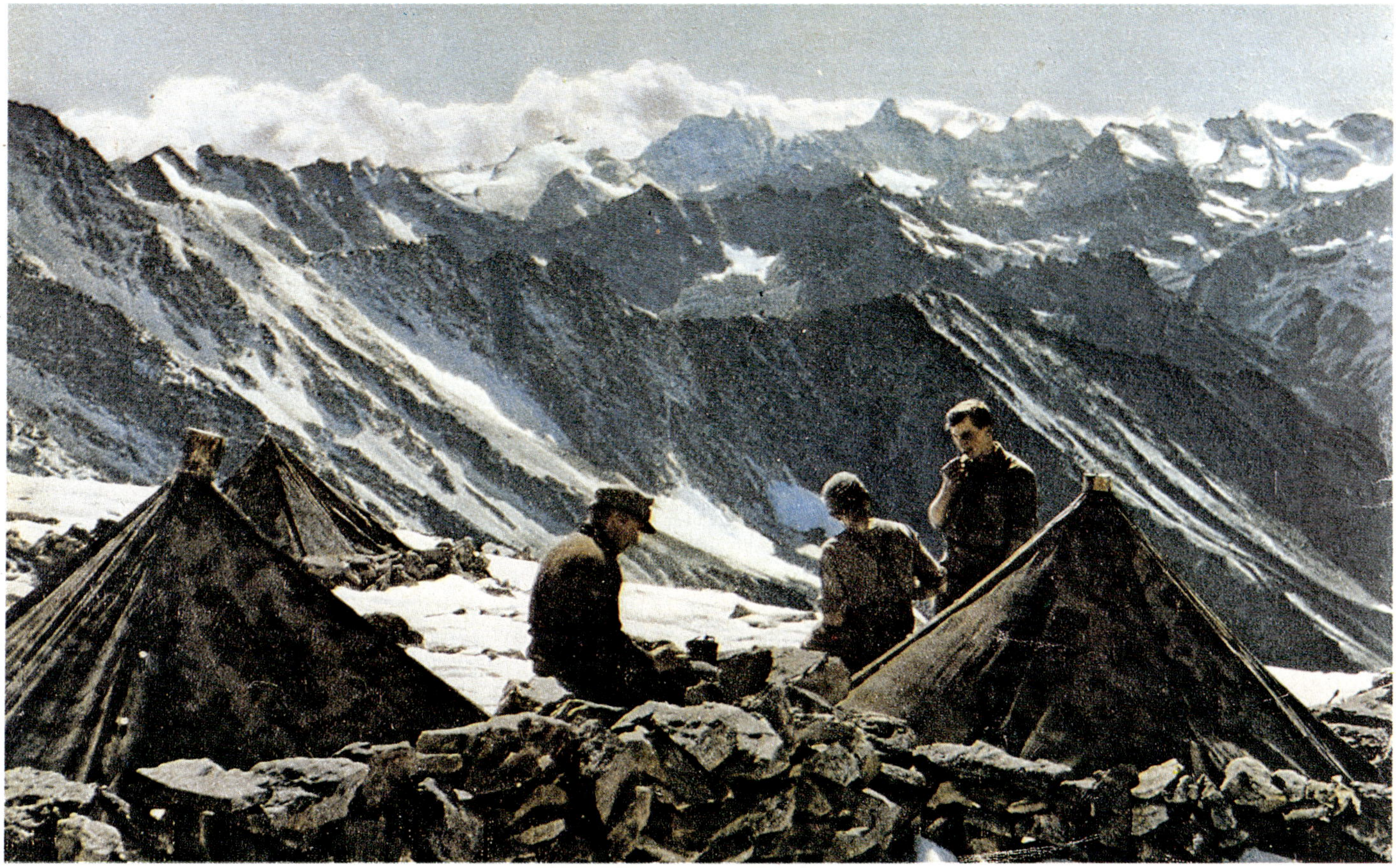

After a rapid crossing of the steppes of the Kuban during the summer of 1942, the German advance slowed down when it reached the foothills of the Caucasus mountains. This was a consequence of the stretching of the lines of communication, the difficulties of the terrain and growing Soviet resistance. Thus General Konrad's mountain corps was unable to control the central mountain passes and to break through in the direction of the Sukhum. However, a detachment of German troops did succeed in planting a German flag on the 18,480 ft (5633 m) high summit of Mount Elbruz on 21 Aug. 1942, but this feat was of propaganda value only.

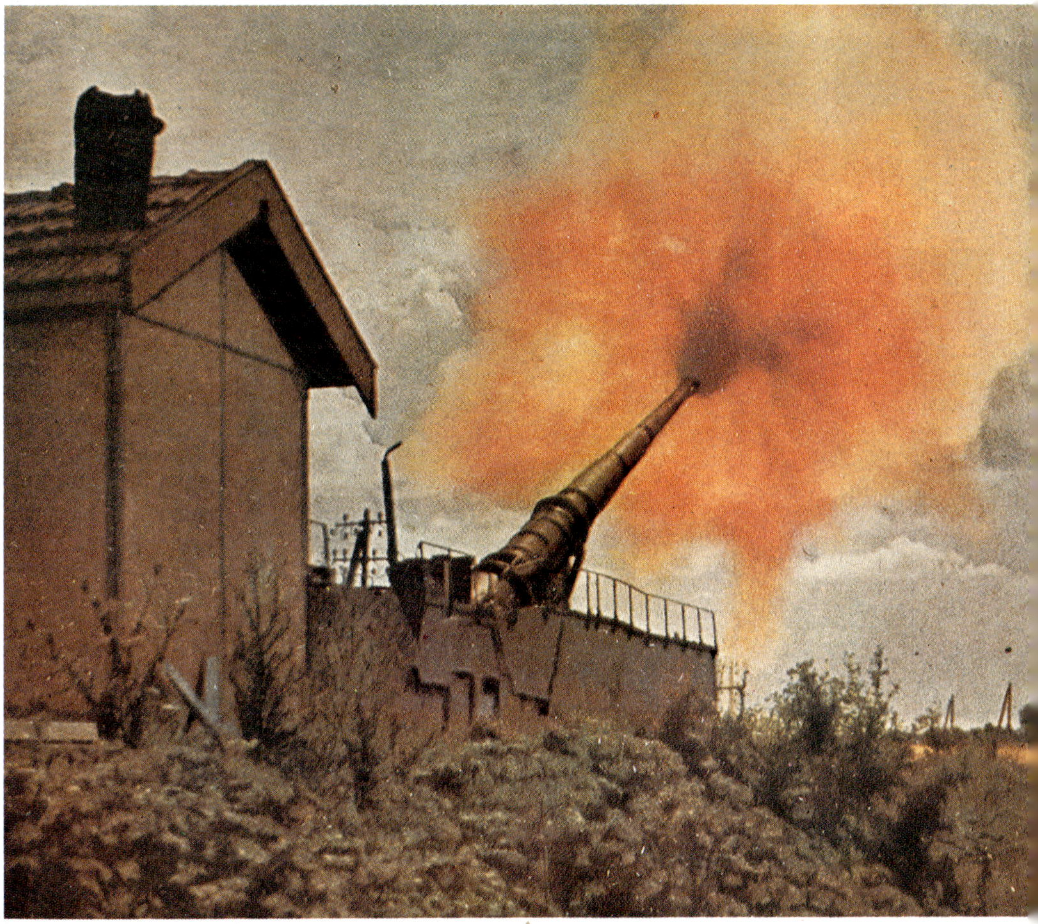

The Channel. Following the armistice of 1940 the coastal areas of northern France were occupied by the Germans and the Channel once more took on the maritime role it had during the 17th and 18th centuries when England and France were frequently at war. Although the Wehrmacht was unable to cross the Channel, it did set up in the Pas-de-Calais impressive emplacements of heavy guns which were capable of bombarding Dover, paralysing the movement of shipping and preventing the passage of the Royal Navy's large vessels. These heavy guns made their presence felt for the last time in Sept. 1944 with an intensive bombardment on the eve of the British army's liberation of the coastal areas of the Pas-de-Calais.

Opposite
The Channel. American soldiers shortly before the Normandy landings.

Right
From 1943, in the expectation of an Anglo-American landing, the Germans began to fortify the Channel coast. At the beginning of the following year the work was speeded up by Rommel, who had been sent to France to prepare the coastal defences against an Allied invasion. Believing that a landing would take place at high tide in order to reduce the vulnerability of the infantry, Rommel arranged for improvised obstacles – tetrapods, which were concrete teeth filled with explosive – to be set up on all beaches at the low tide mark, which would be death traps for landing craft. The discovery of these obstacles led the Allied commanders to modify their plans and to consider a landing at dawn at half-tide.

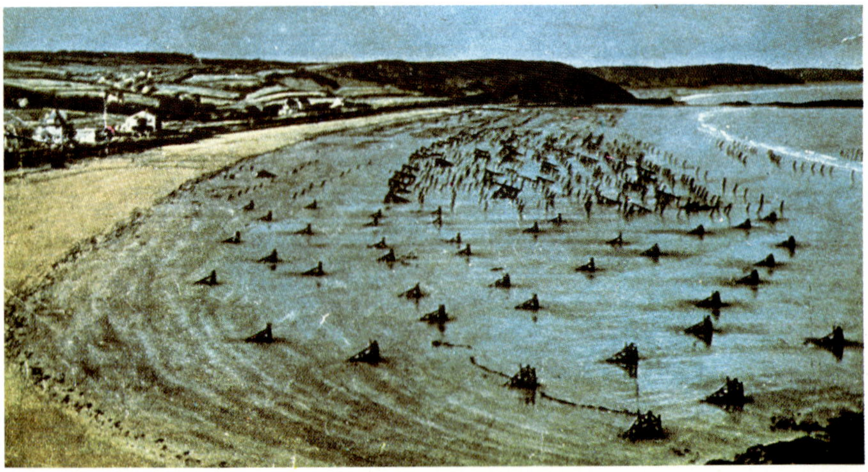

Chiang Kai-shek. The head of the Nationalist party and a bitter opponent of the Communists, he remained in 1941 the symbol of China's struggle against Japanese imperialism. His prestige enabled him to receive considerable aid from the United States, thanks to the airlift over the Himalayas and the Burma road. Chiang Kai-shek, seen here in company with the American general Wedemeyer, Stilwell's successor as deputy supreme Allied Commander in southeast Asia in 1944, proved to be a difficult partner and not very co-operative. Despite the reorganization of his army he showed no inclination to resume a vigorous offensive against the Japanese, preferring to conserve his forces in order to deal with the Communist problem after the war.

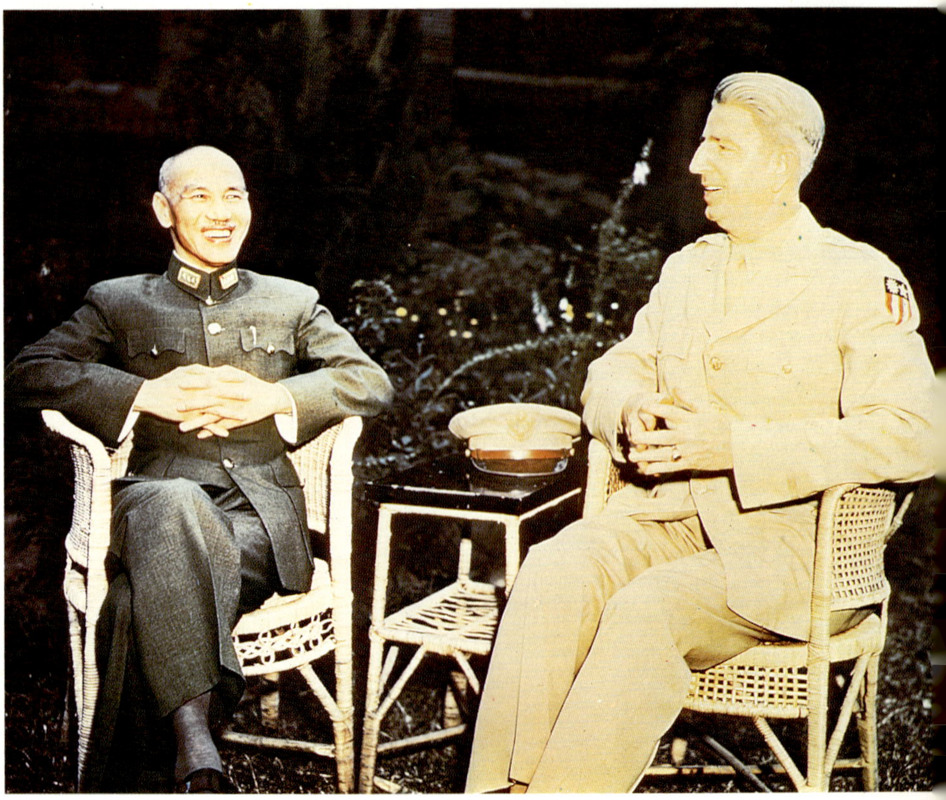

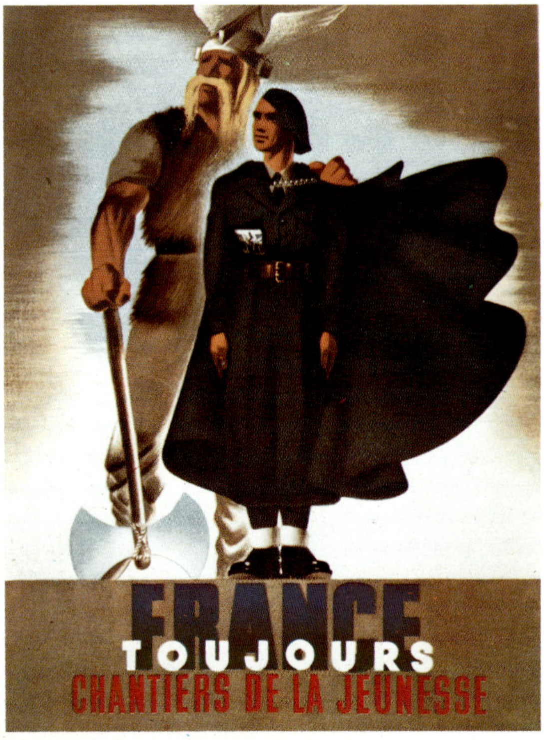

The *Chantiers de la jeunesse* ('Workshops of Youth'). First set up at the time of the armistice between France and Germany in 1940, they became an actual institution in Jan. 1941. They involved all young people aged 20 in the unoccupied zone of France and the period of work and training lasted eight months. These young people, under virtual military discipline, devoted themselves to farm work and also took part in more intellectual activities such as lectures, debates and talks. Directed by General de la Porte du Theil, the Chantiers aimed to foster respect for traditional values and to initiate the young into the cult of Marshal Pétain. The German move into the unoccupied zone and the creation of the *Service du Travail Obligatoire* (Compulsory Labour Service) were a fatal blow to the Chantiers, the last of which were dissolved in June 1944.

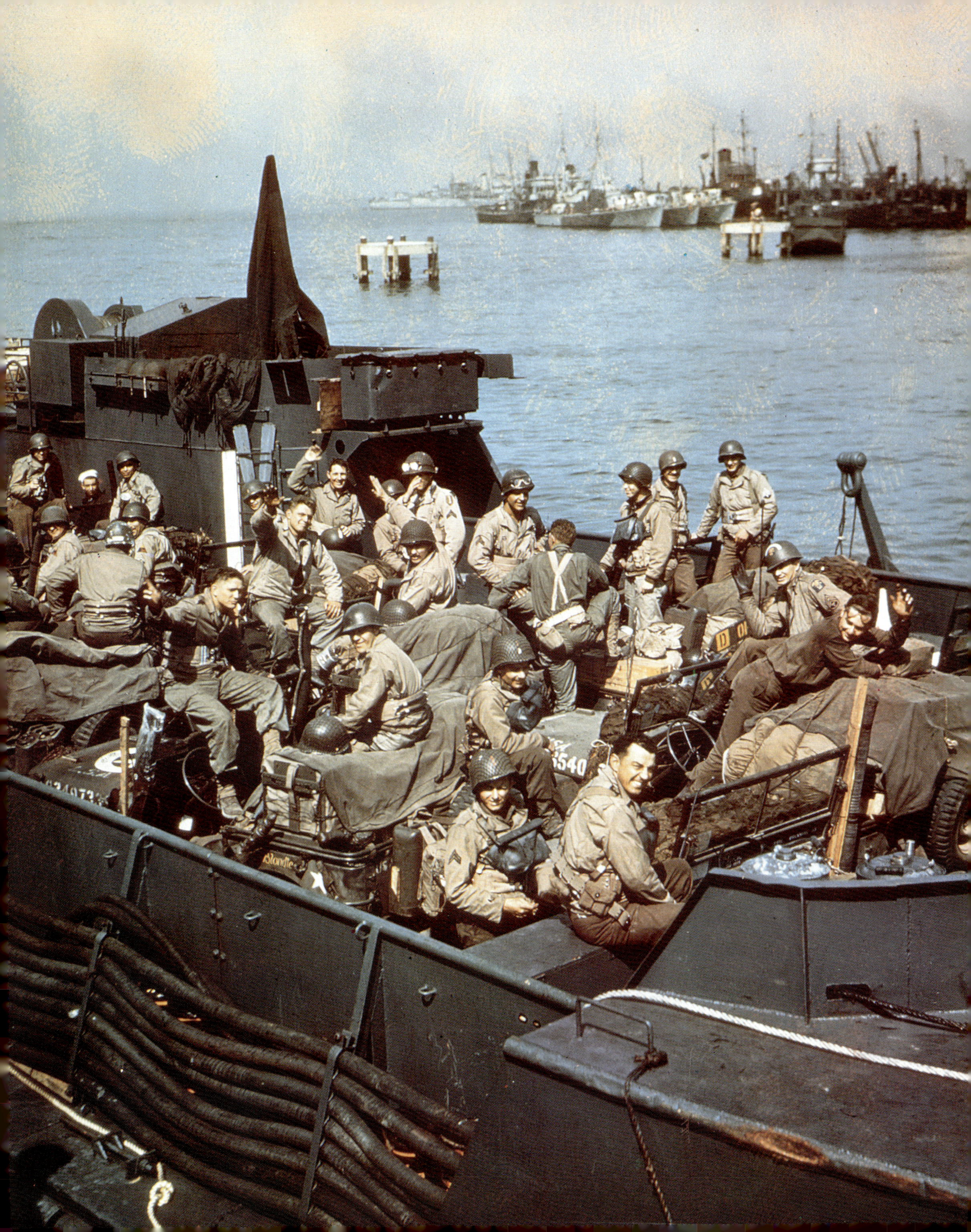

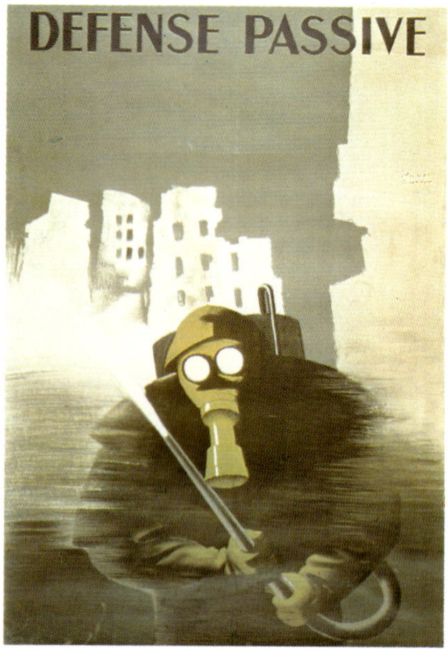

Chemical warfare. On the eve of the conflict all major nations feared an expansion of chemical warfare. Thus in France, Britain and Germany gas masks were distributed not only to fighting troops but also to civilians including children. In fact none of the belligerents risked using gas, although much more effective gas was available than in 1914–18, probably because they feared being unable to control the use of this weapon.

China. Chinese soldiers at a training exercise in 1944. The Chinese army could rely on inexhaustible reserves, mobilized almost 14 million men in more than 300 divisions and benefited from considerable American aid. Thus, at the end of the war, Chiang Kai-shek found himself at the head of an impressive army. However, he maintained a constantly passive attitude, being careful to use his forces economically with a view to re-establishing the authority of the Kuomintang over the whole of China after the war, and this passivity was a great irritant to his chief of staff, the American General Stilwell.

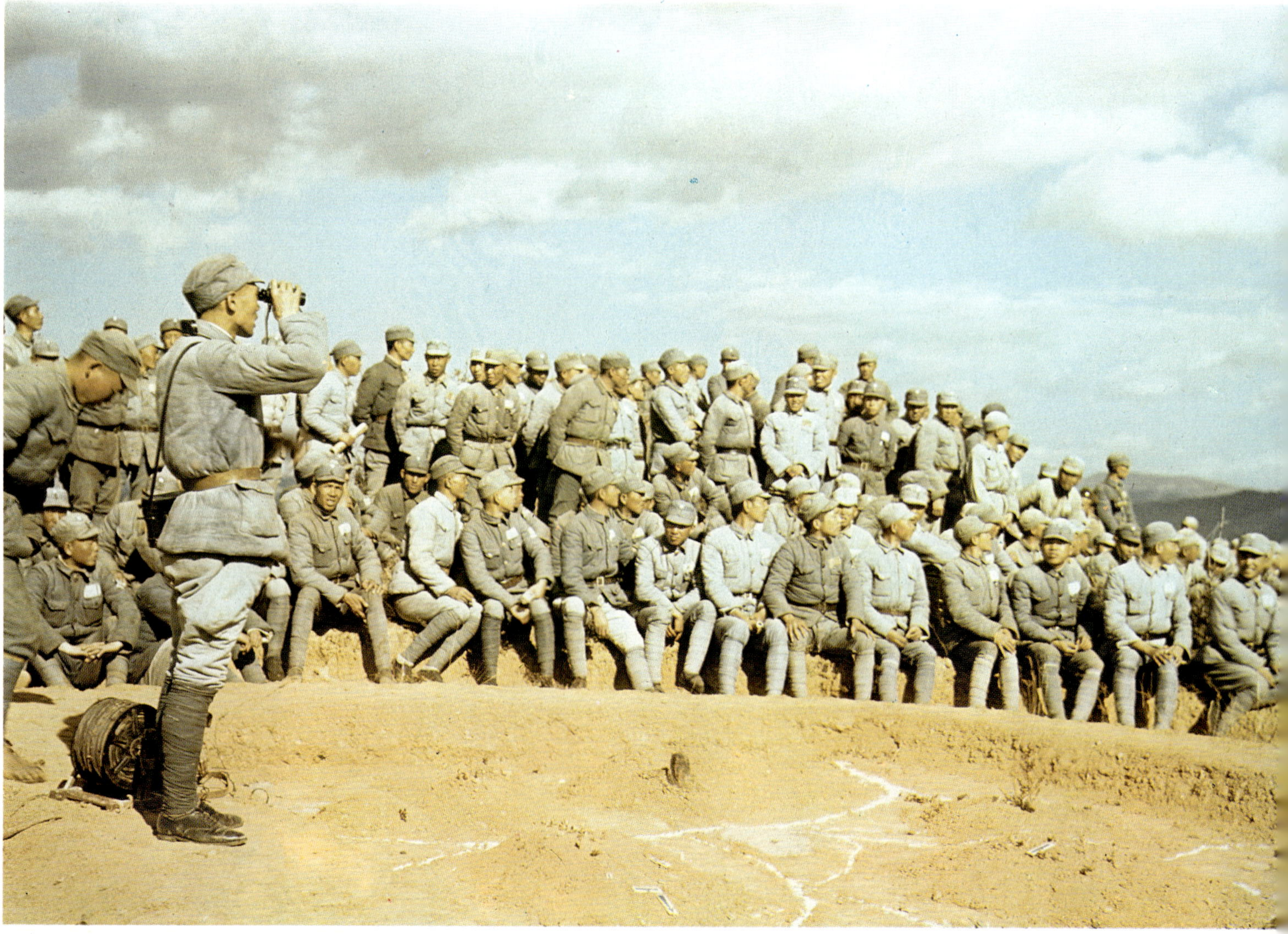

Following the Long March of 1934–35 the Chinese Communists under the leadership of Mao Tse-tung had fallen back into Shensi province in north China. Relying on support among the local population, they were to wage guerrilla war on the Japanese forces up to 1945, at the same time preparing to confront the Kuomintang after the war. This was the origin of the 'third civil war' in China.

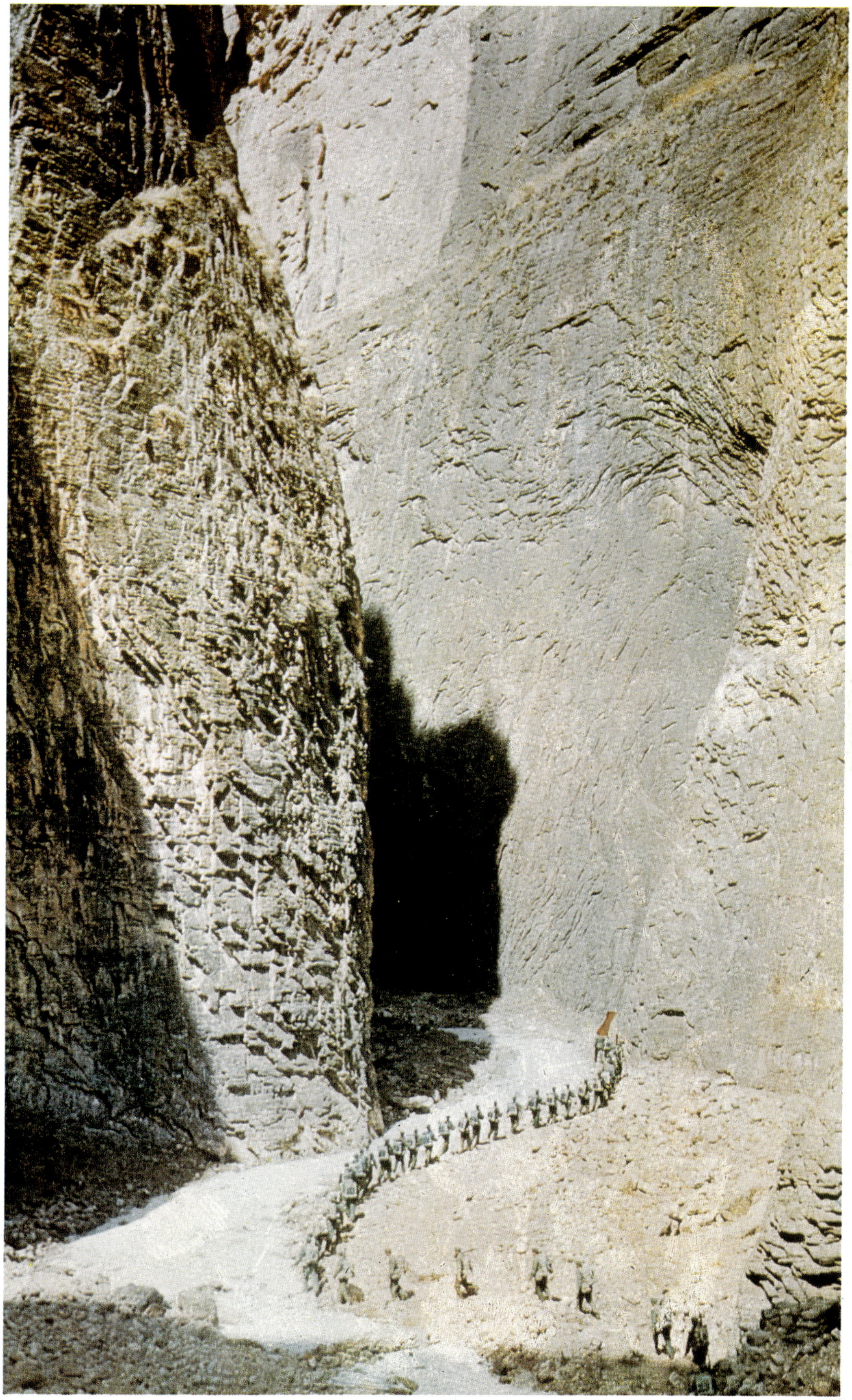

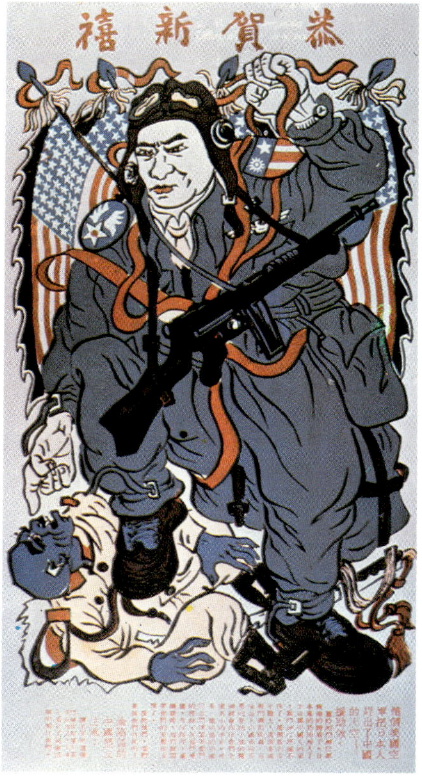

A Chinese poster, the text of which includes the words 'Happy New Year. Your American pilots are fighting for your freedom.' In point of fact American airmen were to play a continual part in the Sino-Japanese conflict. Claire Lee Chennault's volunteers, known as the 'Flying Tigers', began operating in 1941. From 1943 a mixed Chinese-American unit took part in operations, followed by squadrons of the US 14th Air Force which made use of airfields in the south of China and went on to make strategic bombing raids against Japan. Finally, from 1942 onwards American 'Hump' pilots, flying across the Himalayas on the air lift from India, were to contribute to the resupply of the Chinese Nationalist forces.

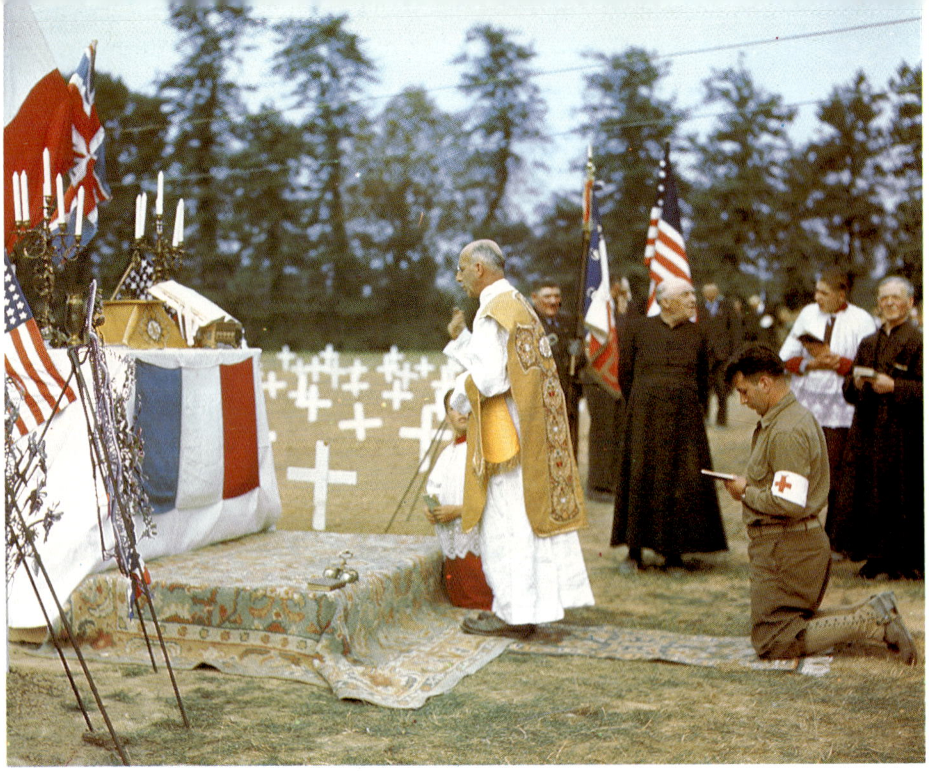

Opposite
The Cinema. Veit Harlan's *Der grosse König* (1942), a German historical film glorifying Frederick II (the Great) of Prussia.

The Churches. A Roman Catholic chaplain in the US army celebrating mass at the Montebourg military cemetery in the Cotentin peninsula in 1944, in honour of the American soldiers killed during the battle of Normandy. Throughout the war the churches faced an exceptionally difficult task: that of preaching the message of Christ in a world beset by national passions and totalitarian systems.

Winston Churchill. Churchill visits Montgomery's headquarters some days after the Normandy landings in June 1944, accompanied by Sir Alan Brooke, the Chief of the Imperial General Staff. Although already written off as a politician by some, Churchill had entered the Chamberlain government in Sept. 1939 as first lord of the admiralty and subsequently became prime minister in May 1940. For five years he was the incarnation of traditional British stubbornness, in spite of terrible difficulties, and led the British people to victory. At the end of the conflict, however, he suffered two great disappointments: his party's defeat in the election of July 1945 and his inability to impose on the Americans his political views with regard to Europe.

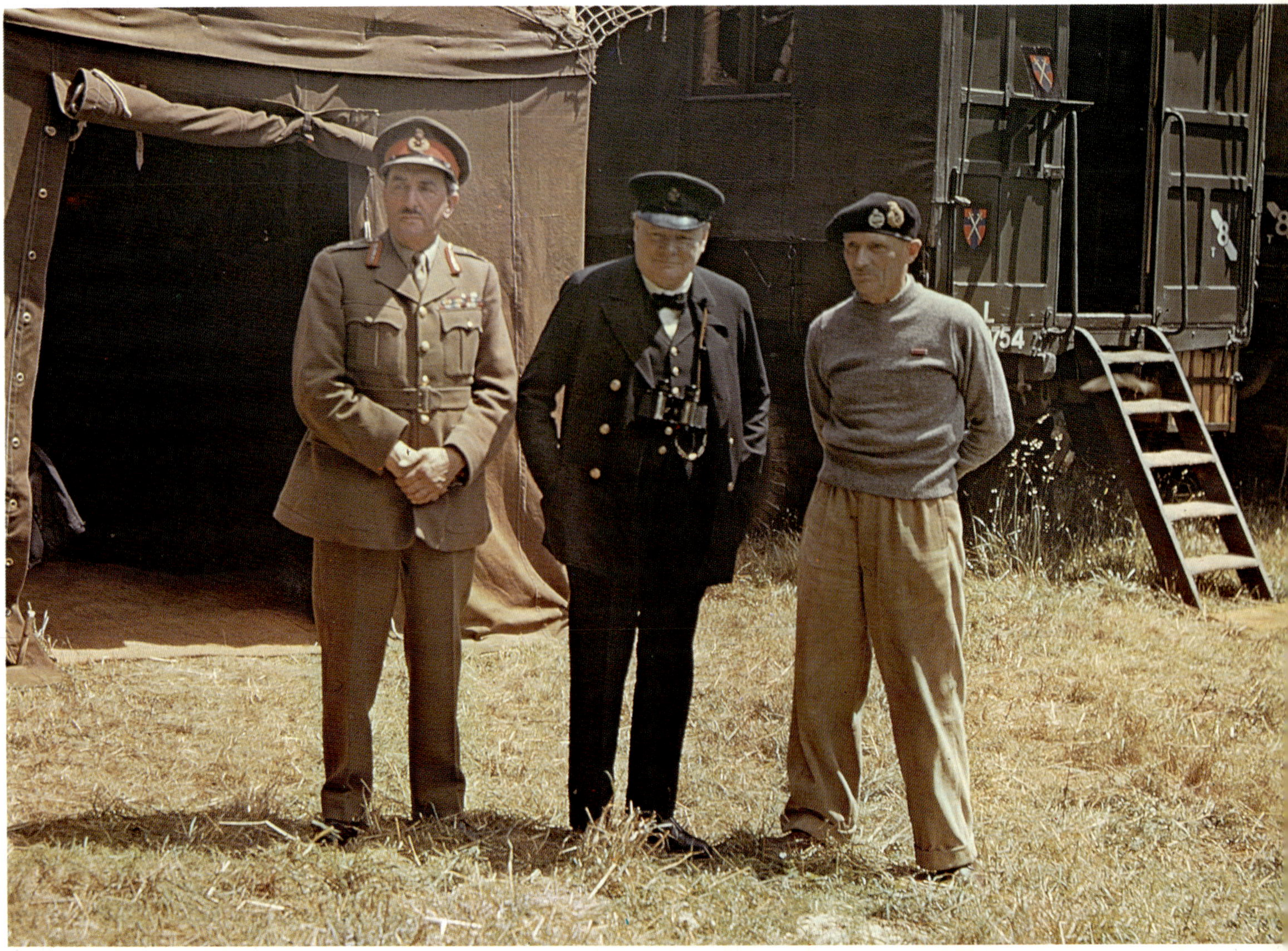

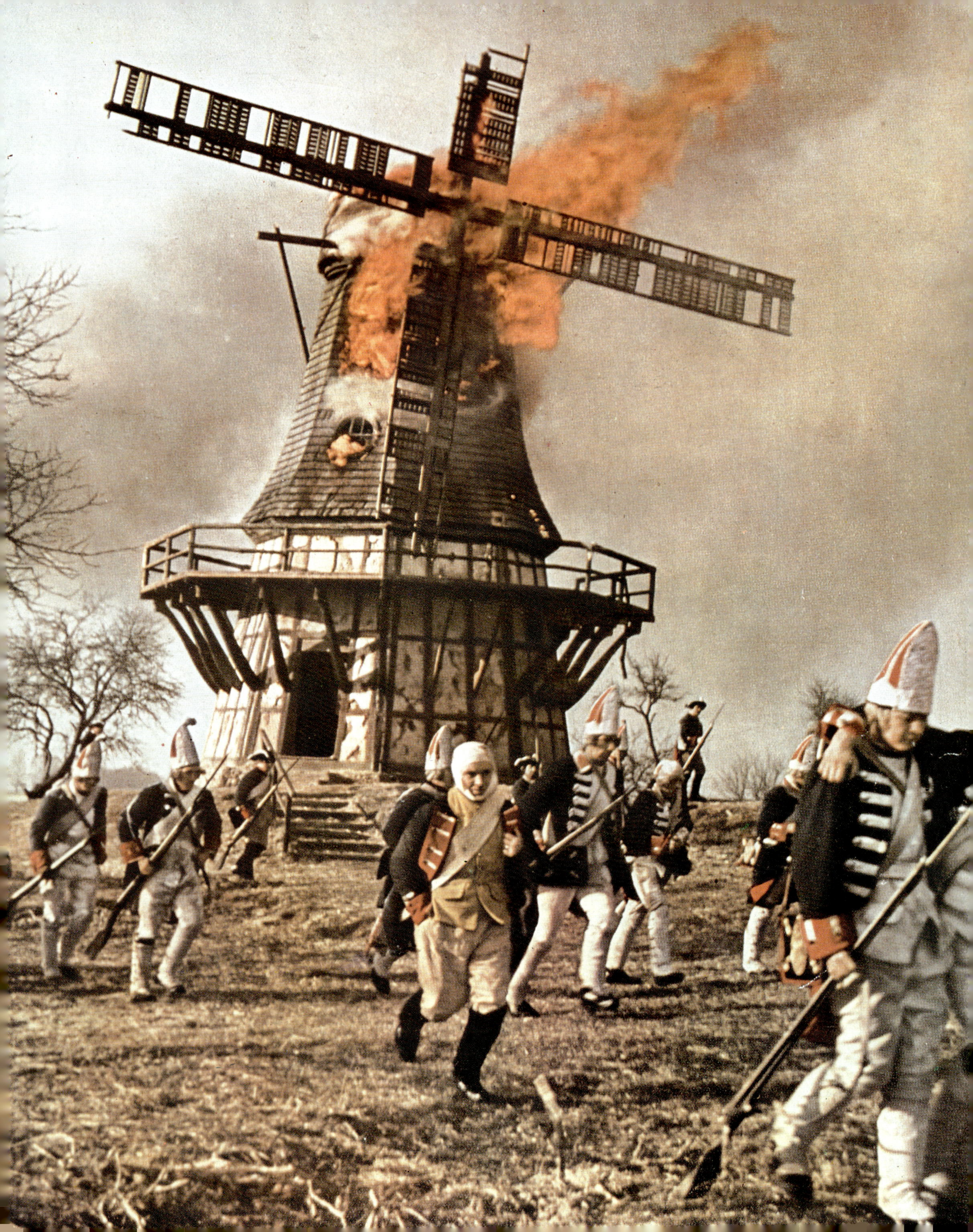

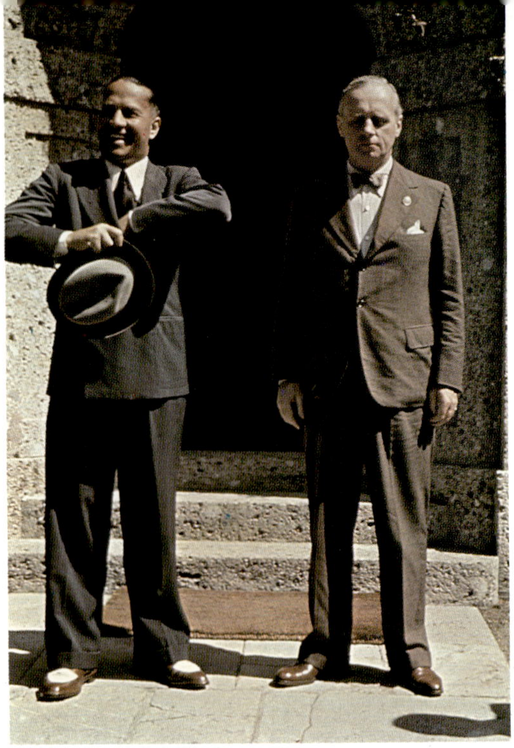

Count Ciano (on the left) with Ribbentrop in 1939. The son of a Fascist dignitary and the husband of Mussolini's daughter, Ciano had a dazzling career in the Fascist regime, becoming Minister of Foreign Affairs in 1936 at the age of 33. Intelligent but lacking in strength of character, at first he completely supported Mussolini's expansionist policy, and boosted the alliance with Germany, before eventually becoming distrustful of Hitler. After the major reverses of 1941–42 he advised the Duce to break with the Reich. He had a hand in the conspiracy of the summer of 1943 and then made the mistake of taking refuge in Germany. Ciano was judged and condemned to death in Verona and shot on 11 Jan. 1944.

The Cinema. *Gone with the Wind* (1939), one of the greatest financial successes of the American cinema, was in essence the work of David O. Selznick, one of the most ambitious of Hollywood producers. After George Cukor was sacked, Victor Fleming directed the film with help from Sam Wood and others. The film of Margaret Mitchell's best-seller enhanced the reputations of Clark Gable, Olivia de Havilland and Leslie Howard and made Vivien Leigh the most acclaimed film actress of the English-speaking world. The most memorable scene of the film was without doubt the burning of Atlanta, filmed with many technical resources and made still more impressive by the use of Technicolor, which until then had been little employed in the cinema.

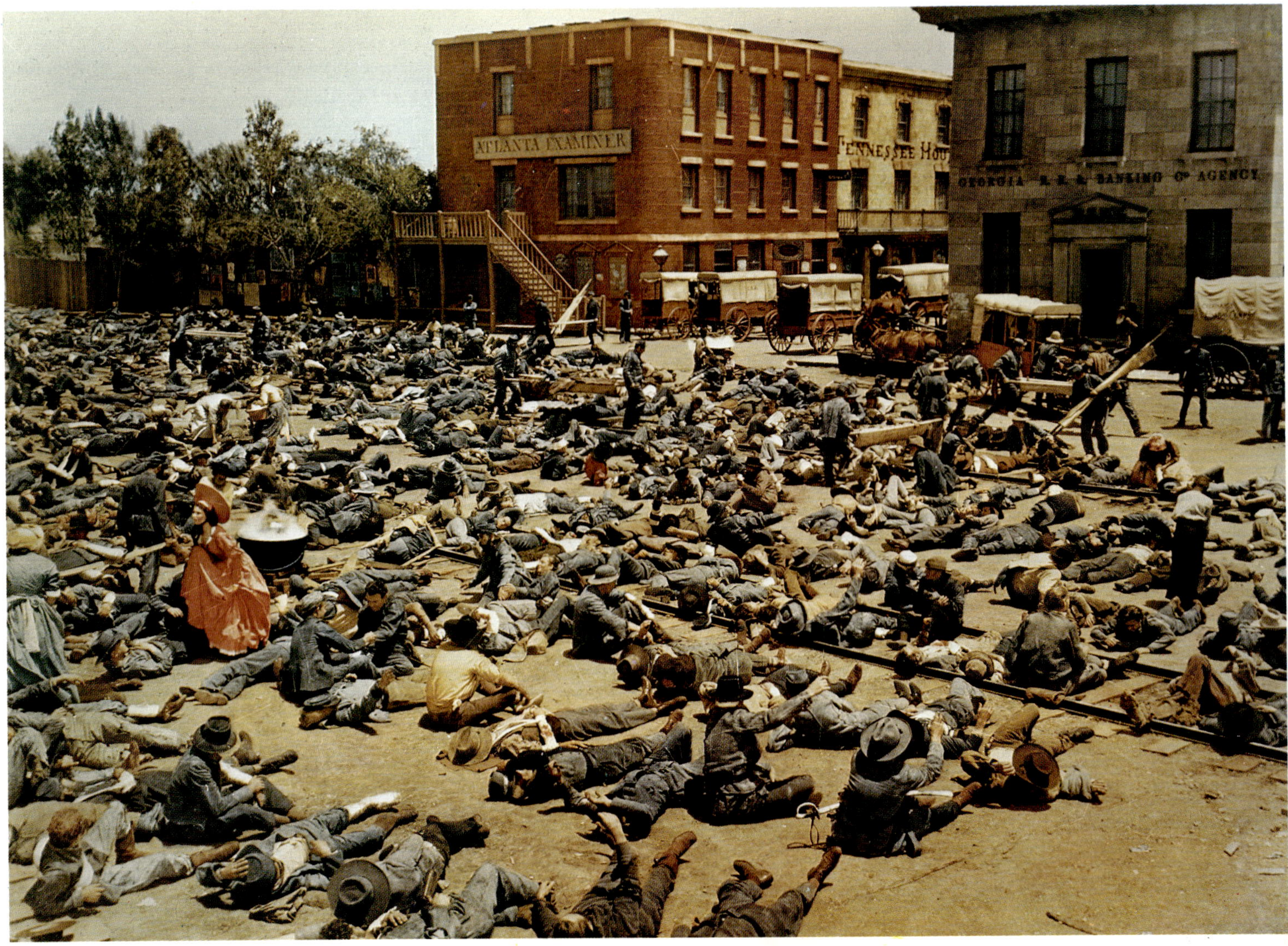

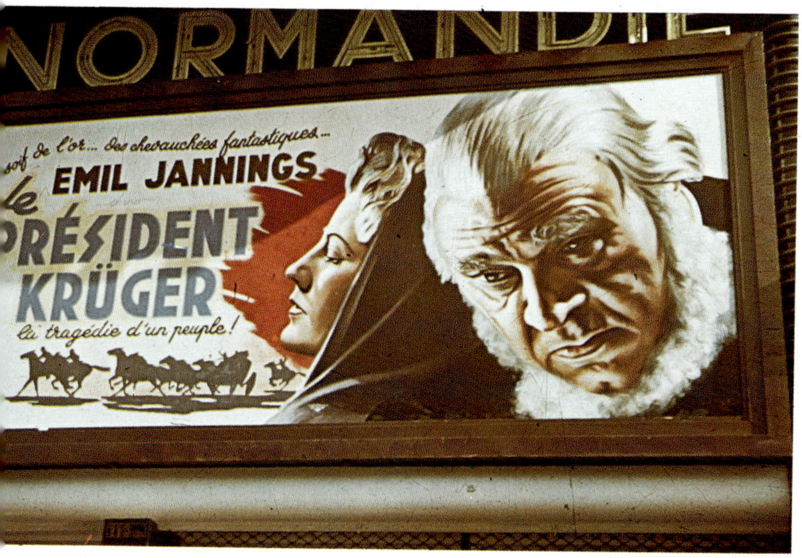

Above
Kruger (1941) was a political propaganda film, a 'state command determined to the smallest details', of which the model was, strangely, Eisenstein's *Battleship Potemkin*, which had impressed Goebbels very strongly. With its budget of 5,400,000 marks, it was the Nazi cinema's most expensive production. Not without certain artistic qualities, this violently anti-British film was a personal triumph for Emil Jannings, who portrayed the Boer leader, and he received the 'Golden Ring of the German Cinema' personally from Goebbels in his capacity as minister of propaganda.

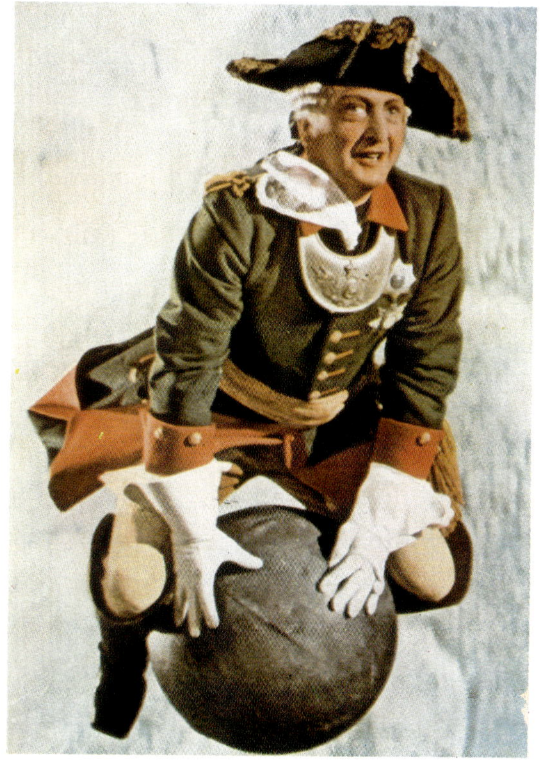

Munchhausen was a 'super-production' intended as a solemn celebration of the 25th anniversary of the setting up of the UFA film studios and the 10th anniversary of the Nazi cinema. It was in fact in 1943 that the director, Josef von Baky, was given the task of recounting – in Agfacolour – the adventures of a boastful baron called Munchhausen. The film was an overwhelming success. Its imagination (for example in the scenes in which the baron travels on a cannon ball or escapes from Venice in a balloon, constantly defying gravity), its humour, its special effects and its skilful production were to make it one of the most durable successes of the German wartime cinema. The baron was played by Hans Albers.

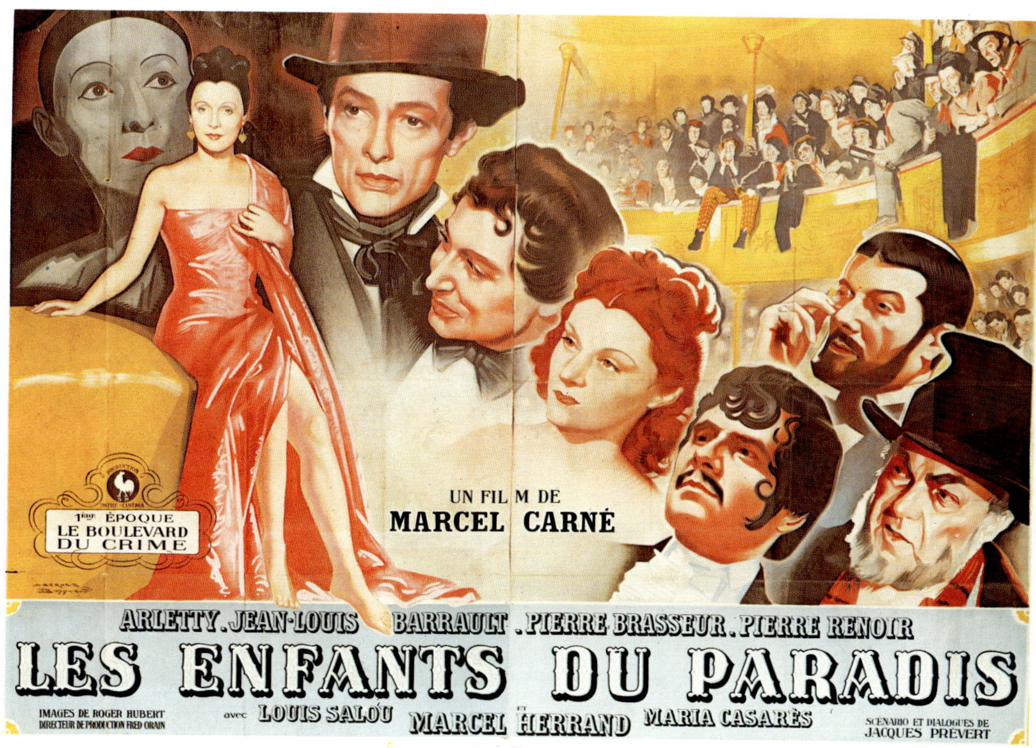

Les Enfants du Paradis, the masterpiece of the Jacques Prévert–Marcel Carné partnership, was not shown in public until after France had been liberated. It had been started as early as Aug. 1943 in the Victorine studios at Nice but had encountered production difficulties which would have discouraged many people. Nevertheless, this panoramic drama in two parts, lasting more than three hours altogether was a complete success. The décor depicting Paris in the Romantic era (the Boulevard du Crime in 1840), the stunning acting (in particular by Jean-Louis Barrault, Arletty, Pierre Brasseur, Marcel Herrand and Maria Casarès), Prevert's ingenious and sparkling dialogue and the masterly skill of Marcel Carné all gave the film an atmosphere which the passing of time has not dispelled.

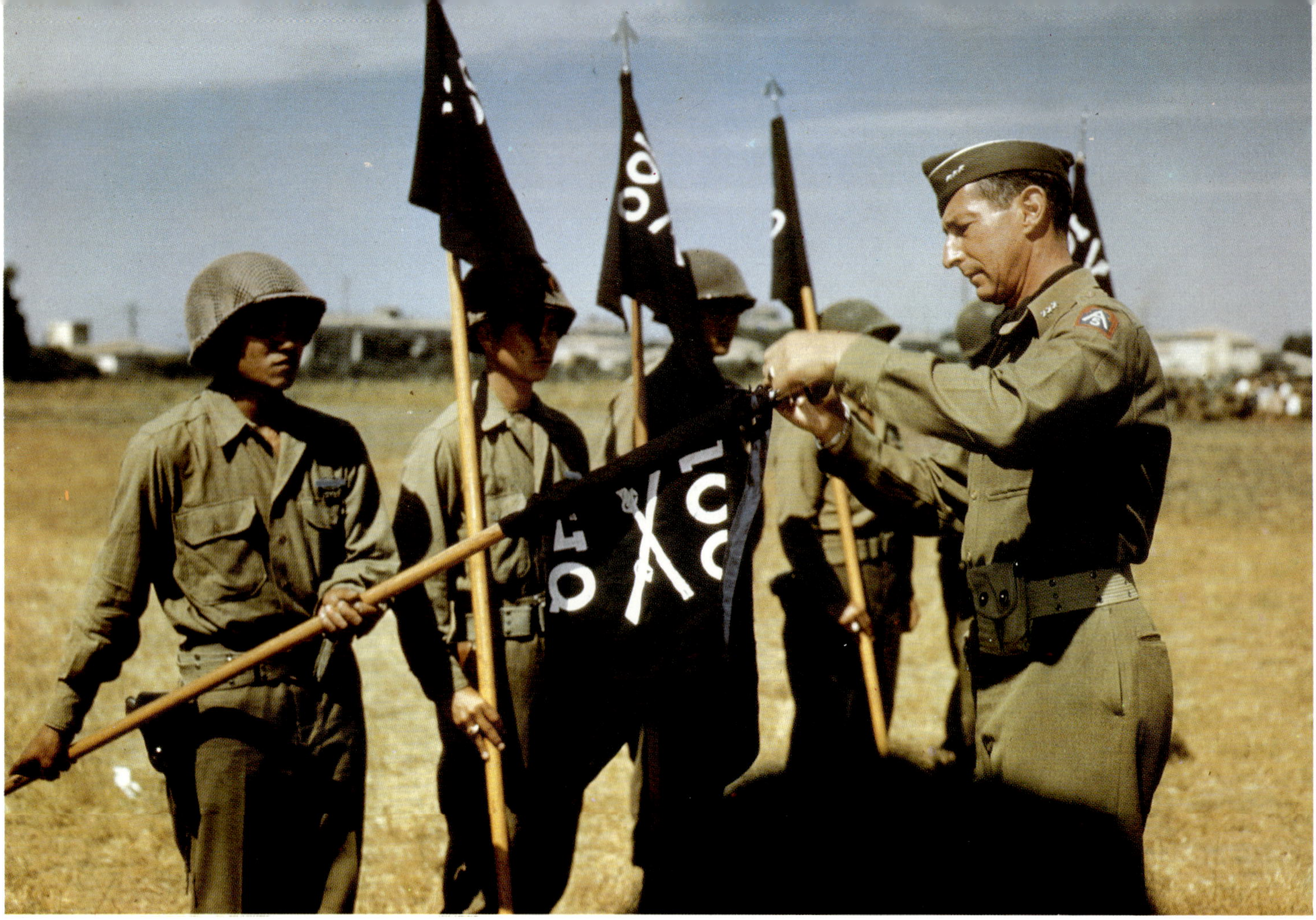

Mark Wayne Clark. Singled out for promotion by General Marshall, Clark was one of the youngest American generals of the Second World War. After helping to organize the Allied landings in North Africa in Nov. 1942 he commanded the American troops in Tunisia and then went on to lead the 5th Army in Sicily and in Italy (where this photograph was taken). Finally, from the end of 1944 he was in command of all the Allied forces in Italy. After the war he continued to have an important diplomatic and military role as commander of the United Nations forces in Korea in 1952–53 (following MacArthur and Ridgeway).

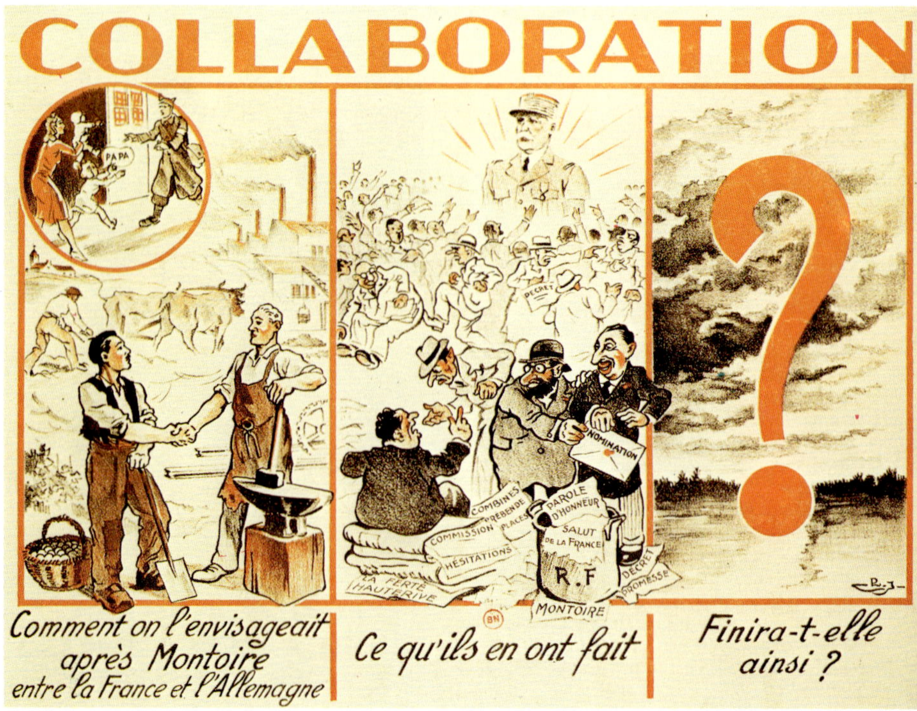

Collaboration in France. By exploiting the ambiguity of the word 'collaboration' pronounced by Pétain following his meeting with Hitler at Montoire in Oct. 1940, certain groups who were completely in favour of a rapprochement with Germany wanted to see in Pétain's statement a confirmation of their own political views, as this poster emphasizes. This rapprochement was intended to involve a rural and agricultural France and a highly industrialized Germany. The idea expressed in the poster offers an opportunity once again to stress the misdeeds of the political parties in the scandal-ridden Third Republic. The people depicted conform to the caricatured view of the Jews which was held in collaborationist circles. (From the Prints Department of the Bibliothèque Nationale).

Cologne. By reason of its importance and relative nearness to England, Cologne had the dubious privilege of being the target of massive RAF raids from 1941 onwards. One of the most destructive of these took place on 30 May 1942. Known as the 'thousand bomber raid', it involved virtually all the forces of Bomber Command and caused the destruction of over 13,000 houses and many thousands of deaths. In 1945 the population of the city had declined to 25,000 from the 700,000 it had on the eve of the war.

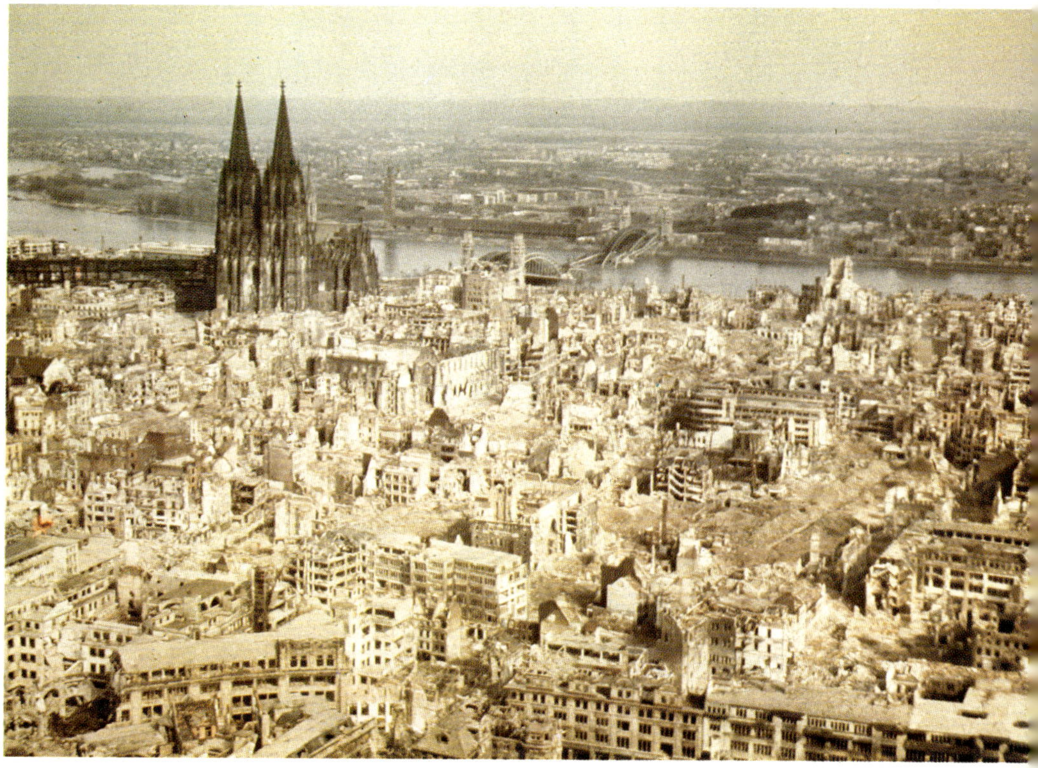

Combined operations. Contrary to the experience in the First World War, in which the Dardanelles operation had been a costly failure, there were numerous successful combined operations during the Second World War. Their success was due firstly to complete air and sea superiority, secondly to the size of the preparatory air and naval bombardments and thirdly to the use of many types of specialized vessels. This picture shows a landing exercise by Australian soldiers under American command on a beach in Queensland in 1943.

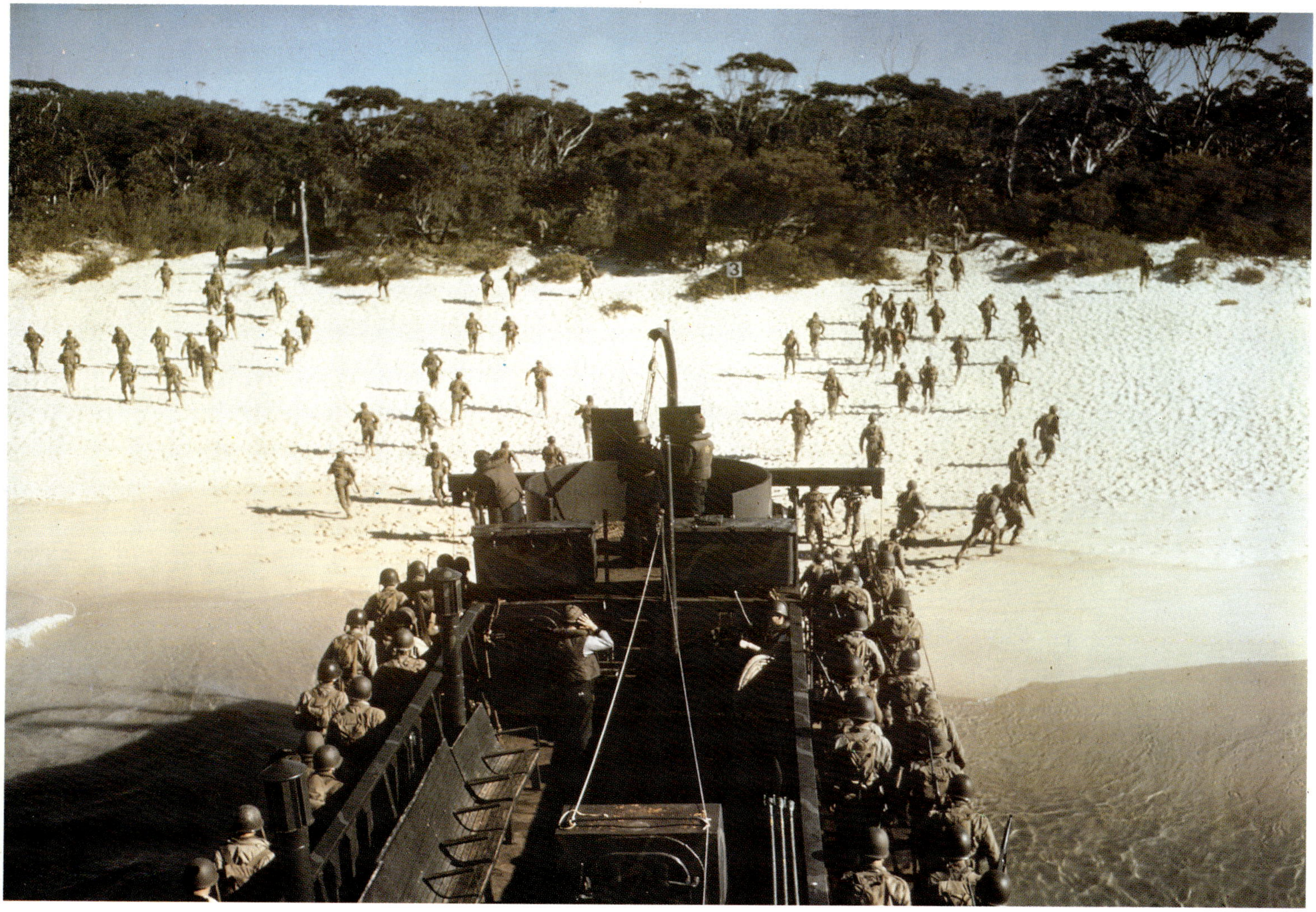

Opposite
Cologne. An American soldier among the ruins of the city.

Commandos. These were created by the British in June 1940 and were destined to have an important part in the war. It was intended that the commandos, who underwent a very tough training, should make 'nuisance' raids on the coast of occupied Europe and should confuse the enemy, destroy specific objectives and bring back prisoners, thus giving proof of continuing British determination while the Allied invasion was awaited. The idea was taken up by the US Army which formed its 'Rangers'. From 1943 the Free French too had their commandos, for example, the Kieffer commando and the Africa commando or 'shock battalion'. This picture shows American soldiers with blackened faces during a training session in anti-tank combat.

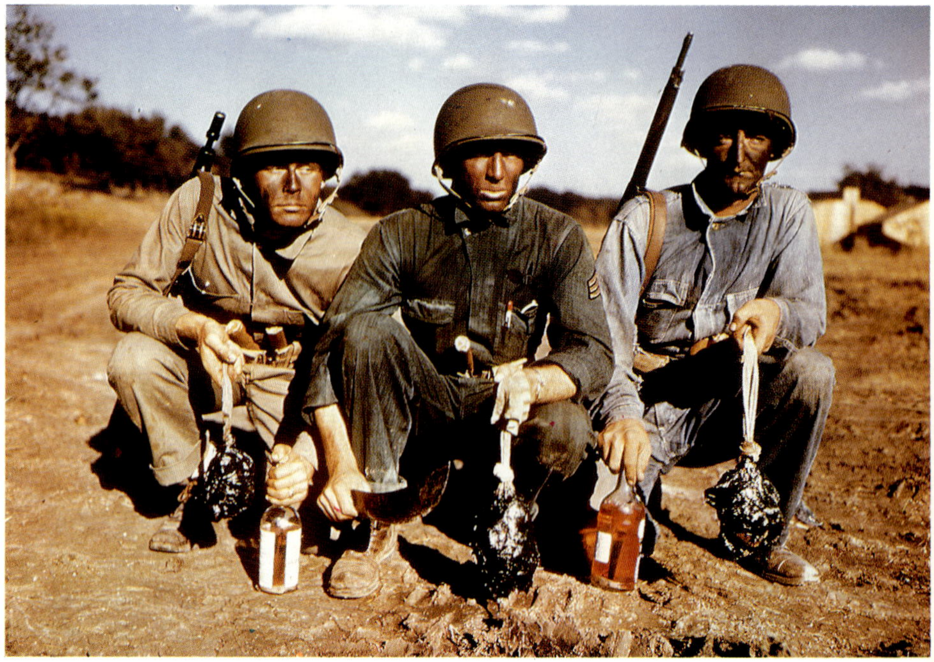

The Germans set up special units in the course of the war which were somewhat similar to the Allied commandos. The 'Brandenburg' Division was thus trained for acts of sabotage and surprise raids and even for espionage. The same was true of the 'Oranienburg' unit, established in 1943. Paratroop units also took part in commando operations, such as the unit (seen in the picture) which succeeded in abducting Mussolini from Gran Sasso in Sept. 1943.

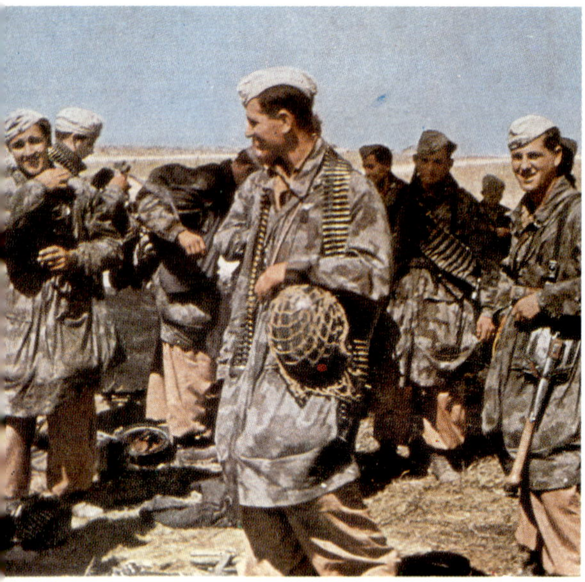

Communism. Following the attack on the Soviet Union and particularly after the Wehrmacht's first defeats in 1942–43, German propaganda continually exploited the theme of the Bolshevik menace threatening western civilization. This theme was disseminated throughout occupied Europe, as is shown by this poster with a caption in Polish.

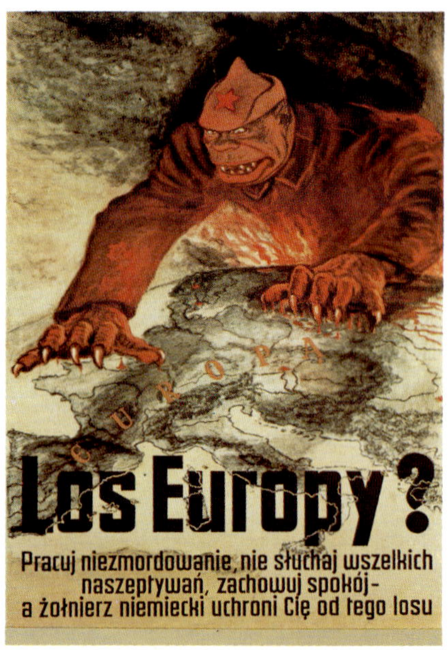

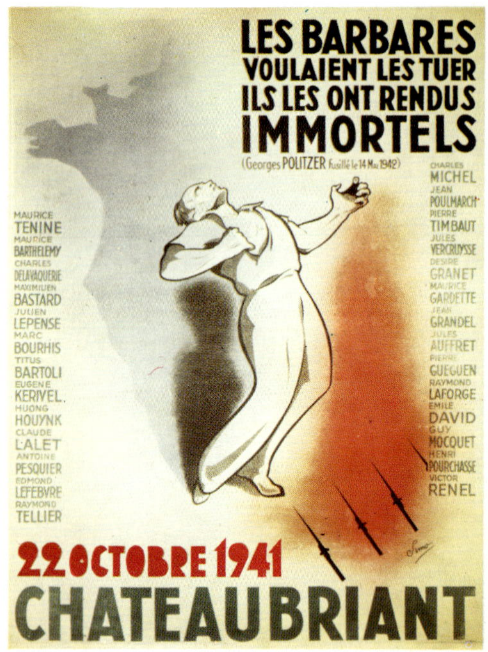

The German attack on Russia released the French Communists from the uncomfortable situation in which the German–Soviet pact had placed them. It was as early as July 1941 that Communist militants first made attacks on German soldiers in the hope that the reprisal measures would cause the population to rise up against the occupying power. In fact the Germans reacted by taking hostages and carrying out executions. In Oct. 1941 the assassination of the German commander at Nantes led to the shooting near Chateaubriant of 50 hostages, the majority of them Communists.

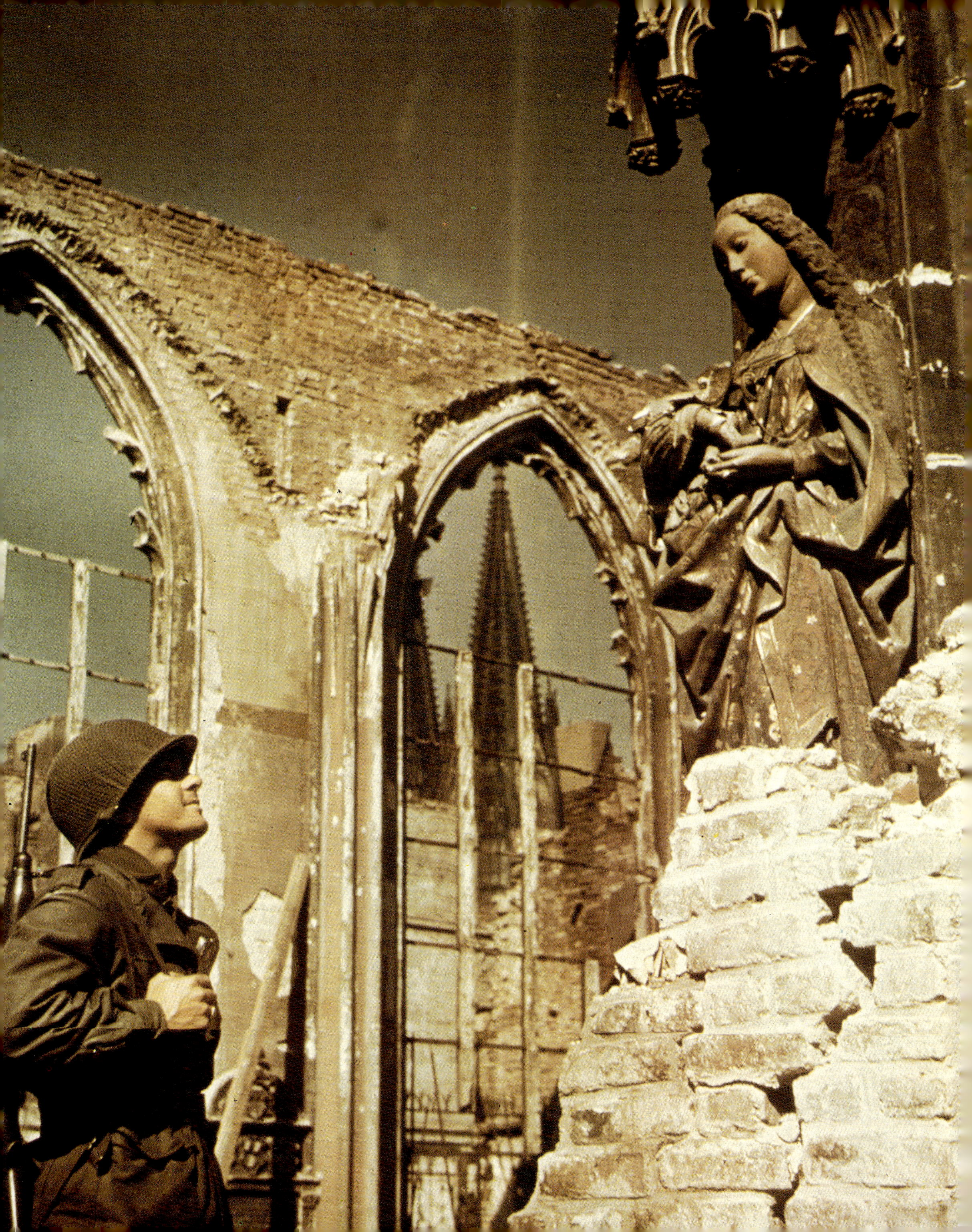

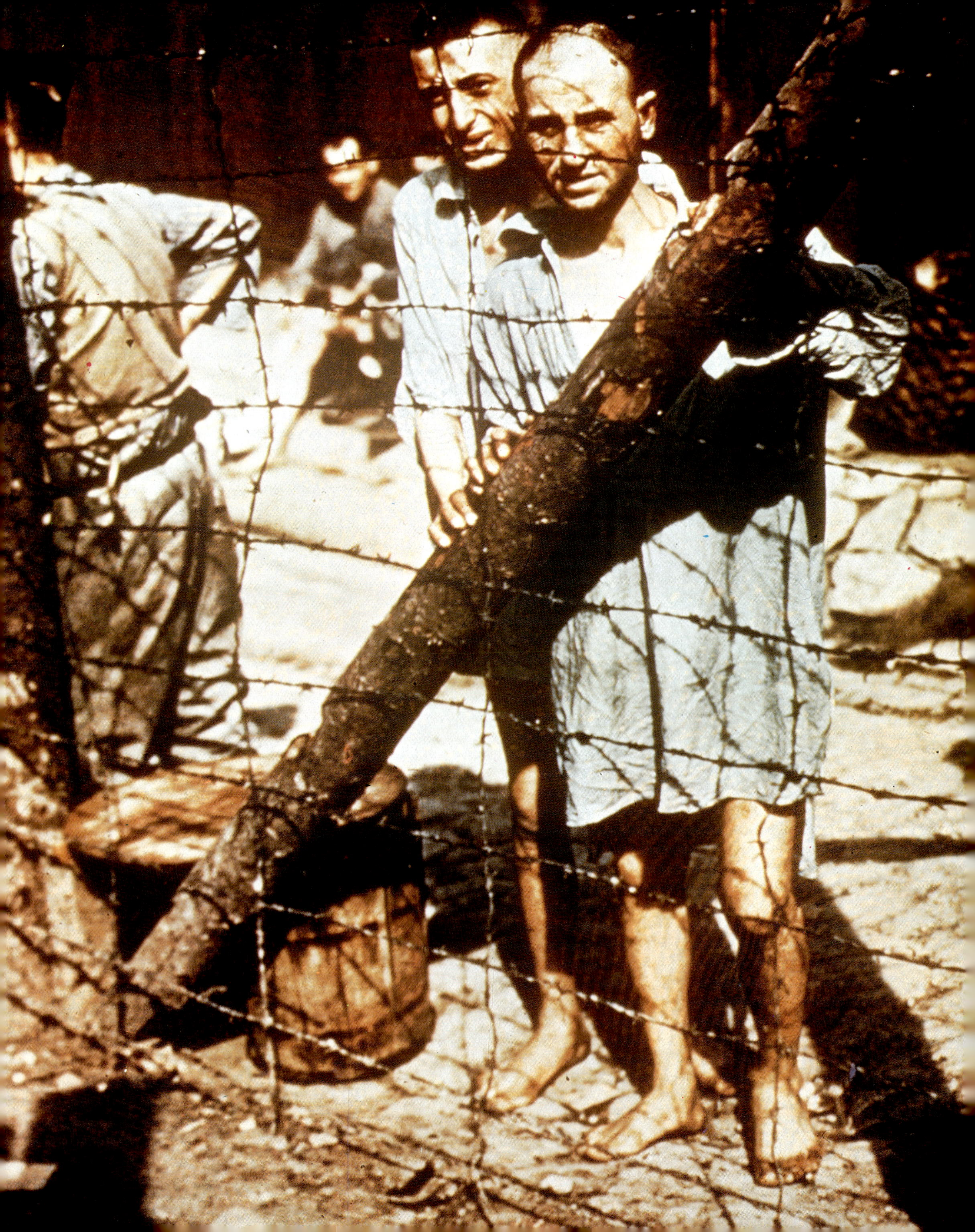

Opposite
Concentration camps. Prisoners in Buchenwald after their liberation.

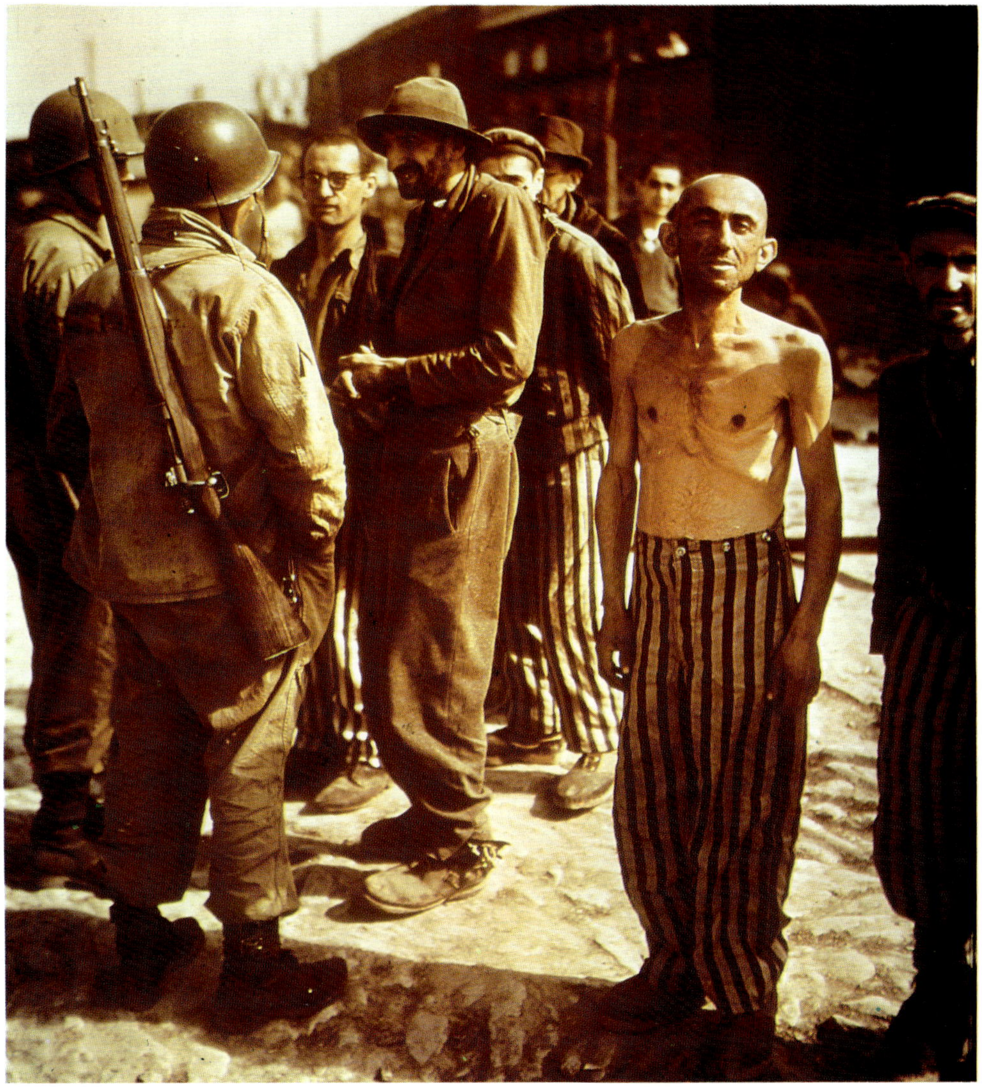

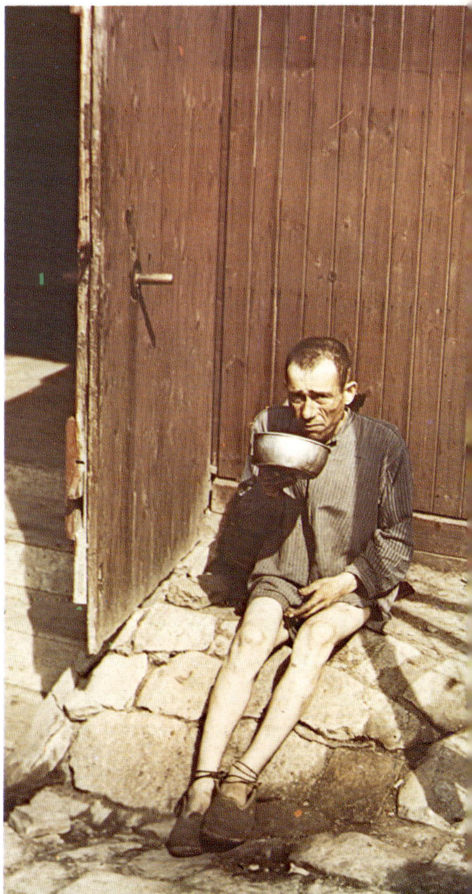

Concentration camps. The first Nazi concentration camp was established at Dachau near Munich in 1933. During the war – with the occupation of a large part of Europe, the decision to annihilate the Jews, the appearance of national resistance movements, the first defeats and the requirements of the war economy – the concentration camp system underwent an enormous expansion. This picture shows the tragic appearance of some of the survivors of Buchenwald a few days after the liberation of the camp. Millions of people died in the concentration camps, including some 6 million Jews who were exterminated in the gas chambers as part of the 'final solution' and many others who succumbed to ill treatment, malnutrition and disease.

In the totalitarian countries the war led to an extension of the system of concentration camps. In them the Nazis exterminated millions of Jews in the 'final solution'. Hundreds of thousands of others from all over occupied Europe – political prisoners, Soviet POWs, forced labourers, etc. – suffered and died in the concentration camps. Here we see a prisoner at Buchenwald several hours after the liberation of the camp by the Americans. In the Soviet camps the inhabitants of annexed regions, such as the Baltic states, or Soviet citizens accused of treason or cowardly behaviour during the German occupation were liquidated en masse.

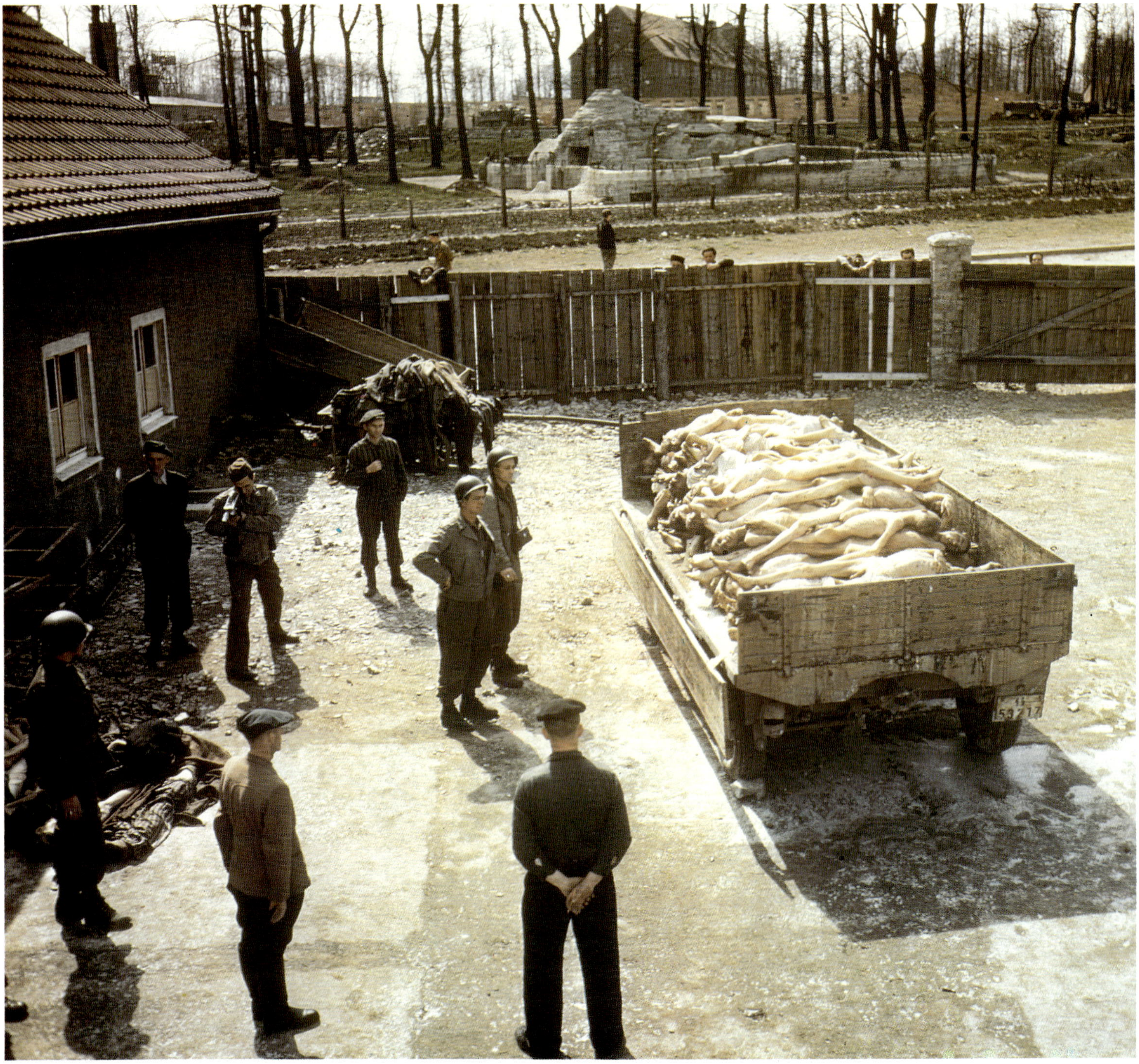

The concentration camp of Buchenwald near Weimar. Opened in 1937, it was first reserved for opponents of the Nazi regime but later people representing all the nationalities of occupied Europe were sent there. During its existence the camp held more than 230,000 prisoners in total and at least 35,000 of these vanished. When the camp was liberated by the Americans on 11 April 1945 21,000 survivors were found there, together with hundreds of corpses.

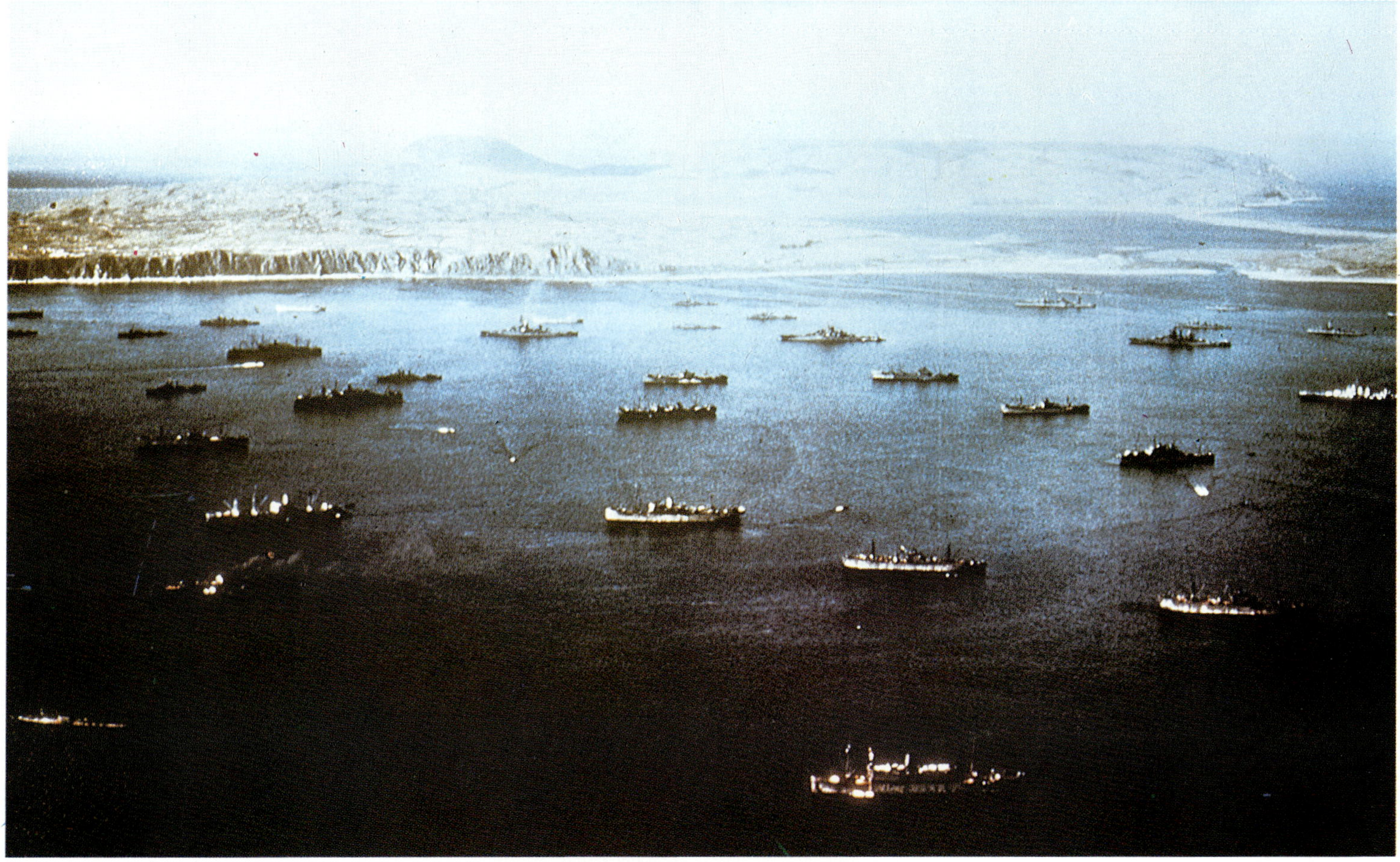

Convoys. An Allied convoy off the coast of Iceland. Throughout the war the belligerent countries, having once again taken up a tactic in use since the 17th century, employed the convoy system to protect their merchant shipping. In spite of its disadvantage – the decline in profitability of merchant shipping – the system did have the advantage of providing defence against aircraft, submarines and surface ships. However, very slow ships and very fast ships, such as liners, the speed of which was a protection in itself, were excluded from convoys.

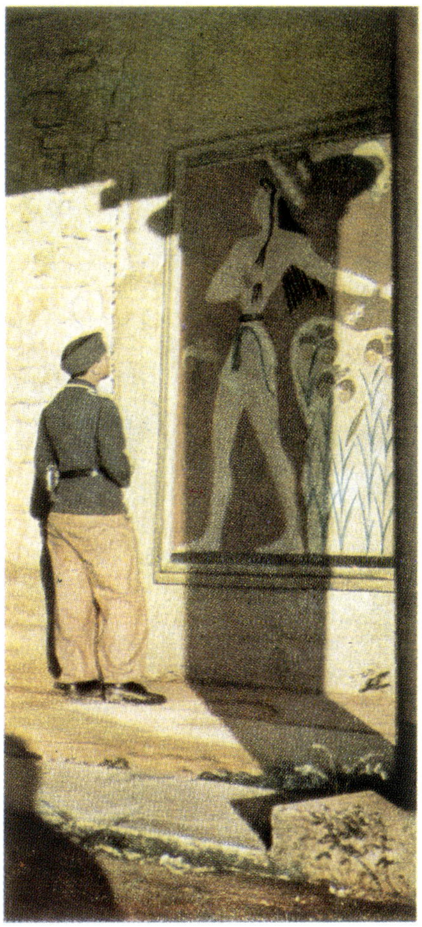

Crete. The picture shows a German soldier visiting the ruins of Knossos and admiring a famous fresco, 'The Prince with the Lilies' dating from the 16th century BC. It was in June 1941, following the conquest of Greece, that General Student's paratroops succeeded in capturing Crete in a brilliantly successful operation, which, however, cost many German lives. While the Allied troops were being evacuated the Luftwaffe inflicted heavy losses on the Royal Navy, sinking two cruisers and several destroyers. The Germans were to occupy Crete right up until May 1945.

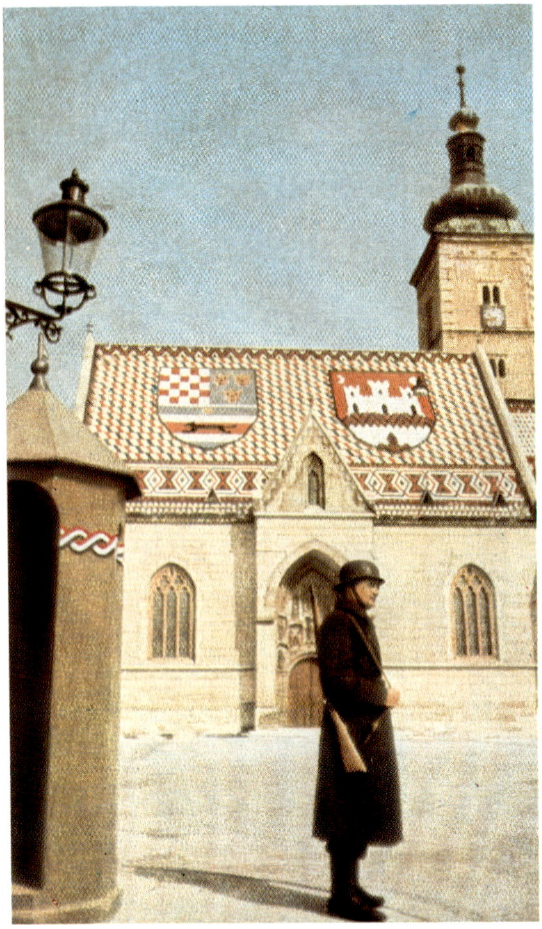

Croatia. The picture shows a sentry outside St Mark's church in Zagreb, the capital of Croatia. Since 1919, when Croatia had become an integral part of Yugoslavia, the Croats had continually claimed autonomous status. The Serbs' refusal to grant this was a factor in the rise of the terrorist Ustashi (rebel) party, which was supported by Italy, Hungary and, before long, by the Third Reich. Hence, after the Germans had overwhelmed Yugoslavia in 1941, they were able to set up a nominally independent Croatia, led by an Ustashi, Ante Pavelič. Obedient to Germany, he pursued a policy of terror against the Jewish and Serbian minorities and this contributed to the rise of resistance groups. After the defeat of Germany the Ustashi regime collapsed and Croatia once again became part of Yugoslavia.

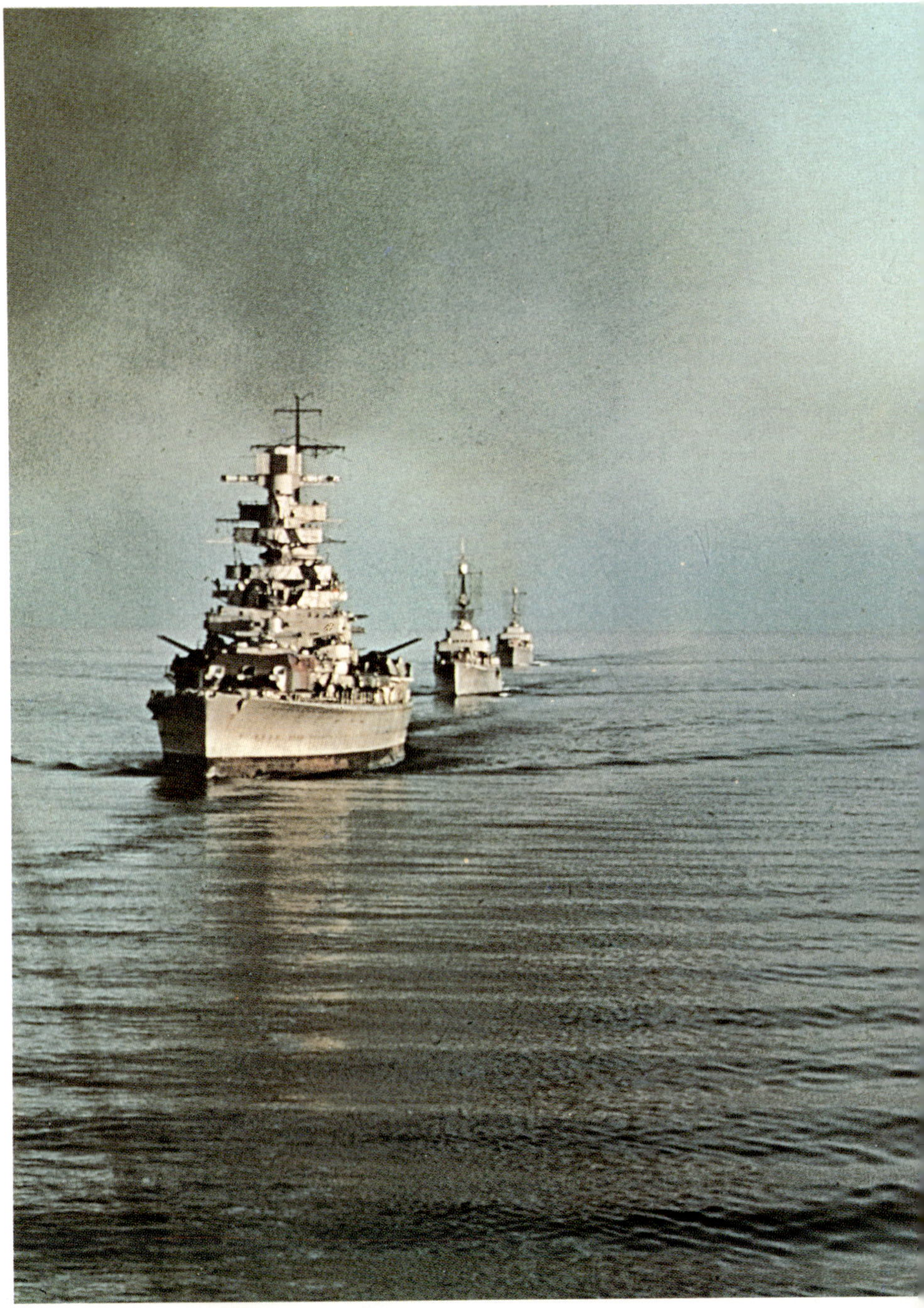

Cruisers. In 1939 there were two types of cruiser in the major navies of the world: heavy cruisers of 10,000 tons or over and light cruisers ranging from about 6000 to 7500 tons. Fast, but lacking protection, these vessels played an essential role in two types of mission: firstly, giving fire support in amphibious operations and secondly providing the air defence for naval formations, which they were able to do since their anti-aircraft armament was much increased. At the end of the war and even before the era of the naval guided missile the cruiser had eclipsed the battleship. This picture shows a German cruiser leading two destroyers on operations in the Atlantic some time in 1941–42.

Sir Andrew Cunningham was undoubtedly the most outstanding British naval commander of the Second World War. In 1939, after a distinguished career which had begun 42 years earlier, he was acting commander-in-chief of the Mediterranean fleet. In spite of the relative weakness of his forces, he was able to gain the initiative over the Italian navy, making a successful air attack on the Italian fleet at Taranto on 11 Nov. 1940 and winning the battle of Cape Matapan in March 1941. Subsequently, in Oct. 1943, he became first sea lord and ended his naval career as an admiral of the fleet.

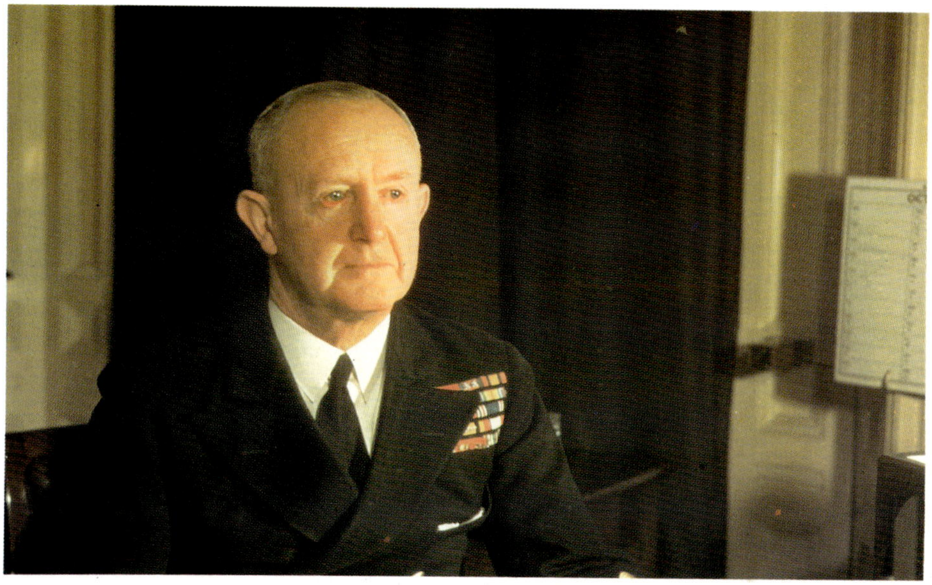

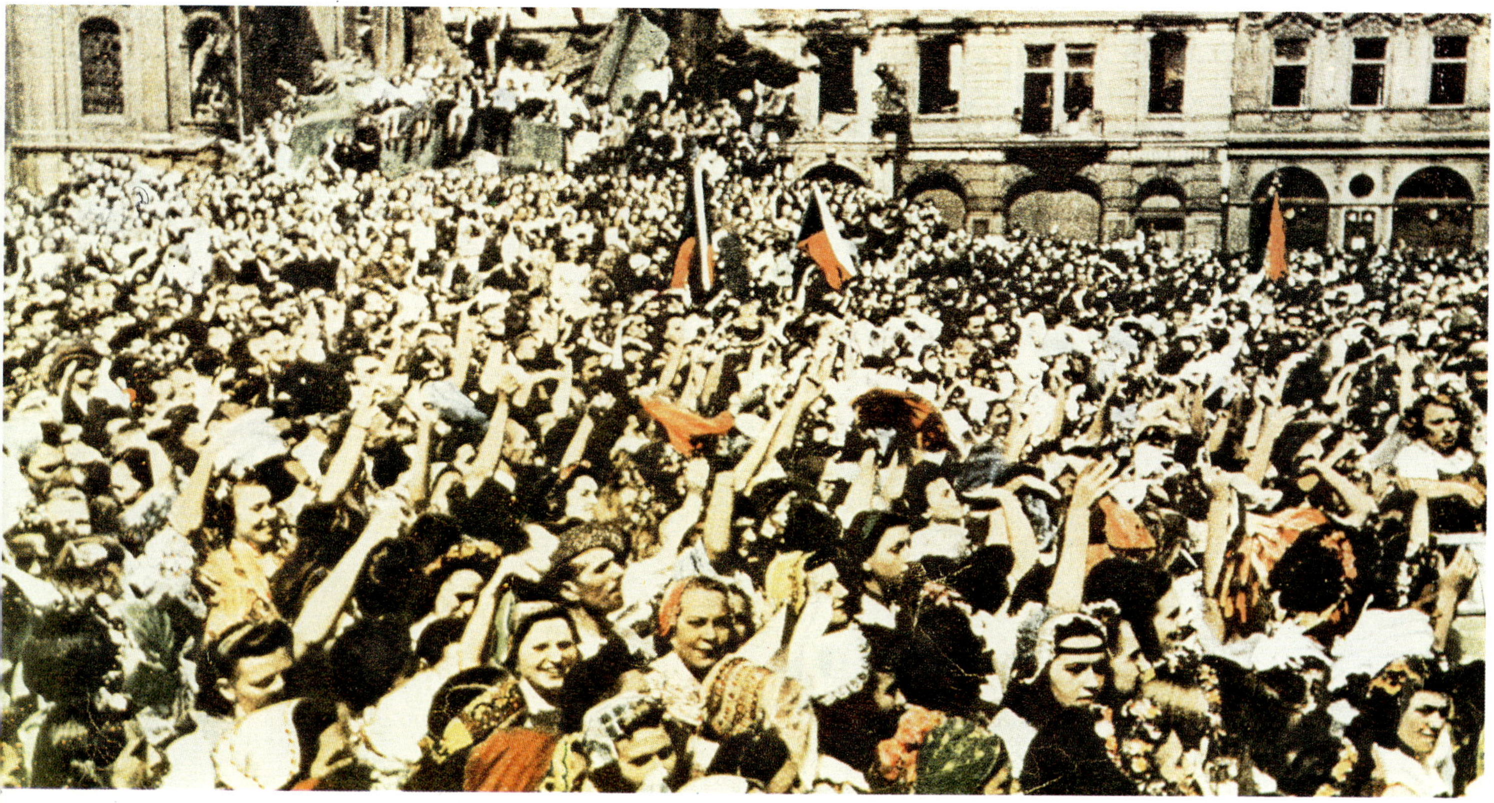

Czechoslovakia. Dismembered after the Munich crisis of Sept. 1938, Czechoslovakia did not begin to reappear on the international scene until 1942, when a government in exile was set up in London. This government, headed by Beneš and Masaryk, obtained from the Allies a promise that Czechoslovakia would be restored to its original state, and it signed a treaty of alliance and mutual assistance with the USSR (Dec. 1943). In 1945 Czechoslovakia was liberated by the Red Army, which made a triumphant entry into Prague on 9 May (photograph) amid the enthusiasm of the majority of the population. In fact, having finally been freed from German domination, three years later Czechoslovakia was swept into the Soviet orbit.

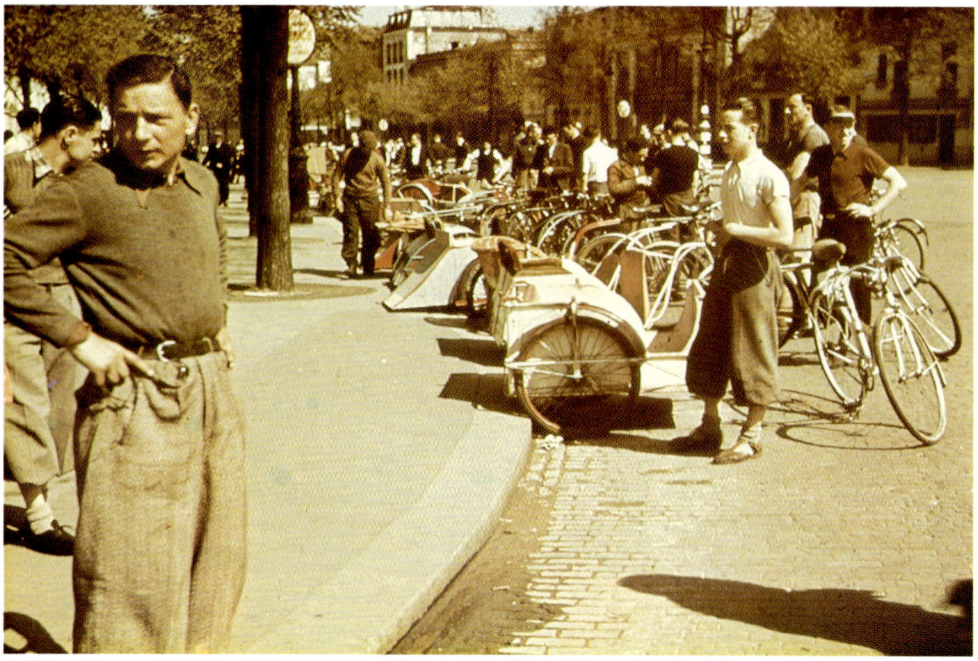

Daily life. In every country in occupied Europe the war was accompanied by a complete disruption of everyday life, because of the petrol shortage caused by German requisitions and the Anglo-American blockade. This disruption was particularly noticeable in the area of transport, with the almost complete disappearance of individual vehicles, taxis and private cars. In France this disappearance led to a great renewal of popularity for the bicycle. In Paris and in all the large towns even cycle-taxis appeared, fitted with a trailer capable of carrying one or two people. Here we see a cycle-taxi rank at Port Maillot in Paris, on a Sunday when there was horseracing at Longchamp.

Throughout the war and even during the succeeding years, the almost complete disappearance of private means of transport led to a great demand for public transport, notably the railways. In Paris the Métro conveyed a record number of passengers in 1943. It carried a considerable quantity of former road-users, owing to the reduction in the numbers of buses. The only buses remaining were those equipped with gas-generators or operating on mains gas. One such bus is shown in this picture, taken in the Place d'Étoile. The refilling of the gas balloons took place at the terminus and the balloons were disguised by a streamlined plywood structure painted white.

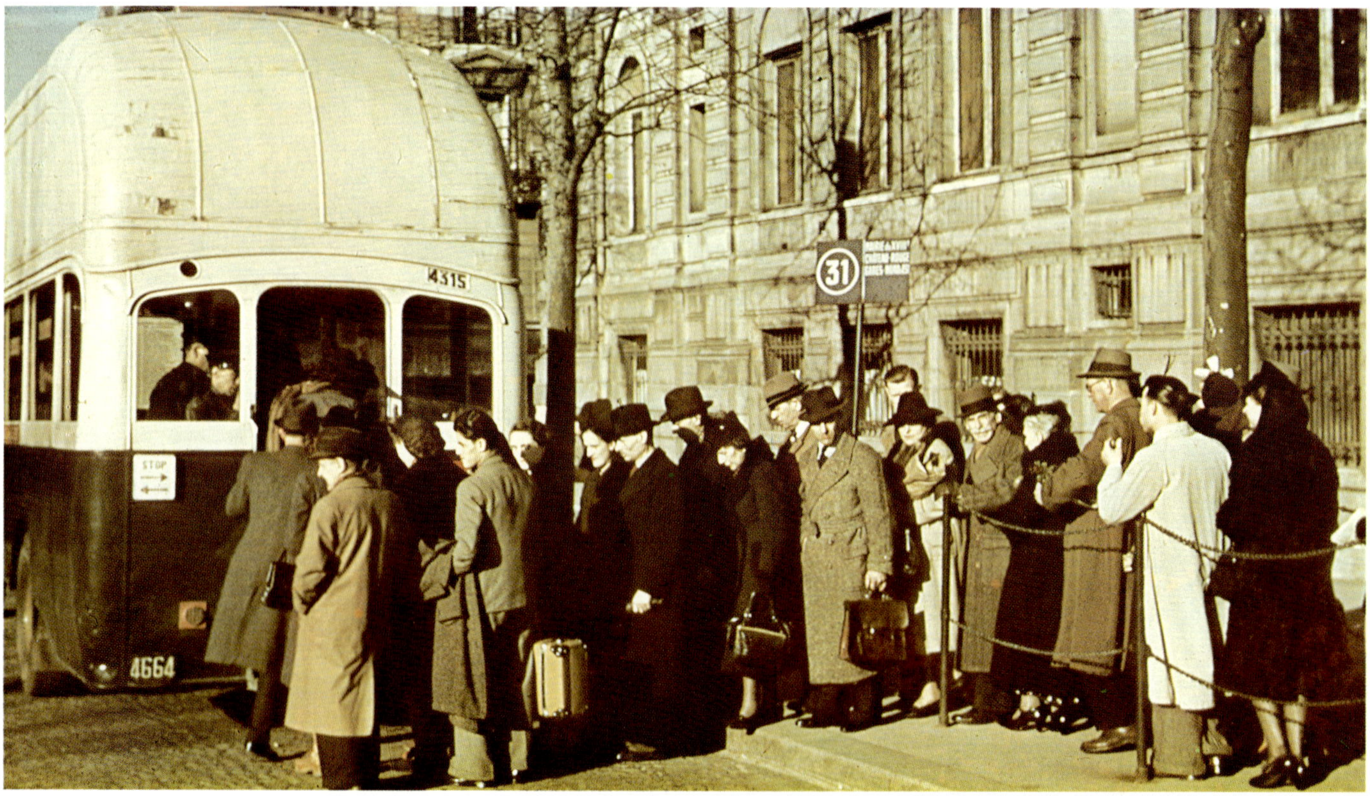

Throughout the conflict daily life in all the countries at war was affected by shortages of food, caused by requisitions, the blockade and the fall in production. Severe in Britain and Germany, these restrictions were distinctly worse in the occupied countries of western Europe. They reached their lowest point in the eastern European states, notably in the Soviet Union, where the standard of living had already been extremely low on the eve of the war. Here, in 1942, during the German occupation, the inhabitants of Kharkov are queuing outside a gastronom – a general grocery store.

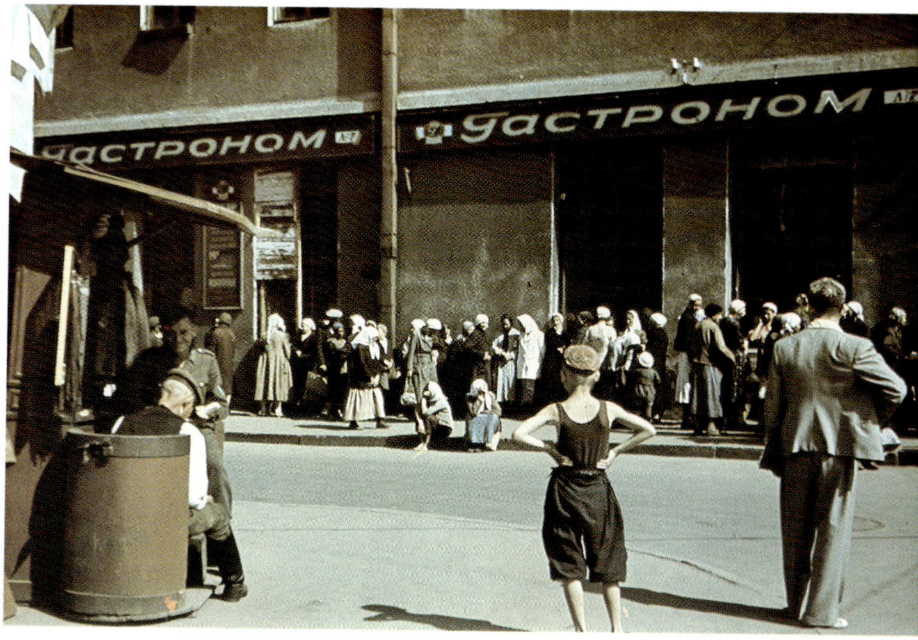

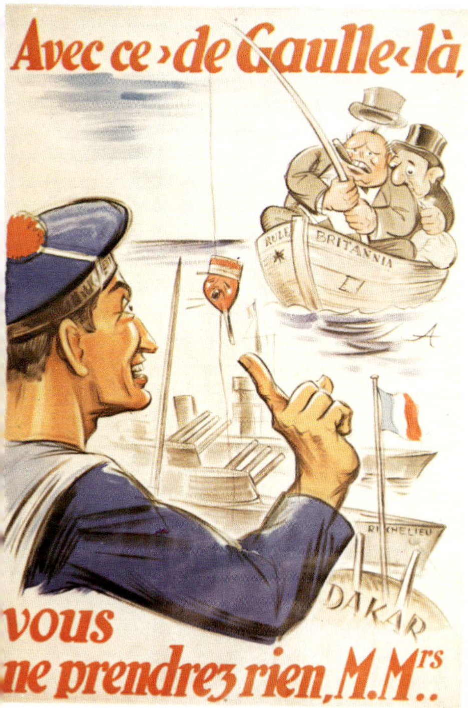

The Dakar expedition. Although carried out with a force of major size – virtually all the Free French forces and Admiral John Cunningham's squadron – the operation of 23–25 Sept. 1940 to bring the Vichy-controlled port of Dakar in French West Africa over to the Allied side ended in failure and there were serious repercussions. Churchill had to face an angry House of Commons, General de Gaulle's prestige was badly damaged and the affair brought an end to the attempts to win France's colonies over to the side of the Free French and the Allies. In France the collaborationist press and anti-British circles thoroughly exploited the 'battle' of Dakar, as this poster emphasizes. It seeks to discredit General de Gaulle and to widen the gulf between France and Britain which had been created by the Mers-el-Kebir operation.

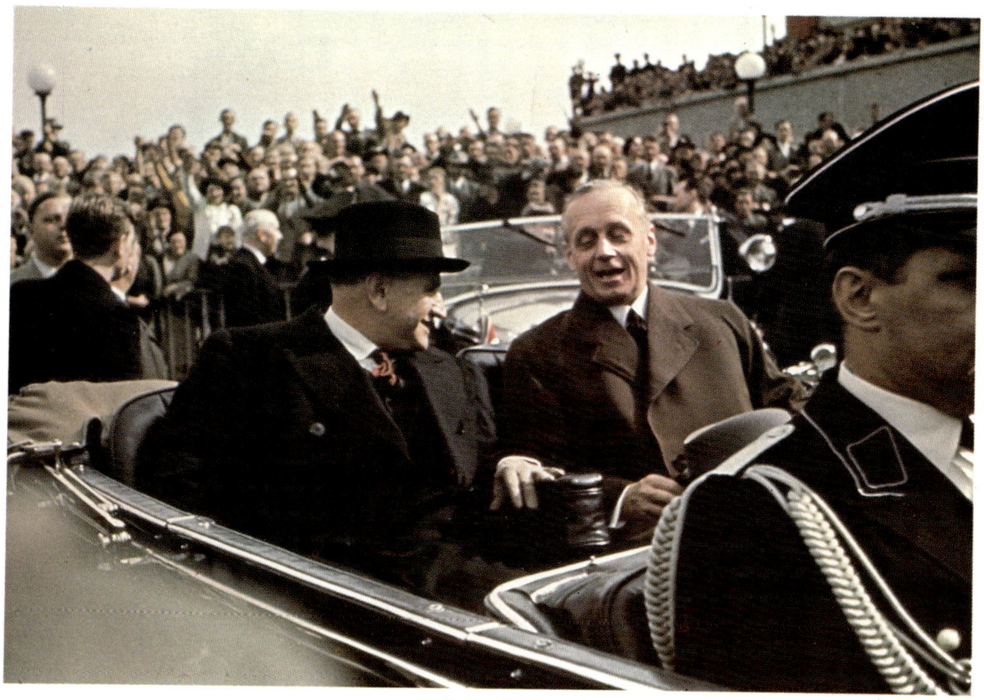

Daladier. Here Daladier, the French prime minister, is seen in the company of Ribbentrop, the Reich foreign minister, on the eve of the Munich conference in Sept. 1938. Daladier's smiling face should not delude anyone. He had been prime minister of France for five months already and was perfectly aware of the risks of giving in to Hitler's threats over the Sudetenland. He was, however, in a very difficult situation. He could not count on British support; the French army, which was intended mainly as a defensive force, was thought to be incapable of going to the help of Czechoslovakia; and, finally, French public opinion remained strongly pacifist. On his return to France, as soon as he got out of his aircraft at Le Bourget, Daladier received a frenzied welcome from a vast crowd, rejoicing that peace had been preserved (as they thought).

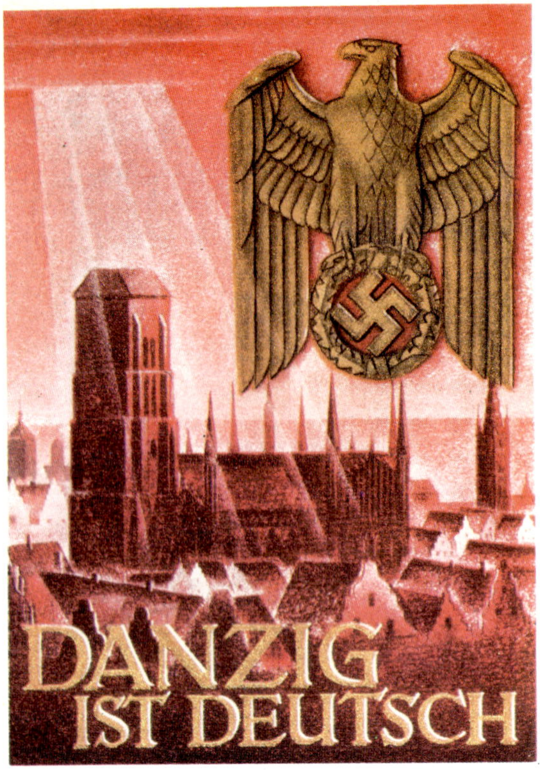

Danzig. An ancient city of Prussia, Danzig had been proclaimed a 'free city' in 1919 as a consequence of the Treaty of Versailles and, together with the Polish Corridor which gave Poland access to the sea, it was intended to serve as an economic outlet for Poland. Hitler demanded the recovery of Danzig in 1939 but in fact the Germans had not accepted the status of the city at any time since 1919. It was at Danzig that the first shots of the Second World War were to be fired. . . The city was occupied by the Red Army on 30 March 1945 and was immediately incorporated into Poland under the name of Gdansk. In a later era it would become known as a centre of opposition to the Communist regime.

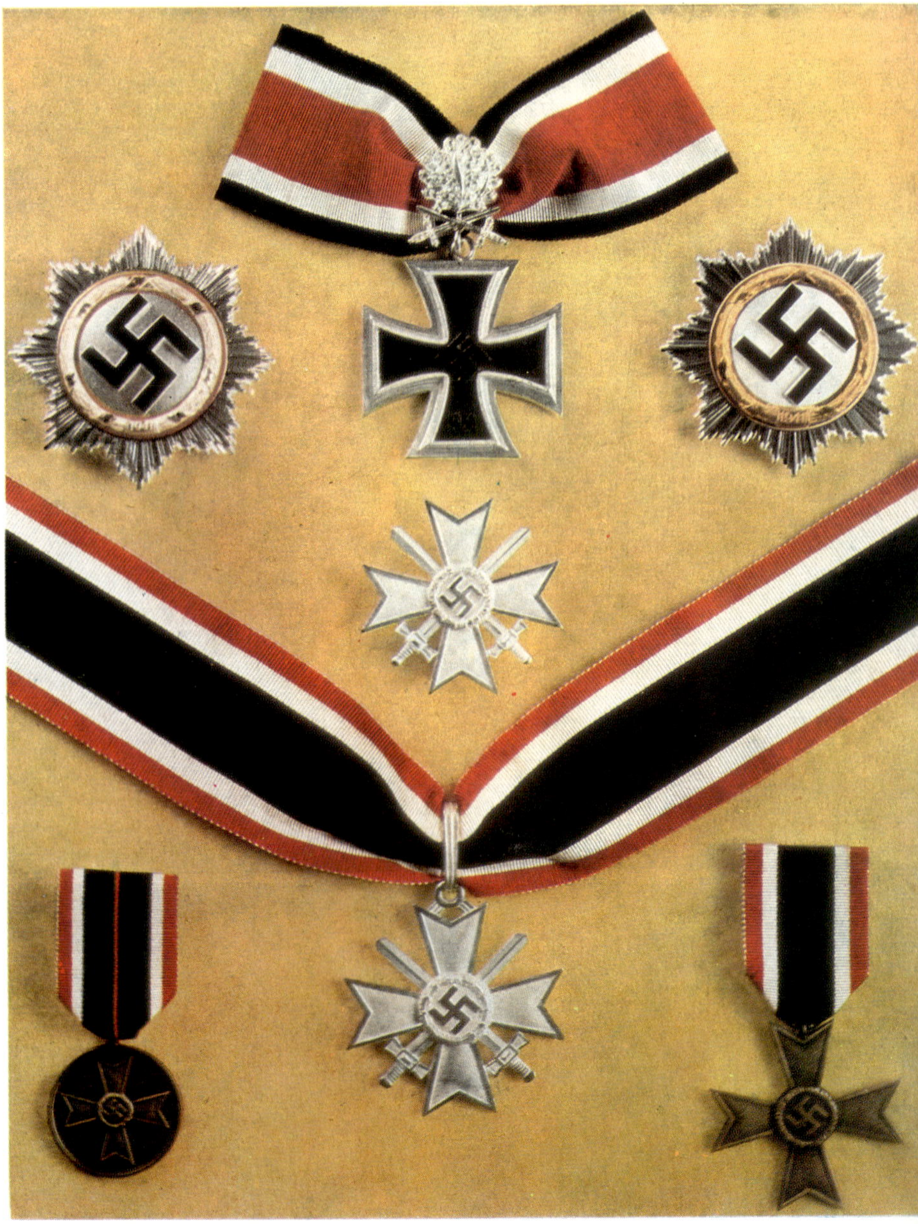

Decorations. Some German military decorations of 1939–45. The Iron Cross, instituted in 1813, remained the major military distinction for the German armed forces of the Second World War. It existed in a number of grades and one of the very highest, which could be awarded in a case of exceptional merit only, was the Ritterkreuz or Knight's Cross (top, centre) with oak leaves, swords and diamonds (brilliants). Among the other decorations are the Kriegsverdienstkreuz or War Merit Medal (bottom, left and right) and the Deutsches Kreuz or German Cross, in gold and silver (top, left and right), which was instituted by Hitler.

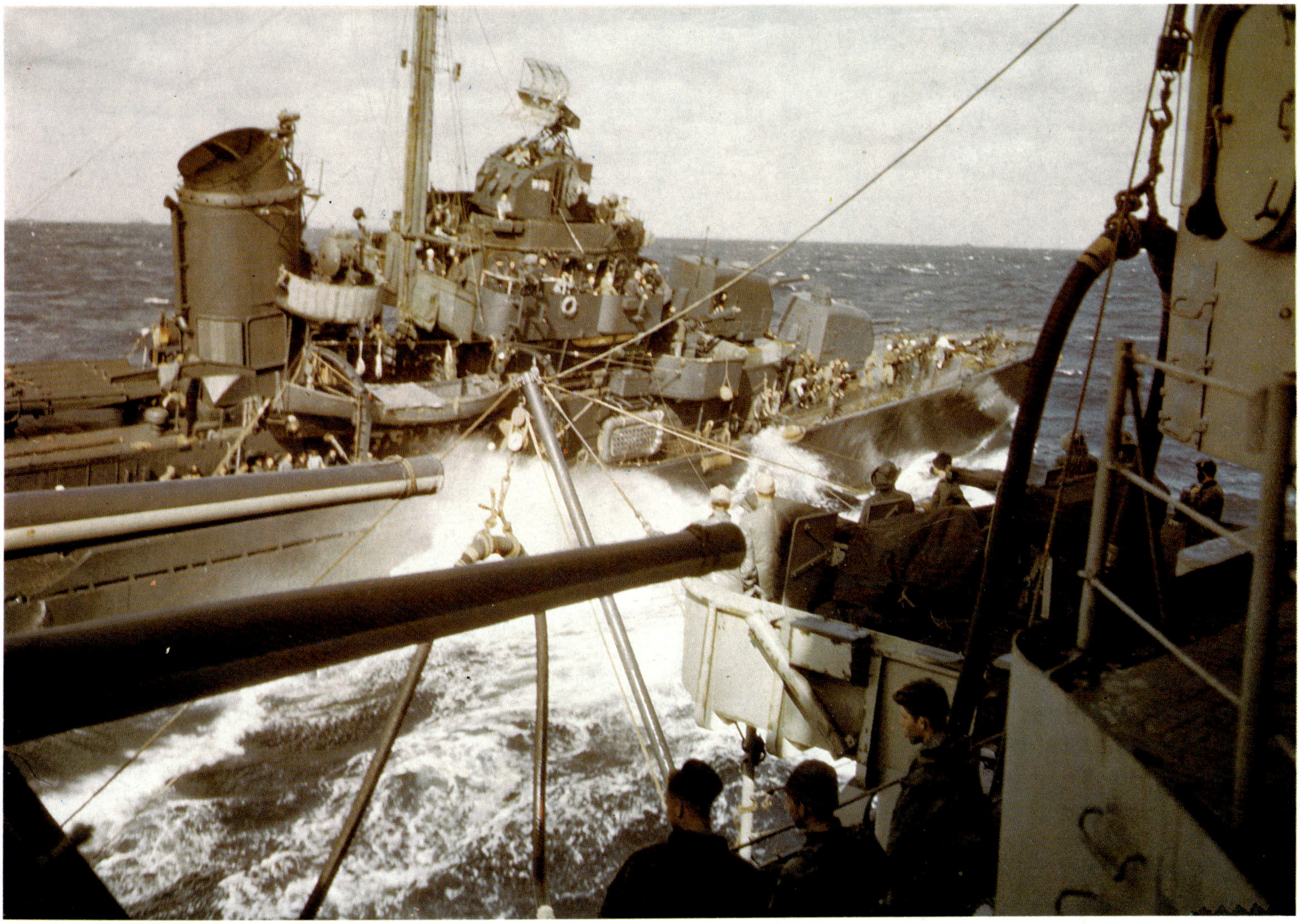

Destroyers. During the war in the Pacific a *Fletcher*-class destroyer of the US navy takes on fuel while sailing beside a *Missouri*-class battleship. These 2000-ton destroyers, armed with five 5-inch guns and several smaller guns or torpedo tubes, acted as watchdogs for the big task forces, providing early-warning radar defence or direct protection against aircraft or submarines.

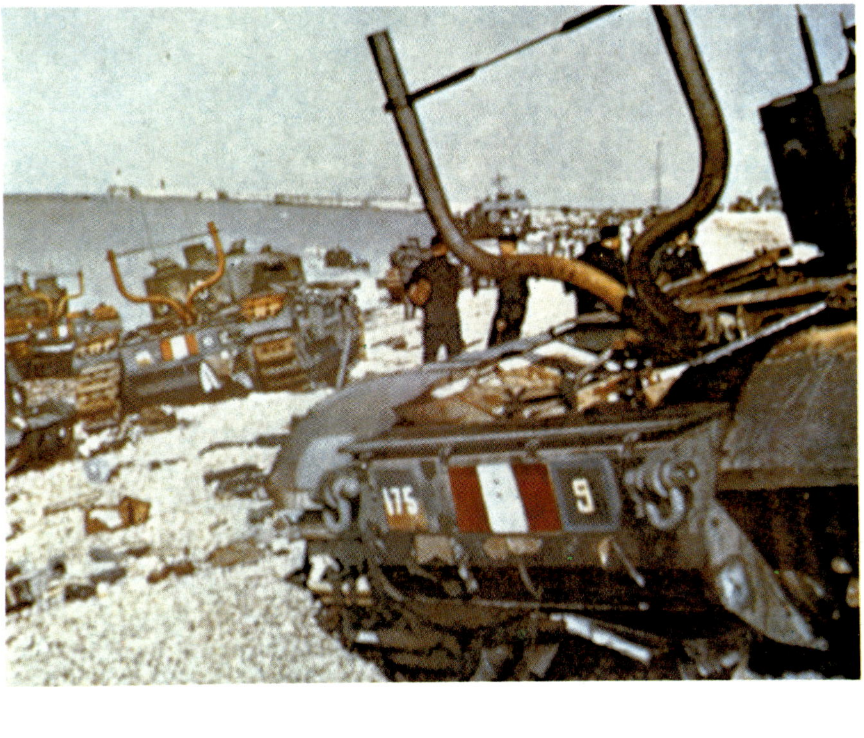

Dieppe. British Churchill tanks abandoned on the sea-front at Dieppe, following the failure of the Allied raid of 19 Aug. 1942. These particular tanks were provided with special exhaust pipes which allowed them to reach the landing beach under their own power, after descending into the water from landing craft. In spite of the severe losses suffered by the Canadian troops the Dieppe raid was not completely without useful result. In anticipation of the invasion planned for 1944, it meant that the Allied supreme command gave up all thought of a direct attack on heavily defended ports and came round to the idea of a landing directly on to beaches using specialized equipment.

Opposite
Desert warfare. A German PzKpfw tank passing alongside an abandoned British bren gun carrier in Libya.

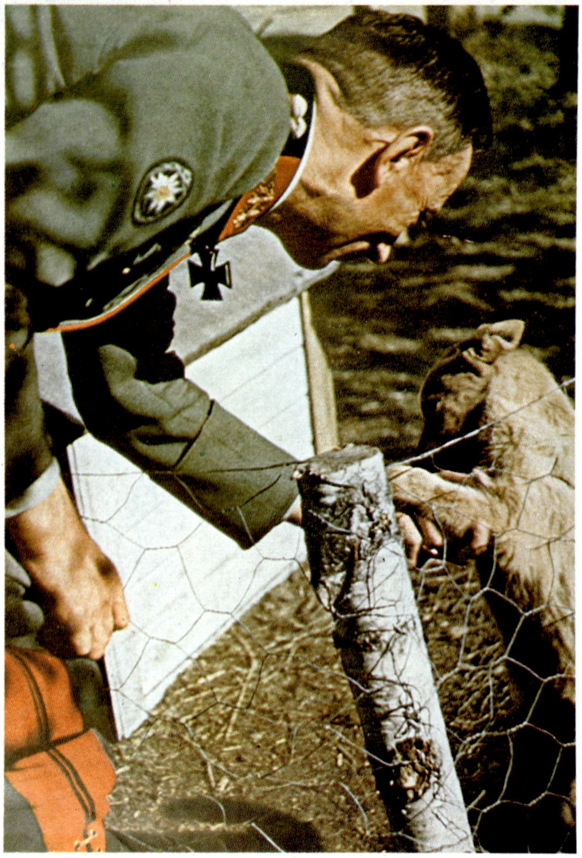

Dietl. General Eduard Dietl, a Wehrmacht specialist in mountain warfare, first came to notice in Norway, at the time of the fighting round Narvik. In 1941, at the beginning of the war on the eastern front, he was put in command of three divisions and given the task of defending the mines of Petsamo and Kirkenes and of capturing Murmansk. Although he was unable to achieve the second objective, he nevertheless made the north of German-occupied Norway secure from attack and held down large numbers of Soviet troops. Dietl lost his life in an aircraft accident on 23 June 1944.

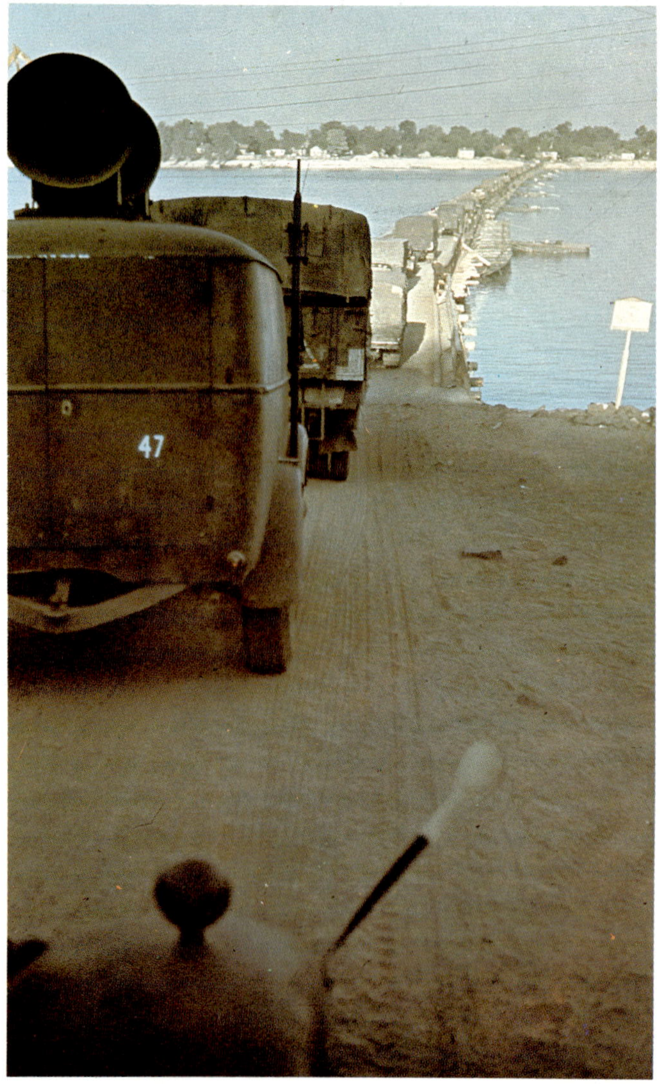

The Dniepr. During the major offensive in the summer of 1941 German troops succeeded in crossing the Dniepr in the first fortnight of September, in spite of the size of this river. This move enabled the Germans to surround several Soviet armies and to capture Kiev. Here a motorized column is seen traversing the river over a pontoon bridge.

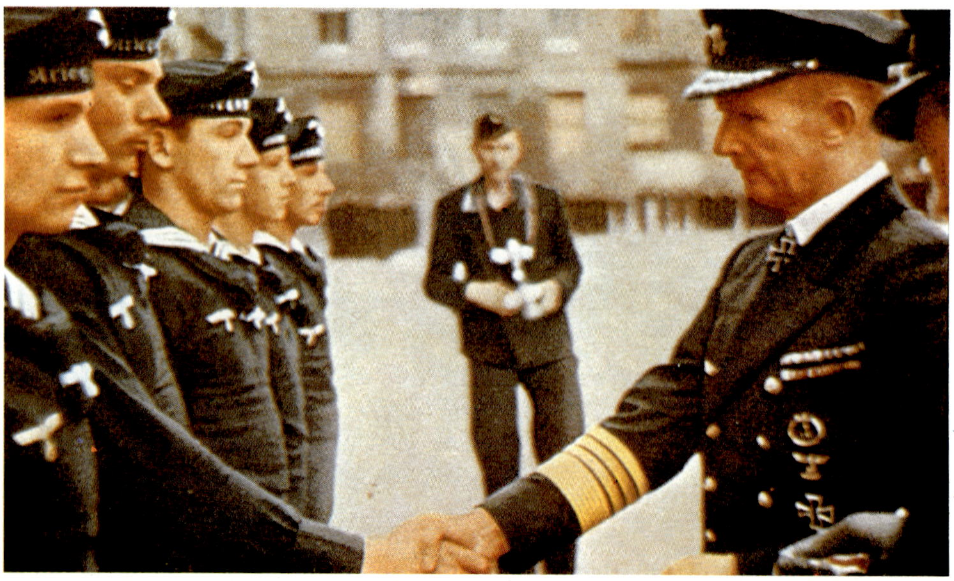

Dönitz. Throughout the war, first as a commander of the U-boat arm and then as commander-in-chief of the German navy, Admiral Dönitz devoted all his energies to submarine warfare. He was in the habit of receiving the U-boat commanders personally on their return from missions. He also had the crews presented to him and would hand over decorations himself.

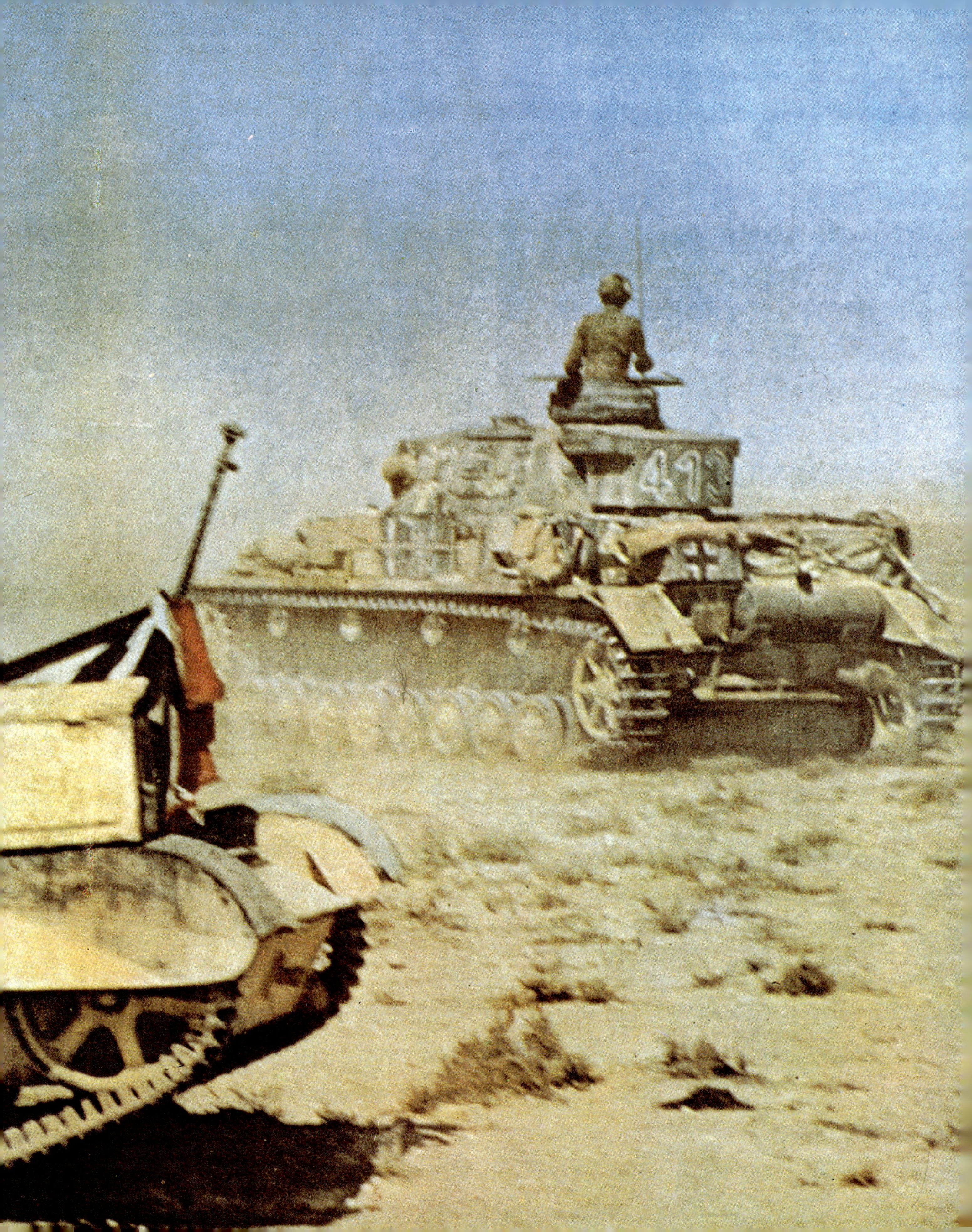

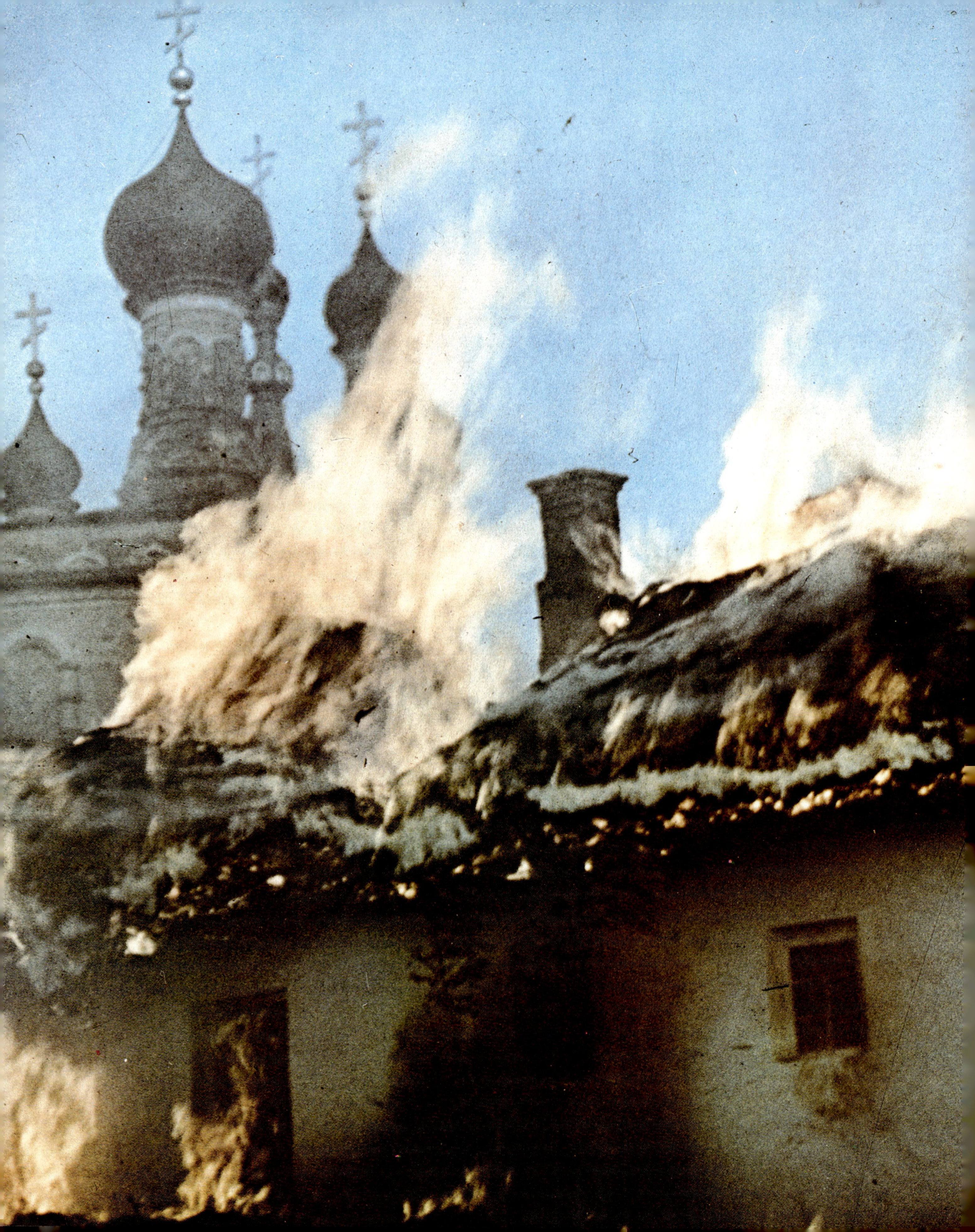

The Dniepr. A town in flames during the German-Soviet war.

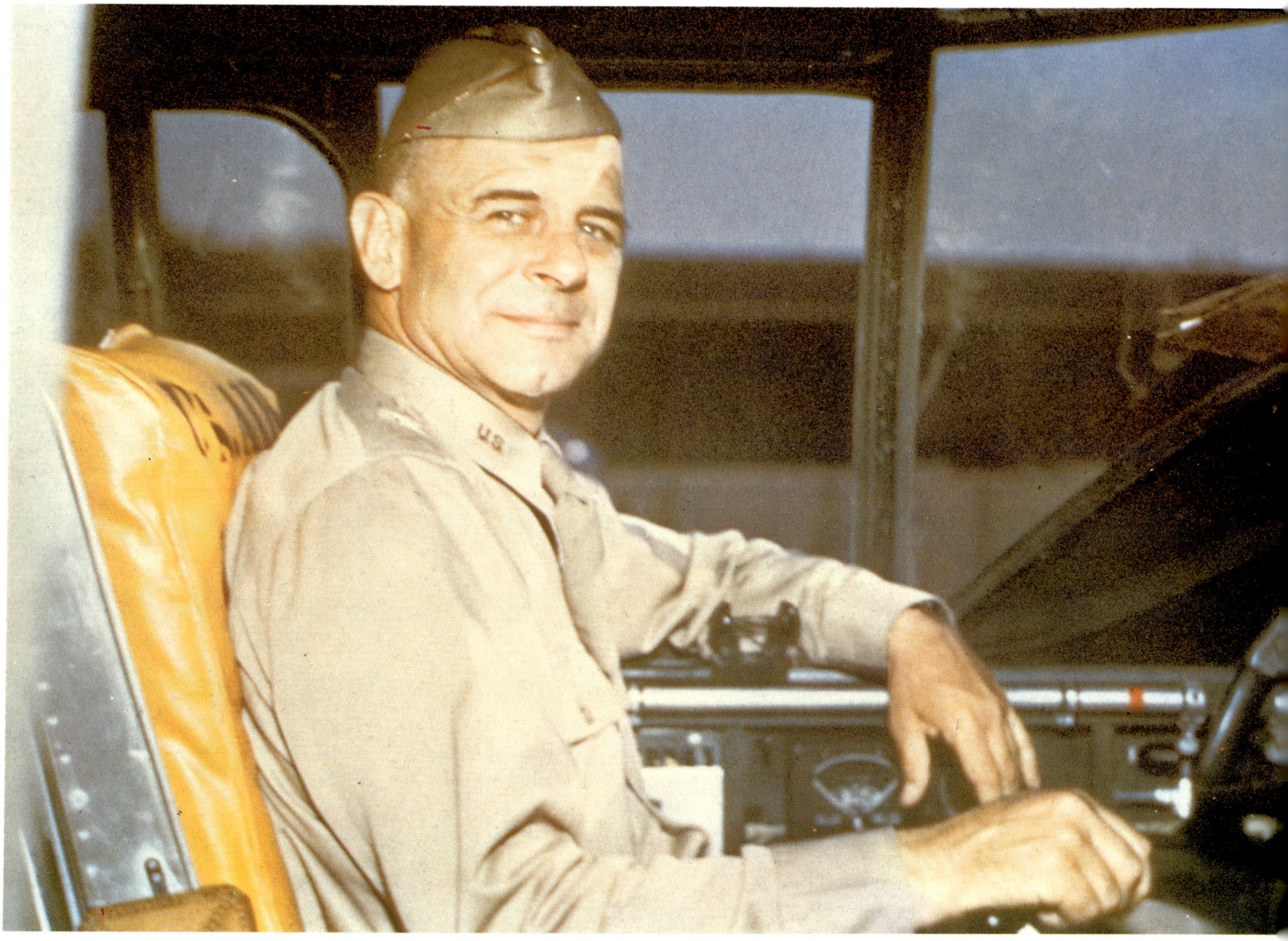

Doolittle. The Tokyo raid, launched on 18 April 1942 from the US aircraft carrier *Hornet*, was to make General Doolittle's name. He is seen here on board one of the 16 North American B-25 Mitchell twin-engined bombers shortly before take-off. Although its actual results were minimal, the Tokyo raid had important consequences. It induced Admiral Yamamoto to undertake the operations which would lead to the Battle of Midway.

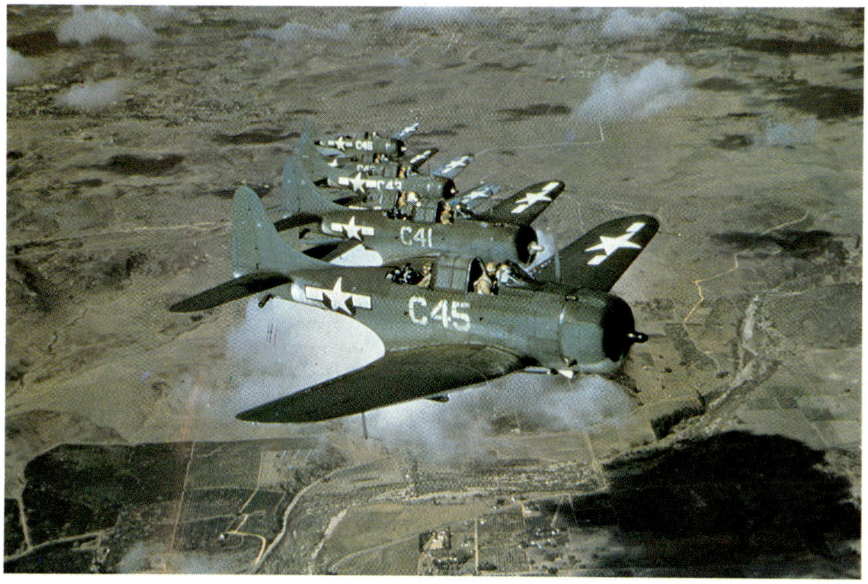

The Douglas Dauntless. The Douglas SBD Dauntless which entered service in 1940 was one of the US navy's best aircraft. Up to 1944 nearly 6000 had been built. With its 1800 horsepower engine the Douglas Dauntless had a top speed of 245 mph (400 km/h). It was armed with four machine guns and carried a 1100 lb (500 kg) bomb below the fuselage and two 110 lb (50 kg) bombs under the wings. It was produced in various versions and its maximum range was 450 mi. (750 km).

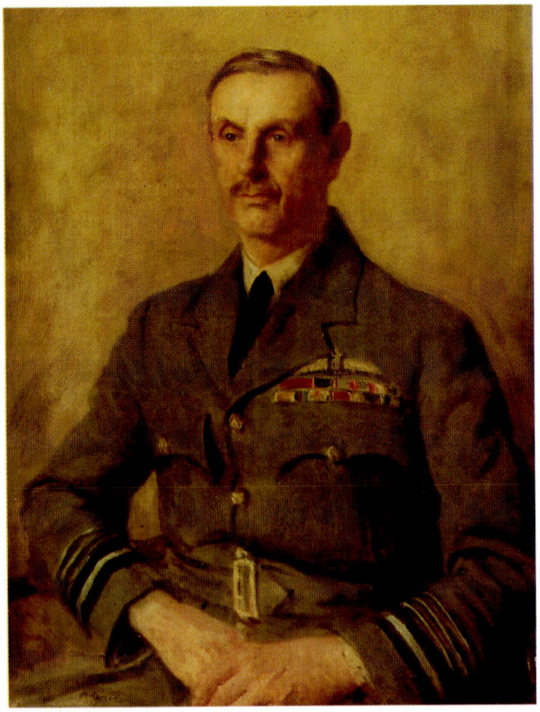

Dowding. Leader of RAF Fighter Command during the Battle of Britain, Air Chief Marshal Sir Hugh Dowding co-ordinated the defence of Britain against the Luftwaffe during the critical summer of 1940. With the help of radio and radar, Dowding developed a system of fighter control which transformed Fighter Command into a highly organized defensive system covering the whole of Great Britain. At the time of the Battle of France he fought to keep his fighter squadrons in Britain, thus bringing him into conflict with the cabinet, but this typical determination was undoubtedly instrumental in saving Britain in July, August and September 1940 during the Battle of Britain. Painting by W. Russell.

Dresden. In Feb. 1945 3000 tons of explosive and incendiary bombs were dropped on this German city by aircraft of the RAF and the US Army Air Force. This bombing of a city almost deprived of air defence, lacking air raid shelters and crowded by the influx of refugees from the east may have caused the heaviest loss of life of any air raid of the war. Estimates of the deaths caused range from 30,000 to 200,000. Figures of both 70,000 and 135,000 are suggested as accurate in different sources. The number of deaths was such that it took days to burn the corpses. Here, Russian auxiliaries of the Wehrmacht, commanded by German officers, are counting the victims while a funeral pyre burns in the background.

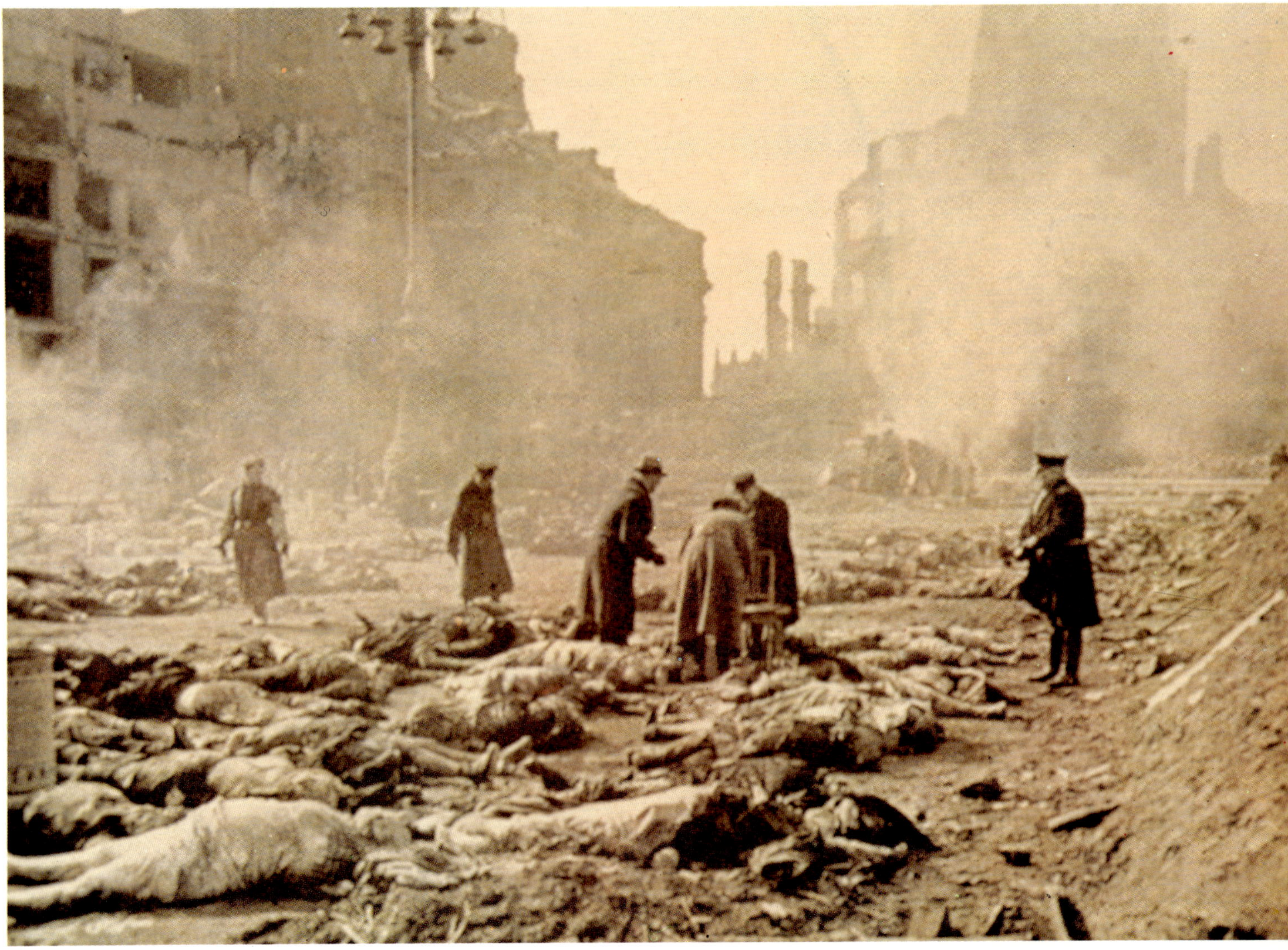

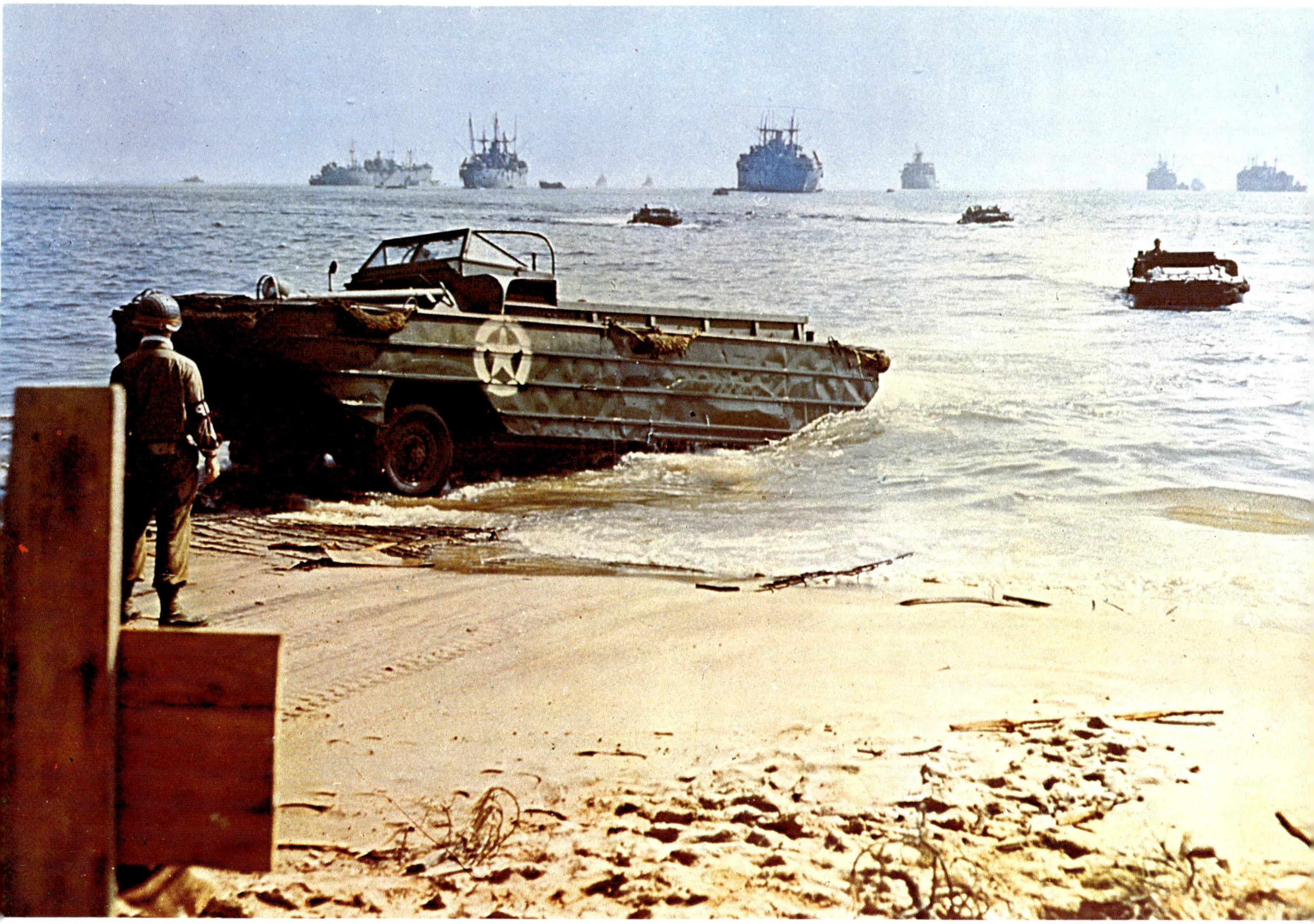

The DUKW. First constructed in 1942, the DUKW was an amphibious vehicle derived from the GMC truck. Intended to carry supplies from ships to the shore without the need for pontoons or landing stages, the DUKW performed an important function during amphibious operations, as is shown by this picture of a scene from the landings in Provence.

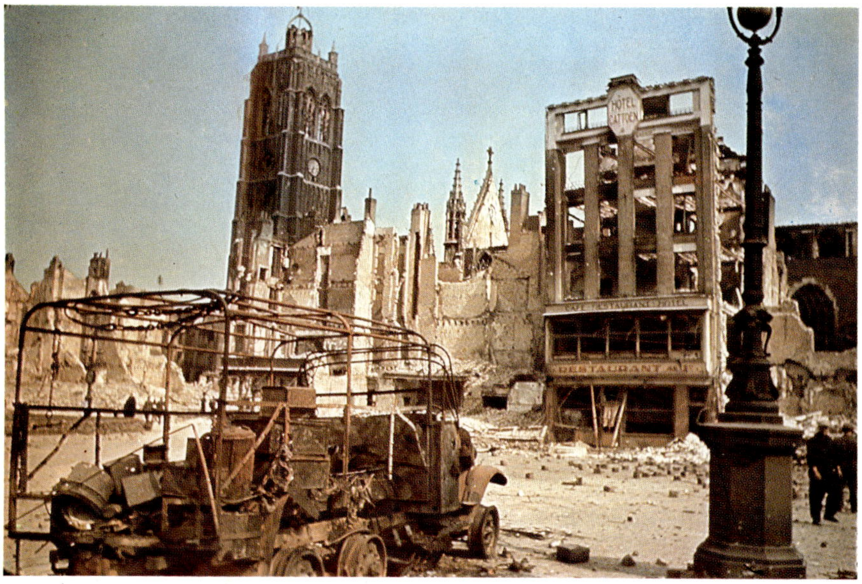

Dunkirk. Dunkirk had been subjected to heavy air and artillery bombardment and when German troops entered the town on 4 June 1940 it was nothing more than an expanse of ruins. An inexplicable delay in the German advance at the end of May had relieved some of the pressure on the British and French troops being evacuated from the beaches at Dunkirk.

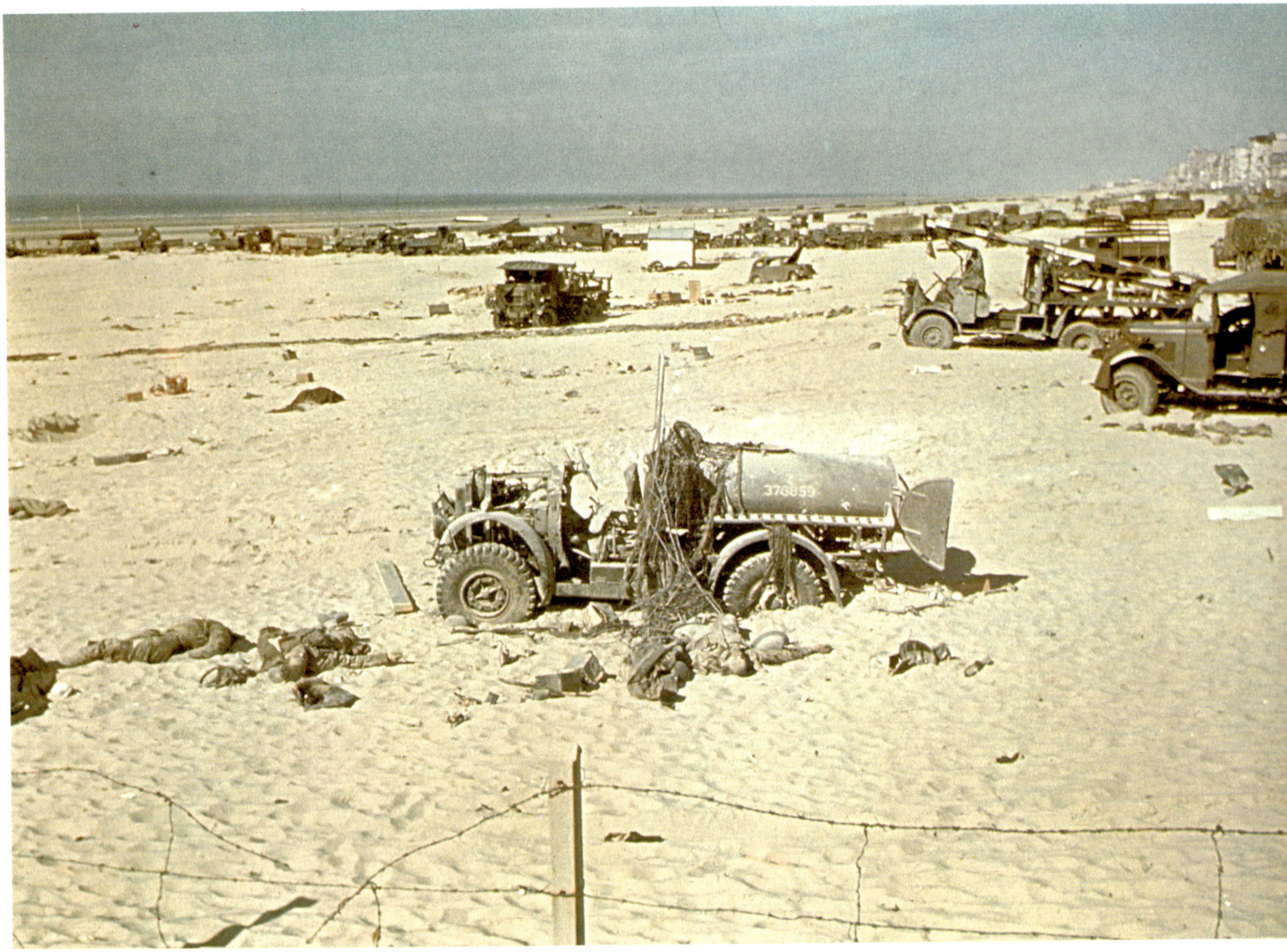

When the Germans reached the sea on the outskirts of Dunkirk they found a scene of desolation. Corpses and abandoned vehicles were scattered on the beaches. In 'Operation Dynamo', as it was code-named, French and British naval forces had indeed successfully evacuated nearly 350,000 men, leaving only 40,000 to the enemy, but almost all their equipment had been left behind.

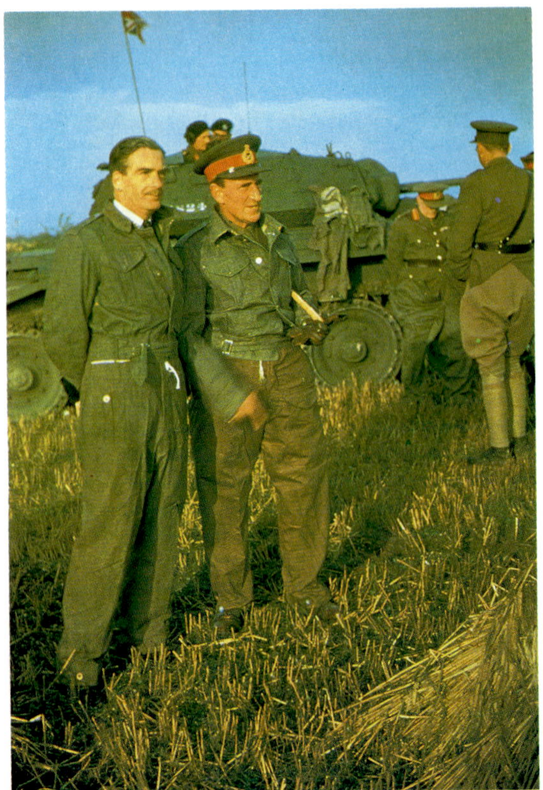

Eden. Eden, a brilliant, elegant personality, had resigned from the post of foreign secretary in 1938, disapproving of Chamberlain's lack of firmness towards Hitler and Mussolini. From 1940 to 1945 he was once again to direct foreign affairs in Churchill's cabinet and this involved him in extensive travel. Here he is seen at military manoeuvres in Yorkshire in 1942.

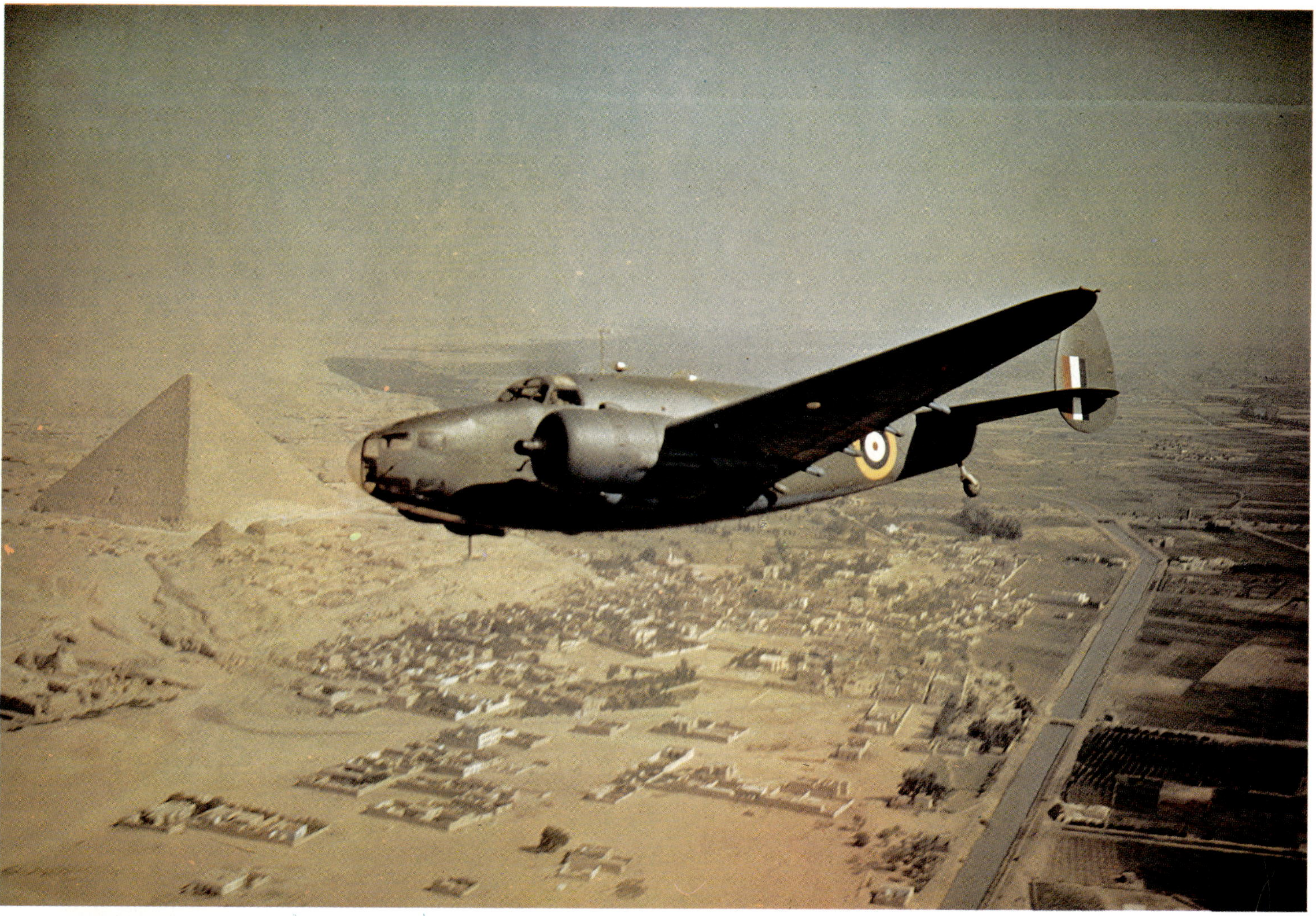

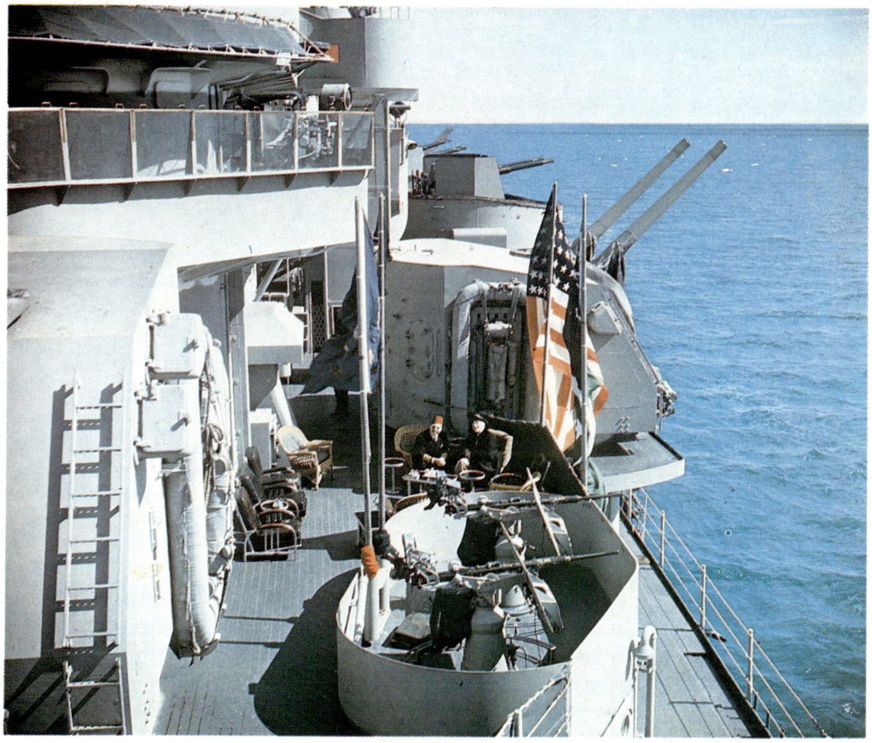

Egypt. Under the term of a treaty made in 1936 Egypt was one of the major bases of British operations throughout the Second -World War. Nearly 500,000 British servicemen were there at various times, carrying on the war against the Italian and German forces in Africa and defending the Suez Canal and the British bases in the Middle East. This picture shows a Hudson bomber of RAF Coastal Command flying over the pyramids.

From 1939 to 1942 relations between Britain and Egypt were strained. Successive Egyptian governments, supported by King Farouk, refused to declare war on the Axis powers and large sections of the public did not hide their pro-German sympathies. In Feb. 1942 the British had to engineer a coup d'état, obliging King Farouk to form a government which would be favourable to the Allies. President Roosevelt, on his return from the Yalta conference in 1945, thought it prudent to invite the Egyptian king for a talk on board the cruiser *Quincy*, which is shown in this picture.

Energy. Jerricans of petrol destined for the Afrika Korps.

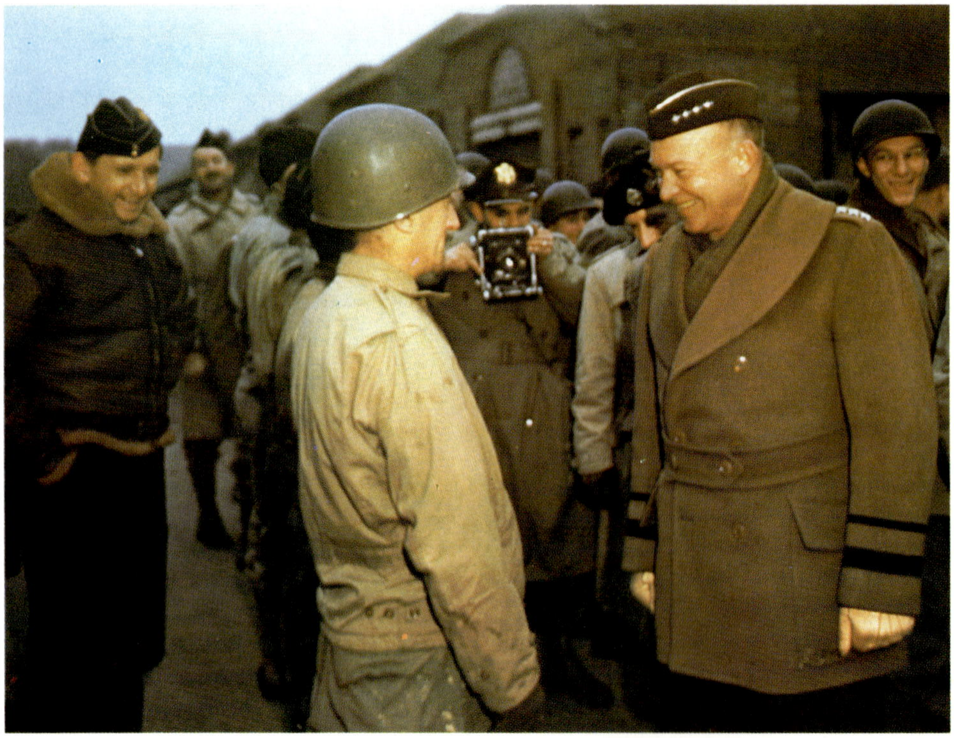

Eisenhower. The favour of the US army's chief of staff, General Marshall, meant that Eisenhower's career advanced at exceptional speed during the war. Thus he was put in command of Operation Torch in North Africa, then of the Mediterranean theatre before, at the end of 1943, becoming supreme allied commander of the forces which were to invade the western European mainland. Eisenhower was not so much a great strategist as a conciliator, an essential quality in a coalition war. Here he is seen in conversation with an American soldier shortly before the Normandy landings.

Energy. From 1939 to 1945 oil was truly the 'sinew of war'. This picture shows an oil tanker on fire after being torpedoed by a U-boat during the German submarine offensive off the Atlantic coast of the United States at the beginning of 1942. This offensive was intended to cut the supply route for the transport of petrol and oil from the Gulf of Mexico to the east coast of the United States.

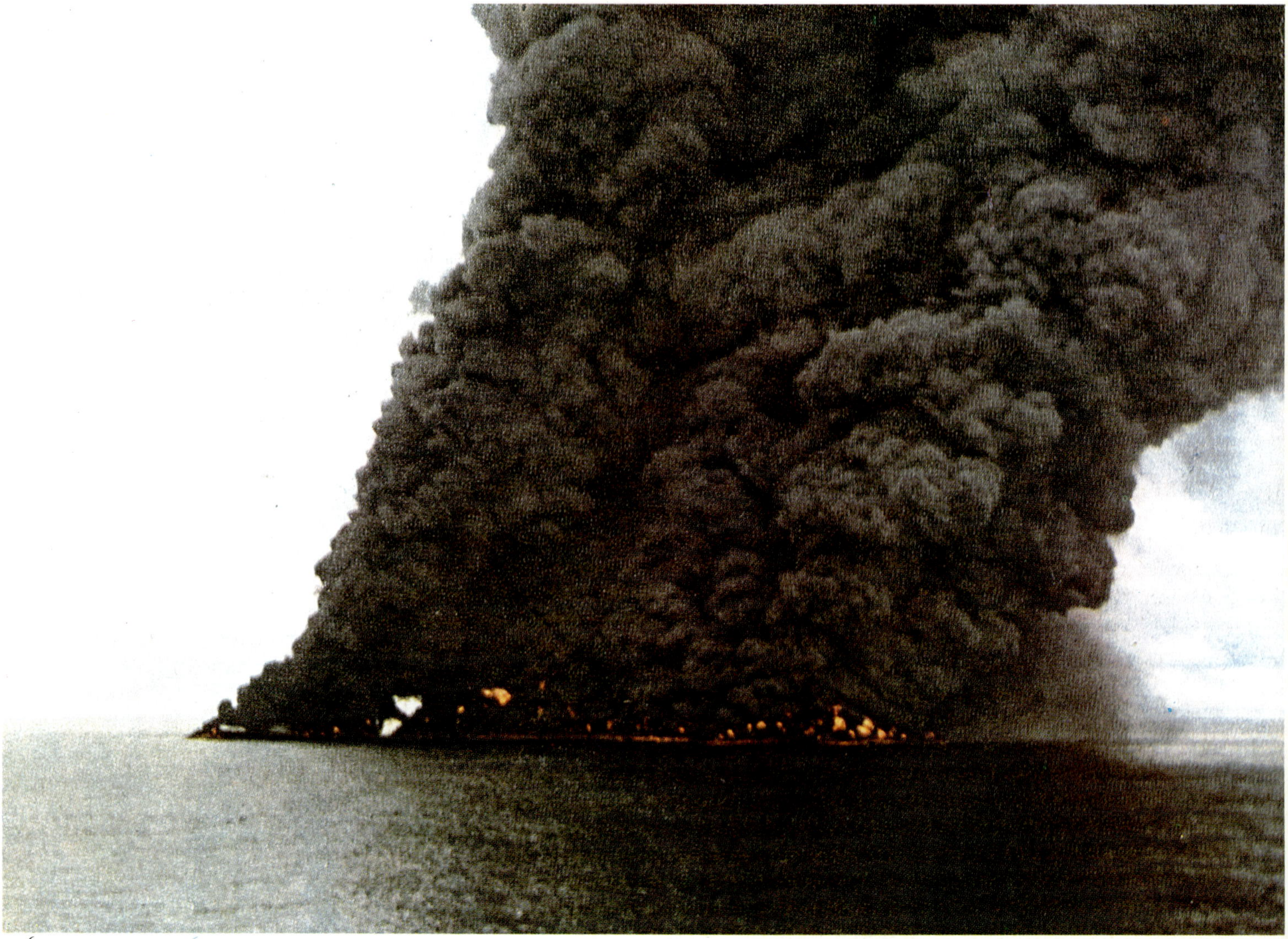

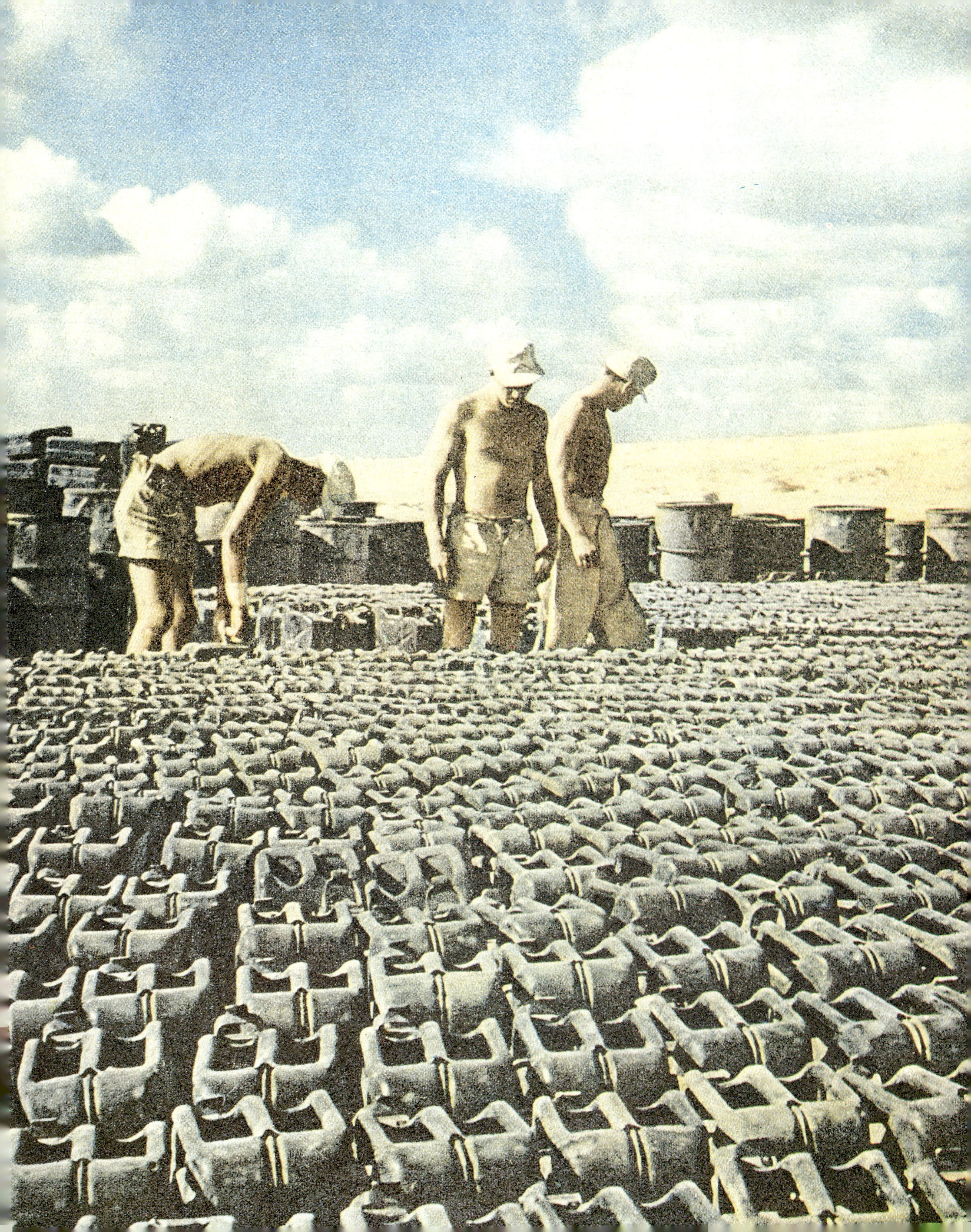

From 1939 to 1944 Germany was able to exploit the oilfields of Ploesti in Romania for its own use. Nevertheless, when faced from 1943 onwards with the threat of Allied bombers operating from southern Italy, the Germans had to strengthen the anti-aircraft defences of the oil wells considerably.

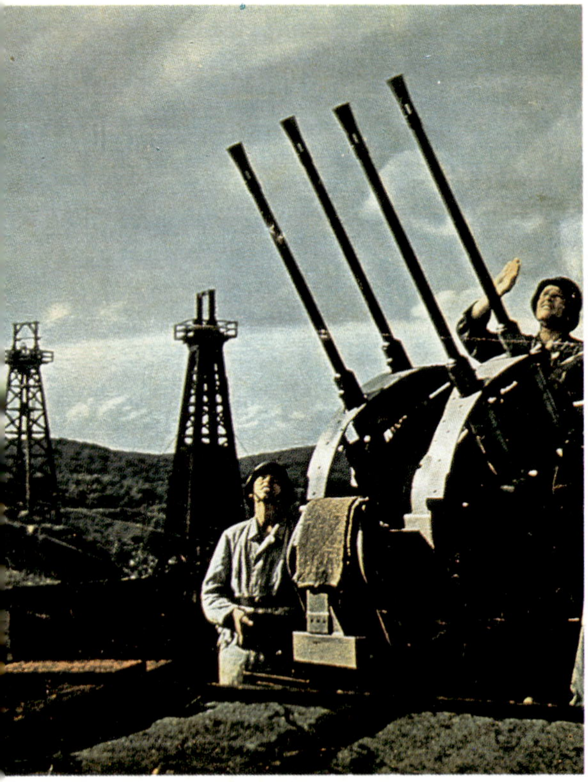

In the autumn of 1944 Allied bombers began a systematic series of raids on all the oil refineries and synthetic fuel plants in Germany, in order to try to paralyse the Reich's war machine. The results of this offensive were spectacular, as this picture of the ruins of the Zeitz refinery shows.

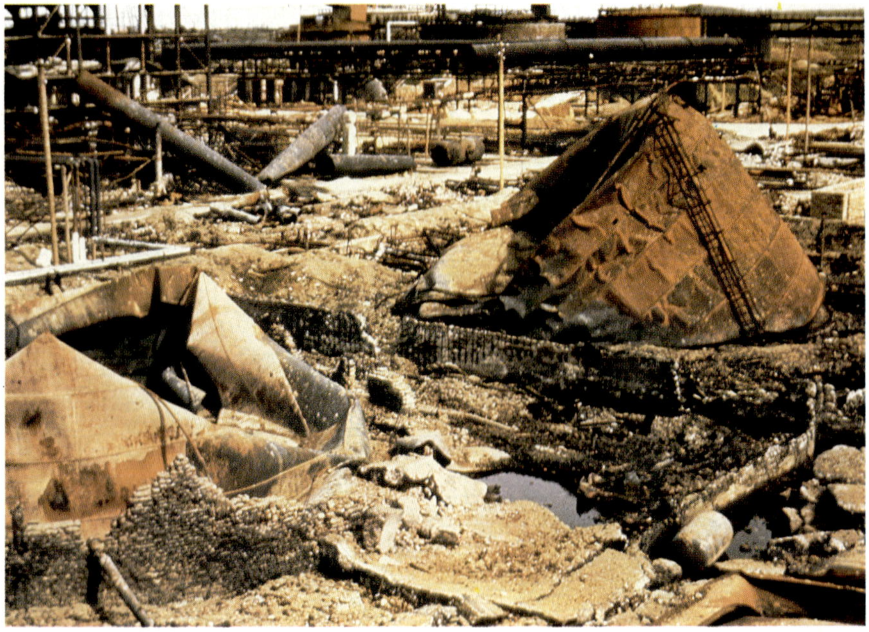

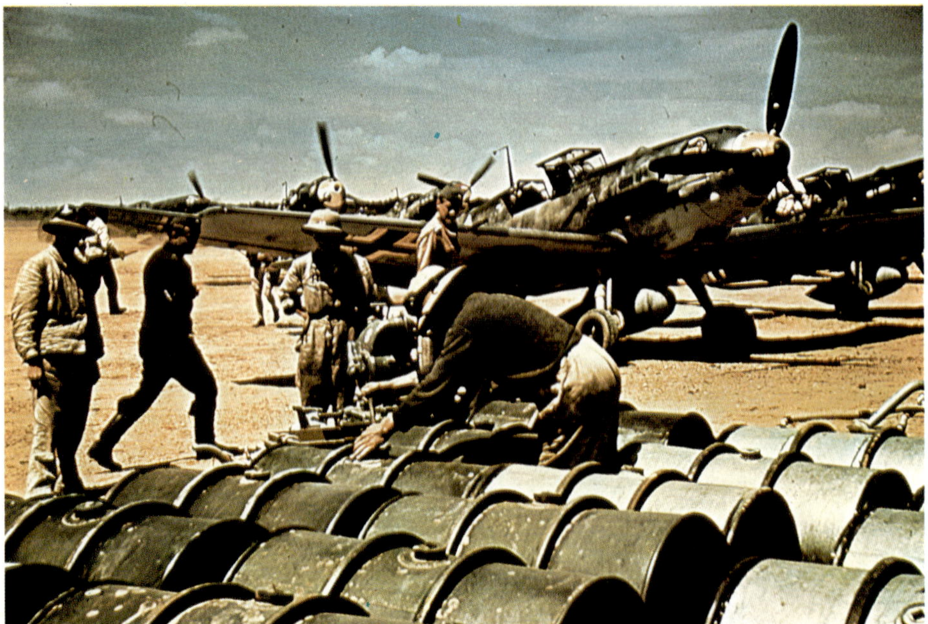

Throughout the conflict the supply of high octane fuel to air forces was one of the major concerns of the supply services. Here, German Messerschmitt Bf-109 fighters are seen refuelling on an airfield in Libya.

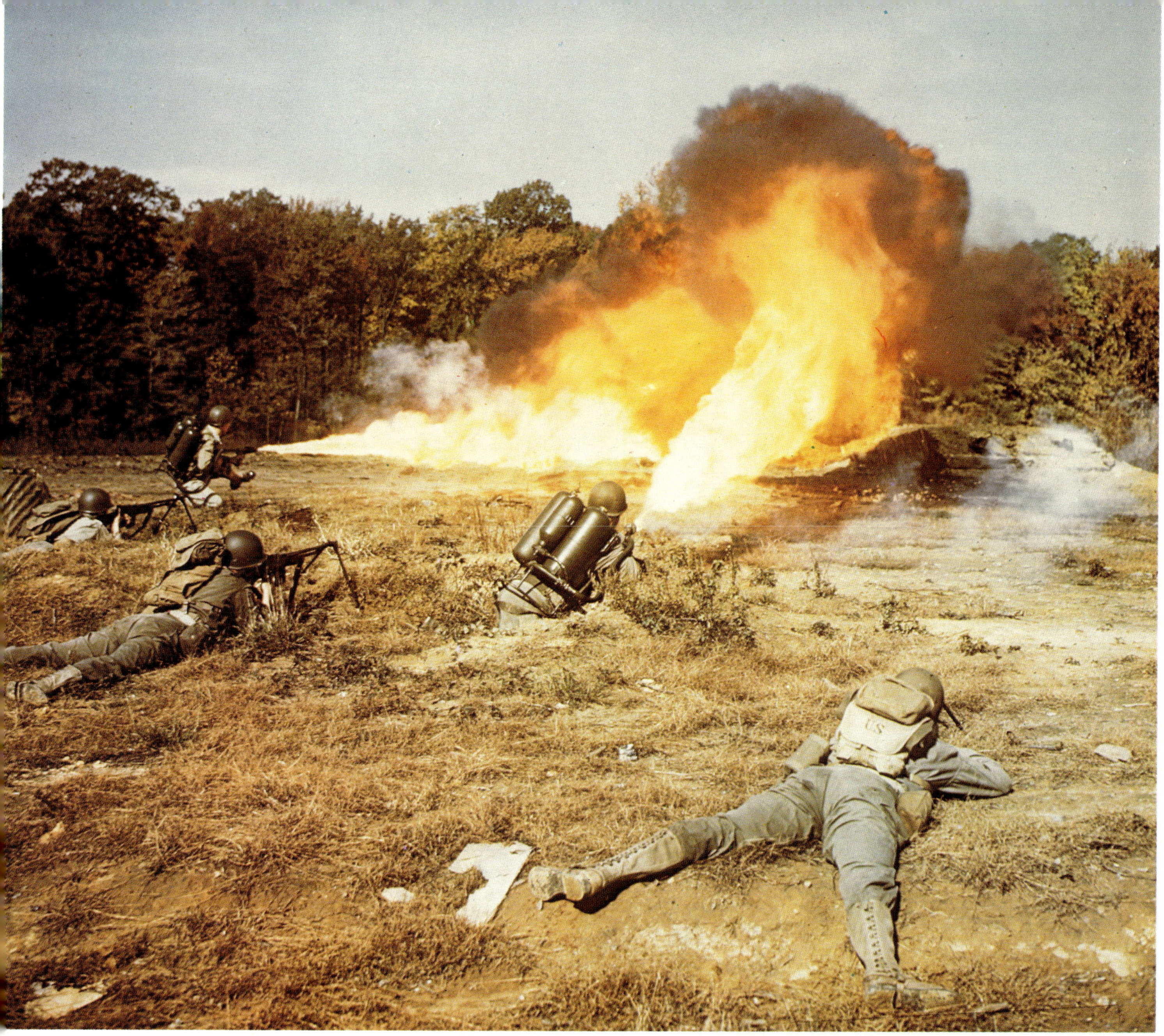

Engineer troops. Engineers armed with chemical weapons fought in the front lines during the war. This picture shows a scene at a US army training camp in Maryland. Two men equipped with the M2-2 portable flame-thrower are protected by two infantrymen firing submachine guns. In use the M2-2 flame-thrower had an immediate destructive effect and was employed particularly in attacks on small fortifications.

Apart from combat missions, the engineers in all the armies carried out their usual tasks, improving roads, setting up pontoon bridges and repairing bridges and tunnels, etc. In this picture teams of US army engineers are repairing a railway bridge in the Belgian Ardennes. These units had at their disposal an impressive amount of equipment and even made use of divers.

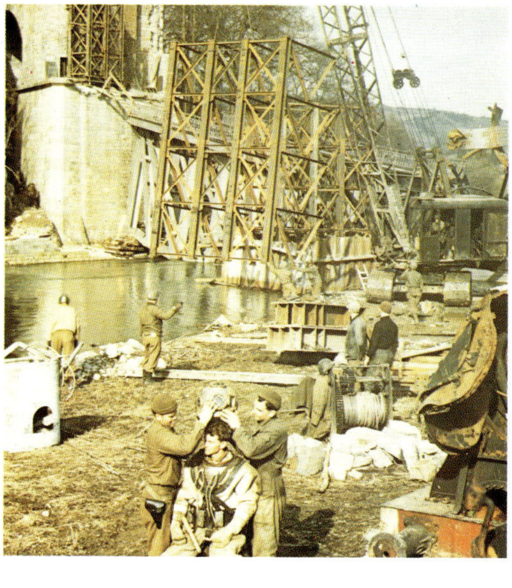

The air offensive over Europe. The air offensive not only against Germany but also against the countries of occupied Europe was one of the major elements of British strategy as early as 1941. The air raids, which were carried out at night, were directed at towns and industrial areas, with the intention of paralysing industrial production and breaking the morale of the German population. Here an RAF officer is seen briefing bomber crews on the eve of an operation.

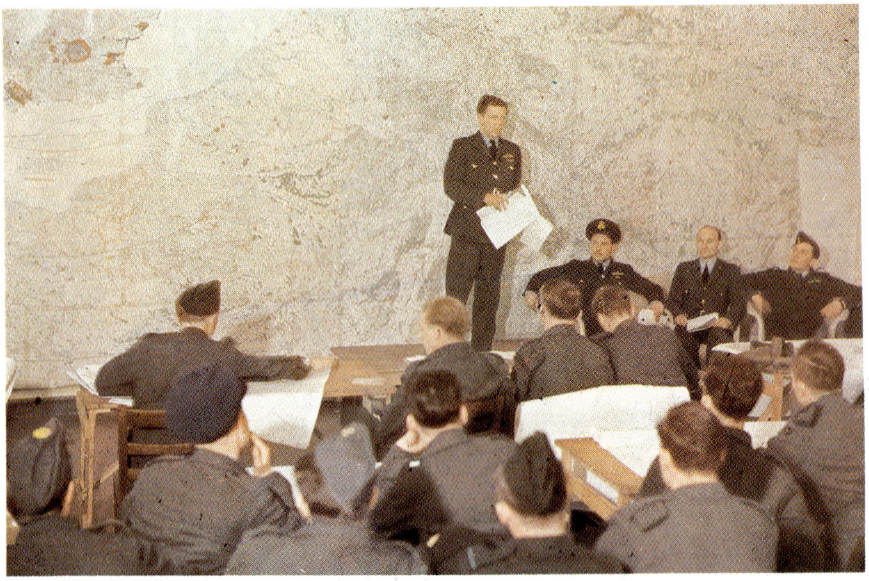

From the summer of 1942 the US 8th Air Force began to take part in the air offensive over Europe. Its specific tactic was to make daylight precision attacks on targets of military or economic importance. This picture shows a formation of Boeing B-17 Flying Fortresses over France at the beginning of 1944: their mission was to bomb the Meulan region (Seine et Oise) where the Germans had set up a repair centre for their Dornier aircraft.

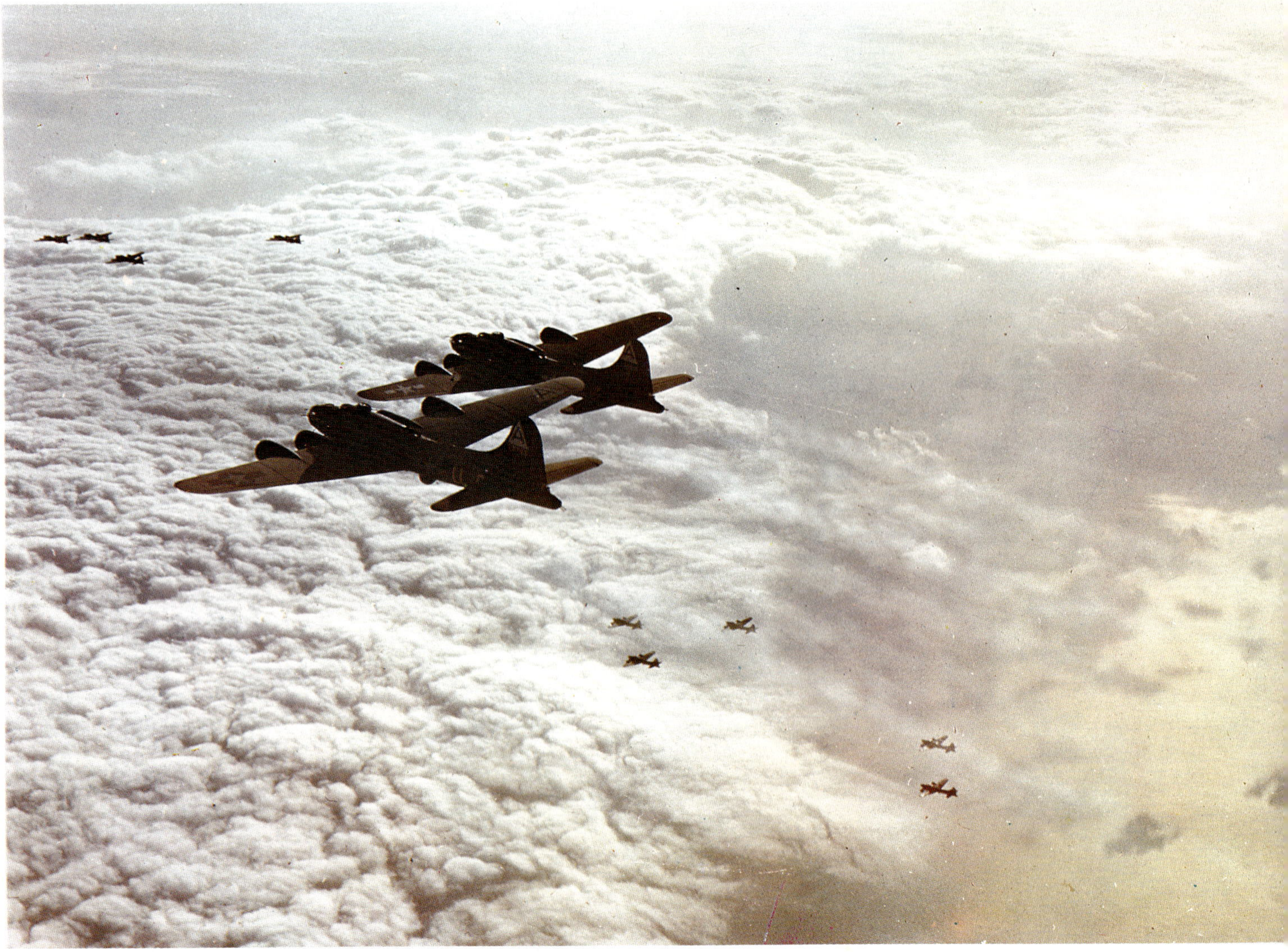

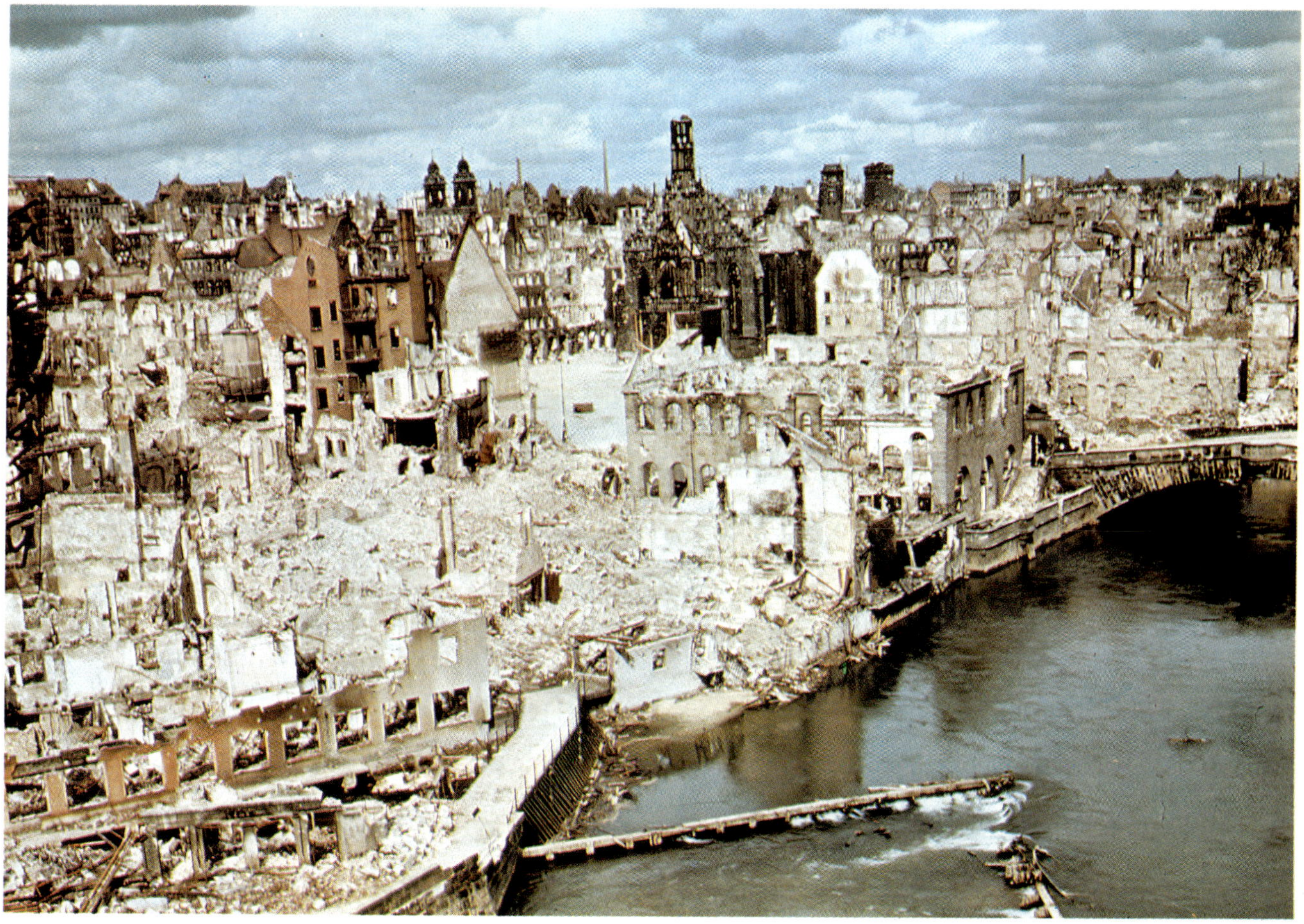

The Allied bombing raids on German cities brought heavy losses for the civilian population and caused terrible destruction. Here the ruins of Nuremberg are seen in 1945. The raid of 30 March 1944 was in its turn very costly for the RAF also. Out of the 795 aircraft carrying a total of 8000 tons of bombs, 95 were shot down and 71 returned seriously damaged. This heavy loss meant that long-range raids on Germany were suspended for several months.

From the spring of 1944 onwards a large part of the British and American bomber force concentrated its efforts on the petroleum industry, attacking the Romanian oilfields and the refineries and synthetic fuel plants of the Reich. More than 230,000 tons of bombs were dropped with devastating effects, as is shown by this picture of a factory at Misburg near Hanover in 1945.

German tank factories were the object of heavy air raids from Aug. to Oct. 1944. Often these had spectacular results, as is shown by this view of an assembly workshop, in which one can make out the unfinished hulk of a Jagdpanther tank. In fact the damage caused by such raids was quickly repaired and the losses in tank production for the year 1944 did not exceed 15%.

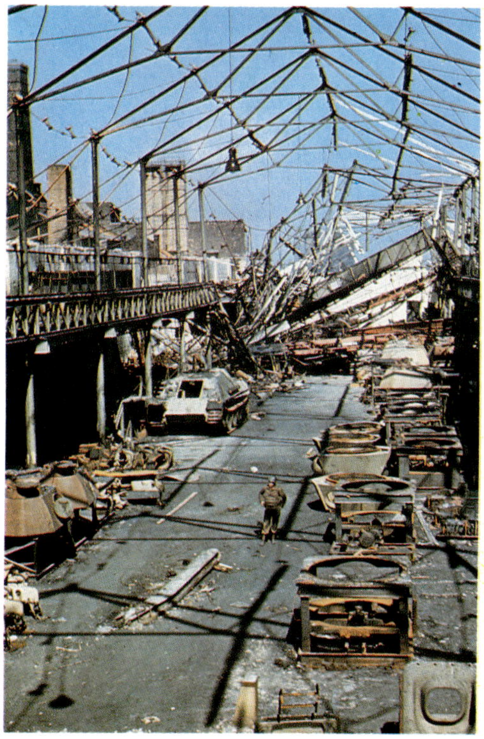

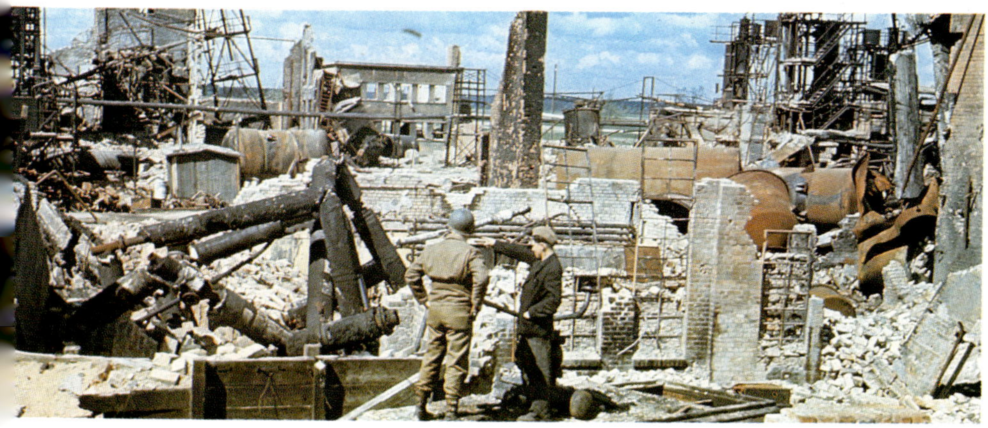

German-occupied Europe. A member of the Wehrmacht's engineer (pioneer) corps in an assault craft.

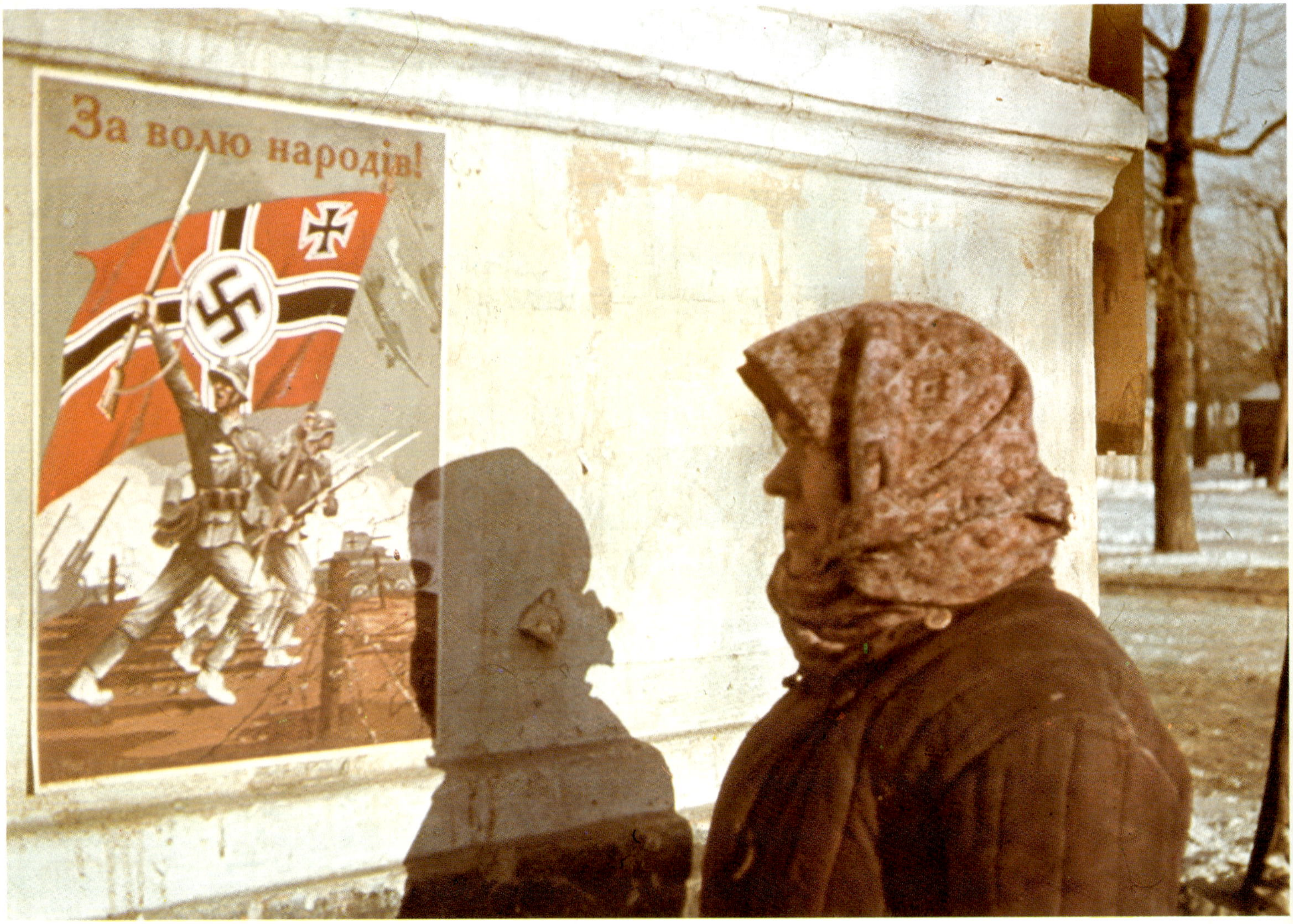

German-occupied Europe. In Kharkov in 1942 a Ukrainian woman studies a poster showing the Wehrmacht's (alleged) struggle for the freedom of the Ukrainian nation. In fact German behaviour in the USSR was to contradict this type of propaganda and General Guderian would say, 'We lost the war on the day when we failed to raise the Ukrainian flag on the cathedral in Kiev'.

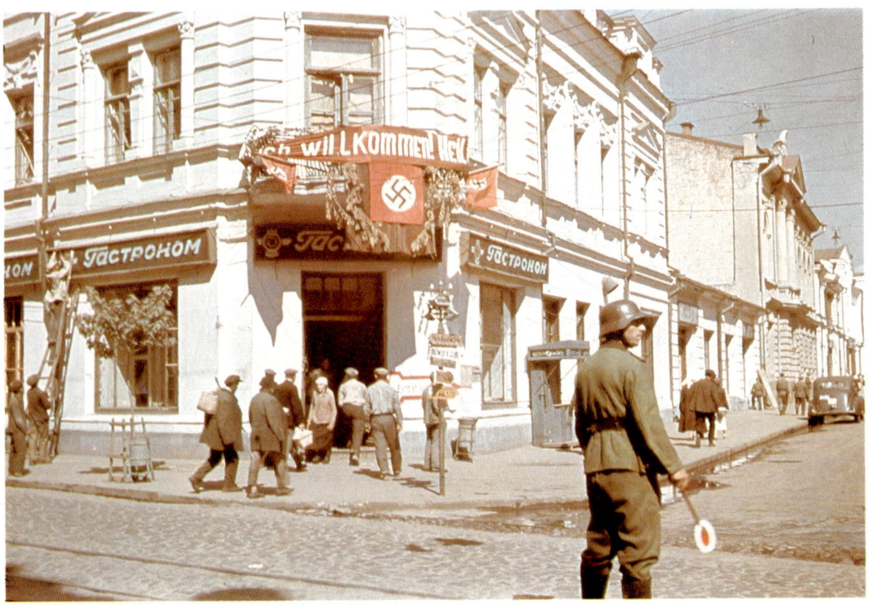

A German soldier directs traffic in a street in Kharkov in 1942. In the background is a food shop (gastronom) with a propaganda banner hung above the entrance. The German occupation of the Ukraine, which was to last nearly two years, was marked by massive requisitions of food and labour and by ruthless repression.

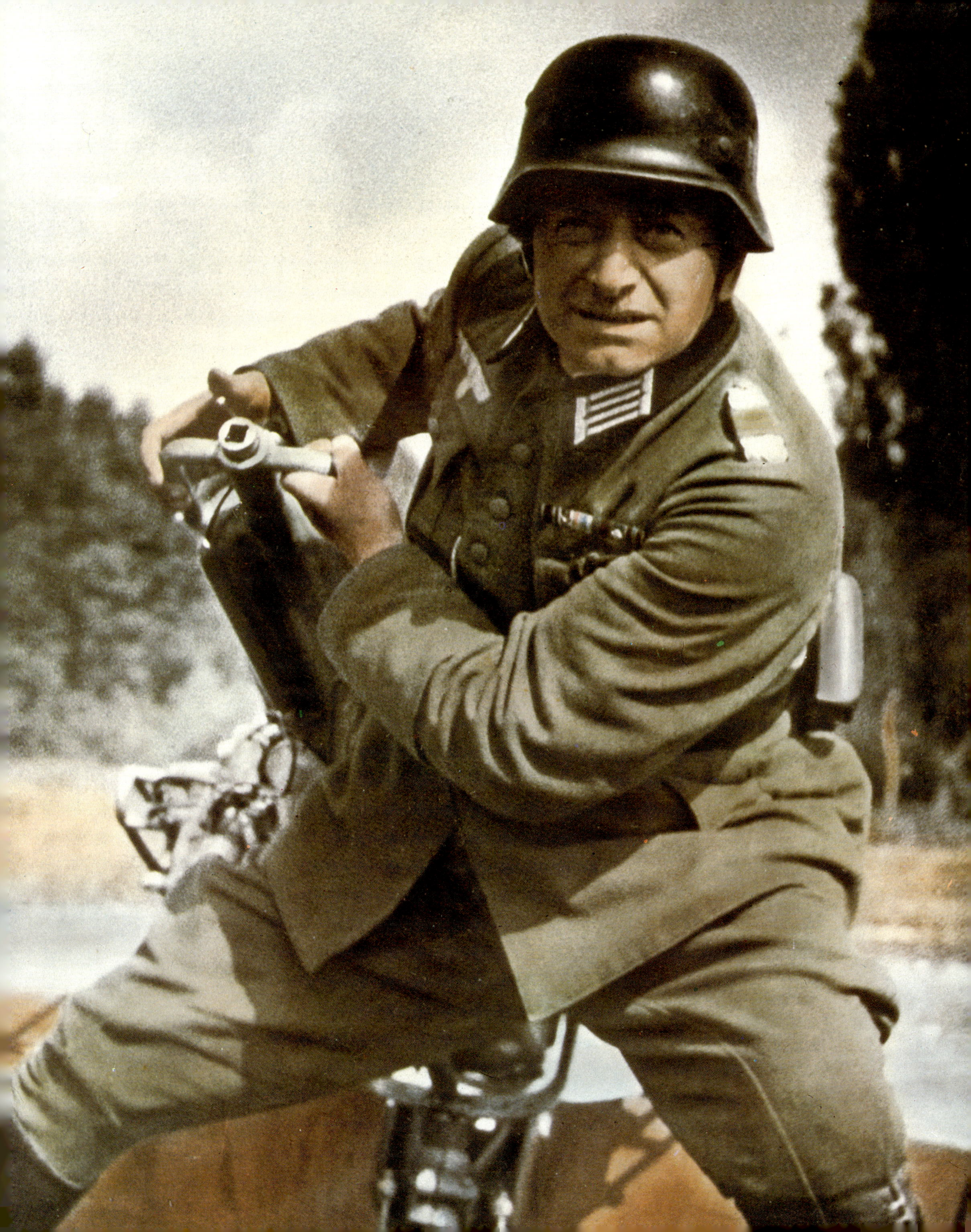

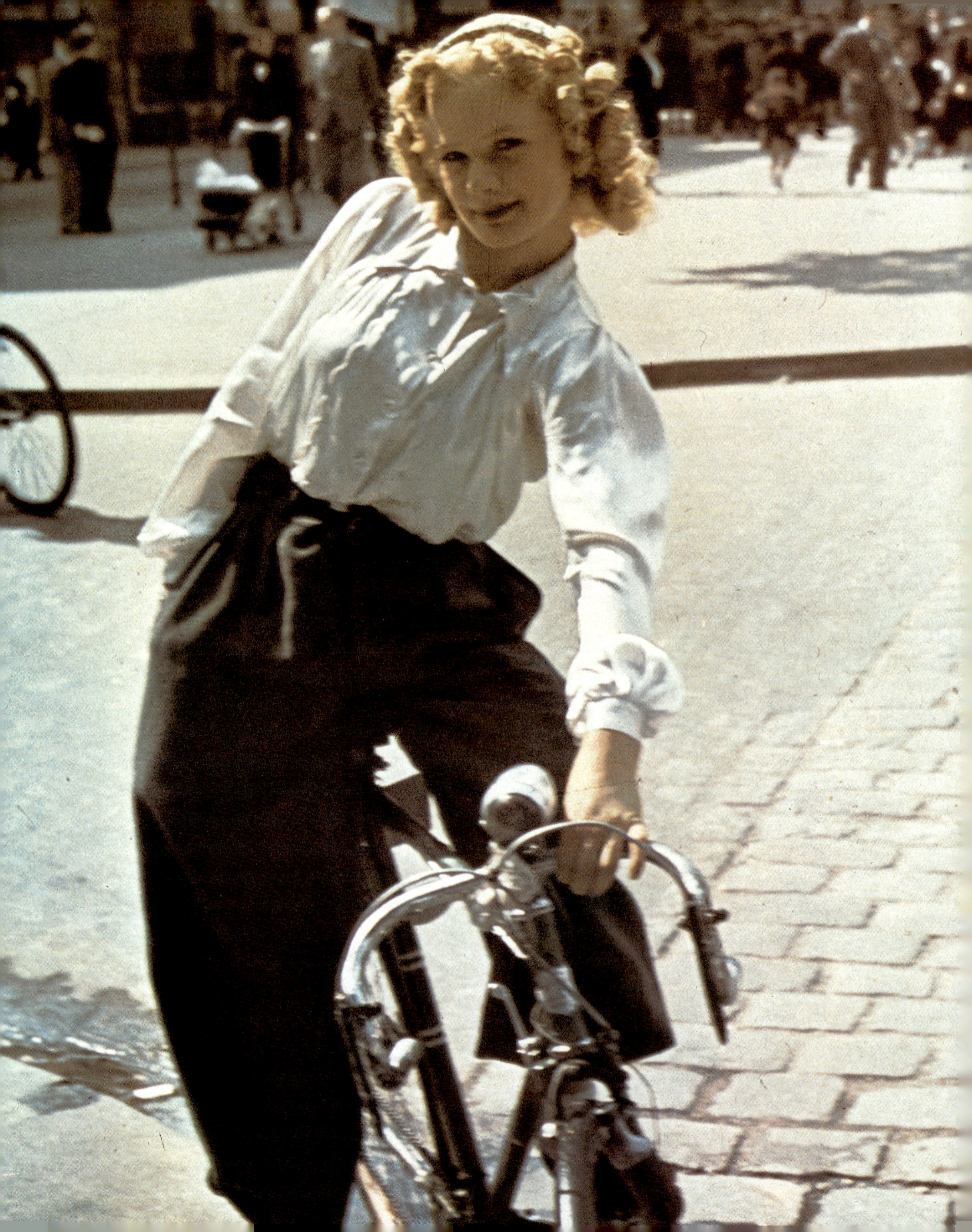

Fashion. A young Parisian on her bicycle during the Occupation.

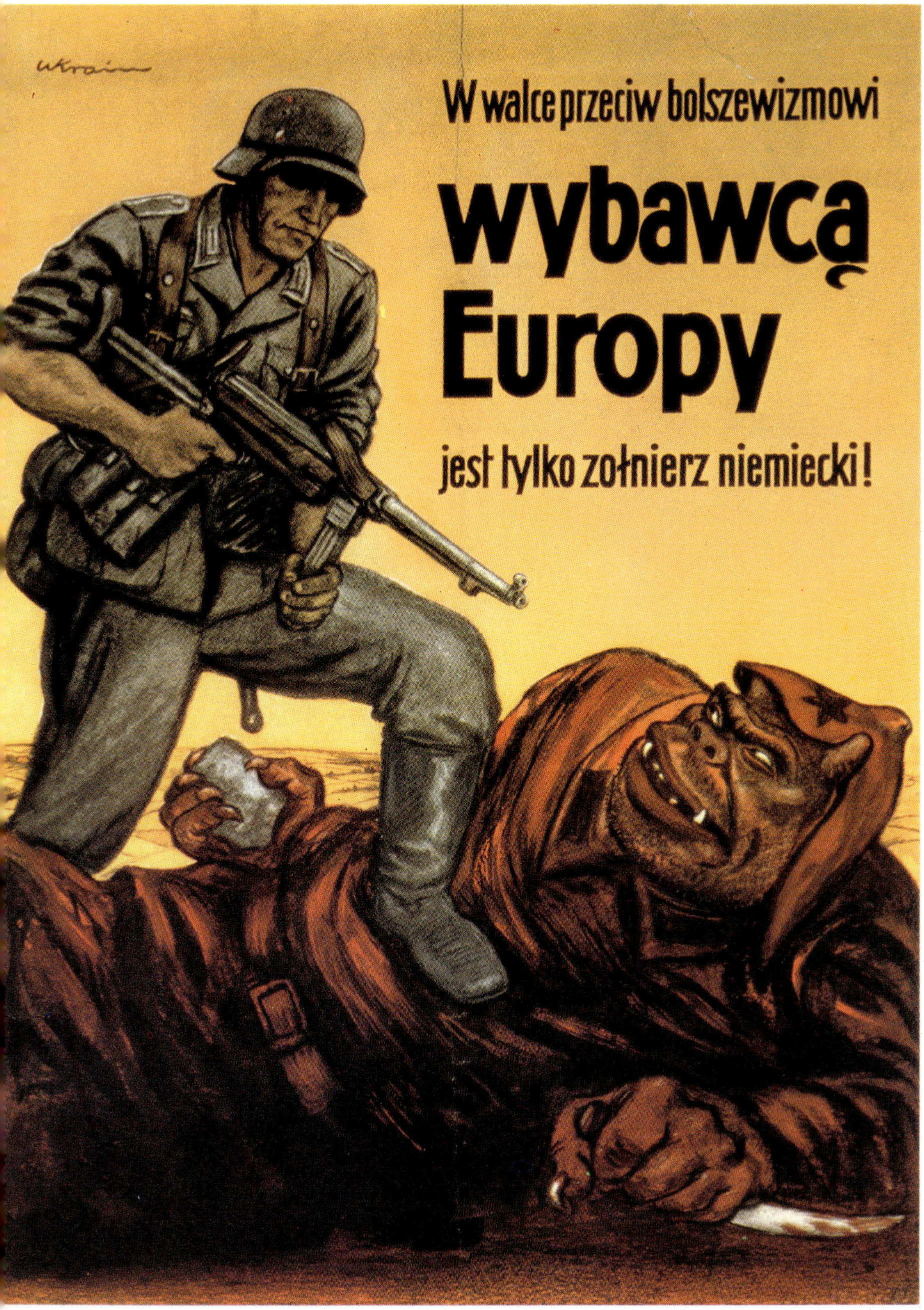

From 1942 German propaganda attempted to exploit the theme of Soviet subversion, in order to combat the growing opposition which was evident in the occupied countries. The theme can be seen in this poster produced for occupied Poland, the caption of which reads, 'In the fight against Bolshevism the German soldier alone is the saviour of Europe!'.

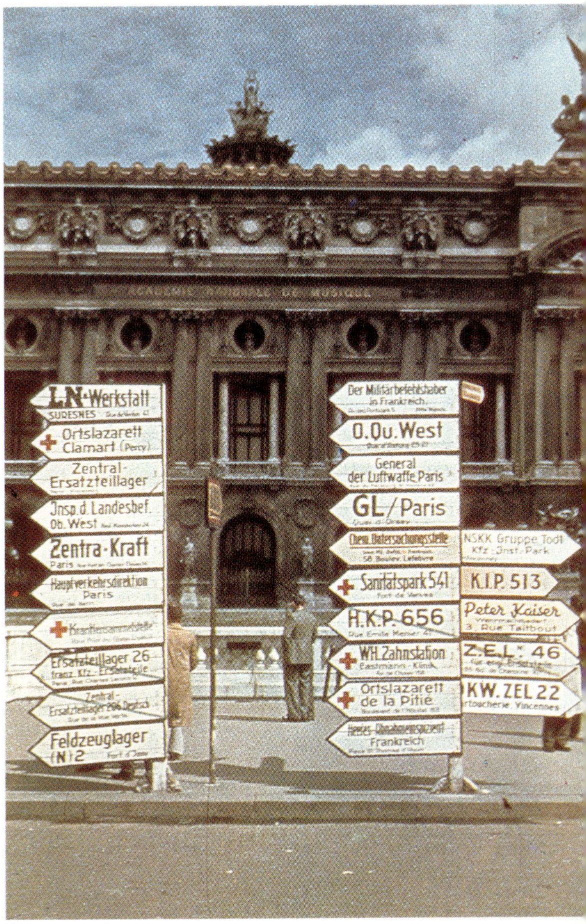

In the occupied countries one of the most characteristic aspects of the street scene was the blossoming of sets of German road signs (those in the Place de l'Opéra in Paris are shown here). Occupation was to take very diverse forms. It was much more harsh and brutal in eastern Europe, particularly in Poland and the Soviet Union, than it was in western Europe.

Fashion. In spite of the occupation the great French fashion designers succeeded in maintaining the tradition of French elegance. Ingenuity made up for the scarcity of leather and dress fabrics. Shoes were made with cork or wooden soles. People used furnishing materials or lace articles rediscovered at the bottom of old chests. Parachute nylon was used to make blouses and underwear. Lacking silk or rayon stockings, women tinted their legs. New themes made their appearance. In 1943, with the success of Marcel Carné's film *Les Visiteurs du soir*, the medieval look was in vogue.

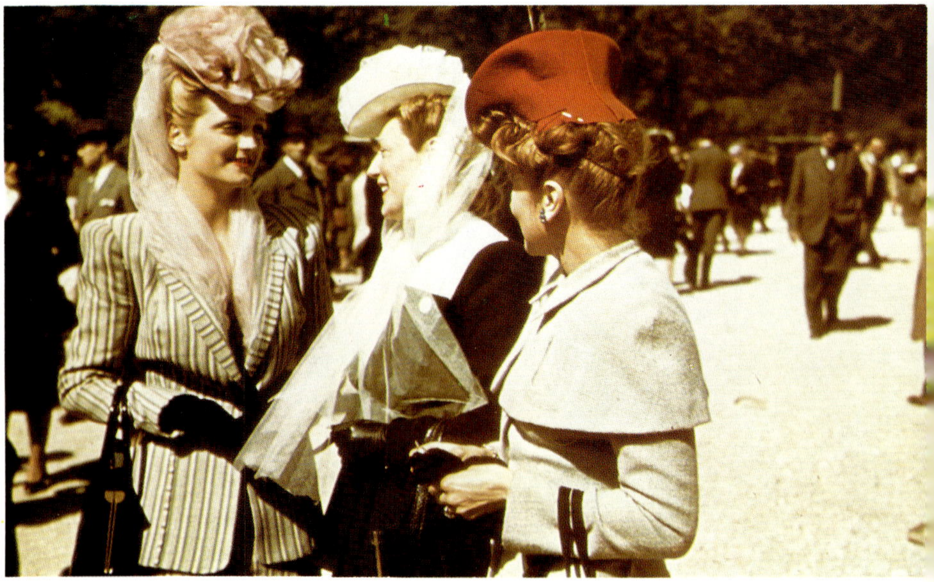

The Fifth Column. This expression, widely used during the period of the Phoney War in 1939–40, dated from the Spanish Civil War. At the time of the attack on Madrid Franco had announced that the city would fall to four motorized columns, acting in liaison with a 'fifth column' which was already in the Spanish capital and was ready to launch attacks involving sabotage and poisoning. Although not completely imaginary, the fifth column idea took on obsessional overtones and affected almost all Germany's opponents. An example is provided by this American poster warning the GIs against making indiscreet remarks which might be picked up by enemy agents.

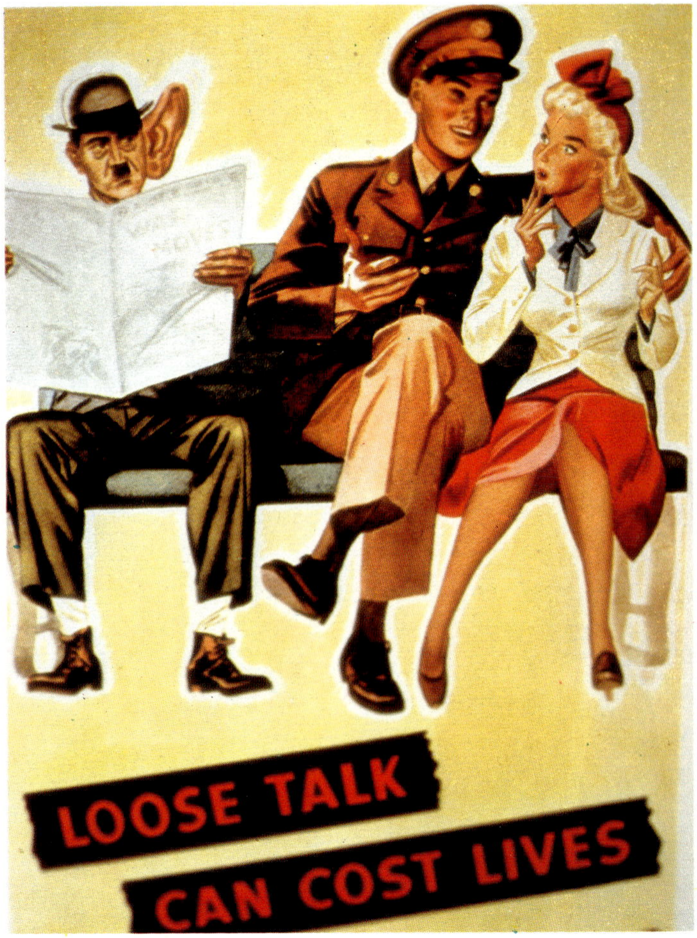

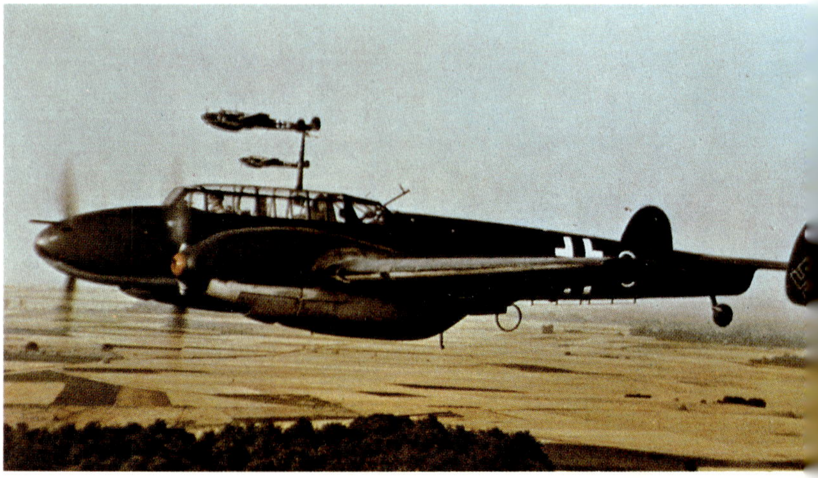

Fighter operations. The Messerschmitt Bf-110, nicknamed 'the Destroyer', was one of the Luftwaffe's standard fighters in 1939. In actual fact this fast twin-engined aircraft, with a top speed of 352 mph (560 km/h), showed itself to lack manoeuvrability and to be very inferior to the Hurricane and Spitfire during the Battle of Britain. Before its replacement by the Me-210 and the Me-410 the Bf-110 was successfully used as a tactical support aircraft and as a night fighter. More than 6000 were built in the course of the war.

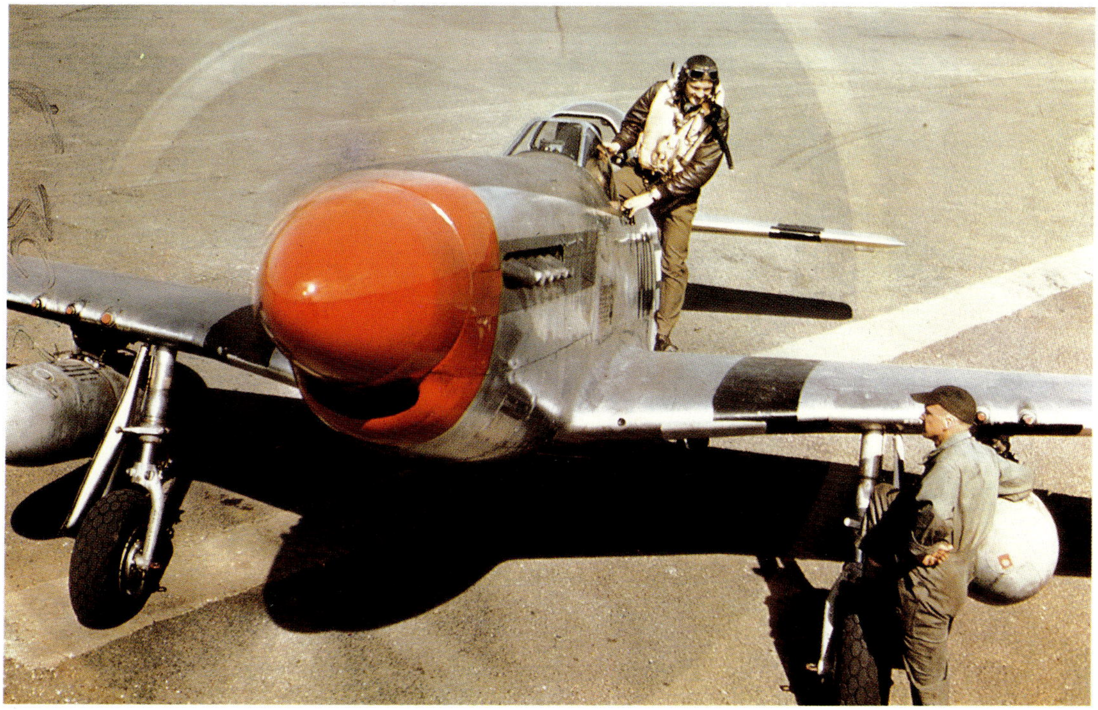

The North American P-51 Mustang fighter was, by the end of the war, one of the US Army Air Force's best aircraft, 6500 of them being built. In its most numerous version it was armed with four 20 mm cannon or six .50 in. machine guns and had a top speed of 437 mph (700 km/h). This aircraft was particularly versatile and operated in various roles – photographic reconnaissance, tactical support and especially bomber escort. Indeed from Jan. 1944 the Mustang, provided with supplementary tanks, accompanied the American bombers on their long-range raids over Europe. These escort missions had a double result: they reduced the bomber losses and inflicted heavy losses on the German fighter force on the eve of the Normandy landings.

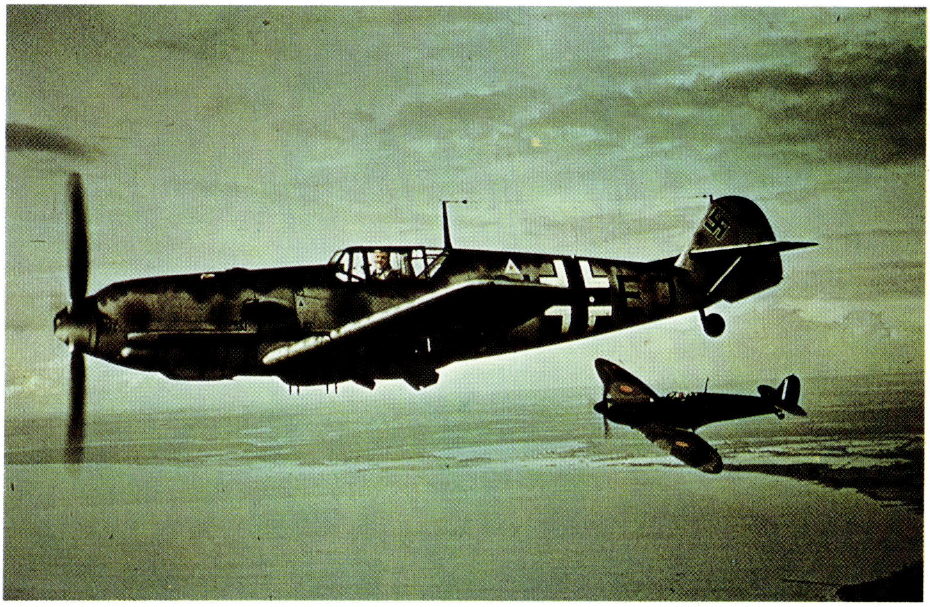

The picture right appears to show a phase in an aerial dog fight between two of the most famous fighters of the early part of the Second World War, the Messerschmitt Bf-109 and the Spitfire. In fact it is a photomontage, produced for propaganda purposes, of an actual Luftwaffe aircraft and an undamaged British Spitfire which had come into the hands of the Germans.

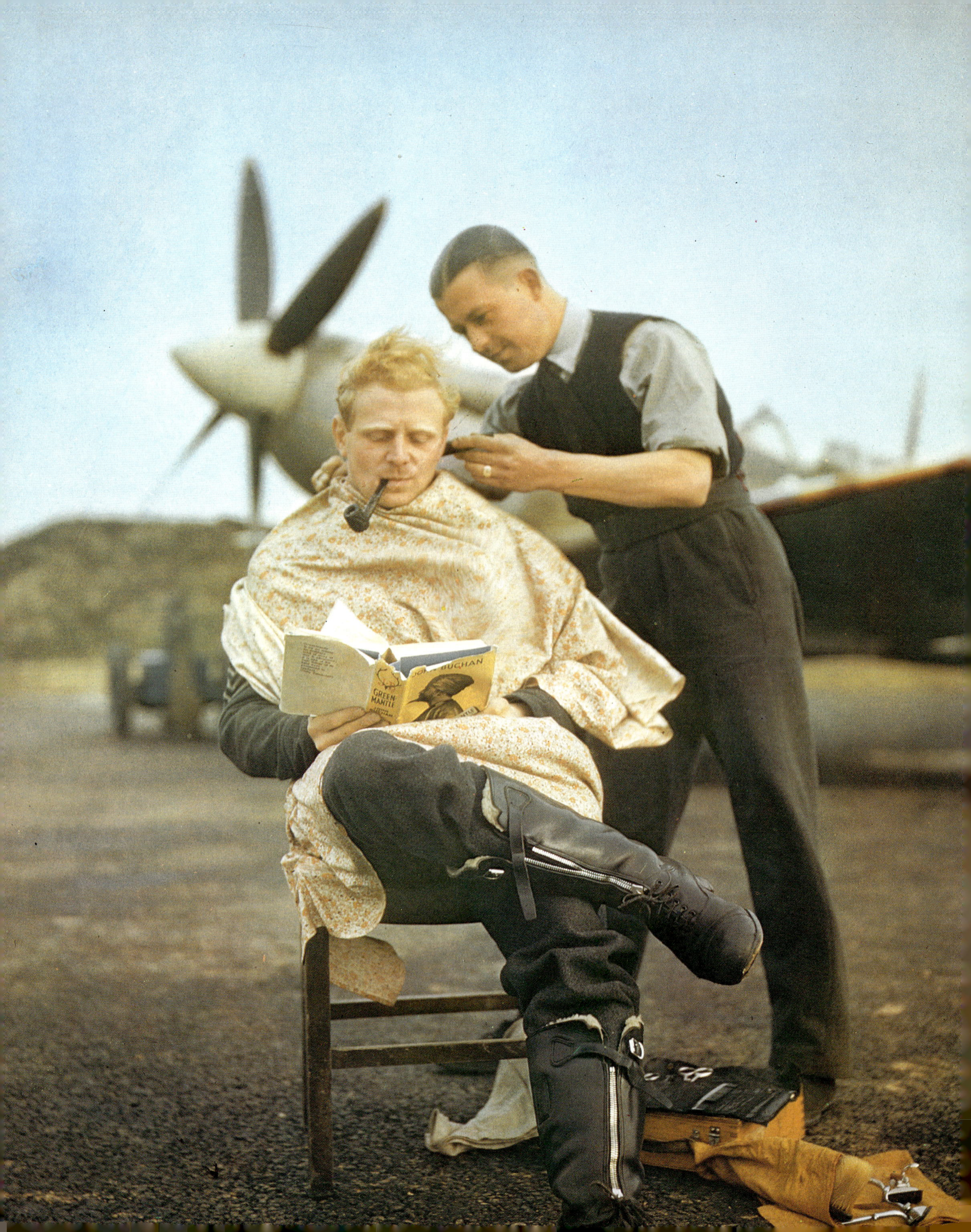
BUCHAN
GREEN MANTLE

Fighter operations. A Spitfire pilot being tended by the station barber in between sorties.

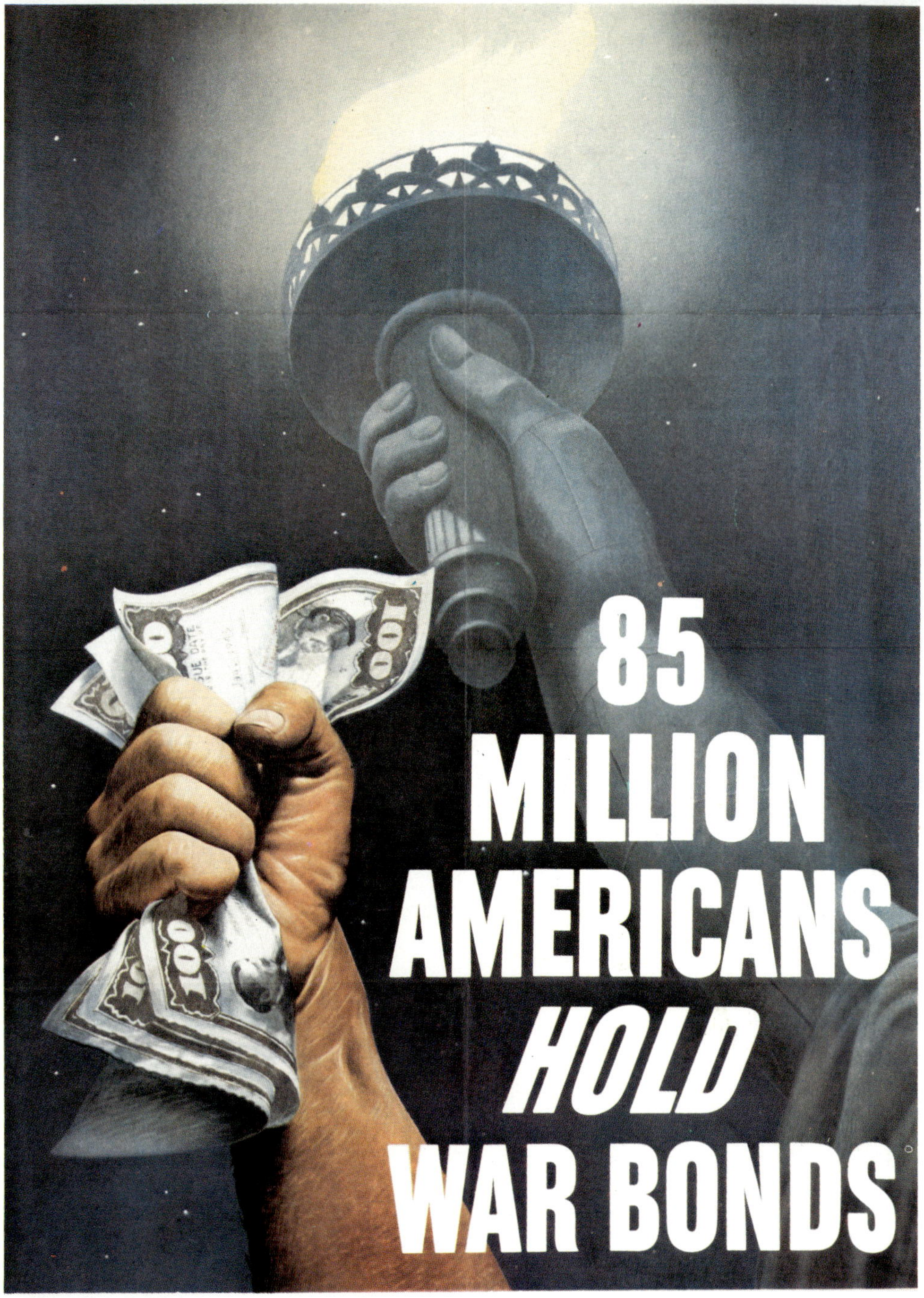

Finance. It was not possible for any of the belligerent countries to cover the enormous expenditure on armaments simply by taxation, and the raising of funds by means of war loans thus became necessary, as this American propaganda poster emphasizes. Between 1941 and 1945 the total amount of the US public debt rose from less than $48,000 million to more than $230,000 million. A poster from the collection of the Musée des Deux Guerres Mondiales – BDIC (Universités de Paris).

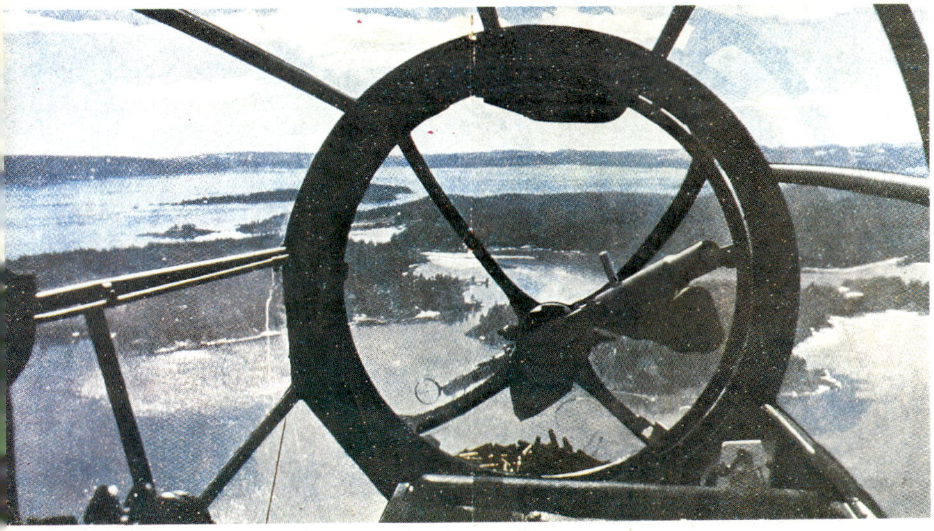

Finland. Finland, a country of large forests and 35,000 lakes, was the scene of two successive wars against the Soviet Union. The first, the 'Winter War' of 1939–40, was followed by the so-called 'Continuation War' from June 1941 to Sept. 1944, intended to recover Finland's lost territories in the favourable circumstances created by the German attack on the Soviet Union. The objective could not be achieved and in the autumn of 1944 the second conflict ended in a harsh armistice with the USSR which nevertheless preserved Finnish independence. In this picture the Finnish landscape is seen from a German medium bomber.

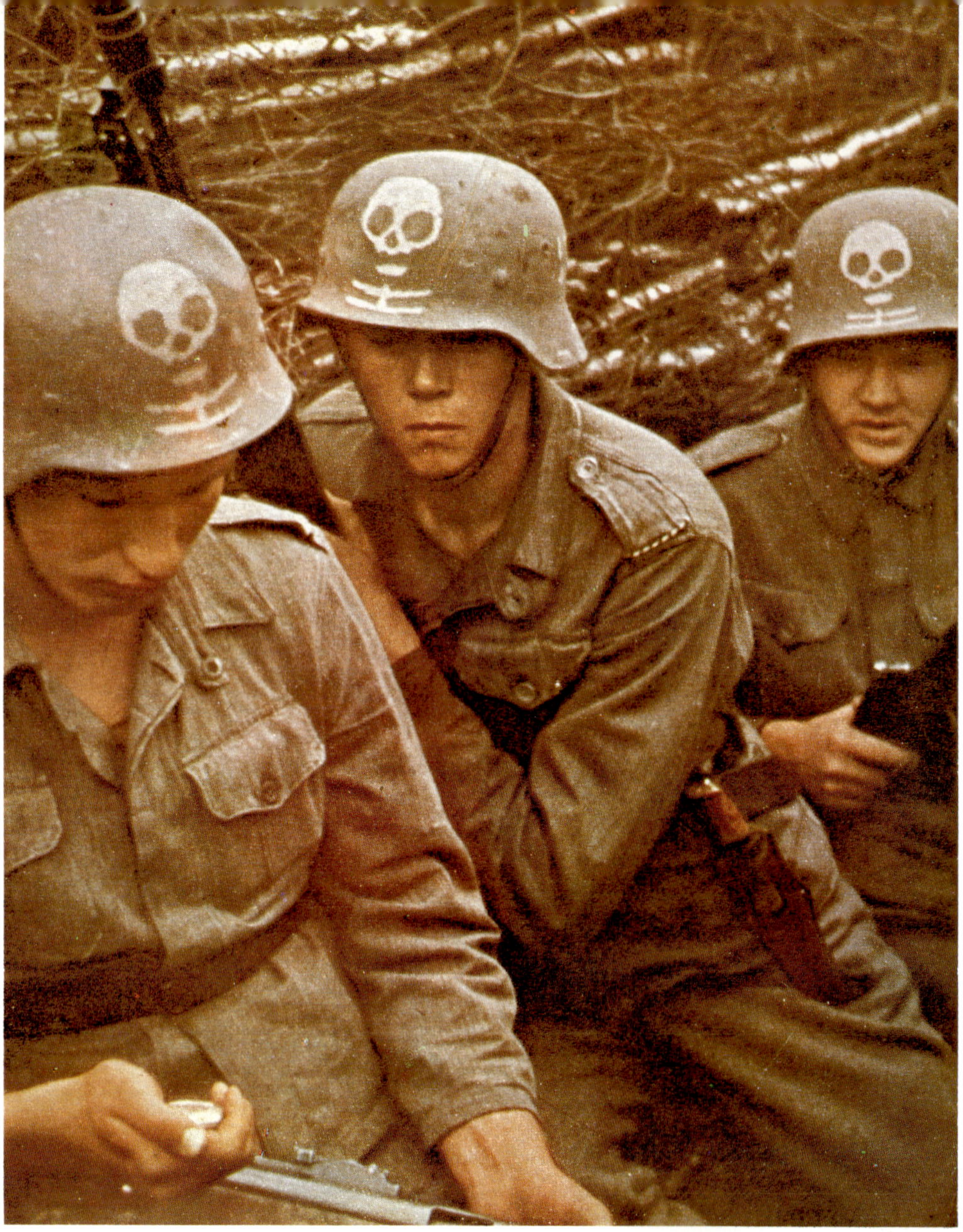

A group of Finnish soldiers seen a few minutes before making an attack. In the conflict with the USSR the Finnish soldier aroused admiration for his courage and skill in using terrain. In spite of the Soviet Union's demands under the armistice – the annexation of territory and a heavy indemnity – the valour of the Finnish nation enabled it to safeguard its national independence and to avoid the fate of the Baltic countries and the other states of eastern Europe.

During the 'Continuation War' German troops carried out operations in Lapland in the far north of the country, in liaison with Finnish units. Here German mountain troops are seen with reindeer.

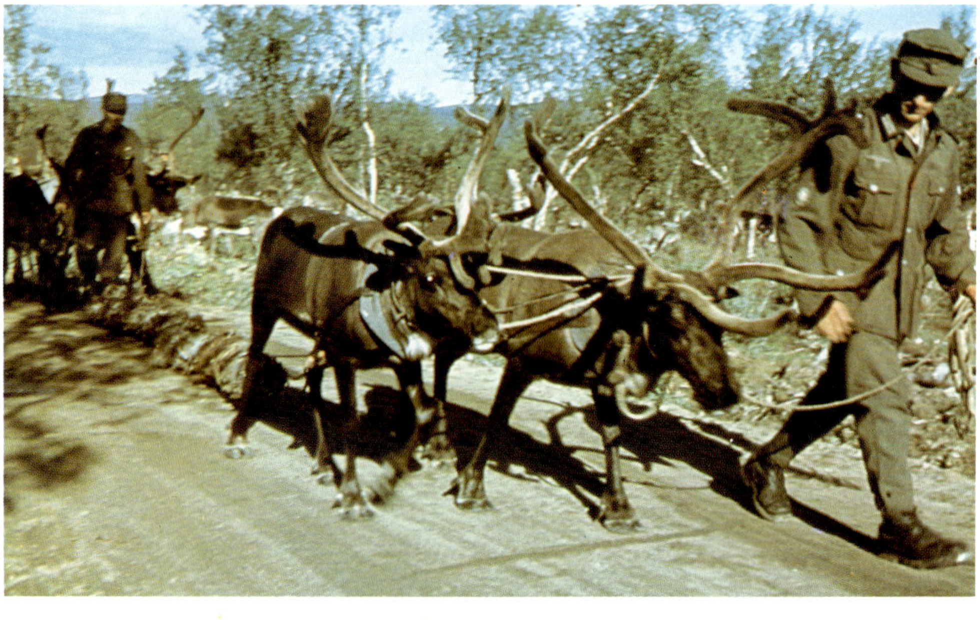

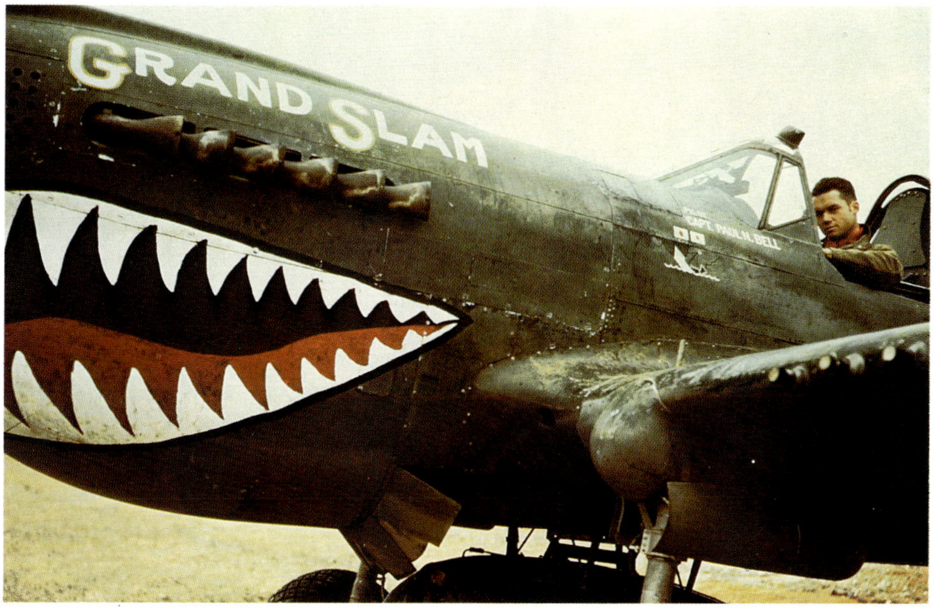

The Flying Tigers. These were a group of volunteer pilots recruited by the American Claire Lee Chennault, who fought alongside the Chinese against the Japanese from 1940 to 1942 in Curtiss P-40 Tomahawk fighters. They also took part in the Burma campaign and in the protection of the airlift over the Himalayas. However, during the summer of 1942 General Stilwell announced that the Flying Tigers were to join the American Army Air Force. This decision, accepted by only five pilots out of nearly 65, marked the end of an astonishing epic, during which Chennault's volunteers had downed 286 Japanese planes.

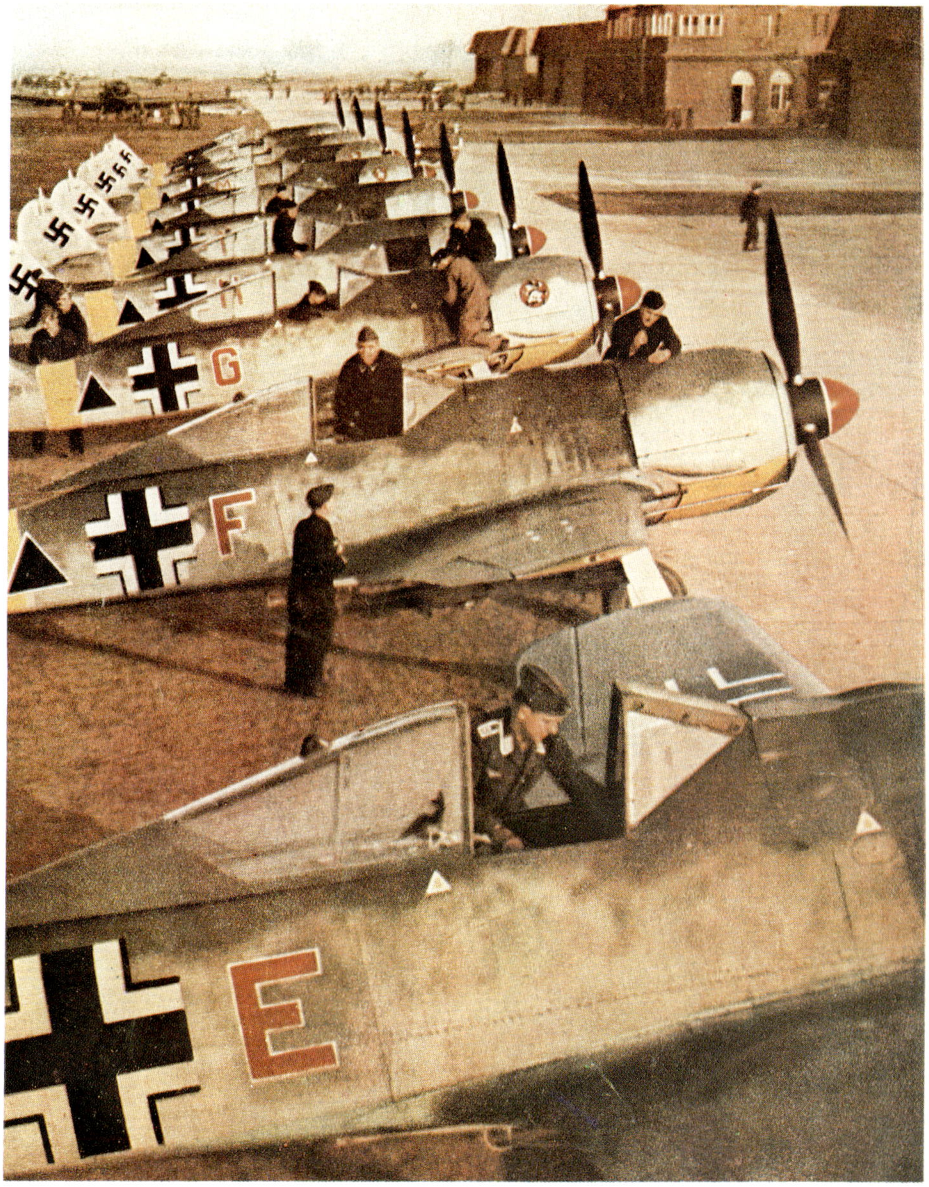

Focke Wulf. The first Focke-Wulf FW 190 fighters were delivered to the Luftwaffe in the summer of 1941. It was a very successful aircraft and when it first appeared it outclassed the Spitfire. More than 20,000 FW 190s were built right up to the end of the war. The mark D9 version shown in the picture was $33\frac{1}{2}$ ft (10.20 m) long, had a wingspan of $34\frac{1}{2}$ ft (10.50 m) and weighed 9500 lbs (4300 kg). Its 1776 hp Jumo 213 engine gave it a top speed of about 440 mph (685 km/h). It was armed with two 20-mm cannon and two machine-guns.

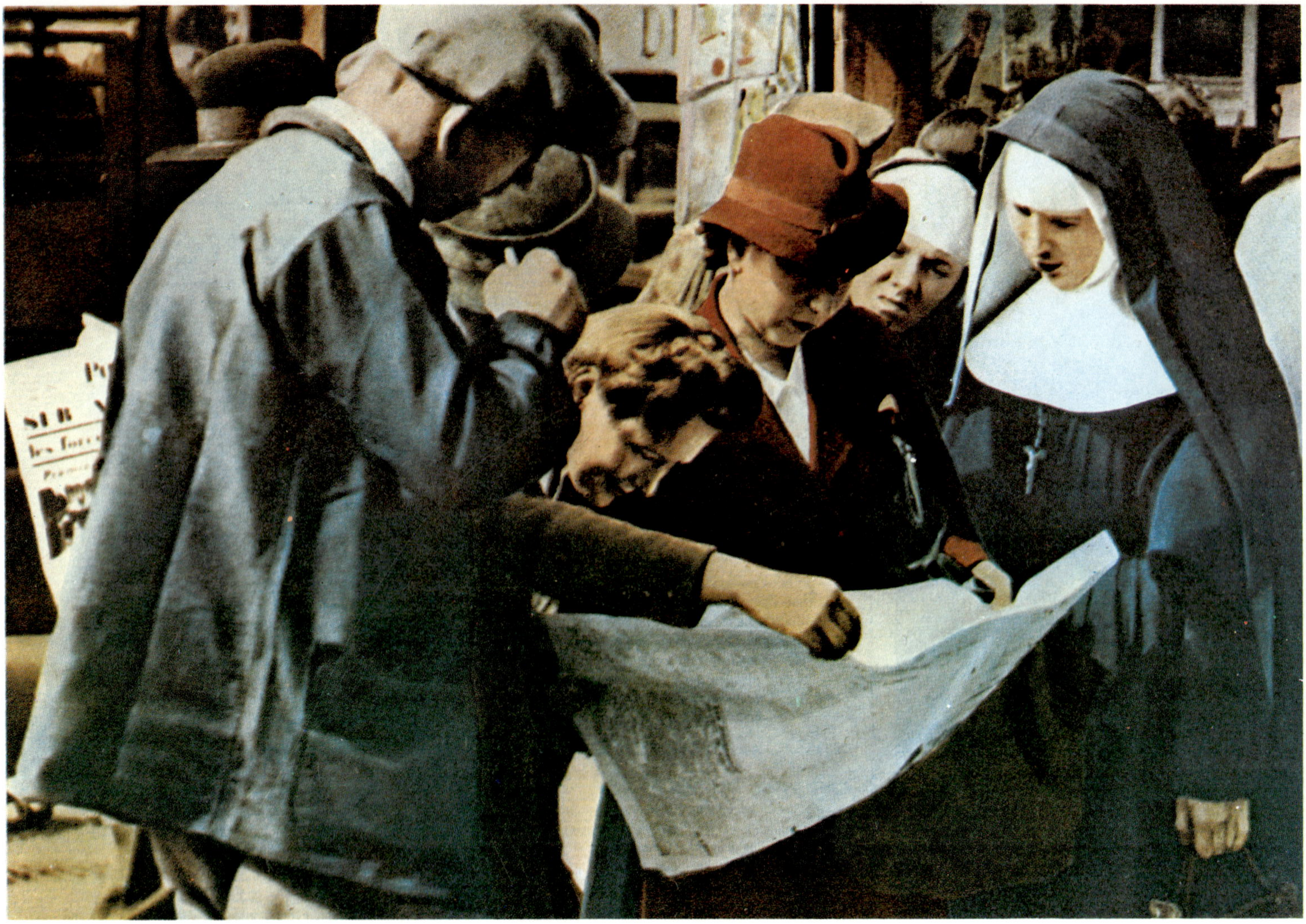

France. During the nine months of the 'phoney war' French public opinion lived in a state of expectation and even of illusion that the country would not be directly affected by the conflict. This picture shows Parisians poring over the newspapers which announce the beginning of the German offensive on 10 May 1940.

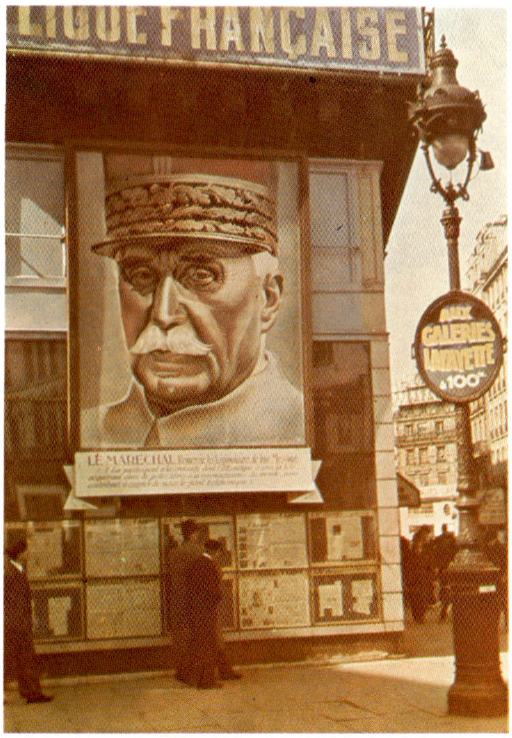

In the period following the collapse and the armistice with Germany in 1940, Marshal Pétain was the object of a veritable cult throughout France. In the occupied zone groups such as Constantini's French League cited certain of the Vichy chief of state's declarations in favour of the League to develop a broad policy of collaboration with the occupying power. The headquarters of the French League and the newspaper *L'Appel* were on a corner of the Rue Chaussée d'Antin in Paris.

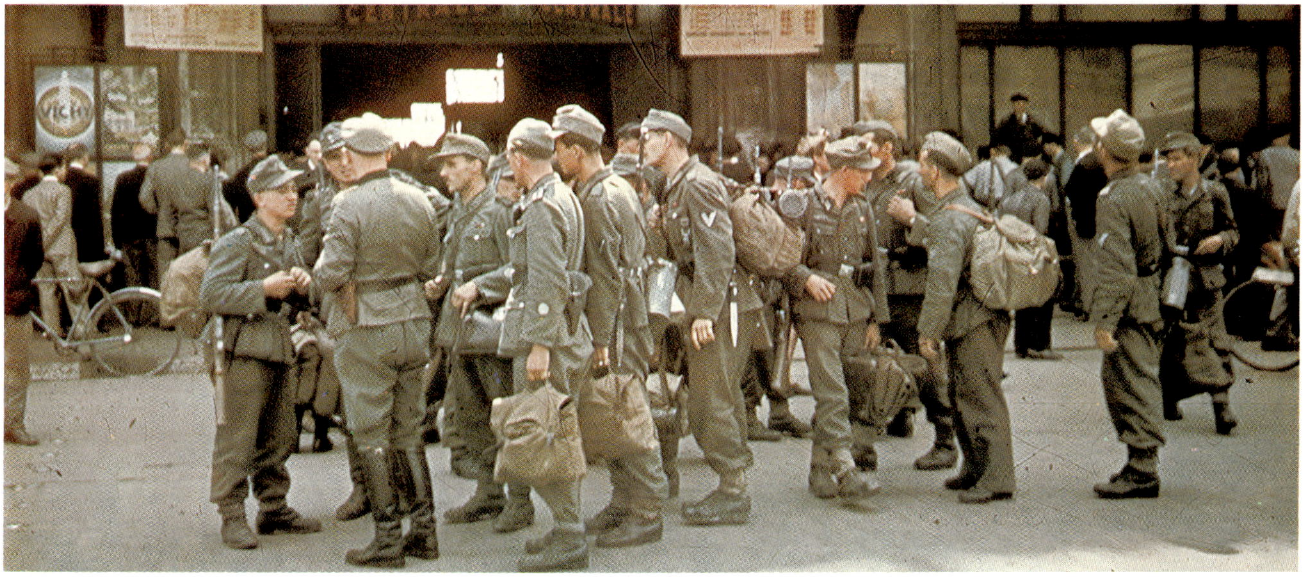

A group of German soldiers outside the Gare de Lyon in Paris. Hundreds of thousands of German soldiers passed through the railway stations of Paris, particularly after the war with the USSR had begun. For Hitler, France and especially Paris figured as an area of diversion and relaxation. From 1943 this situation changed with the increase in resistance activity.

Following the fall of Paris, Hitler was seized with a desire to make a rapid tour of the major sights of the French capital at an early hour in the morning, accompanied by his staff and his architect, Speer. Here Hitler is seen leaving the church of Saint Louis des Invalides, where he had mused over the tomb of Napoleon.

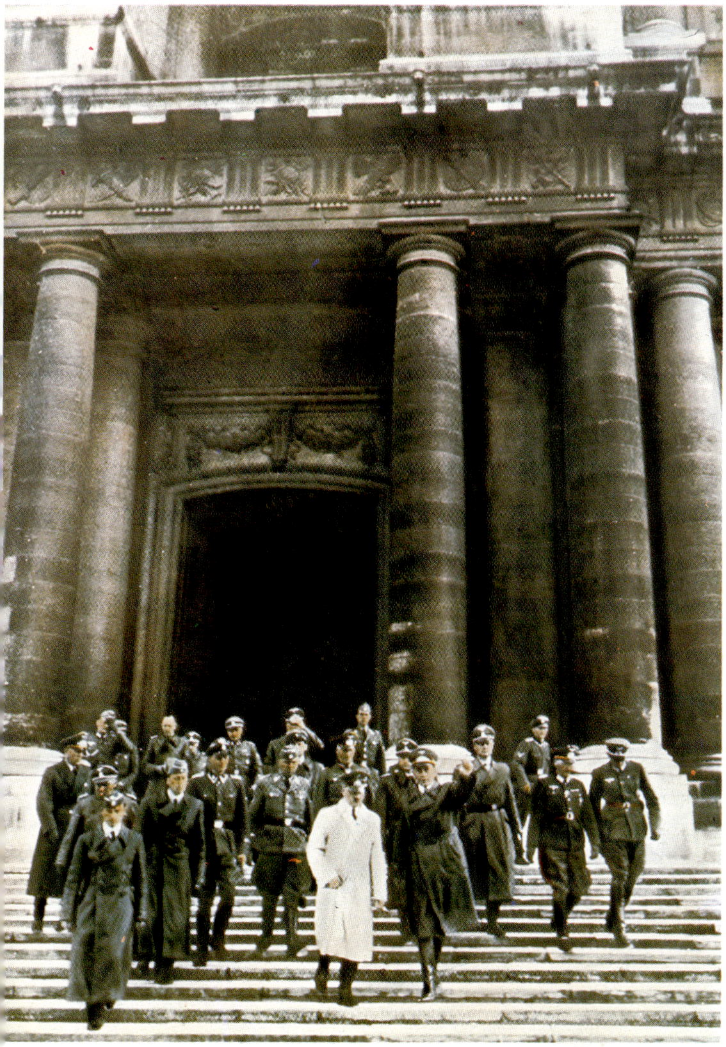

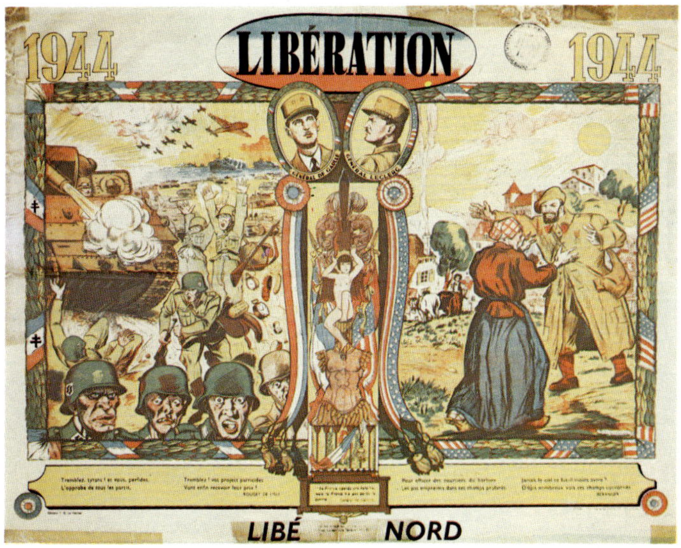

The Liberation of France. This depiction of the liberation, published at Sceaux in Sept. 1944, expresses the myths and the dreams of the French people. The Germans are seen in full flight under heavy attack from tanks and aircraft, abandoning the fruits of their plunder. Also shown are the return of a French prisoner of war and the re-establishment of a completely rural peacetime existence. Inset portraits of de Gaulle and Leclerc, the two architects of the liberation, are also included. (From the collection of the Comité d'histoire de la deuxième Guerre Mondiale.)

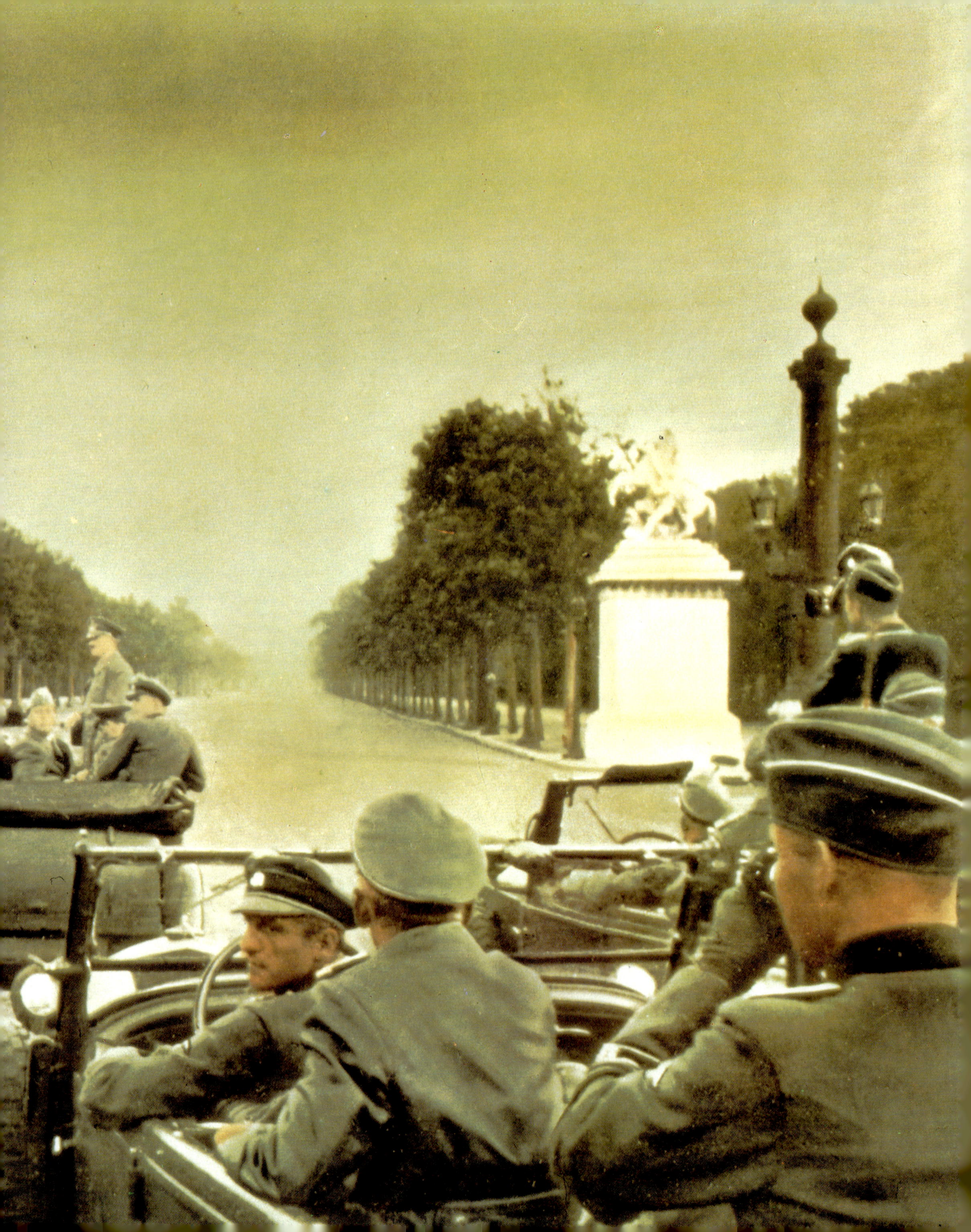

Occupied France. Hitler drives along the Avenue des Champs Elysées during his visit to Paris in June 1940.

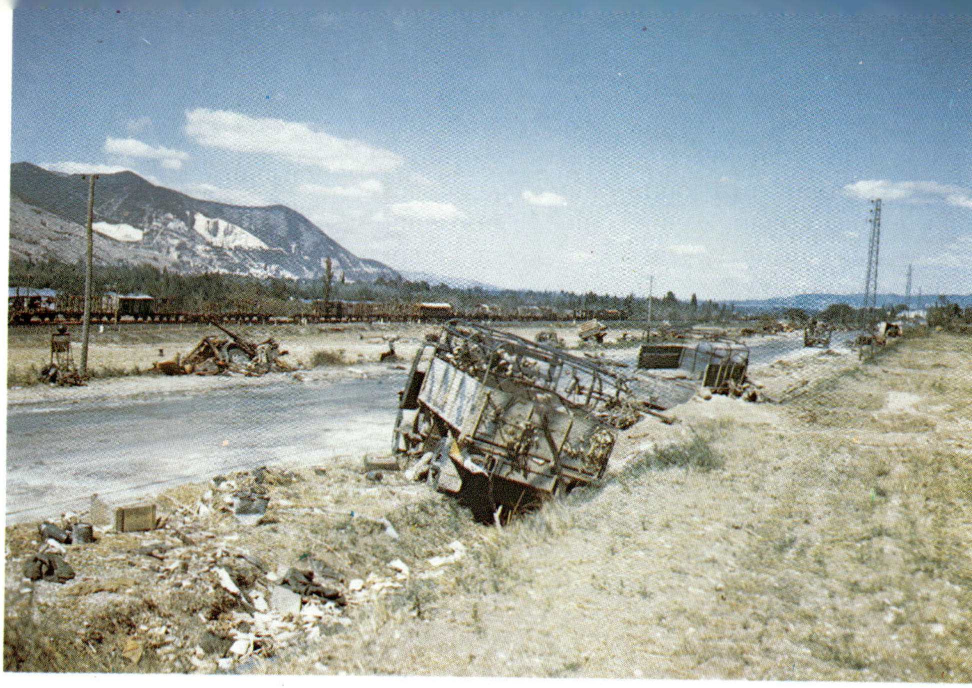

The Liberation of France. Following the landings in Provence on 15 Aug. 1944, the German 19th Army, under General Wiese, was able to withdraw and to retreat northwards up the Rhône valley. However, near Montelimar (photograph) Allied aircraft began to make heavy attacks on the main road and the Marseilles–Lyons railway line, inflicting severe losses of men and supplies on the German forces. One month after the landings the whole of southeast France was liberated.

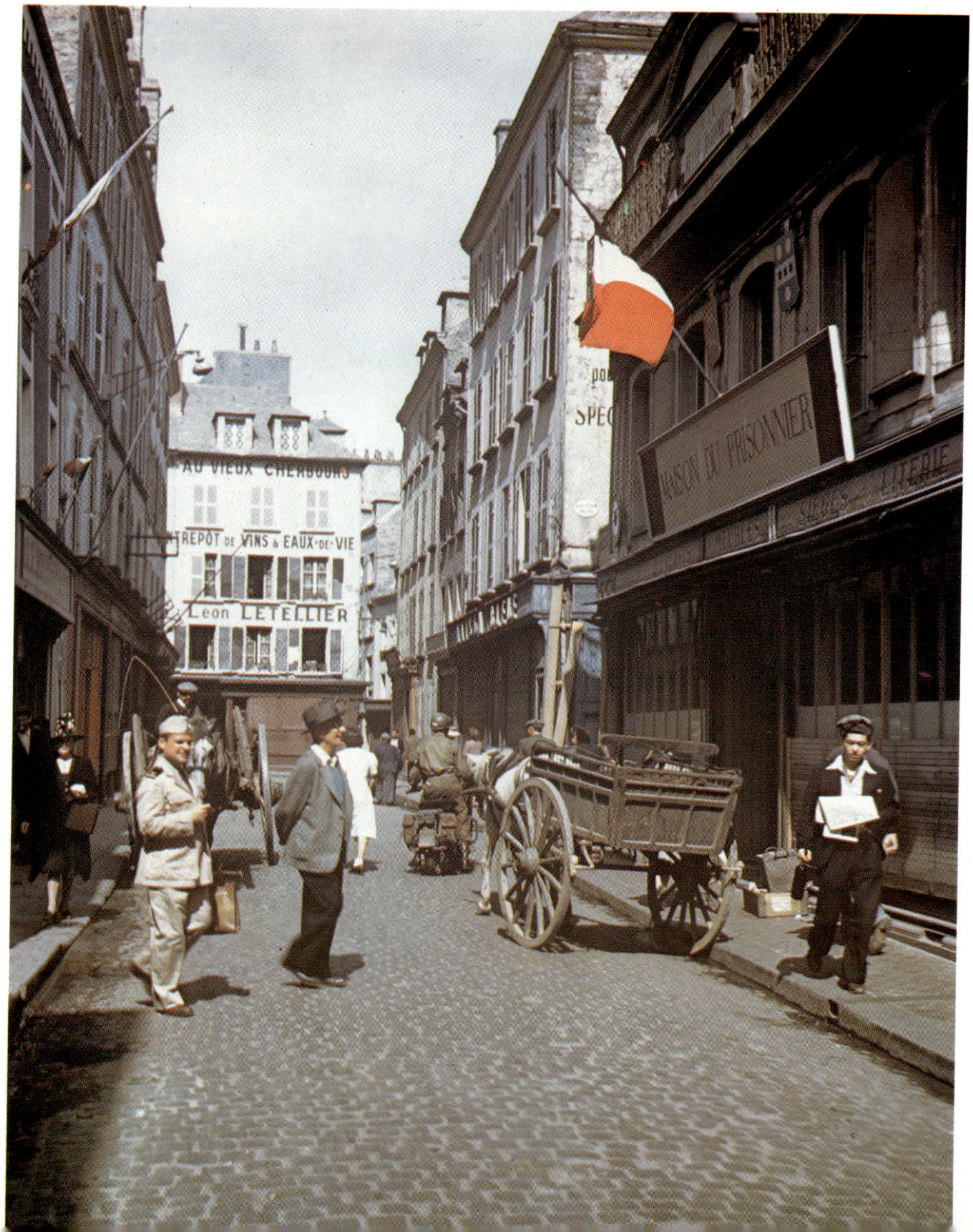

Following the liberation life goes on as usual in a part of Cherbourg which has been spared in the fighting. The change is marked by the presence of several Allied soldiers and the reappearance of the French flag. The very traditional quality of French provincial life at the end of the war (shops, horse-drawn vehicles) can be observed, as can the *Maison du Prisonnier* (POWs' aid centre). The fate of their prisoners of war was one of the French people's main anxieties during the war.

The liberation of Normandy was far more difficult and destructive than that of Provence. The small town of Saint-Lô (photograph) suffered heavy attacks from the air from 6 June onwards and was occupied by American forces only in mid-July. By then the buildings of the town were reduced to heaps of ruins and US army engineers had to clear the roads with bulldozers to allow convoys to pass through.

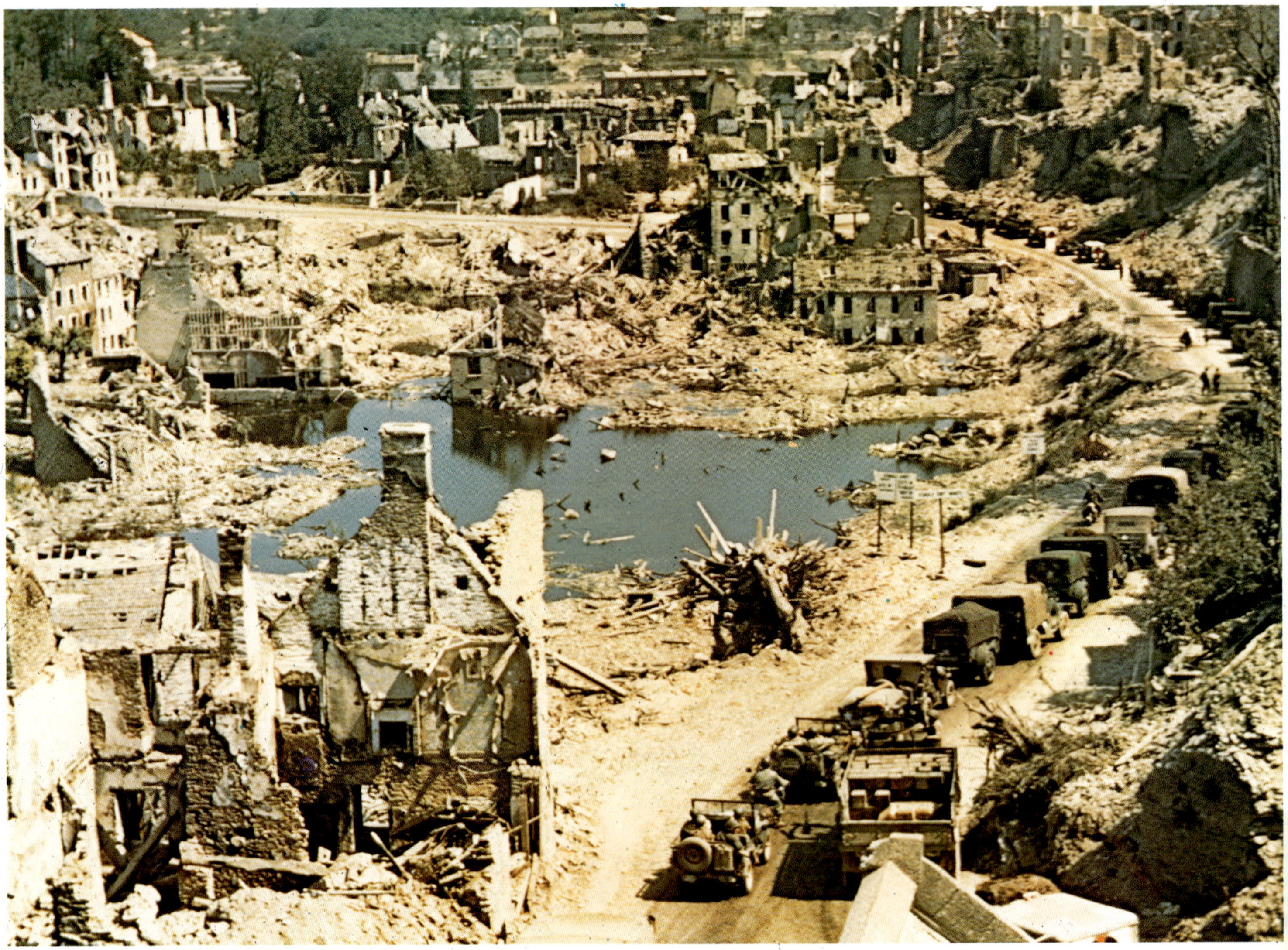

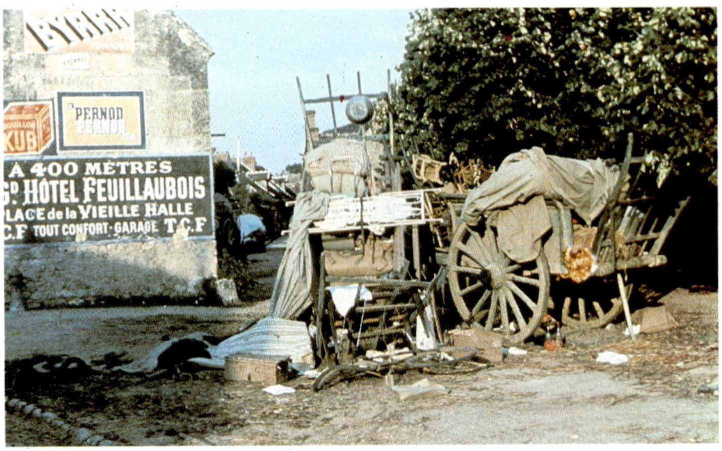

The French campaign of 1940. During this traumatic period the Allied troops made repeated attempts to slow down the enemy advance by putting up improvised barriers at the entrances to towns and villages. These barricades, which were insufficiently defended, proved to be derisory obstacles and had no influence on the course of events.

The campaign of 1940 has been seen subsequently as a tragic illustration of the devastating effect of the Blitzkrieg. The German advance towards the sea proved to be unstoppable as early as 13 May, the day on which German troops crossed the River Meuse. The same phenomenon was repeated in June after the breaking of the front on the Somme and the Aisne. Motor-cyclists went ahead of the advancing columns of tanks and vehicles. Their function was to reconnoitre the advance and to estimate how much opposition would be offered by pockets of resistance.

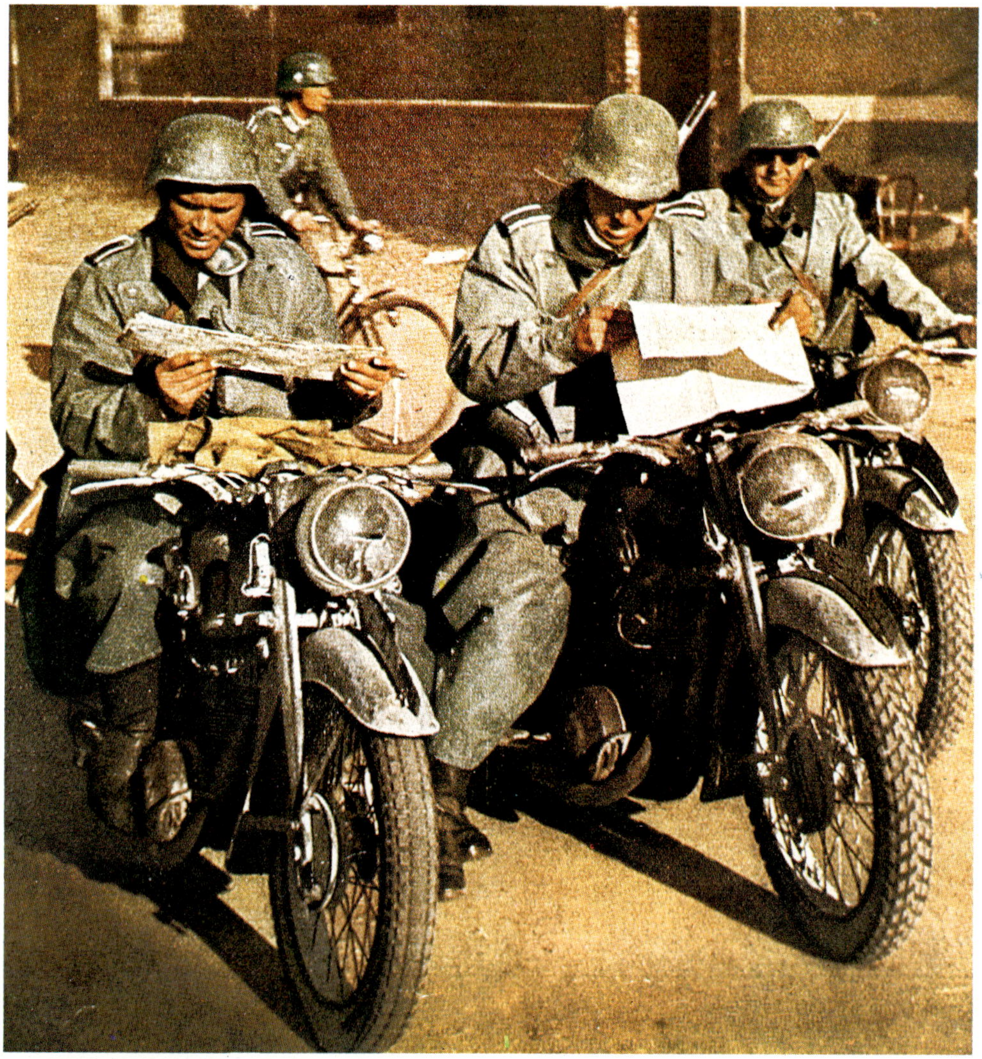

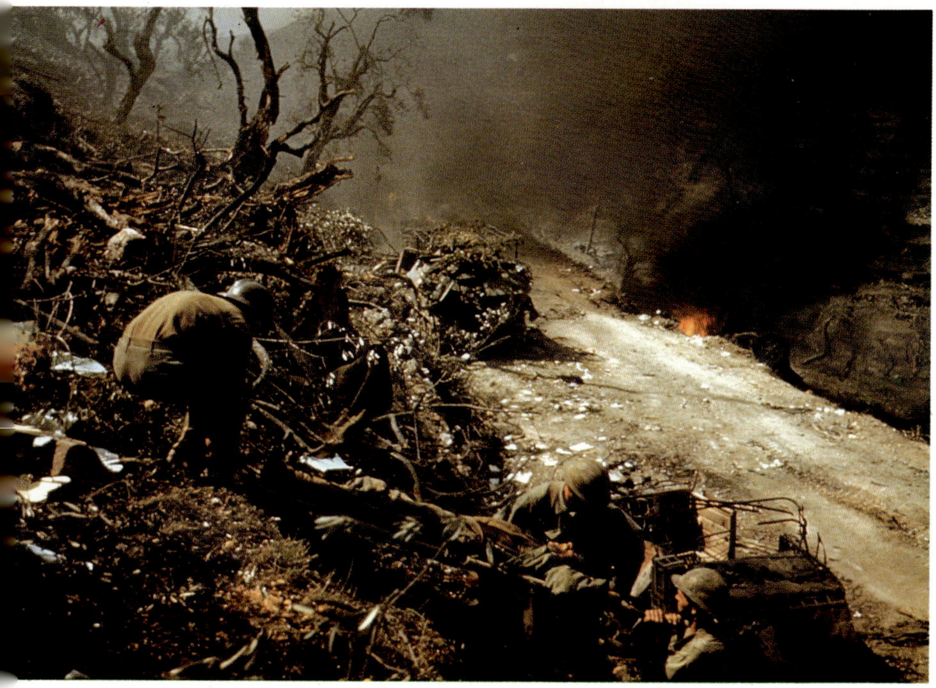

The French Expeditionary Corps. In the spring of 1944 the Corps, stationed in Italy under the command of General Juin, consisted of four divisions. It played a decisive part in the breaking of the German positions on the Gustav Line. The breakthrough in the Aurunci mountains brought about the evacuation of Cassino by the Germans. As it advanced, however, the 3rd Algerian Division ran into an ambush after the capture of Esperia and suffered heavy losses (as can be seen in the picture). The attack on Monte d'Oro allowed the enemy to be cleared from the road and the advance to be resumed.

De Gaulle at the Free French headquarters in Carlton Gardens in London in Feb. 1943.

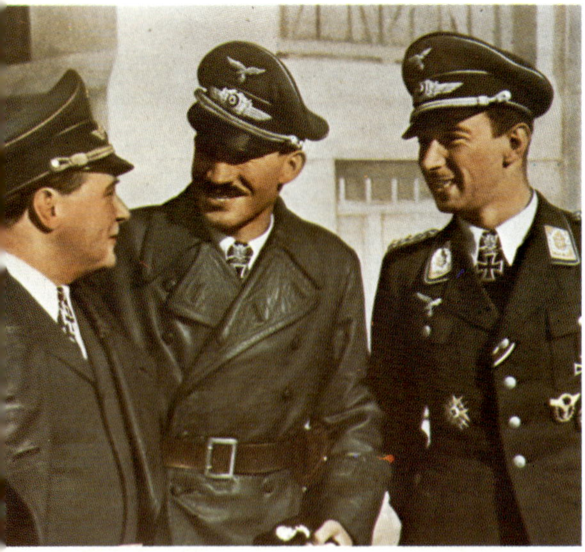

Adolf Galland. He is seen here in the company of Udet (on the left), a German air ace of the First World War and one of the creators of the Luftwaffe, and Molders (on the right), a distinguished fighter pilot who lost his life in 1941. Galland was to play a major role in the Luftwaffe in the course of the war. During the French campaign and the Battle of Britain he became famous as a Messerschmitt Me-109 pilot and the commander of the Gruppe III (3rd Group) of Jagdgeschwader 26. In 1941 he was promoted, as Molders' successor, to be inspector general of fighters and had the task of organizing the defence of the Reich against Allied air raids. In this post, however, he was unsuccessful in getting priority for the production of jet aircraft. He was dismissed in Jan. 1945 and ended the war in a fitting manner as the commander of a squadron of Messerschmitt Me-262 jets.

De Gaulle. From the time of his radio appeal to the French nation, made from London on 18 June 1940, De Gaulle was to embody the spirit of French resistance in the eyes of the world. However, the general wanted to go beyond the military sphere and to make him and his movement, the Free French, recognized straight away as the legitimate French government. He could not make this claim without creating difficulties with the Allies, particularly the Americans, who were fearful of De Gaulle's intransigence and did not wish to prejudge the decisions the French people would have to take after the war. In addition, Roosevelt underestimated the position which the leader of Free France held in an increasingly important segment of French public opinion. De Gaulle's government was not recognized by the great powers until Oct. 1944. Here the general is seen in Aug. 1945, as he is greeted by General George C. Marshall on an airfield in Washington, DC.

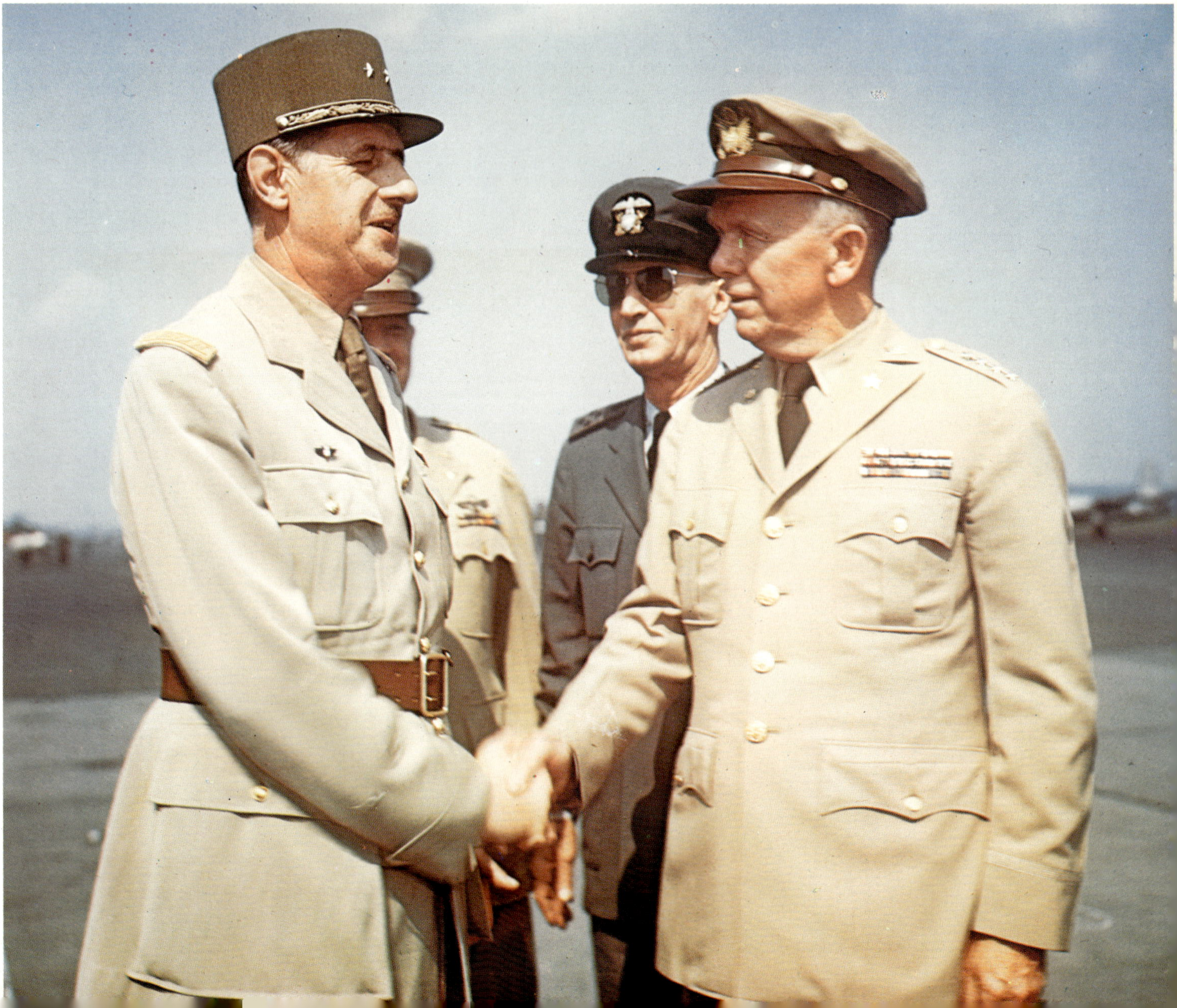

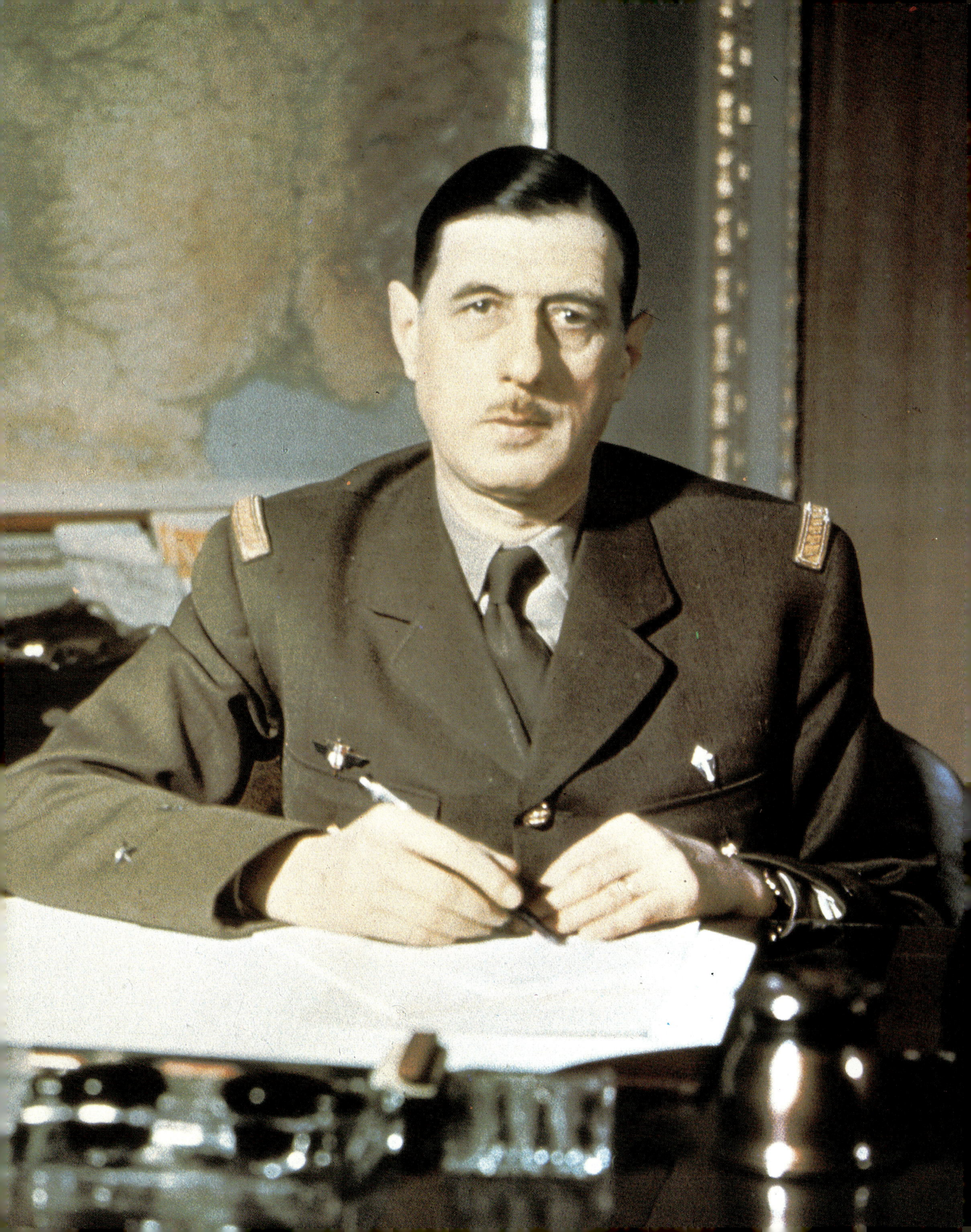

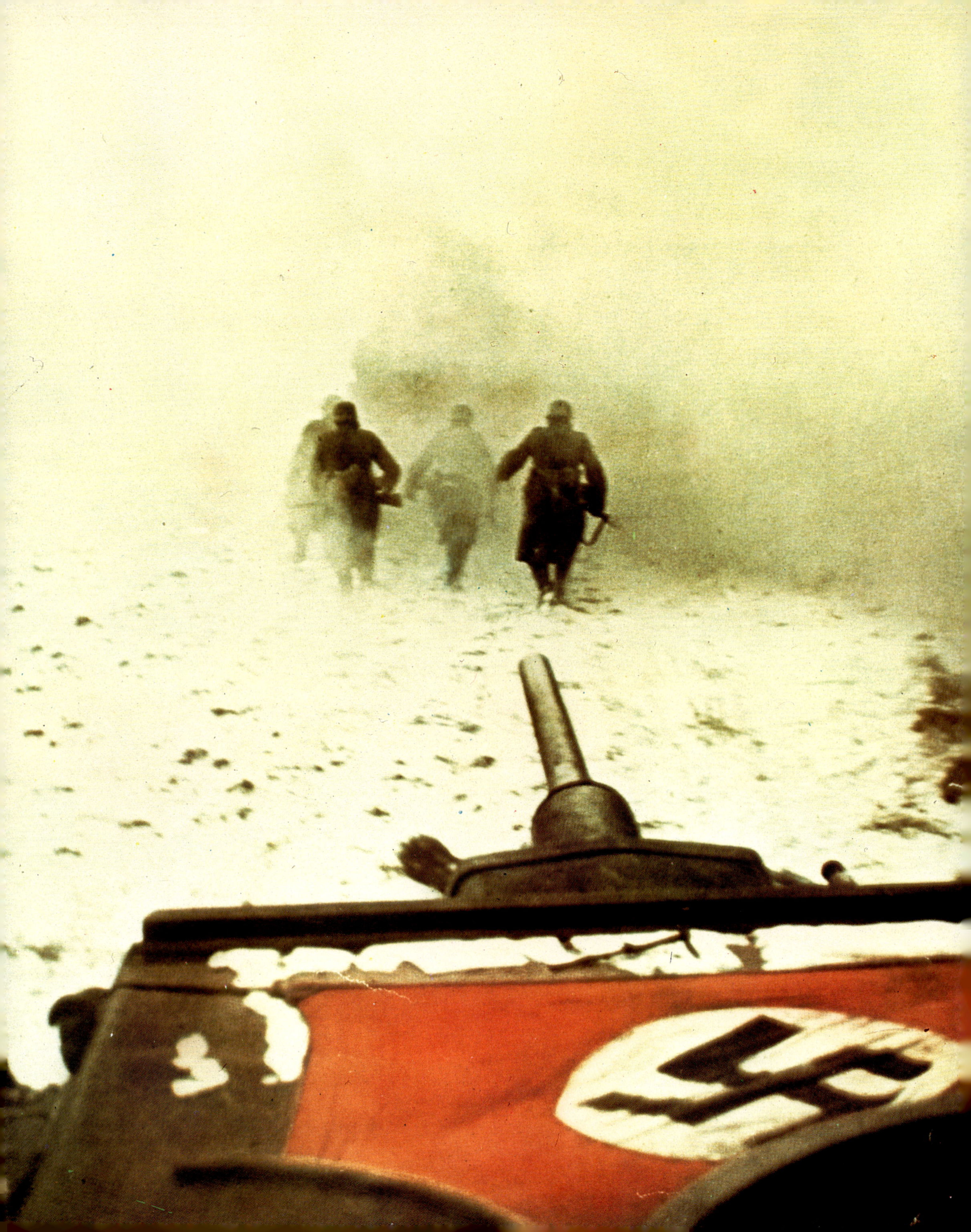

The German-Soviet War. German infantry moving forward under the protection of tanks during the battle for Moscow in Dec. 1941.

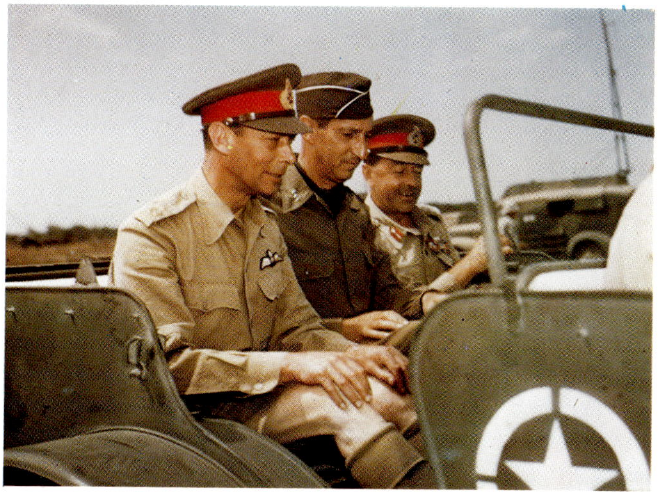

George VI. Throughout the war George VI carried out all the duties of a constitutional monarch punctiliously, overcoming his great natural shyness in order to do so. During the Blitz he shared the trials of the people of London and visited hospitals and bombed areas. He also made visits to the major theatres of war. He is seen here in Italy in the company of Generals Clark and Alexander, before a review of troops. George VI's conduct during the war helped to reinforce the popularity of the British monarchy.

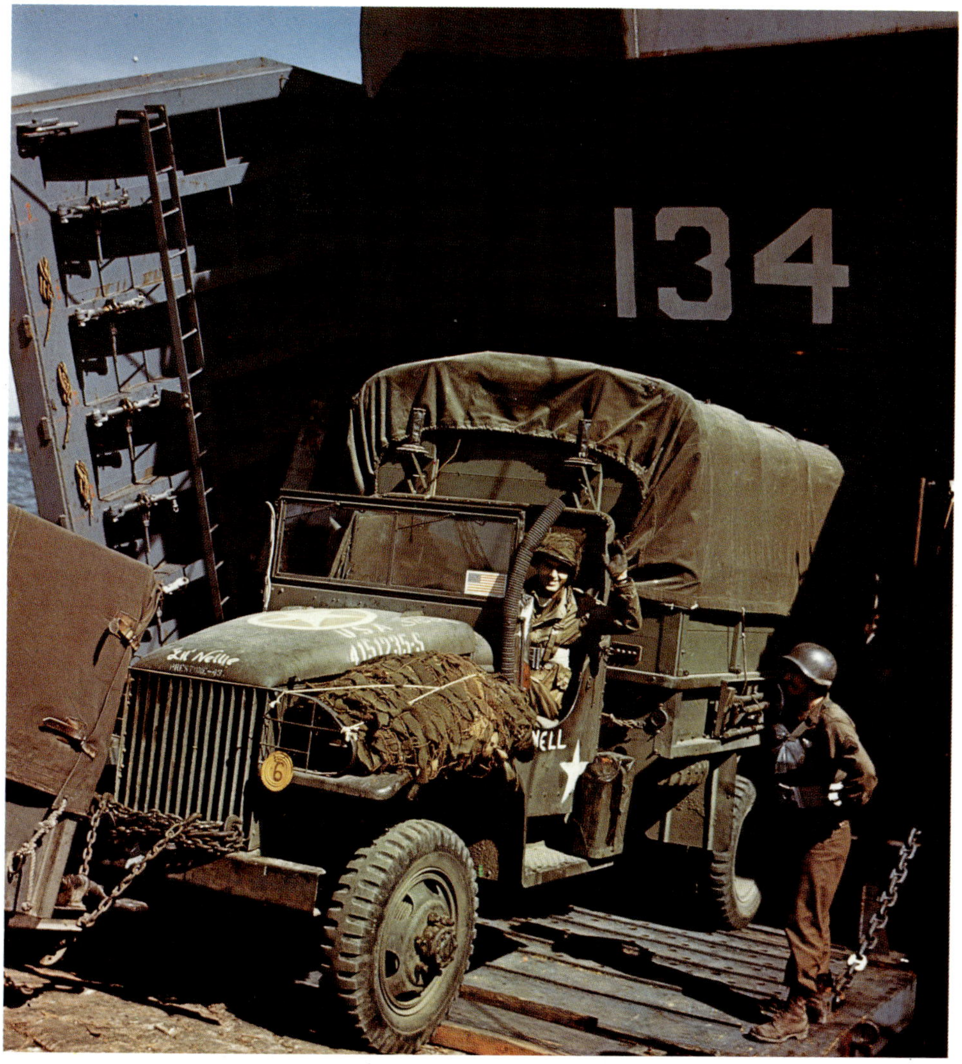

The GMC. This truck, identified with the initials of the General Motors Corporation, was one of the most widely used not only in the American forces but also in those of the other Allies, including the USSR. It had three driving axles, a carrying capacity of 2.5 tons, weighed 4.5 tons, could travel 240 mi. (400 km) on one tank of fuel and was a virtual maid of all work. During the war more than 800,000 GMC trucks were built, 100,000 of these being supplied to the USSR.

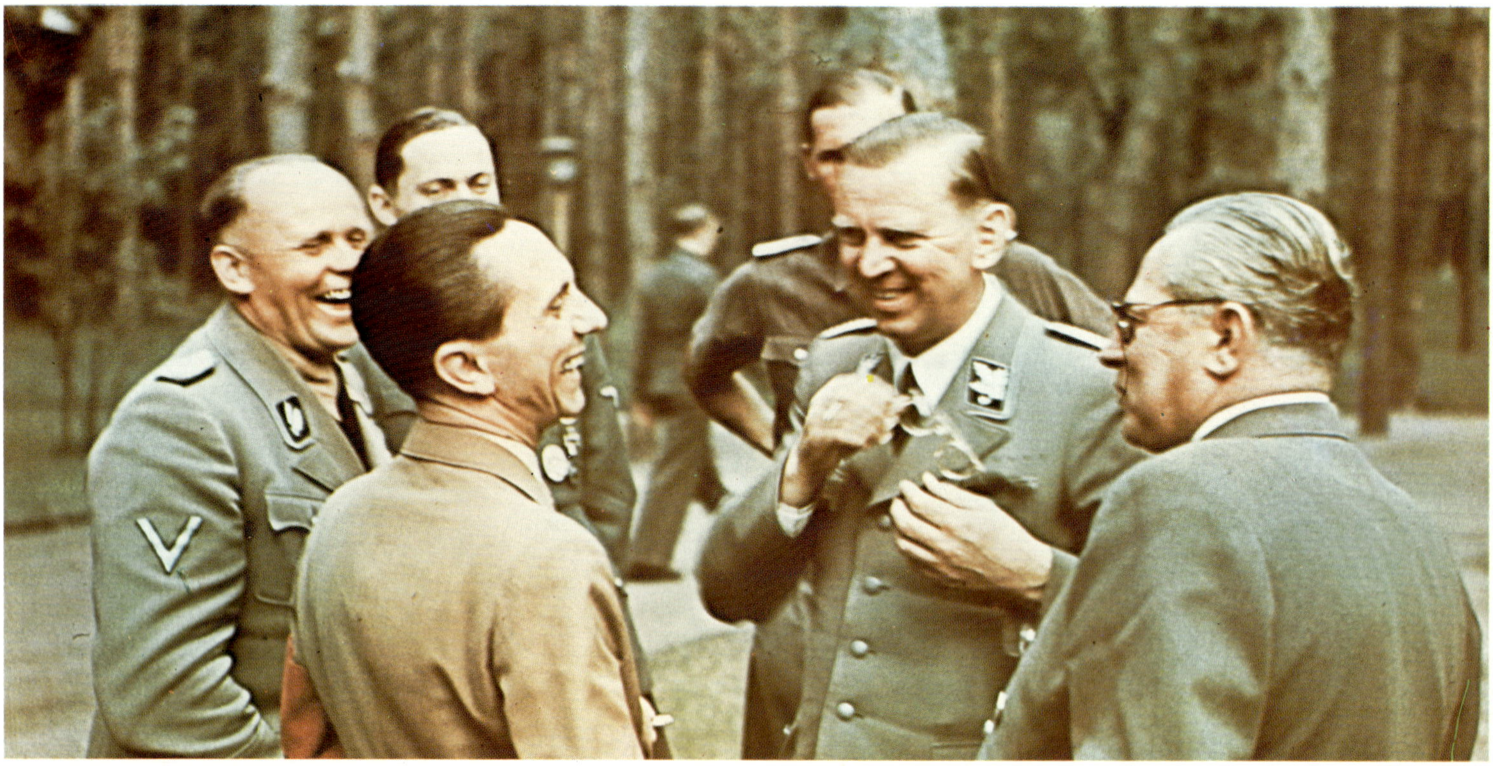

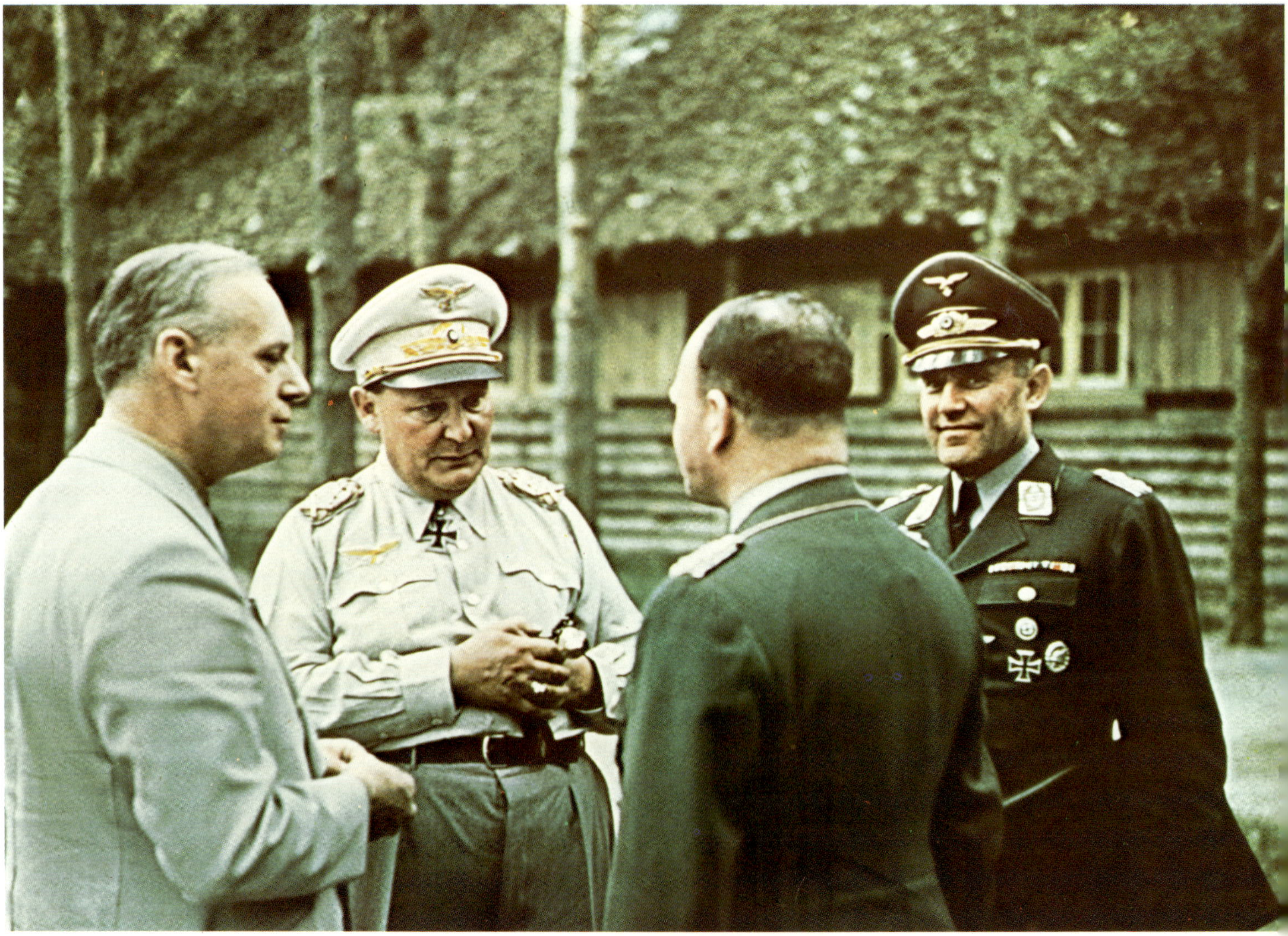

Goebbels. An ambitious, intelligent and cynical man, he was one of the organizers of the Nazi Party and founded the journal *Der Angriff* ('The Attack'). When the Nazis came to power he was made minister of propaganda and information. In this capacity he was able to influence public opinion by means of the press, radio and cinema in particularly effective ways. This effectiveness was seen again during the war, as Goebbels exploited the themes of 'total war', 'Judaeo-Bolshevik conspiracy' or 'secret weapons'. Sufficiently clear-sighted to regret the war on the eastern front, he nevertheless stayed faithful to Hitler until the end, committing suicide, with his wife and children, in the bunker of the Reich Chancellery in Berlin. He is seen here at Hitler's headquarters at Vinnitsa in the Ukraine in 1942, in the company of members of Hitler's personal staff. Hitler's photographer, Heinrich Hoffman, is on the right.

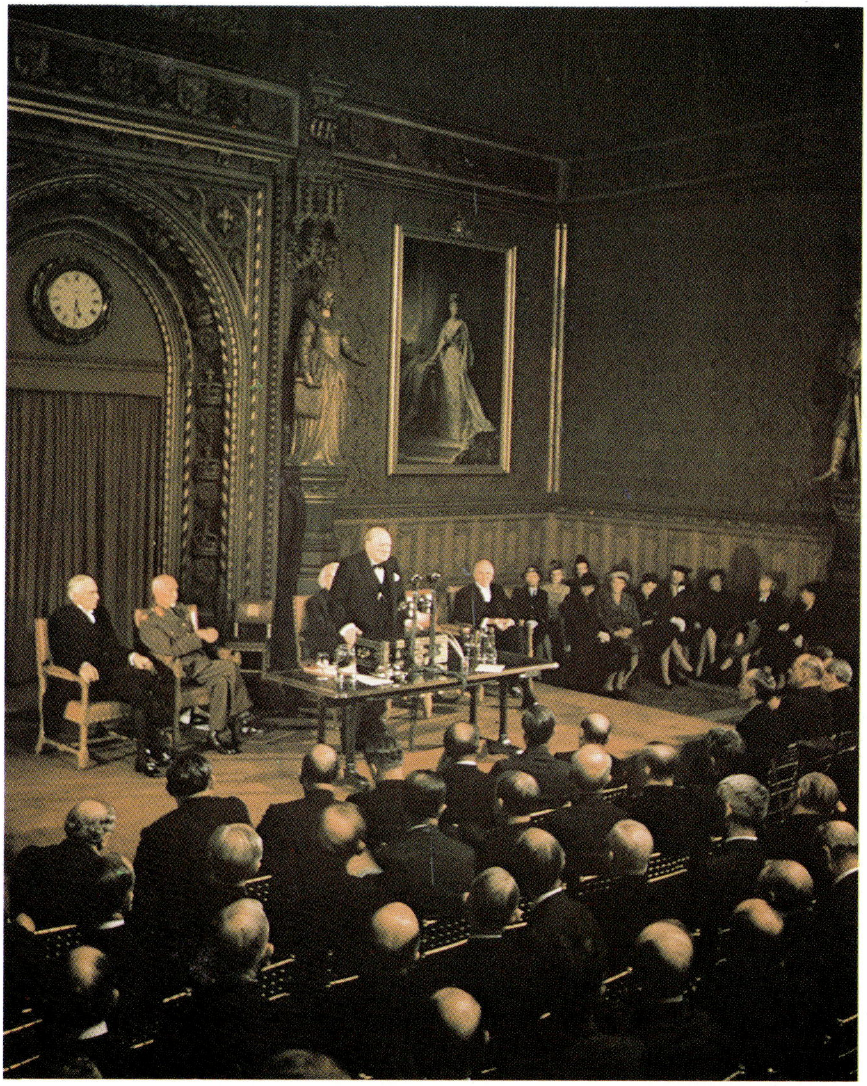

Göring. A former member of the Richthofen squadron during the First World War, he played a major role in the creation of the Nazi Party and its assumption of power. From 1933 he was the second-most important person in the regime. He set up both the political police, which was to become the Gestapo, and the first concentration camps. He was responsible for the four-year plan to mobilize the economy on a war basis and, most importantly, he was Reich air minister. He set up the Third Reich's new Luftwaffe which demonstrated its overwhelming superiority in the campaigns in Poland and France, but suffered its first setback during the Battle of Britain. From 1943 onwards, Göring was in semi-disgrace following the reverses of the Luftwaffe at Stalingrad and in the air battle over Germany. From then on the clear-sighted man who had opposed the idea of war in 1939 sank into drugged reveries in the luxurious surroundings of his house and estate of Karinhall. Arrested by the Allies and tried at Nuremberg, he eventually succeeded in committing suicide and thus avoided death by hanging. Here Göring is seen in company with Ribbentrop (on his right) and Milch (bare-headed, back to camera) at Hitler's headquarters at Vinnitsa in the Ukraine during the summer of 1942.

Great Britain. Britain's democratic institutions continued to function throughout the war and the role of Parliament was considerable. However, from 10 May 1940 onwards political life was dominated by the personality of Churchill. The old warrior, who was truly a charismatic leader, had the merit of never hiding the truth from the British people. He is seen here introducing the South African prime minister, General Smuts, to an assembly of Parliament on 21 Oct. 1942.

Great Britain was spared from invasion during the Second World War. However, contrary to British experience in previous conflicts, the country was to suffer the destructive consequences of war on its own soil. From Sept. 1940 to May 1941, during the Blitz, the Luftwaffe attacked towns in southern Britain and particularly London, inflicting considerable damage on the East End and the City. (The picture shows a scene near St Paul's Cathedral). London and its surrounding areas were to be the target of V1 flying bombs and V2 rockets from June 1944 until March 1945. The total of British civilian deaths caused by the German bombing and V-weapon offensives exceeded 60,000.

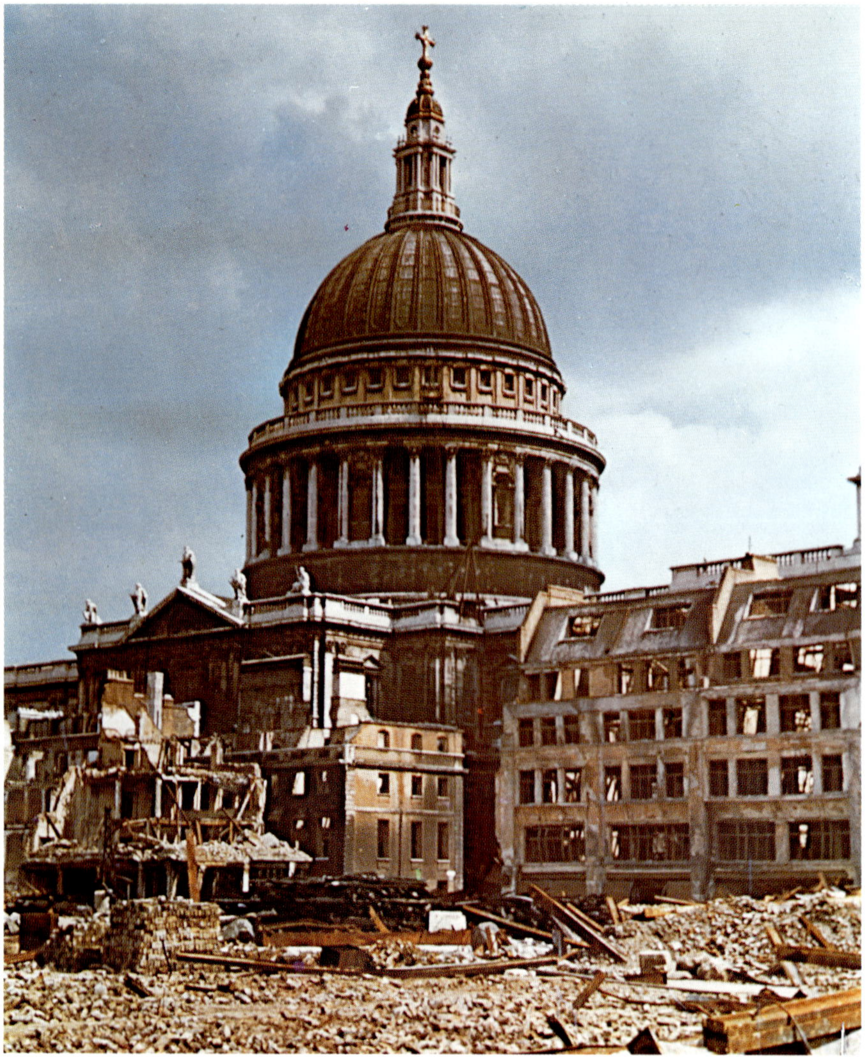

After a belated and timid rearmament programme in the 1930s Britain began to rearm seriously after the Munich Agreement of Sept. 1938. Once the war had begun Britain put its economy on a true war footing from the end of 1939, mobilizing all the country's labour and industrial resources. The effort was particularly concentrated on shipbuilding and aircraft construction, in accordance with the strategic ideas of Britain's political and military leaders. Thus the numbers of aircraft built rose from 8000 in 1941 to 20,000 in 1942 and reached 26,000 per annum in subsequent years. This picture shows De Havilland Mosquito twin-engined fighter-bombers on the assembly line. The Mosquito was among the most successful British aircraft of the war.

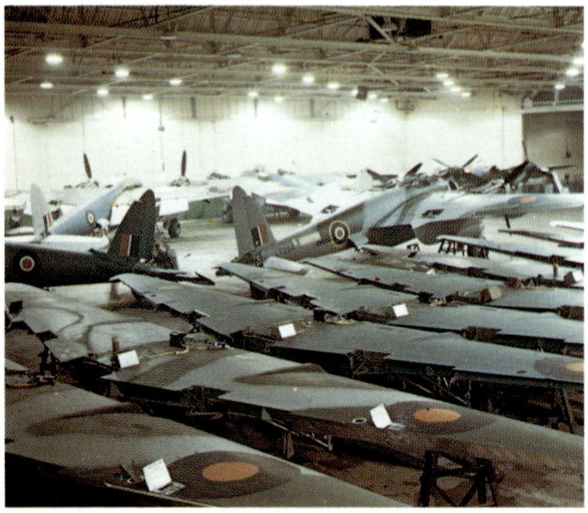

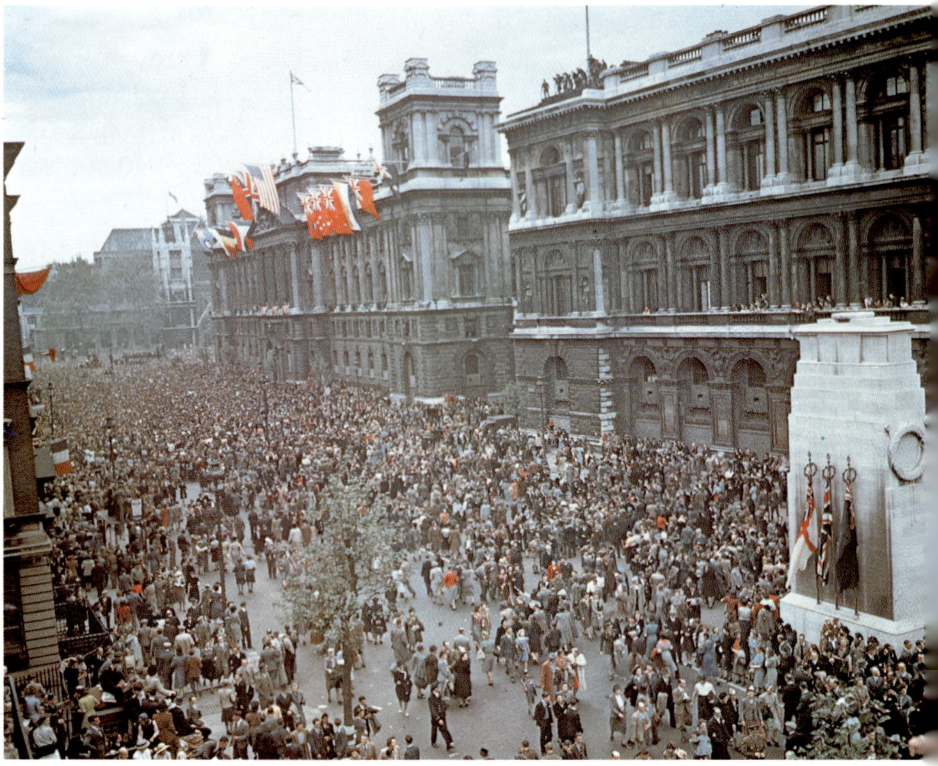

Victory in Europe gave rise to an immense outpouring of joy in Britain. This picture shows the crowds in Whitehall near the Cenotaph in London on 8 May 1945. A feeling of pride was apparent throughout the country which, alone among the Allies, had borne the weight of the struggle right from the beginning to the end. However, in 1945 British morale was not what it had been. The almost sporting zest displayed at the time of the Battle of Britain had been succeeded by weariness and a muted irritation. As is shown by the success of the Beveridge report, the broad mass of the population was expecting an immediate improvement in social conditions. This feeling of expectation is one of the explanations of Churchill's and the Conservatives' defeat in the general election of July 1945.

The Greater East Asia Co-prosperity Sphere. This Japanese version of Hitler's 'New Order', christened 'The Greater East Asia Co-prosperity Sphere', was officially adopted in 1940. It corresponded to Japan's zone of expansion, which the country considered indispensable to its economic and military security, and its rather vague boundaries proved to be adjustable in accordance with the progress of Japanese conquests in Southeast Asia. The name chosen had the advantage of disguising Japanese imperialism and the 'New Order' it proposed to establish. Japanese propaganda thoroughly exploited the theme of Asian solidarity and of the struggle, led by Japan, of a yellow Asia against the white oppressor, a theme which did not find the favourable response which might have been expected from people colonized by the western powers. Such propaganda had in reality very little hold over them, in view of the harshness of Japanese occupation, as this poster printed in Ceylon in 1943 shows: it denounced the co-prosperity imposed on Asia by the Japanese and their puppets.

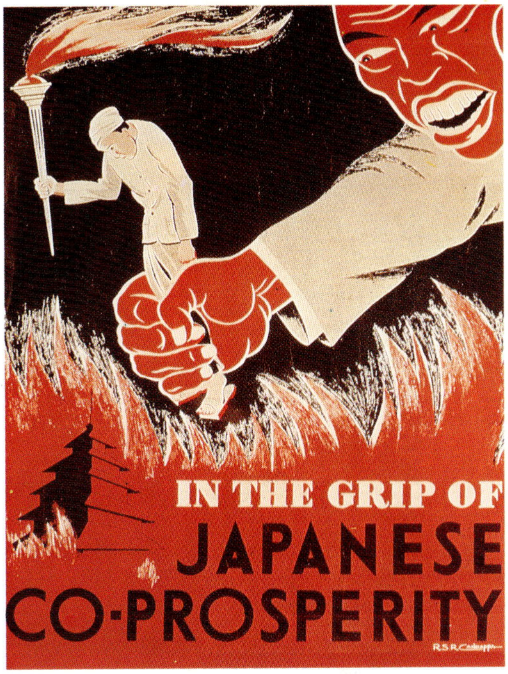

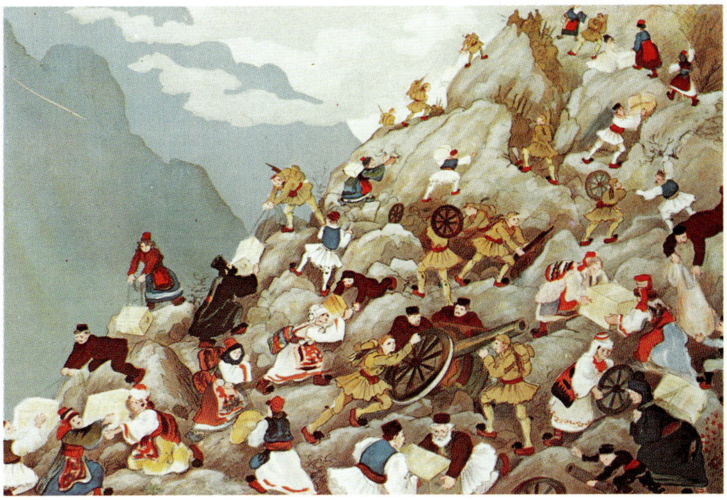

Greece. The attack launched against Greece in Oct. 1940 by Mussolini, who was jealous of Hitler's success, soon faltered. The Italian high command had underestimated not only the difficulties of the terrain and the climate but particularly the surprising resistance offered by the Greek army, which succeeded in going on to the offensive and in pushing back the Italians into Albania. In accordance with an old tradition dating from the time of the struggle against the Turks, the people of Epirus lent their assistance to the army, as is shown in this popular print.

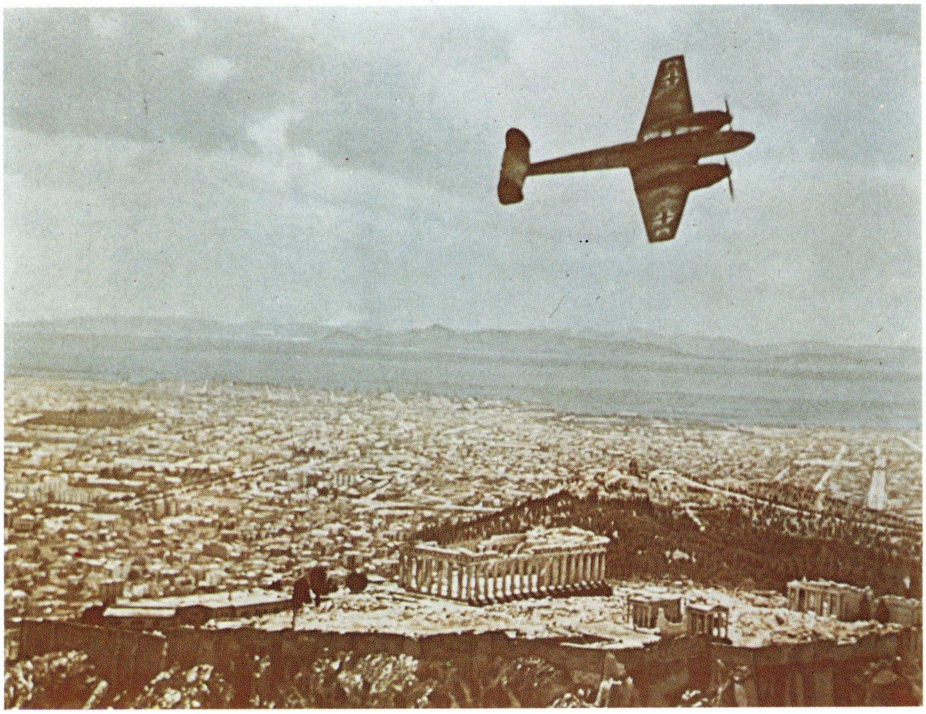

Hitler, who was determined to secure the German rear before the attack on the Soviet Union, and to pull Mussolini out of the Hellenic hornet's nest, decided to intervene in the Balkans at the beginning of April 1941. In spite of British help the Greek forces could not withstand the German attack and their defeat was brought about in less than a month. German troops entered Athens on 27 April. This picture of a Messerschmitt Bf-110 flying over the Acropolis illustrates this stunning German victory, which was the beginning of a period of terrible suffering for Greece.

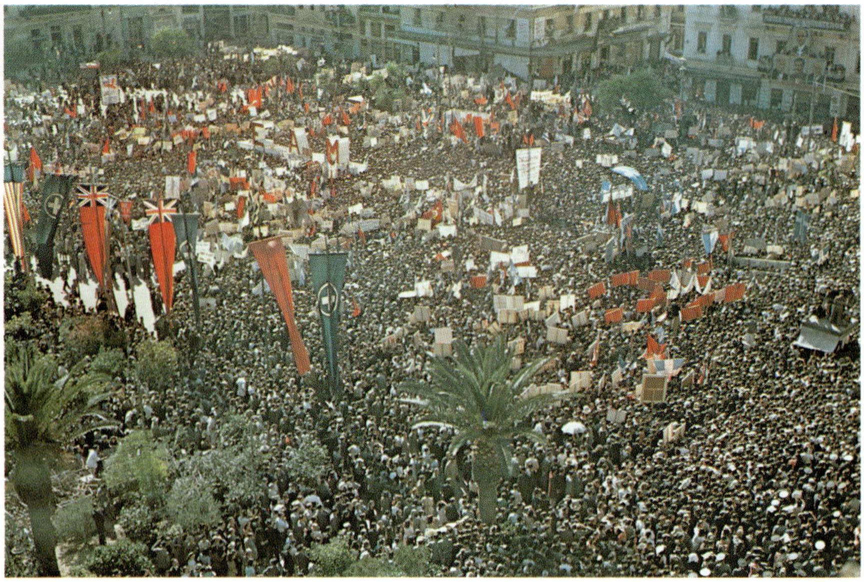

Following the German victory the king of Greece and the Greek government took refuge first in London and then in Cairo, while in Greece itself there appeared several resistance movements against the occupiers. Those movements were, however, deeply divided among themselves as regards the country's political and social future. The EAM (National Liberation Front) which was dominated by the Communists and commanded a people's army, ELAS, was by far the most important. On 18 Oct. 1944, a few days after British troops had entered Athens, EAM organized a mass demonstration (shown in this picture) in celebration of the liberation. Among the mingled Greek and Allied flags a placard bears the inscription 'Welcome British Army'. However, this state of grace would not last long. Churchill's main preoccupation was the disarming of ELAS. The British troops, who had recently disembarked, and who were relying on the support of right-wing forces, prepared for a confrontation. This was the starting point of a terrible civil war which lasted four years.

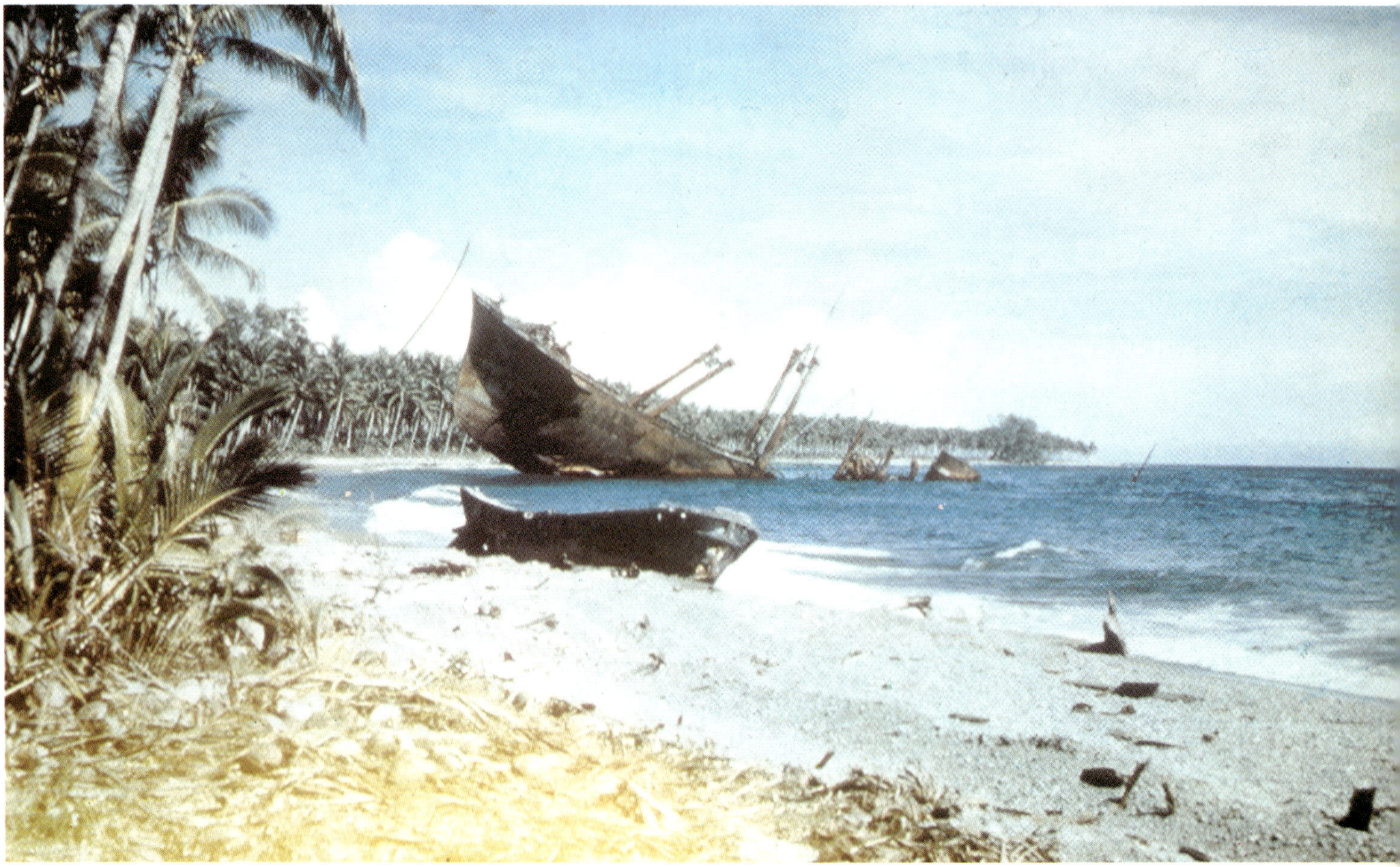

Guadalcanal. Because of the fierceness of the fighting which took place there from Aug. 1942 to Feb. 1943, Guadalcanal may well be called the Stalingrad of the Pacific. By confronting the Japanese at Guadalcanal, the Americans determined to end the offensive with which the Japanese intended to isolate Australia. In addition to the fighting on the island, there were numerous encounters at sea, in which both sides attempted to hinder the resupply of the other's troops on Guadalcanal. This picture shows a Japanese merchant vessel which had been wrecked and run aground as a consequence of a naval action.

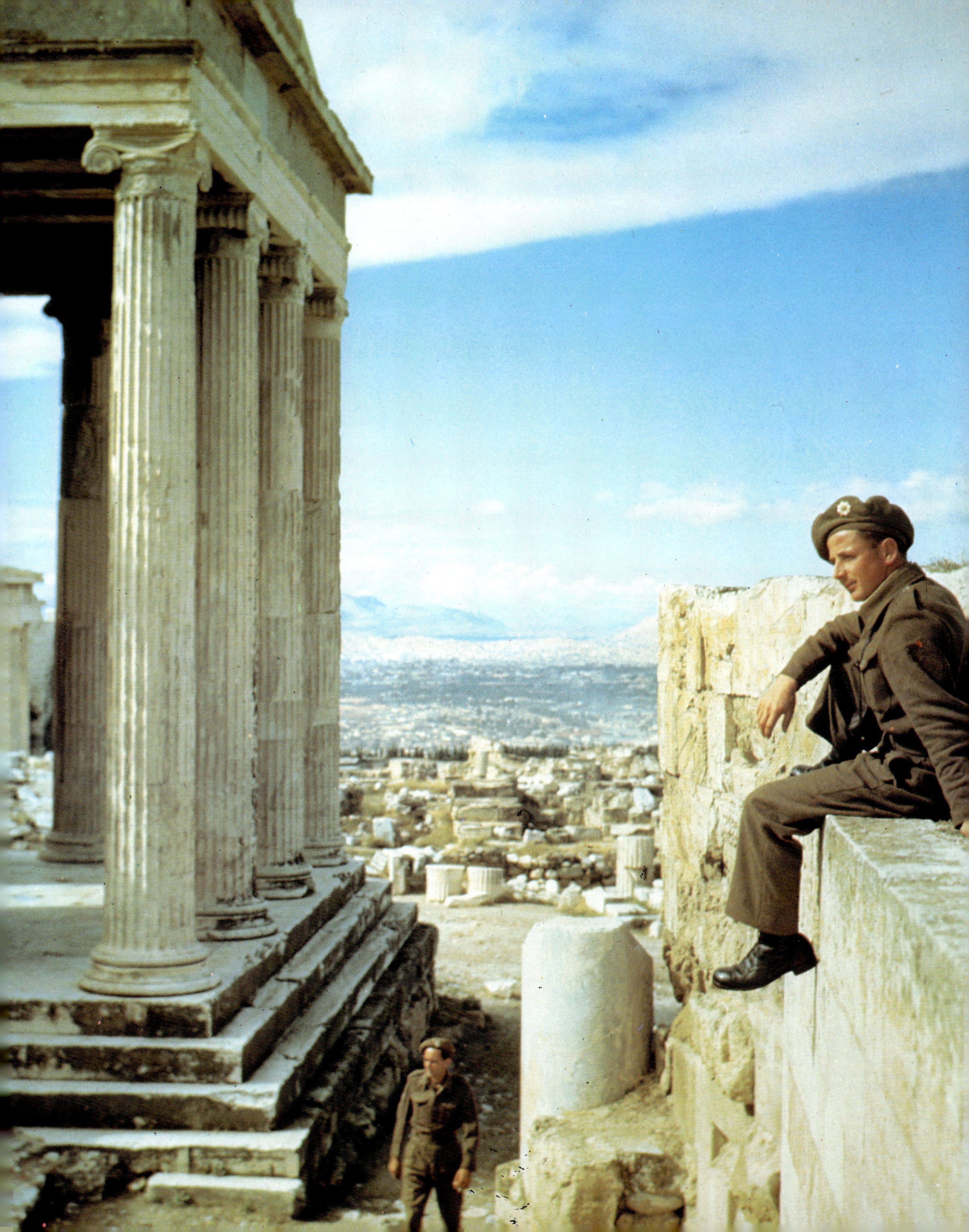

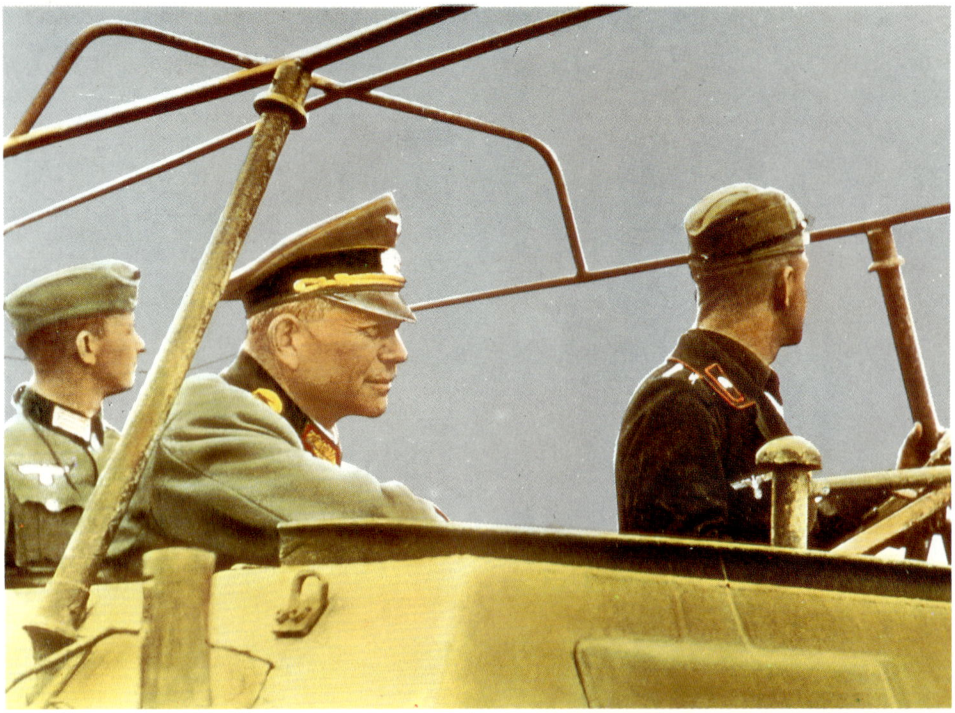

Guderian. In the Reichswehr (the army of Weimar Germany) Guderian was a passionate believer in the importance of tanks, in spite of the fact that Germany was forbidden to possess them by the Treaty of Versailles. He had been impressed with the role that tanks had played in the battle of Cambrai in 1917. When Hitler came to power, Guderian was given the opportunity to organize the first armoured divisions and develop new tactical ideas which were to be the basis of the Blitzkrieg. From 1939 to 1941 he demonstrated the dazzling possibilities of tank warfare, directing operations himself from his command vehicle (in the picture). After a period out of favour in 1942, in Feb. 1943 he was given the title of inspector general of armoured troops and reorganized the German tank forces. Following the bomb plot in July 1944, Guderian became chief of the general staff but was finally dismissed in March 1945 following constant disagreements with Hitler.

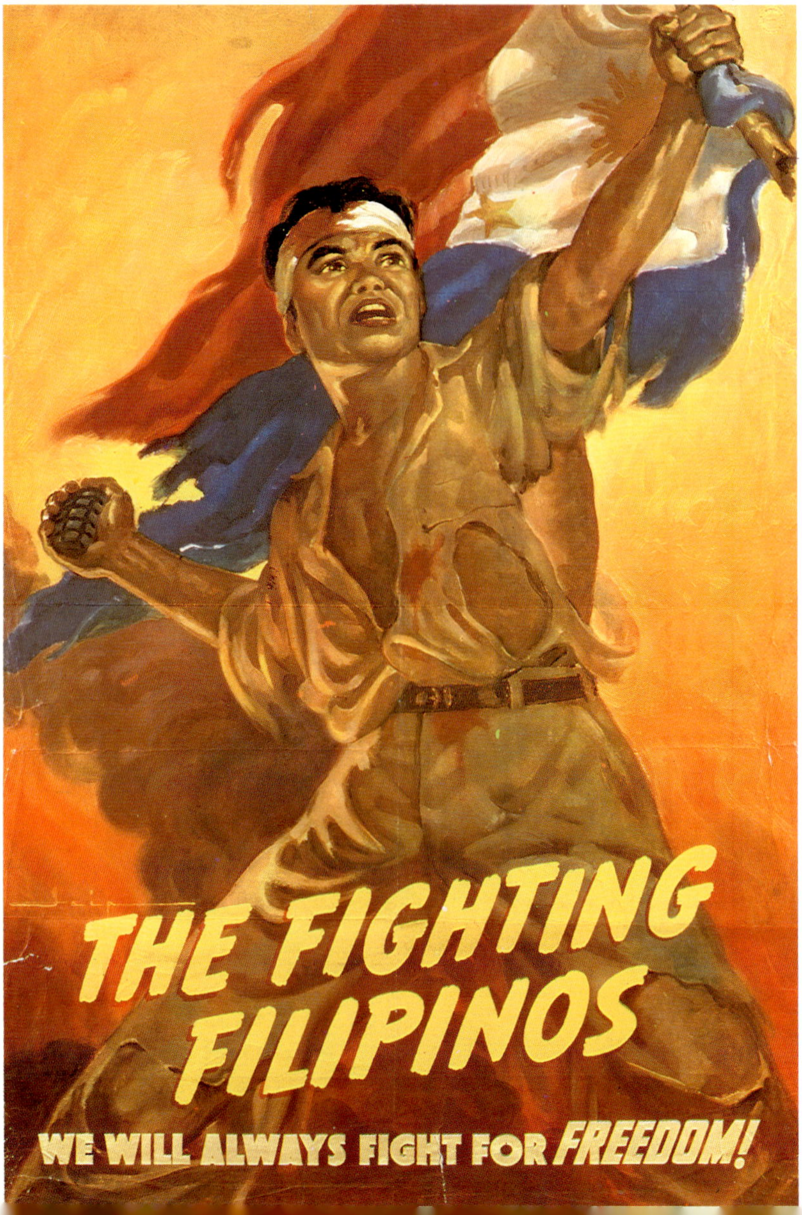

Guerrilla warfare. This became widespread during the Second World War. This was due partly to the size of the territories occupied by the European Axis powers and Japan, partly to the ideological nature of the conflict and partly to the use of modern technology in the form of radios and aircraft. These enabled scattered groups to stay in contact and arms to be dropped from the air. In the Far East the most important guerrilla movement was in the Philippines, as this poster emphasizes, where guerrillas fought against the Japanese from 1942 onwards. This was one of the reasons which induced General MacArthur to advocate the liberation of the Philippines as a way of putting an end to the excesses committed by the Japanese in reprisal for guerrilla activity. (A poster from the collection of the Musée des Deux Guerres Mondiales – BDIC (Universités de Paris)).

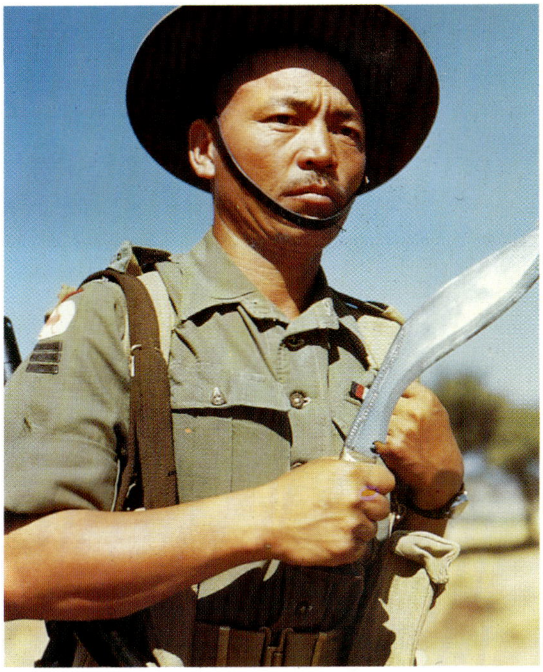

The Gurkhas. The first regiments of Gurkhas from Nepal were formed by Britain early in the 19th century. They proved to be an outstanding fighting force, serving with distinction in various theatres during the Second World War, notably in the Burma campaign. Here a Gurkha is shown with his kukri or fighting knife.

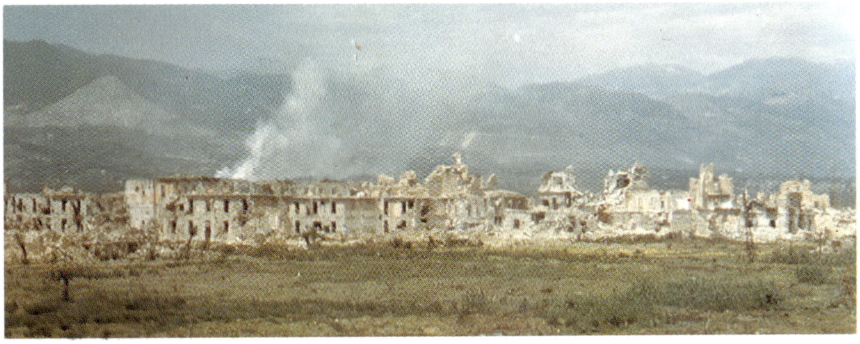

The Gustav Line, which was built by the Germans across the Italian peninsula between Rome and Naples, was the scene of fierce fighting throughout the winter of 1943–44. The Allied armies tried in vain to capture Cassino, both by direct attack and by attempting to outflank it over the mountains. In this picture can be seen the marshy valley of the Rapido river and the ruins of the town of Cassino which had undergone continuous air and artillery bombardment.

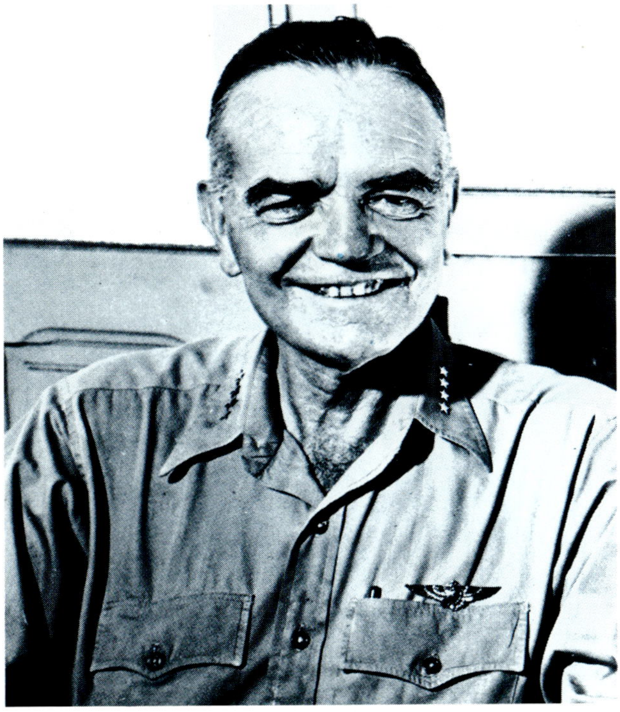

Halsey. He played a leading part in the defeat of Japan in the Pacific War. He was called in by Admiral Nimitz to resolve the stalemate in the Solomons campaign, and helped to draw up guidelines for tactics to counter the night-fighting skills of the Japanese. These tactics later helped to prevent the Japanese resupplying their troops in the Solomon Islands. Halsey's realization that this would provoke stiffer Japanese resistance led to him suggesting the leapfrogging of Japanese troop concentrations by US forces, and this tactic was successfully employed. In Oct. 1944, as commander of the Central Pacific fleet at the Battle of Leyte Gulf, Admiral Halsey managed to sink or damage the remains of the Japanese carrier fleet.

Harris. Sir Arthur Harris, who had joined the Royal Flying Corps during the First World War, did not play any determining role in the evolution of the RAF in the inter-war period. In 1939 he held the relatively minor post of RAF commander-in-chief in Palestine and it was only in Feb. 1942 that he was appointed head of Bomber Command. A tenacious and persuasive man, he aimed to make it the key instrument in the defeat of Germany by means of massive area bombing raids. This strategy, which was relentlessly pursued, was to lead to the destruction of whole towns, without, however, succeeding in breaking the morale of the German population or in disorganizing the economy.

The Heinkel He-111. The Heinkel He-111, the design of which was first planned in 1934, entered squadron service in 1936 and in the Spanish Civil War this fast and powerful aircraft showed itself to be one of the most effective bombers of the era. It was one of the Luftwaffe's standard aircraft up to 1944, in spite of its weak defensive armament which made it vulnerable to fighter attack. This picture shows a crew and their aircraft on a snow-covered airfield in Dec. 1942 at the time of the battle of Stalingrad.

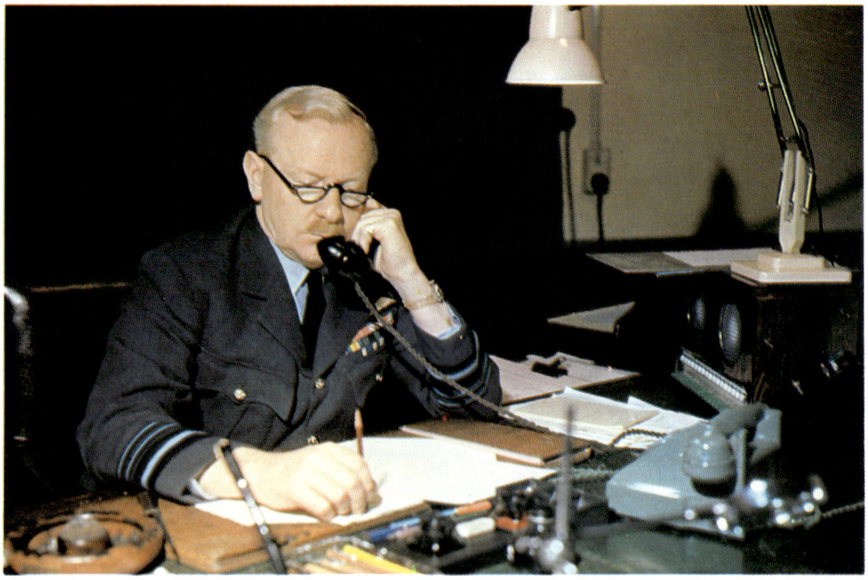

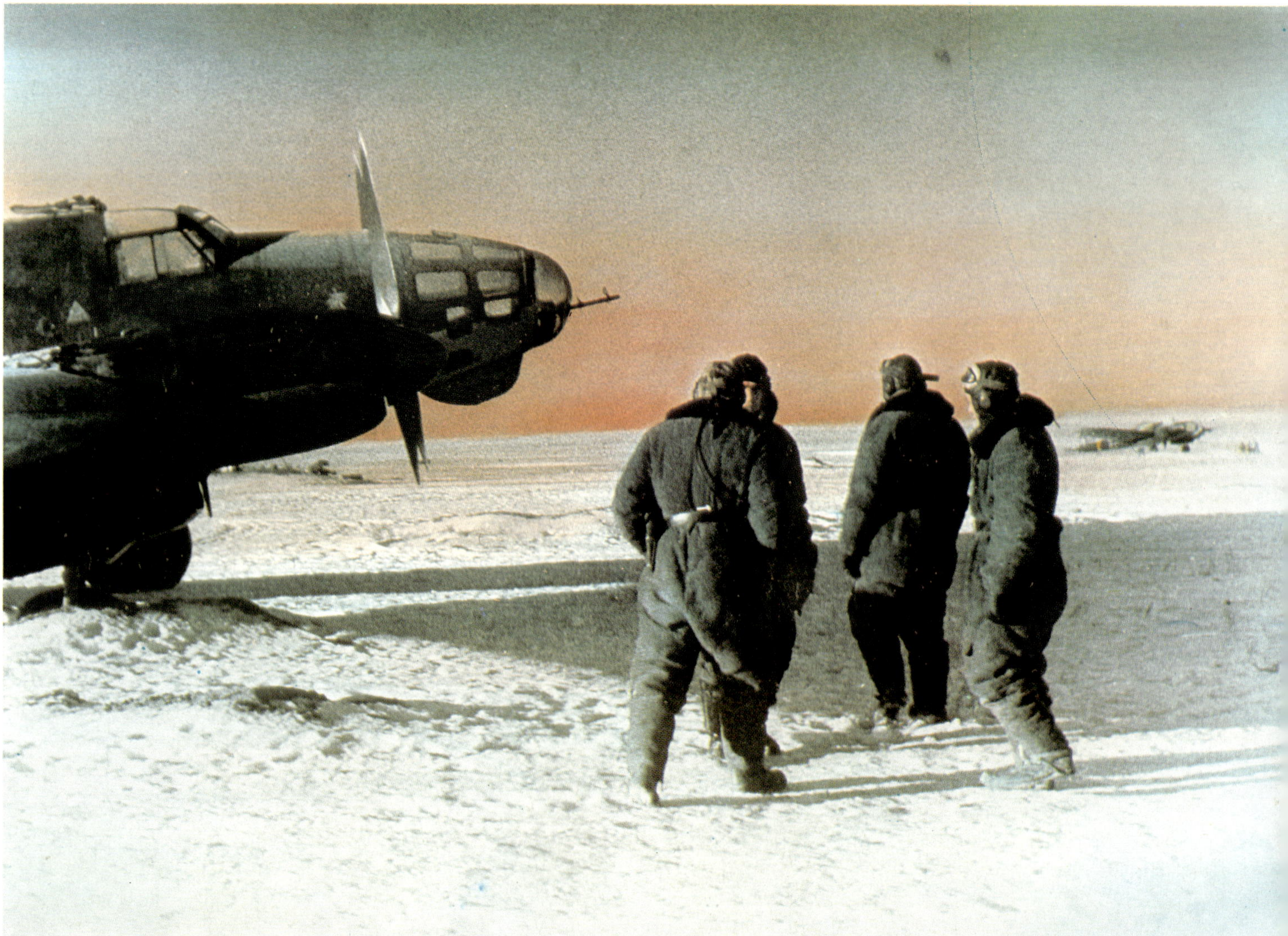

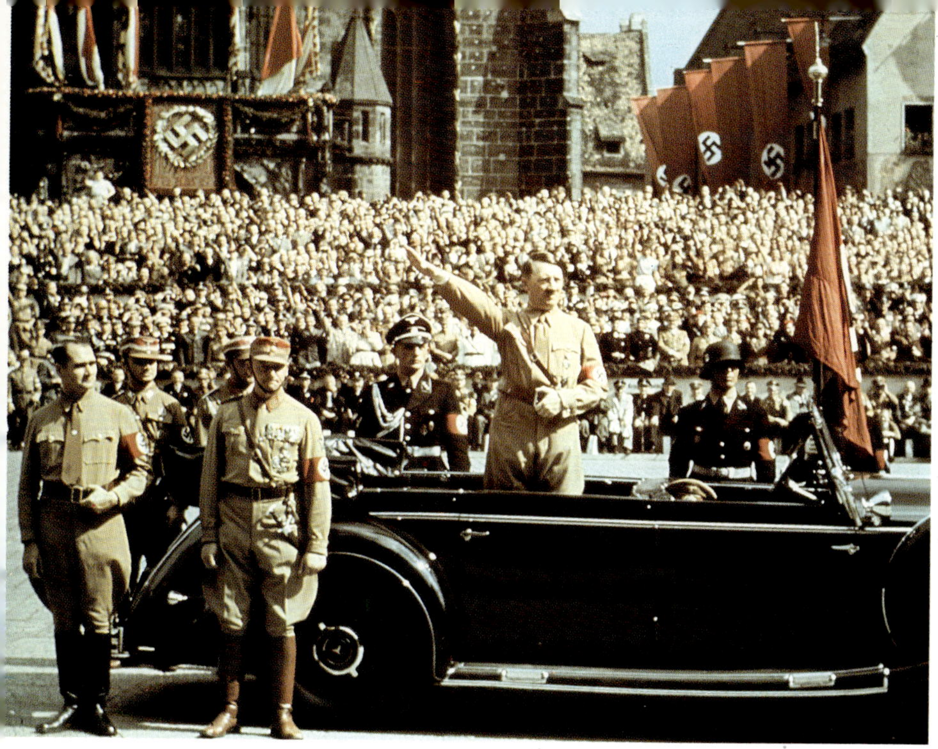

Hess. Having served in in the First World War, Rudolf Hess joined the Nazi Party early on, in 1920. After the Munich Beer Hall putsch in 1923 he became Hitler's friend and faithful confidant. When the Nazis came to power he was figuratively number three in the regime, immediately behind Göring, and had an important role as head of the Nazi Party administration, without real aspirations to power. On the eve of the attack on the USSR, he still thought it would be possible for an agreement to be made between Britain and Germany, which would permit the Reich to concentrate all its strength against its principal enemy, namely Bolshevism. Hess himself flew an aircraft to Scotland, in the hope of making contact with Churchill and concluding a peace agreement with him. When discovered he was at once arrested and treated as a prisoner of war by the British authorities. After the war he was tried at Nuremberg as a major war criminal and condemned to life imprisonment. He is now the last remaining prisoner in Spandau Prison in West Berlin. In this picture Hess stands next to Hitler's car on the far left, bare-headed, during the Nuremberg Nazi party rally of Sept. 1938.

Hiroshima. The atomic bomb was dropped on Hiroshima on 6 Aug. 1945 at 8.15 in the morning. The consequent loss of life and injuries among the population were very high indeed. In 1946 an investigation established the figures as 78,150 killed, 13,982 missing and nearly 40,000 injured. The physical destruction was enormous: 90 % of the buildings in the city were either destroyed or damaged. The Hiroshima raid, followed three days later by that on Nagasaki, did, however, enable the Japanese emperor to compel his country to capitulate and thus to spare the population as a whole from the further suffering which would have been brought by large-scale land fighting on Japanese soil.

Himmler. He had joined the Nazi Party in 1923 and developed a passionate interest in racial purity and anti-semitism. In 1929 he became head of the Schutzstaffel (SS) with the title of Reichsführer SS and proceeded to make of it a virtual state within a state, spreading its tentacles throughout the Reich and later the occupied territories of Europe. Through the SS organization Himmler came to control the criminal and political police, the concentration camps, the implementation of the racial laws and the 'final solution' of the Jewish problem. The war and the German army's defeats further reinforced his power and he was able considerably to increase the importance of the Waffen-SS in relation to the army. He also came to be in charge of the internal intelligence services and extended his control into all areas of national life. When the Reich collapsed Himmler still cherished the hope that a separate peace could be made in the west. He was captured by the British in the disguise of a private soldier but soon after his identity was discovered he committed suicide on 24 May 1945. In this picture he is seen talking to a peasant boy in Byelorussia, during a tour of inspection of the eastern occupied territories.

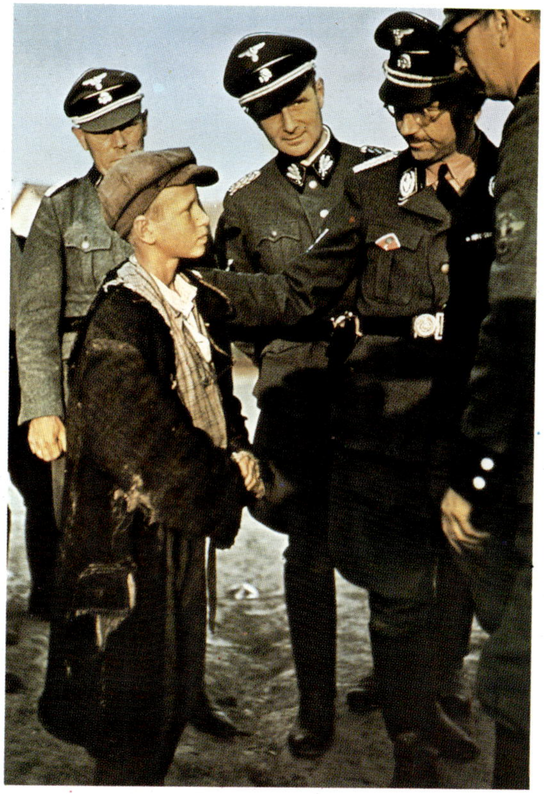

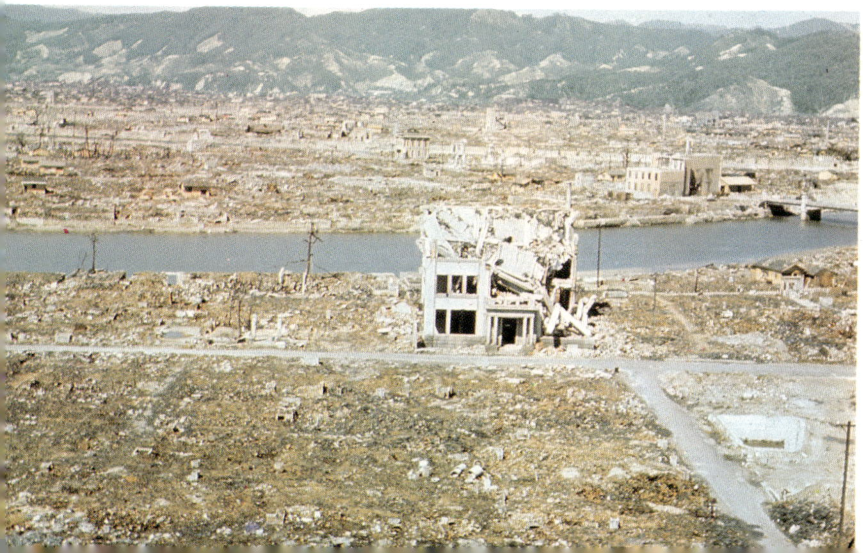

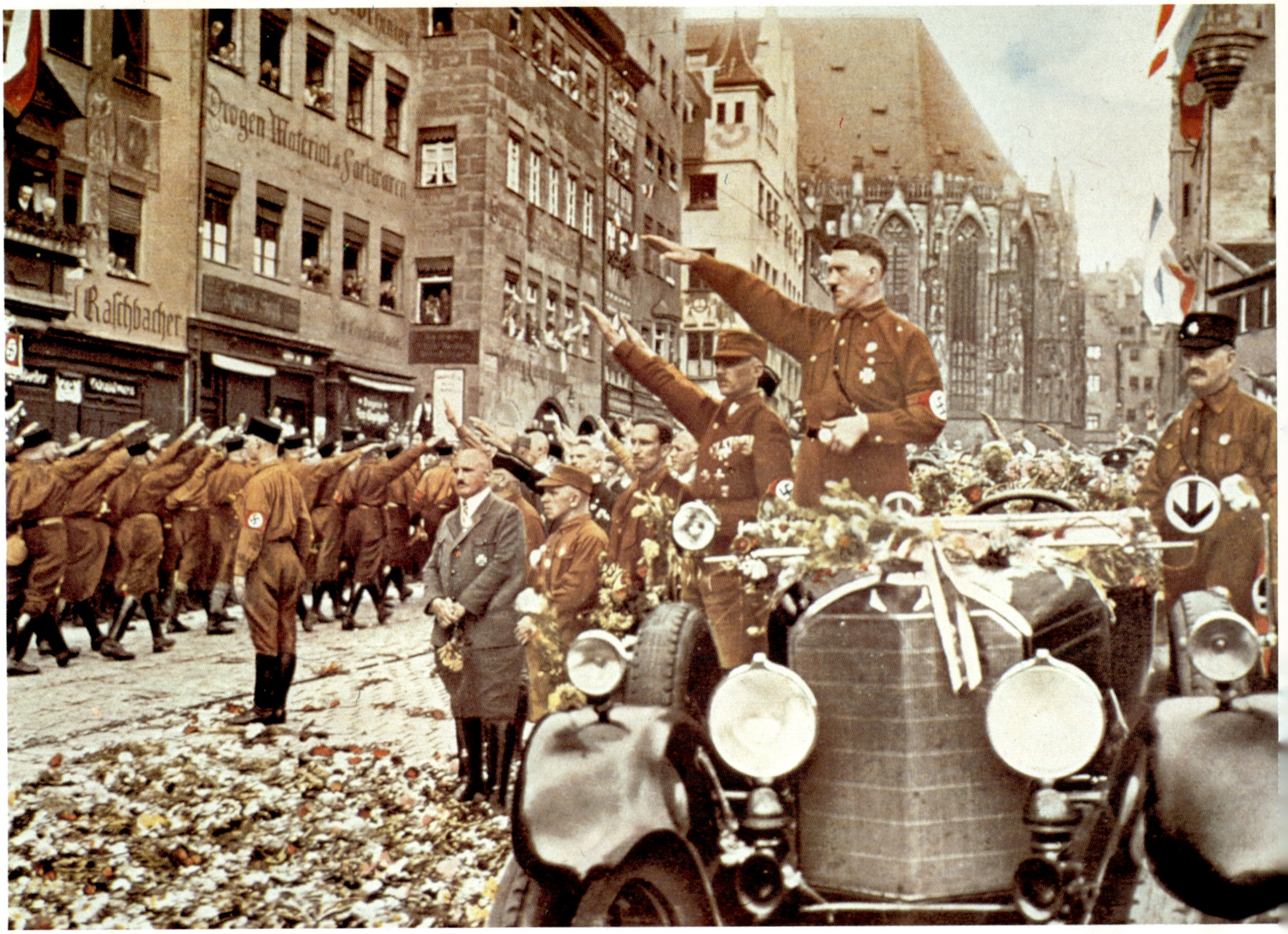

Hitler. Until the Nazis came to power in 1933 Hitler, who had risen from obscurity, was considered a demagogue and a small-time agitator. People hardly saw the qualities of a real political party leader in him. Nevertheless, in his public speaking he could appeal to the deepest aspirations of an ever-greater part of the German people who had been humiliated by the country's defeat in the First World War and the Treaty of Versailles and were then lashed by the consequences of the world economic crisis of 1929. Hitler was able to electrify crowds by stirring up the collective unconscious at military parades or great Nazi rallies. These were staged with a consummate feeling for mass psychology, thus giving to everyone the sense of being part of an irresistible force. In this picture Hitler is seen in Nuremberg in 1927 at the time of the Nazi party rally. He is reviewing one of the SA's first parades after the lifting of the ban placed on this organization following the Munich Beer Hall putsch of 1923. The man in grey with the shaven head is Julius Streicher, the head of the Nazi Party in Nuremberg.

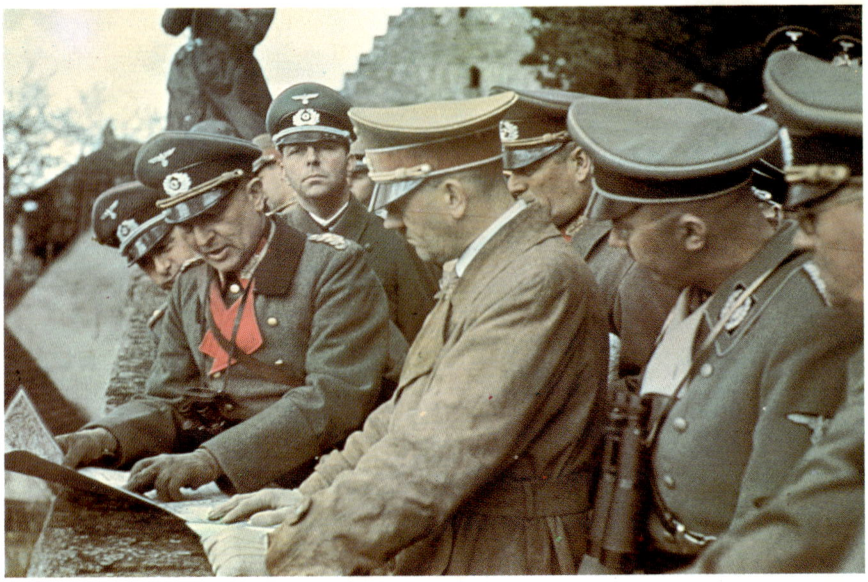

From 1935 onwards, as the pace of German rearmament increased, Hitler's image became increasingly that of a war leader. He is seen here conferring with his generals at army manoeuvres in 1938. The start of the war and the success of the Blitzkrieg would only tend to strengthen the image further. In Dec. 1941, at the time of the defeat outside Moscow, he added to his functions as supreme commander of the armed forces, that of commander-in-chief of the German army, succeeding Brauchitsch who had been obliged to resign by Hitler. From 1942 onwards, however, his insistence that German forces should make last-ditch stands on the field of battle (instead of tactically withdrawing) and his keenness on initiatives that would end in disaster only precipitated the final collapse of Germany.

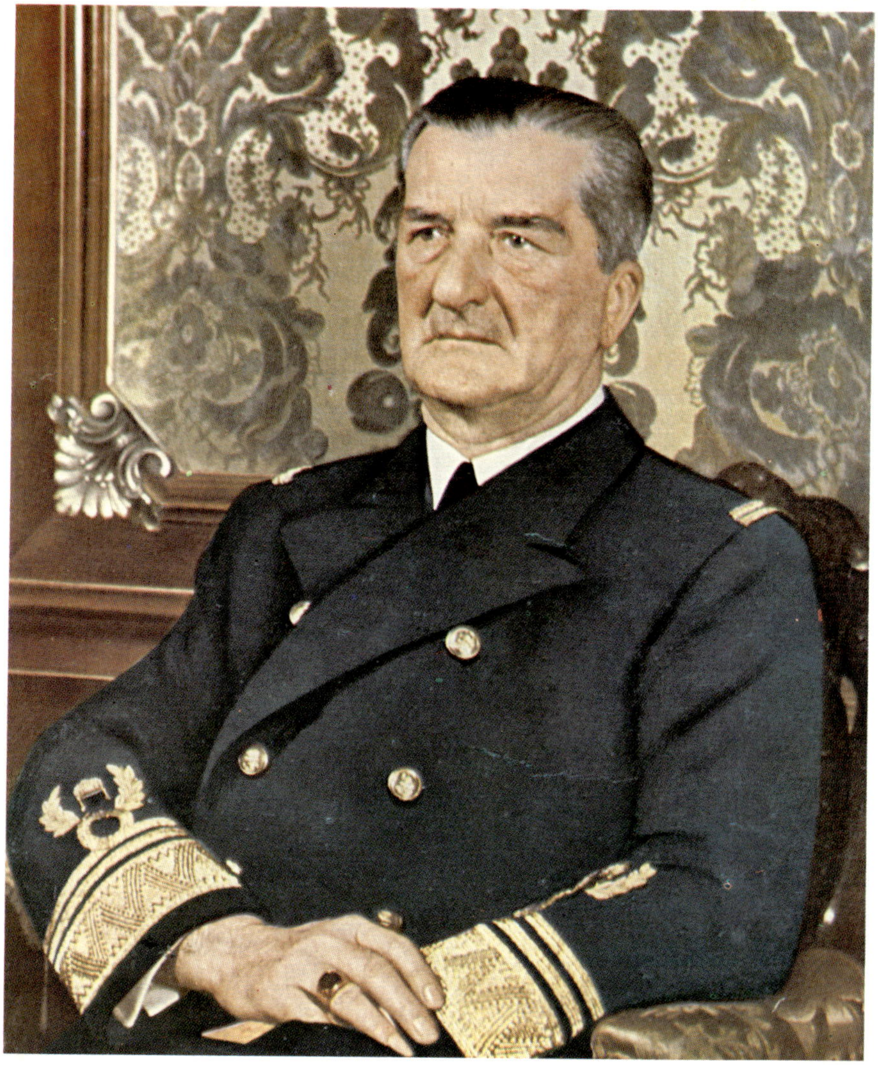

Hungary. Following the defeat of the Central Powers in 1918 the frontiers of Hungary had been much altered, territories with Hungarian populations being given to Romania, Czechoslovakia and Yugoslavia. Under the leadership of Admiral Horthy (who is shown in this picture) who had taken the title of 'regent' in the expectation of the hypothetical election of a new sovereign, the country thus found itself among the 'revisionist' states (i.e., those which did not accept the terms of the peace treaties imposed by the Allies in 1919–20) and was thus brought closer to Italy and Germany. This policy had advantages for Hungary. Under the 'Vienna Awards' of 1938 and 1940 Hungary was able to recover the territories of Carpatho-Ukraine and Transylvania, the majority populations of which were Hungarian. However, the alliance with Germany proved to be disastrous from the time of the attack on the USSR, since Hungary found itself drawn into the conflict.

Peasant women in the streets of Budapest in about 1940. Following the Trianon Treaty of 1920, Hungary as a state was reduced in size, in large part rural and agricultural, and under growing economic pressure from Germany. This pressure, and also real diplomatic advantages, meant that Hungary increasingly became a satellite state of the Third Reich. The country was drawn into the war on the eastern front and had to agree to increasingly heavy sacrifices. From 1944 Hungary was totally subject to the wishes of Hitler, who had removed Horthy from power, and it found itself obliged to continue the struggle on the side of Germany right up until April 1945.

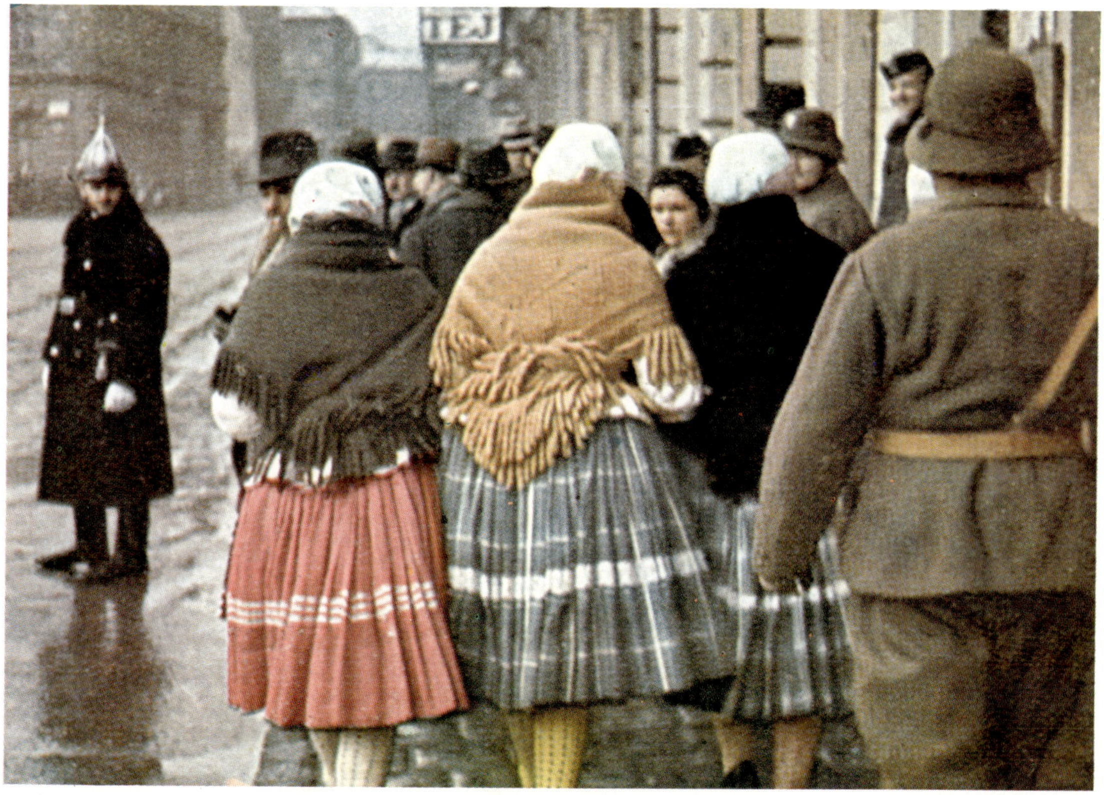

Hungary. Gunboats of the Danube river patrol.

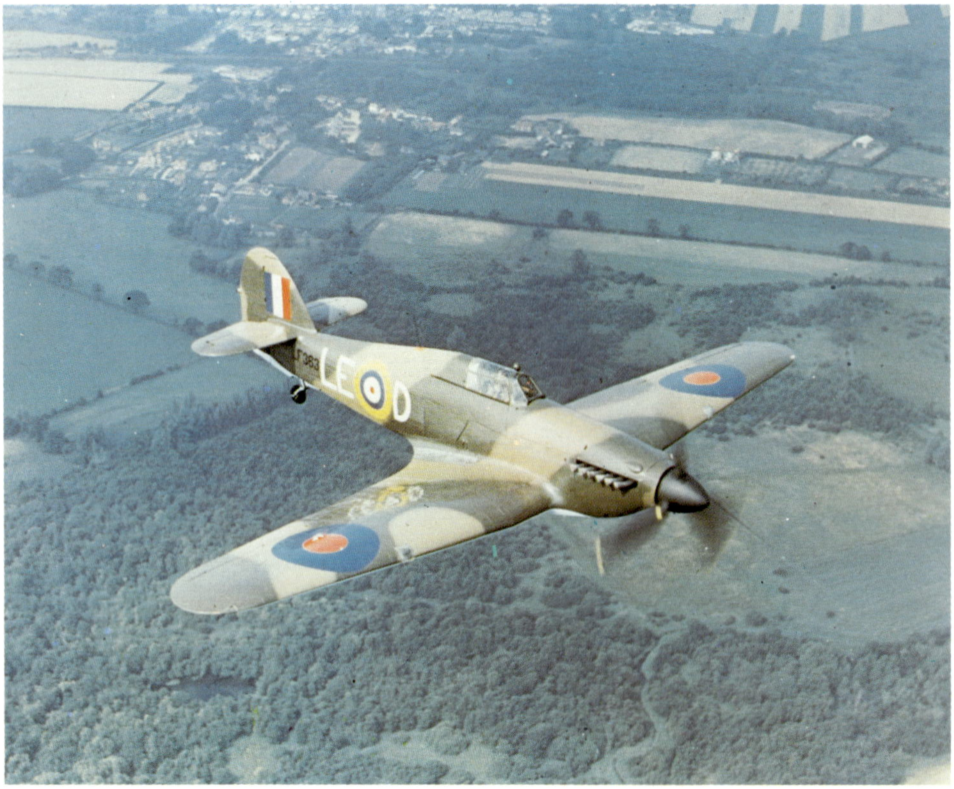

The Hawker Hurricane. As soon as the Hurricane entered service in 1937 it showed itself to be most effective as a fighter aircraft, being fast and manoeuvrable. From 1939 to 1941 the Mark I version, which was armed with eight machine guns, was, with the Spitfire, the backbone of the Royal Air Force's Fighter Command, notably during the Battle of Britain. New versions of the Hurricane appeared from 1942 onwards. The Mark II, which had a 1280 horsepower Merlin engine, could be used as a light bomber, carrying 250 or 500 lb (125 or 250 kg) bombs, or in anti-tank operations with its 40 mm cannon. From 1937 to 1944 a total number of 14,230 Hurricanes were constructed in the Hawker factories.

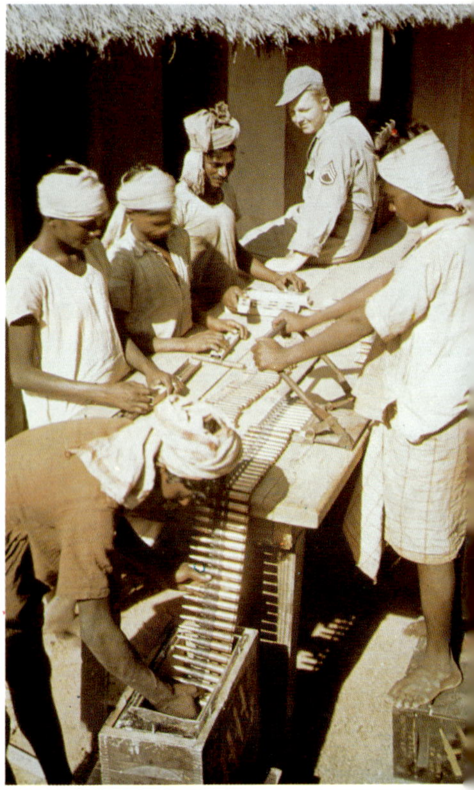

India. The picture shows Indian workers feeding ammunition into a machine-gun belt at a base of the United States 10th Air Force. The 10th Air Force carried supplies to the Allied troops during the campaign to reconquer Burma in 1943–44. India made significant contributions to the war effort in both the military and the economic spheres. However, the war years were also marked by the growing impatience of the nationalists in Gandhi's Congress Party and by the rise of Jinnah's Muslim League. The British authorities succeeded in avoiding a general insurrection by means of strong repressive measures. Nevertheless, in accordance with the promises made in March 1942 by Stafford Cripps on behalf of the Labour Party, the Indian Empire was to gain its independence in 1947 in the form of two separate dominions, India and Pakistan.

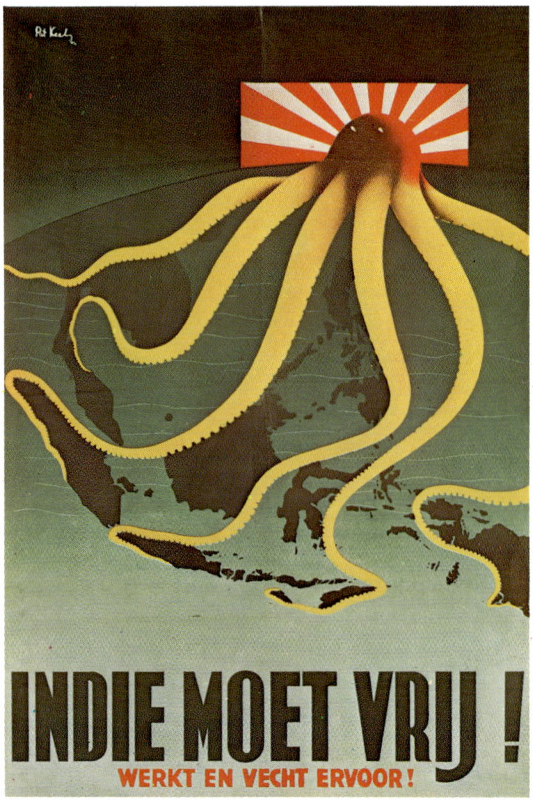

Indonesia. At the beginning of 1942 Indonesia, which at that time was a Dutch possession (the Netherlands East Indies) was occupied by Japanese troops after some resistance by Dutch and British forces and incorporated into the 'Greater East Asia Co-prosperity Sphere'. Although an Indonesian government led by the nationalist, Sukarno, was set up, the Japanese presence soon turned to tyranny and exploitation. This is emphasized in this British poster designed by Pat Keely which was published for the Dutch government in exile. It illustrates the dominance of the Japanese 'octopus' and is intended to support the struggle for the liberation of the Dutch East Indies: 'The East Indies should be free! Work and fight for this!'. However, the fall of Japan was not marked by a return to the old order. On 17 Aug. 1945 Sukarno proclaimed the independence of Indonesia and affirmed the unwillingness of the people to accept the re-establishment of Dutch colonial authority.

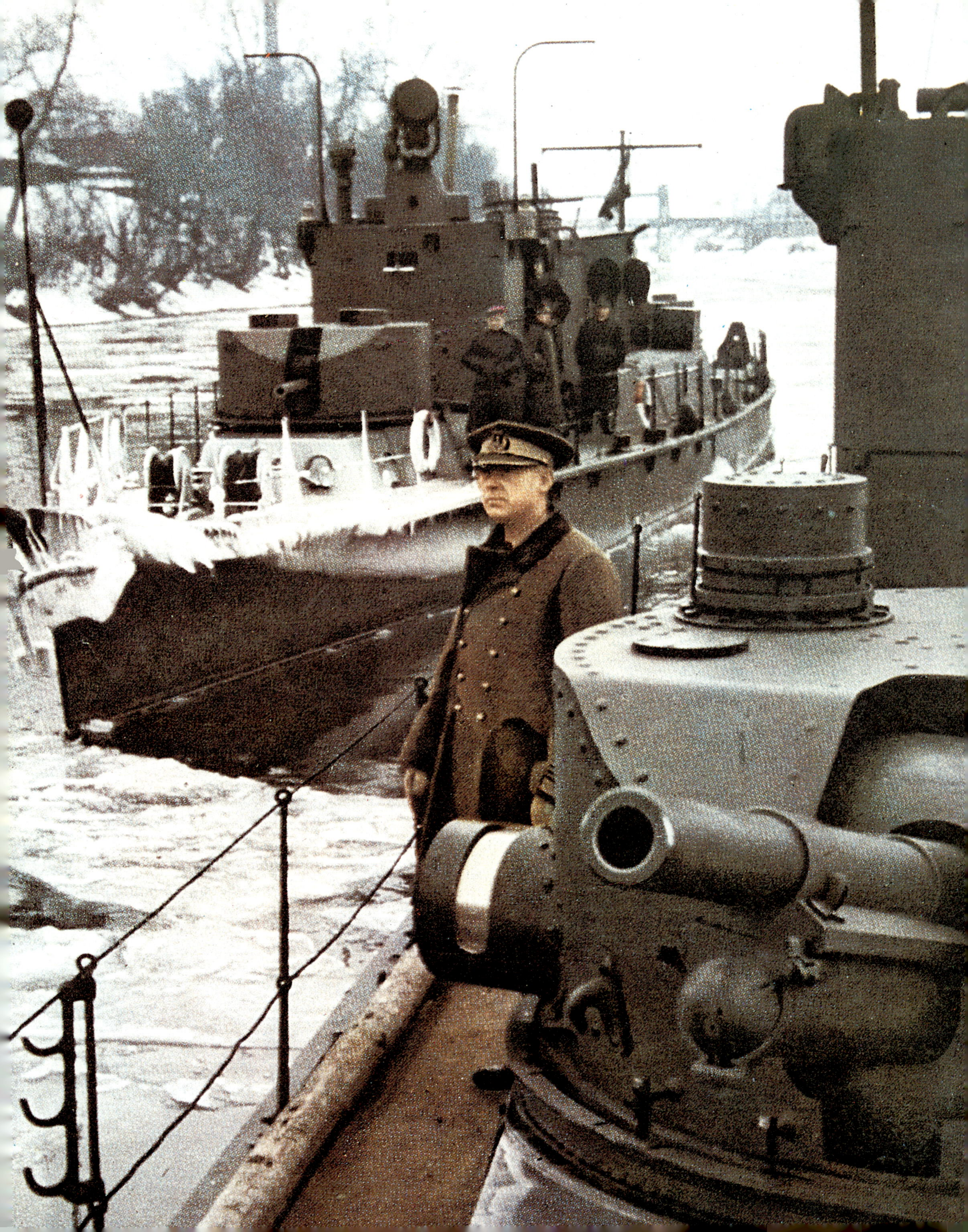

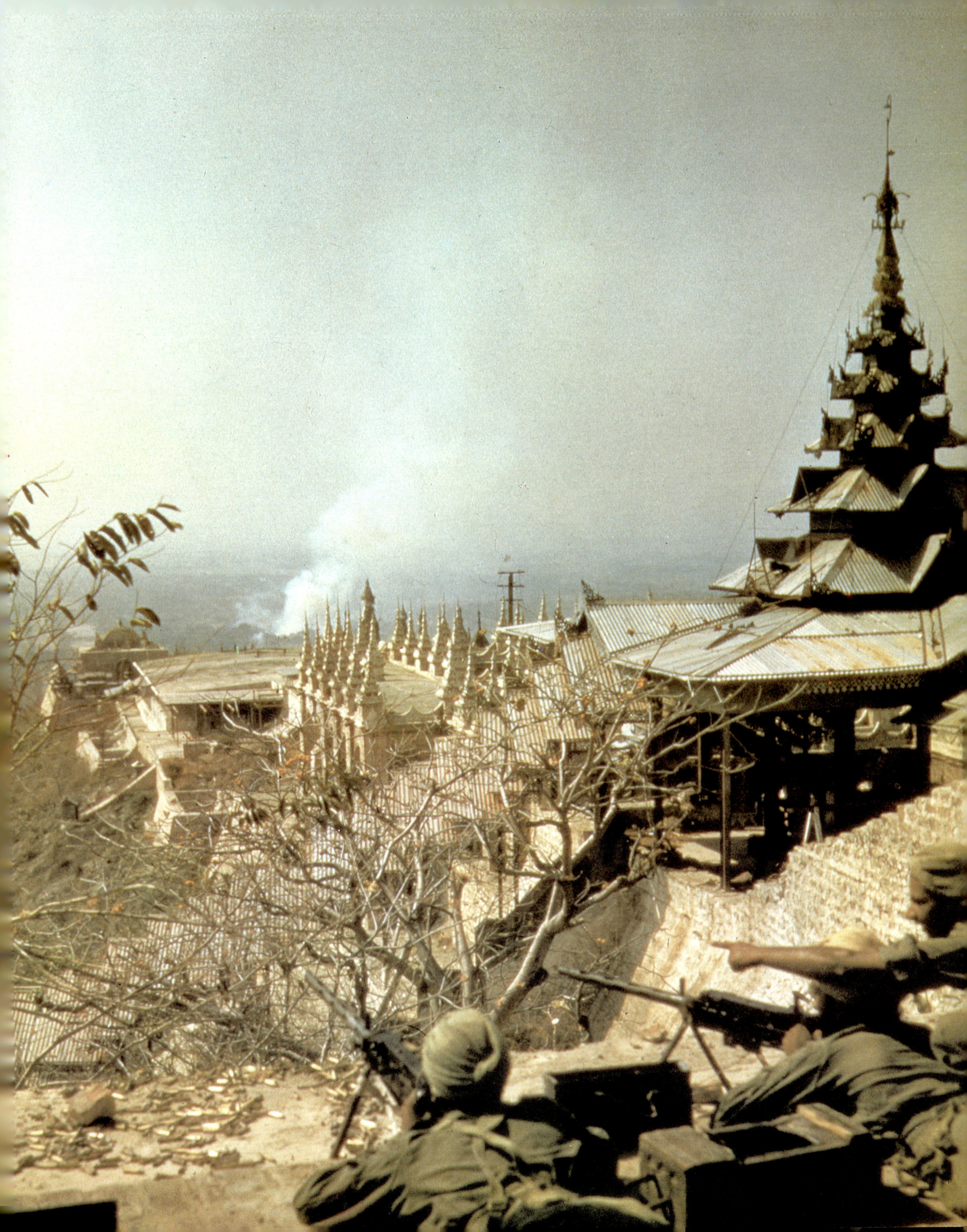

Opposite
India. Sikh machine-gunners on Pagoda Hill during the battle for Fort Dufferin in Mandalay in March 1945.

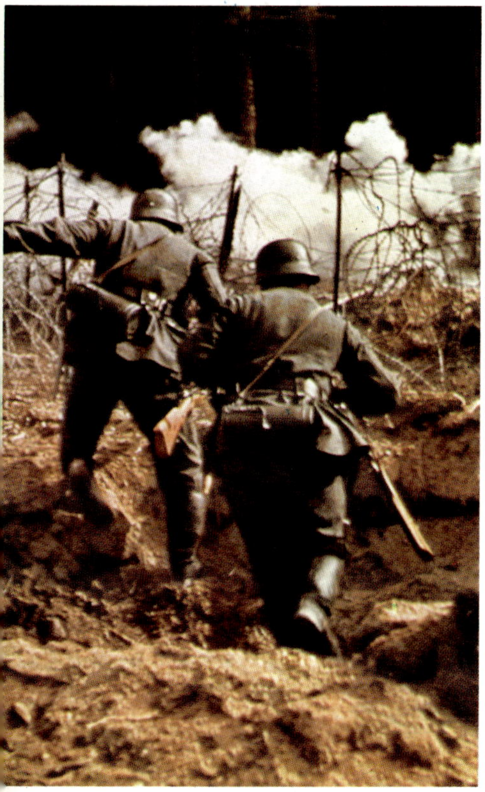

Right
Infantry. At the height of the Blitzkrieg, which was marked by resounding successes of the tank–aircraft combination, it seemed that the infantry had been reduced to a secondary role. In the context of the Blitzkrieg the infantry's role consisted of bringing to an end the resistance of enemy troops encircled by the armoured and motorized columns and in occupying territory, often at the cost of forced marches which in the German army could be as long as 30 mi. (50 km) a day. This picture shows an infantry column of the Wehrmacht in Yugoslavia in April 1941, marching along a road which is little more than a track.

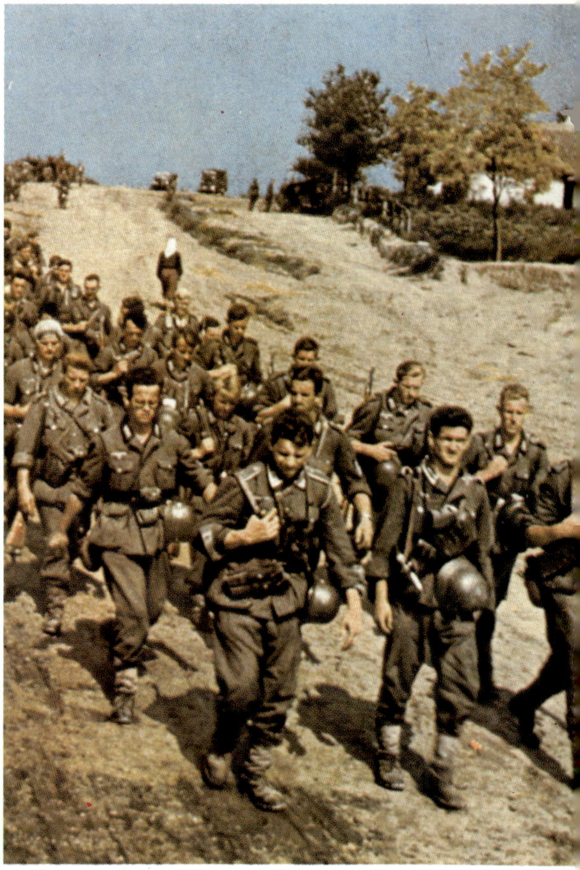

With the stabilization of the Russian front at the end of 1941 the infantry frequently met conditions little different from those of trench warfare during the First World War. This picture shows German infantry moving forward under cover of smoke bombs through a gap made in the barbed wire to attack a Soviet position. The soldiers' equipment – steel helmets, boots, Mauser rifles, gas masks – is not much different from that of 1916–18.

German infantry moving forward in support of a PzKpfw IV tank on the Terek front on the road to the Caucasus in Oct. 1942. From the time they were first formed the German armoured divisions included battalions of infantry whose task was to operate in close liaison with the tanks. The role of the infantryman was to indicate the presence of enemy positions to the 'deaf and blind' tank and to reduce pockets of resistance neglected by the tanks. The infantry also had the task of protecting the tank against well-hidden enemy positions (*i.e.*, which the tank crew could not initially see).

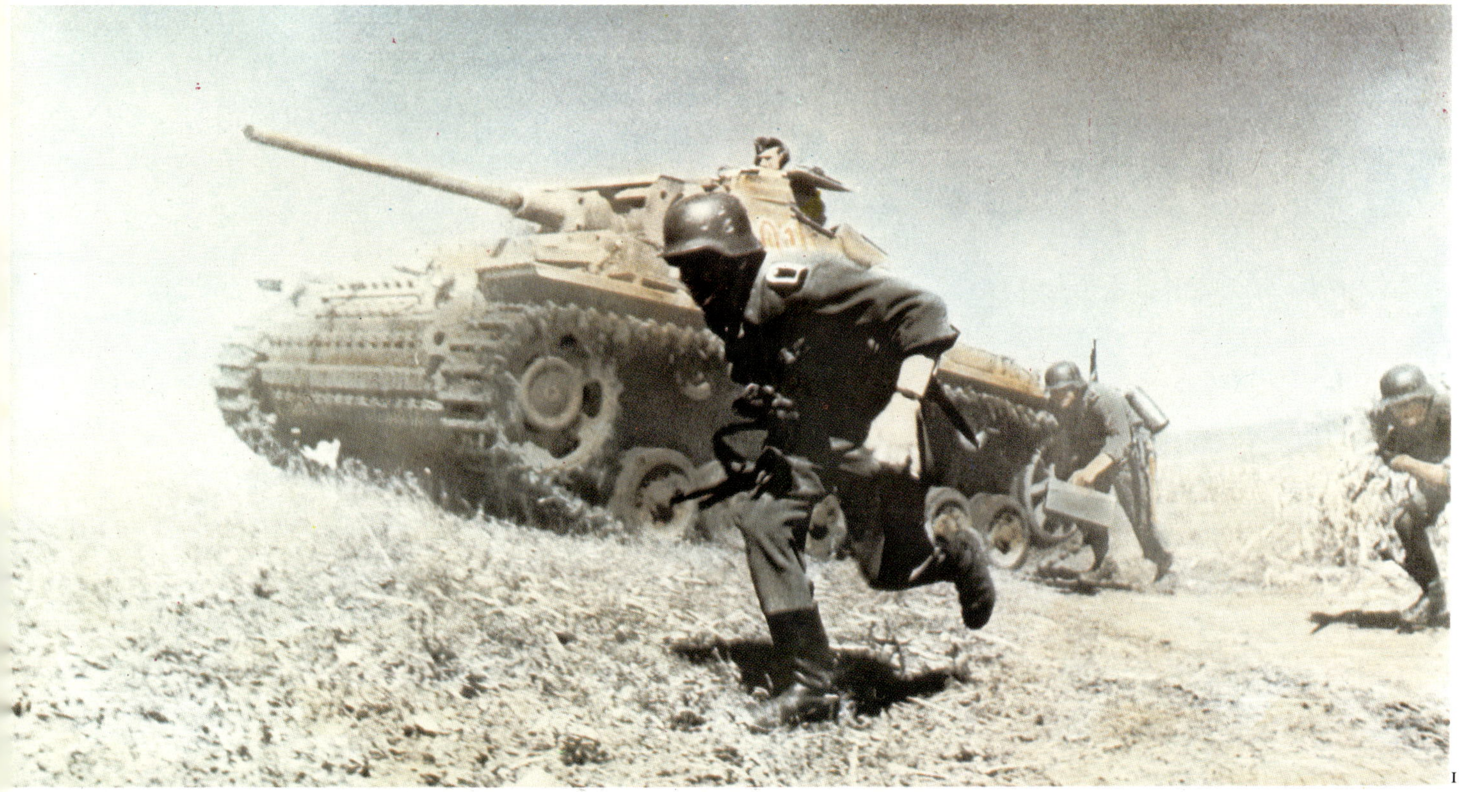

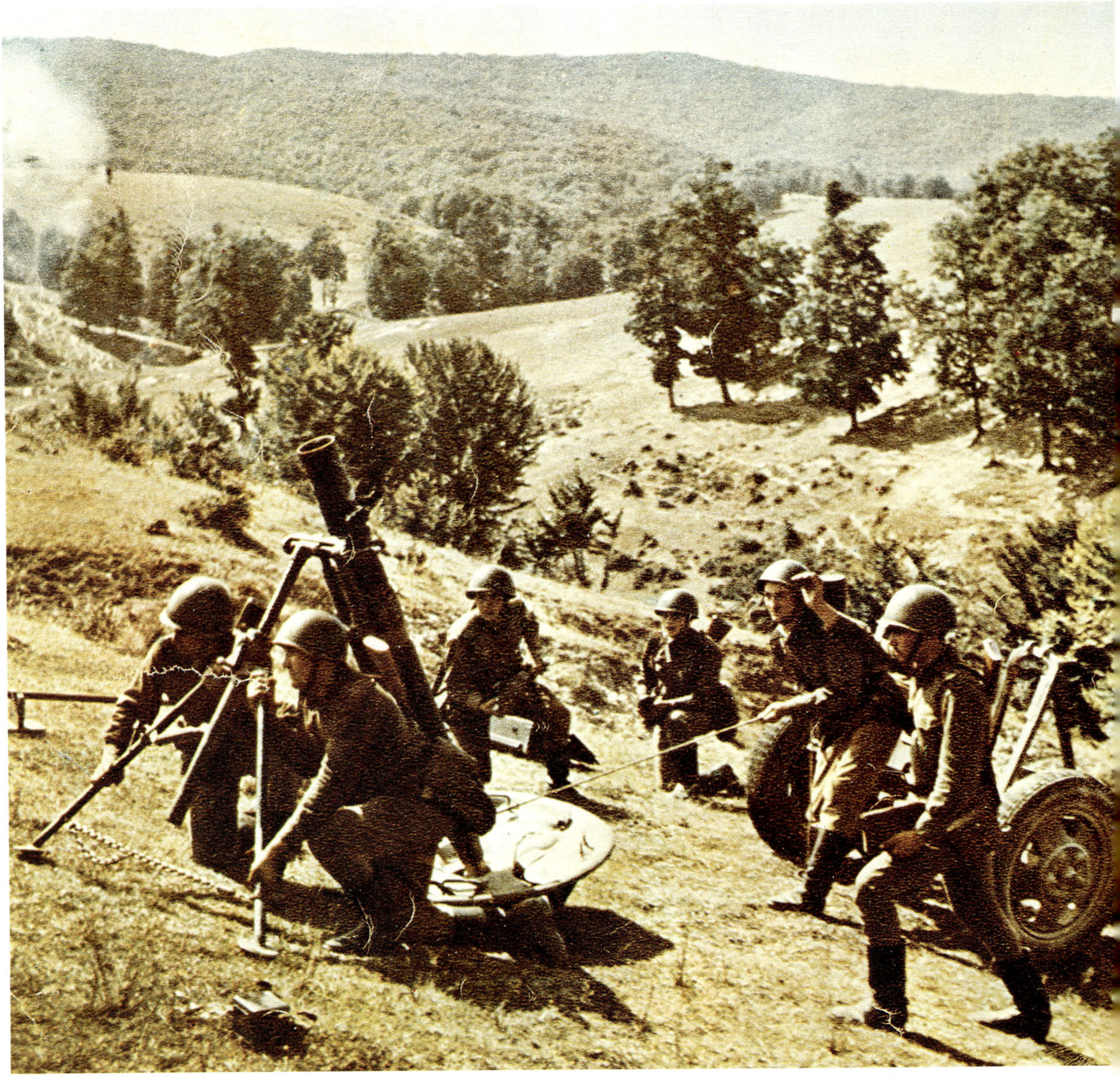

Soviet infantry placing a 120 mm mortar in position. In all infantry forces each battalion included one company whose job it was to operate heavy equipment such as machine-guns, flame-throwers and mortars. The mortar, which had already been widely used during the First World War, showed itself to be a very effective weapon when employed against enemy positions over the brow of a slope, in shell holes or in well-protected positions.

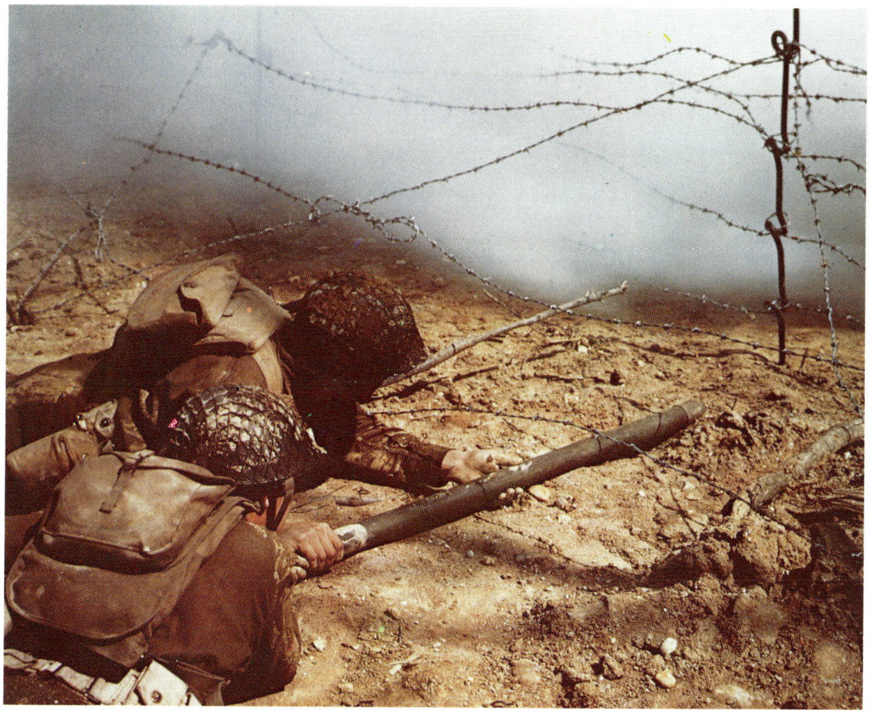

This picture shows Allied infantry using Bangalore torpedoes which are intended to cut through obstacles such as barbed wire. Throughout the war infantry weapons were continually diversified in response to different situations. At the end of the war apart from the standard weapons – rifles, grenades, machine-guns or mortars and so on – infantrymen also had the use of sub-machine guns, flame-throwers, recoil-less guns and a whole range of anti-tank rocket launchers derived from the American Bazooka or the German Panzerfaust.

The rate of fire of automatic weapons was the major obstacle which infantry constantly came up against. If tanks were not available, infantry had to resort to using mortars or light artillery to destroy pockets of resistance. This picture shows a group of American soldiers operating an infantry gun which is firing high-explosive shells. Used with armour-piercing shells, this gun was also an effective anti-tank weapon.

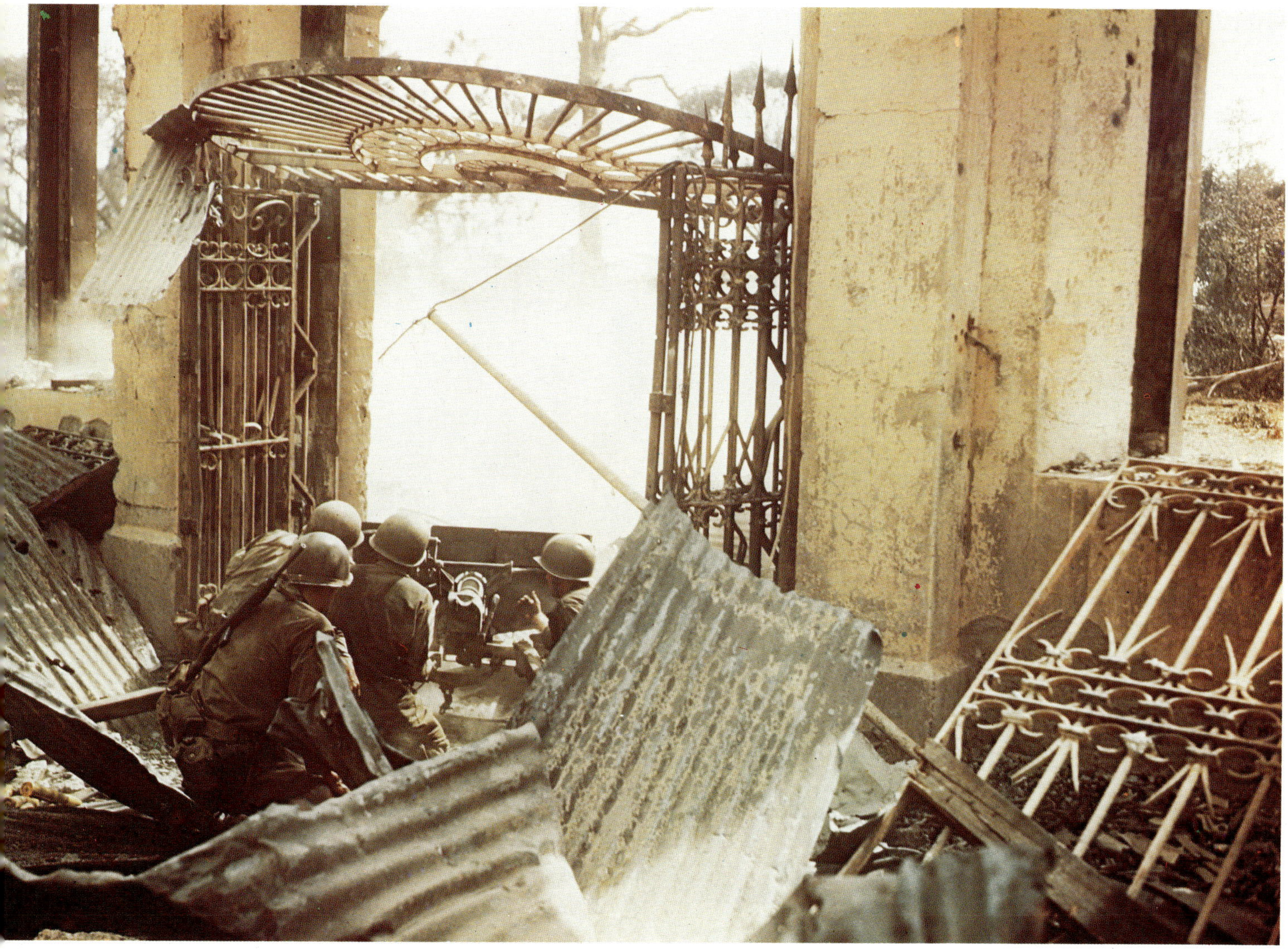

Infantry. American airborne troops manning a machine-gun.

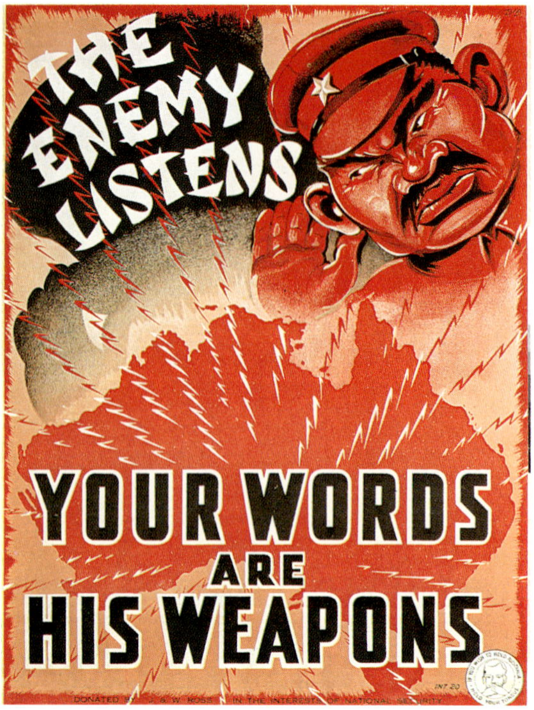

Intelligence. Throughout the war intelligence played an important role and the belligerent countries endeavoured to obtain information by all possible means. They used aerial reconnaissance, the decipherment of coded messages, the infiltration of agents and the assistance of resistance networks. From the very beginning of the conflict the Allied governments were on guard against the risk of careless conversation which could be made use of by an enemy, as shown in this Australian poster of 1942 directed against Japanese espionage.

The Italian campaign. Despite the reservations of the Americans, who had determined upon a landing in France, the British succeeded in winning support for a major operation in 1943 against Italy, considered by Churchill as the 'soft under-belly' of the Axis. After the occupation of Sicily during July–August, the Italian peninsula was, from September onwards, the object of large-scale amphibious operations at Taranto and Salerno. On account of the ferocity of the German opposition, the landing at Salerno in September (seen here) was one of the most difficult of the whole war and nearly ended in disaster.

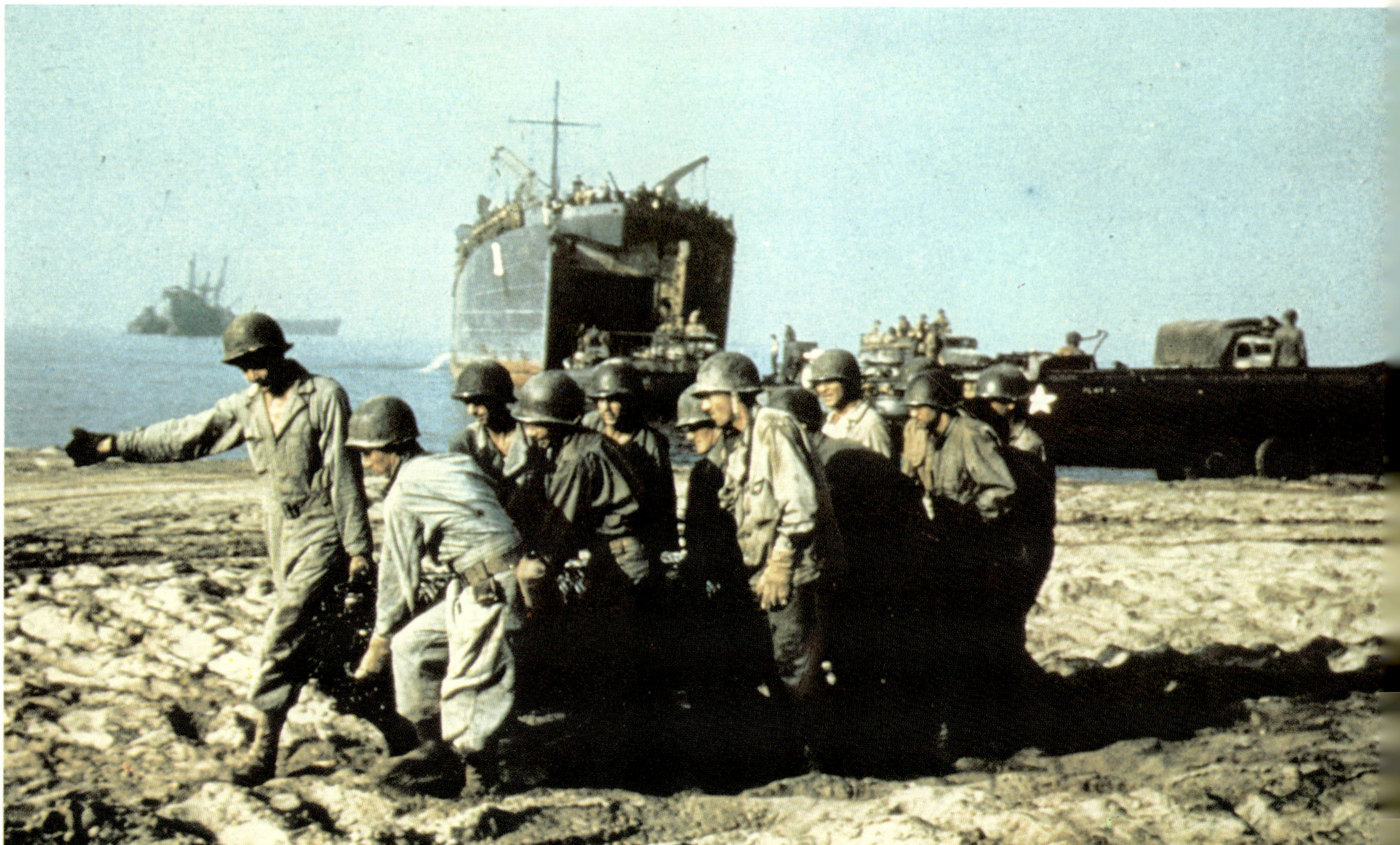

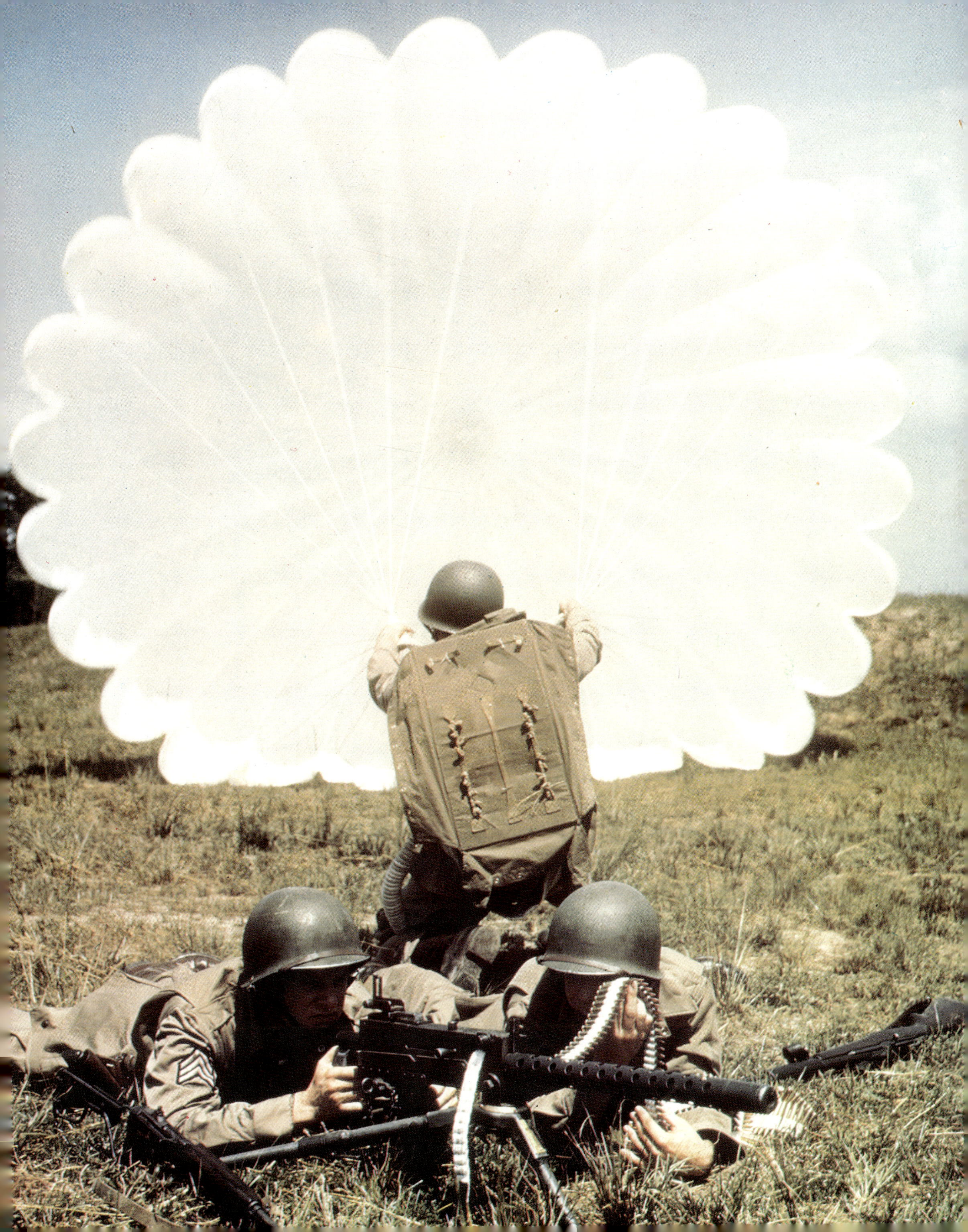

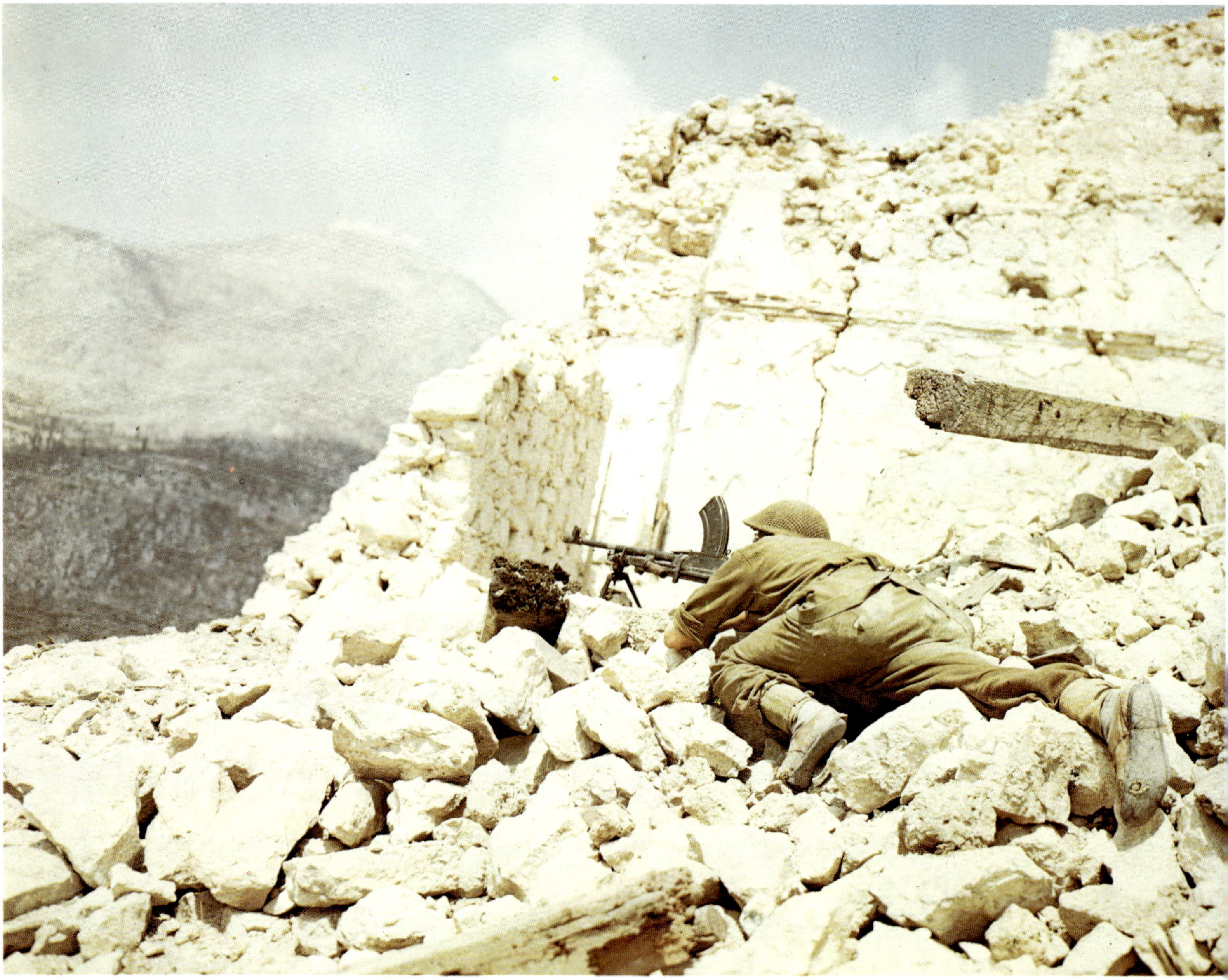

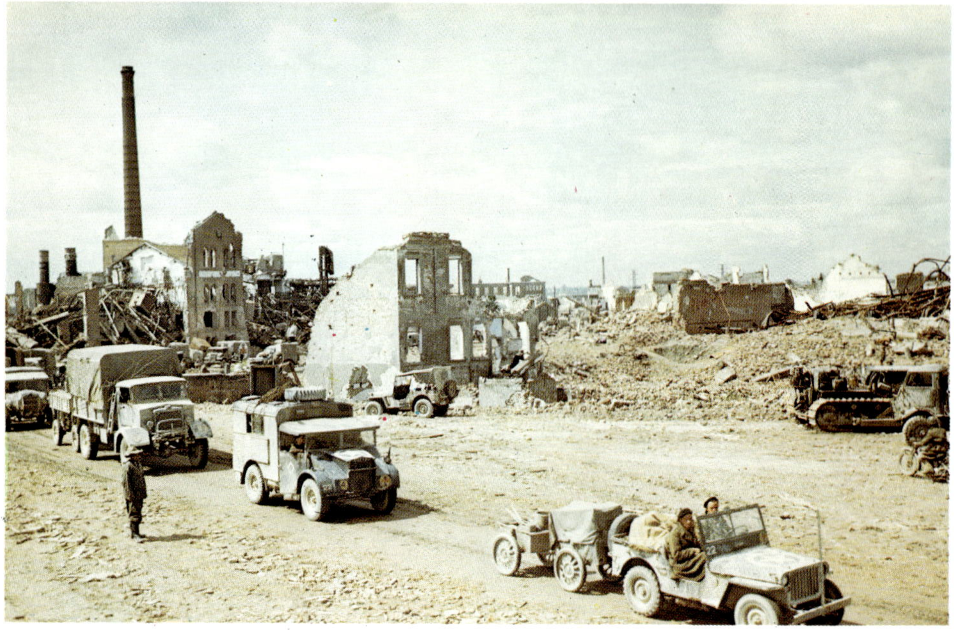

The Italian campaign, about which highly optimistic forecasts had been made, was to prove one of the most unpleasant surprises of the war for the Allies. Quite apart from the stubborn resistance of the Germans, they had to adapt to mountain warfare, becoming acquainted with cold, mud and snow during the harsh winter of 1943–44. The fiercest fighting, in conditions recalling the 1914–18 war, took place at the approaches to Monte Cassino. Here we see a British soldier in the ruins of the little town of Cassino, which had become impassable for tanks or any other kind of vehicle.

In the autumn of 1944 Field Marshal Kesselring's forces were to make a final stand on the Gothic Line, which had been established on the foothills of the Apennines, to the north of Florence. It was only from 9 April 1945 onwards that the Allies broke through and reached the Po valley. In this photograph a British convoy is passing through the ruins of Pontelagoscuro, north of Ferrara, on 28 April. On the following day the German authorities signed the act of surrender of their forces, which came into effect on 2 May.

During the Italian campaign both Germans and Allies did their best to spare the country's artistic treasures. There was, however, considerable destruction which affected more than 300,000 buildings and a large number of installations such as bridges. In the course of their retreat the Germans saved the Ponte Vecchio in Florence but blew up the city's other bridges. Here some inhabitants of Florence are crossing the Arno using the remains of a bridge which has collapsed (Aug. 1944).

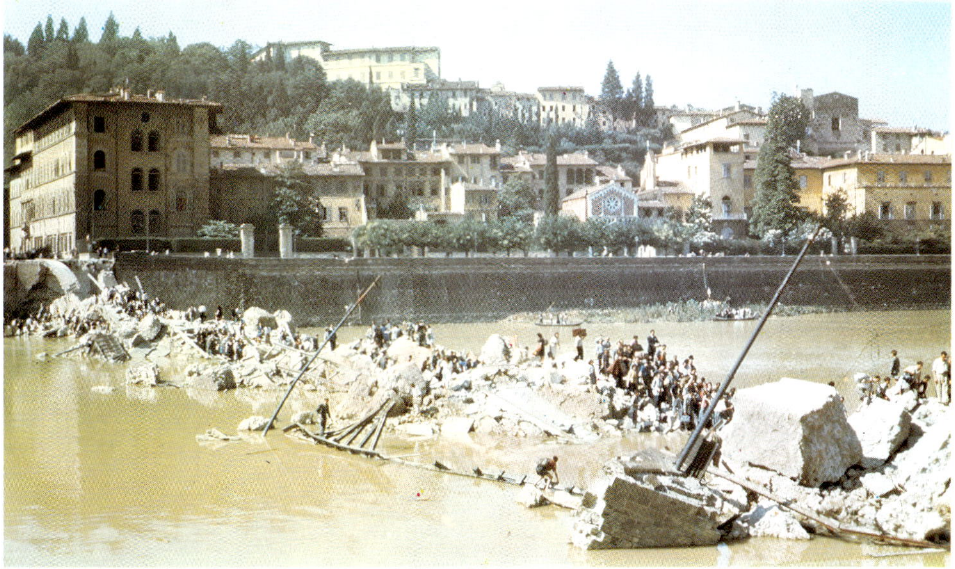

The capitulation in Sept. 1943 did not lead to a rapid liberation of Italy. As part of Operation Achse, Rommel's and Kesselring's divisions succeeded in occupying two-thirds of the peninsula and in blocking the path of the Allies in the heart of the Apennines, between Naples and Rome. For more than 18 months these highly trained troops, making admirable use of the terrain, succeeded in stopping or slowing down the Allied advance. Seen here is a German heavy machine gun in position in a mountainous limestone region.

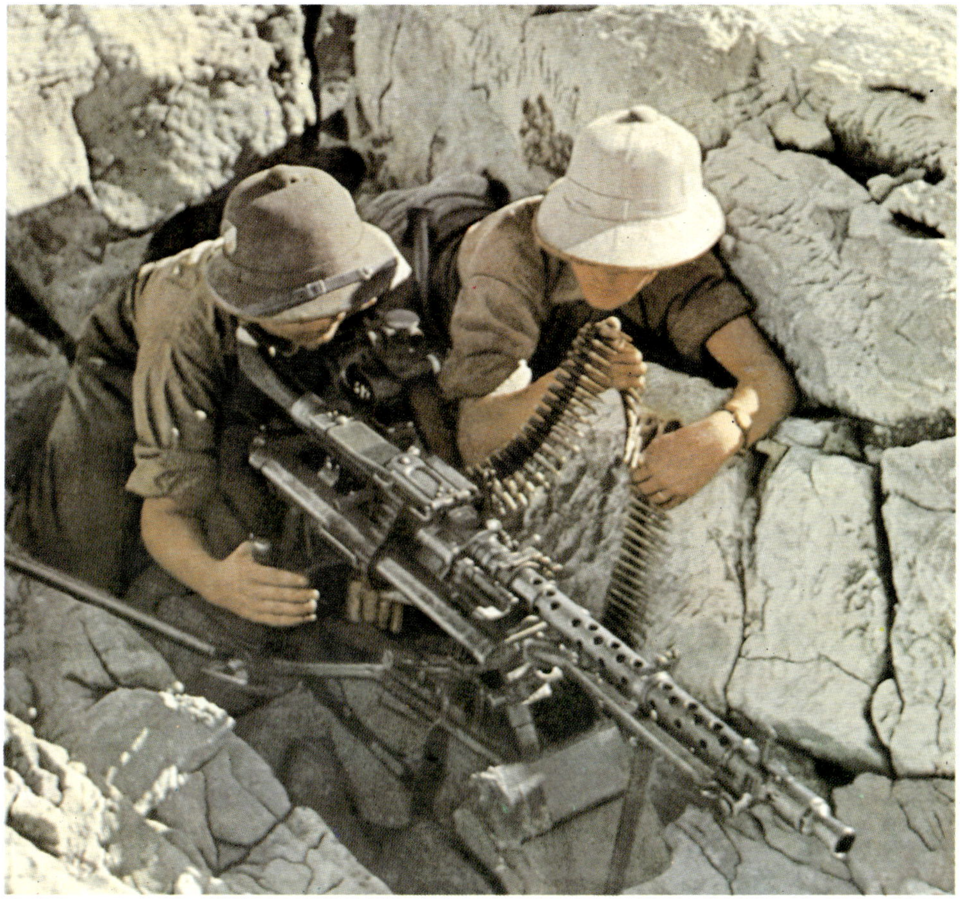

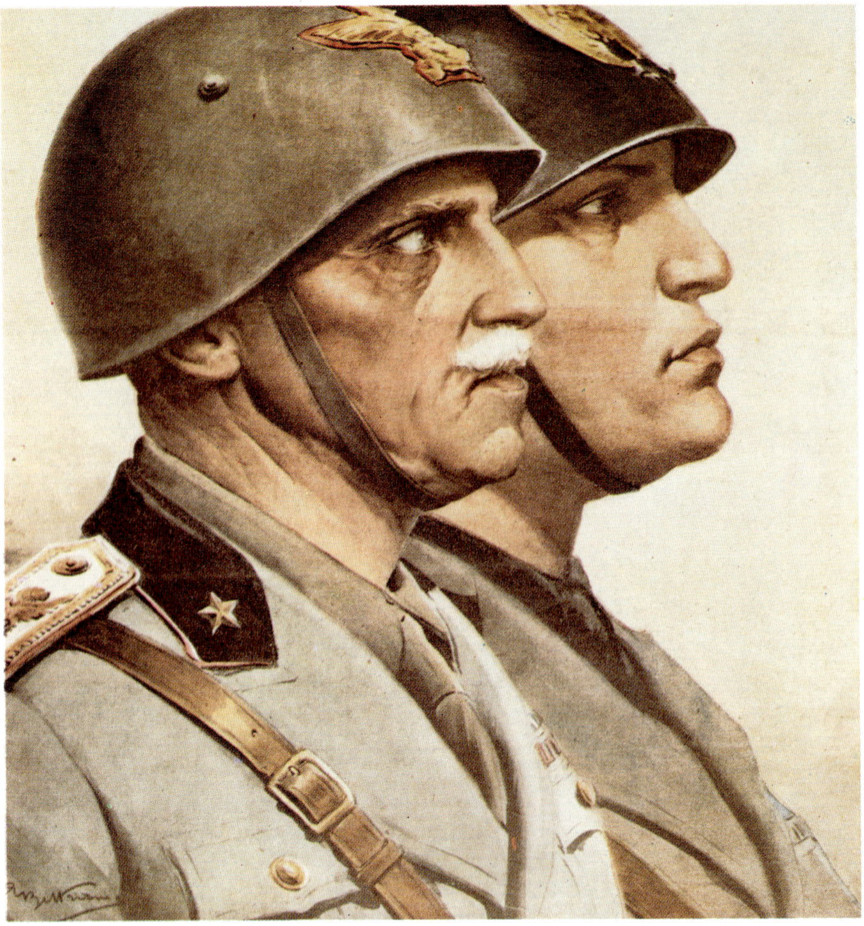

Opposite
Italy. A group of women in front of the ruins of Castelforte in May 1944.

Italy. Although Mussolini himself had considerable powers and the Fascists were the only political party, political opposition having disappeared, he was never the undisputed master of Italy as Hitler was of Germany. He had to take the Church and, especially, the monarchy into consideration. It was King Victor Emmanuel III who had summoned him to take power at the time of the 'March on Rome' and it was he who decided to arrest him and replace him with Marshal Badoglio on 25 July 1943, when faced with the disastrous turn the war was taking for Italy.

Disappointed by the attitude of the western democracies at the time of the Abyssinian war, and committed to the support of the Nationalists in Spain, from 1936 onwards Mussolini drew gradually closer to Hitler, despite the misgivings he felt about the policies of the Third Reich. In May 1938, on the occasion of Hitler's visit to Italy, the Duce was determined to impress the Führer with demonstrations of national unity and large-scale military manoeuvres. All the organizations of the Fascist Party were mobilized for the occasion. Here, at Santa Marinella, near Rome, we see a parade of armed young *balillas* (members of the Fascist youth movement) bearing German and Italian flags.

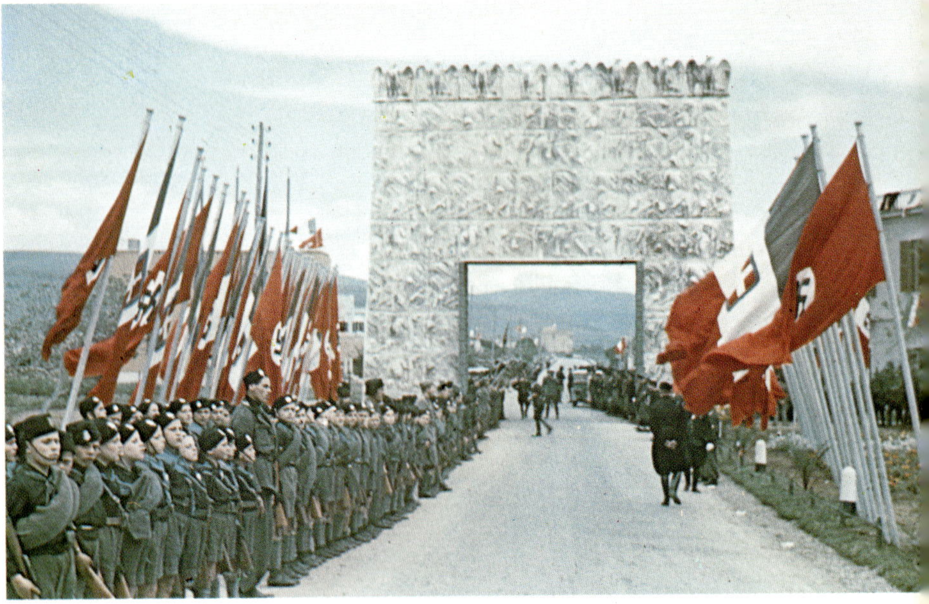

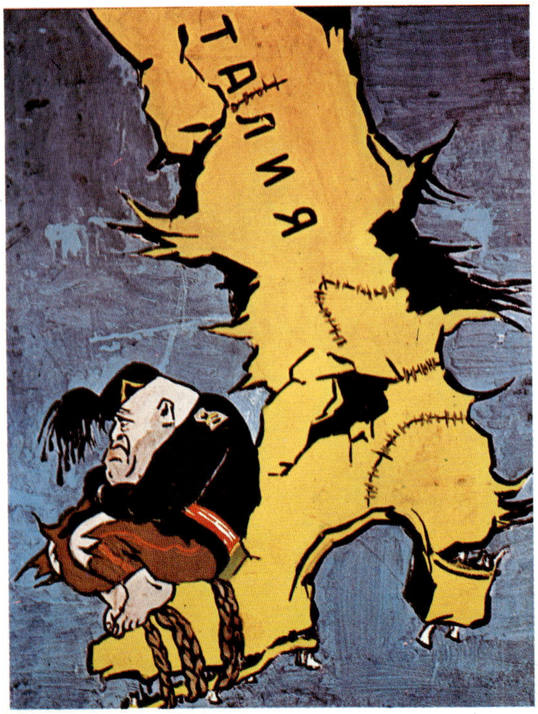

Italy's entry into the war in June 1940 was based upon a gross miscalculation: the certainty that, following the collapse of France, Britain would accept a compromise peace and that Italy would need to do nothing else except take part in the negotiations. British resistance upset all these preconceptions. Italy was shown to be incapable of waging a war concurrently with Germany. It piled up defeats in Libya, in Greece and at sea, and from the beginning of 1941 was compelled to accept the humiliating assistance of the Reich. As this Soviet cartoon emphasizes, at the beginning of 1943 Italy was in an appalling political, economic and military situation. The Duce, overwhelmed by failure, was no more than a shadow of his former self.

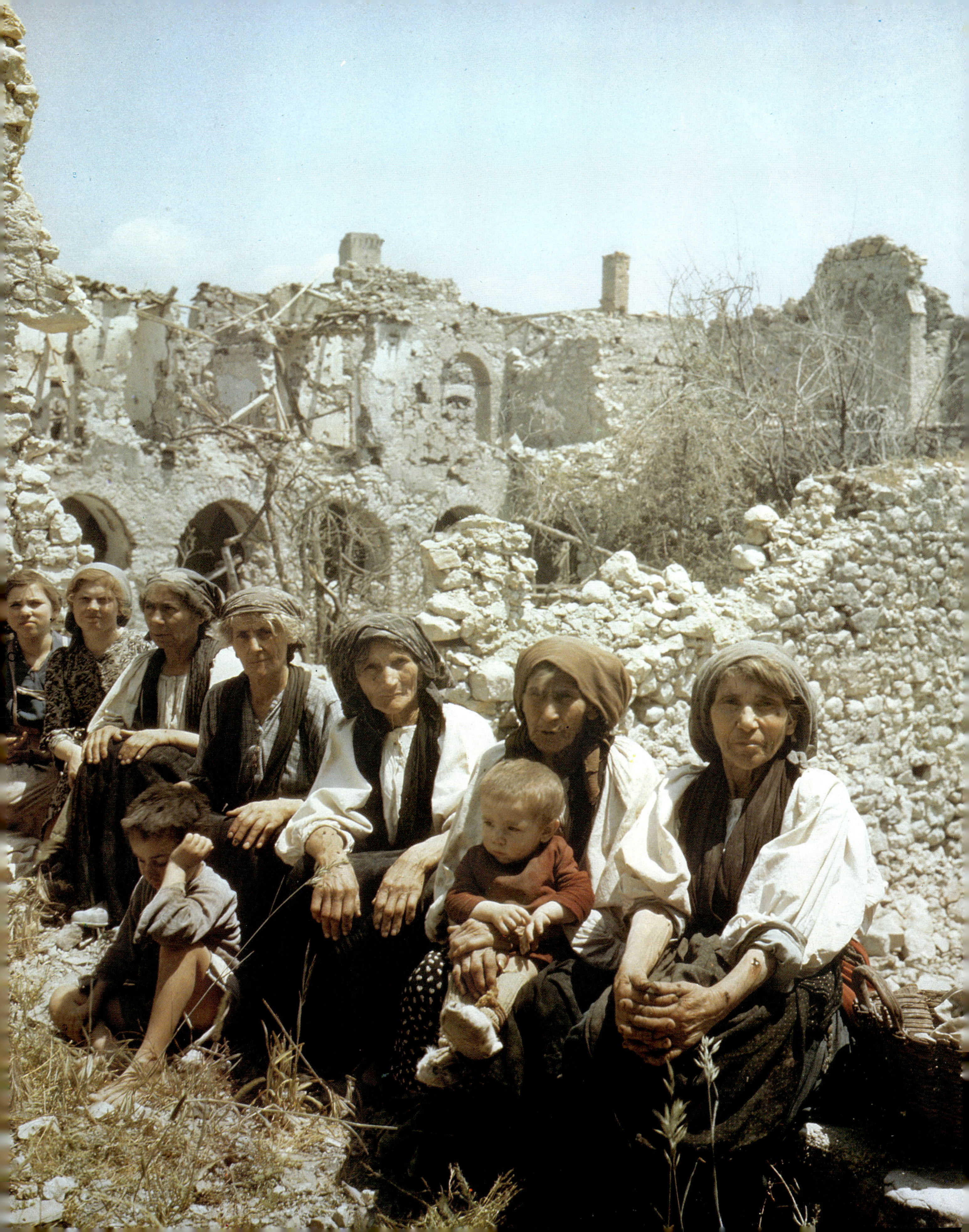

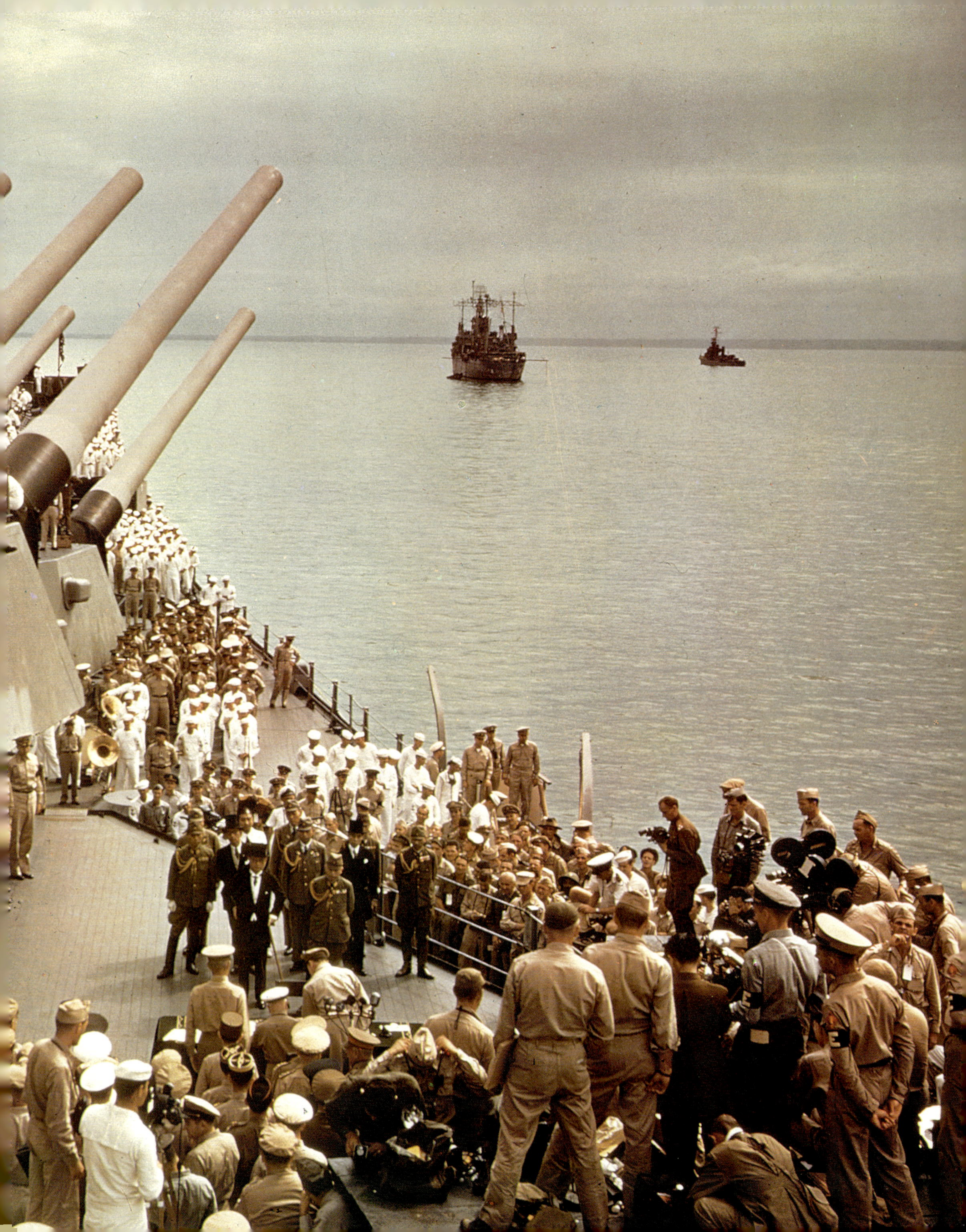

Japan. The surrender on board the battleship *Missouri* on 2 Sept. 1945.

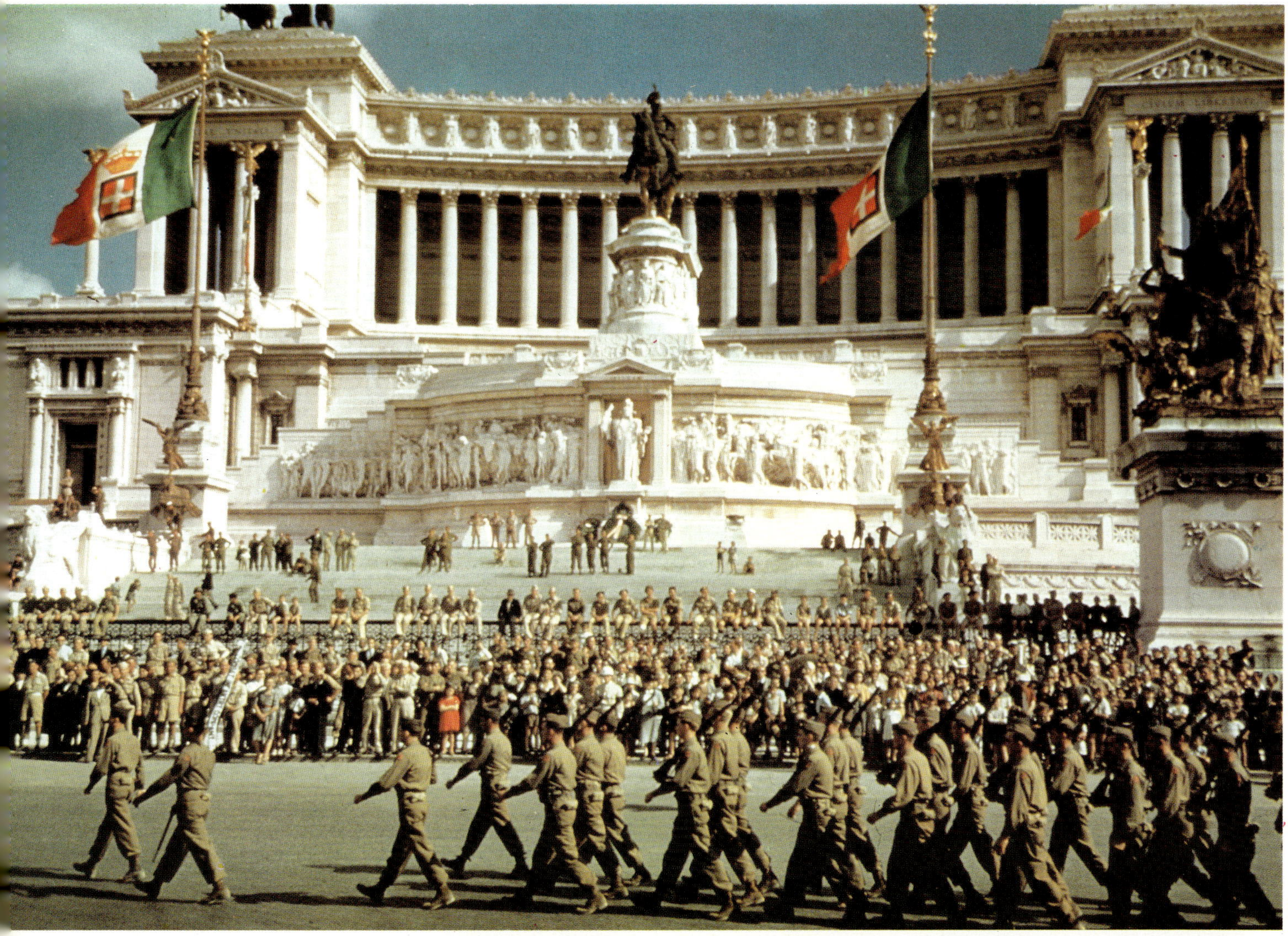

Despite all the forecasts made by the British and American commanders the capture of Rome, initially planned for the autumn of 1943, did not actually take place until 4 June of the following year. Here troops are marching past the memorial to Victor Emmanuel II. The occupation of the Eternal City, which removed it from the nominal authority of Mussolini's Social Fascist Republic, illustrated the ambiguities of Italian political life. The population, just like the royal government which had declared war on Germany, could consider the capture of Rome as a liberation.

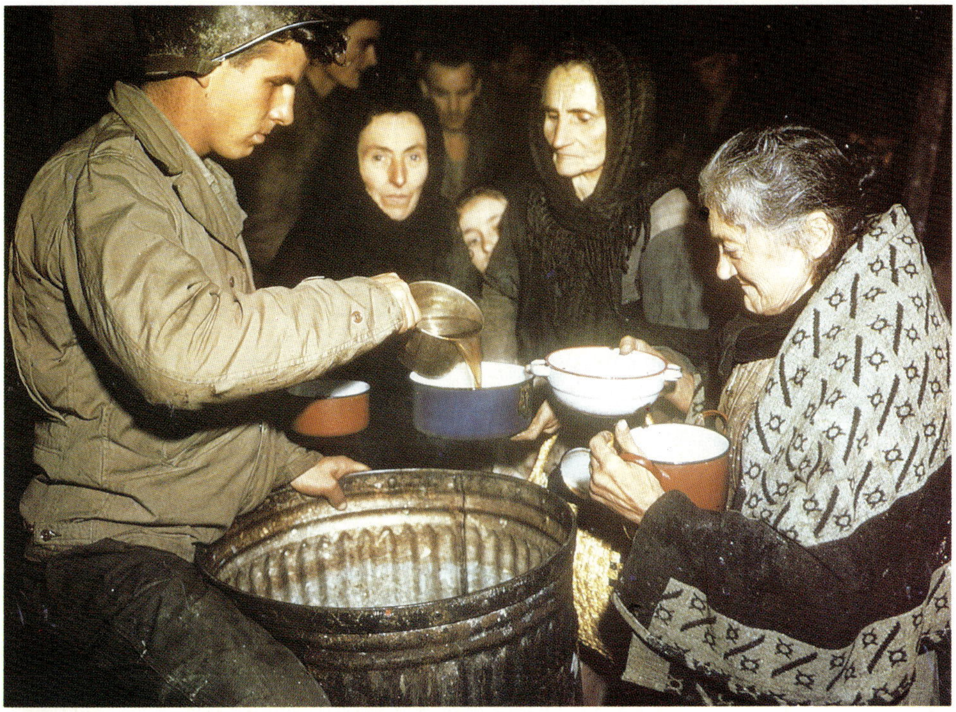

In spite of the hopes of King Victor Emmanuel III and Badoglio, the capitulation of Sept. 1943 could not prevent Italy from becoming a battlefield for the Germans and the Allies throughout a period of more than 18 months. The fighting and the bombardments led to considerable destruction of buildings and means of communication and laid waste large areas of the countryside. In the north as well as in the south the population experienced epidemics, severe cold and food shortages. Here at Bologna an American soldier is serving out coffee to a group of women and children.

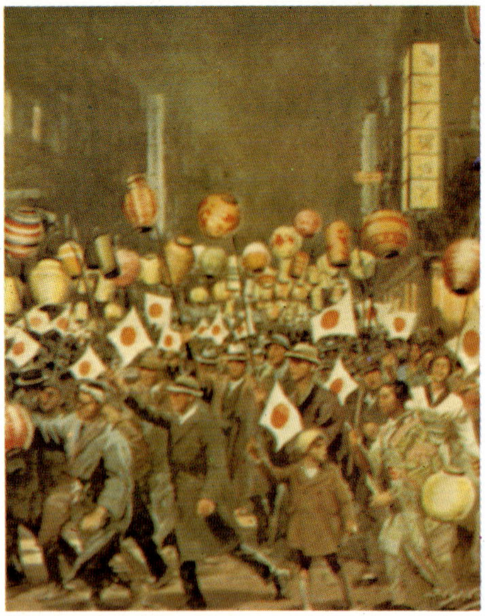

Japan. From 1931 onwards, the Japanese government, coming more and more under military domination, pursued an increasingly expansionist policy in Asia. The occupation of Manchuria – transformed into a puppet state, Manchukuo – in 1932 was followed in 1937 by an undeclared war against China. At the same time Japan drew closer to Germany, signing on 25 Nov. 1936 the Anti-Comintern Pact, and also to Italy which joined the Pact in Nov. 1937. Shortly afterwards Italy recognized Manchukuo, thus setting off a demonstration of nationalist enthusiasm in Tokyo, as this illustration from an Italian magazine shows.

As a sequel to Pearl Harbor the resounding victories won by the Japanese navy and army in the Philippines, Malaya and Indonesia were received with outbursts of joy by an ill-informed population, convinced of its moral superiority over the peoples of the western world. In this painting the artist, Mitsuru Suzuki, has tried to convey the enthusiasm of young Japanese students on their way to war.

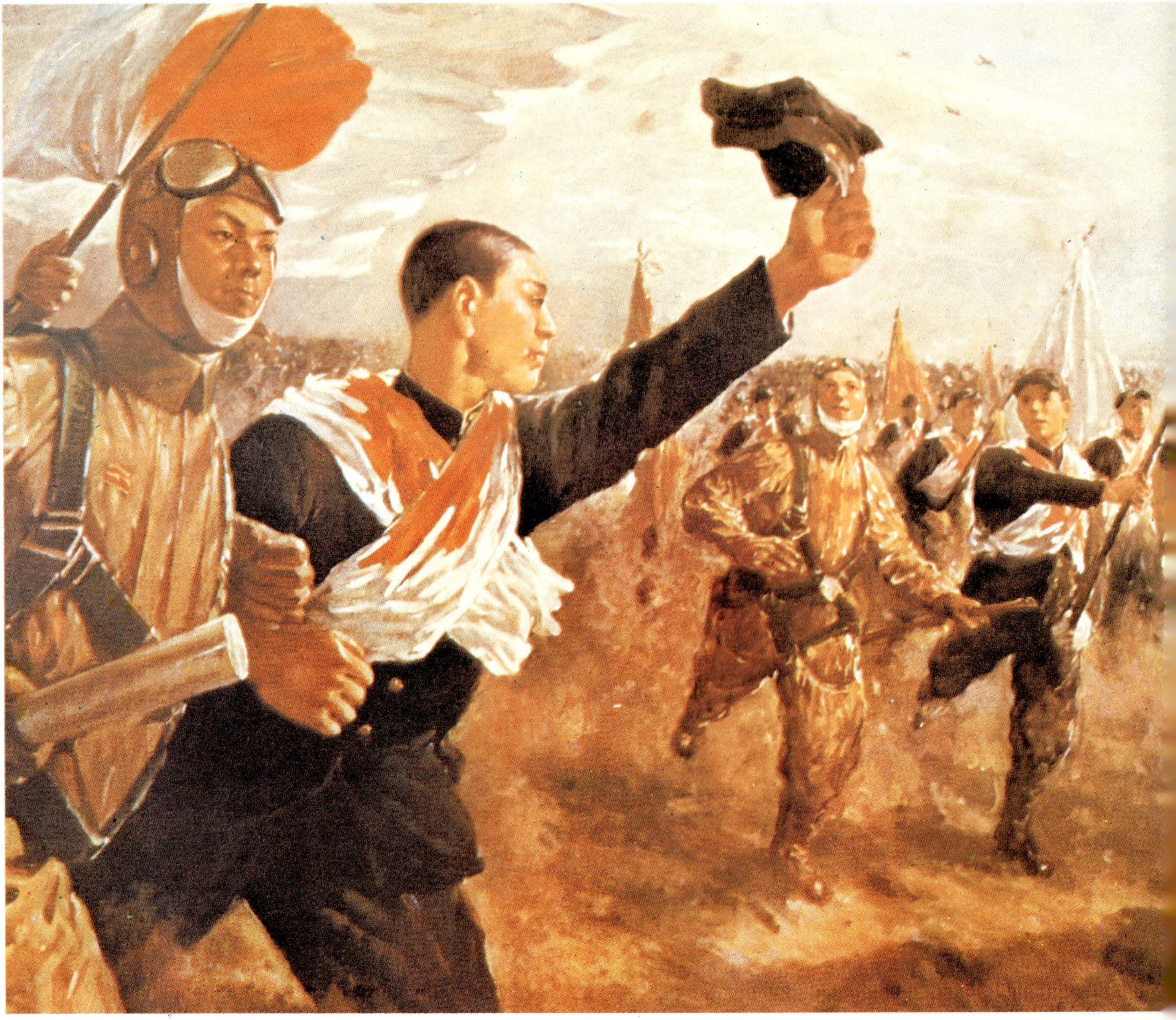

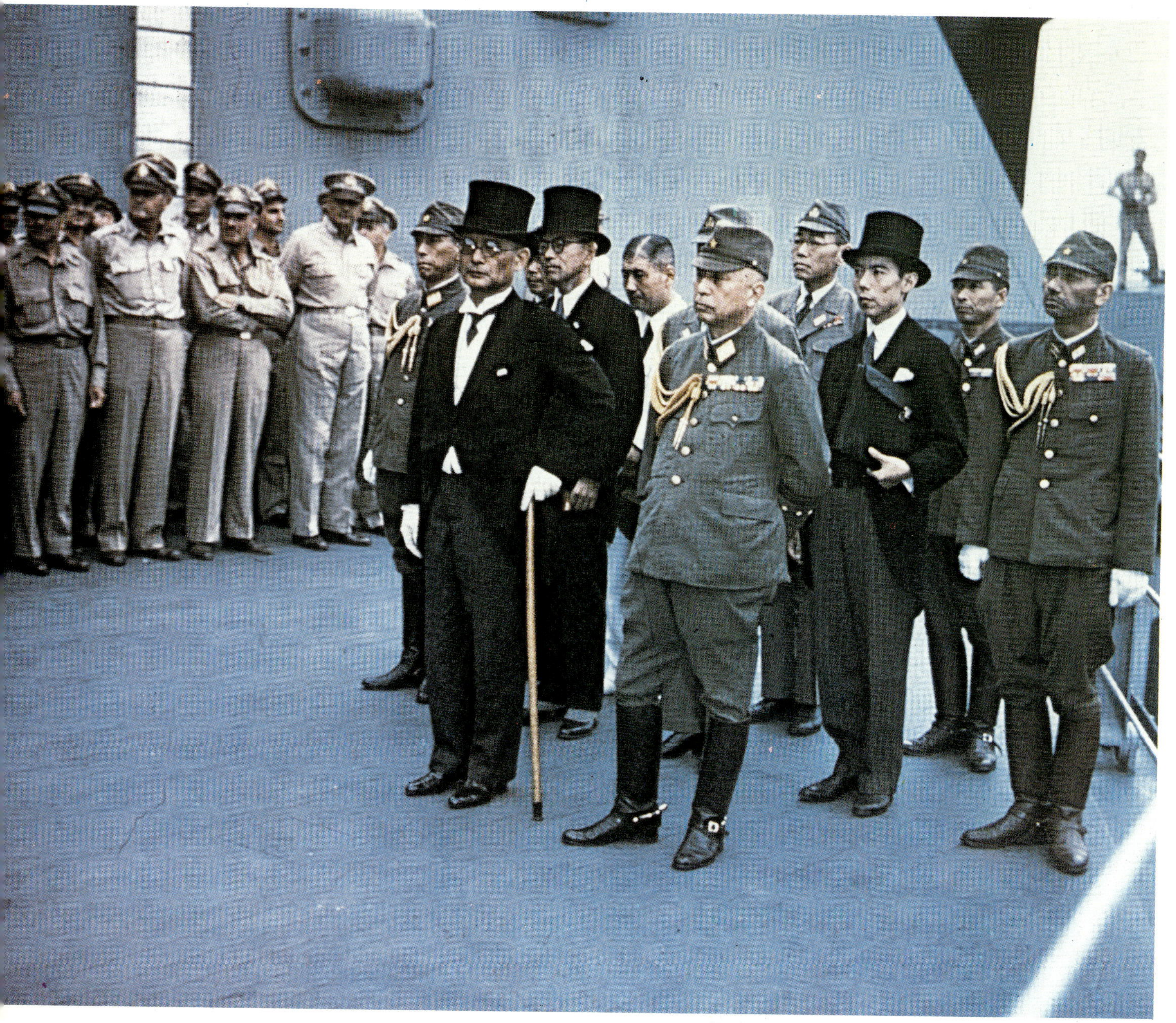

Following the atomic air raids on Hiroshima and Nagasaki and the Soviet intervention in Manchuria, the emperor Hirohito succeeded in making the army accept the principle of surrender and in bringing a disastrous war to an end. The surrender (photograph) was signed on 2 Sept. 1945, in Tokyo Bay, on board the battleship *Missouri*, under the supervision of General MacArthur. Leading the Japanese delegation were the minister of foreign affairs, Shigemitsu, with, on his left, General Umazu, representing the armed forces. Japan lost all its overseas possessions, had to submit to military occupation and accept a virtual American protectorate. The emperor, however, retained his throne.

The Jeep. Brought to perfection by the American company, Wyllys-Overland, the Jeep – of which we see here an example in the ruins of Saint-Lô in 1944 – was the most widely used of all the Allied combat vehicles during the war. Nearly 635,000 were built. Its name was derived from GP (general purpose) and from a popular comic strip character, Eugene the Jeep, Popeye's little rodent pal. The Jeep weighed just over a ton (1100 kg), had a 54 horsepower engine and a range of 220 miles (350 km). It showed a remarkable versatility, being used (among other things) as a reconnaissance and transport vehicle, as an ambulance and for towing light artillery weapons.

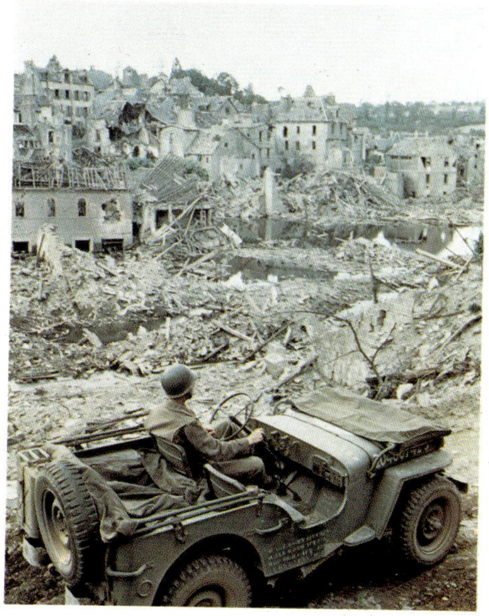

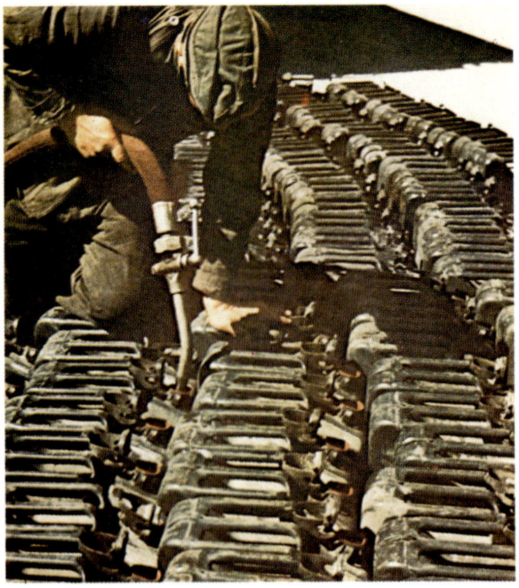

Jerricans. Its widespread use by the Allied armies made the jerrican, or petrol can, very popular. With a capacity of 20 litres, it was in fact copied from the container used by the Wehrmacht from 1939 onwards and designed to facilitate the refuelling of motorized units. Here on the eastern front in 1943 a German soldier is filling several dozen cans. The word jerrican is derived from 'can' and 'Jerry', the nickname given by the British to the German soldiers of the Second World War.

The Jews. The occupation of Europe enabled the Nazis to subject all the Jews in areas under German control to the persecution already undertaken in Germany itself since 1933. It was in the countries of eastern Europe that they suffered their most tragic fate. Having for generations experienced victimization and harassment by the local population, after the conquest of a large part of Poland by Germany in 1939, they began to be confined in huge ghettos. The one at Kutno is shown here. There then began the physical extermination of the Jewish communities, which reached a much greater geographical extent with the invasion of the USSR in 1941. Finally, the decision to destroy completely the whole Jewish population of Europe (the 'final solution') was officially approved by the Nazis at the Wannsee Conference on 20 Jan. 1942.

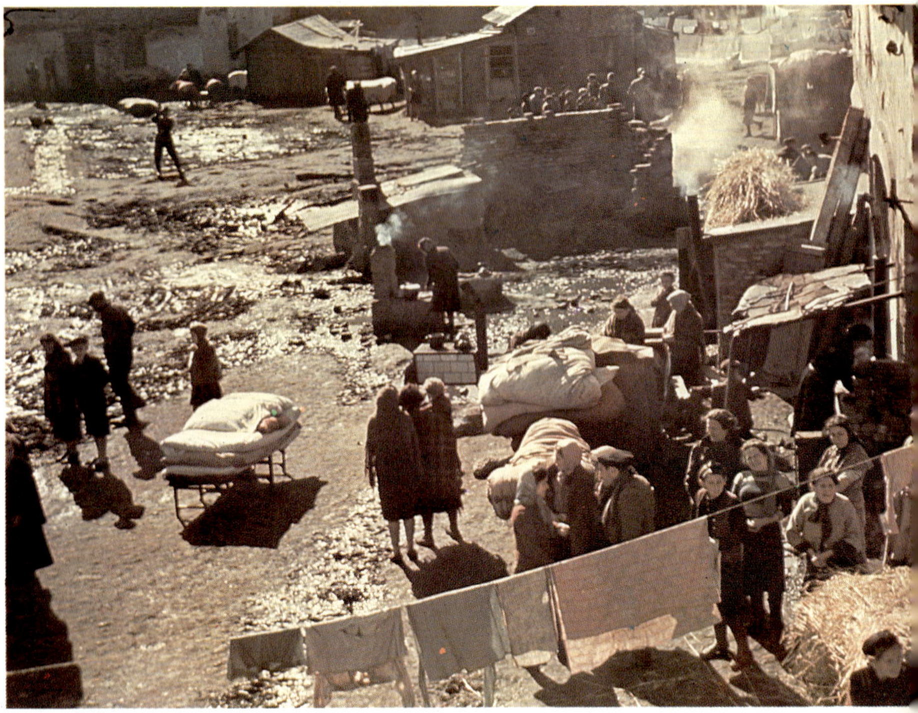

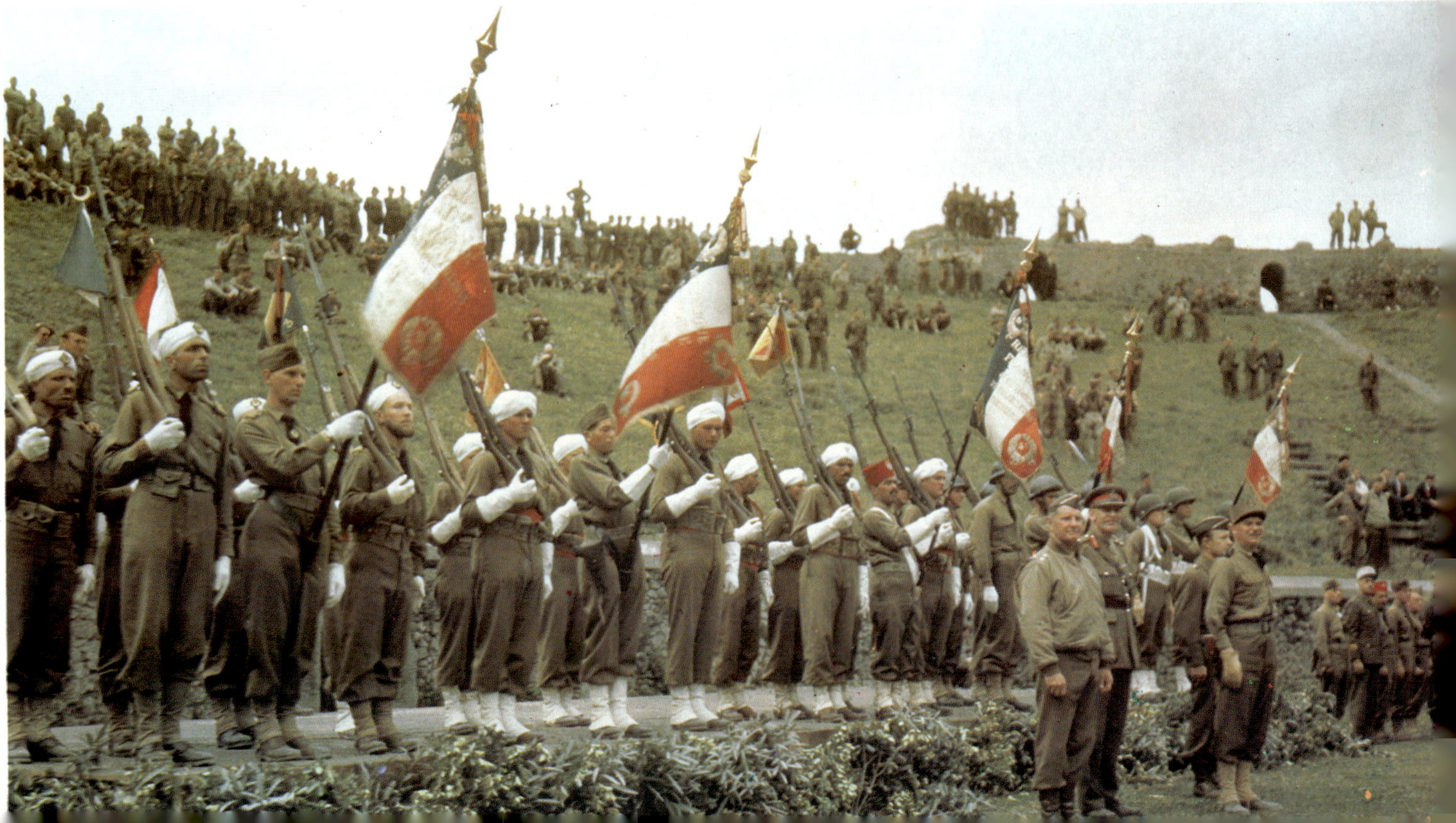

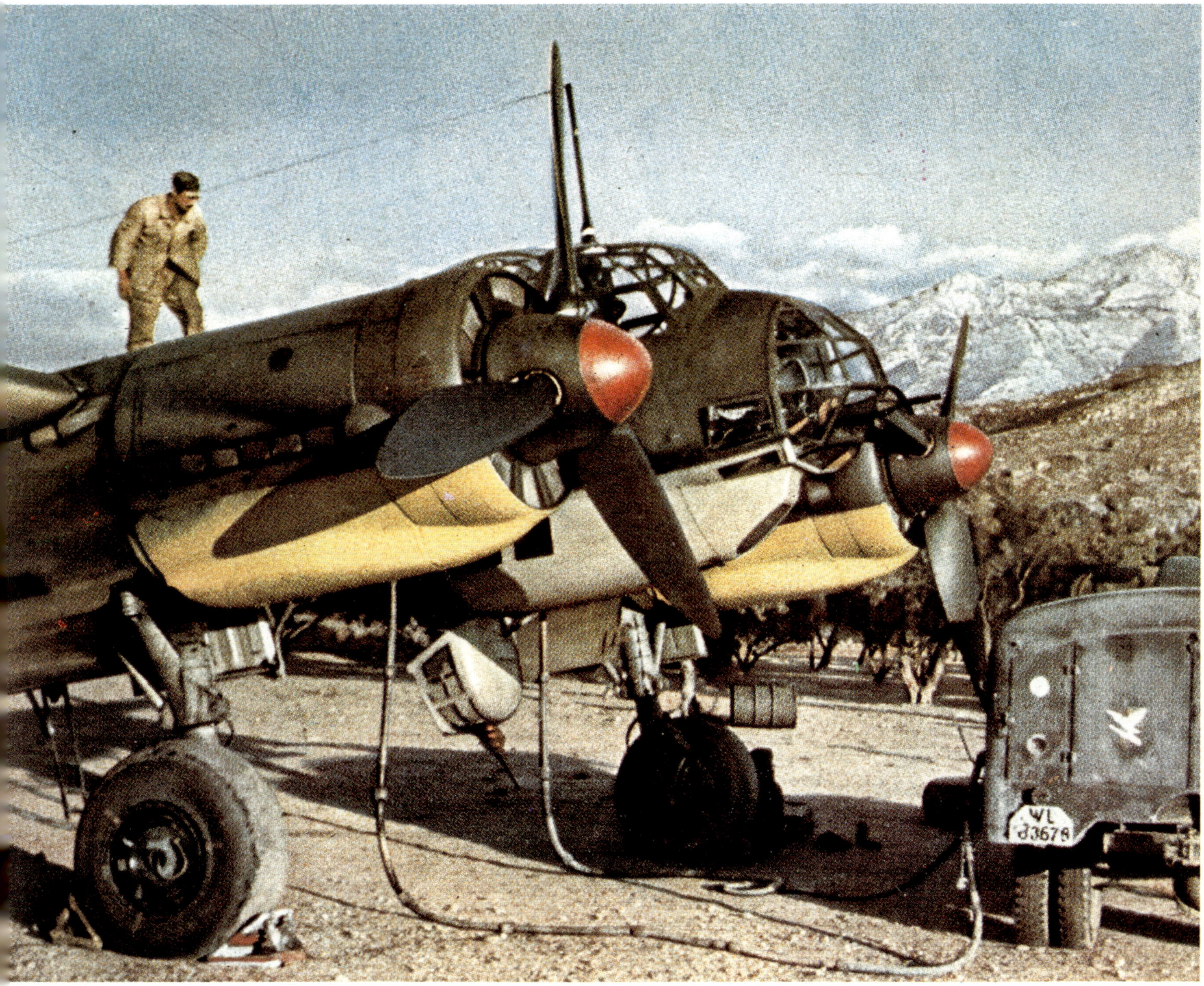

The Junkers Ju-88. Brought into service in 1938, this aircraft appeared in numerous different versions which enabled it to perform a great variety of functions. It was used for conventional and dive bombing, in the ground-support role with anti-tank guns, as a nightfighter, for long-distance reconnaissance and as a training aircraft. In its A4 version, the Ju-88 had a wingspan of 66 ft (20 m) and was 47 ft (14.40 m) long. Its speed was more than 270 mph (430 km/h) and it could carry nearly 1100 lb (500 kg) of bombs. In all 18,000 Junkers Ju-88s were built during the war. Here in April 1941 we see one of these bombers being refuelled with kerosene.

Juin. Of humble origins, General Alphonse Juin had spent most of his career in North Africa, and was commanding the French 15th Motorized Infantry Division when he was taken prisoner near Lille on 30 May 1940. Set free in 1941, he made his way to Africa and took part in the Tunisian campaign, following Operation Torch, before being given command of the French Expeditionary Corps in Italy. In that theatre he showed what he was capable of, revealing remarkable qualities as a tactician, and played a decisive part in the breaking of the Winter Line and the capture of Rome. Here he is seen, on the right, in the first row, (*opposite page*) during a parade by the French Expeditionary Corps in the ruins of Pompeii.

Kharkov. Child in rags begging in the streets o the town in 1942.

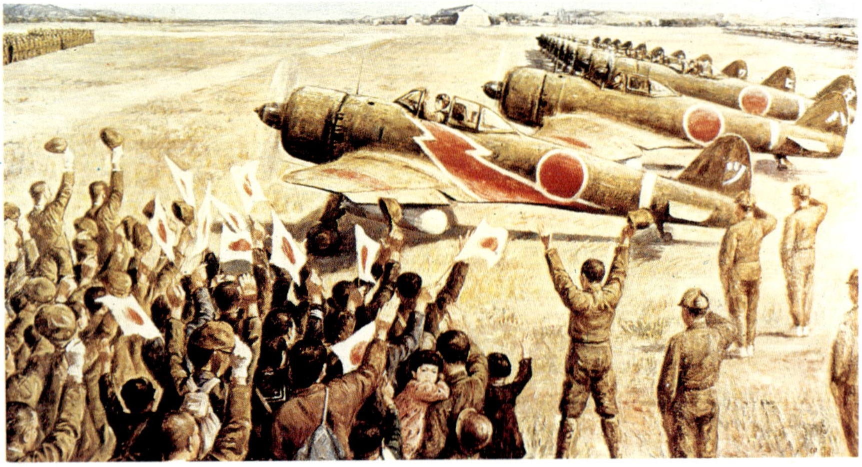

The Kamikazes. Confronted with the disastrous turn of events, in the autumn of 1944 the Japanese high command decided to resort to the desperate solution of a corps of kamikazes, consisting of pilots of suicide planes. Assembled in a few days in the Philippines, the unit was very quickly put to use. In view of the initial success of the operations the imperial general staff encouraged further development. The kamikazes consisted of young, inexperienced pilots, all volunteers, recruited throughout Japan after an unrestrainedly nationalistic propaganda campaign, which affected students and even children at high school. The high command as a rule held in reserve for special missions the all too few experienced pilots that remained. The young kamikazes were trained in a few days. It was during the battle of Okinawa that they were used in mass formations against the American fleet. The departure of the kamikazes took place according to a ritual that the painter, Usaburo Ihara, has endeavoured to capture in this painting, which gives a good indication of the climate of feverish patriotism which prevailed when a suicide squadron was about to set off.

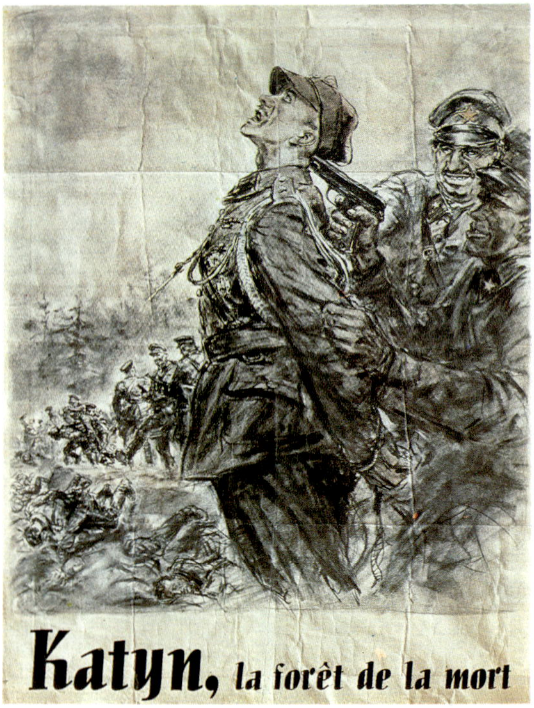

Katyn. In April 1943, in the forest of Katyn, near Smolensk, the Germans discovered in communal graves the bodies of more than 4000 Polish officers, captured by the Red Army in 1939. They had been killed by a bullet in the back of the neck, as shown in this German propaganda poster of 1943 intended for occupied Europe. In spite of all the denials by Moscow there is no doubt whatsoever today about the origins of the massacre, which was ordered by Stalin in 1940 in order to deprive Poland of its military and civilian elite. At the time, the discovery of Katyn only confirmed the suspicions of the Polish government in exile in London, which had been unable to obtain from the Kremlin the slightest information about the 15,000 officers who had been taken prisoner and had vanished in the USSR since 1939.

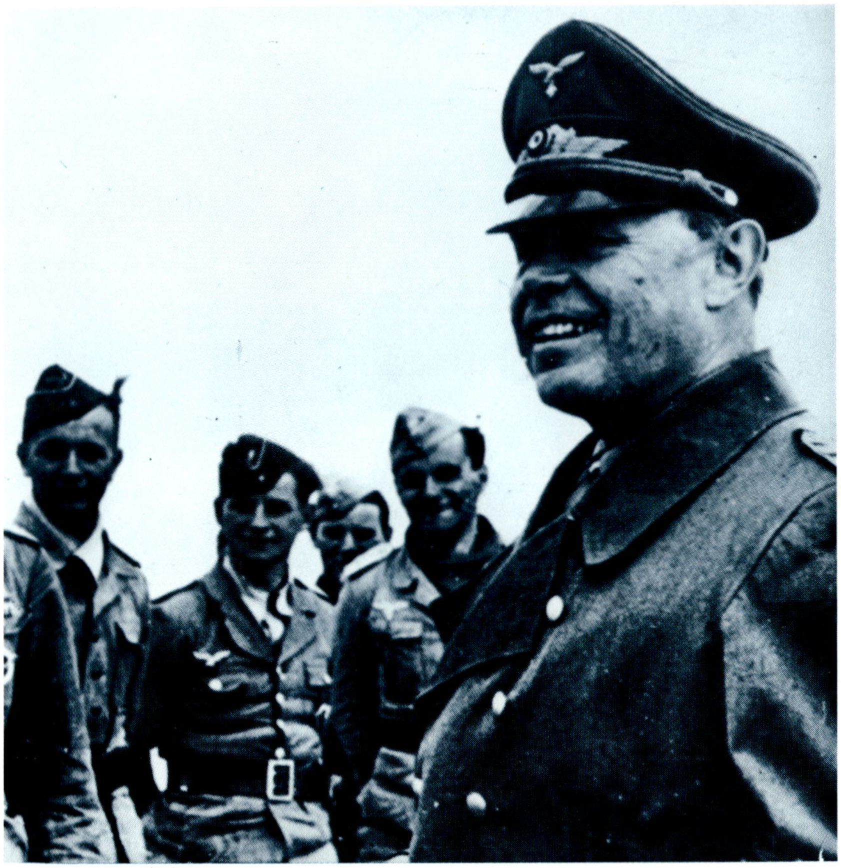

Kesselring. Considered to be one of the most talented commanders of the war, Field Marshal Albert Kesselring held the command of air fleets during the invasions of Poland and France. During the Battle of Britain his air fleet was on the verge of defeating Fighter Command before Göring transferred the bombing offensive to London. In 1941 he was sent to the southern front and shared the direction of the North African campaign with Rommel. Although he was unable to halt the Allied advance in North Africa, Kesselring held up the Allies in Sicily and organized a brilliant defence of the Italian peninsula. In 1945 he replaced Rundstedt as commander of the west, but this came too late to prevent the German collapse.

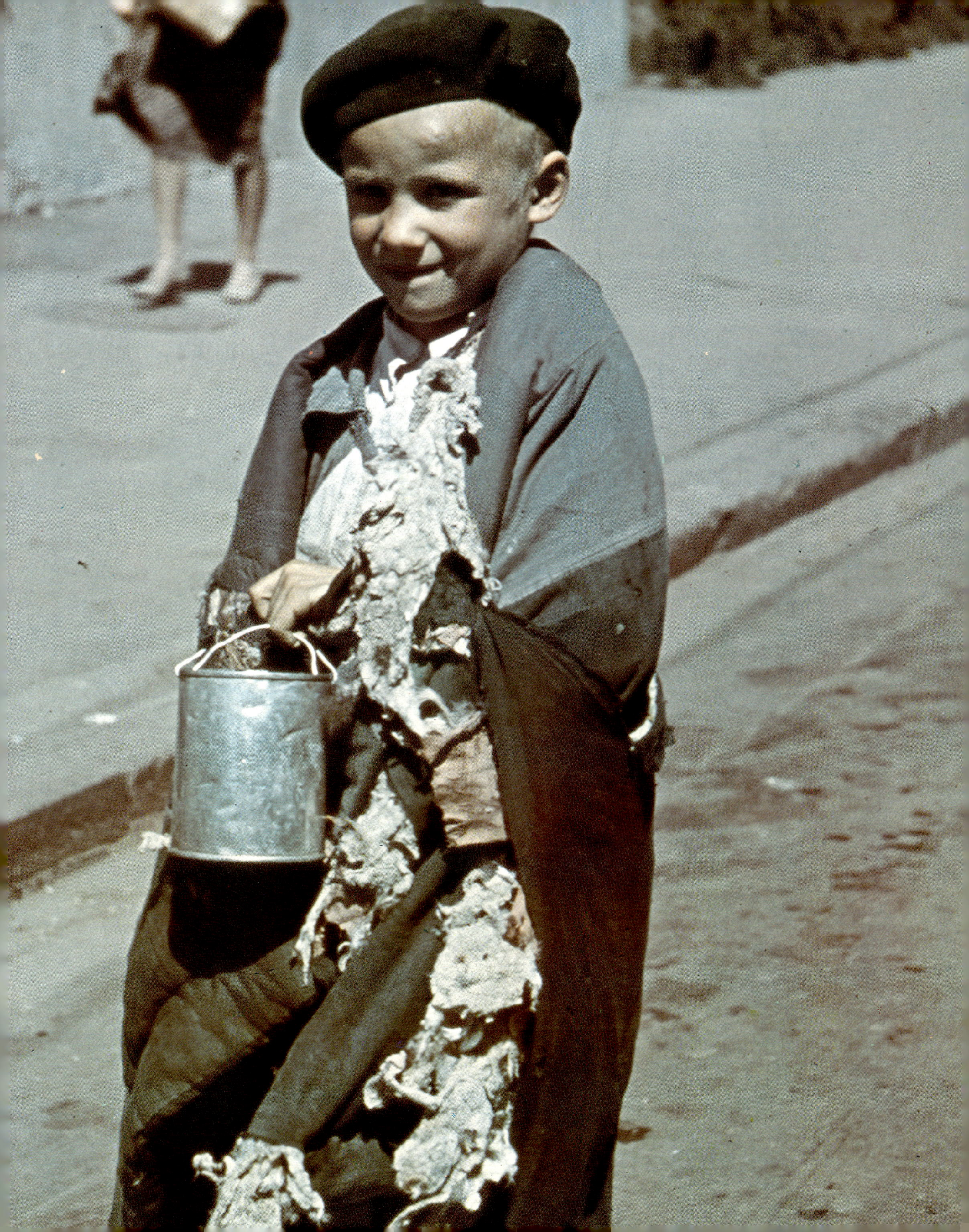

Kharkov. With the exception of a short-lived liberation by the Red Army at the end of the winter of 1942–3, the Germans were to occupy Kharkov, the economic capital of the Ukraine, from Nov. 1941 to Aug. 1943. As this picture shows, the population, already living in wretched conditions as a result of the sacrifices imposed by the Soviet five-year plans, was reduced to further extremes of degradation during the war. With the collapse of production large flea markets were set up on the outskirts of the town for the exchange of basic necessities.

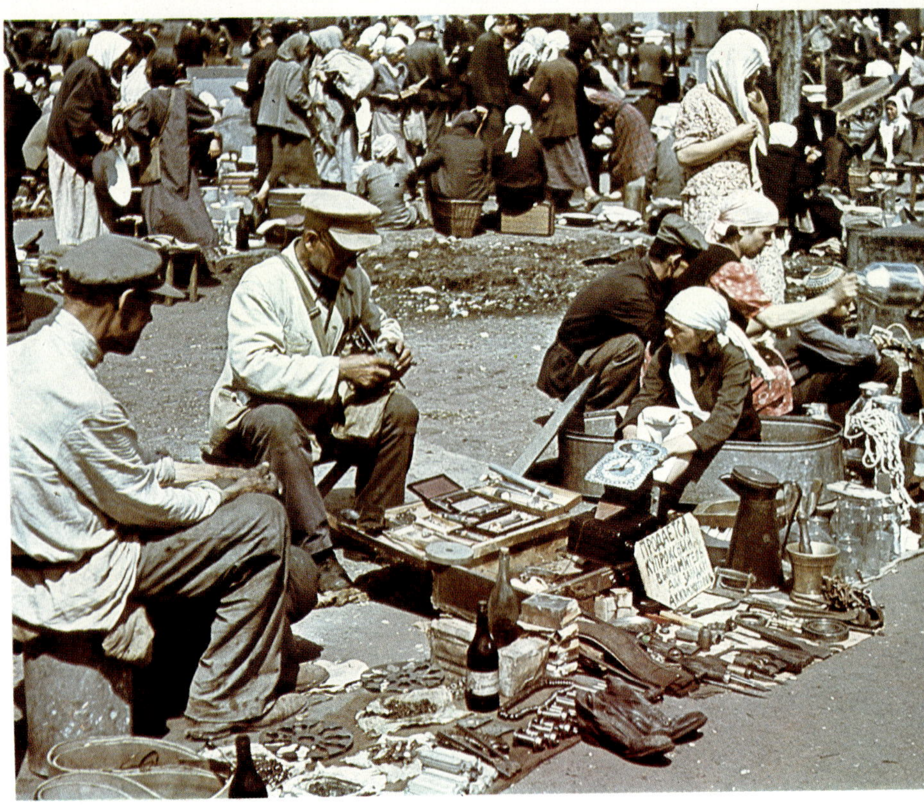

The occupation by the Germans of Kiev, considered the political and spiritual capital of the Ukraine, took place in Sept. 1941 after a battle of encirclement which ended with the destruction of an army of more than a million men. In spite of Kiev's traditional separatism, the Germans did not succeed in winning over the population, because of their deportations of able-bodied men and their refusal to recognize the independence of the Ukraine. The liberation of the town took place in Nov. 1943. Here the direction 'Kiev' can be seen on the German signposts at the centre of the town of Poltava.

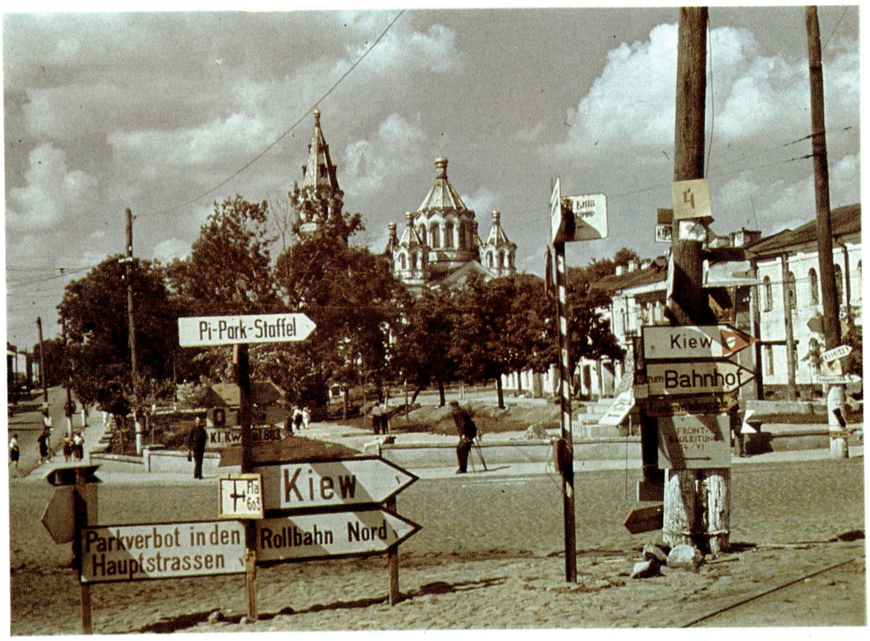

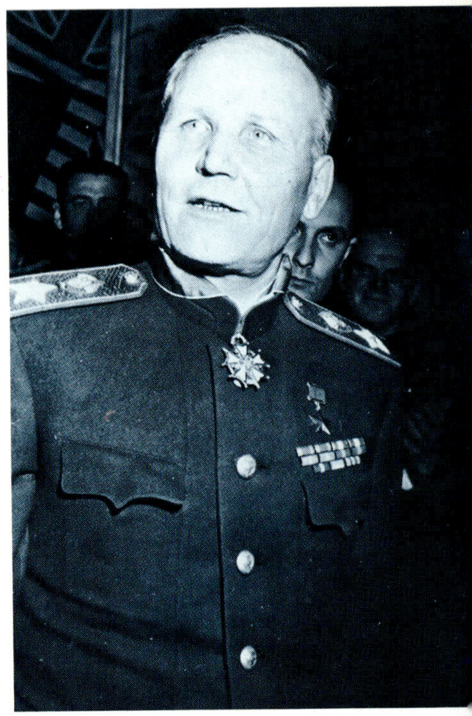

Konev. Having served in the Smolensk region soon after the German attack on Russia in 1941, he was commander of the front which checked the German advance on Moscow. In July 1943 he resisted the attack on Kursk and pushed on to retake several cities. Early in 1944 Konev succeeded in encircling ten German divisions at Korsun, one of the most famous of Russian victories. In Feb. 1944 Ivan Konev became marshal and accompanied Zhukov's advance from the Vistula to the Oder and later to Berlin.

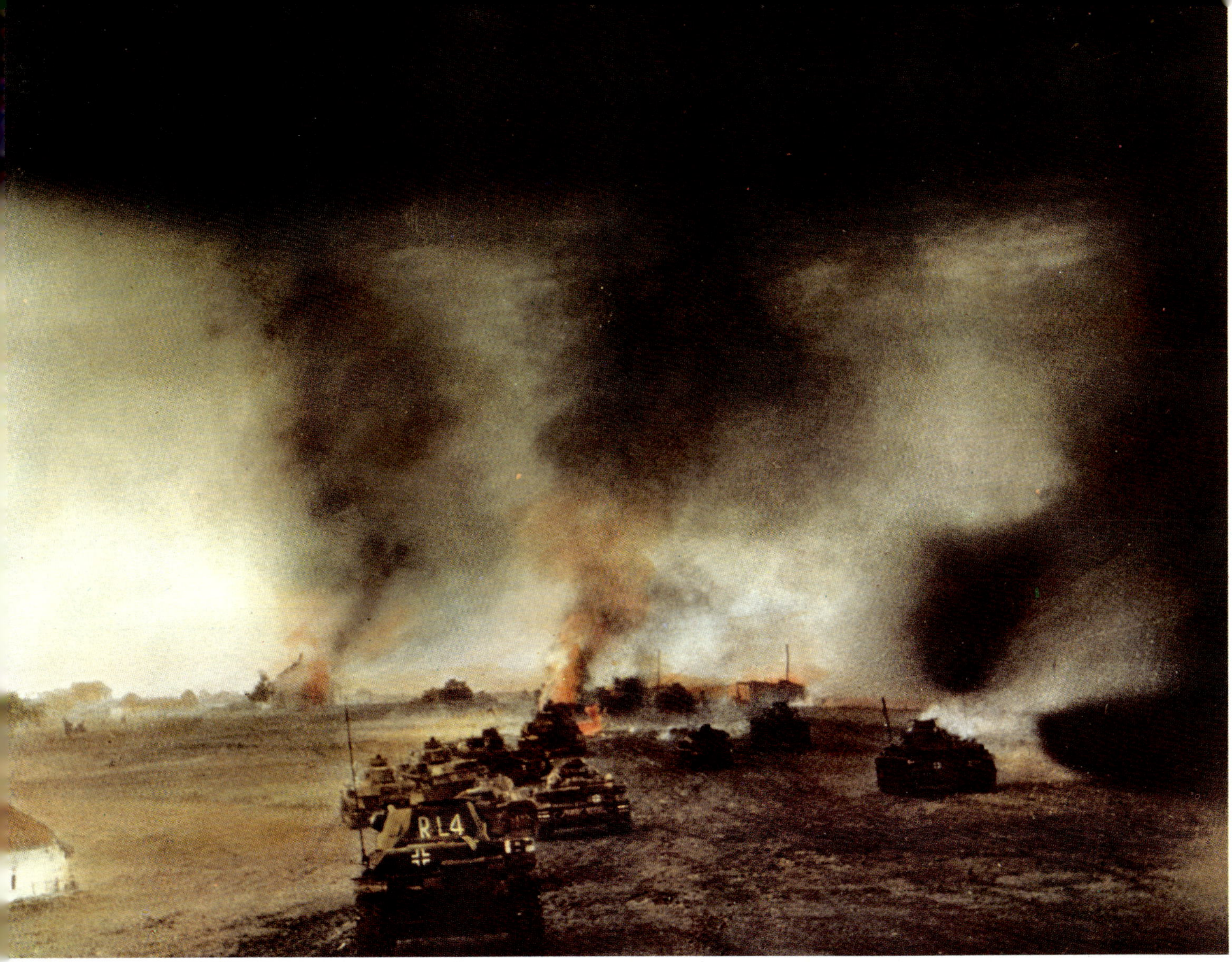

Kursk. The offensive against the Kursk salient in July 1943, as part of Operation Citadel, was the last large-scale operation launched on the eastern front on the initiative of the German high command. In spite of formidable concentrations of armour the Germans did not succeed in penetrating the Russian positions, which had been established in depth, and were themselves subjected to fierce counter-attacks by Russian tanks. After the failure of this offensive, which cost the Wehrmacht nearly 100,000 men (500,000 according to Soviet historians), the initiative passed to the Red Army for good.

Kwajalein. The assault launched against Kwajalein Atoll in the Marshall Islands in Jan. 1944 was an integral part of one of the first stages of Nimitz's counter-offensive against Japan. Carried out with minimum losses, the occupation of Kwajalein was to lead to the neutralization of Truk, the capture of Eniwetok and the offensive against the Marianas. The success of the American operation was largely dependent upon the combined air and naval preparations, which had made possible the destruction of the Japanese defences. Here can be seen the remains of a blockhouse after the battle: its state gives some idea of the ferocity and concentration of the American bombardment.

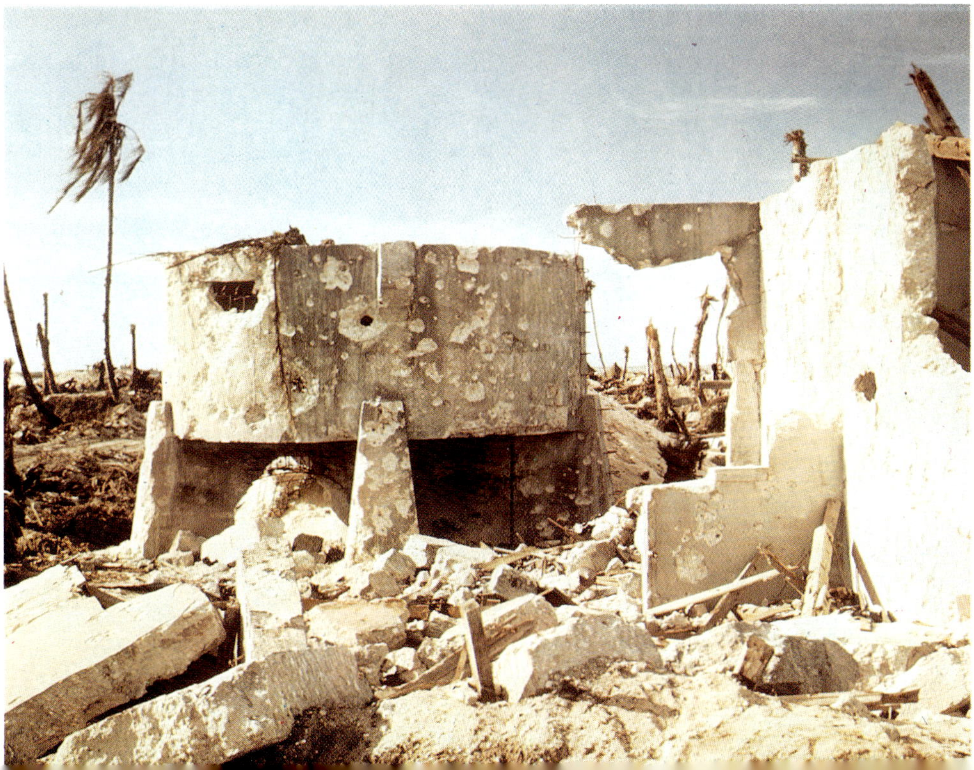

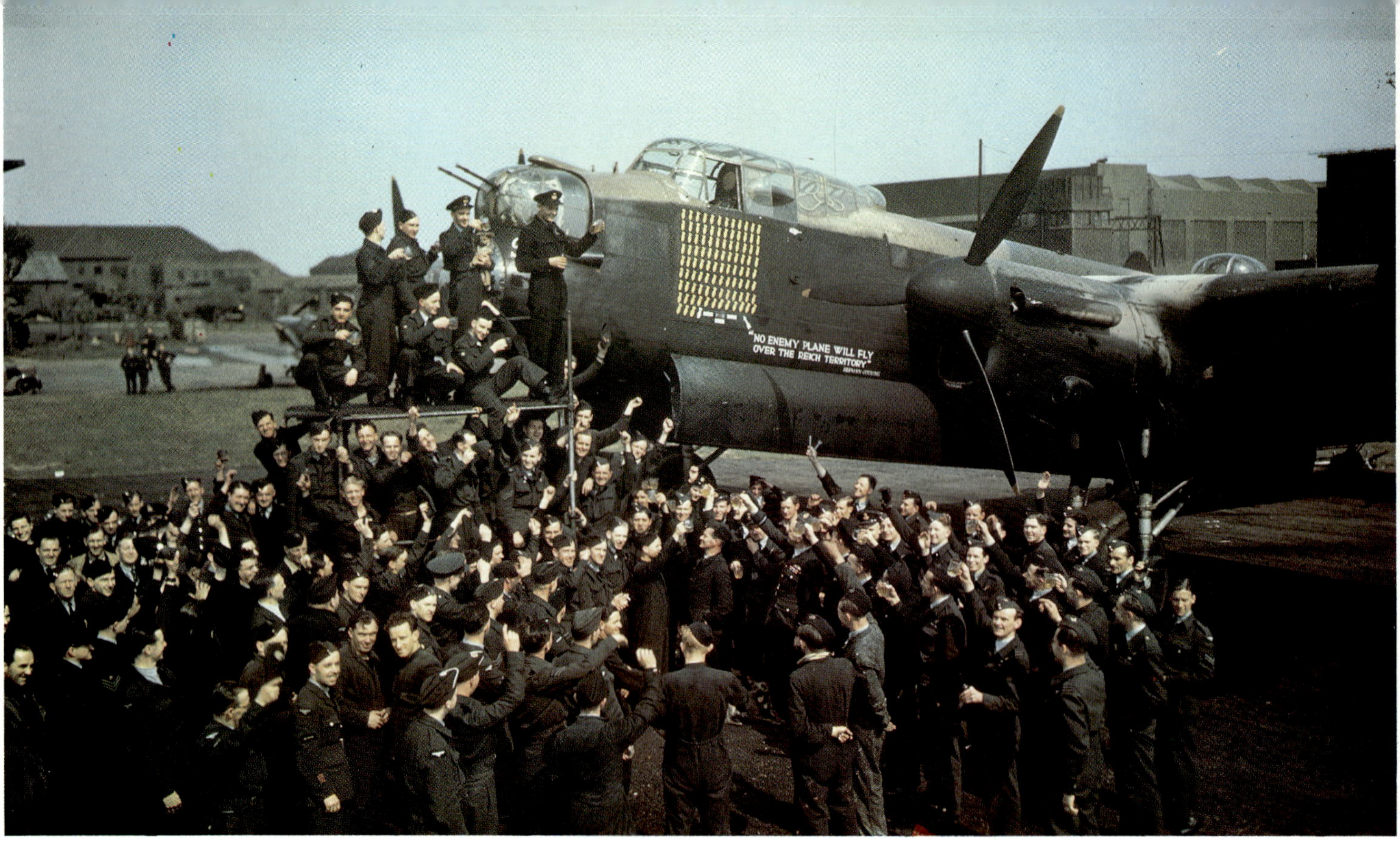

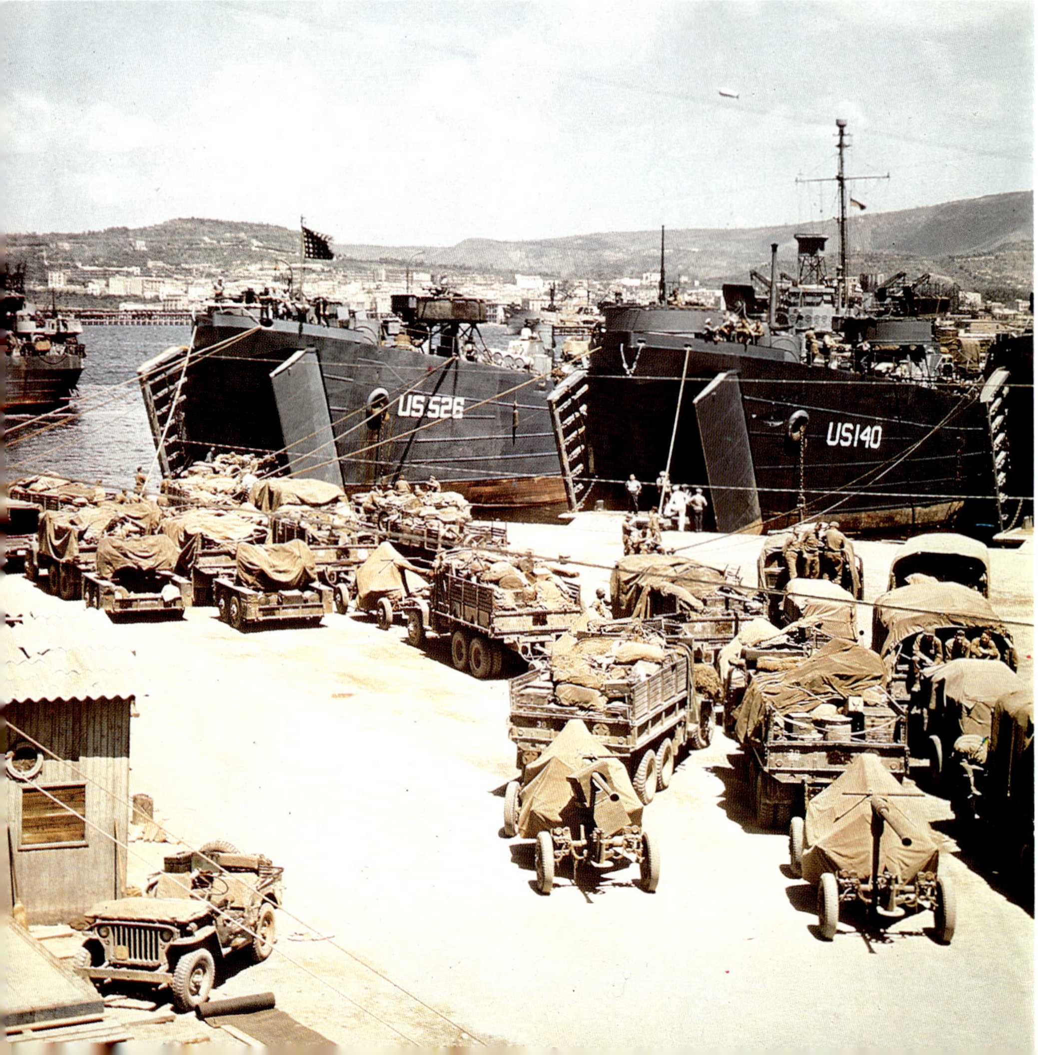

The Lancaster. The Lancaster, which entered service from March 1942 onwards, and of which more than 7400 were built, became the RAF's principal heavy bomber. One of its standard versions had a wingspan of 102 ft (31 m), a length of 69 ft (21 m), a weight of 32 tons (32,000 kg) and a speed of 290 mph (460 km/h). It could carry $5\frac{1}{2}$ tons (5500 kg) of bombs a maximum distance of 1750 miles (2800 km) and its defensive armament consisted of eight machine-guns. In the picture the crew of a bomber are celebrating the return from its 100th mission, indicated by the bombs painted on the fuselage. It also carries Göring's famous quotation: 'No enemy plane will fly over the territory of the Reich.'

Landing craft. Perfected by the Japanese during the conflict with China and developed on a vast scale by the British and, especially by the Americans, landing craft and ships (seen here during the Italian campaign) represented one of the great lessons of the war and assured the success of combined operations. Ranging in scale from the simple landing craft through the LCI and LCT, intended to transport infantry or tanks, to the LST (Landing Ship Tanks) of 4000 tons, landing vessels had the advantage of enabling troops, armour and vehicles to land directly on beaches and they were subsequently able to ensure the resupply of the units which had landed. In 1945 the US Navy alone had more than 50,000 landing vessels, with a tonnage in excess of 2 million.

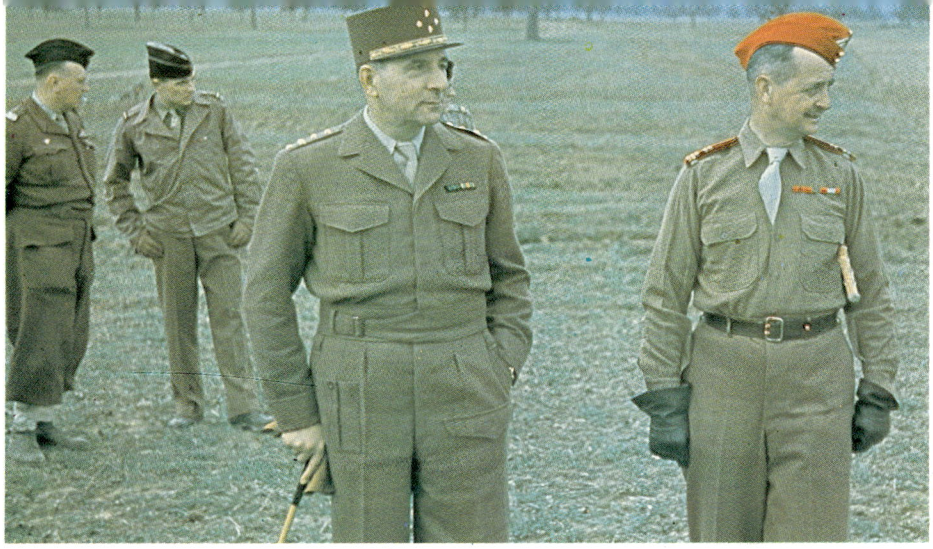

De Lattre de Tassigny. General de Lattre came into prominence when commanding the French 14th Division in 1940, and later by his attempt at resistance in Nov. 1942 at the time of the German takeover of unoccupied France. However, he really made his name as commander of the First French Army in 1944–45. In this capacity de Lattre was to take part in the liberation of southeast France, in the difficult campaign in Alsace and in the advance into southern Germany. On many occasions he had the onerous task of reconciling the orders of the American military commanders with the politically inspired directives of General de Gaulle.

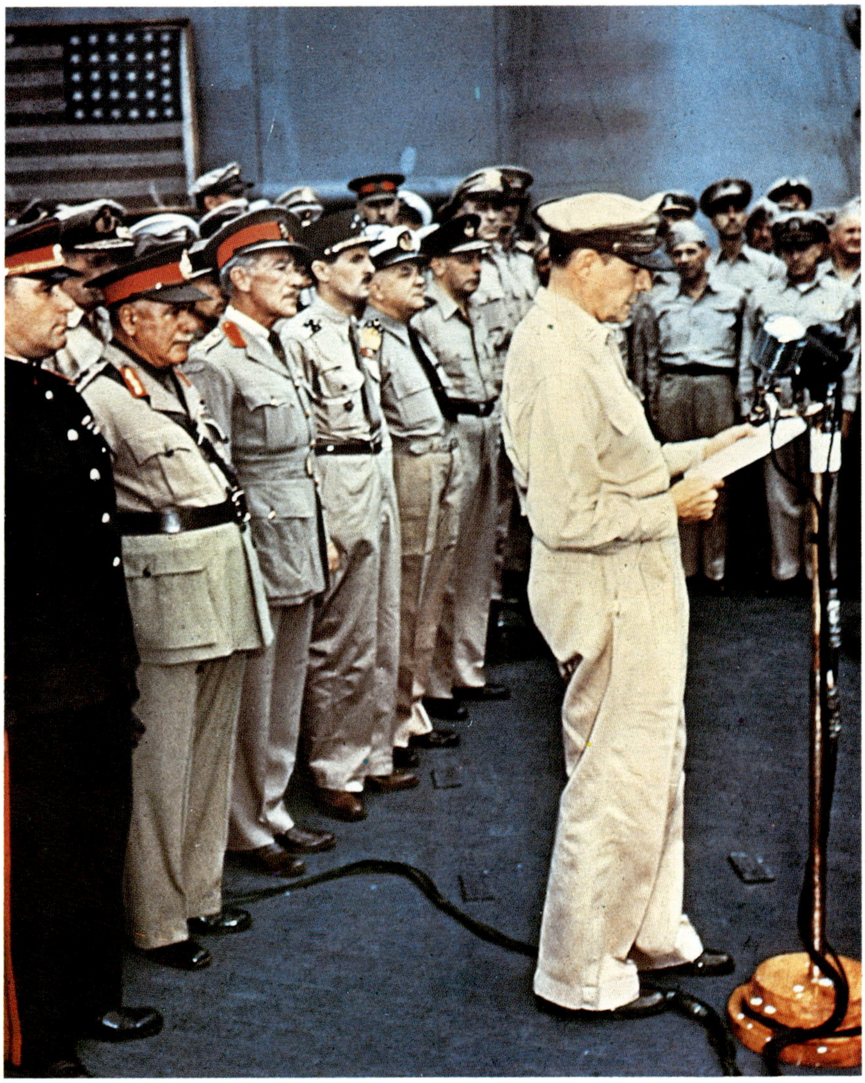

Leclerc. Still a captain in 1939, Philippe de Hauteclocque sided with de Gaulle in 1940 and, under the name of Leclerc, was to acquire an almost legendary reputation during an epic career. He led a Free French force all the way from Lake Chad to Tripoli to assist in the invasion of Tunisia. Subsequently, as commander of the French 2nd Armoured Division, he took part in the invasion of Normandy and the liberation of Paris and Strasbourg before reaching Berchtesgaden on 5 May 1945. He is seen here, fourth from the left, among other Allied officers, as France's representative at the signing of the Japanese surrender on 2 Sept. 1945, on board the battleship *Missouri*.

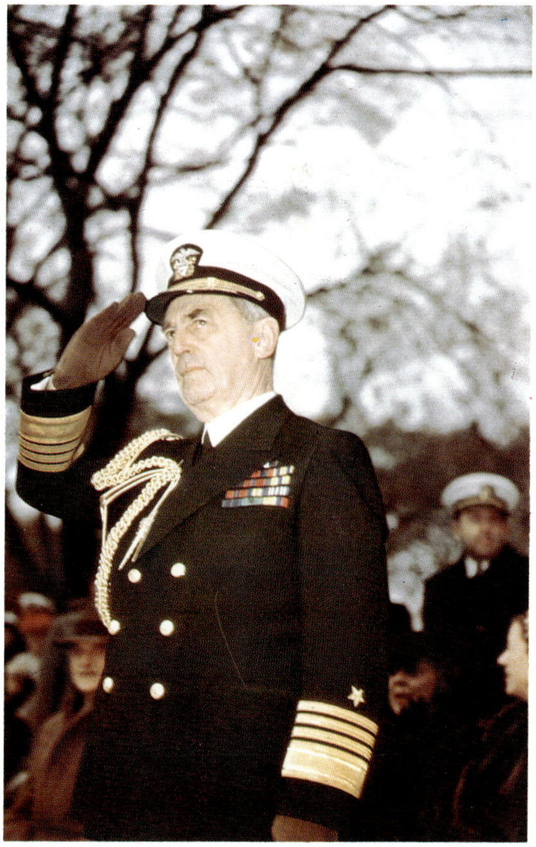

Leahy. Although in 1939 Admiral Leahy had retired from active service with the US Navy, where he had been chief of naval operations, he played an important part during the war, becoming one of Roosevelt's close advisers. The president's confidence won him the position of ambassador to Vichy from Jan. 1941 to May 1942, during which time he tried in vain to check the collaborationist tendencies of the Vichy prime minister, Pierre Laval. Having subsequently been appointed admiral of the fleet, he accompanied first Roosevelt and then Truman to all the big Allied conferences from Casablanca to Potsdam.

The Legion of French Volunteers against Bolshevism. In Aug. 1941, on the initiative of certain collaborationist groups, and with the backing of the Vichy government, a legion of French volunteers was created. Never reaching regimental strength, it first saw action in the battle of Moscow, being subsquently (until 1944) engaged in the fight with partisans behind the German lines. Since France was not at war with the USSR, the volunteers served in Wehrmacht uniform with a simple tricolour badge. In July 1944 the 2000 survivors of the Legion were integrated in the French 'Charlemagne' brigade of the SS.

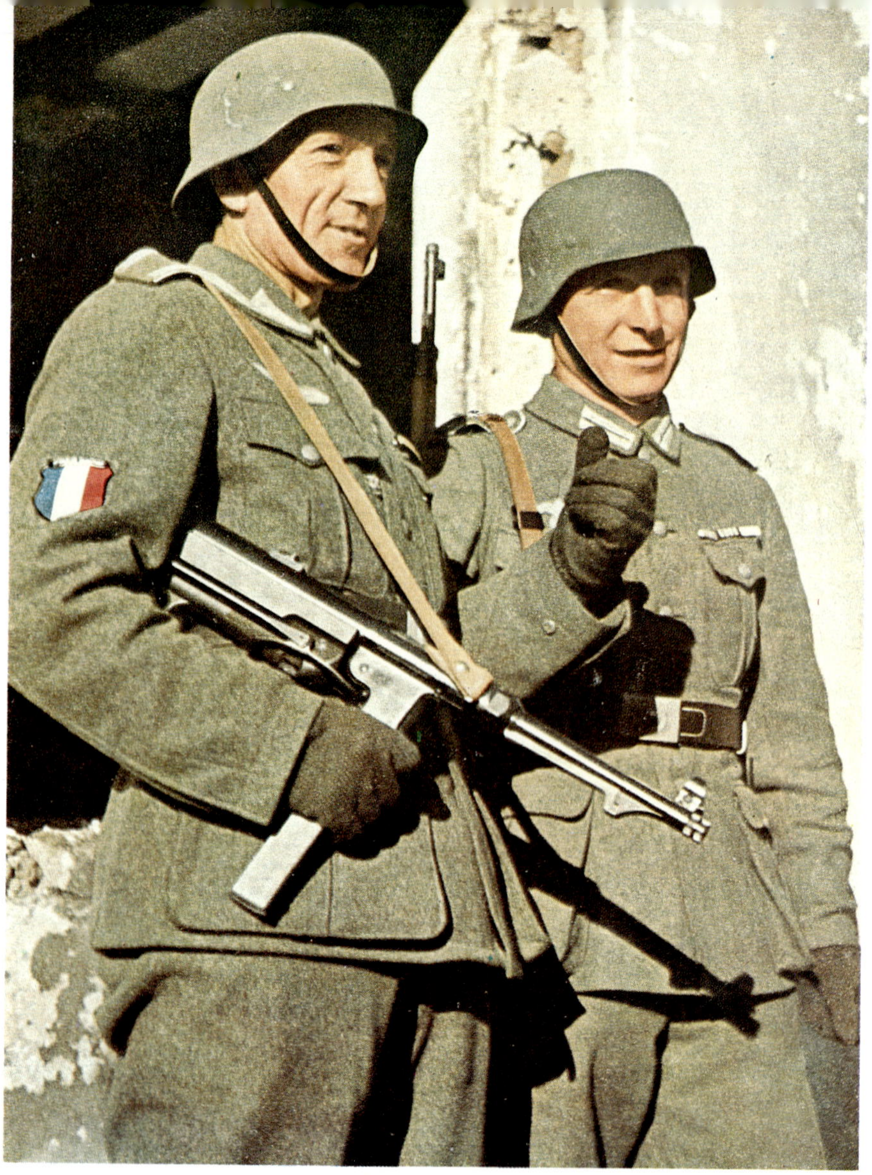

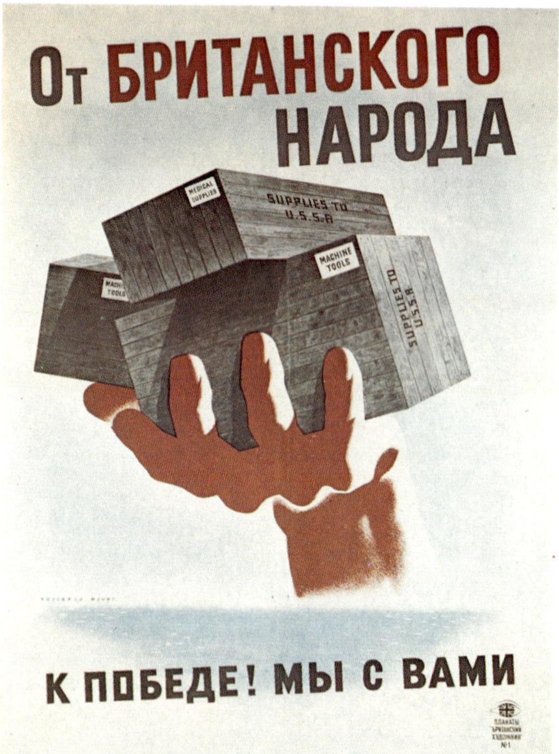

Lend-Lease. From the very beginning of the war in the east, Great Britain was eager to send material help to the Soviet Union, as this British poster written in Russian shows: 'From the British people. On to victory. We are with you.' In fact the main aid to countries fighting the Axis powers came from the United States through the agency of lend-lease devised by Roosevelt and enacted in March 1941 in favour of Great Britain. The Soviet Union was in its turn one of the chief beneficiaries. It received considerable quantities of war materiel, munitions, machine-tools, rolling stock and fuel. Thanks to lend-lease, America really did play the role of the 'arsenal of democracy'. Musée des deux Guerres Mondiales. B.D.I.C. (Universités de Paris).

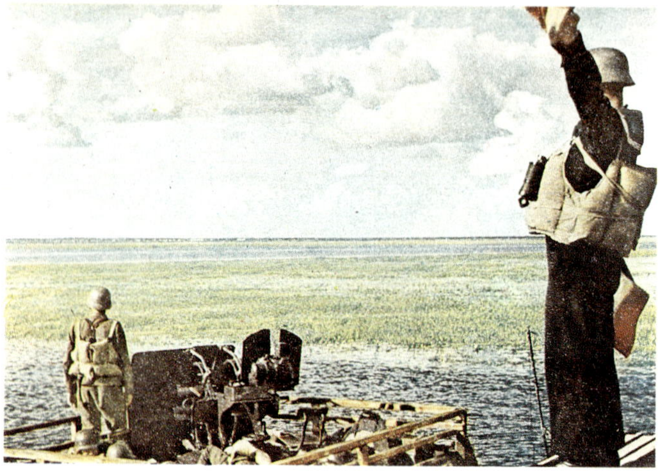

Leningrad. From the beginning of autumn 1941 German troops had in fact won control of the low-lying and often marshy region (photograph) which surrounds Leningrad, thus effectively isolating the city. This encirclement led to a terrible siege, in which the inhabitants, subjected to bombardment, cold and famine (in spite of the supply lifeline across Lake Ladoga), experienced appalling suffering: 900,000 died before Leningrad could be finally relieved at the beginning of 1944. Here we see a German anti-aircraft gun set up on a raft on Lake Ilmen. On the right a German naval signaller is using semaphore flags to convey orders from one side of the lake to the other.

Leyte. In autumn 1944 the twofold American offensive against Japan with MacArthur in the south and Nimitz in the centre, came together in the Philippines and culminated in the first landing in Leyte on 17 Oct. Simultaneously, the American fleet shattered the last resistance of the Imperial Japanese Navy and sank the majority of its warships. The landing at Leyte put the seal on MacArthur's famous promise at Corregidor in March 1942: 'I shall return'. Anxious, as ever, about his public image, the general had himself photographed frequently during the first operations. Here he is about to make a short speech: 'By the grace of the Almighty, our troops are on Philippine soil, this soil bathed in the blood of our two peoples.'

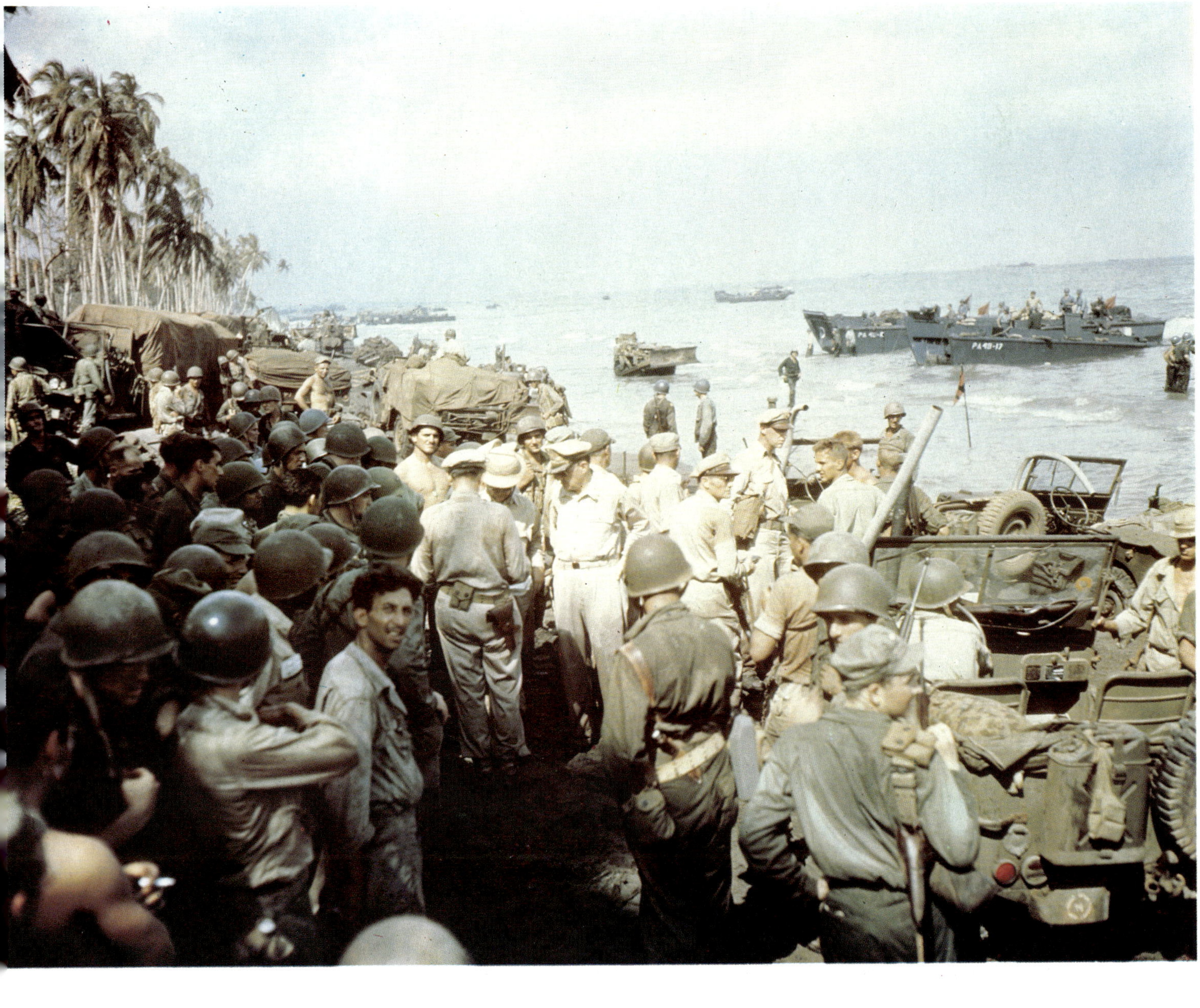

Opposite
Leyte. Douglas Dauntless bombers, one of the standard aircraft of the American Pacific fleet.

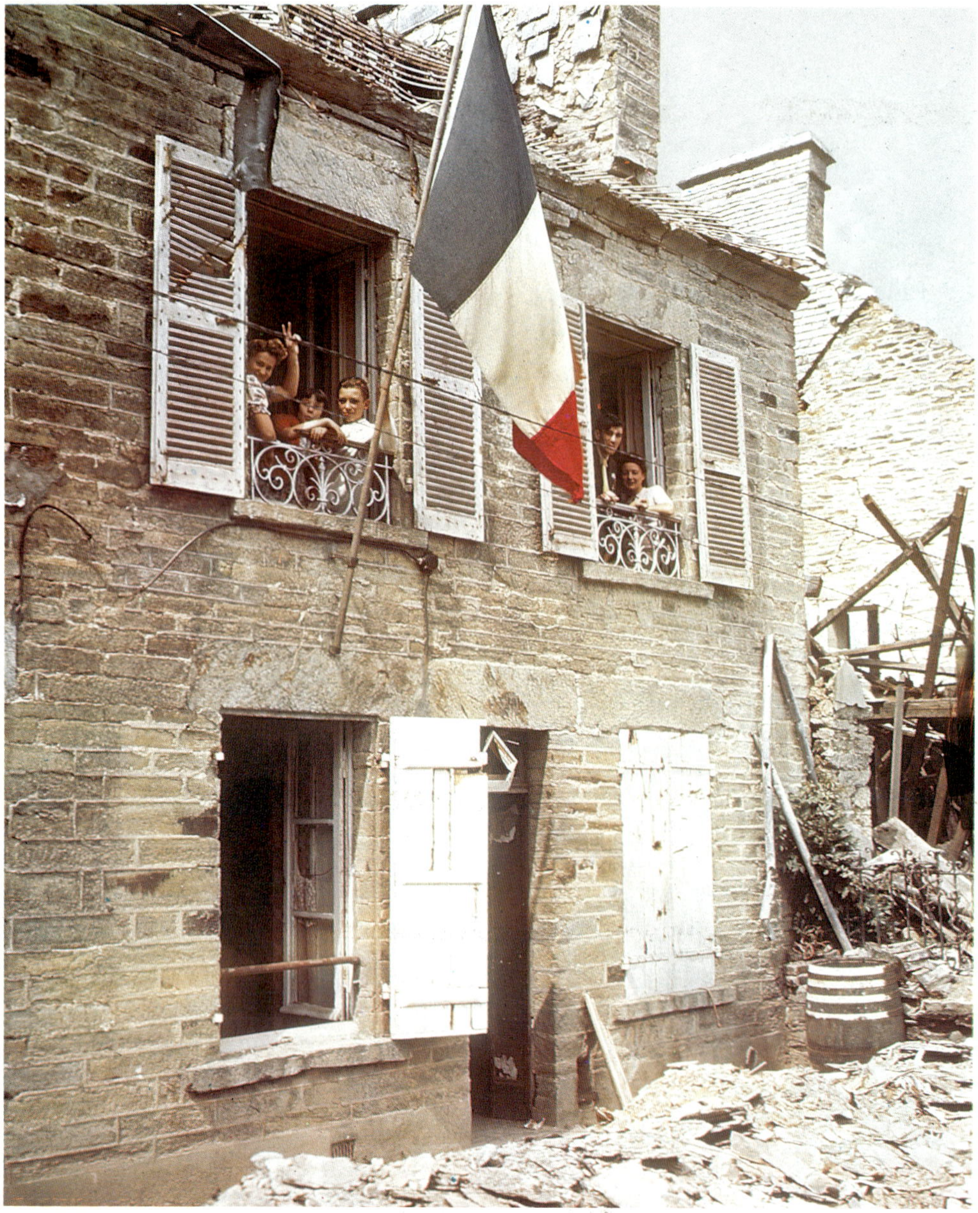

The Liberation. In a house in Cherbourg relatively untouched by the bombardment and the fighting, a family celebrates the liberation of the town by displaying a flag. During the fierce battle for Normandy, which lasted more than two months, the French became rather anxious about the liberation of the country and whether it would bring large-scale devastation. There was also uncertainty about the political future.

After the breaching of the German front in Normandy and the landing in Provence on 15 Aug. 1944 the liberation of the country seemed to take place with miraculous speed. Here we see an American convoy passing through a little town in Normandy. Aided by the FFI (Forces françaises de l'intérieur), in a single month the Allied troops succeeded in driving the Germans out of two-thirds of France.

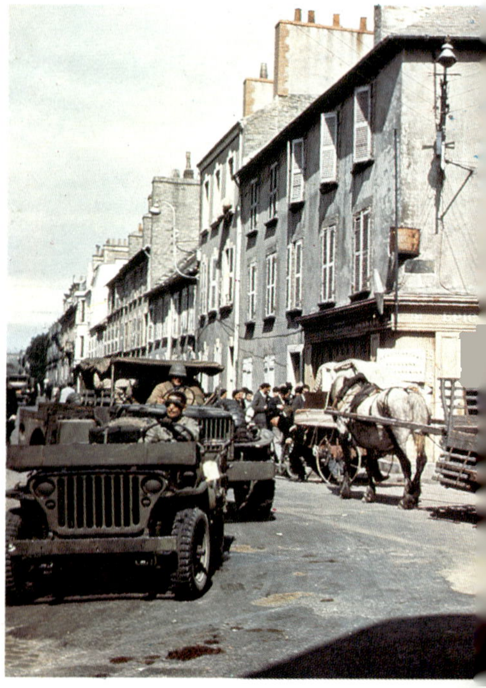

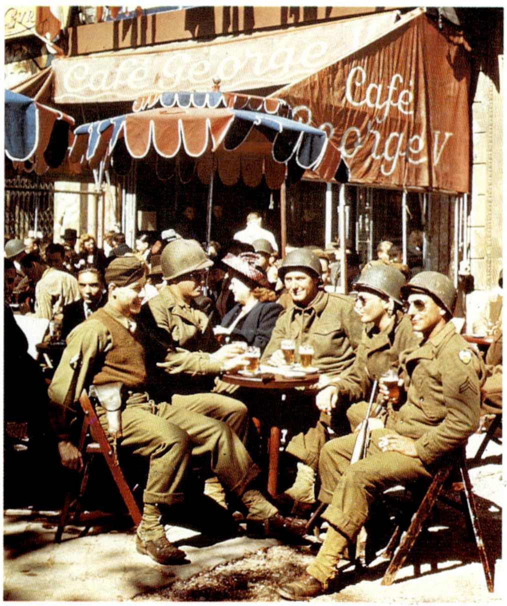

The entry of the Allies into Paris, at the end of Aug. 1944, on a magnificent summer's day marked the high point of the liberation. Here we see a group of American soldiers outside the Café George V, which had still been under German occupation only a few days earlier. The end of the war seemed near, but a mood of disillusionment was becoming apparent before the end of September. The Germans still held on to several pockets on the Channel and on the Atlantic coast and were re-establishing their positions to the east, in the Vosges and near Belfort. Transport and the economy were disorganized and the provision of supplies more difficult than ever. Nearly 2 million French prisoners and deportees were still in Germany.

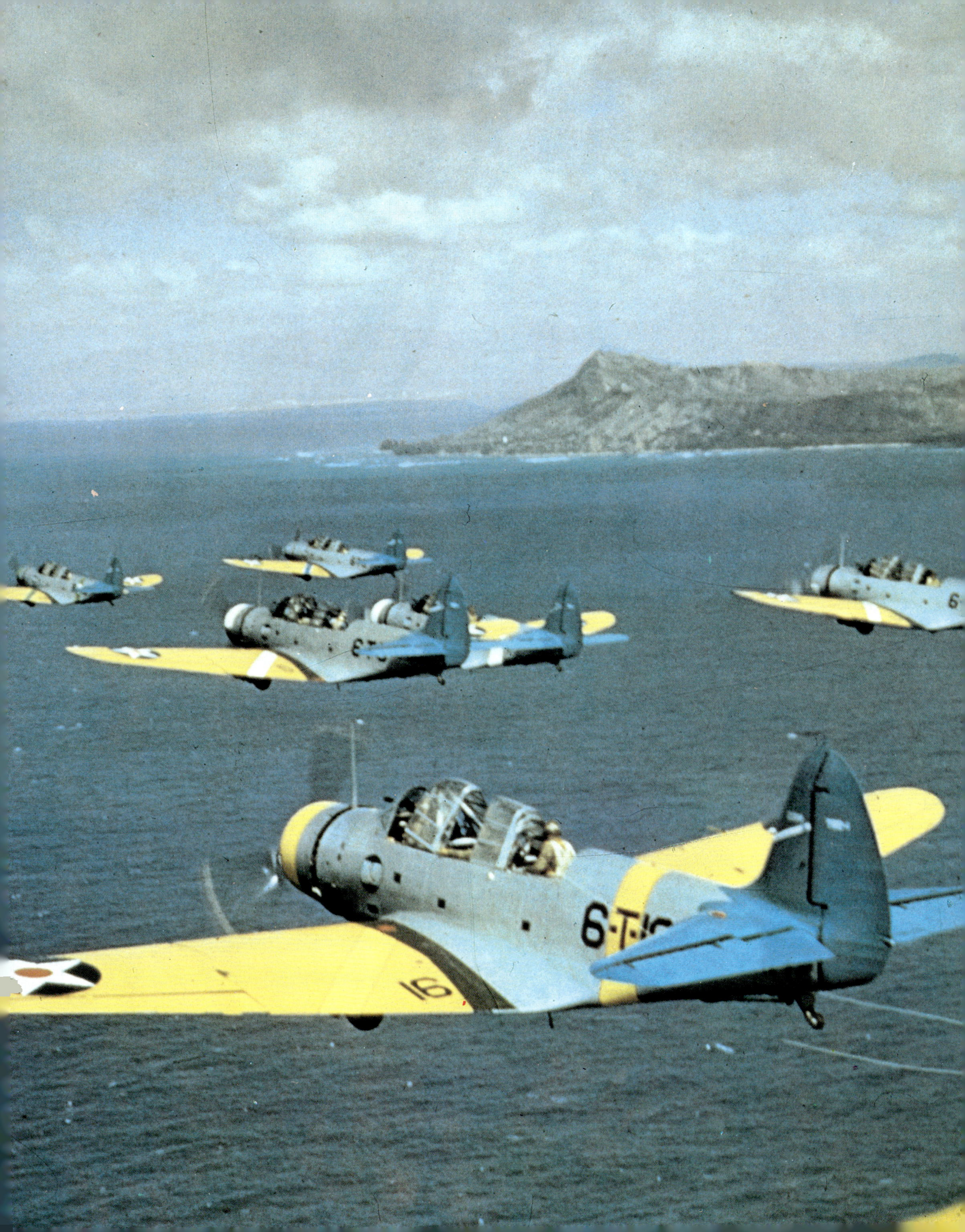
16

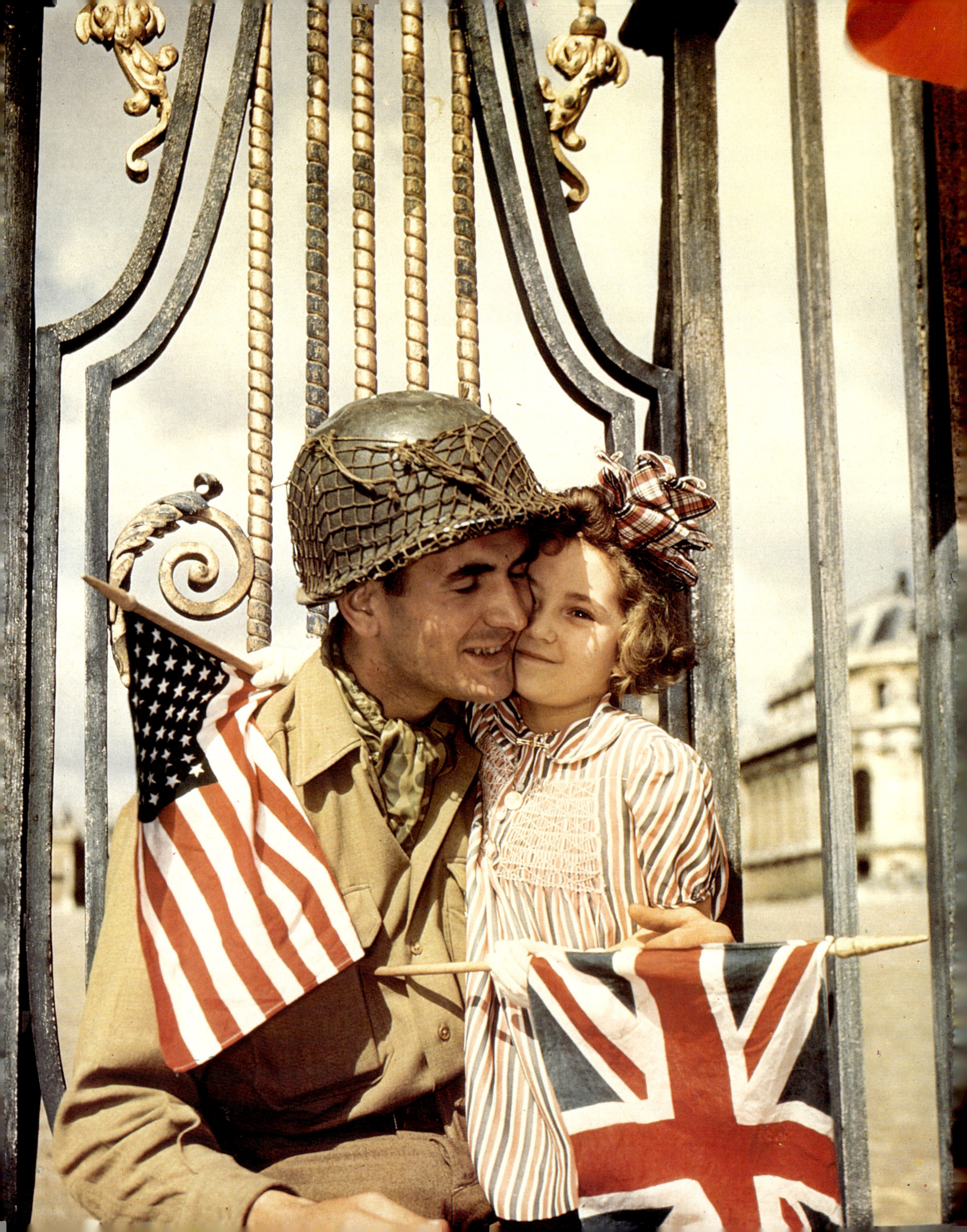

The Liberation. An American soldier in front of the gates of the Palace of Versailles in Sept. 1944.

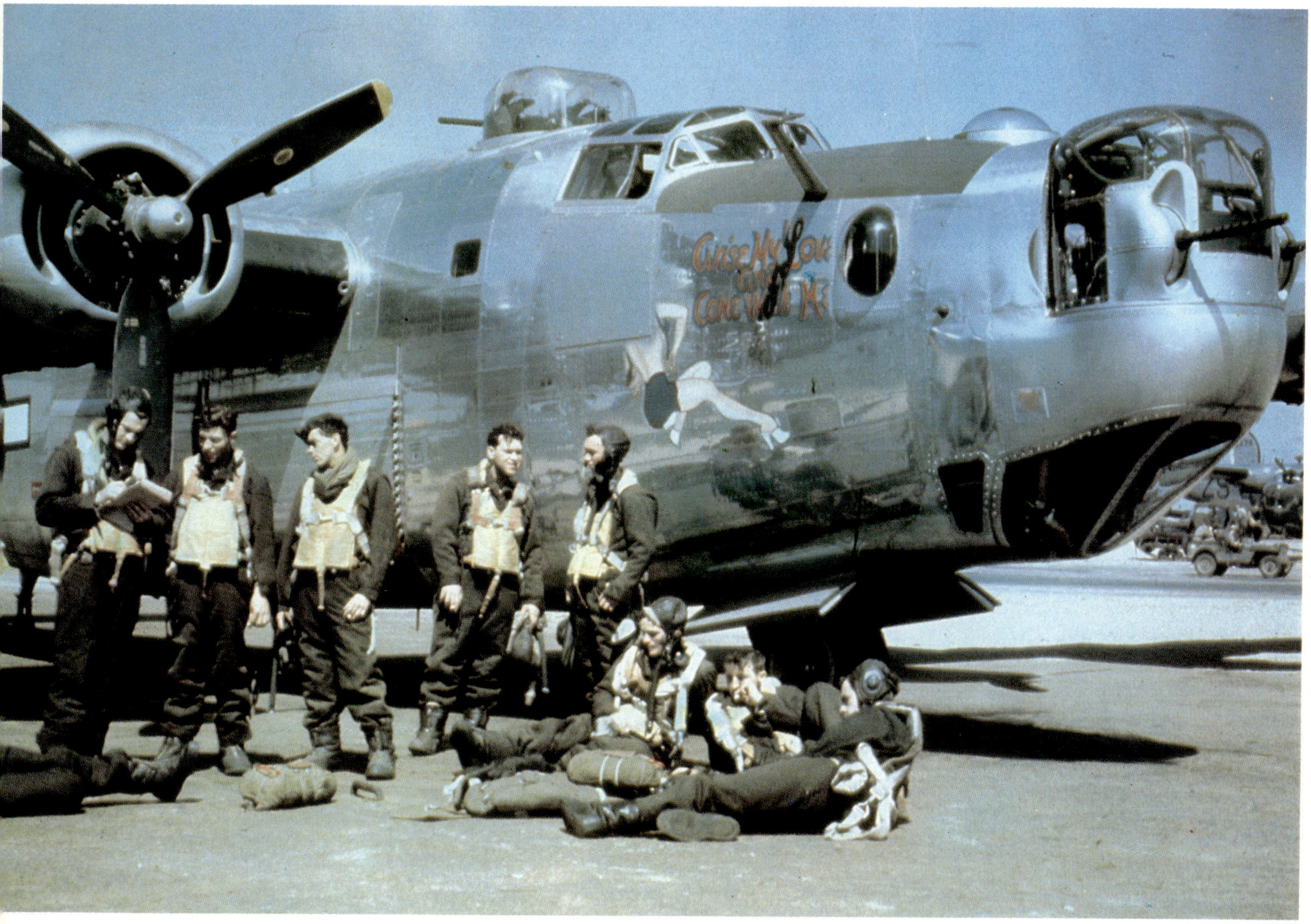

The B-24 Liberator. Together with the Flying Fortress the Consolidated Vultee B-24 Liberator formed the backbone of the American strategic bombing force. Under development by the Consolidated Company since 1932, the Liberator had a wing span of 108 ft (33 m), a length of 66 ft (20 m) and a gross weight of 25 tons (25,000 kg). Its effective range was 2100 miles (3400 km) at 220 mph (350 km/h). With a 12-man crew, the aircraft could carry nearly 5000 lb (2265 kg) of bombs and was armed with 10 heavy machine-guns for close-action defence. More than 18,000 Liberators were built during the war.

The Liberty Ship. To make up for wartime losses and to meet the demands for increased tonnage made necessary by the enormous logistic requirements of the Allies, the American shipyards undertook the mass production of highly standardized cargo ships. The most famous was the Liberty Ship. This very basic vessel, with a deadweight of 10,000 tons, burnt oil, but retained a simple reciprocating engine of 2500 horsepower which did not permit a speed of more than 10 knots. More than 2500 Liberty Ships were built and in 1945 represented nearly 30% of world tonnage.

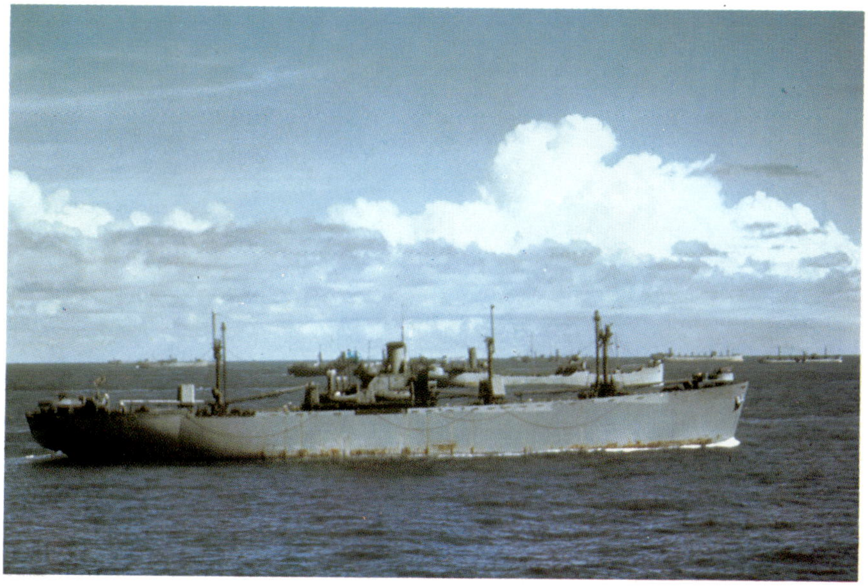

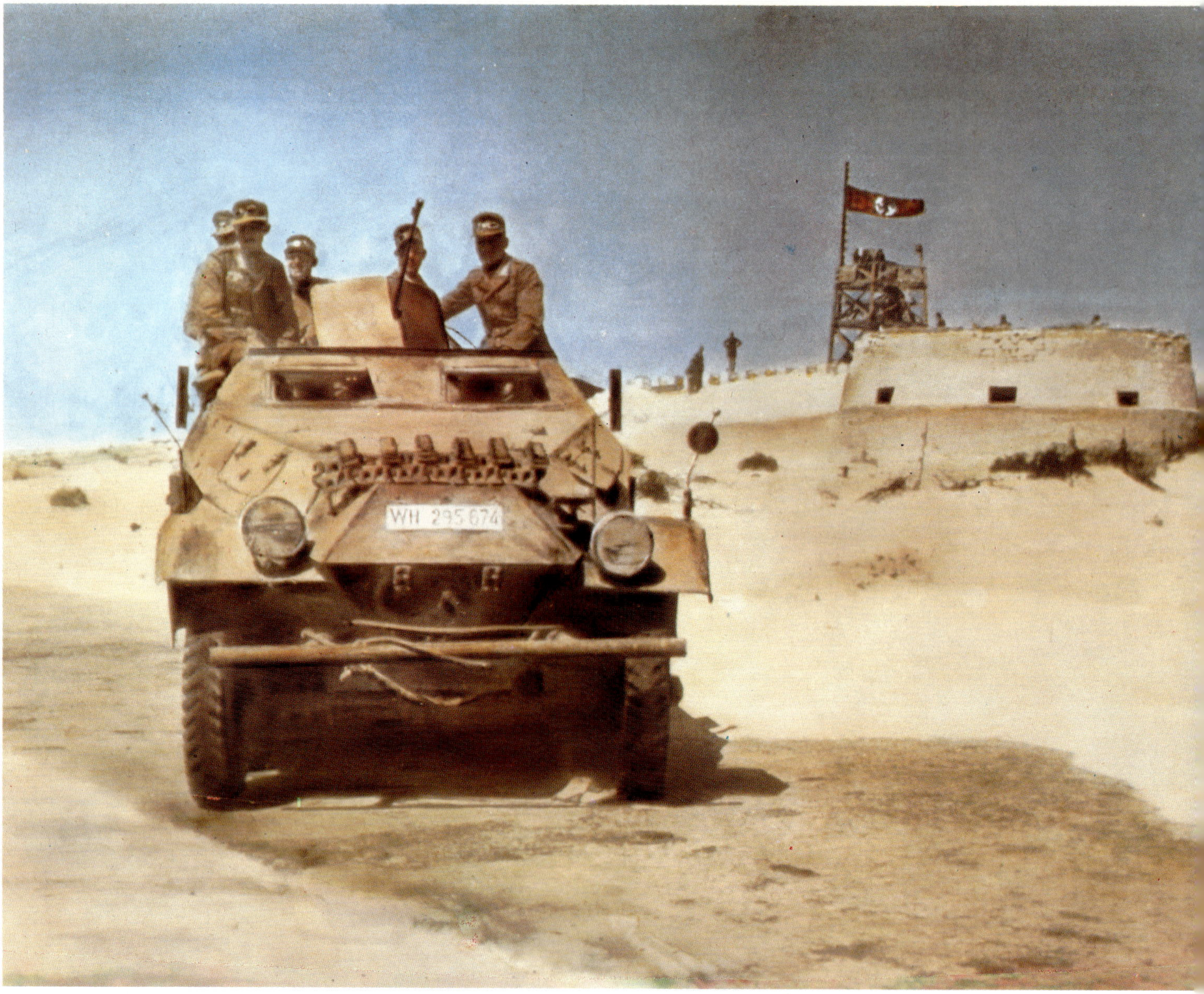

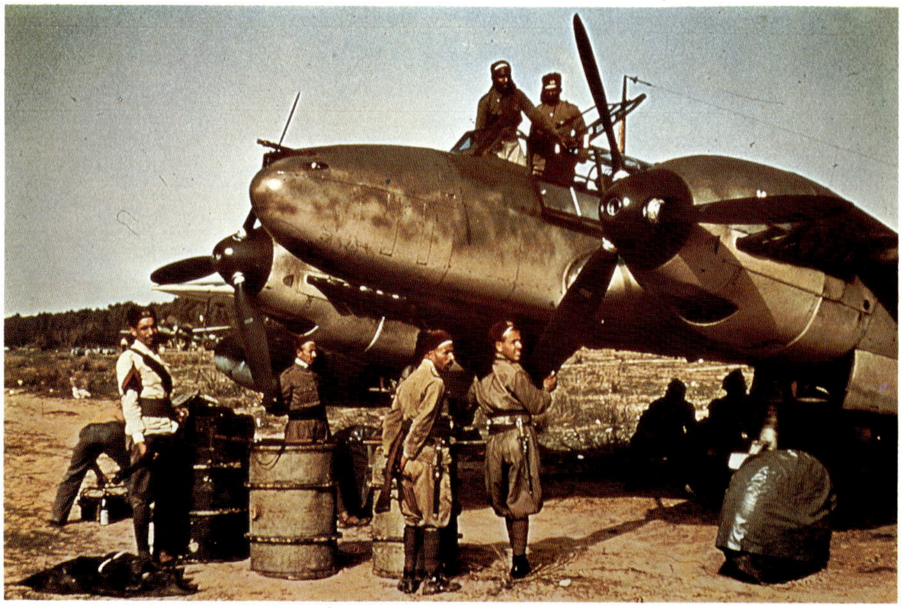

Libya. The arrival in Feb. 1941 of one German armoured and one motorized division, under the command of Rommel, was sufficient to restore the situation in Libya, to inflict serious reverses on the 8th Army and push the British back beyond the Egyptian frontier. Contrary to general belief, the Libyan desert was to be a superb proving ground for tanks, and Rommel soon acquired a reputation as a remarkable tactician. In this picture, taken in 1942, a German armoured reconnaissance vehicle in desert camouflage can be seen outside Fort El Agheila.

As a result of weather conditions which were often exceptional, air power played a decisive role in operations in Libya. Here in June 1941 is a Messerschmitt Bf-110 fighter 'destroyer', surrounded by soldiers belonging to an Italian colonial unit. Axis air power not only gave support to ground forces, but also, by means of intensive bombing, endeavoured to neutralize Malta and to protect convoys of supplies leaving Italy for Africa.

Despite his initial successes in March–April 1941, Rommel had to face renewed offensives by the Eighth Army, notably Operation Crusader in Nov. 1941 which enabled Tobruk to be relieved and pushed the German and Italian armies back to El Agheila. During this offensive Rommel revealed once more his skills as a military leader. Careful use of his resources finally enabled him to bring the Allied forces to a halt. In this picture can be seen the famous 88-mm gun, originally designed as an anti-aircraft weapon, used directly against tanks. At long range it inflicted serious losses on British armour.

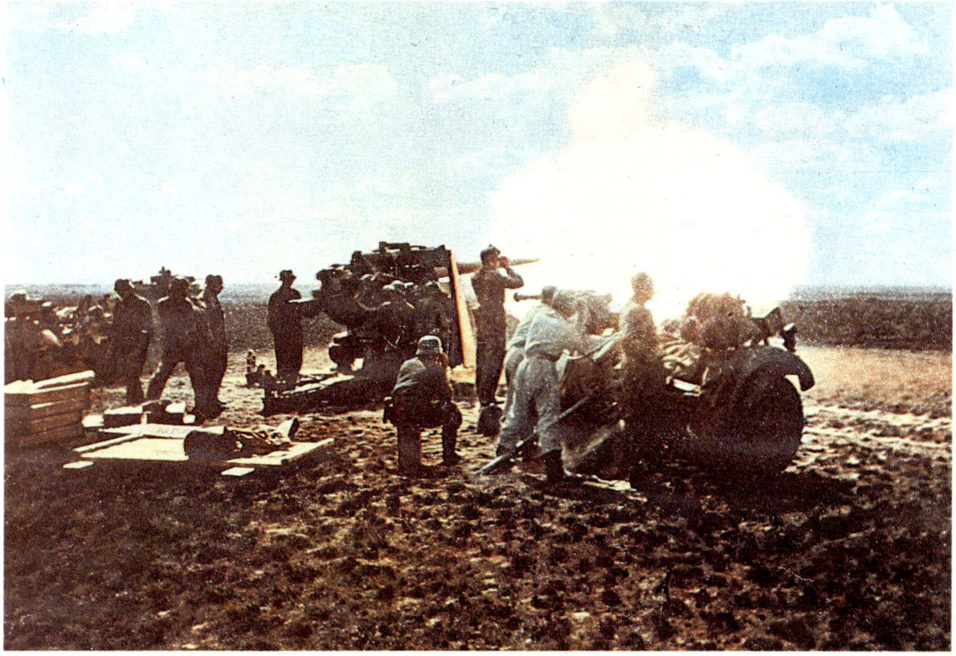

The campaign in Libya was in large measure a war of communications and supplies. After the defeat at Gazala the British stand at El Alamein was made possible by Rommel's logistic difficulties and by reinforcements of tanks and aircraft. In the picture is one of the RAF airfields in Egypt. It was because of his considerable superiority in resources that Montgomery was able, in the autumn of 1942, to take the offensive once and for all against the Axis, in conjunction with the Allied landing in North Africa.

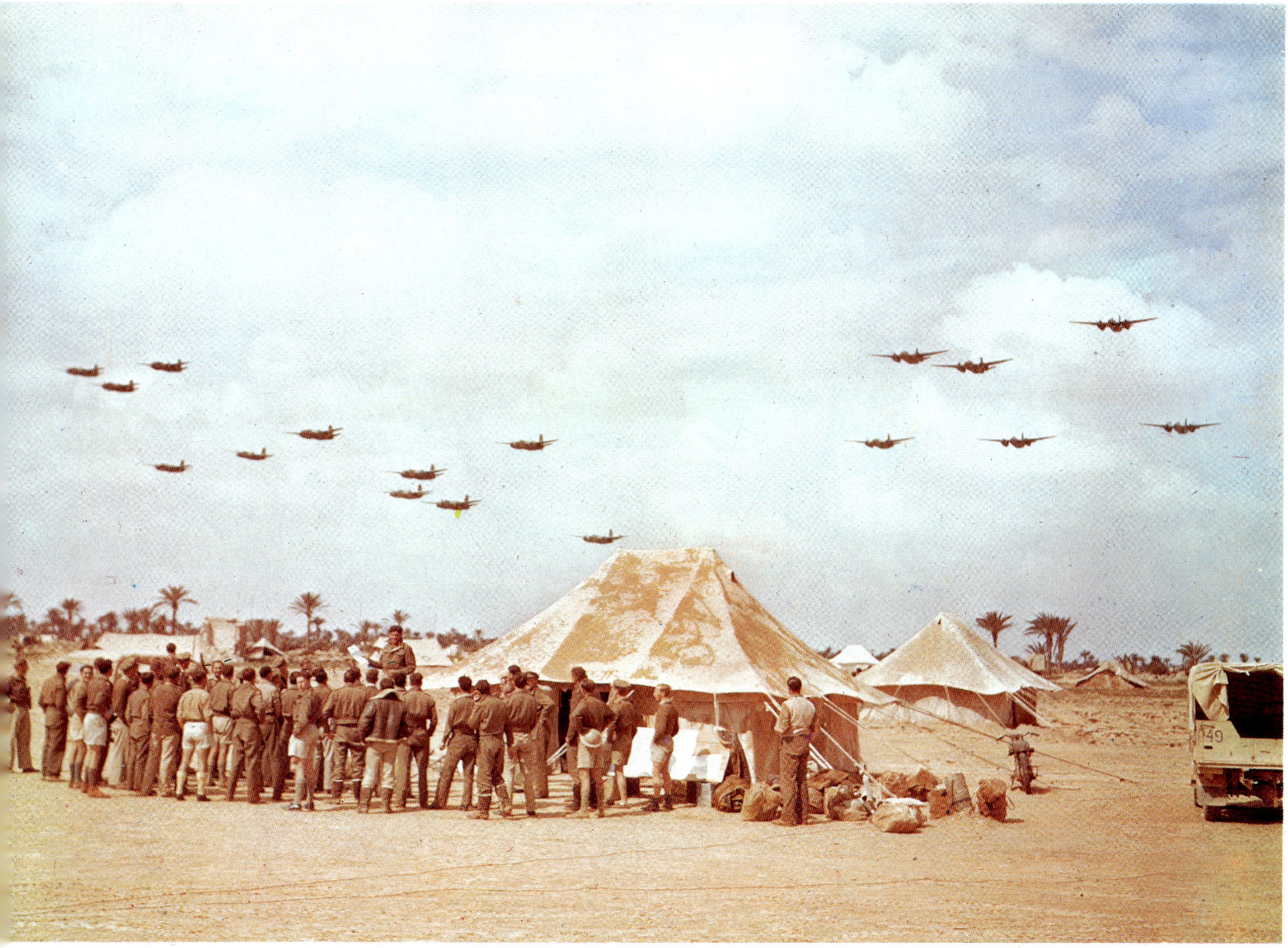

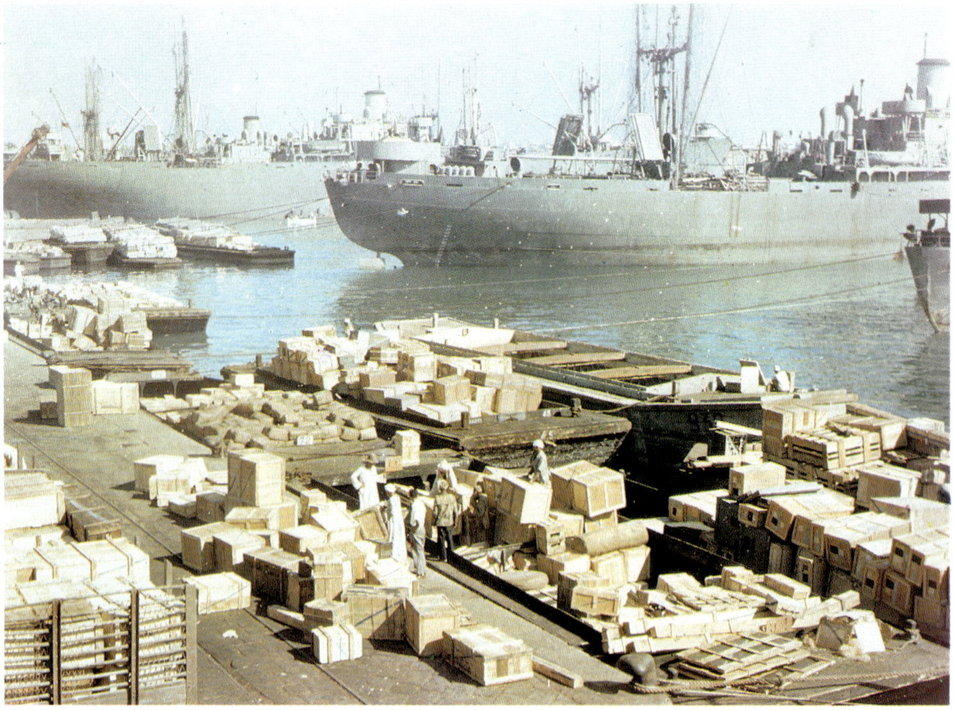

Logistics. British and American Liberty Ship cargo vessels unloading in the port of Alexandria in 1944. Throughout the war the crucial factor in Allied logistics was the conveyance of supplies by sea. In this sphere, the United States, which was centrally placed in relation to the various theatres of war and had become in Roosevelt's words the 'great arsenal of democracy', played a fundamental part. Across the Atlantic alone American ships carried, from 1941 to 1945, nearly 270 million tons of goods of various kinds.

Transporting German tanks on the eastern front in 1943. Throughout the entire course of the war in Russia the Wehrmacht came up against severe problems in logistics. The roads were both few in number and rarely surfaced, and in spring and autumn were transformed into quagmires. They also had to face the difficulties posed by the Soviet Union's railway gauge of 5 ft (1.52 m), which was (and still is) wider than the standard western European gauge of 4 ft $8\frac{1}{2}$ in (1.44 m). On many occasions the Luftwaffe maintained supplies to encircled units. Although this was accomplished successfully at Demyansk during the first winter of the war in the east, it ended in disaster at the siege of Stalingrad.

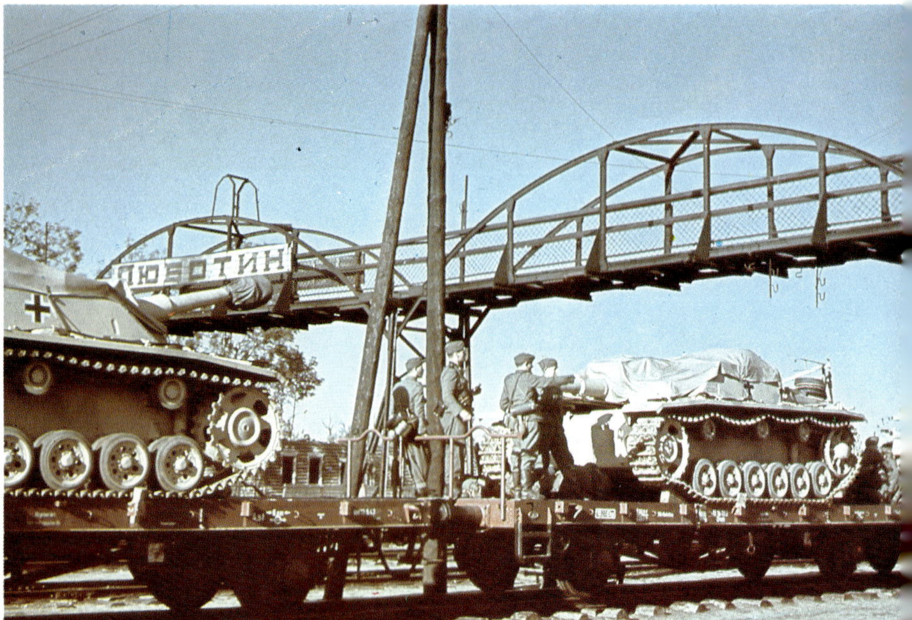

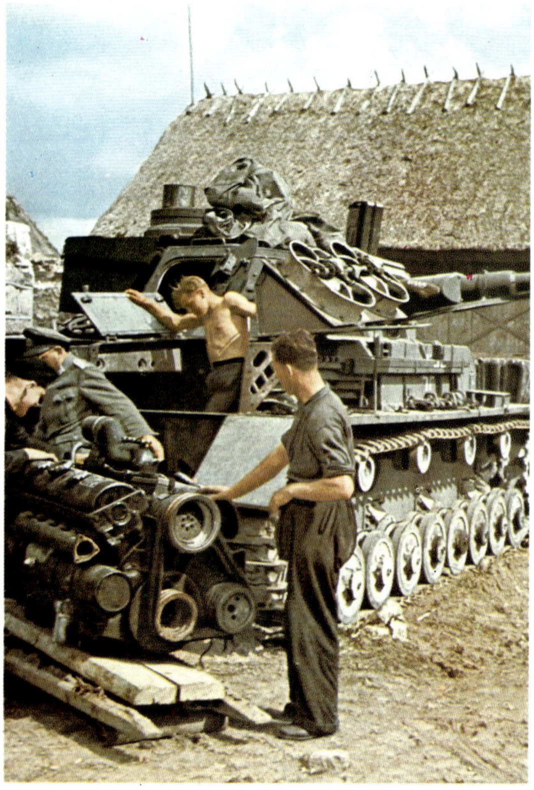

Logistics are not simply a matter of transporting troops, armaments and provisions to various fronts. They are also concerned with the provisioning of all military units with spare parts and the maintenance of supplies to repair shops which have sometimes been set up in the most primitive conditions. Here in a Russian village a group of German mechanics are preparing to change the engine of a self-propelled gun.

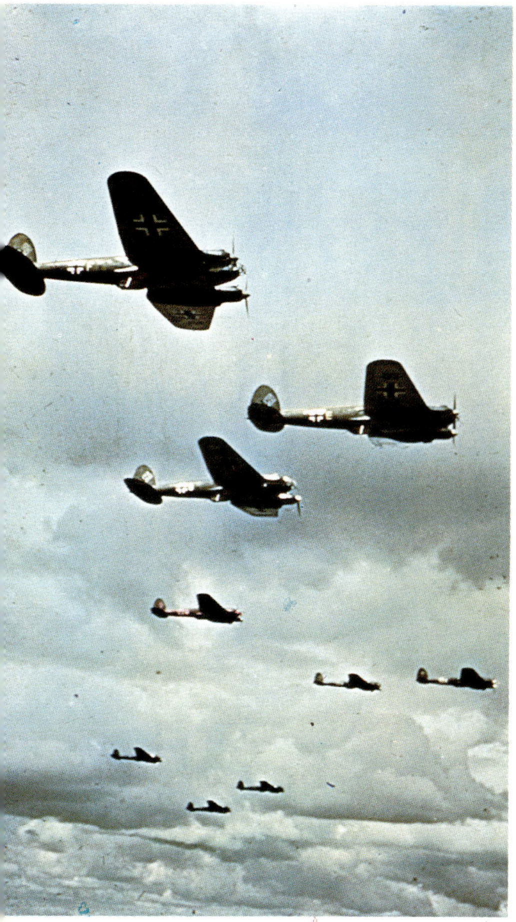

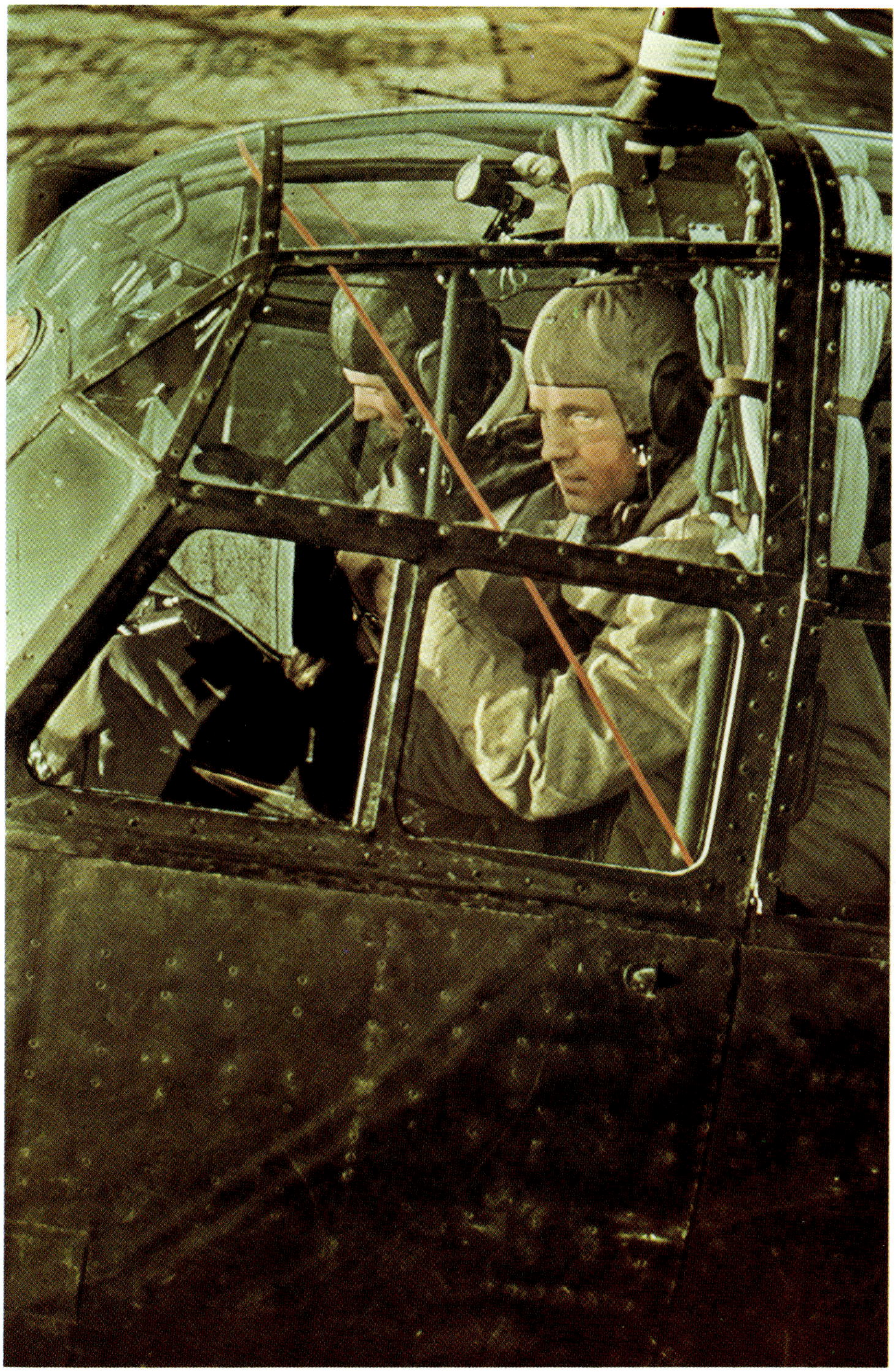

The Luftwaffe. During the early campaigns of 1939–40 the Luftwaffe showed remarkable qualities as an instrument of war and as one of the most important elements of the Blitzkrieg. In powerful fleets of from 500 to 700 aircraft, the bombers, with fighter support, gave direct help to armoured columns by attacking the communications and rear areas of the enemy. Here are a group of Heinkel He-111 bombers in the skies over France in June 1940.

The pilot's seat in a Junkers Ju-88 medium bomber at the time of the Battle of Britain. The Luftwaffe, which had only recently been created and was lacking in heavy bombers, was conceived as a tactical support weapon for armoured divisions in the context of the Blitzkrieg. It was to experience its first setback during the Battle of Britain. Despite its unremitting efforts, it was unable to neutralize the RAF, weaken the morale of the population or disrupt the British economy. This setback, from which the Allies were unable to draw the correct conclusions, proved that, contrary to the ideas of Giulio Douhet, air power alone could not be a decisive factor in time of war.

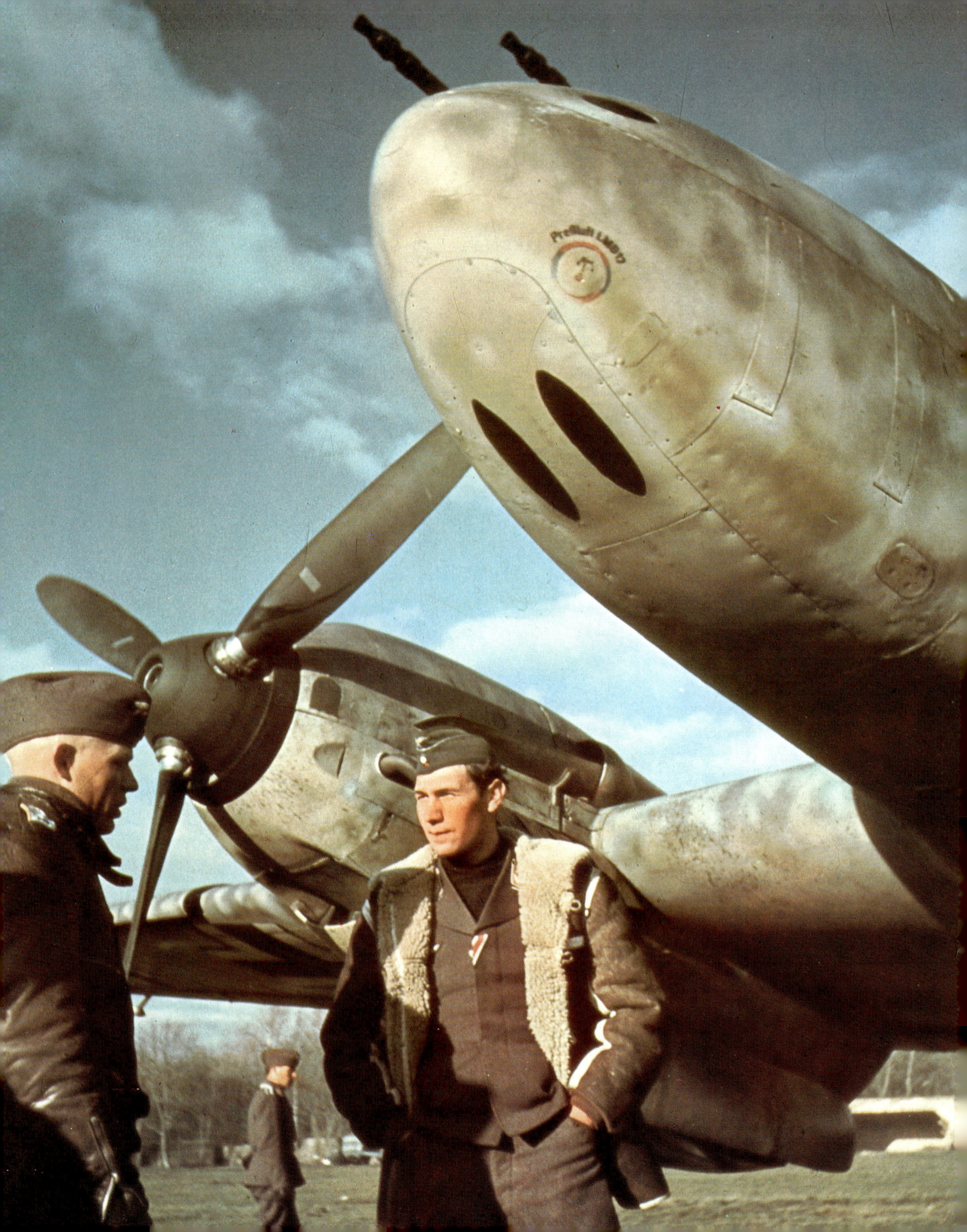

Opposite
The Luftwaffe. Messerschmitt Bf-110 fighter on an airfield at Lille in Aug. 1940.

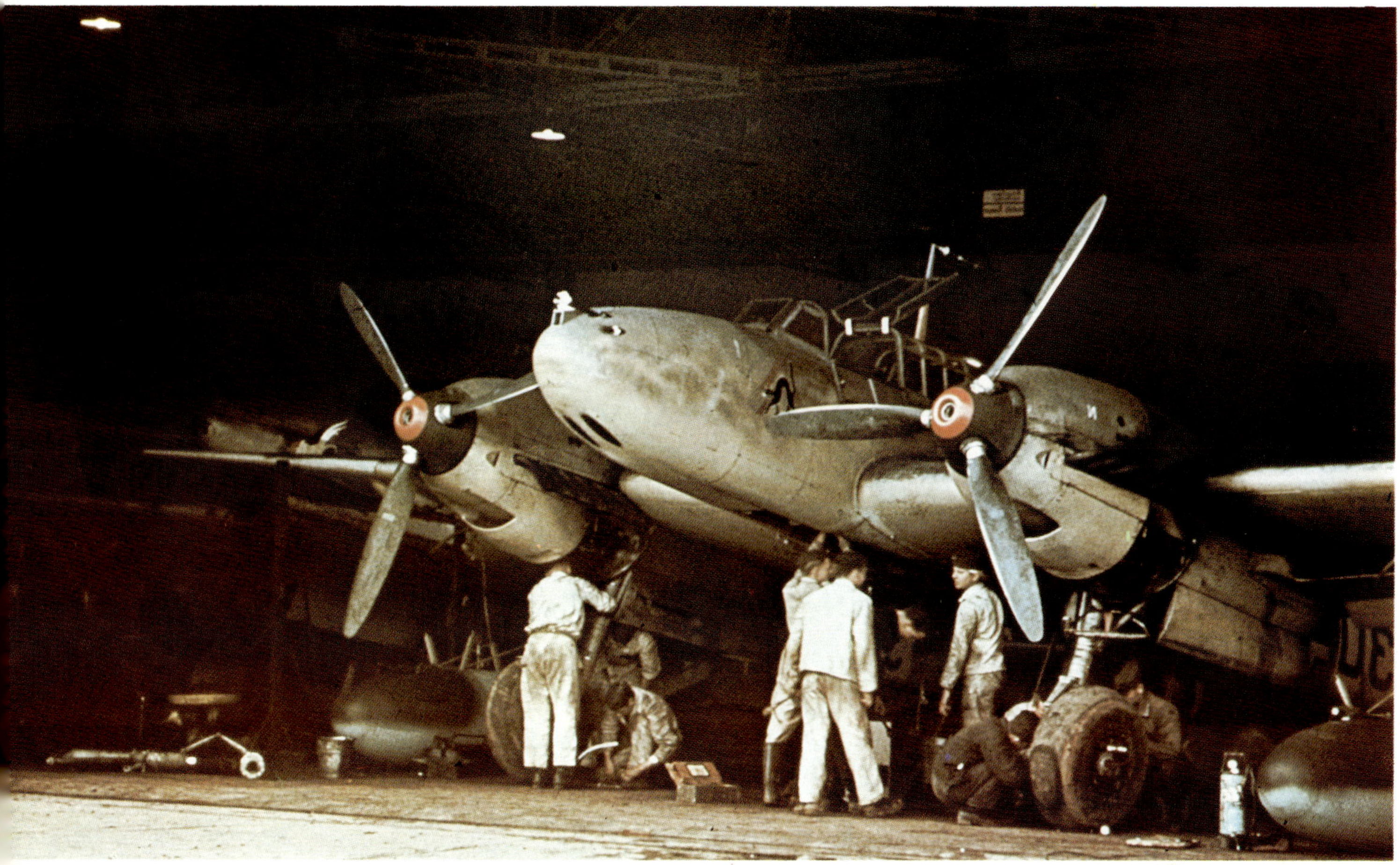

A Messerschmitt Bf-110 fighter destroyer inside the hanger of a Libyan base in 1941. As Göring emphasized at the time, the Luftwaffe was the only arm of the Wehrmacht to have been continuously in action since the beginning of the conflict. After taking part in the campaigns in Poland and France, in the Battle of Britain and in the war in the Balkans and on the eastern front, it played a decisive role in the Mediterranean in 1941–42. From bases in Sicily, Crete and Libya, the Luftwaffe was able repeatedly to neutralize Malta's effectiveness and support Axis operations in North Africa.

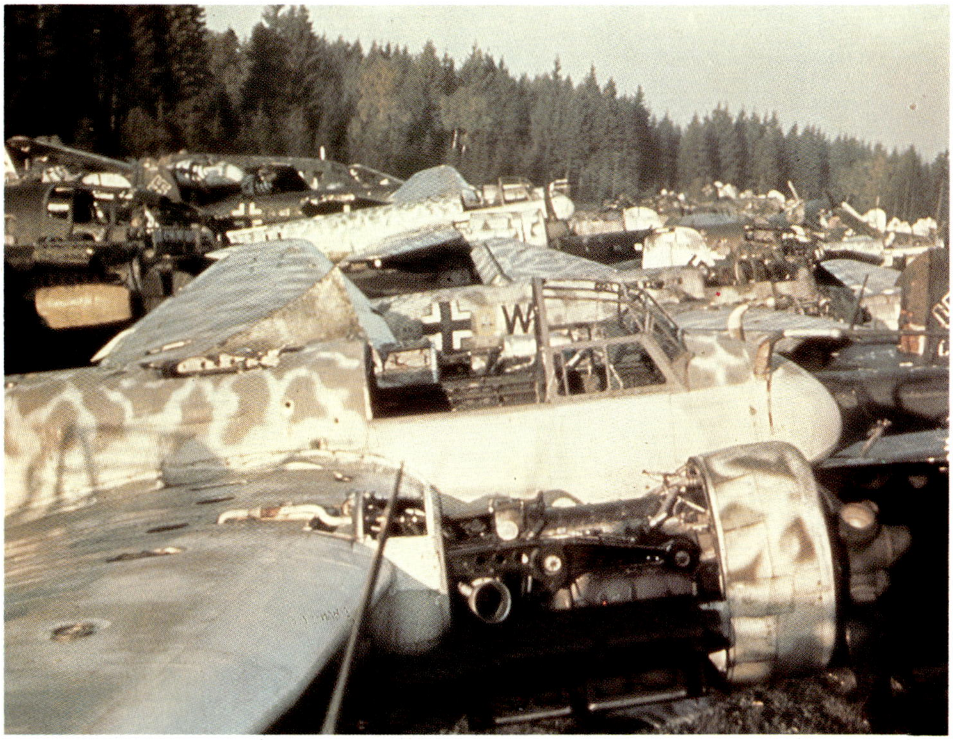

From 1943 onwards the Luftwaffe was reduced to a defensive role – and in the end to almost complete impotence – on all fronts. It was outnumbered by the Anglo-American and Soviet air forces and compelled to assign the majority of its aircraft to the defence of Germany, which was being subjected to heavy strategic bombing. It did, however, maintain a distinct technical lead, with jet planes such as the Messerschmitt Me-262 and the Arado Ar-264. However, Allied raids on aircraft factories and the severe shortage of aviation fuel prevented these aircraft from coming into service in large numbers and thus upsetting the course of events. Here, in May 1945, are a group of sabotaged Luftwaffe aircraft at an airfield at Badkirchen.

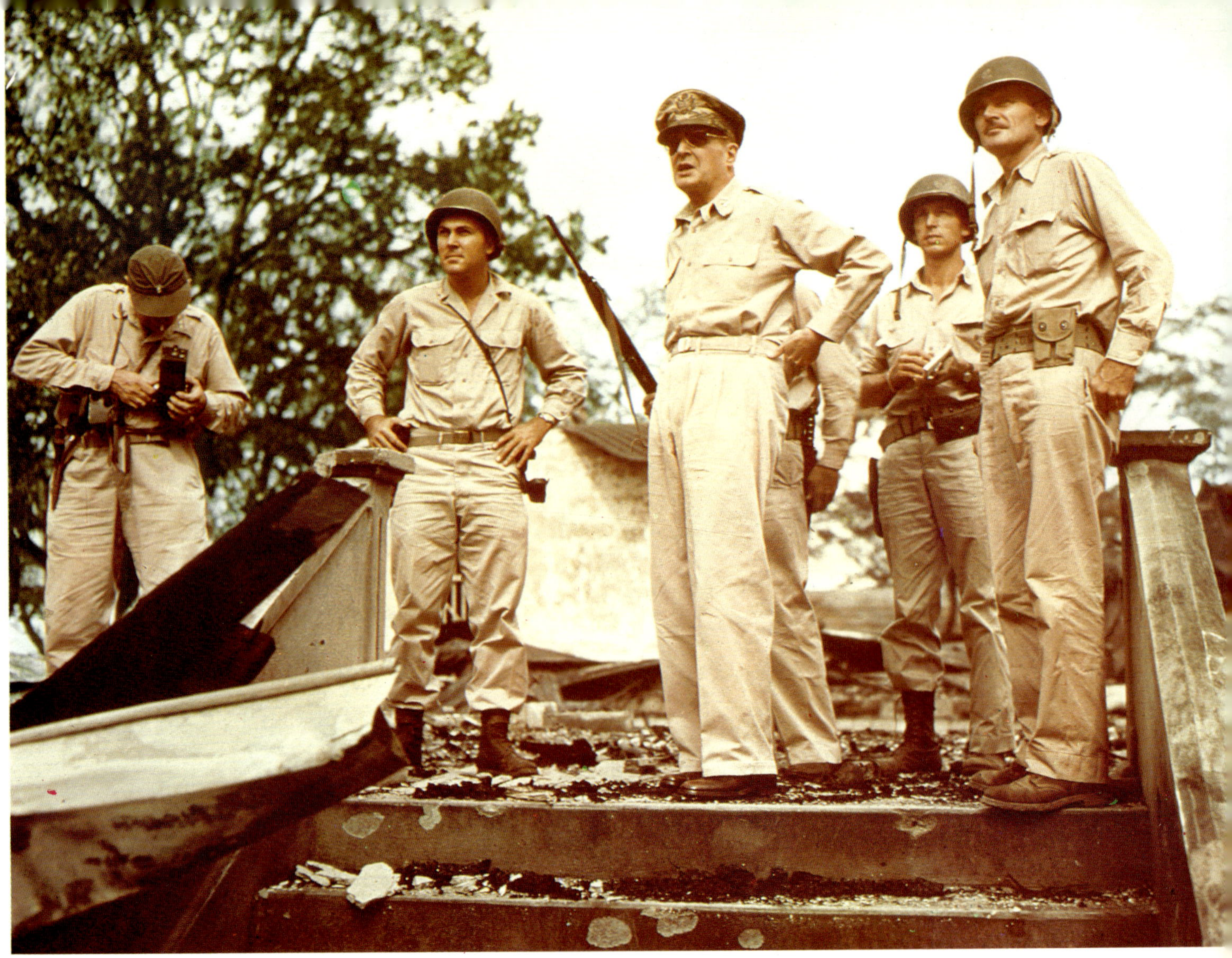

MacArthur. A colourful character and skilful at presenting his public image, MacArthur was one of the most celebrated American leaders in the Pacific War. The early stages of the conflict frustrated his plans for the defence of the Philippines, starting with Bataan and Corregidor, which were compelled to surrender in April 1942. Displaying remarkable energy and with growing resources at his disposal, as commander of the southern Pacific front, MacArthur succeeded in holding on to a fringe of territory north of Australia. He was then able to resume the offensive and from Oct. 1944 onwards was to undertake the reconquest of the Philippines. He is seen here at Fort Stotensburg on Luzon. His reputation reached its highest point in 1945 when he was appointed to command a possible landing on the Japanese mainland. However, without denying the importance of his role, history now acknowledges that Admiral Nimitz was perhaps even more the great victor of the Pacific war.

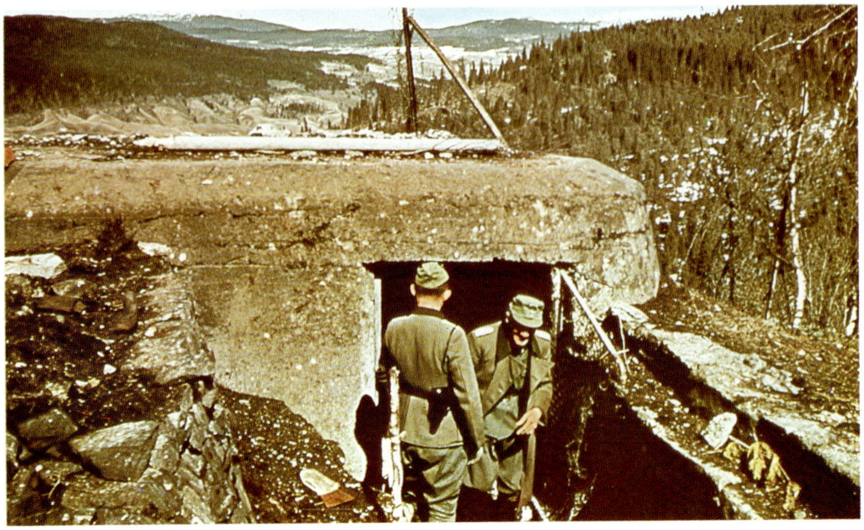

The Maginot Line. Built between 1930 and 1938, the Maginot line provided, from Longuyon to the confluence of the Lauter and the Rhine, about a hundred fortifications of various sizes linked with powerful underground installations. Originally designed to provide protection during mobilization and to serve the armies as an 'instrument of manoeuvre', it ended by being viewed by French public opinion and even by the army high command as an insurmountable barrier. In fact it absorbed an excessive amount of French army manpower, to the point where it contributed to the success of the German offensive of May 1940. German officers are seen here inspecting a blockhouse just after the armistice.

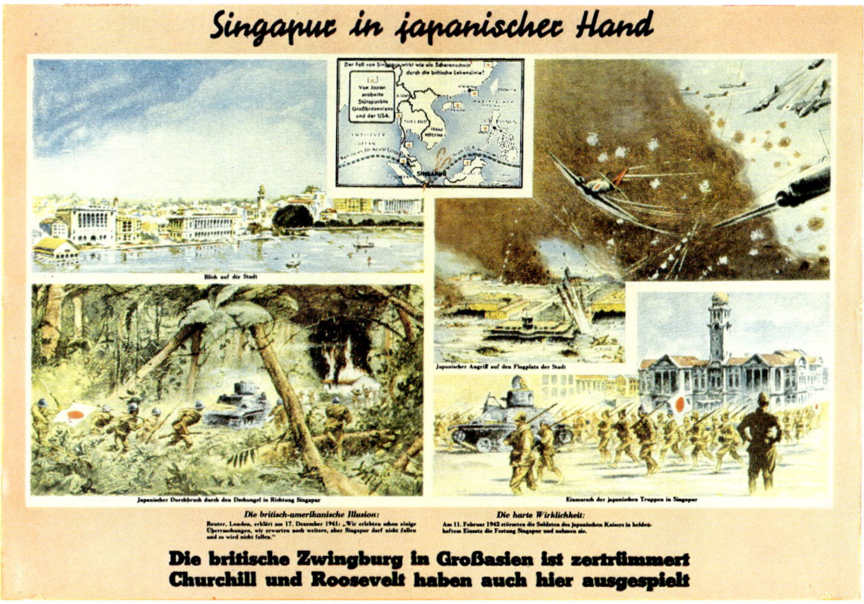

Malaya. The conquest of Malaya, which began on 8 Dec. 1941, and was completed in 73 days, was one of the greatest Japanese victories in the war in Asia and the Pacific. Impelled by an extraordinary fighting spirit, General Yamashita's troops, who had undergone special training in Formosa, showed a remarkable aptitude for jungle warfare, constantly overrunning the British positions. As this German propaganda picture shows, the culminating point of the campaign was the capture of Singapore, whose fortifications, designed exclusively to meet an attack from the sea, proved to be useless. Having swamped the British defences the Japanese secured the surrender of the town on 15 Feb. 1942, taking more than 100,000 prisoners. Great Britain suffered one of its most humiliating defeats of the whole war.

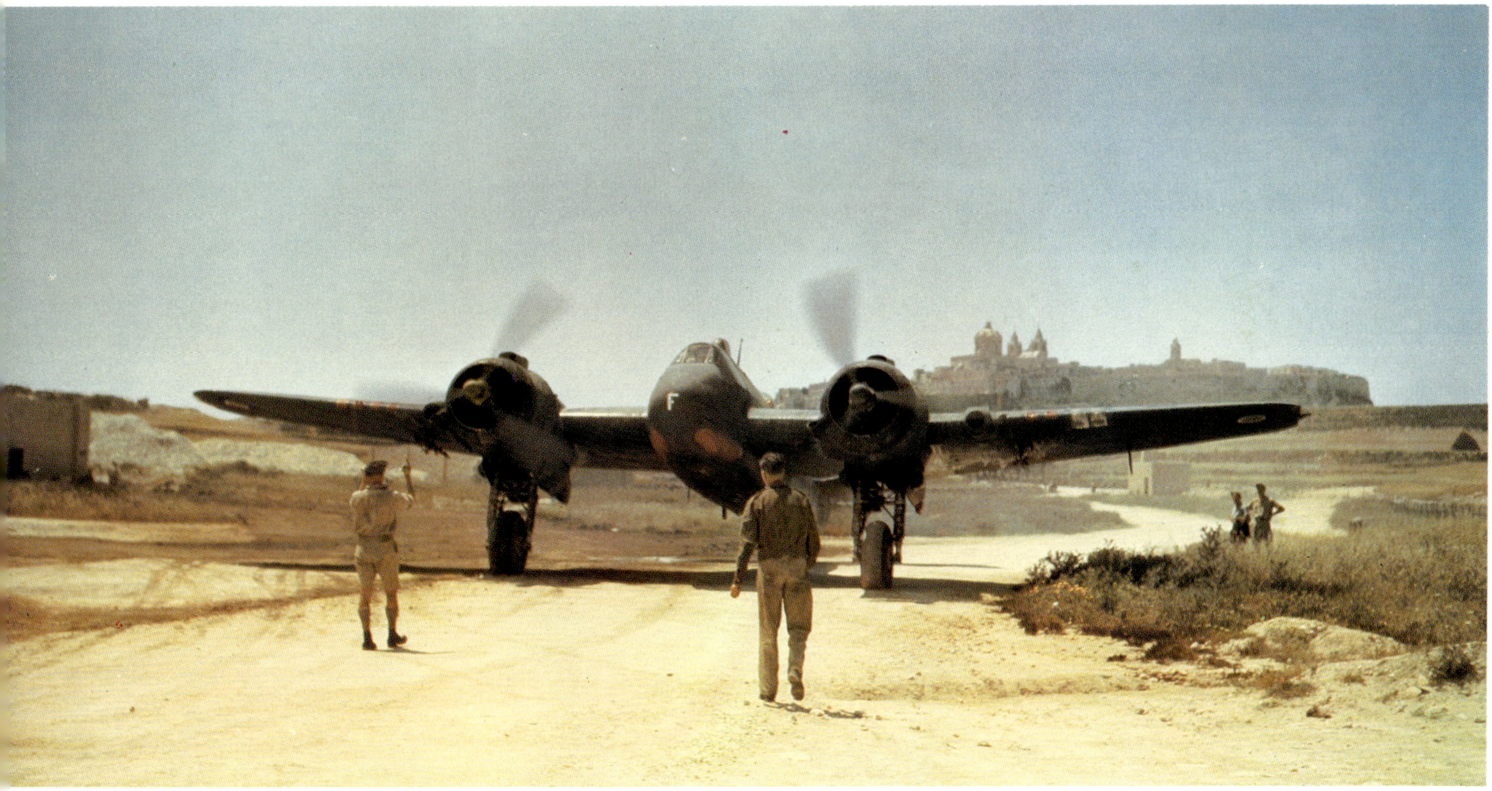

Malta. Owing to its central position, Malta played a decisive role in the war in the Mediterranean. From the autumn of 1940 the British submarines, cruisers and aircraft which were based there were able to disrupt Italian communications with Libya. When the Germans intervened in North Africa the Luftwaffe tried twice, in 1941 and again in 1942, to interrupt British naval shipping in the Mediterranean and to neutralize Malta in order to allow Axis convoys to reach Libya without mishap. However, the British succeeded in reinforcing the defences of the 'aircraft carrier island', which continued its resistance, despite intensive bombardment. It made an important contribution to the cutting off of supplies to German troops in North Africa, thus playing a decisive role in the defeat of Rommel and in the Allied victory in the Mediterranean. Here a British fighter-bomber, the Bristol Beaufighter, used as a torpedo-carrying aircraft against Axis shipping, is seen landing at an airfield near Valletta, at the time of the preparations for the landing in Sicily in June 1943.

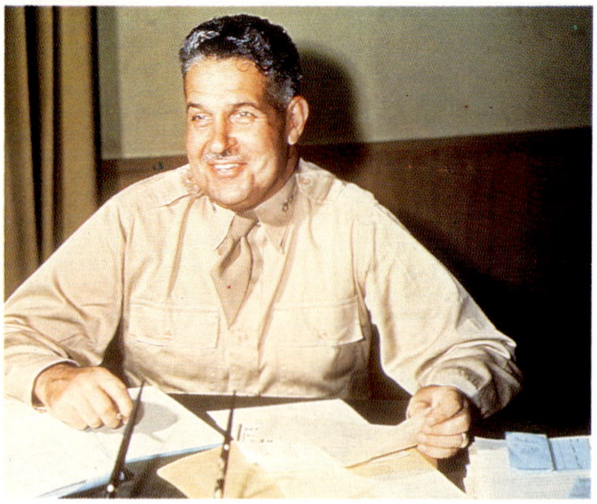

The Manhattan Project. From 1942 to 1945 General Groves, who belonged to the US army's Corps of Engineers, was in charge of the Manhattan Project, which was ultimately to give the Allies the atomic bomb. Mobilizing enormous resources and a whole army of scientists from many different countries, the research took place in various centres, the chief of these being Chicago, Hanford, Los Alamos and Oak Ridge. Two methods were explored, the one involving plutonium and the other uranium 235, leading almost simultaneously in the spring of 1945 to the creation of the first atomic weapons.

Mannerheim. A former Tsarist army officer, who had taken part in the Russo-Japanese War and the First World War, he was to play a decisive role in the creation of an independent Finland after the Bolshevik Revolution. Promoted field marshal in 1933, he commanded the Finnish army during the 'Winter War' of 1940–41 and the 'Continuation War' from 1941 to 1944 in alliance with Germany. A competent military leader, he was also to show – in difficult circumstances when the survival of his country was at stake – skill in diplomacy and a sense of realism which enabled him both to keep his distance from Hitler's Germany and to preserve Finland's independence from the USSR.

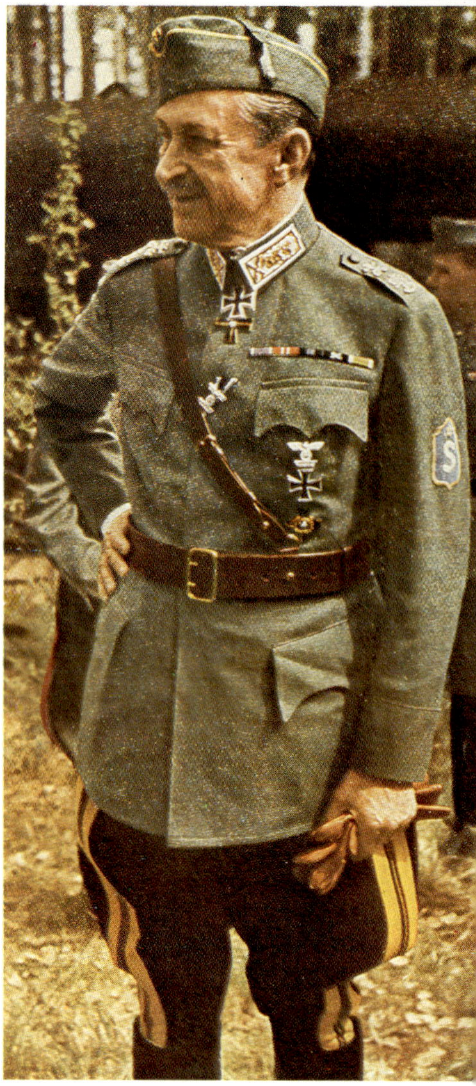

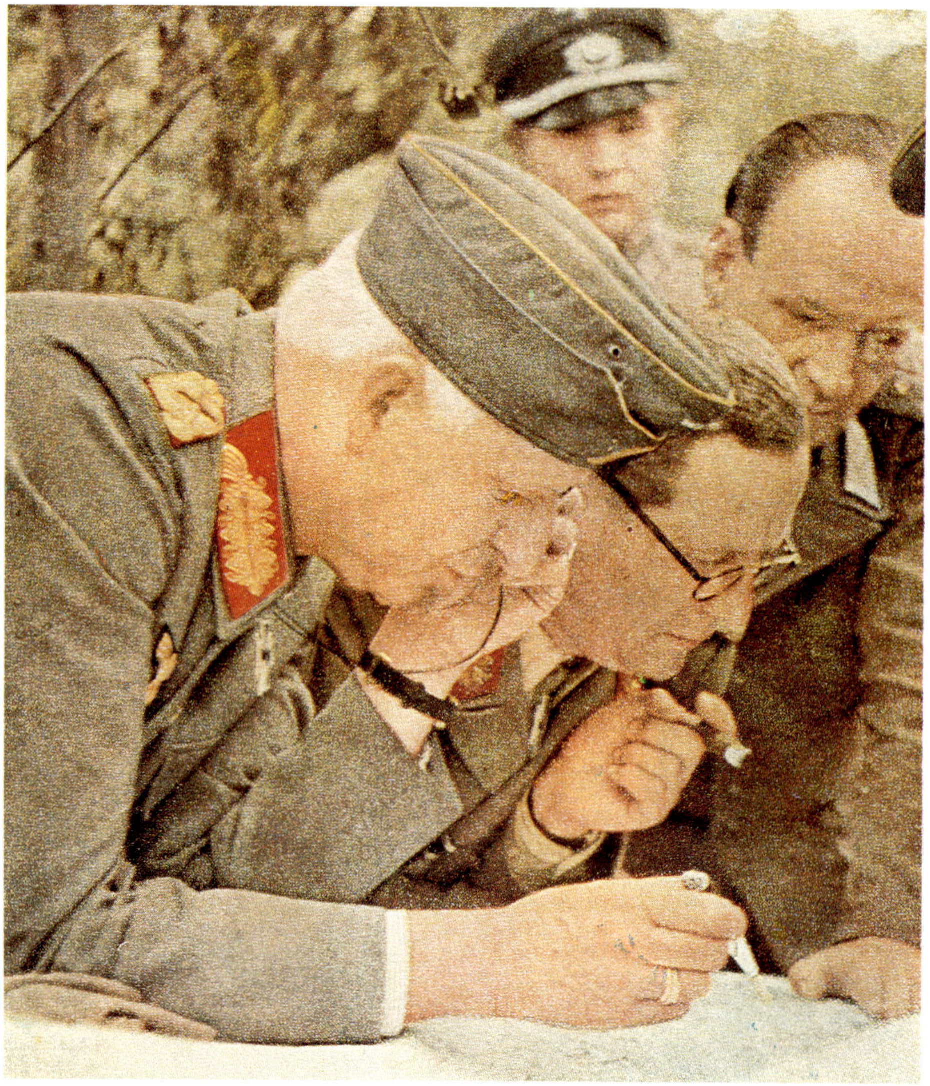

Manstein. As chief of staff of von Rundstedt's Army Group A, at the end of 1939, he advocated the breaching of the western front by way of the Ardennes and the Meuse, a conception which differed fundamentally from the plans of the German general staff. Attracted by Manstein's plan, Hitler compelled the general staff to accept it. During the Russo-German war Manstein (photographed here in 1943) was once more to reveal his exceptional qualities as a tactician, spurred on by a dynamic energy. He succeeded in conquering the Crimea and then in capturing Sebastopol. Although he was unable to extricate the German forces trapped in Stalingrad, he did manage to restore the position on the southern front by recapturing Kharkov in March 1943, also playing a notable part at the battle of Kursk in July of the same year. After carrying out a skilful retreat in the Ukraine, interspersed with counter-attacks, he was relieved of his duties in March 1944, since Hitler considered that he was no longer suited to a war which had become purely defensive. He is considered by many to be one of the best German generals of the Second World War.

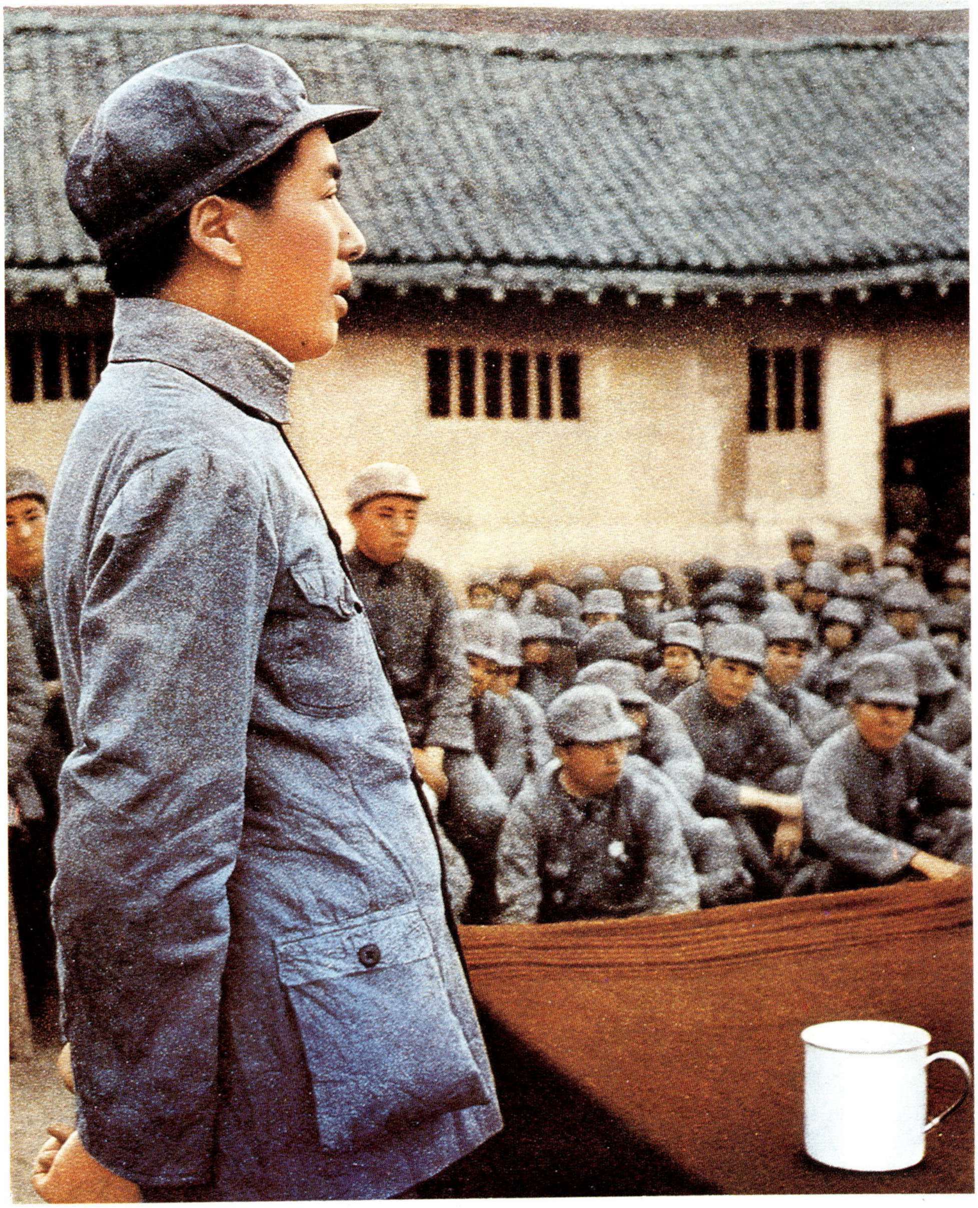

Mao Tse-tung. The war against Japan and the Second World War together constituted a fundamentally important stage in the life of Mao Tse-tung and in the history of China itself. Within the framework of the 'united front', that is, of a truce with the Kuomintang, he directed a partisan war against the Japanese forces, beginning at Yenan in the north of Shensi province, where the Communists had fallen back after the Long March. At the same time he reinforced his authority within the party, ensured the triumph of the 'peasant line' and removed 'bourgeois deviationists'. By 1945 he had become the undisputed leader of the movement. At that time he controlled about 20% of the Chinese population, backed up by a party of 1,200,000 members and a tough, well-organized army of 900,000 men.

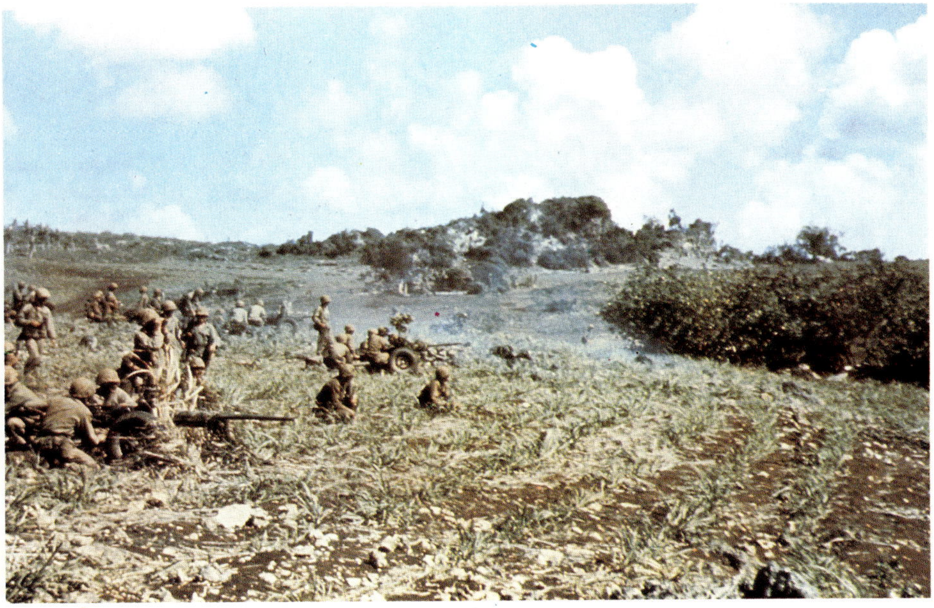

The Mariana Islands. The reconquest of the Marianas archipelago during the summer of 1944, linked with a major Japanese naval defeat, was one of the most important stages in the American counter-offensive in the Pacific. In the picture we see the progress of a unit of US Marines on Guam Island, supported by 1½ in. (37 mm) guns. The occupation of Guam, Saipan and Tinian made a sizable breach in Japan's 'defensive perimeter'. From the autumn of 1944 these islands were to be used as bases for American strategic bombers whose task was the destruction of the large Japanese cities.

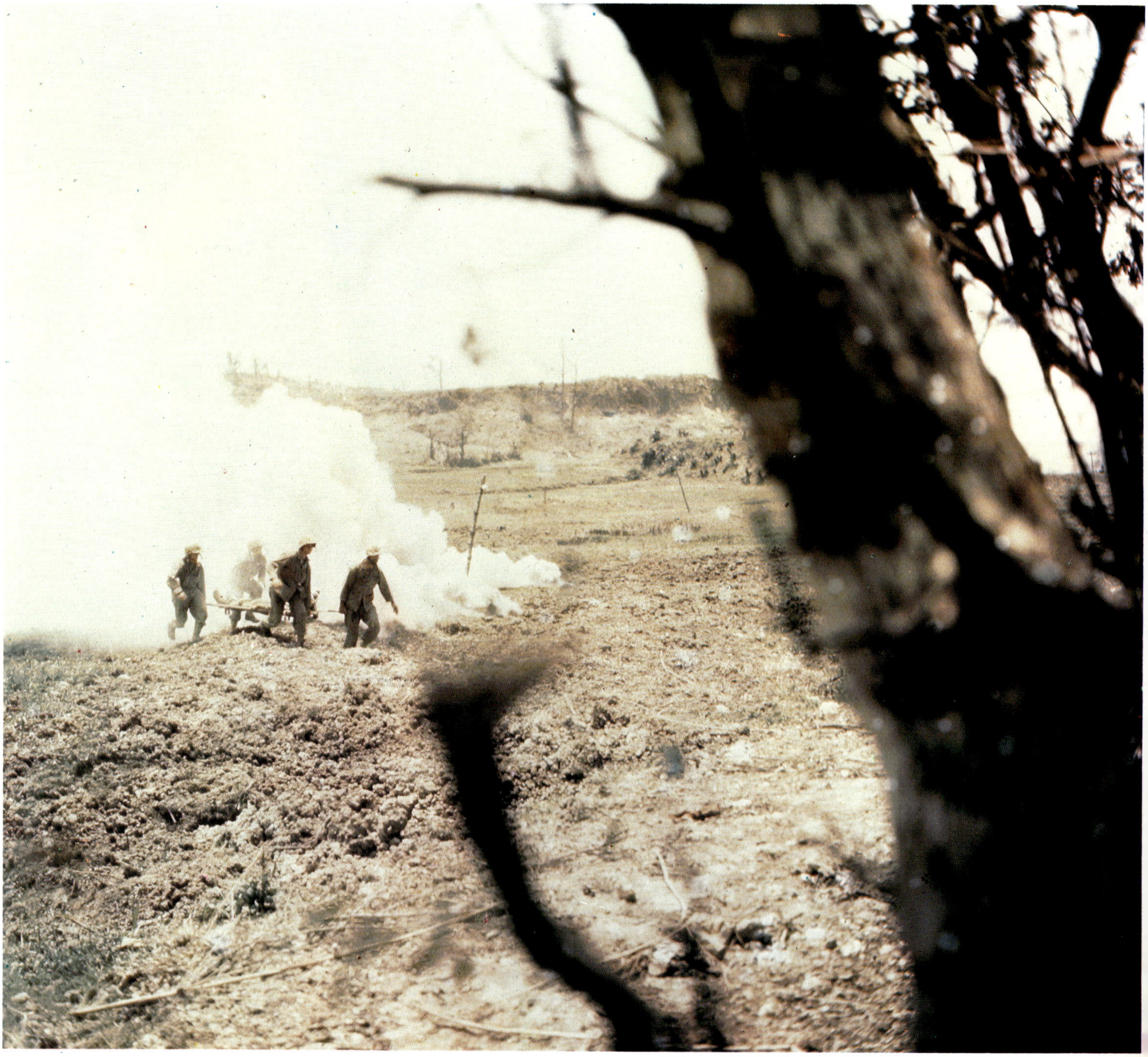

The Marines. Established in 1775, the Marines were a corps of soldiers deployed by the US Navy within the framework of combined operations. During the course of the Second World War, the US Marine Corps underwent a remarkable development, its numbers increasing from less than 20,000 in 1941 to nearly 500,000 in 1945, with six divisions in all. The Marines for the most part served in the Pacific from the time of the first landings on Guadalcanal in Aug. 1942. Their losses amounted to nearly 17,000 dead and more than 60,000 wounded. In this picture stretcher bearers are carrying a wounded marine during the fierce fighting on Okinawa.

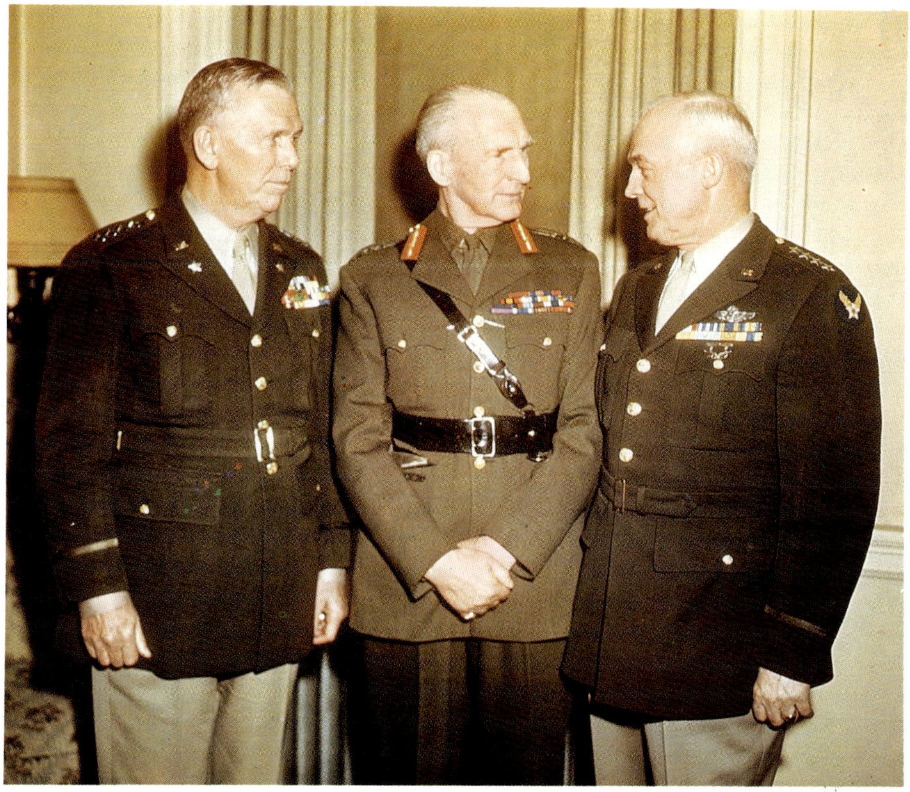

Marshall. Chief of Staff of the US army from the early months of the war, General George C. Marshall revealed himself to be a remarkable strategist and could rightly be considered as the organizer of victory. However, his reputation did not become firmly established until after the war, with his appointment as ambassador to China in 1945 and the plan for the economic reorganization of Europe which was to bear his name. His career culminated in 1951 with his appointment as Secretary of State for defence. Here we see him in 1944 (on the left), in company with the British field marshal, Sir John Dill (centre), the head of the British mission to the United States, and the US general, Henry 'Hap' Arnold.

The Marshall Islands. The conquest of the Marshall Islands in Jan.–Feb. 1944 was to form the first phase of the American counter-offensive in the central Pacific, under the direction of Admiral Nimitz. By taking possession of the islands of Majuro, Roi-Namu, Eniwetok and Kwajalein the Americans were able to breach the Japanese defensive perimeter and provide a springboard for the neutralization of Truk and the attack on the Mariana Islands. In this picture the star-spangled banner flies over the Japanese airfield at Roi, previously bombarded by the American navy and air force and strewn with the wreckage of Japanese planes.

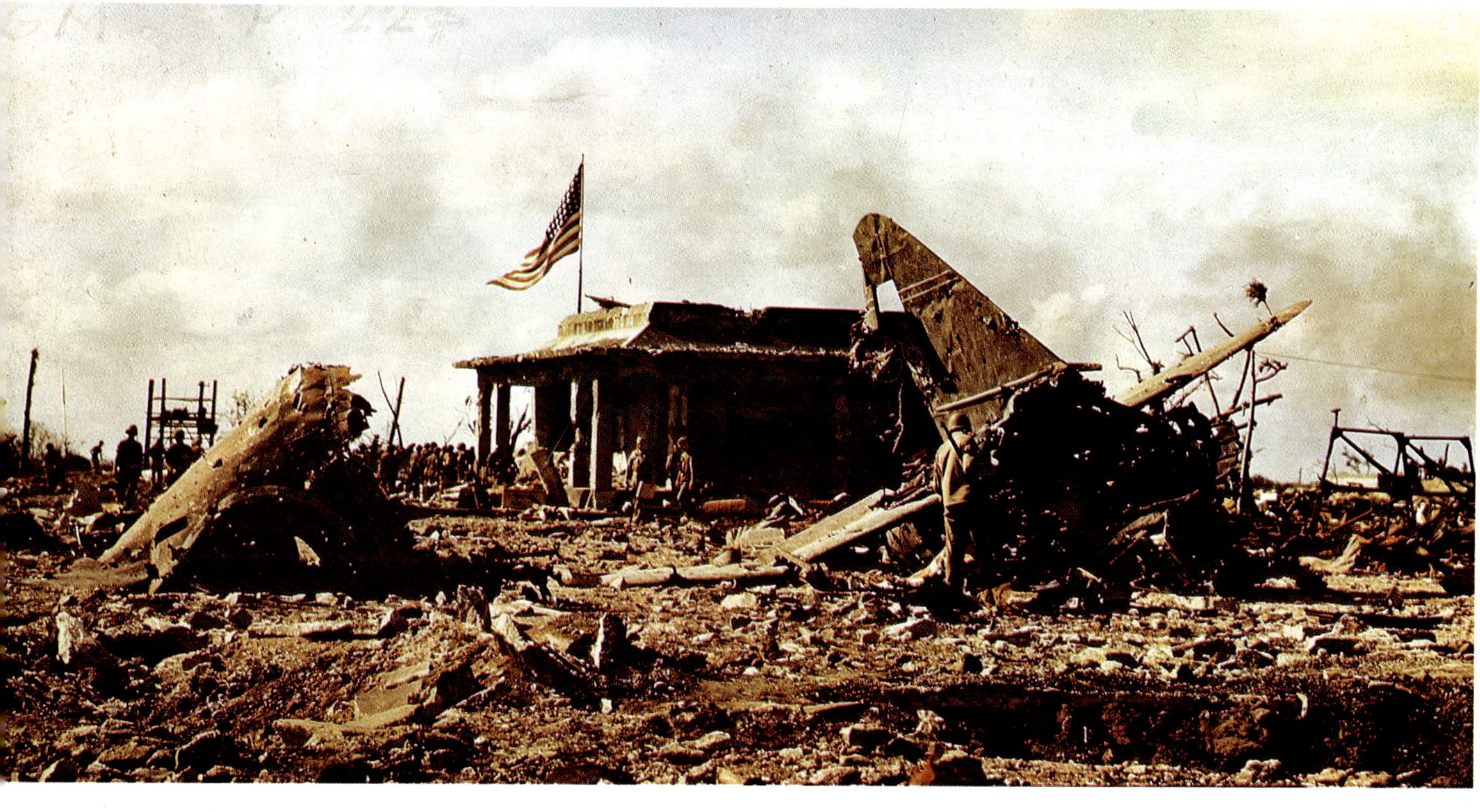

Medicine and health. A captured German airman and a wounded G.I.

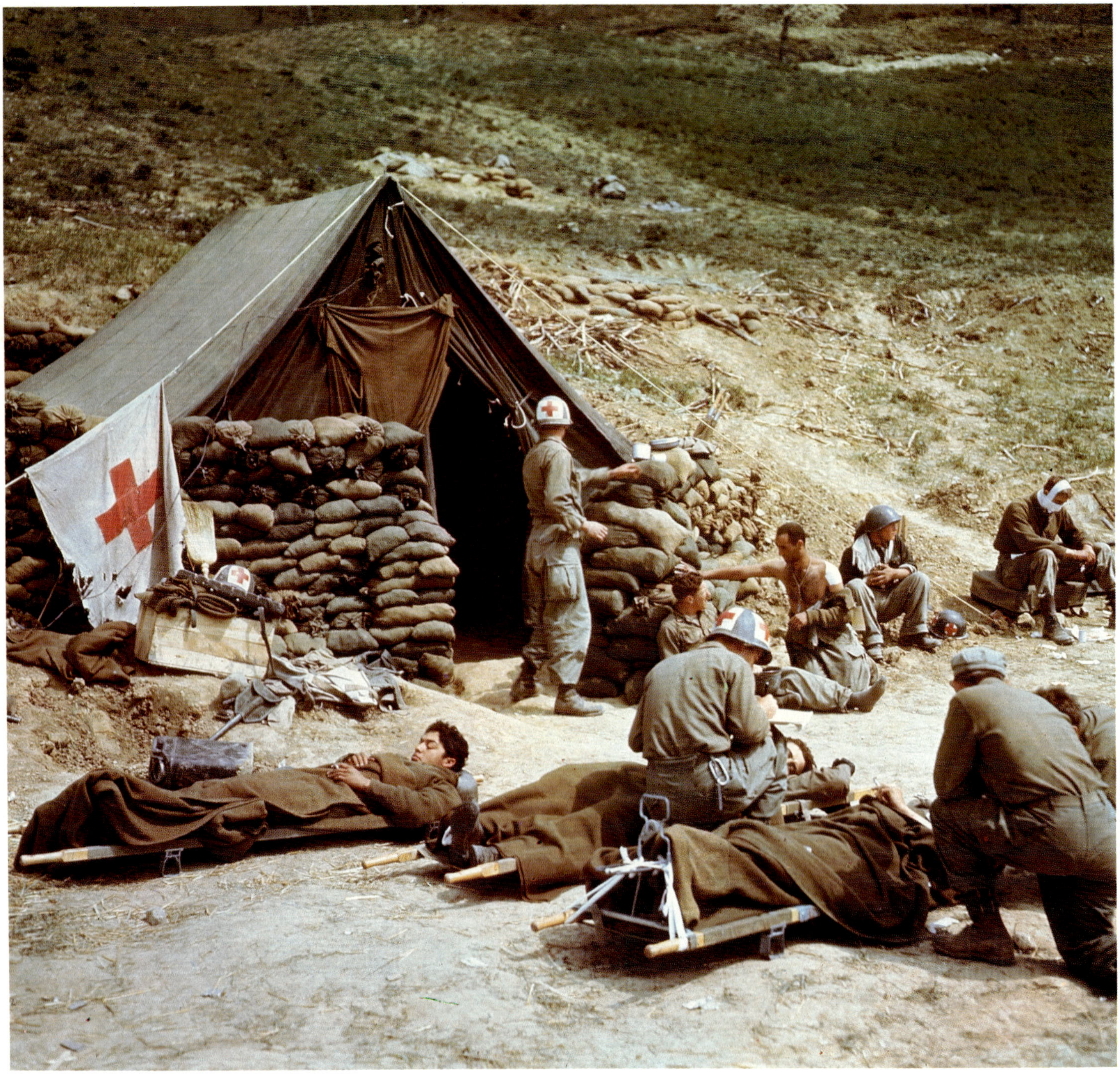

Medicine and health. Throughout the conflict medical services played an invaluable role. In the American army alone the number of wounded exceeded 600,000. There was a whole hierarchy of medical services, from first aid posts in advanced positions providing immediate care and the field stations performing operations to the most advanced hospitals far removed from the front, which treated the most seriously wounded soldiers or provided rehabilitation. Here we see a first aid post belonging to the US 10th Division, north of the Apennines near Bologna.

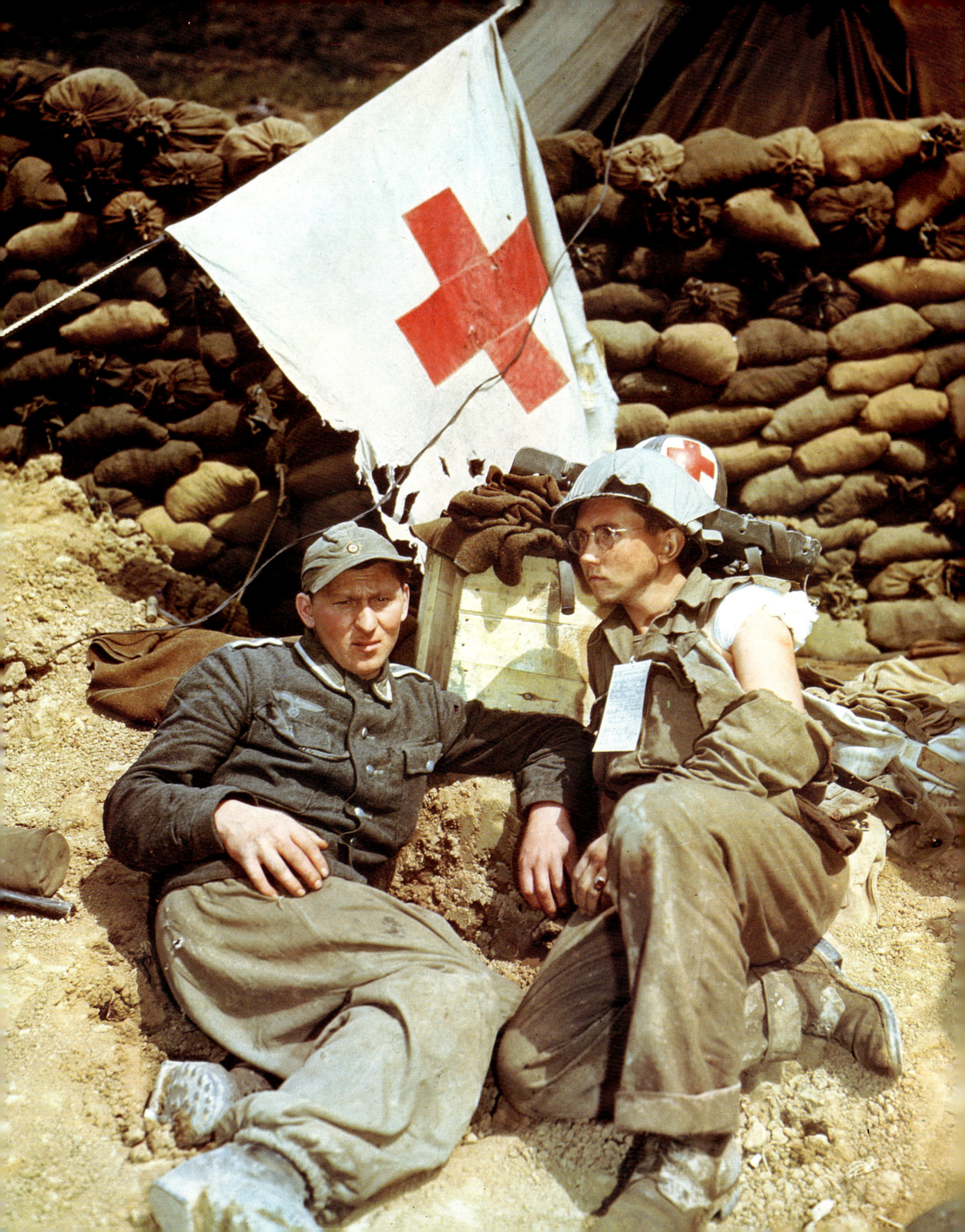

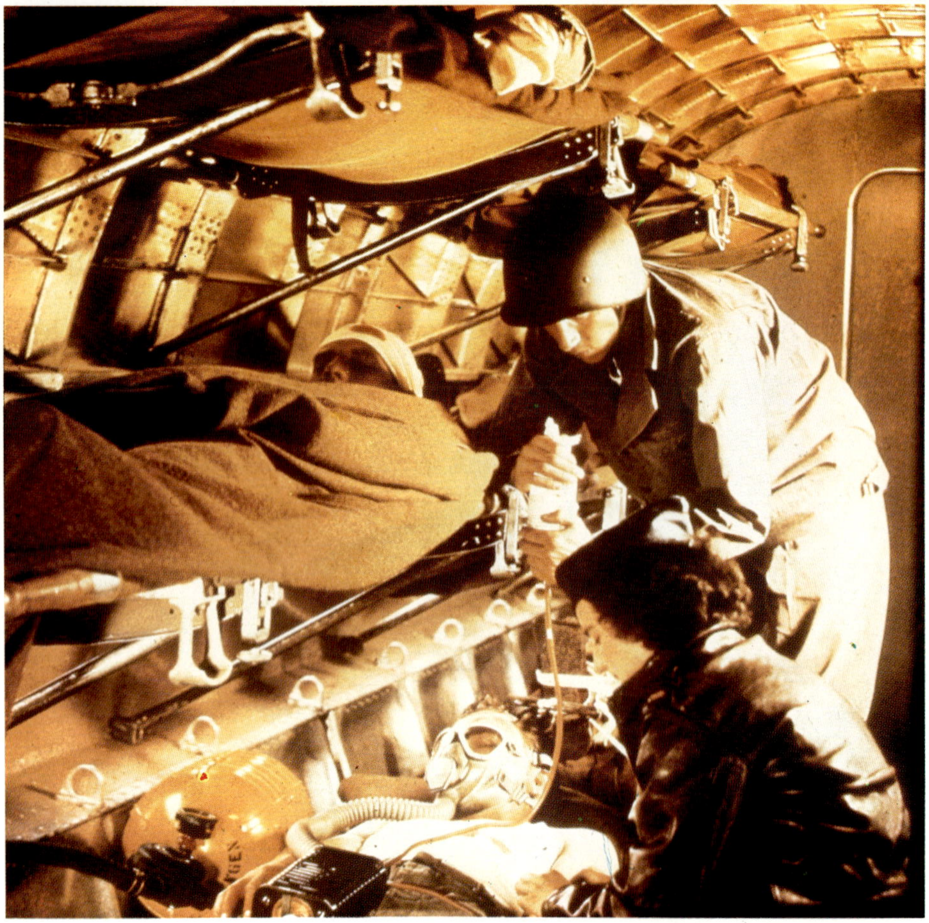

Unlike the First World War the transport of wounded men was not restricted to the roads or the railways. All the large armies used ambulance aircraft supplied with resuscitation equipment, as can be seen in this photograph showing the evacuation of American wounded. Aircraft were to prove invaluable in areas lacking the usual means of transport and especially for the evacuation of gravely wounded men needing treatment which could only be given in particularly well equipped hospital centres.

All the field hospitals possessed the equipment necessary for major operations and for saving the lives of thousands of men. However, because of the flood of wounded, the proportion of amputations remained much higher than had been foreseen, sometimes even exceeding the totals recorded in 1914–18. On the other hand there was a spectacular decrease in postoperative infections, due to the use of sulphonamides and the early antibiotics. Thus gas gangrene vanished for good from Allied hospitals.

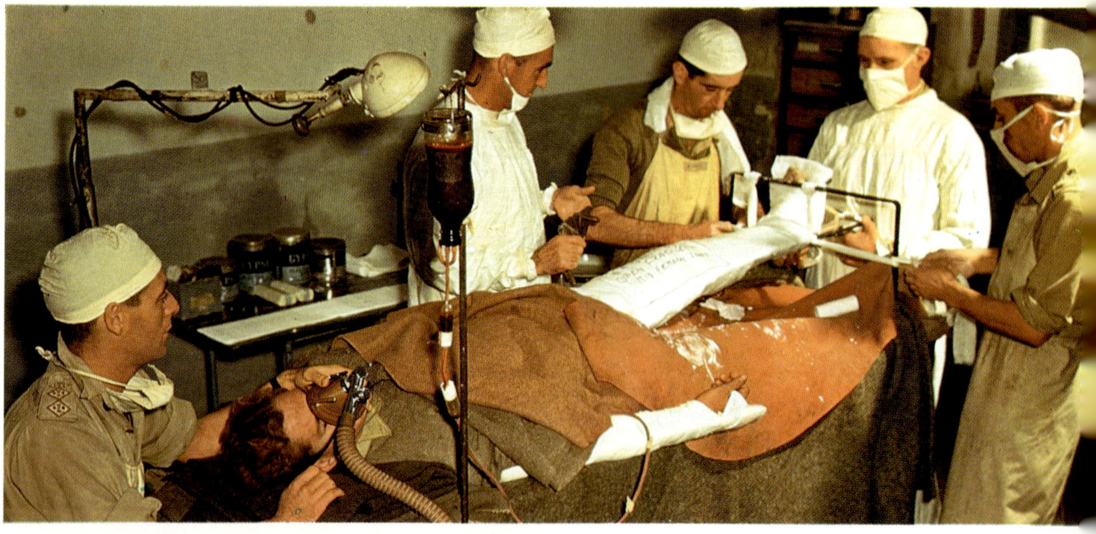

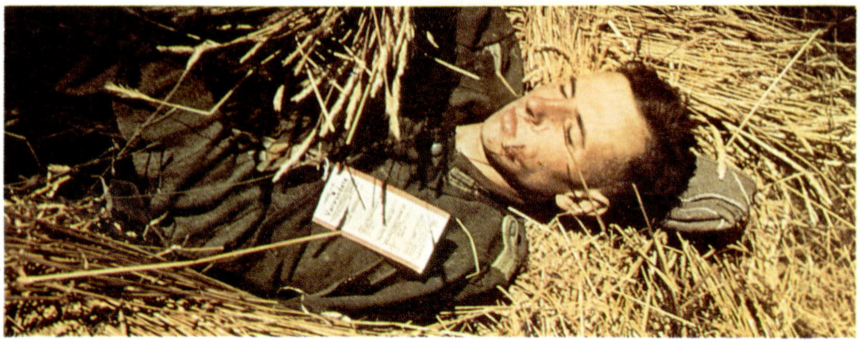

From 1941 onwards, with the beginning of the war in the east, the Wehrmacht's medical services were faced with an enormous task, having to treat hundreds of thousands of casualties under the most difficult conditions. Because of remarkable organization, however, the survival rate remained exceptionally high. Here we see an officer wounded during the fighting in the summer of 1942. The evacuation document describes the nature of the wound and the treatment given. The two strips of colour also indicate that the wounded man is fit to be moved.

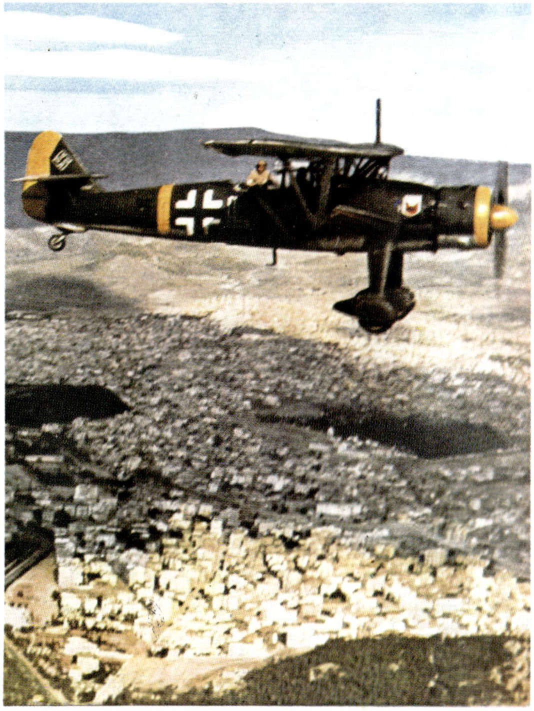

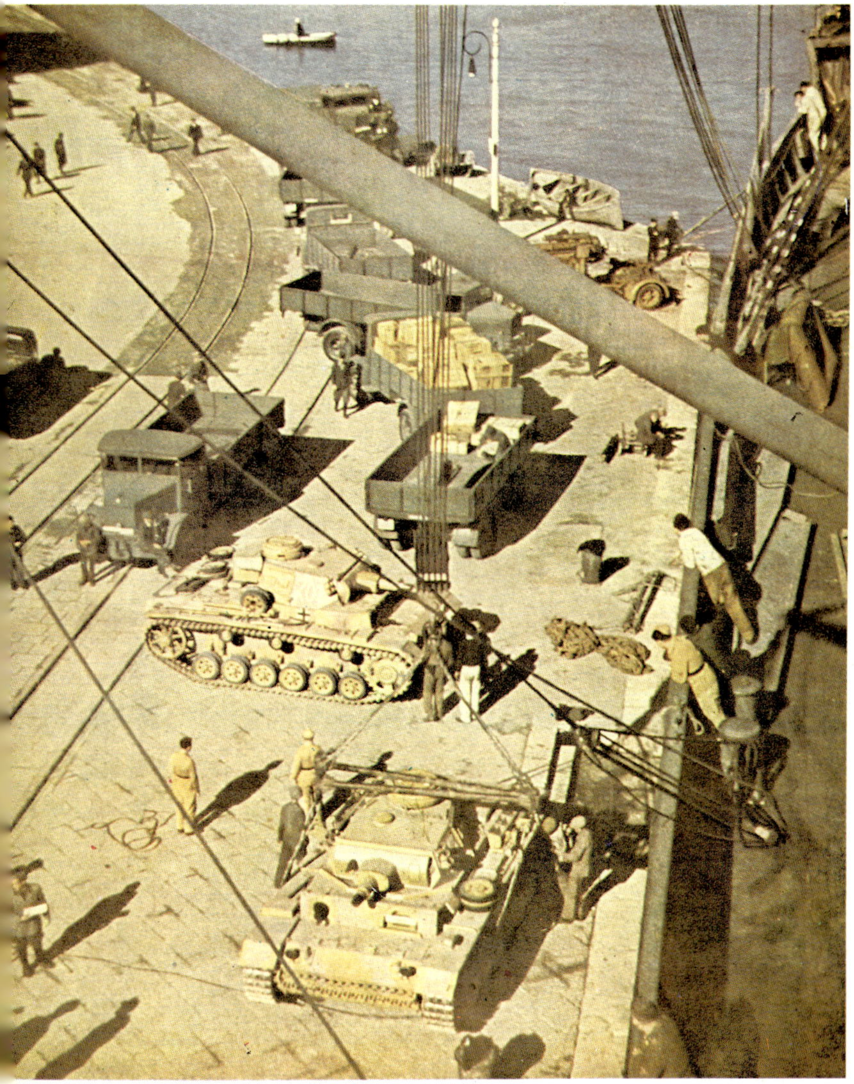

The Mediterranean. Contrary to all expectations, from 1940 to 1944 the war in the Mediterranean took on considerable importance. The inability of Italy to conduct a war along the same lines as Germany led to the intervention of the Wehrmacht in this theatre at the beginning of 1941. This intervention took the following form: the despatch of the Afrika Korps to Libya as well as Luftwaffe units to Sicily and the campaign in the Balkans to extricate the Italian forces trapped in Greece. Here we see a Luftwaffe reconnaissance aircraft flying over a Greek town in April 1941.

Despite the Anglo–American landings in Morocco and Algeria and Montgomery's victory at El Alamein, Rommel's troops succeeded in falling back into southern Tunisia and linking up with other Axis forces which had come from Italy. Here we see the disembarkation at an Italian port of German tanks and Italian lorries. Allied mastery of the air and the sea was sufficient to cut off supplies from the Axis bridgehead and to bring about its surrender in May 1943.

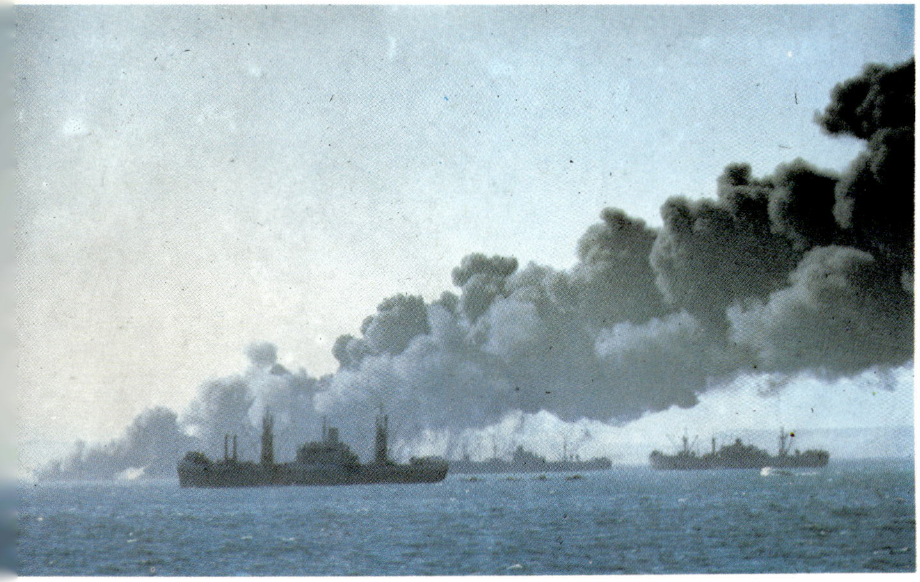

The war in the Mediterranean was not confined to operations in the Balkans, Libya, Tunisia or Italy. It was a struggle for communications. From 1940 onwards the British were attacking the links between Italy and North Africa, while Axis forces attempted to isolate Malta. When the large-scale landings in Sicily and at Salerno took place, the Luftwaffe, despite its numerical inferiority, did its best to attack the Allied supply convoys. Here a cargo vessel is seen on fire off the coast of Sicily during the landing of July 1943.

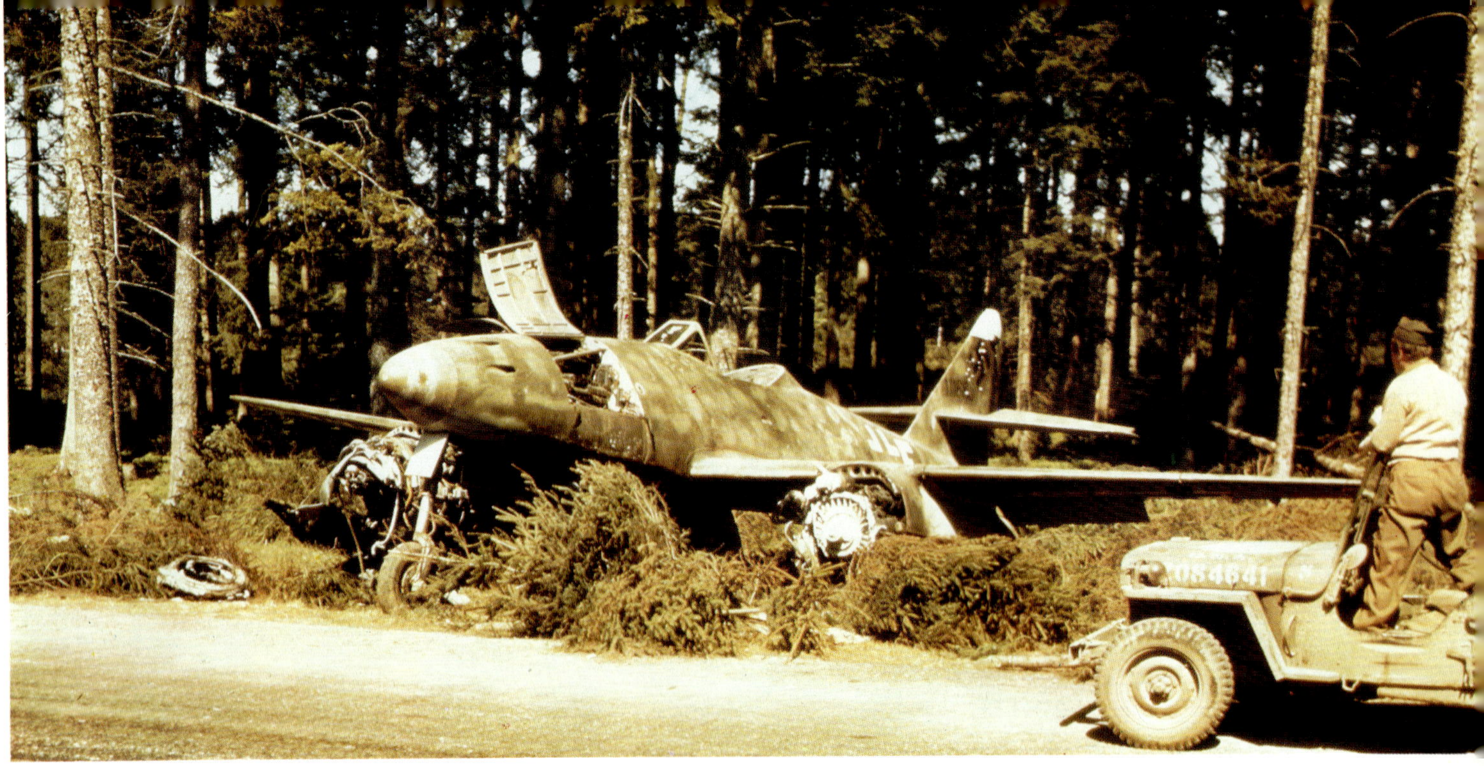

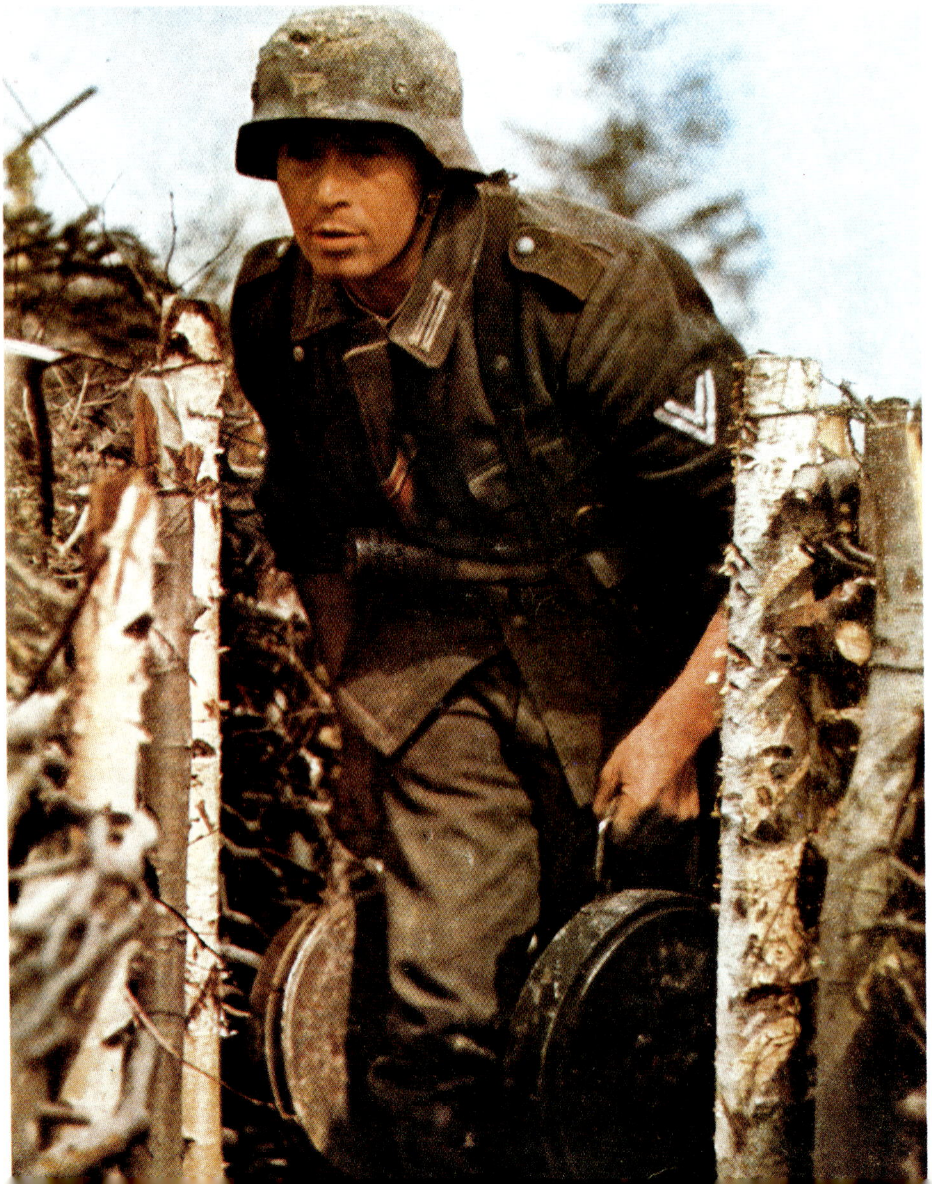

Messerschmitt. Bearing the name of its founder, the Messerschmitt company played a considerable part in German wartime aircraft production. It was responsible for some particularly successful aircraft, such as the single-engined Bf-109 and the twin-engined fighters, reconnaissance and tactical support aircraft, the Bf-110, Me-210 and Me-410. The most spectacular achievements were, towards the end of the war, two aircraft designed to give the Luftwaffe mastery of the air once again. These were the rocket-engined Me-163 interceptor and, especially, the twin-engined Me-262 jet aircraft, which outclassed all Allied aircraft in the same category. Introduced too late, the Me-262 could not affect the outcome of the war. We see here a damaged example on a German airfield captured by American troops.

Mines. Already in use during 1914–18, mines underwent a considerable development during the Second World War. On land the armies employed a great variety – antipersonnel, antitank, etc. When magnetic detectors appeared they had to resort to mines made of bakelite or wood. It was the Germans who, throughout the conflict, showed the greatest expertise in this area. Here, in 1943, on the eastern front, a German soldier is carrying two 'plate' mines which he is preparing to put in position in front of the lines.

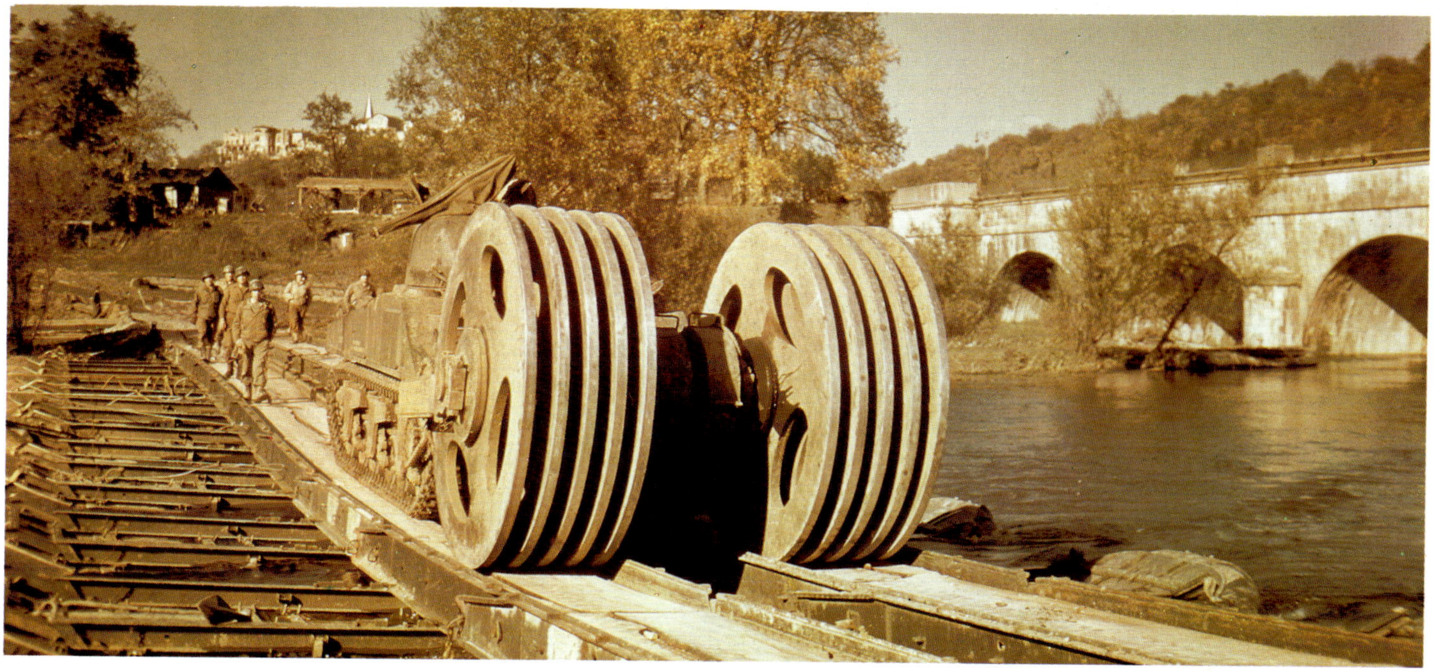

The detection and destruction of mines was an extremely difficult and dangerous task for engineering units, which often had to work under enemy fire. After the Normandy landing, for mine-clearing operations in France the Allies sometimes used some rather unusual contraptions, such as this Sherman M4 tank with its two enormous rollers, designed to set off mines intended for armoured vehicles. These tanks showed themselves to be particularly effective from the time of the Normandy landing until the crossing of the Rhine.

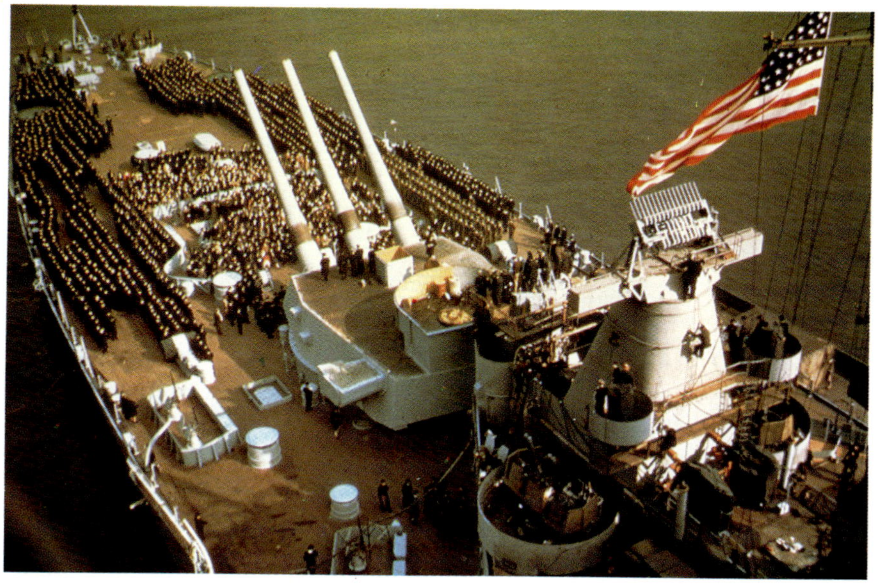

The *Missouri*. Entering service at the end of 1944, this American battleship belonged to a series of four 45,000 ton vessels, capable of 33 knots, heavily protected and equipped with extremely powerful armament, consisting of nine 16 in. (406 mm) guns and numerous 100 anti-aircraft weapons, ranging from 40 to 127 mm. Having carried Admiral Halsey's flag at the battles of Iwo Jima and Okinawa, the *Missouri* was, as the photograph shows, the scene of the Japanese surrender on 2 Sept. 1945, in Tokyo bay.

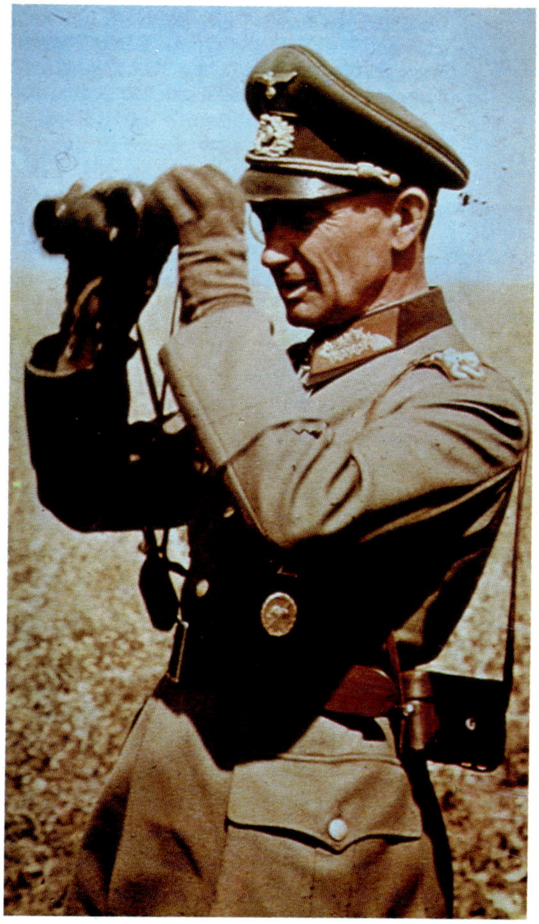

Model. An outstanding commander of armoured units during the campaigns of the Blitzkrieg, he was able to limit the extent of the reverses German forces were to suffer on the various fronts from 1943 onwards. Possessing unusual energy and a great talent for improvisation, he became the man for tackling desperate situations on the eastern front. Promoted field marshal on 1 March 1944, he succeeded von Kluge as commander in the west on 17 Aug. He took part in the Ardennes offensive but could do no more than delay the final collapse. Encircled in the Ruhr, he committed suicide on 21 April 1945.

Morale. British soldiers in Venice after the liberation.

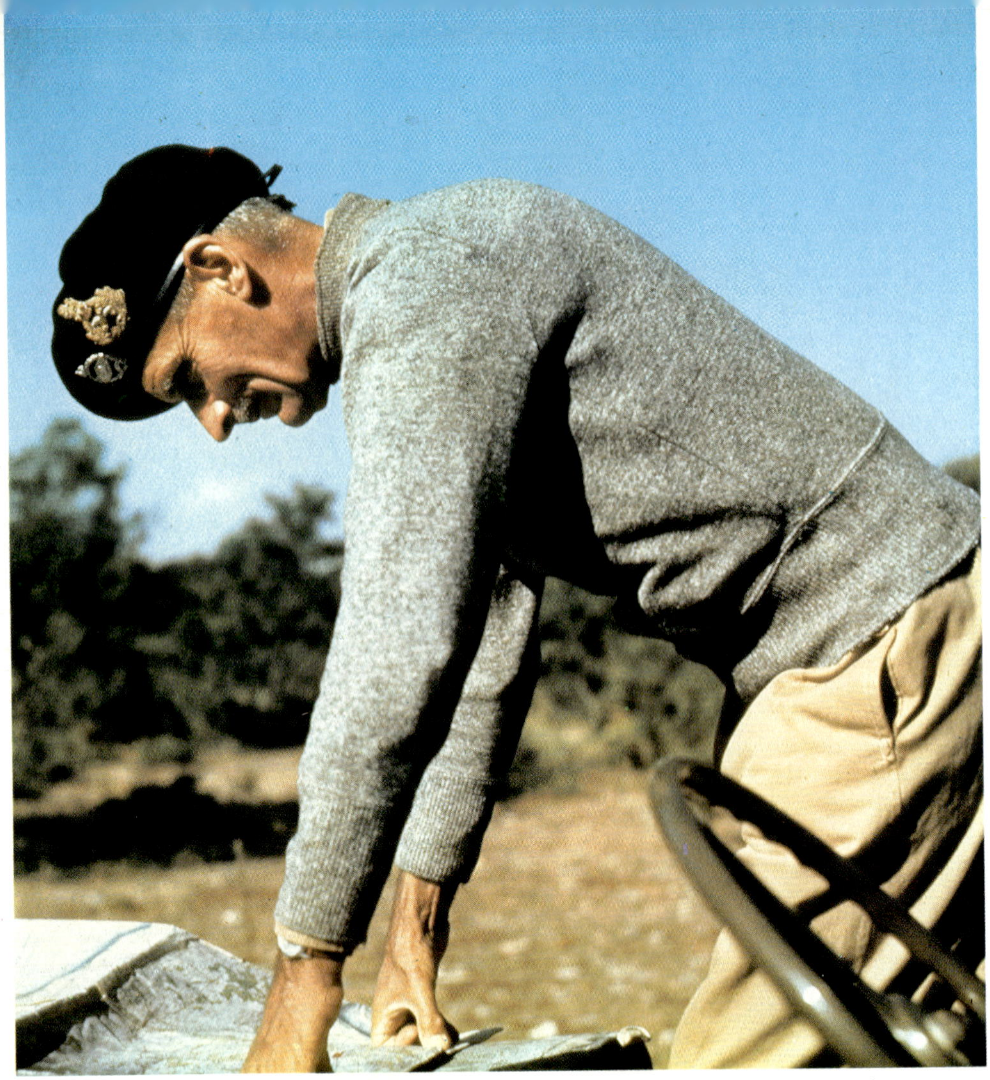

Montgomery. Following the battle of El Alamein, which saw the success of the British 8th Army over Rommel in the autumn of 1942, he became the most famous general in the British army. Puritanical and ascetic, by nature both unbending and unorthodox, he gave the impression not only of a soldier who was very concerned about the morale and material well-being of his men, but also of a great war leader, although often controversial, and certainly a better tactician than he was a strategist. Here we see 'Monty' – Churchill had given the nickname his blessing – with his inevitable pullover, studying a staff map during the Italian campaign.

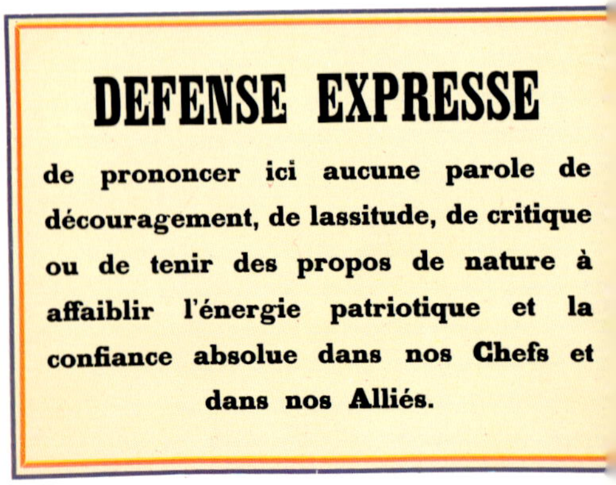

DEFENSE EXPRESSE

de prononcer ici aucune parole de découragement, de lassitude, de critique ou de tenir des propos de nature à affaiblir l'énergie patriotique et la confiance absolue dans nos Chefs et dans nos Alliés.

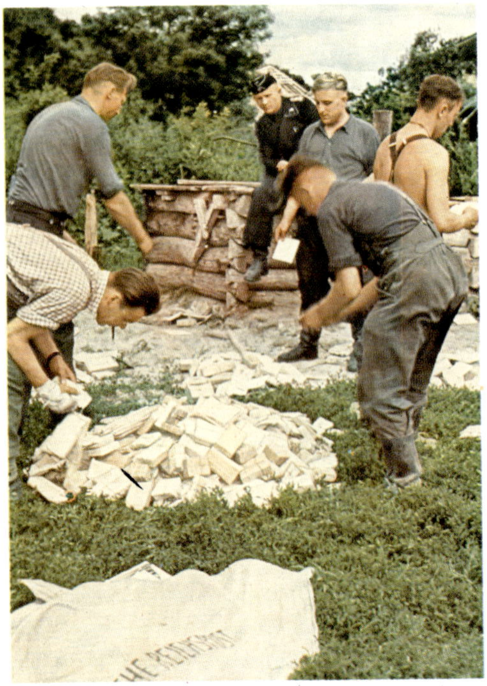

Morale. Throughout an interminable war, the morale of the ordinary soldier remained one of the chief preoccupations of the military authorities. While insisting on a respect for discipline, the high command in all the armies made good use of various honours (decorations, citations, mentions in dispatches) and, as far as circumstances allowed, gave great attention to those factors designed to increase the well-being of soldiers (leave, quality of food, etc). In every army it was recognized that the speed and regularity of the postal services constituted an essential element of morale. Here a group of Wehrmacht postal officers are sorting a sack of mail on the eastern front in the autumn of 1942.

From the outset of the war, governments understood the necessity of maintaining not only the morale of the fighting soldiers, but also that of the civilians often separated from their relatives and facing the difficulties of their material existence, including the threat of air raids. During the 'phoney war' there appeared on walls and in public places in France this kind of notice (photograph) which was aimed, in principle, at averting the harmful effects of a prolonged period of inactivity. The results were poor and in 1940 such attempts did not succeed in preventing a general decline in the morale of the country. (Bibliothèque du Musée de l'Armée.)

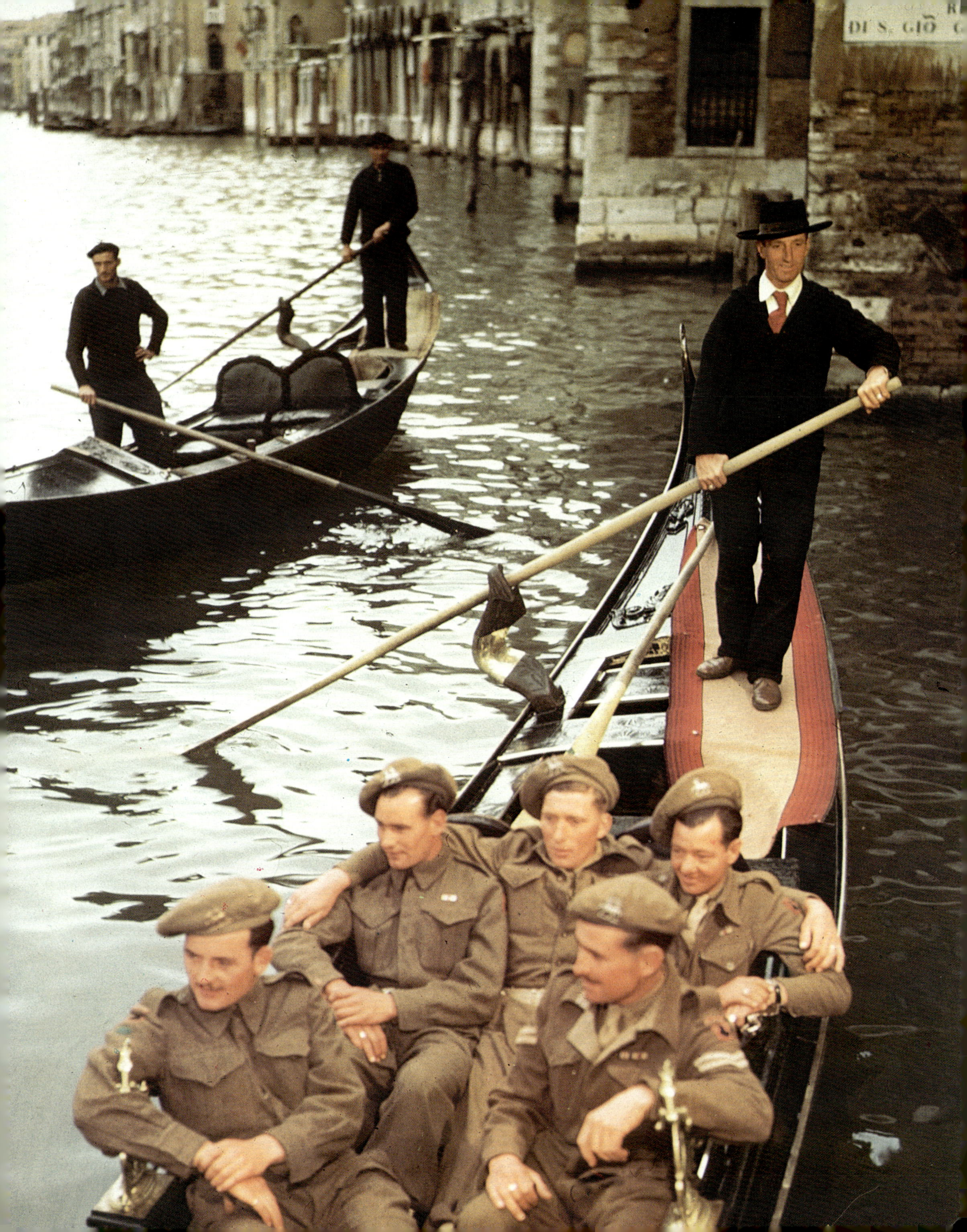
DI S. GIŌ

Moscow. In the autumn of 1941, after the spectacular victories of the summer and the great battle in the Ukraine in which numerous Soviet forces were encircled, Hitler and the Wehrmacht chiefs entertained the hope of finishing the war in the east before the winter with a final devastating blow. Operation Typhoon, the great offensive aimed at Moscow, was launched at the end of September and initially met with some startling successes. However, first the mud, then the cold weather and the growing resistance of the Russians began, during November, to break up its momentum. In this picture, taken at a time when victory still seems in sight, a German armoured car is on reconnaissance at the Mozhaisk crossroads, 62 mi. (100 km) from Moscow and 1820 mi. (2910 km) from Brest.

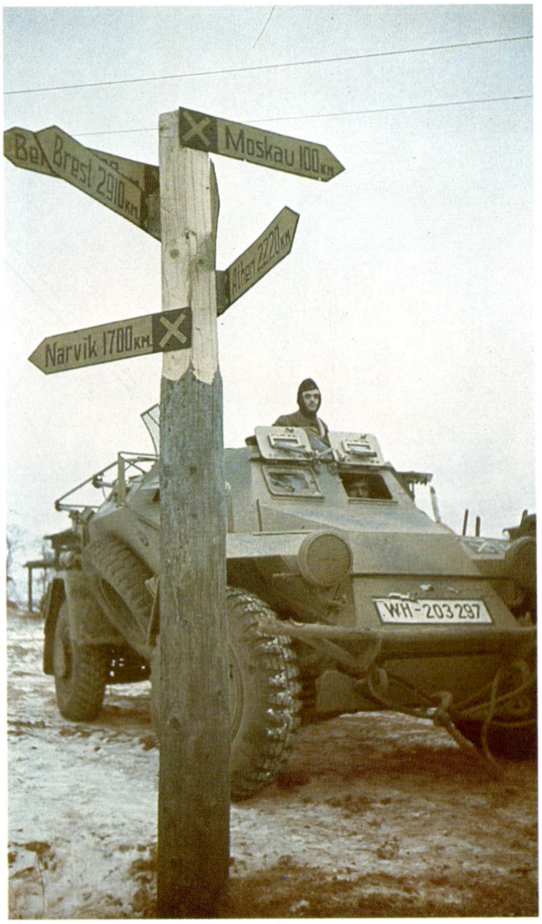

At the beginning of Dec. 1941 the big German offensive against Moscow was virtually at a standstill because of growing logistical difficulties, the intense cold and the fierce resistance of the Red Army. To the west of the capital, less than 60 mi. (100 km) from the Kremlin, heavy fighting took place on the Volokolamsk road (photograph). To the north forward armoured units reached the suburbs of the city but were unable to proceed any further. The German army halted for good on 5 Dec., before suffering the full weight of fierce Soviet counter-attacks.

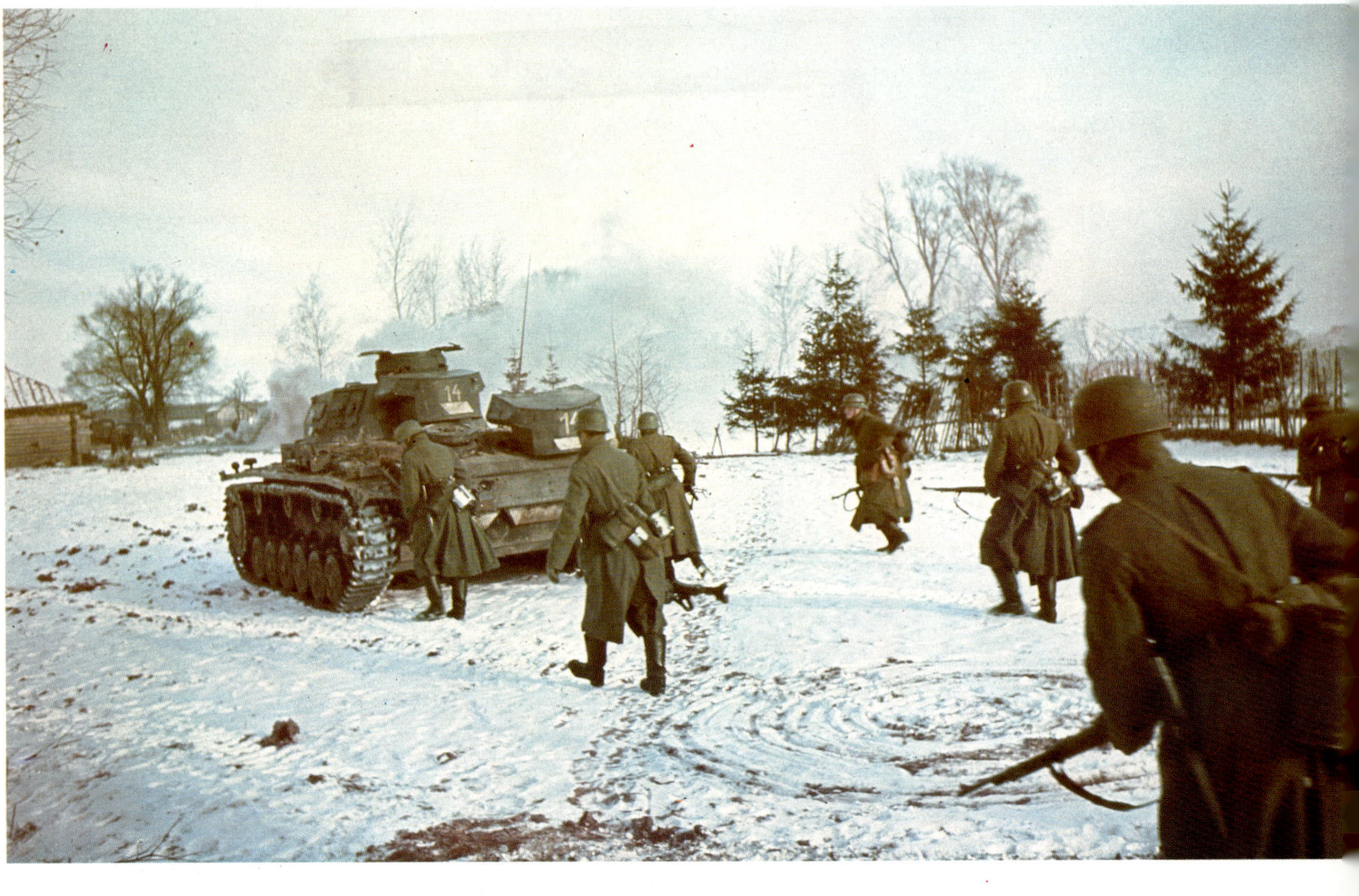

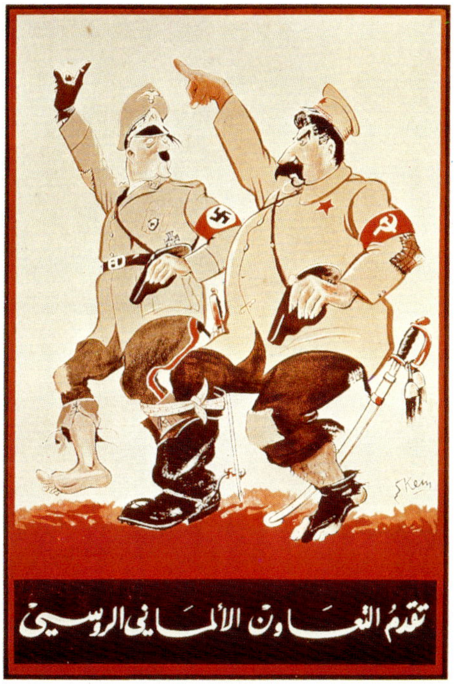

The Russo-German Pact, signed in Moscow on 23 Aug. 1939, produced an amazed reaction throughout the world. It gave the Egyptian-born caricaturist, Kem, the opportunity of displaying his talent while emphasizing the unnatural character of the alliance between two opposing totalitarian systems. Although entangled in the same boot, Stalin and Hitler are here trying, as best they can, to stride off in different directions. With remarkable foresight the cartoon underlined the fragile and temporary nature of the agreement.

The Mosquito. The De Havilland Mosquito, of which more than 7000 were built in different versions, entered service in 1940. It was one of the most successful aircraft of the whole war and one of the finest achievements of the British aircraft industry. Very fast, flying at high altitude, it carried out thousands of reconnaissance and bombing missions over Europe. In addition, it showed remarkable qualities as a day – and night – fighter, and was also used for training purposes.

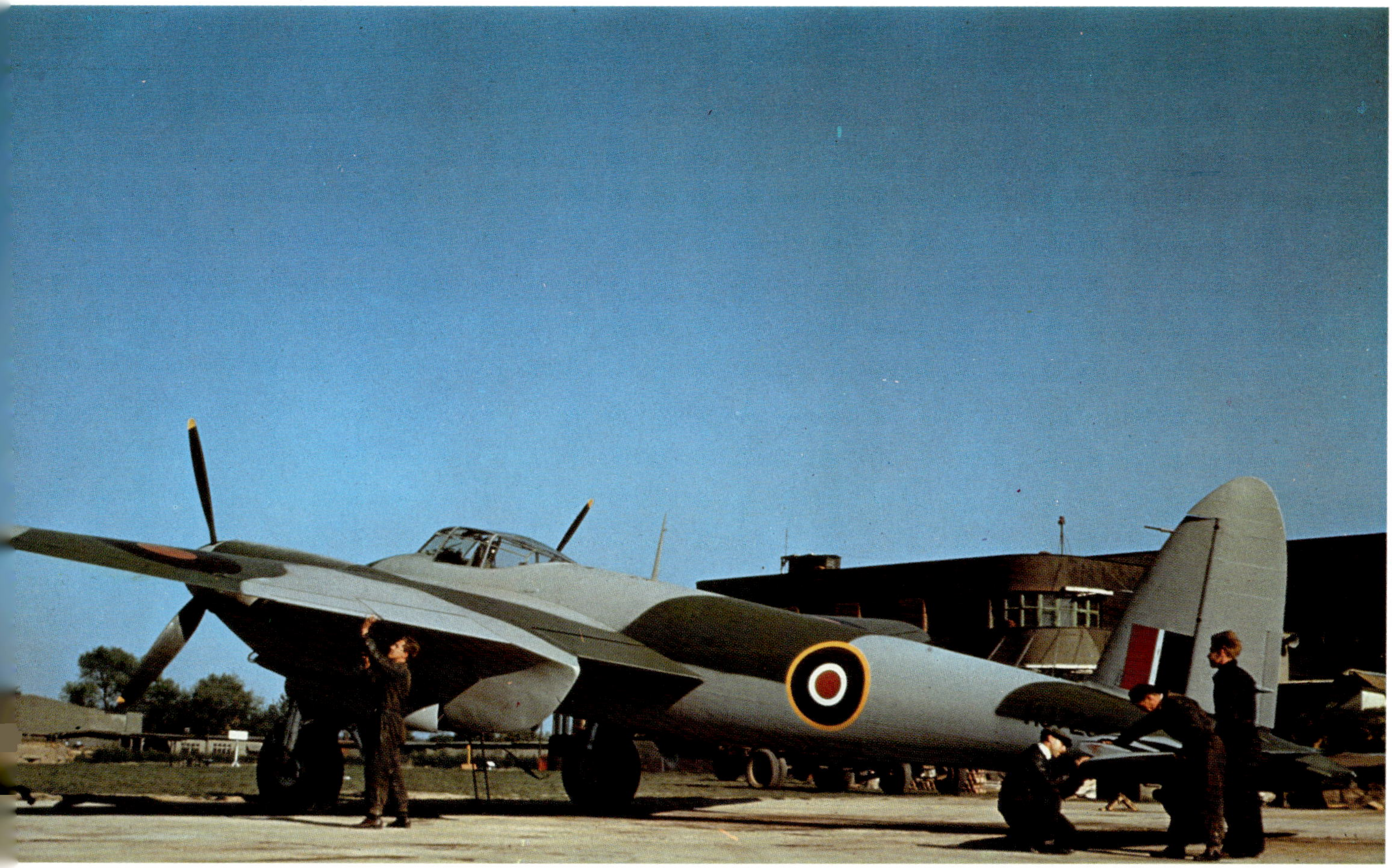

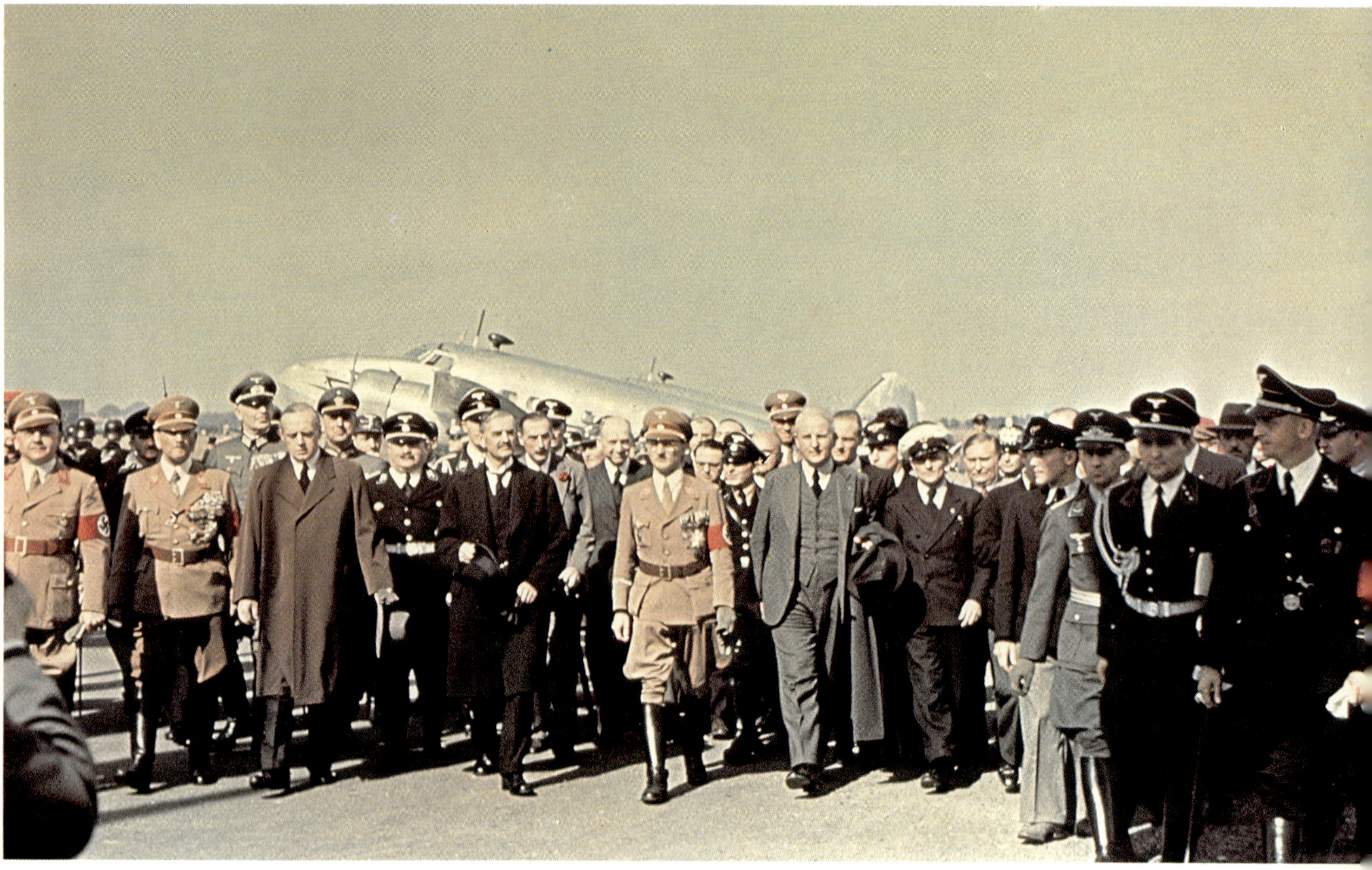

Munich. The Munich crisis in the autumn of 1938 was caused by Hitler's determination to attach to Germany by agreement or by force the Sudeten German minority which formed an integral part of Czechoslovakia. For a week Europe believed itself to be within a hairsbreadth of war. The crisis was resolved only by the capitulation of the western democracies who resigned themselves to abandoning Czechoslovakia. Here Chamberlain is being received at an airfield in Munich on 29 Sept. by the Reich's foreign minister, Ribbentrop, several hours before the opening of the fateful conference.

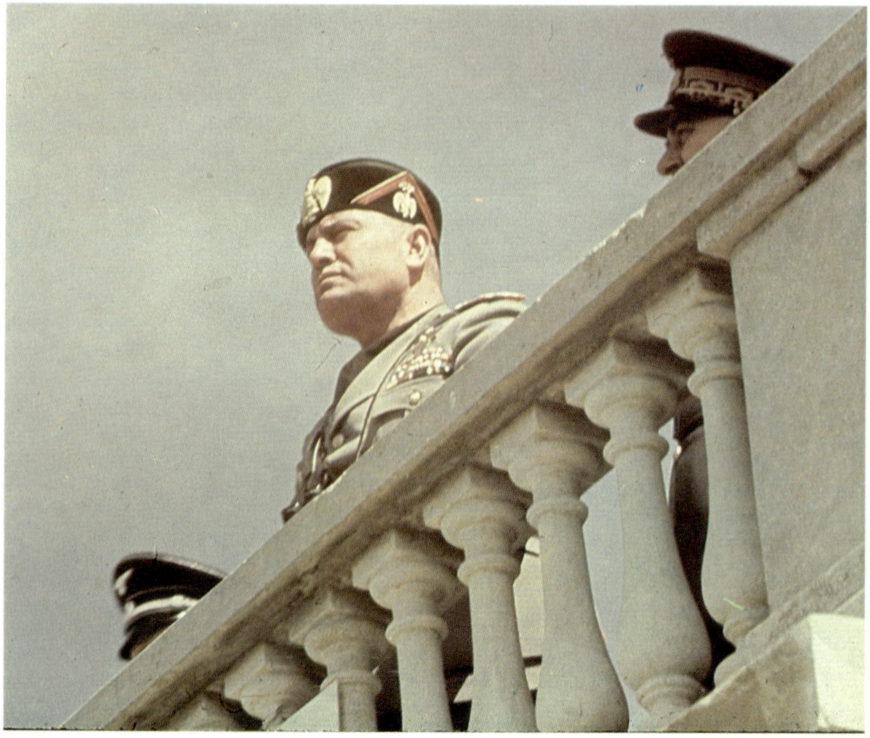

Mussolini. A photograph of the Duce watching manoeuvres by the Italian air force over the beach at Furbara, during Hitler's visit to Italy in May 1938. The alliance with the Third Reich was in the long run to prove disastrous for the Fascist regime. Because of its lack of economic and military resources, Italy was unable to conduct a 'parallel war' with Germany. The defeats mounted up and in July 1943 the regime collapsed. Arrested by the king and then set free by the Germans, Mussolini, now totally dependent upon the Third Reich, played only a minor role as head of the Italian Social Republic before being shot by partisans in April 1945.

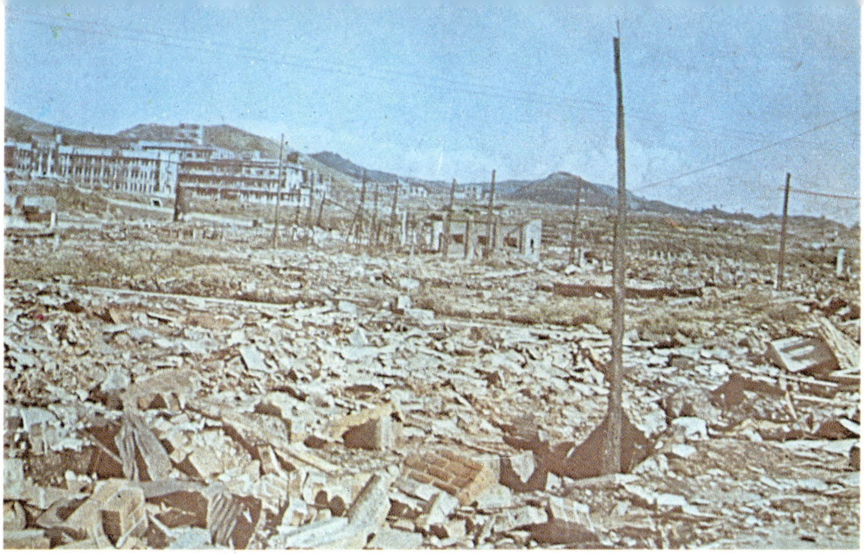

Nagasaki. Three days after Hiroshima, on 9 Aug. 1945, the Americans carried out a second nuclear attack against Japan. Because of adverse weather conditions the bomb was not dropped on the town of Kokura, which had been originally designated as the target, but on Nagasaki. The device caused destruction comparable with that at Hiroshima, although a line of hills, which can be clearly seen in this picture, protected the western part of the town. Nevertheless the estimates of the number of dead range from 24,000 to 30,000 and casualties from 23,000 to 50,000.

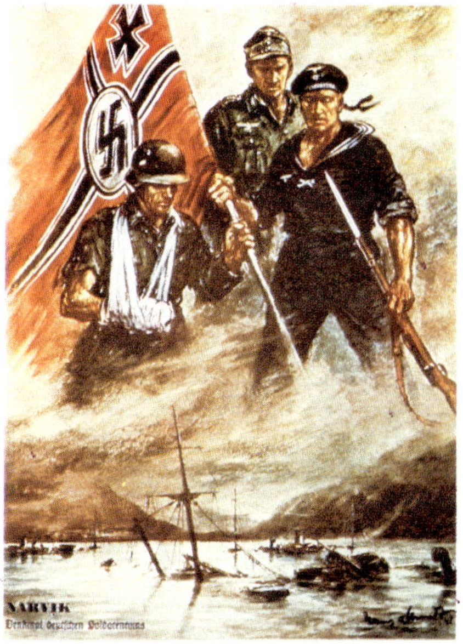

Narvik. The battles at Narvik were the only Allied successes of the campaign in Norway during April–May 1940, in which they were to be heavily defeated. The first success was the destruction on 13 April of a flotilla of German destroyers taken by surprise inside the fjord. The second, a month later, was the combined operation which enabled Narvik to be taken after a hard-fought struggle, which pushed the Germans back towards the Swedish frontier, at the very moment when the disastrous turn taken by the campaign in France compelled the Allies to evacuate their forces. German propaganda (photograph) exploited the event in order to glorify the role of the defenders of Narvik. On this poster, grouped around the flag of the Third Reich, are a wounded infantryman wearing a helmet, a mountain infantryman and a sailor, gun in hand, fighting on land after the destruction of his ship.

Naval bases. At the end of the 19th century Admiral Mahan, the great American theoretician of naval power, had emphasized the importance of naval bases. The Second World War was to illustrate the truth of this proposition on a large scale. Well-equipped naval bases were seen to be indispensable for the re-supply and maintenance of sea-going forces. This picture shows a British submarine flotilla completing the taking on of stores before it sets off on operations.

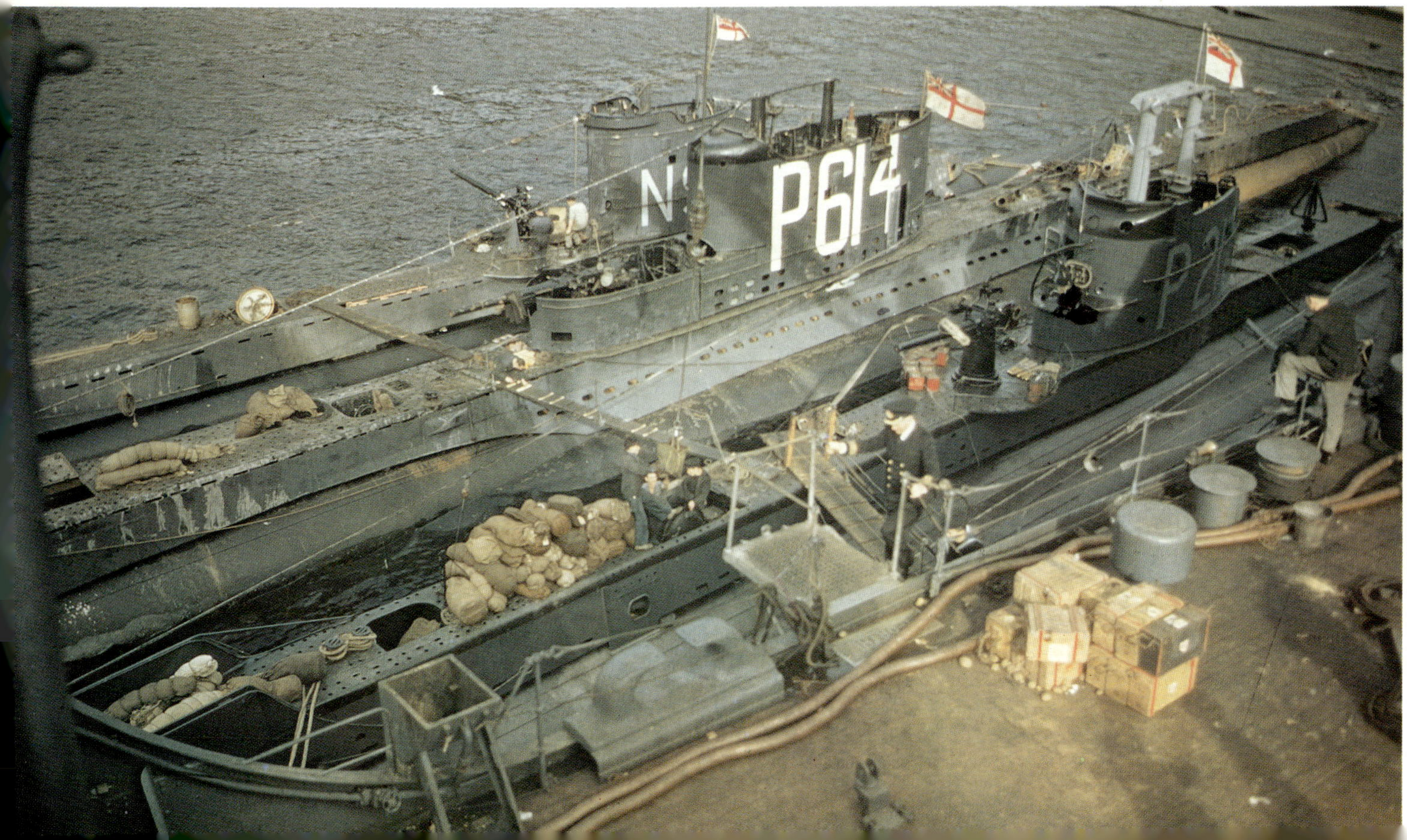

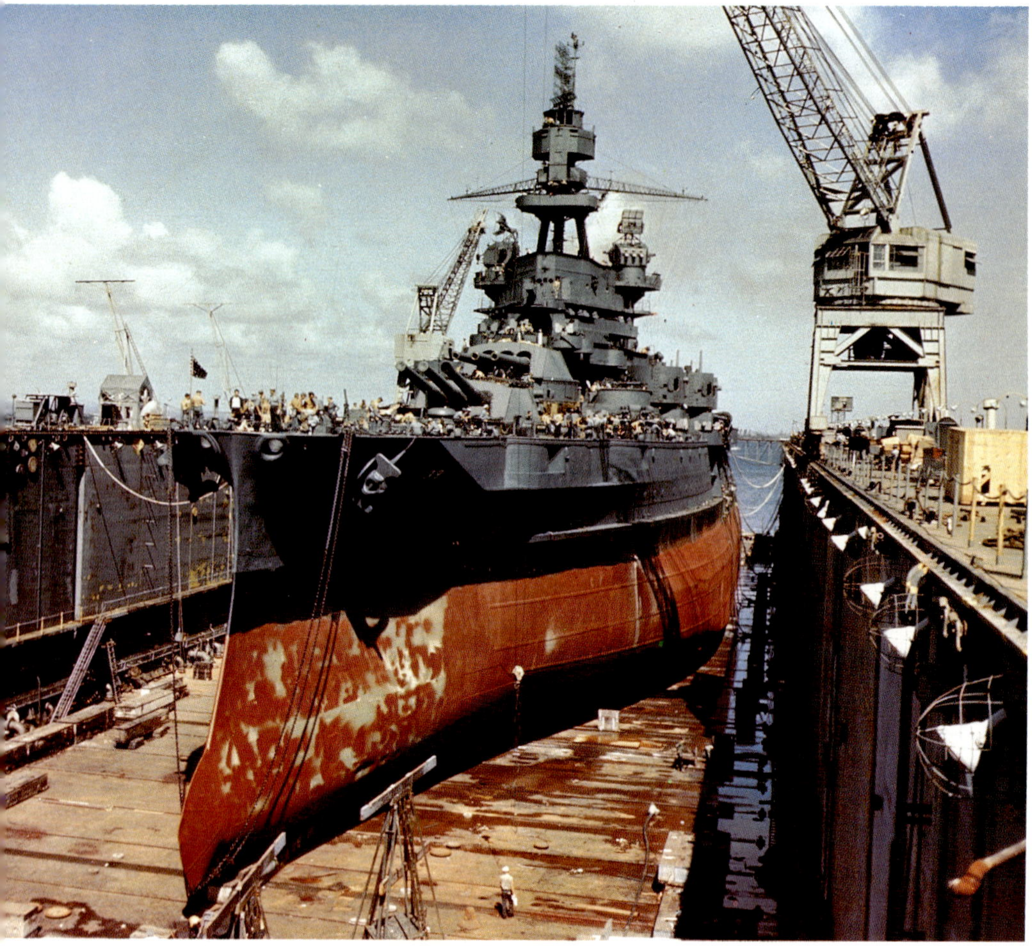

As operations in the Pacific developed the Americans came up against a serious 'base problem'. The west coast naval bases of San Francisco and San Diego and even Hawaii were soon found to be too far from the zones of operations. So the US Navy decided to set up fully equipped forward bases closer at hand, like that of Ulithi in the Mariana Islands. Operated by naval supply and maintenance units, these bases could carry out maintenance operations of all kinds. In this picture the battleship *Pennsylvania*, in a floating dock of 35,000 tons, is having its hull scraped.

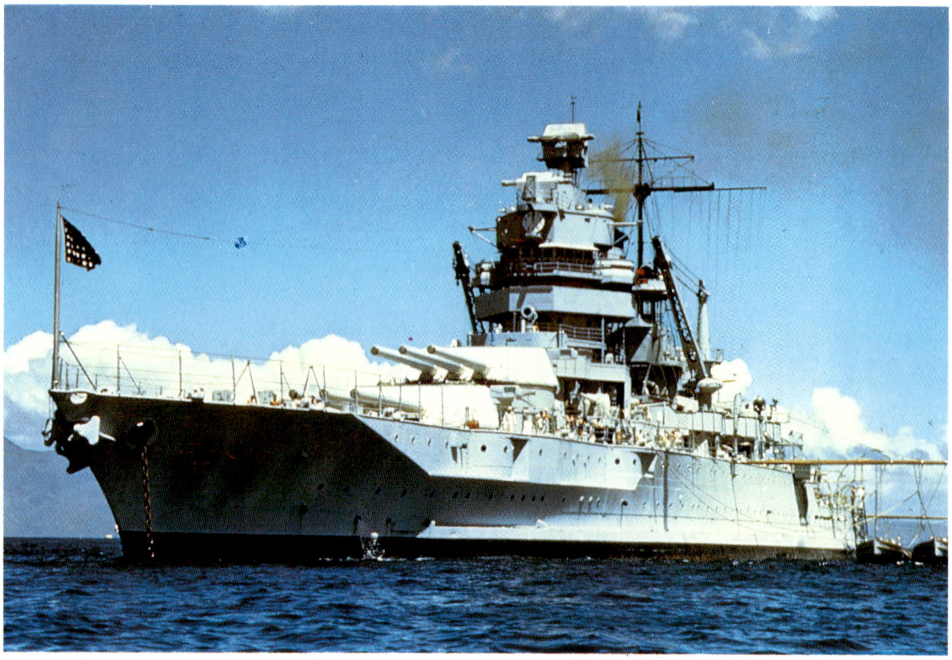

Naval forces. At the beginning of the Second World War, the battleship was still the spearhead of the battle fleets. Most of the warships were relatively old, modernized during the interwar years and conspicuous for their slow speed (20–22 knots), strong protective armour and heavy armament. The gun calibre of such battleships' main armament varied from 12 to 16 in. (300 to 400 mm). Here we see an American battleship of the *Tennessee* class, typical of this generation, riding at anchor in Hawaii in 1943, just after a final refit, which has scarcely altered its general outlines.

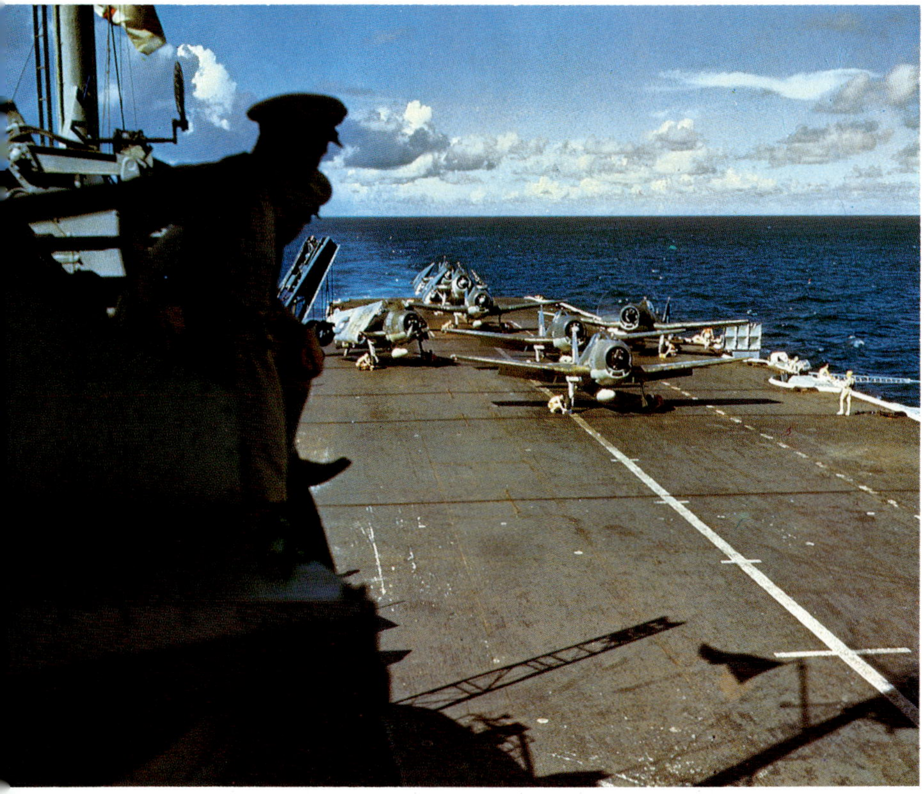

Grumman F6F Hellcats, fighters of American design, on the flight deck of the British aircraft carrier *Indomitable* in Jan. 1944. At the beginning of hostilities the aircraft carrier was still relegated to a subordinate position in the battle fleet. It was employed in reconnaissance operations and, if necessary, could be used to damage or slow down an enemy battleship with bombs or torpedoes in order to bring it within range of the guns of the big ships. It was only from 1942 onwards that the aircraft carrier became the principal warship, with a capacity for action and destruction extending over a radius of 190 miles (300 km).

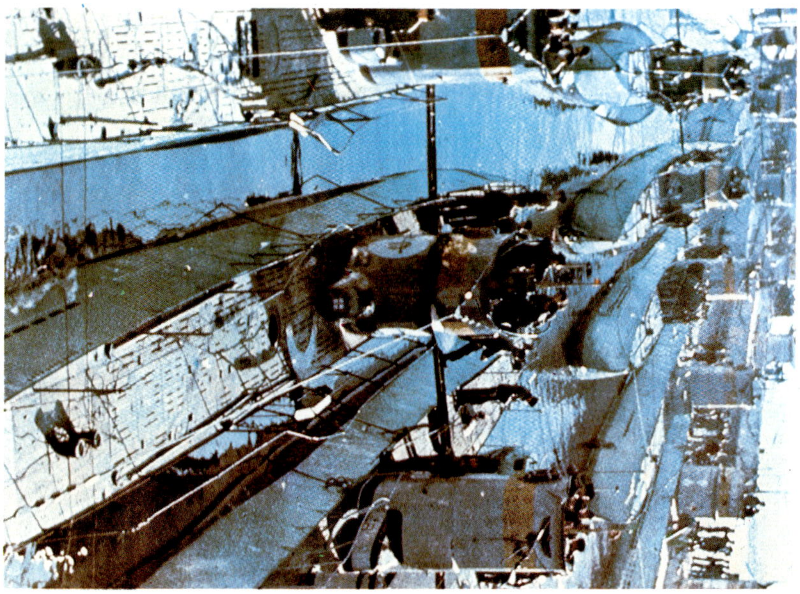

Contrary to the forecasts of the naval high commands, the submarine continued to demonstrate its remarkable qualities throughout the Second World War as an offensive weapon against warships and merchant vessels. It was also used on intelligence missions, for carrying commandos and for transporting supplies. The aircraft proved itself to be a much more deadly enemy of the submarine than the surface vessel. Nevertheless, at the end of the war a new generation of high-performance German submarines, equipped with snorkels, were able to a great extent to neutralize the threat from the air. Here we see a flotilla of Type II German submarines just before the outbreak of war.

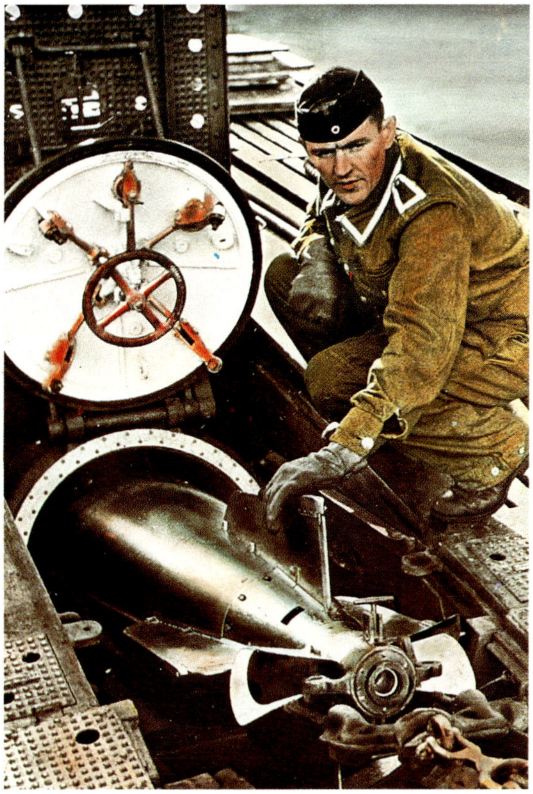

German naval officer supervising the loading of a torpedo into a submarine. During the war the Germans were constantly making improvements to their torpedoes. In 1939 they introduced electrically driven ones with magnetic ignition, but getting them to work properly proved an arduous task. In 1943 they were the first to develop torpedoes with a homing device which automatically made straight for the sound of a ship's propeller. Christened 'destroyer busters', these torpedoes were especially intended for use against convoy escorts. The Allies responded by towing noise-producing devices behind their ships.

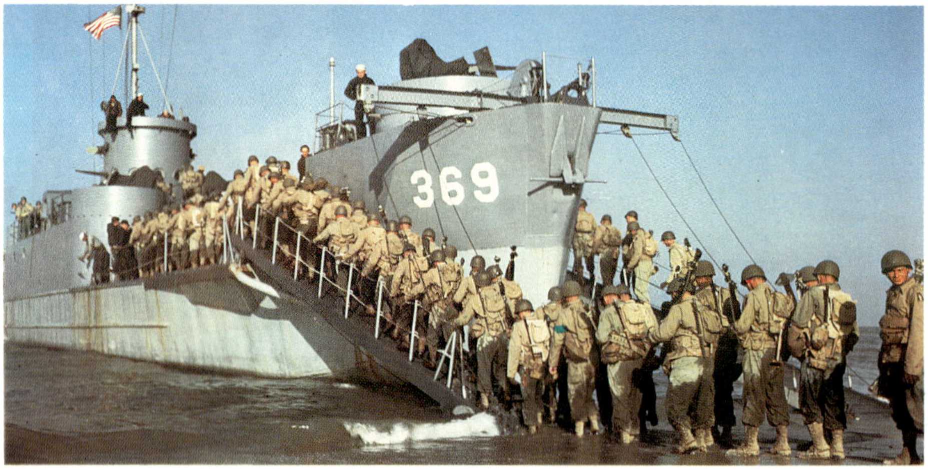

American soldiers in England boarding a barge prior to the invasion of Normandy. The extent of amphibious operations during the Second World War was considerable. Contrary to experience in previous conflicts, the major navies were in a position to land and supply large armies. These landings necessitated the building of a whole auxiliary fleet of more than 50,000 landing vessels, whose tonnage exceeded two million tons for the US navy alone.

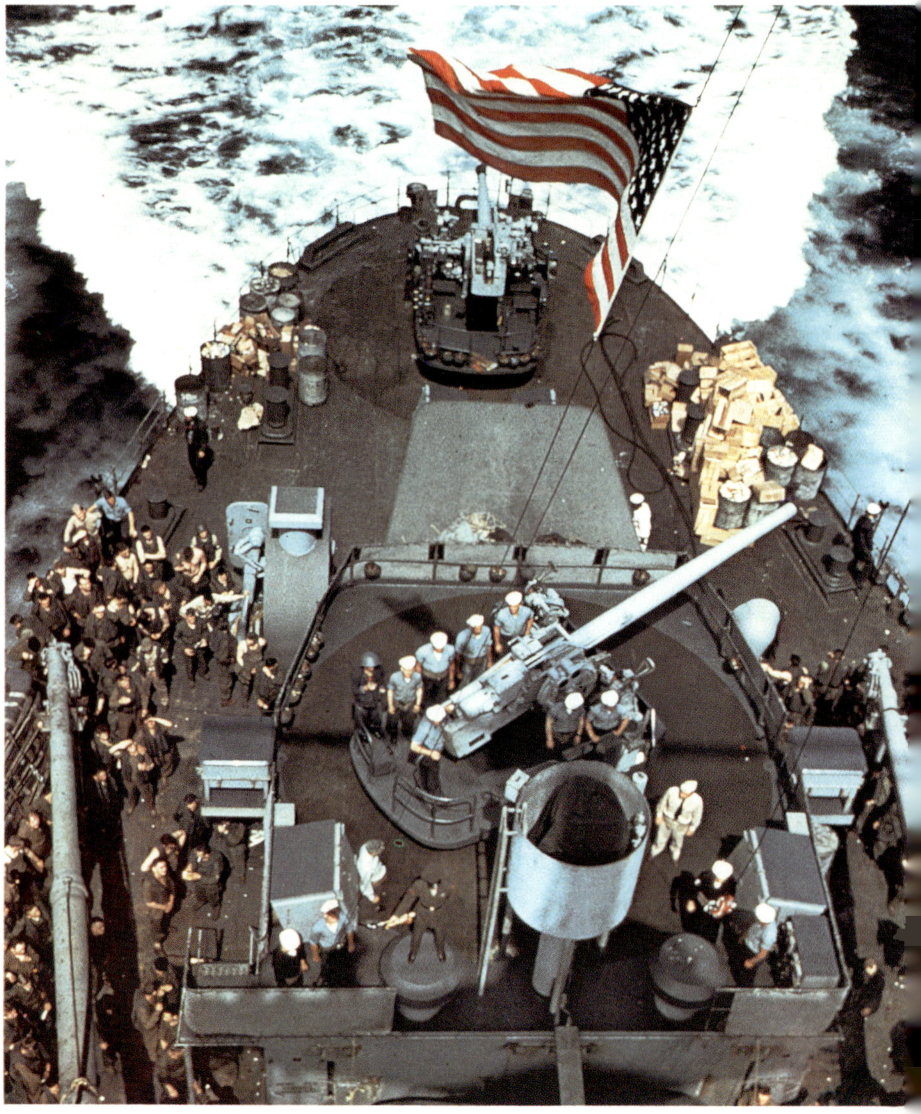

An American transport ship in the Pacific in 1944. During the war the US navy was to undergo a remarkable expansion. Despite losing 600,000 tons, it grew from 1,400,000 tons in 1941 to 4,500,000 tons in 1945. The Pacific fleet alone possessed 23 battleships, 26 combat aircraft carriers, 64 escort aircraft carriers, 52 cruisers, 323 destroyers, 298 escort vessels, 181 submarines and 160 minesweepers, as well as 2783 landing vessels and nearly 15,000 combat aircraft. The total strength of this new navy rose from 350,000 to 3,400,000 men.

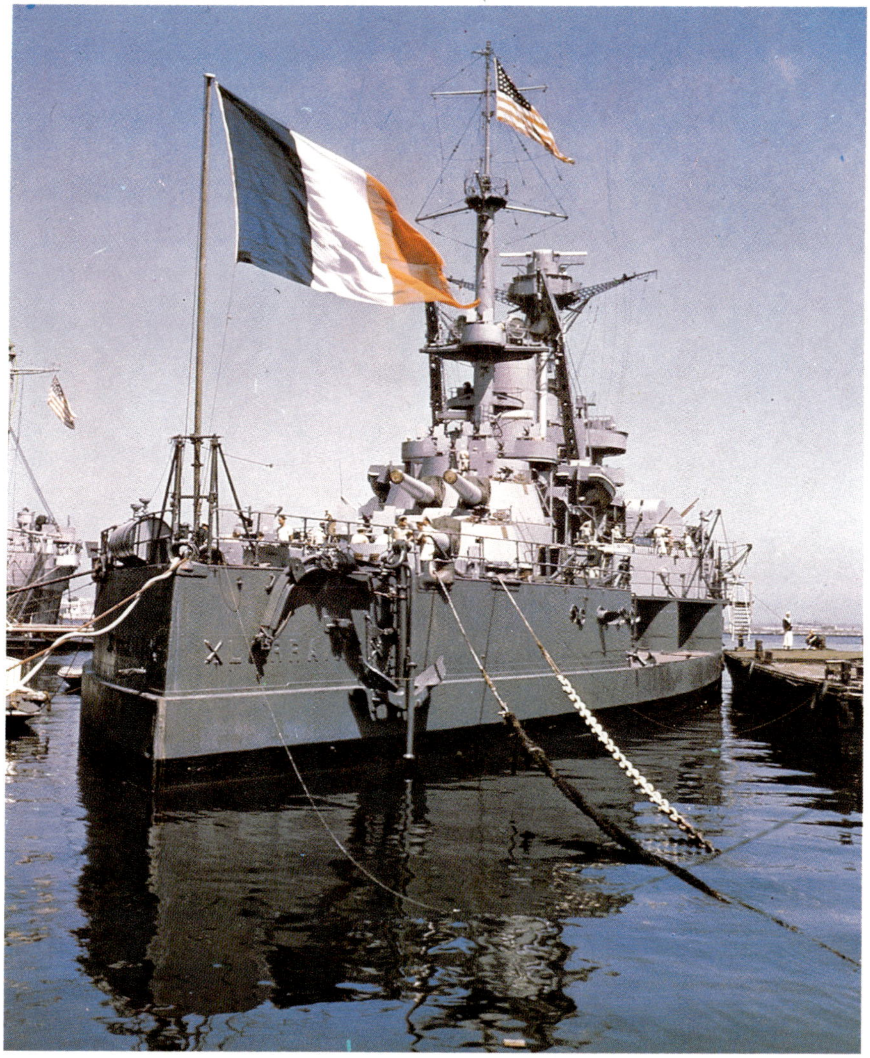

The French Navy. With a tonnage of 750,000 tons, in 1939 the French navy was the fourth largest in the world. Its best ships were the battle-cruisers *Strasbourg* and *Dunkerque* and a recently built uniform class of fast, well-armed cruisers and destroyers. Some old vessels, such as the battleship *Lorraine* of 23,500 tons (photograph), which had entered service in 1916 and had been refitted between the two wars, were to play a quite important role. With its eight 13½ in. (340 mm) guns, the *Lorraine* took part in the bombardment which preceded the landing in Provence.

From 1935, as part of a rearmament programme, the French navy had undertaken the modernization of its battle-fleet by laying down two 35,000 ton battleships, the *Richelieu* and the *Jean-Bart*. These vessels, with a speed of 31 knots and equipped with eight 15 in. (380 mm) guns in two quadruple turrets, were in addition heavily armoured. In June 1940 they succeeded in reaching Dakar and Casablanca respectively. In 1943 the *Richelieu* underwent an important refit in the USA, which mainly involved the strengthening of its anti-aircraft armament. Here she is seen entering New York harbour before reaching the Brooklyn Navy Yard.

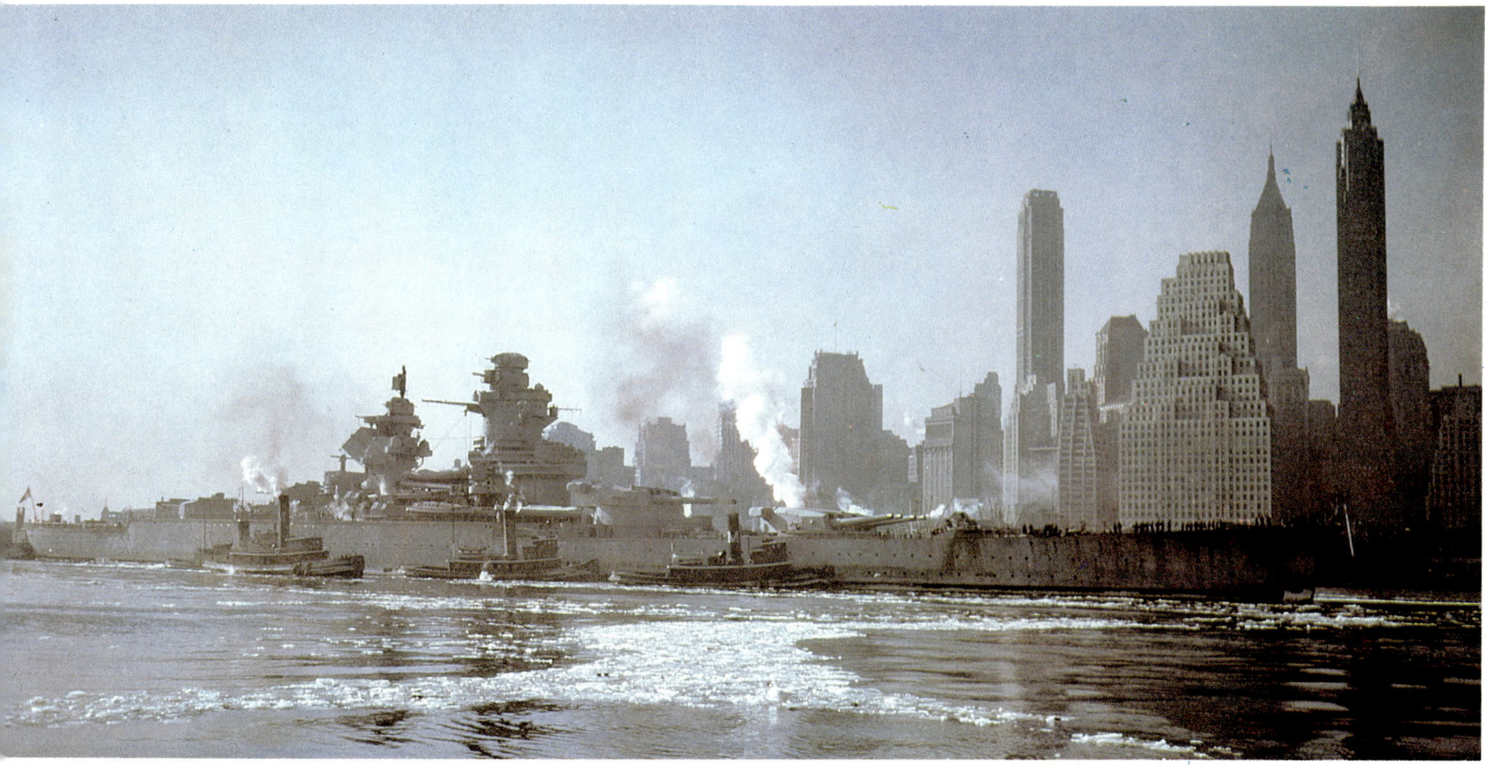

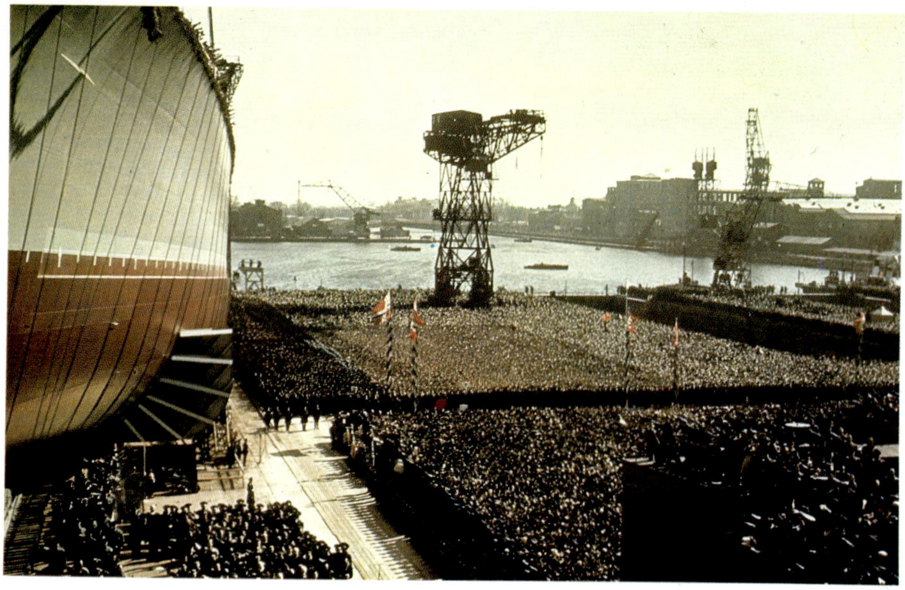

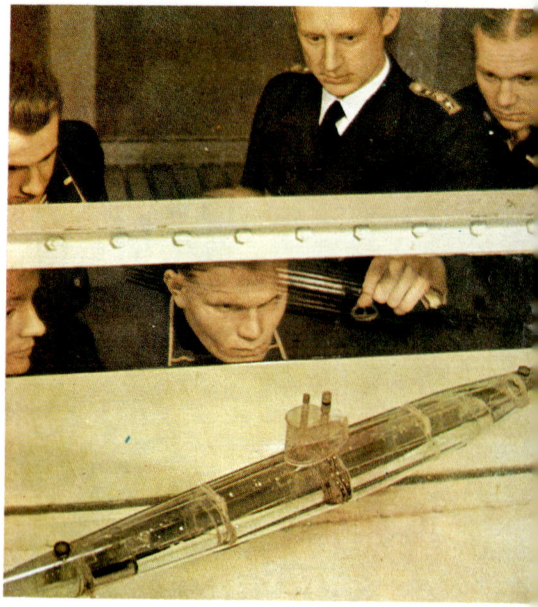

The German Navy. The launching on 1 April 1939 of the 42,000 ton battleship Tirpitz (photograph), sister-ship to the Bismarck, marked an important stage in the recovery of the German Navy. It had been entirely freed from the constraints of the Treaty of Versailles since the Anglo-German Agreement of June 1935, which authorized Germany to possess a navy equal to 35% of the tonnage of the Royal Navy. In accordance with Plan Z, devised by Grand Admiral Raeder, the German Navy had at its disposal a sizable fleet of major surface vessels and submarines with which to attack Britain's lines of communication. However, in 1939 this plan had scarcely yet been realized.

Below
Throughout the war German naval losses were proportionately very heavy. The submarine service alone lost nearly 30,000 men out of a total of 40,000. Unlike the British who, following Drake's example, buried their dead at sea, the Germans, in accordance with what was in fact a fairly recent tradition, endeavoured to bring their dead back home and bury them in military cemeteries. Here, in 1943, at a French port, the burial is taking place of sailors from a destroyer who have been killed in battle.

In the days following the declaration of war the development of Plan Z was virtually brought to a halt and the Reich confined its efforts to completing those vessels already under construction. Its main efforts were concentrated on submarines, whose rate of production eventually reached 25 a month. The sea training of new submarine crews took place in the Baltic, backed up with some sound theoretical instruction on land. In this photograph, at a U-boat Training School, future submariners are taking part in a diving demonstration, using a glass scale model in a water tank.

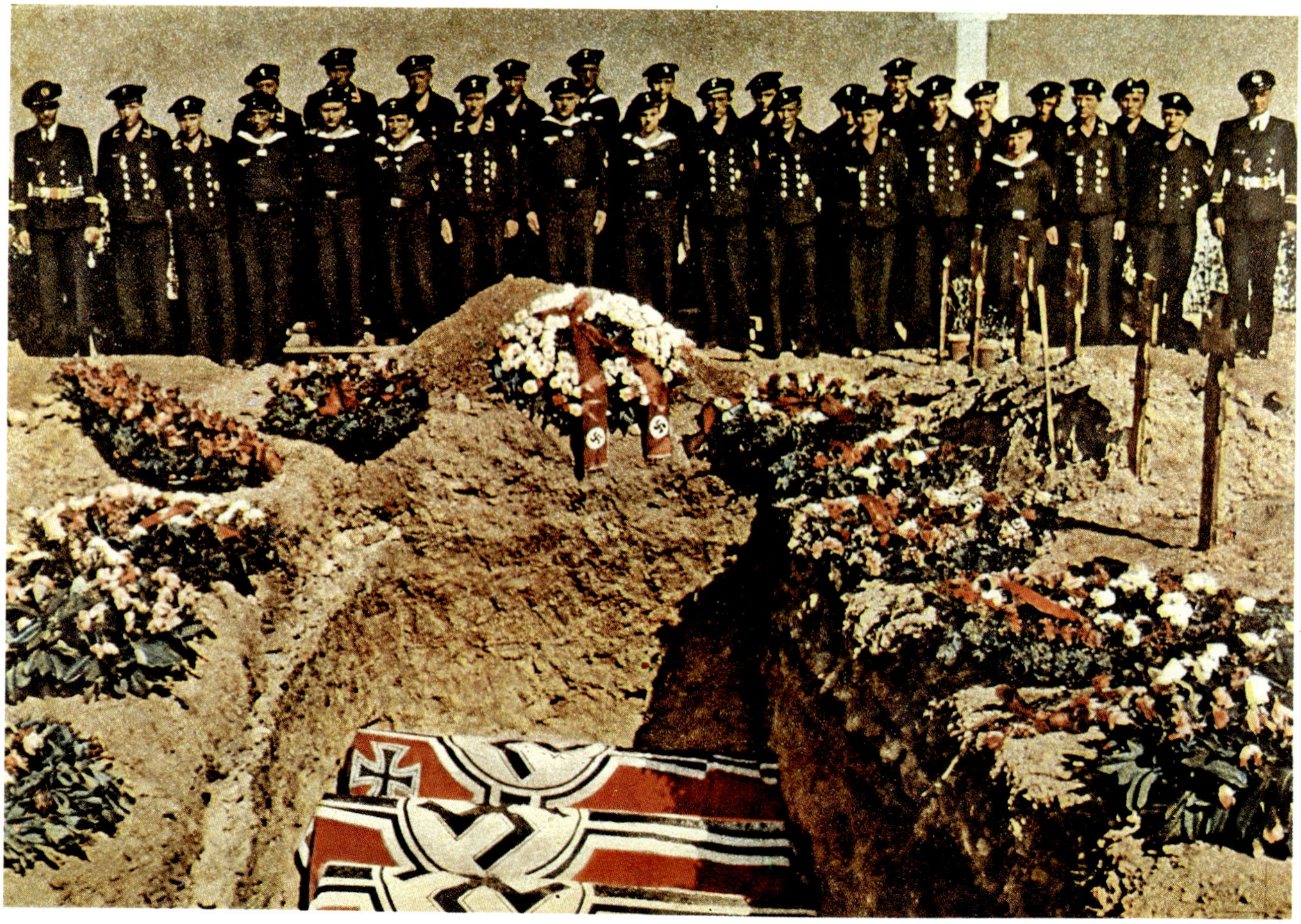

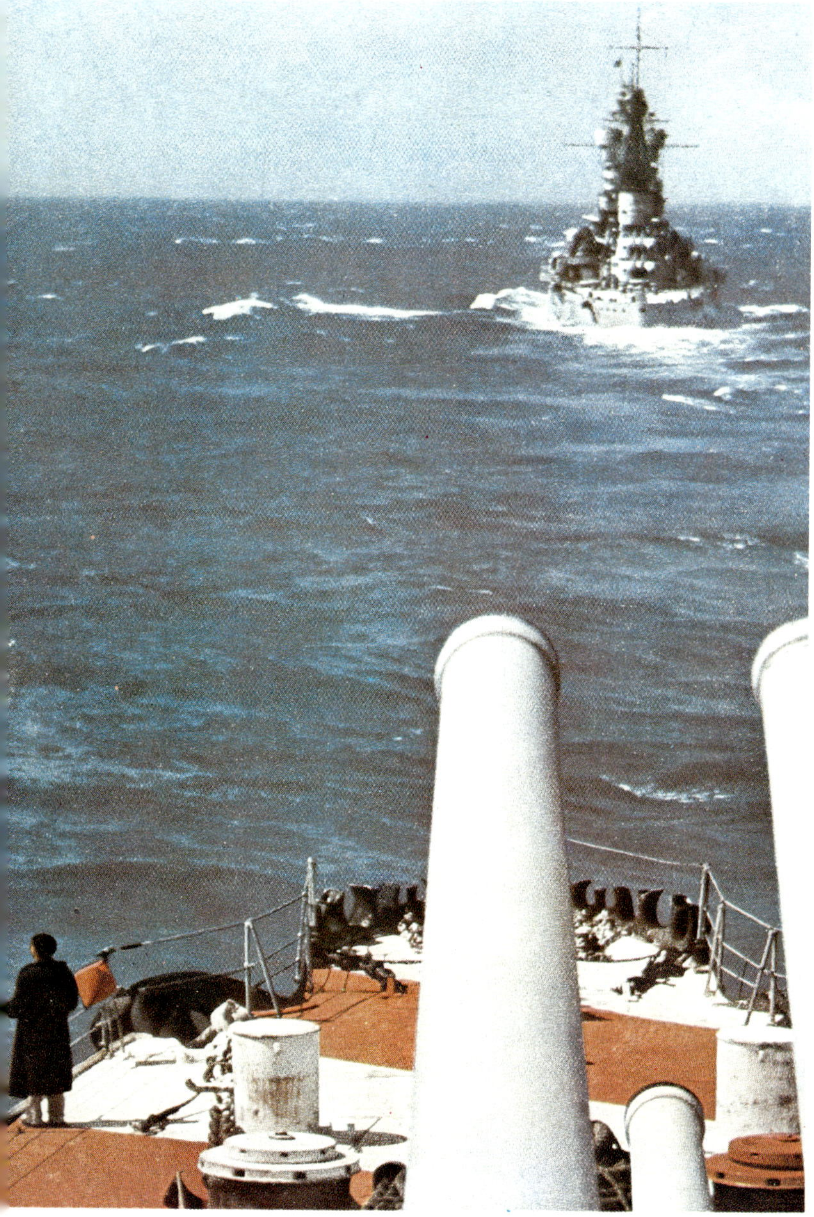

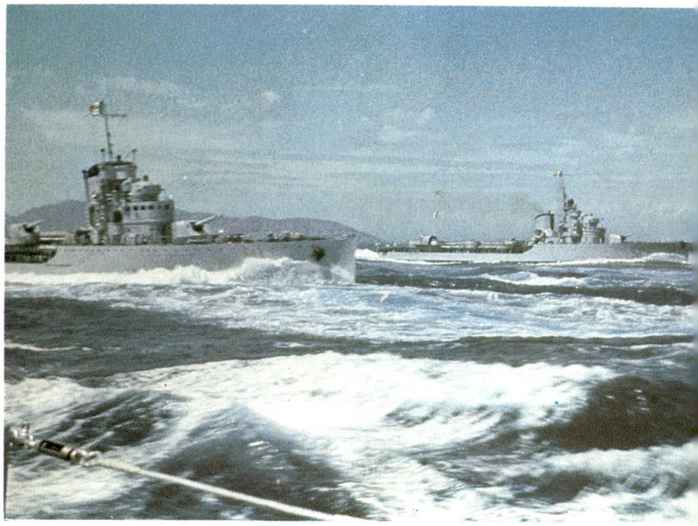

The Italian Navy. In 1939 Italy possessed a navy whose tonnage was scarcely less than that of France. It consisted of battleships, cruisers and fast destroyers, all well armed but relatively lightly protected, and intended for raids against British and French lines of communication in the Mediterranean. In the picture are light Italian warships carrying out displays in the Bay of Naples on the occasion of a big naval review organized by Victor Emmanuel III and Mussolini during Hitler's visit to Italy in May 1938.

Left
An Italian heavy cruiser during an attack on a Malta convoy in the summer of 1942. Although it possessed numerous modern vessels, from 1941 to 1943 the Italian navy experienced a series of reverses in the Mediterranean, at Taranto, at Matapan and when either defending or attacking convoys. The explanation for this failure lies in shortcomings in radar or sonar, in the absence of liaison with the air force and, above all, in the weakness of the high command, which constantly displayed excessive caution and a total lack of offensive spirit.

The Japanese Navy. In 1941 the Japanese navy constituted a remarkable fighting weapon. It had managed to turn to good account the war in China and to learn the lessons provided by the early stages of the Second World War, which had demonstrated that the aircraft had an essential role to play in the war at sea. The Japanese high command had, however, underestimated the enormous capacity for development of the US navy. From 1943 onwards the Japanese fleet found itself more and more outclassed in numbers and in quality of material and suffered a series of disasters which led to its almost complete extinction. In this photograph, taken just after Japan's surrender, three vessels which had escaped destruction can be seen anchored in the naval base of Sasebo: a destroyer and the aircraft carriers *Kasagi* and *Ibuki*.

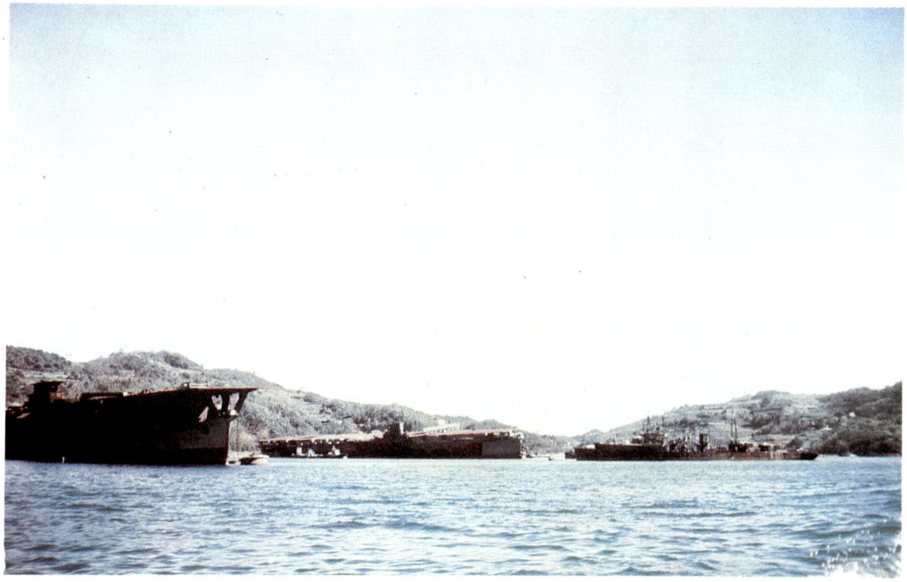

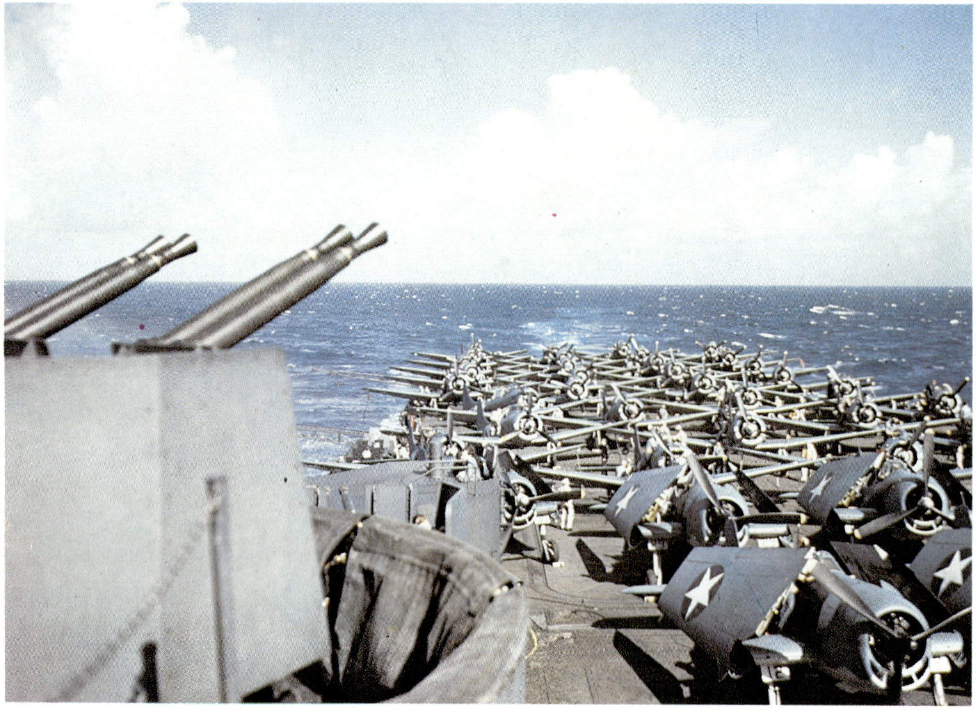

The US Navy. The US navy underwent great development during the Second World War. From 1941 to 1945 its total tonnage increased from 1,400,000 to 4,500,000 tons, not counting 2,000,000 tons-worth of landing vessels. The development was accompanied by a far-reaching transformation. The battleship, which had been the spearhead of the navy at the beginning of the conflict, yielded pride of place to the aircraft carrier. In 1945 the US Pacific Fleet comprised 26 combat aircraft carriers, 64 escort aircraft carriers and only 23 battleships. Here we see the rear of the flight deck of the aircraft carrier *Enterprise*, cluttered with fighter-bombers, some with their wings folded. The only survivor (together with the *Saratoga*) of the American aircraft carriers in service at the time of the attack on Pearl Harbor, it took part in all the major engagements and was nicknamed the 'Survivor of the Pacific'.

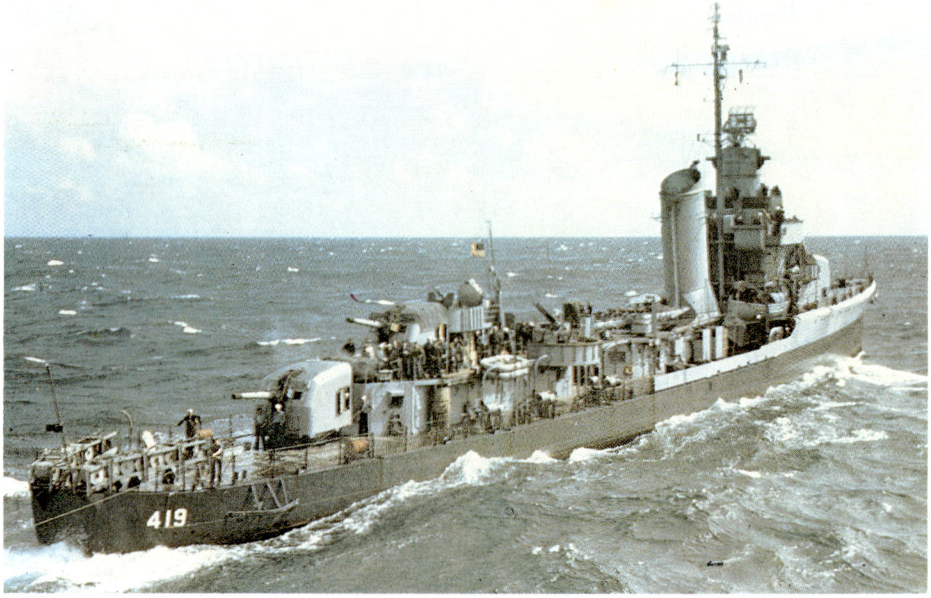

In 1945 the US Navy possessed 323 destroyers. Here one of these vessels, belonging to the *Porter* class, is escorting an Atlantic convoy just before the landing in North Africa in Nov. 1942. Without having the prestige of the aircraft carriers, the destroyers played a major role throughout the conflict, a true jack-of-all-trades of the sea. They protected convoys or big ships against aircraft and submarines. They also served as radar pickets for forward aerial detection, and were even used as troop transports. On the other hand, they had very little opportunity to fulfil their true function, which is the launching of torpedoes.

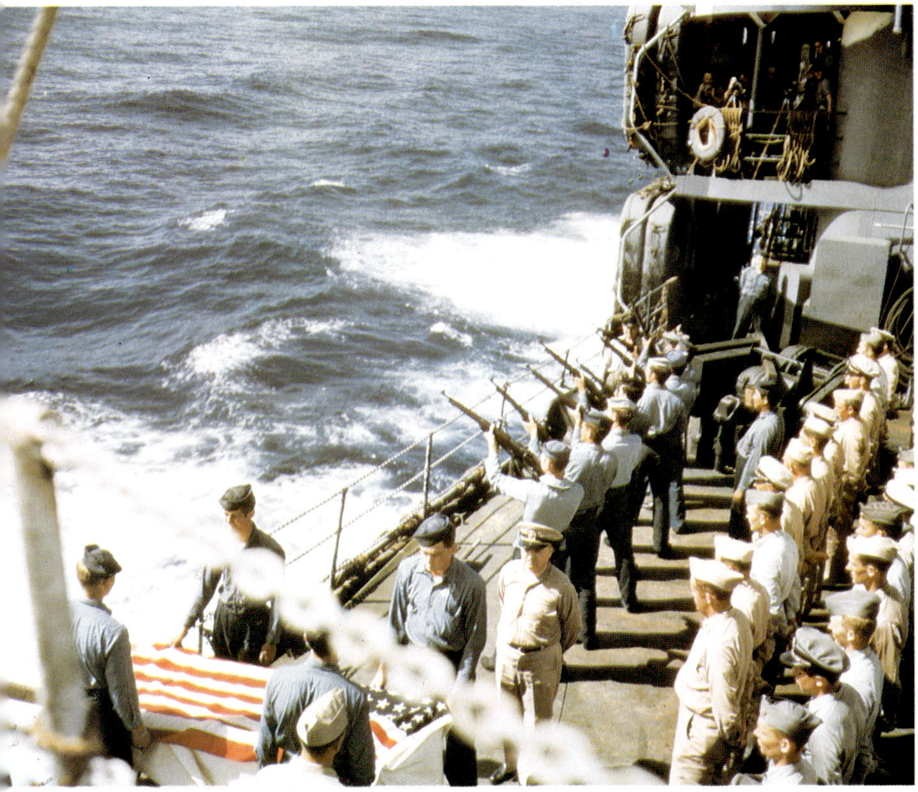

In the British and US navies it is traditional to bury the bodies of dead sailors at sea. In this photograph a squad is preparing to fire a salute at the moment when the body of a sailor covered with the stars and stripes is to be consigned to the waves. The captain of the ship, the chaplain and a section of the crew are taking part in this final ceremony in all its poignant simplicity.

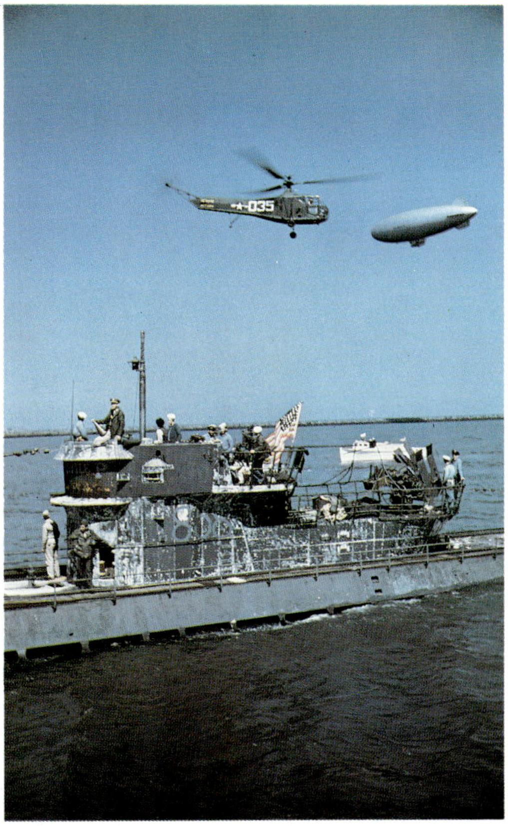

During the Pacific war in particular submarines played a decisive although – quite unjustly – unacknowledged role. After Pearl Harbor they constituted the only American offensive force and Admiral Nimitz, a former submariner, knew well how to use them. From 1942 to 1945 American submarines were responsible for sending a third of Japan's warships to the bottom of the ocean and they also sank two-thirds of its merchant marine. By 1944, as a result of this remarkably successful action, Japan was almost in a stranglehold and could no longer communicate with its occupied territories in southeast Asia. This submarine (photograph) is escorted by an R-4 Sikorsky helicopter and a reconnaissance airship of the US navy.

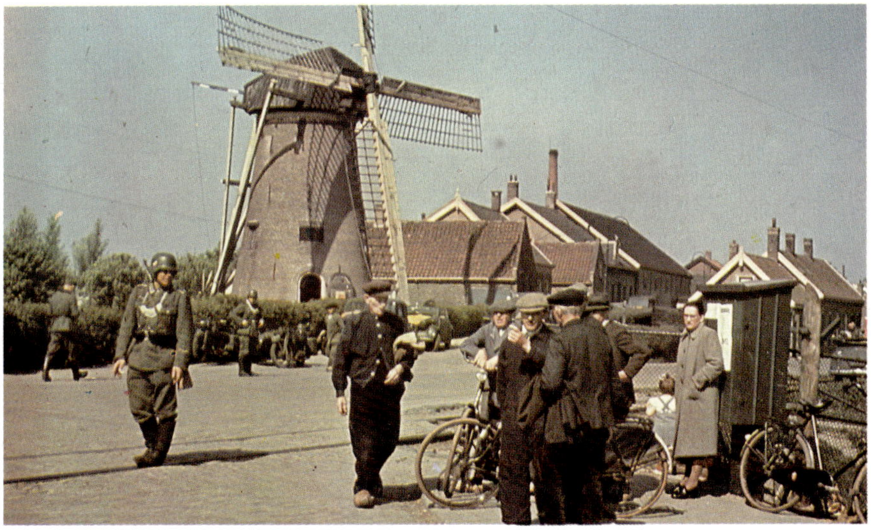

The Netherlands. Because of their own lack of preparation and the extent of the resources available to the Germans, notably airborne troops, the Dutch forces were compelled to surrender on 14 May 1940. Here we see soldiers of a Wehrmacht reconnaissance unit in a typical Dutch village. After the initial shock had worn off, public opinion was for the most part unmoved by the overtures of Reich Commissar Seyss-Inquart who, with the support of Mussert's Dutch National Socialist Party, hoped to integrate the Netherlands within a Greater Germany. Throughout the whole of the occupation, which became progressively harsher and did not end until May 1945, the Dutch people showed by their attitude their refusal to engage in any kind of collaboration.

The liberated Netherlands. American soldier and children.

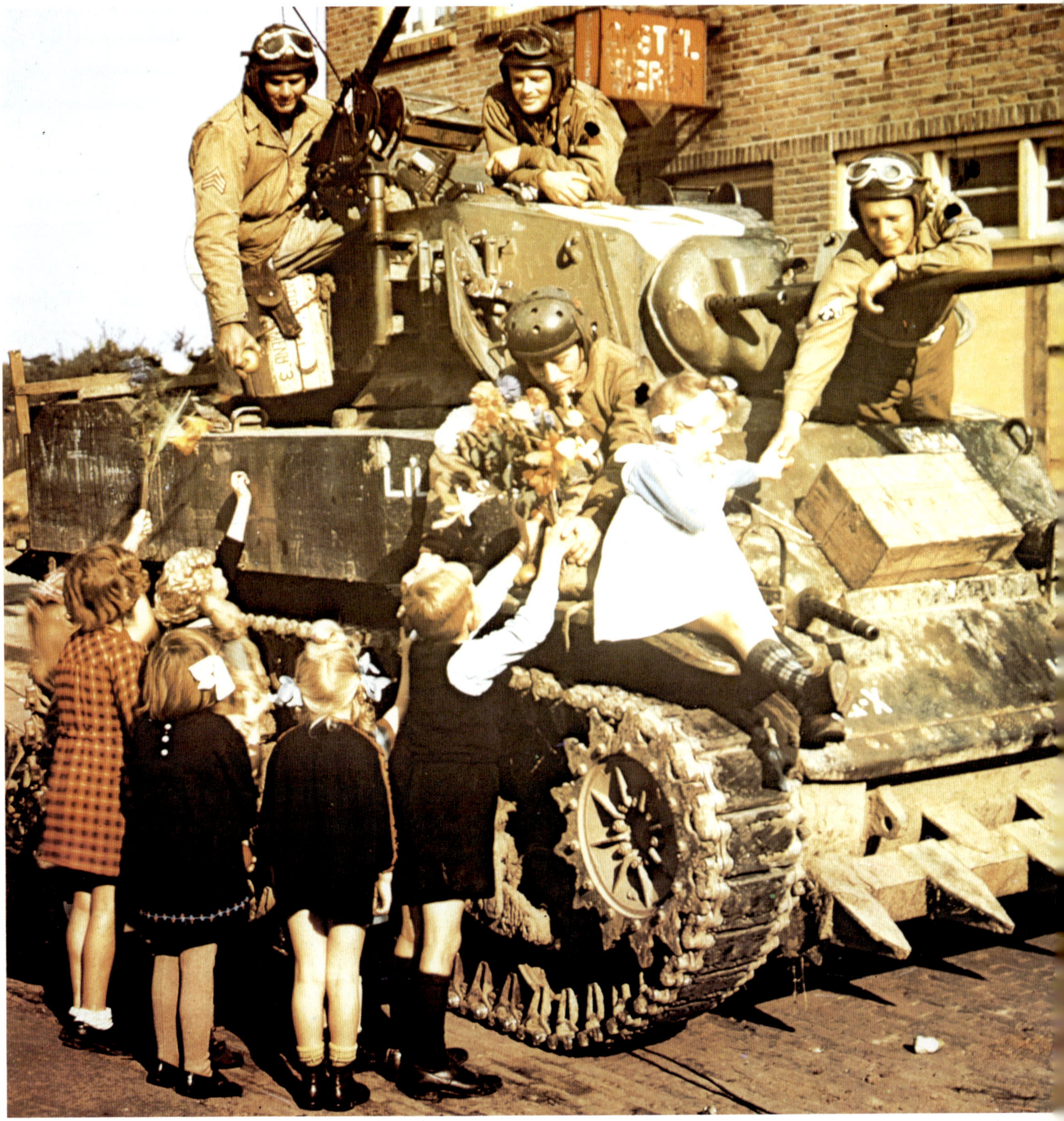

The German surrender in May 1945 saw the liberation of the last areas in Europe which were still occupied – Norway, Denmark and the Netherlands. Here a group of children are enthusiastically greeting the crew of an American light reconnaissance tank. The last months of the war had been particularly grim in Holland, marked by the harshness of winter, severe restrictions and food shortages and the brutality of the occupation.

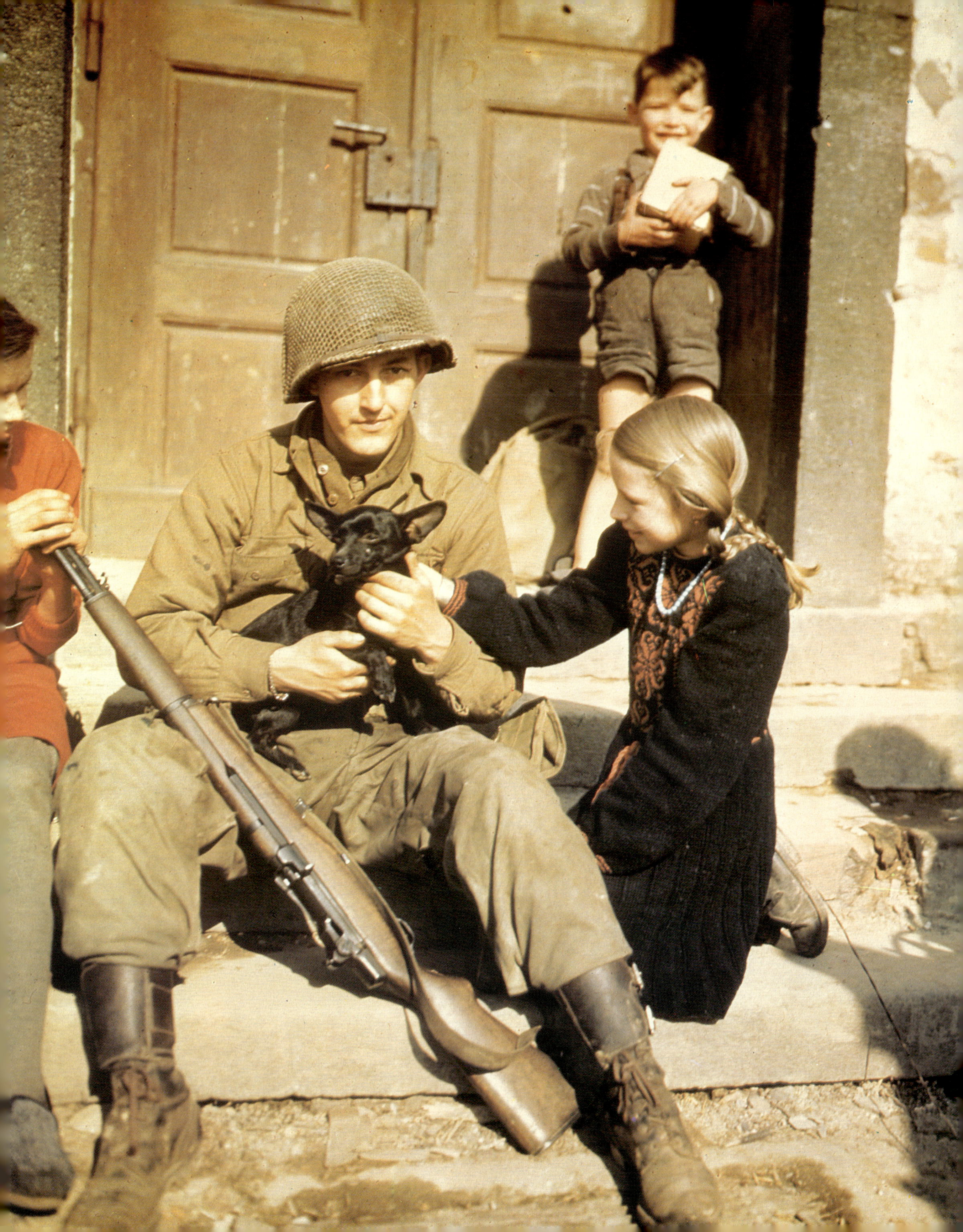

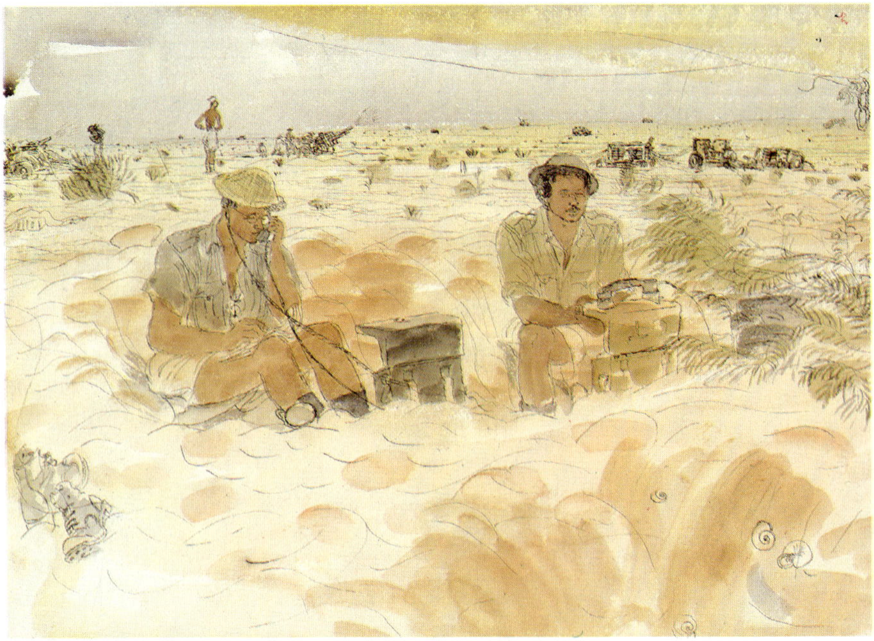

New Zealand. At the outbreak of the Second World War, New Zealand's strong links with Britain were emphasized by the way in which it threw its whole weight into the war effort. Troops were sent to Egypt to train for the European conflict and were involved in the advance on North Africa and the Balkans, and saw action in Greece, Crete and Italy. After the outbreak of the Pacific War, New Zealand was directly threatened by Japan; because it did not withdraw its troops from the European theatre, it came to rely solely on the US forces for its own defence. This painting by A. Gross shows a New Zealand battery in action in Egypt in 1942.

Nimitz. Unaffected, reserved, and lacking the histrionics of a MacArthur, Admiral Nimitz can rightly be regarded as the victor of the war in the Far East. Appointed to the command of the Pacific Fleet after Pearl Harbor, he was to show remarkable strategic and tactical skills at the battles of Midway and Guadalcanal, but above all at the time of the masterly counter-offensive in the central Pacific which, at the beginning of 1945, brought the American forces close to the Japanese archipelago. Here we see him (centre) in company with the US secretary of the navy, James Forrestal, on his right.

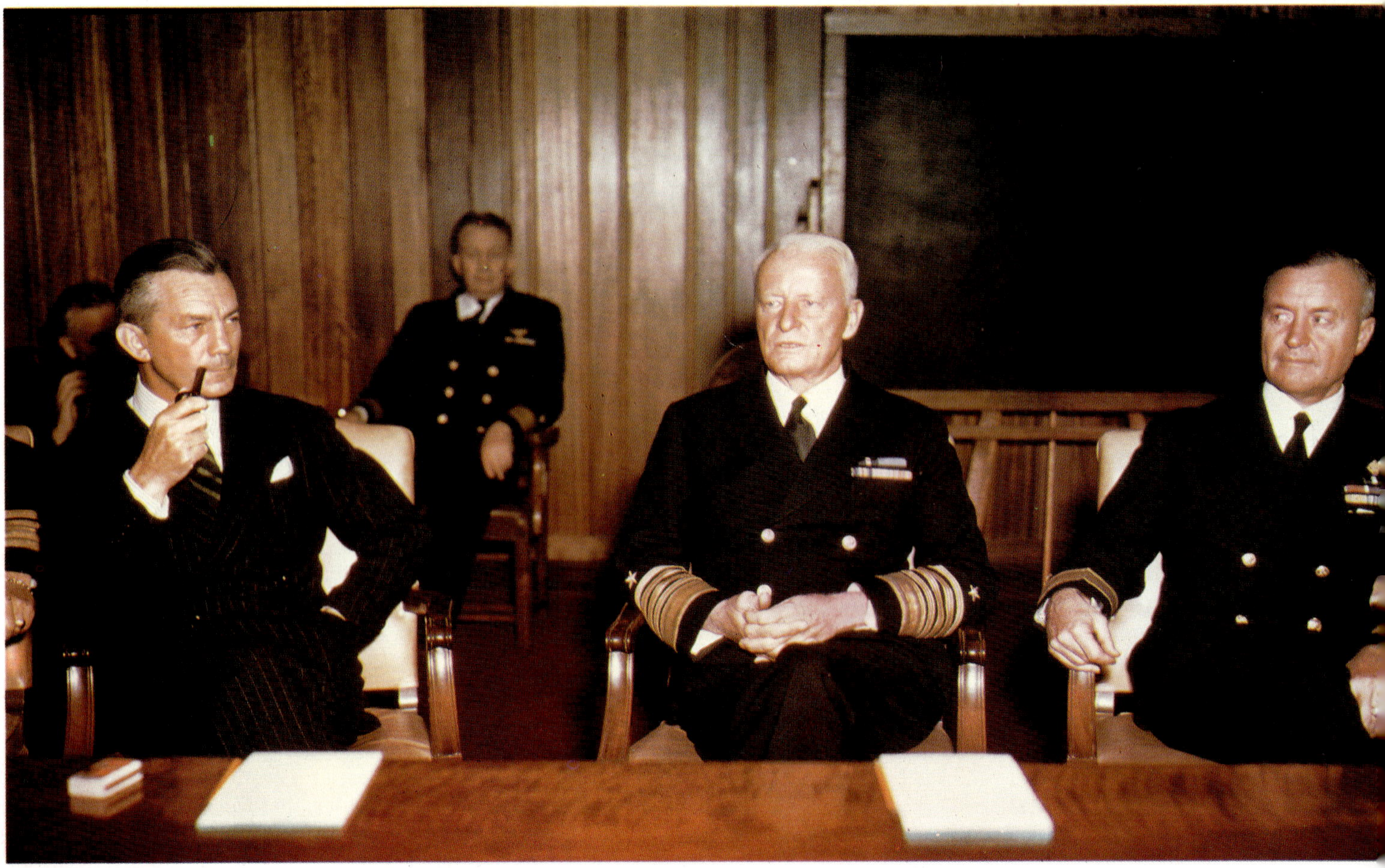

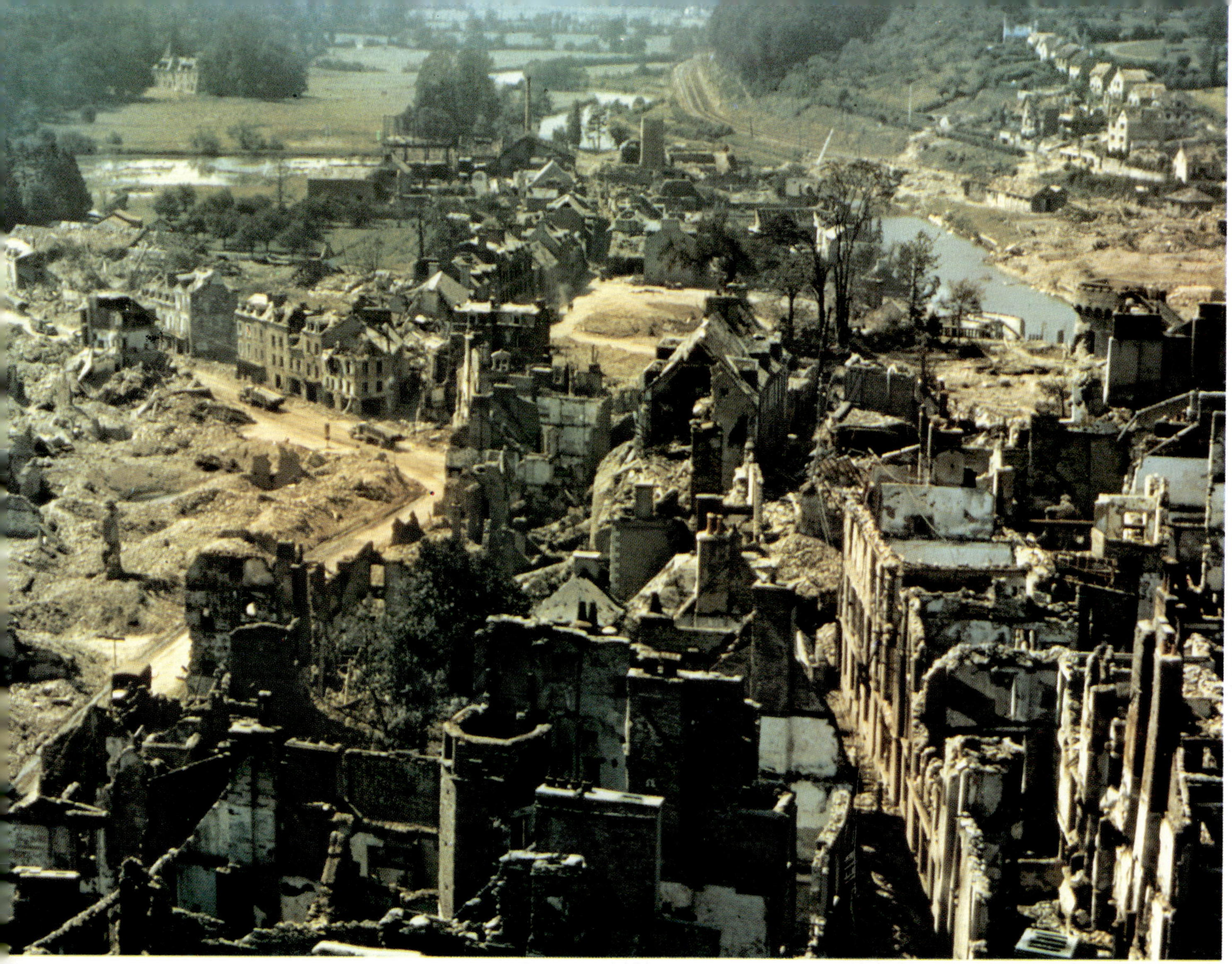

The Battle for Normandy. In spite of the success of the initial landing on 6 June 1944, Normandy was to be the scene of bitter fighting for more than two months. Using all the advantages of a terrain criss-crossed with hedges and trees, the Germans succeeded in holding up the Allied advance in the Caen sector and in the Cotentin peninsula. This fighting had disastrous results for the towns and villages of the area which suffered intensely from bombardments by artillery and aircraft.

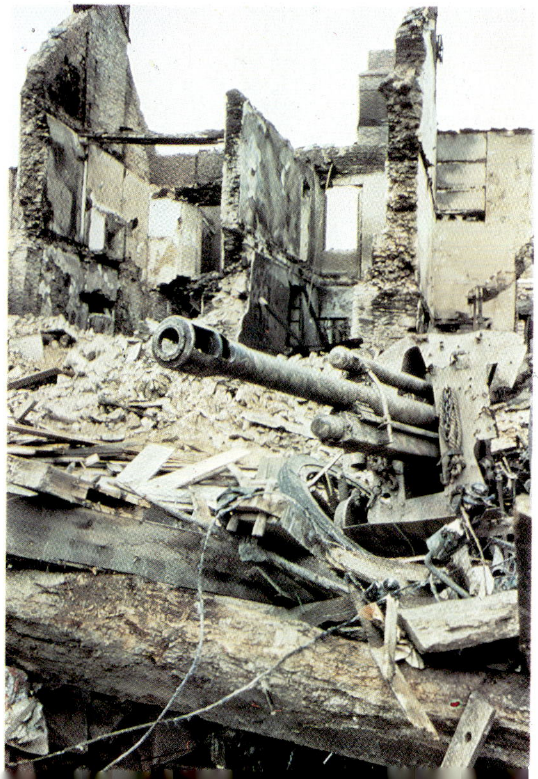

The most critical phase of the battle for Normandy came in the middle of July 1944 with the setback to the British offensive in the Caen sector and the slow and costly advance of the Americans in the centre of the front. The liberation of the ruins of Saint-Lô (photograph), therefore, did not take place until 18 July, and only after considerable losses. The Allies did not succeed in extricating themselves until the end of July, with the breakthrough at Avranches, which Patton exploited so successfully.

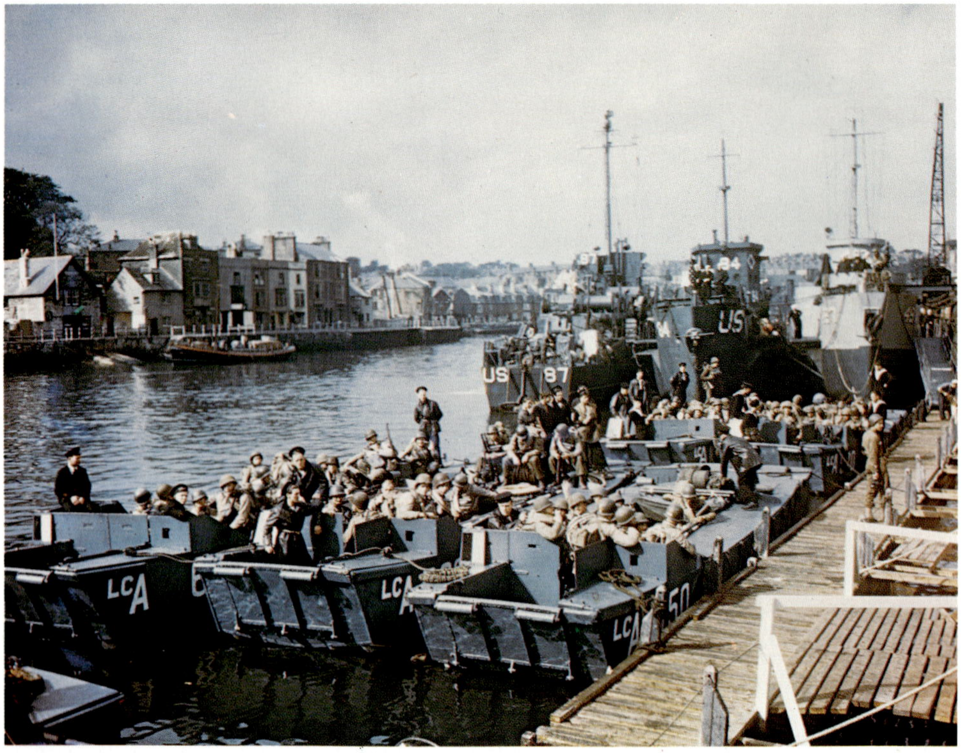

Opposite
The Normandy Landings. Anti-aircraft bal loons in storage in Britain and intended tc protect the Allied fleet on D-Day.

On the eve of Operation Overlord the south of England became a gigantic military depot. Two million men were packed into camps, in the middle of dumps of food and munitions, rows of tanks and vehicles of all descriptions. A huge armada filled the Channel ports and hundreds of landing barges were dispersed around the humblest harbours, as this photograph shows.

The fighting spirit of the Germans, the quality of the defences on the Atlantic Wall, and above all, the weather conditions, were for the Allies the great unknown factors of Overlord. Because of a strong westerly wind it was necessary to put back the launching of the operation, originally scheduled for 5 June, by 24 hours. On the beaches at Omaha, in the Vierville sector (photograph), the Americans encountered keen resistance which could only be broken by naval gunfire and direct attack by aircraft, in spite of low clouds. Here Republic P-47 Thunderbolt fighter bombers are supporting the advance of soldiers under German artillery fire.

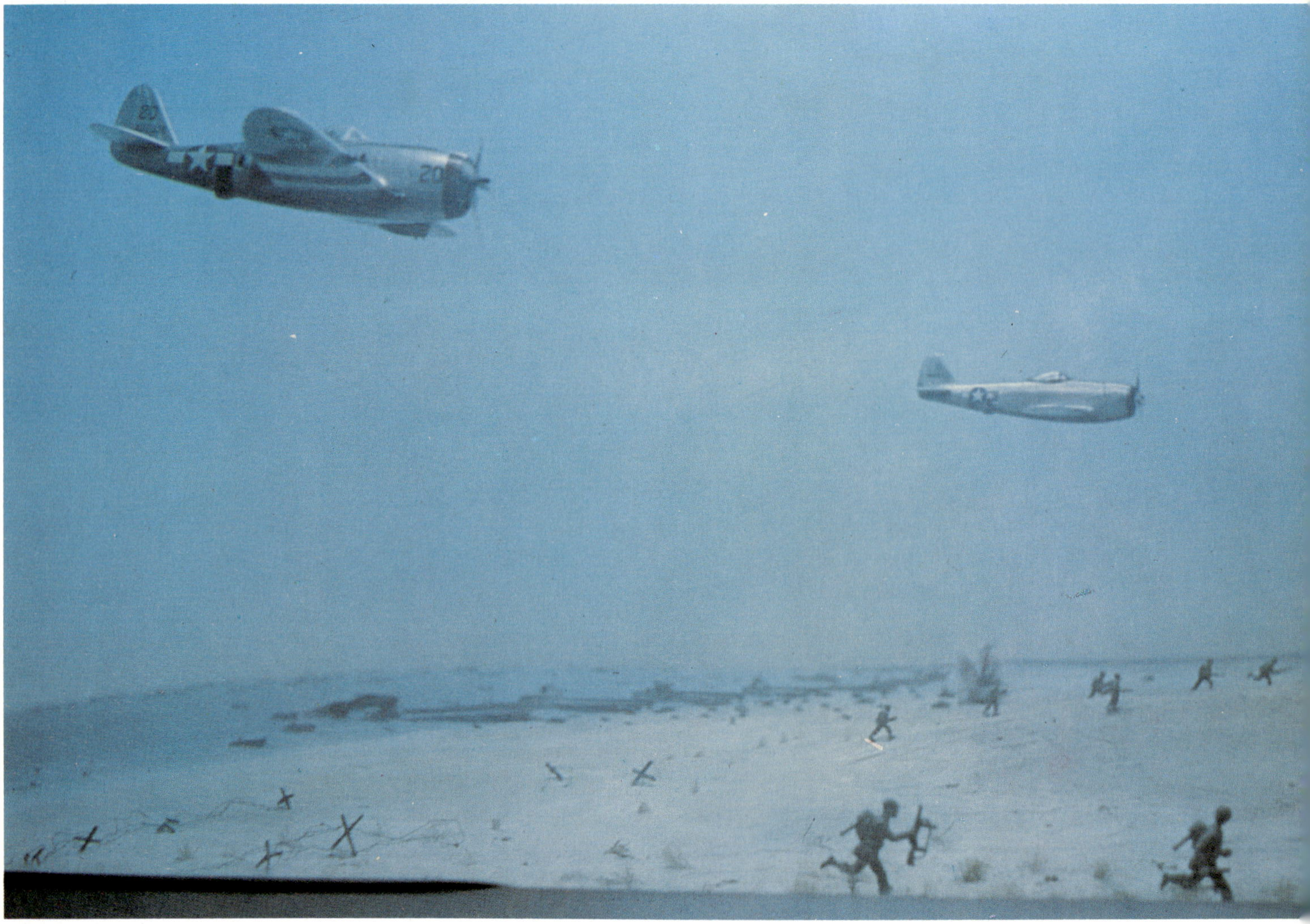

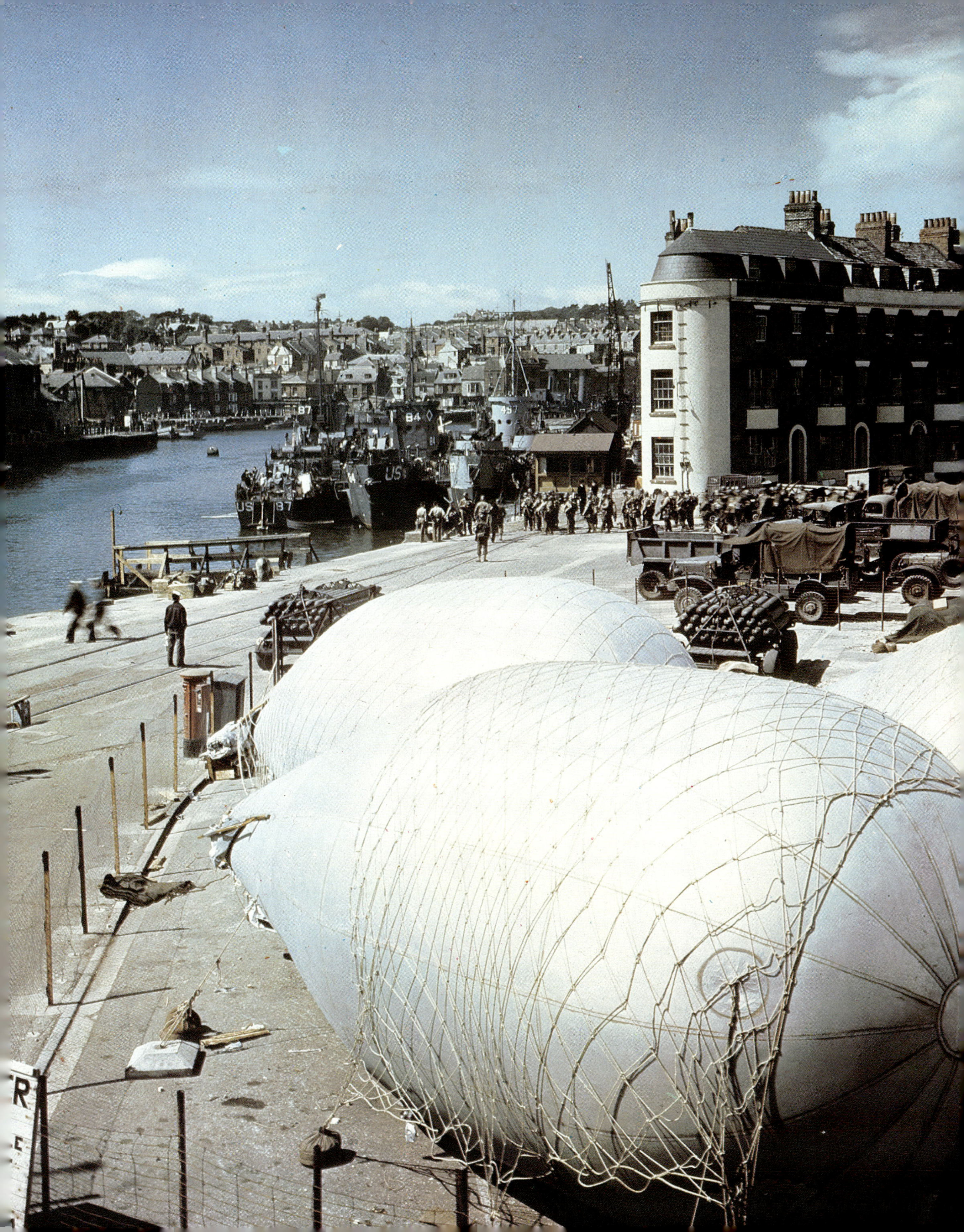

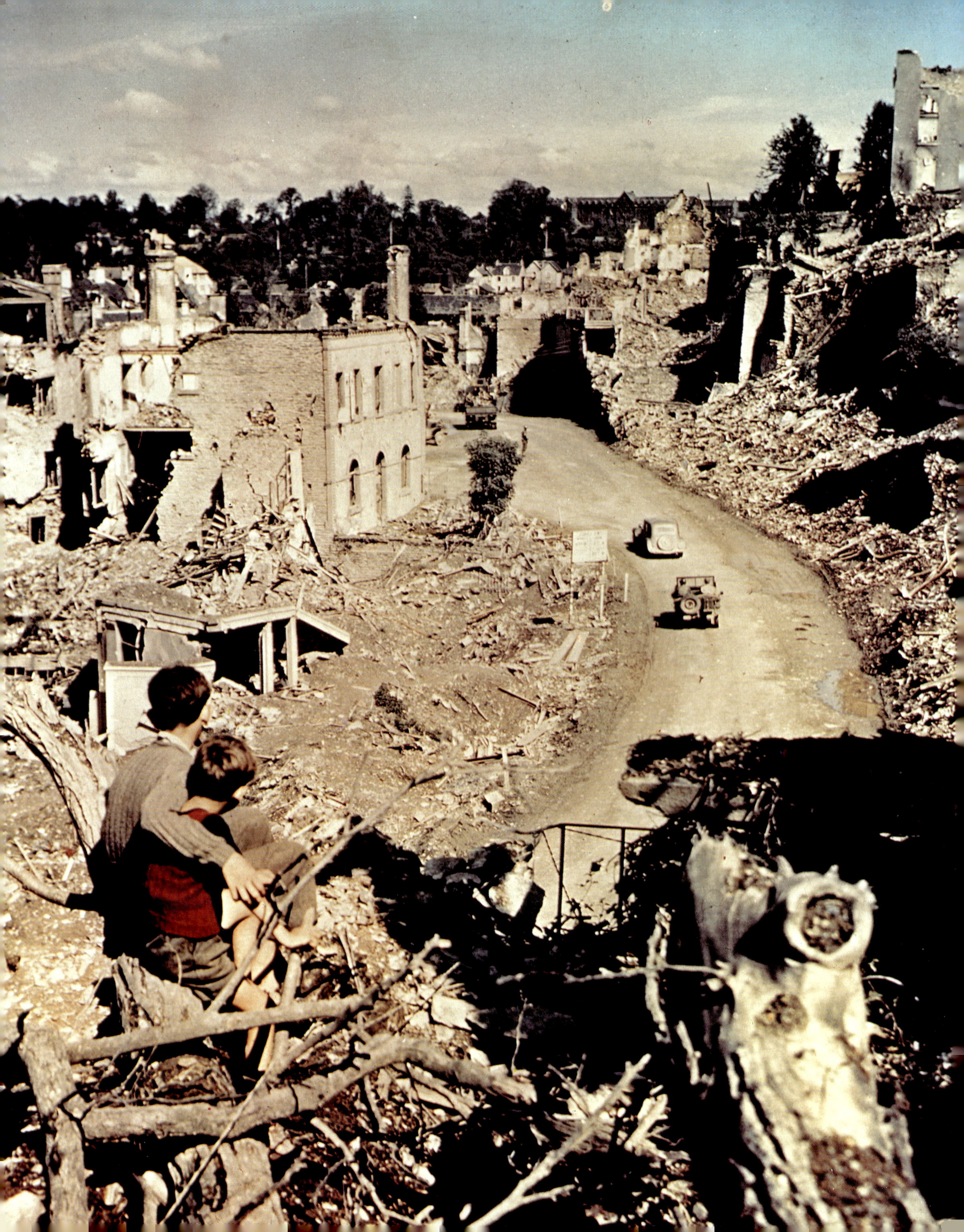

Opposite
The Battle for Normandy. US army vehicles driving through the ruins of Saint-Lô.

The North African landings. American troops disembarking in the course of Operation Torch. Launched in Nov. 1942, this operation marked the starting point of the first stage of the Anglo-American offensive which would eventually be aimed at Europe. Involving 100,000 troops and extensive war supplies, in the short term it permitted the occupation of Morocco and Algeria and enabled the French Army of Africa to get back into the war. However, Operation Torch was also to lead to the gruelling Tunisian campaign which did not end until May 1943.

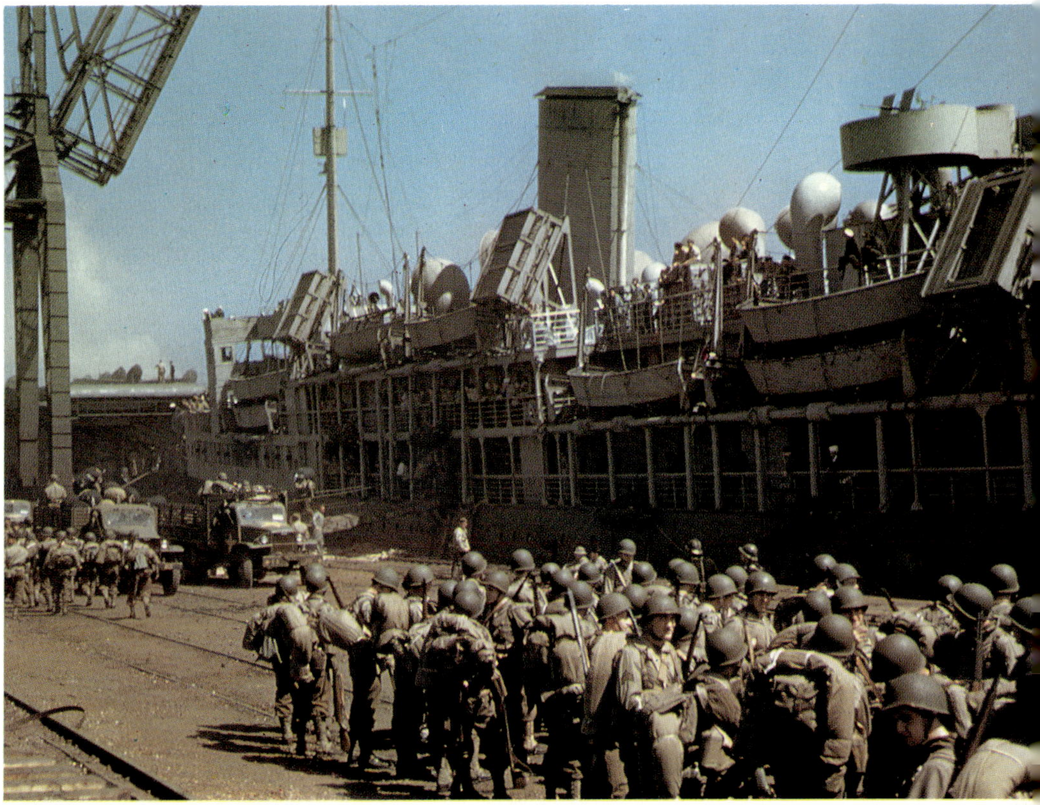

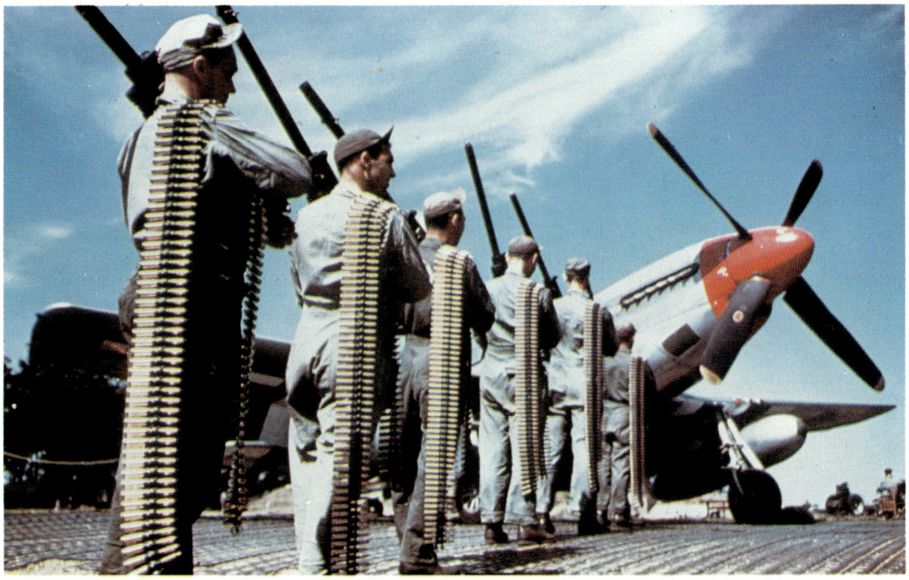

The North American P-51 Mustang. Entering service in 1941, this single-engined American fighter plane did not reach its maximum effectiveness until 1944, when it was equipped with a 1700 horsepower engine. With a speed in excess of 440 mph (700 km/h), it could rival the best fighters in the Luftwaffe. When filled with drop tanks it had the range to accompany strategic bombers from their bases deep into Germany. As this picture indicates the Mustang possessed an armament of six 0.5 in. (12.7 mm) machine guns, which are here being carried by armourers together with their cartridge belts.

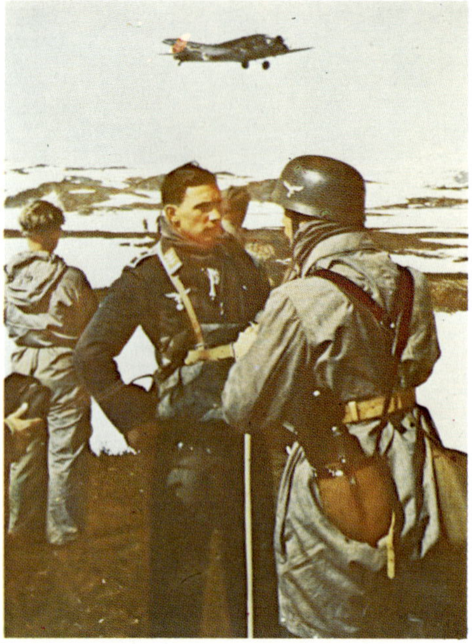

Norway. Launched by Germany on 9 April 1940, the attack on Norway was in fact a preventive operation intended to forestall Allied attempts to cut off Germany's vital supplies of iron-ore from Sweden. Used by the Wehrmacht for the first time, the airborne forces made it possible for the Germans to take Oslo on the very first day. Here a parachutist (seen from behind) is in conversation with a pilot while a Junkers Ju-52 transport aircraft manoeuvres overhead.

The Nuremberg Trial. Following the German surrender, the victors took the unprecedented step of arraigning before an international tribunal on a charge of 'war crimes', the leaders of the Third Reich, seen here in the dock. The trial, which took place at the Nuremberg law courts, lasted 315 days (20 Nov. 1945–1 Oct. 1946) and ended with 12 death sentences, 7 prison sentences and 3 acquittals. Four organizations were condemned: the National Socialist (Nazi) party, the Gestapo, the SS and the SD (Security Service). The verdict enabled the United Nations to define the crime of genocide.

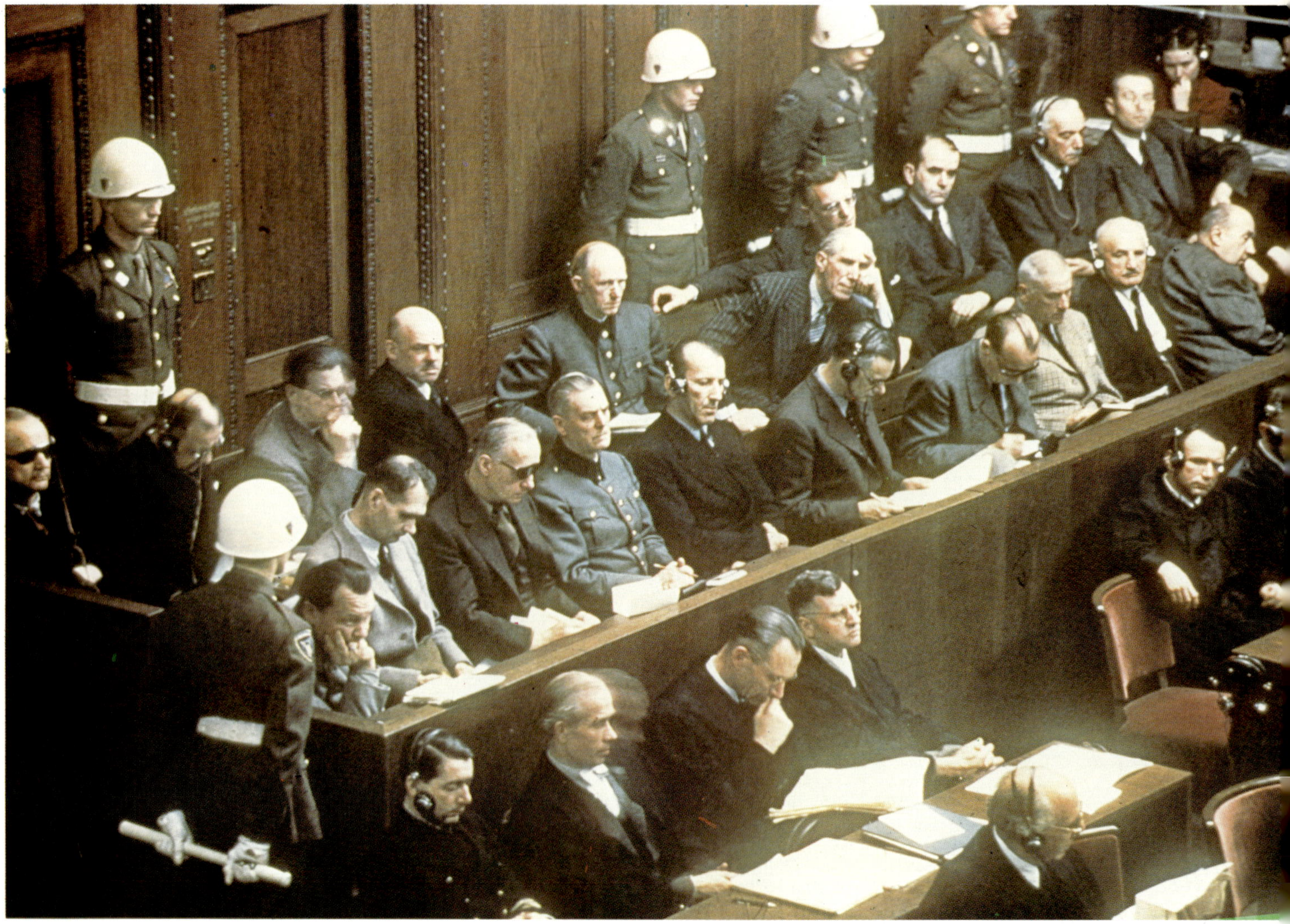

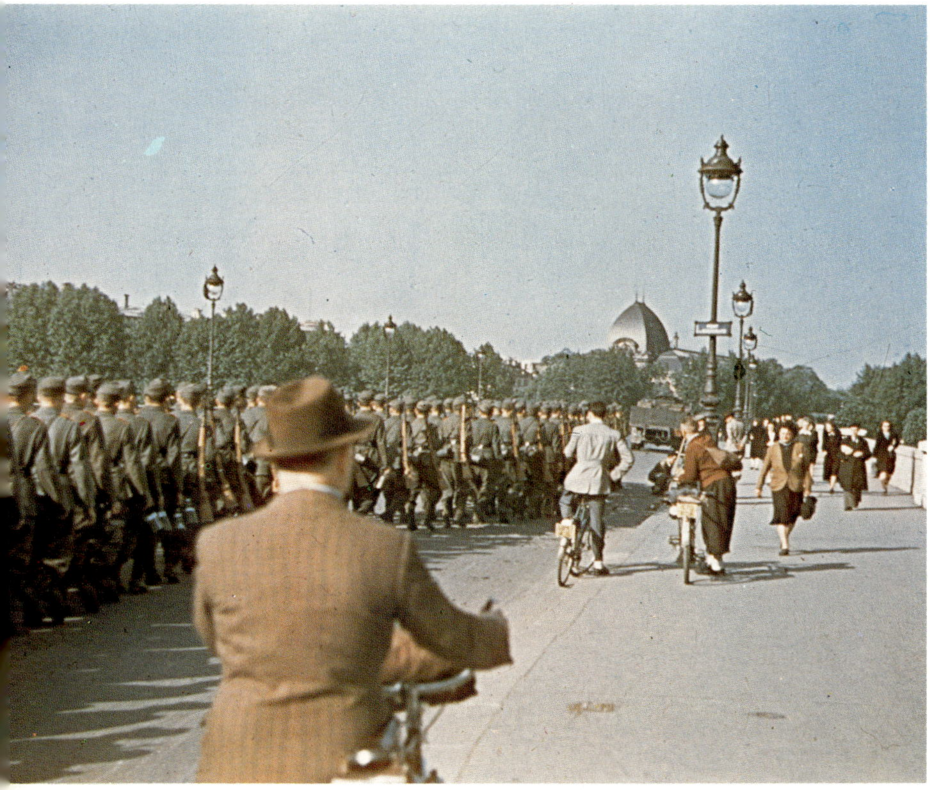

The Occupation. A parade of German soldiers in the streets of the capital was a familiar sight to Parisians for more than four years. Another aspect of daily life was the almost complete disappearance of private cars, replaced by thousands of bicycles, which were compelled to carry a number plate, so that records could be kept. In spite of the humiliation of defeat and various restrictions, Paris still retained much of its old charm, thanks to the variety of its entertainments and the intense activity of its intellectual and artistic life.

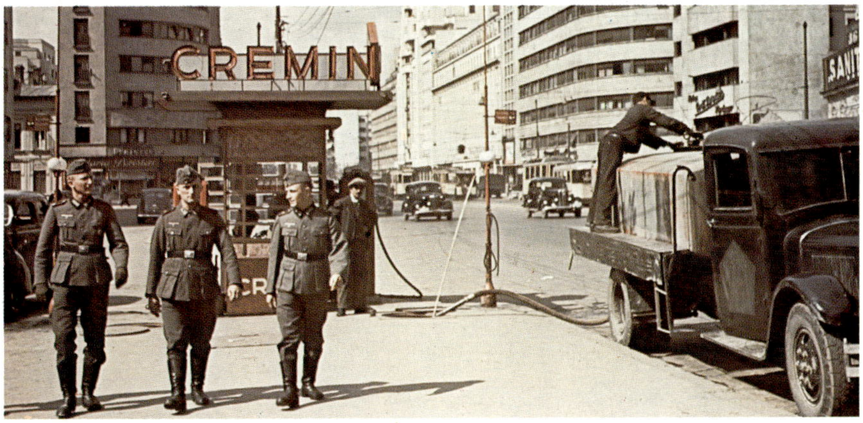

When the Third Reich was at the peak of its power, soldiers of the Wehrmacht were stationed in every country on the European mainland except Portugal, Spain, Switzerland and Sweden. Their presence was the result of resounding defeats, as in the case of France, or because of a policy of gradually turning countries which were supposedly allies, such as Romania, into satellites. Here we see German soldiers strolling along one of the main thoroughfares in the centre of Bucharest.

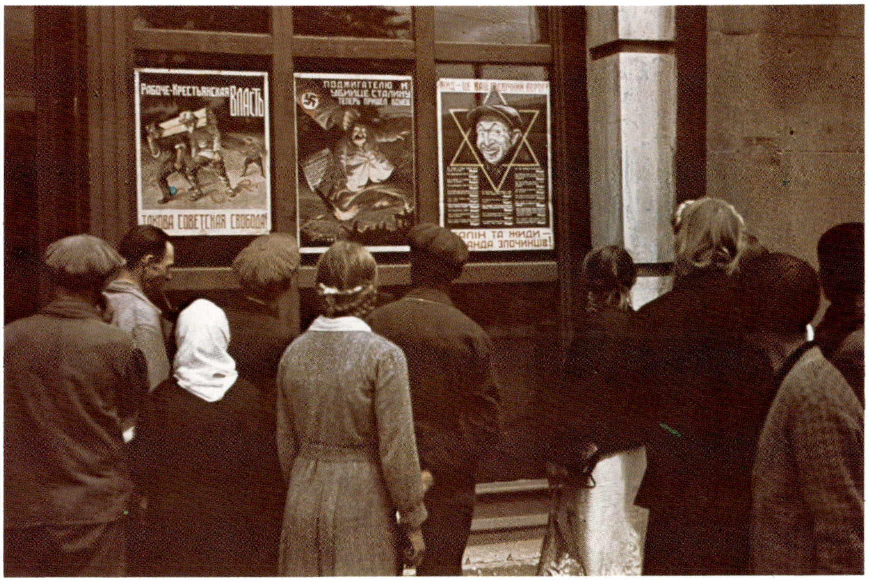

From the end of 1941 almost the whole of the Ukraine was occupied by the forces of the Third Reich. Despite the existence of a strongly separatist feeling, the Germans refused to encourage the idea of independence and systematically exploited the Ukraine. The sole concession was the re-establishment of religious life. As these posters on a wall in Kiev show, German propaganda strove at the same time to exploit the theme of the Judaeo-Bolshevik conspiracy and to remind the population of the excesses of Stalinist tyranny. However, the demands made by the German troops on the civilian population, already regarded as the future subjects of the colonies of the Third Reich, together with the brutal policy of the occupation authorities, which was hostile to any manifestations of nationalism, inevitably made the civilians sympathetic towards the resistance movement.

Nuremberg. The ruins of the town in 1945.

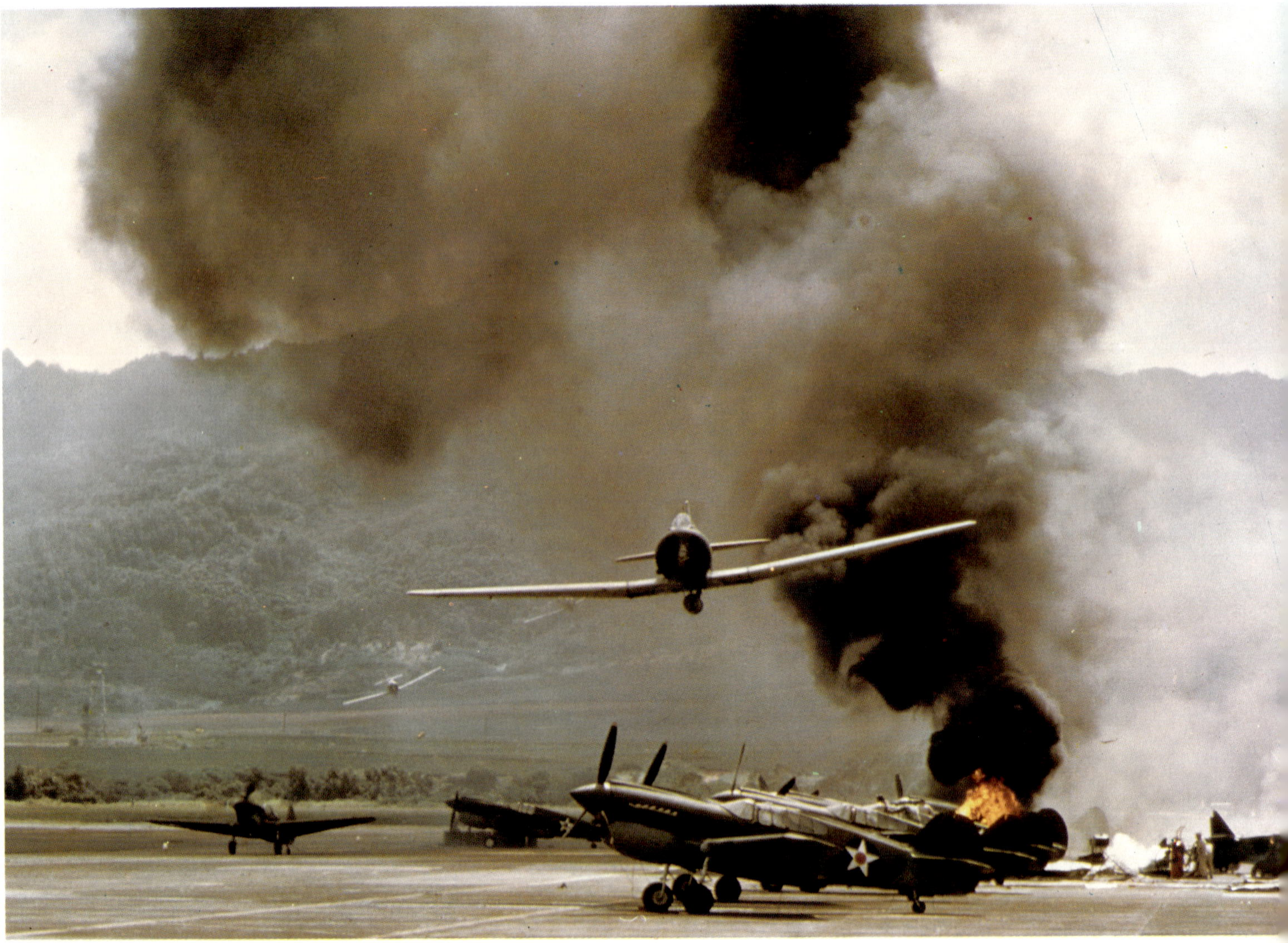

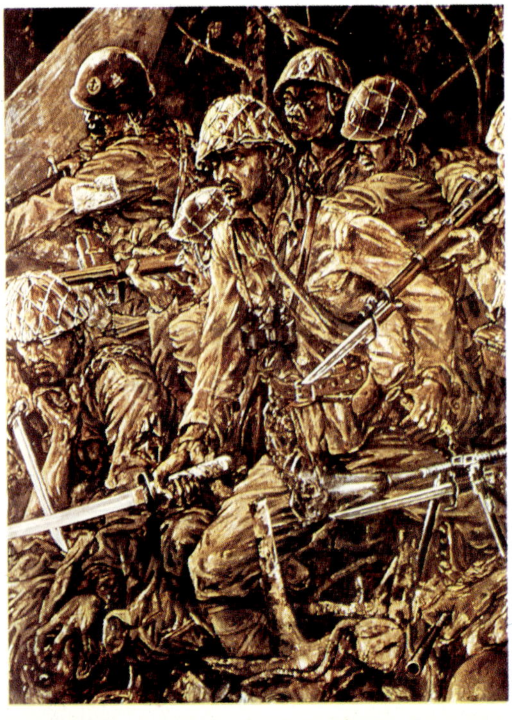

The War in the Pacific. When they attacked Pearl Harbor on 7 Dec. 1941, the Japanese were aiming to put out of action the warships and the aircraft of the great Pacific naval base. In this they were almost completely successful, except as regards the aircraft carriers which, for a variety of reasons, were away at sea. The complete surprise of the operation enabled the Japanese, as this photograph taken from the film *Tora-Tora-Tora* shows, to destroy 160 aircraft on the ground, all the more easily since the planes had been drawn up in the open in order to avoid possible sabotage by members of the Japanese colony in Hawaii.

Following on from Pearl Harbor the Japanese achieved a series of uninterrupted successes as a result of operations against the Philippines, Malaya, Burma and Indonesia. However, the first miscalculation occurred in May 1942. After the battle of the Coral Sea the Japanese high command had to give up the idea of a landing at Port Moresby in New Guinea. Nevertheless, it attempted to get possession of this position by a land attack launched from the north of the island, despite a terrain consisting of high mountains covered with jungle and infested with malaria. This offensive, which was eventually to prove unsuccessful, brought much hardship to the Japanese soldiers, as this detail from a picture by Key Sato attempts to recall.

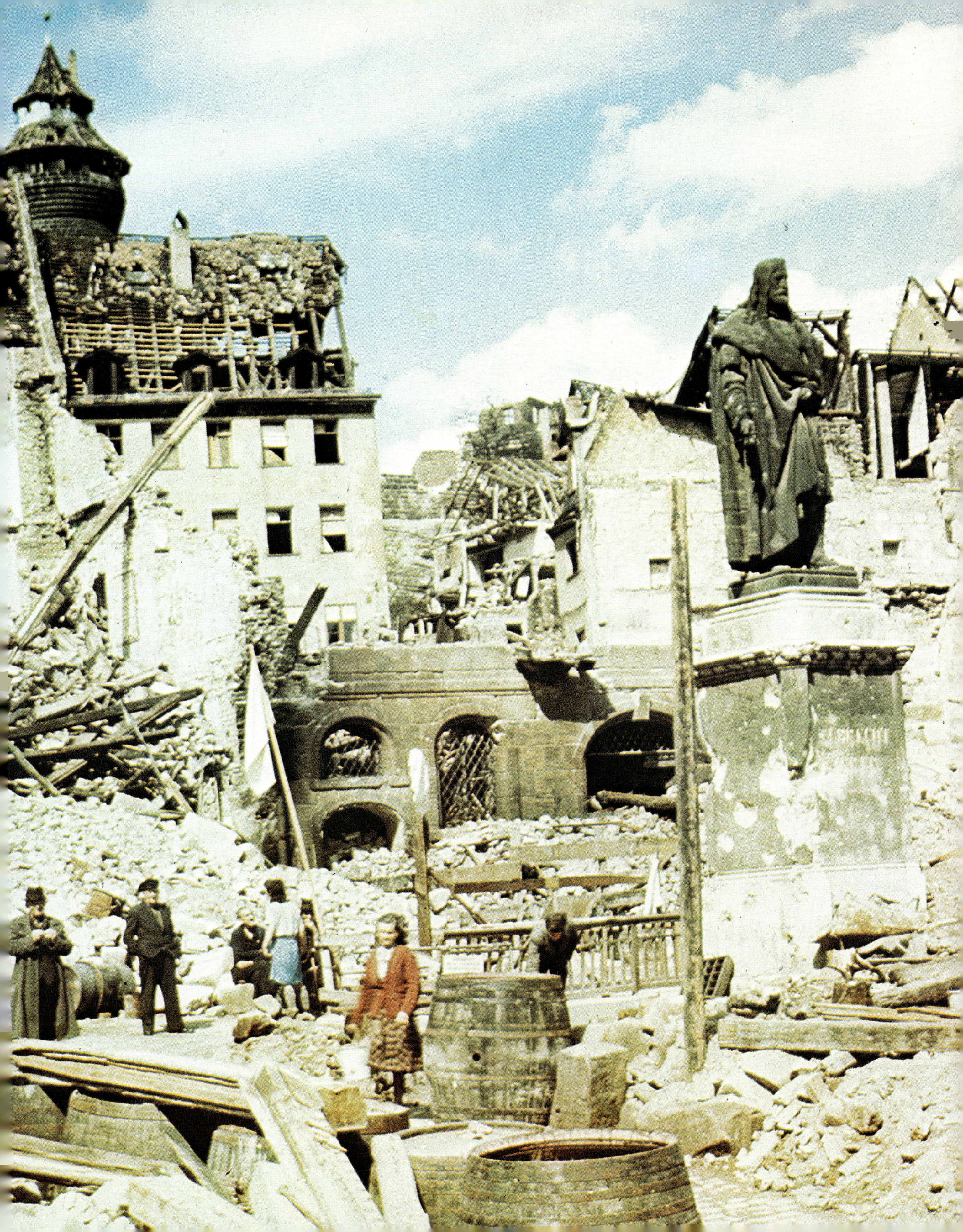

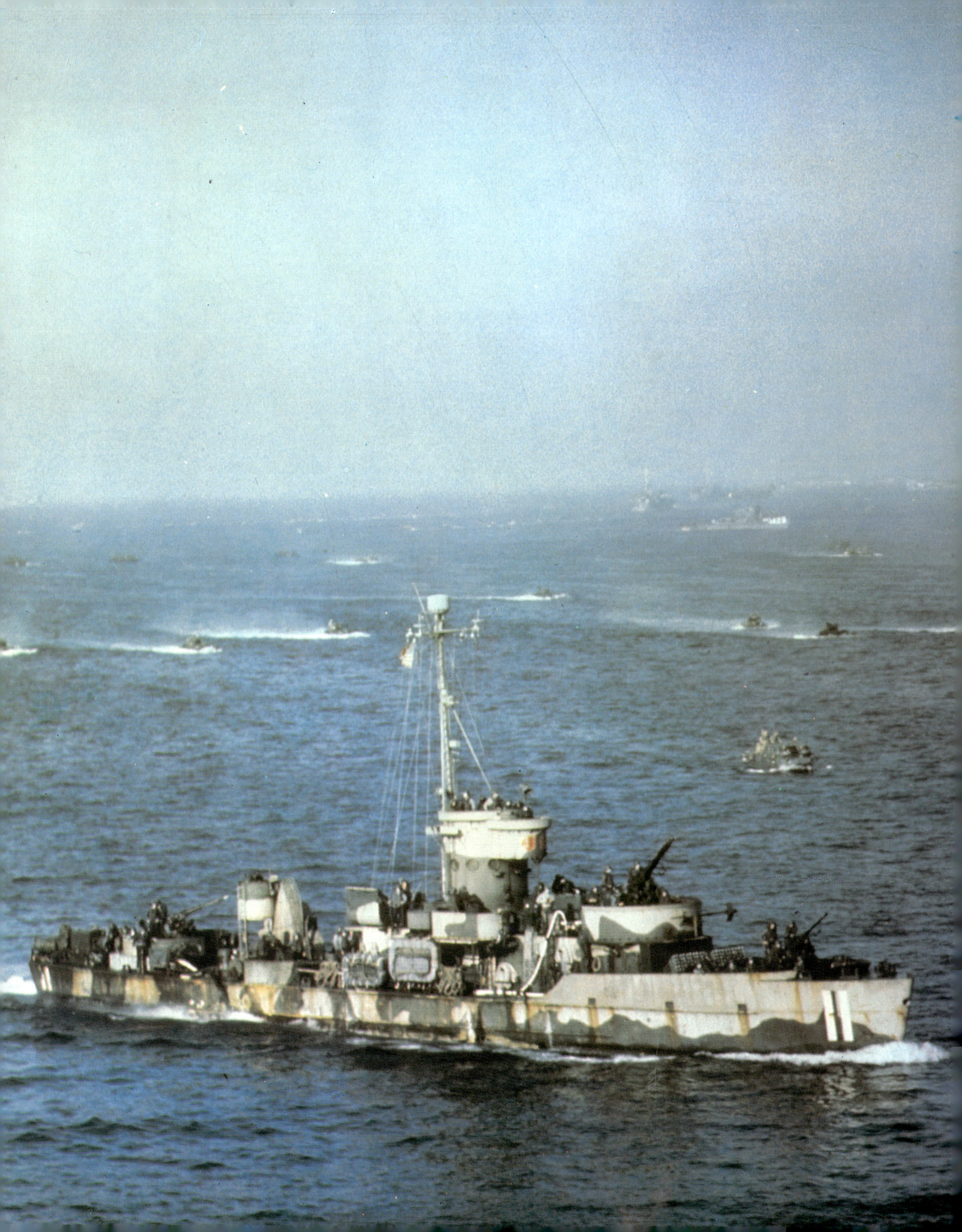

Okinawa. The landing on 1 April 1945.

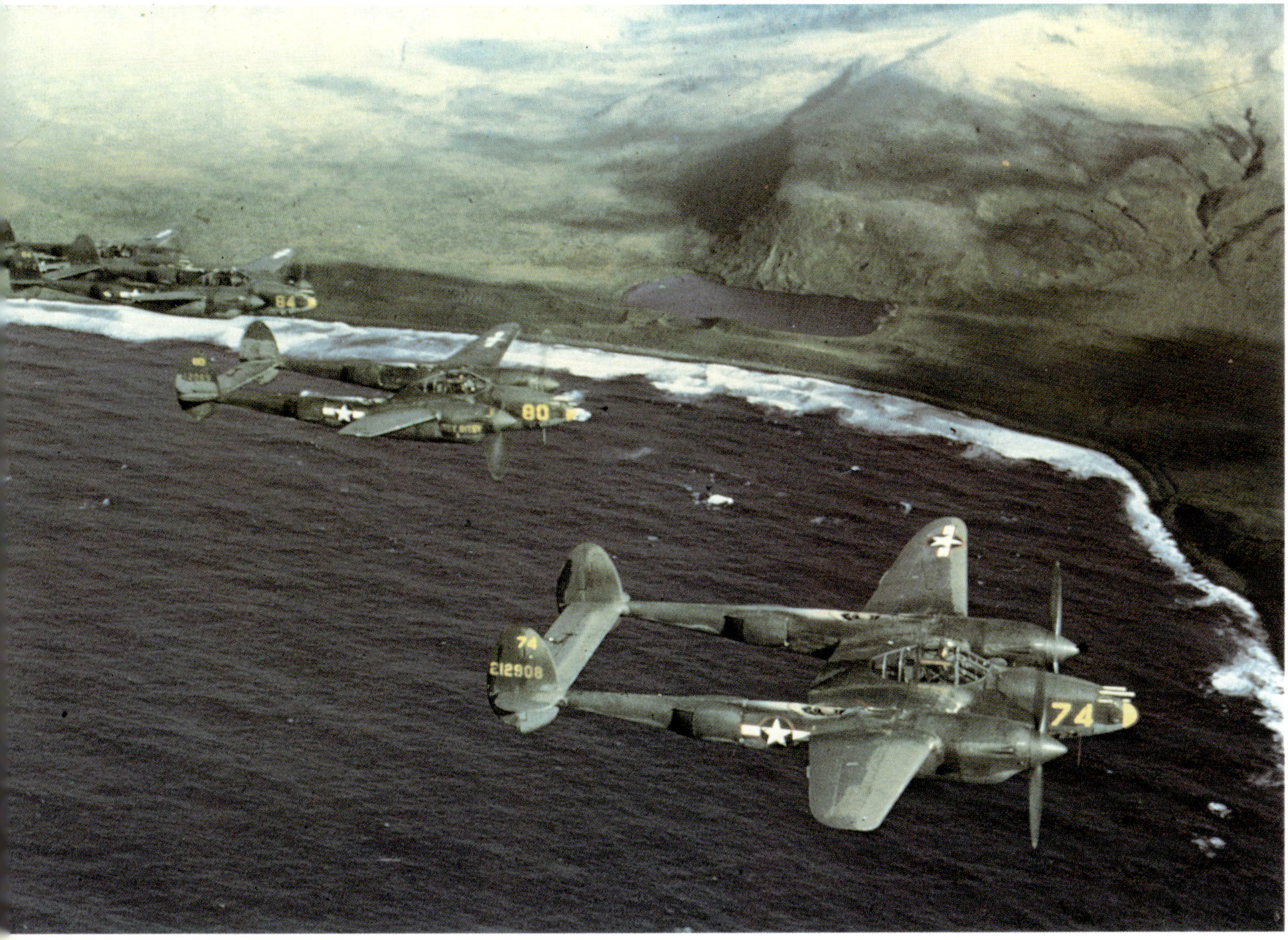

In the spring of 1942 the commander-in-chief of the Japanese navy, Admiral Yamamoto, tried to force a decision by inducing the Americans to give battle off Midway. The affair ended, at the beginning of June, with a severe Japanese defeat. Yamamoto's plan was linked with a diversion in the Aleutians, which ended with the capture of Kiska and Attu, whose strategic value proved to be nil. The Americans were to reoccupy these positions during the summer of 1943. Here a group of Lockheed P-38 Lightning fighters are flying over the southern coast of the Aleutians.

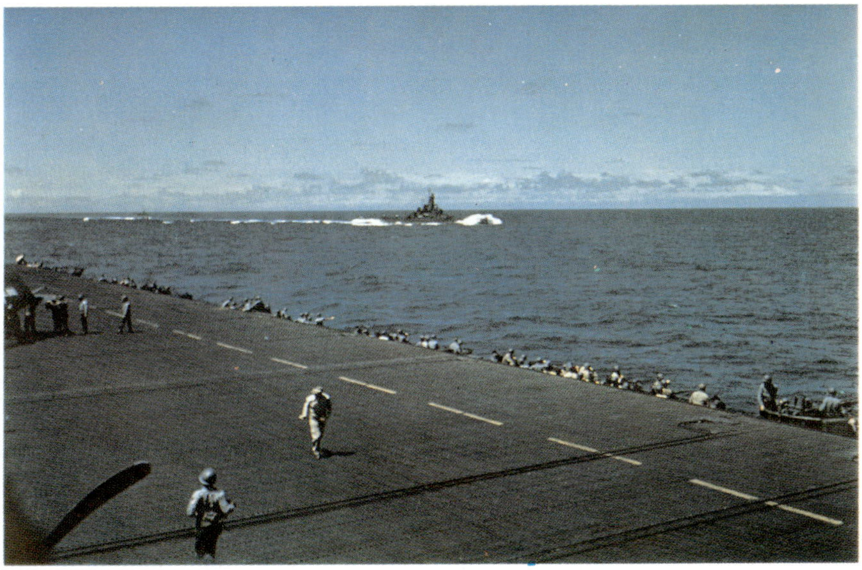

With the entry into service at the end of 1943 of an entirely new fleet from the American shipyards, Admiral Nimitz was in a position to launch a decisive offensive in the central Pacific against the Japanese positions on the Gilbert and Marshall Islands. The preliminary operations were conducted by a task force comprising aircraft carriers and supporting ships. Here, in the background, a heavy cruiser provides protection for the escort carrier *Cowpens* (foreground).

In June 1944, having already captured the Gilbert and Marshall Islands, Nimitz made a second breach in the Japanese defences by taking possession of Guam, Saipan and Tinian in the Marianas. These islands were quickly put into service as bases for the strategic bombers, which at the end of 1944 launched devastating raids on the chief cities of the Japanese mainland. Here a Boeing B-29 Superfortress is taking off from Harmon field on Guam.

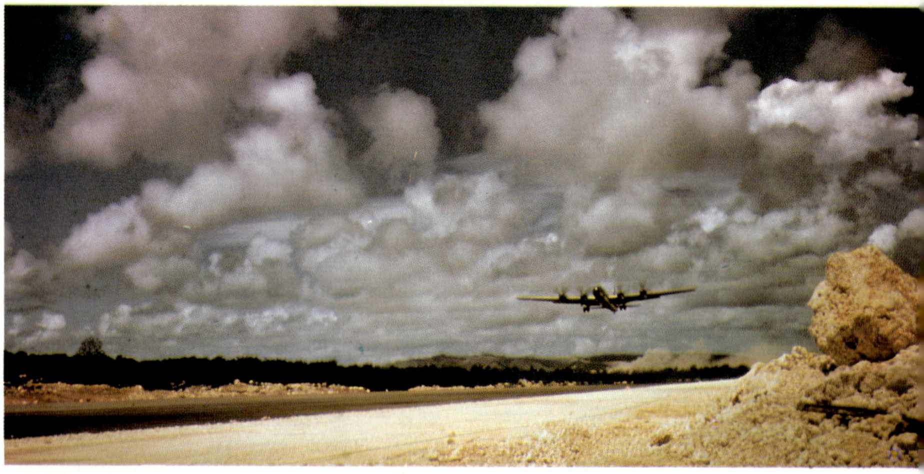

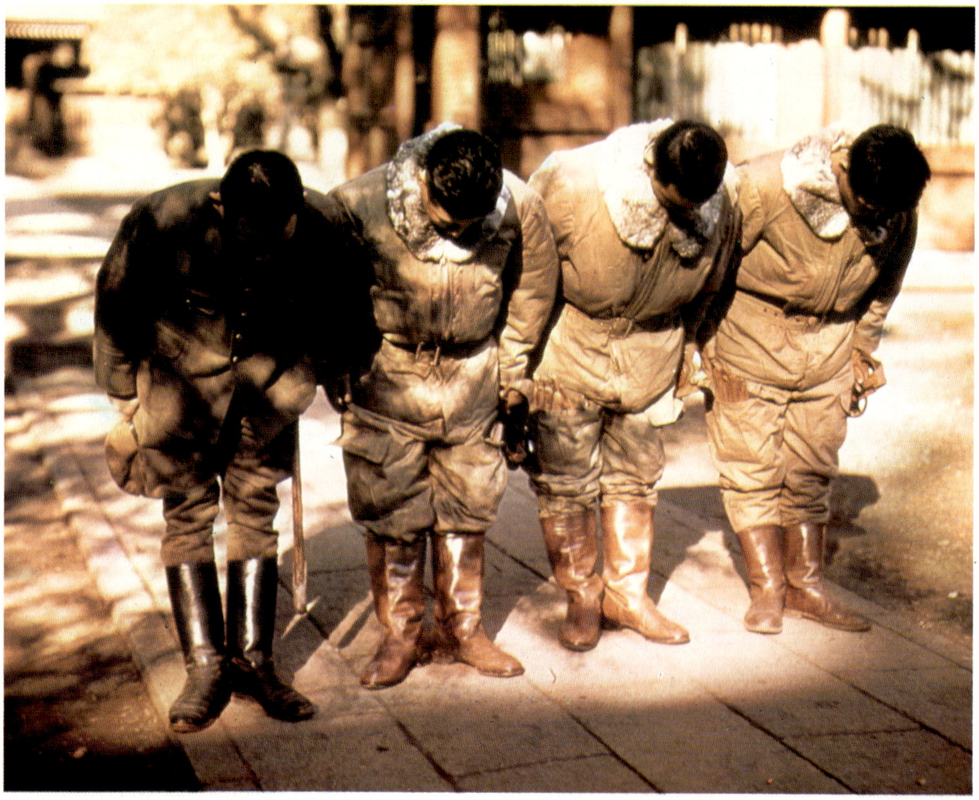

By the summer of 1945 Japan faced a disastrous situation. Subjected to devastating air raids, its supplies cut off as a result of the destruction of its merchant navy, the country was daily under attack by American warships and on the brink of an invasion of its own territory. The Soviet intervention and the two atomic bombs enabled the emperor to compel the army to accept the idea of capitulation and thus spare the population further suffering. As this picture shows, the act of surrender by officers took place according to the rules of the Japanese code of honour.

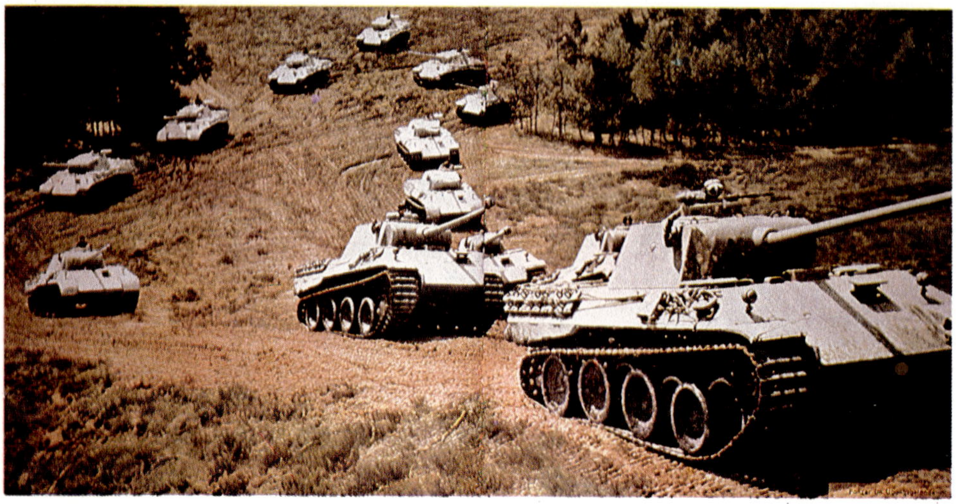

The Panther. Designed in response to the Soviet T-34, the German Panzer (PzKpwv) tank entered service in the spring of 1943 and proved a remarkable success despite some teething troubles. With a weight of 45 tons (45,000 kg), it had frontal armour plating 3 to 4 in. (80 to 100 mm) thick. It possessed a fine 75 mm gun with a high initial rate of fire. Its 700 horsepower Maybach engine permitted a speed of 28 mph (45 km/h) over a range of 125 mi. (200 km). More than 5500 of these machines left the MAN factories and the Panther was engaged in every theatre of operations. Here several Panthers are manoeuvring on a training ground.

Papen. Descended from an old family of Catholic aristocrats, Franz von Papen, whose beliefs were monarchist and ultraconservative, began his political career in 1921. At the height of the crisis of the Weimar Republic, he became chancellor of the Reich in 1932, with the support of General von Schleicher and President Hindenburg. But the government of 'barons' could not halt the rise of the Nazis, with whom Papen finally made a secret agreement, which brought Hitler to power. Contenting himself with the post of vice-chancellor, he had no doubt that he could succeed, with the support of the president and conservative circles, in harnessing the new political force. His hopes disappointed, he was sufficiently sure of himself to publicly denounce the excesses of the regime in a speech at Marburg on 17 June 1934 – a speech the circulation of the text of which was quickly forbidden by Goebbels. On 30 June 1934, the 'Night of the Long Knives', three of his chief colleagues – and the real writers of the speech – were murdered. Papen himself, placed under house arrest, soon gave in, accepting less than a month later the post of ambassador in Vienna, where on 25 July 1934 the Nazis assassinated Dollfuss. He subsequently became ambassador to Turkey, and showed himself to be, right to the end, the willing instrument of the Third Reich. Acquitted at the Nuremberg Trials (1946), he was nevertheless condemned by a German court, being released in 1949. Here he is standing on the left, with arm raised, during a Nazi demonstration in Stuttgart in 1933. On the right, in the foreground, is Goebbels.

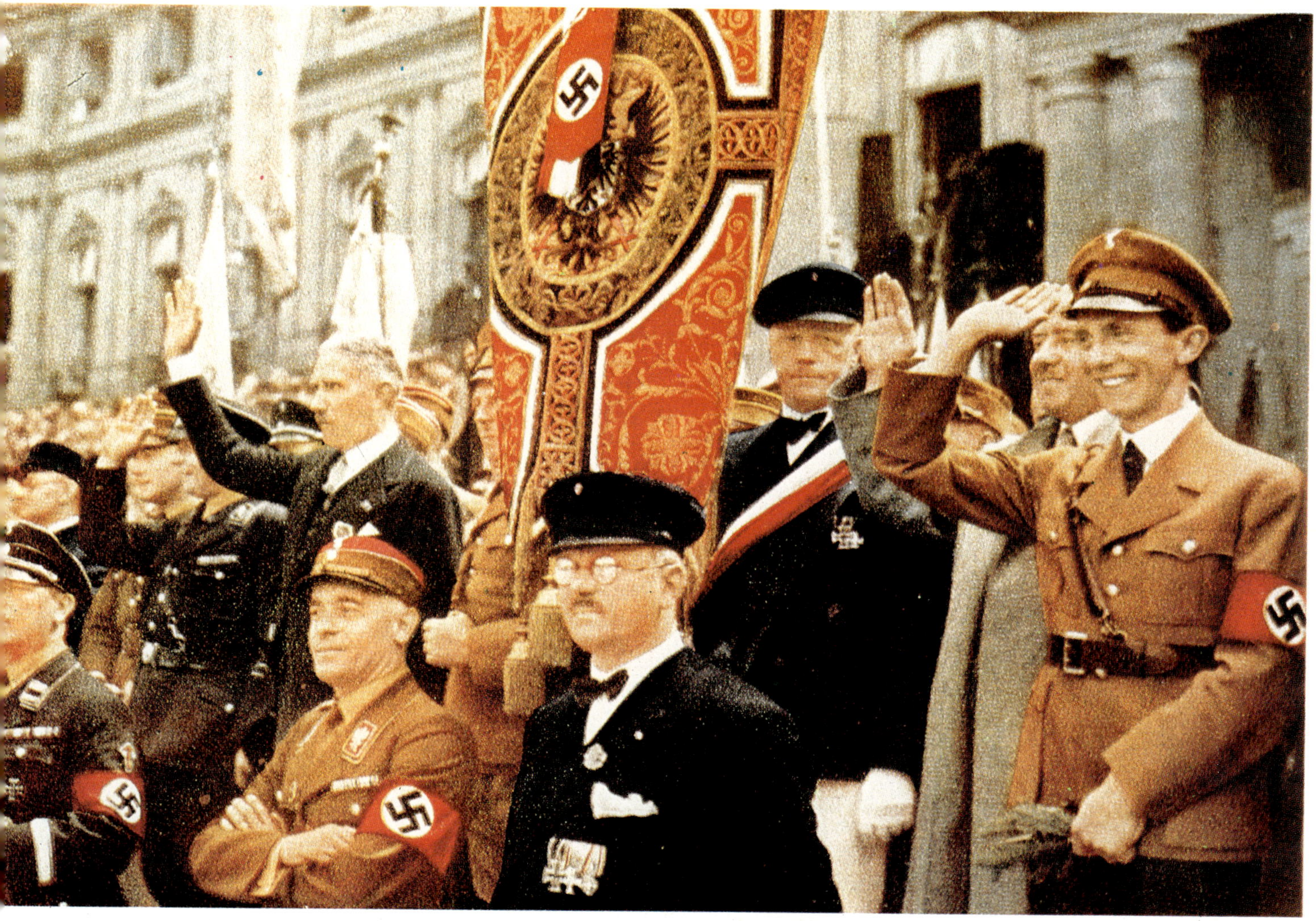

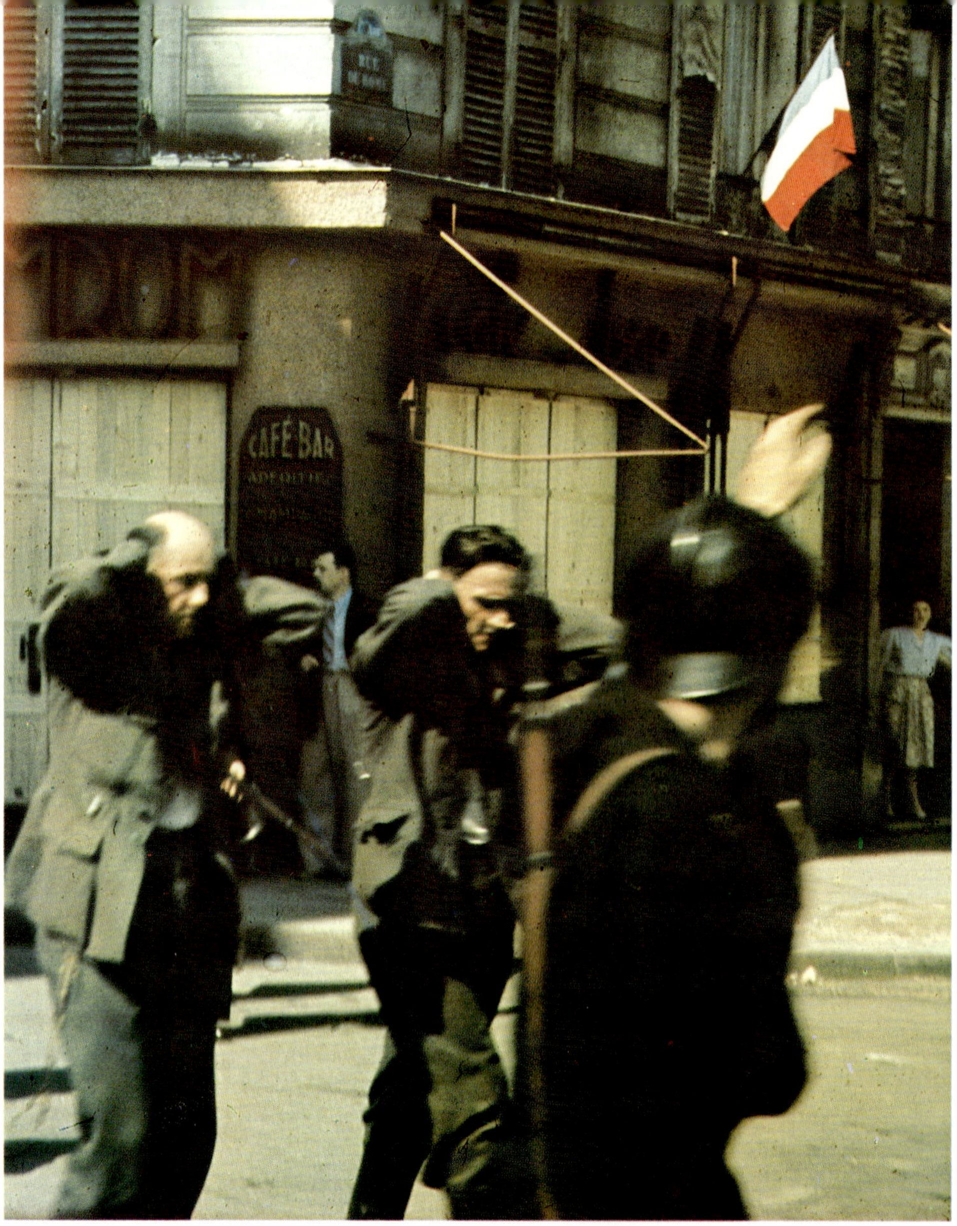

The Liberation of Paris. On 19 Aug. 1944, when it became clear that the Germans had lost the battle for Normandy, the Forces Françaises de l'Intérieur (FFI) began a rising in the capital in answer to the appeal by the Comité Parisien de Libération and the Conseil National de la Résistance. This was despite a recommendation of caution by General de Gaulle's representatives who feared bloody reprisals by the Germans. Interrupted for a week by a short-lived truce (arranged on the initiative of the Swedish consul-general) until the arrival of the 2nd French Armoured Division under General Leclerc, the insurrection took the form of a series of harassing operations against strong points held by the German garrison, commanded by General von Choltitz. As this photograph taken in the Rue de Rome shows, isolated German soldiers were killed or captured during the course of these engagements. The losses sustained by the FFI were heavy, amounting to a total of about 1000 dead and 1500 wounded.

On the evening of Tuesday 22 Aug., when the truce between the German garrison and the various resistance groups had come to an end, de Gaulle obtained permission from the American high command for Leclerc's 2nd Armoured Division to march on Paris, backed up by the US 4th Division. The attack was successful and Choltitz surrendered three days later. On 26 Aug., during a triumphal march from the Arc de Triomphe to Notre Dame (here seen at Place de l'Hôtel de Ville) Leclerc's soldiers and the FFI received a rapturous welcome from the population.

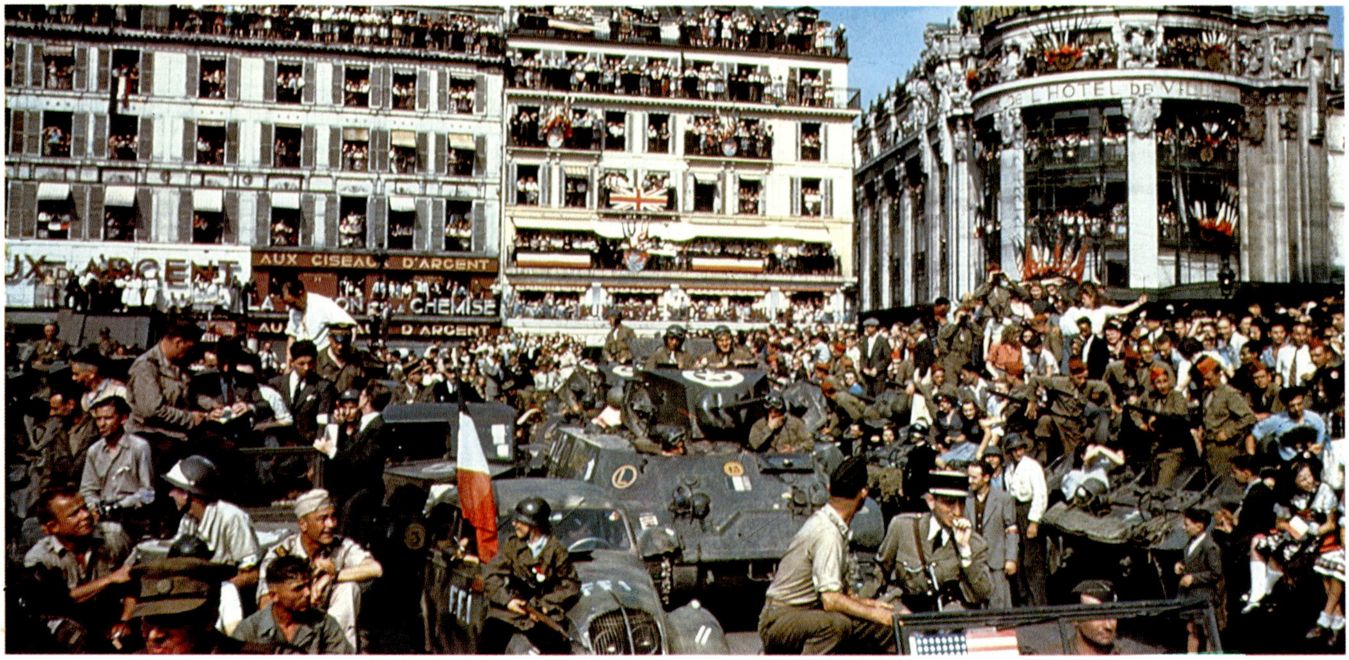

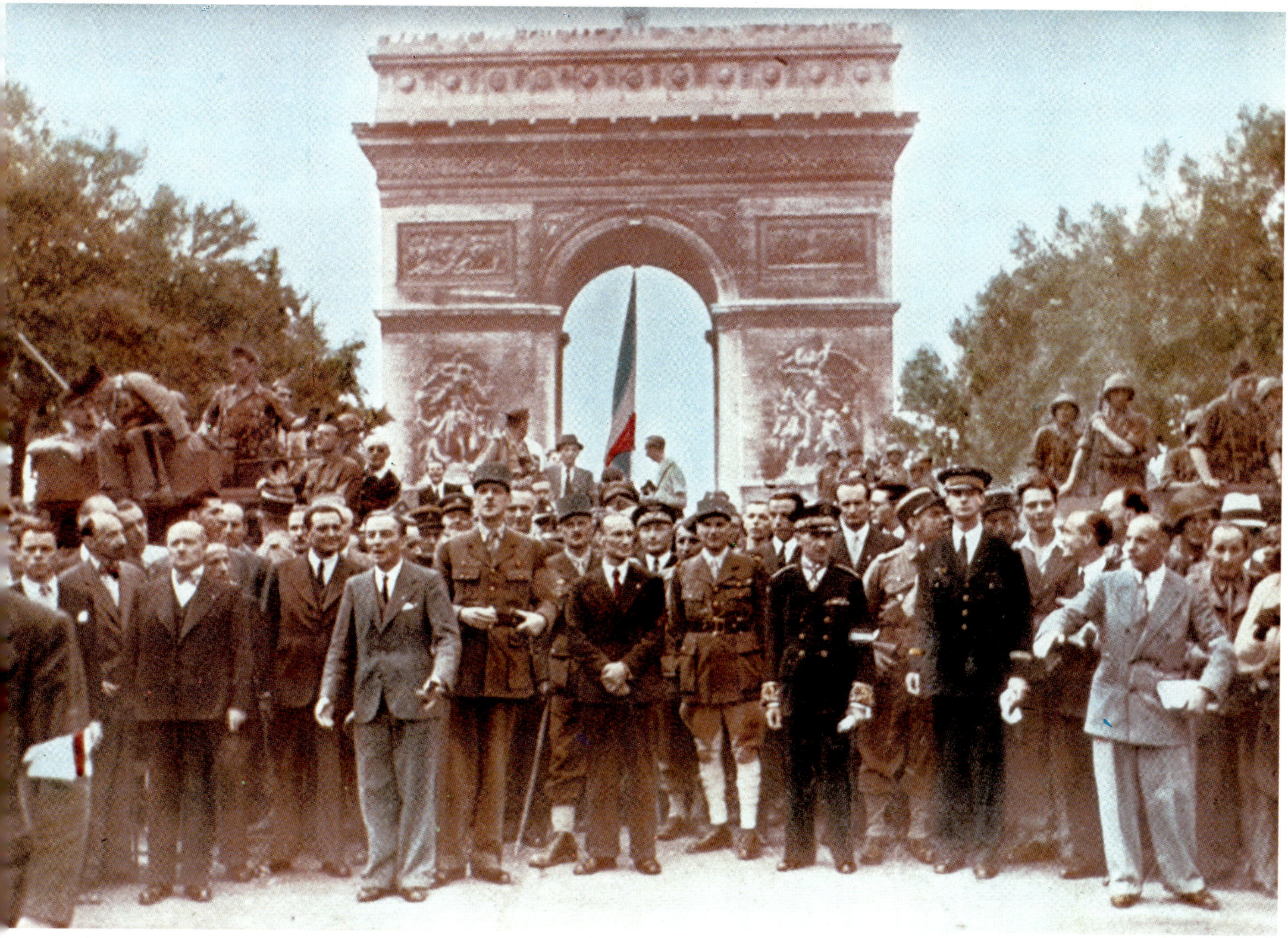

For General de Gaulle the liberation of Paris was a magnificent outcome, the culmination of four years of effort. On the afternoon of 26 Aug. 1944, surrounded by leading political and military members of the Resistance, the General walked down the Champs-Elysées, to the cheers of an enthusiastic crowd. The day, which was to end with a *Te Deum* in Notre-Dame, was marred by shooting in the Place du Parvis, the work of isolated marksmen, which resulted in an unknown number of deaths and more than 300 wounded.

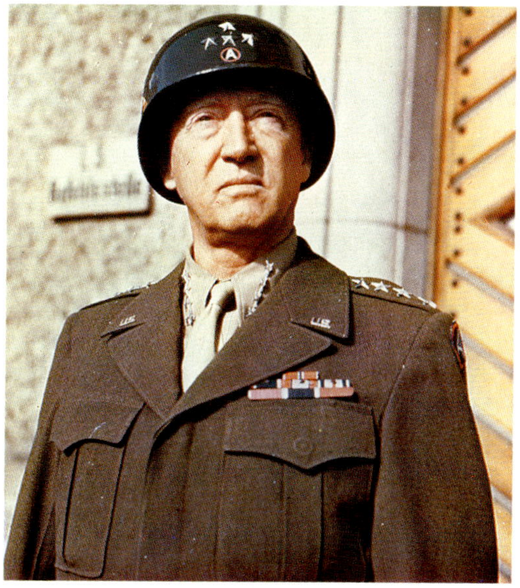

Patton. Aggressive, colourful, a poseur, this fine leader was undoubtedly one of the best Allied tacticians of the Second World War, on the same level as Guderian and Rommel. He had left West Point as a cavalry officer in 1909, and the use of the tank in modern warfare came as a revelation to him at the Battle of the Argonne in 1918. He showed his abilities at the head of the 2nd Corps in Tunisia in 1943, before amply demonstrating his determination and bravery in Sicily as commander of the 7th Army. His career was now overshadowed by a scandal, when he slapped a soldier who was suffering from a nervous disorder. However, in July 1944, Patton was given a new command. At the head of the Third Army, he brilliantly exploited the breakthrough at Avranches and made a decisive contribution to the victory at Falaise, before going on to take part in the campaign in Lorraine, the Battle of the Ardennes and the invasion of Germany. In disgrace once more over some acrimonious remarks made against the Soviet Union, he met his death in a car accident in Germany.

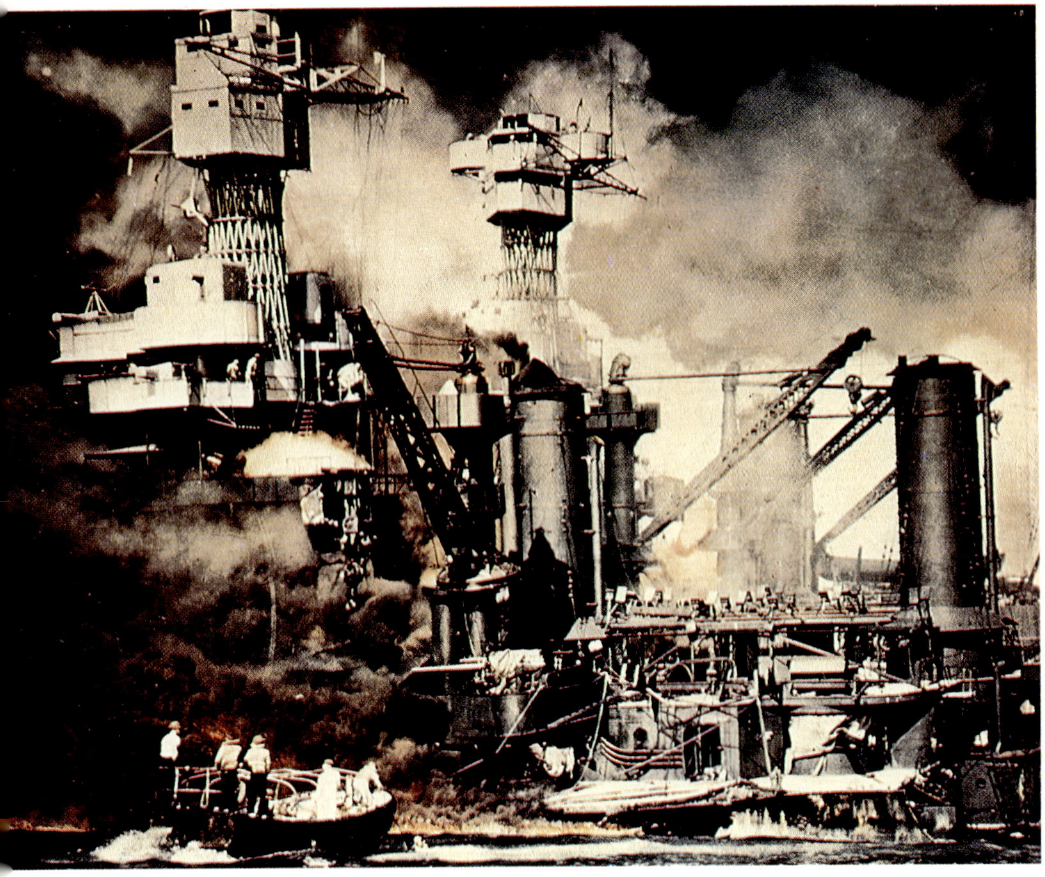

Pearl Harbor. Launched at dawn on 7 Dec. 1941 by planes from the six aircraft carriers in the squadron of the Japanese admiral, Chuichi Nagumo, the surprise attack on the American base at Pearl Harbor, in the Hawaiian archipelago, was to be a tactical success. The eight battleships of the American Pacific fleet were put out of action and 160 aircraft destroyed on the ground. The triumph was, however, incomplete because of the absence of the American aircraft carriers, which were at sea that day. But it was chiefly in the political sphere that the consequences of Pearl Harbor were disastrous for Japan. The 'day of infamy' as President Roosevelt called it, put an end to the isolationism of the United States. It led to a nation-wide surge of enthusiasm among the American people, determined to wage total war against Japan, whereas the Japanese government expected a limited conflict ending in a compromise peace which would leave Japan exercising hegemony over South-East Asia. The picture shows the battleships *Tennessee* and *West Virginia* on fire, while rescue teams try in vain to put out the flames.

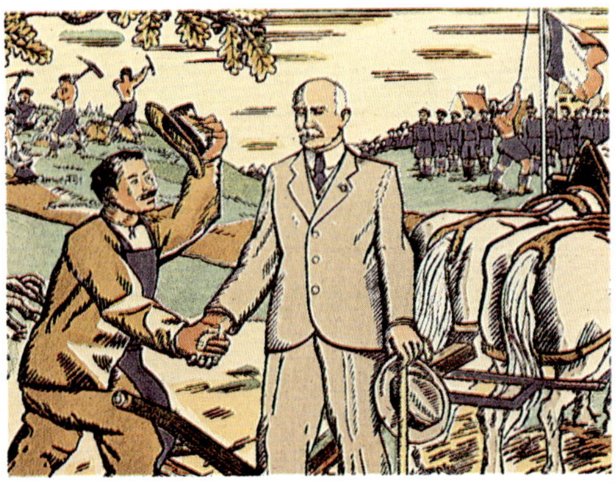

Pétain. To his immense prestige as a great soldier of the First World War, at the time of disaster in 1940 Pétain was to add the image of a father figure and saviour of the country which enabled him to obtain the support of a deeply distressed people. Trying to arouse in them the hope of a national revival based on the themes of work, family and native land, the Marshal was for two years to enjoy the confidence of the nation and acquire an almost mythic status, sustained by an efficient propaganda machine. Despite the complete occupation of the country, the failure of the so-called 'national revolution', the uncertain policy of Laval, and measures and actions which frequently conflicted strongly with national feeling in general, the Marshal remained popular with a section of the population until the end of the Vichy regime. Despite his trial and condemnation for complicity with the enemy, a number of French people remained convinced that in their darkest hour Pétain had held the shield while de Gaulle brandished the sword. This print glorifies the virtues of work, as part of the great Vichy 'back to the land' theme.

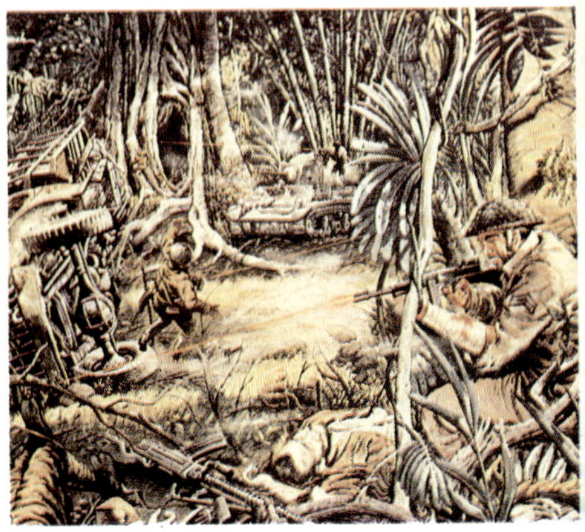

The Philippines. After Pearl Harbor the Japanese embarked upon the conquest of the Philippines, whose position commanded the approach to Indonesia. After landing on Luzon, the chief island, on 10 Dec. 1941, Japanese troops pushed back the American forces commanded by MacArthur towards the Bataan peninsula and the fortress of Corregidor. As this reproduction of a painting by Stanley Dersh shows, American units engaged in fierce fighting in collaboration with Filipino contingents, even, on 15 Feb. 1942, going over to the offensive and obliging the Japanese to mark time while they waited for reinforcements. This resistance delayed the fall of Corregidor by two months.

When he left the Philippines at the end of March 1942 on the personal order of President Roosevelt, MacArthur had spoken the famous words: 'I shall return'. He was to keep his promise two and a half years later. In Oct. 1944, protected by a formidable armada, the Americans in fact landed in Leyte, before setting foot once more on the island of Luzon itself, at Lingayen, in Jan. 1945, as this photograph shows. The liberation of the Philippines proved in the long run to be a slow and costly operation, because of the skilful and stubborn resistance of Yamashita's forces. The Americans had to make an increasing number of landings from the sea in order to outflank enemy positions.

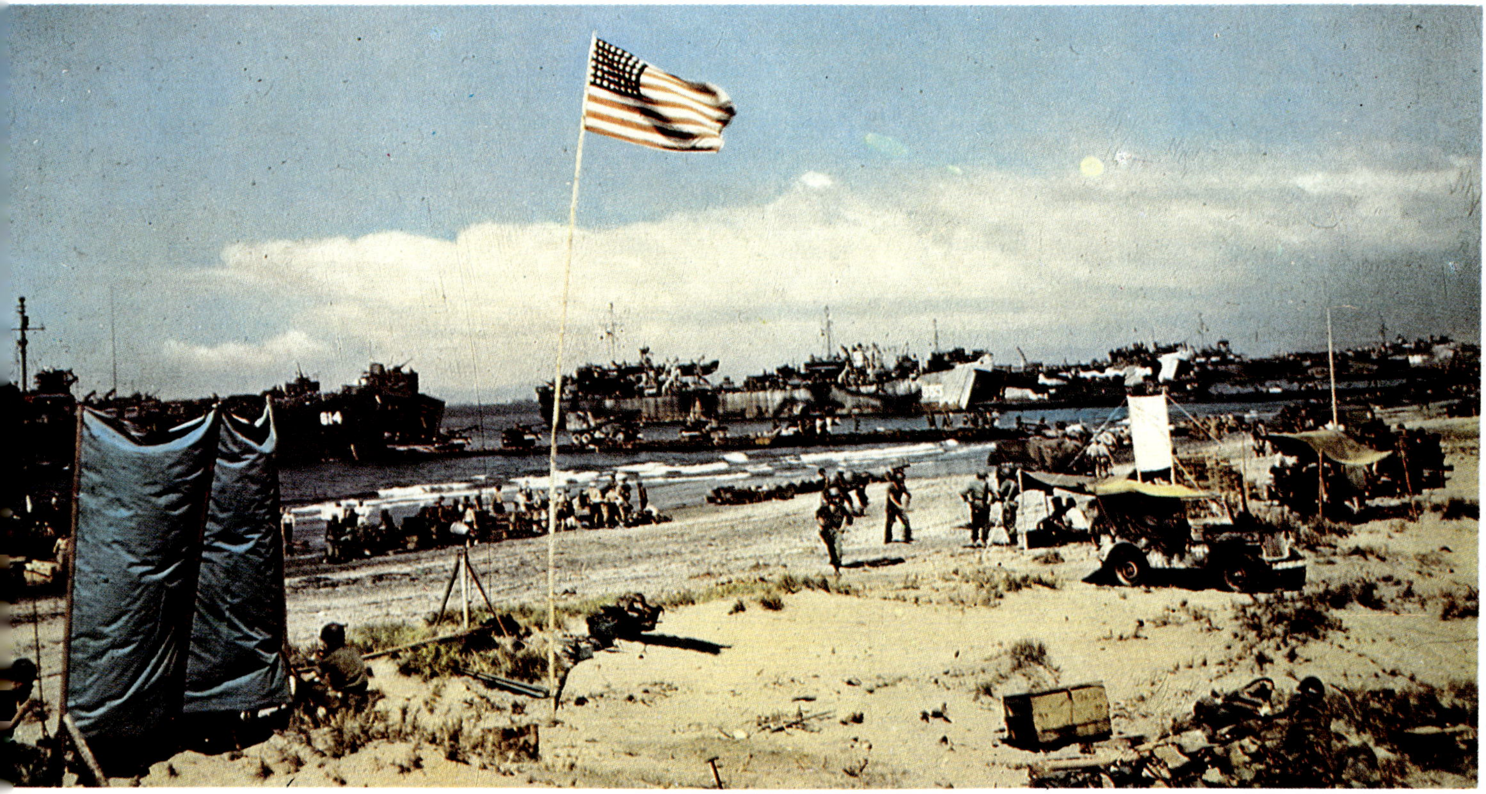

The battle for the recapture of the Philippines reached its climax at the beginning of Feb. 1945, when American troops arrived at the outskirts of Manila. The city, which was defended street by street and house by house by a garrison of 20,000 men, fell only after a month of fighting which cost the Americans more than 8500 dead. Immediately after its liberation the capital of the Philippines, ravaged by aerial bombardment and artillery shelling, was nothing more than an immense expanse of ruins, as this view of the port installations shows.

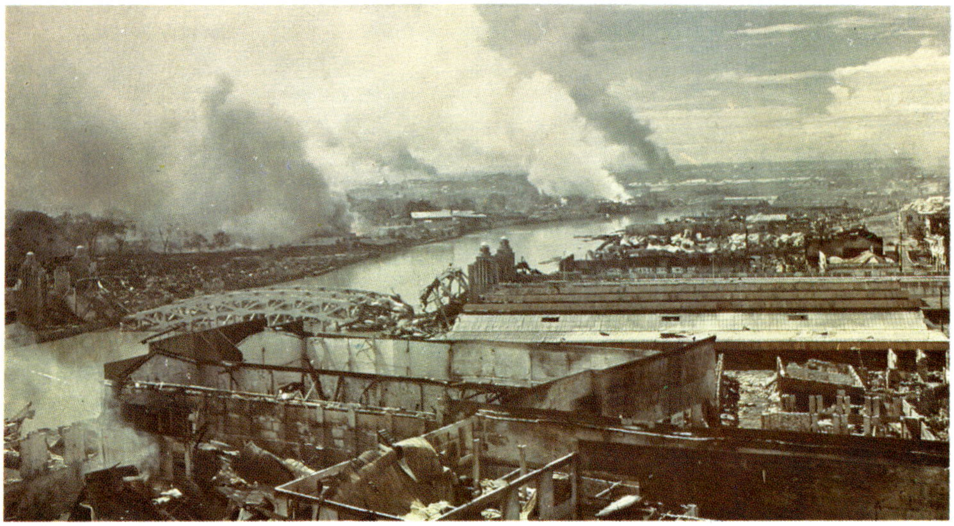

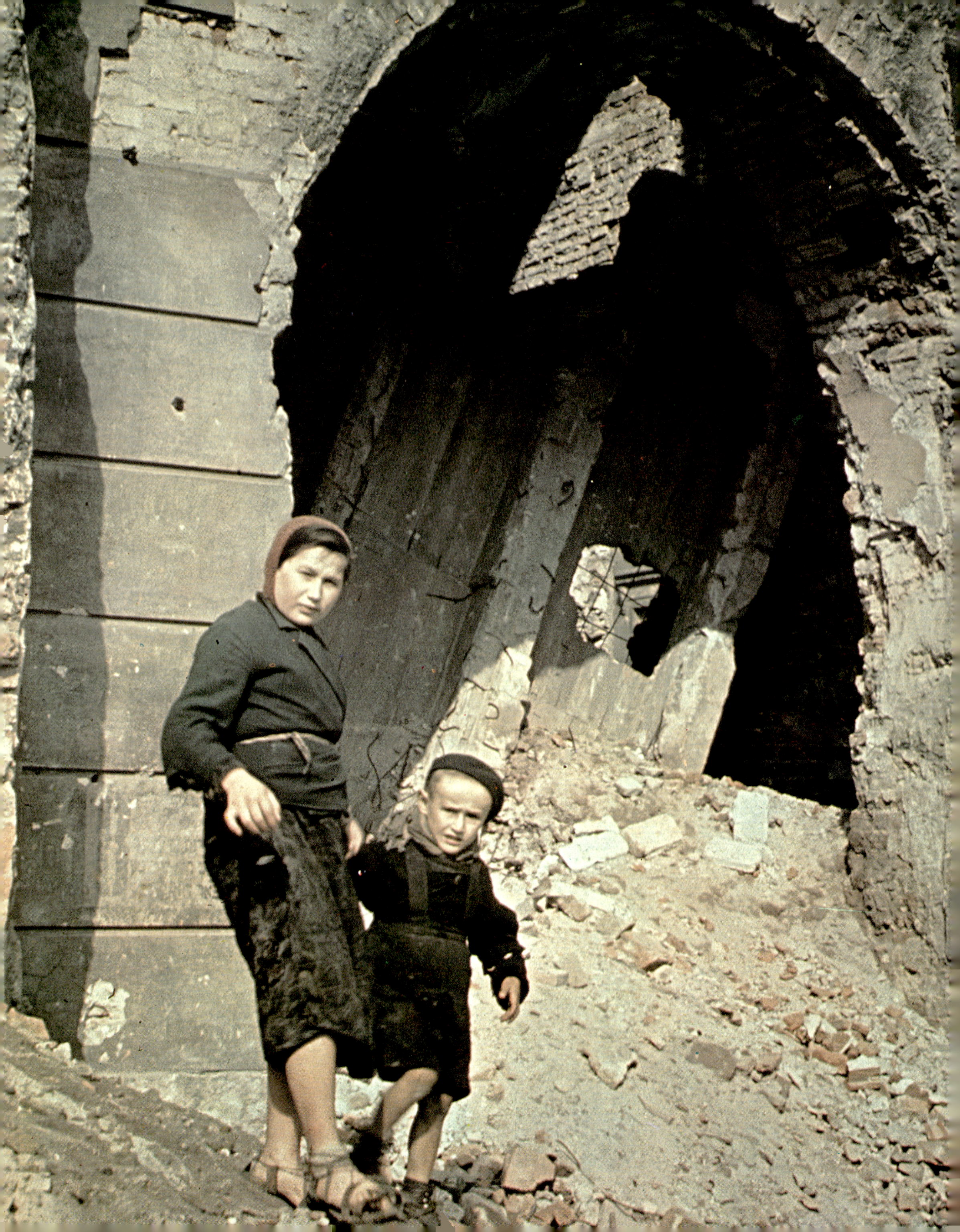

Poland. In the ruins of a town.

Poland. Beginning at dawn on 1 Sept. 1939, the campaign against Poland showed to an astonished world the hitherto unsuspected possibilities of the Blitzkrieg. In less than eight days the combined actions of air and armoured formations, launching large-scale destructive and breaching operations linked with vast encircling manoeuvres, were to prove decisive. Having lost control of its forces, the Polish high command was unable to make a stand of any sort behind the chief rivers. Here, after the fighting, civilians at Ostroleka on the Narew River, are crossing a destroyed railway bridge on which some makeshift repairs have been carried out.

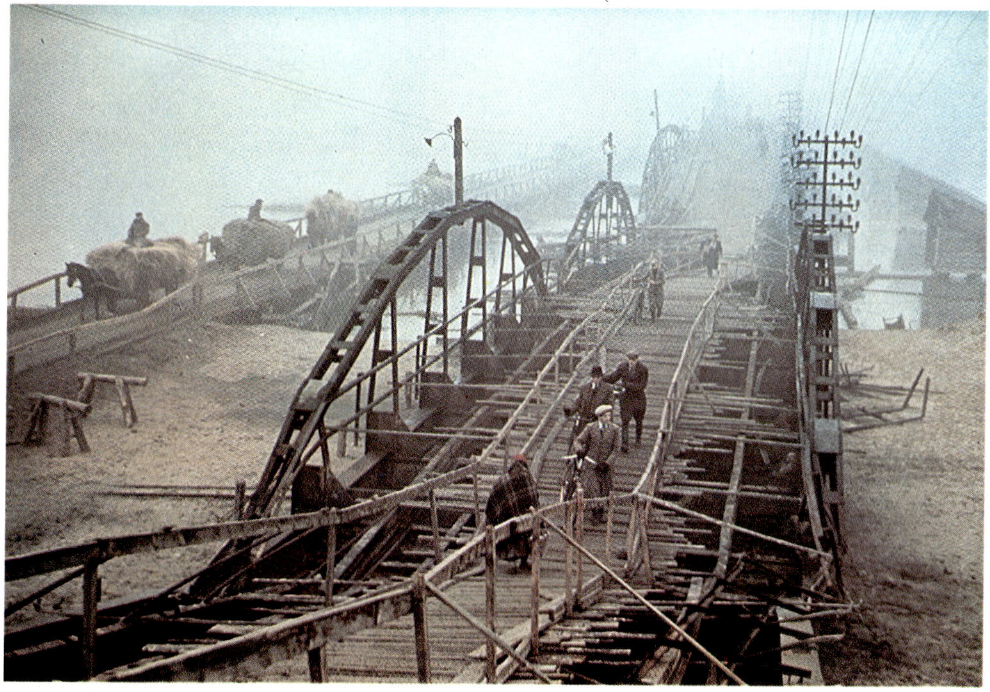

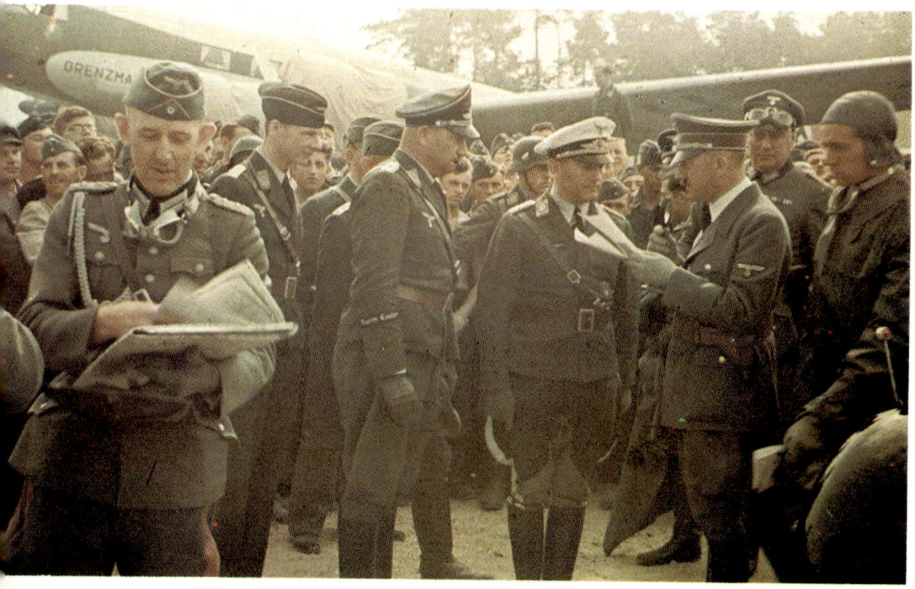

During the Polish campaign Hitler took almost no part in the conduct of operations but visited units at the front on several occasions. Here he is in company with senior officers. During the operations the German air force had, for the first time, the opportunity to try out its potential as a tactical support weapon, acting in direct liaison with the troops on the ground, while still carrying out attacks on lines of communication and airfields, as well as terror raids against towns.

Poland did not suffer the onslaught by the Wehrmacht alone. In accordance with the Russo-German Non-Aggression Pact, the Red Army in its turn went on the attack, without a declaration of war, under the pretext of 'protecting the Ukrainian and Byelorussian population', thus achieving the complete defeat of the Polish army. The link-up between German and Soviet forces took place at Brest-Litovsk and the protocol of 29 Sept. sanctioned once again the partition of Poland. In the photograph can be seen a control post established along the demarcation line which was to serve as a frontier between Germany and the USSR until 22 June 1941.

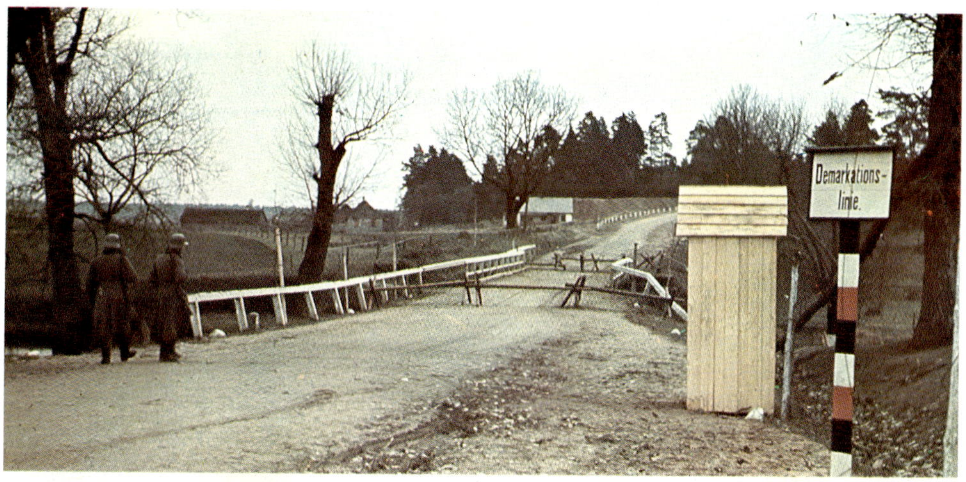

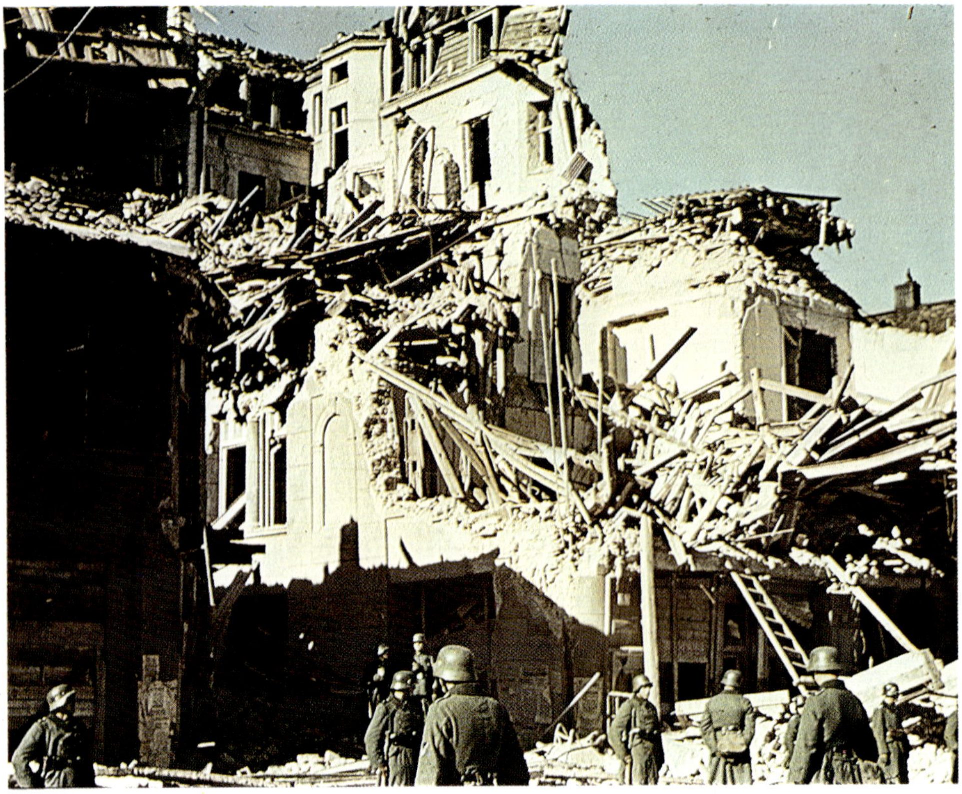

Throughout the campaign the Poles fought with great spirit, not hesitating to launch cavalry units against tanks and refusing to declare Warsaw an open city. In fact, the capital, which had been under attack since 14 Sept., rejected all offers of surrender. In spite of bombardments by artillery and aircraft, the resistance continued for nearly two weeks. The garrison did not capitulate until 27 Sept. and the Germans granted it the honours of war. At the end of the siege, which had hit the civilian population hard, many areas occupied by the Wehrmacht were in ruins.

As early as the winter of 1939–40 Warsaw presented the grim picture of a capital under enemy occupation: less traffic on the roads, much of it horse-drawn, and numerous German propaganda posters. Despite the deportations and a formidable police apparatus, the population was not long in recovering its spirits and resistance took the form of the creation of a secret army. Finally, a clandestine state was established. However, Poland's tragedy was not yet over. It was to culminate in 1944 in the suppression by the Germans of the Warsaw Rising and the liberation of the country by the Red Army, which was to lead to the country becoming a Soviet satellite – contrary to the wishes of the vast majority of the population.

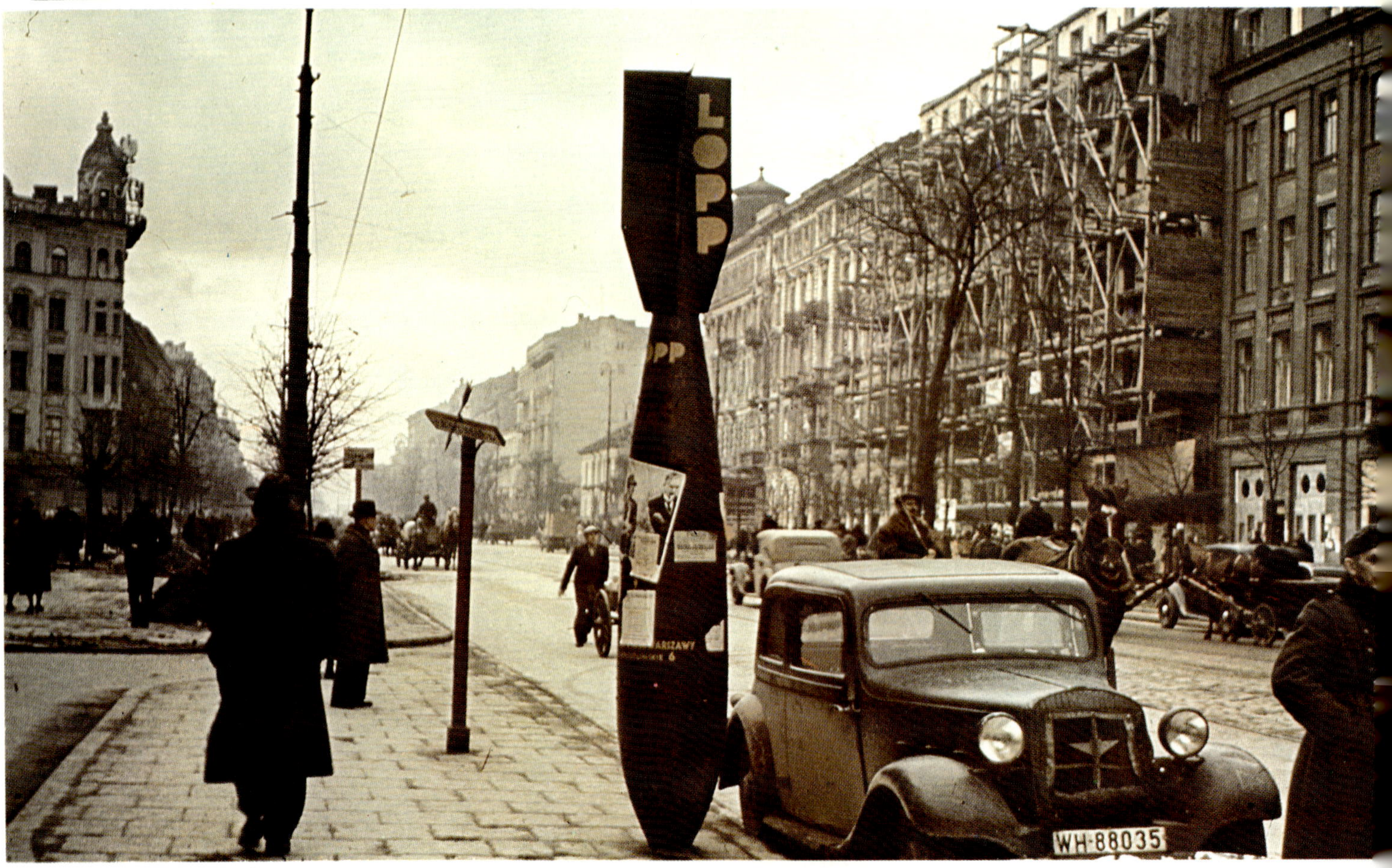

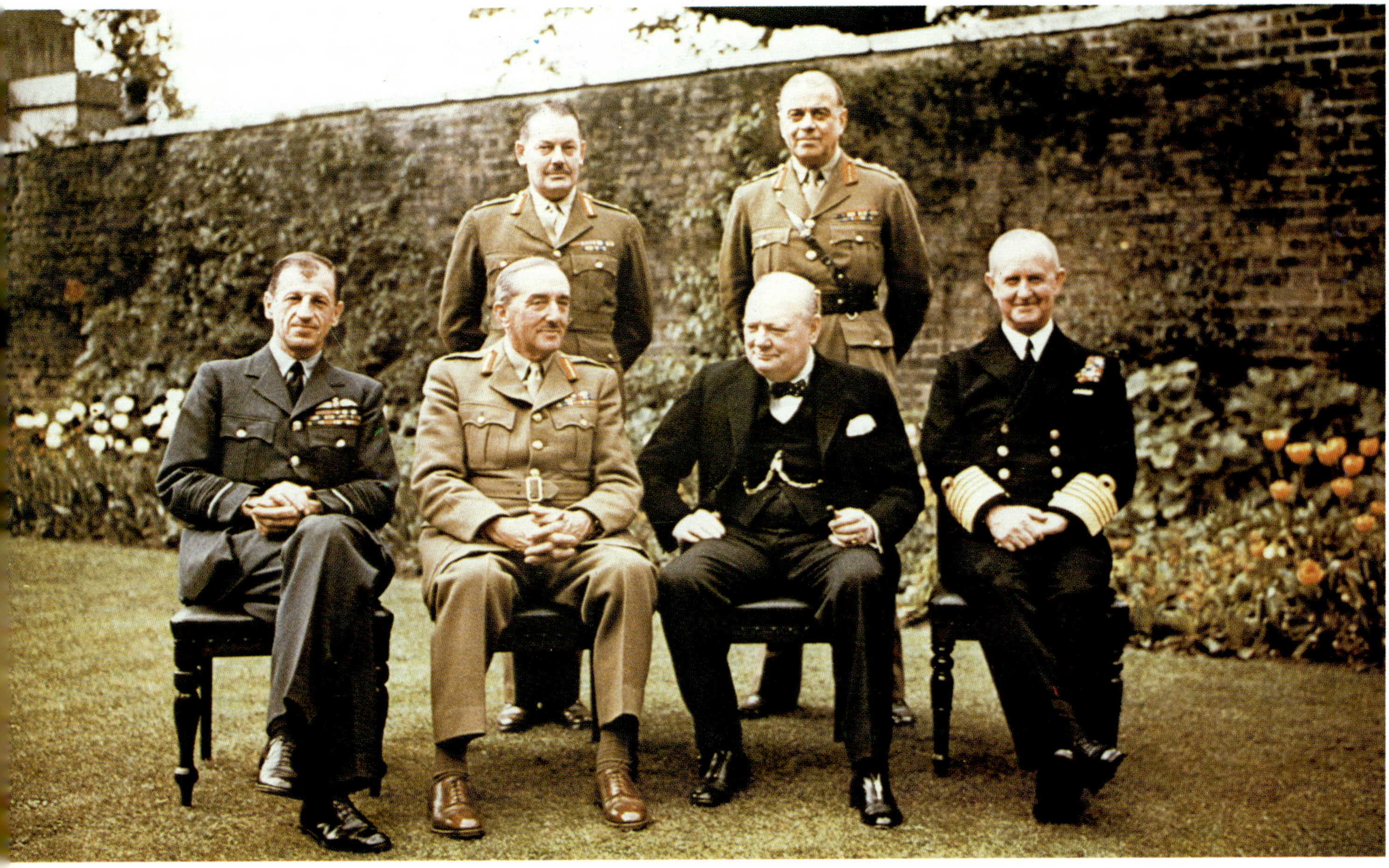

Portal. The photograph shows the chiefs of the British general staff in the garden of 10 Downing Street, on 7 May 1945. Seated with Churchill are, from left to right, Portal, Sir Alan Brooke, and Admiral Cunningham. Profiting from vast experience, acquired during the First World War and in the interwar period, Air Chief Marshal Portal became head of the RAF in Oct. 1940, just after the Battle of Britain. As chief of air staff, he bore the heavy burden of deciding the conduct of British operations, while at the same time establishing the general direction of air strategy. Up to 1943 he was an advocate of raids on urban areas, with the aim of disorganizing German production and of undermining the morale of the civilian population. However, in contrast to Harris, the head of Bomber Command, he realized, from the beginning of 1944, the necessity of directing the efforts of the RAF (in preparation for the landing in France) towards the bombing of targets connected with the petroleum and transport industries.

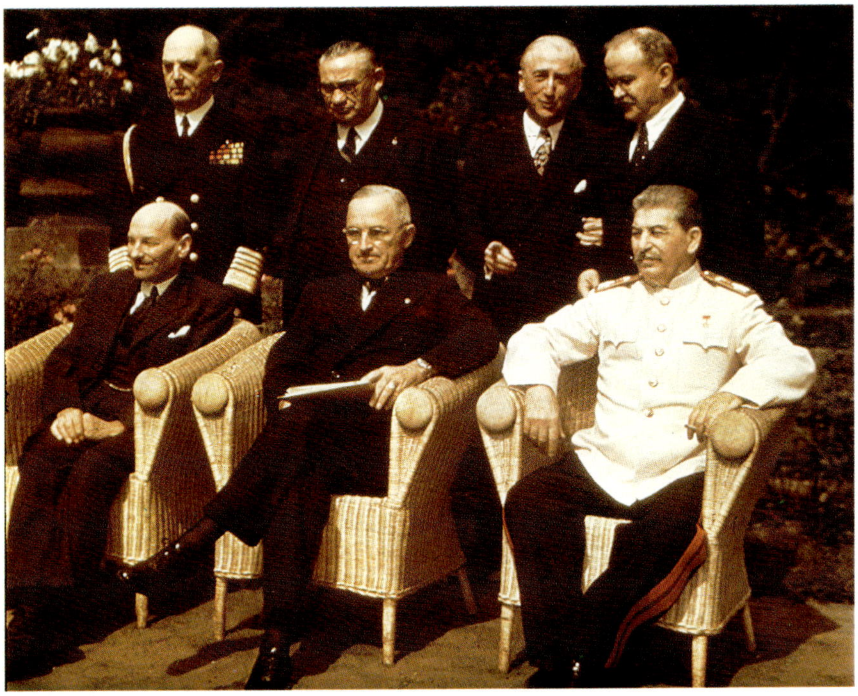

The Potsdam Conference. This took place in July 1945 just after the surrender of Germany. In contrast to Teheran and Yalta, Stalin found himself, as can be seen in this photograph, with two new partners: in the centre, the president of the United States, Harry S. Truman, who had succeeded Roosevelt, and the new British prime minister, the Labour leader, Clement Attlee (left), who came to power after the elections of June 1945 which had seen Churchill and the Conservatives defeated. Despite an apparent air of cordiality the Potsdam Conference carried in it the seeds of the Cold War, with Stalin's declared intention of settling the problems of Eastern Europe without interference by the Western powers. It was at Potsdam that on 26 July, ten days after the first atomic explosion at Alamogordo, that an Anglo-American ultimatum, in which the Russians had joined, was addressed to Japan demanding unconditional surrender.

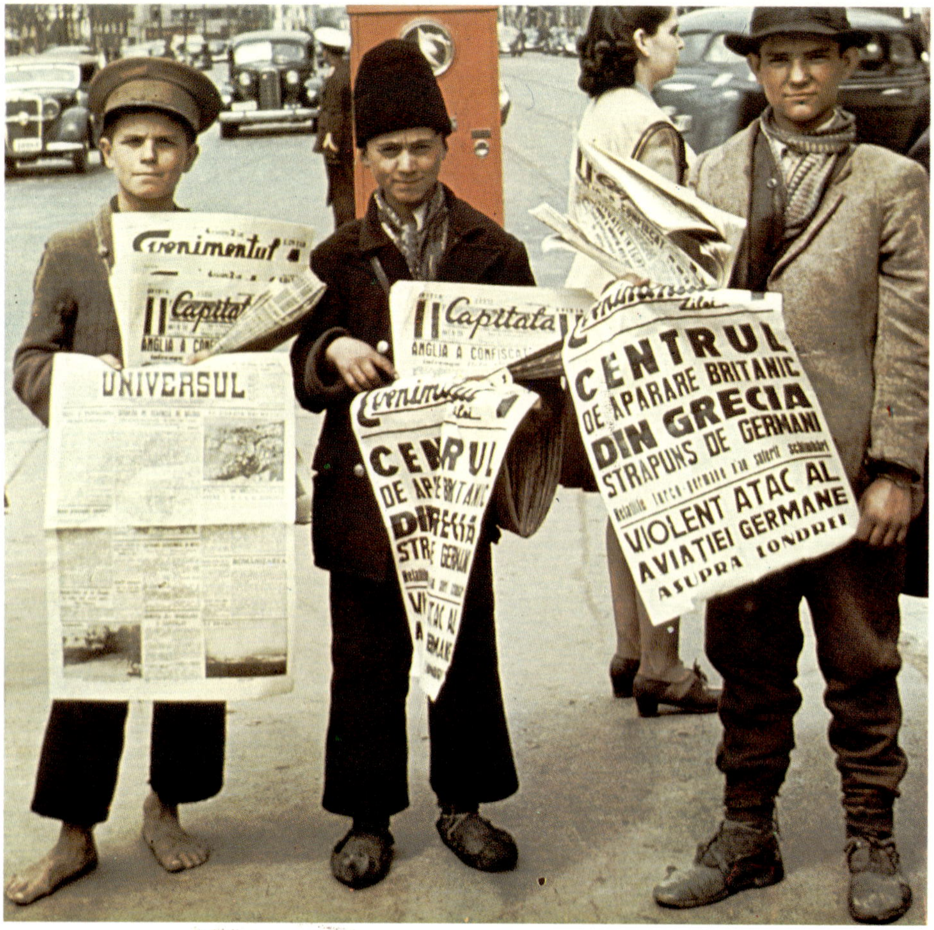

The Press. In the same way as radio, the press was to play an important role during the conflict. In the countries at war it had a twofold objective: to provide information about important political or military events, and at the same time keep up the morale of the population. In spite of censorship, in the western democracies it enjoyed considerable freedom. On the other hand in totalitarian countries, like the Soviet Union, Japan, Germany and Italy, it was reduced to the level of an instrument of the government or the party, at the same time suffering from severe material shortages (this lack of paper led to a reduction in the size of newspapers). In this photograph street sellers in Bucharest are displaying newspapers announcing the German offensive in the Balkans in April 1941.

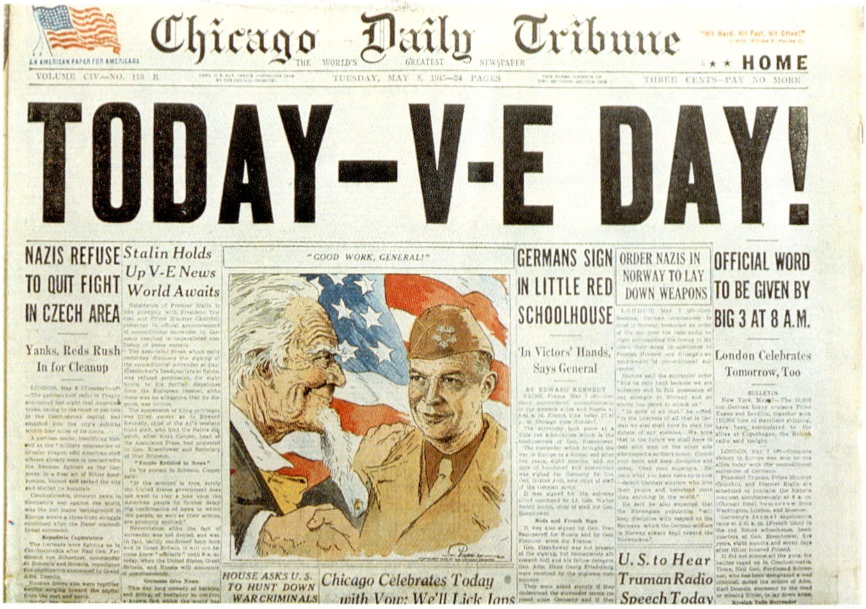

Chicago Daily Tribune

THE WORLD'S GREATEST NEWSPAPER

AN AMERICAN PAPER FOR AMERICANS

★★ HOME

VOLUME CIV.—NO. 110 R

TUESDAY, MAY 8, 1945—24 PAGES

THREE CENTS—PAY NO MORE

TODAY—V-E DAY!

NAZIS REFUSE TO QUIT FIGHT IN CZECH AREA

Yanks, Reds Rush In for Cleanup

Stalin Holds Up V-E News World Awaits

"GOOD WORK, GENERAL!"

GERMANS SIGN IN LITTLE RED SCHOOLHOUSE

'In Victors' Hands,' Says General

ORDER NAZIS IN NORWAY TO LAY DOWN WEAPONS

OFFICIAL WORD TO BE GIVEN BY BIG 3 AT 8 A.M.

London Celebrates Tomorrow, Too

HOUSE ASKS U.S. TO HUNT DOWN WAR CRIMINALS

Chicago Celebrates Today with Vow: We'll Lick Japs

U.S. to Hear Truman Radio Speech Today

Until 1944 the people of western Europe had to content themselves with newspapers controlled by the occupying power or those issued by the resistance press, printed and distributed in the most difficult and dangerous conditions. At the liberation Europeans were at last able to read the great American newspapers, which enjoyed exceptionally easy access to information and encountered only slight material difficulties. This front page from the *Chicago Daily Tribune* of 8 May 1945, is interesting on two counts. It announces not only victory (V-Day) but lays emphasis in the second column on one of the early indications of East–West confrontation – Stalin's reluctance to recognize the surrender at Rheims on 7 May, as marking the end of the war in Europe. For the Soviet authorities it was the ceremony at Berlin, held on the night of 8–9 May, which put the seal on the cessation of military operations and the real collapse of Germany.

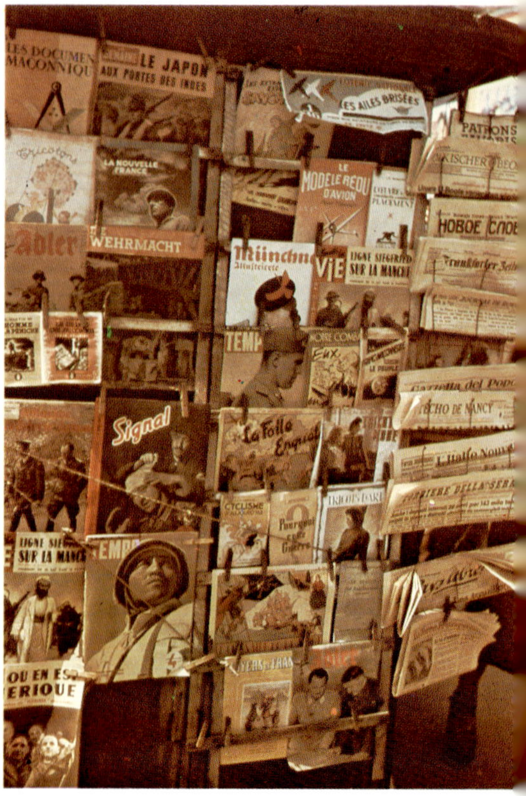

In the countries of occupied Europe, the press was of course under the absolute control of the victor, at the same time facing competition from German or Italian publications. This Parisian kiosk provides a perfect example. Alongside the few French newspapers, such as the *Echo de Nancy*, which was in any case supported by the German authorities, German and Italian newspapers are prominently displayed: the *Völkischer Beobachter* or *Il Corriere della sera*, in company with magazines published in French, such as *Die Wehrmacht*, *Signal* or *Der Adler*, the organ of the Luftwaffe. In unoccupied France, the press enjoyed relatively greater freedom. However, in 1942, with the whole country under occupation, a number of newspapers, for example *Le Figaro* and *Le Temps*, both of which had moved to Lyons, ceased publication.

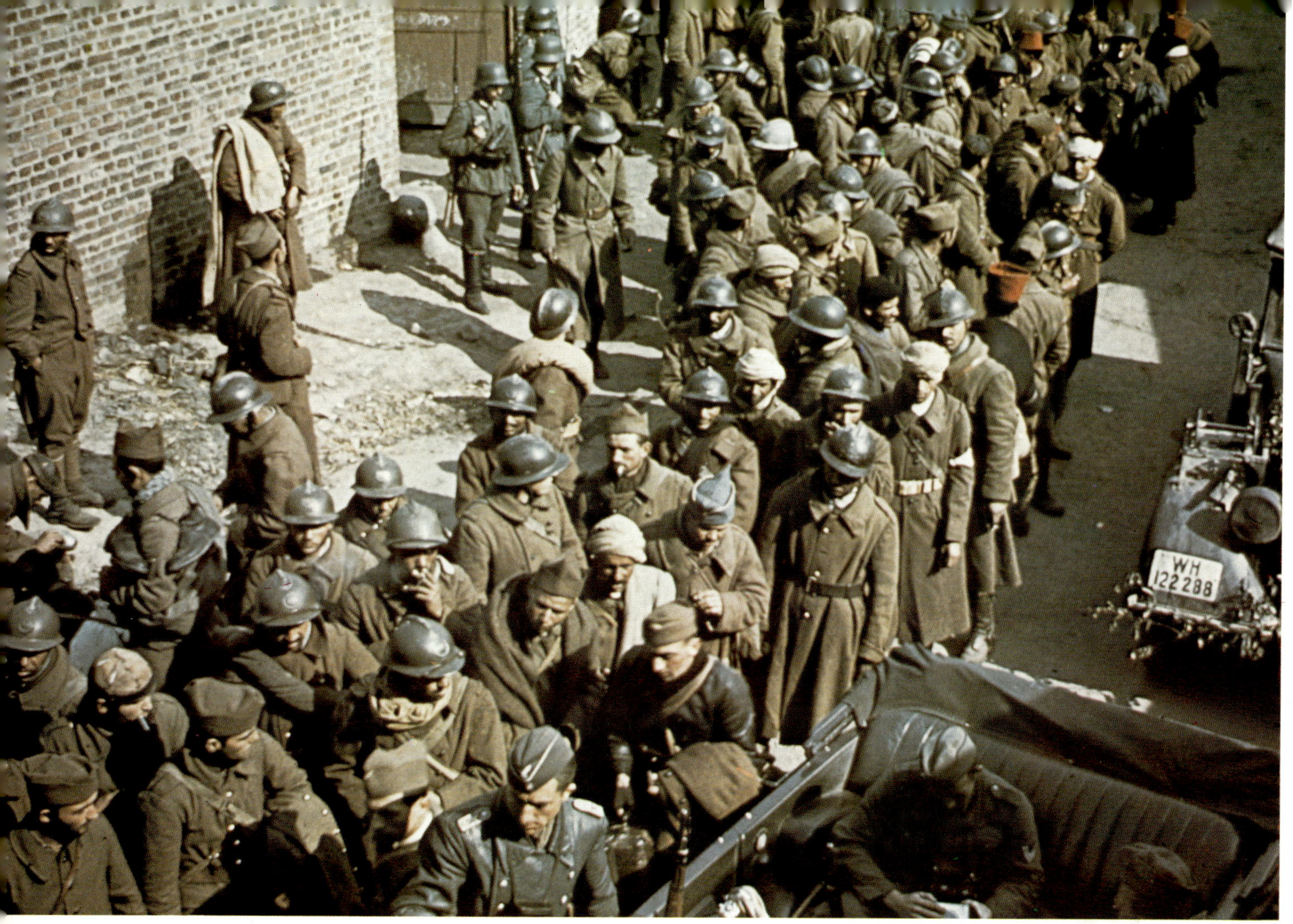

Prisoners of war. The Second World War was characterized, to a much greater extent than in 1914–18, by the magnitude of the problem of prisoners of war. Up to 1942, with the help of the Blitzkrieg, the Germans had captured millions of prisoners, on the western front as well as in the east. Here we see a motley group of French and African (French colonial) soldiers captured during May–June 1940. Prisoners experienced widely varying conditions of internment according to their nationality, as a result of the racial discrimination practised by the Germans. Although soldiers captured on the western front were often subjected to extremely harsh conditions, particularly in the special work units, their fate bore no comparison to that of the Slavs taken prisoner on the eastern front. They were treated by the Nazis as sub-human, and the death of more than half of the 5 million Soviet prisoners is evidence of this.

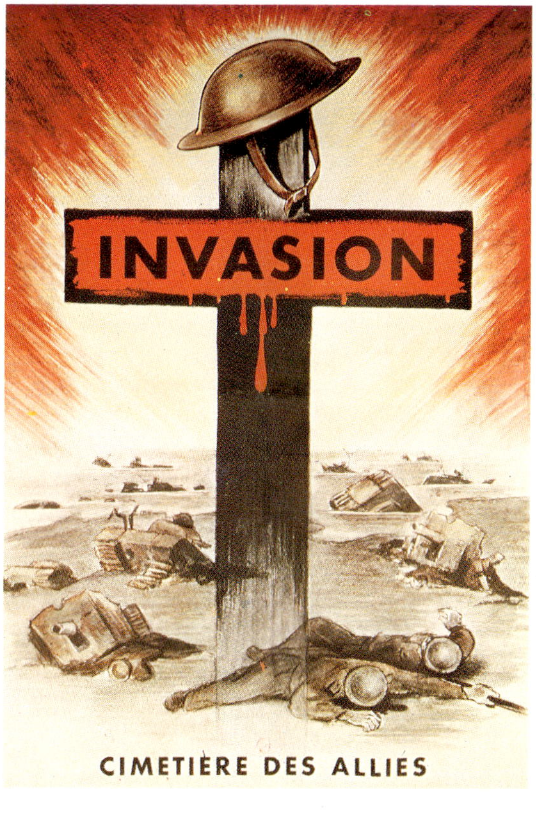

Propaganda. In the context of an exceptionally long and bloody conflict, in which civilians and soldiers were equally involved, propaganda played a notable – and even unprecedented – role, with the help of very sizeable resources and up-to-date techniques. On each side it pursued a twofold objective: to maintain or improve the morale of the population and the fighting men, and to undermine the enemy's. This German poster, intended for occupied France, exploits the failure of the Anglo-Canadian raid on Dieppe in 1942 and is intended to show what the result of a future invasion could be. This kind of propaganda met with only limited success. It was quite otherwise with very suggestive pamphlets showing the soldier's fiancée or wife seeking help and consolation in the arms of a shirker or a profiteer well behind the lines.

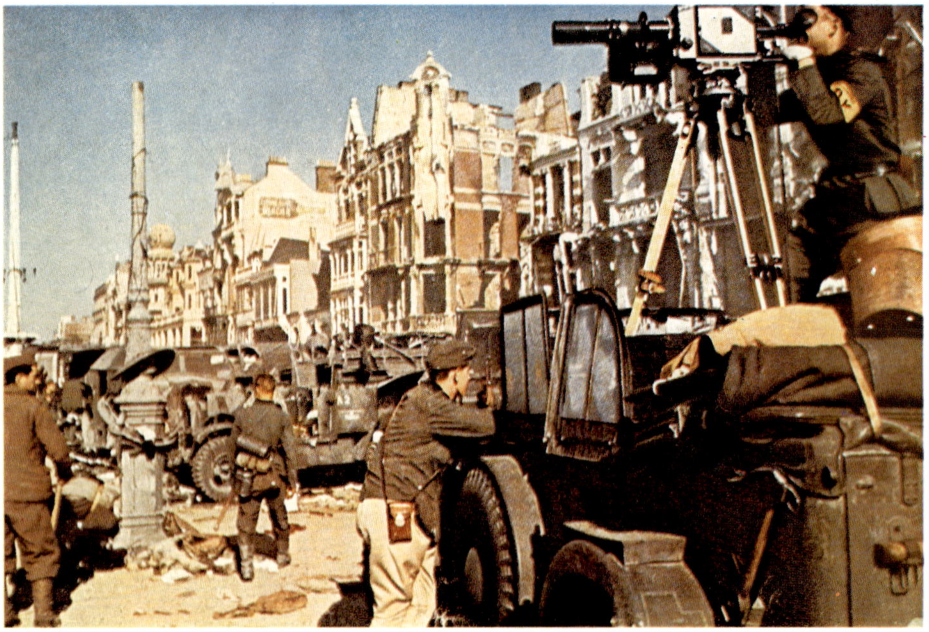

As early as 1939 the Wehrmacht possessed units whose job was to photograph and film military operations. During the dazzling period of the Blitzkrieg, these records were used for the enlightenment of German civilians and the peoples of occupied countries. Here, in June 1940, a member of a Wehrmacht propaganda company is filming, from the back of a vehicle, the remains of the Allied rout on the beaches of Dunkirk, which are cluttered with abandoned war materials.

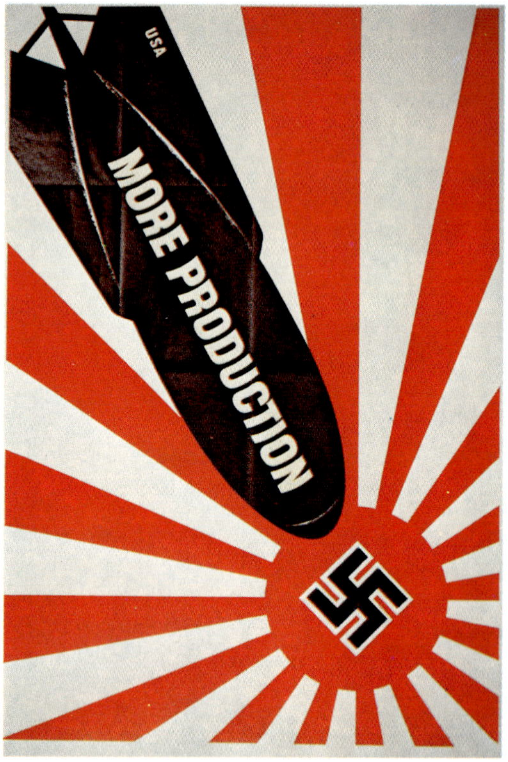

In all the countries at war, propaganda aimed at stimulating production and the war effort, as is shown by this American poster encouraging the development of armaments in order to conquer Germany and Japan. This task was all the more necessary in the United States which was too far away to feel any of the effects of the conflict – either the blockade, bombing or the threat of invasion. The mobilization of the country's economy on behalf of its war effort was to make a powerful contribution to its emergence from an economic crisis to reach an unprecedented level of prosperity.

Following the armistice in 1940, certain French circles attempted to exploit as much as possible the antagonism between France and Britain which arose from the defeat. Thus, this poster recalls firstly Britain's promise to protect French security contained in the Treaty of Versailles. It then recalls Great Britain's refusal to commit the whole of the RAF in the battle for France and the evacuation of the expeditionary force at Dunkirk. In addition it emphasizes the blockade established after June 1940 and the bombing of ports and industrial towns. This kind of propaganda had little effect in occupied France, where hostility to the Germans was continually increasing. On the other hand it obtained, for a time, some results in the 'free zone', where restrictions could not be entirely blamed on German requisitions.

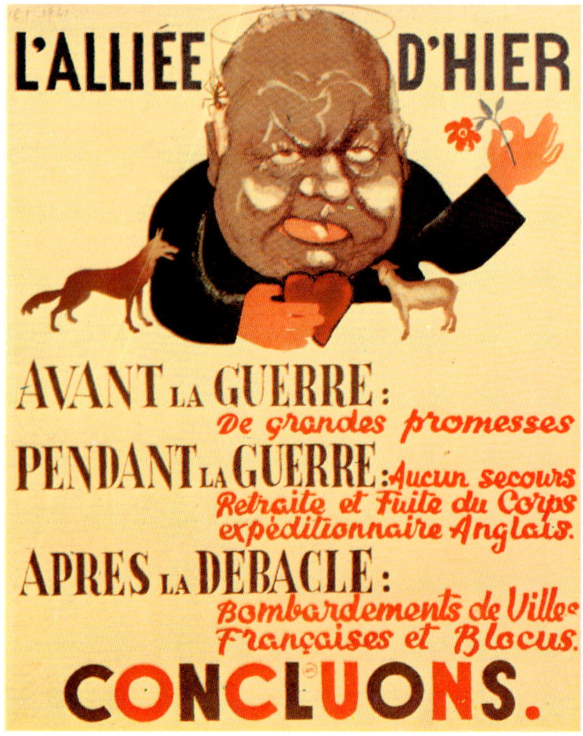

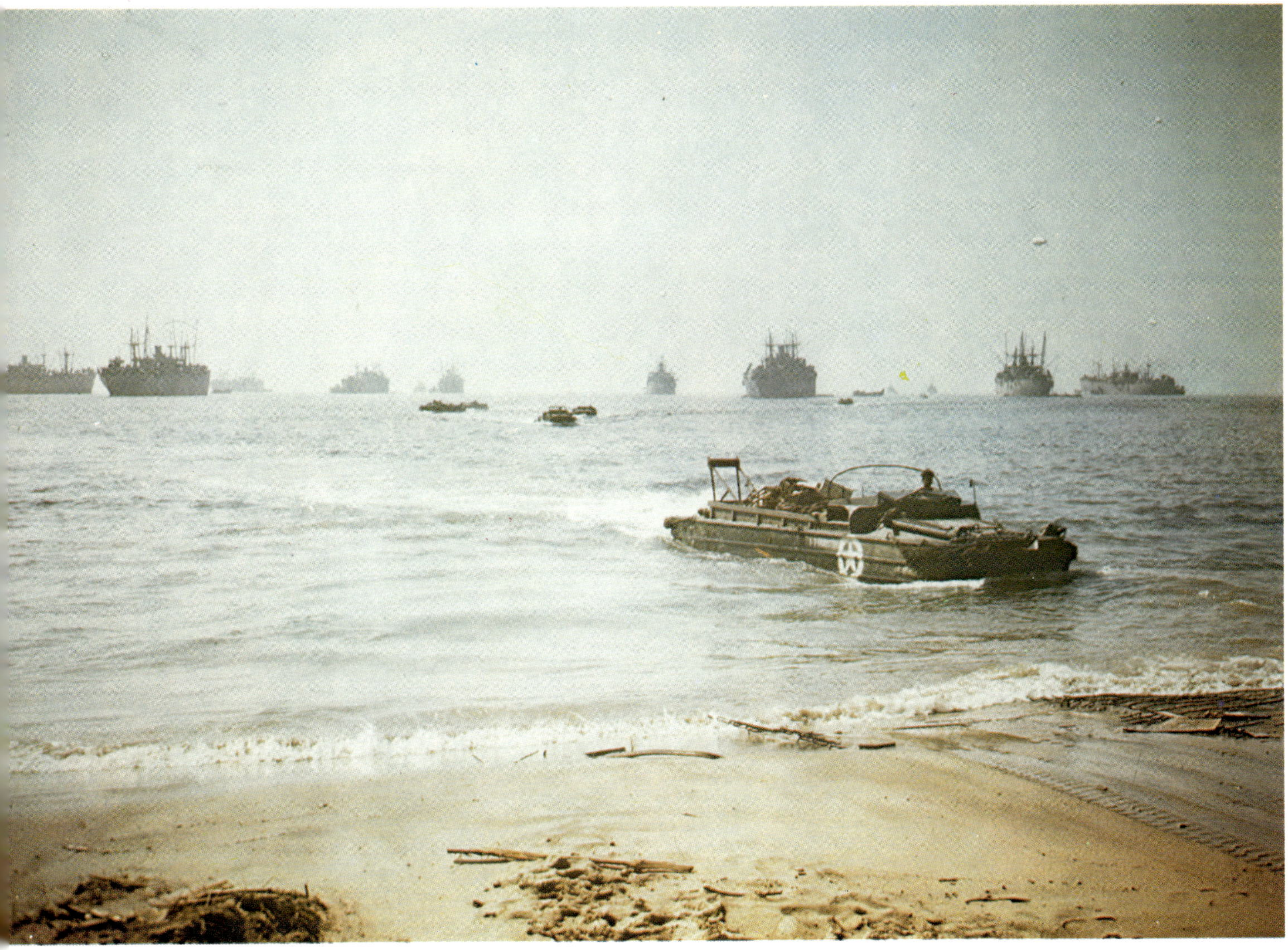

The Landings in Provence. Christened *Anvil* and then *Dragoon*, these were literally imposed on the British and French by the Americans, who considered it to be the essential complement to the operation launched in Normandy. Owing to the weakness of the German defences and the magnitude of the resources deployed by the Allies – four American assault divisions, French Army Group B in reserve, 2000 front-line aircraft, 500 warships – the landings (a scene from which is shown in the photograph) were accomplished without any major difficulties, surprise and fine weather contributing to the success of the operation. By the evening of 15 Aug. the Allies had established two bridgeheads between Cavalaire and Théoule.

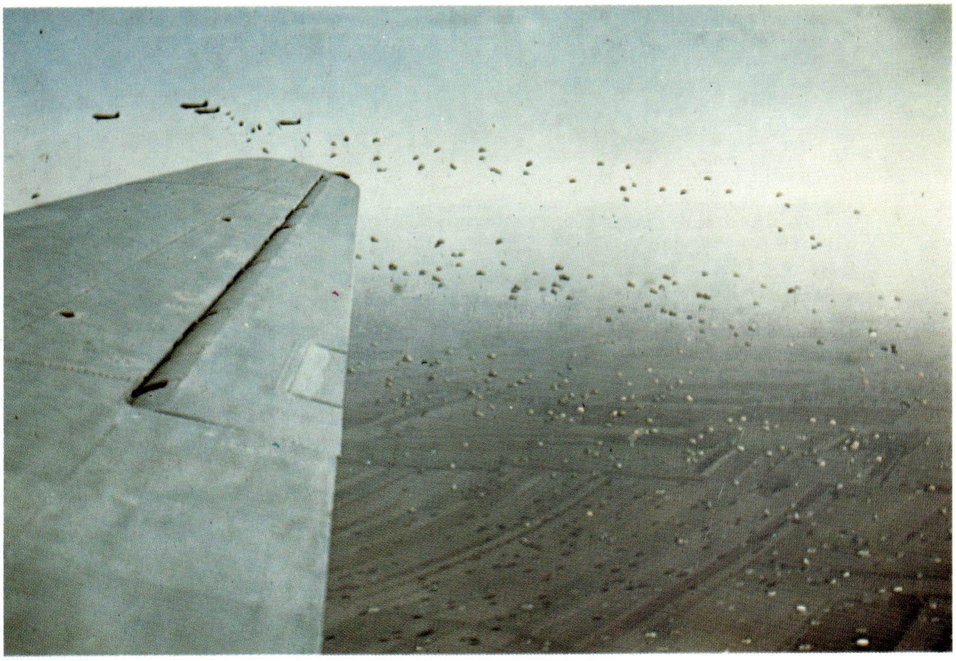

Early on 15 Aug. the landing in Provence was preceded by a large airborne operation behind the German forces in the Muy region. This operation, carried out by Rugby Force, involved the 10,000 men of the American 1st Airborne Division of General Frederick carried by 535 planes and 465 gliders. It proved to be a complete success with relatively few losses, less than 200 dead and wounded. By blocking the approach from the valley of the Argens early on, the operation made the bridgehead secure against German attack.

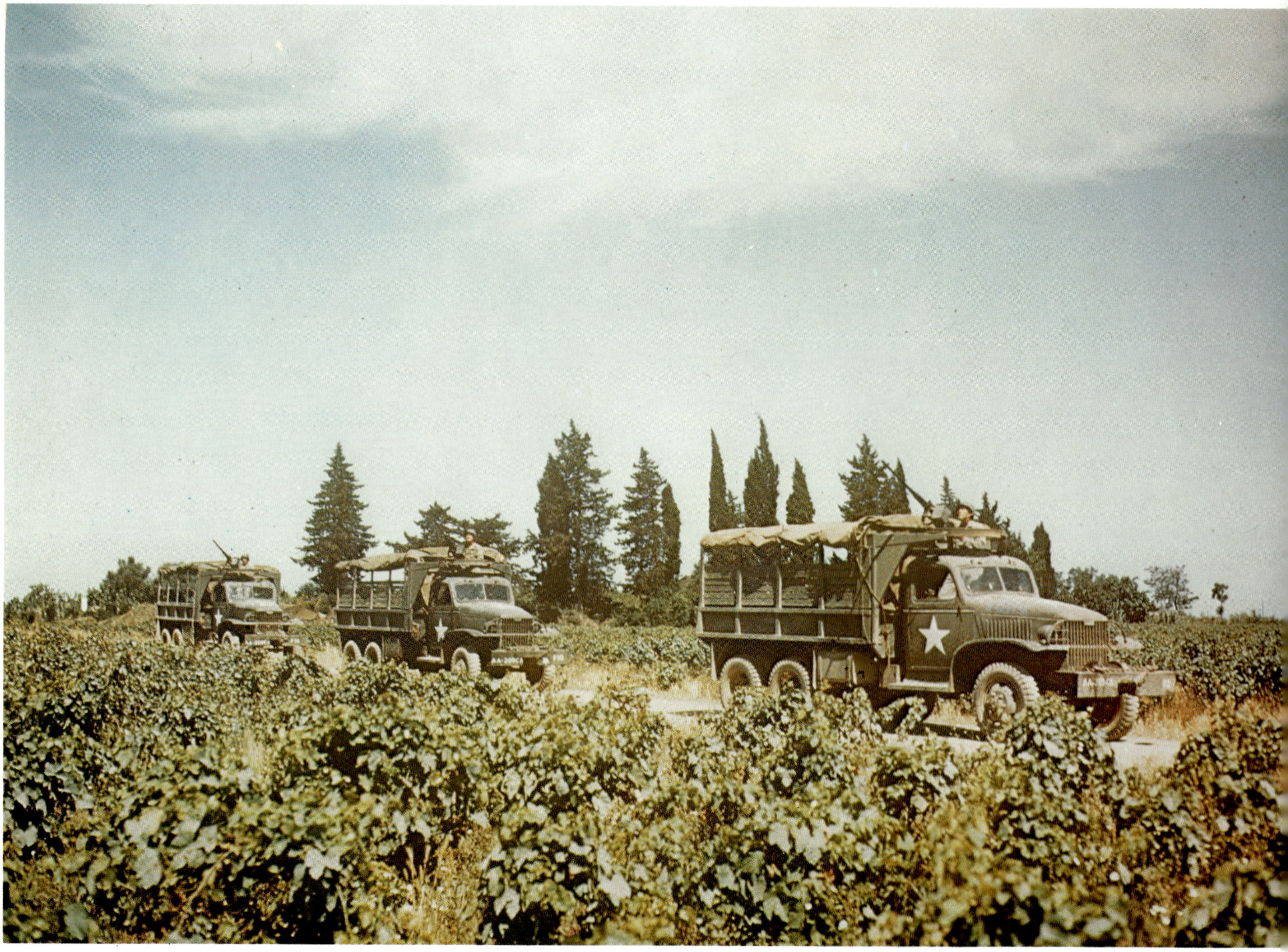

Following the landings in Provence the Allied advance moved at a swifter pace than had been foreseen, owing to the rapid retreat of the German forces. By 17 Aug. American troops were emerging from Les Maures and L'Esterel and marching in the direction of Aix and the valley of the Rhône, while the French divisions, which had started landing on 16 Aug., were moving forward quickly in the direction of Toulon and Marseilles. Despite fierce resistance these two towns were to be liberated on 23 Aug. and 29 Aug. respectively, a considerable advance on the timetable established by the Allied staffs. Here a column of American lorries are passing through a typically Provençal landscape, without encountering the slightest opposition.

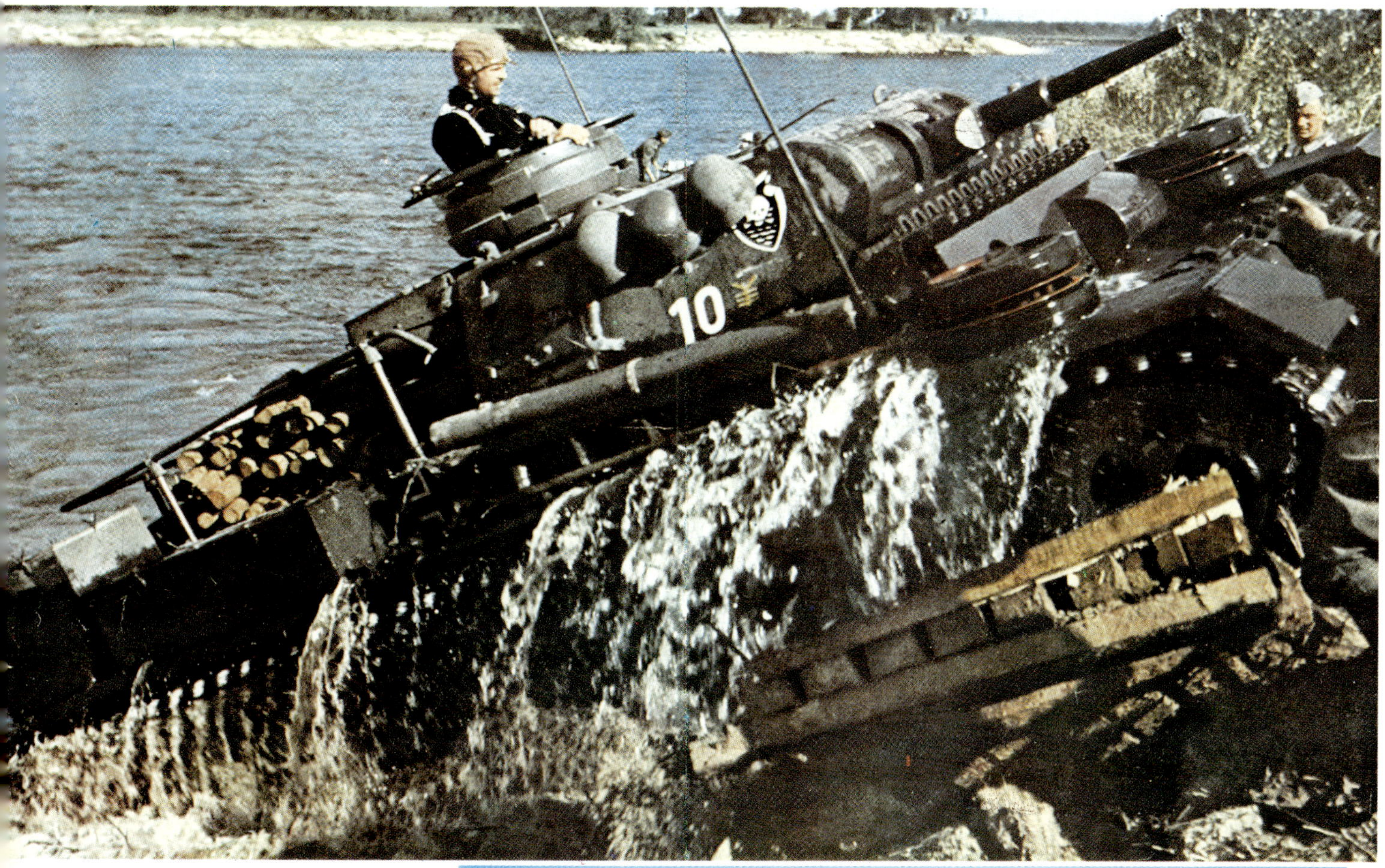

PzKpfw I, II, III and IV. An abbreviation of *Panzerdivision* (armoured division), the word 'Panzer' was to symbolize from 1939 to 1942 the most spectacular results of the Blitzkrieg. Consisting of about 15,000 men, each Panzer division included nearly 250 tanks, as well as battalions of motorized infantry, anti-aircraft units and engineers. Given the task of breaking through the enemy lines and then exploiting the breakthrough, they opened the way for the regular infantry divisions. Here a light tank, the PzKpfw Mark III, is crossing the western side of the Bug, in June 1941, at the beginning of the German offensive in the east. From the beginning of 1943, because of changing circumstances, the Panzer divisions assumed a distinctly more defensive aspect, with an important addition to their equipment in the form of tank destroyers.

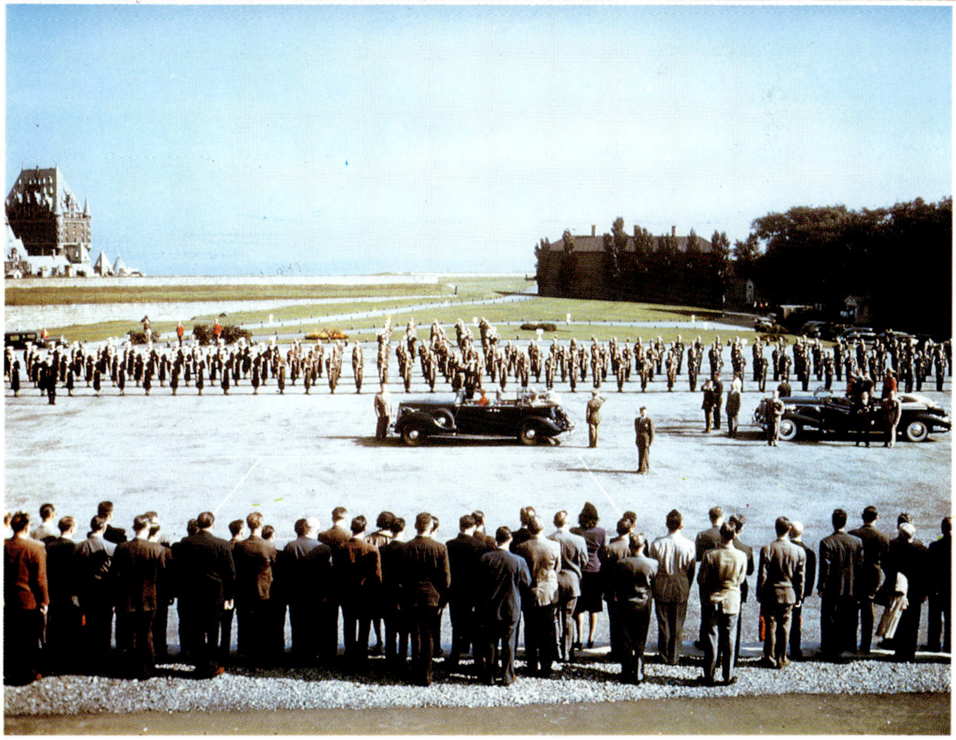

The Quebec Conference. The second Quebec Conference, which brought Roosevelt and Churchill together again, took place in Sept. 1944 at a time when the victory of the Anglo-American forces in France was assured. Here we see the arrival of Roosevelt's car on the esplanade of the citadel of Quebec which towers over the St Lawrence river. The meeting brought out some differences between the two great men. Roosevelt did not evince much enthusiasm for Churchill's proposal that they should open negotiations with Stalin about the allocation of spheres of influence in Europe. However, the two statesmen did agree on the future American and British occupation zones in Germany. The most remarkable outcome of the conference, however, was the decision by Roosevelt and Churchill to adopt the Morgenthau plan which proposed to reduce Germany to a purely agricultural country, given over to stock breeding and crop growing. The plan was, however, to be abandoned by the two leaders a month later.

Opposite
The RAF. A pilot standing in front of a Brist
Beaufighter.

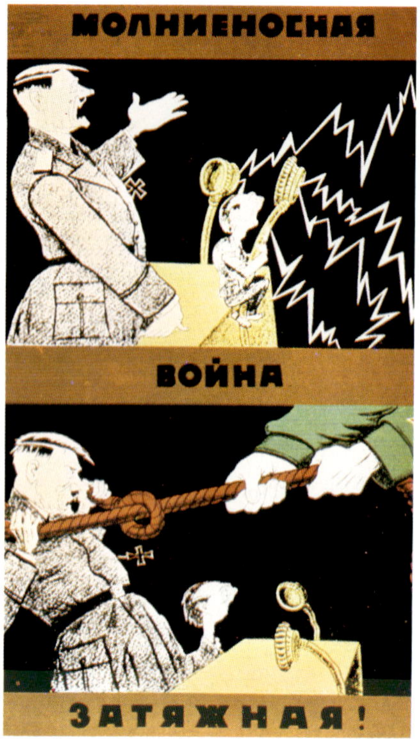

The Radio War. This Soviet caricature of Hitler and Goebbels at the microphone who, having tried to outdo each other in resounding proclamations at the beginning of the war in the east are rendered speechless by their defeats, underlines the importance of the radio war between 1939 and 1945. The radio was not only a propaganda weapon, but also a means of getting round the censorship imposed on the press. With the help of broadcasts from enemy sources, soldiers and civilians of countries at war could get a clearer idea of the political and military situation at the most critical moments. Thus Europeans listened in to Allied or Swiss stations.

Raeder. After a brilliant career in the First World War, Raeder, who became a rear-admiral in 1922 at the age of 46, was named chief of naval command in 1928. Subsequently, when he was appointed commander-in-chief of the German navy in 1933, he embarked upon the development of the new German fleet. An officer of the old school, he devoted all his attention to the big surface vessels and neglected aircraft and submarines. During the war he did not succeed in making his strategic conceptions prevail, notably in the Mediterranean, where he advocated an all-out war against Britain. Finding himself frequently in opposition to Hitler, following the failure of his surface vessels he was induced to retire at the beginning of 1943, and was replaced by Dönitz.

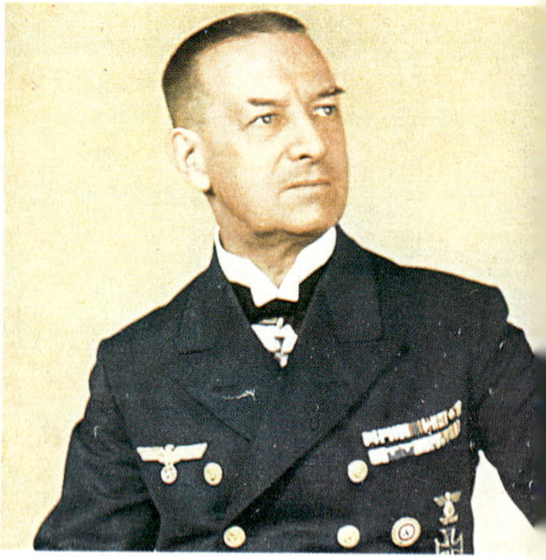

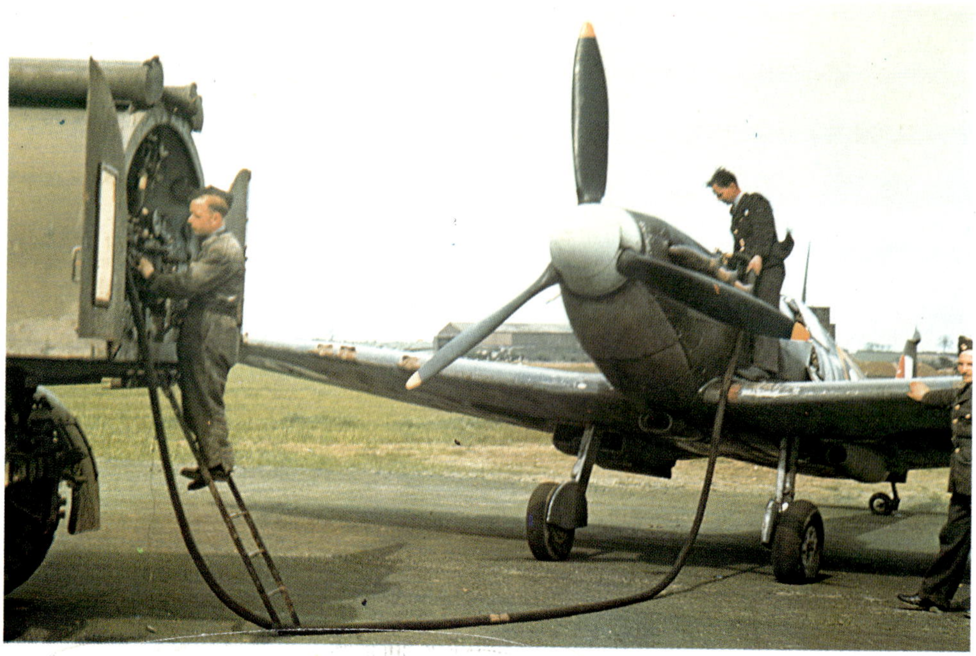

The RAF. At the beginning of the war Fighter Command was the spearhead of the Royal Air Force. With 700 aircraft, the majority Hurricanes and Spitfires, it was to play a decisive role during the summer of 1940, breaking up the attacks by the Luftwaffe and thus dispelling the spectre of invasion. Here, a Spitfire, Fighter Command's most famous aircraft, is being refuelled on an airfield in the south of England.

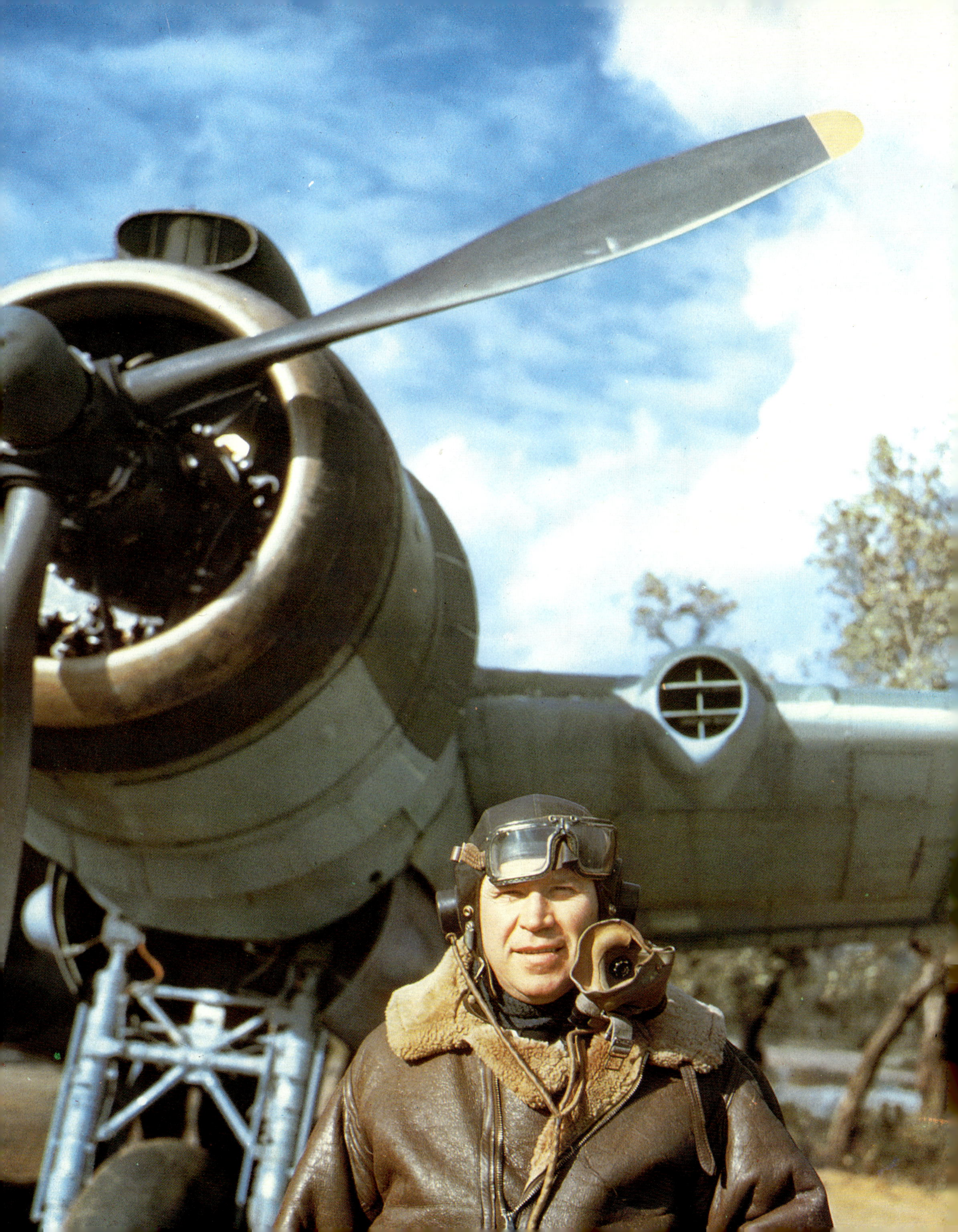

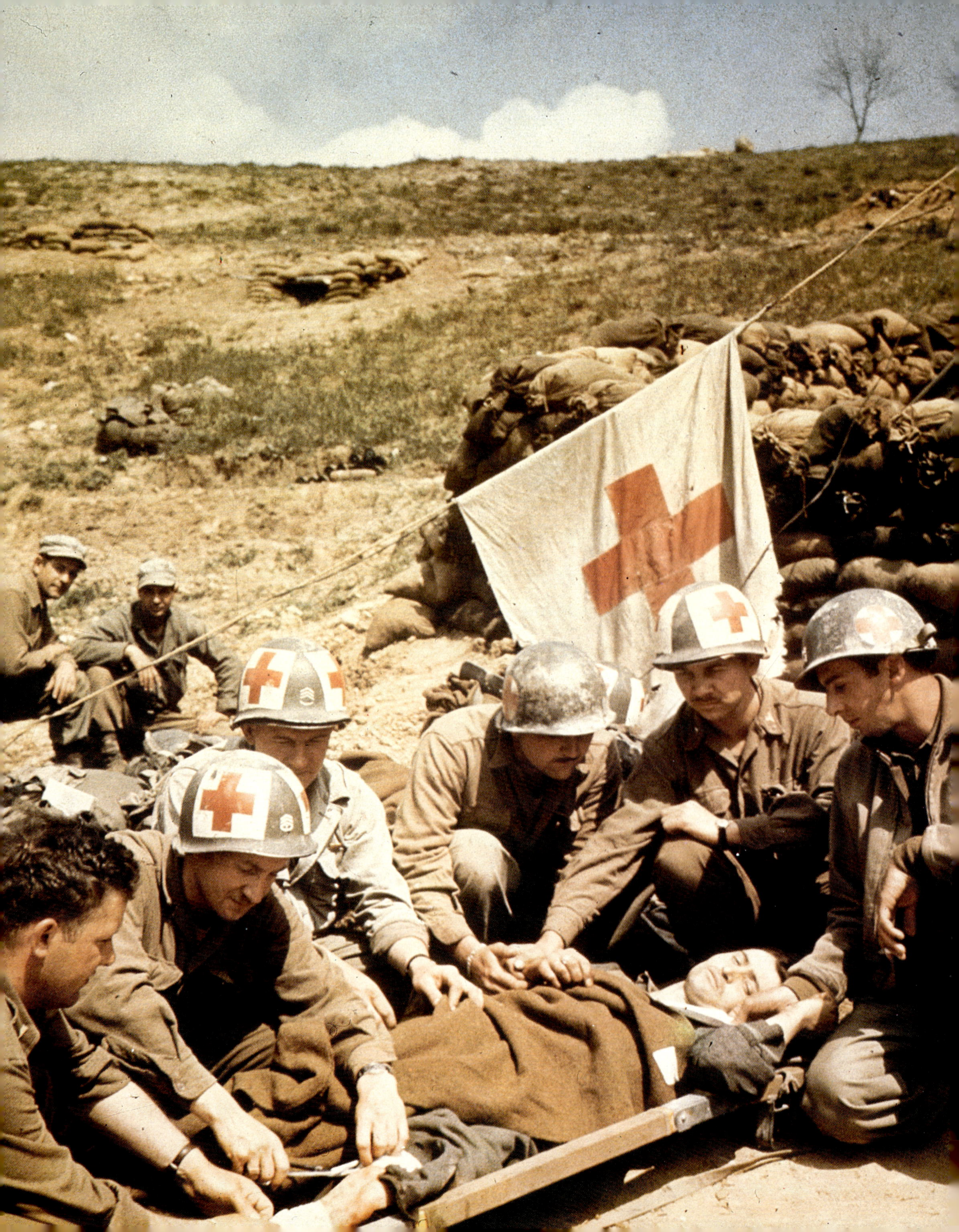

The Red Cross. Soldiers of an American medical unit tending a wounded German.

After the Battle of Britain the RAF increasingly directed its efforts towards the bombing offensive. By means of massive night raids on the main German towns, it hoped to disorganize the economy of the Reich and shatter the morale of the population. Despite spectacular results this objective was not attained and the Allies had to invade in order to bring about a German collapse. Here a group of airmen are passing under the nose of a Short Stirling Mk I heavy bomber, one of the first strategic bombers in service with the RAF.

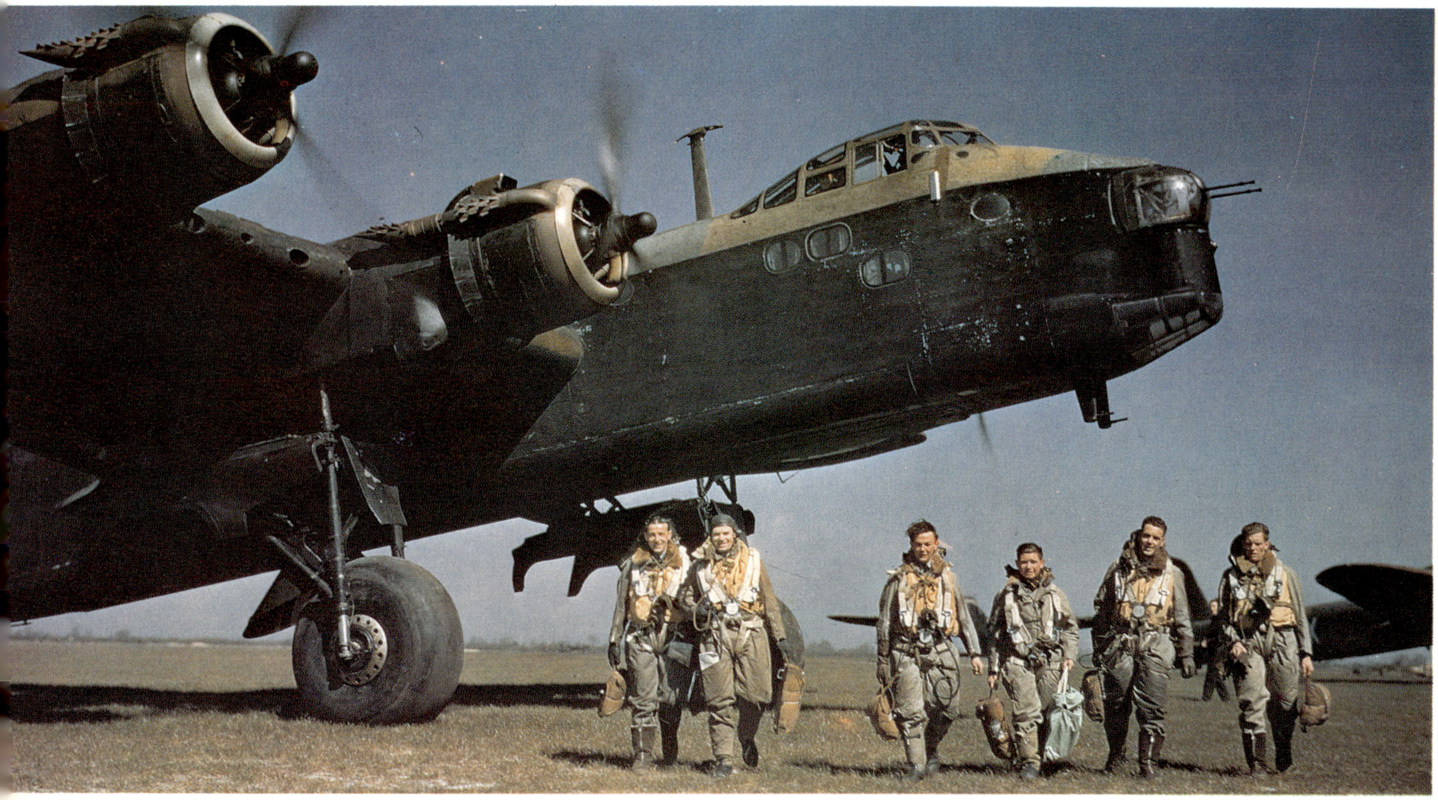

With the growing extent of the conflict, the RAF underwent considerable development and took part in the fighting in every theatre of operation – Europe, North Africa, and the Far East. Here a Bristol Beaufighter fighter bomber is being serviced on an Egyptian airfield. At the end of the war the total strength of the RAF was 9200 aircraft in 487 squadrons. In six years Fighter Command had carried out more than 700,000 sorties and Bomber Command had dropped nearly one million tons of bombs. More than 70,000 aircrew had been killed on all fronts.

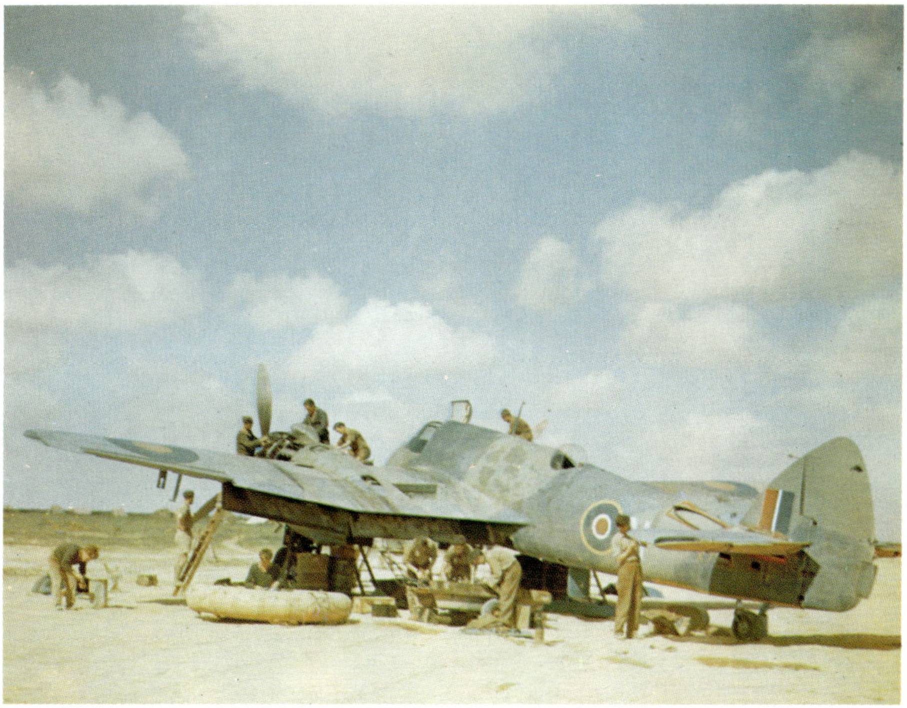

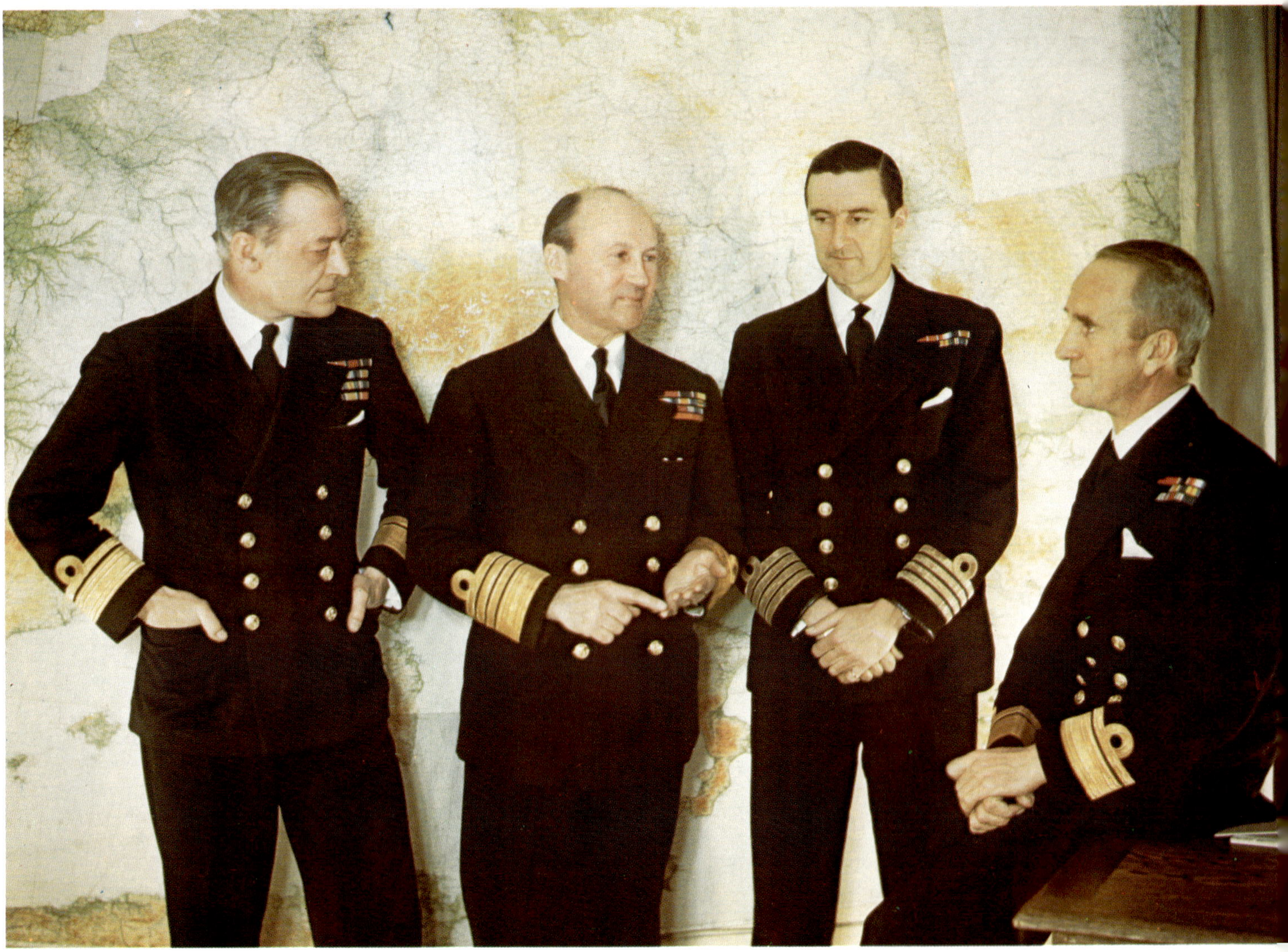

Ramsay. Appointed vice-admiral in 1939, Bertram Ramsay, seen here in the centre, was to play a major role in certain phases of the war. As commander-in-chief at Dover, he directed the evacuation from Dunkirk in May 1940. As assistant to Cunningham, he prepared and put into operation the large-scale landings in the Mediterranean, notably in Sicily. However, it was in 1944 that he was to give the greatest proof of his efficiency by organizing and directing the whole naval side of the Normandy landing, as part of Operation Neptune. He was to die six months later in an aircraft accident.

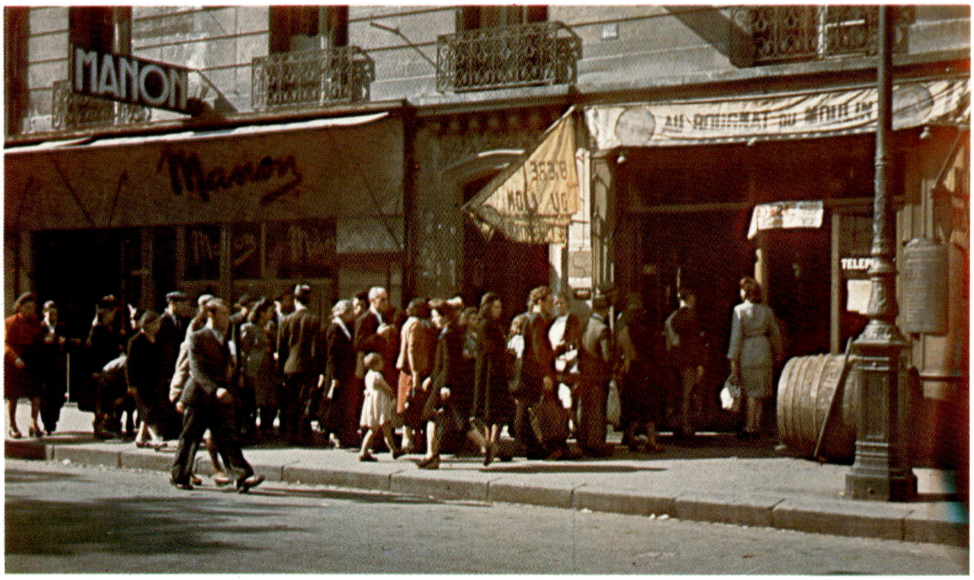

Rationing. During 1939–40, as a result of mobilization, the fall in agricultural production and the reduction in imports, all the countries at war found that they had to introduce rationing in order to allow the population as a whole to obtain essential items at fixed prices. This rationing was accompanied by restrictions which varied greatly from one country to another: insignificant in the United States, bearable in Britain and Germany, very severe in the countries of occupied Europe and even more so in the USSR. As this photograph, taken in the Les Halles district of Paris, shows, rationing often brought lengthy queues with it.

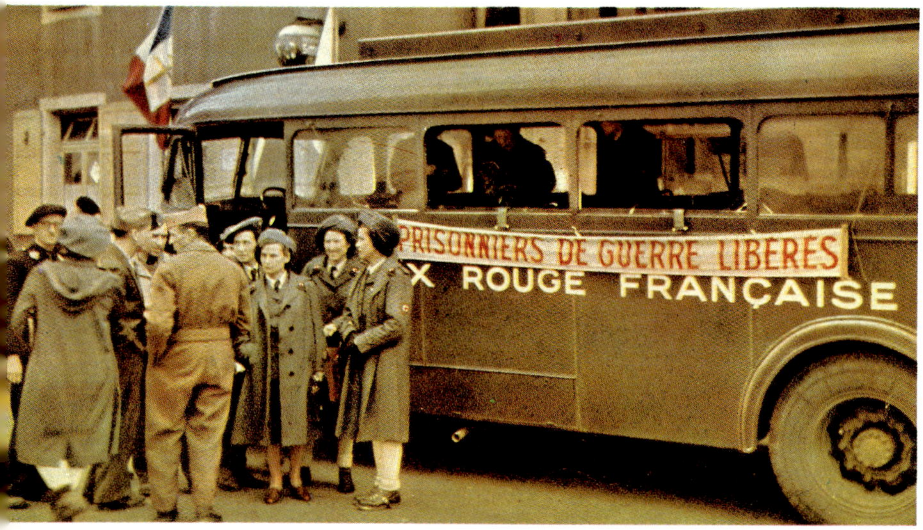

The Red Cross. Founded in 1865, the Red Cross organization played a considerable part throughout the war in trying to see that the Geneva Conventions were observed, particularly as they affected prisoners of war. The International Committee set up a central register, visited 8000 camps, distributed letters and parcels and carried out repatriations. Its actions in regard to civilians and refugees were less effective and it was powerless to help those who had been deported. Likewise, the USSR's refusal to adhere to the convention of 1929 had bad consequences for the prisoners of both sides who were captured on the eastern front. This picture shows a scene at Karlsruhe in Germany, in 1945, during the repatriation of former French prisoners of war.

Refugees. With the defeats of the Allied armies in May and June 1940 came a massive exodus of refugees from northern, eastern and even central France. Those who fled feared bombing attacks or that the front would eventually stabilize, bringing in its turn the hardships of enemy occupation. This exodus, in which the most varied means of transport were used, helped to paralyse Allied troop movements.

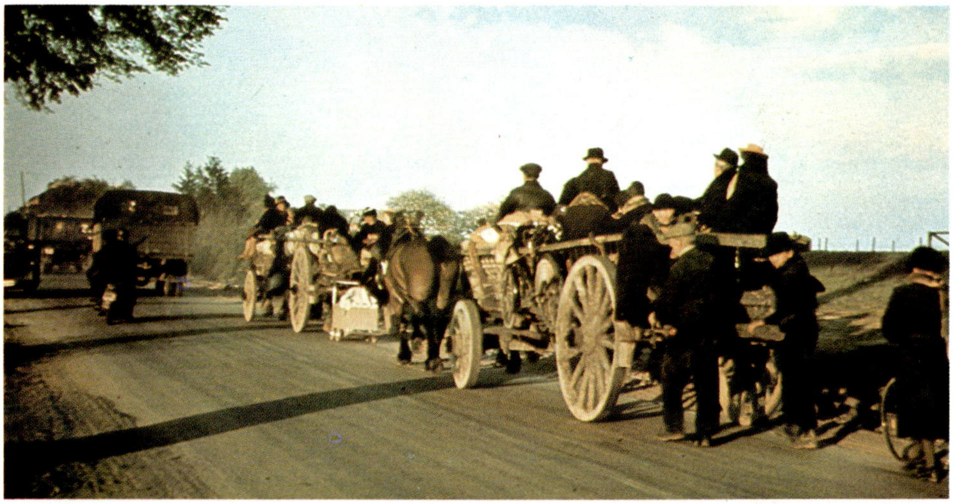

The Reich Chancellery. Hitler's study in the new Reich Chancellery is a perfect illustration of the Führer's intention of creating a grandiose and monumental building in neo-classical style in the heart of a new Berlin, in accordance with the 'will to power' of the new regime. The new building was constructed in a record time of less than one year under the direction of the Führer's personal architect, Albert Speer, and inaugurated on 12 Jan. 1939 with a reception for the diplomatic corps. It was in the bunker beneath the Chancellery that Hitler committed suicide on 30 April 1945. The Chancellery building, which had been badly damaged in air raids, was finally pulled down by the Soviet military authorities and some of the building materials were used in the construction of the Soviet war memorial in Berlin.

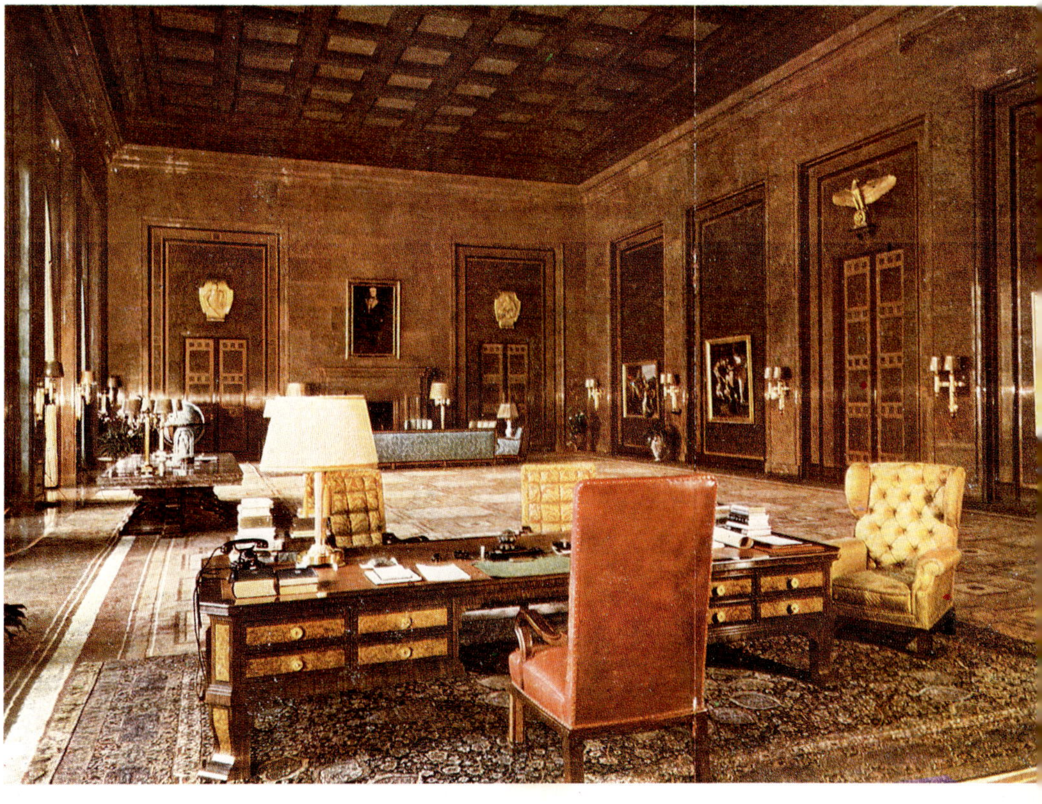

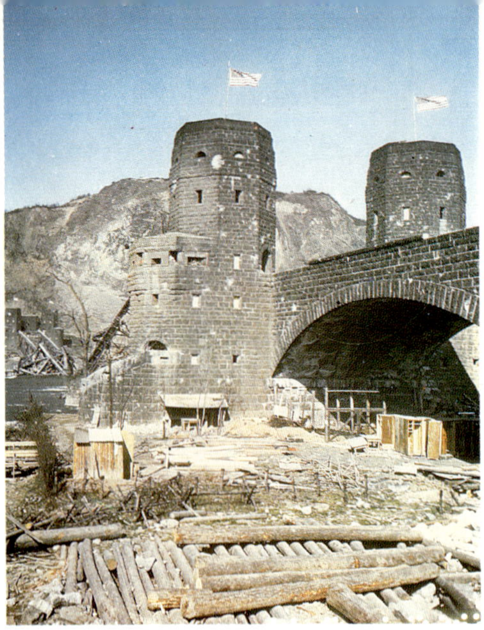

Remagen. The capture on 7 March 1945 at Remagen, of the only bridge left intact on the Rhine – the Germans, in a state of complete disorganization had not succeeded in blowing it up – enabled the Americans to establish a first bridgehead of four divisions on the right bank of the river. In their endeavours to put right a 'national catastrophe' the Germans attempted to destroy the bridge by a wide variety of means: artillery, aircraft, V2s and naval frogmen, but all in vain. Eventually, on 17 March, the structure collapsed, wrecked by explosions and heavy traffic. By then, however, the Americans had had sufficient time to instal two pontoon bridges as a replacement.

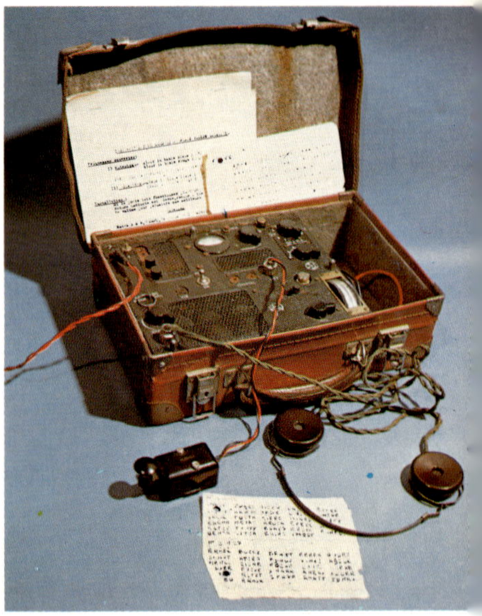

The Resistance. From 1943 onwards the Resistance assumed increasing importance in Europe. There were many reasons: hatred of the occupying power, the requisition of the labour force, the participation of the Communists, and the parachute drops of arms by the Allies. Resistance took a variety of forms: the formation of maquis units, the passing on of intelligence, actual attacks on the enemy and acts of sabotage. These all greatly intensified in 1944 at the time of the Allied offensive in Italy and the landings in France. Here we see the result of the sabotage of a train in northern Italy.

The resistance was strengthened by the use of modern technology: liaison aircraft, parachute drops, explosives, which were easy to use, and most of all, radio transmitters and receivers. At a time when transistors did not yet exist, these sets were sufficiently miniaturized to be hidden in a small suitcase. They enabled an isolated agent to transmit coded messages over a long distance. Here we see an English-made A Mark III set with a range of over 300 miles (500 km), which worked from mains or from batteries. This kind of apparatus was supplied to the resistance in northern France by SOE and British intelligence. Musée de l'Armée.

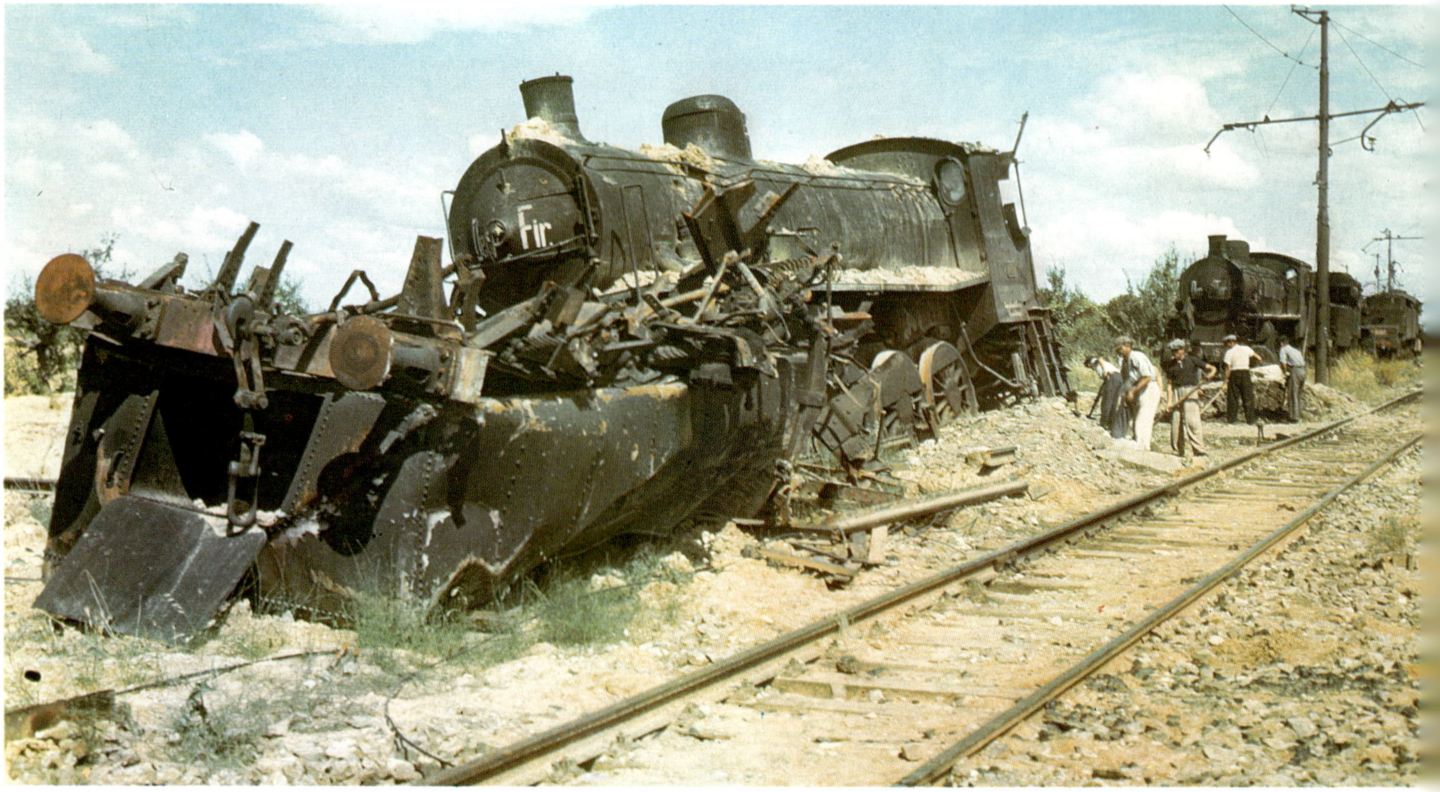

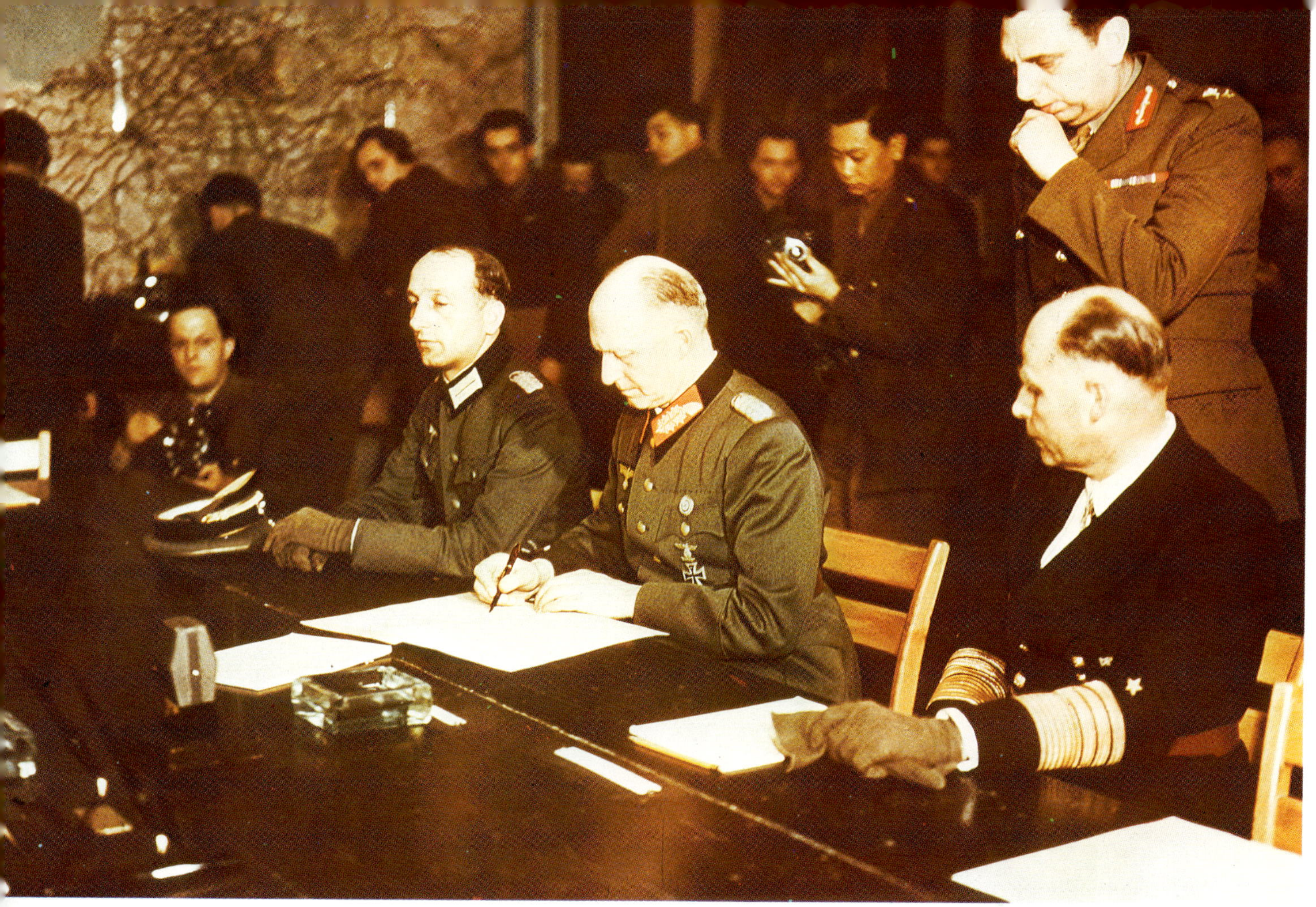

The Surrender at Rheims. The Third Reich's dream of domination over Europe finally collapsed on 7 May 1945, with the signing by General Jodl, accompanied by Admiral von Friedeburg (on the right), of the capitulation of all German forces in the east as well as in the west. The very brief ceremony took place at Rheims, at Eisenhower's headquarters in the visitors' room of a vocational school. The commander-in-chief did not wish to take part and was represented by his chief of staff, Bedell-Smith. Three senior officers, a Briton, a Russian and a Frenchman, were present at the surrender as witnesses. Two days later, during the night of 8–9 May, at a ceremony held in the main hall of the Karlhorst School for Non-Commissioned Officers in Berlin, the German delegation, led by Field Marshal Keitel, acknowledged, for the second time, the unconditional surrender of all the German armed forces.

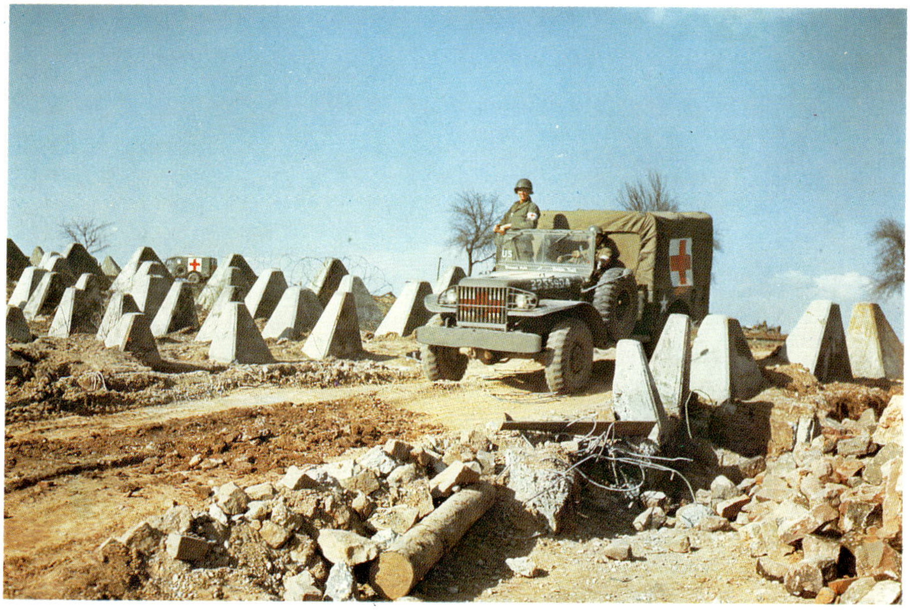

The Rhineland. Following the liberation of Belgium and France the Allied armies attempted to get possession of the Rhineland, cross the Rhine and penetrate into the heartland of Germany before winter. This attempt did not succeed owing to the failure of the airborne operation at Arnhem (Sept. 1944) and to the stiffening of German resistance all along the frontier, particularly on the outskirts of Aachen. During the autumn Allied progress became slow and costly. Quite apart from German resistance, the Allies also had to overcome the defences of the Siegfried Line. Here an ambulance is passing a series of antitank obstacles, known as dragon's teeth.

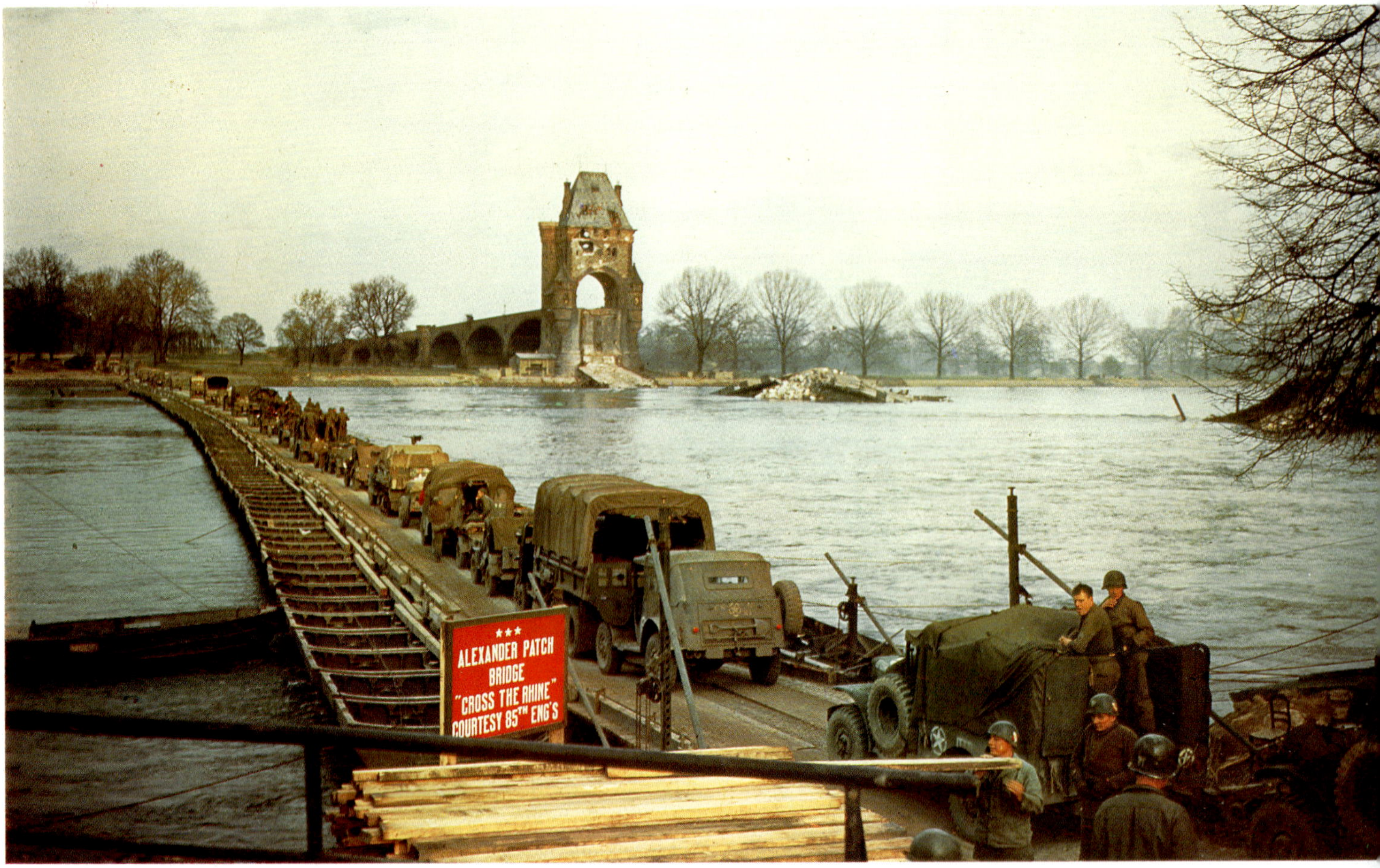

It was only in March 1945, after they had overcome the disorganization caused by the German counter-offensive in the Ardennes and had crushed all resistance on the left bank of the Rhine, that the Allied troops reached the river which denied them access to the heartland of Germany. The Allies possessed considerable resources – 87 divisions and more than 10,000 aircraft – facing an enemy worn down by the recent fighting, for the operation of crossing the Rhine, which had been prepared in minute detail and was to be completely successful everywhere. The much-feared obstacle had been passed by the end of the month. In this photograph units of the 7th US Army of General Patch are crossing the Rhine at Worms on a pontoon bridge, set up by a battalion of engineers alongside the old bridge, which has been destroyed.

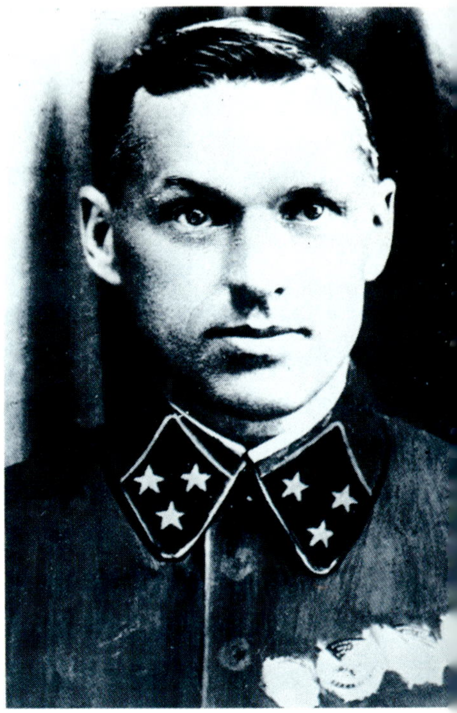

Rokossovsky. Marshal Konstantin Rokossovsky, who had been a victim of the 1938 purges but was later reinstated, led the first Soviet counter-attack against the German invasion of June 1941, later helping the inexperienced Russian armies to force their way out of Smolensk in August. After a notable display in the defence of Moscow, Rokossovsky was involved in defending Stalingrad, where his army broke through decisively, thus enabling Soviet forces to move south and encircle Paulus' Sixth Army. At the Battle of Kursk, Rokossovsky and Vatutin repelled the German onslaught for a week, after which the Germans fell back. In the summer of 1944, Rokossovsky took Lublin, Brest-Litovsk and Bobryusk, before nearly reaching Warsaw in July. With a reorganization of the fronts at the beginning of 1945, he resumed his advance by taking Warsaw and Danzig, thus trapping the Germans in East Prussia.

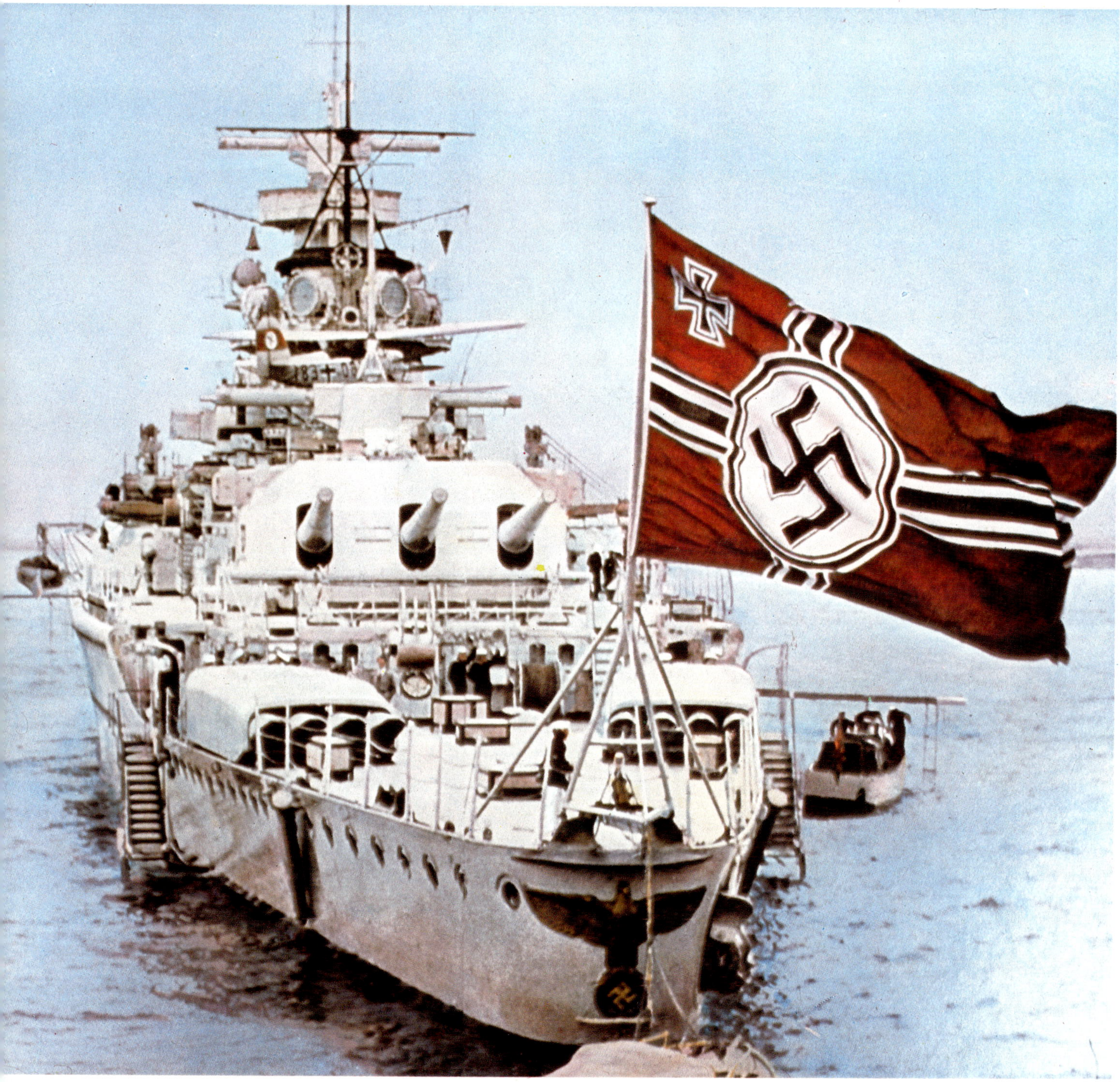

The Battle of the River Plate. This, the first big naval engagement of the war, was a clash between the pocket battleship *Graf Spee* (photograph) and three British cruisers, in Dec. 1939. Although it had put one of its adversaries out of action, the German vessel, whose capacity for action remained unimpaired, took refuge in the port of Montevideo. Under the impression that he was blockaded by vastly superior forces, the commander of the *Graf Spee*, Captain Langsdorff, decided on 17 Dec. to scuttle his ship in the estuary of the River Plate, committing suicide in Buenos Aires on the following day. This dramatic episode led world opinion to the belief that the new German navy was lacking in fighting spirit.

Opposite
Rome. American soldiers in the liberated capital in June 1944.

Rome. According to the plans of the Allied staffs, drawn up at the time of the landing at Salerno, Rome should have fallen before the end of 1943. However, because of the fierce resistance put up by German troops around Cassino, the taking of Rome was delayed by six months. The Eternal City did not fall until 4 June 1944, after the breaching of the Winter Line and following a virtual race between Allied divisions. It was the Americans who won. Here a group of soldiers of the US Fifth Army are moving through the Roman Compagna shortly before entering the capital, which had been proclaimed an 'open city' by the Germans.

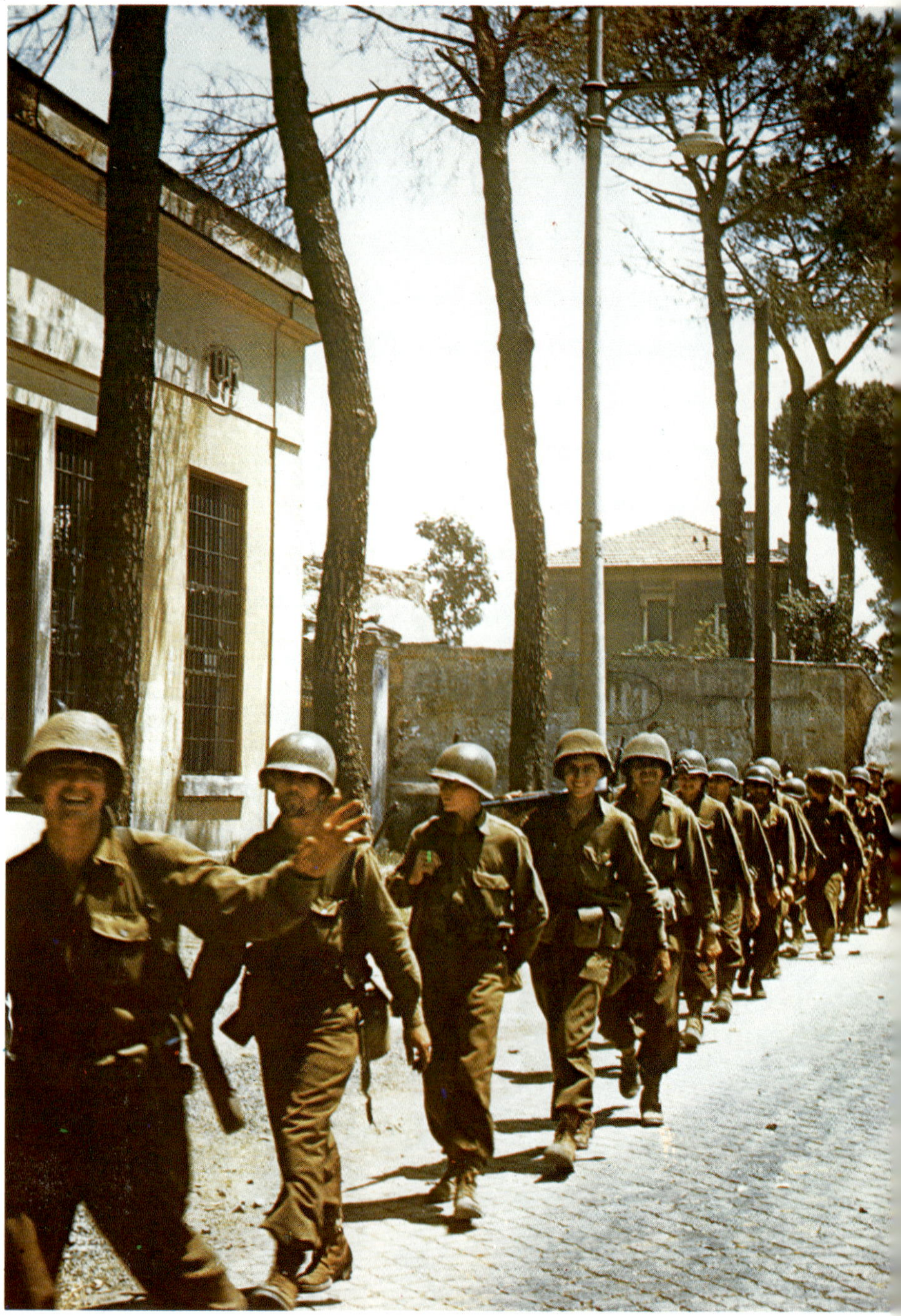

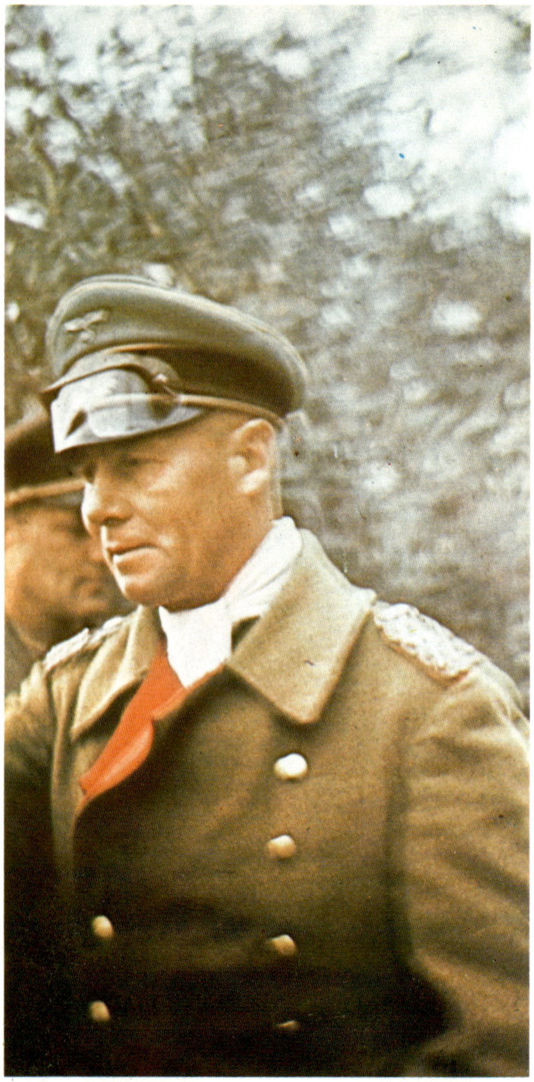

Rommel. An infantry officer during the First World War, his military career underwent a notable change of course when the Wehrmacht was created, and he became a brilliant commander of armoured units. During the campaign in France and the war in North Africa, he showed exceptional qualities as a tactician and as a leader of men, limited at times by a lack of an overall strategic view and a poor evaluation of the logistics of the conflict. For a long time a supporter of the Nazi regime and of its leader, whose complete confidence he enjoyed, he was plagued by misgivings after the Normandy landings and joined, somewhat reluctantly, the conspiracy which was to come to a head with the attempt on Hitler's life in July 1944. Compromised, Field Marshal Rommel was driven to commit suicide in Oct. 1944.

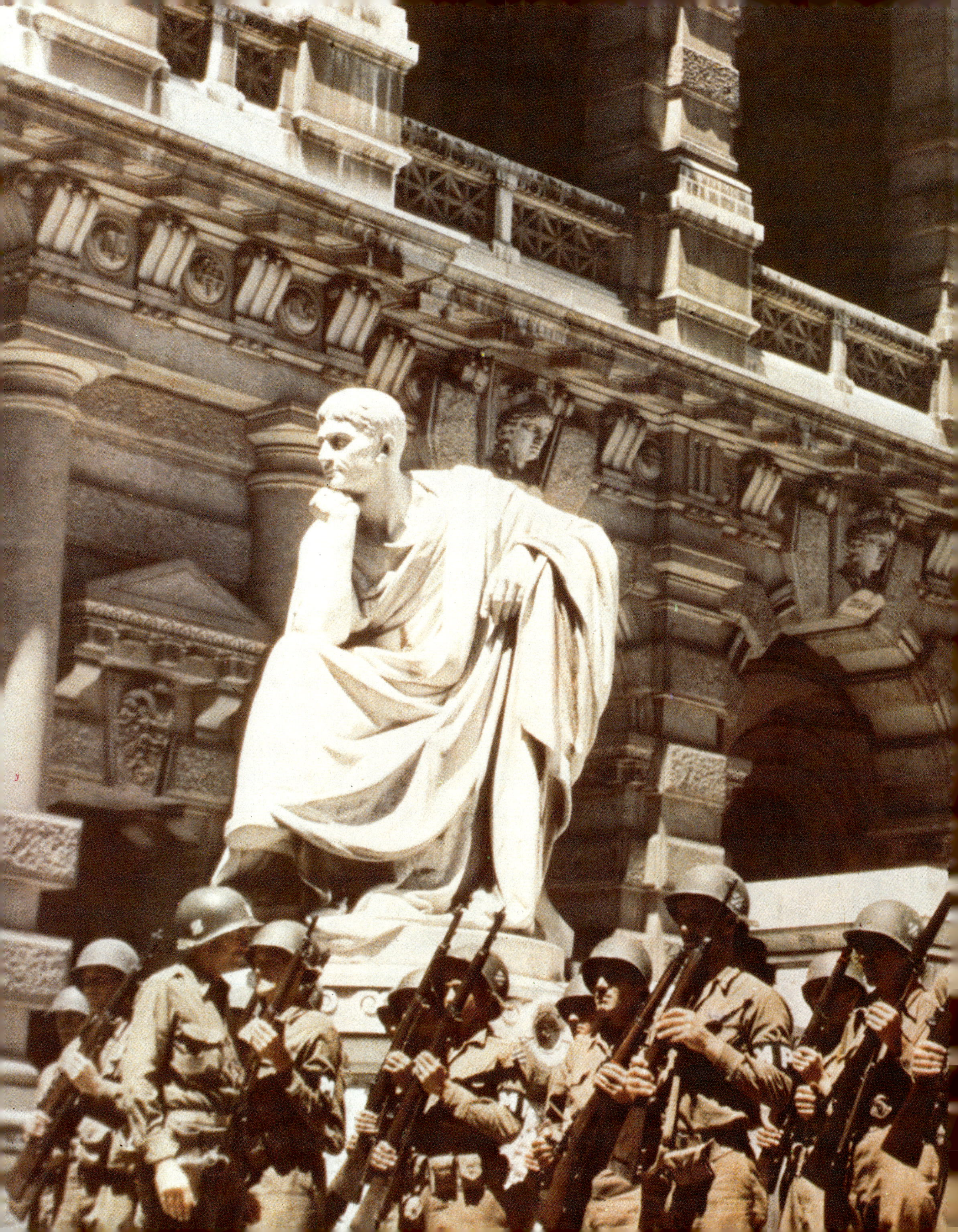

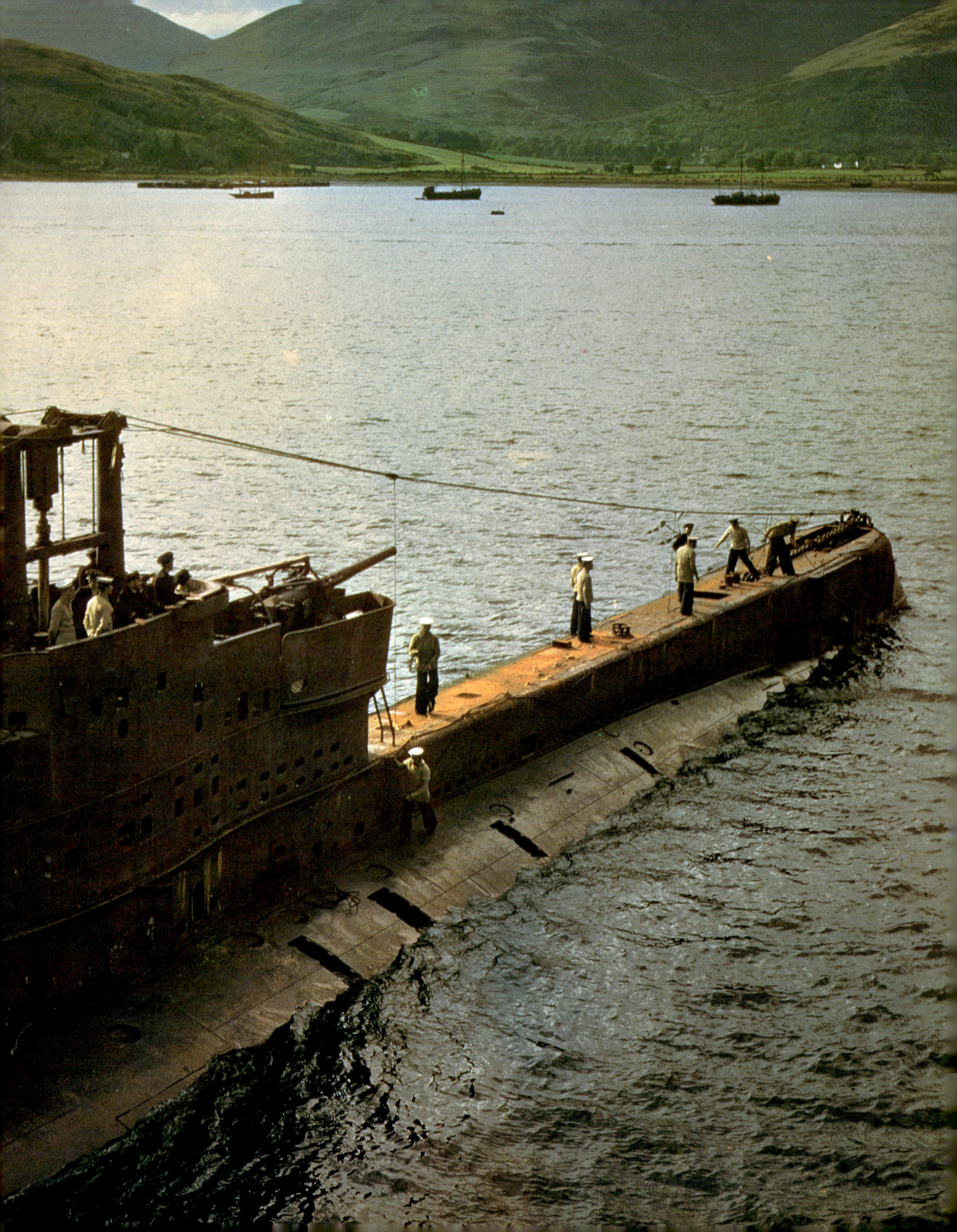

he Royal Navy. A British submarine return-
g to its base in Scotland.

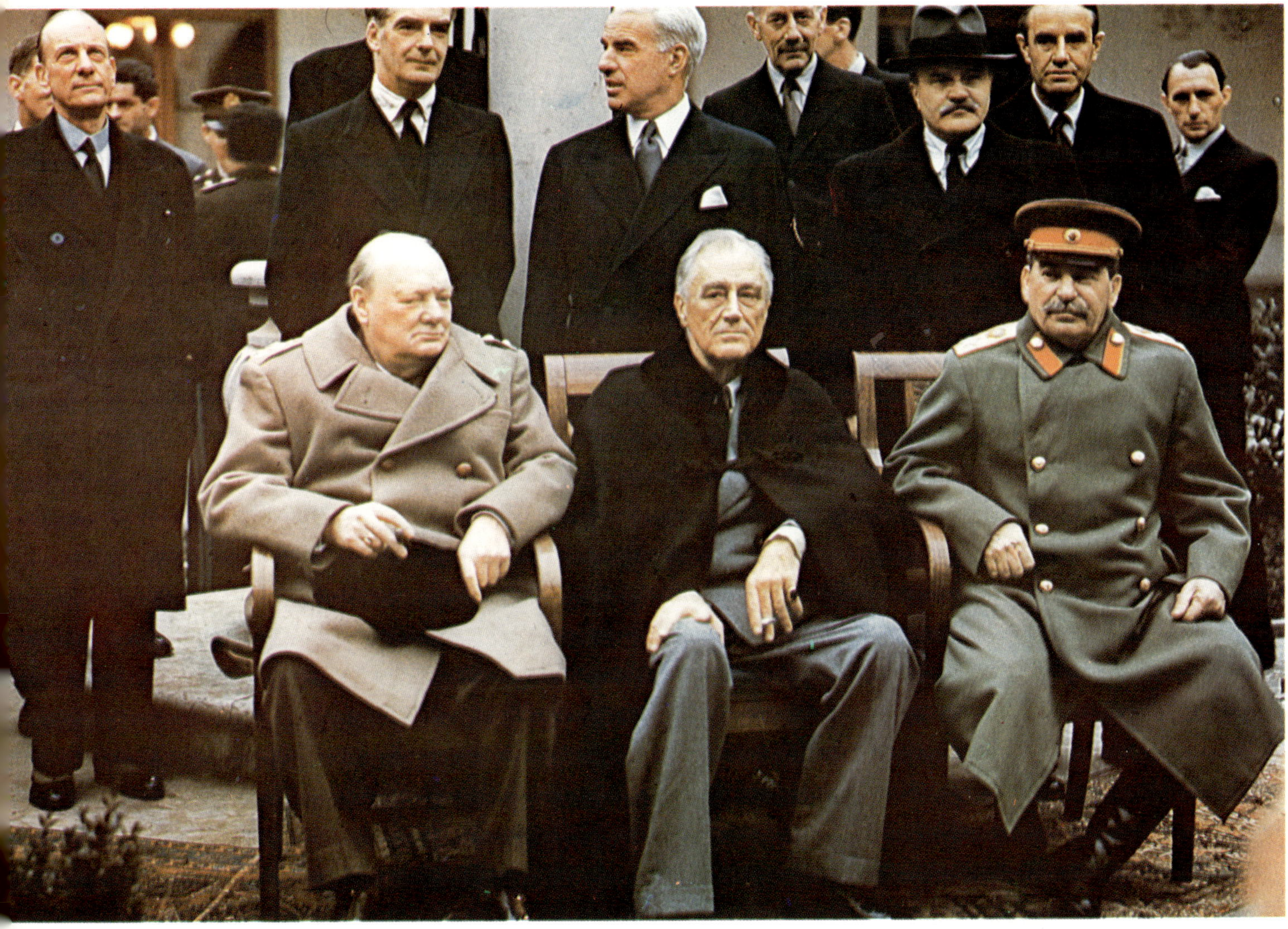

Roosevelt. President of the United States from 1933 to 1945, this great statesman was to have a far-reaching influence on world events during this decisive period and helped to make his country the leading economic and military power. However, the results he obtained sometimes fell far short of his aims and efforts, and his policy was not without its contradictions. It was the war rather than the energetic measures of the New Deal which enabled America to emerge from the economic crisis. A bitter opponent of totalitarian regimes, after Pearl Harbor Roosevelt threw the whole weight of the American forces into the conflict, but victory over Germany could be secured only with the decisive support of the Soviet Union which was subjected to Stalin's brutal tyranny. The dream of maintaining the grand alliance between the USA and the USSR was already fading as early as 1944. Here we see the president at the Yalta conference in Feb. 1945, a few weeks before his death. Worn down by illness, he was only a shadow of his former self.

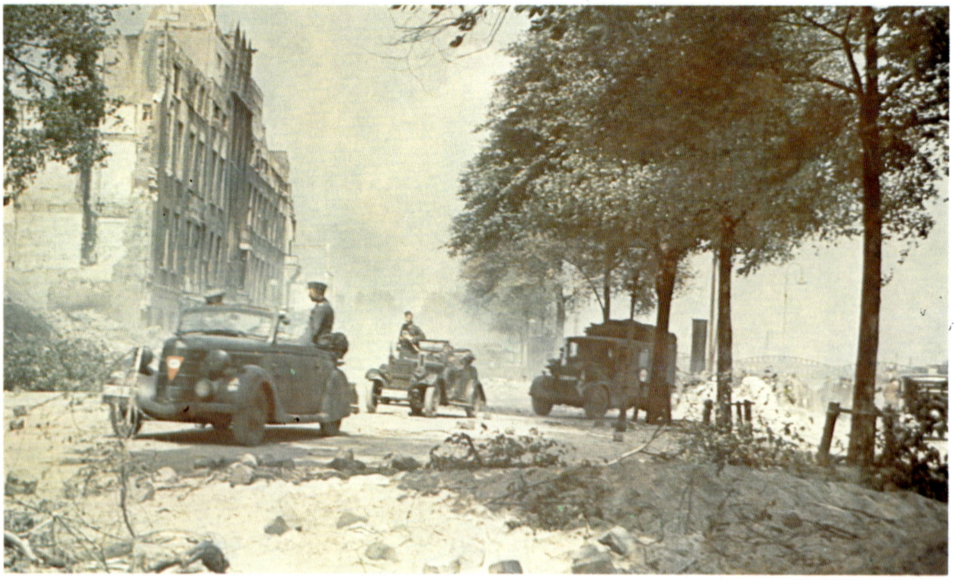

Rotterdam. Launched on 14 May 1940 despite a last-minute countermand the bombardment of Rotterdam by the Luftwaffe had important strategic consequences. Leaving more than 800 dead and 78,000 homeless, it led to the surrender of the city and induced the Dutch army command to order its troops to lay down their arms, for fear of similar raids on other towns. The bombardment of Rotterdam also aroused feelings of panic in Belgium and France, thus adding to the flood of refugees, especially since it was rumoured to have caused the deaths of 35,000 civilians.

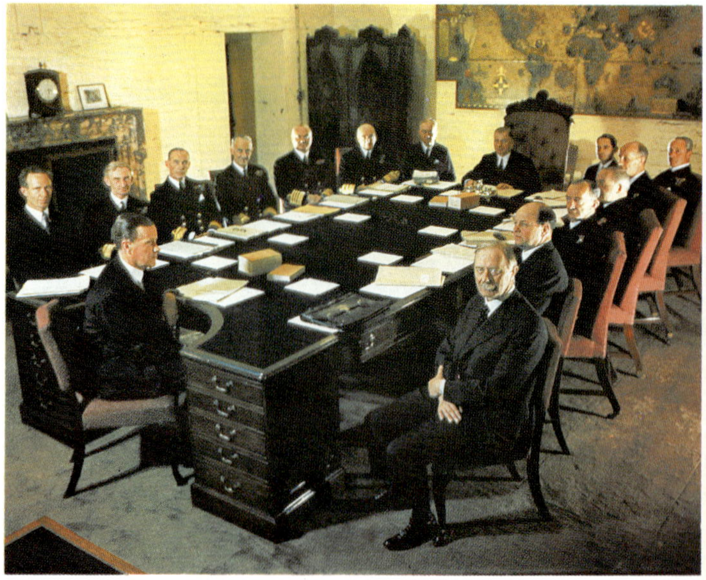

The Royal Navy. This photograph, taken in July 1943, shows a meeting of the Admiralty. Throughout the Second World War, despite belated rearmament, the Royal Navy displayed its traditional qualities of efficiency. It ensured the protection of the British Isles against attack from the sea, the defence of vital lines of communication and the supply of armies engaged in distant theatres of war. In collaboration with the US Navy, it was to play a major role in the landings of 1943–4.

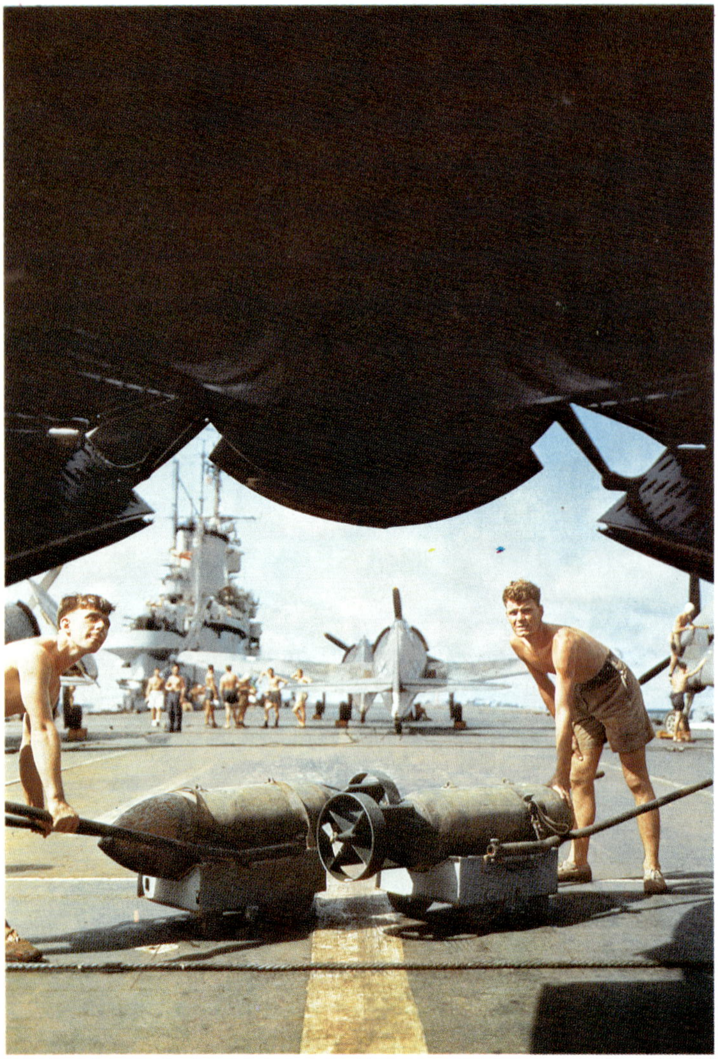

During the conflict the Royal Navy, after having neglected the role of the submarine and, even more, the aeroplane, was to undergo a remarkable transformation. From 1939–40, with the help of a vast programme of escort ships, emphasis was placed on the development of anti-submarine forces. At the same time a special effort was directed towards the building of aircraft carriers which had replaced battleships as the main warships. In this photograph, taken in Jan. 1945 on board the aircraft carrier *Indomitable*, off Sumatra, armourers are preparing to load bombs on to aircraft to be used to attack oil installations.

Following the surrender of Germany the Royal Navy proceeded to reinforce its Far Eastern units in order to be able to play an effective part in the fight against Japan. Under the command of Admiral Rawlings, Task Force 57 comprised four aircraft carriers, two battleships, five cruisers and ten destroyers. In action at the Admiralty Islands, it participated in the Battle of Okinawa by attacking bases in Formosa and the Ryukyu Islands. Here the battleship *Howe* is seen passing through the Suez Canal on its way to the Pacific.

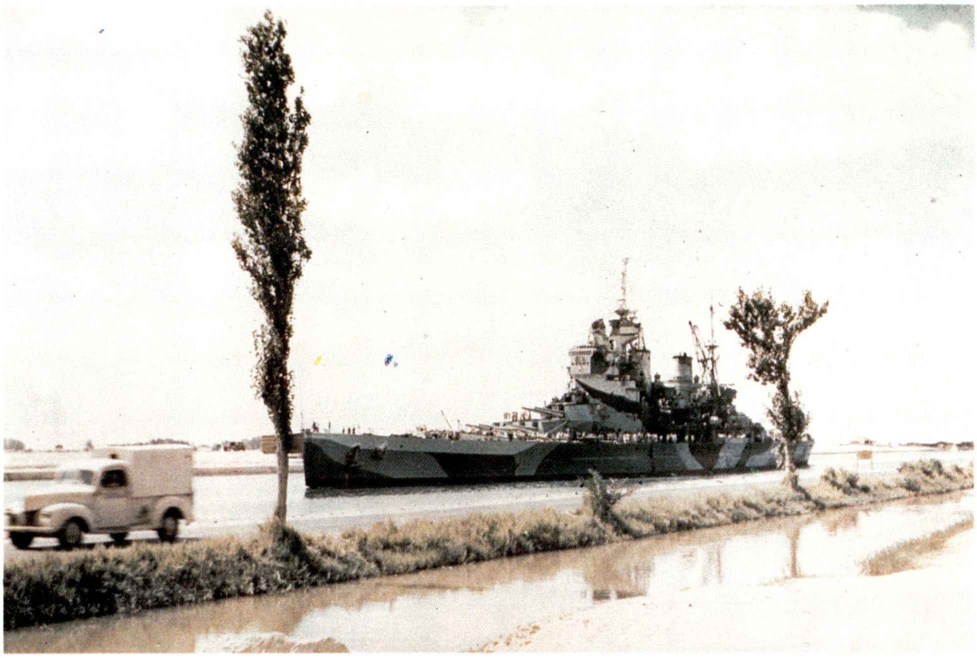

The RSHA. After he had taken power, by a series of decrees Hitler set about the reorganization of the police forces within the Reich and entrusted the task of coordination to the SS. Reichsführer SS Heinrich Himmler was placed at the head of this vast apparatus, while his deputy, Heydrich, was given special responsibility from 1939 onwards for the running of the Reichssicherheitshauptamt or Chief Office of Security of the Reich, which included, in particular, the criminal police and the ruthless Secret State Police or Gestapo. In this photograph, taken on the occasion of manoeuvres in Austria in the spring of 1939, there can be seen together with Hitler and his general staff, the two supreme heads of the new organization: Himmler (in the centre, with folded hands) and Heydrich (in the background, on the right).

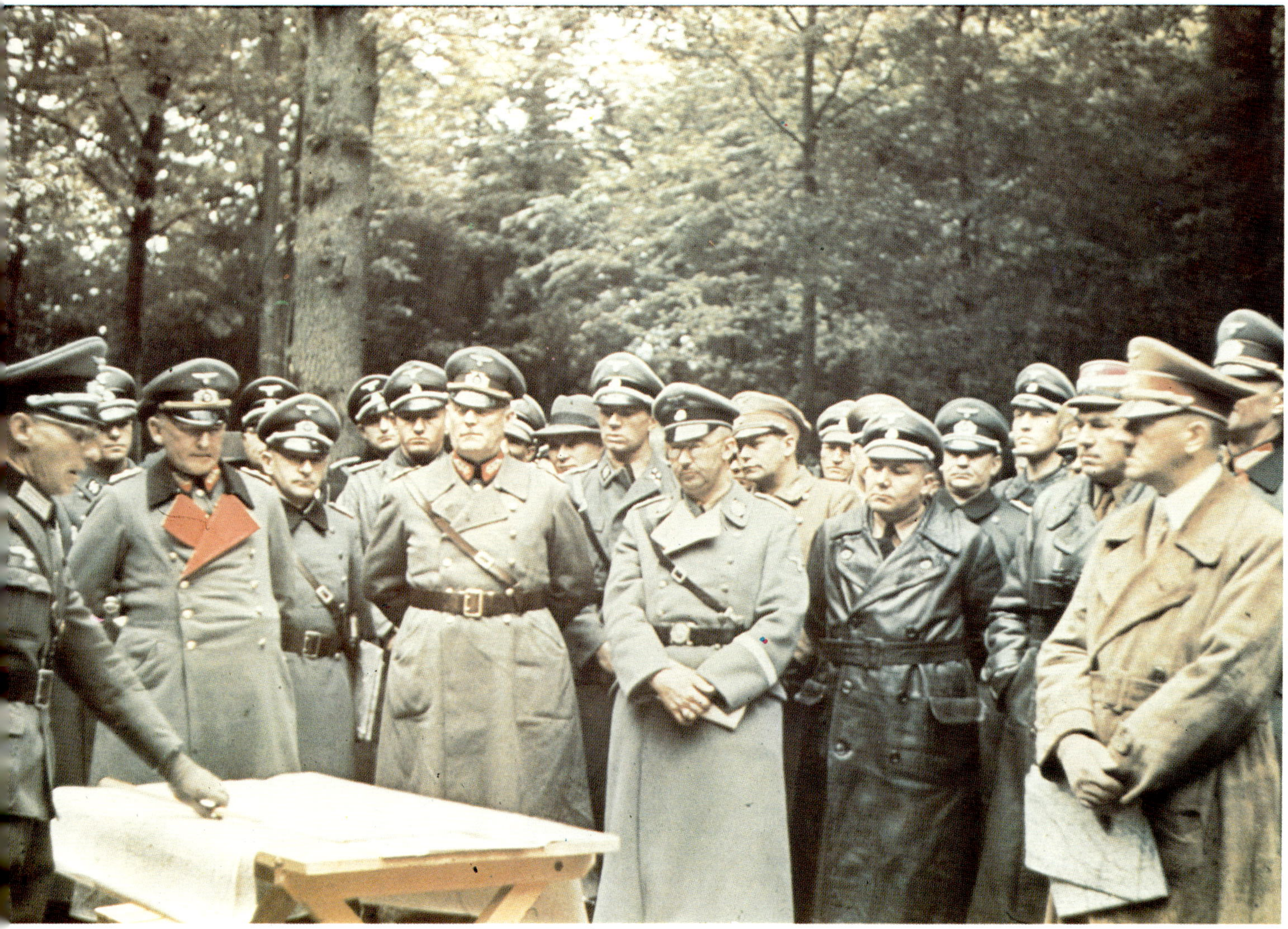

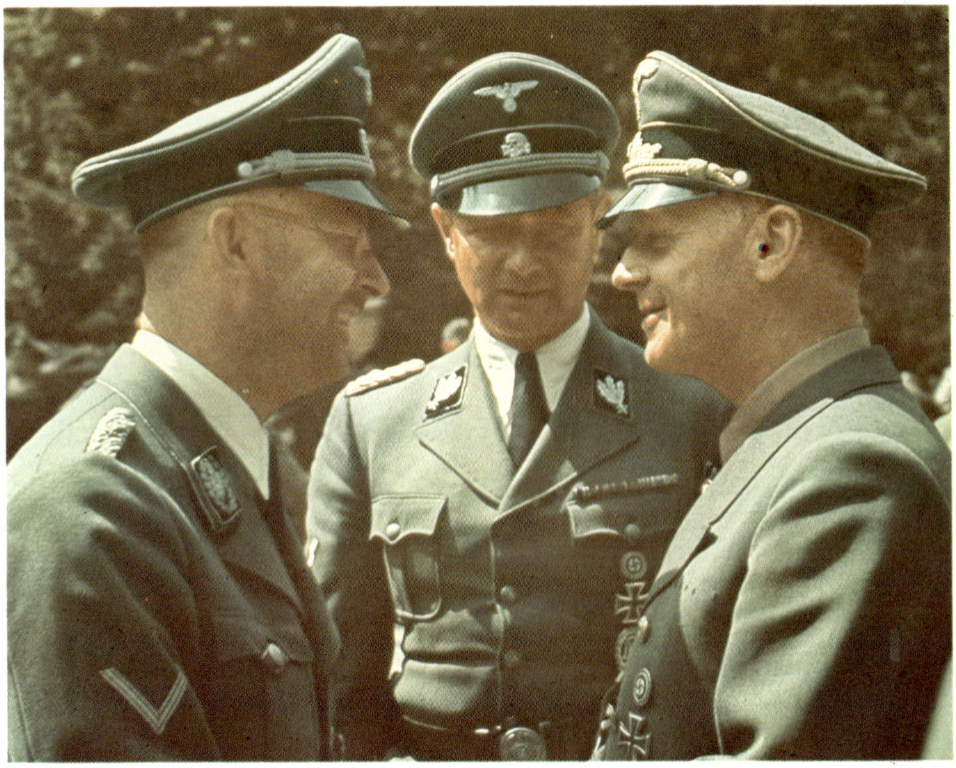

In this picture are Heinrich Himmler (left) in conversation with Ribbentrop and (in the centre) Gruppenführer SS Wolf. With the evolution of the war and the assassination in May 1942 of Heydrich, Himmler was able continually to strengthen and extend the influence of the RSHA. By 1944 it dealt with all activities outside the Third Reich, including the maintenance of order by terror in the occupied countries and, following integration with the Abwehr, with all forms of intelligence and counter-espionage.

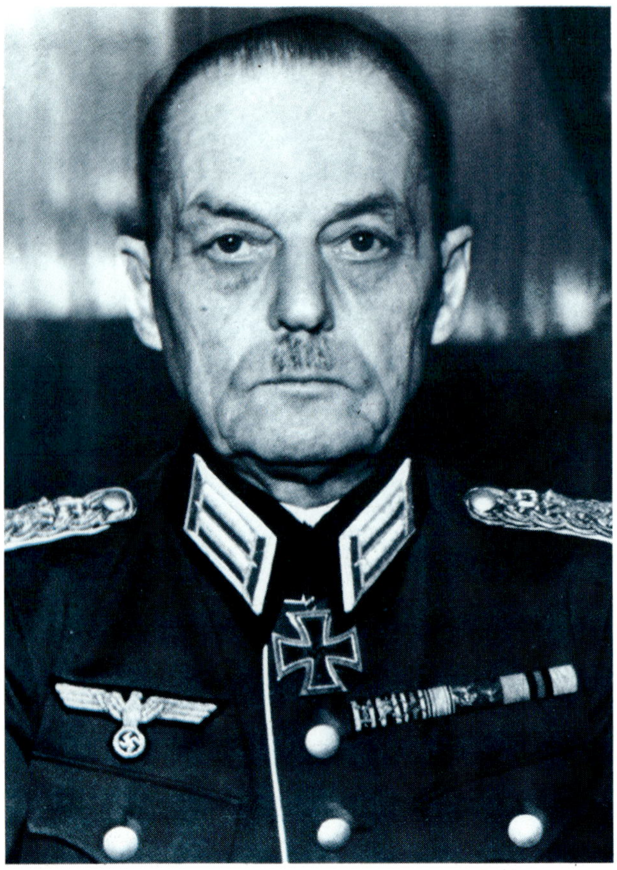

Rundstedt. After commanding a German army group during the invasion of Poland, Field Marshal Gerd von Rundstedt was in overall charge of the forces which broke through the French defences at Sedan in May 1940, cutting off the British Expeditionary Force. During the next two years he was appointed and then relieved of two different commands, Army Group South and Fortress Europe. He was eventually recalled in Sept. 1944 but by that time could do little to halt the Allied advance in north-west France, and he was replaced by Kesselring.

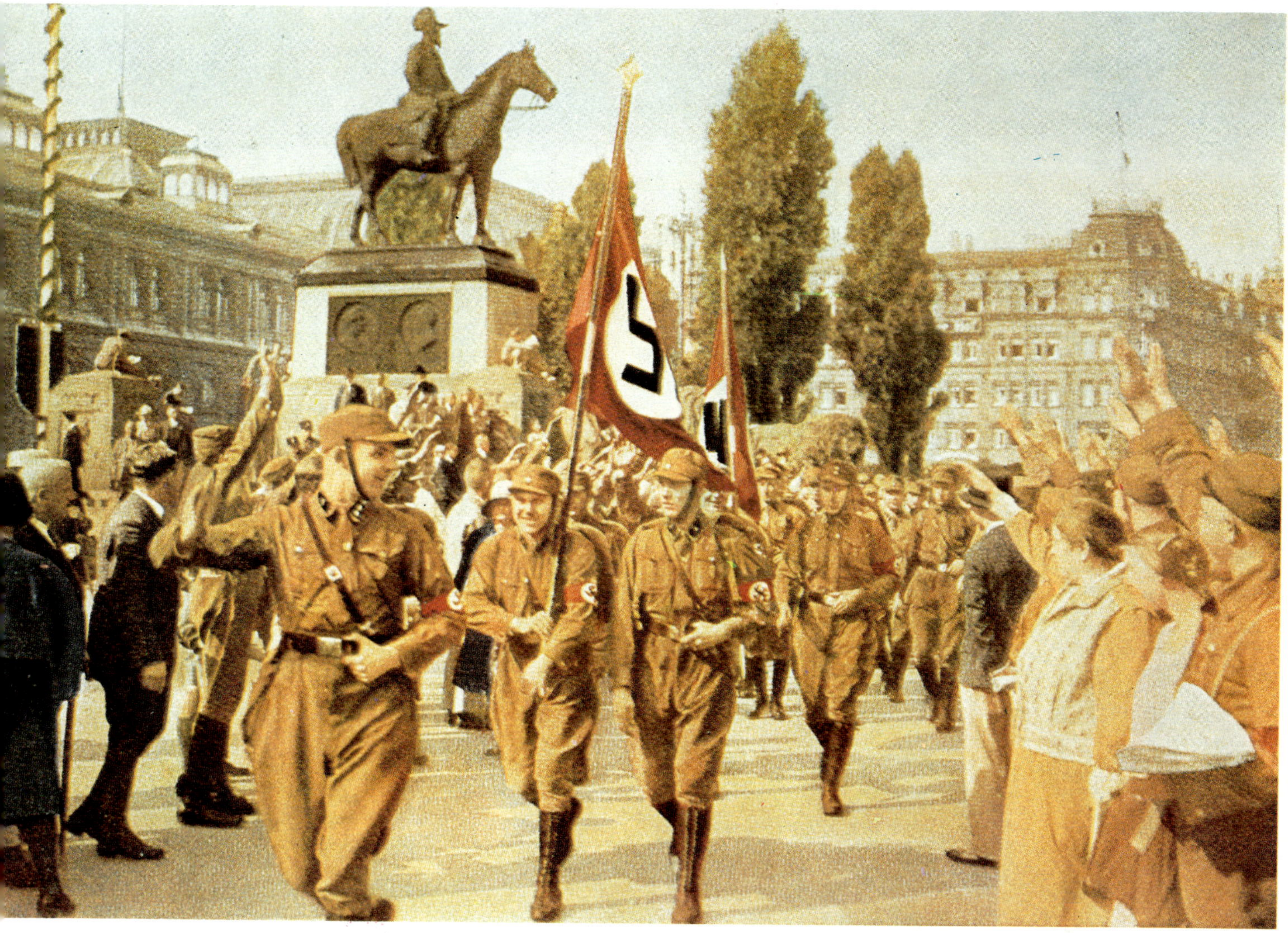

The SA. Created in 1921 in order to maintain order at Nazi rallies and to prevent other parties from meeting by the use of force, the storm troopers (*Sturmabteilungen*) employed intimidation and violence on a large scale in the streets, and did not hesitate to manhandle and even to kill their opponents. Through the impetus given by Röhm, the SA became an enormous paramilitary organization, its numbers growing from about 100,000 in 1930 to 400,000 in 1932, before the presidential elections, and to 4,500,000 in 1934 after the installation of the Nazi regime. This large, unruly force eventually became a source of concern to the army, to rival groups within the Nazi Party and to Hitler himself. On 30 June 1934, in the 'Night of the Long Knives', he purged the movement of its top men and reduced it to a subordinate role. Here in 1929 a group of SA men are parading in Nuremberg behind one of the leaders of the Berlin sections, Horst Wessel, who met his death in Feb. 1930 in one of the frequent street battles between Nazis and Communists. His death, exploited by Goebbels' propaganda machine, was to make him the hero and martyr of the Nazi cause.

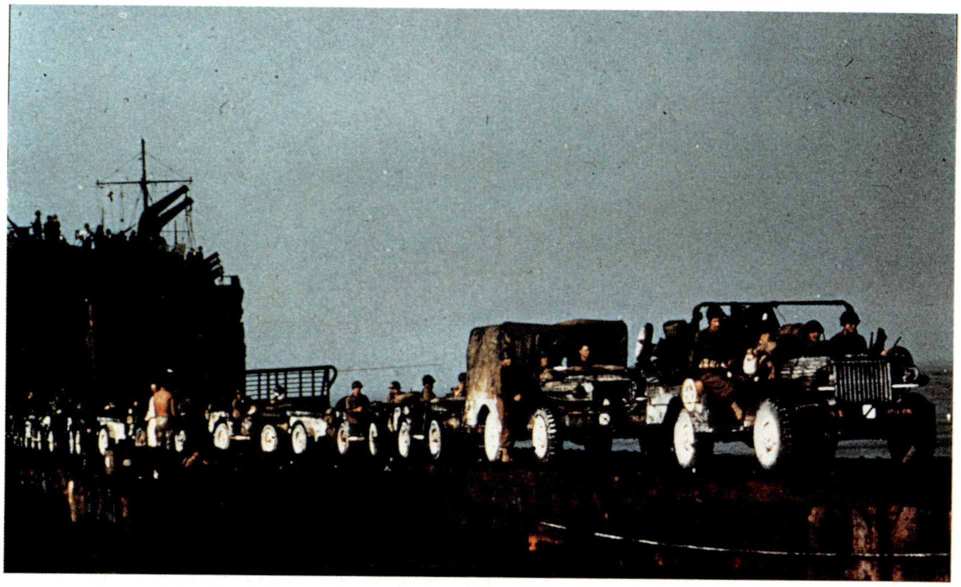

The Landing at Salerno. Launched on 9 Sept. 1943, near Naples, this was the first big Anglo-American amphibious operation carried out on the European mainland. Timed to coincide with the announcement of the Italian capitulation, it was the intention of the Allied high commands that it should be accompanied by a speedy occupation of the whole Italian peninsula, which would constitute a severe threat to Germany's southern borders.

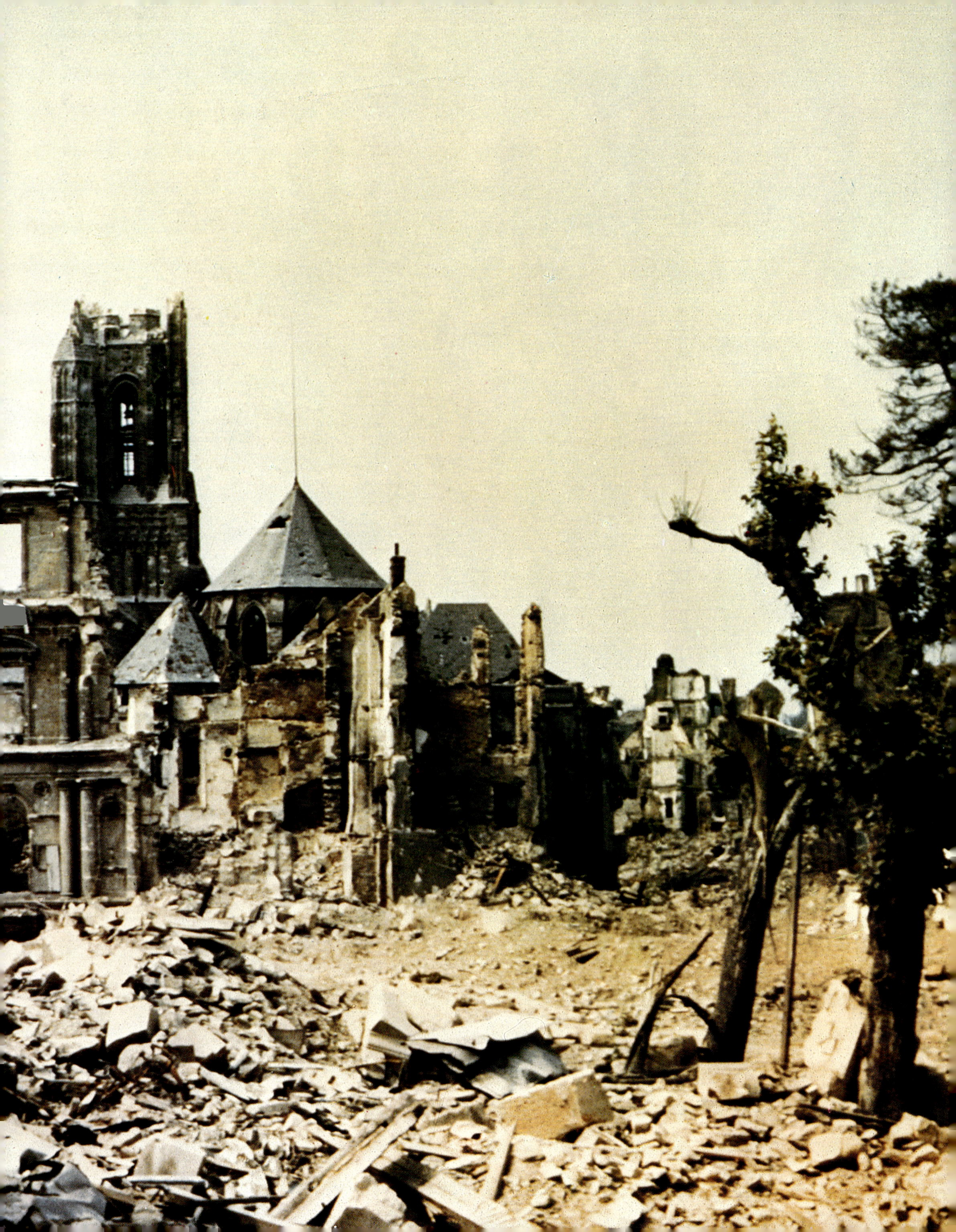

pposite
int-Lô. The ruins of the town after the mbardment of June 1944.

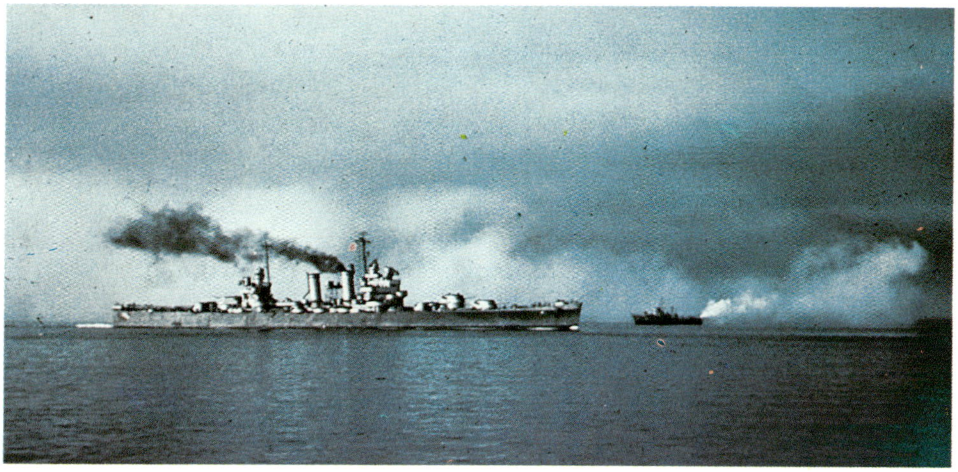

Right
Contrary to Allied expectations the landing at Salerno was to prove extremely difficult. As soon as they landed the British and American forces came up against fierce German opposition, accompanied by dangerous counter-attacks. On 12 Sept. an evacuation was even contemplated. The beachhead was eventually saved only by massive Allied air intervention and in particular by the supporting fire of the guns of the fleet. Here an American heavy cruiser is in action off the beaches of Salerno. In the background a patrol boat is laying down a smokescreen to provide cover for troops who are landing.

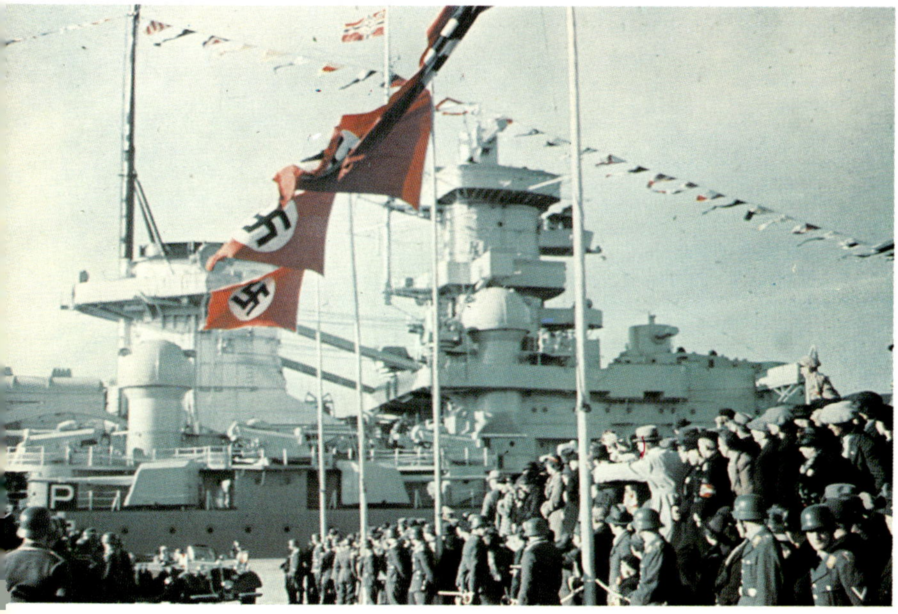

The *Scharnhorst*. Entering service on 7 Jan. 1939, this battle cruiser, armed with nine 11 in. (280 mm) guns, had a displacement of more than 30,000 tons and possessed particularly strong armour plating. In company with its sister ship, the *Gneisenau*, the *Scharnhorst* was to be extremely active during the war, its successes including the destruction of the auxiliary cruiser *Rawalpindi* in 1939 and the aircraft carrier *Glorious* during the Norwegian campaign. Having made several cruises in the Atlantic, the *Scharnhorst* returned to Germany by way of the English Channel in Feb. 1942 and from that time onwards operated from Norway against Allied convoys bound for Murmansk. It was during one of these sorties, on 26 Dec. 1942, that it was to be intercepted and destroyed by the Home Fleet after putting up a fierce struggle.

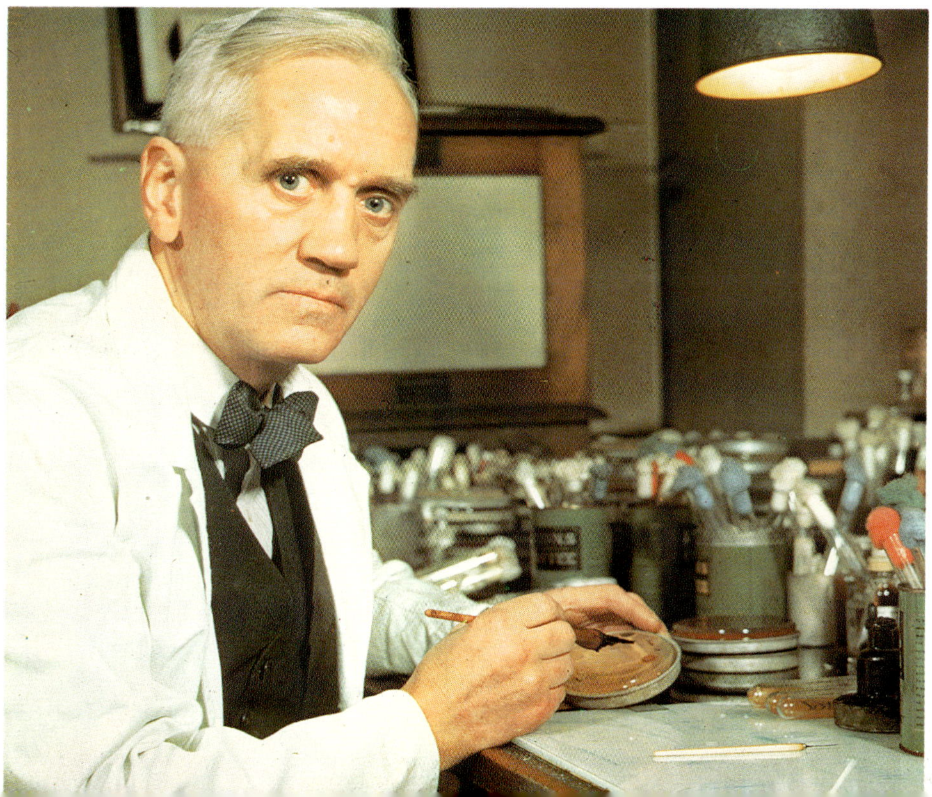

Science. The war provided an opportunity for certain branches of science to make spectacular progress because of their practical applications, notably chemistry, nuclear physics and electronics – which was responsible for the development of radar. The same held true for the first antibiotics, such as penicillin, which was finally isolated in 1942 as a result of work by Fleming, Florey and Chain. At first reserved for wounded airmen and munition workers, thanks to a massive production effort penicillin began to be used on a very large scale by the Allied medical services. Here Sir Alexander Fleming is at work in his laboratory at St Mary's Hospital, London.

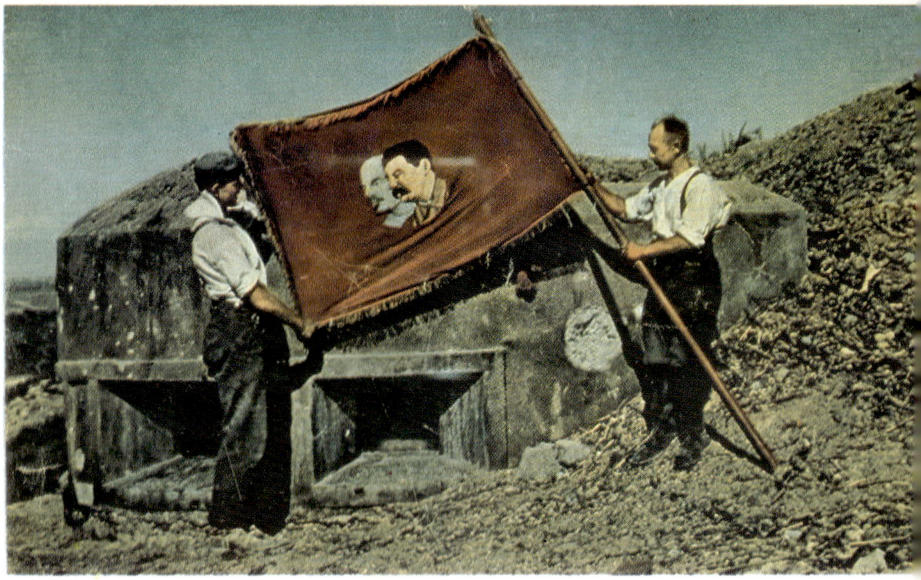

Sebastopol. In the spring of 1942, on the eve of the great offensive in the direction of the Volga and the Caucasus, the German high command considered it necessary to capture the fortified town of Sebastopol, which threatened its right flank. The assault, carried out by Manstein's army, was preceded by massive aerial attacks and the use of heavy artillery, involving gigantic mortars. Despite the size of the Soviet garrison, which was established in positions in depth, the Germans, supported by Romanians, succeeded during the month of June in capturing the main strongholds and in reaching the port and the heart of the town, taking nearly 100,000 prisoners. Here two German soldiers are examining a Soviet flag bearing portraits of Stalin and Lenin, removed from one of the galleries of Fort Maxim Gorki.

SHAEF. Set up in Feb. 1944 with the task of preparing and carrying out the planned landings in France and subsequently of conducting operations leading to the liberation of western Europe, the Supreme Headquarters Allied Expeditionary Force, or SHAEF, was placed under the command of Eisenhower, supported by a combined Anglo-American staff. Here are the leading figures, meeting in London in May 1944 during the final preparations for Operation Overlord. From left to right: General Bradley, commanding American land forces; Admiral Ramsay, the naval commander; Air Chief Marshal Tedder, deputy supreme commander; Eisenhower, supreme commander; Montgomery, the commander of all the land forces; Air Chief Marshal Leigh-Mallory, commander in chief of the air forces; and General Bedell Smith, chief of general staff.

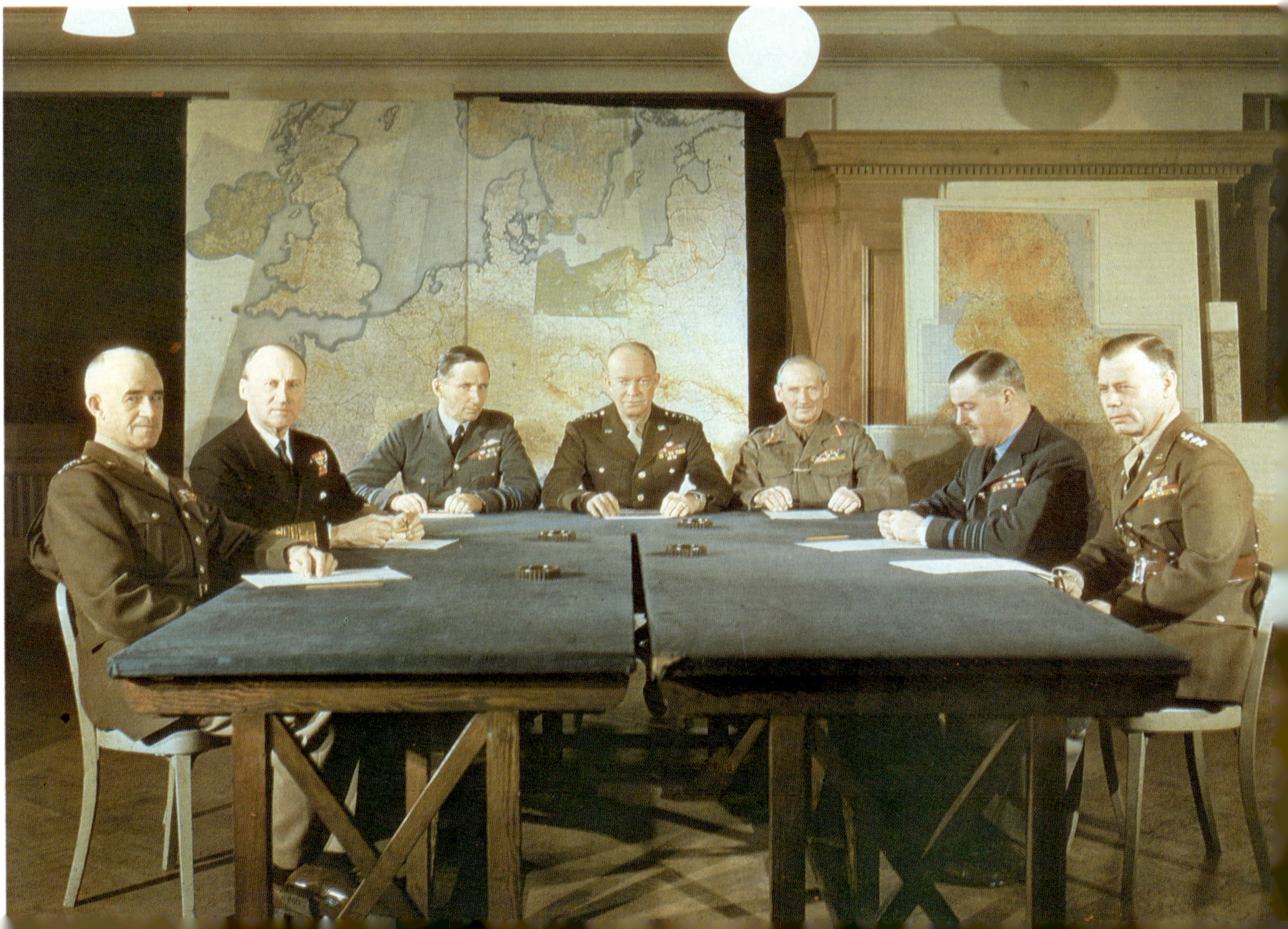

Right
The Sherman Tank. The Sherman tank, which came into service in the autumn of 1942 at the Battle of El Alamein, was the most famous American tank of the whole war and was used by all the Allied armies. Weighing 30 tons and with armour plating up to 3 in (75 mm) thick, it was equipped with a 75 mm gun and three machine guns. It had a crew of five. However, when the landings in France took place, the Sherman proved to be distinctly inferior to the German Tiger and Panther tanks, even the PzKpfw Mark IV. It had to be re-equipped with the long-barrelled 76 mm gun. Nevertheless, the mass production of the Sherman, made easy by the simplicity of its mechanical design, had the advantage of creating uniformity among the armoured units on the western front and of saturating the German defences. In all, nearly 50,000 Sherman tanks emerged from American factories and the Sherman's chassis was to be used as a basis for tank destroyers and for self-propelled 155 mm guns.

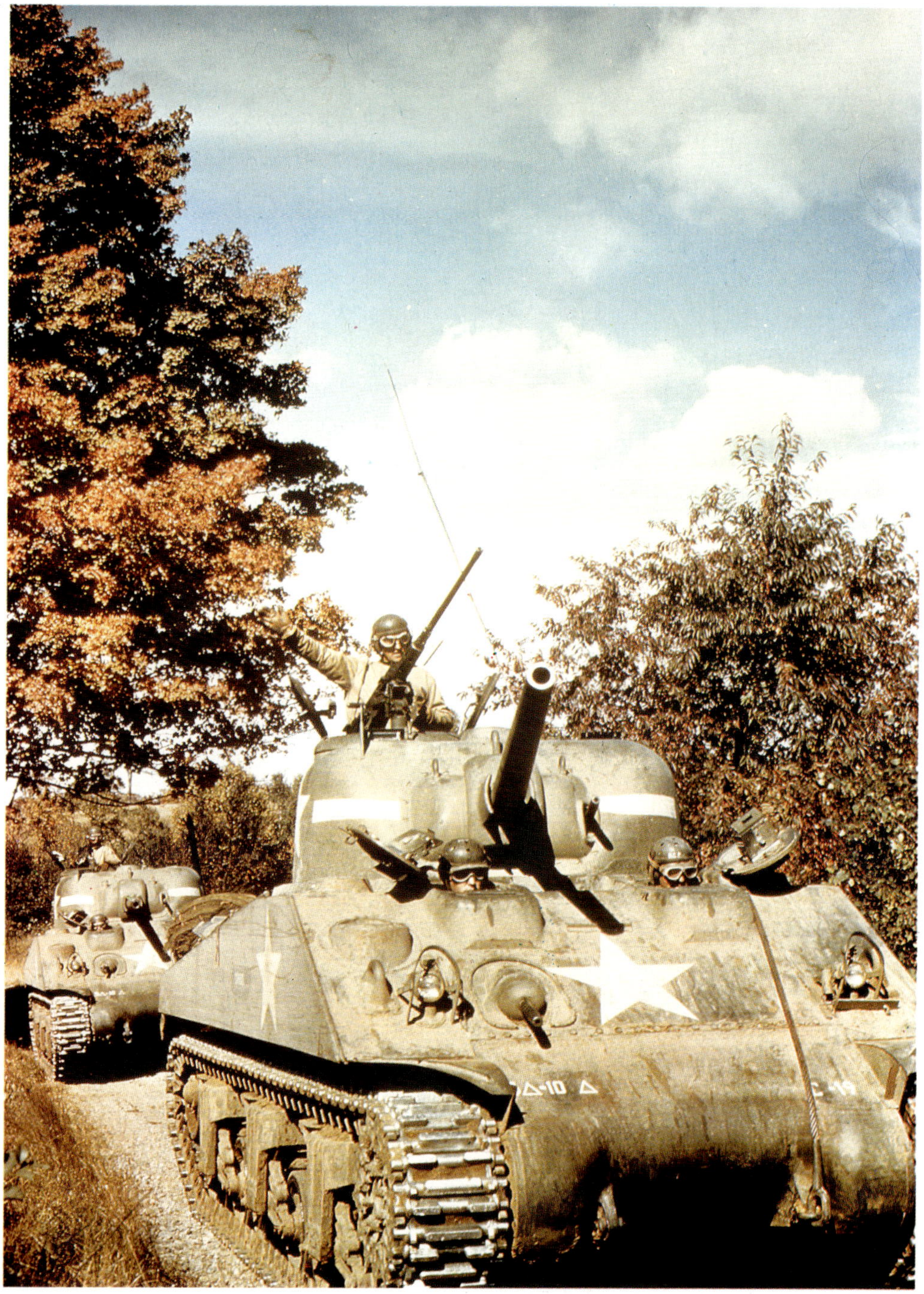

The Short Stirling. Entering service on the eve of war, this four-engined plane was the RAF's first strategic heavy bomber. It took part in the first big raids on Europe in 1941. However, its low service ceiling and the weakness of its defensive armament made it an easy prey for the fighters of the Luftwaffe. For this reason it was progressively replaced by the Lancaster and the Halifax. Here we see a Short Stirling which has had to make a forced landing during a raid on the Reich, standing on a German airfield together with the Messerschmitt Bf-109 which brought it down.

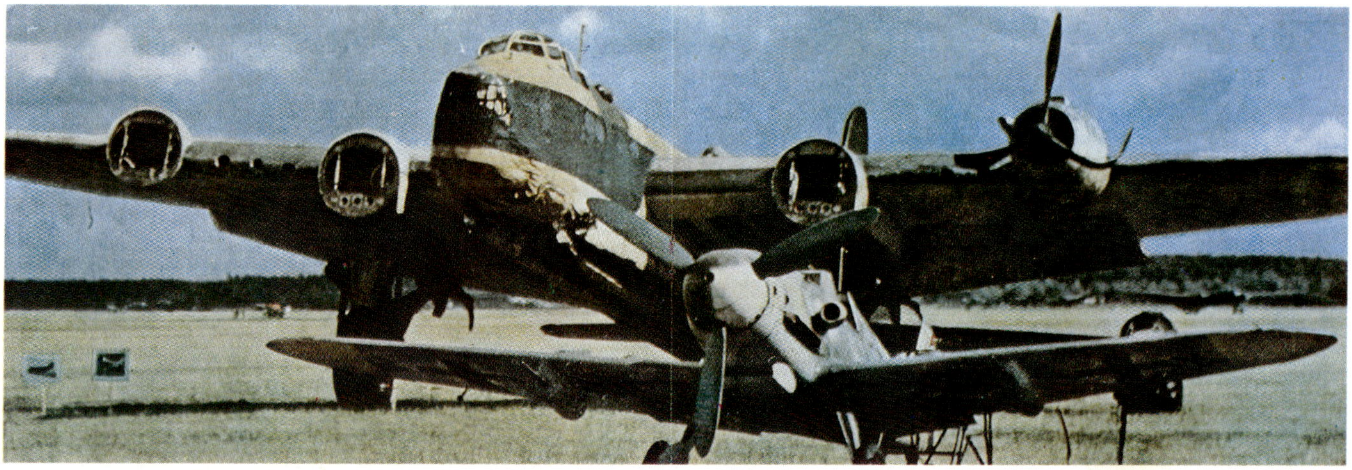

Sicily. Some days after the Allied landir

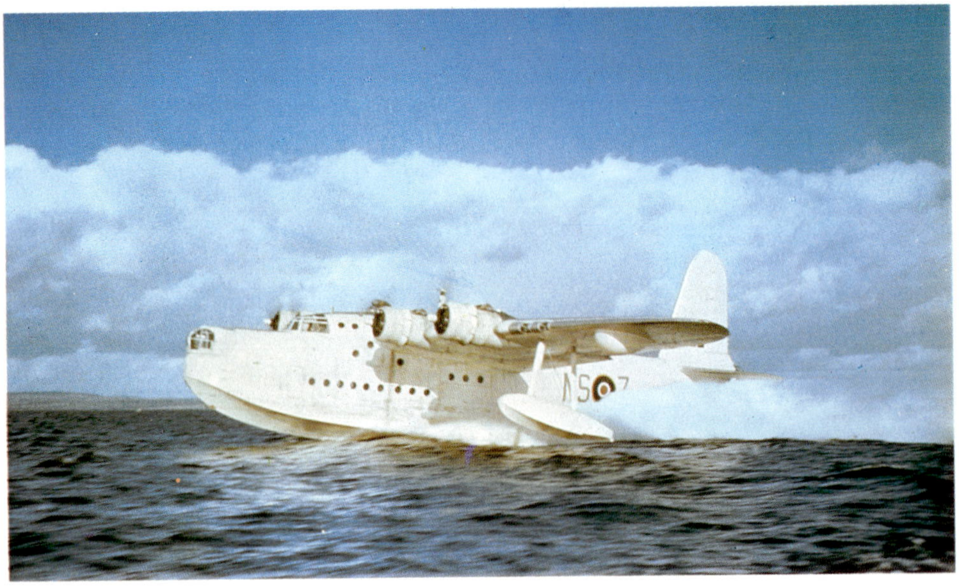

The Short Sunderland. Appearing in its final form in 1937, this heavy four-engined British flying-boat was to prove a remarkable success. With a range of 2900 mi. (4600 km) at a cruising speed of 190 mph (300 km/h) and a powerful defensive armament, it was used to equip several squadrons of Coastal Command. It was employed on long-range reconnaissance missions, in anti-submarine warfare, on rescue missions and even as a transport. Improvements were continually being made to this aircraft, of which 750 were eventually produced.

The Conquest of Sicily. Carried out on 9–10 July 1943, the landings in Sicily were to have momentous strategic consequences for the whole war. They clearly indicated the collapse of the Italian army and led to the fall of the Fascist regime on 25 July, accompanied by the arrest of Mussolini. In spite of the competition between Patton's army (the US 7th) and Montgomery's (the British 8th), the conquest of the island was in the long run to prove slow and difficult. German forces put up a stiff and skilful resistance on both sides of Mount Etna. Messina, of which a view of the main street is shown here, did not fall until 16 Aug. and the Allies were unable to prevent the Wehrmacht's divisions from crossing the straits to the mainland and withdrawing into Calabria with all their equipment.

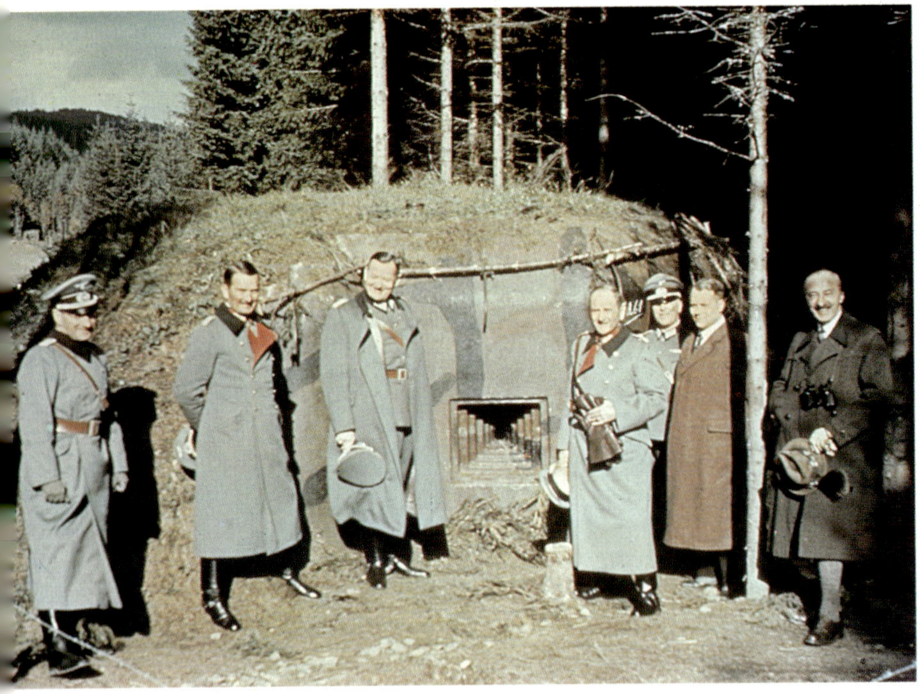

The Siegfried Line. It was after the remilitarization of the Rhineland in 1936 that the Germans embarked upon the construction of the 'West Wall', called the Siegfried Line by the French. Following the western frontier of the Reich from the Netherlands to Switzerland, this system of fortifications did not, like the Maginot Line, consist of large-scale works but of a series of small forts at varying intervals and combined with minefields and antitank obstacles. From the time of its construction the Siegfried Line was to have an important strategic consequence: it reinforced the defensive aspect of French military doctrine and contributed to the passive attitude of the western democracies in 1938 and 1939. In this photograph, taken before the war, a group of high-ranking German officers are posing in front of a blockhouse.

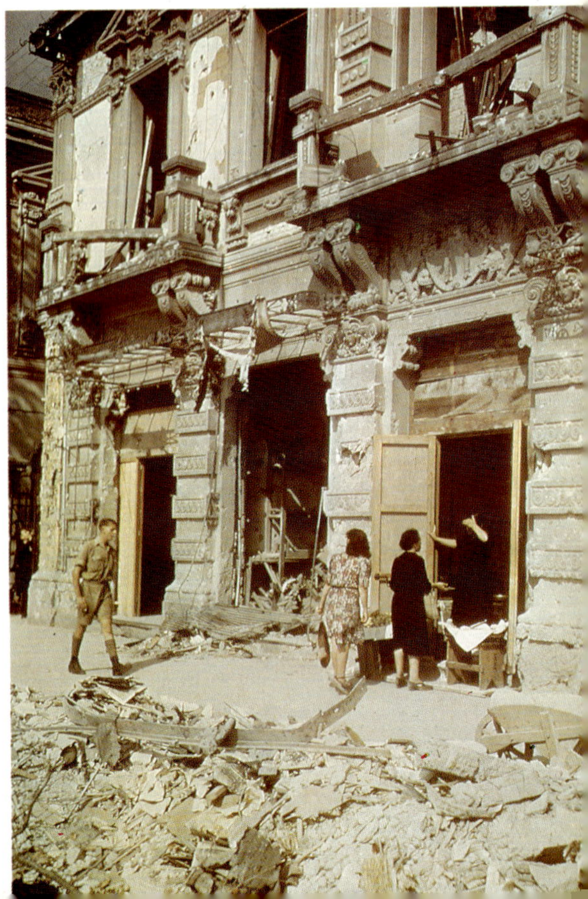

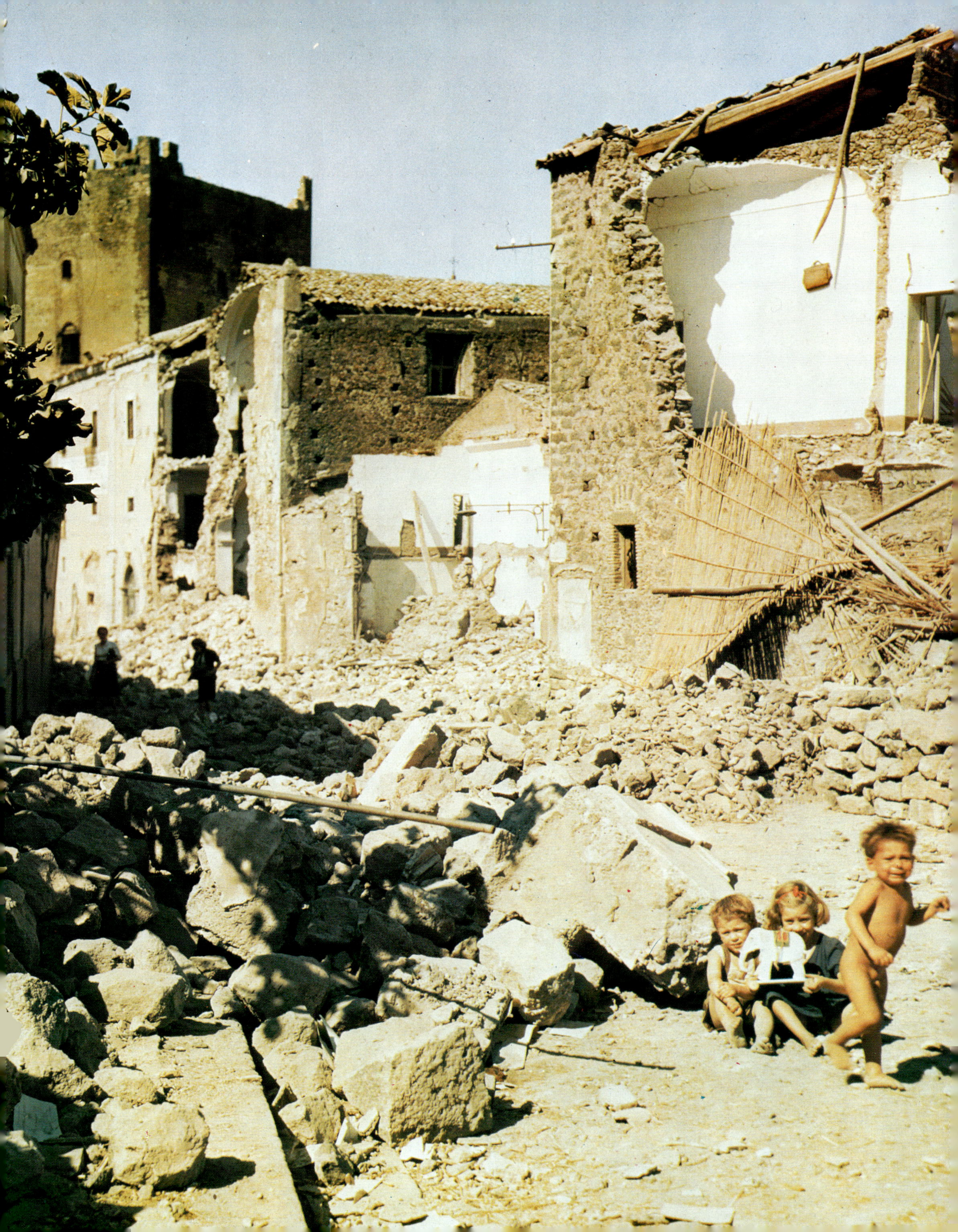

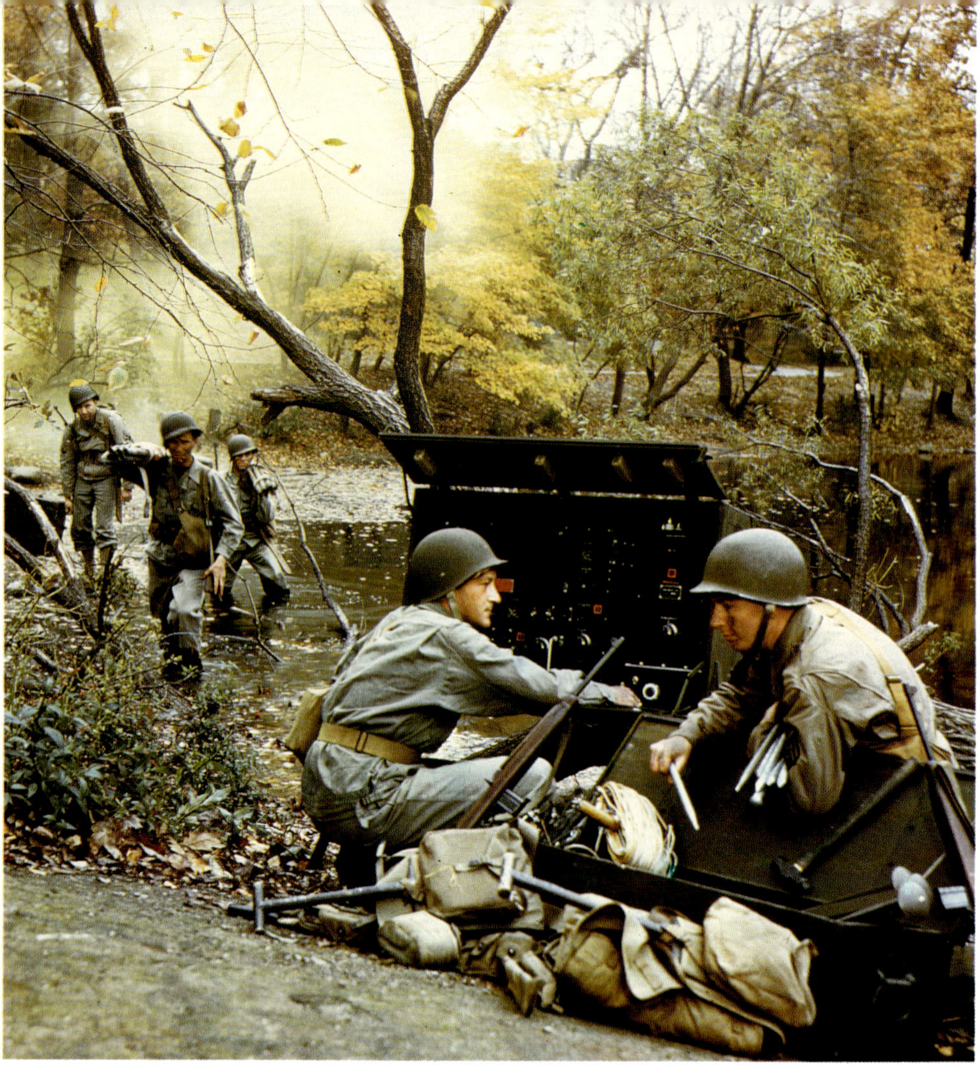

Signals. An American signals post set up in the front line. During the war radio transmissions in particular improved considerably and had a profound influence on the conduct of operations. The higher command could maintain direct contact with forward units much more easily than by using liaison officers, or even by telephone. Likewise, troops in the front line were in a position to send information or request artillery or air support in the shortest possible time.

Silesia. This German province, on either side of the upper part of the Oder river, was in Feb.–March 1945 subjected to a heavy offensive by the Red Army which threatened Berlin from the south and opened the way to Dresden and Prague. German resistance was fierce and the town of Breslau, the capital of the province, did not surrender until 9 May. As this photograph shows, the Soviet attack was preceded, in the depths of winter and in intense cold, by the flight of the population. After the war the Soviet government was to hand over Silesia to the new Poland in exchange for the annexation of those territories lying to the east of the famous Curzon Line.

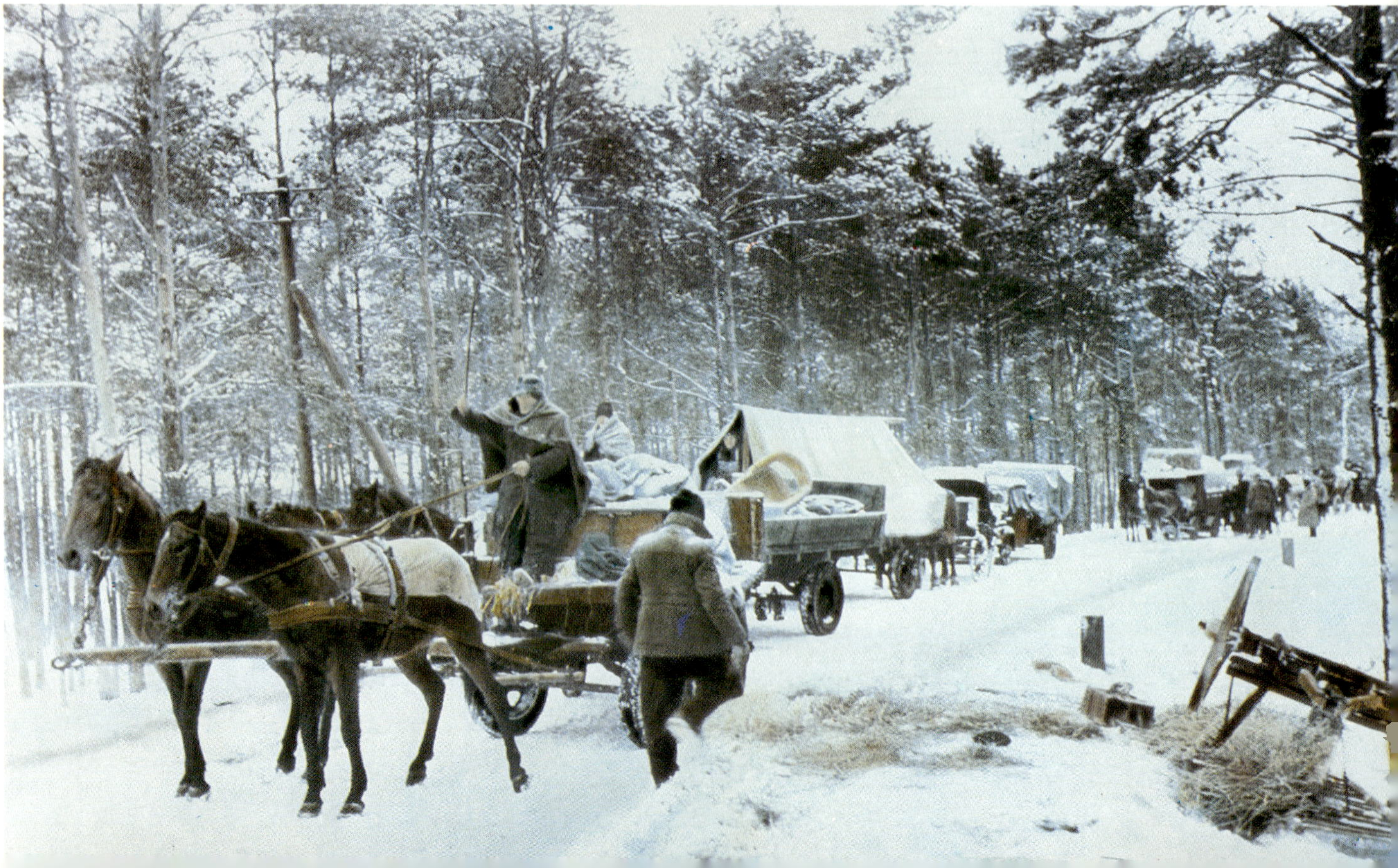

Slim. Slim, who had risen from the ranks, was, with Montgomery, undoubtedly the best British military leader of the Second World War. After the disastrous campaign in Burma in 1942, it was greatly to his credit that he succeeded in re-establishing a British army in India and in training it for jungle warfare. He was able to go over to the offensive in 1944 and the victories of Kohima and Imphal enabled him to reach Mandalay. After the decisive battle of Meiktila (Feb.–March 1945) he was in a position to complete the reconquest of Burma and to capture Rangoon. He ended his career, after the war, as governor general of Australia. He is seen here in March 1945 during the ceremony of raising the colours at Fort Dufferin, in Mandalay, after the capture of the Fort.

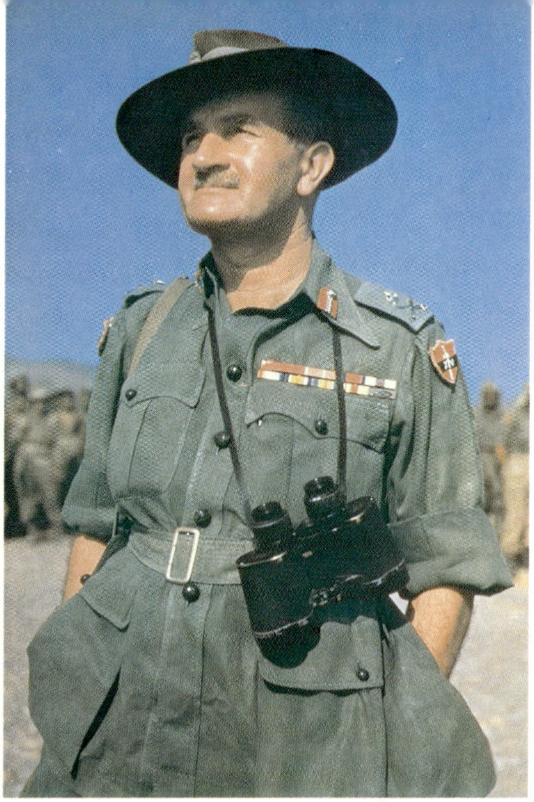

Solomon Islands. After their victory at Guadalcanal, with the support of naval forces under Admiral Halsey, American troops began to clear the area skirting the north of Australia and to neutralize the base at Rabaul by taking possession of the Solomon Archipelago. During 1943 the reconquest proved to be particularly difficult. The Americans confined their activities to the partial occupation of certain islands, isolating the Japanese garrisons and leaving them 'to rot' where they were. Here American assault craft are moving towards the beaches at Bougainville under a smokescreen cover.

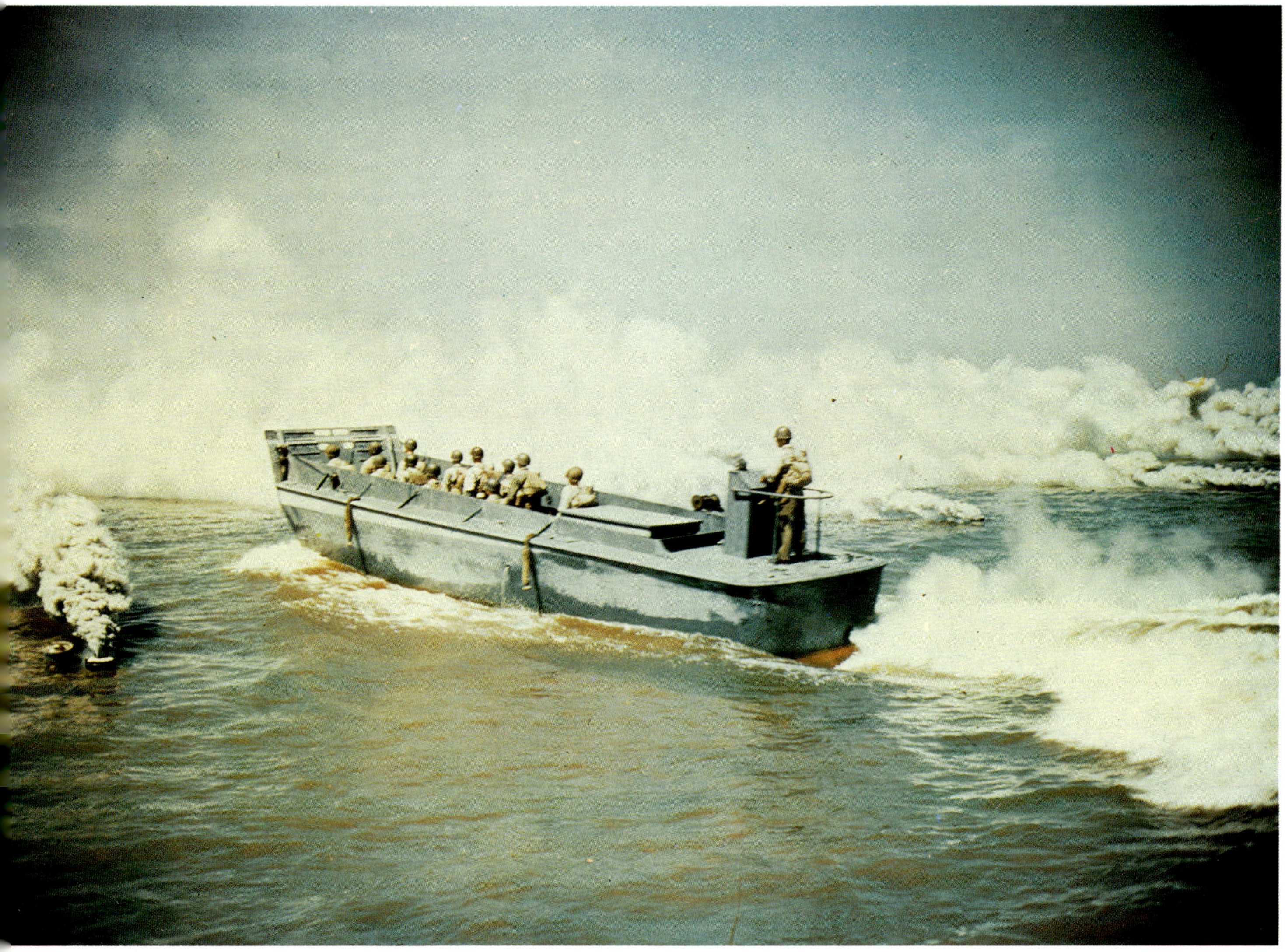

The Battle of the Somme. Following the disastrous battle in the Nord department, marked by the evacuation at Dunkirk, the French high command still nourished the hope of being able to hold the Wehrmacht in check on the Somme and the Aisne, despite the imbalance between the opposing forces. The battle began on 5 June 1940, and for 48 hours the French troops were able to contain the German divisions. However, at the end of two days the Panzers succeeded in making a breakthrough on the Somme front in the direction of Rouen. General Weygand was now compelled to resign himself to a general retreat. Here a horse-drawn German battery of 105 mm guns is crossing the Somme near Picquigny on a bridge of inflatable dinghies.

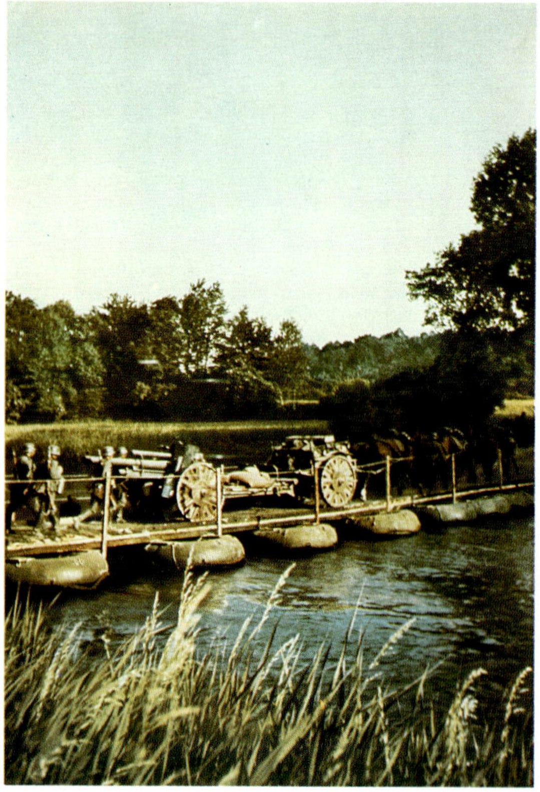

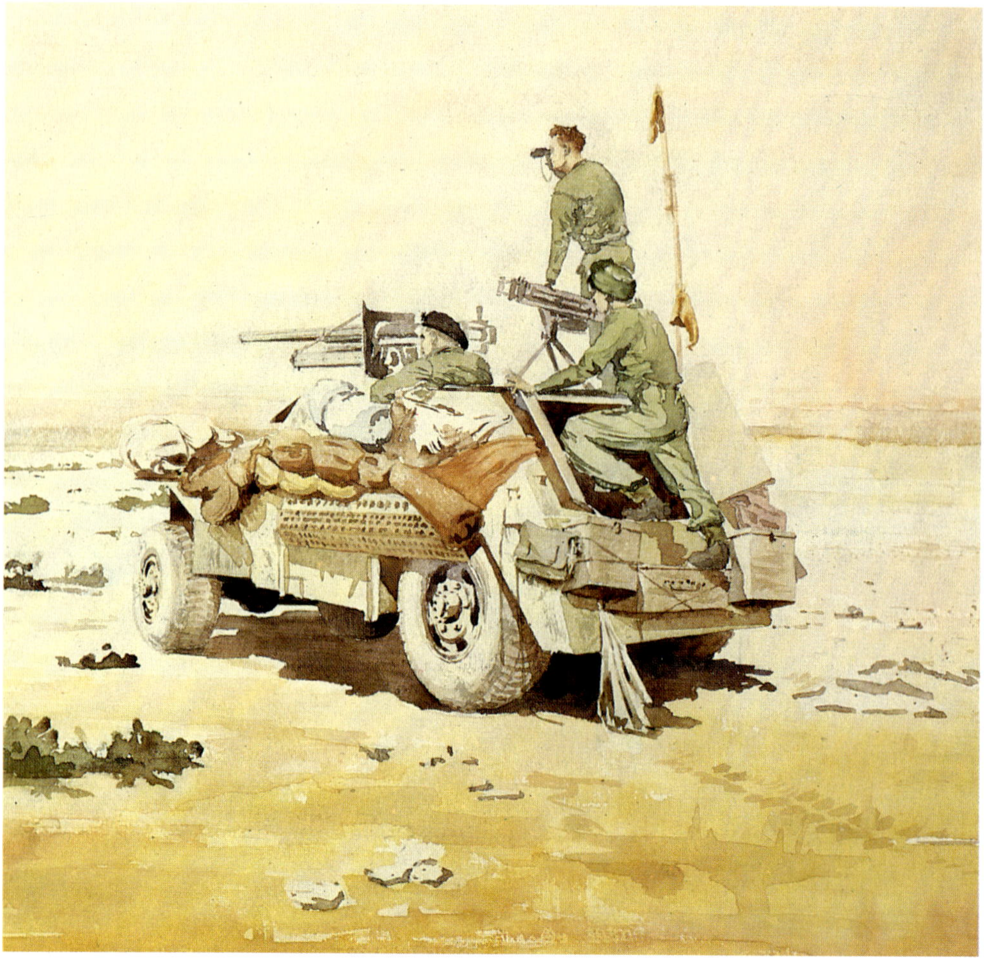

South Africa. After a crisis over what stance it should take, South Africa under Jan Smuts declared war on Germany on 5 Sept. 1939. In all, 325,000 men (whites and non-whites) served in Ethiopia and the Mediterranean with great distinction, and, like the Australians, South Africans served in the RAF. Industry was switched to munitions production and the manufacture of military clothing, and Smuts remained in close contact with Churchill throughout the war. Men of the South African Reconnaissance Regiment firing a captured 37 mm Breda gun. Painting by A. Gregson.

Spain. The triumph of Franco's Nationalist forces in 1939 had been ensured to a large extent by the military support of Germany and Italy. During the war, nevertheless, Franco followed a very circumspect course of action and refused to involve Spain on the side of the Axis powers. In this picture Franco is seen at the parade held in Madrid in 1939 to celebrate the Nationalist victory in the civil war.

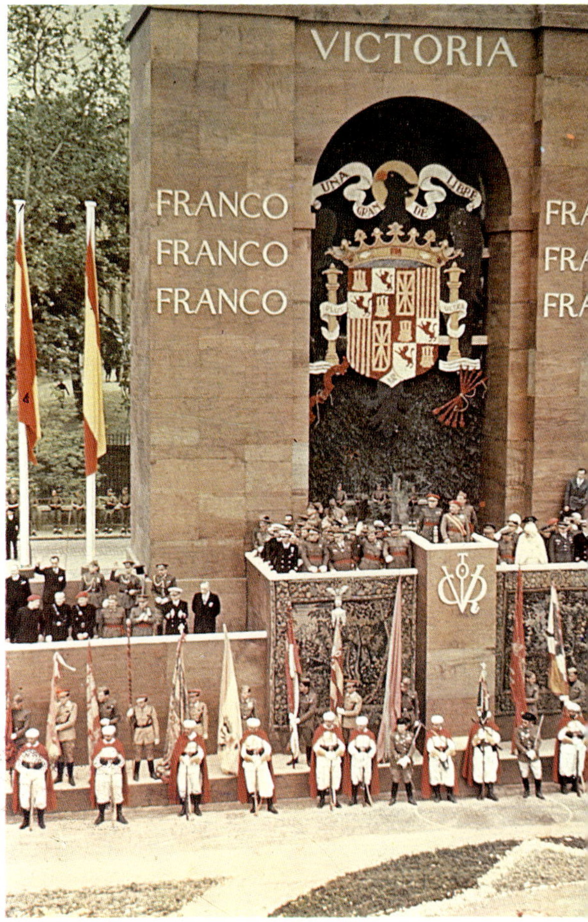

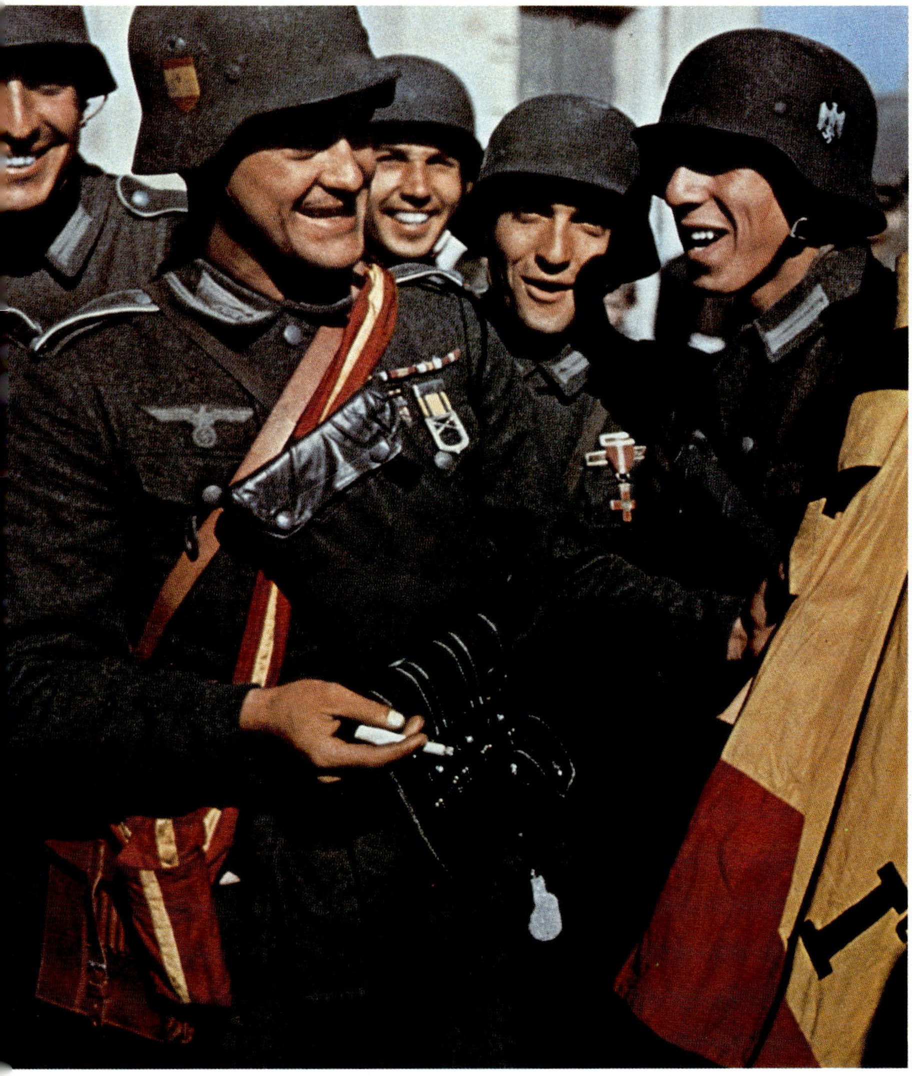

In spite of pressure exerted by Hitler, particularly at their meeting at Hendaye on the border between France and Spain in Oct. 1940, Franco refused to take any part in the conflict on the side of Germany, not even as part of an operation aimed at capturing Gibraltar from the British. In 1941 he merely authorized the sending of a unit of volunteers, the *División Azul* ('Blue Division'), to fight on the Russian front. This picture shows Spanish soldiers of this division who have distinguished themselves in the fighting around Leningrad.

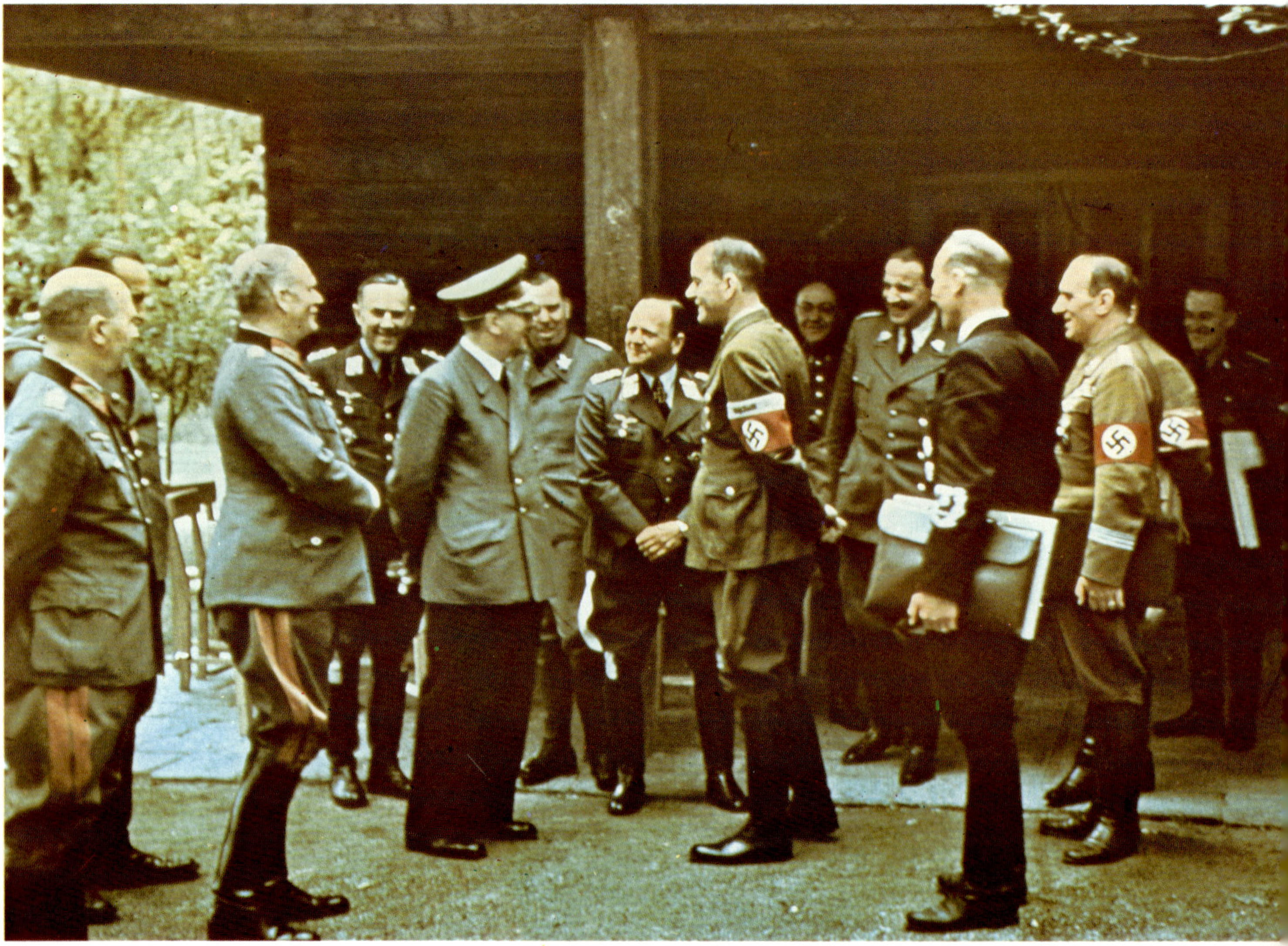

Speer. Between 1932 and 1937 this young architect carried out various design projects for the Nazi party, providing the grandiose settings for Nazi party ceremonies in association with the Ministry of Propaganda. This brought him to the attention of Hitler and in 1937 Speer was appointed inspector-general of buildings in Berlin, with the task of replanning the capital. He was responsible in particular for the building of the new Chancellery in a colossal neo-classical style and also designed the 'Mars Field'. At the height of the war, in 1942, he was appointed minister of armaments and war production in succession to Fritz Todt. He now succeeded in really putting the country's economy on a war footing and in giving German industry a considerable boost by mobilizing the foreign labour force (prisoners of war and deportees) and by the systematic exploitation of the occupied countries. His action was so effective that, despite the Allied bombing and the shrinking of the territory of the Reich, the production of German war industries reached its record level in 1944. Here, wearing a Nazi armband with a white strip bearing the name of the Todt Organization, he is seen in conversation with Hitler and Marshal Milch of the Luftwaffe at the Führer's headquarters on the eastern front at Vinnitsa in the Ukraine, in the early summer of 1942.

Stalin. In spite of the misguided policy which in 1937 led him to purge the Red Army of its senior officers, leaving it disorganized and gravely weakened, and the shortsightedness which made him ignore all the warning signs about Hitler's attack on Russia, Stalin (*opposite*) appeared in 1945 as the great victor of war. After initial heavy defeats he had succeeded in completely re-establishing his authority over the Soviet Union and in leading it to triumph. With the collapse of Germany and the weakening of Britain, which was reduced to a secondary role, he now dominated Europe, the eastern countries of which were in the course of becoming Soviet satellites. Despite the enormous losses in manpower and materials which his country had suffered, the Stalin of Yalta was the embodiment of the world's second largest power – a situation which would have appeared impossible less than four years before.

SS. The origins of the SS appear to have been peculiarly modest. In 1929 the *Schutzstaffeln* ('protection groups') comprised no more than 280 men entrusted, under the direction of Himmler, with the personal protection of Hitler. The build-up of the Black Order began when the Nazis took power and, ten years later, in 1943, it would not be an exaggeration to talk about an actual SS state in Germany, dominating the various police forces and controlling whole sectors of the economy, the diplomatic service, the propaganda machine and the army. With the war, the expedient of the Waffen SS ensured that the Black Order even constituted an army within an army. In 1944 the Waffen SS consisted of 38 large units with a total strength of 600,000 men, of whom half were foreigners. The SS were the Nazi Party's organ of intelligence, entrusted with the task of 'fighting openly and ruthlessly the most dangerous enemies of the state, Jews, freemasons and the political clergy', in collaboration with Gestapo, besides being the pitiless administrators and guards of the concentration camps. In this photograph, taken on the occasion of the Nuremberg congress of 1933, the SS can be seen in the foreground dressed in black, wearing peaked caps with the death's head badge, and still in a minority compared with the SA (in the background), then at the height of its power.

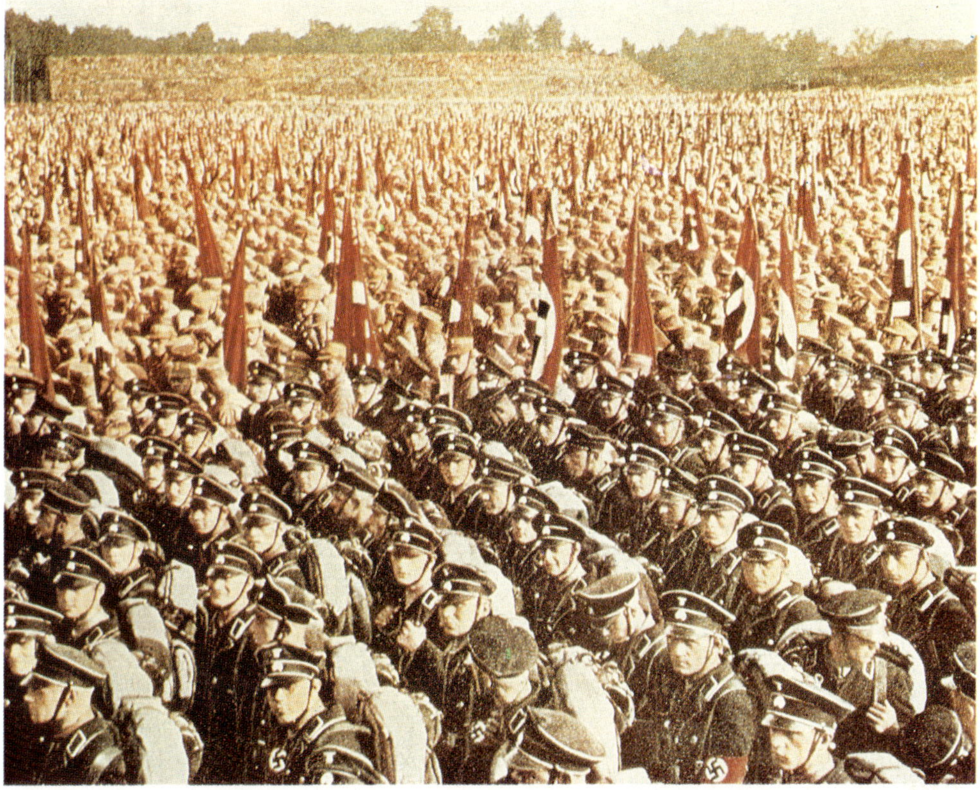

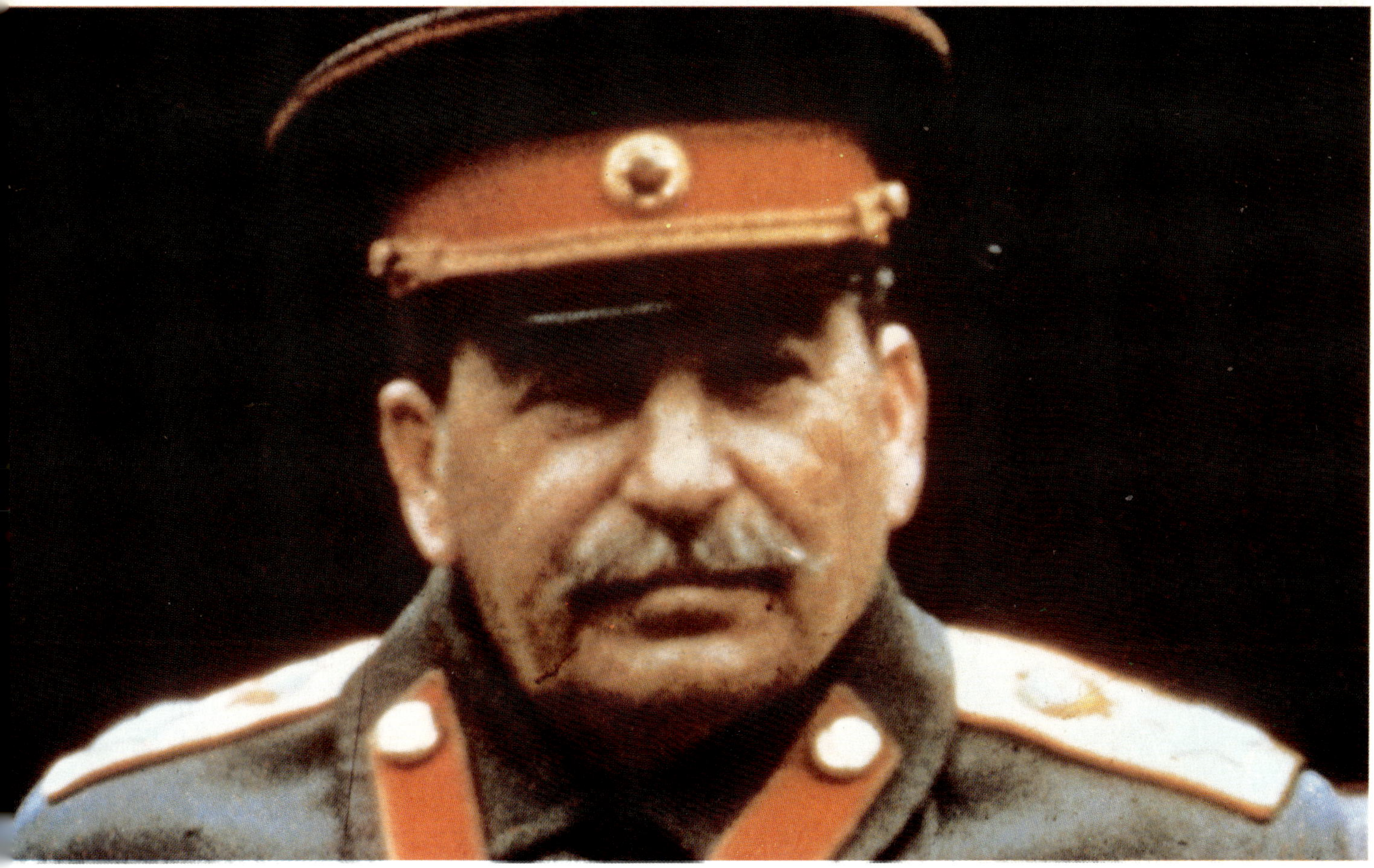

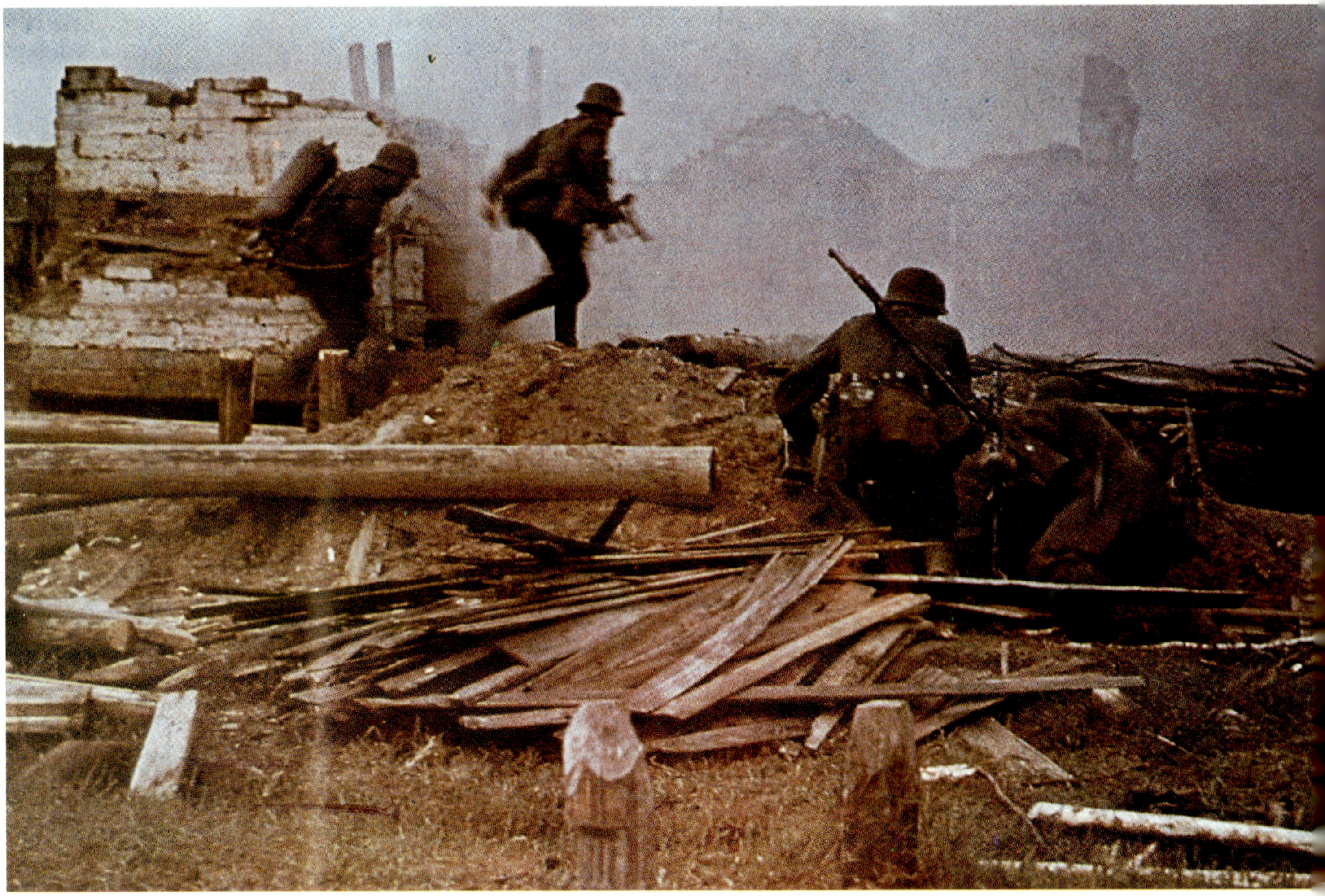

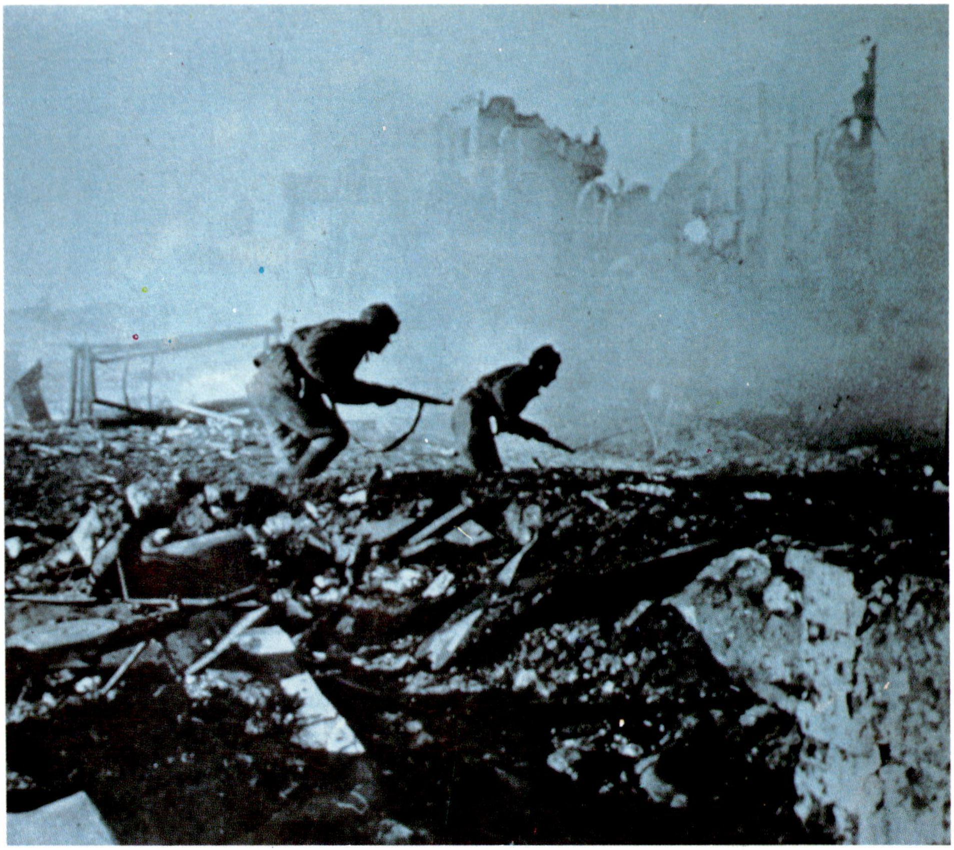

Stalingrad. In committing the German army to fight at Stalingrad in the summer of 1942 Hitler and the Wehrmacht high command committed a fatal error. The battle was to absorb in bloody street fighting units intended for a war of movement and divert the German army from its chief task: the assault upon and capture of the oil-wells of the Caucasus. For soldiers on both sides Stalingrad was hell on earth. Men fought street by street, house by house and floor by floor. In this photograph soldiers of a German engineer unit, armed with automatic weapons, grenades and flame-throwers, are moving through the middle of the debris at Rinok, near the Volga.

The battle of Stalingrad gave the Russian soldier an opportunity to display his traditional qualities of courage and self-denial. Throughout the summer and the beginning of autumn, Chuikov's troops fought in the worst possible conditions, subjected to intense artillery and air bombardment, with their backs to the Volga. The provision of supplies posed terrible problems. Priority was given to ammunition, next vodka and finally food. Because of the shortcomings of the medical services Soviet losses were extremely heavy – far greater than those of the Germans. The photograph shows Russian soldiers making their way through the ruins of Stalingrad.

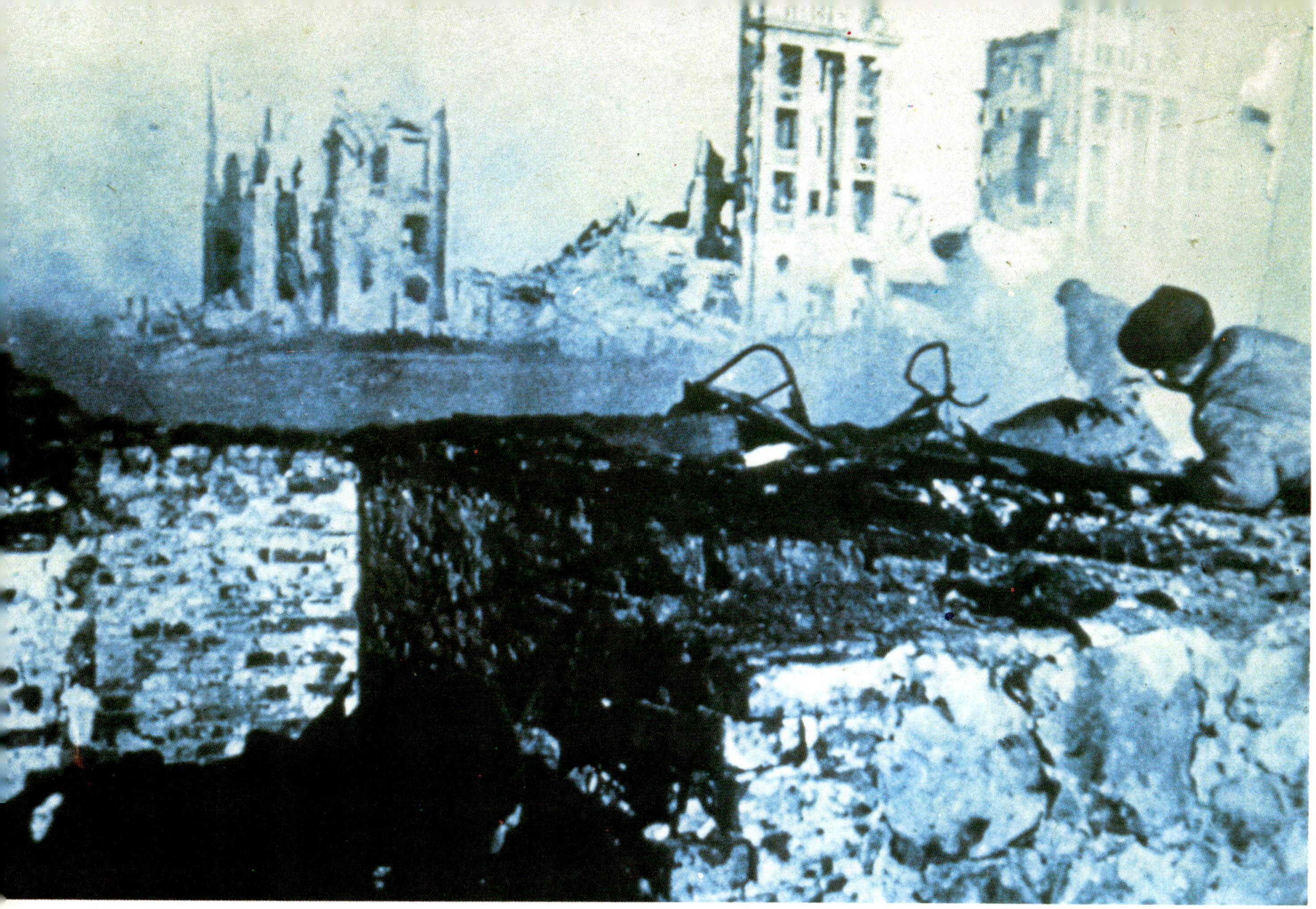

Soviet soldiers fighting in the ruins of Stalingrad. The unrealistic decisions made by Hitler and the German army high command in the summer of 1942 enabled the Russians to wear down the frontline forces of the Wehrmacht in street-fighting of unparalleled ferocity. By resisting inch by inch in the ruins and by means of increasing numbers of counter-attacks, the Soviet forces already in the city gave the Red Army time to put together a main striking force, leading to the victorious November counter-offensive, which ended with the encirclement and destruction of von Paulus' 6th Army.

When the Germans had succeeded in taking possession of almost all the ruins of the town, on 19 Nov. 1942, the second battle of Stalingrad began with a victorious counter-attack by the Red Army, which was to end with the encirclement of von Paulus' 6th Army. Since Göring had assured him that the Luftwaffe would be able to supply the trapped German forces, Hitler refused to order a withdrawal – still possible at this stage. The agony of the 6th Army, short of food, ammunition, fuel and medical supplies, was to endure almost two and a half months, tying down considerable Russian forces. The surrender of the 90,000 survivors took place unit by unit from 27 Jan. to 3 Feb. 1943. Only 8500 were to survive Soviet captivity. Here we see two German soldiers in a trench, at the very beginning of the siege, when they were not yet affected by real hardships.

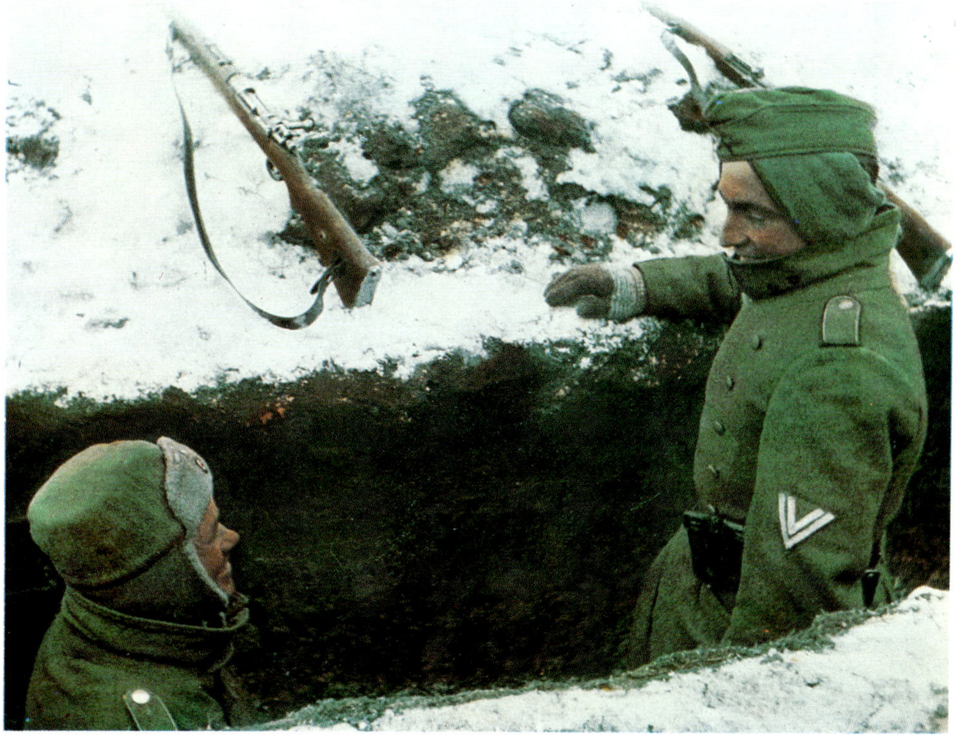

Strategy and tactics. German infantry on th move, protected by tanks, to the north c Moscow, during the winter of 1941.

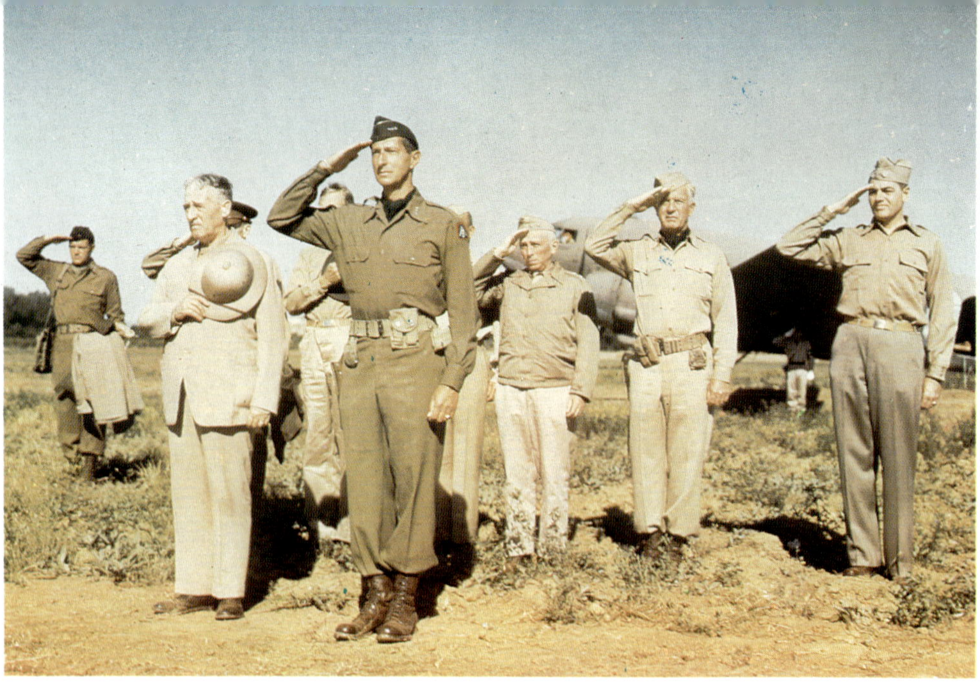

Stimson. He is one of the forgotten personalities of the Second World War. An outstanding lawyer with Republican sympathies, he was appointed secretary of state under Hoover and became noted for his uncompromising opposition to the expansionist policies of the totalitarian powers. In 1940 Roosevelt chose him as secretary for war. It was largely owing to Stimson that his country made such an enormous war effort and achieved the status of a great military power. Together with Truman he was strongly in favour of using the atomic bomb against Japan. Stimpson, who is holding a sun helmet, is seen here in Italy beside General Clark, the commander of the 5th Army.

The STO. In 1940 the government of the Third Reich decided to make use of manpower provided by the occupied countries in order to ensure the smooth running of the German wartime economy. In France at the beginning of 1942 more than 800,000 men were already working on behalf of Germany. However, the Third Reich's manpower requirements, which were steadily becoming more urgent as the war progressed, led it to demand from the Laval government the sending of workers to Germany. Government propaganda at first attempted to encourage the workers to go as volunteers, as this poster appearing on the walls of Paris shows. However, in view of the disappointing results obtained, and urged on by the fresh demands of Gauleiter Sauckel, in 1943 the French state created the 'Service du Travail Obligatoire' (compulsory labour service) and the number of enforced deportations to Germany rapidly increased. In all, nearly 750,000 Frenchmen were conscripted to go and work in the Reich's factories. Many of those who evaded the draft went on to join the resistance.

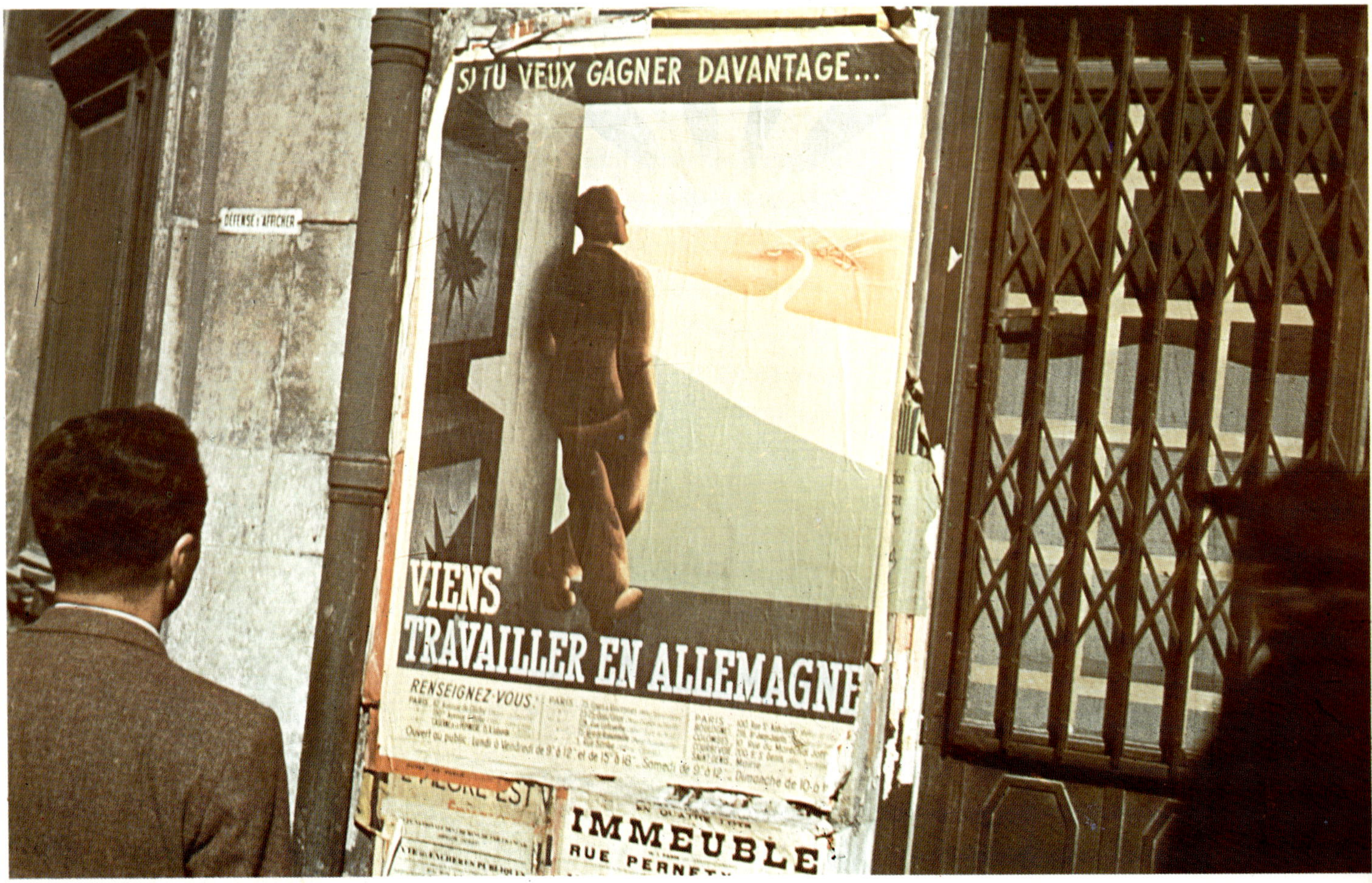

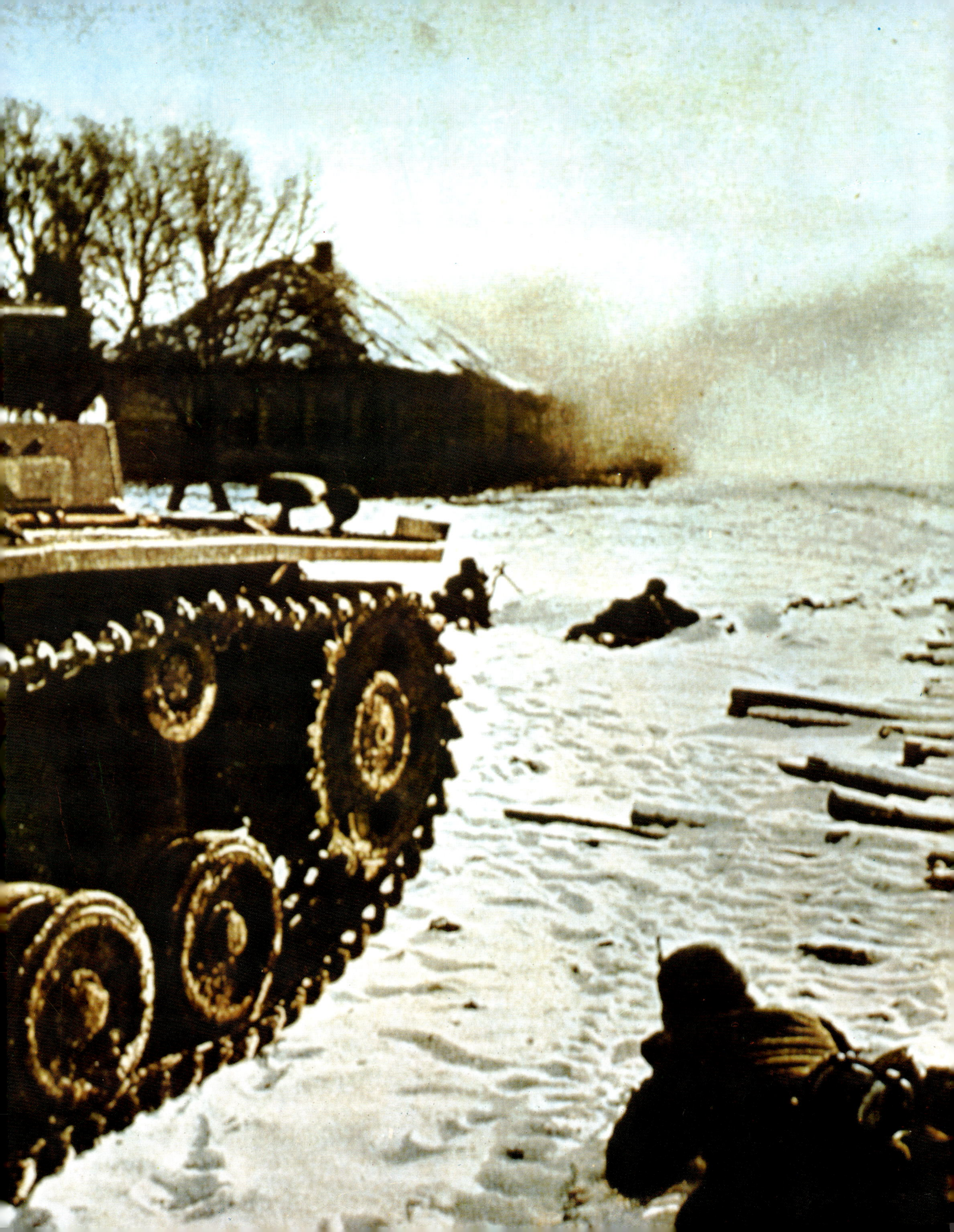

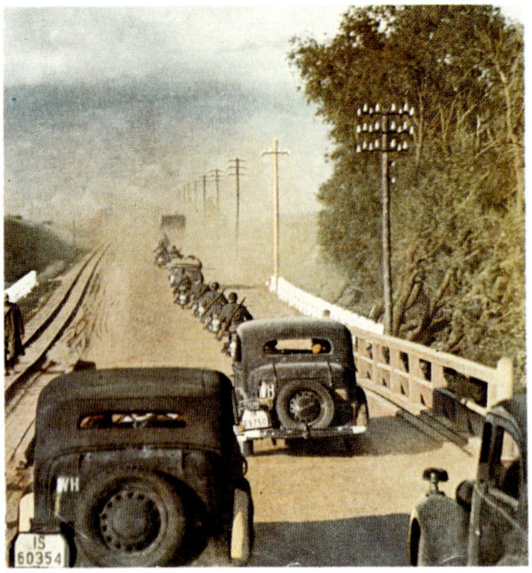

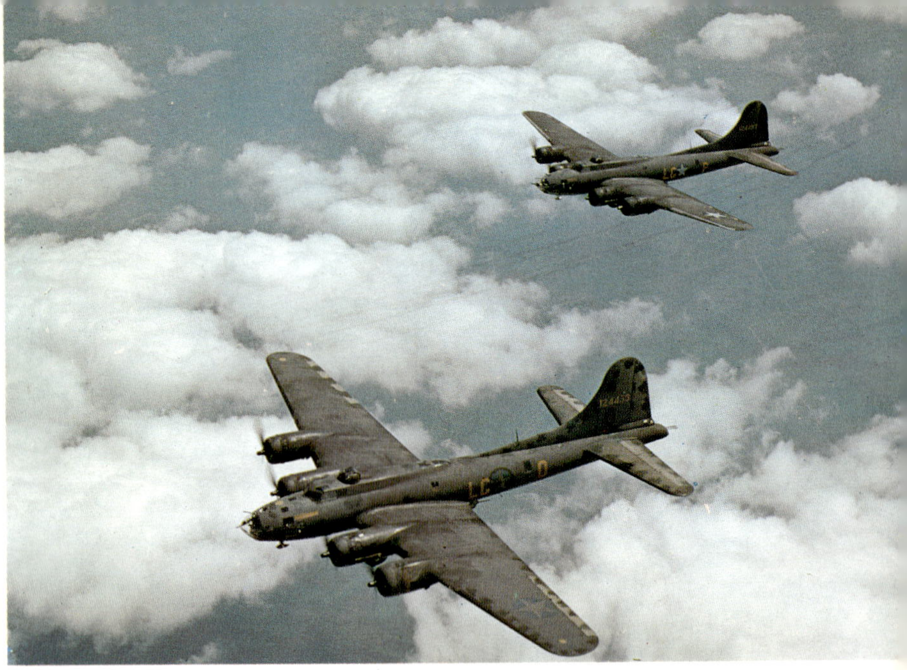

Strategy and Tactics. As a result of new tactical methods, during the course of the Second World War strategy acquired unprecedented importance. The effectiveness of the combination of aircraft and tank facilitated the return to a war of movement, as seen in the Polish campaign, and broke the stalemate imposed by a continuous front line which had paralysed operations during the First World War. The mechanization of armies also permitted the maximum exploitation of breakthroughs made by armoured elements and jeopardized an enemy's chances of re-establishing his position. Here a German column is on the move during the advance in 1941. The war of movement was, however, to find its limitations in the USSR, taking into account the vastness of the country and the fact that the industrial and population centres were widely dispersed.

Above
Apart from the tank and the mechanized unit, one of the great tactical and strategic innovations of the war was the use of aircraft. In fact they played a decisive role, whether directly supporting the forces on the ground or as a weapon to be used behind the lines, attacking staff headquarters, communications and troop concentrations. They also revealed their potential as a strategic instrument in the massive raids on centres of population and armament production. In this respect the aerial offensive conducted by Britain and the USA on Germany achieved devastating results. Nevertheless, despite the hopes of some enthusiastic advocates of air power, these raids could not by themselves bring about the collapse of Germany or Japan. Here four-engined American Boeing B-17s of the 8th Air Force are flying over Europe.

One of the major factors in the Second World War was the sheer scale of combined operations. Unlike the unfortunate precedent provided by the failure of the Dardanelles operation in World War I, most of the landings carried out between 1940 and 1945 by the fighting powers proved to be successful. This success was due to sea and air superiority, to the extent of naval and aerial preparations and to the massive use of landing vessels, enabling armoured elements capable of reducing every defence to be thrown in with the first attacking waves. Here, in the Pacific in Sept. 1944 American landing ships are in a convoy moving towards the Moluccas archipelago.

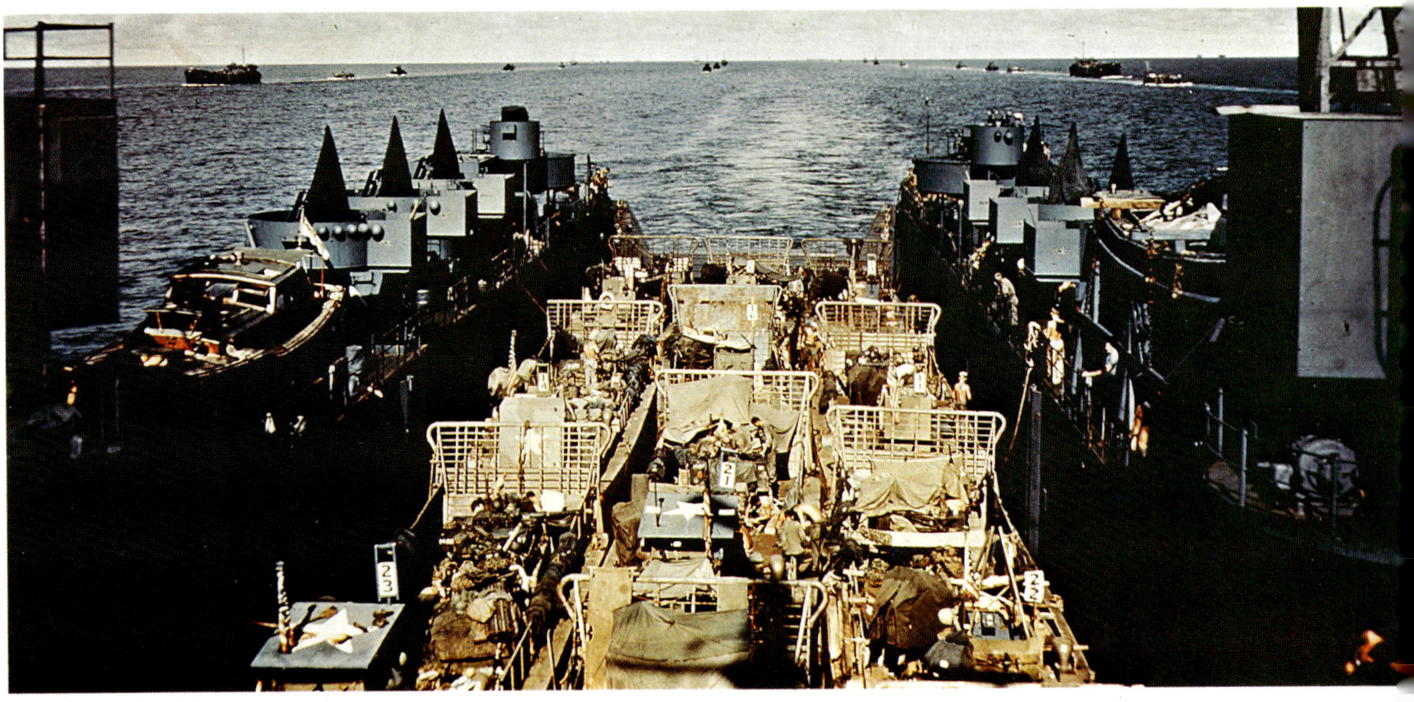

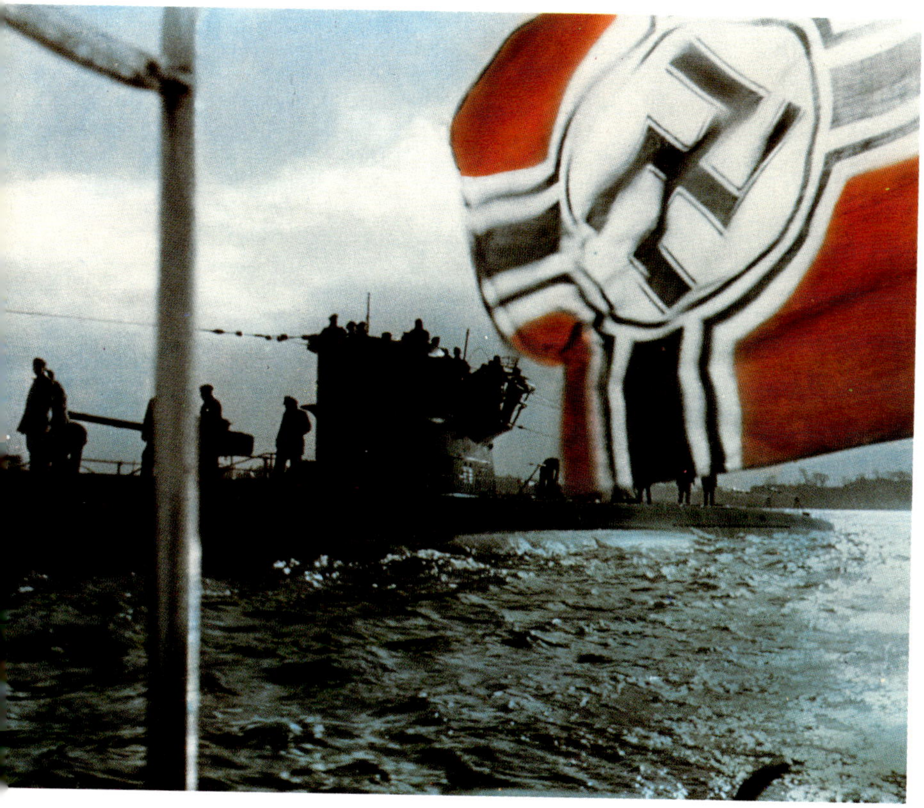

Submarines. A German submarine at the entrance to the base at Lorient in 1940. Contrary to the forecasts of the British Admiralty, convinced of the power of Asdic and the effectiveness of the convoy system, during the Second World War the U-boats displayed even greater efficiency than they had done in 1914–18. Their successes were infinitely greater than those recorded by the large surface vessels and by aircraft. German submarines alone sank more than 2700 merchant vessels, or more than 14 million tons, as well as two battleships, six aircraft carriers and about a hundred destroyers and escort vessels.

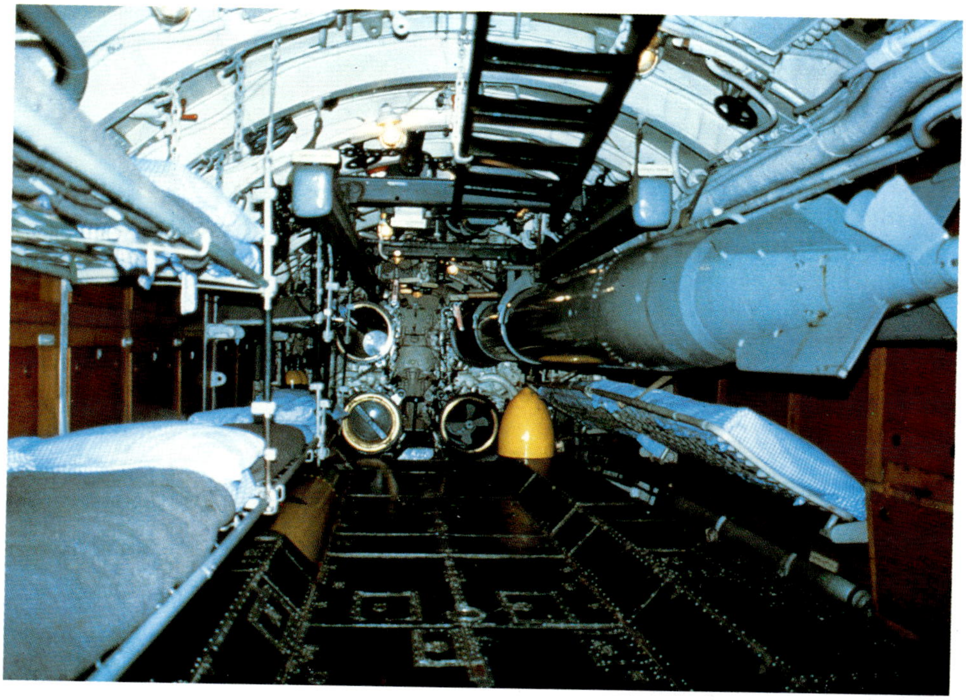

The torpedo room on board the German submarine U-505. The photograph is especially interesting in that it emphasizes the lack of space in such vessels. Folding berths lie close to torpedoes stored in the interior of the boat. The four torpedo tubes can be seen. The lower left tube is closed and the lower right tube is open. A torpedo, whose propeller is clearly visible, has been inserted into it. At the beginning of the war the Germans experienced some setbacks with their magnetically fired torpedoes, which were not finally put right until 1941.

Submarines. An Allied submarine somewh[illegible] in the Atlantic.

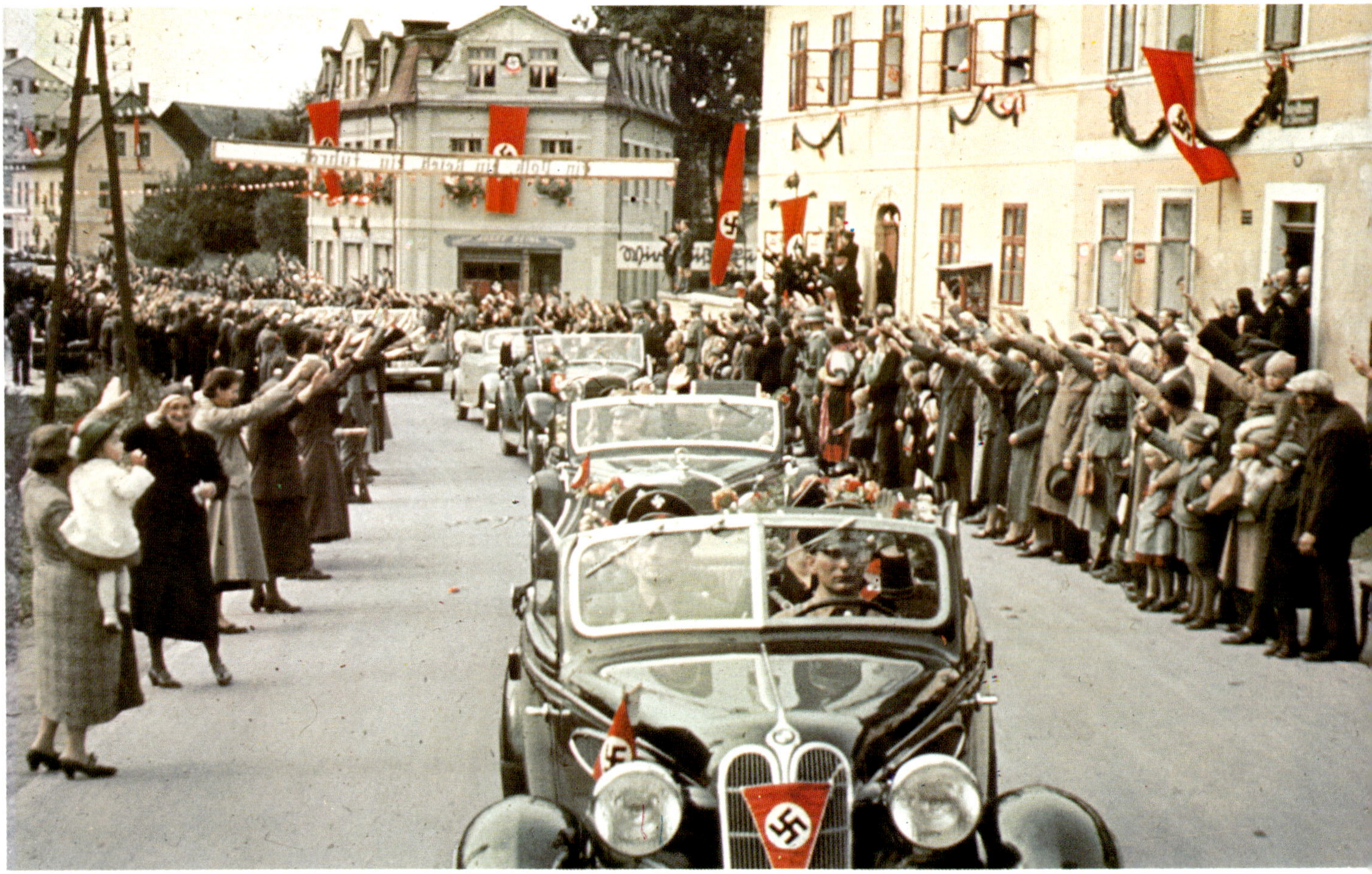

The Sudetenland. The Sudetenlanders were a people of German origin, numbering about 3.5 million, living on the edge of the Bohemian plateau in Czechoslovakia. Making the most of the refusal by the Czechs to grant autonomy to this minority group, in Sept. 1938 Hitler used the Munich crisis to obtain the annexation of the Sudetenland region, at the same time taking the opportunity virtually to break up the Czechoslovak state. Here we see the arrival of Hitler at Eger (now Cheb) in Oct. 1938, where he is greeted by the enthusiastic population.

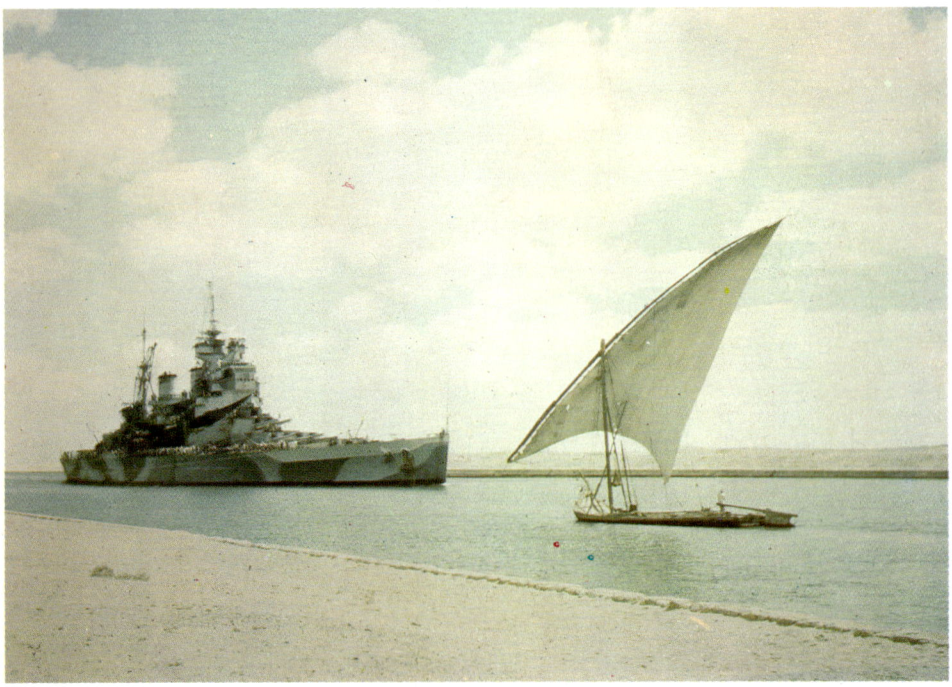

The Suez Canal. In spite of a considerable decrease in the usual commercial traffic, successive closures up to 1943 of the Mediterranean route in favour of the Cape route, and bombing by the Luftwaffe, the Suez Canal played a major strategic role during the conflict. Thanks to security measures taken by the British, it was not closed for more than 76 days in total and only one ship was sunk in the canal. It was by way of the canal that supplies for the 8th Army in Egypt and the landing in Sicily in 1943 were maintained. Here the battleship *Howe* is seen passing through the Canal in 1944 en route for the Pacific.

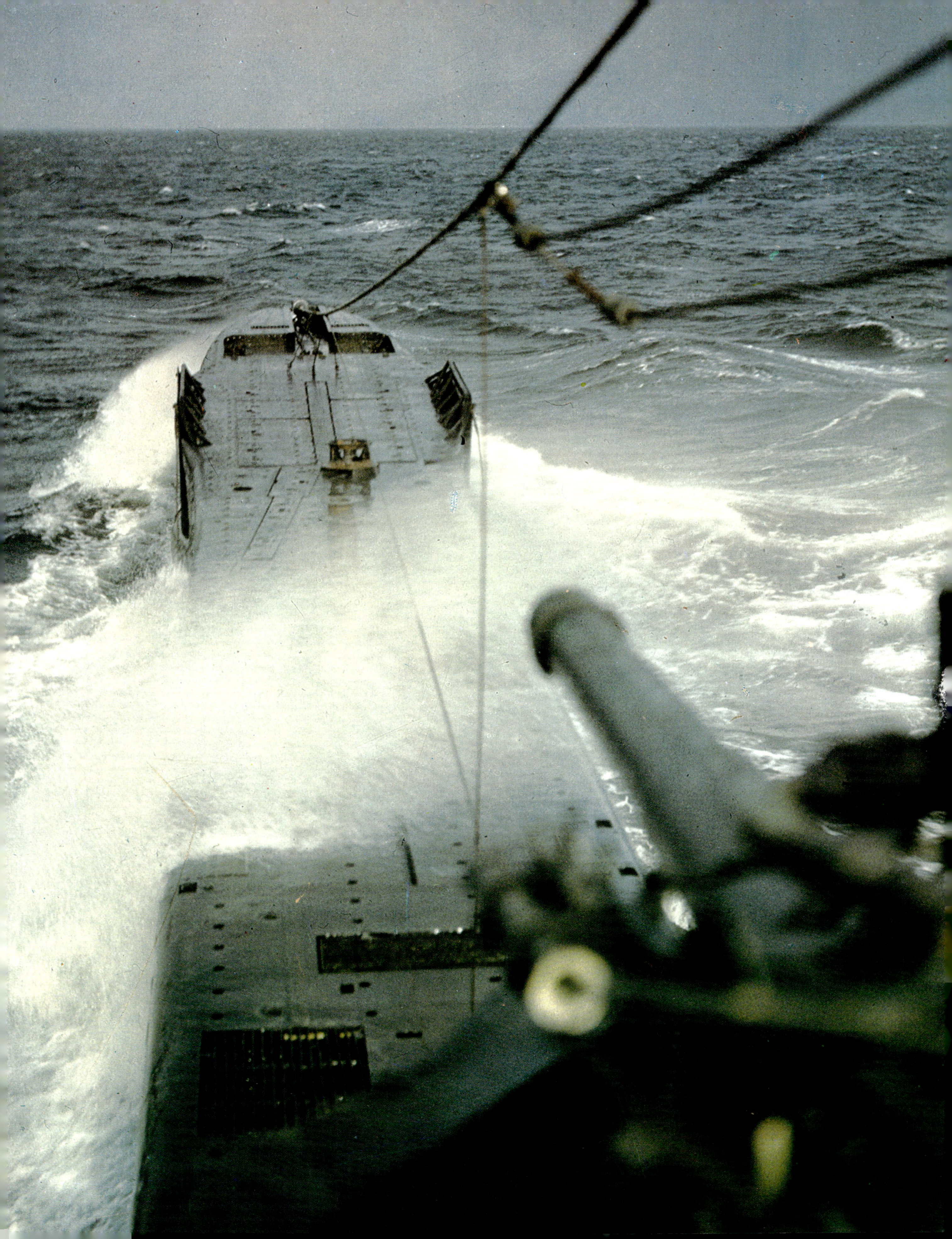

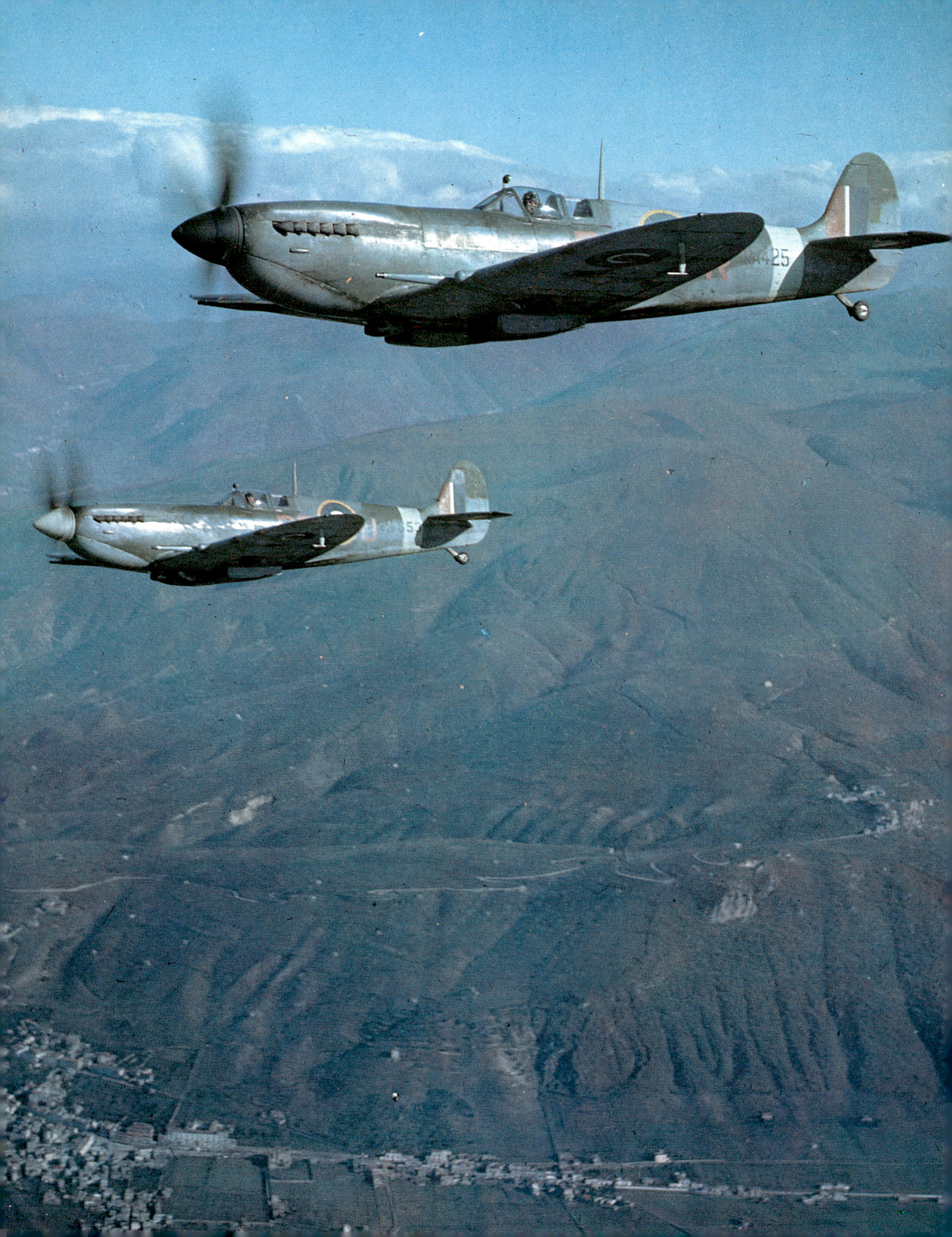

e Supermarine Spitfire. Two of these British
nters to the south of Rome in Feb. 1944.

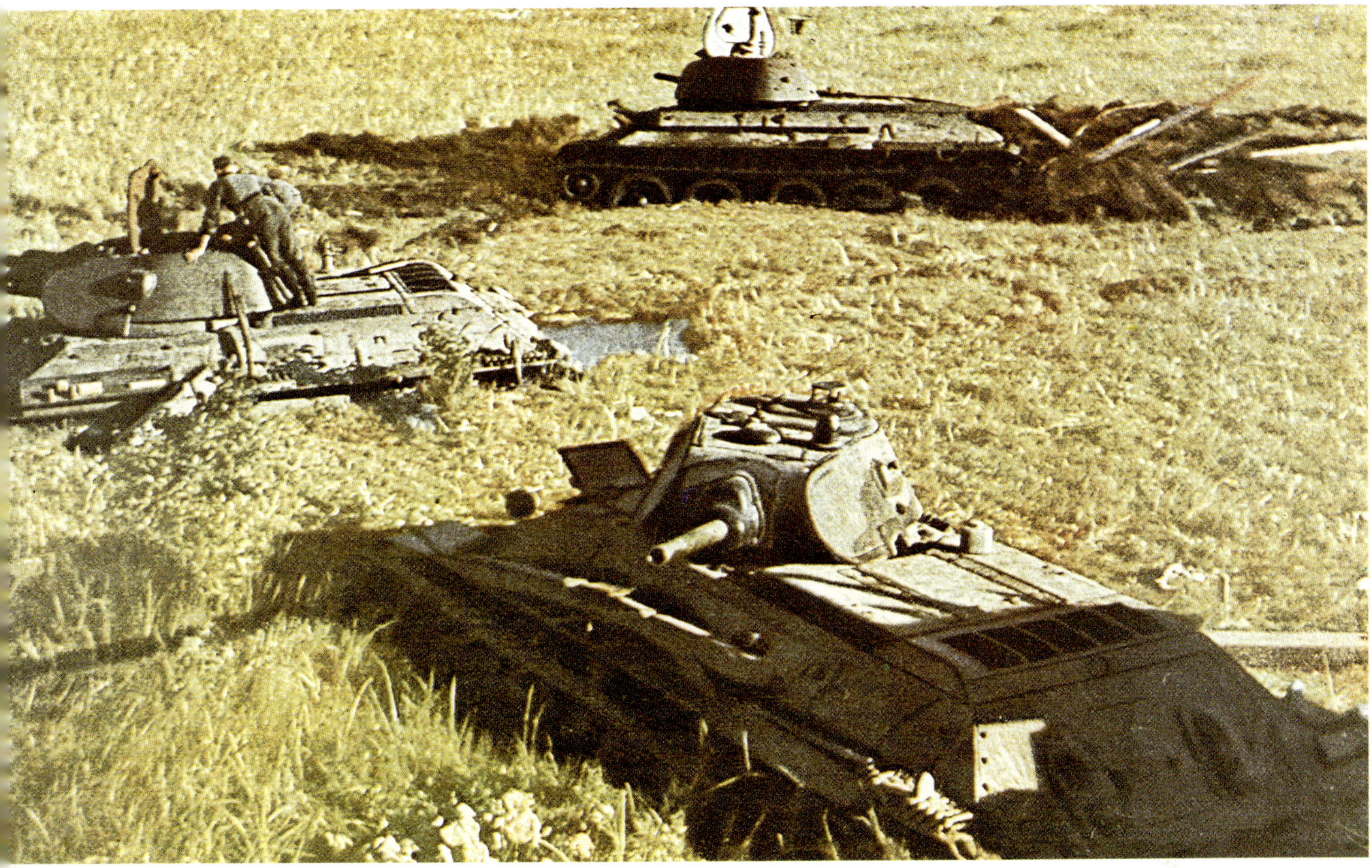

The T-34. From the very beginning of the war on the eastern front the Germans had the unpleasant surprise of coming up against a considerable number of tanks, of which the best, the T-34, made its first appearance as early as June 1941. More adaptable and easier to handle than the enormous KV-1, the T-34 weighed 30 tons, was powered by a diesel engine, heavily armoured and equipped with an excellent 76 mm gun. Continually improved, and from 1943 armed with an 85 mm gun, it remained in service throughout the war. In all, more than 40,000 T-34s were built. Here several of these tanks, which have been abandoned by their crews, having become stuck in the mud in the Drut marshes in Byelorussia, are being carefully examined by the Germans during their offensive in the summer of 1941.

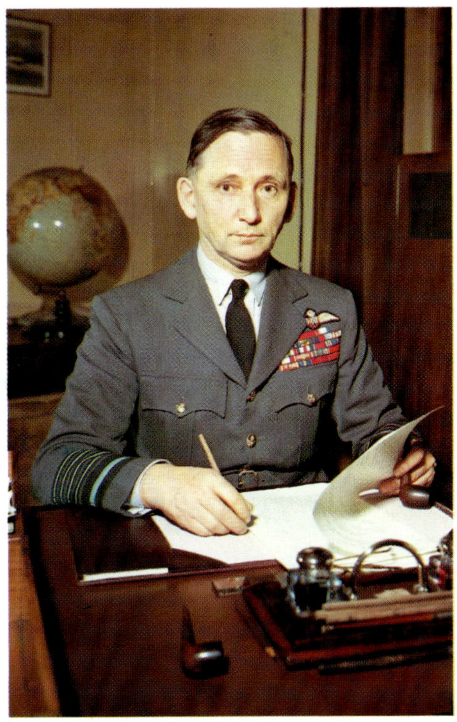

Tedder. Air Chief Marshal Sir Arthur Tedder first became prominent in 1941 as commander of the Middle East Air Force, stressing the importance of air superiority. Despite nearly being dismissed by Churchill in Oct. 1941, Tedder retained his command and managed to achieve air superiority by the time of El Alamein. Having co-ordinated land and air operations in the invasions of Italy and Sicily, he was appointed Eisenhower's deputy in the preparations for the Normandy landings, and, together with Bedell Smith, signed the German surrender document on Eisenhower's behalf in May 1945.

The Third Reich. From the moment it assumed power, the National Socialist regime resolved to keep the working classes under tight control by a whole series of measures. These included a ban on the right to strike, the institution of compulsory work record books, the dissolution of trade unions and their replacement by a single organization grouping together both employees and employers – the German Labour Front – which was simply an instrument of the Nazi Party. At the same time the Third Reich endeavoured, not altogether unsuccessfully, to win over the working people by the progressive reduction of unemployment, a relative improvement in the standard of living, some social benefits (the counterpart to numerous, heavy compulsory contributions) and an intensive propaganda campaign, of which the high spot was the launching of the 'people's car' (the Volkswagen) by Hitler himself, who declared that every German worker should possess a car. The German Labour Front, which was in charge of the project, embarked upon the construction at Fallersleben, near Wolfsburg, 'of the largest motor vehicle factory in the world'. The ceremony of laying the first stone and the display of the various models (our picture) took place in June 1938. However, although the workers themselves had financed the major part of the enterprise by paying in advance threequarters of the price of the car they wished to acquire, no vehicle was ever delivered to them under the Third Reich. At the very beginning of the war the Volkswagen factory was turned over to the production of armaments.

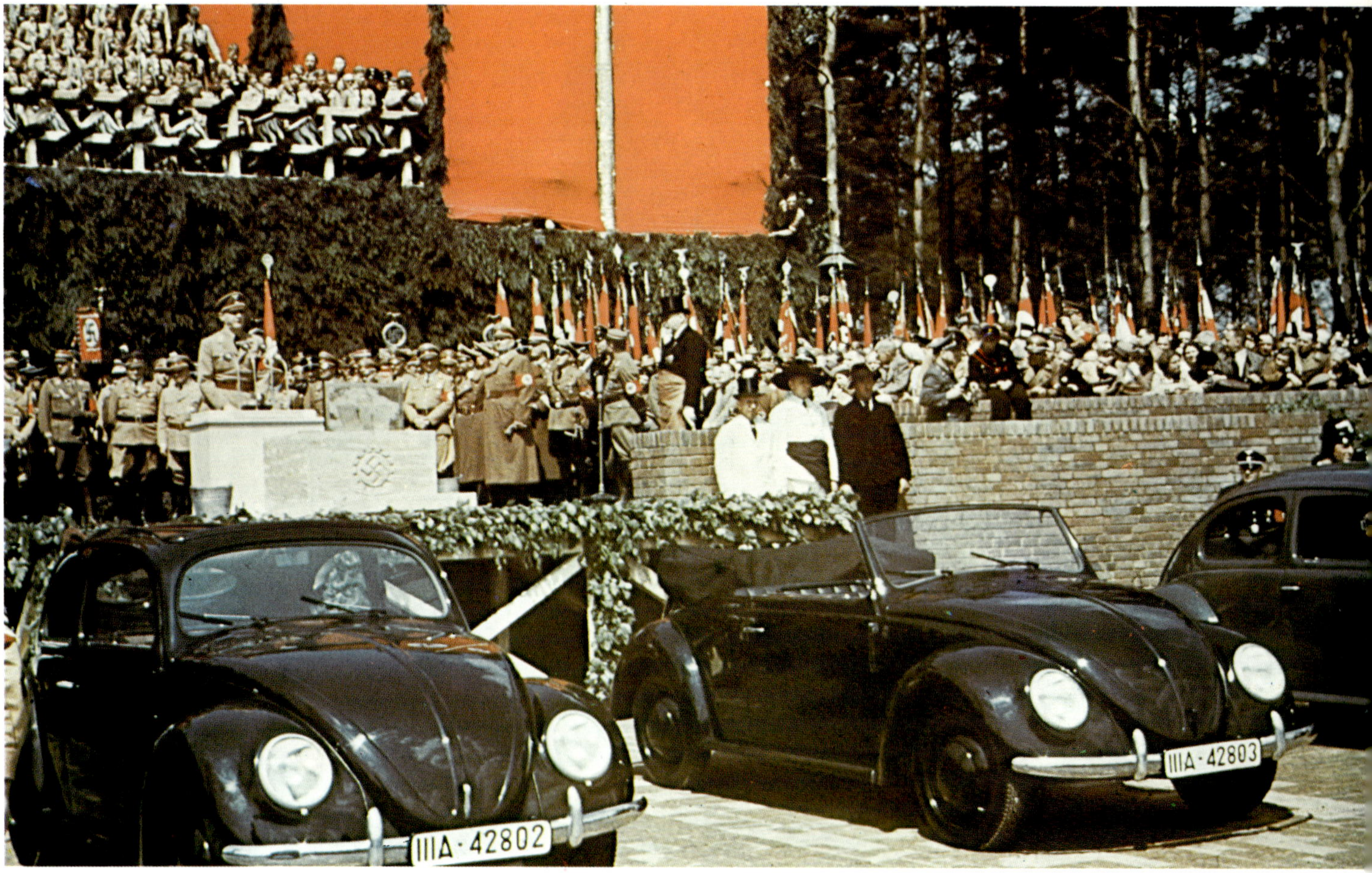

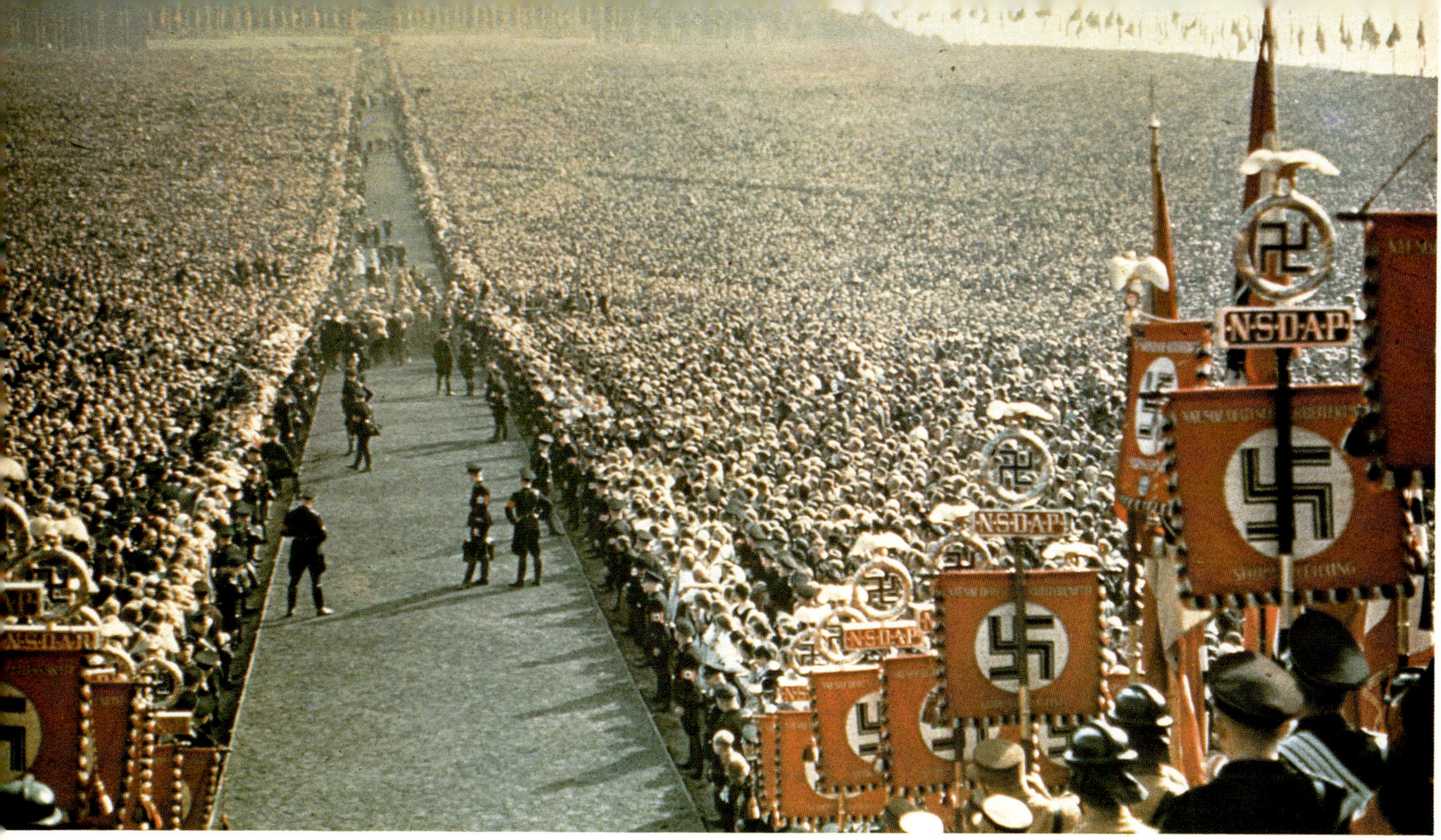

During the Weimar Republic the Nazis had shown their strength, their capacity for organization and their sense of the dramatic, which found expression in parades and mass demonstrations calculated to fire the imagination. After Hitler had taken power these displays took place on an unprecedented scale, reaching their climax every year in September, when the party congress was held in Nuremberg in the presence of the Führer. The huge stadium, with 100,000 places, was then opened. An immense crowd composed of delegations from all the Nazi organizations from every part of Germany demonstrated a flawless unity, a complete confidence in the future of their country and in themselves, and an absolute faith in their leader, whose appearance and speeches produced a delirious enthusiasm. This crowd presented the impressive spectacle of an irresistible force.

From the very beginning of the Third Reich Hitler relentlessly pursued a policy which aimed at the abrogation of all the military restrictions imposed by the Treaty of Versailles. He considered this an indispensable condition for the restoration of Germany's prestige. Freed from the final restraints with the remilitarization of the Rhineland in 1936, the regime could now devote all its efforts to the development of what was to be the essential instrument of Hitler's imperialist policy: a powerful modern army, equipped with tanks and aircraft, and organized on the basis of the existing nucleus of the Reichswehr. The whole economy of the country was geared to production for war and rearmament was pushed to extremes. Several months before the beginning of the conflict, on the occasion of the Führer's 50th birthday, 20 April 1939, the new Wehrmacht was able to display its strength in the course of an immense parade. Here, in Berlin, an infantry unit is goosestepping past the official grandstand.

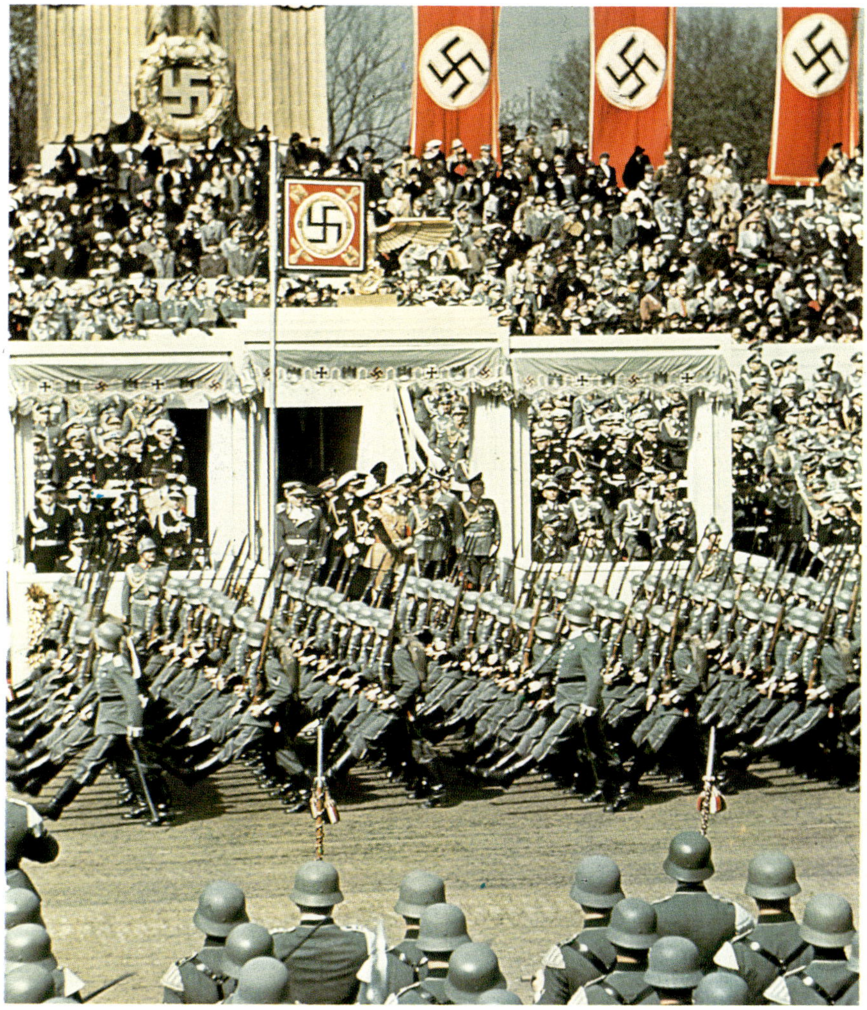

Opposite
The Third Reich. A scene in Berlin after Allie bombing in 1945, with buildings in flames.

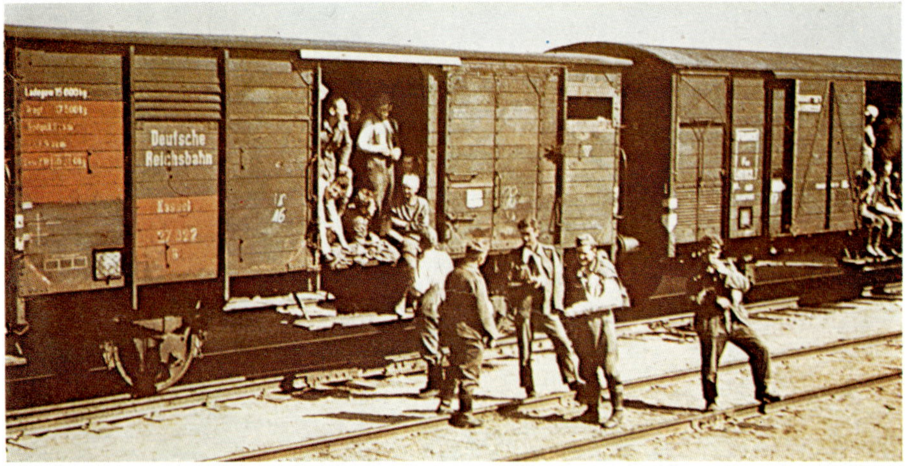

The early campaigns in Poland, in Norway, in the west and in the Balkans were to be for the Third Reich an easy war. The successes were spectacular and the losses small. The real sacrifices only began with the attack on the Soviet Union. During 1941–5 the Wehrmacht lost more than 3 million dead on the eastern front. In this picture, a group of German and Italian wounded returning from the Soviet Union have briefly got out of the train which is transporting them back to Germany.

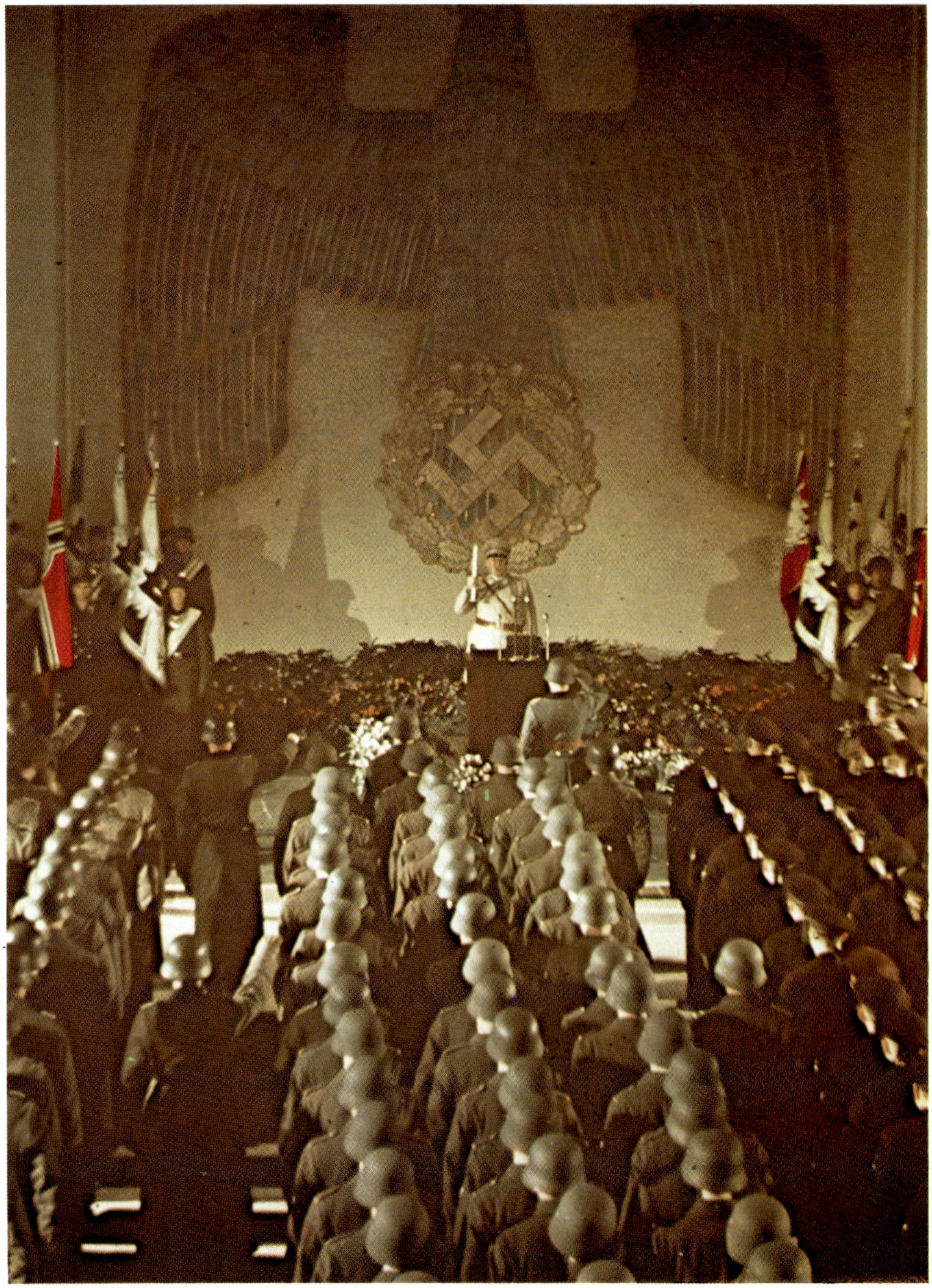

From 1939 the sense of the dramatic, so characteristic of the Third Reich, adapted itself to the evolution of the conflict. It was in a deliberately austere decor that Göring celebrated on 30 Jan. 1943 the tenth anniversary of the assumption of power. Several days later came the surrender of Stalingrad and solemn ceremonies were held throughout Germany in honour of von Paulus' 6th Army. With the first major defeats the Reich began to live in a Wagnerian atmosphere.

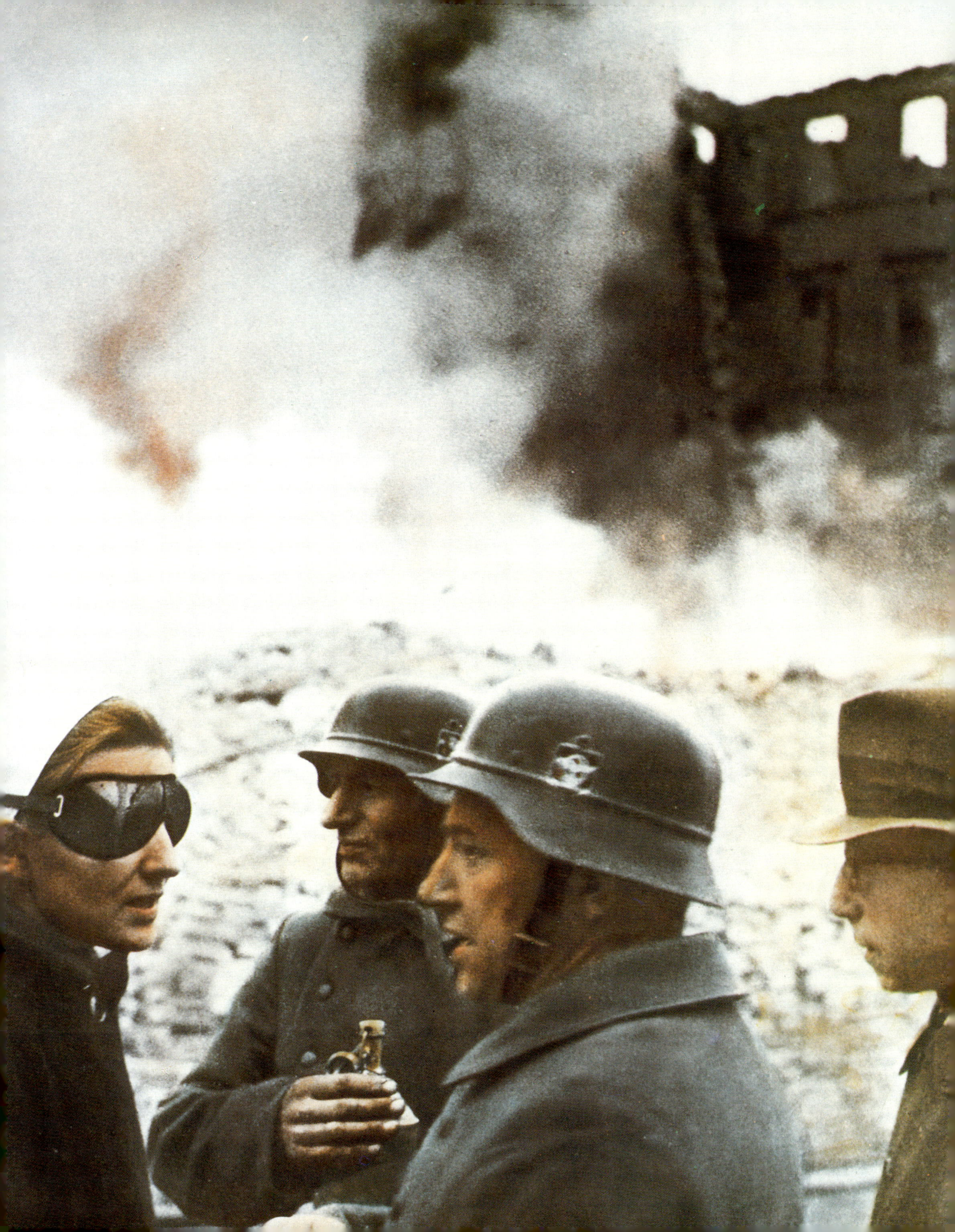

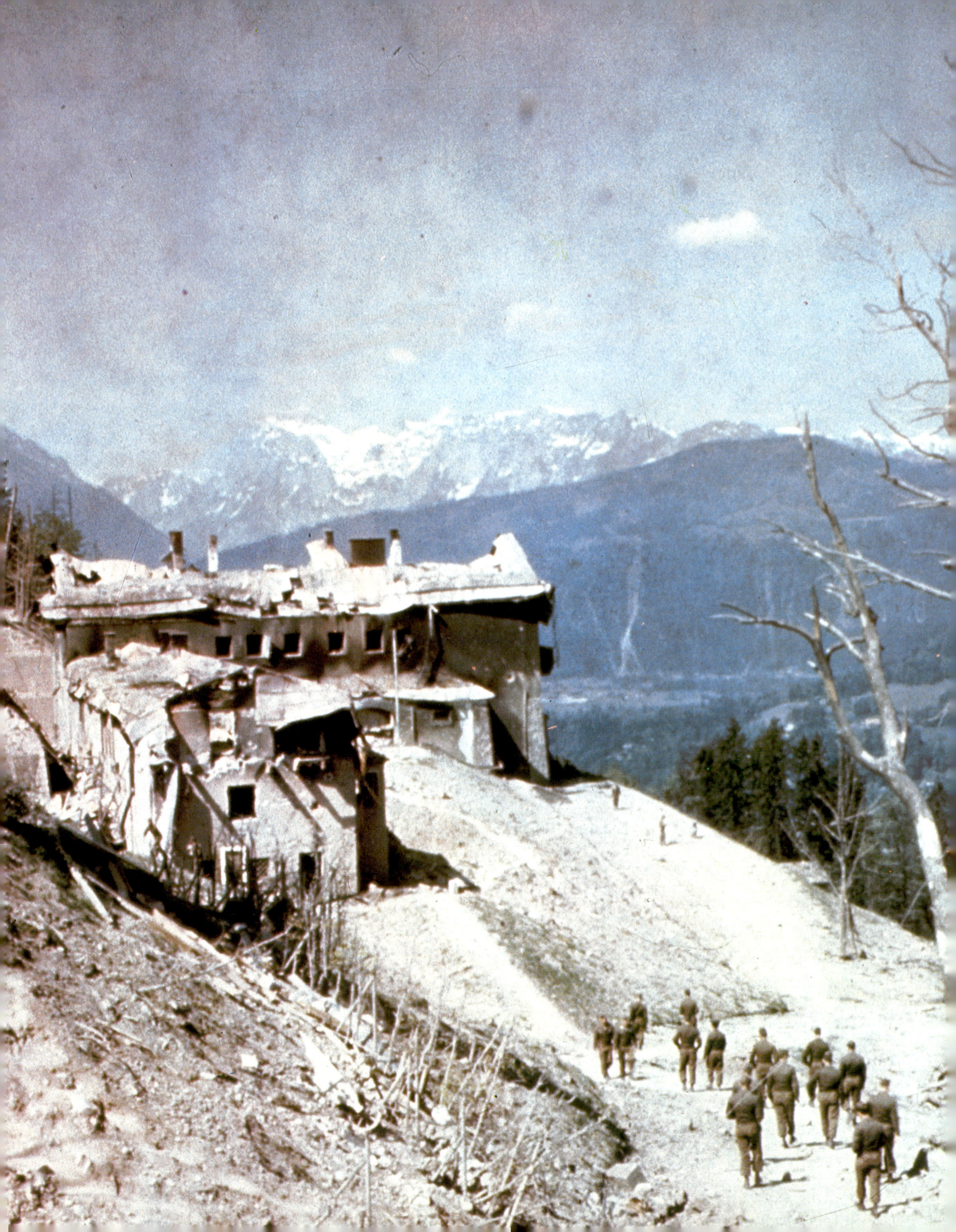

pposite
symbol of the fall of the Third Reich in 1945,
: ruins of the Berghof, Hitler's residence, at
rchtesgaden.

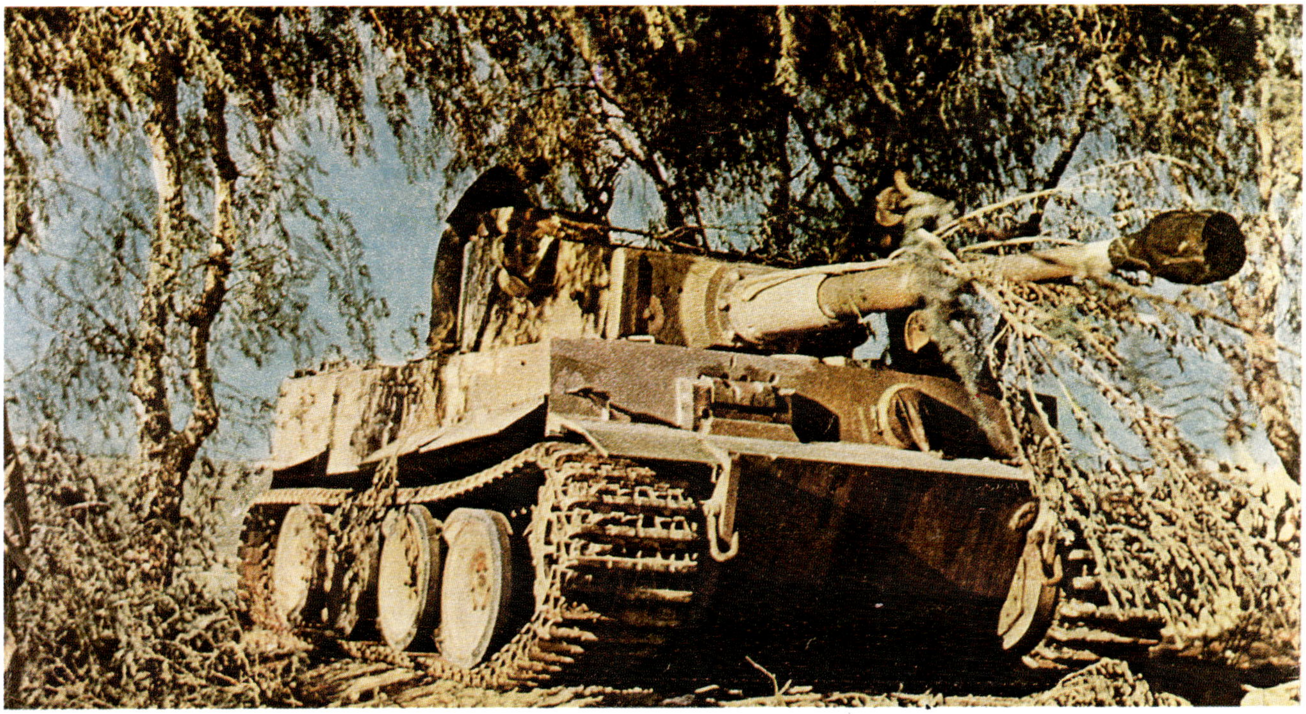

The Tiger. Brought into service in March 1942, the Tiger was the most powerful tank of its time. Weighing 55 tons, it was extremely well armoured and equipped with an excellent 88 mm gun, possessing a high muzzle velocity. Formed into battalions of heavy tanks, which were at the disposal of the German high command, it saw service on all fronts. In 1944 the Tiger II was developed from the Tiger I. Weighing 70 tons and more streamlined, it was more heavily armoured and equipped with an improved gun. Both models, however, suffered from lack of speed and limited range. Here a Tiger I is seen on the Tunisian front in 1943.

The Tirpitz. Brought into service in 1941, this sister ship of the *Bismarck* was one of the most powerful battleships of the Second World War. With a displacement of 45,000 tons, it was extremely well protected and its armament consisted of eight 15 in. (380 mm), twelve 5.9 in. (150 mm) and sixteen 4.1 in. (105 mm) guns, plus powerful anti-aircraft batteries. Based in northern Norway, the *Tirpitz* made only the occasional sortie. However, it presented a constant threat to Allied convoys bound for Murmansk, and helped to tie up several Allied battleships in Scapa Flow until 1944. On several occasions the British tried in vain to destroy it by means of attacks by midget submarines or by aircraft carriers. It was eventually the RAF which succeeded in sinking the *Tirpitz*, on 12 Nov. 1942, with 12,000 lb. bombs. The photograph shows the *Tirpitz* seen from the foredeck of the heavy cruiser, *Admiral Hipper*, on the occasion of one of its infrequent sorties from Altenfjord.

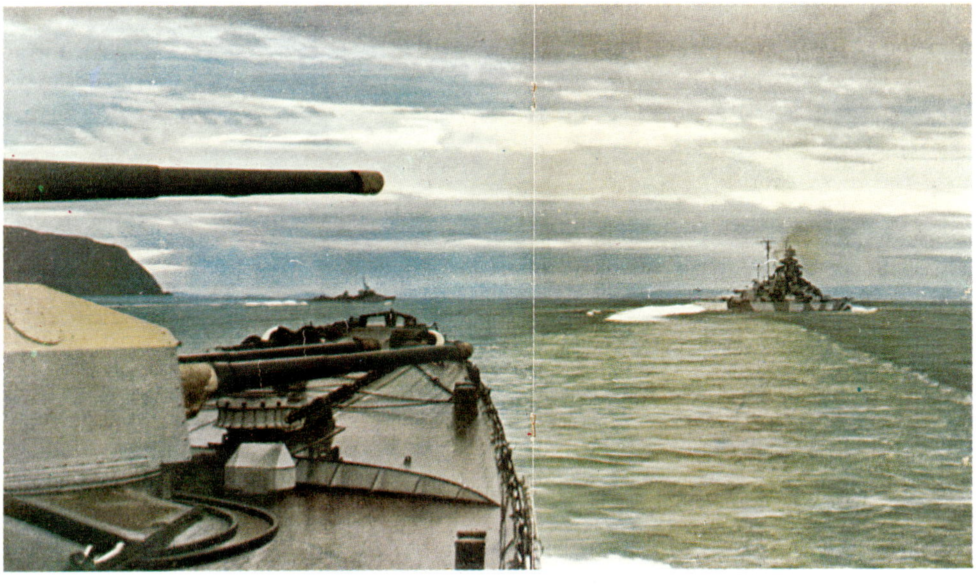

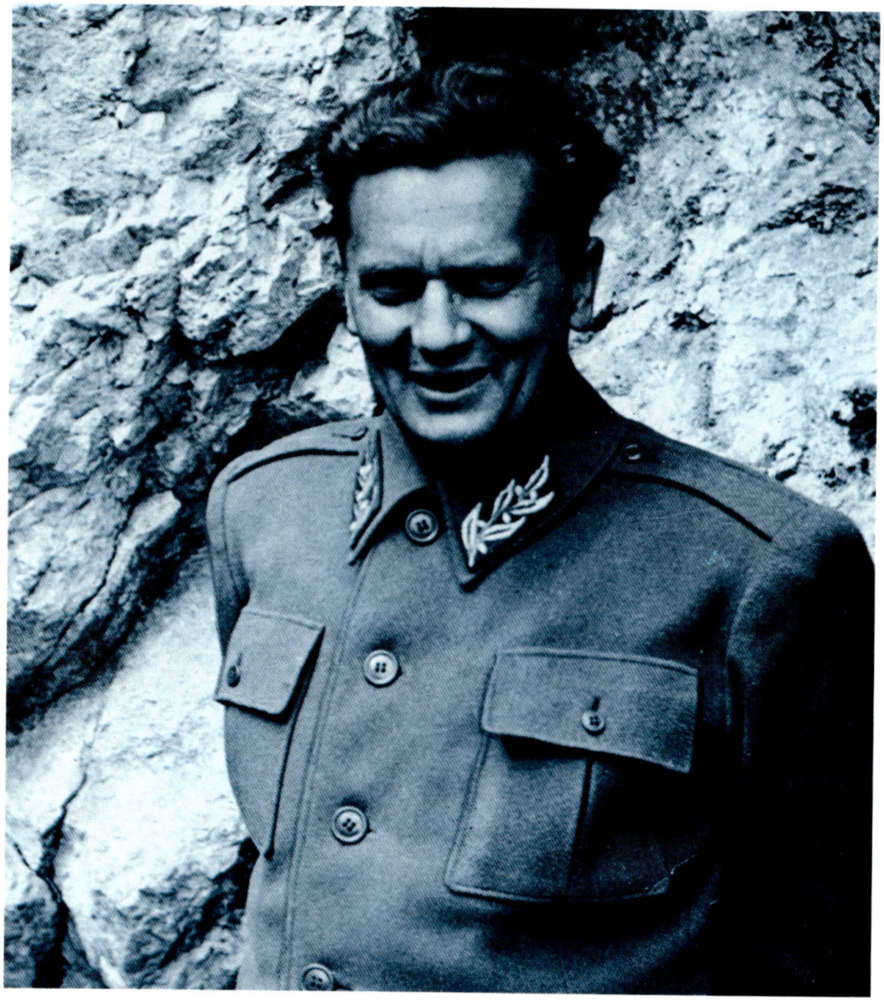

Tito. As Communist leader of the Yugoslav resistance, Tito forced thousands of Axis troops to be tied up fighting the partisans when they were badly needed elsewhere. Having organized an effective resistance he crossed swords with the rival Chetniks, and after defeating them, was driven out of Serbia by the Germans. At the end of 1942, the Allies shifted their support from the Chetniks under Mihajlović to Tito, and this was extended to air support when the Germans launched a large offensive against the partisans. With the Allies' help, Tito managed to take Belgrade by the end of Oct. 1944.

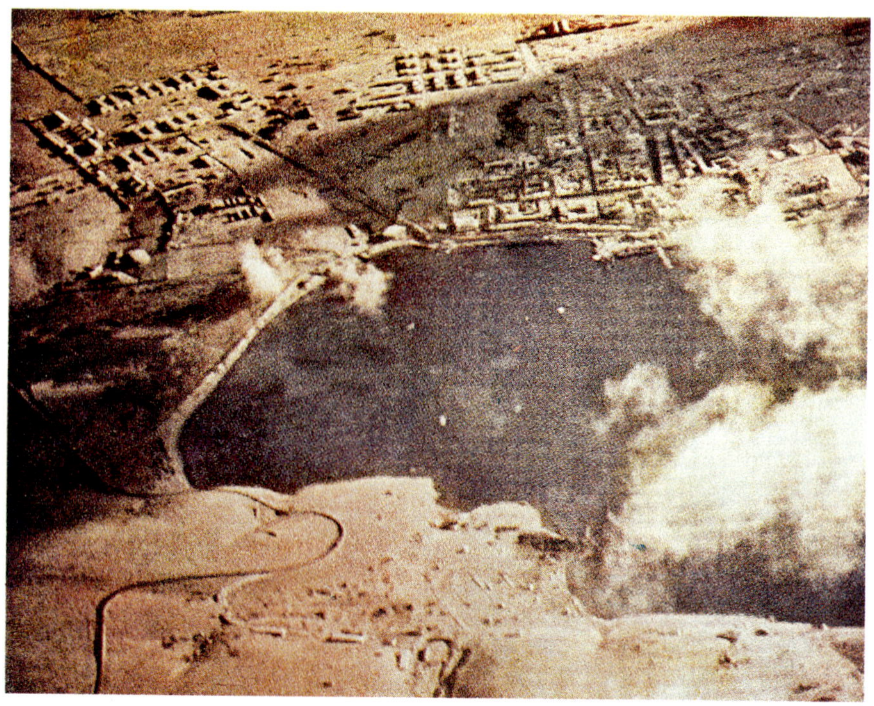

Tobruk. The chief port of Cyrenaica, Tobruk was to play an important part in the course of the war in North Africa. Captured by the 8th Army in Jan. 1941, it was subsequently to be besieged by the Germans and Italians from April to December of that year and subjected to bombardments (photograph). After a 240-day siege the port was relieved as part of the 'Crusader' offensive. Despite all the forecasts, Rommel succeeded in taking Tobruk on 21 June 1942, just after the victory at Gazala. The surrender was accompanied by the capture of a considerable amount of material and 32,000 men. Following the battle of El Alamein Tobruk was reoccupied for good by the British on 12 Nov. 1942. Bibliothèque du musée de l'Armée.

The Todt Organization. Established in 1938 in order to co-ordinate the public works of the Reich, the Todt Organization (from the name of its director) became from 1940 onwards a vast concern, on a European scale, employing more than 2 million people, both Germans and foreigners. Apart from the repair of roads, railways and airfields, it also undertook the building of fortifications, such as the Winter and Gothic Lines in Italy, and the Atlantic Wall which was erected along the whole coast of western Europe. In this picture a group of conscripted North African workers are engaged, under German supervision, on the construction of concrete works intended to provide shelter for submarines.

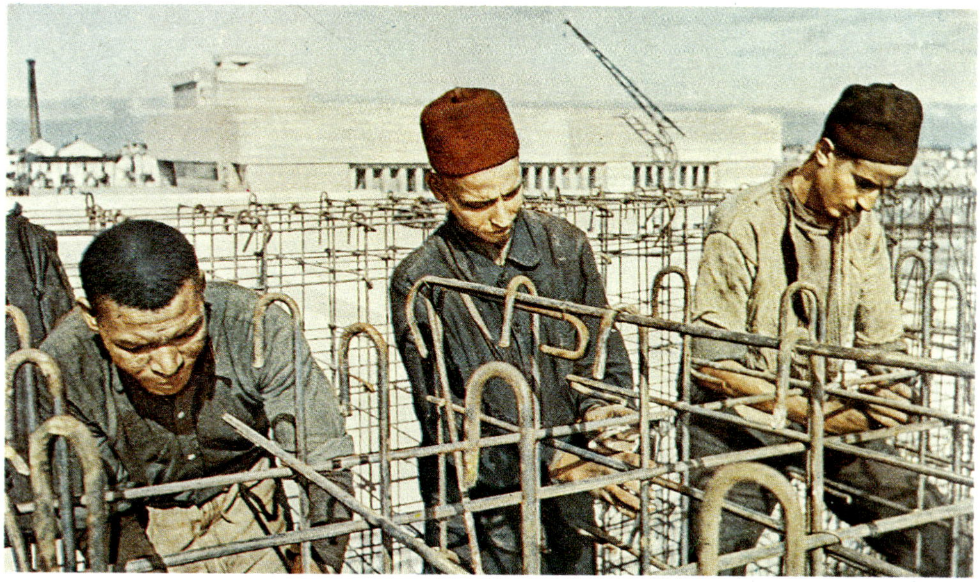

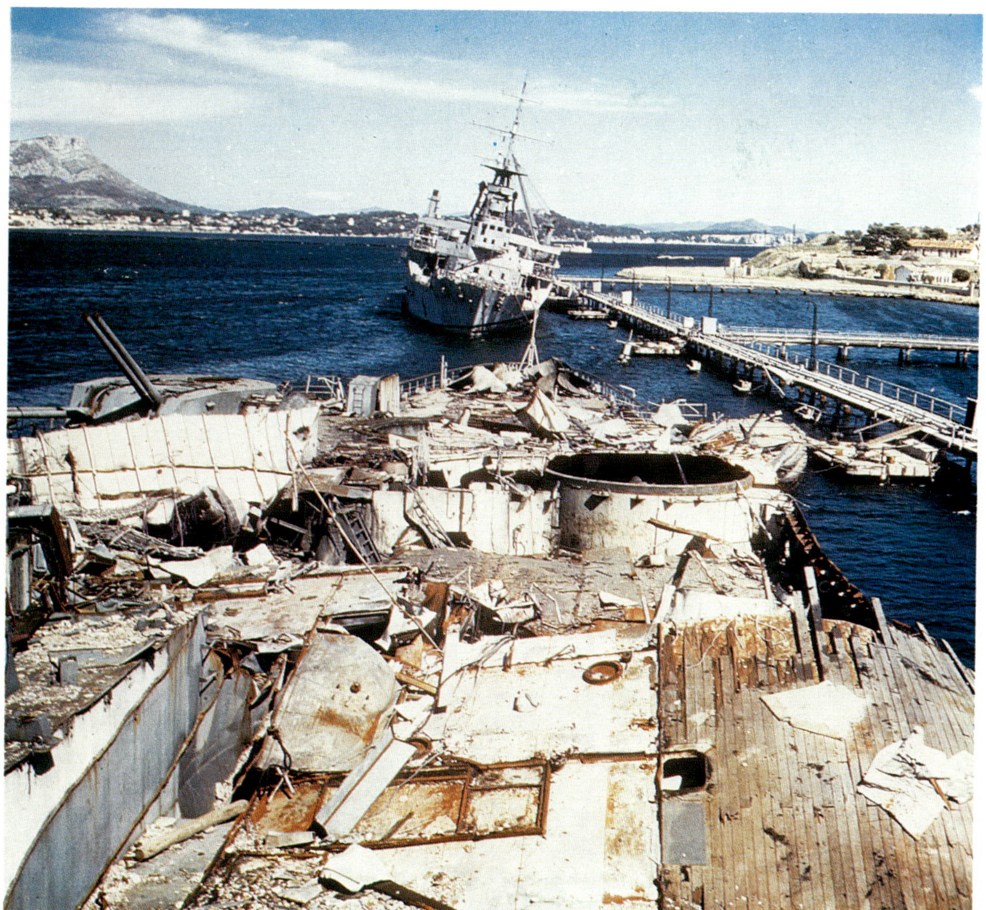

The scuttling of the French fleet at Toulon. At dawn on 27 Nov. 1942, 16 days after the Germans had moved into the unoccupied zone of France, two German divisions took the fortified area at Toulon by surprise and attempted to get possession of the French fleet. Warned at the last minute, Admiral de Laborde succeeded in giving the order to scuttle the ships of the fleet. Nearly 90 vessels were thus destroyed, representing almost half the French navy. Only five submarines succeeded in getting away, three of which reached North Africa. With the scuttling of the fleet the Vichy regime had lost its last asset.

Tojo. He entered the army in 1905 and embarked upon a brilliant career, achieving rapid promotion. In 1936 he became chief of staff of the Manchurian army, being appointed chief of general staff of the Japanese army two years later. In July 1940 he was made minister of war and as such embodied the imperialist element which demanded the creation of a 'new order' embracing China and the Far East. After helping to bring about the fall of the Konoye cabinet in Oct. 1941, Tojo became prime minister and took the decision to attack Pearl Harbor. In 1942 the great Japanese victories seemed to justify his dreams of imperialism. But after the defeats in the Gilbert and Mariana Islands, his position became weaker and he resigned on 18 July 1944. Following Japan's surrender he was arrested, tried and condemned to death, together with other Japanese leaders, as a war criminal, by the international military tribunal in Tokyo in 1948. Here he is seen reading the text of his deposition during the trial.

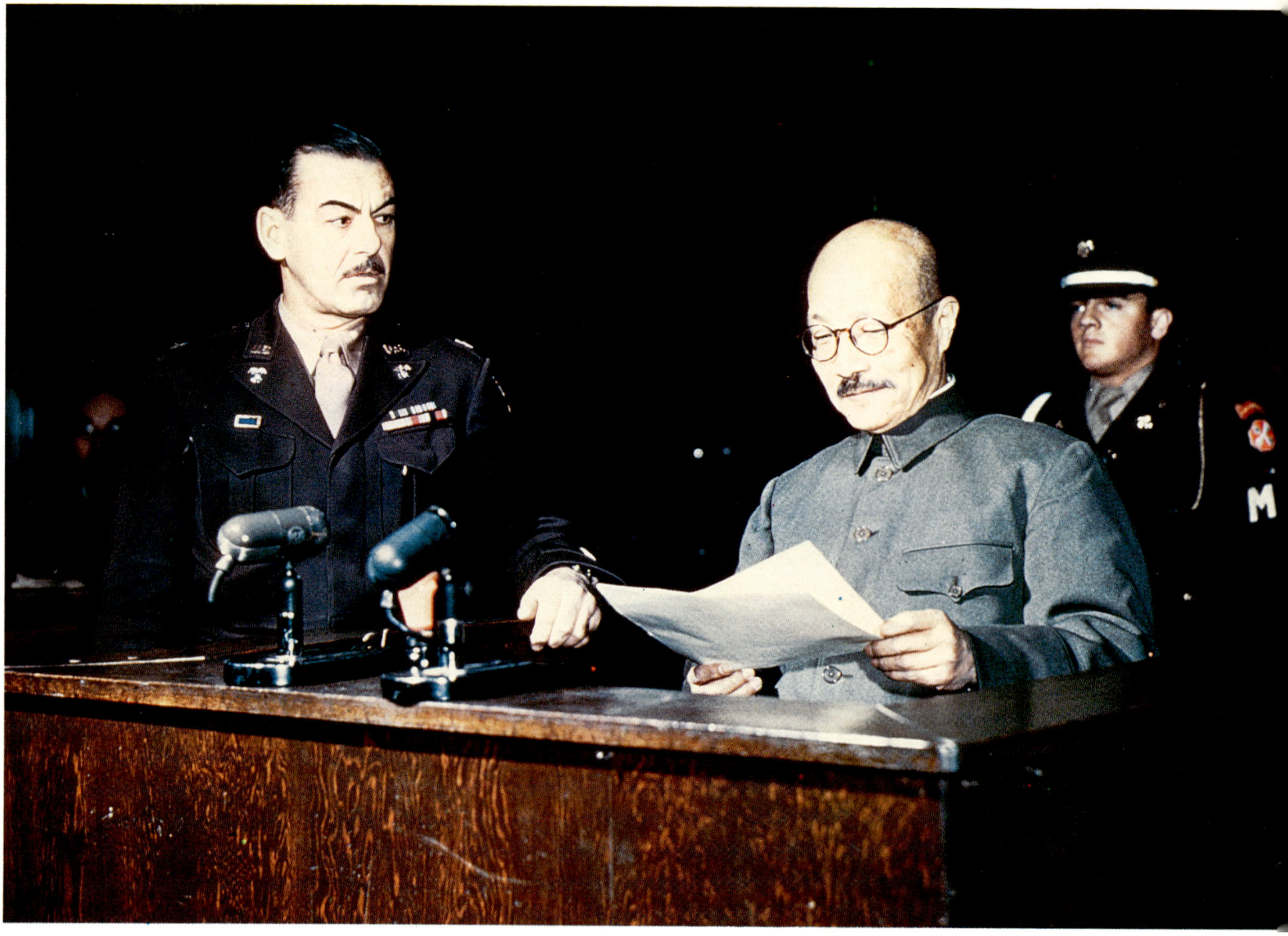

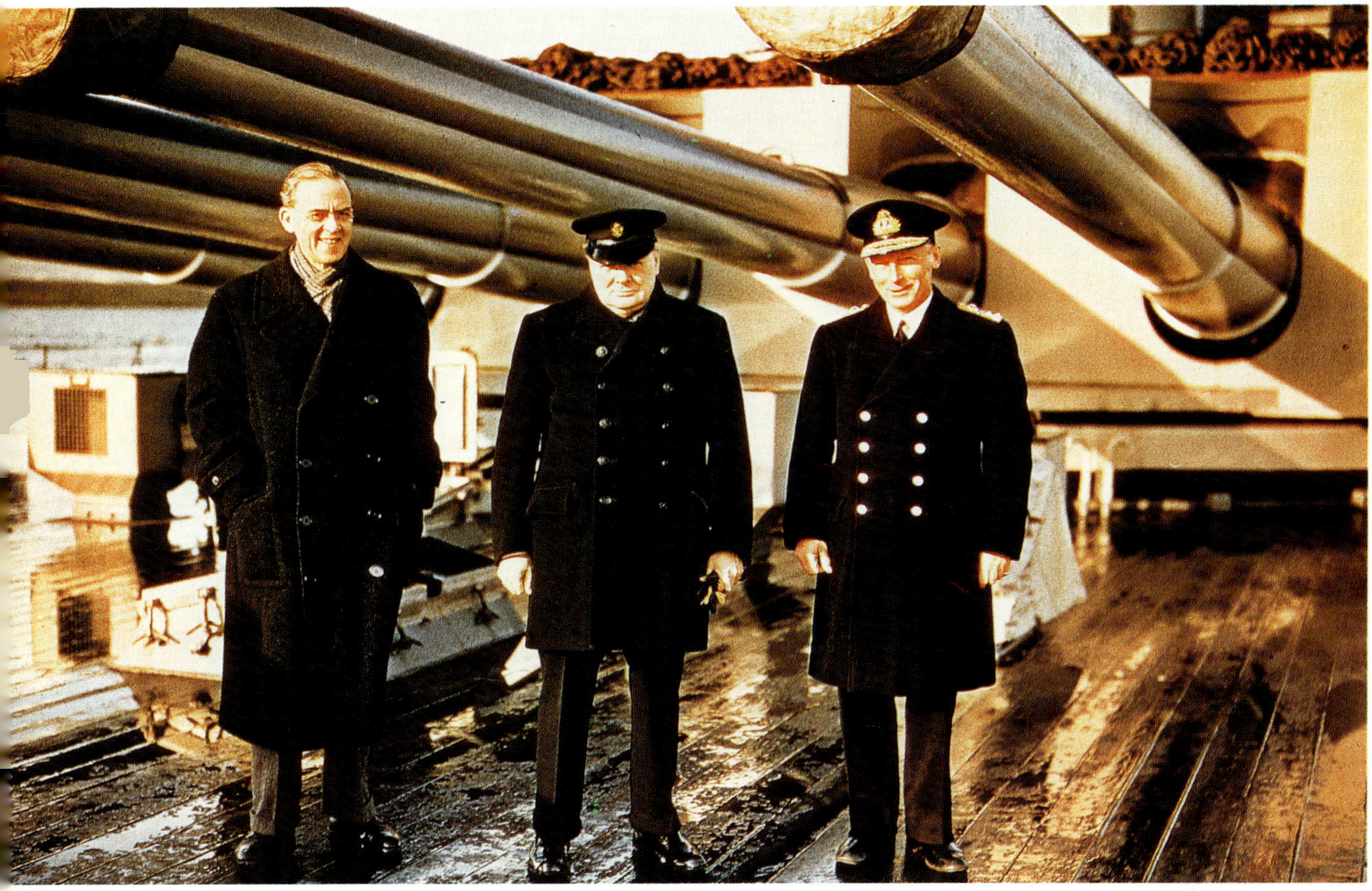

Tovey. Admiral Tovey in company with Winston Churchill and Sir Stafford Cripps, minister of aircraft production, on the deck of a British battleship of the *King George V* class in 1943. Promoted vice-admiral in 1940, Tovey had distinguished himself in the Mediterranean at the head of light naval forces, before being put in command of the Home Fleet from Dec. 1940 to May 1943. In this capacity he took part in the pursuit and destruction of the *Bismarck* and in the protection of convoys bound for Murmansk. Promoted admiral in 1943 and port-admiral of the Nore, he played a major part in the preparations for the Normandy landings.

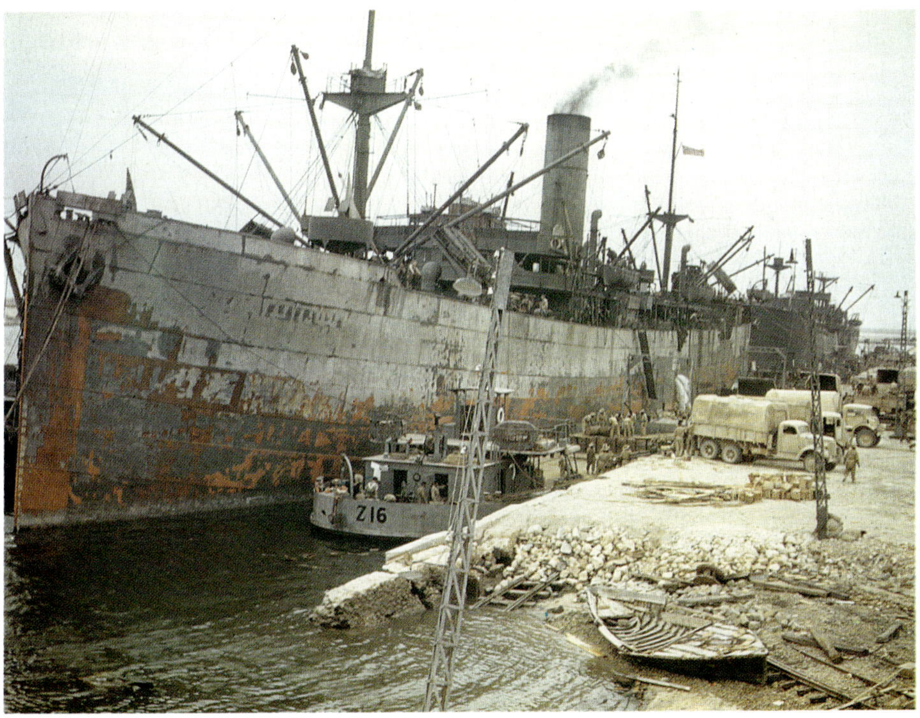

Transport. Throughout the conflict the armies were dependent upon lines of communication by land or sea stretching over thousands of miles. With the help of sea transport the United States was in a position to resupply the war economies of its allies and to put armies into position in the Pacific and European theatres of war. More than 75,000 ships crossed the Atlantic Ocean alone, carrying nearly 270 million tons of material and more than 4 million men. Here in 1943 a Liberty Ship merchant vessel is unloading barrels of petroleum and various other materials at a Tunisian port.

Opposite
Tunisia. Cleaning the gun of a British tank, t
Cruiser Mk VI Crusader.

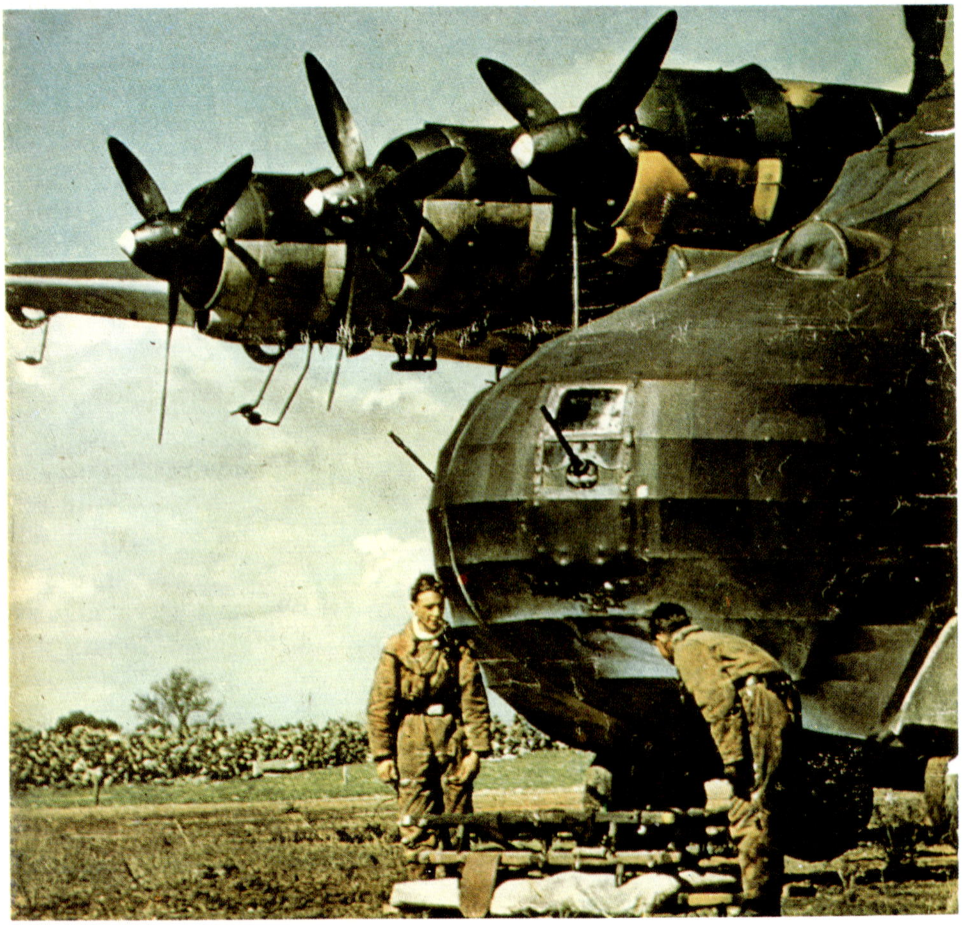

Transport by air. During the first four years of the war the Germans were almost the only combatants to use air transport as part of large-scale operations, such as the Norwegian and French campaigns, the attack on Crete and the supplying of Rommel's Afrika Korps in Libya. During the battle of Stalingrad 6500 tons were airlifted to the German positions and nearly 50,000 wounded evacuated. At this period the Germans used mainly the three-engined Junkers Ju-52, and also formations of He-111s and Ju-86s. From 1943 they also brought into service the six-engined Messerschmitt Me-323 (photograph) which had an enormous carrying capacity.

The Tripartite Pact. This cartoon by Arthur Szyk, published in the United States in 1942, illustrates the tragic fate of the famous signatories of the Tripartite Pact – Germany, Italy and Japan – who, despite their alliance, finally lost the war. Here Mussolini is enslaved by Germany, represented by Göring, and by Tojo, minister of war in the Japanese government. Concluded on 27 Sept. 1940, the pact had a mainly symbolic value. In no way did it deter the United States, as Japan hoped, nor did it serve as an effective coalition against Britain or as a means of isolating the USSR, as Germany calculated. Among other countries Hungary, Romania, Slovakia then Bulgaria and Yugoslavia and, after the dismemberment of the latter, Croatia, eventually gave their adherence to the pact. The most positive result of the treaty was that it induced Germany and Italy to declare war on the United States in Dec. 1941, after Pearl Harbor.

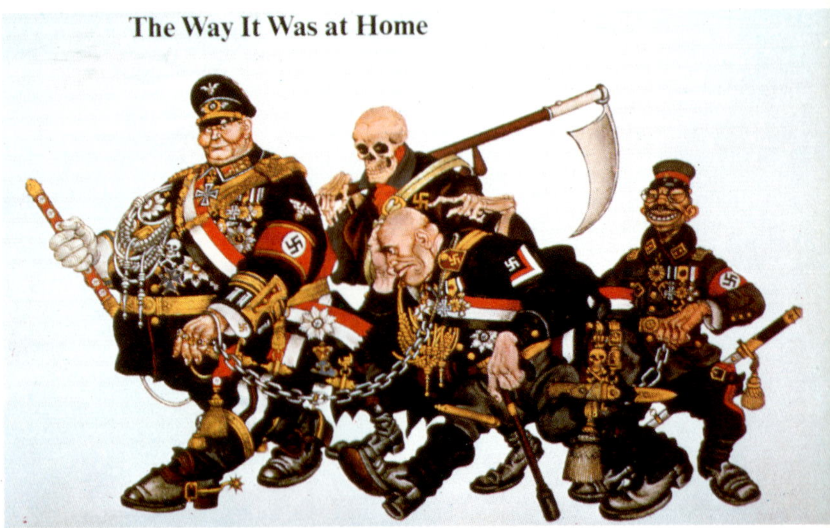

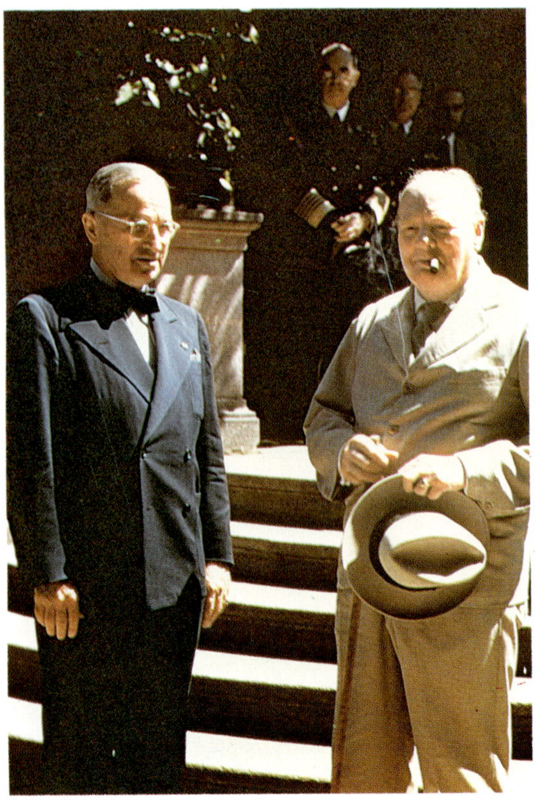

Truman. By virtue of the provisions of the US constitution, Vice-President Truman succeeded Roosevelt following the latter's sudden death on 12 April 1945. He quickly adapted himself to his new role and soon showed his dynamism and efficiency to best advantage. He was confronted with the onerous task of ending the war in Europe, of deciding on the use of the atomic bomb and of dealing with the first serious disagreements between the USA and the USSR. Here he is seen in July 1945 in company with Churchill at the time of the Potsdam Conference.

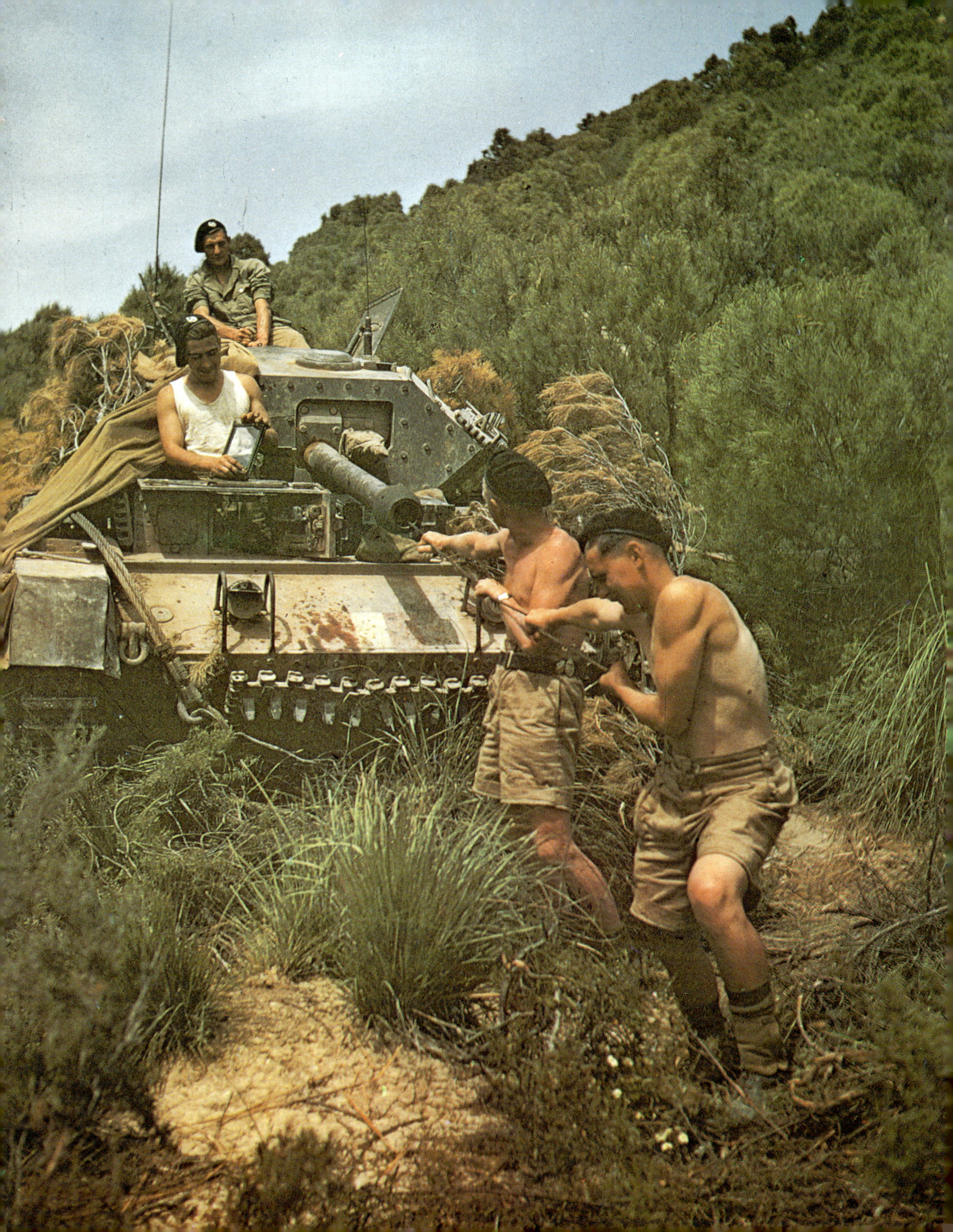

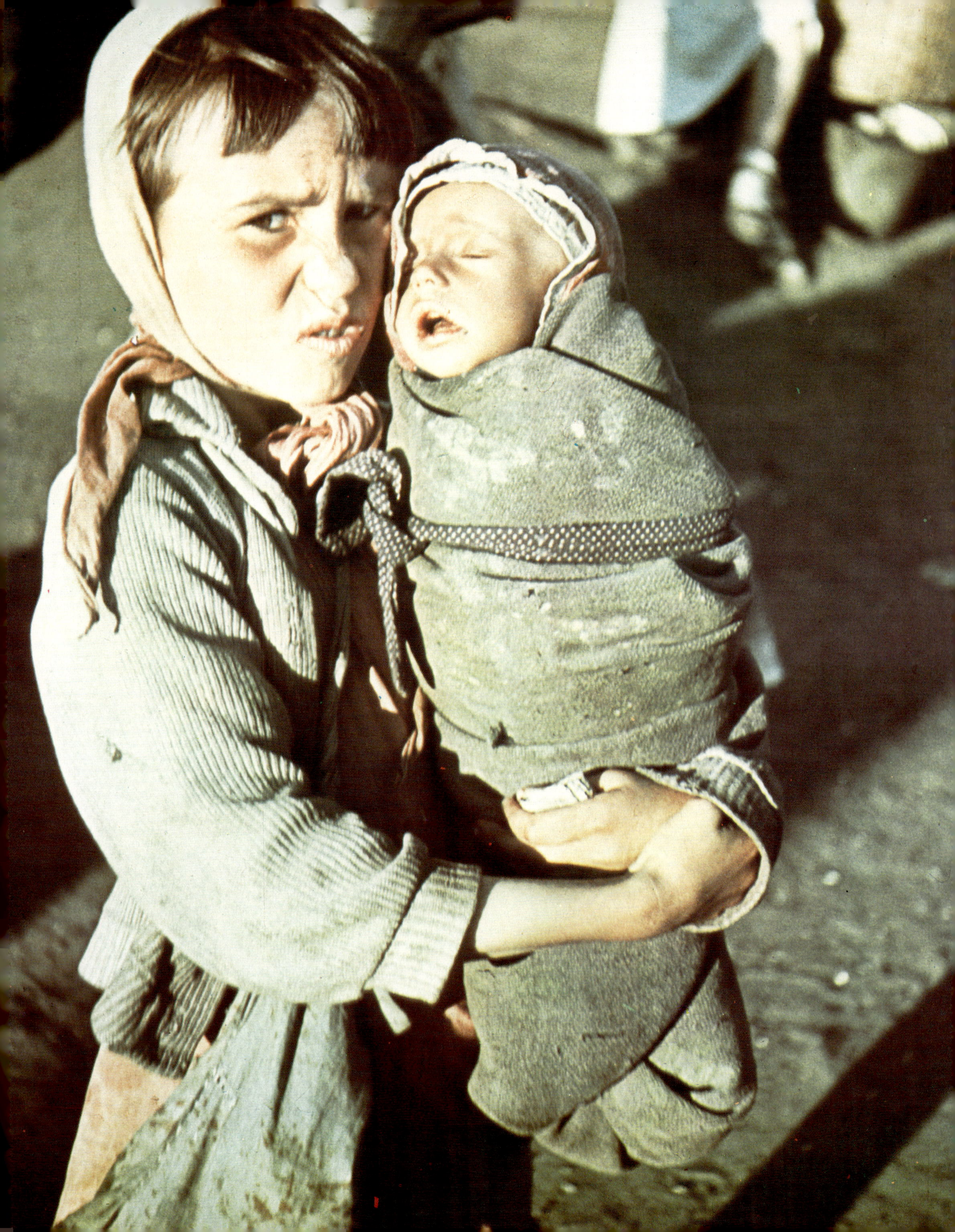

Ukraine. Child carrying a baby in a street
oltava in 1942.

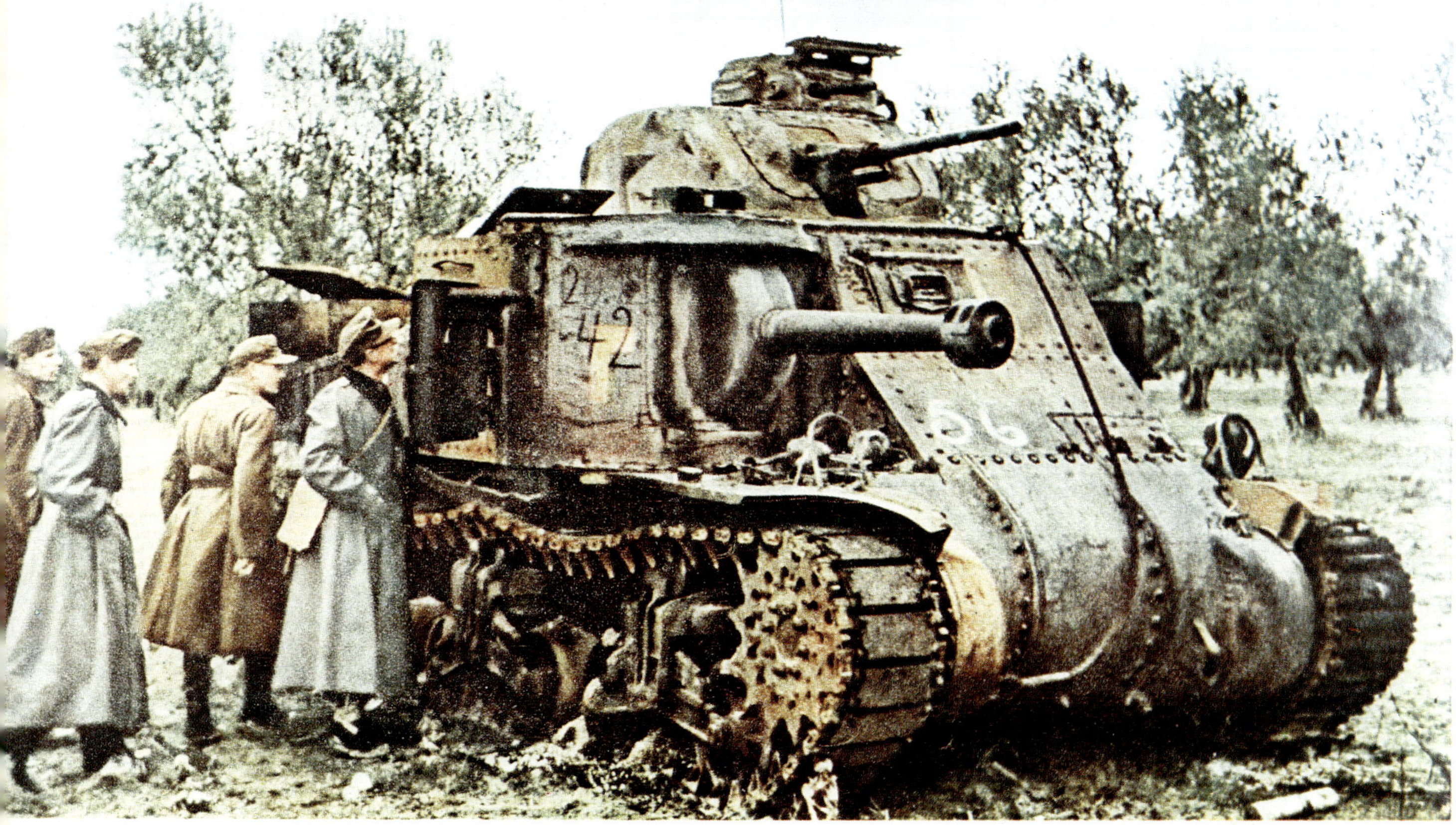

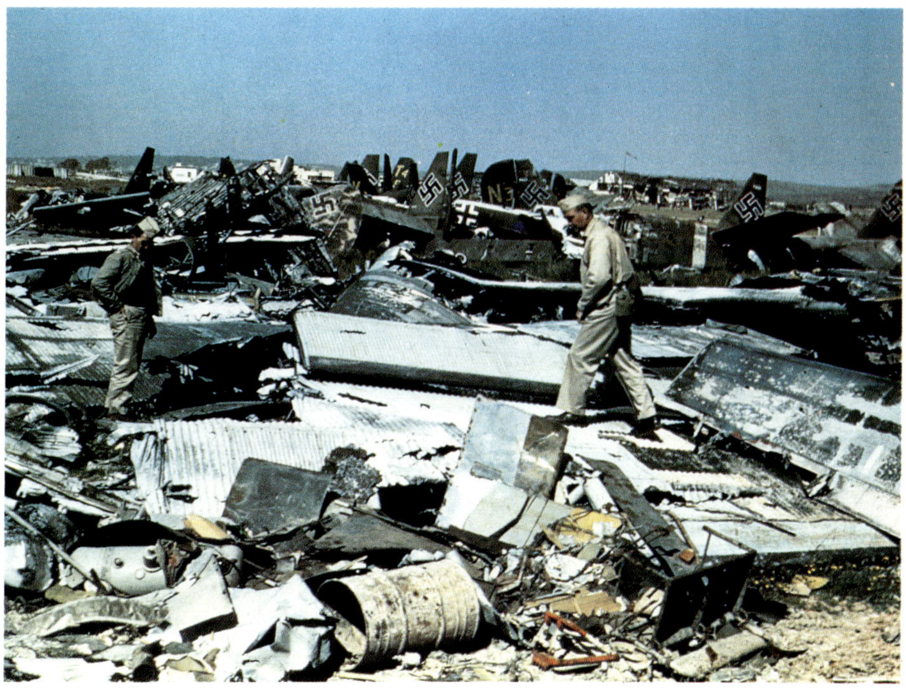

The Tunisian Campaign. Lasting from Nov. 1942 to May 1943, this proved to be far tougher than had been anticipated, because of the terrain, the climate and the fierce resistance of the German and Italian forces led by Rommel, von Arnim and the Italian general Messe, with considerable reinforcements from Europe which were to be absorbed into the fighting. It provided the opportunity for American troops to become seasoned fighters and to test the quality of their equipment. Here German soldiers are examining a wrecked General Grant tank, still of a much poorer quality than the German tanks of the period.

After six months' fighting the Allied armies under Montgomery and Eisenhower succeeded in pushing back the Axis forces into the Tunis area and the Cape Bon peninsula, achieving their final surrender on 13 May 1943, and capturing over 200,000 prisoners. This important Allied victory was due chiefly to their supremacy at sea and in the air, which had gradually worn down the combined German and Italian armies, shut in without any possibility of reinforcements in their bridgehead in the north of Tunisia. In this picture American soldiers are examining the debris of German planes on a Tunisian airstrip.

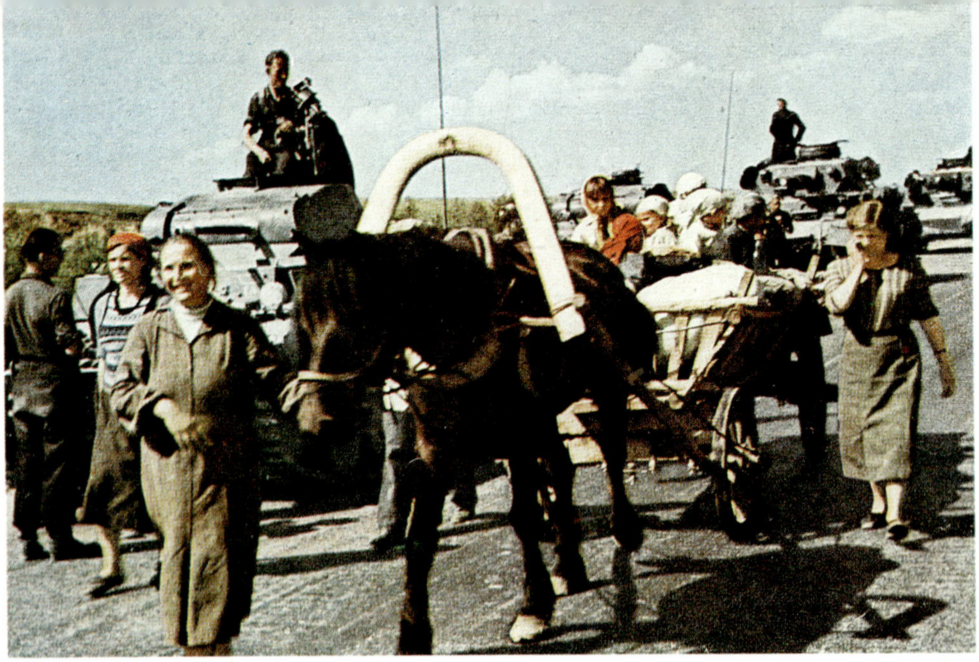

The Ukraine. During the German offensive in the summer of 1941, the Ukraine, with its important agricultural and industrial resources, was the objective of von Rundstedt's Army Group South. In the autumn, after the great encircling battle at Kiev, almost the whole of this Soviet republic – as large as France – was in the hands of the invader. The Russians had, however, succeeded in evacuating the greater part of their industrial plant. Here, near the Dniepr, during the summer operations, refugees returning home encounter a column of German tanks.

The United States. This picture, showing American sailors returning to New York at the end of hostilities, has a symbolic value. It illustrates the vast military effort of the United States, which was shown by the mobilization of 13 million men who fought on the two major fronts in the Pacific and in western Europe.

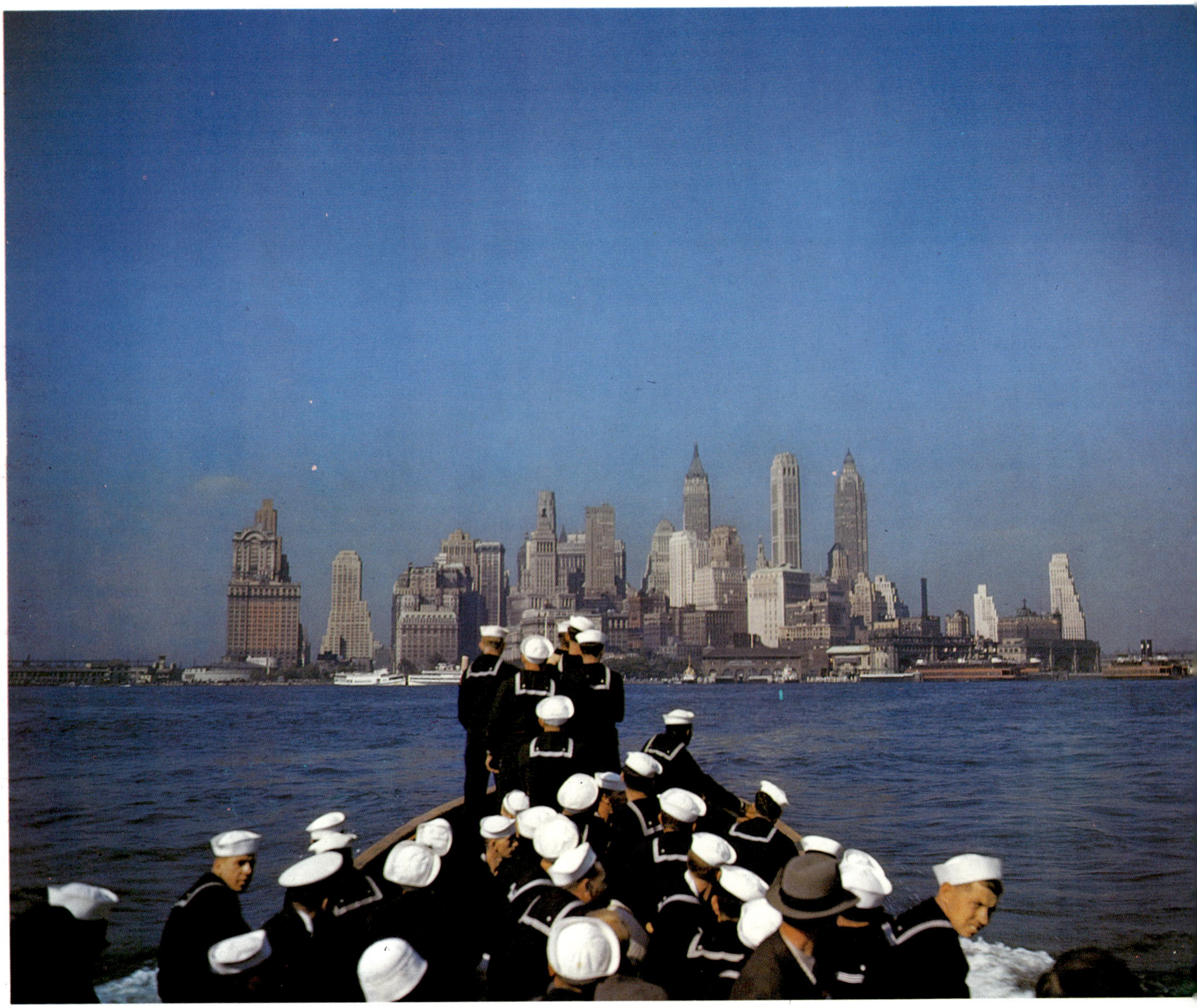

The war brought with it a spectacular increase in the strength of the American army. This picture shows a parade held at the very beginning of the war. The soldiers are still wearing the uniform derived from that of 1917–18 and the British-type steel helmet.

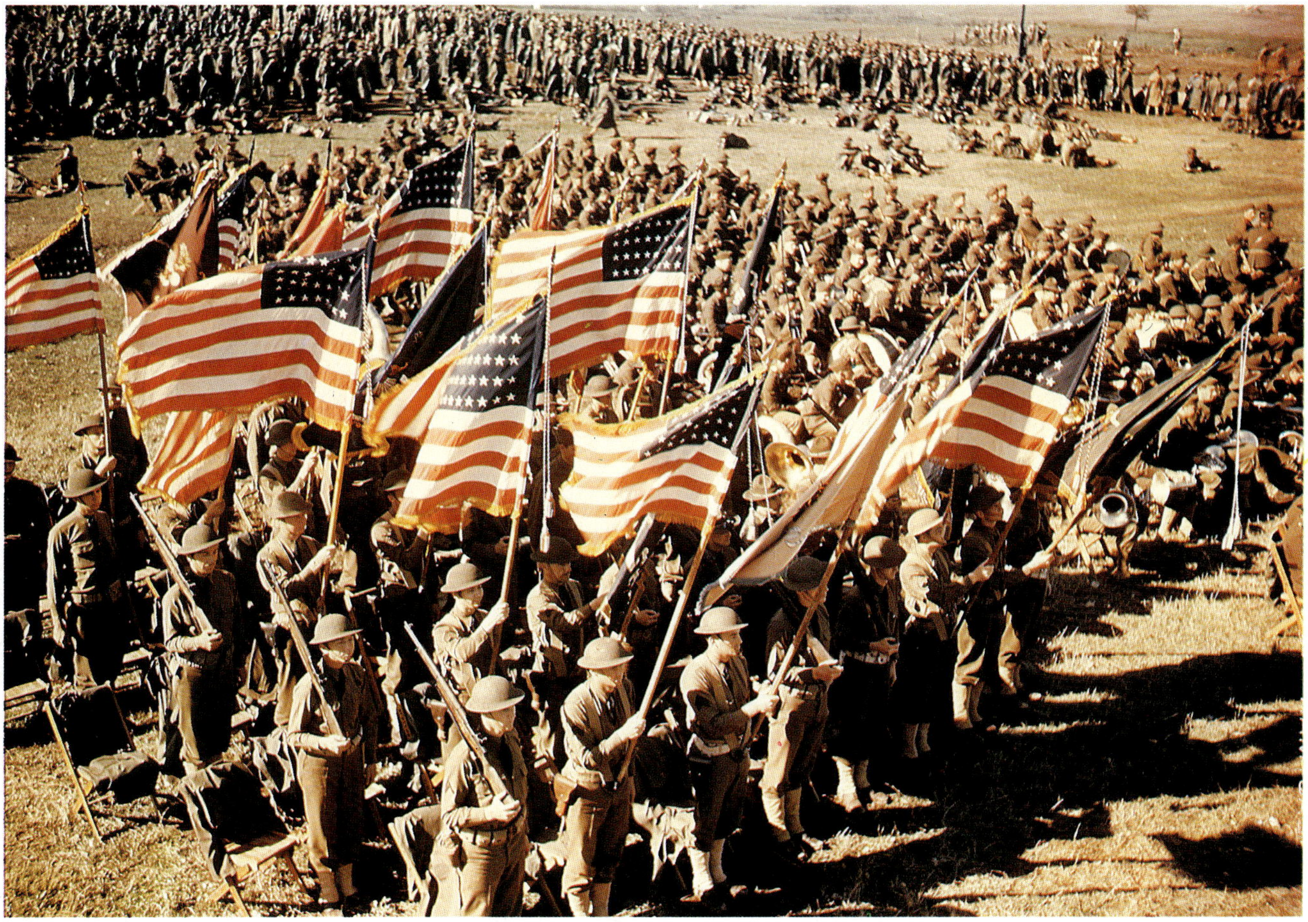

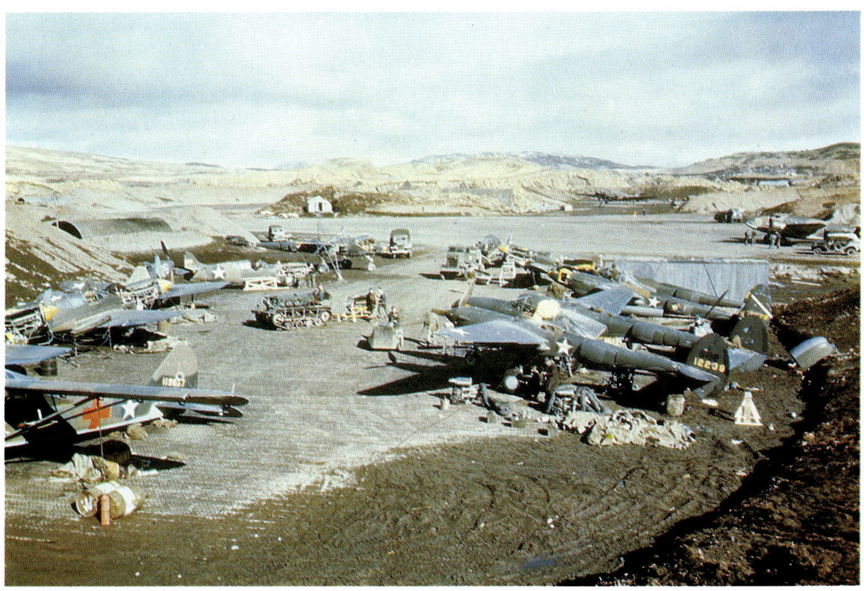

The involvement of American armed forces in these vast theatres of war entailed a major logistic effort. In 1939–40 the Americans had only 69 military airfields but by 1943 they had a network of 1400, 800 of which were situated outside the United States, such as this air base in Alaska. Its runway, made partly of metal grilles, had been constructed in a few weeks by US army engineers.

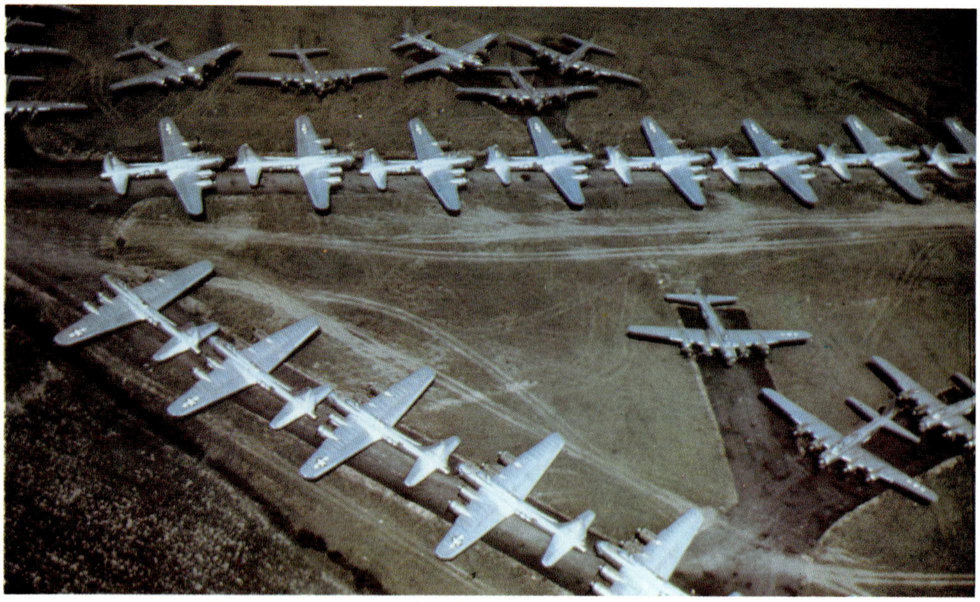

America's industrial effort during the war was truly prodigious. It included the construction of nearly 300,000 aircraft. This picture shows Boeing B-17 Flying Fortress heavy bombers assembled on an airfield in Britain shortly before the Normandy invasion.

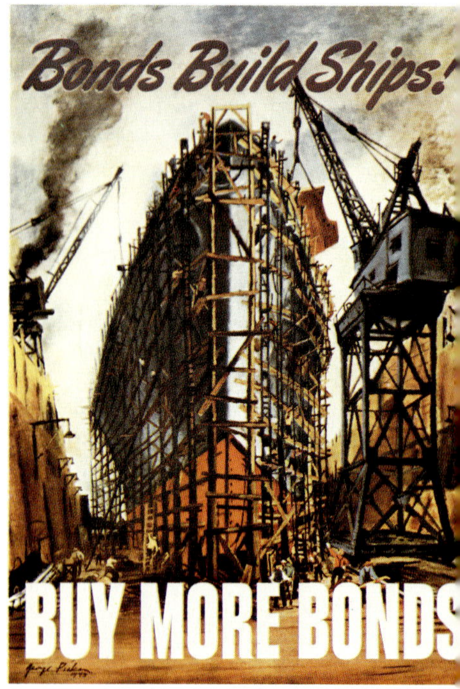

The United States' war effort involved considerable outlay of public funds. 50% of the expenditure came from taxes and the rest was raised by borrowing and by the issue of war bonds, as is shown by this poster which stresses the efforts being made in shipbuilding, in which 6 million tons of warships and nearly 40 million tons of merchant ships were constructed. (A poster from the collection of the Musée des Deux Guerres Mondiales – B.D.I.C. [Universités de Paris]).

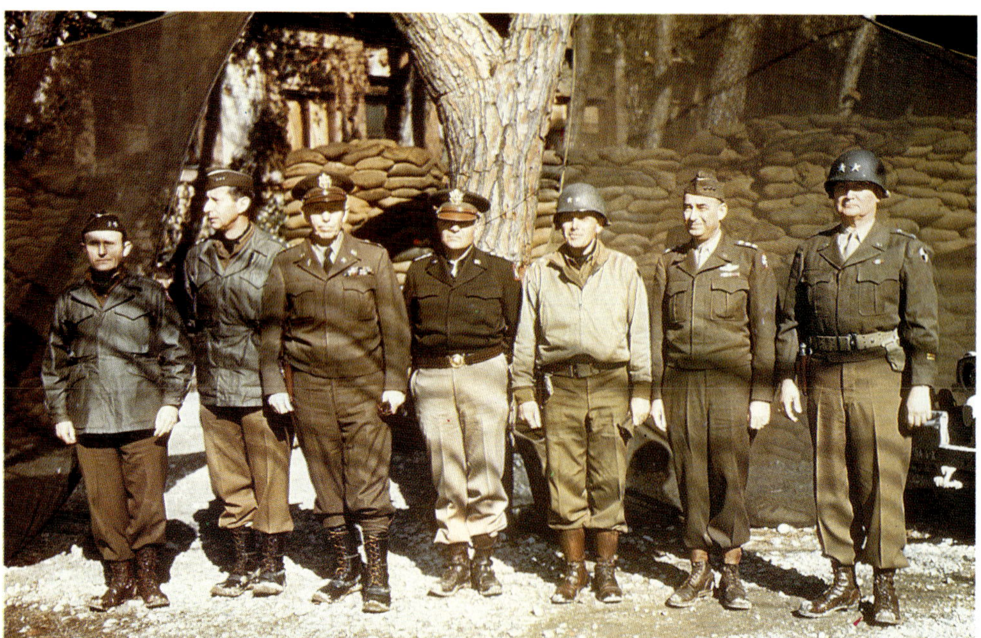

The US commanders. This picture shows a group of high-ranking American officers with General Marshall, the chief of staff of the US Army, during his tour of inspection in Italy in the winter of 1944–45. Mark Clark can be seen on the right of Marshall and Lucian Truscott, commander of the 5th Army, is on his left. Following Pearl Harbor the American high command system was reorganized to make it more flexible and effective. The Joint Chiefs of Staff presided over by Admiral Leahy, Roosevelt's personal representative, consisted of General Marshall, Admiral Ernest J. King, the commander in chief of the Navy and General H. 'Hap' Arnold, the commander of the US Army Air Force. Joining with representatives of the British chiefs of staff, the Joint Chiefs of Staffs formed the Combined Chiefs of Staffs, by whom common Allied strategy was formulated.

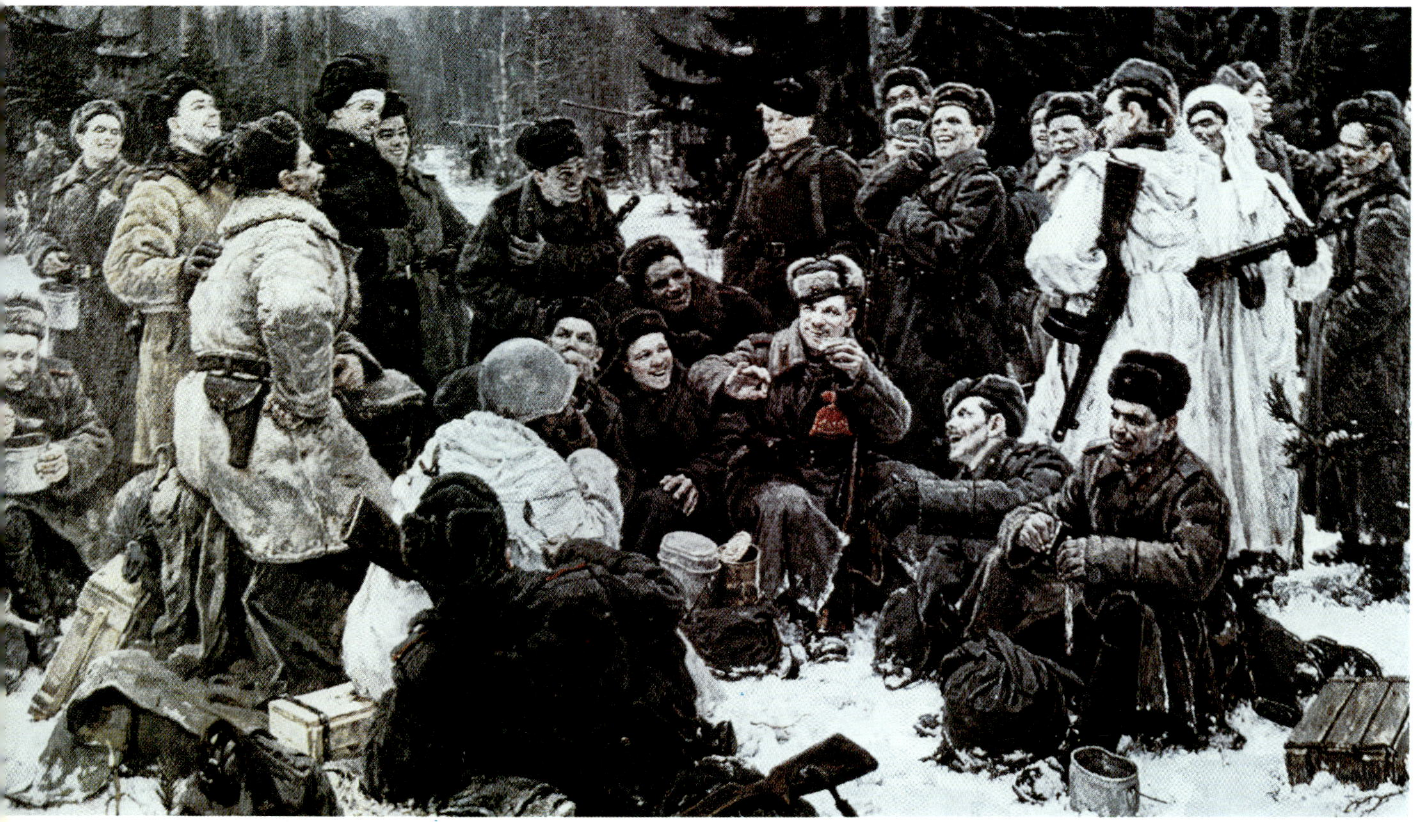

The USSR. A picture by Neprintsev depicting Soviet partisans in the Russian countryside. This painting, which was characteristic of the 'socialist realism' of the Stalinist period, illustrates one of the remarkable phenomena of Russia at war. As early as 1941 thousands of partisans, most often recruited from encircled units, continued the struggle in the rear of the German army, carrying out acts of sabotage and harassing operations. These groups, linked by radio and by aircraft with the Red Army high command, brought it invaluable support, sometimes acting as advance guards or taking part in vast, carefully planned operations against the Wehrmacht's communications.

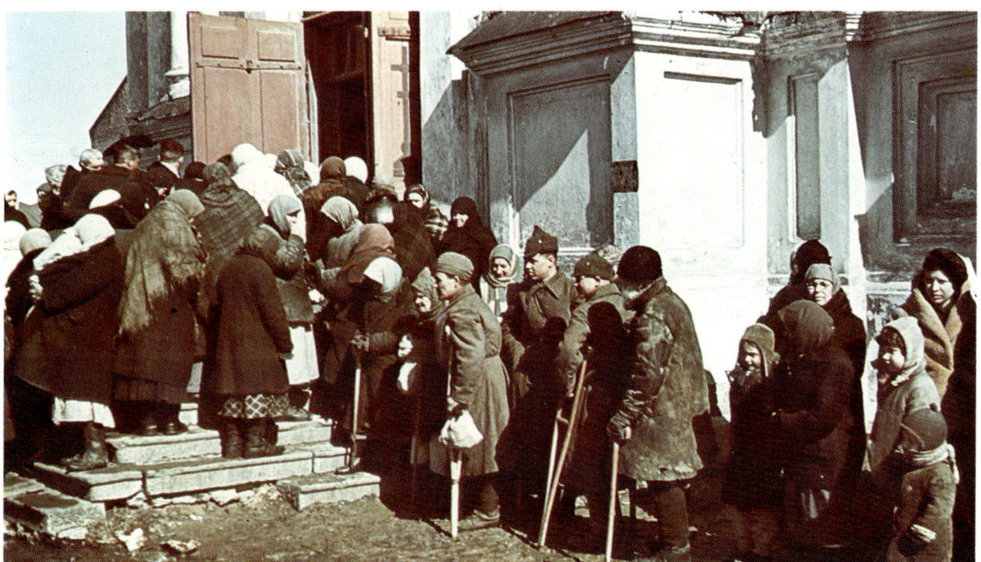

A scene in the Soviet Union under German occupation. A group of worshippers, including some war disabled, are preparing to enter an Orthodox Church in Poltava in 1942. In the occupied regions the Germans had re-opened the churches and re-established the Orthodox religion, which had been virtually banned by the Soviet regime. Large numbers of people at once began flocking to the churches, thus underlining the persistence of religious belief. In those areas which had remained under Moscow's control there was a distinct relaxation in the official attitude towards religion, since Soviet policy emphasized the defence of the traditional values of the Russian people as a factor in the struggle.

The confrontation between Germany and the Soviet Union was to illustrate in a new and dramatic fashion the miseries of war. The people of the Ukraine, already extremely poor in 1941, had to endure a very harsh occupation, which imposed starvation rations and forced labour. In the photograph two civilians, utterly destitute, are seen in the ruins of the city of Kharkov, which was the scene of fierce fighting in 1941 and 1943.

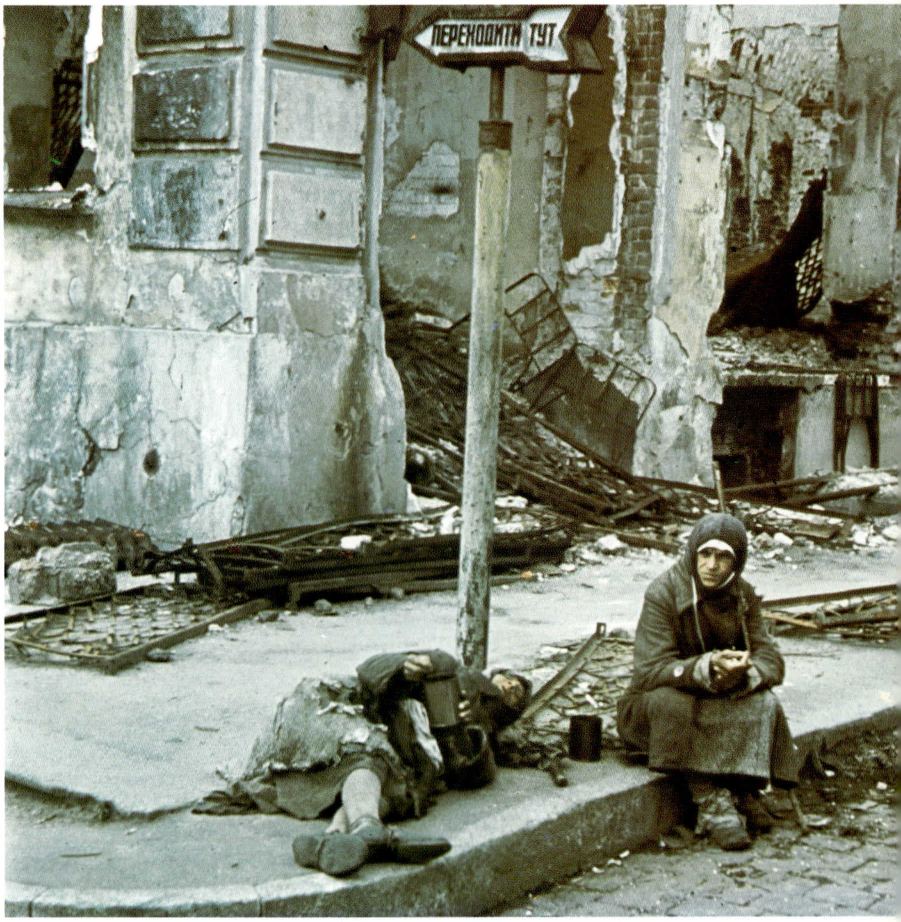

Ukrainian women in a street in Poltava in 1942. When they advanced into the USSR the Germans discovered a population which had remained poor and whose living standards had been sacrificed to the development of heavy industry and armaments. In reaction to the policy of the Soviet regime the Germans authorized the re-establishment of small traders and cottage industries. The poster on the left, in two languages, denotes the presence of a cap maker and the inscription on the shutter on the right, a shop selling perfumes.

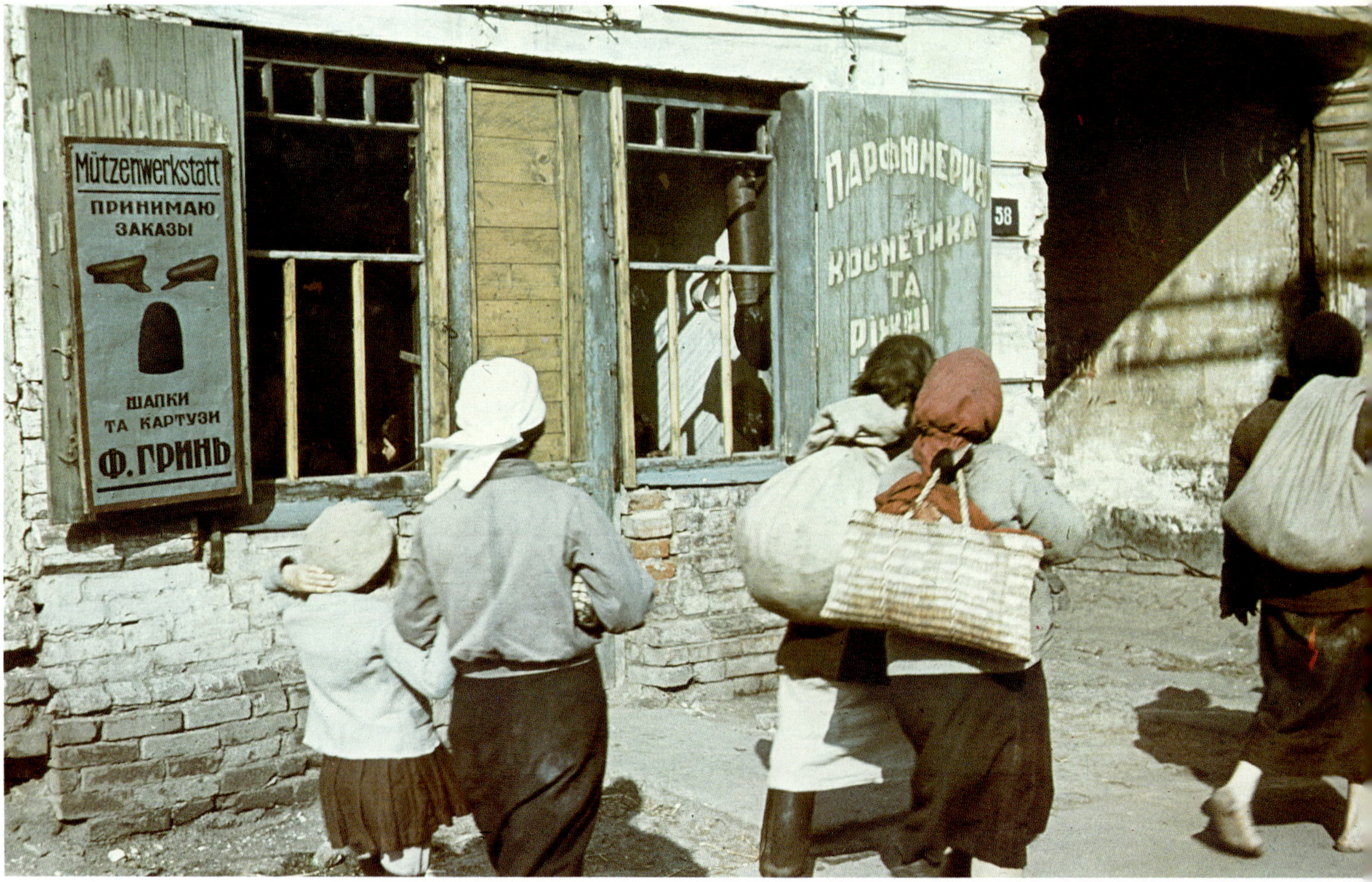

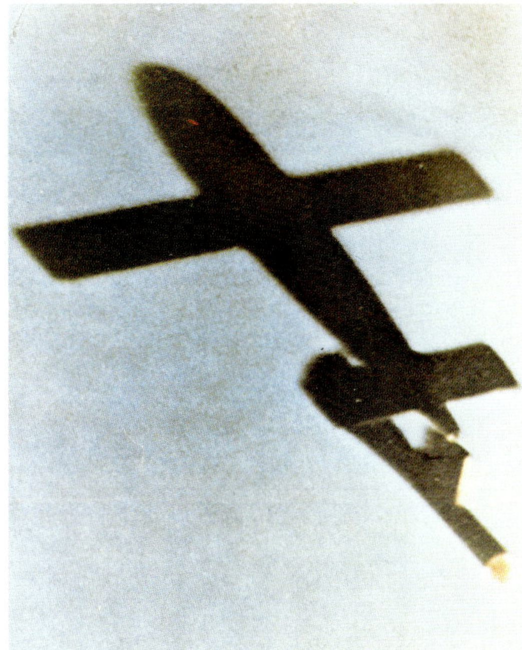

The V1. Faced with the inability of the Luftwaffe to resume strategic raids, from 12 June 1944 the Germans began bombing London by means of pilotless aircraft. The flying bomb, with its Fieseler Fi-103 preset guidance system, of which an example can be seen here several moments after its launch from the testing base at Peenemünde, weighed two tons, reached 375 mph (600 km/h) and had an average range of 150 mi. (240 km). It carried nearly one ton of explosives. Brought into action too late, the V1s were unable to alter the course of the war. They did, however, inflict considerable damage on London, killing more than 5000 people. They compelled the Allies to strengthen their air defences considerably and to allocate a large part of their air power to attacking the launching sites. After the liberation of northern France and Belgium the V1s were used against Antwerp. In all, about 30,000 were produced, of which more than 8000 were launched against London.

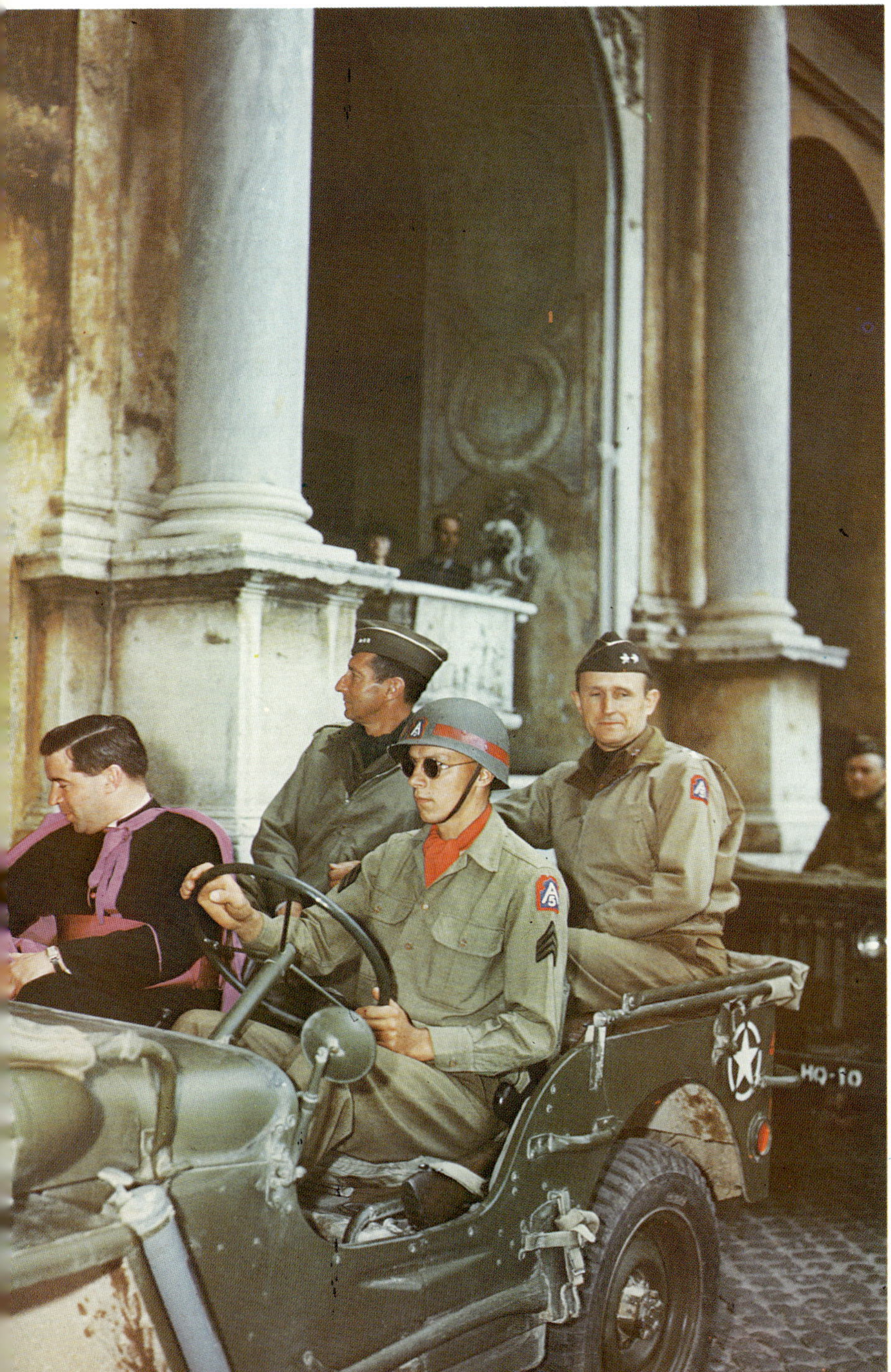

Vatican. Throughout the war the Vatican was confronted by an even more difficult situation than in 1914–18, in a world torn apart by conflicting nationalisms and ideologies and incapable of resisting the appeal or the pressures of totalitarian systems. Although it attempted, with some success, to bring help to a number of victims of the conflict, it was unable to put an end to the most grievous atrocities, and the efforts of Pope Pius XII in favour of peace proved to be tragically ineffective. The liberation of Rome by the Allies enabled the Holy See to express its views more freely. In this photograph, General Clark, the commander of the US Fifth Army and his chief of staff, General Gruenther (on the right), are arriving in the Vatican City with Monsignor Carroll, the day after their entry into the city in June 1944.

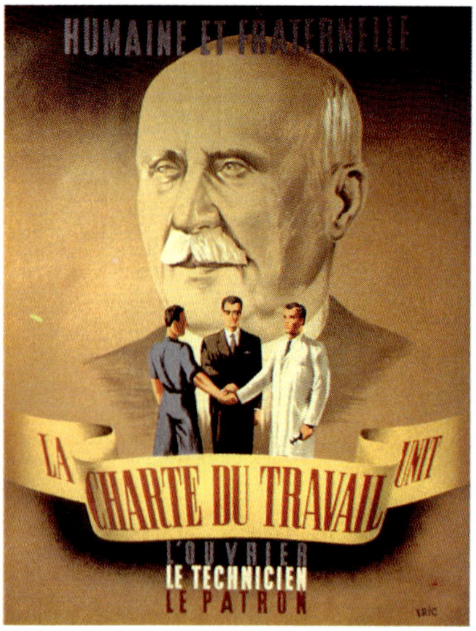

Vichy. Following the defeat of 1940 the vast majority of French people greeted the Armistice with relief and rallied to the new regime, which benefited from the prestige and popularity of Marshal Pétain. The Vichy government, having denounced the failure of the democratic system, replaced it with a hierarchical and authoritarian state, influenced by Franco's regime in Spain and Salazar's Estado Novo in Portugal. The dissolution of all existing groups of affiliated trades unions on 9 Nov. 1940, was followed, as part of the 'national revolution', by the promulgation on 4 Oct. 1941, of the Labour Charter. This aspired to put an end to the class struggle and to reconcile capital and labour by uniting the worker and the technician with the employer under the authority of the head of state, as this Vichy propaganda poster illustrates. The corporatism of Vichy in fact strengthened not only the power of the employer within the firm, but also the control of the state over businesses and trades.

The *Vittorio Veneto*. Laid down in 1934, this battleship, one of a series of four vessels, was the first to be built according to the standards imposed by the Treaty of Washington of 1922. With a theoretical displacement of 40,000 tons, its main armament consisted of nine 15 in. (318 mm) guns in three triple turrets and its secondary armament four triple turrets of 6 in. (152 mm) guns, as well as numerous anti-aircraft guns. It had a speed in excess of 30 knots. The *Vittorio Veneto* took part in many operations in the Mediterranean, notably the battle of Cape Matapan (March 1941). Included in the surrender of the Italian fleet in Sept. 1943, it was broken up after the war.

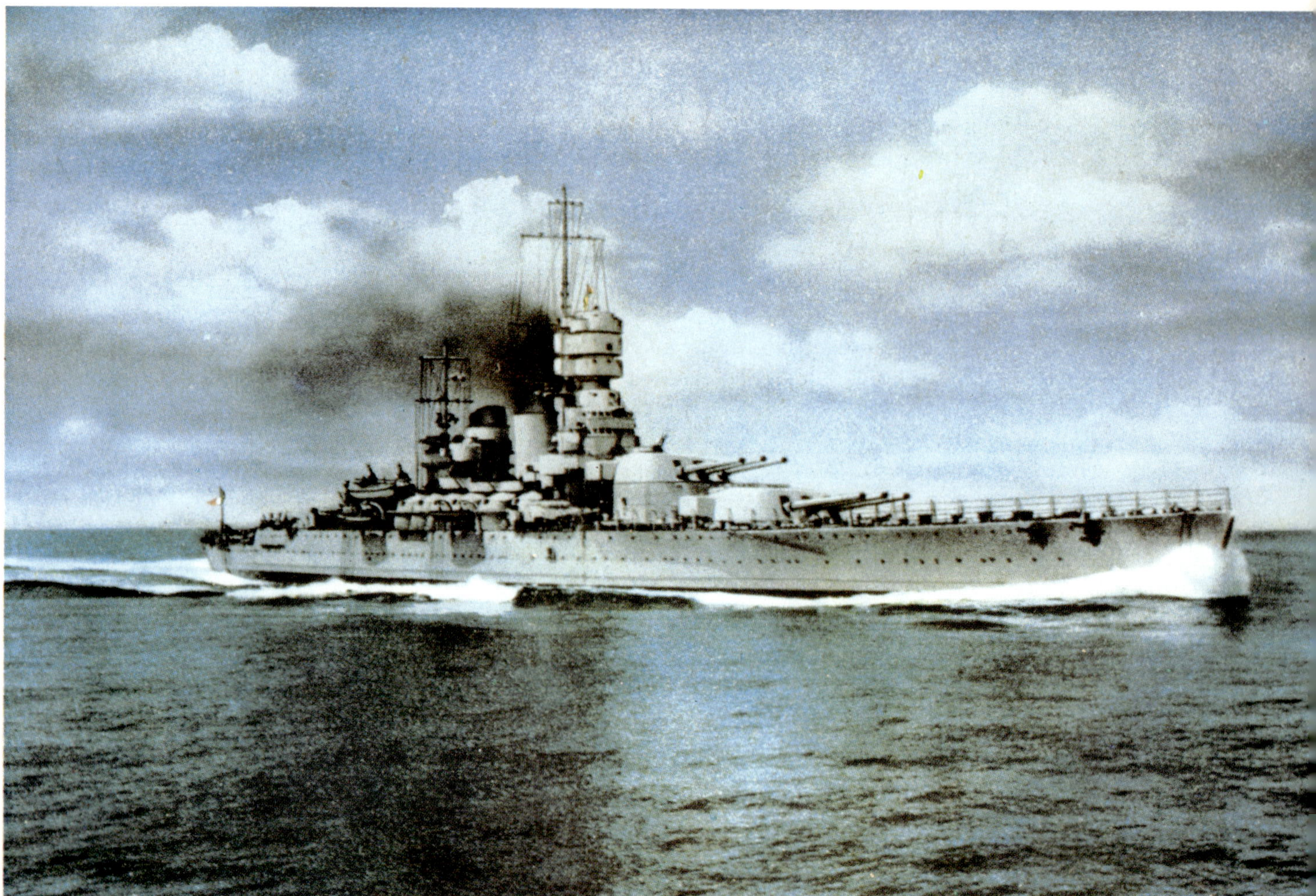

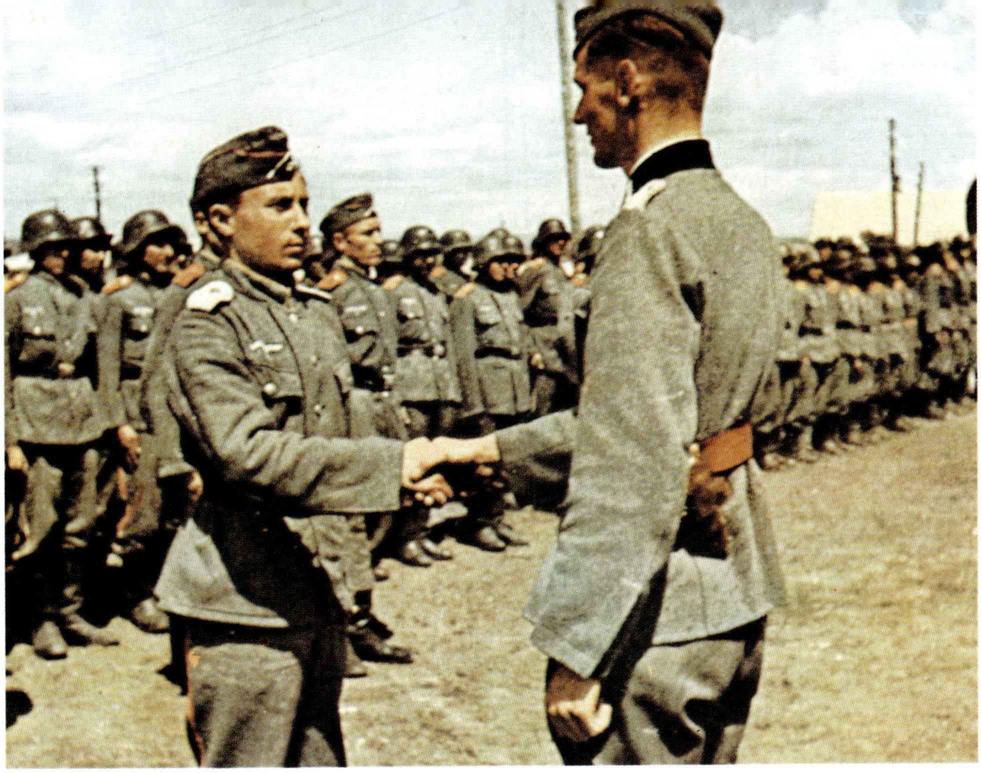

The Vlassov Army. Its advance into the Soviet Union in 1941–42 enabled the Wehrmacht to recruit hundreds of thousands of auxiliary troops, who were impelled to join the German side by hatred of Stalinism or Great-Russian imperialism. These volunteers were particularly numerous in the Ukraine, and among the Cossacks and Caucasians. Some were employed only on duties of an auxiliary nature, but tens of thousands were incorporated into security battalions to fight against the partisans or in national legions, but always under German command. The attempt by General Vlassov to set up a Russian National army, allied to the Third Reich but autonomous, was in fact never really accepted by the Germans, who feared the rebirth of Russian nationalism. In the picture a volunteer from the 'Plato' Cossack regiment, belonging to a so-called 'army of liberation', is receiving his insignia from a German officer.

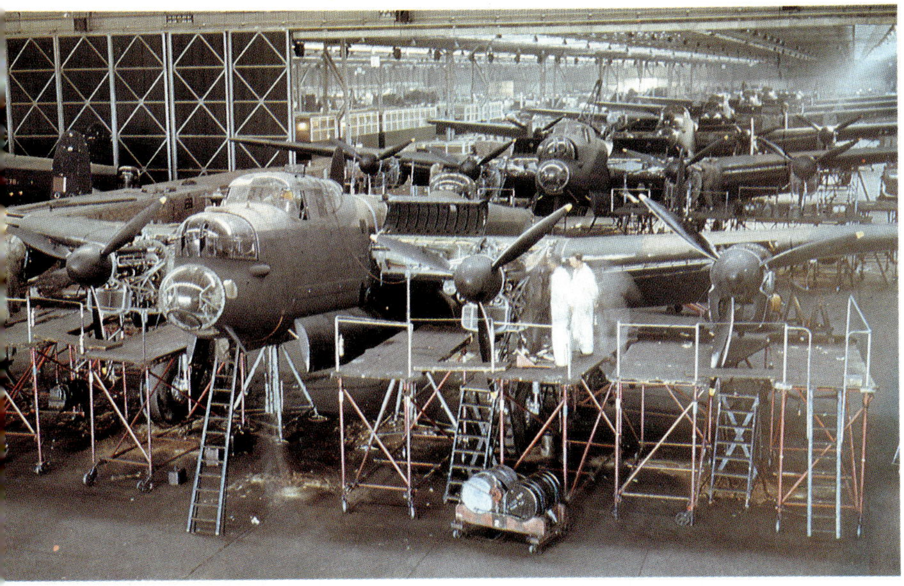

The war economy. Britain's war effort in the economic sphere was one of the most considerable of any of the belligerents. More than 50% of the national income went on war supplies and armaments and priority was given to the aircraft industry, in accordance with strategic thinking. This picture shows Lancaster bombers, intended for raids on Germany, on the assembly line.

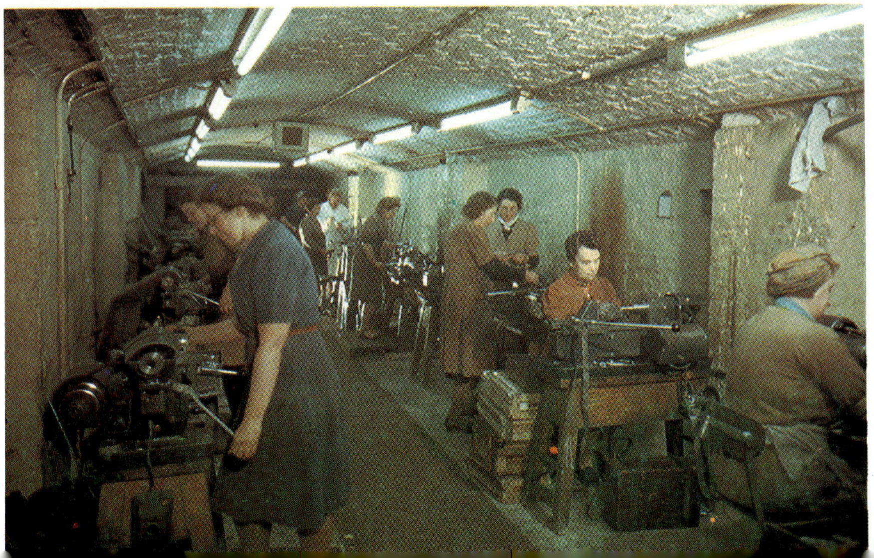

In the course of the conflict all the countries at war had to call on women workers to fulfil the need for increased production and to fill the gaps left by the induction of men into the armed forces. Nazi Germany, however, only followed this course at a late stage and when compelled to do so by the first defeats. In Great Britain, on the other hand, women participated in the war effort on a major scale as early as 1940, as is shown by this machine-tool workshop in a British arms factory, which has been transferred to an underground shelter to escape the effects of bombing.

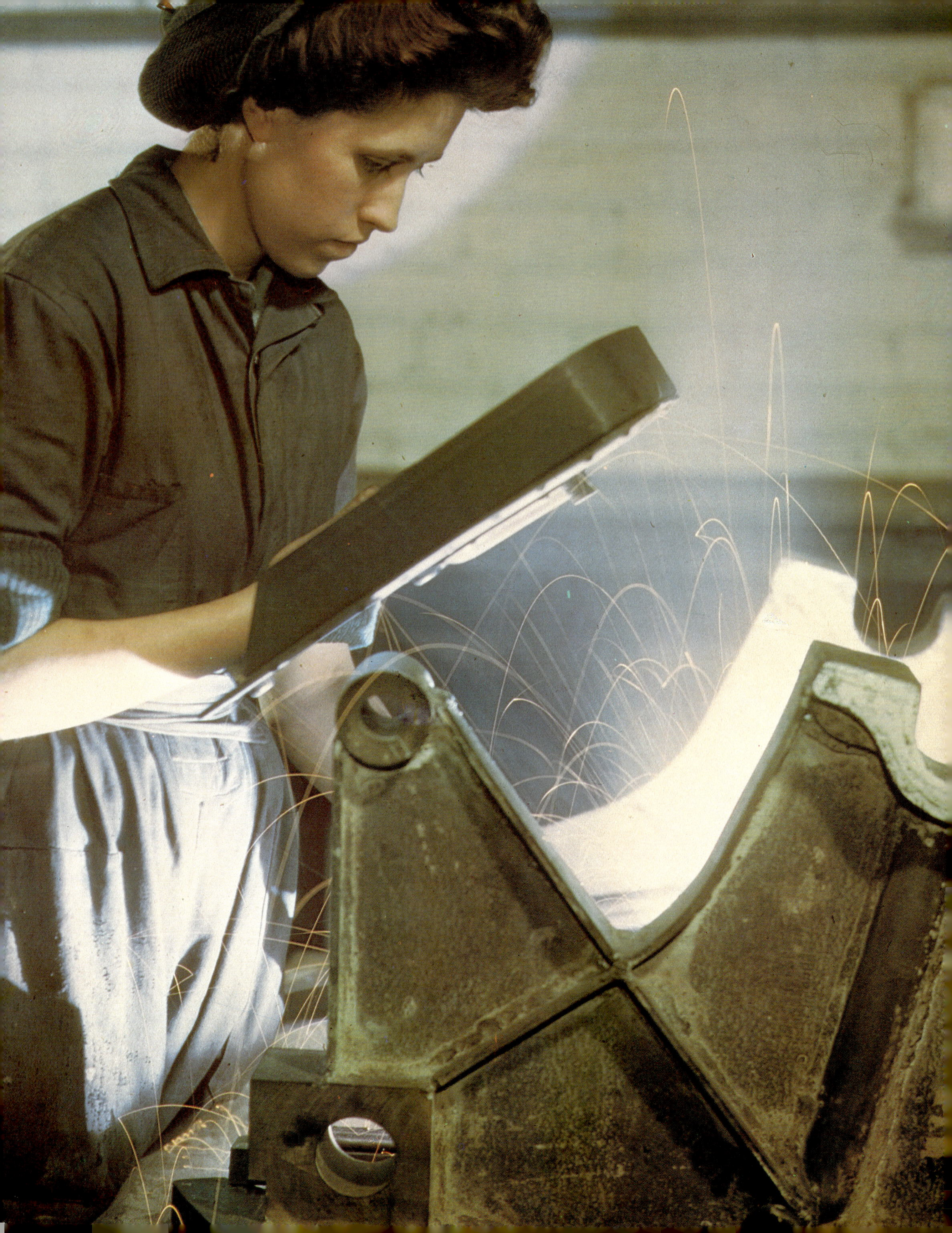

war economy. A woman worker in a
sh arms factory.

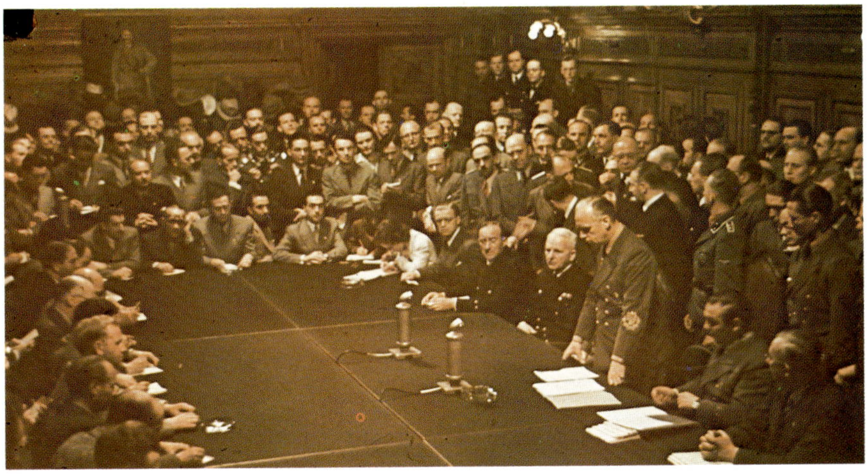

The War in Russia. On 22 June 1941, in the presence of foreign press officials and officials from his own ministry the Reich foreign minister, Ribbentrop, announces the launching of Operation Barbarossa and the opening moves in the war against the Soviet Union, the decision on which had been reached at the end of 1940. In 'opening a doorway on to the unknown' Hitler was pursuing a three-fold plan: first, to avert a surprise attack by the Red Army, which the German leadership believed was a possibility and whose potential strength continued to increase; secondly, to acquire so-called 'living space' for the Reich in the east; and thirdly, to discourage Britain and induce her to seek peace by depriving her of her last potential ally on the European mainland.

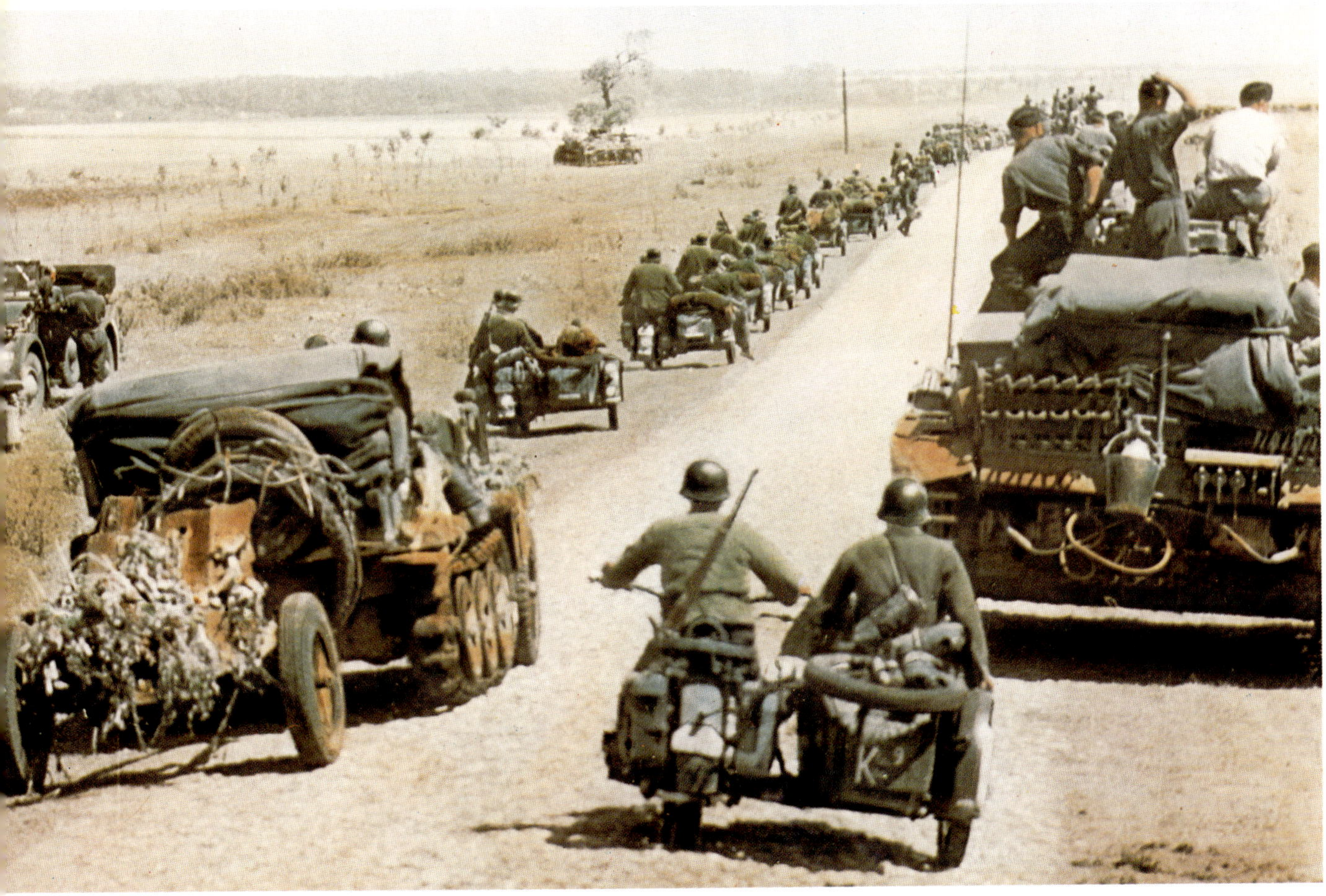

The opening moves of the war on the eastern front once again clearly demonstrated the destructive capacity of the Blitzkrieg and the remarkable qualities of the Wehrmacht as a fighting force. In spectacular encirclements the German armoured divisions captured hundreds of thousands of prisoners and penetrated deep into Soviet territory. This picture shows a motorized column advancing towards Ostrog in the Ukraine. However, the bad state of the roads, the rigours of the climate and the stubborn Soviet resistance were all to contribute to break the impetus of the German advance in the autumn of 1941.

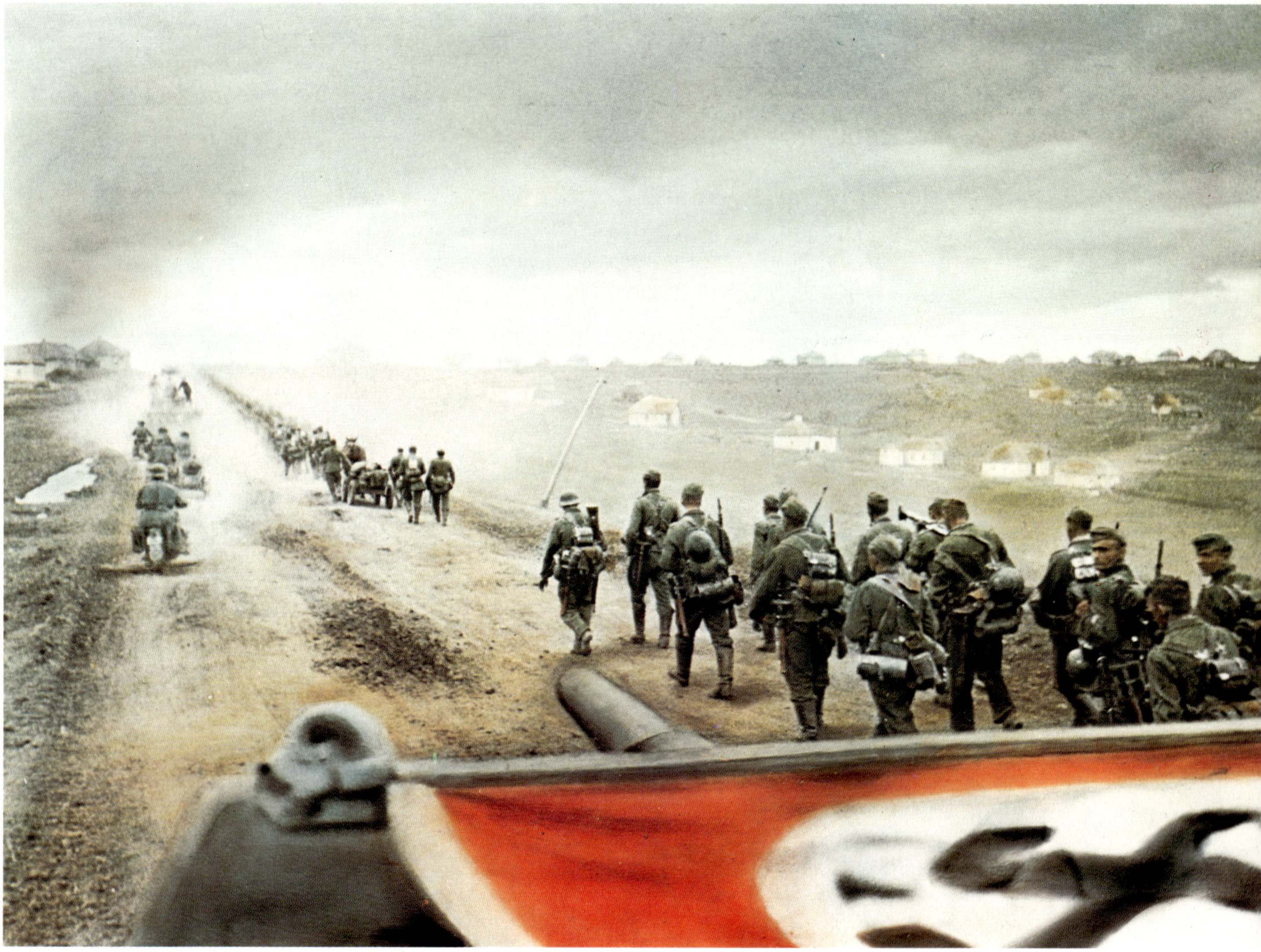

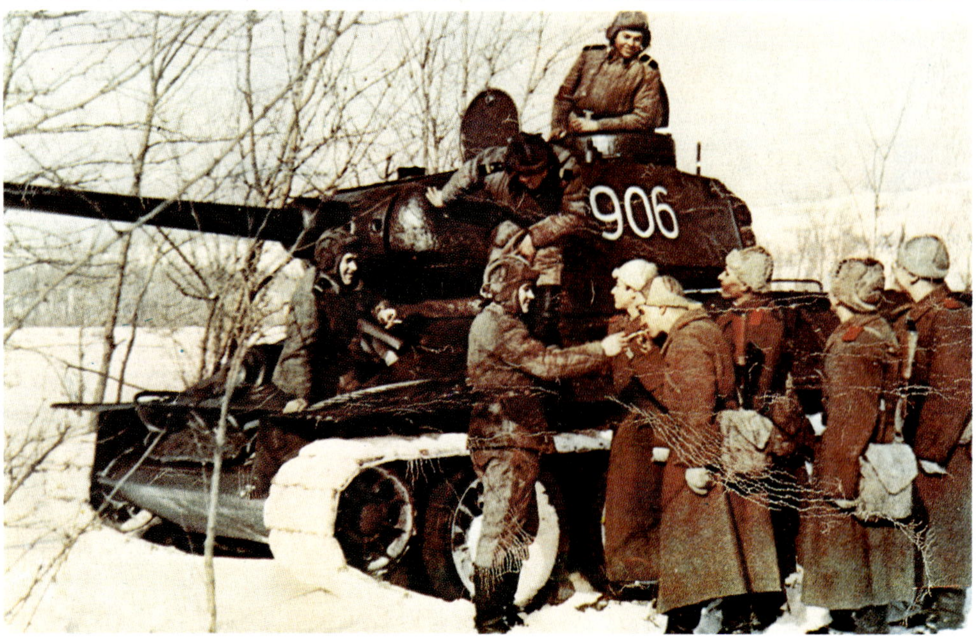

In spite of its defeat outside Moscow in the winter of 1941–42 the German army was still in a position to resume the offensive in the summer of 1942, pushing towards the Volga and the oil-wells of the Caucasus. In this picture an infantry unit is advancing along a road through a dust cloud raised by motor vehicles. In the foreground the swastika flag on top of the tank serves as an identification sign for aircraft, at a period when the Luftwaffe still had air superiority. This summer offensive would in due course come to an end in the disaster of Stalingrad.

The Red Army gained the initiative on the eastern front from 1943 onwards and the instrument of this counter-offensive was the T-34 tank (shown here). This strongly armed and well-armoured tank had wide tracks which permitted it to manoeuvre in mud and snow. Hand rails on its rear allowed a group of infantrymen to ride on the tank's superstructure and thus keep up with the tanks as they advanced, at the same time being protected by them.

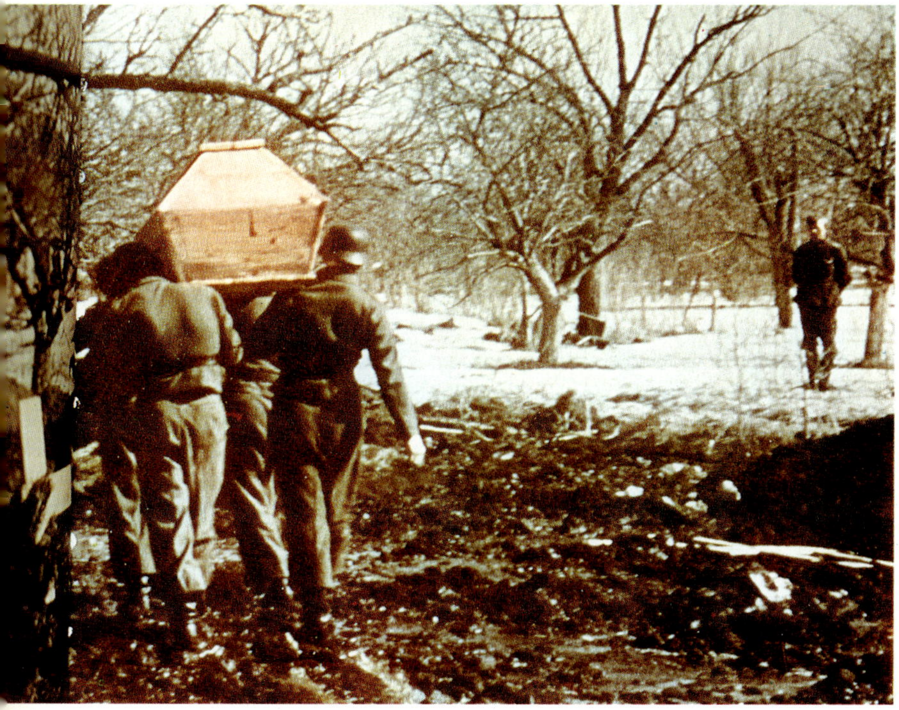

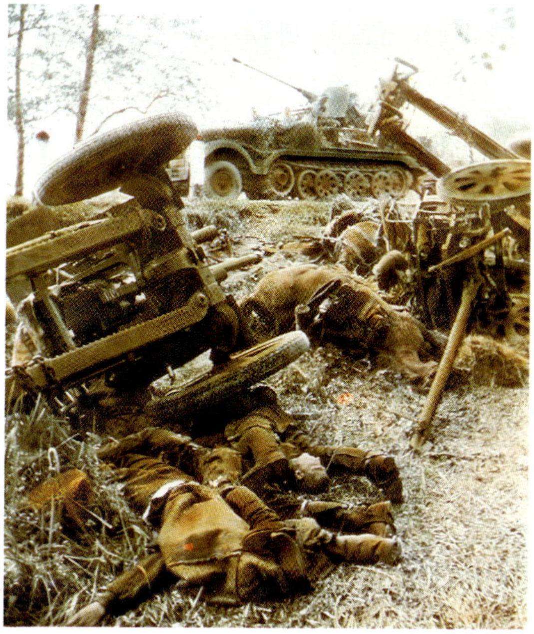

War: the final count. The human cost of the war can of course be limited to dry statistics. More than 20 million combatants lost their lives in the course of the Second World War. The funerals of soldiers in the field tend to have a sort of poignant grandeur, although (and because) they are simple and reduced to essentials. This picture taken on the eastern front during the winter of 1941–42 shows a group of German soldiers accompanying a comrade who has fallen in battle to his last resting place. Behind the coffin a man carries the simple wooden cross which will mark the grave.

As the war on the eastern front progressed the Germans began to suffer rather higher losses than they had in the Polish and French campaigns. This was due to the fierceness of Soviet resistance. This picture shows the identification of the bodies of German soldiers killed during the clearing of the Uman pocket in the late summer of 1941.

In war death often occurs in the most brutal way, as it has for these Soviet artillerymen struck down with their horses beside an overturned gun and ammunition carrier. In the background can be seen a German artillery tractor armed with a 50 mm anti-aircraft gun. The Red Army suffered terrible losses throughout the war on the eastern front. These have been estimated at 12 million men, more than four times higher than those of the Germans.

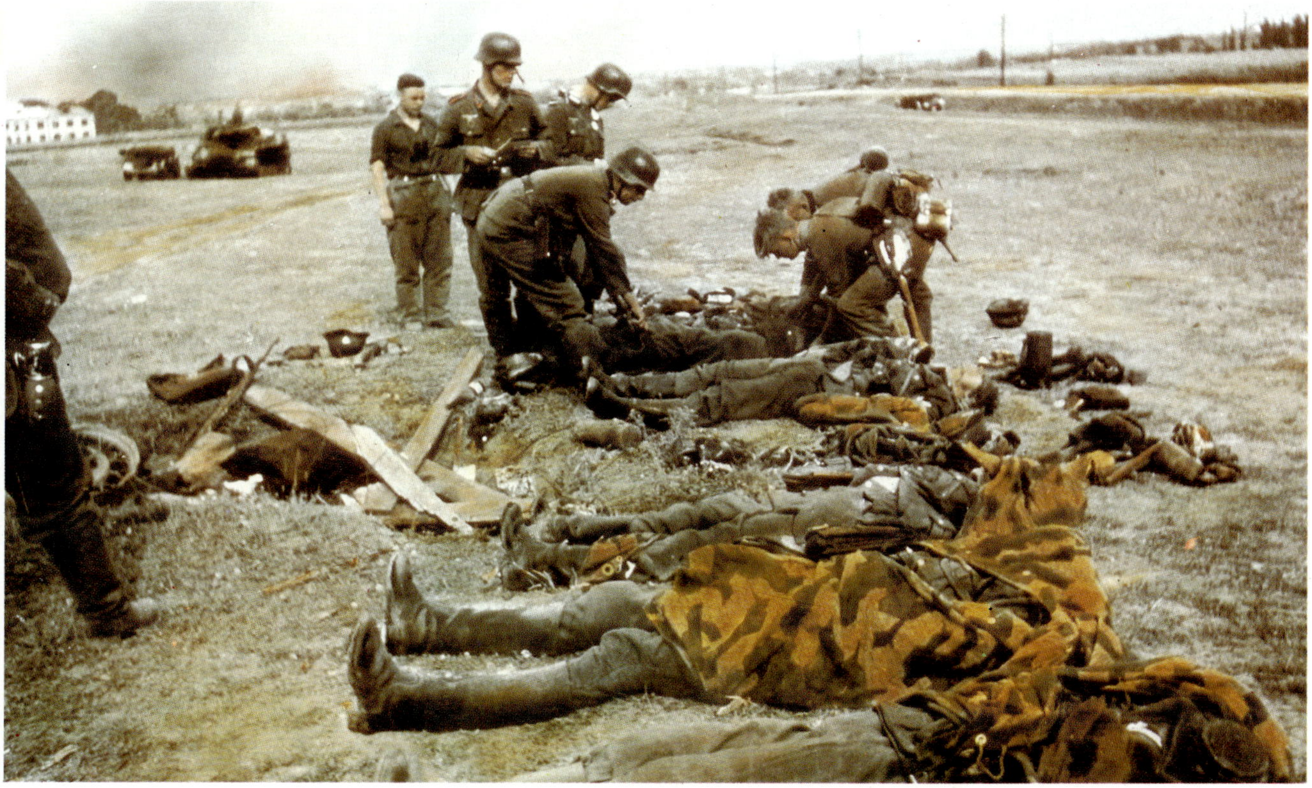

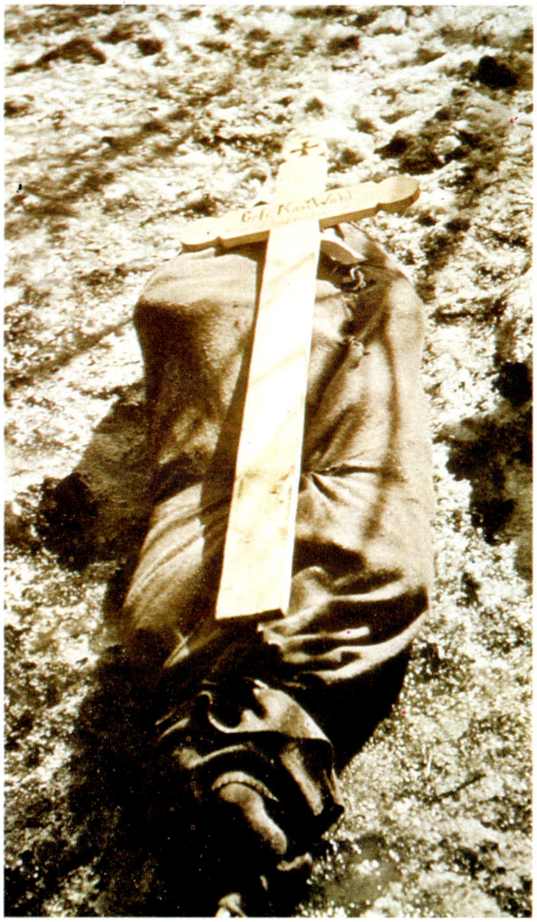

Throughout the war on the eastern front and despite very heavy losses the Germans did their best to bury with dignity soldiers killed in action. This photograph shows the corpse of the soldier Karl Wahl, of the Grossdeutschland Regiment, covered with a simple blanket and the traditional wooden cross. Since the soil was frozen to a considerable depth the corpse would have to wait until the thaw to be buried. Nearly 3 million German soldiers met their deaths in the Soviet Union.

Contrary to the First World War, in the Second World War there was very heavy civilian loss of life, as a result of refugee movements, deportations, organized massacres and, in particular, air raids. This picture shows a scene following an Allied air raid on Berlin in which civilians whose homes are being ravaged by fire are being evacuated from the area. More than 500,000 people were to lose their lives during the air offensive against Germany.

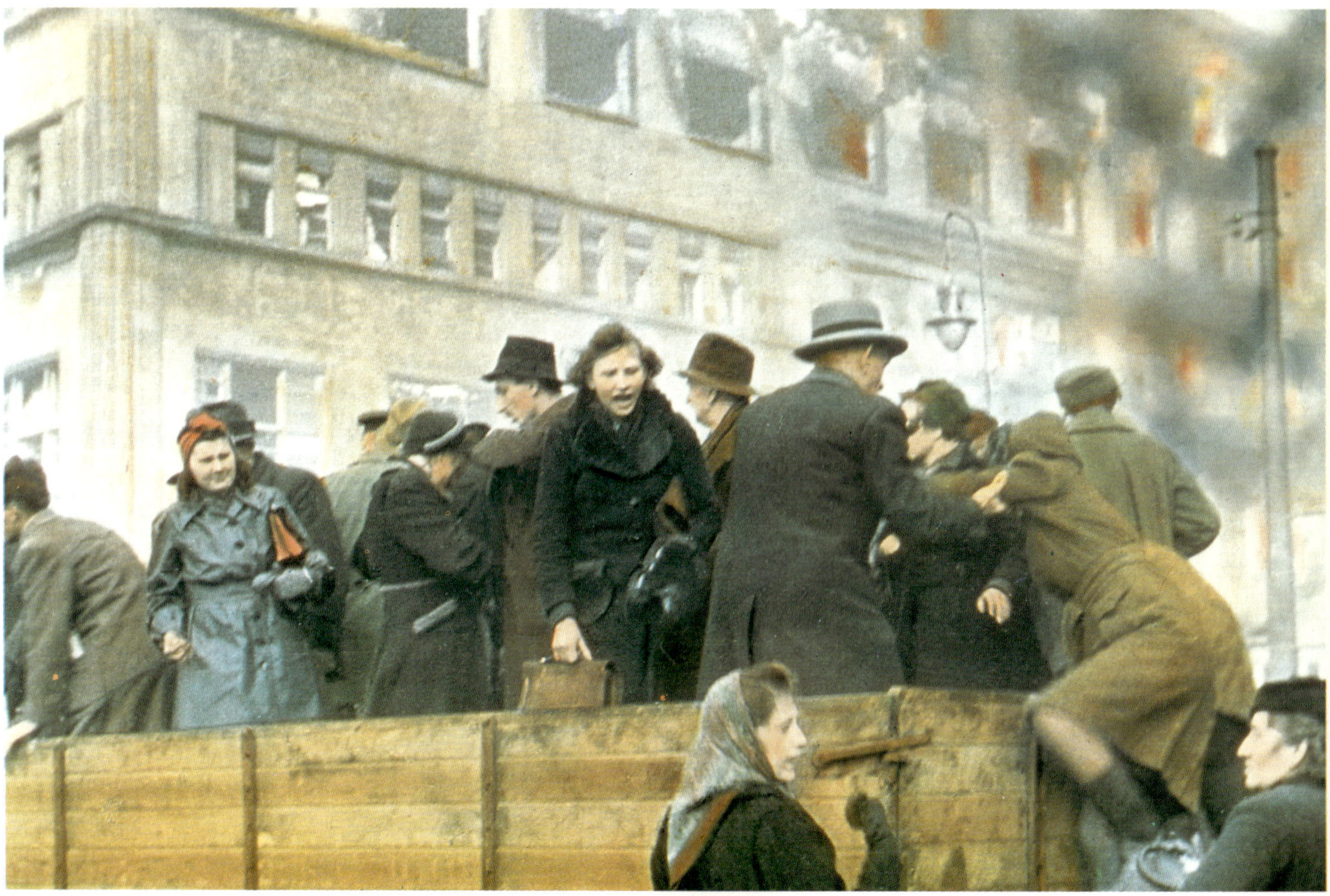

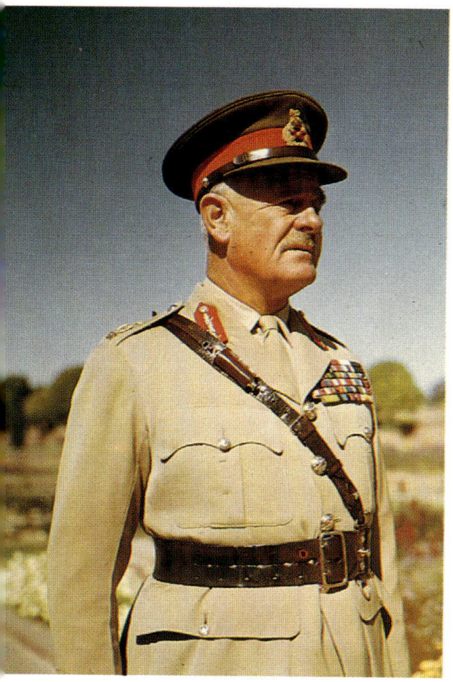

Wavell. Initially Wavell had great success in the North African campaign, driving the Italians out of Egypt and capturing Tobruk and Benghazi by Feb. 1941. However, having agreed to send part of his force to aid the Allies in Greece, Rommel overcame the force that Wavell retained in Cyrenaica, and by April he was at the Egyptian border. Because Churchill was impatient for an offensive against the Germans in North Africa, and had little faith in Wavell's ability, Wavell was transferred in mid-1941 to India. In South-East Asia he was unable to prevent the Japanese victories because his forces were too weak. Having launched an unsuccessful offensive in defence of Burma at the end of 1942, Wavell was transferred to the Indian command and in 1943 was appointed viceroy of India. He was persistently unlucky in having impossible assignments throughout his career.

Weapons. Faced with increasing danger from the air, the armament of surface ships changed radically in the course of the war. No longer limited to heavy guns, it included an increasingly large number of quick-firing, light anti-aircraft guns, such as this eight-barrelled 40 mm weapon, known as the 'Pom-Pom', seen in this photograph. These guns showed themselves to be particularly effective and signalled the end of low-level air attacks from the air. Off Okinawa the heavy cruiser USS *Guam* was able to destroy 82 Japanese aircraft in this way in half an hour.

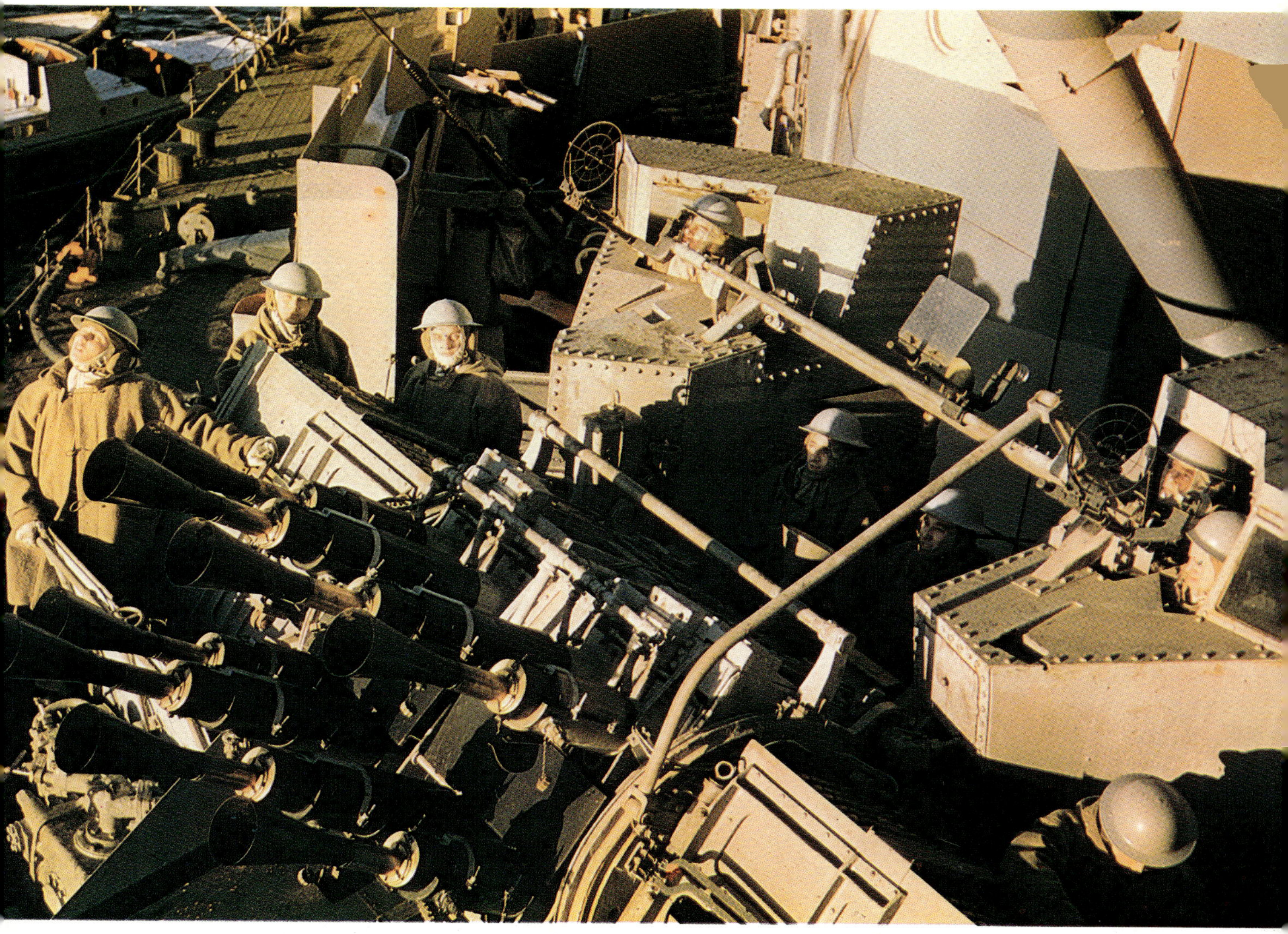

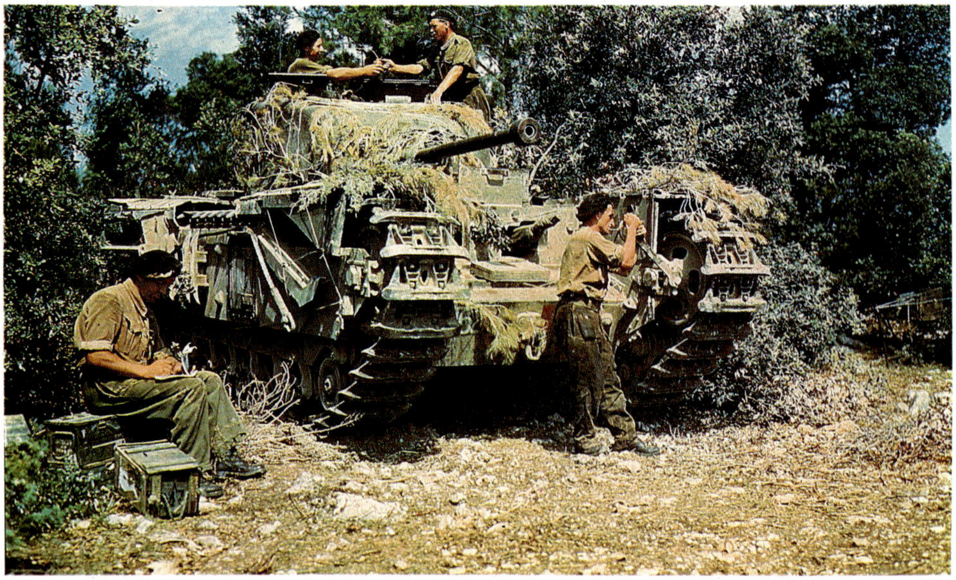

Tank construction was one of the most important branches of the armaments industry. However, theories about tanks varied a great deal. In spite of the lessons of the Blitzkrieg the British remained faithful to the heavy tank used in conjunction with infantry. The Churchill, which entered service in 1942 at the time of the Dieppe raid, illustrates this point of view. With its heavy armour and weight of about 40 tons, it had a top speed of only about 15 mph (25 km/h). The Churchill Mark I was armed with a 2 pdr gun in the turret, intended to destroy field fortifications, and a 3-inch howitzer in the hull front. This armament was found to be very inadequate in combat and it had to be replaced by a 6 pdr and then by a British version of the American 75 mm gun, in order to put the Churchill on an equal footing with the tanks of the Wehrmacht.

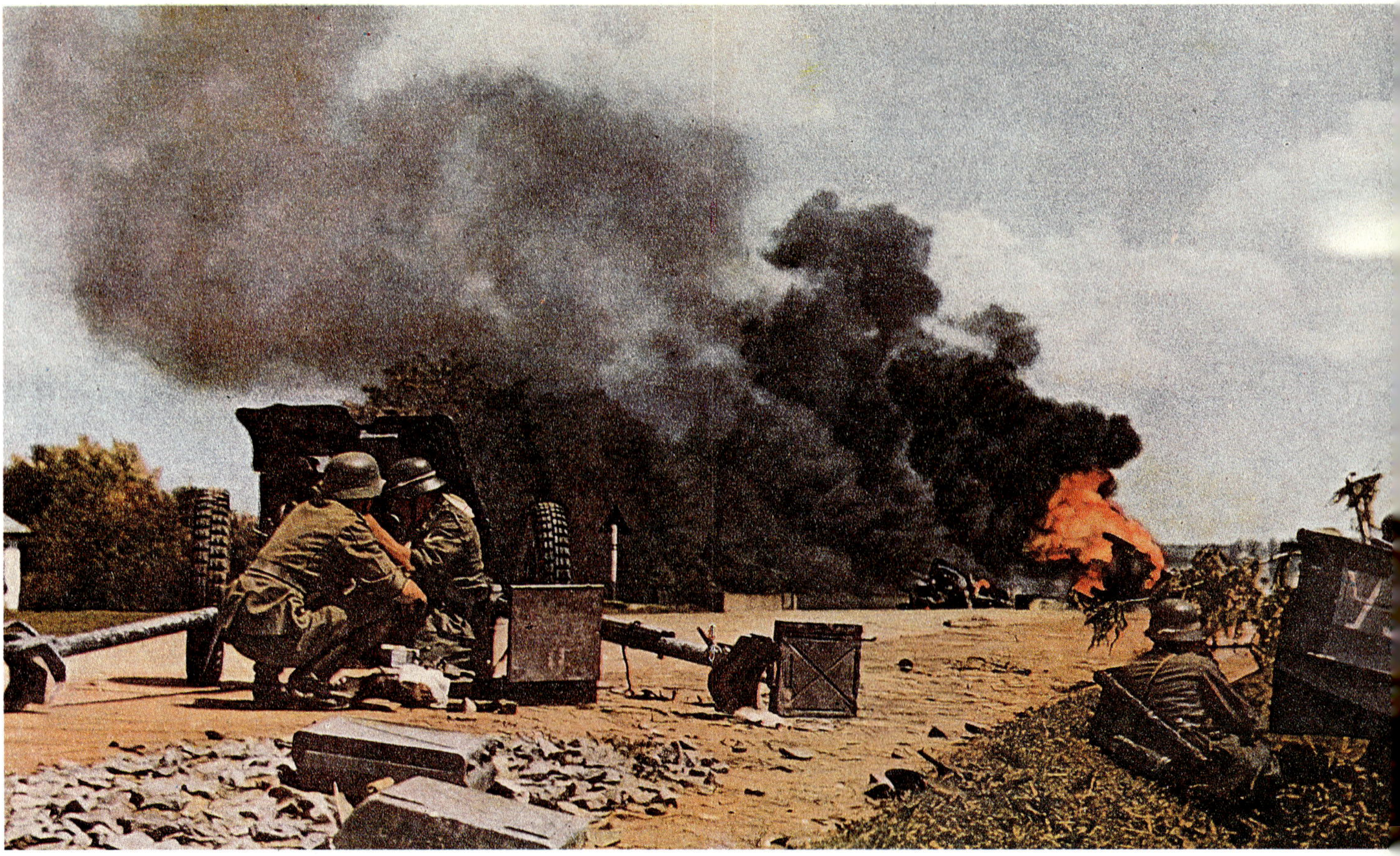

Throughout the first three years of the war the 1.5 in. (37 mm) was the Wehrmacht's basic anti-tank gun. Here a weapon of this type, light and easy to handle, is seen in action on the Russian front in 1942. Later when heavy Soviet type T-34 tanks were increasingly used, the 37 mm had to be replaced by heavier weapons of 2 in. (50 mm) and then of 3 in. (75 mm).

The Weather. Throughout the war the armies involved came up against extremely variable climatic conditions. The Wehrmacht, for example, was to experience both the scorching temperatures of the Libyan desert and the icy cold of the Russian winter. However, on the eastern front the Germans also had to contend with the difficulties of the Russian spring and autumn. Melting snow and torrential rain transformed the roads into quagmires which could bring all troop movements to a complete halt. Here we see the painful progress of a German motorized column.

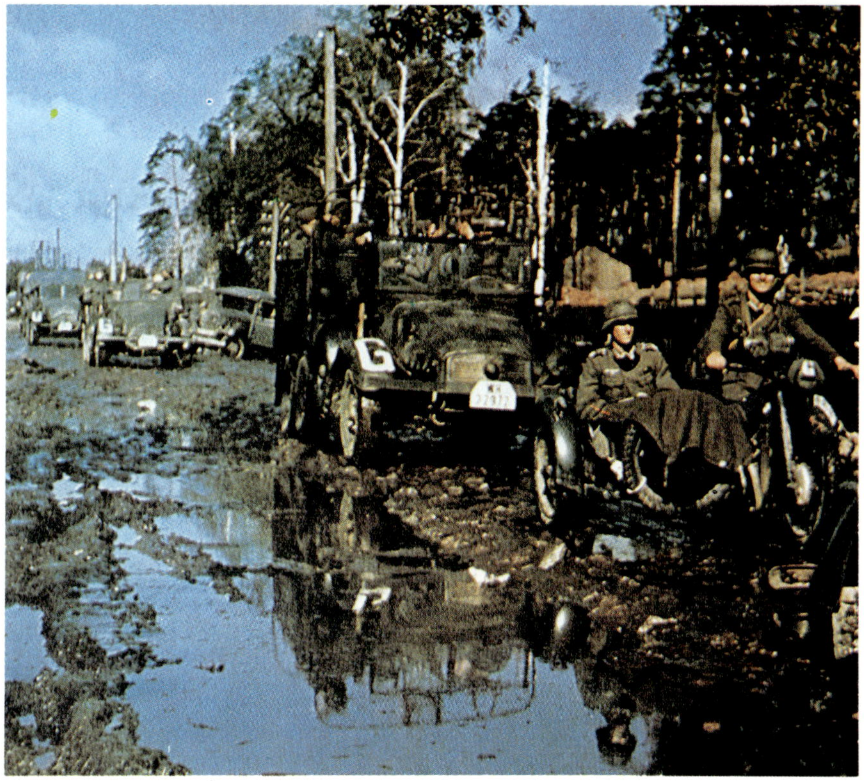

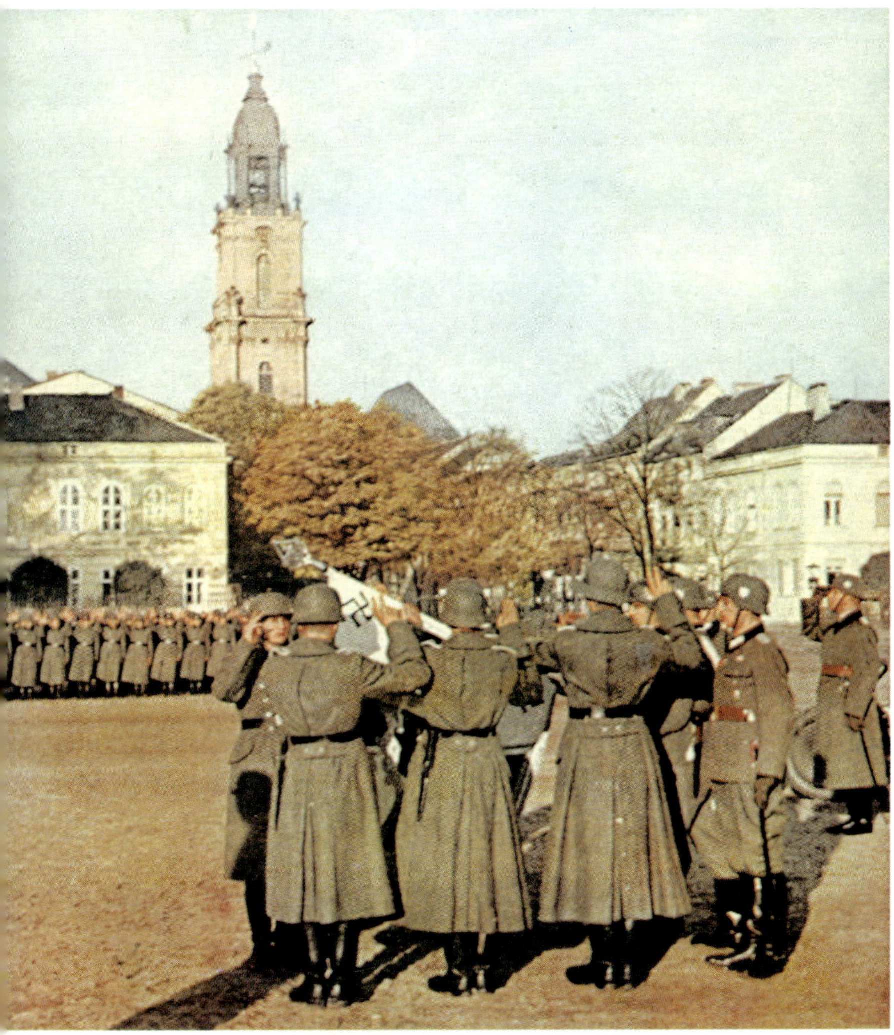

The Wehrmacht. Following the abrogation of the military clauses of the Treaty of Versailles in 1935, the professional Reichswehr was transformed into the Wehrmacht, a national army based on compulsory military service. Hitler made every effort to bind the new army – the only independent force remaining in Germany – closely to himself and to the new regime, while at the same time turning Prussian military traditions to his own advantage. With this aim in mind, when the Nazis took power, Goebbels organized a ceremony in the Garrison Church at Potsdam on 21 March 1933. The barracks square, dominated by the steeple of the chapel where the body of Frederick the Great lay, continued to be the setting for numerous military ceremonies. Recruits (photograph) took an oath of allegiance to the swastika flag and swore to fight to the death for Führer and fatherland.

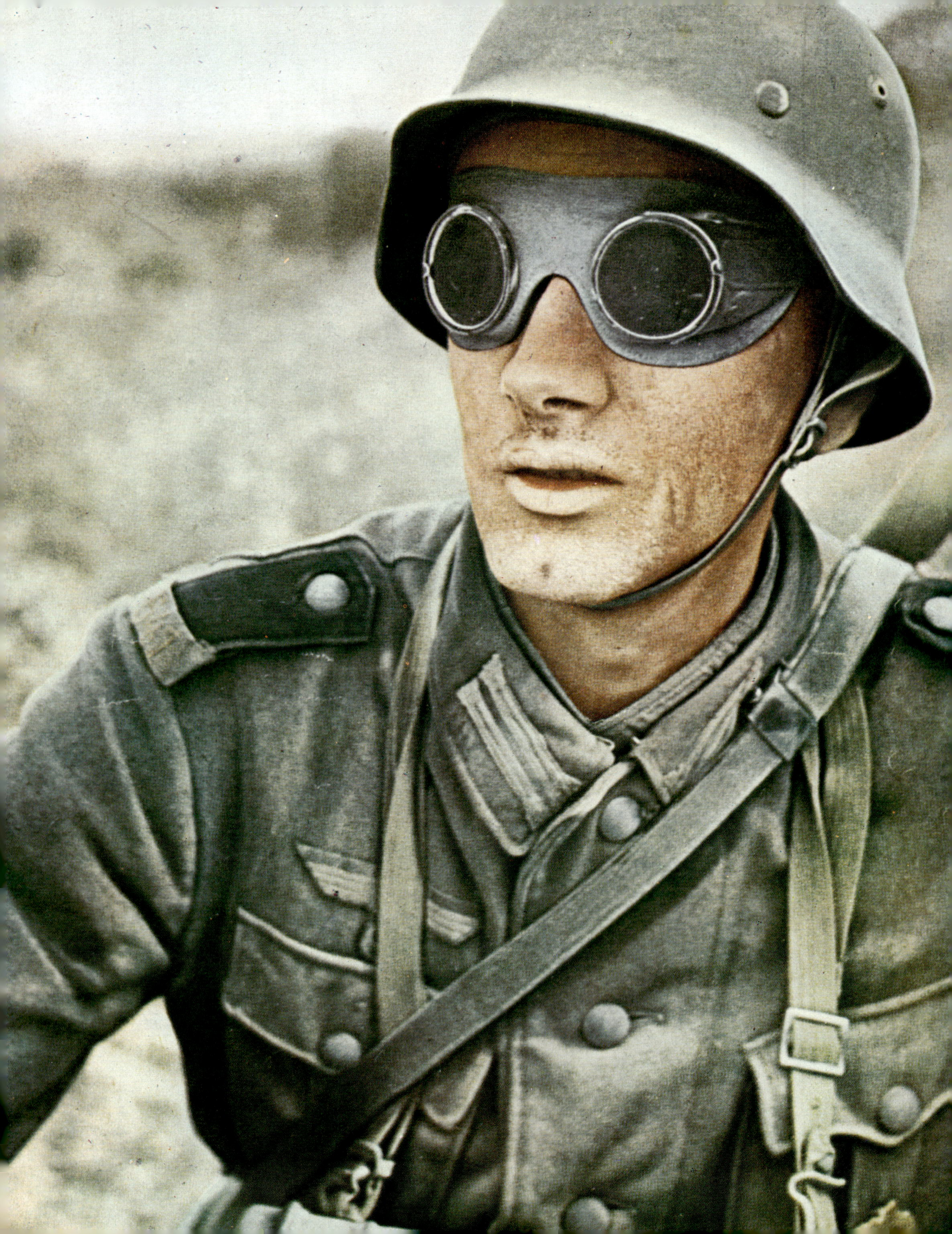

Wehrmacht. A despatch rider in the USSR
ing the summer offensive of 1942.

At the beginning of the war the cohesion, fighting spirit and the quality of its equipment made the Wehrmacht a formidable fighting weapon, distinctly superior to all the other armies. It was to give proof of this in Poland, in France, in the Balkans and in the USSR up to 1942. Its spearhead was made up of a first-rate group of armoured and motorized units, operating en masse and achieving break-throughs in depth in close co-operation with the air force. In this photograph, taken in the USSR during the summer of 1942, an armoured group is preparing to move.

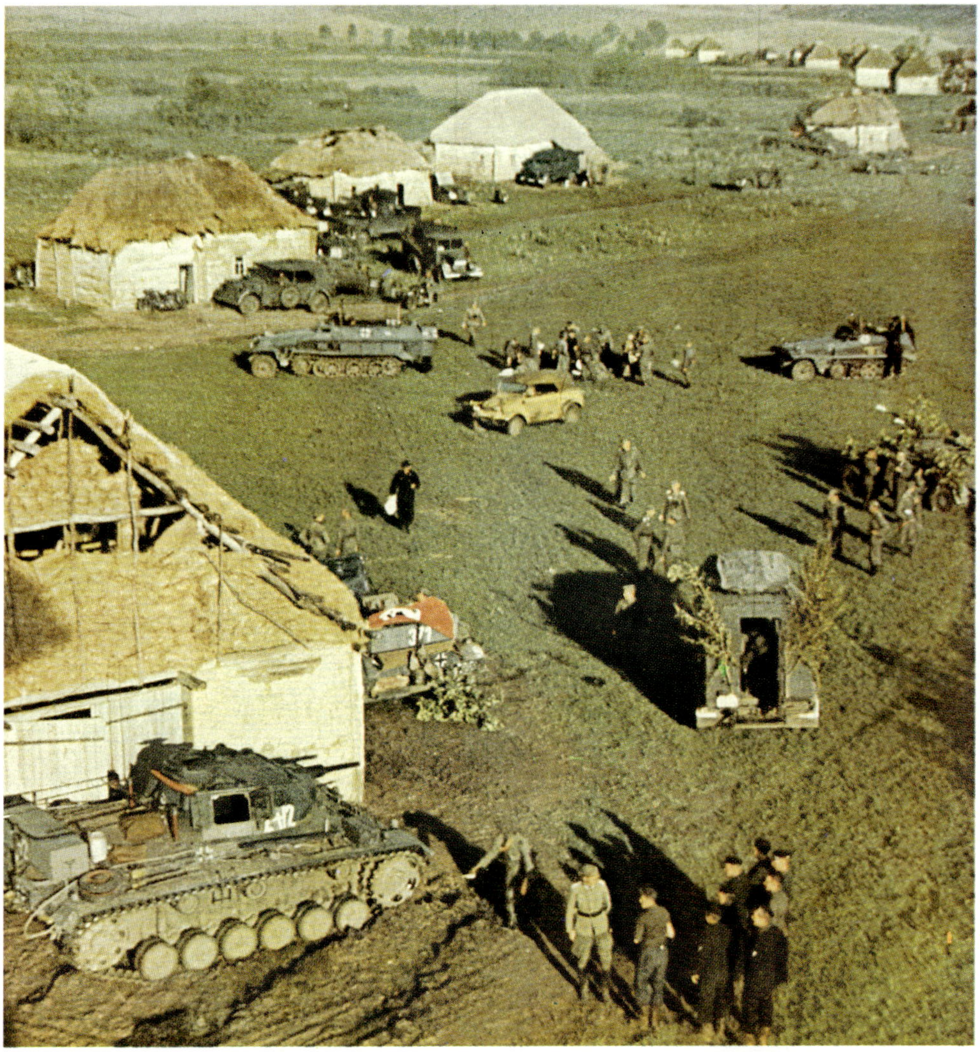

The spectacular victories of the Panzer divisions should not allow one to forget the thankless but decisive role played by the major infantry units in the Wehrmacht at war. By forced marches they had to follow the Panzers and to finish off encircled forces with large-scale enveloping movements. Here we see an infantry column in the Ukraine moving along the left bank of the Dniepr during the battle for Kiev in Sept. 1941. Horse-drawn regimental vehicles are following the foot soldiers.

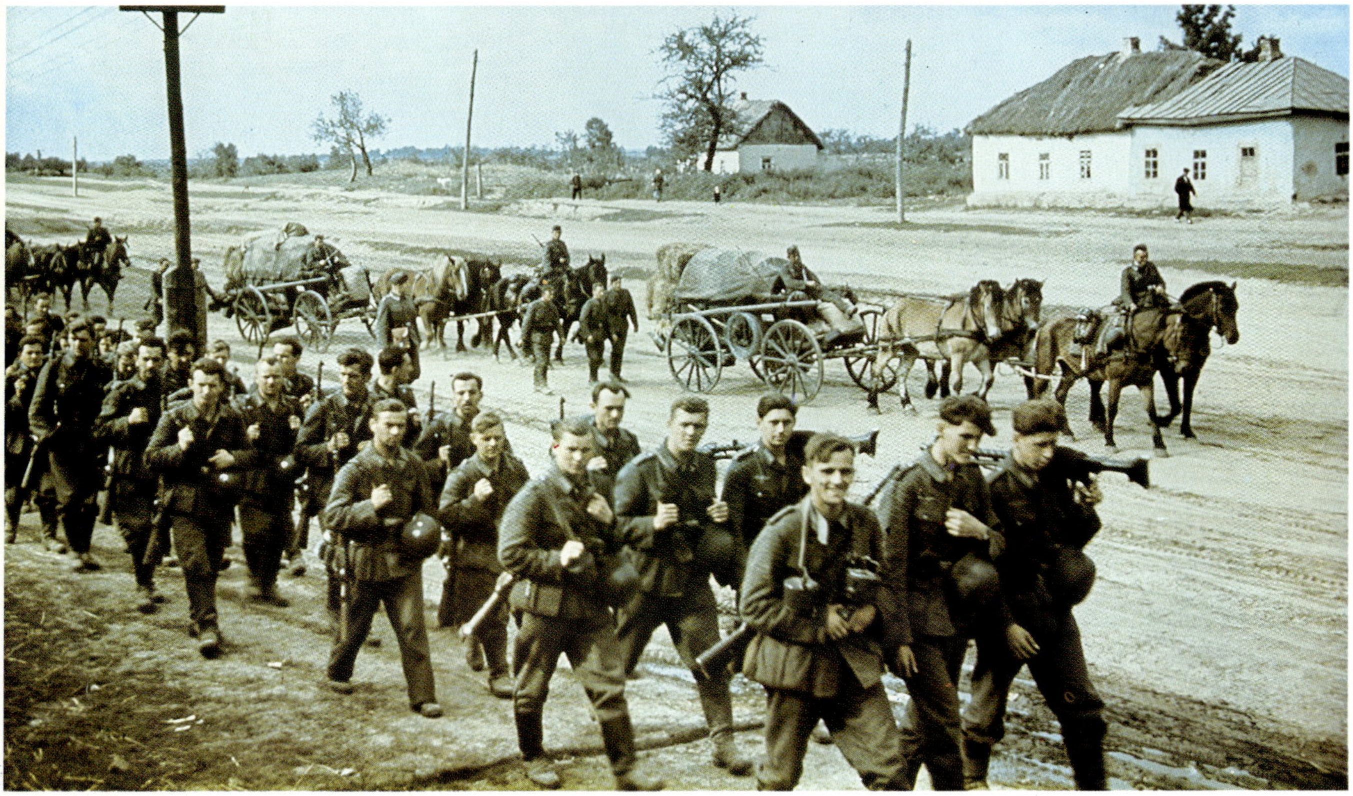

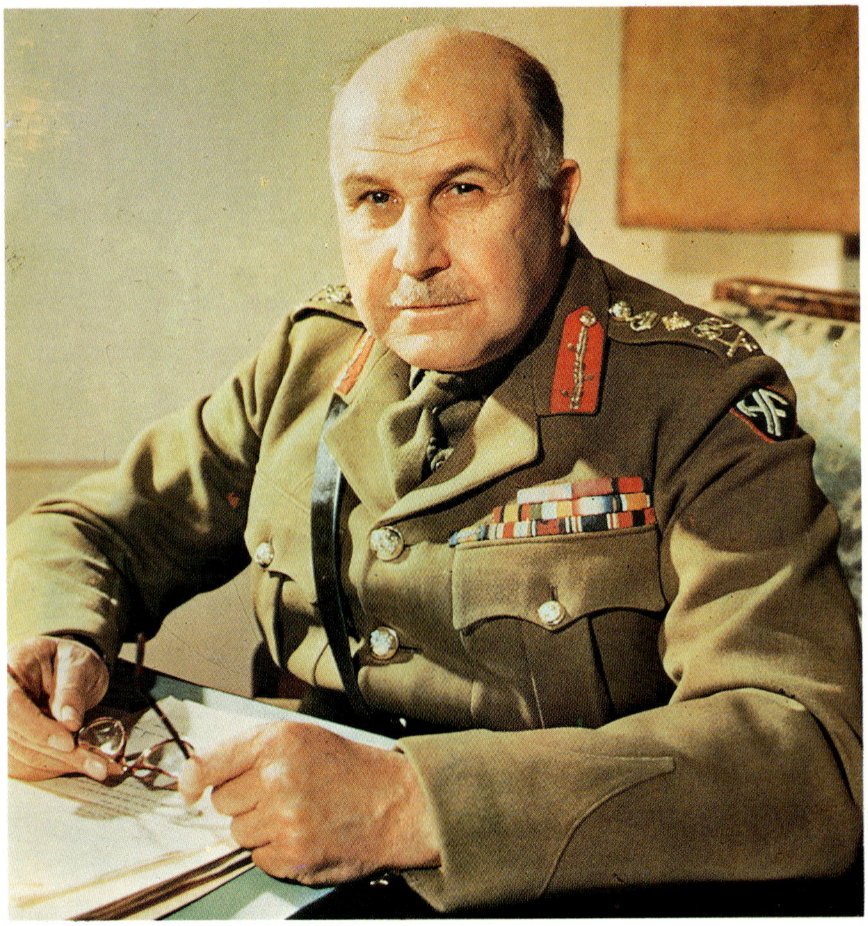

Wilson. Promoted field marshal in Dec. 1944, General Sir Henry Maitland Wilson, seen here several months earlier at the headquarters of the Allied forces in Italy, was among the best British military leaders of the war, being chiefly concerned with the Mediterranean theatre. He thus played a decisive part in the Italian defeat in Libya at the end of 1940. On the other hand he also had to organize, in the most difficult conditions, the re-embarkation of British troops in Greece in April 1941, and subsequently directed the successful campaign in Syria. Having in Feb. 1943 become commander-in-chief in the Near East, in Jan. 1944 he succeeded Eisenhower as Allied supreme commander in the Mediterranean at Algiers. From here he supervised the course of operations in Italy, and the campaign in southern France, having previously prepared the landings in Provence.

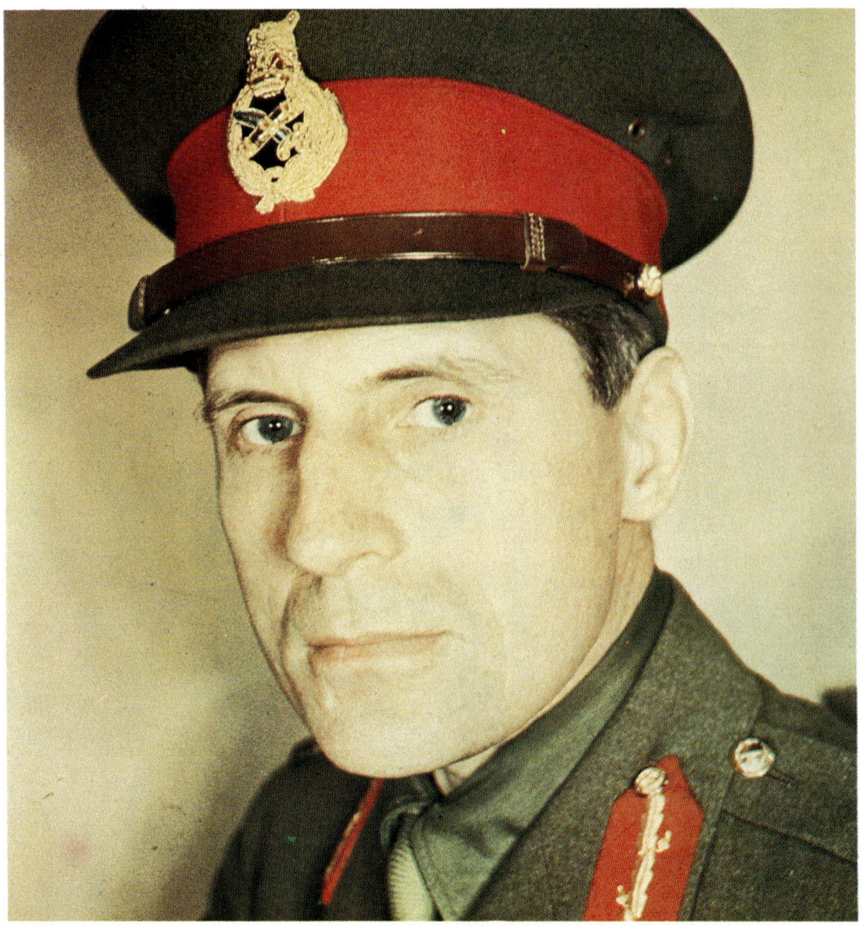

Wingate. A highly educated, anti-establishment figure, he was one of the most innovative British officers of the Second World War. He was well known for his ideas on the use of irregular native troops for attacks deep in the rear of the enemy in order to destroy his communications and to harass him generally. He demonstrated the effectiveness of his methods in Ethiopia, where he made a notable contribution, at the head of his volunteers, to the liberation of the country in 1941. However, it was above all in Burma that he had the opportunity to put his ideas into practice successfully, combining the infantry groups (the Chindits) composed of British, Indians, Gurkhas and Burmese, chosen and trained by him in jungle warfare, with the aircraft responsible for transporting and supplying them. He was killed in 1944 in an aircraft accident on the Burmese frontier, in the course of one of these operations.

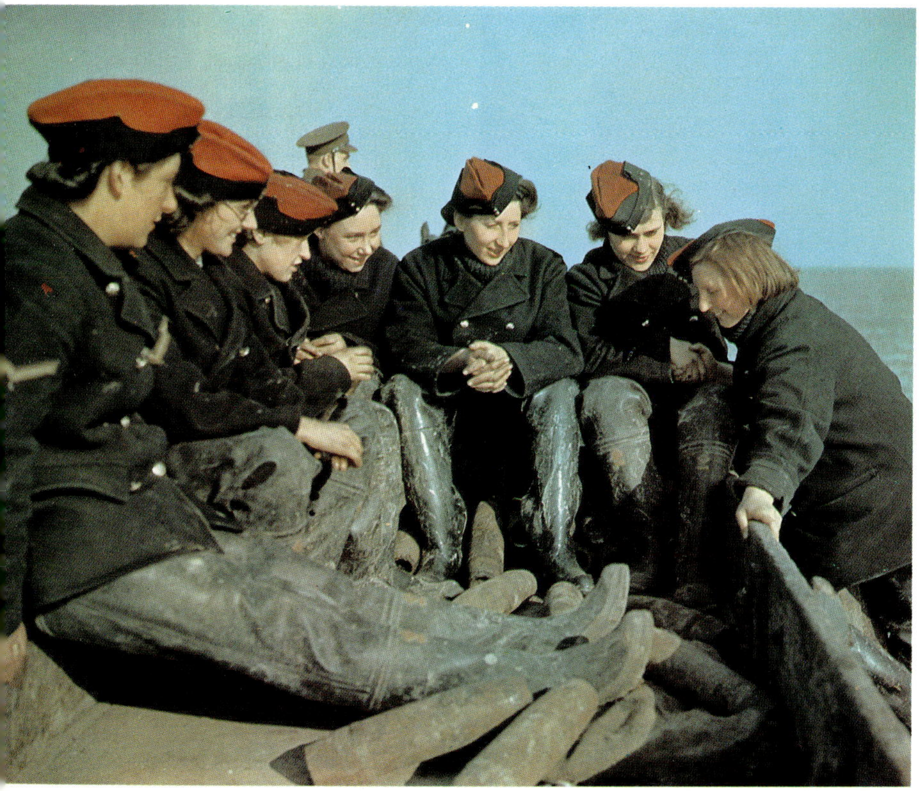

Women. All the belligerent countries used female labour in vast amounts for the most diverse tasks – agriculture, industry, auxiliary military services and units – in order to offset the mobilization of men into the armed forces. Here young British women of the ATS are about to collect artillery shells on a beach at low tide at Shoeburyness in Essex.

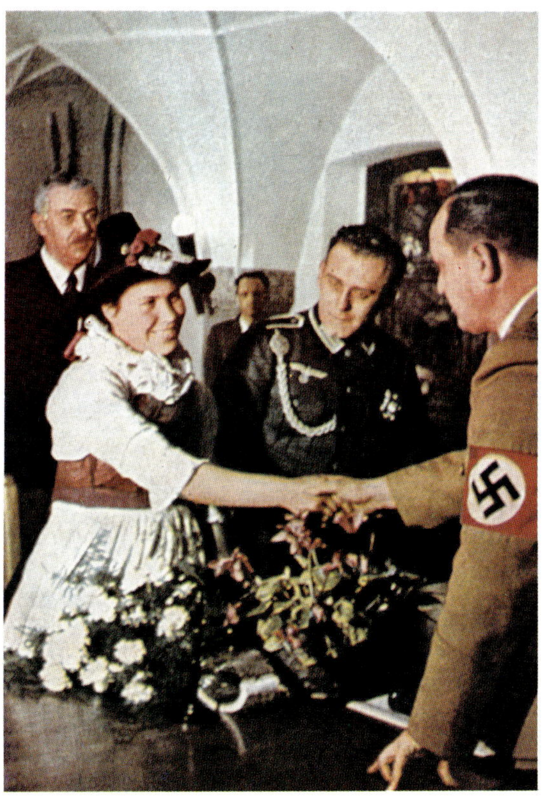

Of all the major powers Germany was paradoxically the slowest in resorting to the mobilization of women for the war effort. Up to 1943 the Reich was able to manage with the labour resources provided by prisoners of war and forced labour from the occupied countries. Hitler was also keen to preserve the stability of family life and to maintain the birth rate by encouraging wartime marriages, as is shown by the scene of this marriage, celebrated at Innsbruck in Austria.

Women. A British WAAF checking off equipment of a lifeboat.

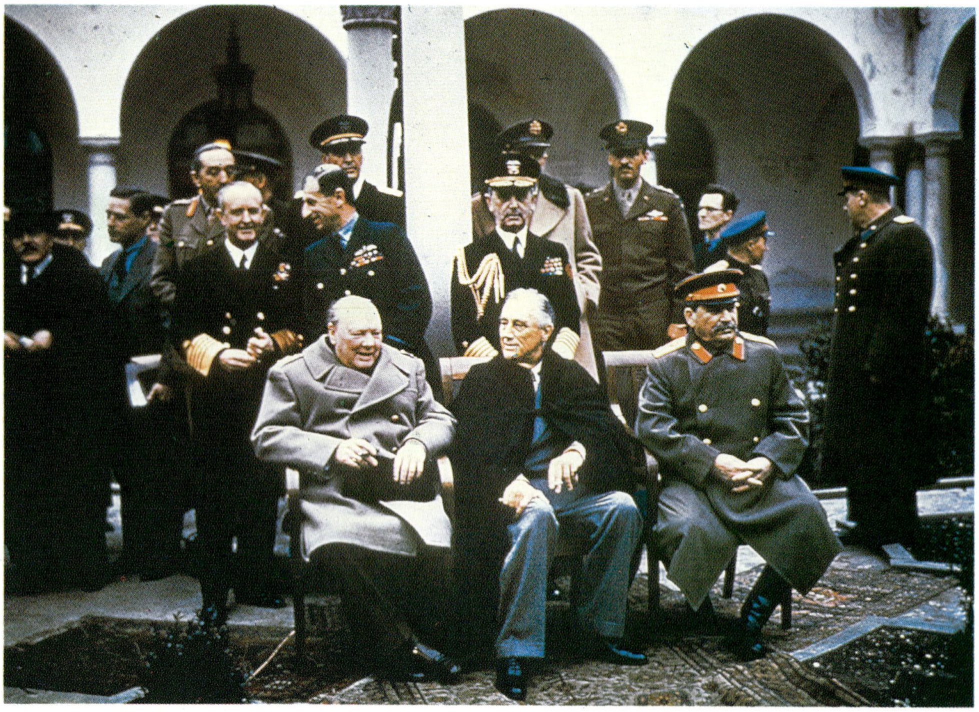

The Yalta Conference. It was at Yalta in the Crimea that, from 4 Feb. to 11 Feb. 1945, the final great wartime summit conference bringing together Roosevelt, Stalin and Churchill took place. Its object was to study the consequences of the imminent defeat of Germany and the conditions under which the struggle against Japan was to be pursued. Contrary to a deep-rooted belief, there was no division of the world at Yalta. As far as eastern Europe was concerned, the western powers refused to admit the idea of a Soviet sphere of influence and tried to establish the principle of the internationalization of problems. In reality Roosevelt and, especially, Churchill knew that the future of eastern Europe would depend essentially on the position of the armies on the ground. In this photograph, taken in the courtyard of the Livadia Palace, Churchill, Roosevelt and Stalin can be seen seated. Behind Roosevelt is Admiral Leahy, and behind Churchill, are Admiral Cunningham and Air Chief Marshal Portal.

Throughout the Yalta Conference Roosevelt did his best to charm Stalin, to the annoyance of Churchill. To re-establish the balance of power in the world, the president of the United States cherished the hope of maintaining the cordial atmosphere of the grand alliance and rejected the idea of establishing spheres of influence. At the end of the conference he believed he had attained his objective. Roosevelt showed himself all the more satisfied for having obtained Stalin's agreement that the USSR should enter the United Nations, and also a commitment to intervene against Japan, considered necessary at a time when the creation of the atomic bomb was not yet a certainty. In reality, undermined by illness, Roosevelt was deeply deluded about Soviet ideology and the character of Stalin.

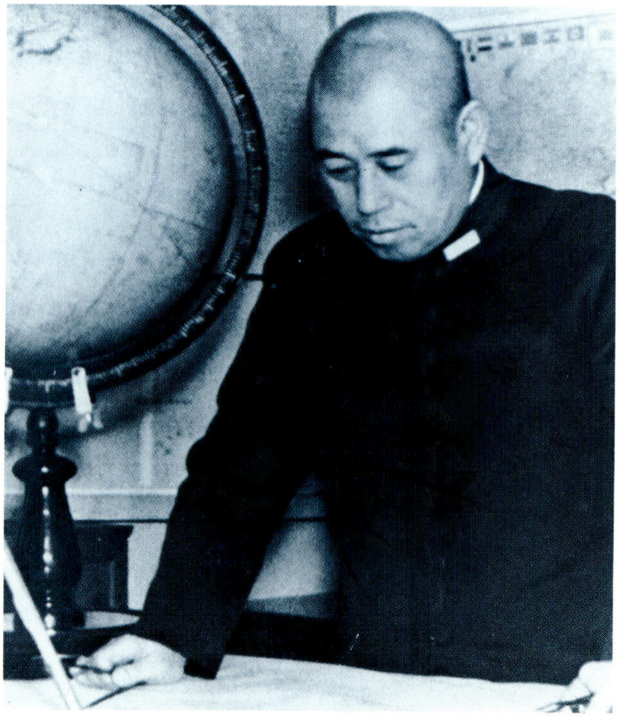

Yamamoto. As Commander of the First Fleet from 1939, Admiral Isoroku Yamamoto was responsible for the attack on the US Pacific Fleet at Pearl Harbor in Dec. 1941. He had realized that the only way to defeat such a powerful force was by a pre-emptive attack. However, the US aircraft carriers were at sea at the time of the assault and so escaped the Japanese attack. Having devised a complex plan to take Midway, Yamamoto was devastated when his scheme failed because the Americans had discovered it in advance, and the Japanese fleet was decimated. Despite this defeat, Yamamoto continued to command Japanese naval forces in the Solomons campaign, but their losses were crippling. He was eventually killed when the Americans shot down the plane in which he was travelling.

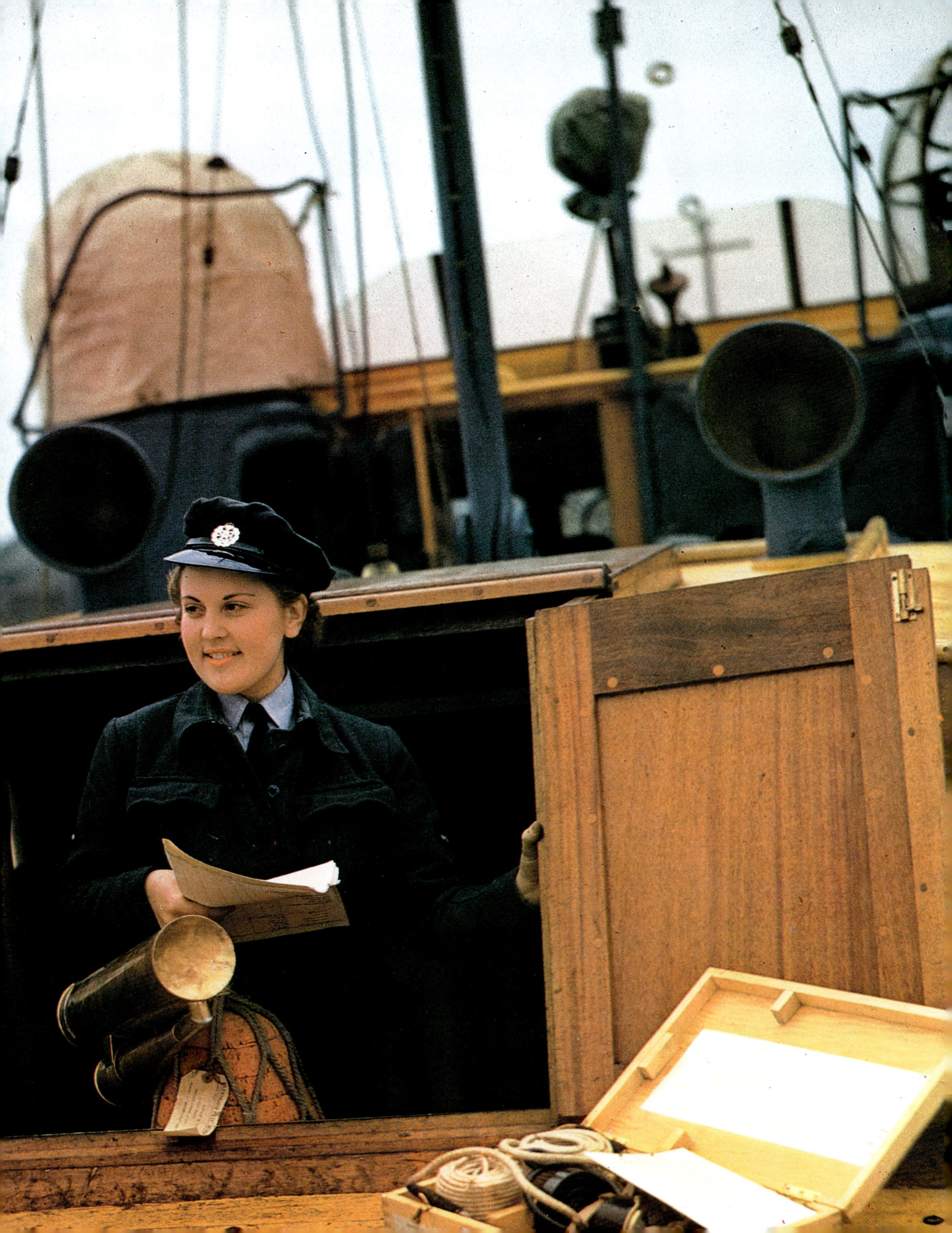

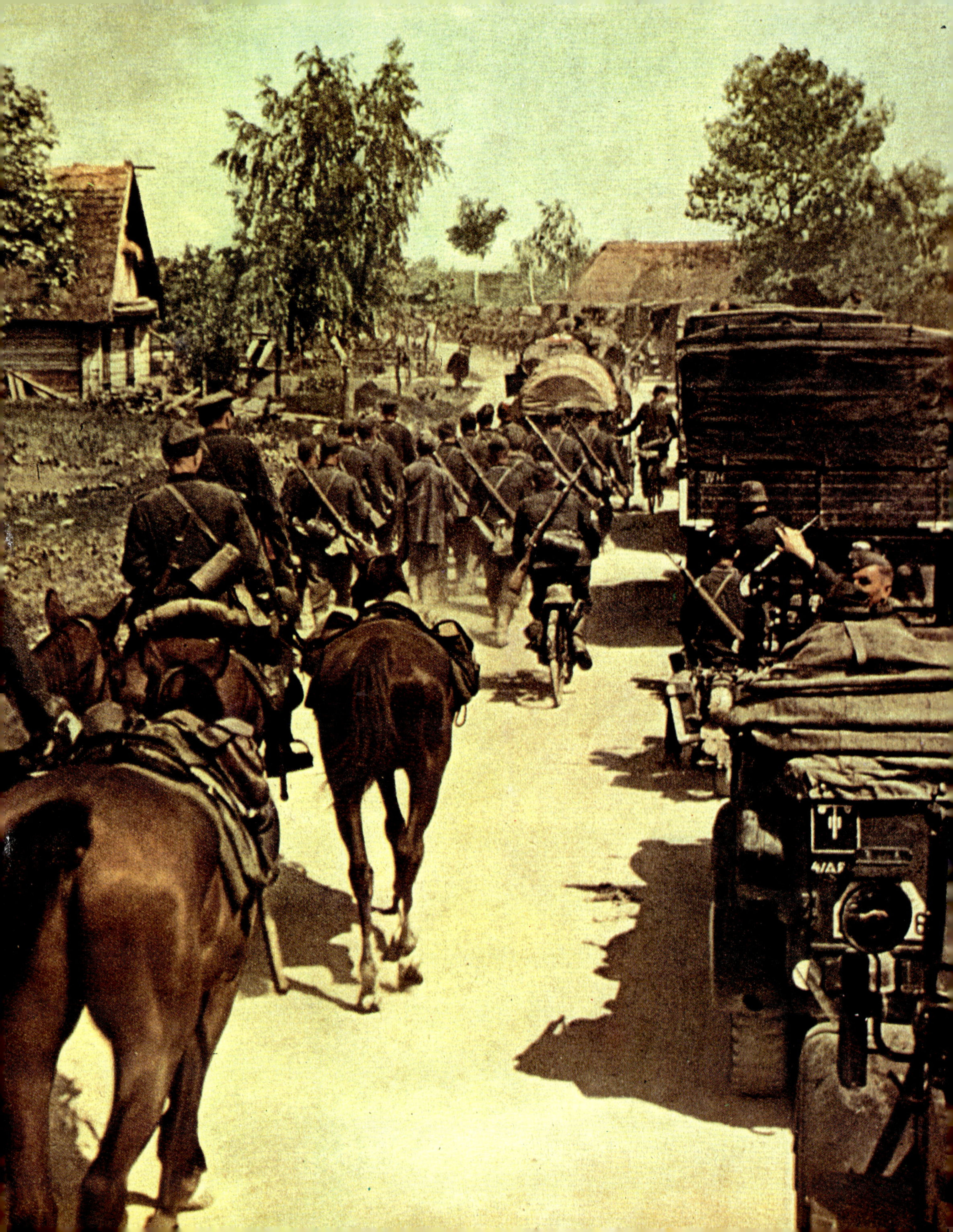

goslavia. German convoys on the move in 41.

Yamashita. As commander of the Japanese 25th Army, Lt-Gen. Tomoyuki Yamashita was responsible for the capture of Malaya and for bluffing the British into surrendering in Singapore. Tojo then retired him to train soldiers in Manchuria, but when Tojo fell in the summer of 1944, Yamashita was appointed to lead the defence of the Philippines. Although obliged to retreat, he continued operations against the Americans, and gave up only when news of the Japanese surrender reached him in early Sept. 1945.

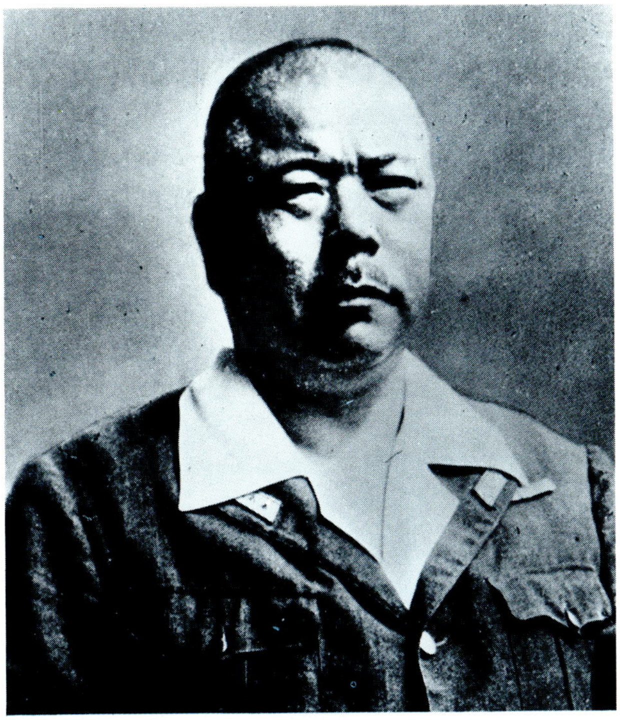

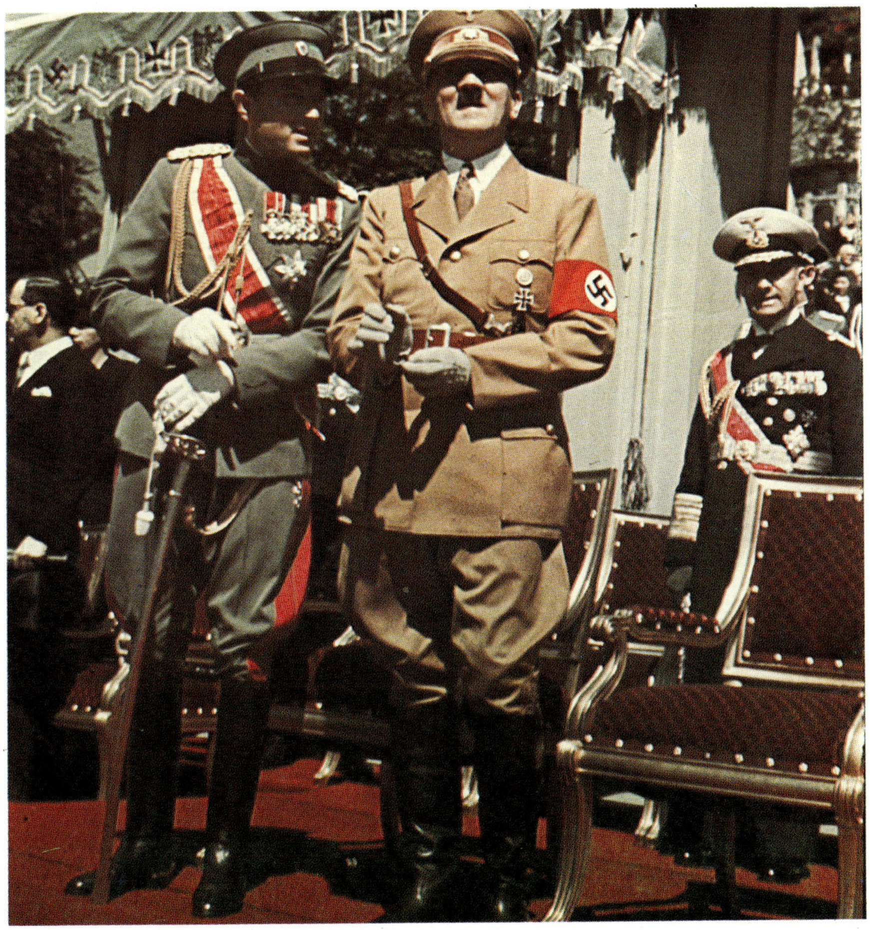

Yugoslavia. From 1937 onwards Hitler entertained the hope of bringing Yugoslavia into the German orbit. He is seen here in Berlin in June 1939 attending a military parade in company with Prince Paul, the regent of Yugoslavia. The Führer's policy was apparently successful. Very much impressed by the power of Germany, the regent had drawn closer to the Axis countries in order to facilitate his dealings with them. In 1941, subjected to strong pressure by Hitler who demanded, together with his adhesion to the Tripartite Pact, the free passage of the Wehrmacht through Yugoslavia, in order to restore the situation in Greece, he finally gave way, and agreed to sign the treaty of alliance at Vienna, which made his country a satellite of the Third Reich.

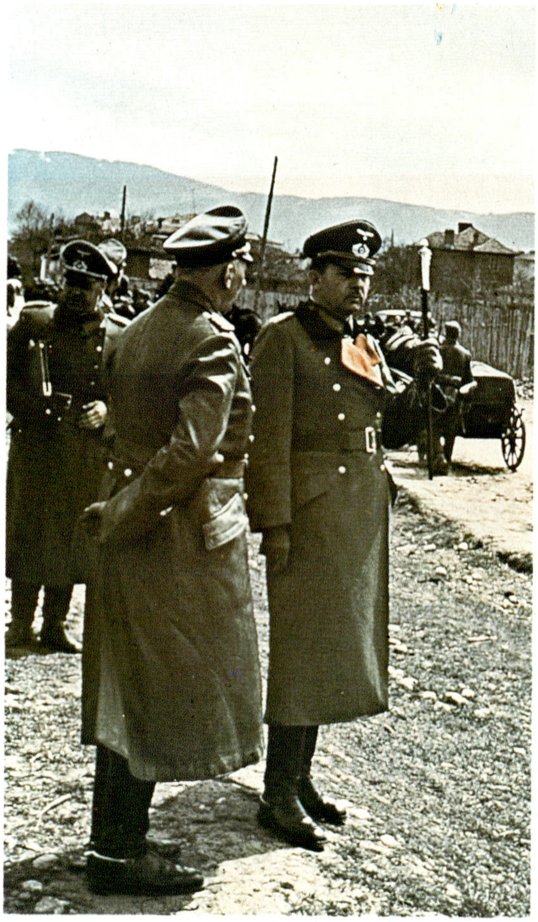

Launched on 6 April 1941, the Yugoslav campaign was to reveal once more the fighting qualities of the German army. By means of a twofold concentric manoeuvre in the direction of Belgrade and Sarajevo the operation was completed in 11 days. Incapable of making a stand in Serbia, the Yugoslav army was compelled to surrender on 17 April. However, King Peter succeeded in escaping to London. Here Field Marshal List, the commander of the German 12th Army, who was also responsible for the invasion of Greece, is watching a convoy of his troops pass by in a village in the south of Yugoslavia.

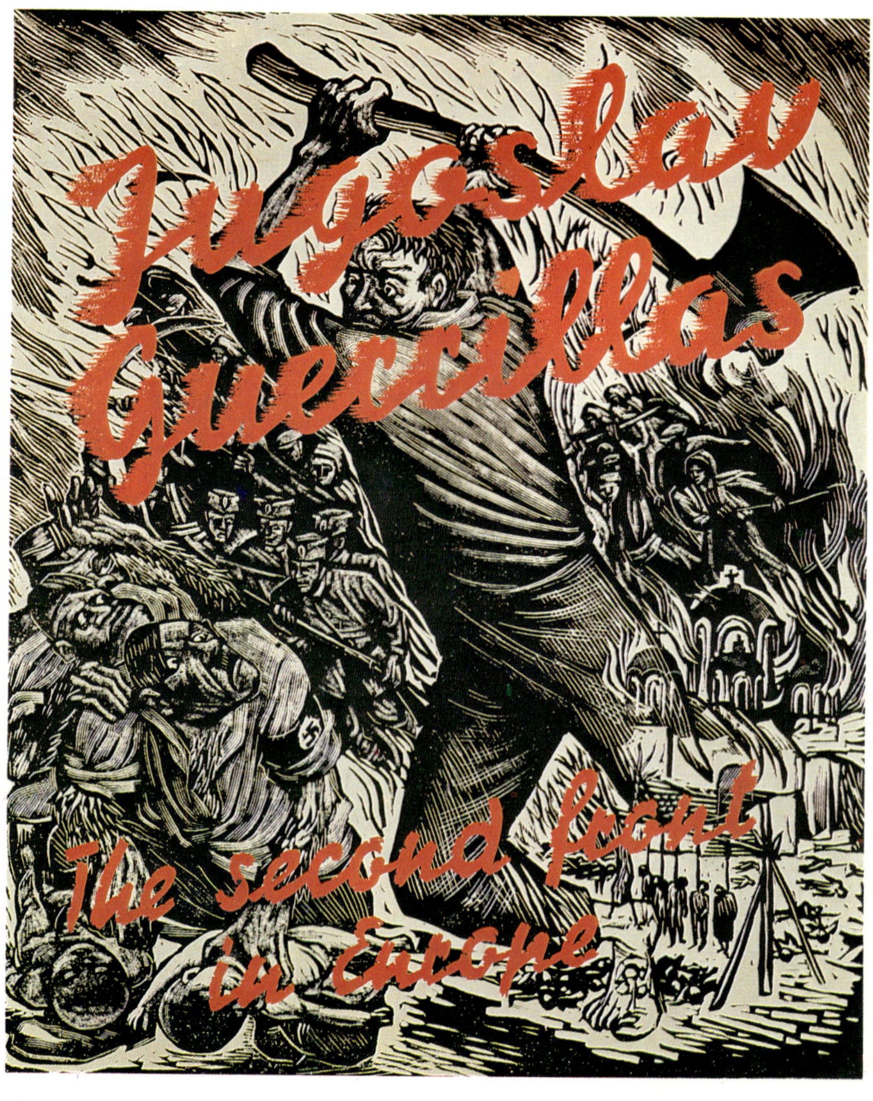

From the moment it capitulated on 17 April 1941, Yugoslavia was divided up, Italy, Germany, Hungary and Bulgaria sharing large portions of its territory between them. Puppet states subject to Mussolini or the Third Reich were established in Montenegro and in a Serbia reduced to its 1913 frontiers. Finally, a Greater Croatia was set up under the bloody dictatorship of Pavelić and his Ustashis, nominally independent but in fact owing complete allegiance to the Axis powers. This dismemberment was the starting point of four years of martyrdom for Yugoslavia, which was to lose 1,600,000 people, a tenth of its population. The massacres of Serbs by Ustashi Croats and the particularly savage repression by the occupying forces led to the development of a very active, but divided resistance movement, which could not avoid bloody confrontations between rival parts of it. In this fratricidal struggle between Mihajlović's Chetniks, who were pan-Serbian nationalists, much too attached to a 'wait and see' policy, and Tito's partisans, who were conducting an active guerrilla warfare and setting up their own administration in liberated zones, the latter were to triumph in the end. The brutality of German and Fascist reactions and the merciless reprisals against the civilian population could not fail to foster the partisan movement as this poster by Leopoldo Mendez demonstrates. In 1944–45 Tito's Army of National Liberation, numbering 450,000 in all, freed by its own efforts a large part of Yugoslav territory.

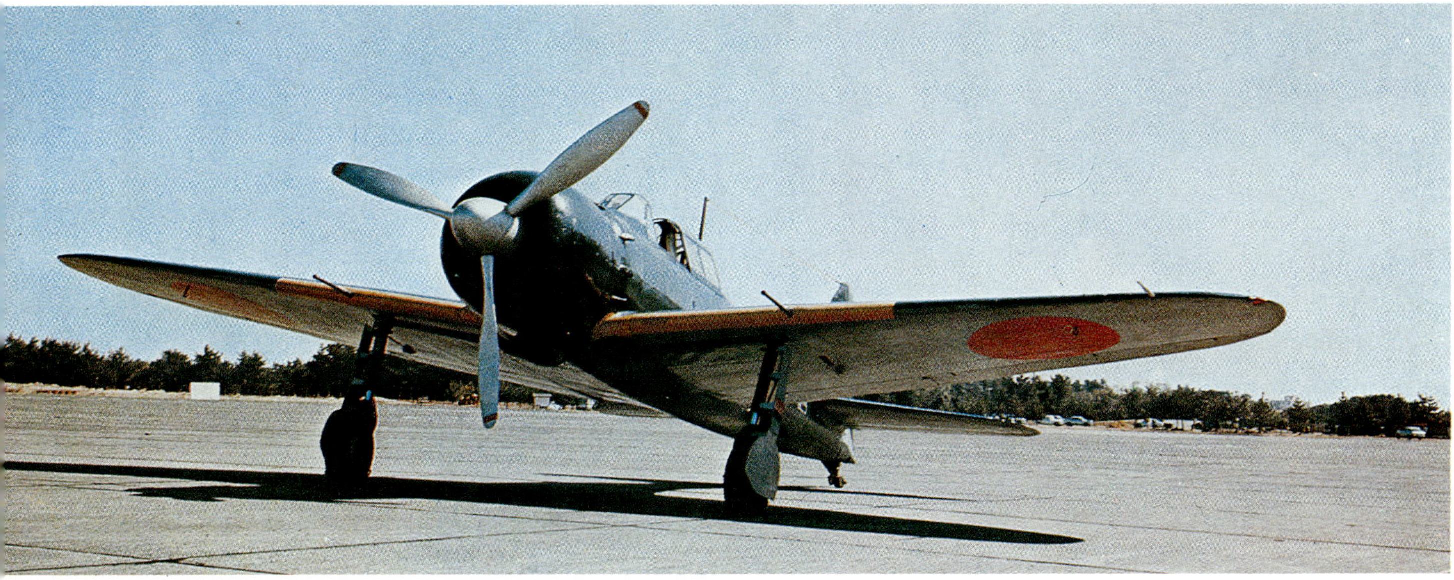

The 'Zero'. In the aftermath of Pearl Harbor the Japanese naval fighter, Mitsubishi 12 Shi A6M, known as the 'Zeke' or 'Zero', was to prove an unpleasant surprise for the Allies. Weighing 6200 lb (2800 kg), with a speed of 345 mph (550 km/h) and highly manoeuvrable, the Zero outclassed all the British and American fighters in service. Its armament consisted of two machine-guns and two 20mm cannon. It was not until 1943, with the appearance of the Corsair and the Hellcat, that the Americans began to get the upper hand. In all, more than 10,000 Zeros were built during the war.

Zhukov. A former Tsarist soldier, he joined the Red Army in 1918 and rapidly achieved distinction as a cavalry officer before becoming one of the first exponents of armoured warfare. A favourite of Stalin, gifted with a remarkable sense of strategy, and extremely tough, he was involved in all large-scale military operations on the eastern front, from the battle for Moscow to the capture of Berlin, including Stalingrad and the liberation of the Ukraine. Here he is seen, on 12 July 1945, in Berlin in front of the Brandenburg Gate, in conversation with Field Marshal Montgomery, who has just presented him with a decoration.

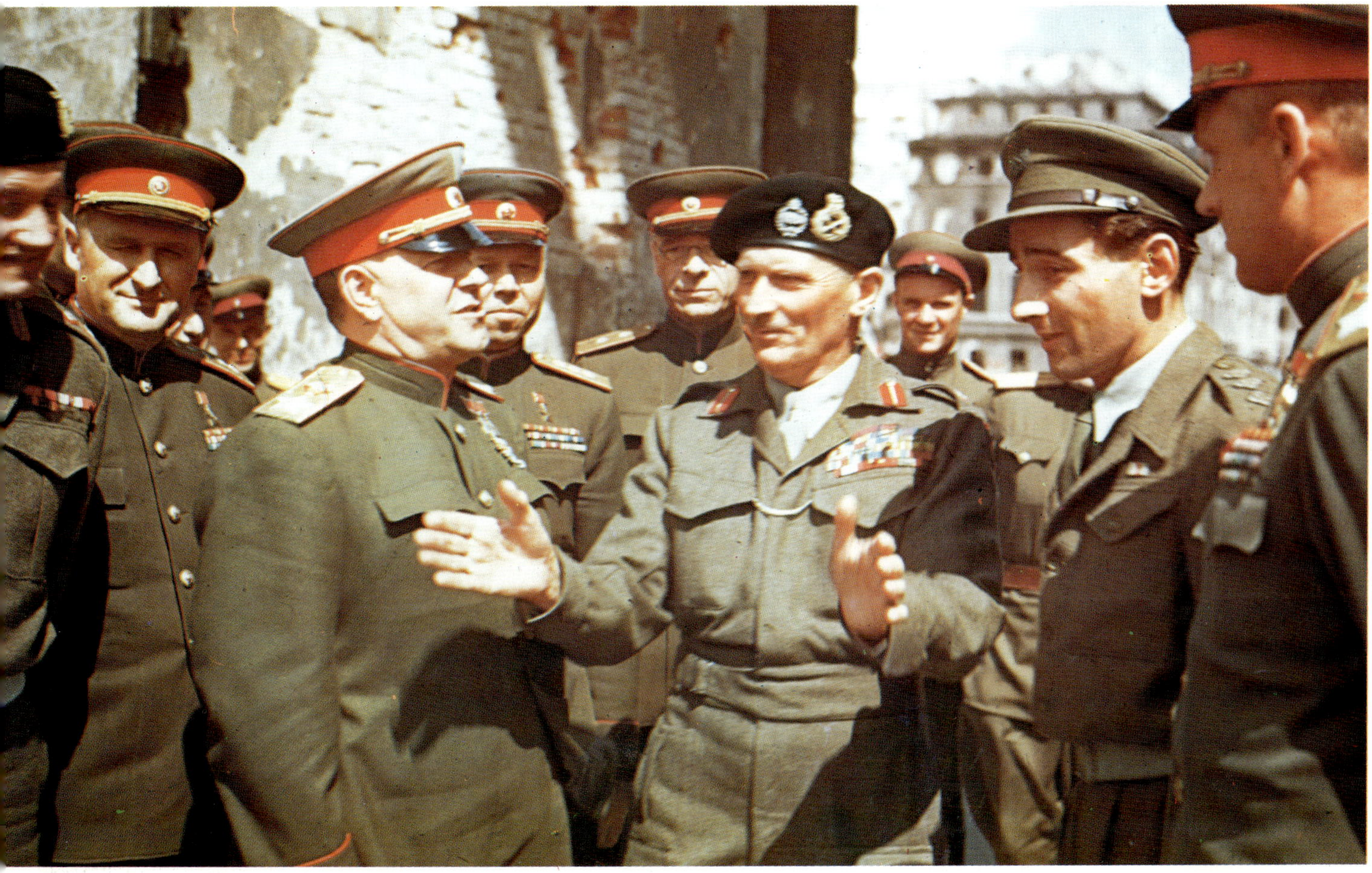